India

a travel survival kit

India - a travel survival kit
3rd Edition

Published by
Lonely Planet Publications
Head Office: PO Box 88, South Yarra, Victoria 3141, Australia
Also: PO Box 2001A, Berkeley, CA 94702, USA

Printed by
Colorcraft, Hong Kong

Photographs by
Peter Campbell (PC), Mark Carter (MC), Geoff Crowther (GC),
Hugh Finlay (HF), Linda Henderson (LH), Prakash A Raj (PR),
Tony Wheeler (TW)

Cover Photographs
Front Cover – City Palace guards, Jaipur (LH)
Back Cover – bathing ghats on the Ganges at dawn, Varanasi (TW)

Illustrations by
Tony Jenkins

First published
October 1981

This edition
June 1987

Although the author and publisher have tried to make the information
as accurate as possible, they accept no responsibility for any loss,
injury or inconvenience sustained by any traveller using this book.

National Library of Australia
Cataloguing-in-publication entry

Crowther, Geoff
India, a travel survival kit.

3rd ed.
Includes index.
ISBN 0 909096 93 8.

1. India – Description and travel – 1981- – Guide-books. I. Raj, Prakash A. II.
Wheeler, Tony. III. Title.

915.4'0452

The Authors

Geoff Crowther was born in Yorkshire, England and started his travelling days as a teenage hitch-hiker. Later, after many short trips around Europe, two years in Asia and Africa and short spells in the overgrown fishing village of Hull and on the bleak and beautiful Cumberland fells, Geoff got involved with the London underground information centre BIT. He helped put together their first, tatty, duplicated overland guides and was with them from their late '60s heyday right through to the end. With Lonely Planet Geoff has written or collaborated on guides to Africa, South America, Malaysia, Korea and Taiwan as well as this book. Geoff now lives with Hyung Pun, whom he met in Korea, on an old banana plantation in the rainforests near the New South Wales/Queensland border. In between travel he spends his time pursuing noxious weeds, cultivating tropical fruits, trying to get a house built and brewing mango wine.

Prakash A Raj was born in Nepal and studied for two years in Varanasi where he learnt to speak fluent Hindi. He later spent five years at university in Michigan, Nevada and Massachusetts in the USA. Following that he studied for a year in the Netherlands, travelled extensively in Europe and then returned to Nepal where he worked on the Kathmandu English-language daily as a journalist and also for the Nepalese government's planning agency. Prakash has also worked for the OECD in Paris and the UN secretariat in New York. He is now working for the UNHCR in Asia. For Lonely Planet he wrote *Kathmandu & the Kingdom of Nepal* and has also written several other books about Nepal and his life there in both English and Nepali.

Tony Wheeler was born in England but spent most of his younger years overseas due to his father's occupation with British Airways. Those years included a lengthy spell in Pakistan, a shorter period in the West Indies and all his high school years in the USA. He returned to England and did a university degree in engineering, worked for a short time as an automotive design engineer, returned to university again and did an MBA. He then dropped out on the Asian trail with his wife Maureen. They've been travelling, writing and publishing travel guidebooks ever since. Now living in Melbourne, Australia, Tony has written a number of the Lonely Planet books including the popular *South-East Asia on a Shoestring*, and today divides his time between travel, writing and running Lonely Planet.

Lonely Planet

Lonely Planet Publications started in the early '70s when Tony and Maureen Wheeler made a lengthy overland trip and turned their experiences and the information they had gathered into the first edition of *Across Asia on the Cheap* (now titled *West Asia on a Shoestring*). Since then Lonely Planet has grown to a list of 50 travel titles and phrasebooks, many of them unique; an office in Melbourne, Australia and (since 1984) a second office in Berkeley, California; and, most important of all, thousands of 'our' travellers out there on the road.

This Book

When the first edition of this book emerged in 1981 it was the biggest, most complicated and most expensive project we'd tackled at Lonely Planet. The preliminary steps were taken when Tony and Maureen made an exploratory trip to south India to see what information would be needed, how long gathering it would take and how big the resulting book would be. It took longer and it turned out bigger.

The following year Geoff, Prakash and Tony – all of whom had visited India on numerous occasions in the past – returned to India and spent a combined total of a year's more-or-less non-stop travel. Back in Australia much additional work went into desk research and producing maps and other illustrations. The end result exceeded all our hopes and expectations – it instantly became our best-selling guide and in Britain it won the Thomas Cook 'Guidebook of the Year' award. In India it became the most popular guide to the country; a book used even by Indians to explore their own country.

This Edition

This is the third edition of *India – a travel survival kit* and once again we returned to India to comprehensively update our work. On this occasion, however, Geoff Crowther was travelling in Africa so the research work was rearranged with Prakash Raj tackling the south of India, which Geoff had previously covered, while Tony Wheeler covered central and north India, the regions covered by Prakash and Tony on the first edition. To get around this vast region in the limited time available Tony made use of an Indrail pass followed by a Discover India airline pass and numerous other bus, train and taxi trips in between. He also bicycled his way around numerous cities and for a few days in Goa even rented an Indian Yezdi motorcycle ('the worst motorcycle I have ever ridden', he reported).

Once again this was not a sponsored or assisted operation – we paid for the airfares to and from India, we paid for our travel, nobody from the Indian tourist office looked after us. There's nobody we have to be nice too! Well, almost nobody; we have to admit that sometimes this book is so well known that it proves virtually impossible to stop hotel owners rolling the red carpet out if they recognise our researchers!

As well as to our three writers, thanks must also go to a long list of additional contributors. The motorcycling in India report is by Australian Roman Wowk, while American Ann Sorrel wrote the equivalent bicycle section. Englishman (but Australian resident) Mark Carter once again updated his article on 'gricing', tracking down old Indian steam engines. The cartoons are by Canadian Tony Jenkins and you can see much more of his work in his book *Traveller's Tales*. The Garwhal Himal trek reports were written for the first edition by Davindra Garbyal. In India during the research phase Tony would once again (as with the two previous editions) like to thank Ashok and Lalita Khanna, with whom he stayed each time he passed through New Delhi.

Back at home base, updating this edition was much easier than before as we now have the book totally on computer and all the updating is done 'on screen'. It was computerised with the last edition but you don't get the full benefit of working on a guidebook in this way until you approach it for the second time. Not only did Tony work on this book at our Australian office on our Kaypro microcomputers, he also took it with him on a month-long visit to our US office where he continued to work on it with his well-travelled Toshiba lap-top computer.

Integration of Prakash's revision work onto the computer disks was tackled by Maureen Wheeler. With this edition we decided to make a major effort to improve many of the maps and also (due to enormous reader pressure!) get north up at the top of most of them! This part was tackled by Fiona Boyes with support from Todd Pierce and Peter Flavelle. Editing was handled by Elizabeth Kim at our US office. Alison Porter did the typesetting, Dennis Sheehan the design and paste up, Sue Mitra and others worked on final final proof reading and indexing.

Finally, but far from least important, a very big thank you to those countless readers and travellers who took the time to tell us where we went wrong; and to Sue Tan who faces the monumental task of sorting through the many letters we receive from 'our travellers' out on the road. To those many travellers a special thank you (and an apology if we've missed any names). A list of people who have written to us is at the back of this book.

And the Next Edition

Things change, prices go up, good places go bad and bad ones go bankrupt. So if you find things better, worse or simply different please write and tell us about it. As usual good letters will be rewarded with a free copy of the next edition or an alternative Lonely Planet guidebook.

A Word About Hotel Classifications

Our classifications are always fuzzy and subjective, but basically 'bottom end' means most double rooms are less than Rs 75 a night. Anywhere in India you should be able to get a decent double with bathroom for that price, usually for much less. At the bottom of bottom end you can get a bed in many places for Rs 10 or less, and many travellers never pay more than Rs 20 a night their whole time in India.

'Middle' means roughly Rs 75 to 200 a night for a double; 'top end' means anything above that. If it's a small place we may combine the middle and top-end categories. In places where prices are very low we may categorise some hotels as 'middle' even though the price falls into our bottom category. Similarly, in a very expensive town like Bombay bottom-end hotels may cost more than Rs 75.

Contents

Introduction

India, it is often said, is not a country but a continent. From north to south and east to west the people are different, the languages are different, the customs are different, the country is different. There are few countries on earth with the enormous variety that India has to offer and it's a place which somehow gets into your blood. Love it or hate it you can never ignore India. It's not an easy country to handle and more than a few visitors are only too happy to finally be getting on that aircraft and flying away. Yet a year later they'll be hankering to get back.

It all comes back to that amazing variety – India is as vast as it is crowded, as luxurious as it is squalid. The plains are as flat and featureless as the Himalaya are high and spectacular, the food as terrible as it can be magnificent, the transport as exhilarating as it can be boring and uncomfortable. Nothing is ever quite the way you expect it to be.

India is far from the easiest country in the world to travel around. It can be hard going, the poverty will get you down, Indian bureaucracy would try the patience of even a Hindu saint and the most experienced travellers find themselves at the end of their tempers at some point in India. Yet it's all worth it.

Very briefly, India is a triangle with the top formed by the mighty Himalayan mountain chain. Here you will find the intriguing Tibetan region of Ladakh and the astonishingly beautiful Himalayan areas of Kashmir, Himachal Pradesh, the Garwhal of Uttar Pradesh and the Darjeeling and Sikkim regions. South of this is the flat Ganges basin with the colourful and comparatively affluent Punjab to the north-west, the capital city New Delhi and important tourist attractions like Agra (with the Taj Mahal), Khajuraho, Varanasi and the holy Ganges

CALCUTTA COPS
A diverse lot in smoggy white. I found them courteous and helpful. They speak softly and do carry a very big stick.

itself. This plain reaches the sea at the northern end of the Bay of Bengal where you find teeming Calcutta, a city which seems to sum up all of India's enormous problems.

South of this northern plain the Deccan plateau rises. Here you will find cities that tell of the rise and fall of the Hindu and Muslim kingdoms and the modern metropolis that their successors, the British, built at Bombay. India's story is one of many different kingdoms competing with each other and this is never more clear than in places like Bijapur, Mandu, Golconda and other centres of central India. Finally there is the steamy south where Muslim influence reached only fleetingly. Here Hinduism was least altered by outside influences and is at its most exuberant. The temple towns of the south are quite unlike those of the north and superbly colourful.

Basically India is what you make of it and what you want it to be. If you want temples there are temples in profusion and with enough styles and types to confuse anybody. If it's history you want India has plenty of it and the forts, abandoned cities, ruins, battlefields and monuments all have their tales to tell. If you want to simply lie on the beach there are enough of those to satisfy the most avid sun worshipper. If walking and the open air is your thing then head for the

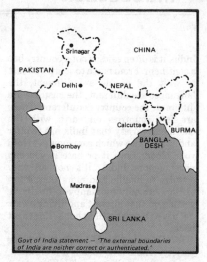

Govt of India statement: — 'The external boundaries of India are neither correct or authenticated.'

trekking routes of the Himalaya; some of them are as wild and deserted as you could ask for. If you simply want to meet the real India you'll come face to face with it all the time – on Indian trains and buses getting there may not always be half the fun but it certainly is half the experience. A visit to India is just that, it's not a place you simply and clinically 'see'. India is a total experience, an assault on all the senses, a place you'll never forget.

Facts about the Country

HISTORY

India is the home of one of the world's 'great' civilisations – its social structure as it exists today can be traced back thousands of years and empires of great size and complexity existed here far earlier than anything comparable in Europe. Yet India as an entity is a comparatively recent invention put together by the British. Even the mightiest of India's ancient civilisations did not encompass all of modern India and today it is still as much a country of diversities as of unities. Few people in the Tamil-speaking south speak Hindi, the national language, for example. Beyond India's own history and development, its role as the birthplace of two of the world's great religions is enough to ensure its historical importance.

Indus Valley Civilisation

India's first major civilisation flourished for a thousand years from around 2500 BC along the Indus River valley in what is now Pakistan. Its great cities were Moenjodaro and Harappa, where a civilisation of great complexity developed. The major sites were only discovered this century but other, lesser, cities have been subsequently unearthed at sites like Lothal, near Ahmedabad in India.

The Indus Valley cities were ruled by a religious group rather than by kings, but the most interesting thing about them is their highly developed engineering. Four thousand years ago they already had a sophisticated drainage system and even organised garbage collection! Despite the extensive excavations conducted at the sites, comparatively little is known about the development and eventual demise of this civilisation. Their script has still not been deciphered, nor is it known why such an advanced civilisation collapsed so quickly with the invasion of the Aryans.

Early Invasions

The early Aryan invasions were vague and disjointed, although the people of north India today are defined as Aryans and those of the south as Dravidians. The Aryans came from the north from around 1500 BC and gradually spread across India from the Punjab and Sind (now in Pakistan) and down the Ganges towards Bengal. Under Darius (521-486 BC) the Punjab and Sind became part of the Persian empire, but this was still peripheral to India itself.

Alexander the Great reached India, in his epic march from Greece, in 326 BC but his troops refused to march further than the Beas River, the easternmost extent of the Persian empire he had conquered, and he turned back without extending his power into India itself. The most lasting reminder of his appearance in the east was the development of Gandharan art, that strange mixture of Grecian artistic ideals with the new religious beliefs of Buddhism.

The Rise of Religions

Two great religions had their birth on the sub-continent – Buddhism and Hinduism. The Hindu religion is one of the oldest in the world. Even the priest-dominated Indus Valley civilisation bears many similarities to Hinduism. The great Hindu books are all thought to refer to actual historical events. The Vedas, written around 1500 to 1200 BC, tell of the victory of Brahma over Indra, the god of thunder and battle. This probably refers to the revival of Brahmanism (the predecessor of Hinduism from which Hinduism evolved) following the Aryan invasions.

Hinduism has had a series of declines and revivals, most recently during the past century, but the greatest challenge it has faced came from India's other great

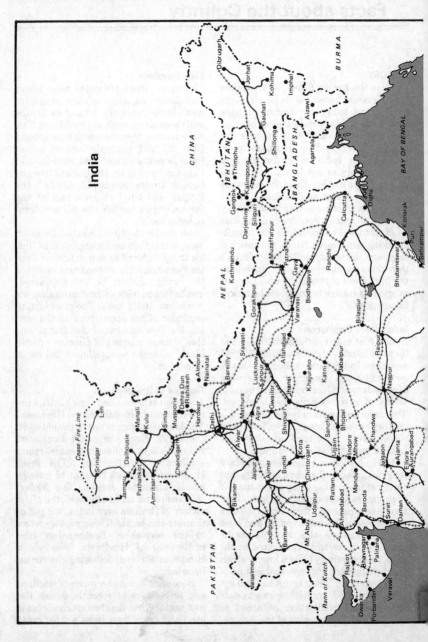

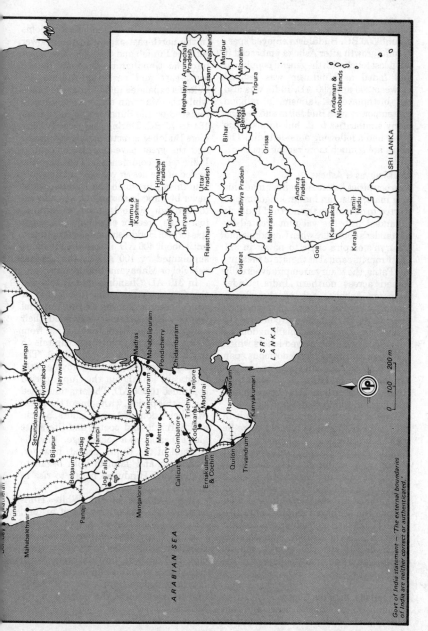

Govt of India statement — 'The external boundaries
of India are neither correct or authenticated.'

religion, Buddhism. First formulated around 500 BC, Buddhism enjoyed spectacular growth after Ashoka embraced it but it lost touch with the general population and faded as Hinduism was revived between 200 and 800 AD. India was also the birthplace of Jainism, a religion contemporary with Buddhism and bearing many similarities to it, but Jainism has never had a following outside India. The Sikhs are a much more recent creation.

The Mauryas & Ashoka

Two centuries before Alexander made his long march east, an Indian kingdom had started to develop in the north of India. It expanded into the vacuum created by Alexander's departure when Chandragupta Maurya's empire came to power in 321 BC. From its capital at the site of present-day Patna, the Mauryan empire eventually spread across northern India. Under Emperor Ashoka, one of the classic figures of Indian history, it reached its peak. In 262 BC Ashoka was converted to Buddhism. Throughout his kingdom he left pillars and rock-carved edicts which delineate to this day the enormous span of his empire. Ashokan edicts and pillars can be seen in Delhi, in Gujarat, in Orissa, at Sarnath in Uttar Pradesh and at Sanchi in Madhya Pradesh.

Ashoka also sent missions abroad; in Sri Lanka his name is revered since he sent his brother as a missionary to carry Buddhism to that land. The development of art and sculpture also flourished during his rule, and his standard, which topped many of his pillars, is now the seal of the modern state of India. Under Ashoka the Mauryan empire controlled more of India than probably any subsequent ruler prior to the British. Following his death in 232 BC the empire rapidly disintegrated and finally collapsed in 184 BC.

An Interlude, then the Guptas

A number of empires rose and fell following the collapse of the Mauryas.

The successors to Alexander's kingdoms in the north-east expanded their power into the Punjab and this later developed into the Gandharan kingdom. In the south-east and east the Andhras or Telugus expanded inland from the coast, while the Mauryan empire was directly replaced by the Sungas, who ruled from 184 to 70 BC. During this period many more Buddhist structures were completed and the great cave temples of central India were commenced. This was the period of the 'lesser vehicle' or Hinayana Buddhism, in which the Buddha could never be directly shown but was alluded to through symbols such as stupas, footprints, trees or elephants. Although this form of Buddhism probably continued until about 400 AD, it was already being supplanted by 100 AD by the 'greater vehicle' or Mahayana Buddhism.

In 319 AD Chandragupta II founded the Gupta empire, the first phase of which became known as the Imperial Guptas. His successors extended their power over northern India, first from Patna and later from other capitals in north India, such as Ayodhya. The Imperial Guptas gave way to the later Guptas in 455 AD but the Gupta period continued to 606 AD. The arts flourished during this period, with some of the finest work being done at Ajanta, Ellora, Sanchi and Sarnath, and poetry and literature also experienced a golden age. Towards the end of the Gupta period, however, Buddhism and Jainism both began to decline and Hinduism began to rise in popularity once more.

The invasions of the White Huns signalled the end of this era of history, although at first they were repelled by the Guptas. They had earlier driven the Gandharas from the north-east region, close to Peshawar, into Kashmir. North India broke up into a number of separate Hindu kingdoms and was not really unified again until the coming of the Muslims.

Meanwhile in the South

A continuing theme of Indian history has been that events in one part of the country do not necessarily affect those in another. The kingdoms that rose and fell in the north of the country generally had no influence or connection with those in the south. While Buddhism, and to a lesser extent Jainism, was displacing Hinduism in the centre and north of India, Hinduism continued to flourish in the south.

The south's prosperity was based upon its long-established trading links with other civilisations. The Egyptians and later the Romans both traded by sea with the south of India and, later still, strong links were formed with South-East Asia. For a time Buddhism and later Hinduism flourished in the Indonesian islands and the people of the region looked towards India as their cultural mentor. The *Ramayana*, that most famous of Hindu epics, is today told and retold in various forms in many South-East Asian countries. Outside influences also came to the south of India. In 52 AD St Thomas the Apostle is said to have arrived in Kerala and to this day there is a strong Christian influence in this region.

Great empires that rose in the south included the Cholas, Pandyas, Cheras, Chalukyas and Pallavas. The Chalukyas ruled mainly over the Deccan region of central India, although at times their power extended further north. With a capital at Badami in Karnataka, they ruled from 550 to 753 AD before falling to the Rashtrakutas – only to rise again in 972 and continue their rule through to 1190. Further south, the Pallavas pioneered Dravidian architecture with its exuberant, almost baroque style. They also carried Indian culture to Java in Indonesia, to Thailand and to Cambodia.

In 850 AD the Cholas rose to power and gradually superseded the Pallavas. They too were great builders, as their temple at Tanjore indicates. They also carried their power overseas with raids into Ceylon and a long-running war with the Sumatran-based Srivijaya empire. At times they actually controlled part of Sumatra and the Malay peninsula.

The First Muslim Invasions

While the Hindu kingdoms ruled in the south and Buddhism was rising and falling in the north, Muslim power was creeping towards India from the Middle East. In 622 AD Mohammed fled from Mecca and in 630 AD marched back in to start Islam's period of rapid expansion. Less than a century later there were raids to the Sind and even to Gujarat by Arabs carrying, as Mohammed had recommended, the Koran and the sword.

Muslim power first made itself strongly felt on the sub-continent with the raids of Mahmud of Ghazni. Today Ghazni is just a grubby little town between Kabul and Kandahar in Afghanistan, but from 1001 Mahmud conducted raids on a virtually annual basis. His army would descend upon India destroying infidel temples and carrying off everything of value that could be moved. In 1033, after his death, one of his successors actually took Varanasi; but in 1038 the Seljuk Turks, also expanding eastwards, took Ghazni and the raids into India soon ceased.

These early visits were no more than banditry and it was not until 1192 that Muslim power arrived on a permanent basis. In that year Mohammed of Ghori, who had been expanding his powers across the Punjab, broke into India and took Ajmer. The following year his general Qutb-ud-din took Varanasi and then Delhi and, after Mohammed of Ghori was killed in 1206, he became the first of the Sultans of Delhi. Within 20 years they had brought the whole of the Ganges basin under their control, but the Sultans of Delhi were never consistent in their powers. With each new ruler the kingdom grew or shrank depending on his personal abilities.

In 1297 Ala-ud-din Khilji pushed the borders south into Gujarat and his general subsequently moved much further south, but did not maintain the extension. In 1338 Mohammed Tughlaq decided to move his capital south from Delhi to Daulatabad, near Aurangabad in Maharashtra, but having marched most of Delhi's population south eventually had to return north. Soon after, the Bahmani kingdom arose here and the Delhi Sultanate began to retreat north, only to be further weakened when Timur made a devastating raid from Samarkand into India in 1398. From then on the power of this Muslim kingdom steadily contracted, until it was supplanted by another Muslim kingdom, the mighty Moghuls.

Meanwhile in the South (again)

Once again events in the south of India took a different path than in the north. Just as the Aryan invasions never reached the south, so the Muslim invasions failed to permanently affect events there. Between 1000 and 1300 AD the Hoysala empire, with centres at Belur, Halebid and Somnathpur, was at its peak but fell to a predatory raid by Mohammed Tughlaq in 1328 and then to the combined opposition of other Hindu kingdoms.

Two other great kingdoms developed in the north of modern-day Karnataka – one Muslim and one Hindu. With its beautiful capital at Hampi, the Hindu kingdom of Vijayanagar was founded in 1336 and was probably the strongest Hindu kingdom in India, during the time the Muslim Sultans of Delhi were dominating the north of the country. Meanwhile the Bahmani Muslim kingdom also developed but in 1489 it split into five separate kingdoms at Berar, Ahmednagar, Bijapur, Golconda and Ahmedabad. In 1520 Vijayanagar took Bijapur, but in 1565 the kingdom's Muslim opponents combined to destroy Vijayanagar in the epic battle of Talikota. Later the Bahmani kingdoms were to fall to the Moghuls.

The Moghuls

Only Ashoka is as giant a figure in Indian history as the Moghul emperors. These larger-than-life individuals ushered in another Indian golden age and spread their control over India to an extent rivalled only by Ashoka and the British. Their rise to power was rapid but the decline was equally quick; there were only six great Moghuls. After Aurangzeb the rest were emperors in name only.

The Moghuls did more than simply rule, however; they had a passion for building which resulted in some of the great buildings in India – Shah Jahan's magnificent Taj Mahal ranks as one of the greatest buildings in the world. Art and literature also flourished under the Moghuls and the magnificence of their court stunned early European visitors.

The six great Moghuls were:

Babur	1527-1530
Humayun	1530-1556
Akbar	1556-1605
Jehangir	1605-1627
Shah Jahan	1627-1658
Aurangzeb	1658-1707

Babur, a descendant of both Timur and Genghis Khan, marched into the Punjab from his capital at Kabul in Afghanistan and defeated the Sultan of Delhi at Panipat. This initial success did not totally destroy opposition to the Moghuls, and in 1540 the Moghul empire came to an abrupt end when Sher Shah defeated Humayun, the second great Moghul. For 15 years Humayun lived in exile until he was able to return and regain his throne. By 1560 Akbar, his son and successor, who had come to the throne aged only 14, was able to claim effective and complete control of his empire.

Akbar was probably the greatest of the Moghuls, for he not only had the military ability required of a ruler in that time, he was also a man of culture and wisdom with a sense of fairness. He saw, as previous Muslim rulers had not, that the number of Hindus in India was too great to simply subjugate them. Instead he integrated them into his empire and made use of many Hindu advisers, generals and administrators. Akbar also had a deep interest in religions and spent many hours in discussion with religious experts of all persuasions, including Christians. He eventually formulated a religion which combined the best points of all those he had studied.

Jehangir followed Akbar but devoted much of his reign to expressing his love for Kashmir and eventually died while en route there. His tomb is at Lahore in Pakistan. Shah Jahan, however, stuck much more to Agra and Delhi and during his reign some of the most vivid and permanent reminders of the Moghuls' glory were constructed. Best known, of course, is the Taj Mahal, but that was only one of Shah Jahan's many magnificent buildings. Indeed some say that it was his passion for building that led to his downfall and that his son, Aurangzeb, deposed his father in part to put a halt to his architectural extravagances.

Aurangzeb was the last of the great Moghuls, and although he extended the empire's boundaries to their furthest he also ensured its downfall by failing to follow the ground rules Akbar had so successfully established. Akbar had combined his flair for magnificence and grandeur with a sense of fairness. He had kept his Hindu subjects 'on side' by including them in the governing process and respecting their beliefs.

In contrast, Aurangzeb was a penny pincher and a religious zealot. His belief in Islam was deep, austere and puritanical, with the result that he soon lost the trust and respect of his subjects and had to cope with revolts on all sides. In many parts of India stand mosques built by Aurangzeb on the foundations of temples destroyed due to his fanatical beliefs. With his death in 1707 the Moghul empire rapidly disintegrated. Although there were 'Moghul emperors' right up to the time of the mutiny, when the British exiled the last one and executed his sons,

they were emperors in name only. In sharp contrast to the magnificent tombs of his Moghul predecessors, Aurangzeb's tomb is a simple affair at Rauza, near Aurangabad.

The smaller states which followed on from the Moghul empire did in some cases continue for a while. In the south the viceroyalty in Hyderabad became one of the British-tolerated princely states and survived right through to independence. The Nawabs of Oudh in north India ruled eccentrically, flamboyantly and badly until 1854 when the British 'retired' the last Nawab. In Bengal the Moghuls unwisely clashed with the British far earlier and their rule was terminated by the Battle of Plassey in 1757.

The Marathas

Moghul power was not simply supplanted by another, greater power. It fell through a series of factors and to a number of other rulers. Not least of these were the Marathas. Throughout the Muslim period in the north of India there were still strong Hindu powers, most notably the Rajputs. Centred in Rajasthan, the Rajputs were a sort of warrior caste, a race of chivalrous princes whose place in Indian history is much like that of the gallant knights of England. The Rajputs opposed every foreign foot that tried to walk into India but were never united or organised in any fashion; when not battling foreign oppression they fought each other. During the Moghul era some of the best military men in the emperor's army were Rajputs.

The Marathas first rose to prominence with Shivaji, who took over his father's kingdom and between 1646 and 1680 performed feats of arms and heroism all over central India. Tales of his larger-than-life exploits are popular with wandering storytellers in small villages. He is a particular hero in Maharashtra, where many of his wildest exploits took place, but is also revered for two other things: As a lower-caste Sudra he showed that great leaders do not have to be Brahmins, and he demonstrated great abilities in confronting the Moghuls. At one time Shivaji was even captured by the Moghuls and taken back to Agra but, naturally, he managed to escape and continue his adventures.

Shivaji's son was captured, blinded and executed by Aurangzeb and his grandson was not made of the same sturdy stuff, but the Maratha empire continued under the Peshwas, hereditary government ministers who became the real rulers. They gradually took over more and more of the weakening Moghul empire's powers, first by supplying troops and then by actually taking control of Moghul land.

When Nadir Shah from Persia sacked Delhi in 1739, the declining Moghuls were even further weakened, but the expansion of Maratha power came to an abrupt halt in 1761 at Panipat. There, where Babur had won the battle that established the Moghul empire over 200 years earlier, the Marathas were defeated by Ahmad Shah Durani from Afghanistan. Their expansion to the west halted, they nevertheless consolidated their control over central India and their region known as Malwa. Soon, however, they were to fall to India's final great imperial power, the British.

Expansion of British Power

The British were not the first European power to arrive in India, nor were they the last to leave – both those honours go to the Portuguese. In 1498 Vasco da Gama arrived on the coast of modern-day Kerala, having sailed around the African Cape of Good Hope. Pioneering this route gave the Portuguese a century of uninterrupted monopoly over Indian trade with Europe. In 1510 they captured Goa, the Indian enclave they controlled right through to 1961, 14 years after the British had left.

In 1612 the British made their first permanent inroad into India when they established a trading post at Surat in Gujarat. In 1600 Queen Elizabeth I had granted a charter to a London trading company giving them a monopoly on British trade with India. For 250 years British power was exercised in India not by the government but by the East India Company which developed from this initial charter. British trading posts were established on the other coast at Madras in 1640, at Bombay in 1668 and at Calcutta in 1690. The British and Portuguese were not the only Europeans in India. The Dutch also had trading posts and in 1672 the French established themselves at Pondicherry, an enclave they, like the Portuguese in Goa, would hold even after the British had finally departed.

Naturally Anglo-French enmity spread to India, and in 1746 the French took Madras only to hand it back in 1749. In subsequent years there was to be much intrigue between the imperial powers. If the British were involved in a struggle with one local ruler they could be certain the French would be backing him with arms, men or expertise. In 1756 Suraj-ud-daula, the Nawab of Bengal, attacked Calcutta and outraged Britain with the 'black hole of Calcutta' incident. A year later Robert Clive retook Calcutta and in the Battle of Plassey defeated Suraj-ud-daula and his French supporters, thus not only extending British power but also curtailing French influence.

India at this time was in a state of flux due to the power vacuum created by the disintegration of the Moghul empire. The Marathas were the only real Indian power to step into this gap and they were more a group of local kingdoms who sometimes cooperated, sometimes did not, than a power in their own right. In the south, where Moghul influence had never been so great, the picture was confused by the strong British-French rivalries with one ruler consistently played off against another.

This was never clearer than in the series of Mysore Wars with that irritation to British power, Tipu Sultan. In the 4th Mysore War in 1789-99, Tipu was killed at Srirangapatnam and British power took another step forward, French influence another step back. The long-running British struggle with the Marathas was finally concluded in 1803, which left only the Punjab outside British control; that, too, came under British control in 1849 after the two Sikh Wars. Britain also took on the Nepalese, whom they defeated but did not annexe, and the Burmese, whom they did.

Rise & Fall of British India

By the early 19th century India was effectively under British control. In part this takeover had come about because of the vacuum left by the demise of the Moghuls, but the British also followed the rules Akbar had laid down so successfully. To them India was principally a place to make money, and the Indians' culture, beliefs and religions were left strictly alone. Indeed it was said the British didn't give a damn what religious beliefs a person held so long as he made a good cup of tea. Furthermore, the British had a disciplined, efficient army and astute political advisers. They followed the policy of divide and rule with great success and negotiated distinctly one-sided treaties giving them the right to intervene in local states if they were inefficiently run; 'inefficient' could be and was defined as the British saw fit.

Even under the British, India remained a patchwork of states, many of them nominally independent but actually under strong British influence. This policy of maintaining 'princely states' governed by Maharajas, Nawabs or whatever, continued right through to independence and was to cause a number of problems at that time. The British interest in trade and profit resulted in expansion of iron and coal mining; the development of tea, coffee and cotton growing; the construction of the basis of today's vast Indian railways network; the

commencement of irrigation projects which have today revolutionised agriculture; and other important and worthwhile developments.

In the sphere of government and law Britain gave India a well-developed and smoothly functioning government and civil service structure. The fearsome love of bureaucracy which India also inherited from Britain may be a down side of that, but overall the country reached independence with a better organised, more efficient and less corrupt administrative system than most ex-colonial countries.

Britain also made some much less helpful moves in India. Cheap textiles from the new manufacturing industry of Britain flooded into India, virtually crippling the local cottage industries. On one hand the British outlawed *sati*, the practise of adding the wife to a husband's funeral pyre, but on the other hand they encouraged the system of *zamindars*. These absentee landlords eased the burden of administrative and tax collection for the British but contributed to an impoverished and landless peasantry in parts of India – a problem which in Bihar and West Bengal is still chronic today. The British also instituted English as the local language of administration; in a country with so many different languages it still partially fulfils that function of nationwide communication today. Nevertheless many British kept themselves to some extent at 'arms length' from the Indians.

In 1857, less than a half century after Britain had taken firm control of India, they had their first serious setback. To this day the causes of the 'Indian Mutiny' are hard to unravel – it's even hard to define if it really was the 'War of Independence' by which it is referred to in India, or merely a mutiny. The causes were an administration which had been run down and other more specific cases. The dismissal of local rulers, inefficient and unpopular as they might have been, proved to be a flashpoint in certain areas but the main single cause was, believe it or not, bullets. A rumour, quite possibly true, leaked out that a new type of bullet issued to the troops, many of whom were Muslim, was greased with pig fat. A similar rumour developed that the bullets were actually greased with cow fat. Pigs, of course, are unclean to Muslims and cows are holy to Hindus.

The British were slow to deny these rumours and even slower to prove that either they were incorrect or that changes had been made. The result was a loosely coordinated mutiny of the Indian battalions of the Bengal Army. Of the 74 battalions, seven (one of them Gurkhas) remained loyal, 20 were disarmed and the other 47 mutinied. The mutiny first broke out at Meerut, close to Delhi, and soon spread across north India. There were massacres and acts of senseless cruelty on both sides, long sieges, decisive victories and protracted struggles, but in the end the mutiny died out rather than conclusively finished. It never spread beyond the north of India, and although there were brilliant self-made leaders on the Indian side, there was never any real coordination or common aim.

The British made two moves with the conclusion of the mutiny. First, they wisely decided not to look for scapegoats or to exact official revenge, although revenge and looting had certainly taken place on an unofficial level. Second, the East India Company was wound up and administration of the country was belatedly handed over to the British government. The remainder of the century was the peak period for the empire on which 'the sun never set' and in which India was one of its brightest stars. Two parallel developments during the latter part of the 19th century gradually paved the way for the independent India of today. First, the British slowly began to hand over power and bring more people into the decision-making processes. Democratic systems began to be implemented in India although the British government retained overall control. In the civil service higher and higher posts were opened up for Indians and not simply retained for colonial administrators.

At the same time Hinduism began to go through another wholesale resurgence and adjustment. The Hindu religion is one of the world's oldest religions but once before, when it shrank before the growth of Buddhism, it had failed to keep in touch with its mass support. Once again it was realised that Hinduism had lost touch with the masses and required a complete shake-up to turn it away from its role as a religion for the priests and high-caste Brahmins. Reformers like Ram Mohan Roy, Ramakrishna and Swami Vivekananda pushed through sweeping changes in Hindu society and paved the way for the Hindu beliefs of today, beliefs which have proved to have an enormous appeal to modern western society.

With the turn of the century, opposition to British rule began to take on a new light. The 'Congress' which had been established to give India a degree of self-rule now began to push for the real thing. Outside of the Congress more hot-blooded individuals pressed for independence by more violent means. Eventually the British mapped out a path towards independence similar to that pursued in Canada or Australia. However, WW I shelved these plans; and the events in Turkey, a Muslim country, alienated many Indian Muslims. After the war the struggle was on in earnest and its leader was Mahatma Gandhi.

Gandhi & Passive Resistance

In 1915 Mohandas Gandhi returned from South Africa, where he had practised as a lawyer and devoted himself to righting the wrongs the country's many Indian settlers had to face. In India he soon turned his abilities to the question of independence, particularly after the massacre at Amritsar in 1919 when a British army contingent opened fire on an unarmed crowd of protestors. Gandhi, who subsequently became known as Mahatma, the 'great soul', adopted a policy of passive resistance or *satyagraha* to British rule. His central achievement was to change the level of the independence struggle from the middle class to the village. He led movements against the iniquitous salt tax and boycotts of British textiles, and for his efforts made a number of visits to British prisons.

Others involved in the struggle did not follow Gandhi's policy of non-cooperation and non-violence, and at times the battle was bitter and bloody. Nevertheless the Congress Party and Mahatma Gandhi were in the forefront, although it was not until after WW II that a conclusion was finally reached. By then independence was inevitable, as the war had dealt a death blow to colonialism and the myth of European superiority. Britain no longer had the power or the desire to maintain a vast empire, but within India a major problem had developed. The large Muslim minority had realised that an independent India would also be a Hindu-dominated India, and that despite Gandhi's fair-minded and even-handed approach others in the Congress Party would not be so willing to share power.

Independence

With the close of WW II it was clear that the European colonial era was over and that independence for India would have to come soon, but how? Congress' refusal to deal with the Muslim League had rebounded on them with the Muslim demand for an independent Pakistan, to be carved out of India. The abrupt end of the war with the atomic bombing of Japan and the July 1945 Labour party victory in the British election made the search for a solution to the Indian problem imperative.

Elections within India revealed the obvious – the country was split on purely religious grounds with the Muslim League, led by Muhammad Ali Jinnah, speaking for the overwhelming majority of Muslims; and the Congress Party, led by Jawaharlal Nehru, commanding the Hindu population. Mahatma Gandhi remained the father figure for Congress but without an official role and, as events were to prove, his political influence was slipping.

'I will have India divided, or India destroyed', were Jinnah's words. This direct conflict with Congress' desire for an independent greater-India was the biggest stumbling block to the British grant of independence, but with each passing day the prospects for inter-communal strife and bloodshed increased. In early 1946 a British mission failed to bring the two sides together and the country slid increasingly towards civil war. A 'Direct Action Day', called by the Muslim League in August 1946, led to a slaughter of Hindus in Calcutta followed by reprisals against Muslims. Attempts to make the two sides see reason had no effect and in February 1947 the British government made a momentous decision. The current viceroy, Lord Wavell, would be replaced by Lord Louis Mountbatten and independence would come by June 1948.

Already the Punjab region of northern India was in a state of chaos and the Bengal region in the east was close to it. The new viceroy made a last-ditch attempt to convince the rival factions that a united India was a more sensible proposition, but they – Jinnah in particular – remained intransigent and the reluctant decision was made to divide the country. Only Gandhi stood firmly against the division, preferring the possibility of a civil war to the chaos he so rightly expected.

As in so many other parts of the world, neatly slicing the country in two proved to be an impossible task. Although some areas were clearly Hindu or Muslim, others had very evenly mixed populations, and still others remained isolated 'islands' of Muslims surrounded by Hindu regions no matter how the country was divided.

The complete impossibility of dividing all the Muslims from all the Hindus is illustrated by the fact that after partition India was still the third largest Muslim country in the world – only Indonesia and Pakistan had greater populations of Muslims. Even today India has a greater Muslim population than any of the Arab countries or Turkey or Iran.

Worse, the two overwhelmingly Muslim regions were on the exact opposite sides of the country – Pakistan would inevitably have an eastern and western half divided by a hostile India. The instability of this arrangement was self-evident, but it took 25 years before the predestined split came and East Pakistan became Bangladesh.

Other problems showed up only after the actual independence. Pakistan was painfully short of the administrators and clerical workers with which India is so well endowed; these were occupations simply not followed by many Muslims. Many other occupations, such as money lenders, were purely Hindu callings and the unfortunate untouchables did the dirty work not only for their higher-caste Hindu brothers but also for the Muslims.

Mountbatten decided to follow a break-neck pace to independence and announced that it would come on 14 August 1947. Historians have wondered ever since if much bloodshed might not have been averted if the impetuous and egotistical Mountbatten had not decided on such a hasty process.

Once the decision had been made to divide the country there were countless administrative decisions to be made, the most important being the actual location of the dividing line. Since a locally adjudicated dividing line was certain to bring recriminations from either side, an independent British referee was given the odious task of drawing the line, knowing that its effects would be disastrous for countless people. The most difficult decisions had to be made in Bengal and the Punjab. In the former, Calcutta, with its Hindu majority, port facilities and jute mills, was divided from East Bengal, with a Muslim majority and jute production as its major industry but without a single jute mill for its processing or a suitable port for its export.

The problem was far worse in the Punjab, where inter-communal antagonisms were already running at a fever pitch. Here one of the most fertile and affluent regions of the country had large percentages of Muslims (55%) and Hindus (30%) but also a substantial number of India's militant Sikhs. The Punjab contained all the ingredients for an epic disaster and with the announcement of the division line, only days after independence, the resulting bloodshed was even worse than expected. Huge exchanges of population took place as Muslims moved to Pakistan and Hindus to India, and in the Punjab the exchange was complete. The dividing line cut neatly between the Punjab's two major cities – Lahore and Amritsar. Prior to independence Lahore's population of 1.2 million included approximately 500,000 Hindus and 100,000 Sikhs. When the dust had finally settled Lahore had a Hindu and Sikh population of only a thousand.

For months the greatest exodus in human history took place east and west across the Punjab. Trainloads of Muslims, fleeing westward, would be held up and slaughtered by Hindu and Sikh mobs. Hindus and Sikhs fleeing to the east would suffer the same fate. The army force sent to maintain order proved totally inadequate and at times all too ready to join the partisan carnage. By the time the Punjab chaos had run its course, over 10 million people had changed sides and even the most conservative estimates calculate that a quarter of a million people had lost their lives. The figure may well have been over a half million. An additional million people changed sides in Bengal, predominantly Hindus since few Muslims migrated from West Bengal to East Pakistan.

Nor was the outright division of the

Punjab to be the only excuse for carnage. Throughout the British era India had retained many 'princely states', and incorporating these into independent India and Pakistan proved to be a considerable headache. Guarantees of a substantial measure of independence convinced most of them to opt for inclusion into the new countries, but at the time of independence there were still three holdouts.

One was Kashmir, predominantly Muslim but with a Hindu Maharaja. In October the Maharaja had still not opted for India or Pakistan and a ragtag Pathan army crossed the border from Pakistan, intent on racing to Srinagar and annexing Kashmir without provoking a real India-Pakistan conflict. Unfortunately for the Pakistanis the Pathans had been inspired to this little invasion by the promise of plunder, and they did so much plundering on the way that India had time to rush troops to Srinagar and prevent the town's capture. The indecisive Maharaja finally opted for India, a brief India-Pakistan war took place, the UN eventually stepped in and Kashmir has remained a central cause for disagreement between the two countries ever since. With its overwhelming Muslim majority and its geographic links to Pakistan, many people are inclined to support Pakistan's claims to the region. But Kashmir is Kashmir and India has consistently evaded a promised plebiscite. India and Pakistan are divided in this region by a demarcation line and to this day neither side agrees on an official border.

The final stages of independence had one last tragedy to be played out. On 30 January 1948 Gandhi, deeply disheartened by partition and the subsequent bloodshed, was assassinated by a Hindu fanatic.

Independent India

Since independence, India has made enormous strides but faced enormous problems. The mere fact that India has not, like so many 3rd world countries,

bowed to dictatorships, military rule or foreign invasion is a testament to the basic strength of the country's government and institutions. Economically it has made major steps forward in improving agricultural output and its industries have expanded to the stage where India is one of the world's top 10 industrial powers.

Jawaharlal Nehru, India's first prime minister, tried to follow a strict policy of non-alignment although India has maintained generally excellent relations with its former coloniser – a fact which has caused some little annoyance to the critics of imperialism. Despite this non-aligned policy India has moved towards the USSR – partially because of conflicts with China and partially because of US support for arch-enemy Pakistan. Since independence, Gandhi's belief in peaceful neutrality has on a number of occasions been thrown out of the window. Three times India has clashed with Pakistan (1948, 1965, 1971) over bitter disputes concerning Kashmir or Bangladesh. Border wars have been fought with China, and India still disputes the area of Aksai Chin in Ladakh which China seized in 1962.

These outside events have taken the attention from India's often serious internal problems. As in any 3rd world country, population growth holds the potential for ultimate disaster. India weathered the first energy crisis of the early '70s remarkably well and no better advertisement could be found for the green revolution, but whether this will continue to be enough is an open question.

Indira's India

Politically India's major problem since independence has been the personality cult that has developed with its leaders. There have only been three real prime ministers – Nehru, his daughter Indira Gandhi (no relation to the Mahatma) and her son Rajiv Gandhi. Having won election in 1966, Indira Gandhi faced serious opposition and unrest in 1975 which she countered by declaring a state of emergency, a situation which in many other countries might quickly have become a dictatorship.

During the 'Emergency' a mixed bag of good and bad policies were followed. Freed of much of the usual parliamentary constraints, Indira was able to control inflation remarkably well, boost the economy and decisively increase efficiency. On the negative side political opponents often found themselves behind bars, India's judicial system was turned into a puppet theatre, the press was fettered and there was more than a hint of personal aggrandizement, as in the disastrous Sanjay Gandhi 'people's car' plan. An equally disastrous programme of virtually forced sterilisations, also masterminded by her son Sanjay, caused much anger. Despite murmurings of discontent Indira decided that the people were behind her and in 1977 called a general election to give credence to her emergency powers. Sanjay had counselled against holding the election and his opinion proved to be a wise one, because Indira and her Congress Party were bundled out of power in favour of the hastily assembled Janata, Peoples' Party.

Janata, however, was a device with only one function, defeating Indira. Once it had won, it had no other cohesive function and its leader, Moraji Desai, seemed more interested in protecting cows, banning alcohol and getting his daily glass of urine than coming to grips with the country's problems. With inflation soaring, unrest rising and the economy stumbling, nobody was surprised when Janata fell apart in late 1979 and the 1980 election brought Indira back to power with a larger majority than ever.

India Today

Mrs Gandhi's political touch seemed to have faded as she grappled unsuccessfully with communal unrest in several areas, violent attacks on untouchables, numerous cases of police brutality and corruption, and the upheavals in the north-east and the Punjab. Then her son and political heir, the none-too-popular Sanjay, was killed in a light aircraft accident and in 1984 Mrs Gandhi was assassinated by her Sikh bodyguards. Her son Rajiv, an Indian Airlines pilot until his younger brother's death, had quickly become the next heir to the throne and he was soon swept into power with an overwhelming majority and enormous popular support.

The Nehru family has now supplied prime ministers to India for three generations and Rajiv Gandhi has brought new and pragmatic policies to the country. Foreign investment and modern technology have been encouraged, import restrictions have been eased and many new industries have been set up. The rise of the Indian middle class under Rajiv has been very noticeable – the number of cars in India has grown enormously in the last few years. Whether these new policies are necessarily in the best interests of India is, however, an open question. Furthermore, the unrest in the Punjab continues to burn and at the other end of the country the turmoil in neighbouring Sri Lanka causes further difficulties. Rajiv is unable to stop Tamil support for the Sri Lankan Tamils because he needs the support of the state government of Tamil Nadu, home for most of India's Tamils. Nor can he tell the Sri Lankan government how to clean up their mess when in the Punjab he has a similar mess of his own.

Despite all these problems, it's worth remembering that of all the people in the world who live in what we know as democratic societies, nearly 50% of them are Indians; as 1977 indicated, it's a democratic society with teeth. Furthermore, India, despite its population problems and vast poverty, manages to do something neither the USSR or China can manage: feed its own people without importing food. Unfortunately the food surplus isn't always where it should be (it stacks up in the Punjab while other areas go hungry) but those old tales of famine and starvation are, hopefully, a thing of the past – at least at the present population levels.

GOVERNMENT

India has a parliamentary system of government with, however, certain similarities to the US government. Basically there are two houses – a lower house known as the Lok Sabha (House of the People) and an upper house known as the Rajya Sabha (Council of States). The lower house has up to 500 members elected on a population basis while the upper has up to 250 members. As in the British House of Commons or the Australian House of Representatives, the lower house can be dissolved but the upper house, unlike Britain's or Australia's, cannot. There are also state governments with legislative assemblies known as Vidhan Sabha. The two national houses and the various state houses elect the Indian president but he or she is a figurehead while the prime minister wields the real power.

There is a strict division between the activities handled by the states and by the national government. The police force, education, agriculture and industry are reserved for the state governments. Certain other areas are jointly administered by the two levels of government. All adult Indians have the vote, and the constitution provides for special facilities and assistance for India's Harijans and for the tribal groups still found in various parts of the country.

POPULATION & PEOPLE

India had a population in 1981 of 687 million. Despite extensive birth control programmes it is still growing far too rapidly for comfort. In the last 20 years it has gone from 439 million at the 1961 census to 547 million at the 1971 census to the present figure. Despite India's many large cities the country is still overwhelmingly rural. It is estimated that only about 100 million of the total population live in cities or towns, but with increasing industrialisation the shift from village to city will continue to grow.

The Indian people are not a homogeneous group. It is quite easy to tell the difference visually between the shorter Bengalis of the east, the taller and lighter-skinned people of the centre and north, the Kashmiris with their distinctly central Asian appearance, the Tibetan people of Ladakh and the north of Himachal Pradesh, and the dark-skinned Tamils of the south. Despite these regional variations, the government has managed to successfully establish an 'Indian' ethos and nationalistic feeling.

Although India is overwhelmingly Hindu, there are large minorities of other religions. These include 76 million Muslims, making India one of the largest Muslim countries in the world, much larger than any of the Arab Middle East nations. Christians number about 19 million, Sikhs 13 million, Buddhists five million and Jains three million. About 7% of the population is classified as 'tribal'. They are found scattered throughout the country although there are concentrations of them in the north-east corner of the country as well as in Orissa and a number of other states.

Birth Control

India's attempts at birth control have been varied, but although there has been some success at slowing the rate of increase the picture is far from happy. Today many international experts feel that the solution to the population increase problem in the third world is not to slow the birth rate, which will then bring prosperity in its wake, but to establish a degree of prosperity which will then bring a desire for fewer children. So long as children are a source of security in old age and so long as male heirs are so avidly desired, it will be difficult to successfully bring population pressures under control.

In the early '70s India had a birth control blitz with slogans and posters appearing all over the country and the famous 'transistor radio in exchange for sterilisation' campaign. More sinister was the brief campaign of the emergency era when squads of sterilisers terrorised half the country and people were afraid to go out after dark. That over-kill campaign probably put the birth control programme in India back by years and it currently enjoys a very low priority in the government's platform, although wall paintings showing the happy two-child family are a familiar sight all over India.

Castes

The caste system is one of India's more confusing mysteries – how it came about, how it has managed to survive for so long, how much harm it causes, are all topics of discussion for visitors to India. Its origins are lost in the mists of history but basically it seems to have been developed at first by the Brahmins or priest class in order to make their own superior position more permanent. Later it was probably extended by the invading Aryans who felt themselves superior to the indigenous pre-Aryan Indians. Eventually the caste system became formalised into four distinct classes, each with rules of conduct and behaviour.

At the top of the heap is the Brahmin class, who are priests and the arbiters of what is right and wrong in matters of religion and caste. Beneath them come the Kshatriyas, who are soldiers and administrators. The Vaisyas are the artisan and commercial class, and finally the Sudras are the farmers and the peasant class. These four castes are said to have come from Brahma's mouth (Brahmins), arms (Kshatriyas), thighs (Vaisyas) and feet (Sudras). Beneath these four castes is a fifth group, the untouchables, who literally have no caste. They perform the most menial and degrading jobs. At one time, if a high-caste Hindu used the same temple as an untouchable, was touched by one, or even had an untouchable's shadow cast across him, he was polluted and had to go through a rigorous series of rituals to be cleansed.

Today the caste system has been much weakened but it still has considerable power, particularly amongst the less educated people. Gandhi put great effort into bringing the untouchables into society, including renaming them the 'Harijans' or 'children of god'. But an untouchable by any other name .... It must be remembered that being born into a certain caste does not limit you strictly to one occupation or position in life, just as being black in the USA does not mean you are poverty-stricken and live in Harlem. Many Brahmins are poor peasants, for example, and hundreds of years ago the great Maratha leader Shivaji was a Sudra. None of the later Marathas, who controlled much of India after the demise of the Moghuls, was a Brahmin. Nevertheless you can generalise that the better-off Indians will be higher caste and that the 'sweeper' you see desultorily cleaning the toilet in your hotel will be a Harijan. In fact when Indian Airlines appointed their first untouchable flight attendant it was front-page news in Indian newspapers.

How do you tell what caste a Hindu is? Well, apart from knowing that if his job is a menial one such as cleaning streets or in some way defiling such as working in leather he is a Harijan, there is not really any way you can tell. If you see a man with his shirt off and he has the sacred thread looped round one shoulder he is a Brahmin, but then Pharsis also wear a sacred thread. Of course if an Indian is a Sikh or a Muslim he will have no caste.

In many ways the caste system today also functions as an enormous unofficial trade union with strict rules to avoid demarcation disputes. Each caste can have many subdivisions so that the servant who polishes the brass cannot, due to his caste, also polish silver. Many of the old caste rules have been considerably relaxed, although less educated or more isolated Hindus may still be worried about pollution from having a lower-caste person prepare their food. Better-educated people probably are not too worried about shaking hands with a caste-less westerner though! Nor does the thought of going abroad, and thus losing caste completely, carry too much weight these days.

The caste system still produces enormous burdens for India, however. During the last few years there have been frequent and violent outbreaks of violence towards lower-caste Hindus. In isolated rural communities higher-caste Hindus have lynched Harijans whom they felt were getting 'uppity', and there are often latent tensions between the castes which can easily spill over into violence. In 1980 in one village a number of Harijans were killed after a riot broke out because a bridegroom didn't dismount from his wedding horse when passing a group of higher-caste men! In 1981 there was a whole series of violent riots in Ahmedabad in Gujarat due to the practice of reserving university places for Harijans, whether or not there were sufficient Harijan applicants for the places. Higher-caste Hindus who could not obtain university places despite having good qualifications prompted these outbreaks.

It's interesting to compare these problems with the situation in the US where, during the desegregation era, many blacks experienced great difficulties in being allowed into 'all-white' schools and restaurants. Similarly in the US today there is a degree of protest about the reservation of college positions for disadvantaged minorities. Going far back into western history, it's interesting that the medieval ideal of heaven was developed in part to keep the peasants in their place – behave yourself, work hard, put up with your lot and you'll go to heaven. Probably caste developed in a similar fashion – your life may be pretty miserable but

that's your caste, behave yourself and you may be born into a better one next time around.

ECONOMY

India is a predominantly agricultural country but it is also one of the world's major industrial powers with important iron and steel works and a growing manufacturing industry. Textiles are still the backbone of India's industrial exports, however. Recently major efforts have been made to launch Indian industry into modern 'high tech' areas, away from the traditional heavy engineering areas. Nevertheless a recent Japanese study indicated that India's policy of protection of local industry from imports rather than a conscious effort to promote exports, even when it meant importing foreign technology, has been far less successful than the opposite policy followed in countries like Japan or South Korea.

The central planning policies and mountains of red tape and paperwork to be surmounted have also held economic development back. It's interesting that China, which followed similar protectionist and isolationist policies under Mao, has made an abrupt about-turn, and India also seems to have become intent upon updating key industries, even if that necessitates importing modern technology.

Despite these industrial and manufacturing activities 70% of India's population is engaged in work on the land – much of it inefficient and unproductive. Small landholdings, poor methods and lack of investment all contribute to this record, although since independence the agricultural production levels have actually increased at a faster rate than the population. The green revolution in India, involving new strains and improved use of fertilisers, has resulted in a food surplus for several years now.

India also has nearly 200 million cattle which in the rural economy are vitally important – pulling the farmer's cart to market or ploughing the fields. Their religious protection probably first developed as a means of protecting them during droughts or famine when the cows might have been killed off and subsequently been hard to replace. There is also some dairy production but nobody would dream of eating a cow, of course. In the cities the cows are totally useless unless you can count scavenging cardboard as a benefit.

GEOGRAPHY

India has a total area of 3,287,782 square km. The north of the country is decisively bordered by the long sweep of the Himalaya, the highest mountains on earth. They run in a south-east to north-west direction, separating India from China. Bhutan in the east and Nepal in the centre actually lie along the Himalaya, as does Darjeeling, the northern part of Uttar Pradesh, Himachal Pradesh and Jammu & Kashmir.

The Himalaya are not a single mountain range but a series of ranges with beautiful valleys wedged between them. The Kulu Valley in Himachal Pradesh and the Vale of Kashmir in Jammu & Kashmir are both Himalayan valleys, as is the Kathmandu Valley in Nepal. Kanchenjunga (8598 metres) is the highest mountain in India although until Sikkim (and Kanchenjunga) were absorbed into India that honour went to Nanda Devi (7818 metres). Beyond the Himalaya stretches the high, dry and barren Tibetan plateau; in Ladakh a small part of this plateau actually lies within India's boundaries.

The final range of the Himalaya, the Siwalik Hills, ends abruptly in the great northern plains of India. In complete contrast to the soaring mountain peaks, the northern plain is oppressively flat and slopes so gradually that all the way from Delhi to the Bay of Bengal it drops only 200 metres. The mighty Ganges River, which has its source in the Himalaya, drains a large part of the northern plain

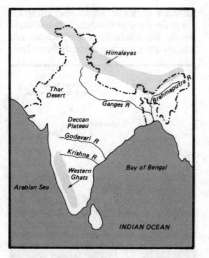

and is the major river of India. The Brahmaputra, flowing down from the north-east of the country, is the other major river of the north. In the north-west the Indus River starts out flowing through Ladakh in India but soon dives off into Pakistani territory and is the most important river of that nation.

South of the northern plains the land rises up into the high plateau known as the Deccan. The Deccan Plateau is bordered on both sides by ranges of hills which parallel the coast to the east and west. The Western Ghats are higher and have a wider coastal strip than the Eastern Ghats. The two ranges meet in the extreme south in the Nilgiri Hills. The southern hill stations are in these hills – Matheran and Mahabaleshwar near Bombay in the Western Ghats, Ooty in the extreme south in the Nilgiri Hills. The major rivers of the south are the Godavari and the Krishna. Both rise on the eastern slope of the Western Ghats and flow across the Deccan into the sea on the east coast.

The eastern boundary of India is also defined by ranges of hills, foothills of the Himalaya, which separate the country

from Burma. In this north-eastern region India bends right around Bangladesh, a low-lying country at the delta of the Ganges, and almost meets the sea to totally surround it.

On the western side India is separated from Pakistan by three distinct regions. In the north, in the disputed area of Kashmir, the Himalaya forms the boundary between the two countries. The Himalaya drops down to the plains of the Punjab, which then merge into the Great Indian Thar Desert. In the eastern part of Rajasthan this is an area of great natural beauty and extreme barrenness. Finally, the Indian state of Gujarat is separated from the Sind in Pakistan by the unusual marshland known as the Rann of Kutch. In the dry season the Rann dries out, leaving isolated salt islands on an expansive plain; in the wet season it floods over to become a vast inland sea.

CLIMATE

India is so vast that the climatic conditions in the far north have little relation to that of the extreme south. While the heat is building up to breaking point on the plains, the people of Ladakh will still be waiting for the snow to melt on the high passes. Basically India has a three-season year – the hot, the wet, the cool.

The Hot The heat starts to build up on the plains of India from around February, and by April or May it becomes unbearable. In central India temperatures of 45°C and above are commonplace. It's dry and dusty and everything is seen through a haze. From the air the country looks parched and barren but usually all you can see below is a blanket of hazy brown from all the dust in the atmosphere. Later in May the first signs of the monsoon are seen – short sharp rainstorms, violent electric storms, dust storms that turn day into night and cover everything with a film of dust. The heat towards the end of the hot season is like a hammer blow; you feel listless and tired and tempers are short. It's said to be the time of year when murders and suicides take place!

The hot season is the time to leave the plains, which are at their worst, and retreat to the hills. Kashmir comes into its own and all the Himalayan hill stations are at their best. The hill stations further south – Mt Abu in Rajasthan, Matheran in Maharashtra, Ooty in Tamil Nadu – are generally not high enough to be really cool but they are better than being down at sea level. By early June the snow on the passes into Ladakh should be all melted and the road will be open. You can also get into Keylong from Manali in Himachal Pradesh. This is the best trekking season in Kashmir and Ladakh.

The Wet When the monsoon finally arrives it's a great relief. As the chart indicates it doesn't simply arrive in one day. After a period of advance warning the rain comes in steadily, starting around 1 June in the extreme south and sweeping north to cover the whole country by early July. The monsoon doesn't really cool things off; at first you simply trade the hot, dry, dusty weather for hot, humid, muddy conditions. Even so it's a great relief, not least for farmers who now have the busiest time of year ahead of them as they prepare their fields for the rice planting. During the monsoon it doesn't simply rain solidly, all day, every day. It certainly rains every day but the water tends to come down in buckets for a while and then the sun comes out and it's quite pleasant.

Some places are at their best during the monsoon – like Rajasthan with its many palaces on lakes. While in Nepal the monsoon is a very bad time to trek, in the north-west Indian Himalayan regions this is a good trekking time. In Nepal the trekking season commences when the monsoon finishes but the regions of Himachal Pradesh, Kashmir and Ladakh in India are further north and the winter is too cold for trekking. Although the monsoon brings life to India it also brings

its share of death. Every year there are many destructive floods and thousands of people are made homeless. Rivers rise and sweep away road and railway lines

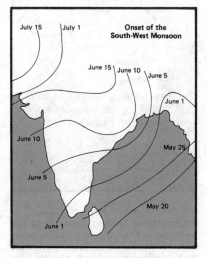

and many flight schedules are disrupted. Travel can definitely be more difficult during the monsoon.

The Cool Finally around October the monsoon ends, and this is probably the best time of year in India. Everything is still green and lush but you don't get rained on daily. The temperatures are delightful, not too hot and not too cool. The air is clear in the Himalaya, and the mountains are clearly visible, at least early in the day. As the cool rolls on it actually becomes cold at night in the north. Delhi and other northern cities become quite crisp at night in December and January.

In the far north it's more than just a little chilly, it's downright cold. The passes into Ladakh are once more snowed in and nobody wants to be staying on a houseboat on Dal Lake in Kashmir when the lake is frozen over. Snow does bring India's small skiing industry into its own, however, so Kashmir has a winter season too. In the far south, where it never really gets less than hot, the temperatures do become comfortably warm rather than hot. Then around February the temperatures start to climb again and before you know it you're back in the hot weather.

Some Regional Variations As in Sri Lanka the south-east coast is also affected by the north-east monsoon and brings rain from mid-October to the end of December. The usual monsoon is the south-west since it comes from that direction. It can get surprisingly wet during the north-east monsoon.

It's easy to forget just how cold it can get in the far north. Even along the Ganges you'll need a sweater or jacket at night and in Kashmir the snow will be up to your neck. Basically the best time to visit India is November through February, except for the northern Himalayan region where April through July is the best time.

RELIGION

India has a positive kaleidoscope of religions. There is probably more diversity of religions and sects in India than anywhere else on earth. Apart from having nearly all the world's great religions represented here, India was also the birthplace of two of the world's greatest (Hinduism and Buddhism), an important home to one of the world's oldest (Zoroastrianism), and home to an ancient religion unique to India (Jainism).

Hindus

India's major religion, Hinduism, is followed by approximately 80% of the population, over 500 million people. Only in Nepal and on the Indonesian island of Bali do Hindus also predominate, but it is the largest religion in Asia in terms of number of adherents. Despite its colourful, comic-book, almost Disneyland appearance it is actually one of the oldest extant religions with firm roots extending back to beyond 1000 BC.

The Indus Valley civilisation developed a religion which shows a close relationship to Hinduism in many ways; later it further developed through the combined religious practices of the southern Dravidians and the Aryan invaders who arrived in the north of India around 1500 BC. Around 1000 BC the Vedic scriptures were introduced and gave the first loose framework to the religion. Hinduism today has a number of holy books, including the *Bhagavad Gita* which is credited to Krishna, the *Mahabharata*, the *Ramayana* – the story of Rama, the *Vedas*, the *Upanishads* and the *Puranas*.

Basically the religion postulates that we will all go through a series of rebirths or reincarnations that eventually lead to *moksha*, the spiritual salvation which frees one from the cycle of rebirths. With each rebirth you can move closer to or further from eventual moksha; the deciding factor is your *karma*, which is literally a law of cause and effect. Bad actions during your life result in bad karma, which ends in a lower reincarnation. Conversely, if your deeds and actions have been good you will reincarnate on a higher level and be a step closer to eventual freedom from rebirth.

Dharma or the natural law defines the total social, ethical and spiritual harmony of your life. There are three categories of dharma, the first being the eternal harmony which involves the whole universe. The second category is the dharma that controls castes and the relations between castes. The third dharma is the moral code which an individual should follow.

The Hindu religion has three basic practices. They are *puja* or worship, the cremation of the dead, and the rules and regulations of the caste system. There are four main castes: the *Brahmin* or priest caste, the *Kshatriyas* or soldiers and governors, the *Vaisyas* or tradespeople and farmers, and the *Sudras* or menial workers and craftspeople. These basic castes are then sub-divided into a great number of lesser divisions. Beneath all the castes are the *Harijans* or untouchables, the lowest caste-less class for whom all the most menial and degrading tasks are reserved.

Westerners have trouble understanding Hinduism principally because of its vast pantheon of gods. In fact you can look upon all these different gods simply as pictorial representations of the many attributes of a god. The one omnipresent god usually has three physical representations. *Brahma* is the creator, *Vishnu* is the preserver and *Shiva* is the destroyer and reproducer. All three gods are usually shown with four arms, but Brahma has the added advantage of four heads to represent his all-seeing presence. The four *Vedas* are supposed to have emanated from his mouths.

Each god has an associated animal known as the 'vehicle' on which he or she rides, as well as a consort with certain attributes and abilities. Generally each god also holds a symbol; you can often pick out which god is represented by the vehicle or symbol. Brahma's consort is *Sarasvati*, the goddess of learning. She rides upon a white swan and holds the stringed musical instrument known as a *veena*.

Vishnu, the preserver, is usually shown in one of the physical forms in which he has visited earth. In all, Vishnu has paid nine visits and on his 10th he is expected as a *Kalki*, riding a horse. On earlier visits he appeared in animal form, as in his boar or man-lion *(Narsingh)* incarnations, but on visit seven he appeared as *Rama*, regarded as the personification of the ideal man and the hero of the *Ramayana*. Rama also managed to provide a number of secondary gods including his helpful ally *Hanuman*, the monkey god. Hanuman's faithful nature is illustrated by the representation of him often found guarding fort or palace entrances. Naturally incarnations can also have consorts and Rama's lady was *Sita*.

On visit eight Vishnu came as *Krishna*, who was brought up with peasants and thus became a great favourite of the working classes. Krishna is renowned for his exploits with the *gopis* or shepherdesses and his consorts are *Radha* the head of the gopis, *Rukmani* and *Satyabhama*. Krishna is often blue in colour and plays a flute. Vishnu's final recent incarnation was on visit nine, as the Buddha. This was probably a ploy to bring the Buddhist splinter group back into the Hindu fold.

When Vishnu appears as Vishnu, rather than one of his incarnations, he sits on a couch made from the coils of a serpent and in his hands he holds two symbols, the conch shell and the discus. Vishnu's vehicle is the half-man half-eagle known as the *Garuda*. The Garuda is a firm do-gooder and has a deep dislike of snakes – Indonesia's national airline is named after the Garuda. His consort is the beautiful *Lakshmi* (Laxmi) who came from the sea and is the goddess of wealth and prosperity.

Shiva's creative role is phallically symbolised by his representation as the frequently worshipped lingam. Shiva rides on the bull *Nandi* and his matted hair is said to have *Ganga*, the goddess of the river Ganges in it. He is supposed to live in the Himalaya and devote much time to smoking dope. He has the third eye in the middle of his forehead and carries a trident. Shiva is also known as *Nataraja*, the cosmic dancer whose dance shook the cosmos and created the world. Shiva's consort is *Parvati*, the beautiful. She, however, has a dark side when she appears as *Durga*, the terrible. In this role she holds weapons in her 10 hands and rides a tiger. As *Kali*, the fiercest of the gods, she demands sacrifices and wears a garland of skulls. Kali usually handles the destructive side of Shiva's personality.

Shiva and Parvati have two children. *Ganesh* is the elephant-headed god of prosperity and wisdom and is probably the most popular of all the gods. Ganesh obtained his elephant head due to his father's notorious temper. Coming back from a long trip, Shiva discovered Parvati in her room with a young man. Not pausing to think that their son might have grown up a little during his absence, Shiva lopped his head off! He was then forced by Parvati to bring his son back to life but could only do so by giving him the head of the first living thing he saw – which happened to be an elephant. Ganesh's vehicle is a rat! Shiva and Parvati's other son is *Kartikkaya*, the god of war.

A variety of lesser gods and goddesses also crowd the scene. Most temples are dedicated to one or other of the gods, but curiously there are very few Brahma temples – perhaps just two or three in all of India. Most Hindus profess to be either *Vaishnavites* (followers of Vishnu) or *Shaivites* (followers of Shiva). The cow is, of course, the holy animal of Hinduism. Hinduism is not a proselytising religion since you cannot be converted. You're either born a Hindu or you are not; you can never become one. Similarly, once you are a Hindu you cannot change your caste – you're born into it and are stuck with it for the rest of that lifetime. Nevertheless Hinduism has a great attraction to many westerners and India's 'export gurus' are many and successful.

A *guru* is not so much a teacher as a spiritual guide, somebody who by his example or simply by his presence indicates what path you should follow. In a spiritual search one always needs a guru. A *sadhu* is an individual on a spiritual search. They're an easily recognised group, usually wandering around half-naked, smeared in dust with their hair and beard matted. Sadhus following Shiva will sometimes carry his symbol, the trident. A sadhu is often someone who has decided that his business and family life have reached their natural conclusions and that it is time to throw everything aside and go out on a spiritual search. He may previously have been the village postman, or a businessman. Sadhus perform various feats of self-mortification and wander all over India, occasionally coming together in great pilgrimages and other religious gatherings. Many sadhus are, of course, simply beggars following a more sophisticated approach to gathering in the paise, but others are completely genuine in their search.

Entry Prohibited

One clear contrast to the general Indian mood of tolerance is the way westerners are not allowed into some Hindu temples. This chiefly applies to the temples in Orissa and Varanasi, and to some temples in the south, particularly in Kerala. It's in complete contrast to Jain and Buddhist temples or to Muslim mosques, where you are almost always allowed to wander at will. These regulations have been much relaxed over the years and there are today far fewer places where an outright ban applies. It's worth noting that it took Mahatma Gandhi to open many temples even to some Hindus. Untouchables were banned from entering temples earlier this century.

An irritation is that in many cases the national or state tourist boards expound at length about the glories of these temples, and never mention even in the smallest print that if you're a westerner you will not be allowed inside. The Orissa publicists are particularly guilty of this. In Tamil Nadu, where there are many wonderful temples, attitudes are fairly relaxed and you can explore all but the inner sanctum at almost any temple; if you're appropriately dressed and sufficiently respectful you may even be invited in there.

Buddhists

Although there are only about five million Buddhists in India, the religion is of great importance because it had its birth here and there are many reminders of its historic role. Strictly speaking Buddhism is not a religion, since it is not centred on a god, but is a system of philosophy and a code of morality. Buddhism was founded in northern India about 500 BC when Siddhartha Gautama, born a prince, achieved enlightenment. Gautama Buddha was not the first Buddha but the fourth, and is not expected to be the last 'enlightened one'. Buddhists believe that the achievement of enlightenment is the goal of every being so eventually we will all reach Buddhahood.

The Buddha never wrote down his *dharma* or teachings, and a schism later developed so that today there are two major Buddhist schools. The *Theravada, Hinayana*, 'doctrine of the elders' or 'small vehicle' holds that the path to *nirvana*, the eventual aim of all Buddhists, is an individual pursuit. In contrast, the *Mahayana* or 'large vehicle' school holds that the combined belief of its followers will eventually be great enough to encompass all mankind and bear it to salvation. To some the less austere and ascetic Mahayana school is a 'soft option'. Today it is chiefly practised in Vietnam, Japan and China, while the Hinayana school is followed in Sri Lanka, Burma and Thailand. There are other, sometimes more esoteric, divisions of Buddhism such as the *Hindu-Tantric* Buddhism of Tibet which you can see in Ladakh and other parts of north India.

The Buddha renounced his material life to search for enlightenment but, unlike other prophets, found that starvation did not lead to discovery. Therefore he developed his rule of the 'middle way', moderation in everything. The Buddha taught that all life is suffering but that suffering comes from our sensual desires and the illusion that they are important. By following the 'eight-fold path' these desires will be extinguished and a state of nirvana, where they are extinct and we are free from their delusions, will be reached. Following this process required going through a series of rebirths until the goal is eventually reached and no more rebirths into the world of suffering are necessary. The path that takes you through this cycle of births is *karma*, but this is not simply fate. Karma is a law of cause and effect; your actions in one life determine the role you will play and what you will have to go through in your next life.

In India Buddhism developed rapidly when it was embraced by the great emperor Ashoka. As his empire extended over much of India, so was Buddhism carried forth. He also sent out missions to other lands to preach the Buddha's word, and his own son is said to have carried Buddhism to Sri Lanka. Later, however, Buddhism began to contract in India because it had never really taken a hold on the great mass of people. As Hinduism revived Buddhism in India was gradually reabsorbed into the older religion.

Today Buddha, to Hindus, is another incarnation of Vishnu. At its peak, however, Buddhism was responsible for magnificent structures erected wherever it held sway. The earlier Theravada form of Buddhism did not believe in the representation of the Buddha in human form; his presence was always alluded to in Buddhist art or architecture through symbols such as the Bo tree under which he was sitting when he attained enlightenment, the elephant which his mother dreamed of before he was born, or the wheel of life. Today, however, even Theravada Buddhists produce Buddha images.

Muslims

Muslims, the followers of the Islamic religion, are India's largest religious minority. They number about 75 million in all, over 10% of the country's population. This makes India one of the largest Islamic nations in the world. India has had two Muslim presidents, several cabinet ministers and state chief ministers since independence. Islam is the most recent and most widespread of the Asian religions; it predominates from the Mediterranean across to India and is the major religion east of India in Bangladesh, Malaysia and Indonesia.

The religion's founder, the prophet Mohammed, was born in 570 AD in Mecca, now in Saudi Arabia. He had his first revelation from God, Allah, in 610 and this and later visions were compiled into the Muslim holy book, the *Koran*. As his purpose in life was revealed to him

Mohammed began to preach against the idolatry for which Mecca was then the centre. Muslims are strictly monotheistic and believe that to search for God through images is a sin. Muslim teachings correspond closely with the Old Testament of the Bible, and Moses and Jesus are both accepted as Muslim prophets although Jesus is not the son of God.

Eventually Mohammed's attacks on local business caused him and his followers to be run out of town in 622. They fled to Medina, the 'city of the prophet' and by 630 were strong enough to march back into Mecca and take over. Although Mohammed died in 632 most of Arabia had been converted to Islam within two decades. The Muslim faith was more than a religion; it called on its followers to spread the word – if necessary by the sword. In succeeding centuries Islam was to expand over three continents. The Arabs, who first propagated the faith, developed a reputation as being ruthless opponents but reasonable masters so people often found it advisable to surrender to them. In this way the Muslims swept aside the crumbling Byzantine empire, whose people felt no desire to support their distant Christian emperor.

Islam only travelled west for a hundred years before being pushed back at Poitiers, in France, in 732, but it continued east for centuries. It regenerated the Persian Empire, which was then declining from its protracted struggles with Byzantium, and in 711, the same year the Arabs landed in Spain, they sent dhows up the Indus River into India. This was more a casual raid than a full-scale invasion, but in the 12th century all of north India fell into Muslim hands. Eventually the Moghul empire controlled most of the sub-continent. From here it was spread by Indian traders on into South-East Asia.

At an early stage Islam suffered a fundamental split that remains to this day. The third Caliph, successor to Mohammed, was murdered and followed by Ali, the prophet's son-in-law, in 656. Ali was assassinated in 661 by the governor of Syria, who set himself up as Caliph in preference to the descendants of Ali. Most Muslims today are *Sunnites*, followers of the succession from the Caliph, while the others are *Shias* or *Shi'ites* who follow the descendants of Ali.

Strangely today Islam, which spread out from its initial foundation with such vigour, has become inertial and unchanging. Women in Islamic society may not exactly be second-class citizens, but they are certainly a second type of citizen. Despite its long period of control over India, Islam never managed to make great inroads into Hindu society and religion. Converts to Islam were principally made from the lowest castes, with the result that at partition Pakistan found itself with a shortage of the educated clerical workers and government officials with which India is so liberally endowed. Although it did not make great numbers of converts, the visible effects of Muslim influence in India are strong in architecture, art and food.

Converts to Islam have only to announce that 'There is no God but Allah and Mohammed is his prophet' and they become Muslims. Friday is the Muslim holy day and the main mosque in each town is known as the Jami Masjid or Friday Mosque. The eventual aim of every Muslim is to make the pilgrimage to Mecca and become a *haji*.

Sikhs

The Sikhs number 13 million and are chiefly found in the Punjab, although they are also all over India. They are the most visible of the Indian religious groups because of the five symbols introduced by Guru Gobind Singh so that Sikh men could easily recognise each other. They are known as the five *kakkars* and are: *kesha* or uncut hair; *kangha* or the wooden or ivory comb; *kachha* or shorts; *kara* or the steel bracelet; and *kirtipan* or

the sword. Because of their kesha Sikh men wear their hair tied up in a bun and hidden by a long turban. Wearing kachha (shorts) and carrying a kirtipan (sword) came about because of the Sikhs' military tradition – they didn't want to be tripping over a long *dhoti* or caught without a weapon. Normally the sword is simply represented by a tiny image set in the comb. The steel bracelet has the useful secondary function of making a good bottle opener. With his beard and turban and his upright, military bearing the 'noble' Sikh is hard to miss!

The Sikh religion was founded by Guru Nanak, who was born in 1469. It was originally intended to bring together the best of the Hindu and Islamic religions. Its basic tenets are similar to those of Hinduism with the important modification that the Sikhs are opposed to caste distinctions and pilgrimages to rivers. They are not, however, opposed to pilgrimages to holy sites. They worship at temples known as *gurdwaras*, baptise their children when they are old enough to understand the religion in a ceremony known as *pahul*, and cremate their dead. The holy book of the Sikhs is the *Granth Sahib* which contains the works of the 10 Sikh gurus together with Hindu and Muslim writings. The last guru died in 1708.

In the 16th century Guru Gobind Singh introduced military overtones into the religion in an attempt to halt the persecution the Sikhs were then suffering. From that time all Sikhs have borne the surname Singh or 'Lion'. Sikhs believe in one god and are opposed to idol worship. They practise tolerance and love of others and their belief in hospitality extends to offering shelter to anyone who comes to their gurdwaras. Because of their get-on-with-it attitude to life they are one of the better-off groups in Indian society. They have a well-known reputation for mechanical aptitude and specialise in handling machinery of every type, from auto-rickshaws to jumbo jets.

At present the Punjab region of India is torn by strife due to a minority of Sikhs demanding greater autonomy for the Punjab or even, at an extreme, an independent state to be called Khalistan. A solution to these problems is still not in sight and visits to the Punjab are restricted.

Jains

The Jain religion is contemporaneous with Buddhism and bears many similarities to it. It was founded around 500 BC by Mahavira, the 24th and last of the Jain prophets known as *Tirthankars* or 'finders of the path'. The Jains now number only about 3½ million and are found all over India but predominantly to the west and south-west. They believe that the universe is infinite and was not created by a deity. They also believe in reincarnation and eventual spiritual salvation or *moksha* through following the path of the Tirthankars. One factor in the search for salvation is *ahimsa* or reverence for all life and the avoidance of injury to all living things. Due to this belief Jains are strict vegetarians and some monks actually cover their mouths with a piece of cloth in order to avoid the risk of accidentally swallowing an insect.

The Jains are divided into two sects, the *Shvetambara* and the *Digambara*. The Digambaras are the more austere sect and their name literally means 'sky clad' since as a sign of their contempt for material possessions, they do not even wear clothes. Not surprisingly Digambaras are chiefly monks who confine their nudity to the monasteries! The famous Sravanabelagola shrine in Karnataka State in south India is a Digambara temple. Jain temples are noted for the large number of similar buildings which are often erected at one place. Their temples also often have many columns, no two of which are ever identical. The Jains tend to be clever and commercially successful and have an influence disproportionate to their actual numbers. Their temples are often extremely well kept. There are many Jains in Rajasthan, Gujarat and Bombay.

Parsis

This is one of the oldest religions on earth and was founded in Persia by the prophet Zarathustra in the 6th or 7th century BC. He was born in Mazar-i-Sharif in what is now Afghanistan. At one time Zoroastrianism stretched all the way from India to the Mediterranean but today is found only around Shiraz in Iran, Karachi in Pakistan and Bombay in India. The followers of Zoroastrianism are known as Parsis since they originally fled to India to escape persecution in Persia.

Zoroastrianism was one of the first religions to postulate an omnipotent and invisible god. Their scripture is the *Zend-Avesta*, which describes the continual conflict between the forces of good and evil. Their god is *Ahura Mazda*, the god of light who is symbolised by fire. Man ensures the victory of good over evil by following the principles of *humata* or good thoughts, *hukta* or good words and *huvarshta* or good deeds.

Parsis worship in fire temples and wear a *sadra* or sacred shirt and a *kasti* or sacred thread. Children first wear these sacred items in a ceremony known as *Navjote*. Flames burn eternally in their fire temples but fire is worshipped as a symbol of God, not for itself. Because Parsis believe in the purity of elements they will not cremate or bury their dead since it would pollute the fire, earth, air or water. Instead they leave the bodies in 'Towers of Silence' where they are soon cleaned off by vultures.

Although there are only about 85,000 Parsis, concentrated in Bombay, they are very successful in commerce and industry and have become notable philanthropists. Parsis have influence far greater than their numbers would indicate and often acted as a channel of communication between India and Pakistan when the two countries were at loggerheads. Because of the strict requirements that a Parsi must only marry another Parsi and children must have two Parsi parents to be Parsis, their numbers are gradually declining.

Christians & Jews

India also has around 18 million Christians. There have been Christian communities in Kerala as long as Christianity has been in Europe, for St Thomas the Apostle is supposed to have arrived here in 54 AD. The Portuguese, who unlike the English were as enthusiastic about spreading their brand of Christianity as making money from trade, left a large Christian community in Goa. Generally though, Christianity has not had great success in India, if success is counted in number of converts. Indians who have become Christians have generally been from the lowest castes.

There are, however, two small states (Mizoram and Nagaland) where Christians form a majority of the population. A quarter of the population of Kerala and a third of Goa are also Christian. There are small Jewish communities in a number of cities but the Jews of Cochin in Kerala are of interest because a group claims to have arrived here in 587 BC.

CULTURE
Painting, Sculpture & Architecture

Indian art and sculpture is basically religious in its themes and developments, and appreciation requires at least some knowledge of its religious background. The earliest Indian artefacts are found in the Indus Valley cities in modern-day Pakistan. Pieces are mainly small items of sculpture and it was not until the Mauryan period that India's first major artistic period flowered. This classical school of Buddhist art reached its peak during the reign of Ashoka. The superb sculpture of this period can be seen at its best at Sanchi. The Sungas, who followed the Mauryas, continued their artistic traditions.

When this empire ended the Gandharan period came into its own in the north-west. Close to Peshawar in today's Pakistan the Gandharan period combined Buddhism with a strong Greek influence from the descendants of Alexander the Great's invading army. During this period the Buddha began to be represented directly in human form rather than by symbols such as the footprint or the stupa. Meanwhile, in India proper another school began to develop at Mathura, between Agra and Delhi. Here the religious influence was also Buddhist but began to be altered by the revival of Brahmanism, the forerunner of Hinduism. It was in this school that the tradition of sculpturing *yakshinis*, those well-endowed heavenly damsels, began.

During the Gupta period from 320 to 600 AD Indian art went through a golden age, and the Buddha images developed their present-day form – even today in Buddhist countries the attitudes, clothing and hand positions have scarcely altered. This was, however, also the end of Buddhist art in India, for Hinduism began to reassert itself. At the same time as the Guptas were bringing Buddhist art to its final zenith in the north, a strongly Hindu tradition was developing in the south. Both schools of art produced metal cast sculptures by the lost wax method as well as larger sculptures in stone.

The following thousand years saw a slow but steady development through to the exuberant mediaeval period of Indian Hindu art. This development can be studied at the caves of Ajanta and Ellora, where there are some of the oldest wall paintings in India and the sculpture can be traced from the older, stiff and unmoving Buddhist sculptures through to the dynamic and dramatic Hindu figures.

These reached their culmination in the period when sculpture became an integral part of architecture and it is impossible to tell where building ends and sculpture begins. Some of the finest examples of this era can be seen in the Hoysala temples of Karnataka, the elaborate sun temple at Konarak and the Chandelas' temples at Khajuraho. In all of these the architecture competes valiantly with the artwork, which manages to combine high quality with quite awesome quantity. An interesting common element is the highly detailed erotic scenes. The heavenly maidens of an earlier period have blossomed into scenes, positions and possibilities that leave little to the imagination. Art of this period was not purely a representation of gods and goddesses. Every aspect of human life appeared in the sculptures and obviously in India sex was considered a fairly important aspect!

The arrival of the Muslims with their hatred of other religions and 'idols' caused enormous damage to India's artistic relics. The early invaders' art was chiefly confined to paintings, but with the Moghuls Indian art went through yet another golden period. Best known of the art forms they encouraged is the miniature painting. These delightfully detailed and brightly coloured paintings showed the events and activities of the Moghuls in their magnificent palaces. Other paintings included portraits, or studies of wildlife and plants.

At the same time there was a massive revival of folk art; some of these developments embraced the Moghul miniature concepts but combined them with Indian religious arts. The popular Rajasthan or Mewar schools often included scenes from Krishna's life and escapades – he's always blue. Interestingly, this school followed the Persian-influenced Moghul school in its miniaturised and highly detailed approach but made no use of the Persian developed sense of perspective, and works are generally almost two-dimensional.

In the north of India – at Jammu, Basohli and Kangra – the Pahari miniatures followed the Moghul school in having a definite sense of perspective, but in their often religious themes were closer to the Rajasthan school. The Basohli paintings are very dark and use much gold colouring, while the Pahari paintings are often pale and delicate.

The Moghuls' greatest achievements were, however, in the architectural field and it is chiefly for their magnificent buildings that they are remembered. After the Moghuls there has not been another major artistic period of purely Indian background. During the British period art became imitative of western trends and ideals. Although there is much British painting in India it is interesting chiefly as an historical record rather than as art itself.

Music

Indian music is in so many ways so unlike the concept of music in the west that it is very difficult for a westerner to appreciate it without a lengthy introduction and much time spent in listening. The two main forms of Indian music are the southern Carnatic and the northern Hindustani traditions. The basic difficulty is that harmony, so important to western music, has no place in Indian music. The music has two basic elements, the *tala* and the *raga*. Tala is the rhythm and is characterised by the number of beats. *Teental* is a tala of 16 beats. The audience follows the tala by clapping at the appropriate beat which on teental is at 1, 5 and 13. There is no clap at the beat of 9 since that is the *khali* or 'empty section' indicated by a wave of the hand.

Just as tala is the rhythm, so is raga the melody; and just as there are a number of basic talas so there are many set ragas. The classical Indian music groups consists of three players who provide the drone, the melody and the rhythm – in other words a background drone, a tala and a raga. The musicians are basically soloists – the concept of an orchestra of Indian musicians is impossible since there is not that harmony that a western orchestra provides – each musician selects his own tala and raga. The players then zoom off in their chosen directions, as dictated by the tala and the raga selected, and, to the audience's delight, meet every once in a while before again diverging.

Yehudi Menuhin, who has devoted much time and energy to understanding Indian music, suggests that it is much like Indian society: a group of individuals not working together but every once in a while meeting at some common point. Western music is analogous to western democratic societies, a group of individuals (the orchestra) who each surrender part of their freedom to the harmony of the whole. Although Indian classical music has one of the longest continuous histories of any musical form, the music has never, until quite recently, been recorded in any written notation. Furthermore, within the basic framework set by the tala and the raga the musicians improvise – providing variations on the basic melody and rhythm.

Best known of the Indian instruments are the *sitar* and the *tabla*. The sitar is the large stringed instrument popularised by Ravi Shankar in the west – and which more than a few westerners have discovered is more than just slightly difficult to tune. This is the instrument with which the soloist plays the raga. Other less popular stringed instruments are the *sarod* (which is plucked) or the *sarangi* (which is played with a bow). The *tabla*, a twin drum rather like a western bongo, provides the tala. The drone, which runs on two basic notes, is provided by the oboe-like *shehnai* or the *tampura*.

Dance

Indian dancing relates back to Shiva's role as Nataraj, the King of Dancers. Lord Shiva's first wife was Sati and when her father, who disliked Shiva, insulted him Sati committed suicide in a sacrifice by fire that later took her name. Outraged, Shiva killed his father-in-law and danced the *Tandava* – the Dance of Destruction. Later Sati reincarnated as Parvati, married Shiva again and danced the *Lasya*. Thus the Tandava became the

male form of dance, the Lasya the female form. Dancing was a part of the religious temple rituals and the dancers were known as *devadasis*. Their dances retold stories from the *Ramayana* or the *Mahabharata*.

Temple dancing is no longer practised but classical Indian dancing is still based on its religious background. Indian dance is divided into *nritta* – the rhythmic elements, *nritya* – the combination of rhythm with expression, and *natya* – the dramatic element. Nritya is usually expressed through eye, hand and facial movements and with nritta makes up the usual dance programmes. To appreciate natya, dance drama, you have to understand and appreciate Indian legends and mythology.

Dance is divided into four basic forms known as *Bharat Natya, Kathakali, Kathak* and *Manipuri*. Bharat Natya is further sub-divided into three other classical forms. One of the most popular, it originated in the great temples of the south and usually tells of events in Krishna's life. Bharat Natya dancers are always women and, like the sculptures they take their positions from, always dance bent-kneed, never standing upright, and use a huge repertoire of hand movements. *Orissi, Mohini Attam* and *Kuchipudi* are variations of Bharat Natya which take their names from the places where they originated.

Kathakali, the second major dance form, originated in Kerala and is exclusively danced by men. It tells of epic battles of gods and demons and is as dynamic and dramatic as Bharat Natya is austere and expressive. Kathakali dancing is noted for the elaborate make-up and painted masks which the dancers wear. Eyedrops even turn their eyes a bloodshot red!

Manipuri dances come, as the name indicates, from the Manipur region in the north-east. These are folk dances and the message is made through body and arm movements. The women dancers wear hooped skirts and conical caps which are extremely picturesque.

The final classical dance type is Kathak, which originated in the north and at first was very similar to the Bharat Natya school. Persian and Muslim influences later altered the dance from a temple ritual to a courtly entertainment. The dances are performed straight-legged and there are intricately choreographed foot movements to be followed. The ankle bells which dancers wear must be adeptly controlled and the costumes and themes are often similar to those in Moghul miniature paintings.

There are many opportunities to see classical Indian dancing while you are in India. The major hotels often put on performances to which outsiders as well as hotel guests are welcome.

FESTIVALS & HOLIDAYS

Due to its religious and regional variations India has a great number of holidays and festivals. Most of them follow the lunar calendar, which differs from the western calendar; thus they fall on a different date each year. Apart from the holidays and festivals celebrated nationally there are many local and regional occasions. PH – public holiday.

January

Sankranti/Pongal Celebrated predominantly in Andhra Pradesh and amongst the Tamil people of the south in Tamil Nadu, this is a harvest festival marking the change of season when the sun is supposed to move to its northern home and the days get longer, the nights shorter.

26 January

Republic Day Celebrates the anniversary of India's establishment as a republic in 1950; there are activities in all the state capitals but most spectacularly in New Delhi, where there is an enormously colourful military parade. (PH)

February-March

Shivaratri This day of fasting is dedicated to Lord Shiva. Processions to the temples are followed by the chanting of mantras and anointing of lingams.

Holi This is one of the most exuberant Hindu festivals, with people marking the end of winter by throwing coloured water or powder at one another – don't wear good clothes on this day! On the night before Holi bonfires are built to symbolise the destruction of the evil demon Holika. It's mainly a northern festival; in the south, where there is no real winter to end, it only takes place in Bangalore. (PH)

March-April

Mahavir Jayanti This major Jain festival marks the birth of Mahavira, the 24th and last Jain Tirthankar. (PH)

Ramanavami In temples all over India the birth of Rama, an incarnation of Vishnu, is celebrated on this day. (PH)

Good Friday This Christian holiday is also celebrated in India. (PH)

May-June

Buddha Purnima The Buddha's birth, enlightenment and reaching of nirvana are all celebrated on this day. The Buddha is supposed to have gone through each of these experiences on the same day but in different years. (PH)

June-July

Festival of the Cars Lord Jagannath's great temple chariot makes its stately journey from his temple in Puri, Orissa. Similar, but far less grandiose, festivals take place in other locations.

July-August

Naga Panchami This festival is dedicated to Ananta, the serpent upon whose coils Vishnu rested between universes. Offerings are made to snake images and snake charmers do a roaring trade. Snakes are supposed to have power over the monsoon rainfall and keep evil from homes.

Janai Purnima After a day-long fast, high-caste Hindus replace the sacred thread which they always wear looped over their left shoulder.

15 August

Independence Day The anniversary of India's independence from Britain in 1947. The prime minister delivers an address from the ramparts of Delhi's Red Fort. (PH)

August

Nariel Purnima A celebration of the official end of the monsoon, observed by sailors and fishermen.

Raksha Bandhan Girls fix amulets known as *rakhis* to their brothers' wrists to protect them in the coming year. The brothers give their sisters gifts.

Pateti Parsis celebrate their migration from Persia on this day but one sect of Parsis sets the date a month earlier. A week later *Khordad Sal* celebrates the birth of Zarathustra.

August-September

Janmastami The anniversary of Krishna's birth is celebrated with happy abandon – in tune with Krishna's own mischievous moods. Although it is a national holiday, Agra, Bombay and Mathura (his birthplace) are the main centres. (PH)

Ganesh Chaturthi This festival is dedicated to the popular elephant-headed god Ganesh. Pune, Madras and Bombay are important centres for its celebration. In Bombay images of the god are carried down into the sea.

Onam Harvest Festival During this Kerala festival the famous snake boat races are held.

September-October

Dussehra (Dassehra in the south) This is the most popular of all the Indian festivals and takes place over 10 days. It celebrates Rama's victory over the demon king Rawana and in many places culminates with the burning of huge images of Ravana and his accomplices in effigy. In Delhi it is known as Ram Lila and there are re-enactments of the *Ramayana* and fireworks. In Mysore and Ahmedabad there are great processions. In West Bengal the festival is known as Durga Puja since Durga aided Rama in his defeat of Ravana. In the north the festival takes place a little later and is a delightful event where the Kulu Valley shows why it is known as the 'Valley of the Gods'. (PH – two days)

2 October

Gandhi Jayanti A solemn celebration of Gandhi's birth-date with prayer meetings at the Raj Ghat in Delhi where he was cremated. (PH)

October-November

Diwali This is the happiest festival of the Hindu calendar and at night countless oil lamps are lit to show Rama the way home from his period of exile. Today the festival is also dedicated to Lakshmi (particularly in Bombay) and to Kali in Calcutta. In all, the festival lasts five days with day one the start of the new business year, day two dedicated to Krishna, day three to Shiva, day four to the friendly (but uppity) demon Bali whom Vishnu put in his place. On the fifth day men visit their sisters to have a tika put on their forehead. (PH)

November

Govardhana Puja A Hindu festival dedicated to that holiest of animals, the cow. (PH)

Pushkar Cattle Fair This incredibly colourful cattle fair in Rajasthan includes camel races amongst other events.

Nanak Jayanti The birthday of Guru Nanak, the founder of the Sikh religion, is celebrated with prayer readings and processions, particularly in Amritsar and Patna. (PH)

December

Feast of St Francis Xavier On 3 December this festival and the feast of Our Lady of the Immaculate Conception are two of the most important festivals in Goa.

25 December

Christmas Day A holiday in India. (PH)

Muslim festivals vary widely in date from year to year, so it is not easy to list what month they will fall in.

Ramadan The most important Muslim festival is a 30-day dawn-to-dusk fast. In Muslim countries this can be a difficult time for travellers since restaurants are closed and tempers tend to run short. Fortunately, despite India's large Muslim minority, it causes few difficulties for visitors.

Id-ul-Fitr This day celebrates the end of Ramadan. (PH)

Id-ul-Zuhara A Muslim festival commemorating Abraham's attempt to sacrifice his son Ishmael, celebrated with prayers and feasts. (PH)

Muharram A 10-day festival commemorating the martyrdom of Mohammed's grandson, Imam Hussain. (PH)

Festival Calendar

Festival	Place	1987	1988	1989
Pongal	Tamil Nadu	15-16 Jan	15-16 Jan	15-16 Jan
Basant Panchami		3 Feb	23 Feb	10 Feb
Republic Day	New Delhi	26 Jan	26 Jan	26 Jan
Shivaratri		26 Feb	16 Feb	6 Mar
Holi		15 Mar	3 Mar	22 Mar
Ramanavami		7 Apr	26 Mar	14 Apr
Buddha's Birthday		13 May	1 May	19 May
Festival of Cars	Orissa	28 June	15 July	5 July
Janmastami		16 Aug	3 Sept	24 Aug
Teej	Rajasthan	27 Aug	14 Sept	3 Sept
Bijya Dasami		2 Oct	20 Oct	10 Oct
Diwali		22 Oct	9 Nov	29 Oct

Months of the Year

		Hindi	English
Spring	Vasanta	Chaitra	March-April
		Baisakh	April-May
Hot Season	Grishma	Jeth	May-June
		Asarh	June-July
Rains	Varsha	Shrawan	July-August
		Bhadon	August-September
Autumn	Sharada	Asvin	September-October
		Kartik	October-November
Winter	Hemanta	Aghan	November-December
		Pous	December-January
Cold Season	Shishira	Magh	January-February
		Phalgun	February-March

WILDLIFE IN INDIA

The following description of India's flora and fauna and its national parks and wildlife sanctuaries was written by Murray D Bruce and Constance S Leap Bruce.

The concept of forest and wildlife conservation is not new to India. Here, since time immemorial, wildlife has enjoyed a privileged position of protection through religious ideals and sentiment. Early Indian literature, including the Hindu epics, the Buddhist Jatakas, the Panchatantra and the Jain strictures, teach non-violence and respect for even lowly animal forms. Many of the gods are associated with certain animals: Brahma with the deer, Vishnu the lion; and Ganesh, the eternal symbol of wisdom, is half man and half elephant. The earliest known conservation laws come from India in the 3rd century BC, when Emperor Ashoka wrote the Fifth Pillar Edict, forbidding the slaughter of certain wildlife and the burning of forests.

Unfortunately, during the recent turbulent history of India, much of this tradition has been lost. Extensive hunting by the British and Indian Rajas, the large-scale clearing of forests for agriculture, the availability of guns and strong pesticides and the ever-increasing population have had disastrous effects on India's environment. In the past few decades the government has taken serious steps toward environmental management and established over 100 parks, sanctuaries and reserves.

A visit to one or more of these wildlife refuges is a must on any traveller's itinerary. Protected areas have been established throughout India, and many, such as the Bharatpur Bird Sanctuary near Agra, are readily accessible. Parks such as Corbett and Manas offer the best opportunity to experience India's outstanding natural scenic beauty and, for abundance and visibility of a variety of wildlife, parks such as Kaziranga compare with the best in East Africa.

Many of the wildlife sanctuaries, and some national parks, are established in the former private hunting reserves of the British and Indian aristocracy. Often the parks offer a speciality, such as the Asian lion in Gir, Indian rhinoceros in Kaziranga, elephant in Periyar, and tiger in Kanha and Corbett; other areas are established to preserve unique habitats such as lowland tropical rainforest or the mangrove forest of the Sunderbans.

Some parks offer modern-style guest houses with electricity, while in others only Dak-style bungalows are available. Facilities usually include van and jeep rides, and at some you can take an elephant ride or boat trip to approach wildlife more discreetly. In addition, watchtowers and hides are often available and provide good opportunities to observe and photograph wildlife at close range.

National parks and other protected areas in India are administered at the state level and are often promoted as part of each state's tourist attractions. To encourage more visitors, road systems, transport, accommodation and other facilities continue to be developed and upgraded. Whenever possible, book in advance for transport and accommodation through the local tourist offices or state departments, and check if a permit is required, particularly in border areas. Various fees are charged for your visit (entrance, photography, etc) and these are usually included with advance arrangements. Meals may also be arranged when you book, but in some cases you must take in your food and have it prepared for you.

The diversity of India's climate and topography, varying from arid desert and tropical rainforest to some of the world's highest mountains, is reflected in its rich flora and fauna, with many species found only in India. Among more than 500 species of mammals, the tiger, elephant and rhinoceros still exist in India and many conservation projects have been established to preserve them. For some species the protection came too late; the Indian cheetah was last recorded in 1948.

A variety of deer and antelope species can be seen, but these are now virtually confined to the protected areas, most recently as a result of competition with domestic animals and the effects of their diseases. They include the graceful Indian gazelle (chinkara); the Indian antelope (blackbuck); the diminutive four-horned antelope (chowsingha); the large and ungainly-looking blue bull (nilgai), capable of great speed; the rare swamp deer (barasingha); the sambar, India's largest deer; the beautiful spotted deer (chital), usually seen in herds; the larger barking deer (muntjac); and the tiny mouse deer (chevrotain).

Also seen are the wild buffalo; massive Indian bison (gaur); shaggy sloth bear; striped hyena; wild pig; jackal; Indian fox; wolf, although much more local in range now; and Indian wild dog (dhole), resembling a giant fox but found in packs in forests. Amongst the smaller mammals are the mongooses, renowned as snake killers, and giant squirrels.

Cats include leopard, or panther; the short-tailed jungle cat; and the beautiful leopard cat. Various monkeys can be seen, with the rhesus macaque, bonnet macaque (south only), and long-tailed Common Languras the most likely.

With over 2000 species and varieties of birds, few countries outside of tropical America can compete with India. The diverse birdlife of the forests includes large hornbills, serpent eagles and fishing owls, as well as the elegant national bird, the peacock. Waterbirds, such as herons, ibises, storks, cranes, pelicans and others, are seen not only in parks but at numerous special waterbird sanctuaries. These sanctuaries contain large breeding colonies, and are also of great importance for the countless numbers of migrating birds which visit India annually.

Among the other wildlife are over 500 species of reptiles and amphibians, including the infamous cobra, other large snakes such as pythons, crocodiles, large freshwater tortoises and monitor lizards (goannas). Then there are the 30,000 insect species, including large and colourful butterflies.

The vegetation types, from dry desert scrub to alpine meadow, comprise some 15,000 species of plant recorded to date.

Geographically, India is divided into three main regions, each with many sub-regions, with distinctive altitudinal climatic variations. From these regions, 24 national parks, wildlife sanctuaries and reserves are listed below.

Northern India

This is a region of extremes ranging from the snow-bound peaks and deep valleys of the Himalaya to flat plains and tropical lowlands.

Dachigam Wildlife Sanctuary (Kashmir) A very scenic valley with a large meandering river. The surrounding mountainsides contain the rare Kashmir stag (hangul), also black and brown bears. A trek to the upper reaches, where you can camp, offers spectacular vistas. There you may also see the musk deer, a small species widely hunted for the male's musk gland, considered valuable in treating impotence and a major export to Europe's perfumeries. The sanctuary is 22 km by road from Srinagar and certainly worth a visit. Best time: June – July.

Flower Valley National Park (Uttar Pradesh) This 'garden on top of the world' is in the north of Uttar Pradesh near Badrinath, at an elevation of 3500 metres. The famous Valley of Flowers is now a national park and, when in bloom, an unforgettable experience. Best time: June – July.

The Gangetic Plain

Some of the most famous parks in Asia are located in this region. It contains the flat, alluvial plains of the Indus, Ganges and Brahmaputra rivers – an immense tract of level land stretching from sea to sea and separating the Himalayan region from the southern peninsula proper. Climate varies greatly, from the arid, sandy deserts of Rajasthan and Gujarat, with temperatures up to 50°C, to the cool highlands of Assam, where rainfall can exceed 15 *metres*, perhaps the wettest place on earth.

Corbett National Park (Uttar Pradesh) The most famous park for the tiger, now rare throughout India, but saved from extinction by India's successful Project Tiger. Other wildlife includes chital and hog deer, also elephant, leopard, sloth bear and muntjac. There are numerous watchtowers, but only daylight photography is allowed. The park has magnificent scenery, from sal forest (giant, teak-like hardwood trees) to extensive river plains. The Ramganga River offers tranquil settings and good fishing. A bit touristy, but worth a visit. Best time: November – May.

Hazaribagh Wildlife Sanctuary (Bihar) An area of rolling, forested hills with large herds of deer, notably sambar; also nilgai and chital, as well as tiger and leopard. Best time: February – March.

Palamau Game Preserve (Bihar) Smaller than Hazaribagh, but with good concentrations of wildlife, including tiger, leopard, elephant, gaur, sambar, chital, nilgai, and muntjac; also rhesus macaque, common langur and (rarely) wolf. It is 150 km south of Ranchi, with bungalows at Betla. Best time: February – March.

Sunderbans Tiger Reserve (West Bengal) These extensive mangrove forests of the Ganges Delta are an important haven for tiger. The reserve is south-east of Calcutta, bordering

Bangladesh. The area protects the largest area of mangroves in India and offers an exceptional chance to see tiger and other wildlife, such as the fishing cat, looking for fish at the water's edge. The only access is by chartered boat (Sunderbans Launch Association, Calcutta). Best time: February – March.

Jaldapara Wildlife Sanctuary (West Bengal) The tropical forests extending from South-East Asia end around here, and if you don't go further east, this is your chance to see the Indian rhinoceros, elephant and other wildlife. The area protects 100 square km of lush forest and grasslands, cut by the wide Torsa River. It is 224 km from Darjeeling, via Siliguri and Jalpaiguri (nearest railhead, Hashimara). There is a rest house at Jaldapara. Best time: March – May.

Manas Wildlife Sanctuary (Assam) This lovely area is formed from the watershed of the Manas, Hakua and Beki rivers and borders with Bhutan. The bungalows at Mothanguri, on the banks of the Manas, offer views of jungle-clad hills. Established trails enter nearby forests and follow the riverbanks. Try to arrange a cruise around by boat. Besides tiger, the grassland is home to wild buffalo, elephant, sambar, swamp deer and other wildlife; the rare and beautiful golden langur may be seen on the Bhutan side of the Manas. Best time: January – March.

Kaziranga National Park (Assam) The most famous place to see the one-horned Indian rhinoceros, hunted almost to extinction for its prize as big game and for the Chinese apothecary trade. The park is dominated by tall (up to six metres) grasslands and swampy areas (jheels). Travelling is best done by elephant, which can be arranged at the park. The first sighting of a rhinoceros is always impressive and awesome, as they can reach a height of over two metres and weigh more than two tonnes. Despite the prehistoric appearance, rhinos are incredibly agile and fast. Spotting them in the tall grass may be difficult. Watch for egrets and other birds who use the rhino's armoured back as a perch, and also listen for the 'churring' sound of a large animal moving through the grass. Best viewing may be by the jheels, where they bathe. Best time: February – March.

Sariska Wildlife Sanctuary; Sawai Madhopur Wildlife Sanctuary (Rajasthan) Both areas provide good opportunities to see the wildlife of the Indian plains. Sariska is notable for night viewing and its nilgai herds. Sawai Madhopur (or Ranthambore) is smaller, which can make seeing animals easier, and has a lake with crocodiles. It is on the Delhi-Bombay railway line, and 160 km south of Jaipur by road. You can stay at the Sawai Madhopur railway retiring rooms. Best time: February – June (Sariska), November – May (Sawai Madhopur).

Keoladeo Ghana Bird Sanctuary (Rajasthan) The best-known and most touristy bird sanctuary (usually just called Bharatpur), this features large numbers of breeding waterbirds and thousands of migrating birds from Siberia and China, including herons, storks, cranes and geese. The network of crossroads and tracks through the sanctuary can increase opportunities to see the birds, deer and other wildlife. It is also on the Delhi – Bombay railway line. Best time: September – February.

Gir National Park (Gujarat) Famous for the last surviving Asian lions (under 200), Gir also supports a large variety of other wildlife, notably the chowsingha. This forested oasis in the desert contains Lake Kamaleshwar, complete with crocodiles. The lake and other watering holes are good places to spot animals. Best time: January – May.

Velavadar National Park (Gujarat) A new park, 65 km north of Bhavnagar, it protects the rich grasslands in the delta region on the west side of the Gulf of Cambay. The main attraction is a large concentration of the beautiful blackbuck. There is a park lodge available for visitors. Best time: October – June.

Little Rann of Kutch Wildlife Sanctuary (Gujarat) A new sanctuary designated for the protection of the desert region of north-west Gujarat, especially the outer rim and a narrow belt of adjacent land. A variety of desert life can be found here, notably the surviving herds of the Indian wild ass (khur); also wolf and caracal (a large, pale cat with tufted ears). Access can be arranged at Bhuj. Best time: October – June.

Shivpuri National Park (Madhya Pradesh) Picturesque, open forests surrounding a lake.

Good for photographing various deer, including chinkara, chowsingha and nilgai; also tiger and leopard. It is close to Gwalior. Best time: February – May.

Kanha National Park (Madhya Pradesh) One of India's most spectacular and exciting parks for both variety and numbers of wildlife and well worth a visit. Originally proposed to protect a unique type of swamp deer (barasingha), it is also important for tiger (about 60). There are large herds of chital, plus blackbuck, gaur, leopard and hyena. Best time: November – March.

Similipal Tiger Reserve (Orissa) A vast and beautiful area protecting India's largest region of sal forest, with magnificent scenery and a variety of wildlife, including tiger, elephant, leopard, sambar, chital, muntjac and chevrotain. Best time: November – June.

Southern India

Here is the Deccan Peninsula, which takes the form of a triangular plateau, ranging in altitude from 300 to 900 metres, intersected with rivers, scattered peaks and hill ranges, including the Western and Eastern Ghats. The Ghats form a natural barrier to the monsoons and have created areas of great humidity and rainfall as on the Malabar Coast, where lush lowland tropical rainforest still occurs, and drier regions on the mountains' leeward sides.

Krishnagiri Upavan National Park (Maharashtra) This park, formerly known as Borivilli, protects an important and scenic area close to Bombay and other attractions. Amongst the smaller types of wildlife to be seen is a variety of waterbirds. Best time: October – June.

Taroba National Park (Maharashtra) A large park featuring mixed teak forests and a lake, with night viewing available to see its large wildlife populations. These include tiger, leopard, gaur, nilgai, sambar and chital. It is 45 km from Chandrapur, south-west from Kanha National Park. You can arrange to stay in the park. Best time: March – May.

Periyar Wildlife Sanctuary (Kerala) A large and scenic park formed by the watershed of a reservoir developed around a large, man-made lake. It is famous for the large elephant population which can easily be seen as you travel by boat along the watercourses leading to the lake. Other wildlife to be seen from the boat are the gaur, Indian wild dog and nilgiri langur, as well as otters, large tortoises, and a rich birdlife, including flights of hornbills. Along the water's edge you may see the flashing, brilliant hues of several kinds of kingfisher, perhaps even a fishing owl. Best time: February – May.

Jawahar National Park This is a recent proposal to cover Bandipur National Park (Karnataka), Nagarhole National Park (Karnataka), Mudumulai Wildlife Sanctuary (Tamil Nadu), and Wynaad Wildlife Sanctuary (Kerala).

Situated at the junction of the Western Ghats, the Nilgiri Hills and the Deccan Plateau, the merging of these contiguous areas protects the largest elephant population in India, as well as one of the most extensive forested areas in the south. The mixed, diverse forests and their terrain also protect a large variety of other wildlife, including many rare species such as leopard, gaur, sambar, chital, muntjac, chevrotain, bonnet macaque and giant squirrels. The very rich birdlife includes many spectacular species such as hornbills, barbets, trogons, parakeets, racquet-tailed drongos and streamer-tailed Asian paradise flycatchers. The two most popular areas are Bandipur and Mudumulai. Not to be missed if you visit the south. Best time: January–June.

Murray D Bruce
Constance S Leap Bruce

Know Your Monkey

Rats apart, the monkey is the most commonly seen wild mammal in India. The common or sacred langur is probably seen most often. This is a large monkey of slender build with pale grey fur and black face, hands and feet. It is often seen in large troops in woods, ruins and even in towns (like Pushkar). Because of its association with the monkey-god, Hanuman, it is venerated by Hindus.

The rhesus macaque is the other common monkey of northern India. The stocky monkey has a pink face, short tail and grey-brown fur tending to reddish on the rump. Again it is found in woods and sometimes towns (as at the Durga Temple in Varanasi). The related bonnet macaque is similar with a longer tail and takes the place of the rhesus in southern India.

Another commonly seen animal is the striped palm squirrel – that cute little fellow with the white back stripes often seen scampering on and about trees.

Lloyd Jones, New Zealand

common langur

rhesus macaque

Tony's Notebook

Communications

Communication in India has special rules, not altogether unlike those in other places in Asia but totally unlike those that prevail in the west. Use any answer rather than a negative one, for example.

'Will the bus stop here?'

'Yes'. Which could equally mean 'No, but I'd hate to disappoint you by telling you so'. Or 'I've got no idea' or 'I simply can't raise the energy to think about that question'.

'Am I heading in the right direction for the Grand Hotel?'

'Yes'. Which might mean 'Good grief, you've come so far in the wrong direction already I'd hate to be the one to tell you'.

The solution is to always word questions so that a commitment must be made. Not 'Is this the way?' but 'Which is the way?'. But then you can fall for the any answer rather than no answer syndrome – 'Down that way and round the corner, then straight for a km' might mean 'I've got no idea at all'. Never ask directions just once.

More annoying than fouled-up communications are no communications at all. Many Indians (and away from the main tourist centres taxi or auto-rickshaw drivers are particularly prone to this) feel that communicating with a foreigner is completely impossible. Hop in an auto-rickshaw and ask for the 'Grand Hotel'. Complete incomprehension. Pronounce 'Grand Hotel' 20 different ways but, despite the fact that the Grand Hotel is the town's number-one landmark, it's not getting through. Eventually an English-speaking passer-by is found. 'Where do you want to go?', he asks. 'Grand Hotel' you tell him, 'Grand Hotel', he says to the auto-rickshaw driver and you're saved.

Even more annoying than that is the precognated communication. The driver knows better than you do what you want. The fact that you're saying airport quietly, loudly or even screaming it has no bearing on his conviction that you really want a hotel and if he can get you into the Hotel Super he'll get a commission!

Facts for the Visitor

VISAS

The Indian visa situaticn has been through major upheavals in the past few years as a result of the crisis in the Punjab. Today virtually everybody needs a visa to visit India, and if you intend to stay longer than 90 days you will also have to go through the paperwork and red tape involved in extending a visa.

Indian visas are available from Indian consular offices and usually cost around US$5 or equivalent. Make sure you know what the price is, though. We've had several complaints from people who sent in the visa fee requested on the form only to discover much later that the fee had been changed and their visa request was on hold until they sent the correct amount. For some reason UK citizens have to pay a much higher visa fee, and many British residents of Australia have been tripped up by this as there is no indication on the form that different fees apply. We've also had a couple of letters from people who when they enquired why their visa was taking so long to issue were told it could be rushed through for an additional fee! Corruption in high places!

Where you apply for a visa also seems to make a difference. Numerous travellers have written to complain that Athens is an absolutely terrible place to get an Indian visa but Ankara, capital of neighbouring Turkey, is no problem at all. In South-East Asia some people say Bangkok is fine, others say that it's chaotic but Chiang Mai in the north of Thailand is a breeze. In some countries (Malaysia and Nepal for example) the Indian consular office insisted that British passport holders supply a letter from the British consular office confirming that they really were British! This costs the unfortunate Brits another US$5 or so! All in all, extending the visa requirements has been the unpleasant time-consuming mess

any India-watcher could have predicted it would be.

If your stay in India is going to be more than 90 days, you have to extend your visa and should set aside at least a day for this little ordeal. If you leave the country and pop across the border to Nepal, for example, after 60 days when you return you will have 30 days left. You do not start the 90 days again. Make sure your visa is a multiple entry if you intend to depart and return. Some people unwittingly end up with single-entry visas which do not permit you to return to India. Also, some offices will not allow you to renew your visa until it is less than 14 days from expiry. The visa-renewal hassles are not due to reluctance to let people stay longer, but to the usual Indian red tape and bureaucracy.

If you stay beyond 90 days you are also supposed to get an income tax clearance before you leave. This is relatively simple in that you just have to show a handful of currency-exchange forms to indicate that you did spend your own money and weren't working while in India. Although it can involve a fair bit of form filling and rubber stamping, a number of travellers have said that it can be done in an hour or less. Even more have written to say that nobody asks for the form when you depart in any case!

Foreigners' Registration Offices

Visa renewals and also permits for Darjeeling are issued by the Foreigners' Registration Offices. The main offices include:

Bombay
    Special Branch II, Annexe 2, Office of the Commissioner of Police (Greater Bombay), Dadabhoy Naroji Rd (tel 268111)
Calcutta
    237 Acharya Jagdish Bose Rd (tel 443301)

New Delhi
  1st floor, Hans Bhavan, Tilak Bridge (tel 272790)
Madras
  13 Victoria Crescent Rd, Egmore (tel 88864)

Special Permits

Even with a visa you are not allowed everywhere in India. Certain places require special additional permits. These are covered in the appropriate sections in the main text, but briefly they are:

Darjeeling Permits can be obtained from consular offices abroad or from the main Foreigners' Registration Offices in Bombay, Calcutta, Delhi or Madras. They cannot be obtained while en route to Darjeeling from Calcutta or at the border if you are coming through Nepal from Kathmandu. The permits are generally valid for an initial stay of 15 days and are easy to obtain. The only exception from the permit system is if you fly to and from Bagdogra, the airport for Darjeeling.

Assam & Meghalaya You must have a permit for these remote north-east states and where you may go is restricted. The permits can be obtained at the offices in Calcutta.

Andaman & Nicobar Islands For these islands you need a permit from an embassy or consulate abroad or from the Ministry of Home Affairs in New Delhi. The application to these places must be made at least six weeks in advance although they recommend you allow 12 weeks. In Madras, however, you can get a permit in just three days and it appears you can now get a permit on arrival at Port Blair if you fly in.

Sikkim You must apply for a permit at least six weeks ahead at a diplomatic office abroad or the Ministry of Home Affairs in New Delhi. Your initial permit allows a stay of only four days but this is easily extended once in Sikkim. You are restricted as to where you may go in Sikkim.

Bhutan Officially this remote Himalayan region beside Sikkim is still an independent entity, although actually India has firm control over foreign policy and most other things in Bhutan. Applications to visit Bhutan must be made through the Director of Tourism, Ministry of Finance, Tachichho Dzong, Thimpu, Bhutan; or through the Bhutan Foreign Mission (tel 74075), Chandragupta Marg, New Delhi 110021, India; or through the Bhutanese mission in New York. Before applying you must have the relevant permits for the restricted areas of India you must pass through in order to get to Bhutan. And don't hold your breath – unless you have high-up Indian connections or a personal friend in the Bhutanese aristocracy, you needn't expect to get a permit. At present permits appear to be issued only to groups, and then generally only for tours costing over US$100 per day.

Other Visas

If you're heading to other places around India the visa stories are as follows:

Afghanistan There is an embassy in Delhi although it may be easier and cheaper to get a visa in Pakistan, but any visit to Afghanistan is likely to be a fly-in fly-out operation and completely restricted to Kabul.

Burma The embassy in New Delhi is fast and efficient – 24 hours, Rs 40 – but the usual 'seven days, no longer' rule applies. There is *no* Burmese consulate in Calcutta although there is one in Kathmandu.

Nepal The Nepalese embassy in New Delhi is on Barakhamba Rd, quite close to Connaught Place, not out at Chanak-yapuri like most other embassies. There is also a consulate in Calcutta. Visas take 24 hours and cost Rs 45. A seven-day visa is available on arrival in Nepal and can be extended, but doing so involves rather a lot of form filling and queueing – better to have a visa in advance if possible.

Sri Lanka Most western nationalities do not need a visa to visit Sri Lanka, but there are diplomatic offices in New Delhi, Bombay and Madras.

Thailand There are Thai embassies in New Delhi and Calcutta. The visa costs about US$10 and is issued in 24 hours. If you are flying in and flying out of Thailand within 15 days, a visa is not required but the 15 days cannot be extended.

Tax Clearance Certificates

If you stay in India for more than three months you need a 'tax clearance certificate' to leave the country. This supposedly guarantees that your time in India was financed by your own money, not by working in India or by selling things. A few years ago getting a tax clearance certificate was a major operation requiring all sorts of forms and lots of time. Today it seems to have become much simpler and more straightforward.

Basically all you have to do is find the local Income Tax Office (sometimes it's handled by the Foreigners' Registration Office) and turn up there with your passport, visa extension form, any other similar paperwork and a handful of bank exchange receipts (to show you really have been changing foreign currency into rupees). You fill in a form and wait for 'only 10 minutes' (say the best-case people) to 'only an hour' (say the worst). You're then given your tax clearance certificate and away you go. Except when you depart the country, nobody even asks for it (reports nearly everybody).

CUSTOMS

The usual bottle-of-whisky-and-200-cigarettes type of duty-free regulations apply in India. If you bring in more than US$1000 in cash and/or travellers' cheques you are supposed to fill in a currency declaration form. You're allowed to bring in all sorts of western technological wonders, but big ticket items are likely to be entered on a 'Tourist Baggage Re-Export' form to ensure you take them out with you when you go. If you wonder why your battered Instamatic has been singled

out to be honoured with a TBRE form perhaps it's because section 3 of customs regulation number 499/15/74 applies to you (our italics):

There is also likelihood of abuse by tourists holding Indian passports and *hippies*. In the case of such tourists therefore, even a camera or transistor radio should be entered on Tourist Baggage Re-Export form before allowing clearance.

MONEY

A$1	= Rs 7.5	Rs 1	= A$0.13
US$1	= Rs 12.5	Rs 1	= US$0.08
£1	= Rs 18.8	Rs 1	= £0.06

The rupee (Rs) is divided into 100 paise (p). There are coins of 5, 10, 20, 25 and 50 paise and notes of Rs 1, 2, 5, 10, 20, 50 and 100. Once upon a time the rupee was divided into 16 annas and you may still hear prices referred to in annas – particularly in markets. Eight annas is half a rupee or 50 paise, four annas is a quarter rupee or 25 paise.

Currency Exchange Forms

You are not allowed to bring Indian currency into the country or take it out of the country. You are allowed to bring in unlimited amounts of foreign currency or travellers' cheques but you are supposed to declare it all on arrival. All money is supposed to be changed at official banks or money changers, and you are supposed to be given a currency exchange form for each transaction. In actual practice you can surreptitiously bring rupees into the country with you – they can be bought at a useful discount price in places like Singapore or Bangkok. Indian rupees can be brought in fairly openly from Nepal and again you can get a slightly better rate there.

Banks will usually not give you a currency exchange form unless you specifically ask for one. It is worth getting them for several reasons. First of all, you will need one for any re-exchange when you depart India. Second, certain official purchases, such as airline tickets, must be paid for either with foreign currency or with rupees accompanied by sufficient exchange forms to account for the ticket price. This is actually a complete waste of time since some little note will be scrawled on the form to the effect that it was sighted when you bought a ticket from A to B. When you buy a ticket from B to C somebody else can quite easily scrawl a similar little note on another corner of the same form! The third reason for saving exchange forms is that if you stay in India longer than 90 days then you have to get an income tax clearance and this requires production of a handful of exchange forms to prove you've been changing money all along and not earning money locally.

Which Currency or TC?

In major cities you can change most foreign currencies or travellers' cheques –

Australian dollars, Deutschmarks, yen or whatever – but out of town it's best to stick to US dollars or pounds sterling. The pound still has a sentimental appeal in India. Thomas Cook and American Express are both popular travellers' cheques and have a number of branches in India. Due to problems of fraudulent use some banks, principally State Bank of India branches, will not accept American Express travellers' cheques. In some town you may find it impossible to cash them at all, so although most of the time they are OK it's probably wise to bring at least a few other travellers' cheques just in case and not to rely totally on American Express.

Many people make the mistake of bringing too many small-denomination cheques. Unless you are moving rapidly from country to country you only need a handful of small denominations for end-of-stay conversions. In between, change

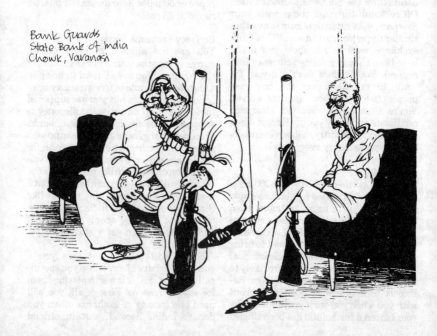

Bank Guards
State Bank of India
Chowk, Varanasi

as much as you feel happy carrying. This applies particularly in India where changing money can be such a time-consuming bore. Even in major cities it sometimes takes a long time. In smaller towns – and that means even quite large places if they have little tourist appeal – changing money can take forever. To change a single travellers' cheque can easily take several hours in some towns. You can also spend a lot of time finding which bank will change money. The answer is to change money as infrequently as possible and to change it only in big banks in big cities.

In some major cities there are now special foreign exchange counters which are more efficient and stay open longer hours. Big hotels also often offer exchange facilities but generally at a poorer rate than the banks.

Money Problems

In the major cities there is a black market for foreign currencies in cash. It seems to vary from city to city but recently it has been very strong in Calcutta. If you have no qualms about dealing with the black market, it's quite accessible, with a little caution it's quite safe, and it does make the money go further. It is, of course, illegal.

A particular catch with Indian currency and declaration forms may arise if you are buying an airline ticket out of India. You can often get tickets at very useful discounts but these sorts of large purchases must be made with a specific bank exchange form. If you are buying a ticket overseas which costs, say, Rs 8000 officially, an agent may be able to offer it to you at Rs 5000. But you must exchange officially Rs 8000 so you get the balance as a Rs 3000 refund from the agent. Since you cannot use your Rs 8000 document to reconvert it (the form specifies it was used to purchase an airline ticket) you're stuck. Two answers – either buy the ticket far enough ahead of your departure that you will use up the money, or else have plenty of

exchange forms saved up to permit you to re-exchange it on departure. Don't plan on showing up at the airport with forms showing you've exchanged US$100 three times over a period of weeks and now want to re-exchange US$299 worth of rupees, though!

Credit Cards

Credit cards are now widely accepted in India, particularly Diners Club. In fact Diners Club has become so widespread in India it's somewhat looked down upon. Credit card acceptability seems to vary with time – one week establishments don't want to know about one variety, the next it's another, depending on how fast the credit card company is paying their bills I guess.

With American Express you can use your card to obtain more funds locally from an Amex office. With their love of forms and carbon paper Indians delight in credit cards. You'll be delighted too when you get back, those bills eventually turn up and you find that the superb splash-out meal at the Ritz actually cost $8 or something equally ridiculous. Note that the warning above on airline tickets also applies to credit card purchases. You can buy an overseas ticket on your card and end up with several thousand rupees in your pocket too.

Cash Problems

When changing money, take two precautions in the rupees you are given. First, don't take it all in larger denominations. Breaking big notes down is always a problem in India and there is a permanent shortage of small change. So always break big notes (Rs 100 in particular) down as much as possible. Secondly, don't accept torn, damaged or dirty notes – when so many are just that it is hard not to, but disposing of a damaged note is always difficult. This particularly applies in small towns where money has to be in better condition than in the big cities to be acceptable.

Transferring Money

Finally, don't run out of money in India. Getting money transferred to India is often a time-consuming, boring, tricky and unpleasant operation. Even transferred by cable it can take weeks and weeks; and by mail it can take forever. Banks have a reputation for not telling people when money has arrived – better in their balance than your pocket, seems to be the mood.

If you must have money sent to you in India, specify the bank, the branch and the address you want it sent to; get it sent by telex or cable rather than by mail; and keep your fingers crossed. Preferably send it to a foreign bank, since they are much more efficient when it comes to overseas transactions than Indian banks. Overseas banks with branches in India include Bank of America, Chartered Bank and, particularly, Grindlays which has many branches in smaller cities as well as in the major cities where Amex also operate. Grindlays has recently been taken over by the Australian ANZ bank. With a European Cheque Card it's possible to cash British Lloyds Bank cheques. Thomas Cook has also been recommended as a good organisation to transfer money through; a New Zealander who was robbed got money transferred through Thomas Cook in less than 24 hours. Other time periods we have had quoted include Citibank – less than one week by cable from the US; State Bank of India – a month by cable; Bank of Baroda – don't even consider it. American Express won't transfer money.

Indian money has its own special angles and curiosities. For a start there is never any change. The restaurant may have been crowded all day but when you give them five rupees for a two-rupee drink they won't have any change. Actually the shortage of change is not quite as bad as they'd like to make out. Often they do have change but are trying to bluff you into parting with yours rather than vice versa. The solution is to always insist that you haven't got any change, then with luck when you meet up with someone who really doesn't have any you will.

Bus conductors never start trips with change. You pay for a Rs 6.60 fare with a Rs 10 note and your ticket is marked to indicate you're owed Rs 3.40. Don't lose it and don't forget to demand your change at the end of the trip.

Giving you change is also open to game playing. Change is never counted out as it is in the west; you're simply handed a handful. Very often if you stand there looking blank you'll be handed some more. Then some more. Post offices are particularly good at this. You ask for a couple of aerograms, a couple of stamps to America, one for a card to England. Total amount, who knows? Everybody behind you in the queue is jostling to get to the front. You can be certain that first handful of change isn't the total due. Wait. This isn't, so I have subsequently been told, necessarily a way of doing you, it's just the way change is given!

The quality of change is also important. Notes circulate far longer than they do in the west and the small notes in particular become very tatty. A note can have holes right through it and be quite acceptable but if it's torn at the top or bottom on the crease line then it's no good and you'll have trouble spending it. The answer to this is to simply accept it philosophically or think of clever uses. Use it for tips, or for official purposes. I'd love to pay the Rs 100 departure tax with 100 totally disreputable Rs 1 notes – although someone who did just that wrote to say he had some trouble getting them to accept it! Of course you could just take it to a bank, but who wants to visit Indian banks more than necessary?

COSTS

It is virtually impossible to say what travelling around India will cost you. It depends on where you stay, what you eat, how you travel and how fast you travel. Two people travelling at exactly the same standard can spend vastly different amounts on a daily basis if one travels twice as fast as the other. A week lying on the beach at Goa watching the waves roll in brings daily costs down very rapidly.

From top to bottom: If you stay in luxury hotels, fly everywhere, and see a lot of India in a very short trip, you can spend a lot of money. India has plenty of hotels at US$50 or more a day and some where a room can cost US$100 plus, more than many people make in a year. At the other extreme, if you scrimp and save, stay in dormitories or the cheapest hotels, always travel 2nd class on trains, and learn to exist on dhal and rice, you can see India on less than US$5 a day.

Most travellers will probably be looking for something between those extremes. If so, you'll stay in reasonable hotels with the sort of standard provided by the tourist bungalows in many states – a clean but straightforward room with fan cooling and an attached bathroom. You'll eat in regular restaurants but occasionally splash out on a fancy meal when you're in a big town. If you mix your travel, you'll try 2nd class sometimes for short trips, opt for 1st class if you're travelling on a long overnight trip. You'll take taxis occasionally rather than always look for a bus or rickshaw. In that case India could cost you something like US$10 to 20 a day on average. It totally depends on what you're looking for.

As everywhere in Asia, you get pretty much what you pay for, and many times it's worth paying a little more for the experience. That old-fashioned Raj-style luxury is part of India's charm and sometimes it's foolish not to lay out the money and enjoy it.

DOCUMENTS

You have to have a passport; it's the most basic travel document. In fact it appears you should have your passport with you all the time. We've had a recent letter from two Australians who spent four days in jail during the Pushkar cattle fair because they'd left their passports for safe-keeping in Jaipur. Two of the four days were after a friend had returned to Jaipur and collected the passports for them! Another traveller was comprehensively ripped off on a day trip to Gwalior, fortunately having left his passport in Agra. The police were more upset about the passport left behind than the theft! The fact that if he had had it with him he would now not have had it made no difference!

A health certificate, while not necessary in India, will probably be required for onward travel. Student cards are not the wonder-workers they once were – many student concessions have either been eliminated or replaced by 'youth fares' or similar age concessions. Nevertheless a student card still can have many uses, so if you can get one then do. Similarly, a Youth Hostel card is not generally required for India's many hostels but you do pay slightly less with one.

There is not much opportunity to get behind the wheel in India, but if you do intend to drive then get an International Driving Permit from your local national motoring organisation. These days motorcycles are becoming more readily available for hire, particularly in Goa, and an International Permit is useful if you rent one. An International Permit can also be used for other identification purposes, such as plain old bicycle hire. It's worth having a batch of 'photo booth' photos for visa applications and other uses. If you run out, Indian photo studios will do excellent portraits at pleasantly low prices.

TIPPING

In most Asian countries tipping is virtually unknown but India is an exception to that rule – although tipping has a rather different role in India than in the west. The term *baksheesh*, which encompasses tipping and a lot more besides, aptly describes the concept in India. You 'tip' not so much for good services but to get things done. A 'tip' to a station porter will ensure you a seat when the train is packed out to the very limit.

Judicious baksheesh will open closed doors, find missing letters, perform other small miracles. Tipping is not necessary for taxis nor for cheaper restaurants, but if you're going to be using something repeatedly an initial tip will ensure the standards are kept up – if you wonder why the service is slower every time in your hotel restaurant for example. Keep things in perspective though. Demands for baksheesh can quickly become never ending. Ask yourself if it's really necessary or desirable before shelling it out.

In tourist restaurants or hotels, where service will usually be tacked on in any case, the normal 10% figure normally applies. In smaller places, where tipping will be optional, you need only tip a few rupees, not a percentage of the bill. Hotel porters usually get about Rs 1 per bag; other possible tipping levels are Rs 1 to 2 for bike watching, Rs 10 to 20 for train conductors or station porters performing miracles for you, Rs 5 to 15 for extra services from hotel staff.

CONSULATES & EMBASSIES

Countries with diplomatic relations with India will generally have their consular offices in New Delhi, the capital, although many also have offices in Bombay and/or Calcutta. See the relevant sections for addresses. Some of the major Indian consular offices overseas include:

Australia
  92 Mugga Way, Red Hill ACT 2603 (tel 062 95 0045)
Burma
  545-547 Merchant St, Rangoon (tel 15933, 16381)
Malaysia
  Asian Bank Berhad Building, 19 Malacca St, Kuala Lumpur (tel 21728)
Nepal
  Lainchaur, Kathmandu (tel 11300)
Singapore
  31 Grange Rd (tel 737 6809)
Sri Lanka
  3rd floor, State Bank of India Building, 18-3/1 Sir Baron Jayatilaka Mawatha, Colombo 1 (tel 21604, 22788)
Thailand
  139 Pan Lane, Bangkok (tel 35065)
UK
  India House, Aldwych, London WC2B 4NA (tel 01 836 8484)

UN
  3 East 64th St, New York NY 10021
USA
  2107 Massachusetts Ave NW, Washington DC 20008 (tel 265 5050)

INFORMATION

The Government of India Tourist Office maintains a string of tourist offices overseas where you can get brochures, leaflets and some information about India. The tourist office leaflets and brochures are often very high in their informational quality and worth getting hold of. On the other hand, some of the overseas offices are not always as useful for obtaining information as those within the country. The overseas offices are listed below; there are also smaller 'promotion offices' in Osaka (Japan) and in Dallas, Miami, San Francisco and Washington DC (all USA).

Australia
  Carlton Centre, 55 Elizabeth St, Sydney NSW 2000 (tel 02 232 1600)
  8 Parliament Court, 1076 Hay St, West Perth WA 6005 (tel 06 321 6932)
Austria
  Opernring 1/E/II, 1010 Vienna (tel 571462)
Belgium
  60 Rue Ravenstein, Boite 15, 1000 Brussels (tel 02 5111796)
Canada
  Suite 1016, Royal Trust Tower (PO Box 342), Toronto Dominion Centre, Toronto, Ontario MSK 1K7 (tel 416 362 3188)
France
  8 Boulevard de la Madeleine, 75009 Paris 9 (tel 265 83 86)
Italy
  Via Albricci 9, 20122 Milan (tel 804952)
Japan
  Pearl Building, 9-18 Ginza, 7 Chome, Chuo ku, Tokyo 104 (tel 571 5062/3)
Kuwait
  Saadoun Al-Jassim Building, Fahad Al-Salem St (PO 4769), Safat (tel 426088)
Singapore
  Podium Block, 4th floor, Ming Court Hotel, Tanglin Rd, Singapore 1024 (tel 235 5737)

Sweden
      Sveavagen 9-11 (Box 40016), S-III-57
      Stockholm (tel 08 215081)
Switzerland
      1-3 Rue de Chantepoulet, 1201 Geneva (tel
      022 321813)
Thailand
      Singapore Airlines Building, 3rd floor, 62/5
      Thaniya Rd, Bangkok (tel 235 2585)
UK
      7 Cork St, London WIX QAB (tel 01 437
      3677-8, 3678)
USA
      30 Rockefeller Plaza, 15 North Mezzanine,
      New York NY 10020 (tel 212 586 4901)
      201 North Michigan Ave, Chicago IL 60601
      (tel 312 236 6899)
      3550 Wilshire Blvd, Suite 204, Los Angeles
      CA 90010 (tel 213 380 8855)
West Germany
      Kaiserstrasse 77-III, 6 Frankfurt Main (tel
      232380)

Within India the tourist office story is somewhat blurred by the overlap between the national and state tourist offices. As well as the national tourist office, each state maintains its own tourist office and this can lead to some confusion. In some cities the national office will be much larger than the state one or the state one will be virtually non-existent. Government of India Tourist Offices include:

Agra
      191 The Mall (tel 72377)
Aurangabad
      Krishna Vilas, Station Rd (tel 4817)
Bangalore
      KFC Building, 48 Church St
Bombay
      123 M Karve Rd (tel 293144)
Calcutta
      4 Shakespeare Sarani (tel 441402)
Cochin
      Willingdon Island (tel 6045)
New Delhi
      88 Janpath (tel 320005)
Gauhati
      B K Kakati Rd, Ulubari
Jaipur
      State Hotel (tel 72200)
Khajuraho
      Near Western Group Temples (tel 47)

Madras
      154 Anna Salai (tel 86240)
Shillong
      Directorate of Tourism, Police Bazaar
Varanasi
      15B The Mall (tel 64189)

The state tourist offices vary widely in their efficiency and usefulness. Some of them are very good, some completely hopeless. In many states the tourist offices also run a chain of Tourist Bungalows which generally offer good accommodation at very reasonable prices. State tourist offices will usually be located in the Tourist Bungalows.

The confusion and overlap between the national and state tourist offices often causes wasteful duplication. Both offices produce a brochure on place A, neither produces anything on place B. More confusion comes in with the division between the Government of India Tourist Office and the Indian Tourism Development Corporation (ITDC). The latter is more an actual 'doing' organisation than a 'telling' one. The ITDC will actually operate the tour bus on the tour for which the tourist office sells tickets. The ITDC also runs a series of hotels and Travellers' Lodges around the country under the Ashok name. States may also have a tourist transport operation equivalent to the national ITDC, so in some cities you can have a national and a state tourist operator as well as a national and a state tourist office!

GENERAL INFORMATION
Postal Services
The Indian postal services and poste restantes are generally excellent. Expected letters almost always are there and letters you send almost invariably get there. American Express, in its major city locations, offers an alternative to the poste restante system. Have letters addressed to you with your surname in capitals and underlined, the poste restante, GPO, and the city in question. Many 'lost' letters are simply misfiled under

given names, so always check under both your names.

You can often buy stamps at good hotels, saving a lot of queueing in crowded post offices.

Posting Parcels from India Most people discover how to do this the hard way, in which case it demands all morning or all afternoon. If you're not that keen to reach a peak of hitherto unknown frustration, then go about it this way:

(1) Take the parcel to a tailor and tell him you'd like it stitched up in cheap linen and the seams sealed with sealing wax. The wax has to be pressed with a seal which cannot be duplicated (if all else fails a non-Indian coin will serve). At some larger post offices this stitching-up service is offered outside. For a small parcel it should cost Rs 4 to 7.

(2) Go to the post office with your parcel and ask for two customs declaration forms. Fill them in and glue one to the parcel. Write your passport number (or any likely looking number) somewhere on the forms together with 'bona fide tourist'. To avoid excise duty at the delivery end it's best to specify that the contents are a 'gift'. The value of the parcel can be up to Rs 1000. (This concession is for tourists only. Internal parcels cannot exceed Rs 500 in value.)

(3) Get the parcel weighed and ask how much it's going to cost.

(4) Buy the stamps (usually not sold at the parcel counter) and stick them on.

(5) Hand the parcel in at the parcel counter and get a receipt for it.

Even if you do it this way it can still take up to two hours. Any other way and you say goodbye to the whole day. That is, if you don't take the easy way out and pay somebody else to do the whole thing! Be cautious with places which offer to mail things home for you after you buy them. Government emporiums are usually OK, but although most people who buy things

from other places get them eventually, some items never turn up (were they ever sent?) or what turns up isn't what they bought.

The other direction (getting parcels sent to you in India), is an extremely hit-and-miss affair. Don't count on anything bigger than a letter getting to you. Don't count on a letter getting to you if there's anything worthwhile inside it.

Telephone
The telephone system in India is hit and miss. Local calls sometimes work, sometimes don't. Trunk calls are even more a matter of chance. Many calls can be dialled direct but if you get through it feels like a pure fluke. It's probably even more flukey if you can actually hear anything. It's more time-consuming but more positive putting trunk calls through the operator, but again there's no guarantee you'll have a clear line.

For long-distance calls within India you can use the operator, or direct dial by STD (Standard Trunk Dialling), or make a Demand Call or Lightning Call. A Demand Call is made faster than a regular call and costs more too. A Lightning Call is supposed to go through (more or less) immediately and costs eight times the regular rate. It's often possible to make phone calls from big hotels far more quickly than from the crowded phone centres.

International calls, however, have improved dramatically in the past few years. You can now generally (but not always) get through quite quickly and the lines are usually remarkably clear. At phone centres in the major towns you can book a call for a couple of hours hence, go away and just turn up a few minutes before your call is due to go through. At big airports you can make international calls from the post office virtually instantly – sometimes you can even dial the call yourself. Big hotels will put through international calls for you and these days a few small ones will too. A typical three-minute overseas call costs about US$7.

Telex
Domestic and international telex services in India are good, reasonably priced and not heavily used like the telephone services. Telex is a good way to reconfirm flights, as you have evidence of having done so. The bigger hotels will sometimes let you use their telex.

Time
India is 5½ hours ahead of GMT, 4½ hours behind Australian Eastern Standard Time, 10½ hours ahead of American Eastern Standard Time.

Business Hours
Indian shops, offices and post offices are not early starters. Generally shops are open from 10 am to 5 pm daily and Saturdays. Some government offices open on alternate Saturdays and some commercial offices are open Saturday mornings. Post offices are open 10 am to 5 pm weekdays and Saturday mornings. Main city offices may be open longer hours, such as 8 am to 6 pm in Delhi.

Banks are open for business between 10 am and 2 pm on weekdays and 10 am and 12 noon on Saturdays. Sunday is the general closing day.

Electricity
230-240 volts, 50 cycles, alternating current. Electricity is widely available in India but breakdowns and blackouts are not uncommon. You can buy small immersion elements, perfect for boiling water for tea or coffee, for Rs 20.

MEDIA
There are a number of daily newspapers in English in India – all of the heavy news variety; there are no tabloids on the subcontinent. The *Times of India, The Statesman* and the *Indian Express* are the best papers; many feel the *Express* is now the best of the bunch. The *Times* is

headquartered in Bombay and *The Statesman* in Calcutta but there are many regional editions in both cases.

The *Illustrated Weekly of India* makes good reading on long train rides and is readily available at train and bus station news-stands. The same applies to the fortnightly *India Today*, a news magazine very *Time*-like in its size, format, approach and layout. The problem with all these Indian publications is that they are so inward looking that you soon become starved for outside news. *India Today*, in particular, is stuffed full of dull stories about state government politics. The strangely named magazine *Gentleman* also makes good reading.

Time and *Newsweek* are readily available throughout India, although once you've become used to Indian prices they seem very expensive! There are all sorts of other Indian magazines in English although many are of very limited interest to western visitors – it takes a long time to build up an interest in Indian movie stars and their film-fan magazines! Indian women's magazines, so alike yet so unlike their western counterparts, are definitely worth looking at. There's even an Indian 'male interest' (we all know what that is) magazine called *Debonair* with photographs of nice ladies discreetly dropping their saris.

India has a wide network of radio stations, and TV stations are becoming increasingly widespread. The TV programmes are very much intended to be educational rather than entertainment, however, and the sheer dreadfulness of Indian TV is a subject of continual discussion.

SPORTS
India follows a variety of sports, including field hockey, in which it is one of the world's leaders with several Olympic golds to its credit. Soccer has a keen following in a number of big cities, particularly Calcutta, where it is a major sport.

India's national sport has to be cricket. There's something about a game with as many idiosyncrasies and peculiarities as cricket which simply has to appeal to the Indian temperament. During the cricket season, if Australia or England are touring India and there is a test match on, you'll see crowds at every street corner in the big cities clamouring to hear what the latest score is from some transistor listener. Test matches with Pakistan, one sign of the thaw in relations between the countries, also have a particularly strong following.

A national pastime Test cricket by transistor radio...

HEALTH

Immunisations

Smallpox has now been totally eradicated worldwide, so apart from yellow fever vaccinations for people coming from infected areas, there are no vaccination requirements for visitors to India. Nevertheless, you may consider protection against the diseases listed below worthwhile.

Cholera is a disease of insanitation and usually occurs in epidemics. Protection against cholera is recommended for India and the vaccination is good for six months. A very useful vaccination, although not required by health authorities, is TABT. This provides protection against typhoid, paratyphoid A and B and tetanus. Typhoid and paratyphoid are both diseases of insanitation, spread by contaminated food. Tetanus is usually caused by a cut or skin puncture. All three are prevalent in hot climates. There are a number of medical centres in India where it is possible to get free or low-cost cholera and other vaccinations.

Polio is also a disease spread by insanitation and found more frequently in hot climates. A booster every five years is recommended by many doctors. The other vaccination you may wish to consider taking is against infectious hepatitis. This disease is, once again, spread by infected water or food and the gamma globulin injection prescribed against it is now thought to give good protection for up to six months.

Malaria

It is not (yet) possible to be vaccinated against malaria but it is absolutely necessary to take precautions against it while you are in India. Malaria is spread by mosquitoes and the disease has a nasty habit of coming back in later years even if you are cured at the time – and it can be fatal. Protection is simple – a daily or weekly tablet depending on which your doctor recommends.

Strains of malaria which are resistant

to chloroquine, the most-used anti-malarial, have become a major problem, but fortunately choloroquine-resistant malaria is not prevalent on the sub-continent.

Pregnant women should not take chloroquine tablets. Some doctors recommend Proguanil as the best anti-malarial for pregnancy – while researching the first edition of this book Maureen was pregnant and used Proguanil without ill effects. Pyrimethamine-sulfadoxine, the anti-malarial once recommended in case of chloroquine resistance (brand names include Fansidar, Faladar, Antemal and Methipox), is generally no longer recommended for anybody, pregnant or not.

When travelling with very small children try to avoid using daily tablets – getting a tablet into a small child every day of the week is not a pleasant task. A syrup form of anti-malarial is available for children. A final quirk of anti-malarials is that they are absurdly expensive in the USA. A course of anti-malarial tablets which might cost US$1 over the shelf in Asia or US$10 in Australia or Europe can set you back US$100 from a US drugstore! In many parts of Asia you can get anti-malarials without even a prescription; if you're an American this can save you a lot of money.

Rabies

Rabies is widespread in India – don't be friendly to India's numerous stray dogs and beware of those picturesque monkeys. The monkeys (particularly macaques) can be very aggressive if you are carrying food. If you are bitten by a possibly rabid animal you should wash the wound thoroughly and then embark on a series of injections which will prevent the disease from developing. Rabies, once developed, is almost always fatal. New rabies vaccines have been developed which have fewer side effects than the older animal-derived serums and vaccines, but head for one of the big cities to get this treatment. Reportedly there is also a rabies vaccination which requires just two shots. If you're going to a very isolated part of India and are worried about rabid animals this might be worth considering.

Stomach Problems

The usual health problem afflicting visitors to India is far more mundane than rabies, hepatitis or malaria. It's simply Delhi belly, the old upset stomach. Often this can be due to a change of diet or a system unused to spicy food. Many times, however, contaminated food or water is the problem.

The primary answer to the upset stomach problem is to avoid getting it in the first place by taking care in what you eat and drink. Uncooked foods are always more likely to harbour germs, but so are cooked foods once they have been allowed to cool. Try to eat only freshly cooked foods and beware of places where food is left sitting around for long periods, particularly if exposed to flies.

The main cause of upset stomachs is probably drinking water – the answer is to drink either hot tea or bottled soft drinks from reputable bottlers. This doesn't always work in the thirsty hot season, so if you must drink water try to either have it boiled or carry water purification tablets. These are available from pharmacies in the west or, with more difficulty, in India. Water is more effectively sterilised by iodine solution than by tablets – it kills amoebic cysts as well but does require practice drinking swimming-pool water! Even in good hotels 'drinking water' may be just filtered, not boiled.

If avoidance fails and you do get a stomach bug, the first thing to do is nothing. If you can simply get back to health by yourself you'll probably build up some immunity against a recurrence. Stick to hot tea and try not to eat too much. People who take antibiotics at the first sign of an upset stomach are only asking for trouble. Not only does it make another assault more difficult to repel, it also kills off the useful organisms in your digestive tract just as efficiently as it kills off the harmful ones. People whose travels in India are one long series of stomach problems are often the people who overdid the modern medicines. India is also a good place to catch the stomach upset known as giardiasis. Tinidazole, a milder sister antibiotic to Flagyl, has been recommended as a cure for this new variation on diarrhoea.

Some advice from two doctors in Nepal on diarrhoea and dysentery:

Diarrhoea is very different from dysentery, and it might be a good idea to define dysentery, which will require good drugs. Dysentery is diarrhoea with blood, pus or fever. Diarrhoea with blood or pus but without fever is usually amoebic dysentery and requires an anti-amoebic drug like metronidazole or flagyl.

Diarrhoea with blood or pus and fever is usually bacillary dysentery and requires antibiotics like tetracycline, or a sulfa drug. None of these drugs need to be given under the supervision of a doctor if a traveller has dysentery, and they can all be obtained in India or from a family doctor before leaving home. Most over-the-counter proprietary stomach-upset cures in India are worthless or dangerous, and if travellers save the drugs suggested above for true dysentery they will avoid one long series of stomach problems.

Most of the diarrhoea that travellers pick up is named appropriately 'travellers diarrhoea' and is without pus, blood or fever. Here the most important advice is to keep drinking to avoid dehydration. Lomotil is neither a heavy gun nor a general cure; it doesn't cure anything but just slows down the guts so that the cramps go away and you don't have to run to the toilet all the time. Lomotil is available over the counter in India but plain codeine is cheaper and works as well.

Hot Season Health

During the hot season there are some additional precautions to take to ensure good health. First of all, protect yourself from the sun as much as possible – it doesn't burn, due to all the dust haze, so you won't get sunburnt, but it certainly does you no good. Secondly, keep your liquid intake up. If you find you are

urinating very infrequently or your urine turns a deep yellow or orange, you're becoming dehydrated. It's very easy to do just that in the hot season.

At times like this you have to balance the dangers of drinking water against the dangers of dehydration. The first is possible, the second is definite, so if necessary throw caution to the winds and drink more water. In good restaurants and hotels drinking water is generally OK anyway and during the dry season water is much less likely to be polluted. It's during the monsoon that you must be especially careful about drinking water. The water is more likely to be polluted in hill resorts or smaller towns; in the big cities the water is now treated and generally is fairly safe. If you can't find purified water, can't face more tea or soft drinks and don't want to risk the water, coconuts and oranges make good thirst quenchers too.

When the sun is shining through loud and clear you can easily get sunburnt, and suntan lotion and sun screen are not widely available in India. Bring some.

Hospitals

Although India does have a few excellent hospitals such as the Mission Hospital in Vellore in Tamil Nadu, the Jaslok Hospital in Bombay and the All India Medical Institute in Delhi, most Indian cities do not have the quality of medical care available in the west. Usually hospitals run by western missionaries have better facilities than government hospitals where long waiting lines are common. Unless you have something very unusual, these Christian-run hospitals are the best places to head for in an emergency. India also has many qualified doctors with their own private clinics which can be quite good. The usual fee for a clinic visit is about Rs 25; Rs 40 for a specialist. Home calls usually cost Rs 50.

General Thoughts

Finally some miscellaneous thoughts:

make sure your teeth are in good shape before departing – dentists' equipment is not always what we've got used to in the west. It's wise to clean your teeth with 'safe' water as well. Always carry a spare pair of glasses or your prescription in case of loss or breakage. It's relatively easy to get glasses made up in an emergency. Don't walk around in bare feet; that is how you get hookworms or worse. Thongs are useful protectors in hotel showers against athlete's foot or other fungal infections. Treat any simple scratch or cut with care – clean it thoroughly with antiseptic and keep it clean. In India's tropical climate it's very easy for the simplest scratch to get infected. 'Wet Ones' or similar pre-moistened towelettes are a convenient aid to keeping things clean.

A straightforward medical kit is a wise thing to carry. Apart from medicines, band-aids, antiseptic and so on, a small clinical thermometer can be very useful. Take extra care in this department if you're travelling with children. You rarely need a prescription to buy medicines in India – if it's available at all it will be available over the counter. Be aware of possible differences in names, however. If you're after a specific drug it's worthwhile knowing the scientific as well as the trade name. Remember that drugs may not be of the same strength as in other countries or may have deteriorated due to age or poor storage conditions. They most probably will, however, be far cheaper than in the west. Prices for common drugs in Europe or the USA are often 10 or more times the retail price in India.

If a simple stomach upset turns out to be real down-to-earth dysentery, the most important thing is to not become dehydrated. Get plenty of liquids. If you get the dreaded hep, rest, good food, no alcohol and generally taking it easy is the cure. Make sure you have a good medical insurance policy, one that covers flying you home in emergencies. If you do need a doctor or other medical help, your embassy or consulate or a good hotel should be able to recommend someone.

It's probably wise to carry your health certificate with you just like your passport. One traveller wrote of having his bus stopped at a 'Cholera Inoculation Checkpoint'. All those who couldn't produce proof of immunisation got a jab on the spot, without benefit of sterilising the needle between goes! The concise and usable *Staying Healthy in Asia* (Volunteers in Asia Publications) or *The Traveller's Health Guide* by Dr Anthony Turner (Roger Lascelles, London) have some good basic advice on staying healthy while travelling. A traveller recommended *In Search of the Masters*, a book about ashrams in India, for its résumé on health problems in India.

It hardly needs saying, but street-corner acupuncturists or ear cleaners (!) are not to be trusted in India. Amazingly, some people do let these folk have a go at them and regret it afterwards!

Most important of all, don't get overly concerned about your health. Most people survive India with very few problems. During the course of researching the first edition of this book Tony and Maureen spent three months in India in one stretch, during the hot season while Maureen was pregnant, with nothing more than a couple of mild stomach upsets between them.

WHAT TO TAKE & HOW TO TAKE IT

The usual travellers' rule applies – bring as little as possible. It's much better to have to get something you've left behind than find you have too much and need to get rid of it. In the south of India you can count on shirtsleeve weather year round, but in the north it can get cool enough to require a sweater or light jacket in the evenings during the winter. In the far north it will get down to freezing and you will need all the warm-weather gear you can muster.

Remember that clothes are easily and cheaply purchased in India. You can buy things off the peg or have clothes made to measure in the small tailor shops found everywhere in India. In the big cities there are plenty of the Indian fashions so popular in the west, and the prices often approximate in rupees what they cost in dollars in the west! One item of clothing to have made as soon as possible is a pair of lightweight pyjama-style trousers. You'll find them far cooler and more comfortable than jeans and they'll only cost a few rupees.

Modesty rates highly in India, as in most Asian countries. Although men wearing shorts is accepted as a western eccentricity, women should dress more discreetly. Even for men, however, wearing shorts or going shirtless in a more formal situation is not very polite. A reasonable clothes list would include:

- underwear & swimming gear
- one pair of jeans, one pair of shorts
- a few T-shirts or short-sleeved shirts
- sweater for cold nights
- one pair of sneakers or shoes
- sandals and/or thongs
- lightweight jacket or raincoat
- a 'dress up' set of clothes

On the non-clothing side take along:

- washing gear
- medical & sewing kit
- sunglasses
- padlock

Other non-clothing items to consider include an umbrella, invaluable in the monsoon.

Sleeping Bag

A sleeping bag can be a hassle to carry but can serve as something to sleep in (and avoid unsavoury-looking hotel bedding), a cushion on hard train seats, a seat for long waits on railway platforms, a bed top-cover (since cheaper hotels rarely give you one) and, of course, as a sleeping bag. If you're going trekking in the north then a sleeping bag will be an absolute necessity. Note that trekking gear cannot

be easily hired in India the way it can be in Nepal. A sheet sleeping bag, like those required by Youth Hostels in the west, can be very useful, particularly if you don't trust a hotel's sheets. Mosquito nets are also rare so your own sheet or sheet sleeping bag will also help to keep mosquitoes at bay and/or keep you warm at night.

Some travellers find that a plastic sheet is useful for a number of reasons, including bed-bug-proofing unhealthy looking beds. Others have recommended an inflatable pillow as a useful accessory.

Toilet Paper

Toilet paper is a necessity if you can't adapt to the Indian method of a jug of water and your left hand. Since not many trees end up as toilet paper in India, the stuff can be very hard to find outside of the big cities and tourist centres. And when you do find it Indian toilet paper is often lousy (either the British masochist-style waxed-paper stuff or a tube of cardboard cms thick with about a metre-and-a-half of paper wrapped around it) and horrendously expensive. One solution is to come to India with an absurd quantity of this western luxury. That makes more sense than it sounds – toilet paper is extremely light and also extremely bulky. Having your pack half full of paper is one way of ensuring that when it's used up you'll have plenty of space for all those interesting things you'll be buying.

Toiletries

Soap, toothpaste and other toiletries are readily available but toilet paper can sometimes be difficult to find outside of major centres. A sink plug is worth having since few cheaper hotels have plugs. A nail brush can be very useful. For women, tampons are not that easy to find in India. Except in 'strange, varied, toxic-shock-inducing forms', wrote one women.

Don't bother taking shaving stuff to India. Every few days pop into one of the barber shops you find in every town. An ordinary shave is quite an experience. First comes the lathering, then the first shave with an ordinary razor blade (which is unwrapped in front of you) fitted into a handle device. Next comes relathering and reshaving followed by an assortment of oils and lotions, some of which sting like hell. Finally, there's the hot, damp towel (and once, some lavender talcum powder!). The total cost of all this, plus interesting advice on where to stay and eat and what to see in town, is Rs 2 to 2.50.

Patrick Hosking, UK

How to Carry It

Where to put all this gear – well, for budget travellers the backpack is still the best carrying container. Adding a little thief-proofing protection by sewing on tabs so you can padlock it shut is worthwhile. A modern variation on the backpack is the travel pack – a backpack with a flap which zips over the shoulder straps to turn it into a soft bag. It looks more presentable that way and is also less prone to damage – the major problem with backpacks. Some airlines will no longer accept responsibility for damage or theft from backpacks.

An alternative is a large, soft, zip bag with a wide shoulder strap. It's not so easy to carry for distances but it is rather more thief proof and less damage prone. Suitcases are only for jet-setters! Lots of plastic bags will keep your gear in some sort of order and will also be invaluable for keeping things dry during the wet season.

Miscellaneous Useful Things

It's amazing how many things you wish you had with you when you're in India. One of the most useful for budget travellers is a padlock. In fact a padlock is a virtual necessity. Many cheaper hotels, in fact most of them, have doors locked by a latch and padlock. You'll find having your own sturdy lock on the door instead of the flimsy thing the hotel supplies does wonders for your peace of mind. Other uses are legion. You can lock a pack onto a railway luggage rack at night, for example.

It may not make it thief proof but it helps. You can buy a good lock in India for Rs 12 to 15. 'Combination locks are relatively unknown so they are very effective', was one reader suggestion.

A universal sink plug is useful since sinks never have them. Ever tried to wash your underwear in a sink without a plug? A knife (Swiss Army for preference) finds a whole field of uses, in particular for peeling fruit. Some travellers rhapsodise about the usefulness of a miniature electric element to boil water in a cup. I carry my Balinese sarong with me everywhere – it's a bedsheet, an item of clothing, an emergency towel, something to lie on at the beach, a pillow on trains!

Insect repellent can also be extremely useful. You may find a clothesline and clothes pegs worthwhile. Power cuts are common in India ('load shedding' as it is euphemistically known) and there's little street lighting at night so a torch (flashlight) and candles can be handy. Clear cellophane tape was one suggestion; it enables you to flawlessly repair torn banknotes! Bring along your spectacle prescription if you're short-sighted. Should you lose or damage your glasses a new pair can be made up very cheaply and in good quality.

Hot-weather survival requires another book of rules in India. First of all a sun hat is essential. Stepping out into the sun in the hot season is like using your head as a blacksmith's anvil. You don't just feel the sun, it reaches out and hits you. Secondly, a water bottle should always be by your side; and thirdly, have water purification tablets. In the heat you need water – cups of tea, fruit and soft drinks are just not going to do the job. Purification tabs are not 100% effective but when it gets really hot you're not going to care how effective they are! You'll also need something with long sleeves, particularly if you're going to ride a bicycle very far.

INDIAN CLOTHING

Many travellers start wearing Indian

clothes while in India – after all, much of it is a lot more appropriate to India's climate than jeans and T-shirts. The best-known Indian clothing style, and one the wearing of which few western women can carry off properly, is the *sari*. This supremely graceful attire is simply one length of material, a bit over a metre in width and five to nine metres long (usually around six metres long). It's worn without any pins, buttons or fastenings to hold it in place so in part its graceful appearance is a necessity. The tightly fitted, short blouse worn under a sari is a *choli*. The final length of the sari, which is draped over the wearer's shoulder, is known as the *pallav* or *palloo*.

There are a number of variations in types of saris and styles of wearing them, but there are also other styles of women's costume in India. Sikh women wear pyjama-like trousers drawn tightly in at the waist and at the ankles. Over these trousers, known as *salwars*, they wear a long, loose tunic known as a *kameez*. This attire is comfortable and 'respectable'. A *churidhar* is similar to the salwar but tighter fitting at the hips. Over this goes a collar-less or mandarin-collar *kurta* – an item of clothing just as popular in the west, where it is worn by men as much as women, as in India.

Although the overwhelming majority of Indian women wear traditional costume, many Indian men wear quite conventional western clothing. Indeed a large proportion of India's consumer advertising appears to be devoted to 'suitings & shirtings' – the material made for tailor-made western-style business suits and shirts. The traditional *lungi* originated in the south and today is worn by women as well as men. It's simply a short length of material worn around the thighs rather like a sarong. The lungi can be rolled up but should be lowered when sitting down or when entering someone's home or a temple. A *dhoti* is like a longer lungi but with a length of material pulled up between the legs, effective but a long way

from elegant! A dhoti is a more formal piece of attire than a lungi, however. Pyjama-like trousers, worn by countryfolk, are known as *lenga*. Regular striped pyjamas are casual and comfortable but they're looked upon as a labourer's outfit, not something to wear to a fancy restaurant or to somebody's home.

There are many religious and regional variations, such as the brightly mirrored Rajasthani skirts and their equally colourful tie-dye materials. In Ladakh the women wear superbly picturesque Tibetan costumes with high 'top hats'. Their men wear long dressing-gown-like coats. Muslim women, of course, wear much more staid and all-covering attire than their Hindu sisters. More traditional Muslims even wear the all-enveloping tent-like *burkha*.

Dhobi Wallahs

Your clothes will undoubtedly become involved at some point in your travels with the Indian ability to make systems of amazing complexity function smoothly. When you travel in India there's hardly any need for more than one change of clothes. Every day there will be a knock on your door and the laundry boy will collect all those dusty, sweaty clothes you wore yesterday, and every evening those same clothes will re-appear – washed and ironed with more loving care than any washing-powder-ad mum ever lavished upon anything. And all for a rupee or two per item. But what happened to your clothes between their departure and their like-new return?

Well, they certainly did not get anywhere near a washing machine. First of all they're collected and taken to the *dhobi ghat*. A ghat is a place with water, a dhobi is a washerman so the dhobi ghat is where the dhobi plies his trade and washes clothes. In big cities dhobi ghats will be huge places with hundreds of dhobis doing their thing with thousands of articles of clothing.

Then the clothes are separated – all the white shirts are washed together, all the grey trousers, all the red skirts, all the blue jeans. By now, if this was the west, your clothes would either be hopelessly lost or you'd need a computer to keep track of them all. Your clothes are soaked in soapy water for a few hours, following which the dirt is literally

INDIANS TRYING TO BREAK
STONES WITH WET WASHING...
RANA GHAT-**VARANASI**

beaten out of them. No multi-programmed, miracle of technology can wash as clean as a determined dhobi, although admittedly after a few visits to the Indian laundry your clothes do begin to look distinctly thinner. Buttons also tend to get shattered, so bring some spares.

Once clean, the clothes are strung out on miles of clothesline to quickly dry in the Indian sun. They're then taken to the ironing sheds where hundreds of ironers wielding primitive irons press your jeans like they've never been pressed before. Not just your jeans – your socks, your T-shirts, even your underwear will come back with knife-edge creases. Then the Indian miracle takes place. Out of the thousands

upon thousands of items washed that day, somehow your very own brown socks, blue jeans, yellow T-shirt and red underwear all find their way back together and head for your hotel room. A system of marking clothes, known only to the dhobis, is the real reason behind this feat. They say criminals have been tracked down simply by those tell-tale 'dhobi marks'.

WOMEN TRAVELLERS

India doesn't present the problems for solo women travellers that some Asian countries can – Pakistan in particular – but some care can help. Since the first edition several women travellers have written with their thoughts and suggestions.

One woman suggested that 'you should keep your upper arms, chest and back covered because these areas are, for some reason, considered erotic. A big shawl of light cloth will provide some privacy. Don't return male stares', she continued, 'it is considered a come-on. Turning away haughtily and draping your shawl over your head will have the desired effect. Getting involved in inane conversations with men is also considered a turn-on. Keep discussions down to a necessary minimum unless you're interested in getting hassled. If you get the uncomfortable feeling he's encroaching on your space, the chances are that he is. A firm request to keep away – use your best memsahib tone – may help. Firmly return any errant limbs, put some item of luggage in between you and if all else fails find a new spot, with offended dignity. You're also within your rights to tell him to push off!'

A couple of women wrote in some anger over the way they were treated in India. It came down, they decided, to a belief that if you're not married there's something wrong with you and if you are married then what are you doing here all alone!

Being a woman also has some advantages. There is often a special ladies' queue for train tickets or even a ladies' quota and ladies' carriages! One woman wrote that these ladies' carriages were often nearly empty – another said that they were full of screaming children. Special ladies' facilities are also sometimes found in cinemas and other places.

Close attention to standards of dress will go a long way to minimising problems for female travellers. The light cotton draw-string skirts that many western women pick up in India are really sari petticoats and to wear them in the street is rather like going out half dressed. Other ways of blending into the Indian background include avoiding sleeveless blouses, skirts that are too short and, of course, the bra-less look. Remember that *lungis* are only acceptable wear for women in the state of Kerala.

FILM & CAMERA

Colour print film is now much more readily available in India, and developing and printing facilities are now easily found. They're usually cheap and the quality is usually (but not always) good. If you're taking slides bring the film with you, and bring plenty – India is a photogenic country. Colour slide film can still be difficult to find and will not be so cheap, although colour slides can be developed and the quality is usually good. Kodachrome or other 'includes developing film' will have to be sent overseas, however. It's up to you whether you send it straight back or carry it back with you at the end of your trip. Film manufacturers warn that once exposed, film should be developed as quickly as possible; in practice the film seems to last, even in India's summer heat, without deterioration for months.

There are plenty of camera shops which should be able to make minor repairs should you have any mechanical problems. Photography itself presents some special problems in India. In the dry season the hazy atmosphere makes it difficult to get sharp shots or to get much contrast between what you are photographing and the background. Everything looks washed out and flat even with a polarising filter. In the mountains you should allow for the extreme clarity of the air and light intensity, and take care not to overexpose your shots.

Be careful what you photograph. India is touchy about places of military importance – this can include train stations, bridges, airports and any military installations. If in doubt ask. In general most people are happy to be photographed, but care should be taken in pointing cameras at Muslim women. Again, if in doubt, ask.

THEFT

Having things stolen is a problem in India, not so much because it's a theft-prone country – it isn't – but because you can become involved in a lot of hassles getting the items replaced. If your passport is stolen you may have a long trip back to an embassy to replace it. Travellers' cheques may be replaceable if stolen, but first of all avoid theft. Always lock your room, preferably with your own padlock in cheaper hotels. Lock it at night as well; countless people have had things stolen from their rooms when they've actually been in them.

Never leave those most important valuables (passport, tickets, health certificates, money, travellers' cheques) in your room; they should be with you at all times. Either have a stout leather passport wallet on your belt, or a passport pouch under your shirt, or simply extra internal pockets in your clothing. On trains at night keep your gear near you; padlocking a bag to a luggage rack can be useful. Never walk around with valuables casually slung over your shoulder. Take extra care in crowded public transport. In Bombay, for example, pickpockets are adept at the 'razor on the back pocket or shoulder bag' technique.

Thieves are particularly prevalent on train routes where there are lots of tourists. The Delhi-Agra express service is notorious; and Delhi-Jammu Tawi, Delhi-Calcutta and Delhi-Bombay are other routes to take care on. Train departure time, when the confusion and crowds are at their worst, is the time to be most careful. Just as the train is about to leave your bags suddenly fly out the window to a waiting accomplice. On the Delhi-Jammu service the 'instant crowd' technique is the usual method. Young men work in teams so that you suddenly find yourself surrounded by jostling people, and your bags disappear in an instant. Airports are another place to be careful, especially for international arrivals which often take place in the middle of the night, when you are unlikely to be at your most wakeful and alert.

Since the previous edition we've had a number of letters from the victims of drugging episodes. They meet somebody on a train or bus or in a town, get to talking and then are offered a cup of tea or something similar. Hours later they wake up with a headache and all their gear gone. The tea was full of sleeping pills. Don't accept drinks or food from strangers no matter how friendly they seem, particularly if you're on your own.

Beware also of your fellow travellers. Unhappily there are more than a few backpackers who make the money go further by helping themselves to other peoples'. At places like Goa be very careful with things on the beach – while you're in the water your camera or money can walk away very fast.

Remember that backpacks are very easy to rifle through. Don't leave valuables in them, especially for flights. Remember also that something may be of little or no value to a thief, but to lose it would be a real heartbreak to you – like film. Finally, a good travel insurance policy helps.

Travellers' Cheques

If you're unlucky enough to have things stolen, some precautions can ease the pain. All travellers' cheques are replaceable but this does you little immediate good if you have to go home and apply to your bank. What you want is instant replacement. Furthermore, what do you do if you lose your cheques and money and have a day or more to travel to the replacement office? The answer is to keep an emergency cash-stash in some totally separate place. In that same place you should keep a record of the cheque serial numbers and your passport number.

American Express make considerable noise about 'instant replacement' of their cheques but a lot of people find out, to their cost, that without a number of precautions it ain't necessarily so. For a start, 'no bank', reported one unhappy traveller, 'will give an instant refund if the amount stolen is over US$1000'. A good reason for carrying more than one brand of cheque. The same person said that it is necessary to get a receipt to prove that you phoned the nearest American Express office after the theft. The receipt should indicate the number you called and the date. 'Keep the original receipt from when you bought the cheques separate from the cheques themselves', he continued. 'Without that, you won't even get a single dollar for weeks and weeks'. However, I met one Briton who had his stolen travellers' cheques (American Express) replaced within 48 hours; according to him he was dressed up like a businessman when he reported the theft. He felt the refund would have taken much longer if he had been dressed as a 'hippie'.

Another traveller wrote that his travellers' cheques were stolen and he didn't discover the loss for a month. They had been left in his hotel room and the thief (presumably from the hotel) had neatly removed a few cheques from the centre of the book. Explaining that sort of theft is really difficult and, of course, the thief has had plenty of time to dispose of them.

We've had a number of letters concerning theft in India, including one from a woman who was so upset when her camera was stolen soon after arrival that she left on the next available flight. Other writers' belongings were ripped off from a beach hut at Goa, on various trains, from the top of the bus to Darjeeling, on internal flights and from their hotel rooms. One man had his camera stolen at knife point by a rickshaw rider who was supposedly about to buy it, and Geoff even had stuff stolen while researching the second edition. What can we say – be careful.

But, of course, there's a reverse side. In many years of travel I (Tony speaking here) have had various things stolen in France, Italy, Thailand (more than once), Malaysia, Indonesia, Peru, the USA and even Australia. On all my visits to India (touch wood) I've never once lost anything. India has no world-exclusive on thieves; it's just a matter of luck.

I'll leave the final word to an elderly visitor (he and two friends who visited India and told us about it had a combined age of 200 years!): 'I have never had anything stolen while in transit or in hotels. I am not a particularly careful person and can only conclude that the risk is exaggerated. We found it only too easy to be suspicious and were frequently humbled by realising that people we thought were trying to con us were only trying to be helpful. Every time we misplaced some item of luggage our first thought was that it had been stolen; but we lost absolutely nothing in that way. On the other hand we were several times followed with things we had inadvertently left in teashops or buses'.

PLACES TO STAY
India has a very wide range of accommodation possibilities apart from straightforward hotels. Some of them include:

Cheap Hotels
There are hotels all over India with conditions ranging from extremely drab and dismal (but prices at rock bottom) up to quite reasonable in both standards and prices. Lazily swishing ceiling fans, mosquito nets on the beds, private toilets and bathrooms are all possibilities even in rooms costing Rs 35 or less a night for a double.

Throughout India hotels are defined as 'western' or 'Indian'. The differentiation is basically meaningless, although expensive hotels are always western, cheap ones Indian. 'Indian' hotels will be more simply and economically furnished but the acid test is the toilet. 'Western' hotels have a sit-up-style toilet; 'Indian' ones usually (but not always) have the traditional Asian squat style. You can find modern, well-equipped, clean places with Indian toilets and dirty, dismal dumps with western toilets, so don't be put off them.

Although prices are generally quoted in this book for singles and doubles, most hotels will put an extra bed in a room to make a triple for about an extra 25%. This is a considerable economy if there are more than two of you. In some smaller hotels it's often possible to bargain a little if you really want to. On the other hand these places will often put their prices up if there's an accommodation shortage.

Expensive Hotels

You won't find 'international standard' hotels throughout India. The big, air-con, swimming-pool places are generally confined to the major tourist centres and the large cities. There are a number of big hotel chains in India. The Taj Group has some of India's flashiest hotels, including the luxurious Taj Mahal Inter-Continental in Bombay, the romantic Rambagh Palace in Jaipur and the Lake Palace in Udaipur. Other interesting hotels are the Taj Coromandel in Madras and the Fort Aguada Resort in Goa. The Oberoi chain is, of course, well known outside India as well as within. Clarks are a small chain with popular hotels in Varanasi and Agra, amongst other places. The Welcomgroup and the Air-India-associated Centaur hotels are other chains.

The chains include the government-operated ITDC group who usually append the name 'Ashok' to their hotels. There's an Ashok hotel in virtually every town in India, so that test isn't foolproof, but the ITDC places include a number of smaller (but higher-standard) units in places like Sanchi or Konarak where accommodation possibilities are limited. The ITDC has been getting a lot of complaints in India recently for its inefficiency and large financial losses. We've also been getting numerous reports from travellers on badly maintained and poorly run ITDC hotels.

The more expensive hotels in India are not the great bargains they might seem at first. Although labour costs in India are low, it takes a lot of people to get anything done. Combine that with high costs for imported equipment and fittings plus the high cost of electricity and power in India, and room costs are certainly not low compared to those in other countries' more expensive hotels.

Beware of extra taxes and charges in the more expensive hotels. There will almost always be a 10% service charge, and in addition there will often be a 'luxury tax'. This tax, which is usually either 5% or 10%, seems to depend on the room cost or other factors like air-conditioning. In some places, where there are different off-season and high-season rates, you may find the luxury tax is higher in the high season – presumably because the higher room rate in season moves it from one bracket to another. Sometimes a room rate will be broken down into individual charges, thereby keeping the basic room rate low enough to avoid luxury tax. Thus you might find the total price is Rs x for the room plus Rs y for the phone (which you never used). On x alone there is no tax but on x plus y there would be. Rates quoted in this book are generally the basic rate only – taxes and charges are additional.

Government Accommodation

Back in the days of the Raj, a whole string of government-run accommodation units were set up with labels like Rest Houses, Dak Bungalows, Circuit Houses, PWD (Public Works Department) Bungalows, Forest Rest Houses and so on. Today most of these are reserved for government officials, although in some places they may still be available for tourists, if there is room. In an approximate pecking order the Dak Bungalows are the most basic; they often have no electricity and only essential equipment in out-of-the-way places. Rest Houses are next up and then come the Circuit Houses, which are strictly for travelling VIPs.

Tourist Bungalows

Usually run by the state government, these often serve as replacements for the older government-run accommodation units. Tourist Bungalows are generally well kept and often excellent value, although in the last few years prices have risen dramatically in some states. They often have dorm beds as well as rooms – typical prices are around Rs 10 to 12 for a dorm bed or Rs 30 to 75 for a double room. The rooms will be well kept and have a fan, double bed and attached bathroom; there may be more expensive air-conditioned rooms. Generally there's a restaurant or 'dining hall'. There are particularly good Tourist Bungalows in Rajasthan and Tamil Nadu, although almost every state has some towns where the Tourist Bungalow is definitely the best place to stay.

In tourist bungalows, as in many other government-run institutions such as the railways in India, you will find a curiously Indian institution, the 'complaints book'. In this you can write your complaints and periodically someone higher up the chain of command comes along, reads the terrible tales and the tourist bungalow manager gets his knuckles rapped. In disputes or other arguments, calling for the complaints book is the angry customer's final weapon. In many places the complaints book can provide interesting and amusing reading. Try the Madurai Tourist Bungalow's complaints book, suggested one traveller.

Railway Retiring Rooms
These are just like regular hotels or dormitories except they are at the railway stations. To stay here you are generally supposed to have a railway ticket or Indrail Pass. The rooms are, of course, extremely convenient if you want to be handy for a train departure, although they can be noisy if it is a busy station. They are often very cheap and in some places they are also excellent value. Some stations have retiring rooms of definite Raj pretensions, with huge rooms and enough furniture to do up a flat or apartment back home.

Railway Waiting Rooms
Emergency accommodation when all else fails or when you just need a few hours' shut-eye before your train departs at 2 am. These are a free place to rest your weary head. The trick is to rest it in the comfortable 1st-class waiting room and not the depressing and crowded lower-class one. Officially you need a 1st-class ticket to be allowed to use the 1st-class room and its superior facilities. In practice, luck, a 2nd-class Indrail Pass or simply your foreign appearance may work.

Youth Hostels
Indian Youth Hostels are generally very cheap and sometimes in excellent condition with superb facilities. They are, however, often inconveniently situated some distance from the town centres. You are not usually required to be a YHA member (as in other countries) to use the hostels, although your YHA card will generally get you a lower rate. Nor do the usual rules about arrival-and-departure times, lights-out times or not using the hostel during the day apply. A list of Government of India hostels includes:

Andhra Pradesh
    Youth Hostel, near Secunderabad Sailing Club, Secunderabad
Goa
    Youth Hostel, Panaji (tel 2433)
Gujarat
    Youth Hostel, Sector 16, Gandhinagar (tel 2364)
Haryana
    Panchkula Youth Hostel, Haryana Tourist Complex, Panchkula, Ambala
Himachal Pradesh
    Youth Hostel, bus stand, Dalhousie (tel 89)
Jammu & Kashmir
    Patni Top Youth Hostel, c/o Tourist Office, Kud (tel 7)
Kerala
    Youth Hostel, Veli, Trivandrum
Madhya Pradesh
    Youth Hostel, North TT Nagar, Bhopal (tel 63671)
Maharashtra
    Youth Hostel, Padampura, Station Rd, Aurangabad (tel 3801)

Orissa
Youth Hostel, Sea Beach, Puri (tel 424)
Punjab
Youth Hostel, Mal Mandi, GT Rd, Amritsar (tel 48165)
Rajasthan
Youth Hostel, SMS Stadium, Bhagwandas Rd, Jaipur (tel 69084)
Tamil Nadu
Youth Hostel, Indira Nagar, Madras (tel 412882)
Youth Hostel, Solaithandam Kuppam, Pondicherry
Uttar Pradesh
Youth Hostel, Malli Tal near Ardwell Camp, The Mall, Nainital (tel 513)
West Bengal
Darjeeling Youth Hostel, 16 Dr Zakir Hussain Rd, Darjeeling (tel 2290)

There are some state government-operated Youth Hostels. In Tamil Nadu, for example, there are state hostels in Mahabalipuram, Rameswaram, Kanyakumari, Kodaikanal and Ooty.

Other

There are YMCAs and YWCAs in many big cities – some of these are modern, well equipped and more expensive (but still good value). There are also a few Salvation Army Hostels – in particular in Bombay and Calcutta. There are a few camping places around India, but travellers with their own vehicles can almost always find hotels with gardens where they can park and camp.

Free accommodation is available at some Sikh temples where there is a tradition of hospitality to visitors. It can be insightful to try one, but please don't abuse this hospitality and spoil it for other travellers. At many pilgrimage sites there are *dharamsalas* offering accommodation to pilgrims, and travellers are often welcome to use these. This particularly applies at isolated sites like Ranakpur in Rajasthan.

Staying with an Indian family can be a real education. It's a change from dealing strictly with tourist-oriented people, and the differences and curiosities of everyday Indian life can be very interesting. 'I was shown great hospitality by Indian friends of friends', wrote one visitor.

Touts

Hordes of accommodation touts operate in many towns in India – Jaipur and Varanasi in particular. Very often they are the rickshaw-wallahs who meet you at the bus or train station. The technique is simple – they take you to hotel A and rake off a commission for bringing you there rather than to hotel B. The problem with this procedure is that you may well end up not at the place you want to go to but at the place that pays the best commission. Some very good cheap hotels simply refuse to pay the touts and you'll then hear lots of stories about the hotel you want being 'full up', 'closed for repairs' or 'no good anymore'. Nine chances out of 10 they will be just that – stories.

Touts do have a use though – if you arrive in a town where some big festival is on (or a cricket test match against England or Australia!), finding a place to stay can be very difficult. Hop in a rickshaw, tell him in what price range you want a hotel, and off you go. He'll know which places have rooms available and unless the search is a long one you shouldn't have to pay him more than Rs 5; Rs 10 at the most. Remember that he'll be getting a commission from the hotel too!

FOOD

Despite the very fine meals that can be prepared in India, you'll often find food a great disappointment. In many smaller centres there is not a wide choice and you'll get bored with rice and *dhal*. When you're in larger cities where the food can be excellent, take advantage of it.

Contrary to popular belief, not all Hindus are officially vegetarians. Strict vegetarianism is confined more to the south, which has not had the meat-eating influence of the Aryan and later Muslim invasions. On the other hand, eating meat is not always a pleasure in India – the quality tends to be low (most chickens give the impression that they died from starvation) and the hygiene is not all that it might be. Beef, from the holy cow, is strictly taboo of course – and leads to interesting Indian dishes like the mutton-burger. Pork is equally taboo to the Muslims. All in all, whether you're vegetarian or not you'll end up eating a lot more vegetarian food in India.

Railway station restaurants are always a good bet here. Their food is generally safe, and if one more curry will kill you they also have a western menu – at higher prices. Of course no culinary achievement awards are ever going to be made to station restaurants, but in general they're not bad. Indian interpretations of western cuisine can be pretty horrific; it's usually best to let them stick to preparing Indian food. Meals served on trains are usually palatable too, and reasonably cheap. At every stop you will be besieged by food and drink sellers. Even in the middle of the night that raucous cry of 'chai, chai' breaks into your sleep. The sheer bedlam of an Indian station when a train is in is a part of India you never forget.

If, after some time in India, you do find the food is getting you down physically or psychologically, there are a couple of escapes. It is very easy for budget travellers to lose weight in India and feel lethargic and drained of energy. The answer is to up your protein intake – eat more eggs, which are readily available; buy bananas, mandarin oranges or peanuts, all easily found at stations or in the markets. Many travellers carry multi-vitamins with them. Another answer, if you're travelling on a budget, is to occasionally splash out on a meal in a fancy hotel or restaurant – compared to what you have been paying it may seem amazingly expensive, but try translating the price into what it would be at home.

There are considerable regional variations from north to south, partly because of climatic conditions and partly because of historical influences. In the north, as already mentioned, much more meat is eaten and the cooking is often 'Moghul style', which bears a closer relationship to food of the Middle East and central Asia. The emphasis is more on spices and less on curry heat. In the north far more grains and breads are eaten and less rice. In the south the food is more strictly vegetarian, more rice is eaten and the curries tend to be hotter. Sometimes very hot. Another peculiarity of southern vegetarian food is that you do not need eating utensils; it is always eaten with fingers (of the right hand only). Scooping up food that way takes a little practice but you soon become quite adept at it. It is said that eating this way allows you to get the 'feel' of the food, as important to south Indian cuisine as the aroma or arrangement are for other cooking styles, but it also offers the added protection that you never need worry if the eating utensils have been properly washed.

In the most basic Indian restaurants and eating places the cooking is usually done right out front so you can see exactly what is going on and how it is done. Vegetables will be on the simmer all day and tend to be cooked out and mushy to western tastes. In these basic places dhal is usually free but you pay for *chappatis, parathas, puris* or rice. *Sabzi* (vegetable stew), dhal and a few chappatis makes a passable meal for around Rs 5. If you order half-plates of the various dishes brewing out front you get half the quantity at half the price and get a little more variety. With chutneys and a small plate of onions, which come free, you can put together a reasonable vegetarian meal for, say, Rs 5, or non-vegetarian for Rs 7 to 10. In railway station restaurants and other cheaper restaurants always check the prices and add up your bill. If it's incorrect query it.

At the other end of the price scale there are many restaurants in India's five-star hotels that border on the luxurious and by western standards are absurdly cheap.

Paying US$10 to 15 for a meal in India seems exorbitant after you've been there for a while, but check what a meal in your friendly local Hilton would cost you. As one traveller put it:

If not on a starvation budget the occasional splurge on a really good meal is very worthwhile in India. Best value are the unlimited 'buffet lunches' which are available at a number of the larger hotels. The *Taj Mahal Inter-Continental* in Bombay is one of the best. A large, opulent dining room complete with orchestra and an astonishing array of every kind of food imaginable.

The *Oberoi Grand* in Calcutta comes a close second – a much smaller dining room here and perhaps not quite so much variety, but the quality is even higher. Where else can you find a tray of steaks to help yourself from? It's slightly more expensive than the Taj, but in Madras the *Connemara* is rather cheaper. The food here is not in quite such abundant variety but you can still eat yourself silly. Extras like soft drinks are very expensive in these hotels – drink water or make yourself a milk shake from the ice cream!

Many other international standard hotels, like the *Oberoi Palace* in Srinagar, offer similar deals. For budget travellers it makes a very pleasant change from dhal and rice.

At small hotels and restaurants you can often get much better food if you order half a day (or more) in advance. Not only does the food improve but you may find that far fewer items on the menu will be 'unavailable'.

Finally, a couple of hints on how to cope with curry. After a while in India you'll get used to even the fiercest curries and will find western food surprisingly bland. If, however, you do find your mouth is on fire don't reach for water. In emergencies that hardly helps at all. Curd (yoghurt) or fruit do the job much more efficiently.

Curry & Spice

Believe it or not, there is no such thing as 'curry' in India. It's an English invention, an all-purpose term to cover the whole range of Indian food spicing. *Carhi*, incidentally, is a Gujarati dish, but never ask for it in Kumaon where it's a very rude word!

Although all Indian food is certainly not curry, this is the basis of Indian cuisine. Curry doesn't have to be hot enough to blow your head off, although it can do that if it's made that way. Curry most definitely is not something found in a packet of curry powder. Indian cooks have about 25 spices on their regular list and it is from these that they produce the curry flavour. Normally the spices are freshly ground in a mortar and pestle known as a *sil-vatta*. Spices are usually blended in certain combinations to produce *masalas*. *Garam masala*, for example, is often a red-hot combination of cloves and cinnamon with peppercorns.

Popular spices include *saffron*, an expensive flavoring produced from flowers. This is used to give rice that yellow biriyani colouring and delicate fragrance. *Turmeric* also has a colouring property, acts as a preservative and has a distinctive smell and taste. *Chillies* are ground, dried or added whole to supply that curry heat. They come in red and green varieties but the green ones are hottest. *Ginger* is supposed to be good for the digestion, while many masalas contain *coriander* because it is said to cool the body. Strong and sweet *cardamom* is used in many desserts and in rich meat dishes. Other popular spices include *nutmeg, cinnamon, poppy seeds, caraway seeds, cummin, fenugreek, mace, garlic* and *cloves*.

Breads & Grains

Rice is, of course, the basic Indian staple, but although it is eaten throughout the country, it's all-important only in the south. The best Indian rice, it is generally agreed, is found in the north where *Basmati* rice grows in the Dehra Dun Valley. It has long grains, is yellowish and has a slightly sweetish or 'bas' smell. In the north (where wheat is the staple) rice is supplemented by a whole range of breads known as *rotis* or in the Punjab by *phulka* (blown up). You can also find western-style sliced bread (*double roti*) in India but it is almost always horrible, sickly sweet and nearly inedible.

Indian breads are varied but always delicious. Simplest is the *chappati*, just flour and water fried up like a thin pancake – it's an English invention. Rotis are flour and water cooked on a hot *tawa* griddle. Direct heat blows them up but how well that works depends on the glutin content of the wheat. Baste your roti in butter or ghee and it becomes a *paratha*. If you deep-fry it you will have a *poori* in the north or a *loochi* in the east. Made of lentil flour it is a *dosa* in the south; dosas are found all over India, and wrapped around curried vegetables you have *masala dosa*, a terrific snack meal. Another type of deep-fried bread with a stuffing is the *kachori*. Bake the bread in an oven and you have *nan*. Whatever you do with them, Indian rotis taste great.

Use your chappati or paratha to mop or scoop up your curry. An *idli* is a kind of rice dumpling, often served with a spicy curd sauce or with spiced lentils and chutney. *Papadums* are crispy deep-fried wafers often served with thalis or other meals.

Outside the Delhi Jami Masjid you may see 'big' chappatis known as *rumali* (handkerchiefs). Note that Hindus use their tawa concavely, Muslims convexly! In some hill stations (like Naini Tal or Mussoorie) you can get quite good western-style bread.

Basic Dishes

Curries can be vegetable, meat (usually chicken or lamb) or fish, but they are always fried in *ghee* (clarified butter) or vegetable oil. North or south they will be accompanied by rice, but in the north the various excellent breads will also come with them. There are a number of dishes which aren't really curries but are close

enough to them for western tastes. *Vindaloos* have a vinegar marinade and tend to be hotter than most curries. *Pork vindaloo* is a favourite dish in Goa. *Kormas*, on the other hand, are rich, substantial dishes prepared by braising. *Doopiaza* literally means 'two onions' and is a type of korma which uses onions at two stages in its preparation.

Probably the most basic of Indian dishes is *dhal*, rather like a thick lentil soup. Lentils are *masoor; malka* is a close relation but the grains are bigger. Dhal is almost always there, whether as an accompaniment to a curry or as a very basic meal in itself with chappatis or rice. In many places dhal and rice is just about all there is on the menu so you'll get heartily sick of it before you leave! The favourite dhal of Bengal and Gujarat is yellow *arhar*; in Bengal *channa* is also yellow, *mung* is green, *rajma* is the Heinz 57 varieties of dhal!

Other basic dishes include *mattar panir* – cheese and peas in gravy; *saag gosht* – meat and spinach; *alu dum* – potato curry; *alu chhole* – spicy-sour chick peas and diced potatoes.

Tandoori & Biriyani

Tandoori food is a northern speciality and refers to the clay oven in which the food is cooked after first being marinaded in a complex mix of herbs and yoghurt. Tandoori chicken is a special favourite. This food is not as hot as curry dishes and usually tastes terrific.

Biriyani (again chicken is a popular biriyani dish) is another northern Moghul dish. Here the meat is mixed with a deliciously flavoured, orange-coloured rice which is sometimes spiced with nuts or dried fruit. A *pulao* is a simpler version of a biriyani and you will also find it in other Asian countries further west. Those who have the idea that Indian food is always curry and always fiery hot will be surprised by tandoori and biriyani dishes.

Regional Specialities

Rogan Josh is a straightforward curried lamb always popular in the north and in Kashmir where it originated. *Gushtaba*, pounded and spiced meat balls cooked in a yoghurt sauce, is another Kashmiri speciality. Still in the north, *chicken makhanwala* is a rich dish cooked in a butter sauce.

Many coastal areas have excellent seafood, including Bombay where the *pomfret*, a flounder-like fish, is popular; so is Bombay duck, which is not a duck at all but another fish dish. *Dhansak* is a Parsi speciality found in Bombay – lamb or chicken cooked with curried lentils and steamed rice. Further south, Goa has excellent fish and prawns; in Kerala State, Cochin is famous for its prawns.

Another indication of the influence of central Asian cooking styles on north Indian food is the popularity of *kababs*. You'll find them all across north India with a number of local variations and specialities. The two basic forms are *sikka* (skewered) or *shami* (wrapped). In Calcutta *kati kababs* are a local favourite. Another Bengali dish is *dahi maach* – curried fish in yoghurt sauce, flavoured with ginger and turmeric. Further south in Hyderabad you could try *haleen*, pounded wheat with a lightly spiced mutton gravy. 'In Tamil Nadu', wrote a visitor, 'I particularly enjoyed *pongal* at breakfast, I think it's made of semolina with whole peppercorns'.

Side Dishes

Indian food generally has a number of side dishes to go with the main meal. Probably the most popular is *dahi* – curd or yoghurt. It has the useful ability of instantly cooling an over-heated curry – either blend it into the curry or, if it's too late, you can administer it straight to your mouth. Curd is often used in the cooking or as a dessert and appears in the popular drink *lassi*. *Raita* is another popular side dish consisting of curd mixed with cooked or raw vegetables, particularly cucumber (just like Greek zatziki) or tomato.

Sabzi are curried vegetables, *bhartha* is pureed or minced vegetables (particularly in the north), *bhujias* are fresh vegetables. *Mulligatawny* is a soup-like dish which is really just a milder, more liquid curry. It's a dish adopted into the English menu by the Raj. *Chutney* is pickled fruit or vegetables and is the standard relish for a curry.

Thalis

A *thali* is the all-purpose Indian vegetarian dish. Although it is basically a product of south India, you will find restaurants serving thalis or 'vegetarian plate meals' all over India. Often the sign will simply announce 'Meals'. In addition, there are regional variations like the particularly sumptuous Gujarati thalis.

The name is taken from the 'thali' dish in which it is served. This consists of a metal plate with a number of small metal bowls known as *katoris* on it. Sometimes the small bowls will be replaced by simple indentations right in the plate; in more basic places the 'plate' will be a big, fresh banana leaf. A thali consists of a variety of curry vegetable dishes, relishes, a couple of papadums, puris or dosas and a mountain of rice. A fancy thali may have a *pata*, a rolled leaf stuffed with fruit and nuts. There'll probably be a bowl of curd and possibly even a small dessert.

Thalis are consistently tasty and good food value, but they have two other unbeatable plus points for the budget traveller – they're cheap and they're usually 100% filling. Thalis can be as little as Rs 4 or 5 and will rarely cost much more than Rs 15 at the very most – big hotel apart. Most are 100% filling because they're normally 'all you can eat'. When your plate starts to get empty they come round, add another mountain of rice and refill the katoris. Thalis are eaten with fingers, although you may get a spoon for the dahi or dhal. Always wash your hands before you eat one – a sink or other place to wash your hands is provided in a thali restaurant.

One enthusiast's findings from four weeks of thalis in the south:

I tried a total of 35 different thalis. The tastiest was probably at the *Mathura Restaurant* in Madras, closely followed by the *Laxmi Vilas* in Bombay and the one in the dining hall at Ranakpur. The best for your money is in the downstairs restaurant at *New College House* in Madurai – very good service and a record 13 side dishes. Second best was the 'special thali' in the back part of *Mamalla Bhavan* in Mahabalipuram. The *worst* was at a small beachfront restaurant in Kovalam; I was in withdrawal and a desperate man. This was closely followed by every thali in Ernakulam.

Ivor McMahen, Canada

Snacks

Samosa, tasty little curried vegetable snacks fried up in a pastry triangle, are found all over India. *Bhelpuri* is a popular Bombay snack peddled across the city. *Chana* is spiced chick peas *(gram)* served with puris. *Sambhar* is a soup-like lentil-and-vegetable dish with a sour tamarind flavour. *Chat* is the general term for snacks and nibbles.

Western Food

Sometimes Indian food simply becomes too much and you want to escape to something familiar and reassuring. It's not always easy, but railway station restaurants often have something palatable and close to 'back home'. The Indian-food blues are particularly prone to hit you at breakfast time – somehow *idlis* never really feel like a breakfast. Fortunately that's the meal where you'll find an approximation to the west most easily obtained. All those wonderful Indian varieties of eggs can be had – half-fried, omelettes, you name it.

Toast and jam can almost always be found, and very often you can get cornflakes and hot milk, although Indian cornflakes would definitely be rejects from Mr Kellogg's production line. The Scots must have visited India too,

Street vendor setting up...

because porridge is often on the breakfast menu and usually is good.

That peculiar Raj-era term for a mid-morning snack still lives – *tiffin*. Today tiffin means any sort of light meal or snack. One western dish which Indians seem to have come 100% to terms with is chips (French fries). It's quite amazing how, if they are available, they will almost always be excellent. To be safe, ask for 'finger chips' or you may end up with what the English know as 'potato crisps' although to Americans they'll be 'potato chips'! Some Indian cooks call French fries 'Chinese potatoes'.

Other Asian foods, apart from Indian, are often available. There's still a small Chinese population, particularly in Calcutta and Bombay, so you can find Chinese food in the larger cities. In the north, where many Tibetans settled following the Chinese invasion of Tibet, you'll find Tibetan restaurants in places like Dharamsala, Manali or Srinagar.

Desserts & Sweets

Indians have quite a sweet tooth and an amazing selection of desserts and sweets to satisfy it. *Kulfi* is a widely available dessert, a sort of Indian interpretation of ice cream. You can, of course, also get normal ice cream all over India. The major brands are healthy and very good. *Rasgullas* are another very popular Indian dessert, sweet little balls of rose-water-flavoured cream cheese.

The desserts are basically rice or milk puddings, various interesting things in sweet syrup or else sweet pastries. *Gulub jamuns* are a typical example of the small 'things' in syrup – they're made of flour, yoghurt and ground almonds. *Jalebi* are pancakes in syrup. Milk dishes are usually boiled until the liquid has been removed and then have various ingredients added to make a dessert like *barfi*, which has coconut with almond or pistachio flavouring. *Sandesh* is another variety of milk dish, a particular favourite in Calcutta. *Payasam* is a southern sweet made from milk simmered with crushed cashews, cereals and sugar, topped with raisins. *Firnee* is a rice-pudding dessert with almonds, raisins and pistachios.

Many of the Indian sweets come covered in a thin layer of silver, as do some of the desserts. It's just that, silver beaten paper thin. Don't peel it off, it's quite edible. There are countless sweet shops with their goodies all lined up in glass showcases. Prices vary from Rs 5 to 10 for a kg but you can order 50 or 100 gm at a time or simply ask for a rupee's worth. These shops also often sell *dahi* (curd), which makes a very pleasant dessert as well as a good curry cooler. Sweets include all sorts of unidentifiable goodies; try them and see. *Halwa* is a translucent, vividly coloured sweet rather like Turkish delight.

Fruit

If your sweet tooth simply isn't sweet enough to cope with too many Indian desserts, you'll be able to fall back on India's wide variety of fruit. It varies all the way from tropical delights in the south to apples, apricots and other temperate-region fruits in the north. Some local specialities include cherries and strawberries in Kashmir, and apricots in Ladakh and Himachal Pradesh. Apples are found all over this north-western region but particularly in the Kulu Valley of Himachal Pradesh.

Melons are widespread in India, particularly watermelons, which are a fine thirst quencher when you're unhappy about the water and fed up with soft drinks. Try to get the first slice before the flies discover it. Coconuts are even better and in the hot season there'll be coconut stalls on many city street corners. When you've drunk the milk the stall holder will split the coconut open and cut you a slice from the outer covering to scoop the flesh out with.

Mangoes and bananas are also found in many parts of India; pineapples are found in Assam and elsewhere. You don't see oranges all over the place (lots in Kerala though), but tangerines are widespread in central India, particularly during the hot season. You can go through an awful lot of them in a day.

Pan

An Indian meal should properly be finished with *pan* – the name given to the collection of spices and condiments chewed with *betel*. Found throughout eastern Asia, betel is a mildly intoxicating and addictive nut, but by itself it is quite inedible. After a meal you chew a pan as a mild digestive.

Pan sellers have a whole collection of little trays, boxes and containers in which they mix either *sadha* (plain or *mitha* (sweet) pans. The ingredient may include, apart from the betel nut itself, lime paste (the chemical not the fruit), the powder known as *catachu*, various spices and even a dash of opium in a pricey pan. The whole concoction is folded up in a piece of edible leaf which you pop in your mouth and chew. When finished you spit the left-overs out and add another red blotch to the sidewalk. Over a long period of time, indulgence in pan will turn your teeth red-black and even addict you to the betel nut. But trying one occasionally won't do you any harm.

Cooking Back Home

There are all sorts of books about Indian cooking should you want to continue the experiment after you leave India. *Indian Cookery* by Dharamjit Singh (Penguin, London, 1970) is a useful paperback introduction to the art.

Drinks – Non-Alcoholic

Surprisingly, tea is not the all-purpose and all-important drink it is in Iran and Afghanistan. What's worse, the Indians, for all the tea they grow, make some of the most hideously over-sweetened, murkily-milky excuses for that fine beverage you ever saw. It may go by the name of *chai*, just like in the rest of Asia, but what a let down. Still, some people like it and it is cheap. 'Don't think of bazaar tea as tea in the western sense', was the advice one traveller gave!

Better tea can be obtained if you ask for 'tray tea', which gives you the tea, the milk and the sugar separately and allows you to combine them as you see fit. Usually tea is 'mixed tea' or 'milk tea', which means it has been made by putting cold water, milk, sugar and tea into one pot and bringing the whole concoction to the boil, then letting it stew for a long time. The result can be imagined.

Tea is more popular in the north, while in the south coffee, which is generally good, is the number-one drink. There are Indian Coffee Houses all over the country. You should not drink water unless you know it has been boiled, but frankly that is often difficult. In the hot season it is

simply too dry not to drink water – if you quenched your thirst all the time on Indian soft drinks you'd drop dead from a sugar overdose.

Water is generally safer in the dry season than in the monsoon (when it really can be dangerous), and adding your own purifying tablets can further improve it. Some travellers report that in the major cities it is 'certainly chlorinated' and can be drunk without ill effect. You can probably count on the water being reasonably safe in big hotels and the better restaurants. Although it is no safer than the water it's made with, lemon squash, *nimbu pani*, is almost always excellent. Plastic bottles of mineral water can now be bought in many centres.

Soft drinks are a safe substitute for water although they tend to have a high sugar content. Coca Cola got the boot from India a few years back for not cooperating with the government, but there are many substitutes with names like Campa Cola, Thums Up, Limca, Fanta, Gold Spot or Double Seven. By Asian standards they are pretty expensive at around Rs 2 to 2.50 for a 190-ml bottle (more in restaurants). They're also sickly sweet if you drink too many of them, as you're virtually forced to in the hot season. One very pleasant escape is the Kashmiri apple juice drink Apco, but unfortunately it's only available in Kashmir. Apple juice drinks are also available in Himachal Pradesh and from Bhutan.

Coconut milk, straight from the young coconut, is a popular streetside drink. Another escape from soft drinks is soda water – Bisleri Soda is widely available and has the further advantage over soft drinks of coming in a larger bottle. With soda water you can get excellent, and safe, lemon squash sodas. Finally there's *lassi*, that oh so cool, refreshing and delicious iced curd (yoghurt) drink.

Drinks – Alcoholic

Alcohol is expensive – a bottle of Indian

beer can cost anything from Rs 8 up to Rs 30 or more in a flashy hotel; Rs 8 to 20 is the usual price range. In some states (like Goa) it is very cheap, some (like Tamil Nadu) very expensive. Indian beers have delightful names like Golden Eagle, Rosy Pelican, Cannon Extra Strong, Kingfisher, Guru or Punjab. They're not too bad if you can find them cold, but all tend to be gassy.

Beer and other Indian interpretations of western alcoholic drinks are known as IMFL – Indian Made Foreign Liquor. Local drinks are known as Country Liquor and include *toddy*, a mildly alcoholic extract from the coconut palm flower, and *feni*, a distilled liquor produced from fermented cashew nuts or from coconuts. The two varieties taste quite different.

Beer Tasting

Travelling English beer enthusiast John Lia sent us his rating of 39 brands of Indian beer ranging from PALS ('the pits, like dog food') to Rosy Pelican ('good and refreshing'). I wasn't totally in agreement with his tastes (good old Kingfisher – 'very weak' he reported – can't be that bad) and a knowledgeable bartender in Bhubaneswar thought his preferences were slanted towards strong or (as he put it) 'kicking' beers. I managed to try about 10 different varieties while I was updating this edition but surprisingly four of them weren't on John's lengthy tasting list! There are a hell of a lot of beer brands in India.

Indian Menus

One of the delights of Indian menus is their amazing English. Start the morning, for example, with corn flaks, also useful for shooting down enemy aircraft. Or perhaps corn flex – Indian corn flakes are often so soggy they'll do just that.

Even before your corn-whatever you should have some tea, and what a variety of types of tea India can offer. You can try bed tea, milk tea, light tea, mixed tea, tray tea, plain tea, half set tea and even (of course) full set tea. Eggs also offer unlimited possibilities: half-fried eggs, pouch eggs (or egg pooch), bolid eggs, sliced omelettes, skerem boil eggs (interesting combination there) or simply

aggs. Finally, you could finish off breakfast with that popular Scottish dish – pordge.

Soup before a meal – how about French onion soup? Or Scotch brath, mughutoni or perhaps start with a parn coactale. Follow that up with some amazing interpretations of western dishes, like the restaurant that not only had Napoleon spaghetti but also Stalin spaghetti! Perhaps a seezling plator sounds more like it? Or simply bum chicken? A light meal – well, why not have a sandwitch? And if you want a drink how about orange squish or that popular Indian soft drink Thumps Up.

Chinese dishes offer a whole new range of possibilities, including mashrooms and bamboo sooghts, spring rolos, plane fried rice and park fried rice. Finally for dessert you could try apple pai or treat yourself to leeches & cream!

Travellers have sent in lots more menu suggestions since the first edition of this book. Like 'tired fruit juice' (tinned you know), 'plane tost' (the stuff they serve on Indian Airlines?), 'omlet & began', 'scrambled eggs', 'banana frilters' and 'chocolet padding'. Or something even Colonel Sanders hasn't thought of yet – 'fried children'.

BOOKS

India is a great place for reading – there's plenty to read about, there's plenty of time to read on those never-ending bus or train trips, and when you get to the big cities you'll find plenty of bookshops to get the reading matter from. The suggested books that follow are only a few interesting ones that should be readily available. Of course there are far more now long out of print. In addition there are many beautiful coffee-table books on India – ideal for whetting the appetite or for conjuring up the magic of India after your return. India has spawned an equally large number of cookery books – if you want to get into curry and all those spices you'll have no trouble finding plenty of instructions. Indian art has also generated a great number of interesting books of all types.

India is one of the world's largest publishers of books in English. After the USA and the UK it's up there with Canada or Australia as a major English-language publisher. You'll find a great number of interesting books on India by Indian publishers, books which are generally not available in the west.

At the other extreme Indian publishers do cheap reprints of western bestsellers at prices far below western levels. A meaty Leon Uris or Arthur Hailey novel, ideal for an interminable train ride, will often cost less than $2. Compare that with your local bookshop prices. The favourite western author is probably P G Wodehouse – 'Jeeves must be considered another incarnation of Vishnu', was one explanation. Recently published British and American books also reach Indian bookshops remarkably fast and with very low markups. If a bestseller in Europe or America has major appeal for India they'll often rush out a paperback in India to forestall possible pirates. The novel *City of Joy* (a European bestseller about Calcutta) was out in paperback in India before even the hardback had reached Australia.

Novels

Plenty of authors have taken the opportunity of setting their novels in a continent as colourful as India. Rudyard Kipling, with books like *Kim* and *Plain Tales from the Hills*, is the Victorian English interpreter of India par excellence. In *A Passage to India* E M Forster perfectly captures that collision of incomprehension in India between the English and the Indians. A very readable book.

Much more recent but again following that curious question of why the English and Indians, so dissimilar in many ways, were so similar in others, is Ruth Prawer Jhabwala's *The Heat & The Dust*. The contemporary narrator of the tale also describes the backpacker's India in a flawless fashion.

Probably the most widely acclaimed Indian novel since the war was Salman Rushdie's *Midnight's Children*, which won the Booker Prize. It tells of the children who were born, like modern India itself, at the stroke of midnight on that August night in 1947 and how the life of one particular 'midnight's child' is inextricably intertwined with events in India itself. Rushdie's follow-up, *Shame*, is set in modern Pakistan.

Paul Scott's *The Raj Quartet* and *Staying On* are other important novels set in India. The big 'bestseller' Indian novel of recent years was the monster tome *Far Pavilions* by M M Kaye. Women's magazine romance in some ways, but some interesting angles on India. *Nectar in a Sieve* by Kamala Markandaya has been recommended as an interesting account of a woman's life in rural India. See the Calcutta chapter for more on *City of Joy*, the 1986 bestseller in Europe and India.

General Interest

John Keay's *Into India* (John Murray, London, 1973) is a fine general introduction to travelling in India. One traveller's observations and perceptions of life in India today provide an illuminating idea of what it's really like.

Paul Theroux's best-selling railway odyssey *The Great Railway Bazaar* takes you up and down India by train (and across most of the rest of Asia) and turns the whole world into a railway carriage. Engrossing, like most such books, as much for insights into the author as into the people he meets. *Slow Boats to China* by Gavin Powell follows much the same path but this time by boat. *Slowly Down the Ganges* by Eric Newby is another boat-trip tale; this one borders, at times, on sheer masochism!

Karma Kola by Gita Mehta is accurately subtitled 'the marketing of the mystic east'. It amusingly and cynically describes the unavoidable and hilarious collision between India looking to the west for technology and modern methods, and the west descending upon India in search of ancient wisdom. *India File* by Trevor Fishlock (Indian paperback by Rupa, New Delhi, 1984) is a very readable collection of articles on India by *The*

Times correspondent. The chapter on sex in India is often hilarious and other sections are equally illuminating.

Ved Mehta has written a number of interesting personal views of India. *Walking the Indian Streets* (Penguin paperback) is a slim and highly readable account of the culture shock he went through on returning to India after a long period abroad. *Portrait of India* is by the same author. Ronald Segal's *The Crisis of India* (Penguin, London, 1965) is written by a South African Indian on the theme that spirituality is not always more important than a full stomach – a counter-argument to all the praise of Hinduism and its spirituality.

Finally, no survey of personal insights into India can ignore V S Naipaul's two controversial books *An Area of Darkness* and *India – A Wounded Civilisation*. Born in Trinidad but of Indian descent, Naipaul tells in the first book of how India, unseen and unvisited, haunted him and the impact upon him when he made the pilgrimage to the motherland. You may well find that much of this book rings very true with your own experiences while in India. In the second book he writes of India's unsuccessful search for a new purpose and meaning for its civilisation.

History

If you want a thorough introduction to Indian history then look for the Pelican two-volume *A History of India*. In volume 1 Romila Thapar follows Indian history from about 1000 BC to the coming of the Moghuls in the 16th century AD. Volume 2 by Percival Spear follows the rise and fall of the Moghuls through to India since independence. At times both volumes are a little dry, but if you want a reasonably detailed history in a handy paperback format they're worth having.

The Wonder that was India by A L Basham gives detailed descriptions of the Indian civilisations, origins of the caste system and social customs, and detailed

information on Hinduism, Buddhism and other religions in India; it is very informative about art and architecture. It has a wealth of background material on ancient India without being overly academic.

Christopher Hibbert's *The Great Mutiny – India 1857* (Penguin, London, 1980) is a recently published single-volume description of the often lurid events of the mutiny. This readable paperback is illustrated with contemporary photographs.

Plain Tales from the Raj, edited by Charles Allen (Futura paperback, London, 1976), is the delightful book derived from the equally delightful series of radio programmes of the same name. It consists of a series of interviews with people who took part in British India on both sides of the table. Extremely readable and full of fascinating little insights into life during the Raj era.

Freedom at Midnight is India's best-selling book of the past decade. Its authors Larry Collins and Dominique Lapierre have written other equally popular modern histories, but you could hardly ask for a more enthralling series of events than those that led to India's independence in 1947. In India you can find *Freedom at Midnight* in a cheap Bell Books paperback (Vikas Publishing, Delhi, 1976).

Religion

If you want to understand India's religions a little better there are plenty of books about them available in India. The English series of Penguin paperbacks are amongst the best and are generally available in India. In particular, *Hinduism* by K M Sen (Penguin, London, 1961) is brief and to the point. If you want to read the Hindu holy books these are available in translations: *The Upanishads* (Penguin, London, 1965) and *The Bhagavad Gita* (Penguin, London, 1962). *Hindu Mythology*, edited by Wendy O'Flaherty (Penguin, London), is an interesting annotated collection of extracts from the Hindu holy books. Convenient if you don't want the whole thing.

Penguin also has a translation of the Koran. If you want to know more about Buddhism, *Buddhism* by Christmas Humphreys (Penguin, London, 1949) is an excellent introduction. *A Handbook of Living Religions* edited by John R Hinnewls (Pelican, London, 1985) provides a succinct and readable summary of all the various religions you will find in India, including Christianity and Judaism.

Guides

First published in 1859, the 22nd edition of *A Handbook for Travellers in India, Pakistan, Nepal, Bangladesh & Sri Lanka* (John Murray, London, 1975) is that rarest of animals, a Victorian travel guide. If you've got a deep interest in Indian architecture and can afford the somewhat hefty price, then take along a copy of this immensely detailed guidebook. Unfortunately its system of following 'routes', in the manner of all good Victorian guidebooks, makes it somewhat difficult to locate things but the effort is worth it. Along the way you'll find a lot of places where the British army made gallant stands, and more than a few statues of Queen Victoria – most of which have been replaced by statues of Mahatma Gandhi.

There are a great number of regional and local guidebooks published in India. Many of them are excellent value and describe certain sites (the Ajanta and Ellora Caves or Sanchi for example) in much greater detail than is possible in this book. The guides produced by the Archaeological Survey of India are particularly good. Many of the other guides have a most amusing way with English.

Books on wildlife are difficult to get, but birdwatchers may find the *Collins Handguide to the Birds of the Indian Subcontinent* useful. It doesn't cover all the birds by any means but it does have the best illustrations and text, and if you're not a very serious bird-watcher you will probably find it useful. Visitors to Kashmir can use *Birds of Nepal*, which includes notes on Kashmir and Sikkim.

Other Lonely Planet Regional Guides

It's pleasant to be able to claim that for more information on India's neighbours and for travel beyond India most of the best guides come from Lonely Planet! If you're heading north to Nepal then look for *Kathmandu & the Kingdom of Nepal*, with complete information on the mountain nation. If you're planning on trekking in Nepal or simply want more information on trekking in general, then look for *Trekking in the Nepal Himalaya* and *Trekking in the Indian Himalaya*. Or you can cross right over the Himalaya with our *Tibet – a travel survival kit*.

For other Indian neighbours there are other Lonely Planet guides. *Pakistan – a travel survival kit* is our guide to the 'unknown land of the Indus'. We also have a guide to India's other Muslim neighbour – *Bangladesh – a travel survival kit*. *Burma – a travel survival kit* covers that thoroughly delightful and totally eccentric country. If your travels take you south to Sri Lanka then you need *Sri Lanka – a travel survival kit*, whether you're planning to explore the ancient cities or laze on the beaches. Finally, if you want more information on the north-west of India then look for our comprehensive guide to *Kashmir, Ladakh & Zanskar*.

If you're travelling further than India across Asia to Europe (Iran permitting), then our book is *West Asia on a Shoestring*. If it's further east you want then look for *South-East Asia on a Shoestring*.

Also Recommended

Readers have recommended numerous other books such as *Eating the Indian Air* by John Morris; *The Gorgeous East* by Rupert Croft-Cooke; *Delhi is Far Away* and *The Grand Trunk Road* by John

Wiles; and books by Jan and Rumer Godden. *A Princess Remembers* by Gayatri Devi is useful if you're going on to Jaipur. *Train to Pakistan* by Kushwant Singh is an excellent novel on the traumas of partition. Irish wanderer Dervla Murphy heads south in her book *On a Shoestring to Coorg*. There are some wonderful Indian comic books dealing with Hindu mythology and Indian history.

FILMS

Once you've read all you can about India, keep your eyes open for a showing of Louis Malle's two-part film *Phantom India*. Running about seven hours in all, this is a fascinating in-depth look at India today. At times it's very self-indulgent, but as an overall view it can't be beaten – and it has been banned in India. The Australian ABC TV channel has produced two excellent documentary series on India, one titled *Journey into India*, the other *Journey into the Himalayas*. Both of them, but particularly the former, are worth seeing if you get a chance.

Of course the epic *Gandhi* has been the major recent India film, spawning a host of new and reprinted books on the Mahatma. *Heat & Dust* has also been made into an excellent film, as has *A Passage to India*.

MAPS

Bartholomew's map of *India, Pakistan, Nepal, Bangladesh & Sri Lanka* is probably the most useful general map of India. It gives you plenty of detail of small towns and villages to help speed along those long bus or train trips. If it has any fault for the traveller, it is that it does not always include places of great interest but small population. The map is widely available in India as well as overseas.

Locally, the Government Map Office produces a series of maps covering all of India. In Delhi their office is opposite the tourist office on Janpath. It's upstairs, above the cafeteria beside the Central Cottage Industries Emporium. The maps are not all that useful since they will not allow production of anything at a reasonable scale which shows India's sea or land borders. It is illegal to take any Survey of India map of larger than 1:250,000 scale out of the country.

The Government of India Tourist Office has a number of excellent give-away city maps and also a reasonable all-India map. State tourist offices do not have much by the way of maps, but the Himachal Pradesh office has three excellent trekking maps which cover the trekking routes in that state.

THINGS TO BUY

India is packed with beautiful things to buy – you could easily load yourself up to the eyeballs with goodies you pick up around the country. The cardinal rule of purchasing handicrafts is to bargain and bargain hard. You can get a good idea of what is reasonable in quality and in price by visiting the various state emporiums, particularly in New Delhi, and the Central Cottage Industries Emporiums. Here you can inspect items from all over the country at fixed prices which indicate fairly well what you can knock the regular dealers down below.

As with handicrafts in any country, don't buy until you have developed a little understanding and appreciation. Rushing in and buying the first thing you see will inevitably lead to later disappointment. In touristy places, particularly places like Varanasi, take extreme care with the commission merchants – these guys hang around waiting to pick you up and cart you off to their favourite dealers where whatever you pay will have a hefty margin built into it to pay their commission. Stories about 'my family's place', 'special deal at my friend's place', are just stories and nothing more.

Carpets

It may not surprise you that India produces and exports more hand-crafted carpets than Iran, but it probably is more of a surprise that some of them are of virtually equal quality. In Kashmir, where India's best carpets are produced, the carpet-making techniques and styles were brought from Persia even before the Moghul era. The art flourished under the Moghuls and today Kashmir is packed with small carpet producers. There are many carpet dealers in Delhi as well as in Kashmir. Persian motifs have been much embellished on Kashmiri carpets, which come in a variety of sizes – three by five feet, four by six feet and so on. They are either made of pure wool, wool with a small percentage of silk to give a sheen (known as silk touch) or pure silk. The latter are more for decoration than hard wear. Expect to pay from Rs 5000 for a good-quality four-by-six carpet and don't be surprised if the price is more than twice as high.

Other carpet-making areas include Badhoi and Mirzapur in Uttar Pradesh or Warangal and Eluru in Andhra Pradesh. In Kashmir and Rajasthan the coarsely woven woollen *numdas* are made. These are more primitive and folksy than the fine carpets. Around the Himalaya and Uttar Pradesh *daris*, flat-weave cotton-warp-and-weft rugs, are woven. In Kashmir *gabbas* are appliqué-like rugs. The many Tibetan refugees in India have brought their craft of making superbly colourful Tibetan rugs with them. A three-by-five Tibetan rug will be less than Rs 1000.

Unless you're an expert it is best to have expert advice or buy from a reputable dealer if you're spending large amounts of money on carpets. Check prices back home too; many western carpet dealers sell at prices you would have difficulty matching even at source.

Papier Mâché

This is probably the most characteristic Kashmiri craft. The basic papier-mâché article is made in a mould, then painted and polished in successive layers until the final intricate design is produced. Prices depend upon the complexity and quality of the painted design and the amount of gold leaf used. Items made include bowls, cups, containers, jewel boxes, letter holders, tables, lamps, coasters, trays and so on. A cheap bowl might cost only Rs 10, a large, well-made item might approach Rs 1000.

Pottery

In Rajasthan interesting white-glazed pottery is made with hand-painted blue-flower designs – attractively simple. Terracotta images of the gods and children's toys are made in Bihar.

Metalwork

Copper and brass items are popular throughout India. Candle holders, trays, bowls, tankards, ashtrays are made in Bombay and other centres. In Rajasthan and Uttar Pradesh the brass is inlaid with exquisite designs in red, green and blue enamel. *Bidhri* is a craft of Andhra Pradesh and particularly Hyderabad, where silver is inlaid into gunmetal. Hookah pipes, lamp bases and jewellery boxes are made in this manner.

Jewellery

Many Indian women put most of their wealth into jewellery, so it is no wonder that so much of it is available. For western tastes the heavy folk-art jewellery of Rajasthan has particular appeal. You'll find it all over the country, but in Rajasthan in the greatest profusion of all. In the north you'll also find Tibetan jewellery, even chunkier and more folk-like than the Rajasthan variety.

Leatherwork

Of course Indian leatherwork is not made from cow-hide but from buffalo-hide or some other substitute. *Chappals*, those basic sandals found all over India, are the most popular purchase. In craft shops in Delhi you can find well-made leather bags, handbags and other items. In

Kashmir leather shoes and boots, often of quite good quality, are made, along with coats and jackets of often abysmally low quality.

Textiles
This is still India's major industry and 40% of the total production is at the village level where it is known as *khadi*. Bedspreads, table cloths, cushion covers or material for clothes are all popular purchases. There is an amazing variety of styles, types and techniques around the country. In Gujarat and Rajasthan heavy material is embroidered with tiny mirrors and beads to produce the mirror-work used in everything from dresses to stuffed toys to wall hangings. Tie-dye work is also popular in Rajasthan.

In Kashmir embroidered materials are made into shirts and dresses. Fine shawls of *pashmina* goats' wool also come from Kashmir. *Phulkari* bedspreads or wall hangings come from the Punjab. *Batik* is a recent introduction from Indonesia but already widespread; *kalamkari* cloth from Andhra Pradesh and Gujarat is an associated but far older craft.

Bronze Figures
In the south delightful small images of the gods are made by the age-old lost-wax process. A wax figure is made, a mould is formed around it and the wax is melted and poured out. The molten metal is poured in and when it's solidified the mould is broken open. Figures of Shiva as dancing Nataraj are amongst the most popular.

Woodcarving
In the south, images of the gods are also carved out of sandalwood. Rosewood is used to carve animals – elephants in particular. Carved wooden furniture and other household items, either in natural finish or lacquered, are also made in various locations. In Kashmir intricately carved wooden screens, tables, jewellery boxes, trays and the like are carved from Indian walnut. They follow a similar pattern to that seen on the decorative trim of houseboats. Old temple carvings can be delightful.

Clothes & Saris
In Bombay and Delhi in particular you can find many readymades exactly like those you'll find from India in western boutiques. Indeed they're most probably the rejects from some export order or other. The prices are so low you need hardly worry, but as usual it's wise to check the quality. Saris, the most Indian of women's outfits, are made in various styles and types of material around the country. In Varanasi they're made of silk, often with gold edging.

Paintings
Reproductions of the beautiful old miniatures are painted in many places, but beware of paintings claimed to be antique – they're highly unlikely to be so. Also note that quality can vary widely; low prices often mean low quality and if you buy before you've had a chance to look at a lot of miniatures and develop some appreciation you'll inevitably find you bought unwisely.

Other
Marble inlay pieces from Agra are pleasant reminders of the beauty of the Taj. They come as either simple little pieces or larger items like jewellery boxes. Appliqué work is popular in many places such as Orissa. In the Kutch region of Gujarat interesting stuffed toys are made. Indian musical instruments always have an attraction for travellers, although you don't see nearly as many backpackers lugging sitars around as you did 10 years ago. A more sensible Indian music buy might be records or tapes. You can always take back Indian tea, food products like mango pickles or papadums, packs of beedies.

At the many Bata shoe shops in India western-style shoes are cheap and reasonably well made. Their best-quality men's shoes are about US$20 to 25, far less than shoes of similar quality in London or New York.

A Warning!

Lots of people want to buy things in India but aren't keen on carting them all around the country with them and then back home. *No problem* say the shops. We'll mail it for you. We've been doing it for years, never had a problem, *trust us*. People trust them and nine times out of 10 there is no problem, the goods turn up *eventually* and everyone is happy. The other 10 times out of 100 you never see the goodies again. Maybe they got lost in the post, maybe they never got sent in the first place, maybe they never had any intention of sending them, who knows? Since the first edition of this book we've had lots of letters from unhappy people who have paid for crafts that have never turned up and want us to do something about it. There is no room in this book to list all the names of shops who were going to send something but didn't. The message? Take it with you, send it yourself, or don't tell us about it!

Antiques

Articles over 100 years are not allowed to be exported out of India. If you have doubts about some item and think it could be defined as an antique, you can check with:

Bombay
    Superintending Archaeologist, Antiquities, Archaeological Survey of India, Sion Fort
Calcutta
    Superintending Archaeologist, Eastern Circle, Archaeological Survey of India, Narayani Building, Brabourne Rd
New Delhi
    Director, Antiquities, Archaeological Survey of India, Janpath
Madras
    Superintending Archaeologist, Southern Circle, Archaeological Survey of India, Fort St George
Srinagar

Superintending Archaeologist, Frontier Circle, Archaeological Survey of India, Minto Bridge

THINGS TO SELL

All sorts of western technological items are good things to sell in India, but cameras, tape recorders, typewriters and the like will most probably be entered into your passport to ensure they leave the country with you. Particularly in Calcutta, Delhi and Madras there is a good market for your bottle of duty-free whisky (say Rs 250). The same applies in Patna if you fly down from Nepal. It has been suggested that prices are even better in smaller towns.

Pocket calculators and watches are popular things to sell and are less likely to be recorded in your passport. The best market is for high-quality watches, not cheap digital things. Don't try and bring several of the same items through customs – it's a bit obvious. Make sure they have 'made in ... ' prominently marked on them. Japan or West Germany are preferable to Taiwan, Korea, etc. Your selling price will be much better if you can supply original boxes, instruction manuals and the lot. It's necessary to bargain hard. In Delhi the underground market is a good place to sell, in Bombay along D Naoragi Rd between Victoria Terminus and Flora Fountain, in Calcutta the New Market.

Be very wary of the buying-to-sell-later game – most people buying things in India to sell elsewhere know what they are about and have spent a lot of time testing the market and establishing good relations with suppliers. Buying precious stones in Agra and Jaipur to sell in Nepal is a favourite game which is unlikely to return the average traveller any profit. We regularly get letters from unfortunate travellers who have been talked into buying precious stones which they are assured can be sold in the west for several times the purchase price. Don't believe it, that story simply isn't true.

LANGUAGE

There is no 'Indian' language, which is part of the reason English is still widely spoken over 30 years after the British left. The country is divided up into a great number of local languages and in many cases the state boundaries have been drawn on linguistic lines. In all there are 14 major languages in India and probably over two hundred minor languages and dialects. The scope for misunderstanding can be easily appreciated!

The most important Indian language is Hindi, spoken by about 50% of the population. In recent years major efforts have been made to promote Hindi as the national language of India and to gradually phase out English. A stumbling block to this plan is that while Hindi is the predominant language in the north – and also related to other northern languages such as Punjabi, Gujarati, Oriya and Bengali – it bears little relation to the Dravidian languages of the south; and in the south very few people speak Hindi. Tamil is the most important Dravidian language, while others include Telugu, Kanada and Malayalam. It is from the south and particularly the state of Tamil Nadu that the most vocal opposition to the adoption of Hindi comes, along with the strongest support for the retention of English.

For many educated Indians, English is virtually their first language and for a great number of Indians who speak more than one language it will be their second language rather than another Indian language. Thus it is very easy to get around India with English – after all, many Indians have to speak English to each other if they wish to communicate. Nevertheless it's always nice to know at least a little of the local language, so the following words and phrases are in Hindi:

where is a hotel (tourist office)?
hotal (turist afis) kahan hai?
how far is .... ?   *.... kitne dur hai?*

how do I get to .... ?
   .... kojane ke liye kaise jana parega?

hello, goodbye	*namaste*
yes/no	*han/nahin*
please	*meharbani se*
thank you	*shukriya, dhanyawad*
how much?	*kitne paise?*
this is expensive	*yeh bahut mehnga hai*
what is your name?	*apka shubh nam?*
what is the time?	*kya baja hai?*
come here	*yahan ao*
show me the menu	*mujha minu dikhao*
the bill please	*bill lao*
big	*bara*
small	*chota*
today	*aaj*
day	*din*
night	*rat*
week	*saptah*
month	*mahina*
year	*sal*
medicine	*dawa*
ice	*baraf*
egg	*anda*
fruit	*phal*
vegetables	*sabzi*
water	*pani*
rice	*chawal*
tea	*chai*
coffee	*kafi*
milk	*dudh*
sugar	*chini*
butter	*makkhan*

Beware of *acha*, that all-purpose word for 'OK'. It can also mean 'OK, I understand what you mean, but it isn't OK'. As in 'Have you got a room available?' to which the answer 'Acha' means 'I understand you want a room but I haven't got one'.

Tamil

Although Hindi is being promoted as the

'official' language of India, it won't get you very far in the south, where Tamil reigns supreme. Tamil is a much more difficult language to master and the pronunciation is not easy. The following words and phrases are in Tamil:

I want to go to ....
   naan ... kku poka-vendum
how do I get there?
   naan anke eppadi povathu
where is ....?
   .... *yenge irukkirathu*

good morning/	
good night	*vanakkam*
good bye	*poi varukiren*
good bye (to you)	*poi varungal*
how do you do	*nalama*
yes/no	*aam/illai*
thank you	*nandri*
how much?	*vilai enna*
too expensive	*athika vilai*
big	*perithu*
small	*siriyathu*
good	*nallathu*
bad	*kettathu*
today	*aaj*
day*	*naal*
day**	*pahal neram*
night	*iravu neram*
week	*vaaram*
month	*maatham*
year	*varudam*
eat	*sappidu*
drink	*kudi*

Numbers

A peculiarity of Indian numbers is that whereas we count in tens, hundreds, thousands, millions, billions, the Indian numbering system goes tens, hundreds, thousands, hundred thousands, ten millions. A hundred thousand is a *lakh* and ten million is a *crore*.

These two words are almost always used in place of their English equivalent. Thus you will see ten lakh rather than one

million and one crore rather than ten million. Furthermore, the numerals are generally written that way too – thus 3,00,000 (three lakh) not 300,000 (three hundred thousand) or 1,05,00,000 (one crore, five lakh) not 10,500,000 (ten million, five hundred thousand). If you say something costs five crore or someone is worth 10 lakh it always means 'of rupees'.

	Hindi	Tamil
1	*ek*	*onru*
2	*do*	*irandu*
3	*tin*	*moonru*
4	*char*	*naangu*
5	*panch*	*ainthu*
6	*chhe*	*aaru*
7	*sat*	*ezhu*
8	*ath*	*ettu*
9	*nau*	*onpathu*
10	*das*	*paththu*
100	*sau*	*nooru*
1000	*hazar*	*aayiram*
100,000	*lakh*	
10,000,000	*crore*	

Phrasebooks

A Hindi and Urdu phrasebook and a Bengali phrasebook will soon be added to the Lonely Planet *Language Survival Kit* series. There are also many phrasebooks and teach-yourself books available in India for Hindi and the other major languages, if you want to learn more of the language. Some of them are typically and amusingly Indian. A section on a visit to the doctor in one phrasebook included the following useful series of phrases, the first of which is quite unlikely in India:

I suffer from severe constipation
I am feeling a bit out of sorts today
The patient is sinking fast
He has much run down
The patient is in a precarious condition
Cholera has broken out in the city
He is dying by inches

WHERE TO FIND WHAT

India can offer almost anything you want, whether it's beaches, forts, amazing travel experiences, fantastic spectacles or a search for yourself. Below are just a few of those possibilities and where to start looking.

Beaches

People generally don't come all the way to India to laze on a beach – but there are some superb beaches here if you're in that mood. On the west coast, at the southern end of Kerala, there's Kovalam; further north, Goa has a whole collection of beautiful beaches complete with the soft white sand, gentle lapping waves and swaying palms of postcards. Over on the east coast you could try the beach at Mahabalipuram in Tamil Nadu. From the Shore Temple the beaches stretch north towards Madras and there are some fine places to stay. In Orissa the great temple of Konarak is only a couple of km away from another superb, and virtually deserted, beach.

beach	state	page
Kovalam	Kerala	697
Goa		573
Mahabalipuram	Tamil Nadu	723
Konarak	Orissa	518
Puri	Orissa	513
Waltair	Andhra Pradesh	666

Faded Touches of the Raj

Although the British have been gone from India for over 30 years, there are many places where you'd hardly know it. Of course much of India's government system, bureaucracy, communications, sports (the Indians are crazy over cricket) and media are British to the core, but you'll also find the British touch in more unusual, enjoyable and amusing ways. For example, the Fairlawn Hotel in Calcutta where the Raj definitely lives in totally unfaded glory. The imposing Victoria Memorial, also in Calcutta, where they tried to build an imitation British Taj Mahal. The Maharajah's Palace in Mysore, rebuilt after it burned down earlier this century.

Could anything be more British than the Dal Lake houseboats, all chintz, overstuffed armchairs and understatement? Or the Residency at Lucknow where with stiff upper lip the British held out against those pesky mutineers in 1857. Or relax in true British style for afternoon tea at Glenary's Tea Rooms in Darjeeling; come to think of it, all of Darjeeling is a touch of the Raj.

sight	place	page
Fairlawn Hotel	Calcutta, West Bengal	323
Victoria Memorial	Calcutta, West Bengal	317
Maharajah's Palace	Mysore, Karnataka	614
houseboats	Dal Lake, Kashmir	217
The Residency	Lucknow, Uttar Pradesh	260
Glenary's Tea Rooms	Darjeeling, West Bengal	345

Freak Centres

India has been the ultimate goal of the on-the-road hippy dream for years and somehow the '60s still continues in India's kind climate. From the clothes, the attitude and the music, Woodstock lives and the Beatles haven't even broken up yet. Goa has always been a great freak centre, the beaches are an attraction at any time of the year and every full moon is the occasion for a great gathering of the clans – but Christmas is its peak period when half the freaks in India seem to flock to its beaches.

In Rajasthan the holy lake of Pushkar has a smaller, but semi-permanent, freak population. Or south at Kovalam the fine beaches attract a steady clientele. The technicolour Tibetan outlook on life (they've got a way with hotels and restaurants too) works well in Kathmandu so why not in India – you'll find Dharamsala and Manali, both in Himachal Pradesh, also have longer-term populations of visitors. Hampi, capital of the Vijayanagar kingdom, is very small in terms of number of visitors but definitely on the circuit. Finally, Puri in Orissa and Mahabalipuram in Tamil Nadu both have temples and beaches, a sure-fire combination.

centre	state	page
Goa		573
Pushkar	Rajasthan	388
Kovalam	Kerala	697
Dharamsala	Himachal Pradesh	186
Manali	Himachal Pradesh	197
Hampi	Karnataka	636
Puri	Orissa	513
Mahabalipuram	Tamil Nadu	723

Great Places to Stay

India has some superb hotels – it's also got a large number of bug-infested filthy dumps and a fair number of 'international class' hotels which are mediocre in standards and service but decidedly first class in price. But it's hard to think of a more enchanting hotel than the *Lake Palace* in Udaipur – it's far more than merely a palace; elegant, whimsical and romantic are all labels that can be applied to it. Or in Kashmir, staying on a houseboat is half the fun of going there; they come in all price ranges, from the rock-bottom 'doonga boats' to 'five-star' luxury complete with television.

The *Fairlawn Hotel* in Calcutta is Raj-style elegance totally untarnished by time – a shame if this one ever fades. In Bombay the elegant *Taj Mahal Inter-Continental Hotel* is probably the best in India – even if you don't stay there its air-conditioned lounge and strategic location are a magnet for everyone from back-packers on up. There are some very fine Tourist Bungalows, run by the state government tourist offices, scattered around India. They're often in fine locations and usually great value.

Backpackers' favourites include the wonderful old *Broadlands* in Madras and the equally well-kept *Z Hotel* in Puri. In

Cochin the *Bolghatty Palace Hotel* is an old Dutch Palace built in 1744 and later a British residency – now a cheap hotel. Or try the *Bikaner Palace Hotel* with its quite amazing suites. Finally the *Naggar Castle*, high up on the valley side between Kulu and Manali, is a fairy-tale eagle's nest and so romantic it's ridiculous!

hotel	place	page
Lake Palace Hotel	Udaipur, Rajasthan	401
houseboats	Dal Lake, Kashmir	217
Fairlawn Hotel	Calcutta, West Bengal	323
Taj Mahal Inter-Continental	Bombay, Maharashtra	535
Broadlands Hotel	Madras, Tamil Nadu	708
Z Hotel	Puri, Orissa	515
Bolghatty Palace Hotel	Cochin, Kerala	678
Bikaner Palace Hotel	Mt Abu, Rajasthan	408
Naggar Castle	Naggar, Himachal Pradesh	196

Getting There is Half the Fun

A lot of travel in India can be indescribably dull, boring and uncomfortable. Trains take forever, buses fall apart and shake your fillings loose, even Indian Airlines sometimes manages to make your delay time far longer than your flying time. Despite the hassles there are a fair number of trips where getting there is definitely half the fun. Trains, of course, are the key to Indian travel and elsewhere in this book you'll find a section on India's unique and wonderful old steam trains. The Darjeeling Toy Train, which winds back and forth on its long climb up to the hill station, is half the fun of visiting Darjeeling. Other 'toy trains' include the run up to Matheran, just a couple of hours outside of Bombay, and the 'rack train' which makes the climb to Ooty from Mettupalayam in Tamil Nadu.

Then there is the delightful backwater trip through the waterways between Alleppey and Quilon – not only is the trip fascinating, it's absurdly cheap. Indian buses are generally a refined form of torture but the two-day trip between Srinagar in Kashmir and Leh in Ladakh is too good to miss. Finally, there could hardly be a more spectacular flight in the world than the Srinagar-Leh route which crosses the full width (and height) of the Himalaya.

trip	state	page
Siliguri-Darjeeling (toy train)	West Bengal	346
Neral-Matheran (toy train)	Maharashtra	547
Mettupalayam-Ooty (rack train)	Tamil Nadu	771
Allepey-Quilon (back – water trip)	Kerala	691
Srinagar-Leh (bus or jeep)	Jammu & Kashmir	236
Srinagar-Leh (Indian Airlines)	Jammu & Kashmir	234

Places to be/When to be there

India is a country of festivals and there are a number of places and times not to be missed. They start with the Independence Day festival in New Delhi each January – elephants, procession and military might with Indian princely splendour. In June-July the great Festival of the Cars at Puri is another superb spectacle as the gigantic temple car of Lord Jagannath makes its annual journey, pulled by thousands of eager devotees. September-October is the time to head for the hills to see the delightful Festival of the Gods in Kulu. That is part of the Dussehra festival which in the south is known as Dassehra and is at its most spectacular in Mysore. November is the time for the huge and colourful Cattle Festival at Pushkar in Rajasthan. Finally, at Christmas where else is there to be in India than Goa?

festival	place	page
Republic Day Parade	New Delhi	41/131
Festival of the Cars	Puri, Orissa	41/513
Festival of the Gods	Kulu, Himachal Pradesh	42/193
Dassehra	Mysore, Karnataka	42/613
Cattle Festival	Pushkar, Rajasthan	42/388
Christmas	Goa	43/573

Deserted Cities

There are a number of places in crowded India where great cities of the past have been deserted and left. Fatehpur Sikri, near Agra, is the most famous since Akbar founded, built and left this impressive centre in less than 20 years. Hampi, the centre of the Vijayanagar Empire, is equally impressive. Not too far from there are the ancient centres of Aihole and Badami. Some of the great forts that follow are also really deserted cities.

site	state	page
Fatehpur Sikri	Uttar Pradesh	254
Hampi	Karnataka	636
Aihole & Badami	Karnataka	641

Great Forts

India has more than its share of great forts – many of them now deserted – to tell of its tumultuous history. The Red Fort in Delhi is one of the most impressive but Agra Fort is an equally massive reminder of Moghul power at its height. A short distance south is the huge, impregnable-looking Gwalior Fort. The Rajputs in Rajasthan could build forts like nobody else and they've got them in all shapes and sizes and with every imaginable tale to tell. Chittorgarh Fort is tragic, Bundi and Kota forts whimsical, Jodhpur Fort huge and high, Amber Fort simply beautiful.

Further south there's Mandu, another fort impressive in its size and architecture but with a tragic tale to tell. Further south again at Daulatabad it's a tale of power, ambition and not all that much sense with another immense fort (they went in for large size) which was built and soon deserted. Important forts in the south include Bijapur and Golconda.

Naturally the European invaders had their forts too. You can see Portuguese forts in Goa and at Daman. The British too built their share – Fort William in Calcutta is, unfortunately, not open to the public, but Fort St George in Madras certainly is and has a fascinating museum.

fort	state	page
Red Fort	Delhi	136
Agra	Uttar Pradesh	246
Gwalior	Madhya Pradesh	473
Chittorgarh	Rajasthan	393
Bundi	Rajasthan	391
Kota	Rajasthan	390
Jodhpur	Rajasthan	410
Amber	Rajasthan	382
Mandu	Madhya Pradesh	471
Daulatabad	Maharashtra	563
Bijapur	Karnataka	643
Golconda, Hyderabad	Andhra Pradesh	654
Goa		573
Daman	(Gujarat)	446
Diu	(Gujarat)	450
Fort William, Calcutta	West Bengal	316
Fort St George, Madras	Tamil Nadu	704
Warangal	Andhra Pradesh	662

Where Gandhi Went

Following the success of the film *Gandhi* you might be interested in making a Gandhi trek round India, starting at Porbandar where he was born and Rajkot where he spent the early years of his life. From his period in South Africa he returned to India at Bombay and visited that city on numerous occasions. The massacre of 2000 peaceful protesters, one of the seminal events in the march to independence, took place in Amritsar. For many years Gandhi had his ashram at Sabarmati, across the river from Ahmedabad. The British interned him in the Aga Khan's Palace in Pune. Finally he was assassinated in the garden of the wealthy Birla family in New Delhi and his cremation took place at Raj Ghat.

event	place	page
Kirti Mandir	Porbandar, Gujarat	462
Kaba Gandhi	Rajkot, Gujarat	464
Mani Bhuvan	Bombay, Maharashtra	527
Jalianwala Bagh	Amritsar, Punjab	171
Sabarmati	Ahmedabad, Gujarat	435
Sevagram	Wardha, Maharashtra	571
Aga Khan's Palace	Pune, Maharashtra	554
Raj Ghat	New Delhi	140

Gurus & Religion

With India's great importance as a religious centre it's no wonder that so many people embark on some sort of spiritual quest there. There are all sorts of places and all sorts of gurus. One of the best known would have to be the Bhagwan Rajneesh and his orange folk, but of course he's scouring the earth for a new home these days.

Rishikesh has been a guru centre ever since the Beatles went there with the Maharishi Mahesh Yogi; it's still popular today. Vrindaban near Mathura, which is between Delhi and Agra, is the centre for the Hare Krishna movement. Muktananda had his ashram at Ganeshpuri but since his death there has been a bitter battle for the succession. The Theosophical Society is headquartered in Madras. The Ramakrishna Mission has centres all over India although Calcutta is its headquarters.

Sai Baba is in Bangalore while Brahma Kumaris' Raja Yoga (Prajapita Brahma) is based in Mt Abu. Raja Yoga followers wear all white. There are plenty of other centres but one guru you won't find in India is the Divine Light Mission's Muharaj ji; when he's there he stays in a hotel, his followers report.

movement	place	page
various	Rishikesh, Uttar Pradesh	287
Krishna Consciousness	Vrindaban, Uttar Pradesh	243
Swami Chidvilasananda	Ganeshpuri, Maharashtra	-

Satyananda	Monghyr, Bihar	
Theosophical Society	Madras, Tamil Nadu	702
Ramakrishna	Calcutta, West Bengal	310
Sri Aurobindo	Pondicherry, Tamil Nadu	730
Sai Baba	Bangalore, Karnataka	605
Raja Yoga	Mt Abu, Rajasthan	405

Holy Cities

Yes, in amongst all India's holy cities there are seven of particular holiness. Some of them, like Varanasi, are obvious while some, like Dwarka, are not so straightforward. Three of them are dedicated to Shiva, three to Vishnu;

Kanchipuram covers both gods. India's richest temple, however, is the Tirupathi and Tirumula complex in Andhra Pradesh. Other particularly holy cities include Rameswaram in Tamil Nadu, Puri in Orissa and Badrinath in Uttar Pradesh. A pilgrimage to Badrinath, Puri, Rameswaram and Dwarka covers the four corners (north, east, south and west) of India.

city	state	page
Varanasi	Uttar Pradesh	270
Hardwar	Uttar Pradesh	286
Ujjain	Madhya Pradesh	487
Mathura	Uttar Pradesh	241
Ayodhya	Uttar Pradesh	269
Dwarka	Gujarat	462
Kanchipuram	Tamil Nadu	721

Tony's Notebook

Sleeping In

Windowless rooms are not recommended for those without a digital watch, as we found at the Carlton Hotel in Bombay. After arriving at 8 in the evening and suffering from gross jet lag we crashed out in our room, intending that we would get up at 9 am to make tracks for Goa. At 8.45 we woke, got dressed, put on our backpacks and walked out into the corridor only to find it was dark. Suddenly we realised that we hadn't been sleeping 12 hours but only 45 minutes! We were suitably pissed off.

Asim Butt, England

Electricity

Indian hotels often have amazingly complicated switch panels with switches for fans, bells, lights in bathrooms, entrance-ways, over the beds, mirrors and so on. Generally three-quarters of them don't work, since failed light bulbs are rarely replaced as long as there is at least one still working. At a small restaurant in Aurangabad I counted a panel with nine fan controls, seven fuses and 46 switches plus assorted plugs, bulb holders and the like.

Flat on the Road

I arrived in Patna one evening and there, severely dead on the road outside my hotel, about a metre or two from the nearest fruit stall, was a dog. When I went out to dinner it was still there; another car or two had gone over it. When I came back from dinner it was looking very secondhand. By breakfast time it was pretty well flat. Even worse by lunchtime. By the time I left Patna that night it was more or less imprinted into the road surface. By the end of the week you could probably walk over it without even noticing it was there.

Getting There

FROM THE UK

Various excursion fares from London to India are available, but cost-wise you can easily do considerably better through London's many cheap ticket specialists or 'bucket shops'. Check the travel page ads in *The Times, Business Traveller* and the weekly 'what's on' magazine *Time Out*; or check giveaway papers like the *Australasian Express* and *LAM*. Two reliable London bucket shops are Trailfinders at 46 Earls Court Rd, London W8; and STA Travel at 74 Old Brompton Rd, London SW7 or 117 Euston Rd, London NW1.

Typical fares being quoted range from around £225 one way or £325 to £440 return. Fares depend very much on the carrier. The cheapest are likely to be on Middle Eastern or Eastern European airlines that nobody much wants to fly on. You'll also find very competitive fares to the sub-continent with Bangladesh Biman or Air Lanka. Thai International always seems to have competitive fares despite their high standards.

If you want to stop in India en route to Australia you're looking at around £500. You might find fares via Karachi (Pakistan) or Colombo (Sri Lanka) slightly cheaper than fares via India.

FROM THE USA

From the west coast the cheapest return fares to India are around US$1000. Another way of getting there would be to fly to Hong Kong and tag on a ticket from there. Hong Kong costs about US$300 one way (just under US$600 return) from San Francisco or Los Angeles. From Hong Kong you can find one-way flights to Bombay for US$230 to 280 depending on the carrier. Alternatively, you can fly to Singapore for around US$500 one way (US$775 return) or to Bangkok for US$425 one way (US$850 return).

From the east coast you can find return tickets to Bombay or Delhi for around US$900 to 1200. The cheapest one-way tickets will be around US$550 to 600. An alternative way of getting there from New York would be to fly to London and pick up a cheap fare from there.

Check the Sunday travel sections of papers like the *New York Times, San Francisco Chronicle/Examiner* or *Los Angeles Times* for adverts for cheap fares. Good low-cost agents include the student travel chains STA or CIEE.

FROM CANADA

Fares from Canada are very similar to those from the states. From Vancouver the route will be like that from the US west coast, with the option of going via Hong Kong. From Toronto it is likely to be easier to travel eastbound via London.

FROM AUSTRALIA & NEW ZEALAND

Advance-purchase return fares from the east coast to India range from around A$1050 to 1350 depending on the season and the destination in India, but you should be able to get tickets for around A$900 to 950 from co-operative travel agents. Fares are slightly cheaper to Madras or Calcutta than to Bombay or Delhi. From Australia fares are less from Darwin or Perth than from the east coast. The low travel period is March to September; peak is October to February.

Tickets from Australia to London or other European capitals with India as a stopover are available for around A$1400 return.

Return advance-purchase fares from New Zealand to India range from around NZ$1800 to 2100 depending on the season.

ROUND THE WORLD FARES

Round-the-world (RTW) fares have

become all the rage in the past few years. Basically they're of two types – airline tickets and agent tickets. An airline RTW ticket usually means two airlines have joined together to market a ticket which takes you round the world on their combined routes. Within certain limitations of time and number of stopovers you can fly pretty well anywhere you choose using their combined routes so long as you keep moving in the same direction. Compared to the full-fare tickets, which permit you to go anywhere you choose on any IATA airline so long as you do not exceed the 'maximum permitted mileage', these tickets are much less flexible. But they are also much cheaper.

Quite a few of these combined-airline RTW tickets go through India, including ones in combination with Air India which will allow you to make several stopovers within India. RTW tickets typically cost from around £1000 (US$1500) for northern hemisphere routes. If you want to include the southern hemisphere (ie Australia) then you're probably looking at around US$2000.

The other type of RTW ticket, the agent ticket, is a combination of cheap fares strung together by an enterprising agent. These will probably be cheaper than an airline RTW ticket but the choice of routes may not be so wide.

OVERLAND – FROM EUROPE

The classic way of getting to India has always been overland, but sadly the events in Iran and Afghanistan have turned the cross-Asian flow into a trickle. In the old days you travelled through Europe to Greece, crossed from Europe into Asia at Istanbul in Turkey, crossed Turkey by a number of routes to Iran. You then continued to Tehran, possibly made a loop down to see Isfahan and Shiraz, and went on to Mashed and finally Afghanistan. In that magical country you followed the well-beaten track through Herat, Kandahar and Kabul with possibly an excursion further north to the Bamiyan Valley and then Mazar-i-Sharif. From Kabul you crossed the Khyber Pass into Pakistan, then followed the Grand Trunk Road through Peshawar to Lahore and eventually into India near Amritsar in the Punjab.

Today Afghanistan is virtually completely off limits and Iran is certainly difficult, although it's only really impossible for Americans. Despite the tensions and uncertainties, many overlanders did continue to go through Iran right through the year of the US hostage drama, and even Iraq has not stopped intrepid travellers. The Iraq situation has also made the alternative route of going down through the Middle East to the Arabian Gulf and then flying or shipping from there to either Pakistan or India more difficult, but again travellers are still managing it. In all, the Asia overland trip is certainly not the breeze it once was but people continue to do it. Many travellers combine the sub-continent with the Middle East by flying between India or Pakistan and Amman in Jordan or one of the Gulf cities. A number of the London-based overland companies still operate their bus or truck trips across Asia on a regular basis. Check with Exodus, Encounter Overland, Top Deck or Hann Overland for more information.

For more detail on Asia overlanding see the Lonely Planet guide *West Asia on a Shoestring*.

OVERLAND – THROUGH SOUTH-EAST ASIA

In contrast to the difficulties in central Asia, the South-East Asian overland trip is still wide open and as popular as ever. From Australia the first step is to Indonesia – either Bali or Jakarta. Although most people fly from an east coast city or from Perth to Bali, there are also flights from Darwin and from Port Hedland in the north of Western Australia. Recently flights have recommenced between Darwin and Kupang on the Indonesian island of Timor. From Bali you head north through Java to Jakarta, from where you either ship or fly to Singapore or continue north through Sumatra and then cross to Penang in Malaysia. After travelling around Malaysia you can ship or fly from Penang to Madras in India or, more popularly, continue north to Thailand and eventually fly out from Bangkok to India, preferably via Burma.

An interesting variation on the straightforward route is to start out from Australia to Papua New Guinea and from there cross to Irian Jaya, then Sulawesi in Indonesia. There are all sorts of travel variations possible in South-East Asia; the region is a delight to travel through; it's good value for money; the food is generally excellent and healthy; and all in all it's an area of the world not to be missed. For full details see the Lonely Planet guide *South-East Asia on a Shoestring*.

TO/FROM THE MIDDLE EAST

There are many flights between Bombay and the Gulf states. There may still be ships operating between Bombay and Kuwait – the route would probably be Bombay-Karachi-Port Qaboos-Dubai-Doha-Bahrain. The trip takes about six days Bombay-Kuwait but about 13 in the opposite direction. Fares from Bombay to Kuwait are approximately US$175 in bunk class, US$250 in cabin class. Check with the shipping agents in Bombay. Boats between Karachi and the gulf are probably more frequent.

TO/FROM AFRICA

There are plenty of flights between East Africa and Bombay due to the large Indian population there. Typical fares from Bombay are around Rs 3000 student fare (Rs 4000 full fare) to Nairobi with Ethiopian Airlines or Kenya Airways. The shipping services between Africa and India will now only carry freight, including cars, not passengers.

TO/FROM PAKISTAN

Relations between India and Pakistan have certainly improved if travel connections between the two countries are anything to go by. After the Bangladesh war they were limited to one road crossing point which was open for one morning each week. Today there are a variety of direct flights but land crossing is still difficult because of the Punjab unrest. There may be a second border crossing point open between the two countries, see below.

Air

Pakistan International Airlines and Indian Airlines operate flights Karachi-Bombay (daily for each airline) for approximately US$70 (depending on exchange rates), Karachi-Delhi (four times weekly) for about US$90 and Lahore-Delhi (four times weekly) for about US$60.

Land

Amritsar-Lahore Due to the unrest in the Punjab the situation at this border crossing changes regularly. At present it appears you can cross by road at Wagah on the 3rd, the 13th and the 23rd of each month only. The train service operates three times a week on Tuesdays, Thursdays and Saturdays. You will need a special permit to enter the Punjab. In Pakistan you must check with the Indian Embassy & in Islamabad. In New Delhi permits are issued by the Home Ministry.

For the Lahore (Pakistan) to Amritsar (India) train you have to buy one ticket from Lahore to Attari, the border town, and another from Attari to Amritsar, but the total fare is only about Rs 10. The train departs Lahore at 2 pm and you get to Amritsar around 6 pm after a couple of hours at the border passing through immigration and customs. Going the other way, you leave Amritsar at 9.30 am and get to Lahore at 2 pm. Pakistan immigration and customs are handled at Lahore station. Sometimes border delays can make the trip much longer.

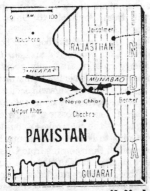

Khokhrapar rail link being reopened

ISLAMABAD. Feb. 15 (PTI)— Pakistan's decision to reopen the Khokhrapar rail and road link with India after a gap of 20 years would be a big step towards easing travel between the two countries.

At present, the residents of Sind and Baluchistan have to travel all the way to Lahore to catch a train to India. Those intending to visit western or southern states of India are compelled to travel via the Indian state of Punjab.

From Amritsar you cannot buy a ticket until the morning of departure and there are no seat reservations. So arrive early and push. Money changers offer good rates for Pakistan rupees on the platform but you cannot get Indian rupees coming the opposite way. Travellers have reported that whichever direction you're travelling, the exchange rate between Indian and Pakistan rupees is more advantageous to you on the Pakistan side of the border, but you can change Indian rupees to Pakistani or vice versa at Wagah and in Amritsar – no matter what the Pakistanis may tell you! Overall the crossing is trouble free with no hassles from officials on either side.

Since the rail route opened far fewer travellers use the old route. It's mainly of interest to people with vehicles or on overland buses. By public transport the trip entails taking a bus to the border at Wagah, again between Lahore and Amritsar, walking across the actual border and then taking another bus into Amritsar. Border formalities here are quite fast so going this way can be less time consuming than by rail, where the train takes a long time at the border.

From Lahore buses and minibuses depart from near the General Bus Station on Badami Bagh. The border opens at 9.15 am and closes at 3.30 pm. If you're stuck on the Pakistan side you can stay at the *PTDC Motel*, where there are dorm beds and double rooms.

Hyderabad-Barmer In early '86 it was announced that the old railway line between Hyderabad in the Sind region of Pakistan to Barmer in Rajasthan would be re-opened. There has been reports that it actually opened in August '86 but as of yet we have not heard from anybody who has used this route. If it is open this will be a fascinating new route across the Thar Desert and a considerable shortcut between Bombay and Karachi.

Other Routes Prior to partition there were, of course, many more routes, but the roads have been cut, the railway lines torn up. The old road connection from Rawalpindi in Pakistan to Srinagar in Kashmir used to be the main route to Kashmir and was much more heavily used than the Jammu-Srinagar route. There was also a route into Kashmir and Ladakh from Skardu to Kargil on the Srinagar-Leh road.

TO/FROM BANGLADESH
You can either fly to or from Bangladesh or cross by land. Unfortunately most land entry and exit points are closed so the choice is much more limited than a glance at the map would indicate. You do not need an exit permit to leave Bangladesh on the Calcutta route; you may need one

on the Darjeeling route. You will need a permit for Darjeeling if you're going to enter India by this latter route.

Air

Bangladesh Biman and Indian Airlines fly from Calcutta to Dhaka (about US$30) and Chittagong (about US$36) in Bangladesh. Many people use Biman from Calcutta through to Bangkok – partly because they're cheap and partly because they fly through Rangoon in Burma. Biman should put you up overnight in Dhaka on this route but be careful – it appears they will only do so if your ticket is specifically endorsed that you are entitled to a room. If not, tough luck – you can either camp out overnight in the hot transit lounge or make your way into Dhaka on your own, pay for transport and accommodation and get hit for departure tax next day. Don't believe that when you buy the ticket you will get accommodation; this only happens if your ticket specifically says so.

Land

Calcutta The Calcutta-Dhaka route is the one used by the overwhelming majority of land travellers. Stage one is a train from Sealdah Station to Bongaon, the end of the line. The trip takes about 2¼ hours and the fare is about Rs 7; the train is all 2nd class. From the station it's about 10 km by rickshaw to the border at Haridaspur on the Indian side. A space in an auto-rickshaw will cost about Rs 10 or 7, the whole vehicle Rs 35. Remember that in Bangladesh auto-rickshaws (also known as scooters in India) are called 'baby taxis'. It's possible to change money at the border.

Crossing the actual border takes an hour or two with the usual form filling and stamping. From the actual border it's about 10 minutes by rickshaw to Benapole on the Bangladesh side. Standard fare seems to be Tk 5 per person either two to a rickshaw or three to a 'van', a sort of freight rickshaw.

It's then about an eight– or nine-hour bus trip from Benapole to Dhaka, a distance of 291 km at a fare of Tk 75. The first leg of the trip takes about 1½ hours to Jessore from where it's an hour to a small ferry crossing. It's only about 10 minutes across the river but with waiting, loading and unloading this will occupy an hour or two. Another 1½ hours takes you to a larger ferry crossing at Aricha. Getting across the river takes a couple of hours. Going to Dhaka takes about half an hour longer than coming from Dhaka, as the crossing is made upstream. Finally it's another 1½ hours to Dhaka. Coming from Dhaka it's wise to book your seat on the bus at least a day in advance.

The easiest buses operate overnight between Dhaka and the border. Coming from Dhaka you can take a bus at 8 to 11 pm and arrive in Benapole at dawn. From Calcutta, if you leave in the early afternoon you should be in Benapole in time for the bus departures at 6 to 8.30 pm. In day time there are no direct buses so you have to take a 'coaster' between the border and Jessore (Tk 10) and a Jessore-Dhaka bus (Tk 55). The last 'direct' buses from Jessore leave around 1 to 2 pm.

Darjeeling From New Jalpaiguri it's about 2½ hours by train at a fare of Rs 4 to Haldibari. The Indian border checkpoint is here but you have got a little travelling yet before you reach Bangladesh. It's a seven-km walk along the disused railway line from Haldibari to the Bangladesh border point at Chiliharti! 'It's here you discover how much excess baggage you're carrying', wrote one traveller. You should be able to find someone to carry your pack for you. There's a train station at Chiliharti from where you can set off into Bangladesh. Bring some takkas into Bangladesh with you. This is officially illegal but changing money in Chiliharti is virtually impossible. You should be able to change some at Haldibari.

Other All other routes are closed.

TO/FROM SRI LANKA

Far fewer travellers are continuing on from India to Sri Lanka due to the level of unrest and violence in that unhappy country, and also because the ferry service is out of operation so flying is now the only way to get there.

Air

There are flights to and from Colombo (the capital of Sri Lanka) and Bombay (US$168), Madras (US$78), Tiruchirapalli (US$55) or Trivandrum (US$53). Flights are most frequent on the Madras-Colombo route.

Sea

The ferry service from Rameswaram at the southern end of India to Talaimannar in Sri Lanka is currently suspended due to the unrest in Sri Lanka. This was a favourite route for shipping arms and equipment to the Tamil guerrilla forces in the north of the country.

TO/FROM NEPAL

There are a number of road crossings into Nepal and also a variety of air links with India.

Air

You can fly to Kathmandu, the capital of Nepal, from Delhi (US$142), Calcutta (US$96), Varanasi (US$71) or Patna (US$41). Note that flying Delhi-Patna and Patna-Kathmandu is much cheaper than flying Delhi-Kathmandu direct.

Land

For full details on the land routes into Nepal see the appropriate sections in the book. The most popular land routes to Nepal are from Raxaul (near Muzaffarpur) and Sunauli (near Gorakhpur). If you are heading straight to Nepal from Delhi or elsewhere in western India then the Gorakhpur-Sunauli route is the most convenient. From Calcutta, Patna or eastern India, Raxaul to Birganj is the best entry point. Finally there is the crossing from Darjeeling, which then involves a lengthy bus trip along the southern lowlands known as the Terai before you intersect the Birganj-Kathmandu road. See Darjeeling in West Bengal for details. There are other roads into Nepal from northern Bihar to the east of Birganj but they are rarely used by travellers.

TO/FROM THE MALDIVES

Trivandrum-Male costs US$63, Madras-Male US$124. The Trivandrum flight is cheaper than flying from Colombo in Sri Lanka.

TO/FROM MALAYSIA

Not many travellers connect between Malaysia and India because it is so much cheaper from Thailand, but there are flights between Penang and Madras. You can generally pick up tickets for the Malaysian Airlines Systems flight from Penang travel agents for around M$500 to 600, rather cheaper than the regular fare.

The *MV Chidambaram*, which used to operate a shipping service between Penang and Madras, no longer operates. The Shipping Corporation of India has indicated it intends to restart the service but it's unknown when that will happen, if at all.

TO/FROM SINGAPORE

Singapore is a great cheap-ticket centre and you can pick up Singapore-Bombay tickets for about S$700, Singapore-Madras for about S$600.

TO/FROM THAILAND

Bangkok is the most popular jumping-off point from South-East Asia into Asia proper because of the flights from there to Calcutta or to Rangoon in Burma, Dhaka in Bangladesh or Kathmandu in Nepal. The popular Bangkok-Kathmandu flight is about US$170. You can make a stopover in Burma on this route and do the seven-day circuit of that fascinating country. Bangkok-Calcutta is about US$130, Bangkok-Delhi about US$175.

TO/FROM BURMA

There are no land crossing points between Burma and India, or any other country for that matter. If you want to visit Burma your only choice is to fly there. Burma Airways Corporation flies Calcutta-Rangoon; Bangladesh Biman flies Dhaka-Rangoon.

CHEAP TICKETS IN INDIA

Although you can also get cheap tickets in Bombay and Calcutta, it is in Delhi that the real wheeling and dealing goes on. There are countless 'bucket shops' around Connaught Place, but enquire with fellow travellers about their current trustworthiness! With most cheap tickets you will have to pay the full official fare through a bank – the agent gets you a bank form stating what the official fare is, you pay the bank, the bank pays the agent. You then receive a refund from the agent, but in rupees. So it is wise either to buy your ticket far enough ahead that you can use those rupees up, or have plenty of bank exchange certificates in hand in order to change the rupees back. This also applies to credit card purchases.

Some typical fares from India are Delhi-Australia for about Rs 6000, Delhi to various European capitals for around Rs 4000 to 5000 or a bit less from Bombay. The cheapest flights to Europe are with airlines like Aeroflot (Rs 4500), LOT (Rs 4300), Kuwait Airways, Syrian Arab Airways (Rs 4000) or Iraqi Airways. Officially Aeroflot is not allowed to sell

tickets in India. In fact they do and the tickets are stamped as having been issued in Moscow or Singapore. You can fly with nice airlines like Thai International for Rs 4750. Delhi-Hong Kong-Vancouver and down to the US west coast (San Francisco or Los Angeles) will cost around Rs 6200.

Despite Delhi's strength in the cheap-ticket business, Bombay is the place through which most flights between Europe and South-East Asia or Australia pass. It's also the place for flights to East Africa. Furthermore, if you're heading east from India to Bangladesh, Burma or Thailand you'll probably find much better prices in Calcutta than in Delhi, even though there are fewer agents. Calcutta-Bangkok with a stop in Rangoon is about Rs 1600.

AIRPORT TAX

India now has one of the higher airport taxes in the world for international flights. For flights to neighbouring countries (Pakistan, Sri Lanka, Bangladesh, Nepal) it's Rs 50, but to more distant countries it's a hefty Rs 100. India's neighbours are also getting into rip-off airport taxes; it's Rs 100 in Nepal and Sri Lanka, although fortunately that's a fair bit less than Indian Rs 100 in both cases. This airport tax applies to everybody, even to babies who do not occupy a seat – in most countries airport tax applies only to seat occupants or adults. The method of collecting the tax varies but generally you have to pay it *before* you check in, so look out for an airport tax counter as you enter the check-in area.

Getting Around

TRAIN

The Indian Railways system is the fourth largest in the world, with a route length of over 60,000 km and nine million passengers every day. The first step in coming to grips with Indian Railways is to get a timetable. *Trains at a Glance* (Rs 3.50) is a handy guide which in around 100 pages covers all the main routes and trains in more than sufficient detail for most travellers. It should be available at any reasonably sized station newsstand. If you can't find it, a regional timetable will provide much the same information with more local train services and also a pink section giving the timetables for the major mail and express trains (the fast ones) throughout the country. There is an *Indian Bradshaw* which covers every train service throughout the country but that's probably too much detail for almost anybody, even if you could find a copy. Thomas Cook's *Overseas Timetable* has good railway timetables for India.

The timetables indicate the km distance between major stations; a table in front shows the equivalent fares for distances from one km to 5000 km for the various train types. With this information it is very easy to calculate the fare between any two stations. The fares quoted in this guide are simply approximations of the fares on the faster trains. Travel times vary widely between trains and the times indicated are usually for the faster mail or express services. In any case Indian trains often suffer delays.

There are a number of factors to be considered with Indian railways. First of all, getting there may not always be half the fun but it is certainly 90% of the experience. Indian rail travel is unlike any other sort of travel in any other place on earth. At times it can be incredibly frustrating (since the trains are not exactly fast) or uncomfortable, but an experience it certainly is. Money aside, if

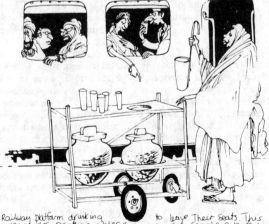

Railway platform drinking water vendor. Drinking water is available at most platforms from faucets but some people prefer not to leave their seats. This car-side service extends to food, drink, newspapers and holy men's blessings.

you simply want to get from A to B then fly. If getting from A to B is as much a part of India as what you see at both ends, then take the train.

During and shortly after the monsoon, rail services can be drastically affected by floods and high rivers. This particularly applies in low-lying areas along the Ganges basin or where major rivers run to the sea, such as the north coast region of Andhra Pradesh.

Classes

There are generally two classes – 1st and 2nd – but there are a number of subtle variations on this basic distinction. For a start there is 1st class and 1st class air-conditioned. The air-con carriages only operate on certain trains and routes. Train travel in India is always more comfortable if you can travel reserved, but in general, reservations are only made for sleepers – an exception is the 1st-class air-con 'chair car'. Although 1st-class day travel is generally unreserved it is rarely crowded – unlike 2nd class, which almost always is. In 2nd class unreserved the train carries as many people as can be crammed on board, which usually means there is not a square cm of sitting, standing, squatting or hanging space left.

Types

What you want is a mail or express train. What you do not want is a passenger train. No Indian train travels very fast, but at least the mail and express trains do keep travelling more of the time. Passenger trains spend a lot of time at a lot of stations, which quickly becomes very boring unless you have a keen interest in small-town stations. Passenger trains are usually 2nd class only; 2nd-class fares on passenger trains are less than on a mail or express train over the same route. Recently 'superfast express' services have been introduced on certain main routes, and due to tighter scheduling and fewer stops they are much faster.

Gauge

What you want nearly as much as a mail or express train is broad gauge. There are three gauges in India; well, three types of gauges. In broad gauge the rails are 1.676 metres apart. Metre gauge is, as it says, one metre wide. Narrow gauge is either 0.762 metres (2 feet 6 inches) or 0.610 metres (2 feet).

Broad gauge has a major advantage – it is much faster. The carriages are much the same between broad gauge and metre gauge, but on narrow gauge they are narrower and the accommodation less comfortable. In areas where there are no broad-gauge lines it is always worth considering taking a bus, which will usually be faster. These areas include Rajasthan and the northern Bihar and Uttar Pradesh areas towards the Nepalese border.

Life on Board

It's India for real on board the trains. In 2nd class, unreserved travel can be a nightmare since the train is always hopelessly crowded – and not only with people; Indians seem unable to travel without the kitchen sink and everything that goes with it. There's an ongoing campaign to educate people not to carry so much junk but it doesn't seem to have much effect.

Combined with the crowds, the noise and the confusion there's the discomfort. Fans and lights have a habit of failing when trains are stationary for prolonged stops and there's no air moving through the carriage. Toilets are often so dirty as to be unusable, and in any case there'll be somebody asleep in it. Worst of all are the stops. Trains seem to stop often, interminably and for no apparent reason. Often it's because somebody has pulled the emergency stop cable because he's close to home – well, so it's said; some people deny this. Still, it's all part of life on the rails.

Costs

Fares operate on a distance basis. The timetables indicate the distance in km between the stations and from this it is simple to calculate the cost between any two stations. If you have a ticket for at least 400 km you can break your journey at the rate of one day per 200 km so long as you travel at least 300 km to the place you first leave the train. This can save a lot of hassle buying tickets and also, of course, results in a small cost saving. Rail fares were increased considerably in early '86. Costs and distances are listed below for mail and express trains; passenger trains are cheaper.

km	air-con	1st class	air-con chair	2nd class
50	Rs 70	Rs 34	Rs 20	Rs 5
100	Rs 110	Rs 53	Rs 30	Rs 11
200	Rs 170	Rs 86	Rs 47	Rs 23
300	Rs 239	Rs 120	Rs 66	Rs 30
400	Rs 306	Rs 154	Rs 84	Rs 38
500	Rs 361	Rs 181	Rs 99	Rs 45
1000	Rs 619	Rs 312	Rs 170	Rs 76
2000	Rs 1042	Rs 522	Rs 285	Rs 126

Reservations

The cost of reservations is nominal – it's the time it takes which hurts! Reservations can be made up to six months in advance and the longer in advance you make them the better. Your reservation ticket will indicate which carriage and berth you have, and when the train comes into the station you will find a sheet of paper affixed to each carriage listing the names of the various passengers beside their appropriate berth number. Sometimes this information is posted on noticeboards on the platform. It's Indian rail efficiency at its best. Reservation costs are Rs 10 in air-con class, Rs 4 in 1st class, Rs 2 in air-con chair class, Rs 2 in 2nd-class sleeper and Rs 1 in 2nd-class sitting. There are very rarely any 2nd-class sitting compartments with reservations. There are also now some 'Superfast Express Trains' for which there is an additional supplementary charge.

If you've not had time to get a reservation or been unable to get one, it's worth just getting on the train in the reserved carriage. If there are spare seats the ticket inspector will come round and charge you an extra reservation fee. If they are taken, or will be taken at a station down the line, you'll simply be banished back to the crush and confusion in the unreserved carriages. This trick only works for day travel. At night sleepers are booked out well in advance so if you can't get one then sitting up in 2nd class is your only choice.

If you can plan your trip well ahead, you can avoid all the hassles by booking in advance from abroad. A good Indian travel agent (Cox & Kings has been recommended) will book and obtain tickets in advance for you and have them ready at your hotel when you arrive.

Sleepers

There are 2nd-class and 1st-class sleepers, although by western standards even 1st class is not luxurious and you usually don't get bedding. First-class sleepers are generally private compartments with two or four sleepers in them, sometimes with a toilet as well. Usually the sleeping berths fold up to make a sitting compartment during the day. First-class air-con sleepers are more luxurious, and more expensive, than regular 1st-class sleepers. Sleeping berths are only available between 9 pm and 6 am.

There is no additional sleeper charge in 1st class but there is an additional charge in 2nd. The charge of Rs 10 is on top of the sleeper reservation charge and is a once-only charge irrespective of the number of nights the trip lasts. For any sleeper reservation you must book at least several days ahead. At busy times, such as on the Delhi-Jammu route for Kashmir during the hot season, you need to plan weeks ahead. There is usually a board up in the station indicating what is available or how long before the next free sleeper comes up on the various routes. You have to fill in a sleeper reservation form, so save time by doing this before you get to the front of the queue. They're usually found in boxes around the reservation hall. The demand for 1st-class sleepers is generally far less than for 2nd class.

Two-Tier vs Three-Tier

Second-class sleepers are of two sorts: two-tier and three-tier. Superficially the padded two-tier sleepers seem more comfortable than the hard wooden three-tier ones, although on many broad-gauge routes three-tier sleepers are padded now. During the day the three-tier sleepers are folded up to make seats for six or eight. At night they are folded down, everybody has to bed down at the same time, and a guard ensures that nobody unreserved gets into the carriage.

In the two-tier compartments there are still regular seats below the padded bunks, so people get on and off and it's noisier and more difficult to sleep. In any case the racket and noise from the chai-wallahs and other merchants operating at every station can make sleeping on Indian trains a pretty hit-and-miss affair.

Getting a Space Despite Everything

If you want a sleeper and there are none left then it's time to try and break into the quotas. Ask at the tourist office if there is a tourist quota on that train. Ask the stationmaster, usually a helpful man who speaks English, if he has a station quota or if there is a VIP quota. The latter is often a good last bet because VIPs rarely turn up to use their quotas.

If all that fails then you're going to be travelling·unreserved and that can be no fun at all. To ease the pain get yourself some expert help. For, say, Rs 10 to 15 baksheesh you can get a porter, or the tourist officer may find one for you, who will absolutely ensure you get a seat. If it's a train starting from your station, the key to success is to be on the train before it arrives at the station. Your porter will do

just that so when it rolls in you simply dawdle on board and take the seat he has warmed for you. If it's a through train then it's every man for himself, and you can be certain he'll be better at it than you are – he'll also not be encumbered with baggage or backpacks.

Women can ask about the Ladies' Compartments which many trains seem to have and are often a refuge from the crowds in other compartments.

Left Luggage

Most stations have a left-luggage facility where backpacks can be left for Rs 1 per day. This is a very useful facility if you're visiting (but not staying in) a town, or if you want to find a place to stay, unencumbered by your gear.

Special Trains

A special 'Palace on Wheels' makes a regular circuit around Rajasthan – you not only travel by train, you stay in the 'fit for a Maharaja' carriages. See the Rajasthan section for more details. The English travel agent Trailfinders operates a regular train tour of India using a special carriage in which you travel, eat and sleep. It's known as the 'Indian Rail Rover'. The carriage is hooked on to regular trains from town to town, then disconnected and left on a siding while you visit the town. The accommodation facilities are basic – this is no palace on wheels – but you cover a lot of India. Tours from 18 to 32 days are available and prices ex-Delhi are around £380.

Indrail Passes

The very popular Indrail Passes permit unlimited travel on Indian trains for the period of their validity. Their costs have not gone up with recent fare increases, so it is likely the US$ costs listed below may rise soon:

days	air-con	1st class	2nd class
7	160	80	35
15	200	100	45
21	240	120	55
30	300	150	65
60	450	225	100
90	600	300	130

Children aged five to 12 years pay half the above fares. Indrail tickets can be bought overseas through travel agents or in India at certain major railway offices. Payment in India must be made in either US dollars or pounds sterling, cash or travellers' cheques. Indrail passes cover all reservation and berth costs at night. They can be extended if you wish to keep on travelling. The main offices in India which handle Indrail passes are:

New Delhi
  Railway Tourist Guide, New Delhi Railway Station
  Central Reservation Office, Northern Railway, Connaught Place
Bombay
  Railway Tourist Guide, Western Railway, Churchgate
  Railway Tourist Guide, Central Railway, Victoria Terminal
Calcutta
  Railway Tourist Guide, Eastern Railway, Fairlie Place
  Central Reservation Office, South-Eastern Railway, Esplanade Mansion
Madras
  Central Reservation Office, Southern Railway, Madras Central

They are also available from Central Reservation Offices at Secunderabad-Hyderabad, Rameswaram, Bangalore, Vasco-da-Gama, Jaipur and Trivandrum, as well as at certain 'recognised Tourist Agencies'.

Is the Indrail Pass worth having? – well, yes and no. In purely financial terms it's probably not. Unless you're travelling very heavily, on the go nearly every day, it's virtually impossible to cover enough distance to make the pass worthwhile *if*

you're looking at it on a purely cost basis. The shorter the length of the pass the less sense it makes costwise. The 1st-class passes are also far better value than the 2nd-class ones. Although there is an air-con Indrail pass as well as a 1st-class one, you only find air-con carriages on certain main routes. You might find it disappointing to invest in an air-con pass and then find you travel by regular 1st class anyway.

That's the downside of Indrail passes, but pure cost isn't all there is to it. First of all you never need to join the interminable queues to buy tickets. You already have your ticket, so if you're travelling unreserved you simply hop aboard. If you are travelling reserved then you still have to get a reservation, and that's where the second advantage comes in. Train reservations aren't just issued from A to Z and in this way used up. There is always a tourist quota, a VIP quota, a stationmaster's quota and so on. Indrail pass users report that when the train is 'full', production of their pass often results in another quota making a miraculous appearance.

One traveller reported that 'I always went round the back to the Chief Reservations Office instead of queueing up; he usually shook my hand and came back in five minutes with the reservations. Only in Bombay did this method not succeed'. Another traveller reported this series of steps for breaking into the tourist quota:

If the train is fully booked go directly to the area officer or station superintendent and ask for 'special permission' to get a berth on the train. You will have to fill out a form and then be given a note to take to the reservation counter where your berth is allocated. Sometimes you're told that your berth is booked and there is nothing further to do. Always insist that they write the berth number on your ticket (especially if you have a tourist quota berth) because your name may not appear on the train listings. If you do not have booking proof you have no recourse with the conductor.

Your Indrail pass also allows you use of the station waiting rooms, often a peaceful haven in the 1st-class variety, and makes it easier to get into the retiring rooms. The retiring room dormitories are often used by Indian travelling salesmen who speak English and know all the best local places to eat. The main virtue of the Indrail Pass, however, is its ability to produce a seat or a sleeper when there isn't one. That can be worth far more than mere money, so overall, yes an Indrail Pass can be a good buy, but convenience and simplicity (both very important features in India) are the plus points, not cost saving. In particular, short-term passes are not so worthwhile, especially the 2nd-class ones. If you're going to travel by Indrail then go the whole hog and get a 1st-class pass.

Other Considerations

In New Delhi and Madras there are now special tourist booking offices at the main stations. These are for any foreign tourists,

not just Indrail Pass holders, and they make life much easier. The people at these offices are generally very knowledge-able but you will be surprised how often you find railway booking clerks who really know their stuff. They will often give you excellent advice and suggest connections and routes which can save you a lot of time and effort.

As an alternative to an Indrail Pass or buying tickets as you go along, it's possible to buy a ticket from A to Z with all the stops along the way prebooked. It might take a bit of time sitting down and working it out at the start, but if your time is limited and you can fix your schedule fairly rigidly this can be a good way of going.

If you arrive too late to get a ticket for a train or the queues are too horrendous, don't despair. Get a ticket, any ticket – even a platform ticket will do – and get on board. When the conductor comes around you can then pay the additional cost plus a small extra charge. If you get on without any ticket at all the fine for riding without a ticket is much higher, though not as high as for riding without a ticket and with the intention of not paying at all!

Gricing

For some travellers, India's rail system is more than just public transport:

Just what gricing is should become apparent over the next few pages, though don't go rushing to find the word in the Oxford Dictionary. Used loosely, it identifies the antics of that strangest of breeds, the railway enthusiast – or gricer! Amongst the temples, villages, gurus and instant karma of India is found the world's second largest treasure trove of steam locomotives. Over 6000 of them still at work at chores long given over to the infernal combustion engine in the western world. Only in China, and only in the last few years, have these numbers been exceeded.

Three gricers, including myself, spent five months travelling the length and breadth of India tracking down the rarest and most obscure of these steel behemoths. The stations and locomotive sheds became our temples, the locomotives the gods we worshipped and our tributes were not measured in gold or silver, but in the profits of Kodak and Agfa. It's unlikely you will be able to match this enthusiasm for steam, but many of the locomotives are real museum pieces and are definitely worth checking out. Some of you have probably never even seen a steam locomotive, or travelled on a train for that matter. A passing interest in India's railways will also give you some idea of what helped hold the Raj together for so long, and continues to play a major role in India's development.

Gricing need not necessarily extend to just the locomotives. There's also the 40-year-old Bengal & Nagpur Railway teacups in the refreshment rooms at Kharagpur; the magnificent station architecture of Lucknow, Bombay and Madras; the mass of humanity that keeps Calcutta's Howrah terminus buzzing 24 hours a day; or the stationmaster's clock at Kalabagh in Pakistan – built in Croydon, England in 1911 and still ticking today!

The first railways in India appeared during the mid-19th century, usually financed by London-based companies that raised funds with a return on invested capital guaranteed by the Indian government. All lines were initially built to the somewhat arbitrary width of 5 feet 6 inches – or broad gauge. Remarkably, this gauge was adhered to for all the early, major routes. Unlike Australia, for example, where separate development of major railway routes by individual colonies caused break of gauge problems that still hinder rail operations in Australia. In India it was not until the financial burden of railway building became too great for the government that an alternative gauge was sought. A track width of one metre was chosen, obviously cheaper and quicker to construct than broad gauge. It was used on many routes of secondary importance, except in Assam and what is today Bangladesh, where it predominates. India's burgeoning 20th-century population means there is a continuous programme of converting heavily trafficked metre-gauge lines to broad gauge. A number of narrow-gauge lines (2 feet and 2 feet 6 inches) were also built as short feeder routes to the main lines.

The railways of India are now divided into nine zonal systems, a result of amalgamations and nationalisations over the years of the various London-based and state concerns. The old romantic company names such as The Great Indian Peninsular Railway and The Oudh & Rohilkhand have long faded into obscurity.

The uniformity of gauge adopted by this patchwork of companies was not mirrored in their steam locomotive designs, leading to problems in operation and with the locomotive builders back in Britain. An attempt was made, starting in 1903, by the British Engineering Standards Association (BESA) to achieve some degree of standardisation. This was only partially successful and a further list of standard designs was drawn up in the 1920s, known as the Indian Railway Standard (IRS). Nearly all the BESA and IRS designs were of British construction and when locomotives had to be ordered from foreign manufacturers because of full order books in Britain, angry questions were asked in parliament.

During WW II large numbers of American locomotives were brought in to cope with increased traffic and these had a profound influence on the post-war designs. These were of a highly standardised nature, incorporating many interchangeable parts. Although Britain was involved in the design and manufacture of the post-war locomotives, well over half of those now remaining are home grown, while builders from America, Germany, Japan,

A Swiss-built X class locomotive on the narrow gauge 'rack' line to Ootacamund.

Built in 1906 in Glasgow this CC class locomotive is on the narrow-gauge line from Rupsa to Bangriposi.

An American-built broad gauge WP class passenger locomotive.

'Tweed', probably the oldest regularly working engine in the world.

Eastern Europe and Canada are also represented. Recent upheavals within the Ministry of Railways have produced a more youthful management structure. The first casualties of these moves were the ageing BESA and IRS designs, which apart from a few isolated examples had completely disappeared by the early 1980s.

Fortunately representatives of most major designs have been preserved in the Rail Transport Museum at Shantipath, New Delhi, near the Chanakyapuri diplomatic enclave. Locomotives from all three gauges have been beautifully restored, many in their original railway company colours. Amongst those on show are the oldest surviving engine in India, built in 1855, and a diminutive 2-foot-gauge loco from Darjeeling, making a stark contrast beside a 234-ton Beyer Garratt locomotive.

With the withdrawal of the older non-standard classes, the remaining 3000 broad-gauge steam locomotives are of only two basic and rather austere designs. The more attractive of the two is the distinctive semi-streamlined WP class introduced in 1947. Although similar in appearance to the American streamliners of the '30s and '40s, these bullet-nosed passenger locomotives never attain speeds they look capable of, and rarely exceed 80 kph. All require a crew of four – driver, two firemen and a workman – to break up the large lumps of coal. Around 700 remain and while their use on express trains is now limited they are used on stopping passenger trains all over the country, except in the south, which is too far away from the coalfields. The 2350 members of the WG class were originally built for heavy freight traffic, but as most of these duties are now worked by diesel and electric traction, the WGs have been allotted such menial tasks as shunting, local freight and slow passenger trains. There's plenty of room on the footplate of these broad-gauge giants and many of the crew are not averse to having you aboard; it's always worth asking.

Although the older BESA designs are no longer seen in India, a few hundred remain on secondary duties in Pakistan. They are usually away from the main travel corridors, but if you pass through Quetta, Peshawar or Lahore there should be a few of these veterans puffing around.

The metre-gauge system has been built up since 1873. The system is not as extensive as broad gauge although it is still possible to travel from the east of Assam to within 80 km of Cape Comorin by metre gauge. The locomotives are generally cleaner than their broad-gauge counterparts, though once again variety has suffered with the withdrawal of older locomotives. The mainstays of the metre gauge are the post-war YP (passenger) and YG (freight) designs which are found everywhere. A large number were built in India, the last YG not appearing until 1972. A handful of the attractive IRS classes YD and YB have managed to survive. The YD still slog their way up the ghats east of Goa on local passenger trains, while the last few YBs are found on the Western Railway in Gujarat.

The star metre-gauge attraction is the rack railway from Mettupallayam to the hill resort of Ootacamund in the Nilgiri Hills. Smart blue engines, built in Switzerland to a 1914 design, push their trains of blue and white coaches through quite spectacular scenery. This was graphically highlighted by the acrobatics of Dr Aziz when the railway featured in the film *Passage to India*. When the gradient becomes too steep a second pair of cylinders activates a mechanism beneath the locomotive which engages a toothed rail in the middle of the track, providing that extra 'push'. Wellington is a good place to watch the train climbing both sides of the valley, and opposite the station at Coonor they serve some of the best masala dosas in India.

It is on the narrow-gauge lines that the real adventure is found; nothing can compete with the Darjeeling Himalayan Railway, arguably the most famous and most spectacular steam railway in the world. The line was opened in 1880 and the oldest engine, 779 'Mountaineer', was built in 1892, others of the same design following until 1927. The bus from Siliguri to Darjeeling takes 3½ hours, the train may take all day but you'd never know what you're missing. There are loops and spirals, Z reverses, and sheer drops where you can look down to see where you were half an hour ago. Batasia loop between Darjeeling and Ghoom is a popular morning viewpoint, and you may be lucky enough to photograph the morning school train from Kurseong with snow-capped Kanchenjunga as a backdrop!

Two other spectacular hill railways run from Kalka to Simla and from Neral (near Bombay) to Matheran, although both are unfortunately worked by diesels. The first narrow-gauge railways in India were built by the Gaekwar of Baroda in 1873 and these lines still exist south of Baroda. The network is centred on Dhaboi, which still sees 44 steam trains a day, though with the arrival of the first of a new generation of narrow-gauge diesels this situation will change rapidly.

Two lines on the east coast appealed to me. The first runs from seemingly nowhere to nowhere, from Naupada on the main line to Gunupur. Originally known as the Parlakimedi Light Railway, the diminutive locomotives were built in Stoke on Trent, England between 1903 and 1931. Further north runs the line from Rupsa to Bangriposi through the land of the Sontal tribe. Immaculate red and black engines, decorated with paintings of peacocks, run on this line. All were built between 1906 and 1908 by the famous North British Company of Glasgow. The majority of narrow-gauge lines are found on the Western, Central and South Eastern Railways.

Finally, India boasts perhaps the greatest steam gem of all – 'Tweed', a metre-gauge relic built by Dubs of Glasgow in 1873. It is still at work at the Saraya Sugar Mills near Gorakphur and is probably the oldest steam engine in the world still in regular use. Two other centenarians are used occasionally at the mill and until recently 'Mersey', a sister engine to Tweed, was at work at Hathua sugar mill.

Although steam locomotives will be around in India well past the year 2000, the variety and colour that remain, especially on the narrow gauge, will certainly have disappeared before then. But before you point that camera, a word of warning. Indian authorities can go a bit overboard when it comes to railway security, so try and ensure that no police or other officials are around. Better still, get a permit from the Indian consular office before you leave home. If it sounds silly the joke's on you when you face a railway policeman threatening to burn your film and smash your camera. Luckily I talked my way out of it – Happy Gricing!

Mark Carter

BUS

Travelling around India by train has such an overpowering image – those up-and-down mail trains, the sights, sounds and smells of the stations, the romantic names and exotic old steam engines – that people forget there is also an extensive and well-developed bus system.

In many cases this simply extends from the railway system – fanning out from railhead stations – or goes where the railways do not or cannot go – up to Kashmir for example. There are, however, many places where buses offer a parallel service to the railways and in some cases a better or faster one. In places where the only railways are on the narrower gauges it will often be much faster to take a bus – this includes the routes in northern Bihar and Uttar Pradesh up to the Nepal border. Agra-Jaipur, Delhi-Jaipur and Bombay-Goa are other examples of routes where buses are faster and more convenient than the trains.

Buses vary widely from state to state, although you can make the general observation that travel by bus is crowded, cramped, slow and none too comfortable. In some states there is a choice of buses on the main routes – thus in Jammu & Kashmir there are A and B class buses, even deluxe and air-conditioned buses on the popular Jammu-Srinagar run. There is also a variety of buses in Haryana, particularly on the Delhi-Chandigarh run. Video buses have become the rage on some routes where there is a variety of buses, but in most cases there is no choice – they will all be equally bad.

There is generally a state-operated bus company in each state, but in some (Orissa, Jammu & Kashmir for example) this is backed up by privately operated buses – although they may only operate on certain routes. Despite the extra speed buses often offer (and lesser safety), they generally become very uncomfortable sooner than trains. If it's a long trip, and particularly one involving overnight travel, you're generally best opting for a train. On many private buses a constant barrage of loud and discordant Hindi pop music is another disadvantage – 'as if the roads aren't rough enough'.

As long as there's two of you, it's worth working out a bus-boarding plan where one of you can guard the gear while the other storms the bus in search of a seat. The big advantage of buses over trains is that they go more frequently and getting one involves comparatively little pre-departure hassle. You can, however, often make advance reservations for a small additional fee – usually Rs 0.50 or Rs 1. Waving that magic ticket in front of you can sometimes get you on board when space is at a premium or can get you a better seat – not at the back, not over a wheel, on the scenic side. On some routes the booking system (so long as you start at the beginning of the route) is efficient and works well although you may find your seating space disappearing as the trip wears on.

At many bus stations there is a separate women's queue. You may not notice this because the sign indicating it will not be in English and there may not

be any women queueing in any case. Usually the same ticket window will handle the male and the female queue, taking turn about. What this means is that women can usually go straight up to the front of the queue (ie straight up beside the front of the male queue) and get almost immediate service.

Baggage is generally carried on the roof of buses, so it's an idea to take a few precautions. Make sure it's tied on properly and that nobody dumps a tin trunk on top of your fragile backpack. At times a tarpaulin will be tied across the baggage – make sure it covers your gear adequately. Theft is sometimes a problem so keep an eye on your bags at chai stops. Having a large, heavy-duty bag into which your pack will fit can be a very good idea, not only for bus travel but also for air travel. On long-distance bus trips chai stops can be far too frequent or, conversely, agonisingly infrequent. They can be a real hassle for women travellers – toilet facilities will generally be inadequate to say the least.

There are extensive local bus routes in all the major cities. These vary from city to city – in Bombay they're surprisingly good, in Delhi they're surprisingly crowded, in Calcutta they are also very crowded but they are backed up by a more expensive and marginally less crowded minibus service.

AIR

The Indian domestic airline, Indian Airlines, operates an extensive service throughout the nation as well as connections to neighbouring countries. Air India also operates a number of domestic services, principally on the Bombay-Delhi, Bombay-Calcutta and Bombay-Madras routes. Indian Airlines is the largest regional carrier in South Asia, with a fleet of A300 Airbuses and Boeing 737s. In recent years the expansion of the fleet together with some hefty fare increases has made getting a seat on Indian Airlines flights much easier.

Recently a second airline called Vayudoot commenced operations with small twin-engined Dornier aircraft. Vayudoot flies to many small centres previously not covered by Indian Airlines and this opens up new possibilities for visitors whose time is limited – or whose patience has run out. Vayudoot will soon have taken over all of Indian Airlines' turboprop services as well, leaving the larger airline only on the more important routes operated by jet aircraft.

Booking Flights

Indian Airlines finally have their computerised booking system in operation at all the larger and many of the smaller stations, making air travel in India much simpler than before. Previously Indian Airlines operated multi-million wide-body jets with a booking system more suitable for a Victorian railway service. Computers have even considerably shortened the 'chance list', which was what the waiting list was more appropriately known as in India.

If you want to know what pre-computer air travel was like, however, Vayudoot can show you. Getting a seat on a Vayudoot flight is still a fraught and problematical affair not helped by some of their agents, who are complete idiots.

Tickets

All Indian Airline tickets must be paid for with foreign currency, travellers' cheques or bank proof-of-exchange forms. Infants up to two years of age travel at 10% fare, but only one infant per adult. Children two to 12 travel at 50% fare. There is no student reduction for overseas visitors but there is a youth fare for people aged 12 to 30. This allows a 25% reduction, but on the dollar tariff. Since the dollar tariff is much higher than the rupee tariff converted into dollars, youth fares are not such a bargain – in fact 25% off the dollar fare is likely to be more than the full fare in rupees! Neat trick, huh? If you book Indian Airlines tickets overseas you have

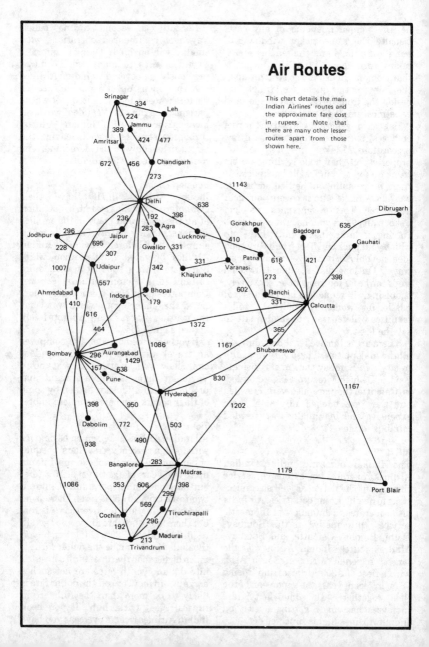

Air Routes

This chart details the main Indian Airlines' routes and the approximate fare cost in rupees. Note that there are many other lesser routes apart from those shown here.

to pay the more expensive dollar tariff fares.

There are heavy penalties for cancellations or no-shows on IA flights. If you cancel more than 48 hours ahead the charge is Rs 20, 24 to 48 hours it is 10%, one hour to 24 hours it is 25%, and if you change your mind in the last hour or fail to show up you can throw the ticket away. These penalties do not apply, however, if you've bought your tickets overseas on the more expensive dollar tariff. Unlike almost every other airline in the world, IA accepts no responsibility if you lose your tickets. They absolutely will not replace lost tickets, so treat them like cash, not travellers' cheques.

Fares

The accompanying chart details the main IA domestic routes and fares.

Indian Airlines also have a 21-day 'Discover India' fare which costs US$375 and a 14-day version called 'Tour India' which costs US$300. These allow unlimited travel on their domestic routes and can be reasonable value if your time is very limited.

Indian Airlines have a number of excursion-fare circuit trips which give you a 20 or 30% discount on the normal fare. These usually link domestic travel with an Indian Airlines overseas route.

In Flight

IA flights usually have a choice of vegetarian or non-vegetarian meals; unless you request otherwise, westerners will always be assumed to be non-veg. The food is usually not very good in either case and IA's stewardesses can make even Aeroflot's mighty ladies look smiling and

happy. Other minor IA irritations are the complete lack of effort to keep you informed of the whys and wherefores of delays, check-in counters are rarely open as far ahead as the requested reporting times, and at the end of flights luggage is often unloaded at a real snail's pace.

Offices
The Indian Airlines office addresses are listed below together with the distance from the office to the airport:

Agartala (12 km)
Khosh Mahal Building, Central Rd (tel 60)

Agra (7 km)
Hotel Clarks-Shiraz, 54 Taj Rd (tel 73434, 72421)

Ahmedabad (10 km)
Airlines House, Lal Darwaja (tel 391736, 391797, 391619)

Allahabad (12 km)
18 Tashkant Marg, Tata Auto Sales Building (tel 42607, 61633)

Amritsar (11 km)
48 The Mall (tel 42607)

Aurangabad (10 km)
Anvikar Building, Adalat Rd (tel 4864)

Bagdogra (14 km)
Hotel Sinclairs, Mallaguri PO Pradhanagar, Siliguri (tel 20692)

Bangalore (13 km)
Karnataka Housing Board Building, District Office Rd (tel 75911, 29769, 76851)

Belgaum (14 km)
Hotel Sanman Deluxe, College Rd (tel 20801, 25898)

Bhavnagar (8 km)
Diwanpara Rd (tel 27144, 23214)

Bhopal (11 km)
Bhadbhada Rd, TT Nagar (tel 61633, 61155)

Bhubaneswar (4 km)
V11-C/8 Raj Path, Bapuji Nagar (tel 50533, 50544)

Bhuj (6 km)
Outside Waniawad Gate, Station Rd (tel 34)

Bombay (26 km)
Air-India Building, 1st Floor, Madam Cama Rd, Nariman Point (tel 233031, 233521, 233154)

Calcutta (16 km)
Airlines House, 39 Chittaranjan Ave (tel 263135, 260730, 260731, 263390, 262954)

Chandigarh (11 km)
SCO-186-187-188 Sector 17C (tel 28721, 26443)

Chittagong
Hotel Agrabad (tel 838542)

Cochin (6 km)
Durbar Hall Rd, Ernakulam (tel 32065, 33826)

Coimbatore (11 km)
503 Trichy Rd (tel 22743, 22208)

Colombo (18 km)
95 Sir Baron Jayatilaka Mawatha (tel 23136)

Dabolim (37 km)
Dempo House, Campal, Panaji (tel 3826, 4190)

Delhi (13 km)
Kanchenjunga, Barakhamba Rd (tel 40052, 40071)

Dhaka (7 km)
Hotel International (tel 231687)

Dibrugarh (26 km)
CIWTC Bungalow, Assam Medical College Rd (tel 114)

Dimapur (5 km)
Dimapur-Imphal Rd (tel 2375)

Gauhati (22 km)
Paltan Bazar (tel 23128, 26655, 23734)

Gorakhpur (7 km)
Park Rd (tel 3940)

Gwalior (12 km)
Tansen Marg, Barrar (tel 21773)

Hyderabad (9 km)
Saifabad, opposite Ravindra Bharati (tel 36902, 77531)

Imphal (7 km)
Mahatma Gandhi Rd (tel 28/1377)

Indore (9 km)
164/1 Rabindranath Tagore Marg (tel 7069)

Jabalpur (15 km)
Chadha Travels, Jackson Hotel, Civil Lines (tel 21324, 22178, 21320)

Jaipur (15 km)
Mundhara Bhawan, Ajmer Rd (tel 72940, 74500)

Jammu (7 km)
Tourist Reception Centre, Veer Marg (tel 42735, 47577)

Jamnagar (10 km)
Indra Mahal, near Bhind Bhanjan Temple (tel 4285)

Jodhpur (5 km)
  Rupali Tourist Bungalow, High Court Rd (tel 20909)
Jorhat (6 km)
  Garhali (tel 11)
Kabul (7 km)
  Chanrahi Malick, Asghar Desh (tel 31469, 32920)
Kanpur (13 km)
  15/69 Civil Lines (tel 63356, 65042)
Karachi (15 km)
  Hotel Inter-continental (c/o PIA) (tel 511577, 515021, 522034)
Kathmandu (8 km)
  Durbar Marg (tel 11198, 13053)
Keshod (3 km)
  Rajmahal Plot, New Railway Station (tel 344)
Khajuraho (5 km)
  Khajuraho Hotel (tel 35)
Lahore (10 km)
  33 Falletis Hotel, Eagerton Rd (tel 305712)
Leh (8 km)
  Ibex Guest House (tel 76)
Lucknow (15 km)
  Clarks Avadh, 5 Mahatma Gandhi Marg (tel 48081)
Madras (16 km)
  19 Marshalls Rd, Egmore (tel 848711, 848712, 847098, 847522)
Madurai (12 km)
  Pandyan House, 7A West Veli St (tel 26795, 415987, 26707)
Male (3 km)
  Beach Hotel (tel 2106, 3003, 3004)
Mangalore (20 km)
  Moti Mahal, Falnir Rd (tel 23504, 27207, 21300, 24669)
Nagpur (10 km)
  242A Manohar Niwar, Rabindranath Tagore Rd, Civil Lines (tel 23186, 25057)
Patna (8 km)
  South Gandhi Maidan (tel 54984, 25936)
Porbandar (5 km)
  Harish Mansion, opposite Indian Oil petrol pump (tel 18)
Port Blair (4 km)
  Middle Point G-55 (tel 208)
Pune (8 km)
  15 Sadhu Vaswani (tel 28179, 24940)
Raipur (19 km)
  Natraj Hotel, GE Rd (tel 26460)
Rajkot (4 km)
  Angel Chamber, Jhabar Rd (tel 23306, 24857, 34122)

Ranchi (7 km)
  Nataya Flat 4, Kedru, B/258 Sector 3 (tel 23350, 21841)
Silchar (25 km)
  Red Cross Rd (tel 72)
Srinagar (13 km)
  Tourist Reception Centre (tel 73538, 73270, 73271)
Tezpur (18 km)
  Jankin Rd (tel 83, 162)
Tiruchirapalli (8 km)
  Southern Railway Employees Co-op Credit Society Building, Dindigul Rd (tel 23116)
Tirupati (15 km)
  Room 9 & 10, TT Devasthanam Guest House (tel 2818, 2884, 2732)
Trivandrum (7 km)
  Air Centre, Muscat Junction (tel 60181, 62288, 66923, 60070, 62110, 61776, 63965, 66370)
Udaipur (25 km)
  LIC Building, outside Delhi Gate (tel 3952)
Vadodara (Baroda) (6 km)
  University Rd, Fateh Ganj (tel 63868, 65677)
Varanasi (22 km)
  Mint House Motel, opposite Nadesar Palace, Cantonment (tel 64146, 66116)
Vijayawada (22 km)
  Shriniketan 27-1-26, Eluru Rd, Covernorpet (tel 72218)
Visakhapatnam (14 km)
  Jeevan Prakash, LIC Building Complex (tel 64665, 62673)

DRIVING

There are no car-rental systems along the lines of those in the west in India, but it is possible to hire chauffeur-driven cars quite easily. This tends to be a little expensive, not because of the chauffeur but because of the cost of the cars, fuel and upkeep. All are very expensive in India by western standards. Basically a chauffeur-driven car is just a long-distance taxi. In some places they run fairly regular services, such as Chandigarh-Manali or Jammu-Srinagar in the north-west. It is also possible to hire jeeps for the two-day run from Srinagar to Leh in Ladakh. Typically, hiring a car and driver might cost around Rs 250 to 350 a day depending on the length of hire and the distance covered.

Fewer people bring their own vehicles to India since the overland trip became so curtailed because of the Russians in Afghanistan and the current situation in Iraq and Iran. If you do decide to bring a car or motorcycle to India it has to be brought in under a carnet, a customs document guaranteeing you will remove the car at the end of your stay. Failing to do so will be very expensive.

Driving in India is a matter of low speeds and great caution. Indian roads are narrow and crowded. At night there are unlit cars and ox carts and in daytime there are fearless bicycle riders. Day and night there are the crazy truck drivers to contend with. A loud horn definitely helps since the normal driving technique is to put your hand firmly on the horn, close your eyes and plough through regardless. Vehicles always have the right of way over pedestrians and bigger vehicles always have the right of way over smaller ones. On the Indian roads might is right.

Because of the extreme congestion in the cities and the narrow bumpy roads in the country, driving is often a slow, stop-start process – hard on you, on the car, on your fuel economy. Service is so-so in India, parts and tyres are hard to obtain. All in all driving is no great pleasure.

People driving across India on the overland trip will most likely be starting out either from Calcutta, Madras or Bombay. The route from Madras crosses the country to Bombay, then heads north to Delhi and on out to Pakistan.

From Madras & Bombay

Route A47	sector km	total km
Madras-Chittoor	157	157
Chittoor-Bangalore	174	331
Bangalore-Chitradurga	202	533
Chitradurga-Hubli	206	739
Hubli-Belgaum	94	833
Belgaum-Kolhapur	103	936

Kolhapur-Pune	234	1170
Pune-Bombay	185	1355
Bombay-Nasik	197	1552
Nasik-Malegan	106	1658
Malegan-Indore	310	1968
Indore-Shivpuri	376	2344
Shivpuri-Gwalior	113	2457
Gwalior-Agra	117	2574
Route A1		
Agra-Delhi	204	2778
Delhi-Ambala	294	3072
Ambala-Jullundur	174	3246
Jullundur-Amritsar	77	3323
Amritsar-Wagah (border)	26	3349

From Madras the road crosses a plain, then climbs up to Bangalore. Karnataka between Bangalore and Belgaum is heavily cultivated and part of the Deccan Plateau. From Belgaum the road leaves the hilly Deccan area and runs down to the coast at Bombay. Leaving Bombay it climbs up over the hill range known as the Western Ghats, then traverses a number of hill ranges through Dhulia, Indore and Shivpuri; at times the road is very winding. At Shivpuri you can diverge east and visit Khajuraho, then rejoin the route at Gwalior, adding 422 km to the trip. At Agra the route meets the busy Grand Trunk Road and continues to Delhi, then crosses the flat Punjab region to Amritsar and the border with Pakistan.

From Calcutta

Route A1	sector km	total km
Calcutta-Asansol	222	222
Asansol-Varanasi	454	676
Varanasi-Allahabad	128	804
Allahabad-Kanpur	192	996
Kanpur-Agra	288	1284
Agra-Wagah (border)	775	2059

From Calcutta the road crosses the heavily populated and fertile West Bengal plain. Traffic all the way is heavy and slow as this route traverses the most densely populated part of India. From Agra the route is the same as from Madras or Bombay.

Road Safety

India suffers about 60 road deaths a day, 20,000 or so a year – an astonishing total in relation to the number of vehicles on the road. The reasons are numerous and many of them fairly obvious – starting with the congestion on the roads and the equal congestion in vehicles. When a bus runs off the road there are plenty of people stuffed inside to get injured and it's unlikely too many of them will be able to escape in a hurry if need be.

Many of the deaths are pedestrians involved in hit-and-run accidents. The propensity to disappear after the incident is not wholly surprising – lynch mobs can assemble remarkably quickly, even when the driver is not at fault! Most accidents are caused by trucks, for on Indian roads might is right and trucks are the biggest, heaviest and mightiest. You either get out of their way or get run down. As with so many Indian vehicles they're likely to be grossly overloaded and not in the best of condition. Trucks are actually licensed and taxed to carry a load 25% more than the maximum recommended by the manufacturer!

The karma theory of driving also helps to push up the statistics – it's not so much the vehicle which collides with you as the events of your previous life which caused the accident.

Indian Vehicles

The Indian vehicle manufacturing industry has gone through an explosion in the last few years and the number of cars and motorcycles on the road has increased dramatically. The old totally Indian Hindustan Ambassador, a copy of an early '50s British Morris Oxford, are still the everyday vehicle on the Indian roads but there are now several more modern ones. These include licence-manufactured Rover 2000s (for the Indian executive), Datsun-engined Fiat 124s and a version of the British Vauxhall – but the big story is the Maruti.

The Maruti is a locally assembled Japanese Suzuki minicar, put together in the abortive Sanjay Gandhi 'peoples car' factory near New Delhi. They've swept the country and you now see them everywhere in surprisingly large numbers. Whether they will have the endurance of the rock-solid (and rock-heavy) old Ambassador is a different question. Whether abandoning the old 'All Indian' policy in favour of assembly operations is a good idea is another moot point.

India's truck and bus industry was always a more important business, with companies like Tata and Ashok Leyland turning out sturdy trucks which you see all over India. Here too there has been a Japanese onslaught; modern Japanese trucks are starting to appear and the tiny Maruti-Suzuki minivans are very popular.

The active motorcycle and motor-scooter industry has also experienced rapid growth. The motorcycles include the splendid Enfield India – a replica of the old British single-cylinder 350 cc Royal Enfield Bullet of the '50s. Enthusiasts for the old British singles will be delighted to see these modern-day vintage bikes still being made. Motor-scooters include Indian versions of both the Italian Lambretta and the Vespa. When production ceased in Italy, India bought the manufacturing plant from them lock, stock and barrel.

There is a variety of mopeds but in the last few years assembly of small Honda, Suzuki and Yamaha motorcycles has also started and they are rapidly becoming as familiar a sight on the roads of India as in South-East Asia. The arrival of Japanese manufacturing companies in India has provided some insightful culture clashes. A recent *Time* magazine article noted that Honda had found it impossible to instill the Japanese-style team spirit at the Hero-Honda plant near New Delhi. Workers didn't mind rubbing shoulders with the management – but not with the untouchables, please. And despite having quality inspectors, unknown in Japanese plants where everybody is a quality inspector, the rejection rate at the end of the assembly line was 30% against 3% in Japan.

TWO-WHEELED EXPERIENCES

The following descriptions of two different ways of travelling independently in India were contributed by Roman Wowk and Ann Sorrel. Motorcycling around India has become much more feasible and much more popular in the last few years and Roman's comments have been updated accordingly, particularly the Which Motorcycle? section.

INDIA ON AN ENFIELD

The possibility of touring India on an Indian motorcycle started as a wild brainstorm with three friends. We jetted into India from Europe via Karachi and first made our way by bus, train and taxi to the snow-covered slopes of Gulmarg in Kashmir. There we met our long-lost Scottish companion who had spent six months getting there from Europe via Turkey, Iran and Pakistan on a custom-built touring bicycle. From Kashmir we headed back across the mountain passes to Amritsar on the plains. For a change I relieved my friend of the bicycle and chased the others back south.

We had decided that the Enfield Bullet (350 cc, single-cylinder, four-stroke, vintage British design) was the only feasible machine for our trip and started looking for suitable machines to purchase at the army depots in Jammu and Pathankot. New ones, at around Rs 15,000, were out of the question as this would have left us with no money to pay for the petrol and running costs. So for three weeks we resided at the Golden Temple in Amritsar, courtesy of the ever-hospitable Mr Singh, while we surveyed the used-motorcycle scene.

Having tried and tested what felt like every Enfield Bullet for sale in the city and having even stretched the patience of many an Indian, we finally purchased two 1971 models and took them on a trial run over the plains and up the mountains to Dharamsala and back. After some incredibly cheap major repairs and adjustments to the machines by a befriended mechanic we were finally ready to go. We grabbed our packed lunch and compass, adjusted our goggles, pointed the bikes in the general direction of east (bearing north-east to south!), kicked them over and took off.

A single-cylinder, 350cc Enfield India

Some 8000 km and 16 weeks later, after innumerable adventures, misadventures, pleasures, trials, punctures, repairs, rip-offs and arguments we had traversed India, visited Nepal and ended up in Calcutta, the end of the road and of our money. Here our patience and the Indians' was tested once again as we bartered the Enfields for a healthy bundle of rupees and departed in different directions.

Perhaps the only better and less obtrusive way to enjoy the kaleidoscopic activity of India would have been by bicycle. But for this you must be willing to expend a much greater amount of physical energy and have much more time, although you would also need much less money in the pocket. We found that the feeling of participation offered by this method of travel was much preferable to crowded buses.

Costs

It's possible to fully recover your initial expenditure on a motorcycle if you have the time, patience and some knowledge of prices. We purchased two 1971 models for Rs 6000 and 6500 and managed to sell them for the same price, having spent around Rs 6500 in running and repair costs over four months and 8000 km. Divided by four people, this came to a cost of around Rs 1600 each over the period, much less than a rupee a km. Of course the costs are double if you ride solo. As a second example another couple we met in Calcutta paid Rs 14,000 for their almost new Bullet, sold it three months later for Rs 10,500 but spent almost nothing on repairs.

Which Motorcycle?

There are far more motorcycles available in India than a few years ago. Perhaps because of this, seeing western visitors exploring India by motorcycle is becoming reasonably common. The new locally assembled Japanese 100 cc motorcycles (Suzukis, Yamahas and Hondas) are available for virtually immediate delivery if you pay in foreign currency. They typically cost around Rs 14,000. Otherwise there are various scooters, several single-cylinder two-strokes of around 175 or 200 cc, the 250 cc Yezdi, and the fastest two-wheeler in India – the 350 cc twin-cylinder Rajdoot Yamaha. Of course true enthusiasts still turn towards the wonderful old Enfield India Bullet, which is also possibly the best motorcycle for long-distance touring.

Price

New Bullets cost over Rs 15,000. One under three years old and in as-new condition should cost around Rs 14,000. Older bikes up to around six years old in original condition will be in the Rs 12,000 to 13,000 range. The price of older models depends more on condition than age. If it's very good expect to pay Rs 8000 to 10,000; if it's just good Rs 7000 to 8000. A reasonably well-kept bike should cost Rs 6000 to 7000 while a very scrappy example will be Rs 5000 to 6000.

For the smaller two-stroke motorcycles and scooters you can expect to pay Rs 2000 or 3000 less for older models. The price will also depend on availability. For example, in Amritsar, where the majority of the traffic is two-wheeled due to the narrowness of the streets, the prices may be lower than in other cities.

Where & How to Purchase

India does not have used-vehicle dealers, motorcycle magazines or weekend newspapers with pages of motorcycle classified advertisements. To purchase a second-hand machine one simply needs to enquire. A good place to start is with mechanics. They are likely to know somebody who is selling a bike. Also there are a number of commission agents who act as middlemen to bring buyers and sellers together. They will usually be able to show you a number of machines to suit your price bracket. These agents can be found by enquiring or may sometimes advertise on their shop fronts.

The commission to these agents is usually Rs 100 each from buyer and seller. For an additional fee, which usually covers a bribe to officials, they will assist you in transferring the ownership papers through the bureaucratic system. Without their help this could take a couple of weeks. If you intend to purchase a new machine this can be done directly through the dealer in the capital city of any state.

Ownership Papers

A needless hint perhaps, but do not part with your money until you have the ownership papers, receipt and affidavit signed by a magistrate authorising the owner (as recorded in the ownership papers) to sell the machine. Not to mention the keys to the bike and the bike itself!

Each state has a different set of formalities regarding transfer of ownership. Assistance may be obtained from the agent through whom you are purchasing the machine or from one of the many 'attorneys' hanging around under tin roofs by the Motor Vehicles Office. They will charge you a fee of up to Rs 100, which will consist largely of a bribe to expedite matters.

Alternatively you could approach one of the many typing clerk services and request them to type out the necessary forms, handling the matter yourself at a much cheaper rate – but with no guarantee of a quick result. Remember to dress very neatly to transact this business as Indian officials have a great contempt for dirty foreigners, and inversely great respect for a well-dressed, well-spoken one. If you are female or there is a female in your party send her to do it, especially if she is blonde!

Check that your name has been recorded in the ownership book and stamped and signed by the head of the department. If you intend to sell your motorcycle in a different state then you will need a 'No Objections Certificate'. This confirms your ownership and is issued by the Motor Vehicles Department in the state where you bought it, so get it immediately when transferring ownership papers to your name. The standard form can be typed up for about Rs 10 or more speedily and expensively through one of the many attorneys. We were unaware of the necessity of obtaining this certificate and discovered that nobody was willing to risk purchasing our machines without it. I had the pleasure of the return train trip from Calcutta to Amritsar (2000 km each way) to collect these pieces of paper!

Other Formalities You can obtain an Indian licence on application, but it is more convenient if you have an international driving permit or a licence from your country of residence, even if it is out of date or does not cover riding a motorcycle. It is sufficient if it has 'driver's licence' written on it, and your name. In some states (for example the Punjab) it is forbidden for females to ride a motorcycle (chauvinists!); they can travel only as the pillion passenger. Also in the Punjab it is against the law for two males to ride together on one motorcycle. This is to reduce the number of armed holdups as motorcycles, being the fastest things on the road, are used as getaway vehicles. Being a foreigner, however, this law will not necessarily apply to you.

As in most countries it is compulsory to have third-party insurance. The New India Assurance Company or the National Insurance Company are just two of a number of companies who can provide it. The cost will be approximately Rs 60 for a year or Rs 45 for six months. Road tax must also be paid and costs around Rs 16 per quarter. Delhi is the only place in India where the wearing of crash helmets is enforced.

Repairs & Maintenance

Anyone who can handle a screwdriver and spanner in India can be called a mechanic or 'mistri', so be careful. If you have any mechanical knowledge it may be better to buy your own set of tools and to learn how to do your own repairs. This will save a lot of arguments over the price. If, however, you are in need of a mechanic, try to find a Mr Singh (look for the tell-tale turban, beard and steel bangle!). He may charge a little more but you can be assured of proud work at a non-rip-off price.

Original Enfield parts purchased from an 'Authorised Enfield Dealer' can be rather expensive in comparison to the copy parts available from your spare parts wallah. Again a Mr Singh can be trusted and is not impartial to a little bargaining. Some costs of typical spare parts or labour include an air filter element for around Rs 5, a battery for Rs 50 on exchange or Rs 100 new, and a battery recharge for Rs 2. Cables are Rs 7, clutch plates Rs 30 (and Rs 10 to fit them), chains Rs 75 front and rear. A new carburetor is Rs 100 but a Japanese one will cost Rs 350. Front fork oil seals are Rs 6 and Rs 4 to fit. You can have a complete engine overhaul for Rs 350 to 400. Points are Rs 20, piston rings Rs 25 (Rs 40 for genuine Enfield), a head gasket Rs 8. Wheel bearings cost Rs 40, a rear-wheel sprocket Rs 25.

These prices are only approximate and as a foreigner you're an obvious target for a quick rupee for a not-so-honest mechanic. Beware of 15-minute jobs, which should cost about Rs 10 for labour, taking three hours and costing nearly Rs 100. A good mechanic makes about Rs 50 per day, so calculate your labour costs on this.

If you purchase an older machine you would do well to check and tighten all nuts and bolts every few days. Indian roads and engine vibration tend to work things loose and constant checking could save you rupees and trouble. Check the engine and gearbox oil level regularly. With the quality of oil it is advisable to change it and clean the oil filter every couple of thousand km.

Punctures Either you're lucky or you're not. One of our bikes did not have a single puncture the whole trip. The other had innumerable punctures, including three in one day! In some places I even suspected (paranoia?) nails being scattered on the road to boost business. Pushing a loaded motorcycle is hard enough; with a flat tyre it's like pushing a tractor. Puncture wallahs are quite frequent (you'll be surprised where you find them), but it's advisable to at least have tools sufficient to remove your own wheel and take *it* to the puncture wallah (*punkucha wallah* in Hindi).

To remove the rear wheel a pair of adjustable multigrips is the only tool necessary, although spanners may be easier to work with. First remove the brake adjusting nut, then the brake cover plate anchor nut. Loosen but do not remove the hub spindle nuts on either side, disconnect the chain at the spring link and disconnect the speedo cable (in the unlikely event that it's currently connected!). Finally loosen the exhaust and silencer nuts if necessary, and off comes the wheel.

A puncture repair will cost Rs 5 for one hole while a new tube will cost Rs 15. Tyres are Rs 100 to 150 retread or Rs 250 to 350 new. When replacing the rear wheel ensure that the chain connecting link fastener has its split end pointing in the opposite direction to that in which the chain travels. Adjust the chain with the cam-shaped adjusters so that the chain tension allows about three cm of up-and-down movement. Check that each cam plate is set on the same number of notches. Finally adjust the footbrake.

Fuel

Petrol is relatively expensive compared to that in the west and compared to the cost of living in India. An Enfield Bullet petrol tank holds 14.5 litres (good for 300 to 400 km), so when the pump reading shows 18 litres you can safely assume the meter has been fixed!

Petrol is usually readily available in all larger towns and along the main roads so there is no need to carry spare fuel. Should you run out, try flagging down a passing car (not a truck or bus since they use diesel) and beg for some. Most Indians are willing to let you have some if you have a hose or syphon and a container in which to pour it. Alternatively you could hitch a ride on a truck to the nearest petrol station.

Maps

Bartholomew's Indian Subcontinent is probably the best road map, although it's not really detailed enough and not readily available outside the larger cities. Alternatively, tourist maps of each state, available from tourist offices, are quite good. If you have no maps then ask the locals. Tell them in which direction you're heading and they will probably give you a list of every town, together with distances between each one from here to there. Then again, you can work out your general direction from the sun and head off that way. We found this the most adventurous.

Truck or Train Transport

If you break down well away from a mechanic and spare parts wallah, it is possible to catch a ride with a truck for around Rs 5 per 10 km. For the price the driver will drop you off at the doorstep of the nearest mechanic. It's also possible to transport a motorcycle by train over longer distances. As an example, a trip of nearly 2000 km costs about Rs 130 for a passenger in 2nd class, Rs 60 for a bicycle or Rs 200 for a motorcycle.

Going Abroad

No special permission is needed to take your motorcycle into Nepal so long as you have your normal visa and you are the registered owner. The motorcycle is declared at customs at the border on entry and is free for the first 15 days. Thereafter it costs Nepalese Rs 15 per day. Before you can take a motorcycle on to the ferry to Sri Lanka (assuming it's running) you have to obtain special permission in Madras.

Selling It

Selling is really a matter of waiting. The better your patience and the more time you have available the better price you will get, or rather the closer you will get to the market value. You will undoubtedly be offered ridiculous prices; your first counter-offer is likely to be half what you ask, so when questioned for the selling price ask the prospective purchaser whether he wants the 'Indian price' or the 'English price'. The Indian price being twice the English!

If you have time it is well worth dressing the machine up, particularly if it looks scrappy. A paint job for Rs 120 to 500 (depending on the number of coats of paint) will more than likely recover its cost. You can get new mudguards for Rs 45, mirrors for Rs 20, a seat cover for Rs 25. Word spreads quickly that you have a machine to sell and if the bike 'looks nice' you'll soon get offers.

Roman Wowk

AND INDIA ON A BICYCLE

Every day millions of Indians pedal along the country's roads. If they can do it so can you. India offers an immense array of challenges for a long-distance bike tourer/traveller – there are high-altitude passes and rocky dirt tracks; smooth-surfaced, well-graded highways with roadside restaurants and lodges; coastal routes through coconut palms; and winding country roads through coffee plantations. Not to mention city streets with all manner of animal and human-powered carts and vehicles as well as the spectacle of the Asian bazaar. Hills, plains, plateaus, deserts – you name it, India's got it!

As elsewhere in the world, long-distance cycling is not for the faint of heart or weak of knee. You'll need physical endurance to cope with the roads and the climate, plus you'll face cultural challenges which I called 'the people factor'.

Books to Read

Before you set out, read some books on bicycle touring like *Bike Touring* by Raymond Bridge (Sierra Club, 1979), *Bike Tripping* by Tom Cuthbertson (10 Speed Press, 1972) or *The Bicycle Touring Book* by Tom and Glenda Wilhelm (Rodale Press, 1980). Cycling magazines in your own country will provide useful information and addresses of spare-parts suppliers which may be vital if you have to send for a part. They're also good places to look for a riding companion. For a real feel of the adventure of bike touring in strange places there's Dervla Murphy's classic *Full Tilt – From Ireland to India on a Bike* now available in paperback, or Lloyd Summer's *The Long Ride*. Look for *Riding the Mountains Down* for a recent 'biking through India' adventure.

Bring Your Own Bike

Bringing your own lightweight touring bicycle will give you lots of mechanical advantages and make mountainous areas much more approachable, but it does have disadvantages. Your machine is likely to be a real curiosity and subject to much pushing, pulling and probing. If you can't tolerate people touching your quality bicycle don't bring it to India!

There are also technical problems, so have a working knowledge of your machine and bring any special tools with you. Bring a compact bike manual with lots of diagrams and pictures in case the worst happens and you need to get your rear derailleur or another strategic part remade – the right Indian mechanic/tinkerer can do wonders and illustrations help break down language barriers.

Either bring a good quality bicycle equipped with top-line touring components or a no-name 10-speed that you won't regret parting with due to damage, theft or sale. Make sure it's a machine that you're comfortable with.

Spare Parts If you bring a bicycle to India, apart from all the normal tools and spares (plenty of spokes) bring a good wire cutter to cleanly cut brake and gear cables. Finding a suitable tool or chisel always seems to be difficult. Long, thin cables for derailleurs aren't available outside major cities so bring enough spares. Bike or moped brake cables bought in India (Rs 30) have to be modified to fit brake levers correctly – I found a spoke nipple threaded through the cable is perfect. Be ready to make do and improvise. Roads don't have paved shoulders and hence are very dusty so take care to keep your chain lubricated.

Although India is theoretically metricated, tools and bike parts are 'standard' or 'English' measurement. Thus don't expect to find tyres for 700c rims, although 27 x 1¼ tyres are produced in India by Dunlop and Sawney. Indian cycle pumps cater to a tube valve different from the Presta and Schraeder valves common on bikes in the west. If you're travelling with Presta valves (most high-pressure 27 x 1¼ tubes) bring a Schraeder (car type) adapter. In India you can then obtain another adapter to Indian pumps, which means you'll have an adapter on your adapter! But bring your own pump as well; most Indian pumps require two or three men to get air down the leaky cable.

In big cities Japanese tyres and components (derailleurs, freewheels, chains) can be obtained though they're pricey – but then so are postage costs, and transit time can be considerable. If you receive bike parts from abroad beware of exorbitant customs charges. Say you want the goods as 'in transit' to avoid these charges. They may list the parts in your passport!

There are a number of shops where you may locate parts. Try Metre Cycle, Kalba Devi Rd, Bombay or their branch in Trivandrum; the cycle bazaar in the old city around Esplanade Rd, Delhi; Popular Cycle Importing Company on Broadway, Madras; Nundy & Company, Bentinck St, Calcutta. Or locate the cycle market and ask around with your bike, and someone will know which shop is likely to have things for your 'special' cycle. Beware of Taiwanese imitations and do watch out for old rubber on tyres which may have been sitting collecting dust for years.

Luggage Your cycle luggage should be as strong, durable and waterproof as possible. I don't recommend a set with lots of zippers, as it makes pilfering of contents easier. As you'll frequently need to remove luggage to bring cycles into lodge rooms (*never* leave your cycle in the lobby or outside – take it to bed with you!), a set designed to easily remove from racks is a must and the less the number of items the better. Think about a large-capacity handlebar bag and a rear pannier set. Front bags mean two more items to haul about. Richard Jones, PO Box 919, Fort Collins, Colorado 80522, USA makes a set of bike luggage that can be easily reassembled into a backpack. Just the thing when you want to park your bike and go by train or on a trek.

Theft If you're on an imported bike try to avoid the loss of your pump (and the water bottle from your frame) – they're popular items for theft because of their novelty, and their loss is of great inconvenience. Don't leave anything on your bike that can be easily removed when it's unattended. Don't be paranoid about theft – outside of the four big cities it would be well-nigh impossible for a thief to resell your bike as it'll stick out too much. And not many folk have the wherewithal to figure out quick-release levers on wheels. In that sense your bike is safer in India than in cities in the west.

Buying a Bike in India

Finding an Indian bike is no problem, every Indian town will have at least a couple of cycle shops. Shop around to find the prices and remember to bargain. Try to get a few extras – bell, stand, spare tube – thrown in. There are many different brands of Indian clunkers – *Hero, Atlas, BSA, Raleigh, Bajaj, Avon* – but they all follow the same basic, sturdy design. *Raleigh* is considered the finest quality, followed by *BSA* which has a big line of models including some sporty jobs. *Hero* and *Atlas* both claim to be the biggest seller but basically you can look for the cheapest or the one with the snazziest plate label.

Once you've decided on the bike you have a

choice of luggage carriers – most of the rat-trap type but varying in size, price and sturdiness. There's a wide range of saddles available but all are equally bum-breaking. A stand is certainly a useful addition and a bell or airhorn can be considered an absolute necessity in India. An advantage of buying a new bike is that the brakes actually work when they're brand new. Centre-pull and side-pull brakes are also available but at extra cost and may actually make the bike more difficult to sell at the end. The average Indian will prefer the standard model.

Spare Parts As there are so many repair 'shops' (some consist of a pump, box of tools, tube of rubber solution and water pan under a tree) there is no need to carry spare parts, especially as you'll only own the bike for a few weeks or months. Just take a roll of tube-patch rubber, a tube of Dunlop patch glue, two tyre irons and a wonderful 'universal' bike spanner for Indian bikes which will fit all the nuts. There are plenty of puncture wallahs in all towns and villages who will patch tubes for Rs 1, so chances are you won't have to fix a puncture yourself anyway. Besides, Indian tyres are pretty heavy duty so with luck you won't have a flat during the time you own the bike.

Luggage Easiest is to simply get a rack modified to suit your pack or travel bags. You may want to have special canvas bags for your rear pannier or adopt the popular green canvas school bags for the job.

Selling It Reselling the bike is no problem. Ask the proprietor of your lodge if they know anyone who is interested in buying a bike. Negotiate a price and do the deal personally or through the hotel. Most people will be only too willing to help you. Count on losing Rs 50 to 100 depending on local prices. Retail bike stores are not usually interested in buying or selling second-hand bikes. A better bet would be a bike-hire shop, which may be interested in expanding their fleet at less cost than for a new bike.

On the Road

The 'people factor' makes a bike ride in India both rewarding and frustrating. It is greatly reduced for those with Indian bikes and can be a decisive element in opting not to bring a 10-speed sports bike. Mob scenes are likely to occur. A halt for tea can bring a crowd of 50 men and boys to encircle you and your machine, offer comments to one another about its operation – one points to the water-bottle saying 'petrol', another twists shifter lever saying 'clutch', another squeezes tyres saying 'tubeless' or 'airless', yet others nod knowingly as 'gear system', 'automatic' and 'racing bike' are mouthed. You may even get 'disco bike'!

Worst is on a city street when you stop for a banana, look up as you are about to push off and find rickshaws, cyclists, pedestrians all blocking your way! At times the crowd may be unruly – schoolboys especially. If the mob is too big just request a lathi-wielding policeman to come. The boys scatter pronto! Sometimes hostile boys may throw rocks. Best advice is to keep pedalling, don't turn around or stop, don't leave your bike and chase them as this will only incite them further. Appeal to adults to discipline them. Children, especially boys seven to 13 years old, aren't disciplined and are dangerous in crowds. Avoid riding by a boys' school at recess.

Routes You can go anywhere on a bike that you would on trains and buses with the added pleasure of seeing all the places in between. Those in great shape and with good cycles may want to ride the Jammu-Srinagar-Leh road, which appears to have become the ride 'to do' if you're a long-distance cyclist in India.

Try to avoid the major highways up north like NH1 through Haryana and NH2 – the Grand Trunk (GT) between Delhi and Calcutta. They're plagued by speeding buses and trucks. Other national highways can be pleasant, often lonely country roads and are very well marked with a stone every km. Learn the Hindi script to read signs, although at least one marker in five will be in English.

Distances If you've never cycled distances before, start with 20 to 40 km per day and build up as you gain stamina and confidence. Cycling long distances is 80% determination and 20% perspiration. Don't be ashamed to push up steep hills either. For an eight-hour pedal a serious cyclist and interested tourist will average 125-150 km a day on undulating plains or 80-100 km in mountainous areas.

Accommodation There's no need to bring a tent, as cheap lodges are available almost everywhere and a tent pitched by the road would draw crowds. There's also no need to bring a stove and cooking kit (unless you cannot tolerate Indian food), as there are plenty of tea stalls and restaurants (called 'hotels'). When you want to eat ask for a 'hotel', when you want a room ask for a 'lodge'. On big highways stop at *dhabhas*, the Indian version of a truck stop. The one with the most trucks parked in front has the best food (or serves alcohol). Dhabhas have *charpois* (string beds) to serve as tables and seats or as beds for weary cyclists. They're not recommended for single women riders and you should keep your cycle next to you throughout the night. There will be no bathroom or toilet facilities and plenty of road noise.

This is the best part of travelling on a bike – finding places to stay between the cities or touristically important places. You get to meet Indians in places like Iglas, Hunsur, Santoli, Ramdeora, Cuddalore or Nandyal – places that may only be whistle stops or small hamlets which the buses speed straight through. First, to make it understood that you're seeking a place to stay, use the expression 'night halt'. Then go down the following list: dak bungalow, PWD resthouse, inspection bungalow, travellers bungalow, municipal or panchayat guest house. These are dirt-cheap (Rs 4 to 10) government accommodation.

Circuit houses are more expensive while *dharamsalas* (lodges for pilgrims) offer primitive conditions (furniture-less rooms) – some can be pleasant, and for just Rs 3 to 5 or free they can't be beat. Ashrams and meditation centres are good bets for lodging and a meal for wandering cyclists. In a village off the road you may end up with a teacher or bank clerk (the most likely people to speak English). They may put you in the school building or simply invite you home to stay with their families. Accommodation will always turn up in some manner or form.

Towns will have lodges and real hotels – start looking near the bus and train stations.

Directions Asking directions can be a real frustration. Approach people who look like they can speak English and aren't in a hurry. Always ask three or four different people just to be certain, use traffic police only as a last resort. Try to be patient; be careful about 'left' and 'right' and be prepared for instructions like 'go straight and turn here and there'!

Maps The most detailed maps are the *Travel & Tourism* plates of the National Atlas prepared by the National Atlas Organisation, 1 Acharya Jagadish Bose Rd, Calcutta 20 and available at most major Automobile Association offices. The AA has other road maps too. The plates mark places of historic and architectural interest, indicating types of roads, temples, mosques and dak bungalows. India is covered in 15 plates costing approximately Rs 4 to 5 each; their weight and bulk is the major disadvantage.

A small, light book entitled *The Maps Road Atlas of India* costs Rs 12 and is highly recommended. It's published by Tamilnad Printers & Traders, Chrompet, Madras 600044. It includes street maps of major cities, distance charts and an excellent concise guide to the states. The Government of India Tourist Information booklets not only have fairly good road maps of each state but also road distances to places of tourist interest and break-up distances. They issue certain road route maps specially meant for tourists with vehicles. Bartholomew's Indian Subcontinent map includes roads and can be useful in some areas because it includes small town maps and gives an idea of geographic features. It's best to have two or three different maps of the same region.

Transporting Your Bike Sometimes you may want to quit pedalling – for sports bikes air travel is easy. With luck airline staff may not be familiar with procedures, so use this to your advantage. Tell them it doesn't need to be dismantled and you've never had to pay for it. Remove all luggage and accessories and let the tyres down a bit.

Bus travel with a bike varies from state to state. Generally it goes free on the roof. If it's a sports bike stress that it's lightweight. Secure it well to the roof rack, check it's in a place where it won't get damaged and take all your luggage inside.

Train travel is more complex – pedal up to the railway station, buy a ticket, explain you want to book a cycle for the journey. You'll be directed to the luggage offices or officer where a triplicate form is prepared. Fill out and note down your bike's serial number and a good description of it. Again only the bike, not luggage or accessories. Your bike gets decorated with one copy of the form, usually pasted on the seat, and you get another. God only knows what happens to the other. The minimum rate is Rs 8 but overall it's not too expensive. Produce your copy of the form to claim the bicycle from the luggage van at your destination. If you change trains en route, *personally* ensure the cycle changes too!

Final Words

Just how unique is a cycle tourist in India? I'd venture to guess about 500 foreign cyclists each year go on a month-long or more ride somewhere on the sub-continent. And the number's rapidly growing. Perhaps 5000 Indians do tours too – mostly young men and college students. 'Kashmir to Kanyakumari' or a pilgrimage to holy places are their most common goals. For your ego, newspaper attention is there for the asking.

If you're a serious cyclist or amateur racer and want to contact counterparts while in India there's the Cycle Federation of India; contact the Secretary, Yamun Velodrome, New Delhi. Last words of advice – make sure your rubber solution is gooey, all your winds are tailwinds and that you go straight and turn here and there.

Ann Sorrel

BOAT

Apart from ferries across rivers – of which there are a great number – there are not many boat trips to be made in India, although a couple are really good. One is the popular trip between Bombay and Goa; since rail connections between the two places are not particularly good this shipping service is very popular. It is suspended during the monsoon, however. Further south the backwater trip in Kerala is an excellent way of not only getting from A to B but also experiencing Kerala as you travel – a not-to-be-missed trip.

HITCH-HIKING

Possible but not always easy. There are not that many private cars streaking across India so you are likely to be on board trucks. You are then stuck with the old 'do they understand what I am doing, should I be paying for this, will the driver expect to be paid/unhappy if I don't offer to pay/unhappy if I do or simply want too much' quandary. But it is possible.

LOCAL TRANSPORT

Although there are comprehensive local bus networks in most major towns, unless you have time to familiarise yourself with the routes you're better off sticking to taxis, auto-rickshaws and rickshaws. In the big cities the buses are usually so hopelessly overcrowded that you can only really use them if you get on at the starting point – and get off at the terminus!

A basic ground rule applies to any form of transport where the fare is not ticketed or fixed (like a bus or train), or metered – agree on the fare beforehand. If you fail to do that you can expect enormous arguments and hassles when you get to your destination. And agree on the fare clearly – if there is more than one of you make sure it covers both of you. One writer suggested an alternative plan of attack with drivers who will not use the meter – jump aboard without agreeing on any fare and at the end of the trip pay what you think it should be. If he doesn't agree then suggest he calls the police to settle the matter. In that traveller's experience agreement usually quickly resulted! If you have baggage make sure there is no extra charge. If you don't you can be certain there will be more extra charges than you could dream of.

In almost all forms of powered transport in India, from taxis and auto-rickshaws to jet aircraft, note how a disproportionate number of the operators are Sikhs. In India's chaotic traffic conditions a martial background helps.

Airport Transport

There are official buses, either government operated, Indian Airlines or some local co-operative, to most airports in India. Where there isn't one there will be taxis or auto-rickshaws. There are even some airports close enough to town to get to by cycle-rickshaw! The bus services keep other operators reasonably honest so it is not difficult to get to or from any of India's airports.

Taxi

There are taxis in most towns in India, most of them (certainly in the major cities) metered. Getting a metered fare is rather a different situation. First of all the meter may be 'broken'. Threatening to get another taxi will usually fix it immediately, except during rush hours.

Secondly the meter will certainly be out of date. Fares are adjusted upwards so much faster and more frequently than meters are recalibrated that drivers almost always have 'fare adjustment cards' indicating what you should pay compared to what the meter indicates. This is, of course, wide open to abuse. You have no idea if you're being shown the right card or if the taxi's meter has actually been recalibrated and you're being shown the card anyway. The only answer is to try and get an idea of what the fare should be before departure (ask information desks at the airport or your hotel). You'll soon begin to develop a feel for what the meter says, what the cards say and what the two together should indicate.

Auto-Rickshaw

An auto-rickshaw is a noisy three-wheel device powered by a two-stroke motorcycle engine with a driver up front and seats for two passengers behind. They're generally about half the price of a taxi, are usually metered and follow the same ground rules as taxis. Because of their size they are often faster than taxis for short trips and their drivers are decidedly nuttier – glancing-blow collisions are not infrequent. Also known as scooters or motor trishaws.

Tempo

Somewhat like a large auto-rickshaw, these ungainly looking devices operate rather like minibuses or share-taxis along fixed routes. In Delhi there are three-wheeler vehicles pulled by old Harley Davidson motorcycles which perform the same function.

Cycle-Rickshaw

Also known as a trishaw or a pedicab, this is effectively a three-wheeler bicycle with a seat for two passengers behind the rider. Although they no longer operate in the big cities, you will find them in all the smaller towns where they're the basic means of transport. Fares must always be agreed on in advance with a trishaw rider; about a rupee a km is a good-rule-of-thumb rate. In places like Agra, where there are a lot of them, the riders are as talkative and opinionated as any New York cabbie. Once upon a time there used to be the old man-powered rickshaws but today these only exist in Calcutta.

It's quite feasible to hire a rickshaw-wallah by time, not just for a straight trip. Hiring one for a day or even several days can make good sense. One traveller commented how, when taking on a rickshaw for several days, the rider would insist that he should 'pay as you like, I just want to please' but, he continued, 'no matter where we went, no matter how generous we were, we were always told at leaving that we had not given them enough'. Settle a price beforehand, no matter how much they insist they don't want to.

Hassling over the fares is the biggest difficulty of cycle-rickshaw travel. They'll often go all-out for a fare higher than it would cost you by taxi or auto-rickshaw. Nor does actually agreeing on a fare always make a difference; there is a greater possibility of a post-travel fare disagreement when you travel by cycle-rickshaw than by taxi or auto-rickshaw – metered or not.

Other

In some places, tongas (horse-drawn two-wheelers) and victorias (horse-drawn carriages) still operate. Calcutta has an extensive tramway network and India's first underground railway. Bombay has suburban trains.

Bicycle

India is a country of bicycles – an ideal

way of getting around the sights in a city or even of making longer trips – see the section on touring India by bicycle. Bicycle shops in most commercial centres will have bicycles for hire; you can often find them even in quite small villages. They charge from around Rs 0.50 an hour or Rs 4 or 6 per day. In some places they may be unwilling to hire to you since you are a stranger, but you can generally get around this by offering some sort of ID card as security. Check the time they put in the log book before you pedal off.

If you should be so unfortunate as to get a puncture, you'll soon spot men sitting under trees with puncture-repair outfits at the ready – less than a rupee to fix it. If you're asking distances you'll often be told in furlongs – eight to a mile, five to a km.

If you're travelling with small children and would like to use bikes a lot, consider getting a bicycle seat made up. If you find a shop making cane furniture they'll quickly make up a child's bicycle seat from a sketch. Get it made to fit on a standard-size rear carrier and it can be securely attached with a few lengths of cord. Tony's two children, Tashi and Kieran, have both done a bit of travelling on the back of Indian bicycles.

TOURS

At almost any place of tourist interest in India, and a good few places where there's not much tourist interest, there will be tours operated either by the Government of India Tourist office, the state tourist office or the local transport company – sometimes by all three. These tours are usually excellent value, particularly in cities or places where the tourist sights are widespread. You probably could not even get around the sights in New Delhi on public transport as cheaply as you could on a half-or full-day tour of that city.

These tours are not strictly for western tourists; you will almost always find yourself far outnumbered by local tourists, and in many places just a little off the beaten track you will often be the only westerner on the bus. Despite this the tours are usually conducted in English – which is possibly the only common language for the middle-class Indian tourists in any case. These tours are an excellent place to meet Indians.

If they have a drawback it is that many of them try to cram far too much into too short a period of time. A one-day tour which whisks you from Madras to Kanchipuram, Tirukalikundram, Mahabalipuram and back to Madras is not going to give you time for more than the most fleeting glimpse. If a tour looks too hectic, you're better off doing it yourself at a more appropriate pace or taking the tour simply to find out what places you want to devote more time to.

Stop Press

We've had a number of complaints recently about 'straight through' tickets to Kathmandu, Nepal from India. These principally operate from Delhi, Varanasi and Darjeeling and nowhere are they particularly good value. The buses are often no more comfortable than any other Indian bus. They are not 'straight through' since you have to change to a Nepali bus at the border. Taking them limits your choices since you could opt for another bus at the border or decide to take a break mid-way. And they're more expensive than doing it yourself, sometimes much more expensive.

New Delhi

Population: 4.5 million
Area: 1485 square km
Main languages: Hindi, Urdu & Punjabi

New Delhi is the capital of India and the third largest city. The city actually consists of two parts. Delhi or 'old' Delhi was the capital of Muslim India between the 12th and 19th centuries. In old Delhi you will find many mosques, monuments and forts relating to India's Muslim history. The other Delhi is New Delhi, the imperial city created as a capital of India by the British. It is a spacious, open city and contains many embassies and government buildings. New Delhi has a third important factor apart from its historic interest and role as the government centre – it is a major travel gateway. New Delhi is one of India's busiest entrance points for overseas airlines, is on the overland route across Asia and is the hub of the north Indian travel network.

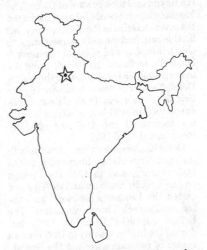

History

Delhi has not always been the capital of India but it has played an important role in Indian history ever since the epic *Mahabharata*, 5000 years ago. Over 2000 years ago Pataliputra, near modern-day Patna, was the capital of the emperor Ashoka's kingdom. More recently the Moghul emperors made Agra the capital through the 16th and 17th centuries. Under the British, Calcutta was the capital until the construction of New Delhi in 1911. Of course, it is only comparatively recently that India as we know it has been unified as one country. Even at the height of their powers the Moghuls did not control the south of India, for example. But Delhi has always been an important city or a capital of the northern region of the sub-continent.

There have been at least eight cities around modern Delhi. The first four were to the south around the area where the Qutab Minar stands. The earliest-known Delhi was called Indraprastha and was centred near present-day Purana Qila. At the beginning of the 12th century AD the last Hindu kingdom of Delhi was ruled by the Tomar and Chauthan dynasties and was also near the Qutab Minar and Suran Kund, now in Haryana.

This city was followed by Siri, constructed by Allah-ud-Din near present-day Hauz Khas in the 12th century. The third Delhi was Tughlaqabad, now entirely in ruins, which stood 10 km south-east of the Qutab Minar. The fourth Delhi dates from the 14th century and was also a creation of the Tughlaqs. Known as Jahanpanah, it also stood near the Qutab Minar.

The fifth Delhi, Ferozabad, was sited at Ferozshah Kotla in present-day old Delhi. Its ruins contain an Ashoka pillar, moved here from elsewhere, and traces of a mosque in which Tamerlane prayed during his attack on India.

Emperor Sher Shah created the sixth Delhi at Purana Qila, near India Gate in New Delhi today. Sher Shah was an

Afghan ruler who defeated the Moghul Humayun and took control of Delhi. The Moghul emperor Shah Jahan constructed the seventh Delhi in the 17th century; his Shahjahanabad roughly corresponds to old Delhi today and is largely preserved. His Delhi included the Red Fort and the majestic Jami Masjid. Finally the eighth Delhi, New Delhi, was constructed by the British – the move from Calcutta was announced in 1911 but construction was not completed and the city officially inaugurated until 1931.

Delhi has seen many invaders through the ages. Tamerlane plundered it in the 14th century, and in 1739 the Persian emperor Nadir Shah sacked the city and carted the Kohinoor Diamond and the famous Peacock Throne off to Iran. The British captured Delhi in 1803, but during the Indian mutiny in 1857 it was a centre of resistance against the British. Prior to partition Delhi had a very large Muslim population and Urdu was the main language. Now Punjabis have replaced many of the Muslims, and Hindi predominates.

Orientation

Delhi is a relatively easy city to find your way around although it is very spread out. The section of interest to visitors is on the west bank of the Yamuna River and is divided basically into two parts – old Delhi and New Delhi. Desh Bandhu Gupta Rd and Asaf Ali Rd mark the boundary between the tightly packed streets of the old city and the spaciously planned areas of the new capital.

Old Delhi is the 17th-century walled city with city gates, narrow alleys, the enormous Red Fort and Jami Masjid of Shah Jahan, temples, mosques, bazaars and the famous street known as Chandni Chowk. Here you will find the Delhi Railway Station and, a little further north, the Interstate Bus Terminal near Kashmiri Gate. Near New Delhi Railway Station, and acting as a sort of 'buffer zone' between the old and new cities, is

Paharganj. There are a number of popular cheap hotels and restaurants in this area.

The 'hub' of New Delhi is the great circle of Connaught Place and the streets that radiate out from it. Here you will find most of the airline offices, banks, travel agents, the various state tourist offices and the national one, more budget accommodation and several of the big hotels. The Regal Cinema, at the south side of the circle, and the Plaza Cinema, at the north, are two important Connaught Place landmarks and are very useful for telling taxi or auto-rickshaw drivers where you want to go.

Janpath, running off Connaught Place to the south, is one of the most important streets with the Government of India Tourist Office, the Student Travel Information Centre in the Imperial Hotel and a number of other useful addresses. New Delhi is a planned city of wide, tree-lined streets, parks and fountains. It can be further sub-divided into the business and living areas around Connaught Place and the government areas around Raj Path to the south. At one end of Raj Path is the India Gate memorial and at the other end is the Indian Parliament building.

South of the New Delhi government areas are Delhi's more expensive residential areas with names like Defence Colony, Lodi Colony or Friend's Colony. Delhi airport is to the south-west of the city, and about half-way between the airport and Connaught Place is Chanakyapuri, the diplomatic enclave. Most of Delhi's embassies are concentrated in this modern area and there are also a number of the major hotels here.

Information

The Government of India Tourist Office (tel 43005-8) at 88 Janpath is open from 9 am to 6 pm Monday to Friday, 9 am to 1 pm Saturday, closed Sunday. The office has a lot of information and brochures on destinations all over India but none of it is on display – you have to know what you want and ask for it. They have a good give-away map of Delhi and New Delhi. The Tourist Office can also assist you in finding accommodation. At the airport there is a tourist counter open around the clock for domestic and international arrivals. Here, too, they can help you find accommodation although, like many other Indian tourist offices, they may tell you the hotel you choose is 'full' and steer you somewhere else when actually your selected hotel is not full at all.

There is also a Delhi Tourism Corporation office (tel 46356) in N Block, Connaught Place. Most of the state governments have information centres in New Delhi. The offices for Andhra Pradesh, Assam, Bihar, Karnataka, Maharashtra, Orissa and West Bengal are all in the State Emporia Building on Baba Kharak Singh Marg. The offices for Haryana, Rajasthan and Uttar Pradesh are in the Chandralok Building, 36 Janpath. Jammu & Kashmir, Gujarat, Himachal Pradesh, Punjab, Kerala and Madhya Pradesh have their offices in the Kanishka Shopping Centre between the Ashok Yatri Niwas and Kanishka hotels.

Visa Renewals & Permits Hans Bhawan, near the Tilak Bridge Railway Station, is where you'll find the Foreigner's Registration Office. Come here to renew visas or to get permits for restricted areas such as Darjeeling. It's chaotic and confused as ever with no organisation or plan, but surprisingly with a little push and shove you can get visas renewed or permits issued remarkably quickly. Two photos are required for visa renewals, four if you're already beyond 90 days; a photographer outside the building will do them on the spot at Rs 20 for four. The office is closed 1 to 1.30 pm.

If you need a tax clearance certificate before departure, the Foreign Section of the Income Tax Department is around the corner from Hans Bhawan in the Central Revenue Building. Bring exchange certificates with you, though it's quite

likely nobody will ask for your clearance certificate when you leave the country. The office is closed 1 to 2 pm. Permits to visit the Punjab are issued by the Home Ministry, Lok Nayak Bhawan near Khan Market in New Delhi. It's open Monday to Friday from 2 to 4 pm.

Travel Agencies Tripsout Travel at 72/7 Tolstoy Lane behind the Government of India Tourist Office on Janpath is popular, appears to be trustworthy and seems to offer discounts which match (or beat) the many Connaught Place agencies. Lots of travellers use the place.

In the Imperial Hotel the Student Travel Information Centre is also used by many travellers and is the place to renew or obtain student cards, although their tickets are not usually as cheap as elsewhere. Some of the ticket discounters around Connaught Place are real fly-by-night operations so take care.

There are all sorts of stories about the best deals on offer, but Aeroflot, various Eastern European airlines and the less popular Middle Eastern airlines still seem to offer the best deals to Europe. The cheapest tickets usually entail hassles like overbooking and long waits for flights; Syrian Arab Airlines has been notorious.

Banks In New Delhi there are major offices of all the Indian banks and overseas ones operating in India. As usual, some branches will change travellers' cheques, some will not. If you need to change money outside regular banking hours the Ashok Hotel has an efficient 24-hour service but it means trekking out to Chanakyapuri. The Bank of America on Barakhamba Rd and the Central Bank of India on Connaught Place are reportedly the only places where you can buy US$ travellers' cheques with rupees.

American Express have their office in A Block, Connaught Place, and although they are usually crowded their service is very fast. If you want to replace stolen or lost American Express travellers' cheques, you need a photocopy of the police report and one photo as well as the proof-of-purchase slip and the numbers of the missing cheques. If you don't have the latter they will insist on telexing the place where you bought them before re-issuing. If you've had the lot stolen they are empowered to give you up to US$200 while all this is going on.

Post Offices There is a post office at 9A Connaught Place but New Delhi's efficient poste restante is on Market St (officially renamed Bhai Vir Singh Marg), some distance from Connaught Place. Poste restante mail addressed simply to 'Delhi' will end up at the inconveniently situated old Delhi post office. Some people also send mail to the Tourist Office on Janpath or the Student Travel Information Centre. Of course American Express have their clients' mail service.

Phone Calls The Overseas Communications Service (OCS) office is on Bangla Shahib Rd – more or less directly behind the poste restante which is on Market Rd. You can make overseas phone calls here fairly quickly and efficiently – if you book the call ahead of time you can usually return just before it's due to go through and not have to hang around. At the other extreme of Indian phone efficiency one visitor reported that the Ashok Yatri Niwas hotel has pay phones on every floor, 'and not one of them from floor 13 on down was working'.

Bookshops There are a number of excellent bookshops around Connaught Place – a good place to look for interesting Indian books or stock up with hefty paperbacks to while away those long train rides. Some of the better shops include the New Book Depot at 18 B Block, Connaught Place; the English Book Depot; the Piccadilly Book Store; the Oxford Book Shop in N Block, Connaught Place; and the Cottage Goods Emporium bookshop just off Janpath. Book World has shops in Palika Bazaar (the underground bazaar on Connaught Place) and at the Ashok Hotel. There are lots of books for sale near the Regal Cinema. The Soviet Bookshop on Connaught Place sells Russian classics and illustrated children's books (fairy tales, etc) at knock-down prices.

Libraries & Organisations The US Information Service is at 24 Kasturba Gandhi Marg and is open from 11 am to 6 pm, but their range of books is very limited. The British Council's Library is open from 10 am to 7 pm and is in the AIFACS Building, Rafi Marg. It's much better than its US equivalent but you officially have to join to get in. There are also cultural centres from France, Bulgaria, Italy, Japan and the USSR.

Sapru House on Barakhamba Rd is an institution devoted to the study of people of the world and has a good library. The India International Centre, beside the Lodi Tombs, has lectures each week on art, economics and other contemporary issues by Indian and foreign experts.

Airlines Addresses of airlines that fly to Delhi include:

Aeroflot
BMC House, 1st floor, N-1 Connaught Place (tel 3310426)
Air France
Ashoka Hotel, Chanakyapuri (tel 604691)
Air India
Scindia House, Connaught Place (tel 3311225)
Air Lanka
Hotel Imperial, Janpath (tel 344965)
Alitalia
19 Kasturba Gandhi Marg (tel 3311020)
British Airways
1A Connaught Place (tel 343428)
Indian Airlines
Kanchenjunga Building, Barakhamba Rd (tel 3310052)
Japan Airlines
Chandralok Building, 36 Janpath (tel 322122)

KLM
9A Connaught Place (tel 343998)
Lot Polish Airlines
Hotel Imperial, Janpath (tel 344789)
Lufthansa
56 Janpath (tel 310554)
Pan Am
Chandralok Building, 36 Janpath (tel 357542)
Royal Nepal Airlines
44 Janpath (tel 321572)
SAS
12A Connaught Place (tel 343638)
Thai International
12A Connaught Place (tel 343608)
Vayudoot
Malhotra Building, F-Block, Janpath (tel 3312587)

Embassies Addresses of some of the embassies in Delhi include:

Australia
1/50G Shantipath, Chanakyapuri (tel 601336)
Bangladesh
56 Ring Rd (tel 615668)
Bhutan
Chandra Gupta Marg, Chanakyapuri (tel 609217)
Burma
3/50F Nyaya Marg, Chanakyapuri (tel 600251)
Canada
7/8 Shantipath, Chanakyapuri (tel 608161)
China
50D Shantipath, Chanakyapuri (tel 609503)
Denmark
2 Golf Links (tel 616273)
Finland
25 Golf Links (tel 616006)
Germany (West)
6/60G Shantipath, Chanakyapuri (tel 604861)
Indonesia
50A Chanakyapuri (tel 602352)
Iran
5 Barakhamba Rd (tel 385491)
Ireland
13 Jor Bagh (tel 617435)
Japan
4/50G Chanakyapuri (tel 604071)
Malaysia
50M Satya Marga, Chanakyapuri (tel 601291)

Nepal
Barakhamba Rd (tel 381484)
Netherlands
6/50F Shantipath, Chanakyapuri (tel 609511)
New Zealand
Taj Palace Hotel, 2 Sardar Patel Marg (tel 3010101)
Norway
50C Kautilya Marg, Chanakyapuri (tel 605982)
Pakistan
2/50G Shantipath, Chanakyapuri (tel 605982)
Singapore
E6 Chandragupta Marg, Chankayapuri (tel 604162)
Sri Lanka
27 Kautilya Marg, Chanakyapuri (tel 3010201)
Sweden
Nyaya Marg, Chanakyapuri (tel 604961)
Thailand
56N Nyaya Marg, Chanakyapuri (tel 605679)
UK
Shantipath, Chanakyapuri (tel 601371)
USA
Shantipath, Chanakyapuri (tel 600651)
USSR
Shantipath, Chanakyapuri (tel 606026)
UN
56 Lodi Estate (tel 690410)

New Delhi is a good place for getting visas. In particular Thai visas are issued with less fuss here than in Kathmandu.

Other Information If Delhi's summer heat (night temperatures in June average 37°C after days in the 41 to 45°C bracket) gets too much, hotel pools are a good retreat and a number of the international hotels will let you use theirs for around Rs 30 a day.

Delhi Architecture

The various periods of Delhi's history can be traced in the many historic buildings around the city. These can be roughly divided into early, middle and late Pathan periods followed by early, middle and late Moghul periods.

Early Pathan (1193-1320) The Qutab Minar complex dates from this period, which was characterised by a combination of Hindu designs with those of the Muslim invaders. Domes and arches were the chief imported elements.

Middle Pathan (1320-1414) The Tughlaqabad buildings date from the beginning of this period. Later buildings include the Feroz Shah Kotla Mosque, the Hauz Khas tomb, the Nizam-ud-din Mosque and the Khirki Mosque. At first local stone and red sandstone were used, later giving way to stone and mortar walls with plaster facing. Characteristic design elements include sloping walls and high platforms for the mosques.

Late Pathan (1414-1556) The Sayyid and Lodi tombs and the Purana Qila date from this period. The impressive domes and coloured marble or tile decorations are characteristic of this period.

Moghul (1556-1754) During the early Moghul period buildings were of red sandstone with marble details; Humayun's and Azam Khan's tombs are typical examples. During the middle period much more use of marble was made and buildings had bulbous domes and towering minarets. The Red Fort, the Jami Masjid and the Fatehpuri Mosque are all good examples, but the supreme building from this period is, of course, the Taj Mahal in Agra. In the later Moghul period the style became over-elaborate; good examples of this decadent period are the Sunehri Mosque on Chandni Chowk in old Delhi and the Safdarjang tomb, probably the last notable Moghul building.

Old Delhi

The old walled city of Shahjahanabad stands to the west of the Red Fort and was at one time surrounded by a sturdy defensive wall, only fragments of which now exist. The Kashmiri Gate, at the northern end of the walled city, was the scene for desperate fighting when the British retook Delhi during the Mutiny. West of here, near Sabzi Mandi, is the British-erected Mutiny Memorial to the soldiers who lost their lives in the events of the uprising. Near the monument is another Ashoka pillar. Like the one in Feroz Kotla, it was brought here by Feroz Shah Tughlaq.

The main street of old Delhi is the colourful shopping bazaar known as Chandni Chowk. It's hopelessly congested day and night, a very sharp contrast to the open, spacious streets of New Delhi. At the east (Red Fort) end of Chandni Chowk, and north of the Jami Masjid, there is a Jain temple with a small marble courtyard surrounded by a colonnade. Next to the Kotwali (police station) is the Sunehri Masjid. In 1739 Nadir Shah, the Persian invader who carried off the Peacock Throne when he sacked Delhi, stood on the roof of the mosque and watched while his soldiers conducted a bloody massacre of the Delhi inhabitants.

The west end of Chandni Chowk is marked by the Fatehpuri Mosque which one of Shah Jahan's wives erected in 1650.

Red Fort

The red sandstone walls of Lal Qila, the Red Fort, extend for two km and vary in height from 18 metres on the river side to 33 metres on the city side. Shah Jahan commenced construction of the massive fort in 1638 and it was completed in 1648. He never completely moved his capital from Agra to his new city of Shahjahanabad in Delhi because his son Aurangzeb deposed him and imprisoned him in Agra Fort.

The Red Fort dates from the very peak of Moghul power. When the emperor rode out on elephant back into the streets of old Delhi it was a display of pomp and power at its most magnificent. The Moghul period at the top was a short one, however. Aurangzeb was the first and last great Moghul emperor to rule from here.

Today the fort is typically Indian with would-be guides leaping forth to offer their services as soon as you enter. It's still a calm haven of peace if you've just left the frantic streets of old Delhi. The city noise and confusion are light years away from the fort gardens and pavilions. If you look out over the fort wall towards the Yamuna River there will probably be assorted musicians, contortionists, rope climbers, magicians, dancing bears and rope climbers down below. Entry to the fort is Rs 0.50, free on Fridays.

Lahore Gate The main gate to the fort takes its name from the fact that it faces towards Lahore, now in Pakistan. You enter the fort here and immediately find yourself in a vaulted arcade, now given over to small shops. This was once the Meena Bazaar – the shopping centre for ladies of the court. The arcade of shops leads into the Naubat Khana, which used to be a gallery for musicians but is now just an open courtyard.

Diwan-i-Am The 'Hall of Public Audiences' was where the emperor would sit to hear complaints or disputes from his subjects. His alcove in the wall was marble panelled and set with precious stones – many of which were looted following the Mutiny. This elegant hall was restored by Lord Curzon.

Diwan-i-Khas The 'Hall of Private Audiences' was the luxurious chamber where the emperor would hold private meetings. Centrepiece of the hall, until Nadir Shah carted it off to Iran in 1739, was the magnificent Peacock Throne. The solid gold throne had figures of peacocks standing behind it, their beautiful colours coming from countless inlaid precious stones. Between them was the figure of a parrot carved out of a single emerald. This masterpiece in precious metals, sapphires, rubies, emeralds and pearls was broken up, and the so-called Peacock Throne displayed in Tehran simply utilises various bits of the original.

In 1760 the Marathas also removed the silver ceiling from the hall so today it is a pale shadow of its former glory. Inscribed on the walls of the Diwan-i-Khas is that famous Persian couplet:

*If there is a paradise on earth
it is this, it is this, it is this*

Royal Baths Next to the Diwan-i-Khas are the *hamams* or baths – three large rooms surmounted by domes, with a fountain in the centre. One of the baths was set up as a sauna!

Moti Masjid Built in 1659 by Aurangzeb, the small and totally enclosed Pearl Mosque is next to the baths and made of marble.

Other The Rang Mahal pavilion or 'Painted Palace' took its name from the painted interior which is now gone. The Khas Mahal was the emperor's private palace, divided into rooms for worship, sleeping and living. There is a small Museum of Archaeology in the Mumtaz Mahal. The Delhi Gate to the south of the fort led to the Jami Masjid.

Sound & Light Show Each evening a *son et lumie're* show re-creates events of India's history, particularly those connected with the Red Fort. There are shows in English and Hindi and tickets are available from the ITDC in L Block, Connaught Place (tel 42336, 40982), or at the fort. They cost Rs 4 and Rs 8. Timings vary with the season so check at the Tourist Office. One of the slogans in the fight for independence was that the tri-coloured Indian flag would replace the Union Jack over the Red Fort.

Jami Masjid
The great mosque of old Delhi is both the largest in India and the final architectural extravagance of Shah Jahan. Commenced in 1644, the mosque was not completed until 1658. It has three great gateways, four angle towers and two minarets

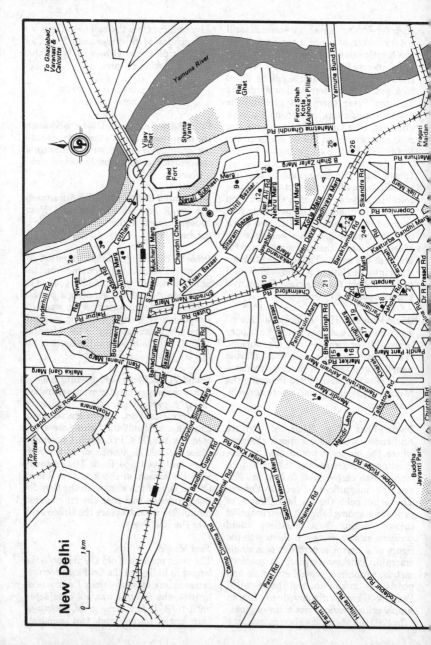

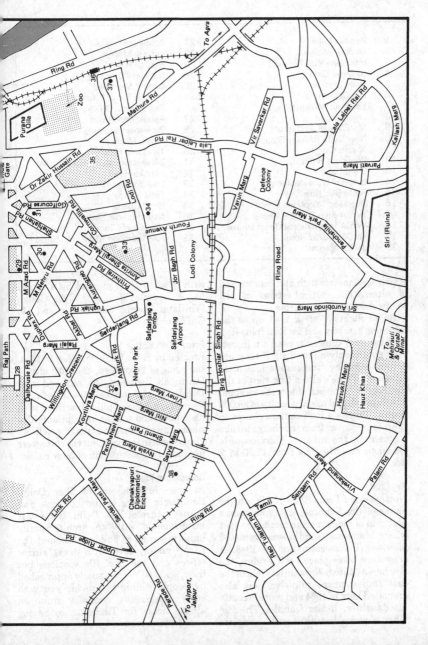

1	Ashoka Pillar	21	Connaught Place
2	Qudsia Gardens	22	Bengali Market
3	Interstate Bus Terminal	23	Natural History Museum
4	Kashmir Gate	24	Nepalese Embassy
5	Delhi Station	25	Gandhi Memorial
6	Old Delhi GPO	26	Income Tax & Foreigner's
7	Fatehpur Mosque		Registration Office
8	Jami Masjid	27	Ashok Yatri Niwas
9	Moti Mahal Restaurant	28	Parliament Building
10	New Delhi Railway Station	29	Indian Museum
11	Tourist Camp	30	Taj Mahal Hotel
12	President Hotel	31	Bikaner House – Jaipur Buses
13	Delhi Gate	32	Ashoka Hotel
14	Lakshmi Narayan Temple	33	Lodi Tombs
15	Poste Restante	34	Tibet House
16	Overseas Telephone Office	35	Hotel Oberoi
17	YWCA Blue Triangle Hostel	36	Nizam-ud-din Station
18	YWCA International Guest House	37	Humayun's Tomb
19	YMCA Tourist Hotel	38	Rail Transport Museum
20	Jantar Mantar		

standing 40 metres high and constructed of alternating vertical strips of red sandstone and white marble.

Broad flights of steps lead up to the imposing gateway and for Rs 2 (plus Rs 2 for a camera) you can ascend a minaret. Women are only allowed up if they are accompanied by 'the responsible male relatives'. There's also a fine view of the Red Fort from the east side of the mosque. The Jami Masjid has a capacity of 25,000 people. There's a Rs 1 camera charge to the mosque, apart from the charge to take a camera up the minaret. The mosque is closed to non-Muslims from 12.30 to 2 pm.

Raj Ghat

North-east of Feroz Shah Kotla, on the banks of the Yamuna, a simple square platform of black marble marks the spot where Mahatma Gandhi was cremated following his assassination in 1948. A ceremony takes place each Friday, the day he was killed. Jawaharlal Nehru, the first Indian prime minister, was also cremated here in 1964 and more recently his daughter, Indira Gandhi. The Raj Ghat is now a beautiful park, complete with labelled trees planted by a mixed bag of notables including QE2, Gough Whitlam, Dwight Eisenhower and Ho Chi Minh!

Feroz Shah Kotla

Erected by Feroz Shah Tughlaq in 1354, the ruins of Ferozabad, the fifth city of Delhi, are between the old and new Delhis. In the fortress-palace is a 13-metre-high Ashoka pillar inscribed with his edicts (and a later inscription). The ruins of an old mosque and a fine well can also be seen in the area, but the ruins were used for the construction of later cities.

Connaught Place

At the northern end of New Delhi, Connaught Place is the business and tourist centre of New Delhi. It's a vast traffic circle with an architecturally uniform series of buildings around the edge - mainly devoted to shops, airline offices and the like. It's spacious but busy, and you're continually approached by people willing to provide you with every imaginable necessity from an airline ticket for Timbuktu to having your fortune read.

Jantar Mantar

Only a short stroll down Parliament St from Connaught Place, this strange collection of salmon-coloured structures is another of Maharaja Jai Singh II's observatories. The ruler from Jaipur constructed this observatory in 1725 and it is dominated by a huge sundial known as the 'Prince of Dials'. Other instruments plot the course of heavenly bodies and the paths of stars, and predict eclipses.

Laxmi Narayan Temple

Due west of Connaught Place, this garish modern temple was erected by the industrialist Birla in 1938. It's dedicated to Vishnu and his consort Laxmi, the goddess of wealth.

India Gate

The 42-metre-high stone arch of triumph stands at the eastern end of the Raj Path. It bears the name of 90,000 Indian Army soldiers who died in the campaigns of WW I, the North-West Frontier operations of the same time and the 1919 Afghan fiasco.

Rashtrapati Bhavan

The official residence of the president of India stands on Raisini Hill, at the opposite end of the Raj Path to India Gate. Completed in 1929, the palace-like building has an elegant Moghul garden and occupies 130 hectares. Prior to independence this was the Viceroy's House, the residence of the viceroy of India. At the time of Mountbatten, India's last viceroy, the number of servants needed to maintain the 340 rooms and its extensive gardens was enormous. There were 418 gardeners alone, 50 of them boys whose sole job was to chase away birds!

Parliament House

Sansad Bhavan, the Indian Parliament Building, stands at the end of Sansad Marg, Parliament St, just north of the Raj Path. This is one of the key elements in the design of New Delhi. A straight line drawn from the parliament building, down Parliament St, passes through the centre of Connaught Place and extended beyond it intersects the Jami Masjid. The

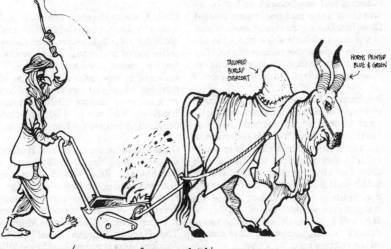

TAILORED BURLAP OVERCOAT

HORNS PAINTED BLUE & GREEN

lawn mower, Parliament Buildings, NEW DELHI.

building is a circular colonnaded structure 171 metres in diameter.

Museums

Delhi has a wide range of museums and galleries. Some of the most interesting include:

National Museum On Janpath just south of Raj Path, the National Museum has a good collection of Indian bronzes, terra cotta and wood sculptures dating back to the Mauryan period (2nd-3rd century BC), exhibits from the Vijayanagar period in south India, miniature and mural paintings and costumes of the various tribal peoples. The museum is definitely worth visiting and is open from 10 am to 5 pm daily, but closed on Mondays. The small entry fee varies through the week; it's free Saturday and Sunday. There are film shows most days of the week.

Nehru Museum On Teen Murti Rd near Chanakyapuri, the diplomatic enclave, the residence of the first Indian prime minister has been converted into a museum and has fascinating but badly organised items and documents related to his life. During the tourist season there is a sound-and-light show about his life and the independence movement. The museum is open from 10 am to 5 pm daily, closed on Mondays. Admission is free.

Rail Transport Museum Located at Chanakyapuri, the railway museum will be of great interest to anyone who becomes fascinated by India's exotic collection of railway engines. The collection includes an 1855 steam engine, still in working order, and a large number of oddities such as the skull of an elephant that charged a mail train in 1894, and lost. There are many steam locomotives on display in very well kept condition. See the introductory Gricing section for more details on the engines here.

The museum is open 9.30 am to 1 pm,

1.30 to 5 pm, closed on Mondays. Admission is Rs 2 and an additional Rs 5 for taking photographs.

Tibet House This small museum has a fascinating collection of ceremonial items brought out of Tibet when the Dalai Lama fled the Chinese. Downstairs is a shop selling a wide range of Tibetan handicrafts. There are often lecture/discussion sessions and there's also a nice little museum. It's at 16 Jorbagh, near the Oberoi New Delhi Hotel. Hours are 9.30 am to 1 pm and 2.30 to 6 pm, April-September; and 9 am to 1 pm and 2 to 5 pm the rest of the year. It's closed Sundays and admission is free.

International Dolls Museum Located in Nehru House on Bahadur Shah Zafar Marg, the museum displays 6000 dolls from 85 different countries. Over a third of them are from India and an exhibit is being prepared that will show 500 dolls in the costumes worn all over India. The museum is open from 10 am to 6 pm daily, closed Mondays. Admission is Rs 0.50, half price for children.

Crafts Museum Recently relocated to the Aditi Pavilion at the Exhibition Grounds, Mathura Rd, this museum contains a collection of traditional Indian crafts in textiles, metal, wood and ceramics. The museum is now part of a 'village life' complex where you can visit rural India without ever leaving Delhi. Opening hours are 9.30 am to 4.30 pm, closed Sundays. Admission is free.

Other The Museum of Natural History is opposite the Nepalese Embassy on Barakhamba Rd. Fronted by a large dinosaur model, it has a collection of fossils, stuffed animals and birds and a 'hands on' discovery room for children. It's open 10 am to 5 pm, closed Mondays. The Gandhi Balidan Sthal in Tees January Marg is where Gandhi was killed and has a display on his life.

There is a National Philatelic Museum at Dak Tar Bhavan, Sardar Patel Square on Parliament St. It's closed on Saturdays and Sundays. At Palam Airport there is an Air Force Museum open from 10 am to 1.30 pm, closed Tuesdays. Admission is free.

Purana Qila

Just south-east of India Gate and north of Humayun's Tomb and the Nizam-ud-din Railway Station is the old fort, Purana Qila. This is the supposed site of Indraprastha, the original city of Delhi. The fort has massive walls and three large gateways. Sher Shah, who briefly interrupted the Moghul empire by defeating Humayun, built the fort during his period of rule from 1538 to 1545 before Humayun wrested control of India back.

Entering from the south gate you'll see the small octagonal red sandstone tower, the Sher Manzil, later used by Humayun as a library. It was in this tower that he slipped, fell and received injuries from which he died. Just beyond it is the Qila-i-Kuhran Mosque or Mosque of Sher Shah.

Humayun's Tomb

Built in the mid-16th century by Haji Begum, wife of Humayan, the second Moghul emperor, this is an early example of Moghul architecture. The elements in its design – a squat building, lighted by high arched entrances, topped by a bulbous dome and surrounded by formal gardens – were to be refined over the years to the magnificence of the Taj Mahal in Agra. This earlier tomb is thus of great interest for its relation to the later Taj. Humayun's wife is also buried in the red-and-white sandstone, black-and-yellow marble tomb.

Other tombs in the garden include that of Humayun's barber, while to the right is the tomb of Isa Khan, a good example of Pathan (Afghan) architecture from the time of the Lodi dynasty. Entry to Humayun's tomb is Rs 0.50, except on Fridays when it is free. There's a fine view over the surrounding country from the terraces of Humayun's Tomb. One traveller noted that just up the main stairs of the tomb building, to the left, are the graves of the five engineers who built it – 'Old Haji Begum had a strange way of saying thank you for a job well done'.

Zoo

The Delhi Zoo on the south side of the fort is not terribly good. The cages are poorly labelled and in winter many of the animals are kept inside. There is a white tiger though. The zoo is open from 8 am to 6 pm in summer, 9 am to 5 pm in winter. Entry is Rs 0.50.

Hazrat Nizam-ud-din Aulia

Across the road from Humayun's Tomb is the shrine of the Muslim saint Nizam-ud-din Chisti. He died in 1325 aged 92, and his shrine, with its large tank, is only one of a number of interesting tombs here. They include the later grave of Jahanara, the daughter of Shah Jahan who stayed with him during his imprisonment by Aurangzeb.

Mirza Ghalib, a renowned Urdu poet, also has his tomb here as does Azam Khan, a favourite of Humayun and Akbar, who was murdered by Adham Khan in Agra. In turn Akbar had Adham Khan terminated and his grave is near the Qutab Minar. The construction of Nizam-ud-din's tank caused a dispute between the saint and the constructor of Tughlaqabad further to the south of Delhi – see Tughlaqabad for details. The tomb of a modern Sufi saint, the Hazrat Inayat Khan, is also near here and every Friday evening about 7 pm Kawali singers perform at it.

Lodi Tombs

About three km to the west and adjoining the India International Centre are the Lodi Gardens. In these well-kept gardens are the tombs of the Sayyid and Lodi rulers. Muhammad Shah's tomb (1450) is a prototype for the later Moghul-style tomb of Humayun, a design which would eventually develop into the Taj Mahal. Other tombs include those of his predecessor Mubarak Shah (1433), Ibrahim Lodi (1526) and Sikander Lodi (1517). The Bara Gumbad Mosque is a fine example of its type of plaster decoration.

Safdarjang Tomb
Beside the smaller Safdarjang airport, where Indira Gandhi's son was killed in a light plane accident in 1980, is the Safdarjang Tomb. It was built in 1753-54 by the Nawab of Oudh for his father Safdarjang and is one of the last examples of Moghul architecture before the final remnants of the great empire collapsed. The tomb stands on a high terrace in an extensive garden. There are good views from the roof. Entry is Rs 0.50; free on Fridays.

Moth ki Masjid
South again from the Safdarjang Tomb, this mosque is said to be the finest in the Lodi style. It was around this area that Timur defeated the forces of Muhammad Shah Tughlaq in 1398.

Hauz Khas
About midway between Safdarjang and the Qutab Minar, this area was once the reservoir for the second city of Delhi, Siri, which lies slightly to the east. Interesting sights here include Feroz Shah's Tomb (1398) and the remains of an ancient college.

Khirki Masjid & Jahanpanah
This interesting mosque with its four open courts dates from 1380. The nearby village of Khirki also takes its name from the mosque. Close to the mosque are remains of the fourth city of Delhi, Jahanpanah, including the high Bijai Mandal platform and the Begumpur Mosque with its multiplicity of domes.

Tughlaqabad
The massively strong walls of Tughlaqabad, the third city of Delhi, are east of the Qutab Minar. The walled city and fort with its 13 gateways was built by Ghiyas-ud-din Tughlaq and its construction involved a legendary quarrel with the saint Nizam-ud-din. When the Tughlaq ruler took the workers whom Nizam-ud-din wanted for work on his shrine, the saint cursed the king with the warning that his city would be inhabited only by Gujars (shepherds). Today that is indeed the situation.

The dispute between king and saint did not end with curse and counter-curse. When the king prepared to take vengeance on the saint, Nizam-ud-din calmly told his followers, in a saying that is still current in India today, 'Delhi is a long way off'. Indeed it was, for the king was murdered on his way from Delhi in 1325.

The fort walls are constructed of massive blocks and outside the south wall of the city is an artificial lake with the king's tomb in its centre. A long causeway connects the tomb to the fort, both of which have walls that slope inward.

Qutab Minar Complex
Situated 15 km south of New Delhi, the buildings in this complex date from the onset of Muslim rule in India, and are fine examples of early Afghan architecture. The Qutab Minar itself is a soaring tower of victory which was commenced in 1193, immediately after the defeat of the last Hindu kingdom in Delhi. It reaches 73 metres high and tapers from a 15-metre-diameter base to just 2.5 metres at the top.

The tower has five distinct storeys, each marked by a projecting balcony. The first three storeys are made of red sandstone, the fourth and fifth of marble and sandstone. Although Qutab-ud-din commenced construction of the tower, he only got to the first storey. His successors completed it, and in 1368 Feroz Shah

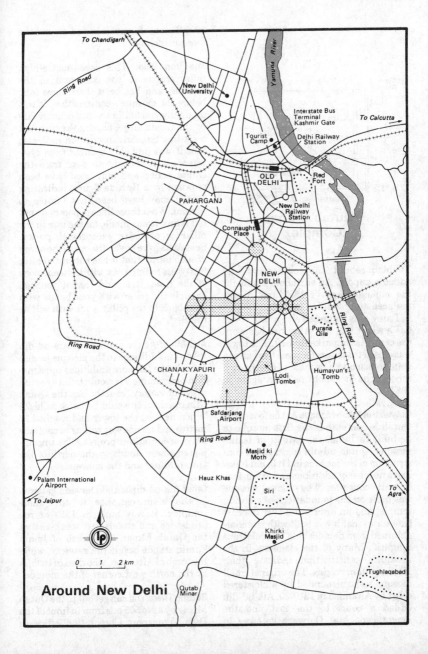

Around New Delhi

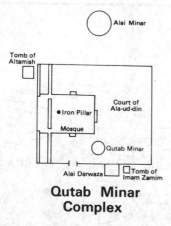

Alai Minar

Tomb of
Altamish

Court of
Ala-ud-din

Iron Pillar

Mosque

Qutab Minar

Alai Darwaza

Tomb of
Imam Zamim

Qutab Minar Complex

Tughlaq rebuilt the top storeys and added a cupola. An earthquake brought the cupola down in 1803 and it was replaced and modified in 1829.

Today this impressively ornate tower has a slight tilt, but otherwise has worn the centuries remarkably well. The tower was closed to visitors for some time after a stampede led to a number of deaths on a school trip. It should be open again in 1987.

Quwwat-ul-Islam Mosque At the foot of the Qutab Minar stands the first mosque to be built in India, the 'Might of Islam' mosque. Qutab-ud-din commenced construction of the mosque in 1193, but it has had a number of additions and extensions over the centuries. The original mosque was built on the foundations of a Hindu temple, and an inscription over the east gate states that it was built with materials obtained from demolishing '27 idolatrous temples'. Many of the elements in the mosque's construction indicate their Hindu or Jain origins. The original small mosque was surrounded by a cloistered court by Altamish in 1210-20. Ala-ud-din added a court to the east and the magnificent Alai Darwaza gateway in

1300. Points of interest in and around the mosque include:

The Iron Pillar This seven-metre-high pillar stands in the courtyard of the mosque, and has been there since long before the mosque's construction. It was originally erected in the 5th century AD by the Hindu king Chandra Varman, but a six-line Sanskrit inscription indicates that it was probably brought from elsewhere. It is thought to date from the Gupta period and may once have been crowned by a Garuda figure, indicating that it may have been in a temple to Vishnu. What those lines of poetry do not tell is how it was made, for the iron in the pillar is of quite exceptional purity. Scientists have never discovered how iron of such purity that it has not rusted after 2000 years could be cast with the technology of the time. It is said that if you can encircle the pillar with your hands with your back to the pillar, your wish will be fulfilled.

Alai Minar At the same time Ala-ud-din made his additions to the mosque he also conceived a far more ambitious construction programme. He would build a second tower of victory, exactly like the Qutab Minar except it would be twice as high! When he died the tower had reached 27 metres and no-one was willing to continue his over-ambitious project. The uncompleted tower stands to the north of the Qutab Minar and the mosque.

Other Ala-ud-din's Alai Darwaza gateway is the main entrance to the whole complex. It was built in 1310 of red sandstone and stands just south-east of the Qutab Minar. The tomb of Imam Zamin stands beside the gateway, while the tomb of Altamish, who died in 1235, is by the north-west corner of the mosque.

Getting There You can get out to the Qutab Minar by a No 505 bus from in front of the Delhi Transport Corporation office in

Connaught Place, or by minibus from in front of the Super Bazaar. The cost is about a rupee in either case.

Around the Qutab

There are a number of other points of interest around this complex. West of the enclosure is the tomb of Adham Khan who, amongst other things, drove Rupmati to suicide following the capture of Mandu (see Mandu). When Akbar became displeased with him he ended up being heaved off a terrace in the Agra Fort.

There are some summer palaces in the area and also the tombs of the final kings of Delhi, who succeeded the final Moghuls. An empty space between two of the tombs was intended for the last king of Delhi, who died in exile in Rangoon, Burma, in 1862, following his implication in the 1857 Indian Mutiny.

Tours

Delhi is very spread out, so taking a city tour makes a lot of sense. Even by public transport getting from, say, the Red Fort to the Qutab Minar would be comparatively expensive.

Three major organisations arrange Delhi tours – beware of agents offering cut-price (and sometimes inferior) tours. The ITDC (Indian Tourism Development Corporation) have tours which include guides and a luxury coach. Their office is in L Block, Connaught Place but their tours also start from the major hotels. Delhi Tourism, a branch of the city government, arrange similar tours and their office is in N Block. Finally, the Delhi Transport Corporation tours do not always include guides but are cheaper than the others and exceptionally good value.

A four-hour morning tour costs Rs 20 with the ITDC, Rs 14 with Delhi Tourism. Starting at 9 am the morning tour includes the Qutab Minar, Humayun's Tomb, India Gate, the Jantar Mantar and the Laxmi Narayan Temple. The similarly priced afternoon tour covers the Red Fort, Jami Masjid, Raj Ghat, Shantiban and Feroz Shah Kotla. If you take both tours on the same day it costs Rs 40 with the ITDC, Rs 25 with Delhi Tourism.

Tours further afield include Delhi Tourism day tours to Agra for Rs 150 or weekend tours to Hardwar and Rishikesh for Rs 150.

There are various cultural performances in Delhi at night. 'Dances of India' takes place from 7 to 8 pm every night at Parsi Anjuman Hall on Bahadurshah Zafar Marg at Delhi Gate. It's 'well worth the entry charge'.

Places to Stay – bottom end

Delhi is certainly no bargain when it comes to cheap hotels. You can easily pay Rs 40 for the most basic single – a price that elsewhere in India will generally get you a reasonable double with attached bathroom. There are basically two areas for cheap accommodation in Delhi. The first is around Janpath at the southern side of Connaught Place in New Delhi. The second is Paharganj near New Delhi Railway Station – this is about midway between old and New Delhi.

There are also a number of rock-bottom hotels in old Delhi itself – they're colourful but too far away from the agents, offices, airlines and so on of New Delhi for most travellers, given Delhi's difficult public-transport situation. Some other possibilities are scattered around Delhi, such as the two popular Tourist Camps and the Youth Hostel in the Chanakyapuri diplomatic quarter.

Janpath Area There are a number of cheaper 'lodges' or 'guest houses' near the Indian Government Tourist Office. They're often small and cramped but you meet lots of fellow travellers, they're conveniently central and there are often dormitories for shoestring travellers. Since many of these places are so popular you may find that your specific choice is full. If that's the case simply stay at one of the others until a room becomes available – it's unlikely you'll have to wait more than a day. For accommodation information in the Janpath area check with the Tourist Office at 88 Janpath, or try the helpful Student Travel Information Centre at the Imperial Hotel.

High on most people's list is the well-known *Ringo Guest House* (tel 3310605) at 17 Scindia House, round Scindia House behind Air India. It has dorm beds for Rs 20, singles/doubles with common bath for Rs 40-45/60 and doubles with attached bath for Rs 75 to Rs 110. The rooms are very small but the management are very friendly, it's clean and the showers and toilets are well maintained. Meals are available in the rooftop courtyard, although at a higher price than in the nearby restaurants, and there are always interesting people to talk to in the afternoons and evenings.

Other places with similar prices include the nearby *Sunny Guest House* (tel 46033) at 152 Scindia House with singles at Rs 35 to Rs 40, doubles at Rs 55 to Rs 90. The somewhat spartan *Asian Guest House* (tel 43393), 14 Scindia House, has singles/doubles with bath for Rs 70/110 as well as a number of more expensive air-con rooms. The *Gandhi Guest House* at 80 Tolstoy Lane is in this same area and has singles at Rs 45 to Rs 50, doubles at Rs 75 – basic but OK.

Still on the east side of Janpath, the *Royal Guest House* (tel 353485) is up four flights of gloomy steps at 44 Janpath, near Nepal Airlines. The rooms are reasonable and cost Rs 80 or with bath Rs 120. *R C Mehta* on the 3rd floor at 52 Janpath, next to the Lufthansa office, is inconspicuously signposted and reasonably cheap.

On the west side of Janpath along Janpath Lane are several places which have been minor legends among travellers for well over a decade now. *Mrs Colaco's* at No 3 is the first one you'll come to. The dormitory costs Rs 20 and there are singles/doubles for Rs 45/55 with common bath. There's a safe deposit for valuables, a laundry service and baggage storage. The place is run with determination and a certain degree of firmness by a lady of the same name, and one can only admire her tenacity at keeping it together for what must be approaching 20 years now. It's basic, crowded, rather hard on the nerves and may soon be closing due to the lease ending.

Round the corner, *Mr S C Jain's Guest House* at 7 Pratap Singh Building is also on Janpath Lane and is yet another legend. Extremely plain rooms with common bath cost Rs 50, 60 and 70. The *Soni Guest House* on Janpath Lane has similar prices.

Across the other side of Connaught Place is the *Hotel Bright* (tel 350444), M-85 Connaught Circus, opposite the Super Bazaar. It's not that bright at all but rooms cost Rs 60 to Rs 80 depending on whether they have attached bathrooms. Air cooling is available for another Rs 15, air-con for Rs 60. Breakfast in the attached vegetarian restaurant is Rs 12. At the same location is the *Hotel Blue* which has rooms at Rs 50/80, one of the cheapest around Connaught Circus.

Paharganj Area Directly opposite New Delhi Railway Station is the start of Main Bazaar, which stretches due west for about a km. There are any number of cheap hotels along this road, offering varying degrees of quality. Many are very popular with budget travellers. Other than the general air of decay and neglect, the problem with the ultra-cheap places here is that they are subject to police raids. Don't let this put you off – there are plenty of places offering excellent value for money without the indignity of being searched for narcotics. The raids can always provide some amusement too, as one traveller reported: 'While being raided by the drug squad no amount of warnings would stop them all from tasting the dessicating crystals (silica?) I used to keep my films dry which had

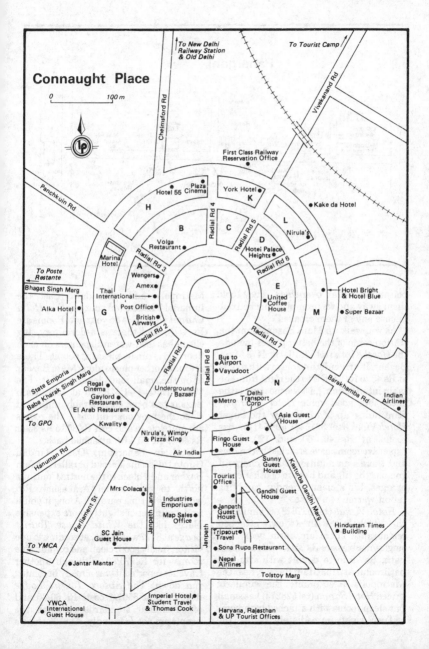

Connaught Place

0   100 m

To New Delhi
Railway Station
& Old Delhi

To Tourist Camp

Chelmsford Rd

Vivekanand Rd

Panchkuin Rd

First Class Railway
Reservation Office

Hotel 55

Plaza
Cinema

York Hotel

K

Kake da Hotel

H

Radial Rd 4

B

C

Radial Rd 5

L

Nirula's

Volga
Restaurant

Marina
Hotel

Radial Rd 3

A

Wengers

D

Hotel Palace
Heights

Radial Rd 6

To Poste
Restante

Bhagat Singh Marg

Thai
International

Amex

E

Hotel Bright
& Hotel Blue

Alka Hotel

Post Office

G

British
Airways

United
Coffee
House

M

Super Bazaar

Radial Rd 2

Radial Rd 7

Radial Rd 1

Radial Rd 8

F

Bus to
Airport

Vayudoot

State Emporia

Baba Kharak Singh Marg

Regal
Cinema

Underground
Bazaar

N

Barakhamba Rd

Gaylord
Restaurant

El Arab Restaurant

Metro

Delhi
Transport
Corp

Indian
Airlines

To GPO

Kwality

Asia Guest
House

Hanuman Rd

Nirula's, Wimpy
& Pizza King

Ringo Guest
House

Air India

Sunny
Guest
House

Kasturba Gandhi Marg

Parliament St

Mrs Colaca's

Janpath Lane

Tourist
Office

Gandhi Guest
House

Industries
Emporium

SC Jain
Guest House

Map Sales
Office

Janpath
Guest
House

Janpath

Tripsout
Travel

Hindustan Times
Building

To YMCA

Jantar Mantar

Sona Rupa Restaurant

Nepal
Airlines

Tolstoy Marg

YWCA
International
Guest House

Imperial Hotel
Student Travel
& Thomas Cook

Haryana, Rajasthan
& UP Tourist Offices

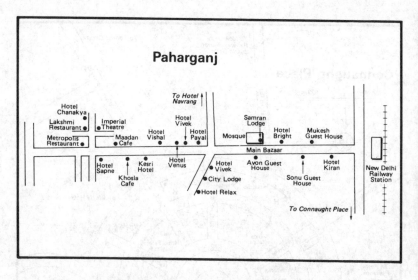

Paharganj

poison written all over them. They took them away and we promptly checked out in case any of them croaked'.

As you walk up Main Bazaar from the station some of the better places include the *Hotel Kiran* (tel 526104) at 4473 Main Bazaar. It's friendly and clean with rooms at Rs 45 to Rs 65. Off to the right from the main intersection, past the mosque, is the cheap but good value *Hotel Navrang*. Continuing up Main Bazaar the larger *Hotel Vivek* (tel 521948) at 1541-50 has rooms at Rs 40, 60 and 120. More expensive rooms have attached bathrooms and there's an additional 10% charge if you use the lift and beware of other extra charges. It's a clean, friendly, rambling rabbit warren of a place.

Hotel Vishal (tel 527629) is similar to the Vivek but with its own attached restaurant. There are dorm beds, and singles/doubles are Rs 35/45 with common bath, Rs 75 for a double with attached bathroom. At 5153 Main Bazaar, near the Metropolis Restaurant, the similarly priced *Hotel Sapna* (tel 528273) has small but clean rooms with attached bathroom.

Turn right immediately before the Metropolis and walk down past the Imperial Theatre (on your right) to *Hotel Chanakya* at 1634 on your left. Rooms are Rs 45/55 and there is a dormitory. It's clean, has iced-water dispensers on each floor and is run by pleasant people. There are many other places along Main Bazaar or on the small roads leading off it. The *Venus Hotel* (tel 526256) at 1566 Main Bazaar has been considerably improved since the previous editions – the rooms are quite clean and cost Rs 30 to Rs 35 or Rs 45 to Rs 60 with attached bath.

Still in Paharganj, Desh Bandhu Gupta Rd is a major road parallel to Main Bazaar and a block to the north. Continue north to the smaller Arakashan Rd, which again runs parallel. Along it you'll find a number of slightly more expensive places like the *White House Tourist Lodge* at 8177 which has, according to one visitor, 'really good, clean and comfortable rooms' for Rs 70/80, although another traveller reported it was already becoming run down. The *Apsara Tourist Lodge* next door at 8501/1 costs Rs 60/80 and offers similar standards although the people are not so friendly. At 8126 there's the slightly more expensive *Hotel Crystal* run by the same people. The old-fashioned and rather drab *Hotel Airlines* (tel 517571-73) is in this same area, directly opposite the New Delhi Railway Station, and has rooms at Rs 90/135.

Between Main Bazaar and Desh Bandhu Gupta Rd, at the station end, *Hotel Little Star* (tel 777819) at 2721 Chowk Sangtrashan is another relatively new cheapie with rooms from Rs 40.

Old Delhi The *Khushdil* and *Crown* hotels are to the left at the west end of Chandni Chowk near the Fatehpuri Mosque, an easy walk from old Delhi Station. The Crown has better facilities than the rather more spartan Khushdil and charges Rs 40 for a single. It used to be the old hippy Mecca in the flower power days, but has now been 'cleaned up'. These old Delhi places certainly have character but you've got to be aware of bed bugs and other nasties in some of the more dive-like places.

Other Places Out at Chanakyapuri (where most of the embassies are) is the *Vishwa Yuvak Kendra* or *International Youth Centre* (tel 3013631) on Circular Rd. Dorm beds are Rs 12; doubles are Rs 50 with commmon bath, Rs 60 with attached bath. There's an additional 'admission fee' of Rs 5 per person in the dormitory or Rs 15 per person in rooms. This one-time charge is valid for a month. The rooms are excellent and there's a cafeteria with good food at low prices. It's a good place to stay if you don't mind the 20-minute bus trip or shorter auto-rickshaw ride from Connaught Place. To get there take a No 620 bus from the Plaza Cinema in Connaught Place and get off near the Indonesian Embassy. Or take a No 662 from old Delhi Station and get off at the Ashok Hotel. It's right behind the Chinese Embassy and near the Chanakyapuri Police Station.

Also in Chanakyapuri is a *Youth Hostel* (tel 376285) at 5 Nyaya Marg where there

are dorm beds at Rs 15 for members, Rs 18 for non-members. Bring your own padlock. There's a bank and a travel agency which will arrange trips to Agra, Jaipur, Delhi and so on. The location is quiet, peaceful and, of course, good for the embassies.

If you want to camp there are several possibilities in Delhi. The *Tourist Camp* (tel 278929) is one of the cheapest places to stay and very popular. Most of the overland operators stay here and it's also the starting point for the overland Magic Bus. Run by retired Indian Army officers, the camp is actually in old Delhi, near Delhi Gate on Jawaharlal Nehru Marg, across from the J P Narayan Hospital (Irwin Hospital), only two km from Connaught Place. You can camp with your own tent for Rs 10 plus Rs 5 per person; vehicles cost Rs 10. Or there are basic rooms with shared bathrooms for Rs 24/38 or deluxe rooms at Rs 32/48. They're spartan but OK; this place generally gets good recommendations from travellers. There's a restaurant and a left luggage room where you can leave your accumulated junk for up to four months. You can reach the camp by taking a six-seater from the Regal Cinema at Connaught Place.

There is a second camping site, the *Qudsia Gardens Tourist Camp*, right across the road from the Interstate Bus Terminal. Camping here costs Rs 8 for the tent plus Rs 3 per person; vehicle charge is Rs 8. The rooms are Rs 24/34 for singles/doubles; bedding is an additional Rs 5.

If all else fails there are *Railway Retiring Rooms* at both railway stations (Delhi and New Delhi), with prices for both 24-hour and 12-hour periods. Dorm beds are Rs 10 (Rs 6 for 12 hours). Deluxe dorm beds are Rs 20 (Rs 12). At New Delhi only there are non-air-con rooms at Rs 50 (Rs 30) while both stations have air-con rooms at Rs 75 (Rs 45) and deluxe air-con rooms at Rs 160 (Rs 100). There are also *Airport Retiring Rooms* at the airport so long as you have a confirmed ticket. They're booked through the Airport

Manager (tel 391351) and cost Rs 75 for a four-bed dorm or Rs 75/150 for singles/doubles.

Places to Stay - middle

There are a number of middle-bracket hotels around Janpath and Connaught Place, including the popular ITDC *Ashok Yatri Niwas* (tel 344511) just 10 minutes' walk from Connaught Place on Ashoka Rd at the intersection with Janpath. This huge hotel (556 rooms) has been something of a political football, but prices have been pushed up sufficiently that it's no longer the astounding bargain it was when it first opened and, therefore, it's no longer always full. The rooms are very plain and spartan; with bathroom singles/doubles are Rs 85/115. Four-bed rooms are Rs 140. Rooms above the 8th floor seem to be better maintained, but then the lifts aren't very reliable or fast. In fact they're so unreliable and so slow that people report walking up even to the 14th floor rather than waiting! Foreigners must pay their bills in foreign currency. There's a good restaurant, a bad cafeteria and a TV lounge. The airport hotel booking desk and the airport bus are both reluctant to book you in or to take you here – probably a question of commissions! This is another of those many Indian hotels which upon completion start a rapid downhill run due to miserable upkeep and maintenance. 'A general air of approaching squalor', was one prediction.

The *Janpath Guest House* (tel 321935-7) is a few doors down from the Tourist Office at 82-84 Janpath. It's popular with travellers, reasonably well kept and clean, and the staff are friendly; the rooms, though, are claustrophobically small and most don't have a window to talk of. Singles/doubles cost Rs 85/120, more if you want air-con.

There are lots of places around Connaught Place. *Hotel Fifty Five* (tel 321244) at H-55 Connaught Circus, near the Nirula restaurants, is well designed with air-con throughout. Rooms with balcony and attached bathroom are Rs 195/250, but we've had a couple of recent reports of drastically declining standards at this nicely situated hotel.

Hotel Palace Heights (tel 351361) in D Block, Connaught Place is a moderately priced place close to Nirula's. Situated on the 3rd floor of an office building, it has a huge verandah overlooking Connaught Place – great for breakfast or afternoon tea. Rooms cost from Rs 52, Rs 74/99 with bathroom, Rs 109 for a double with air-con. It's a bit scruffy and indifferently kept but the location is great and the prices reasonable.

The *Alka Hotel* (tel 344328) is also centrally located at 16/90 Connaught Circus and has air-con singles/doubles at Rs 225/335-420. *Hotel Metro* (tel 48905) on N Block is better than initial impressions might indicate, with rooms for Rs 105/165 or with air-con for Rs 200/250.

Moving away from Connaught Place, the small but popular *Roshan Villa Guest House* (tel 3311770) is at 7 Babar Lane, close to the Bengali Market. To get there go down Barakhamba Rd from Connaught Place, turn left on Tolstoy Marg but go under the flyover to find Babar Rd. It's very clean and well kept, the owners are friendly and hospitable, and it's quiet. There's a Rs 30 dorm and rooms at Rs 80, 100 and 120. Middle-priced rooms share a bathroom with one other room; the top-priced rooms have their own bathrooms. Meals are available and there's hot water in the bathrooms. The only catch is that you have to keep track of how many cups of tea or snacks you have – or be surprised by the final bill.

The *Puri Yatri Paying Guest House* (tel 525463) is at Yatri House, 3/4 Rani Jhansi Rd (at the junction of Panchkuin Rd and Mandir Marg, near Connaught Place). It's calm, secure and moderately priced. The *Ekant Boarding House* (tel 527783) is also at this junction. Just south of the Purana Qila in Sunder Nagar there are a number of better class guest houses with rooms for around Rs 250 a double, such as *La Sagrita*, the *Maharini* and the *Kalash*.

There are several YMCA and YWCA places, all of which take either sex. The *YMCA Tourist Hotel* (tel 311915) is very central, near the Regal Cinema on Jai Singh Rd and opposite the Jantar Mantar. It's excellent value with rooms with hot and cold water, showers, gardens, lounges and a restaurant with western, Indian and Mughlai cuisine. Including breakfast, rooms with common bath are Rs 70/130; with attached bath and air-con they're Rs 150/250. There's a 5% service charge and a transient membership fee of Rs 5 valid for 30 days.

The *YWCA International Guest House* (tel 311561) at 10 Parliament St (Sansad Marg) has singles/doubles at Rs 120/200 (plus 10% service charge), and all rooms have bath and air-con. It's convenient for Connaught Place and has a restaurant. There's a second, lesser-known, YWCA, the *YWCA Blue Triangle Family Hostel* (tel 310133, 310875) on Ashoka Rd just off Parliament Rd (Sansad Marg). It's clean and well run and has a restaurant. Rates, including breakfast, range from Rs 135 to Rs 240 for singles, Rs 175 to Rs 260 for doubles, all with attached bathroom. There are rooms with and without air-con and there's also an expensive dormitory for Rs 60. There's a Rs 5 temporary membership fee and a 5% service charge. The newer Blue Triangle Y is run by the Delhi YWCA; the International Y is run by the national organisation.

A good place for a longer stay in Delhi is the *India International Centre* (tel 619431) beside the Lodi tombs in the south of New Delhi. It is a good place to meet people involved with international aid agencies and each week there are lectures on art, economics and other contemporary issues by Indian and foreign experts. The centre, which is near the UN offices in Delhi, has air-con rooms, but you must be a centre member or a guest of a member before you can stay here. Members pay Rs 145/170, non-members Rs 275/375.

Places to Stay – top end

There has been a spate of top-end hotel construction in Delhi, much of it for the 1984 Asian Games although some of the hotels were still being finished in 1986. Delhi does not have a glut of hotels but it's now much easier to find a room. Many of the 'tourist class' hotels are at Chanakyapuri, where the foreign embassies are chiefly located. This is about midway between the airport and the New Delhi city centre. There are, however, now more places around the centre as well. In these international hotels there will often be a 10 to 15% 'luxury tax' and 5 to 10% 'service charge'.

More moderately priced top-end hotels include *Nirula's Hotel* (tel 352419) on L Block, Connaught Place, right beside the Nirula restaurants and snack bars. Singles/doubles range from Rs 365/465 in this small but good standard hotel.

Hotel Marina on the outer circle of Connaught Place in G Block is surprisingly good inside; the outside is drab. Rooms are Rs 350/390. The *Lodhi Hotel* (tel 619422) is in south Delhi on Lala Rajput Rai Marg, rather a long way from Connaught Place, and has air-con rooms at Rs 300/450.

Some new top-end hotels are still under construction or in '86 were just opening – they include the glossy *Meridien* which reportedly has very good food at reasonable prices. Other top-end hotels:

Ambassador Hotel (tel 690391) is a small hotel at Sujan Singh Park. There are just 73 rooms costing Rs 350/525 and a noted vegetarian restaurant.

Ashok Hotel (tel 600121) is at 50B Chanakyapuri and is the 589-room flagship of the ITDC hotel fleet. It offers everything from restaurants, coffee shops, bars, discos, conference rooms and swimming pool to full air-conditioning. Singles/doubles cost Rs 800/900.

The Centaur Hotel (tel 391411) is on Gurgaon Rd at the airport. It's a big new hotel with rooms from Rs 580/660.

Claridges Hotel (tel 370211) is at 12 Aurangzeb Rd, south of the Raj Path in New Delhi. Singles/doubles cost from Rs 575/675 in this older hotel.

Hotel Hans Plaza (tel 3316861), 19 Barakhamba Rd, is conveniently central but otherwise not very good value. Rooms are Rs 395/520.

Hyatt Regency (tel 609911) is another big new hotel with 535 rooms. It's on Bhikaji Cama Place and costs from Rs 900/1000.

Hotel Imperial (tel 311511) is conveniently situated on Janpath near the centre. It's an old-fashioned hotel with a very pleasant shopping arcade and gardens. Singles/doubles cost Rs 500/600.

Hotel Janpath (tel 350070) is beside the Imperial and is run by the ITDC. Rooms cost from Rs 400/550.

Hotel Kanishka (tel 343400), next to the Hotel Janpath, is a new ITDC hotel with rooms at Rs 590/690.

Hotel Maurya Sheraton (tel 370271) is on Sardar Patel Marg at Chanakyapuri and has 500 rooms costing from Rs 900/1000. The Bukhara is one of the best restaurants in Delhi.

Hotel Oberoi New Delhi (tel 699571) is on Dr Zakir Hussain Rd in the south of New Delhi, near the Purana Qila. This hotel has a good reputation and there are 350 rooms costing Rs 975/1075.

The Taj Mahal Hotel (tel 386162) is at 1 Man Singh Rd. This luxurious hotel is fairly central but fairly quiet. Singles/doubles cost from Rs 850/950.

Places to Eat

Like its places to stay, Delhi's many restaurants and snack bars can be divided by price range and location.

Janpath & Connaught Place

There are now numerous Indian-style fast-food places in this area. Their plus point is that they have good food at reasonable prices and they're clean and healthy. A minus point for some of them is they have no place to sit – it's stand, eat and run. They serve Indian food (from samosas to dosas) and western (burgers to sandwiches). Ice cream parlours have also hit Delhi with a vengeance; nice ice cream.

Nirula's is probably the most popular and long running of these places and does a wide variety of excellent light snacks, both Indian and western. They've also got good cold drinks, milkshakes and ice cream, or they will pack you a box lunch, ideal to take on train trips. The main Nirula's is on L Block on the outer circle, and there's a second snack bar on N Block where Janpath runs into the circle.

Next door to the L Block snack bar on one side is an ice cream parlour and on the other it's pizzas. Above the ice cream bar there's the fourth part of Nirula's, a sit-down restaurant called *Pot Pourri* with appetising food including a Rs 27 eat-all-you-like salad smorgasbord. They've also got pizzas for Rs 20 (from Rs 4 for extras), chili con carne with rice for Rs 25 and a good range of soups and sweets. It's a good place for breakfast from 7.30 am; you can have an all-American breakfast of pancakes, eggs and bacon for Rs 20, omelets for Rs 18 or cereal for Rs 7.50. It's a very pleasant place to eat and the service is good; all in all it's probably the number one place for a minor splurge.

Opposite the main Nirula's is the *National Restaurant*, clean with excellent non-vegetarian food and somewhat lower prices than Nirula's. Also near Nirula's is *The Embassy*, with a kitsch 'airport lounge' decor but good food – excellent korma and biriyani.

On Janpath at N Block, opposite the underground bazaar, there is a small string of fast-food places including the already mentioned Nirula's. At the outer end is *Pizza King* with surprisingly good pizzas to eat there or take away. Next to it is a branch (believe it or not) of the British *Wimpy* hamburger chain. This is the closest you're going to get to a Big Mac (100% lamb!) in India. The 'lamburgers' are fair imitations costing Rs 8 to Rs 16, French fries are Rs 4. It even operates like a western fast-food place – somehow they've resisted the urge to have people writing out chits in quadruplicate.

Other places around Connaught Place include *Sona Rupa* on Janpath with very good south Indian vegetarian food – a Rs

15 thali or a Rs 22 all-you-can-eat lunch buffet with dessert and coffee. The *United Coffee House* on Connaught Place is pleasantly relaxed and popular although it may be closing down.

There's a good collection of cheap restaurants and food markets in Mohan Singh Place, in the same block as the Regal Cinema in Connaught Place. Look for fresh and dried fruits, curd, sweets and so on. Upstairs in the market *Ding Dong* serves good Chinese food for prices reasonable for Delhi.

The fresh milk is excellent at *Keventers*, the small milk bar at the corner of Connaught Place and Radial Rd Number 3, round the corner from American Express. If you just want a cheap soft drink and somewhere cool to drink it, descend into the air-conditioned underground market between Janpath and Parliament St (Sansad Marg) at Connaught Place.

Moving up a price category, there are several higher-price restaurants worth considering on Parliament St (Sansad Marg) and by the Regal Cinema. The *Kwality Restaurant* on Parliament St is spotlessly clean and very efficient but the food now is just average. The menu is the almost standard non-vegetarian menu you'll find at restaurants all over India. Main courses are mainly in the Rs 18 to Rs 22 range. This is also a good place for non-Indian food if you want a break; or you can have breakfast here for Rs 20.

El Arab, right on the corner of Parliament St (Sansad Marg) and the outer circle of Connaught Place, has an interesting Middle Eastern menu with most dishes in the Rs 25 to Rs 35 bracket and a Rs 35 buffet lunch or dinner. Underneath El Arab is *The Cellar*, where breakfast costs Rs 14 to 18 or main courses cost Rs 18 to 25. Round the corner is the more expensive *Gaylords* with big mirrors and chandeliers and excellent Indian food. Also on Connaught Place you can find good vegetarian food at the *Volga*; it's a little expensive but it's air-conditioned, and the food and service are excellent.

Right across the street from Nirula's on the outer circle are a string of popular small *dhaba* places. The famous *Kake da Hotel* here doesn't seem to have been discovered by westerners at all. Despite having no atmosphere whatsoever, it is crowded most of the time. Try the excellent butter chicken, but note the warning sign that there will be 'no extra gravy'!

Finally there's one Delhi food place that should not be forgotten. *Wenger's* on Connaught Place is a cake shop with an awesome range of little cakes (Rs 3 to Rs 5 each) which they'll put in a cardboard box, tie up with a bow and you can self-consciously carry back to your hotel room for private consumption. Take care, reported one hungry traveller – 'In great anticipation as about to devour a famous Wenger's cake this bloody hawk deftly lifted my cake out of my hands and near gave me a heart attack in the process'.

Paharganj Towards the end of Main Bazaar, in the Paharganj area near New Delhi Station, is the long-running and ever-popular *Metropolis Restaurant*. The food is mainly Chinese and western and a little expensive, but it has been a travellers' hangout for years and the food is not bad. Underneath the Hotel Sapna is the considerably cheaper *Restaurant Light* where you can get very good vegetarian food for just a few rupees per dish. It's popular with budget travellers in the evenings. The *Khalsa Punjabi Hotel*, on the left side of Main Bazaar Rd towards the station, beyond the Vishal and Venus hotels, also has good food.

Gobind is a narrow-fronted place on the opposite side towards the Metropolis and is good for lassi or espresso coffee. Breakfast places and stalls offer cheap and tasty food just off Main Bazaar towards the Chanakya Hotel. The popular *Lakshmi Restaurant* in this area has a cheap breakfast including fantastic porridge.

Old Delhi In old Delhi there are numerous places at the west end of Chandni Chowk. The *Inderpuri Restaurant*, around the corner to the right, has a good selection of vegetarian dishes. *Giani*, just before it, has good masala dosas. *Ghantewala*, near the Siganj Gurdwara on Chandni Chowk, is reputed to have some of the best Indian sweets in Delhi.

The stalls along the road in front of the Jami Masjid are very cheap. In the interstate bus station the *ISBT Workers' Canteen* has good food at low prices. Delhi Tourism's *Nagrik Restaurant* is here.

At the other end of the price scale there are two well-known tandoori restaurants in old Delhi. The *Tandoor* at the *Hotel President* on Asaf Ali Rd near the Tourist Camp is an excellent place with the usual two waiters-per-diner service and a sitarist playing in the background. The tandoor kitchen can be seen through a glass panel.

Round the corner on Netaji Subhash Marg in Darayaganj, the famous old *Moti Mahal* is noted for its tandoori dishes including murga musalam, but it seems to live more on reputation than actual ability these days. Quantities are large, however.

Other Places The *YWCA International Guest House's* restaurant has good food, or if you are out at Chanakyapuri (waiting for a visa perhaps), good and inexpensive Indian food can be had in the *International Youth Centre* near the Indonesian Embassy. On Connaught Place the *Marina Hotel* has an air-con coffee bar which does good snacks and excellent coffee.

Not far from Connaught Place the *Ashok Yatri Niwas* has a not-very-good cafeteria (meals Rs 16 to Rs 22) but also a restaurant where you can get a complete and very good vegetarian buffet for Rs 25. Near the Bengali Market at the traffic circle where Tan Sen Marg meets Babar Rd, the neat and clean *Bengali Sweet*

House is a good place for sweets or for a meal of the snacks known as *chat*. You could try *cholaphatura* (puffed rotis with a lentil dip), *tikkas* (fried stuffed potatoes), *papri chat* (sweet/hot wafers, or *golguppas* (hollow puffs you break open and use as a scoop for a peppery liquid accompaniment). They also do good masala dosas.

International Hotels Many Delhi residents reckon that the best food to be found in the capital is at the large five-star hotels. At the Maurya Sheraton the *Bukhara* has many central Asian specialities, including tandoori cooking and dishes from the Peshawar region in the north-west of Pakistan. This is a place for big meat eaters and you can expect to pay around Rs 80 to Rs 100 per person. Main courses are generally around Rs 50, some Rs 75 to Rs 80; the rotis are excellent. It's so successful it's even got a branch in New York.

The *Haveli* at the Taj Mahal Hotel is also popular. Here the food is more mainstream Indian but the quality is high and there is Indian music and dancing as entertainment. Prices are similar to the Bukhara's. Other popular restaurants at the large hotels include the *Peacock* at the Ashok Hotel and the *Mughal Room* at the Oberoi.

Rather lower priced, several hotels have noted vegetarian restaurants. Thalis are Rs 28 at *Dasaprakash* at the Hotel Ambassador, general dishes Rs 8 to Rs 10. The Lodhi Hotel is noted for the thalis at the *Woodlands Restaurant*. The old *Imperial Hotel* is great for an al fresco breakfast in the pleasant garden.

Getting There
Delhi is a major international gateway to India; for details on arriving from overseas see the introductory Getting There section. At certain times of year international flights out of Delhi can be heavily booked so it's wise to make reservations as early as possible. This particularly applies to some of the airlines heavily discounted

out of Europe – double-check your reservations and make sure you reconfirm.

Delhi is also a major centre for domestic travel, with extensive bus, rail and air connections.

Air Indian Airlines flights depart from Delhi to all the major Indian centres. Some important connections include Bombay (Rs 1007, around eight flights daily), Madras (Rs 1429), Calcutta (Rs 1143, three daily), Srinagar (Rs 672), Jaipur (Rs 236), Agra (Rs 192) and Varanasi (Rs 638).

India is not a great place for air-fare bargains on domestic flights – Indian Airlines fly too close to 100% capacity to worry about the hard sell. The Indian Airlines Office in Delhi (tel 3310084-6 enquiries, 3310071-2 reservations) is in the Kanchenjunga Building on Barakhamba Rd. The office occupies a large open area upstairs around the back of the building – you wouldn't know it was there, if you didn't know it was there! Reservations can be made for flights all over India, and with the new computer system you can now make them quickly and reliably.

Rail Delhi is an important rail centre and an excellent place to make bookings. There is now a special foreign tourist booking office in New Delhi Station. This is a haven of calm, quiet and efficiency where you can buy tickets and make reservations all in one go for 1st and 2nd class. They also sell Indrail passes and can give advice on all classes of rail travel.

Remember that there are two main stations in Delhi – Delhi Station in old Delhi, and New Delhi Station at the northern end of New Delhi, more or less on the old Delhi border. The latter is much closer to Connaught Place, and if you're departing from Delhi Station you should allow adequate time to wind your way through the traffic snarls of old

Delhi. Between the Delhi and New Delhi stations you can take the No 6 bus for just Rs 1. There's also the Nizam-ud-din Station south of the New Delhi area where some trains start or finish. It's worth getting off here if you are staying in Chanakyapuri or elsewhere south of Connaught Place.

There are several tourist special trains operating from Delhi. The Taj Express is ideal for day-tripping to Agra, 199 km south. The train departs from and returns to the New Delhi Station and takes three hours each way. The fare is Rs 63 in 1st class, Rs 19 in 2nd. The tourist quota on this service is limited, but it's generally possible to get a seat.

The Pink City Express is a direct train from Delhi Station to Jaipur, departing at 5.50 am and arriving five hours later. Fare for the 308-km trip is Rs 124 in 1st class, Rs 27 in 2nd.

Some other important connections by mail or express train include:

		1st class	2nd class
Amritsar	from 8 hours	Rs 168	Rs 43
Bombay	from 17 hours	Rs 428	Rs 97
Calcutta	from 17 hours	Rs 405	Rs 102
Jammu Tawi	from 13 hours	Rs 206	Rs 52
Madras	from 40 hours	Rs 563	Rs 139
Varanasi	from 12 hours	Rs 253	Rs 63

Bus The large Interstate Bus Terminal is at Kashmiri Gate, north of the Delhi Railway Station in old Delhi. Buses depart from here for locations all around Delhi – ring 229083 for details. State government bus companies operating from here are:

Haryana Government Roadways (tel 221292), bookings 6 am to 12 noon & 1.30 to 9 pm.
Jammu & Kashmir Government Roadways (tel 224559), bookings 10 am to 5 pm but only on air-con buses.

Rajasthan Roadways (tel 222276), bookings 6 am to 8 pm.
Uttar Pradesh Roadways (tel 226175, 273379), bookings 8 am to 4 pm.

Popular buses include the approximately hourly buses to Agra which cost Rs 24. There is also a frequent and fast service to Jaipur for Rs 35 to Rs 40. For Chandigarh, from where you can bus or take the narrow-gauge train up to Simla, the regular buses cost Rs 28.50. There are deluxe video buses for Rs 55 and even an air-con video bus for Rs 96 where you can completely forget you're in India. You can also get buses direct to Simla (10 hours) for Rs 47, Dharamsala Rs 61 and Kulu Rs 57. Buses to Amritsar cost Rs 43.50, to Jammu (for Srinagar) Rs 54.50. To northern Uttar Pradesh buses cost Rs 28 for Hardwar or Rs 30 for Dehra Dun.

The large Dhaula Kuan bus stop is south of the city near the airport. Catching buses here can save you the trip to the station in old Delhi and then the long journey through the centre.

In the popular travellers' hangouts there are adverts for a four-times-weekly bus service to Kathmandu which takes about 36 hours and costs Rs 350. There are also super-deluxe buses to Simla for Rs 130, Srinagar Rs 230, Udaipur Rs 150 and other destinations. The Europe-bound Magic Bus service operates two or three times a month from the Tourist Camp in New Delhi and costs US$150 to Istanbul, US$190 to Munich, US$210 to Paris or Amsterdam, US$230 to London.

Getting Around

Distances in Delhi are large and the buses are generally hopelessly crowded, although there is a more expensive deluxe bus service. The alternative is a taxi or auto-rickshaw.

Airport Delhi's somewhat chaotic, confusing and tatty Palam airport is now officially the Indira Gandhi International Airport. The domestic terminal is only a few minutes' walk away. Fortunately airport-to-city and vice-versa transport is relatively simple. EATS, Ex-Servicemen's Air Link Transport Service, have a regular bus service between the airport and their office in Connaught Place. The fare is Rs 10 and they will drop off or pick up at most of the major hotels en route if you ask. Departures, from opposite the underground bazaar, are from before 5 am through to nearly midnight. Departures from the airport to the centre are timed according to aircraft arrivals. There is also a regular Delhi Transport Corporation bus service which runs through to New Delhi and Delhi Railway Stations and to the Interstate Bus Terminal and costs Rs 5.

A taxi costs about Rs 50 to Rs 60 from the airport to Connaught Place, although they frequently ask for considerably more. Auto-rickshaws will run out to the airport too, although your teeth will be shaking by the time you get there! If you can find a driver willing to use the meter it should cost about Rs 20 to Rs 25. There is a public bus service to the airport (780) from the Super Bazaar at Connaught Place but it can get very crowded.

If you're arriving at New Delhi airport from overseas, the State Bank foreign exchange counter is within the arrivals hall, after you've gone through customs and immigration. Once you've left the arrivals hall you won't be allowed back in. The service is fast and efficient. Many international flights to Delhi arrive and depart at terrible hours in the early morning. Take special care if this is your first foray into India and you arrive exhausted and jet-lagged. If you're leaving Delhi in the early hours of the morning, book a taxi the afternoon before. They'll be hard to find in the night. See the accommodation section for information about the retiring rooms at the airport.

Bus Avoid buses during the rush hours when the situation is hopeless, and whenever possible try to board (and leave) at a starting or finishing point – more chance of a seat, less chance of being trampled. The Regal and Plaza cinemas in Connaught Place are such places. There are some seats reserved for women on the left side of the bus. The Delhi Transport Corporation (DTC) run the buses and you can get a route guide from their office in Scindia House.

Buses include the 504 to the Qutab Minar from the Super Bazaar, and the 502 from the Red Fort. The 101 runs between the Interstate Bus Terminal and Connaught Place. A 620 or 630 will take you between Connaught Place and Chanakyapuri. The 101, 104 and 139 run between the Regal Cinema bus stand and the Red Fort. A short bus ride (like Connaught Place-Red Fort) will only be about Rs 0.50. Buses to New Delhi Railway Station from Connaught Place (Regal Cinema) include the 157 and the R40. A 51, 101 and 104 will take you from the Regal Cinema to the Tourist Camp.

Taxi & Auto-Rickshaw All taxis and auto-rickshaws are metered but the meters are invariably out of date, allegedly 'not working' or the drivers will simply refuse to use them. It matters not a jot that they are legally required to do so. A threat to report them to the police results in little more than considerable mirth, so you will often have to negotiate a price before you set out. Naturally, this will always be more than it should be. There are exceptions; occasionally a driver will re-set the meter without even a word from you. At places like New Delhi Station or the airport, where there are always plenty of police hanging around, you can generally rely on the meter being used because it's too easy to report a driver. Trips during the rush hour or middle-of-the-night journeys to the airport are the times when meters are least likely to be used.

At the end of a journey you will have to pay according to a scale of revised charges or simply a flat percentage increase. Some drivers display these cards in the cab; others consign them to the oily-rag compartment; still others feed them to the cows. So if you do come across a legible copy it's worth noting down a few of the conversions, paying what you think is the right price and leaving it at that. You may rest assured that no-one is going to be out of pocket, except yourself, despite hurt or angry protestations to the contrary.

Flag fall is Rs 2.80 in taxis, Rs 2 in auto-rickshaws. Connaught Place to the Red Fort could be, depending on traffic, around Rs 14 by taxi, Rs 7 by auto-rickshaw. There are also old Harley Davidson 'four-seater' or 'six-seater' auto-rickshaws running fixed routes at fixed prices. From Connaught Place their starting point is by the Regal Cinema and your Sikh driver will chop his way through the traffic as far as the fountain in Chandni Chowk via the Red Fort in old Delhi. They cost less than Rs 2 each and are good value, especially during rush hours.

Bicycle & Cycle-Rickshaw Unlike many Indian cities, New Delhi is not a good place for bicycles – too much high-speed motorised traffic and too great distances. Nevertheless you can hire bicycles for Rs 6 a day near the Bengali Market. Cycle-rickshaws are banned from New Delhi but you still find them in the more crowded and slower-moving streets of old Delhi.

Things to Buy

Good buys include silk products, precious stones, leather and woodwork, but the most important thing about Delhi is that here you can find almost anything from anywhere in India. If this is your first stop in India, and you intend to buy something while you are here, then it's a chance to compare what is available from all over India. If this is your last stop and there was something you missed elsewhere in the country, it's a last chance to find it.

Two good places to start are in New

Delhi near Connaught Place. The Central Cottage Industries Emporium is on Janpath, right across from the Tourist Office. In this large building you will find items from all over India, generally of good quality and reasonably priced. Whether it's woodcarvings, brasswork, paintings, clothes, textiles or furniture, you'll find it here. Along Baba Kharak Singh Marg, two streets round from Janpath, are the various State Emporiums run by the state governments. Each displays and sells handicrafts from their state. There are many other shops around Connaught Place and Janpath. By the nearby Imperial Hotel there are a number of stalls and small shops run by Tibetan refugees selling carpets, jewellery and many (often instant) antiques.

In old Delhi, Chandni Chowk is the famous shopping street. Here you will find carpets and jewellery but you have to search the convoluted back alleys. In the narrow street called Cariba Kalan, perfumes are made as well. You can find an interesting variety of perfumes, oils and soaps at Chhabra Perfumery at 1573 Main Bazaar, Paharganj, near the Vivek Hotel. More than a hundred oils are available in small bottles at Rs 3 or Rs 4 each.

Just south of the Purana Qila, beside Dr Zakir Hussain Rd and across from the Oberoi New Delhi Hotel, is the Sunder Nagar market, a collection of shops selling antiques and brassware. The prices may be high but you'll find fascinating and high-quality artefacts. Shops in the major international hotels also often have very high-quality items, at equally high prices.

Tony's Notebook

Ganja

Yes, there's an awful lot of that well-known weed in India. Shiva, the most worshipped of gods, is supposed to devote a fair amount of time to smoking dope in his remote Himalayan home so it would be pretty difficult to ignore it. In fact there are government hashish shops in places like Varanasi, Puri and Jaipur, but effectively it's illegal unless you happen to be a Hindu sadhu or someone similar who clearly needs it!

If you want to find it you'll have little problem anywhere in India. Goa with its large resident travellers' population, Kashmir and the Kulu Valley, where it grows in profusion, and Varanasi, with its religious connections, are all good places. Discretion is the key word wherever you are. Don't smoke in public and don't leave it lying around hotel rooms.

The places to avoid it include the airports and a number of railway stations. Often dope searches are simply ways of extracting a little baksheesh, but it's still wise not to get involved. Along the popular Delhi-Bombay railway route, at Allahabad, in Manali in the Kulu Valley, from Patna up to the Nepalese border, are all places where dope searches have been known to take place. In Delhi there are occasional dope raids on the cheaper hotels, particularly around Paharganj, and in Agra in the cheap hotels just south of the Taj.

Beware of the concentrated powers of bhang-lassi or other mixtures of bhang with foodstuffs. A German traveller wrote to us describing the two-hour search she and some friends made for their hotel in darkest Jaisalmer after partaking of bhang-pakora!

Tolerance

For all the aggravations and annoyances India can throw in your path, there's one factor which almost every visitor praises about the country and that is its tolerance. In part it's related to the Hindu religion – its followers make no effort to go out and convert people and other religions are happily accepted; it already has so many gods that other people's gods are quite welcome to join the happy band. In India anything seems to go down. If an Indian wants to leave his job, family and comfort to don a loincloth and wander the country as a sadhu, that's considered quite normal. Similarly, if western visitors want to dress up in '60s flower-power gear and wander the country they're quite welcome. If they want to take all their clothes off and lie on the beach at Goa it's considered strange, but most of the time that's OK too.

New Delhi Top: The Jantar Mantar Observatory near Connaught Place (PC)
Left: Looking down from the minaret of the Jami Masjid, old Delhi (TW)
Right: The Moti Masjid or 'Pearl Mosque' from the Diwan-i-Khas in Delhi's Red Fort (TW)

Punjab, Haryana & Top: The Kulu Valley from the Naggar Castle (TW)
Himachal Pradesh   Left: Sikh guard at the Golden Temple, Amritsar (PC)
                   Right: Strange figures at the Rock Garden, Chandigarh (TW)

Punjab & Haryana

Haryana
  Population: 10 million
  Area: 44,222 square km
  Capital: Chandigarh
  Main language: Hindi

Punjab
  Population: 15 million
  Area: 50,362 square km
  Capital: Chandigarh
  Main language: Punjabi

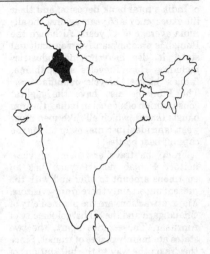

The Punjab was probably the part of India which suffered the most destruction and damage at the time of partition, yet today it is far and away the most affluent state in India. No natural resource or advantage gave the Punjabis this enviable position; it was sheer hard work. Prior to partition the Punjab extended across both sides of what is now the Pakistan-India border. Its capital was Lahore, which today is the capital of the Pakistan state of Punjab. But the population of the Punjab was split between Muslims and Sikhs and by the grim logic of partition that meant slicing the region in two. As millions of Sikhs and Hindus fled eastward and equal numbers of Muslims fled west, there were innumerable atrocities and killings on both sides. More recently Sikh political demands have wracked the state, particularly Amritsar, with violence which looks as insoluble as ever in 1986. The demands are somewhat vague and difficult for outsiders to understand, but the escalating violence between Sikh and Hindu factions has made the Punjab an uncomfortable place of late.

The major city in the Punjab is Amritsar, the holy city of the Sikhs, but it is so close to the Pakistan border that it was thought wise to build a safer capital further within the borders of India. At first Simla, the old imperial summer capital, served as capital but Chandigarh, a new planned city, was conceived and built to serve as the capital of the new Punjab. In 1966, however, the Punjab was to undergo another split. This time it was divided into the predominantly Sikh and Punjabi-speaking state of Punjab and the state of Haryana. At the same time some of the northern parts of the Punjab were hived off to Himachal Pradesh. Chandigarh, on the border of Punjab and Haryana, remained the capital of both states until 1986 when it was handed over completely to Punjab as an attempt to placate the Sikhs. This has left Haryana without a state capital although Chandigarh continues to fulfil that role at present.

At the time of partition the Punjab was devastated but the Sikhs' no-nonsense approach to life has won for it a position that statistics sum up admirably. The Punjab's per capita income is 50% higher than the all-India average (in second place is Haryana). Although Punjabis comprise less than 2½% of India's population, they provide 60% of India's wheat surplus and 50% of its rice surplus. The Punjab provides a third of all the milk produced in India. Punjabis have 5% of India's total bank deposits, and their life expectancy is 65 years against the all-India average of 47 years. Although the Punjab is predominantly an agricultural state, it also has thriving industries including Hero Bicycles at Ludhiana, India's biggest bicycle manufacturer. The Punjabis also have the highest consumption of alcohol in India – the iron bangle (*kara*), which all Sikh men must wear, is an ideal instrument for taking the caps off beer bottles!

From the traveller's point of view, neither Punjab nor Haryana has an enormous amount to offer and with the present uncertainty there are few visitors. Major attractions are the planned city of Chandigarh and the Sikhs' golden city of Amritsar. Those cities apart, the two states are mainly places of transit. Since they're on the way to the hill stations of Himachal Pradesh and the delights of Kashmir, a lot of people do pass through them.

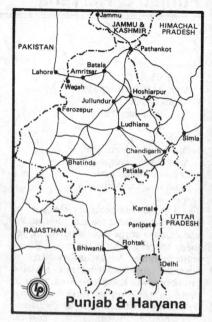

Punjab & Haryana

The Sikhs

The Sikhs are the reason for the Punjab's success story and they're amongst the most interesting people in India. See the introductory section on religions for a description of their religion and customs. Apart from anything else, the Sikhs are the most instantly recognisable people in India. The requirement that they do not cut their hair (*kesh*) ensures that all Sikh men are bearded and turbaned. For some reason they all look big, bulky men too – you never see a weedy-looking Sikh. Sikh women also have a unique costume – the *salvar-kamiz*: wide pyjama-style trousers fastened at the ankles, topped by a long shirt which almost reaches the knees. All Sikhs have the surname Singh, 'lion'.

Curiously, despite their undoubted success the Sikhs have a reputation in India, rather like the Irish in the west. The Indians have as many Sikh jokes as the west has Irish jokes. Not many translate very well but they basically follow the same line, which is strange since the stereotyped Sikh is quite unlike the stereotyped Irishman. The Irish-joke Irishman is supposed to be all thumbs; the Sikhs have a reputation for great dexterity and mechanical ability – they've always been at home with machines, and in India any activity with machines, from driving an auto-rickshaw to piloting a 747, will employ a disproportionate number of Sikhs. Despite this, other Indians mock Sikhs as being blunt and straightforward to the point of stupidity!

Punjab Permits

Officially all foreigners must have a permit to visit the Punjab. In practise this rule seems to require interpretation. Chandigarh, although officially in the Punjab, does not seem to require a permit. Nor do you need a permit if you're simply transitting the Punjab – going to Pathankot en route to Kashmir or going

Sikhs, always very dapper...

almost any major attraction in the north – Jaipur, Agra, Kashmir, Amritsar – you go through Haryana. So they've built a series of 'service centres' along the main roads – the sort of motel-restaurant-service station complexes which in the west are quite common, but in India are all too rare. They're clean and well kept and, if you're after a place to stay, make travelling through Haryana a pleasure. Typically the complexes may have a camping site, camper huts (usually Rs 20 to Rs 30) and rooms (usually in the Rs 75 to Rs 150 range if they have air-con, cheaper without). The main complexes with their distance from Delhi are:

Badkhal Lake (tel 2202-04, 32 km) restaurants, swimming pool, boating, air-con rooms, camper huts.

Sunbird, Surajkund (tel 5357, 18 km) swimming pool, boating, air-con rooms, camper huts.

Magpie, Faridabad (tel 3473, 30 km) air-con rooms.

Dabchick, Hodal (tel 91, 92 km) elephant rides, boating, children's playgrounds, air-con rooms, camper huts with & without air-con.

Barbet, Sohna (tel 56, 56 km) restaurant, café, bath complex, swimming pool, air-con rooms, camper huts.

Jangle Babbleng, Dharuhera (tel 25, Rewari, 70 km) restaurant, café, camel riding, air-con & non-air-con rooms.

Rosy Pelican, Sultanpur (46 km) restaurant, bird-watching facilities, camping site, air-con rooms, camper huts.

Shama Restaurant (tel 2683, 32 km) restaurant, non-air-con rooms.

Mor Pankh (70 km) restaurant, non-air-con rooms.

Ulchana, Karnal (tel 2179, 124 km) restaurant, café, kebab corner, boating, air-con rooms, camper huts.

Parakeet, Pipli (tel 250, 152 km) restaurant, café, camping facilities, air-con rooms, camper huts.

Blue Jay, Samalkha (tel 10, 60 km) restaurant, air-con & non-air-con rooms, camper huts.

Yadavindra Gardens, Pinjore (tel 155, 281 km) at the Moghul gardens, restaurant, open-air café, dosa shop, mini-zoo, children's games, air-con rooms, camper huts.

Panchkula Youth Hostel (270 km) dorm beds.

from Chandigarh to Dharamsala. If, however, you intend to actually stay in the Punjab or will be going through Amritsar en route to Pakistan, you will need a permit. They're obtainable from the Home Ministry in New Delhi.

HARYANA

The state of Haryana has one of the most successful tourist departments in India, which is very interesting when you consider how few tourist attractions the state has. What the clever Haryanans have done is take advantage of their position – if you're going from Delhi to

Skylark, Panipat (tel 3579, 90 km) restaurant, air-con rooms.

Tilyar, Rohtak (tel 3966, 70 km) restaurant, boating, air-con & non-air-con rooms.

Myna, Rohtak (tel 2394, 72 km) restaurant, camper huts.

Flamingo, Hissar (tel 2602, 160 km) restaurant, air-con rooms.

Bulbul, Jind (127 km) restaurant, camper huts.

Kala Teetar, Abubshehr (325 km) restaurant, boating, air-con rooms.

SULTANPUR

There are many birds, including flamingos, at the bird sanctuary here. September to March is the best time to visit. You can stay at the *Rosy Pelican* complex (see above). To get there take a blue Haryana bus to Gurgaon (buses every 10 minutes from Dhaula Kuan), and then take a Chandu bus (three or four times a day) to Sultanpur, 46 km from Delhi.

DELHI TO CHANDIGARH

There are a number of sites of interest along the 260-km route from Delhi to Chandigarh. The road, part of the Grand Trunk Rd, is one of the busiest in India with a lot of traffic of all types.

Panipat

Panipat, 92 km north of Delhi, is reputed to be one of the most fly-infested places in India – due, it is said, to a Muslim saint buried here. He is supposed to have totally rid Panipat of flies, but when the people complained that he had done too good a job he gave them all the flies back, times a thousand.

It is also the site of three great battles, although there is nothing much to be seen of these today. In 1526 Babur defeated Ibrahim Lodi, king of Delhi, at Panipat and thus founded the Moghul empire in India. In 1556 Akbar defeated the Pathans at this same site. Finally in 1761 the Marathas, who had succeeded the Moghuls, were defeated here by the Afghan forces of Ahmad Shah Durani.

Gharaunda

The gateways of an old Moghul *sarai* (rest house) stand to the west of this village, 102 km north of Delhi. Shah Jahan built *kos minars*, 'milestones', along the road from Delhi to Lahore and *sarais* at longer intervals. Most of the kos minars still stand but there is little left of the sarais.

Karnal & Kurukshetra

Events in the *Mahabharata* are supposed to have occurred here, 118 km from Delhi, and also at the tank of Kurukshetra, a little further north. It was at Karnal that Nadir Shah, the Persian who took the Peacock Throne from Delhi, defeated the Moghul emperor Muhammed Shah in 1739. The Kurukshetra tank has attracted as many as half a million pilgrims at times of eclipses – for at these times the water in the tank is also said to contain water from every other sacred tank in India. Thus its ability to wash away sins is unsurpassed – during the eclipse. Kurukshetra also has an interesting small mosque, the Lal Masjid, and a finely designed tomb.

CHANDIGARH (population 250,000)

Construction of Chandigarh from a plan by the French architect, Le Corbusier, commenced in the '50s. Although to many western visitors it appears to be a rather sterile city and hopelessly sprawling, Indians are very proud of it and Chandigarh's residents feel that it is a good place to live.

Chandigarh is a truly dreadful piece of town planning. It's a car city in a country where the general population doesn't own cars. It's as if Le Corbusier sat down and laid the city out having never visited India and without giving a second's thought to what India was like. The end result is a city where walking is a near impossibility, where bicycle rickshaws look lost and spend half their time taking shortcuts the wrong way around sweeping traffic circles, where the huge expanses of road space in the shopping centre would be fine as car parks in the west but here are simply empty. Between the city's scattered buildings are long, ugly, barren stretches of wasteland. In Le Corbusier's home environment they might be parks or gardens, but in India empty ground is obviously doomed.

Orientation & Information

Chandigarh is on the edge of the Siwalik Hills, the outermost edge of the Himalaya. It is divided into 47 numbered sectors, separated by broad avenues. The bus station and modern shopping centre are in Sector 17. The railway station is a long way out of Chandigarh so buses are much more convenient than trains, but you can make rail bookings from the office above the central bus terminus.

The Secretariat and other important government buildings are in Sector 1, to the north. The museum is in Sector 10 and the Rose Garden in Sector 16, next to the bus station. The shopping centre has restaurants, ice cream parlours, book shops and a wide variety of other retail outlets. The Tourist Office is upstairs in the bus station.

Government Buildings

The Secretariat and the Legislative Assembly buildings are in Sector 1. Between 10 am and 12 noon you can go to the top of the Secretariat, where there is an excellent view over Chandigarh. Eventually a huge revolving hand will be built here as the centrepiece of the government sector and the symbol of Chandigarh.

Rock Garden

Close to the government buildings is a not-to-be-missed attraction, the bizarre Rock Garden – a sort of concrete maze with a lot of rocks and very little garden. This strange and whimsical fantasy has grown and grown over the years and is now very extensive. It's open 9 am to 1 pm and 3 to 7 pm from 1 April to 30 September. The rest of the year it opens and closes an hour earlier in the afternoons. Entry is Rs 0.50.

Close by is the artificial Sukhna Lake, where you can rent the rowboats or just stroll round its two-km perimeter.

Museum & Art Gallery

In Sector 10 and open daily except Mondays, the art gallery contains a modest collection of Indian stone sculptures dating back to the Gandhara period, together with some miniature paintings and modern art. The adjacent museum has fossils and implements of prehistoric man found in India. Opening hours are 10 am to 5 pm, Wednesday to Sunday.

Rose Garden

The Sector 16 Rose Garden is claimed to be the biggest in Asia and contains more than a thousand varieties of roses.

Places to Stay – bottom end

There are no great bottom-end bargains in Chandigarh. The *Youth Hostel* is at Panchkula, between Chandigarh and the Pinjore Gardens – a little way out of town, but there are many buses and the hostel is good value.

Much more central is the *Chandigarh Yatri Niwas* at the corner of Sector 24. It's rather anonymous, hidden behind the block of flats at the roundabout nearest the bus station – about 10 minutes' walk. It's a bit hostel-like and all the rooms have common bathrooms, but there seems to be one bathroom for every two rooms. There's hot water and a cafeteria (vegetarian dinner for Rs 7) with hopelessly slow service. Although fairly new, it's already suffering from that Indian instant decay – wiring tumbling out of the walls and so on – but it's clean and at Rs 37/52 for singles/doubles the best value in town.

There are two Tourist Bungalows in Sector 19 – both somewhat inconspicuous although the bus station rickshaw wallahs certainly know how to find them. The *Haryana Tourist Bungalow* (tel 43684) at 3293 in 19D has rooms at Rs 75 or with attached bathroom for Rs 125. The

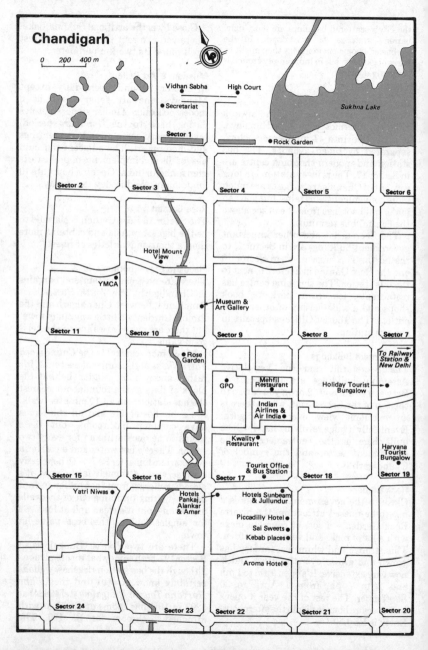

Chandigarh

0   200   400 m

Vidhan Sabha   High Court

Secretariat

Sukhna Lake

Sector 1

Rock Garden

Sector 2   Sector 3   Sector 4   Sector 5   Sector 6

Hotel Mount
View

YMCA

Museum &
Art Gallery

Sector 11   Sector 10   Sector 9   Sector 8   Sector 7

Rose
Garden

*To Railway
Station &
New Delhi*

GPO   Mehfil
             Restaurant   Holiday Tourist
                                 Bungalow

Indian
Airlines &
Air India

Kwality
Restaurant   Haryana
                                                 Tourist
Tourist Office   Bungalow
& Bus Station
Sector 15   Sector 16   Sector 17   Sector 18   Sector 19

Yatri Niwas   Hotels   Hotels Sunbeam
                     Pankaj,   & Jullundur
                     Alankar
                     & Amar   Piccadilly Hotel

                                     Sai Sweets

                                     Kebab places

                                     Aroma Hotel

Sector 24   Sector 23   Sector 22   Sector 21   Sector 20 bathrooms are poorly kept and it's not very good value. All the rooms at the privately run *Holiday Tourist Bungalow* at Kothi 78, 19A are without bath; it's also grubby and poor value even though it's cheaper at Rs 45/65.

Opposite the bus station towards the Sector 21 roundabout is the *Hotel Jullundur* with rooms at Rs 60/70 and up. Travellers have recommended the *Maharajah Tourist Lodge*, just a Rs 2 cycle-rickshaw ride from the bus stand. It's clean and cheap although the guys who run it are 'a real hassle'. The *YMCA* (tel 26532) is in Sector 11 and costs Rs 15.

Places to Stay – top end

Opposite the bus station on Udyog Path in Sector 22 there are three bottom to middle-range hotels side by side at the roundabout towards Sector 23. *Hotel Pankaj* (tel 24792) has comfortable rooms at Rs 145/155 or deluxe rooms at Rs 180/195. The *Alankar* (tel 21303) is cheaper at Rs 75 for singles, Rs 105 or Rs 120 for doubles. The *Amar* (tel 26608) is cheaper still with rooms at Rs 80 to Rs 90.

Several modern top-end hotels have been built in the last few years. Opposite the bus station in Sector 22 by the Sector 21 roundabout is the *Hotel Sunbeam* (tel 32057) with air-con rooms costing Rs 240/310. Turn the corner and there are several hotels along Himalaya Marg in Sector 22. *Hotel Piccadily* (tel 32223) has rooms at Rs 240/320.

Continuing along Himalaya Marg, the more moderately priced *Hotel Divyadeep* has rooms at Rs 70/90 or with air-cooling at Rs 100/120 and with air-con at Rs 140/160. Finally, just past the traffic lights is the long-running *Hotel Aroma* (tel 23359), still only about 10 minutes' walking distance from the bus stand. Rooms with bathroom cost Rs 90/110 and it's clean and well kept.

Finally the *Mount View* (tel 212577, 21583) in Sector 10 is Chandigarh's top hotel. It's less central than the other main hotels but has pleasant gardens and costs Rs 250 to Rs 275 for singles, Rs 320 to Rs 345 for doubles.

Places to Eat

Chandigarh has plenty of places to eat, including a recent proliferation of fast-food ones. Beside the Sunbeam Hotel in Sector 22 is the neon-lit *Traffic Jam* with masala dosas, pizzas, ice creams and even 'Donald Burgers'. There are a bunch of fast-food places in the Sector 17 shopping centre. They include *Piccad's, Hot Millions* and the engagingly named *Food Fight* – conjures up images of your stomach in turmoil. The menu includes not only the inevitable muttonburgers but also a 'brahmin burger'. Presumably it's held together with a sacred thread. There's also an *Indian Coffee House* in the shopping centre.

Along Himalaya Marg from the Sunbeam Hotel at the roundabout to the Aroma Hotel there are a number of places to eat in Sector 22. At the Hotel Divyadeep the *Bhoj Restaurant* serves slightly expensive vegetarian food in glossy surroundings. Further along is *Sai Sweets* at 1102, where they serve the snacks known as *chat*, dosas and, of course, a wide variety of excellent Indian sweets. Continuing along Himalaya Marg there is a group of open-air kebab places, all called *Singh* something or other. Strictly for meat eaters but good value.

Finally, back in the Sector 17 shopping centre there's a street with a cluster of top-end restaurants, including the *Mehfil Restaurant*. This tandoor specialist looks flashy – white tablecloths, soft music, etc – but is actually not too extravagantly priced. Main courses are Rs 16 to Rs 25, desserts Rs 8 to Rs 10. The menu is the standard mix of continental, Chinese and Indian dishes. Close by are the *Ghazal* and the *Mughal Mahal*, and there is a *Kwality* in the shopping centre.

Getting There

Air There are daily Indian Airlines flights

between Delhi and Chandigarh for Rs 273. Five days a week the flight continues to Jammu (Rs 424) and Srinagar (Rs 572). Two days a week the flight continues to Leh for Rs 477. Three times a week Vayudoot fly Delhi-Chandigarh-Kulu.

Rail Buses are more convenient than trains to or from Chandigarh, but reservations can be made at the booking agency in Sector 22 (tel 29117) or at the office above the central bus station. Enquiries can be made by phoning 27605. Delhi-Chandigarh is 245 km and costs Rs 27 in 2nd class, Rs 101 in 1st.

Bus Buses depart regularly from the Interstate Bus Terminal in Delhi (near Kashmir Gate) for the five-hour trip to Chandigarh. Regular buses cost Rs 28; there are also deluxe video buses (Rs 55) and even air-con deluxe video buses (Rs 96) which completely insulate you from any connection with India.

There are regular and deluxe buses to other places such as Simla (Rs 20 standard, Rs 35 deluxe), Dharamsala (Rs 36 to 40 standard), Manali (Rs 50 standard) and Jaipur (Rs 105 deluxe). It takes about 14 hours to Manali by bus, only nine by taxi. It's five hours to Simla, 12 hours to Kulu, six hours to Amritsar, 10 hours to Dharamsala and seven hours to Pathankot.

Getting Around

Chandigarh is much too spread out to get around on foot, but a day is certainly sufficient to see all it has to offer. The extensive bus network is the cheapest way of getting around – Bus No 1 runs by the Aroma Hotel as far as the government buildings in Sector 1. Bus Nos 6, 6A and 6B all run to the railway station.

Cycle-rickshaws operate on the normal bargaining basis but Chandigarh is a bit big even for them – if you're planning a longer trip across the city consider an auto-rickshaw, of which there aren't so many. They're metered but drivers

positively refuse to use them. If you do want to try walking, start off at Sector 1 and stroll back through Sector 10 (Museum & Art Gallery) and 16 (Rose Garden) to the bus station and shopping centre in Sector 17.

Things to Buy

Woollen sweaters and shawls from the Punjab are good buys, especially in the Government Emporium. The Chandigarh shopping centre is probably the most extensive in India.

NEAR CHANDIGARH
Pinjore

The Moghul gardens at Pinjore were designed by Fidai Khan, Aurangzeb's foster brother, who also designed the Badshahi Mosque in Lahore, Pakistan. Situated 20 km from Chandigarh, the gardens include the Rajasthani-Moghul-style Shish Mahal palace. Below it is the Rang Mahal and the cubical Jal Mahal. An otter house and other animals can be seen in the mini-zoo near the gardens. The fountains only operate on weekends.

Places to Stay The rest house here has air-con rooms for Rs 80 to Rs 150 and one camper hut for Rs 10 to Rs 15.

DELHI TO AMRITSAR
Patiala (population 160,000)

A little south of the road and rail lines from Delhi to Amritsar, Patiala was once the capital of an independent Sikh state. There is a museum in the Moti Bagh and the palaces of the Maharaja in the Baradari Gardens.

Sirhind

This was once a very important town and the capital of the Pathan Sur dynasty. In 1555 Humayun defeated Sikander Shah here and a year later his son, Akbar, completed the destruction of the Sur dynasty at Panipat. From then until 1709 Sirhind was a rich Moghul city, but clashes between the declining Moghul and rising Sikh powers led to the city's sacking in 1709 and complete destruction in 1763.

The Pathan-style Tomb of Mir Miran and the later Moghul Tomb of Pirbandi Nakshwala, both ornamented with blue tiles, are worth seeing. The mansion or *haveli* of Salabat Beg is probably the largest private home remaining from the Moghul period. South-east of the city is an important Moghul *sarai*.

Ludhiana (population 450,000)

An important textile centre, Ludhiana was the site of a great battle of the First Sikh War. Hero bicycles are manufactured here.

Jullundur (population 325,000)

Only 80 km from Amritsar, this was once the capital of an ancient Hindu kingdom. It survived a sacking by Mahmud of Ghazni nearly a thousand years ago and later became an important Moghul city. The town has a large *sarai* built in 1857 and is a good place to get out and see some Sikh farming villages.

Places to Stay Not far from the bus stand, the *Skylark Hotel* (tel 75891) has good rooms at Rs 65/95 or Rs 120/195 with air-con and very good food. Other places are the *Plaza Hotel* and the *Hotel Ramji Dass*.

Getting There Trains take about six hours from Delhi and there's also a bus stand from where frequent services run to other northern centres.

AMRITSAR (population 500,000)

Until a second India-Pakistan border crossing is open, travellers heading overland have to go through Amritsar, close to the only land crossing open to Pakistan. Founded in 1577 by Ram Das, the fourth guru of the Sikhs, Amritsar is both the centre of the Sikh religion and the major city of Punjab state – where the majority of Sikhs live. The name Amritsar translates as 'pool of nectar', the name of the sacred pool by which the Sikhs' golden temple is built.

The original site for the city was granted by the Moghul emperor Akbar, but in 1761 Ahmad Shah Durani sacked the town and destroyed the temple. The temple was rebuilt in 1764; in 1802 it was roofed over with copper gilded plates by Ranjit Singh and became known as 'the golden temple'. During the turmoil of the partition of India in 1948, Amritsar was a flashpoint for the terrible events that shook the Punjab. The region's recovery has been remarkable and today Amritsar even looks better off than other parts of India. You see few beggars in the streets.

At present you cannot visit Amritsar without a permit and it receives few visitors. Although the whole state is wracked by political violence, travellers have commented on the friendliness and helpfulness of the Sikhs.

Orientation & Information

The old city is south of the main railway station and is surrounded by a circular road which used to contain the massive city walls. There are 18 gates still in existence but only the gate to the north, facing the Ram Bagh gardens, is original. The Golden Temple and the narrow alleys of the bazaar area are in the interior of the old city.

The more modern part of Amritsar is north-east of the railway station, where you will also find the beautiful gardens known as Ram Bagh, the Mall and 'posh' Lawrence St. The bus station is a km east of the railway station on the road to Delhi. The Tourist Office is opposite the railway station. At present Amritsar is still pretty much off-limits to foreigners except for those in transit. Reportedly foreigners can only stay overnight if they're journalists – 'and who can prove you're not?' asked a Netherlander.

The Golden Temple

The holiest shrine of the Sikh religion is in

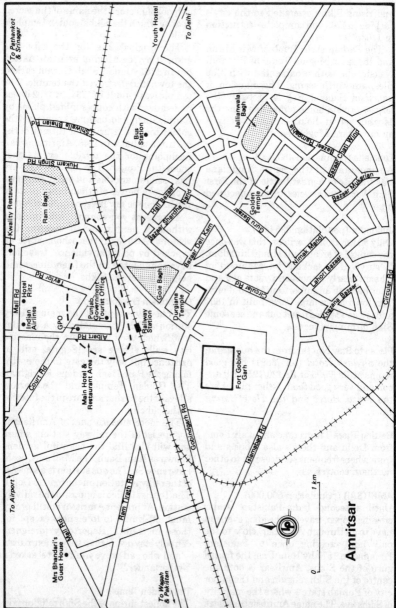

Amritsar

To Pathankot & Srinagar

To Delhi

Youth Hostel

Shivwala Bhairan Rd

Hukam Singh Rd

Bus Station

Jallianwala Bagh

Bazaar Chari Wind

Bazaar Hanuman

Bazaar Mukarian

Kwality Restaurant

Ram Bagh

Hall Bazaar

Bazaar Shardine Mand

Golden Temple

Guru Bazaar

Nimak Mandi

Bazaar Deli Kan

Taylor Rd

Mall Rd

Hotel Ritz

Indian Airlines

GPO

Punjab Government Tourist Office

Gole Bagh

Circular Rd

Lahori Bazaar

Khazana Bazaar

Circular Rd

Albert Rd

Durgiana Temple

Main Hotel & Restaurant Area

Railway Station

Court Rd

Fort Gobind Garh

Gobindgarh Rd

To Airport

Mall Rd

Ram Tirath Rd

Islamabad Rd

Mrs Bhandari's Guest House

To Wagah & Pakistan

0   1 km

the centre of the old part of town. The temple itself is surrounded by the pool which gave the town its name and reached by a causeway. A loudspeaker broadcasts a continuous reading of the *Granth Sahib* in Punjabi. The high priest who reads from the Sikh's holy book sits on the east side of the temple. The original copy of the *Granth Sahib* is kept in the Golden Temple and is occasionally taken out on procession. To the south of the temple enclosure is a garden in which stands the Baba Atal Tower. The tall Ramgarhia Minars stand outside the temple enclosure.

Earlier in the Punjab unrest the Golden Temple was occupied by Sikh extremists who were only evicted by the Indian Army in 1984 with much bloodshed. This action was a contributing factor to Indira Gandhi's subsequent assassination. The temple was again occupied by extremists in 1986.

If the temple is open, pilgrims and visitors to the Golden Temple must remove their shoes and cover their heads before entering the precincts. An English-speaking guide is available at the clock tower which marks the temple entrance. The Central Sikh Museum is upstairs in the clock tower.

The Old City

A 15-minute walk from the Golden Temple, through the narrow alleys of the old city, brings you to the Hindu Durgiana temple. This small temple, dedicated to the goddess Durga, dates back to the 16th century. A larger temple, built like the Golden Temple in the centre of a lake, is dedicated to the Hindu deities Laxmi and Narayan.

There are a number of mosques in the old city, including the mosque of Muhammad Jan with three white domes and slender minarets.

Jalianwala Bagh

This park is just five minutes' walk from the Golden Temple and commemorates

the 2000 Indians who were killed or wounded at this site, shot indiscriminately by the British in 1919. This was one of the major events in India's struggles for independence and was movingly re-created in the film *Gandhi*. Bullet marks and the well into which some people jumped to escape can still be seen. Officially, over 300 were killed.

Ram Bagh

This beautiful garden is in the new part of town and has a museum in the small palace built there by the Sikh Maharajah Ranjit Singh. The museum contains weapons dating back to Moghul times and some portraits of the ruling houses of the Punjab. It's closed on Wednesdays.

Other

The Govindgarh Fort is south-west of the city centre. It was built in 1805-09 by Ranjit Singh, who was also responsible for the city walls. Tarn Taran is an important Sikh tank, about 25 km south of Amritsar. There's a temple and tower on the east side of the tank, also constructed by Ranjit Singh. The temple pre-dates Amritsar. It's said that any leper who can swim across the tank will be miraculously cured.

Places to Stay – bottom end

The *Tourist Guest House*, across from the railway station and near Hotel Airlines, has rooms from Rs 30 and is popular with shoestring travellers. *Hotel Temple View* has rooms at Rs 25 a double – 'clean, real Sikh friendliness and one of the best views of the Golden Temple in town'.

Station Links Rd, opposite the railway station, has three moderately priced hotels. *Hotel Skylark* (tel 46738) and *Hotel Chinar* (tel 33455) cost from Rs 60. *Hotel Palace*, which also houses the state tourist information office, has some cheaper rooms.

If you're on a really tight budget, the state government-operated *Youth Hostel* (tel 48165) is three km out of town on the

Delhi road. There are dorm beds (Rs 8, cheaper for YHA members) and also Rs 20 (but doorless!) doubles. The hotel has hot showers and good, albeit expensive, food. It's one of the better Youth Hostels in India and has camping facilities.

If peace returns to the Punjab and if you'd really like to come to grips with the Sikh religion, you can stay for a few days for free at the guest house of the Golden Temple. Be considerate, don't smoke and don't complain if the standards are not what you expect. Accommodation is dormitory style and mattresses can be loaned for a returnable Rs 10 deposit. There are many cheap hotels around the temple such as the *Vikas Guest House* or the slightly cheaper *Amritsar Majestic Hotel*.

Places to Stay - middle

On The Mall, in the new area of the city and about a km from the railway station, you'll find the pleasant *Hotel Blue Moon* (tel 33416) with rooms at Rs 70/110 or at Rs 110/150 with air-con. In the same area the *Hotel Odeon* (tel 43474) is rather cheaper. This is also the area for a number of restaurants, including a Kwality branch opposite the Ram Bagh.

On Queens Rd, opposite the railway station, is the *Grand Hotel* (tel 33821) with rooms at Rs 50/85; with air-con at Rs 125/150. Other more expensive hotels include the *Airlines Hotel* (tel 44545) on Cooper Rd where air-cooled rooms are Rs 75/100 or with air-con Rs 125/150. It too is near the railway station. Or there's the *Astoria* (tel 48479) on Queens Rd with rooms at Rs 55/95 or with air-con at Rs 115/145.

Places to Stay - top end

Built by the Punjab state government, the centrally air-conditioned *Amritsar International Hotel* (tel 31991) is a modern building near the bus station. Rooms cost from Rs 175/200. On Albert Rd the smaller *Mohan International Hotel* (tel 34146) has rooms at Rs 250/350

and a swimming pool, and is also centrally air-conditioned.

The *Ritz Hotel* (tel 44199) is near the railway station at 45 The Mall. Singles/doubles, all air-con, are Rs 225/300 and there's a swimming pool.

Places to Eat

There are a number of more expensive restaurants in the new part of town such as *Napoli, Kwality* and *Crystal*. There's an ice cream parlour near the Kwality restaurant.

Amritsar also has a number of cheaper and locally popular places such as *Kasar de Dhawa* near the Durgiana Temple and the telephone exchange in the old town. Parathas and other vegetarian dishes are the speciality here, and you can eat well for around Rs 10. *Kundan di Dhawa* near the railway station and *Mangal de Dhawa* are other popular cheapies. *Sharma Vaishna Dhaba*, near the temple, has good vegetarian food too. Also near the temple entrance, the *Losy Restaurant* has 'superb, real Punjabi food'. The railway restaurant is good.

Getting There

Air There's a daily flight from Delhi to Amritsar continuing on to Srinagar, twice a week via Jammu. The fares to or from Amritsar are Delhi Rs 456, Jammu Rs 213, Srinagar Rs 389.

Rail & Bus Amritsar is 447 km from Delhi and takes seven hours by mail or express train (Rs 43 in 2nd class, Rs 92 in 1st). It's rather less comfortable by bus, which takes 10 hours. Amritsar is a jumping-off point to other places in north-west India – Pathankot (on the way to Kashmir) is three hours away by bus and Chandigarh is four. Jammu takes five hours (fast for 215 km) and costs Rs 22. Dharamsala takes 6½ hours (250 km) for Rs 28.

See the introductory Getting There chapter for details on the Amritsar-Atari-Lahore trip by rail or Amritsar-Wagah-Lahore road route. It's only 30 km from

Amritsar to Wagah, on the Pakistan border.

Things to Buy
Woollen blankets and sweaters are supposed to be cheaper in Amritsar than in other places in India, as they are locally manufactured. Katra Jaimal Singh, near the telephone exchange in the old city, is a good shopping area.

PATHANKOT
In the extreme north of the Punjab, 107 km from Amritsar, the town of Pathankot is important to travellers purely for its crossroads function. It's the gateway to Jammu in the state of Jammu & Kashmir, which in turn is the jumping-off point for the bus trip up to Srinagar. Pathankot is also the bus centre for departures to the Himachal Pradesh hill stations – particularly Dalhousie and Dharamsala. Otherwise it's a dull little place, although there's the picturesque Shahpur Kandi Fort, about 13 km north of the town on the River Ravi.

Places to Stay & Eat
The *Gulmohar Tourist Bungalow* (tel 292) has rooms for Rs 30/55 or with air-con for Rs 95/120. There's a dormitory for Rs 8 (Rs 15 with bedding). Pathankot has a rest house and cheap hotels like the *Green Hotel* and the *Imperial Hotel*.

There's reasonable food in the railway station restaurant.

Getting There
The dusty bus station and the railway station are only a hundred or so metres apart. Buses to Jammu take about three hours and cost Rs 10. To Dalhousie it's Rs 13 and about four hours, to Dharamsala Rs 14 and five hours. You can also get taxis for these longer trips from beside the railway station.

DELHI TO FEROZEPORE
This route takes you through Haryana and the Punjab, further south than the Delhi-Chandigarh and Delhi-Amritsar routes. From Delhi the railway line runs through Rohtak, 70 km out, which was once a border town between the Sikhs and Marathas and the subject of frequent clashes.

Bhatinda, 296 km from Delhi, was an important town of the Pathan Sur dynasty. Sirsa, to the south of Bhatinda, was an ancient city but little remains apart from the city walls. Hansi, southeast of Sirsa, towards Rohtak, was where Colonel Skinner (of the legendary regiment 'Skinner's Horse') died. Faridkot, 350 km from Delhi, was once the capital of a Sikh state of the same name. It has a 700-year-old fort. Ferozepore is 382 km from Delhi; the railway line continued to Lahore from here until partition.

Himachal Pradesh

Population: 3.5 million
Area: 55,673 square km
Capital: Simla
Main languages: Hindi, Pahari

The state of Himachal Pradesh came into being in its present form with the partition of the Punjab into Punjab and Haryana in 1966. Himachal Pradesh is essentially a mountain state – it takes in the transition zone from the plains to the high Himalaya and in the trans-Himalayan region of Lahaul & Spiti actually crosses that mighty barrier to the Tibetan plateau. It's a delightful state for visitors, particularly during the hot season when people flock to its hill stations to escape the searing heat of the plains.

High points for the visitor include Simla, the 'summer capital' of British India and still one of India's most important hill stations. The Kulu Valley is simply one of the most beautiful areas on earth – a lush, green valley with the sparkling Beas River running through it and the snow-capped Himalayan peaks forming the background. Then there's Dharamsala, home-in-exile for the Dalai Lama; and a host of other hill stations, lakes, walks and mountains. In the far north of the state the winter snow melts, permitting visitors to explore for a few brief summer months the Tibetan culture of Keylong in Lahaul & Spiti.

Trekking & Mountaineering
See Lonely Planet's *Trekking in the Indian Himalaya* for more information on trekking in this region. The Himachal Pradesh Tourist Office have a brochure on trekking which briefly details a number of treks in the state. They also have three excellent large-scale maps of Himachal Pradesh invaluable for trekkers. The trekking season in Himachal Pradesh runs from mid-May to mid-October. In

Manali there is a Department of Mountaineering & Allied Sports (tel 42) which can advise you on trekking possibilities in the state and also on the numerous unscaled peaks. Unlike in Nepal, no trekking permits are necessary in Himachal Pradesh and this helps to make trekking here relatively cheap.

Equipment and provisions will depend very much on where you trek. In the lower country in the Kulu or Kangra valleys, or around Simla, there are many rest houses and villages. On the other hand, in Lahaul & Spiti the population is much less dense and conditions more severe. You will need to be better equipped in terms of cold-weather gear, food and provisions. Some of the better-known treks are detailed in the appropriate sections. There are a great number of Forest Rest Houses, PWD Rest Houses and other semi-official accommodation possibilities along the Himachal Pradesh trekking routes. Enquire at local tourist offices about using these places before setting off.

The HPTD's *Trekking Guide* lists 136 mountains over 5000 metres high. The majority of them are unclimbed, most not even named. It's virgin territory for mountaineers.

Wildlife

There are fishing possibilities in many places in Himachal Pradesh and a number of trout hatcheries have been established. The various local tourist offices can advise you on where to fish and how to obtain fishing licences. These are much cheaper than in Kashmir.

Some of the state's deer, antelope, mountain goats and sheep are now rather rare. Himalayan black bears and brown bears are found in many parts of the state; the black bear is fairly common but the brown bear is usually only found at higher elevations. Wild boar are found at lower elevations in certain districts. Snow leopards are now very rare and only found at high elevations in the most remote parts of the state. Panthers and leopards are, however, still found in many forested regions. Himachal Pradesh has numerous kinds of pheasants and partridges and many mountain birds.

Temples

Although Himachal Pradesh does not have any particularly renowned temples, at least touristically, it does have many interesting and architecturally very diverse ones. In the Kangra and Chamba valleys there are several 8th to 10th-century temples in the Indo-Aryan shikhara style. Pagoda-style temples with multi-tiered roofs are found in the Kulu Valley. There are many temples of purely local design, often with interesting woodcarvings, particularly in the Chamba region.

In the south of the state there are numerous temples with elements of Moghul and Sikh design, while in several locations there are cave temples. Finally the Tibetans, who came to the state following the Chinese invasion of their country, have built colourful *gompas*

(monasteries) and temples. The people of Lahaul & Spiti in the north of the state are also of Tibetan extraction and have many interesting gompas.

Things to Buy

The Kulu Valley is full of spinners and weavers, mostly men, and their fine shawls are very popular. These are made from the fleece shed in the summer by mountain goats. The shawls made from pashmina hair from the pashmina goat are the finest. Chamba is well known for its leather *chappals* (sandals). In the high Himalaya fleecy soft blankets known as *gudmas* are woven, as well as traditional rugs and *namdas*. In the bazaars you can find locally made jewellery and metalwork. Tibetan handicrafts include coral jewellery, carpets and religious paraphernalia.

Transport

Apart from two railway lines which are both narrow gauge and hence rather more 'fun' than 'transport', getting around Himachal Pradesh means taking a bus – unless you can afford a taxi. The two trains run from Kalka – just north of Chandigarh – to Simla, and from Pathankot along the Kangra Valley to Jogindarnagar.

Himachal Pradesh buses are generally the Indian norm – slow, crowded, uncomfortable and tiring. Things are made a little worse by the mountainous terrain. If you can manage to average 20 kph on a bus trip you're doing well. Taxis are readily available but rather expensive. One way you can make a saving is to find a taxi on a return trip – in that case you can often knock the price down a bit. Ask the people running your hotel; they often know who is going where.

The HPTDC have a number of deluxe tourist bus services. They often operate overnight but usually only in the high seasons or on demand. Typical fares are Delhi-Manali 16 hours, Rs 250; Simla-Manali 10 hours, Rs 100; Chandigarh-Manali 11 hours, Rs 125.

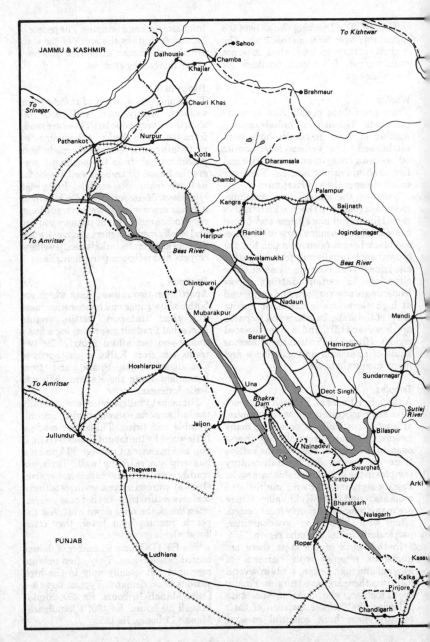

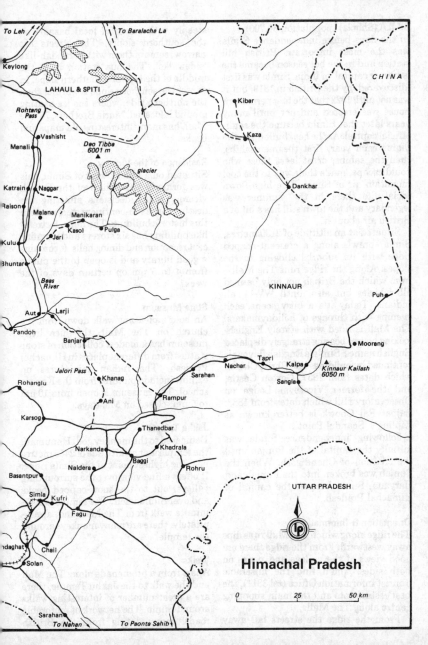

To Leh

To Baralacha La

Keylong

LAHAUL & SPITI

CHINA

Rohtang Pass

Vashisht

Kibar

Manali

Deo Tibba 6001 m ▲

Kaza

Katrain Naggar

glacier

Raison

Dankhar

Malana

Manikaran

Kulu Kasol Pulga

Jari

Bhuntar

Beas River

KINNAUR

Aut Larji

Puh

Pandoh

Banjar

Moorang

Jalori Pass

Tapri Kalpa Kinnaur Kailash 6050 m

Rohanglu

Khanag

Nachar

Sangla

Sarahan

Ani Rampur

Karsog

Thanedbar

Narkanda Khadrala

UTTAR PRADESH

Basantpur Naldera Baggi

Rohru

Simla

Kufri

Fagu

ndaghat Chail

Solan

Himachal Pradesh

0   25   50 km

Sarahan

To Nahan To Paonta Sahib

SIMLA (Shimla) (population 60,700)

In the days before independence Simla was the most important British hill station and in the hot season became the 'summer capital' of India. Simla was first 'discovered' by the British in 1819, but it was not until 1822 that the first permanent house was erected and not until many years later that Simla became the semi-official capital. As the heat built up on the plains each year, first the memsahibs, then the sahibs, or at least those who could escape, made their way to the cool mountain air of Simla. The high-flown social life there in the summer was legendary and the town still has a bit of a British air about it.

Situated at an altitude of 2130 metres, Simla sprawls along a crescent-shaped ridge with its suburbs clinging to the slopes. Along the ridge runs The Mall – from which the British not only banned all vehicles but also, until WW I, all Indians. Today it's a busy scene each evening with throngs of holidaymakers. The Mall is lined with stately English-looking houses bearing strangely displaced English names. Simla's English flavour is continued by buildings like Christ Church which dates from 1857, Gorton Castle, and the former Viceroyal Lodge on Observatory Hill which dates from 1888. Lajpat Rai Chowk is better known as Kipling's 'Scandal Point'.

Following independence Simla was initially the capital of the Punjab until the creation of Chandigarh. When the Punjab was broken into the Punjab and Haryana, Simla became the capital of Himachal Pradesh.

Orientation & Information

The ridge along which The Mall runs dips away westward. From the ridge there are good views of the valleys and peaks on both sides. You'll find the miserable Tourist Information Office (tel 3311), the best restaurants and the main shopping centre along The Mall.

From the ridge the streets fall away steeply with colourful local bazaars on the southern slopes. The streets are narrow, some of them with verandah-like 'sidewalks'. The bus station is in the middle of the crowded southern slope. In winter the southern slope is warmer than the northern side, where the ice-skating ground is located. Maria Brothers, 78 The Mall, has many interesting old maps and books.

Residence of the Viceroy

Situated on a hillock west of Simla, this was formerly the palace of the British viceroy. Many decisions affecting the destiny of the sub-continent were made in this historic building. The huge, fortress-like building has six storeys and magnificent reception and dining halls. It contains a good library and is open to the public from 4 to 5 pm on certain days of the week.

State Museum

An hour's pleasant walk down from the church on The Mall, the nice little museum has a modest collection of stone statues from different places in Himachal Pradesh. The Indian miniatures on exhibit include pictures from the Kangra school. The museum is open from 10 am to 5 pm, closed on Mondays.

Jakhu Temple

Dedicated to the monkey god, Hanuman, the temple is at an altitude of 2455 metres near the highest point of the Simla ridge. It offers a fine view over the surrounding valleys, out to the snow-capped peaks and over Simla itself. The temple is a 45-minute walk from The Mall and, appropriately, there are many monkeys around the temple.

Walks

Apart from a promenade along The Mall and the walk to the Jakhu Temple, there are a great number of interesting walks around Simla. The network of motorable roads, many dating from the British

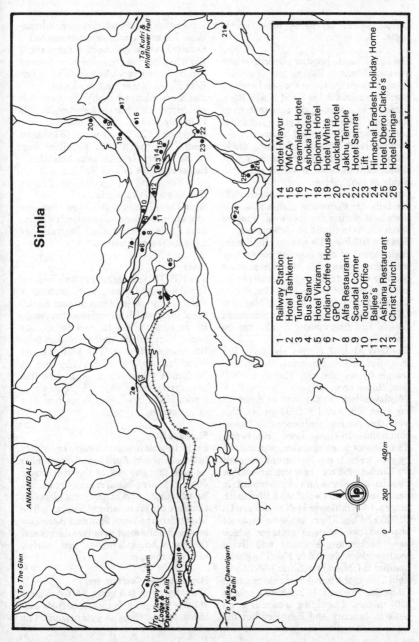

Simla

To Kufri &
Wildflower Hall

ANNANDALE

To The Glen

To Viceroy's
Lodge &
Chadwick Falls

Museum

Hotel Cecil

To Kalka, Chandigarh
& Delhi

0   200   400 m

1	Railway Station
2	Hotel Tashkent
3	Tunnel
4	Bus Stand
5	Hotel Vikram
6	Indian Coffee House
7	GPO
8	Alfa Restaurant
9	Scandal Corner
10	Tourist Office
11	Baljee's
12	Ashiana Restaurant
13	Christ Church
14	Hotel Mayur
15	YMCA
16	Dreamland Hotel
17	Ashoka Hotel
18	Diplomat Hotel
19	Hotel White
20	Auckland Hotel
21	Jakhu Temple
22	Hotel Samrat
23	Lift
24	Himachal Pradesh Holiday Home
25	Hotel Oberoi Clarke's
26	Hotel Shingar

period, offers access to other scenic spots.

The Glen This is a popular picnic spot four km from Simla at 1830 metres. A stream flows through the forest here and you can reach the glen via the Cecil Hotel. It's a four-km walk if you take care to keep to the road. Take the path going right just past the brightly painted house.

Summer Hill There are pleasant, shady walks in this Simla suburb on the Simla-Kalka railway line. It's five km from Simla at 1983 metres.

Chadwick Falls Reached via Summer Hill, the falls are 67 metres high and are at their best during the monsoon. They're seven km from Simla at 1586 metres.

Prospect Hill It's a 15-minute climb from Boileauganj to this popular picnic spot with fine views over the surrounding country and a temple of Kamna Devia. It's five km from Simla at 2145 metres.

Sankat Mochan Seven km from Simla at 1875 metres, this spot, with its Hanuman temple and fine view of Simla, can be reached on foot or by car.

Tara Devi At 1851 metres and seven km from Simla, you can reach this hilltop temple by rail and car. There's a *PWD Rest House* here.

Wildflower Hall On the road to Kufri, 13 km from Simla and at 2593 metres, this was the former residence of Indian commander-in-chief Lord Kitchener. The present huge mansion, surrounded by pine trees, is not the actual one built for Kitchener. From here you have a fine view back to Simla and out to mountain peaks in the Pir Panjal and Badrinath ranges. In Wildflower Hall rooms are Rs 75/125 and up. There are some separate one and two-bedroom cottages which have bathrooms, kitchens and living rooms and cost Rs 200 to 350. The phone number is Chharabra (Simla) 8/212.

Kufri This is the best-known ski resort in Himachal Pradesh, 16 km from Simla at 2501 metres. The skiing season is at its peak in January and February but the snow cover can sometimes be problematical. An annual winter sports festival is usually held the first week of February. If you'd like to try skiing in India, equipment can be rented very cheaply. The *Indira Rest House* is two km from Kufri.

Mashobra Also accessible by car, this picnic spot has pleasant forest walks. It is 13 km from Simla at 2149 metres.

Craignano At 2279 metres and 16 km from Simla, Craignano, with its hilltop *Rest House*, is only three km from Mashobra.

Naldera At 2044 metres Naldera is 23 km from Simla and has a golf course, *Tourist Bungalow* and cafeteria.

Fagu There is a very fine view from this spot and a lot of snow in winter. It's 22 km from Simla at 2510 metres. Fagu also has a potato research centre.

Tours

The HPTDC (Himachal Pradesh Tourism Development Corporation) conducts a number of tours to places around Simla. Local tours, which are run more frequently in the summer season, cost Rs 40, last from 10 am to 5 pm, and are booked from the tourist office on The Mall. Longer tours include the 64-km trip out to Narkanda where there is a very fine panoramic view of the Himalaya. Narkanda is now being developed as a skiing centre.

Places to Stay

Prices in most places in Simla vary widely between the mid-April to mid-September 'season' and the rest of the year. From June to September accommodation can be difficult to find at any price although there are a great number of hotels. As The Mall offers the best views and is the city centre, it's the most popular address and the cost of hotels is highest here, particularly at the top.

Places to Stay – bottom end

The very clean and quiet *YMCA* is good value – you get a fireplace, carpets and blankets, and there's a gymnasium! The food is reportedly good also. Singles are Rs 20, 25 and 30 while doubles are Rs 30, 35 and 45. There's also a Rs 5 temporary membership charge. The YMCA is above Christ Church behind the big Hotel Mayur.

The *Tashkent Hotel*, just down the north side from The Mall and virtually above the Victory Tunnel, has rather primitive rooms with bath for Rs 20/30. On the south side of the ridge there are a number of cheap hotels around the bus station, including the very basic but clean enough *Hotel Vikrant*, where windowless and bathless singles cost Rs 35, singles with a window are Rs 40 and there's an extra Rs 4 charge for bedding. Doubles are Rs 50, 60 and 100.

Up from the The Mall the *Hotel Ashoka* is good value with reasonable rooms with bath at Rs 40 to Rs 70. Not to mention monkeys clattering around on the corrugated iron roof at 6 am! On the way up to the Ashoka from The Mall you pass *Hotel Dreamland*, which is a bit cheaper with rooms from Rs 40 – good value for Simla.

Places to Stay – top end

Just beyond the 'lift' and Hotel Clarkes at the eastern end of The Mall is the *Hotel Shingar* (tel 2881) with rooms at Rs 150, 190 and 210. It's of reasonable middle-price standard. Just beyond the Shingar is the cheaper *Hotel Samrat* where rooms cost Rs 95 to Rs 150.

If you take the road off to the north-east from the open area in front of Christ Church on The Mall, you'll soon come to the *Hotel Diplomat* (tel 3033). It's a relatively modern building but already showing serious signs of Indian decline. The rooms start from around Rs 120 but that's for a windowless little box. Better rooms with a view are Rs 175 and go up to Rs 195 to Rs 275, even more for suites. There's hot water in the bathrooms.

Just beyond the Diplomat, *Hotel White* (tel 6136) is similar in standard but a bit cheaper. Typical prices for rooms start from around Rs 100 for rooms with balcony and bathroom. It's reasonably well kept, bright and airy and has good views from the rooms looking out from the hill. Down the hill on the Circular Rd is *Auckland* (tel 6315), a modern place a notch up-market from the Diplomat and the Hotel White. Rooms in this hotel are Rs 150/175.

You can't miss the sign for the big *Hotel Mayur* (tel 6047-49), which is just above Christ Church. Rooms cost Rs 150 to Rs 200 depending on their size and the view. It's a good standard middle-range Indian hotel. On Circular Rd down below The Mall ridge on the north side is *Lord's Grey Hotel* (tel 5146) where rooms are Rs 110 to Rs 165.

Simla's top hotel is the *Oberoi Clarkes* (tel 6091-95) on The Mall at the eastern end. Rooms are Rs 445/625 including meals. The other Oberoi hotel, the Cecil along The Mall to the west, is very permanently closed at present. On Cart Rd on the south-eastern side of the slope, down below Clarke's, is the state government's *Holiday Home* (tel 6031-38) where doubles are Rs 150 to Rs 250, deluxe doubles Rs 250 to Rs 350. Beyond here is the *Himland Hotel* (tel 3595) on Circular Rd. Rooms cost from Rs 100/175 but it's so far round the road you'd need a car to stay there.

Places to Eat

Curiously Simla is not as well endowed with restaurants as other hill stations – it's a long way behind Darjeeling for example. All the better-known restaurants are along The Mall. *Baljee's* is often crowded in the evening – it has the standard Indian non-vegetarian menu, zero decor and reasonable food. Upstairs there is an associated restaurant known as *Fascination*. Count on around Rs 40 for a meal.

A little further down The Mall the *Alfa Restaurant* also has the standard non-vegetarian menu. Just beyond the Alfa there are two *Indian Coffee Houses* with south Indian food and snacks at reasonable prices. There are various small restaurants in the bazaar area on the southern slopes. The *Sher-e-Punjab* on The Mall near the lift is pretty good.

The State Tourism Department has two restaurants at the main square on the ridge, close to the Tourist Office. The *Ashiana* upstairs is much brighter than the gloomy *Goofa* down below. Prices are much the same in both restaurants although the ritzier Ashiana is supposed to be a cut above the café-like Goofa. The food is fairly mediocre; Simla is not going to be anybody's culinary highlight.

Getting There

Rail By rail to Simla involves a change from broad gauge to narrow gauge at Kalka, a little north of Chandigarh. The narrow-gauge trip to Simla takes nearly six hours. Add on two or more hours to change trains at Kalka plus the trip from Delhi, and you'll find it much faster by bus. On the other hand the rail trip is great fun! Total distance is 364 km from Delhi and the fare is Rs 35 in 2nd class, Rs 142 in 1st.

Bus A bus from Chandigarh is the easiest way to get to Simla. The 117-km trip takes four hours and costs Rs 19 in an ordinary bus or Rs 41 in a deluxe bus. You can reach Chandigarh from Delhi by a variety of buses and by air. A bus straight from Delhi takes around 10 hours and costs Rs 49, Rs 96 in a deluxe bus.

There are buses north from Simla to other hill stations in Himachal Pradesh such as Dharamsala or the Kulu Valley. From Simla to Manali costs Rs 48 and takes 11 hours. On alternate days there's a deluxe bus which costs Rs 100. To Dharamsala costs Rs 44 to 47 and takes 10 to 12 hours. To Mandi it's about six hours for Rs 25. Dehra Dun is a weary nine-hour trip for Rs 38. A taxi to Manali would cost about Rs 800 to Rs 900.

Getting Around

Local bus services operate from the Cart Rd bus stand. A bus runs from the bus station to Boileauganj in the west. Apart from that the best way around Simla is to walk. A little east of the bus stand a two-part 'tourist lift' takes you up to The Mall for Rs 1. It saves a long and tedious climb and it's the only lift I've ever seen with a fire to keep the operator warm!

AROUND SIMLA

Kalka

The narrow-gauge railway line from Kalka to Simla was built in 1903-04. Although going by road is cheaper and quicker, the rail trip is fun. Pinjore, 21 km south-east of Kalka near Chandigarh, has a Moghul summerhouse and garden, built by Fidai Khan, who also built the Badshahi Mosque in Lahore, Pakistan.

Chail

This was once the summer capital of the princely state of Patalia – today the old palace is a luxurious hotel. Chail is 45 km from Simla via Kufri, or you can reach it via Kandaghat on the Simla-Kalka road or narrow-gauge rail line. Chail, at an altitude of 2250 metres, is built on three hills, one of which is topped by the Chail Palace, and one by the ancient Sidh temple. Chail also boasts a temple of quite another religion – cricket. Here you will find the highest cricket pitch in the world!

Places to Stay In the *Chail Palace Hotel* (tel Chail 43 & 47) rooms are Rs 175 to Rs 450 but the Maharaja and Maharani suites are Rs 600 and Rs 700. Chail also has a number of HPTDC cottages and log huts from Rs 200 to Rs 375, and the *Himneel Hotel* with rooms from Rs 35 to Rs 75. There are also a number of local hotels.

Getting There There are direct buses to Chail from Kalka and Simla.

Kasauli

This pleasant little hill station at 1927 metres is only a bit north of Kalka. It's an interesting 15-km trek from Kalka to Kasauli, or you can get there from Dharampur, which is on the Kalka-Simla railway line. Only four km from Kasauli is Monkey Point, a picnic spot and lookout with a very fine view over the plains to the south and to the mountains in the north. Sabathu, 38 km from Kasauli, has a 19th-century Gurkha-built fortress.

Places to Stay & Eat There is a *PWD Rest House* and a number of private guest houses such as the *Alasia, Morris* and *Kalyan. Hotel Ros Common* has rooms from Rs 200. In Dharampur the simple *Mazdoor Dhaba* restaurant near the station has good (and cheap) vegetarian meals and a dormitory upstairs.

Solan

Between Kalka and Simla, on both the railway line and the road, this town is named after the Soloni Devi temple at the southern side of the town. There are pleasant picnic spots and streams around this 1350-metre hill station.

Places to Stay & Eat The *HPTDC Tourist Bungalow* has rooms from Rs 30 to Rs 100 and dorm beds as well as the *Talk o' Town Cafeteria* – they have some names!

Narkanda

At 2700 metres, 64 km from Simla, this is a popular spot for viewing the Himalaya, particularly from the 3300-metre Hattu Peak. Narkanda has recently been developed as a skiing centre. The season lasts from late December to early March and you can take 10-day courses which include your room and board.

From Narkanda you can make trips to Baggi and Khadrala, which are on the Hindustan-Tibet road leading to the Tibetan border. Or you can visit the apple-growing area around Kotgarh or continue to the Kulu Valley via Luhri.

Places to Stay The HPTDC *Hotel Himview* has doubles at Rs 60 and dorm beds for Rs 15. Reservations are made through the Tourist Office in Simla. There's also a *PWD Rest House*.

Tattapani

There's a direct bus to these popular sulphur hot springs, 51 km from Simla and at only 655 metres. Doubles in the *Tourist Bungalow* are Rs 45.

Chabba

Five km from Basantpur, which is on the road to Tattapani, it's a pleasant walk to this *Rest House*, 35 km from Simla.

Thanedhar

This is a centre for apple growing, 82 km from Simla on the route past Narkanda.

Baggi & Khadrala

Also past Narkanda there are *Rest Houses* in both these places. Baggi is 82 km from Simla at 2648 metres, Khadrala is 11 km further on at 2987 metres.

Rohru

Situated 129 km from Simla, this is the site for the Rohru Fair which takes place two days each April. The temple of Devta Shikri is the centre for this colourful fair. The Pabar River, which runs through Rohru, is noted for its trout; there's a trout hatchery 13 km upstream at Chirgaon. Haktoti, a little before Rohru, has an interesting ancient Hindu temple dedicated to the goddess Durga. The temple contains a metre-high image of the eight-armed goddess made of copper and bronze.

Places to Stay There's a *Rest House* in Rohru, a small *Forest Rest House* (booked in Rohru) at Chirgaon and log cabins at Seema, eight km upstream towards Chirgaon.

OTHER PLACES IN THE SOUTH

There are a number of other places of

interest in the south of the state, where Himachal Pradesh borders Uttar Pradesh and Haryana. This district is known as Sirmur.

Paonta Sahib

Situated on the Yamuna River, on the border with Uttar Pradesh, Paonta Sahib is a transit point for travellers from the hill stations of northern Uttar Pradesh to Simla and other hill stations in Himachal Pradesh. It is linked with Gobind Singh, 10th of the Sikhs' gurus who lived here. At Bhangani, 23 km away, he achieved a great military victory when his forces defeated the combined might of 22 hill country kingdoms. His weapons are displayed in the town and his gurdwara still overlooks the river.

Places to Stay There's an HPTDC *Hotel Yamuna* with doubles at Rs 60 to Rs 150. There are also local hotels.

Renuka

North-west of Paonta Sahib a major festival is held each November at this lake. There's a small zoo and a wildlife sanctuary with deer and many water birds.

Places to Stay The HPTDC have a *Tourist Inn* at the lake with rooms for Rs 15, and the *Hotel Renuka* with rooms from Rs 60 to Rs 125.

Nahan

Situated at 932 metres, Nahan is in the Shivalik hills, where the climb to the Himalayan heights commences. There are a number of interesting walks around the town, including the trek to Choordhar (3647 metres) from where there are fine views of the plains to the south and the Sutlej River. Saketi, 14 km south of Nahan, has a fossil park with life-sized fibreglass models of prehistoric animals whose fossilised skeletons were unearthed here.

Places to Stay There are a number of *Rest Houses* and local hotels.

IN THE SOUTH-WEST
Bhakra-Nangal

The giant Bhakra Dam, one of the largest in the world, provides irrigation water for a vast area of the Punjab and also produces hydro-electric power. The public relations office at the dam arranges permits to inspect this major project.

Bilaspur & Naina Devi

On the shore of the Gobindsagar Lake the interesting Vyas Gufa, Lakshmi Narayan and Radhashyam temples are at this town on the Chandigarh-Mandi route. There are fine views over the lake from Naina Devi.

MANDI

The town of Mandi, on the Beas River, is the gateway to the Kulu Valley. From here you climb up the narrow, spectacular gorge of the river and emerge from this grey and barren stretch into the green and inviting Kulu Valley. At an altitude of only 760 metres temperatures are higher here and Mandi mainly serves as a travel crossroads, as its name, which means 'market', might suggest.

The town is famous for its beautiful stone-carved temples – Bhutnath, Triloknath, Panchavaktra, Ardhanari and Shyamakli.

Mandi is 202 km north of Chandigarh and 110 km south of Manali. The road from Pathankot and Dharamsala (150 km away) also meets here whether you are going south to Chandigarh or north to the Kulu Valley.

Rewabar Lake

The Rewabar Lake, a pilgrimage centre for Hindus, Buddhists and Sikhs, is 24 km south-east. There is a mountain cave-refuge for many foreign Buddhists near here. You can stay in the Tibetan Buddhist monastery for Rs 2 and there's also a hotel.

Places to Stay & Eat

Mandi has a *Tourist Bungalow* with a variety of rooms from Rs 50 to Rs 100 or deluxe rooms at Rs 150. There are also dorm beds at Rs 15. For real Maharaja standards try the *Raj Mahal*, a wonderful old palace hotel. It's run down, but at Rs 36/78 for singles/doubles who cares. There's a pleasant garden, strange old rooms and large, ancient bathrooms. Next to it, the palace itself is a crazy Moghul-Chinese mix and well worth a quick look.

There are also a number of cheap hotels in the town. The *Adarsh Hotel*, second hotel on the right over the bridge, has big clean doubles with bathrooms for Rs 35 and a good restaurant. *Café Shiraz* is run by the state tourist office.

KANGRA VALLEY

The beautiful Kangra Valley starts near Mandi, runs north, then bends east and extends to Shahpur near Pathankot. To the north the valley is flanked by the Dhauladhar mountain range to the side of which Dharamsala clings. There are a number of places of interest along the valley, including the popular hill station Dharamsala. The main Pathankot-Mandi road runs through the Kangra Valley and there is a narrow-gauge railway line from Pathankot as far as Jogindarnagar. The Kangra school of painting developed in this valley.

Baijnath

Only 16 km from Palampur, the small town of Baijnath is an important pilgrimage place due to its very old Shiva temple. The temple is said to date from 804 AD and Baijnath has a *PWD Rest House*.

Palampur

A pleasant little town surrounded by tea plantations, Palampur is 35 km from Dharamsala and stands at 1260 metres. The main road runs right through Palampur and there are some pleasant walks around the town.

Places to Stay The HPTDC *Hotel T-Bud* is about a km from the bus station and has rooms for Rs 75, 125 and 150 and dorm beds for Rs 15.

Kangra

There is little to see in this ancient town, 18 km almost directly south of Dharamsala, but at one time it was a place of considerable importance. The famous temple of Bajreshwari Devi was of such legendary wealth that every invader worth his salt took time to sack it. Mahmud of Ghazni carted off a fabulous fortune in gold, silver and jewels in 1009. In 1360 it was plundered once again by Tughlaq but it was still able to recover and, in Jehangir's reign, was paved in plates of pure silver.

The disastrous earthquake which shook the valley in 1905 destroyed the temple, which has since been rebuilt. Kangra also has a much-ruined fort on a ridge overlooking the Baner and Manjhi rivers. It too was sacked by Mahmud, captured by Jehangir in 1620 and severely damaged in the 1905 quake.

Kangra has a *PWD Rest House*.

Jawalamukhi

In the Beas Valley, 34 km south of Kangra, the temple of Jawalamukhi is famous for its eternally burning flame. It's the most popular pilgrimage site in Himachal Pradesh.

Places to Stay The HPTDC *Hotel Jwalaji* (tel 80) has rooms at Rs 100, Rs 125 with air-cooling, Rs 175 with air-con; and there's a Rs 20 dorm. There's also a *PWD Rest House*. Nadaun, south of Jawalamukhi on the Beas River, has another *Rest House*.

Chintpurni

Near Bharwain, 80 km south of Dharamsala and across the Beas, this town has an important temple.

Masrur

Three km from Haripur, about 15 km south of Kangra, Masrur has 15 rock-cut temples in the Indo-Aryan style and richly carved. They are partly ruined but still show their relationship to the better-known and much larger temples at Ellora in Maharashtra.

Nurpur

Only 24 km from Pathankot on the Mandi-Pathankot road, the town acquired its name in 1622 when Jehangir named it after his wife, Nurjahan. Nurpur fort is now in ruins but still has some finely carved reliefs. A ruined Krishna temple, also finely carved, stands within the fort. Nurpur has a *PWD Rest House*.

TREKS FROM KANGRA VALLEY

From Baijnath you can make an interesting trek to Dharamsala, Chamba or Manali. The first day's trek to Bir Khas can be done by bus. At Bara Bhangal, reached on Day 6, you can choose to go east to Manali or west to Dharamsala or Chamba.

Day 1	Baijnath- Bir Khas	1600 m	26 km
Day 2	Bir Khas- Rajgaunda	2500 m	13 km
Day 3	Rajgaunda- Palachak Deota	2750 m	8 km
Day 4	Palachak Deota- Panardu Got	3700 m	8 km
Day 5	Panardu Got- Thamsar Jot	4750 m	6 km
Day 6	Thamsar Jot- Bara Bhangal	2541 m	14 km

From here you can turn west and in four days reach Chanota which is on the Chamba-Dharamsala trek – see Treks from Chamba for details. The days' walks are:

Day 7	Bara Dhangal-Dhardi	21 km
Day 8	Dhardi-Naya Graun	24 km
Day 9	Naya Graun-Holi	16 km
Day 10	Holi-Chanota	13 km

Alternatively you can turn east, and a day's trek will bring you to the Manali Pass treks described under Treks from Manali. There are a number of possible routes down to Manali.

DHARAMSALA (population 12,000)

The hill station of Dharamsala is actually split into two totally separate parts. Close to the snowline the town is built along a spur of the Dhauladhar range and varies in height from 1250 metres at the Civil and Depot Bazaar up through Kotwali Bazaar and Forsyth Ganj to McLeod Ganj at close to 1800 metres. There's quite a temperature variation between the top and bottom.

As in other hill stations there is a wide variety of short and long walks, but Dharamsala has the additional attraction of its strong Tibetan influence. It was here that the Dalai Lama and his followers fled after the Chinese invasion of Tibet. For the serious student of Tibetan culture there's the monastery up at McLeod Ganj and the school of Tibetan studies and its library, one of the best in the world for studying Tibet and its culture, about midway between McLeod Ganj and the lower town.

For the not so serious, McLeod Ganj is a small freak centre with lots of Tibetan-run hotels and restaurants, all the menu favourites, low prices, crowds of western travellers – another Kathmandu in fact. McLeod Ganj is full of colour and energy: those little Tibetan terriers (yappy but spry) scoot around everywhere; in the middle of the main street there's a small temple with a giant prayer wheel; and you may even catch a glimpse of the Dalai Lama cruising by in his Mercedes.

Of course Dharamsala was originally a British hill resort and one of the most poignant memorials of that era is the pretty Church of St John in the Wilderness. It is only a short distance below McLeod Ganj and has beautiful stained glass windows. Here Lord Elgin, viceroy of India, was buried after his death in 1863.

There are many fine walks and even finer views around Dharamsala. The sheer rock wall of Dhauladhar rises behind McLeod Ganj. From the road up from the lower town it seems just an arm's length away.

From McLeod Ganj interesting walks include the two-km stroll to Bhagsu where there is an old temple, a spring, slate quarries and a small waterfall. It's a popular picnic spot and you can continue on beyond here on the ascent to the snowline. Dal Lake is a bit brown and dull; it's about three km from McLeod Ganj, just beyond the Tibetan Children's Village School. A similar distance from McLeod Ganj takes you to the popular picnic spot at Dharamkot where you'll also enjoy a very fine view.

An eight-km trek from McLeod Ganj will bring you to Triund at 2827 metres. Situated at the foot of Dhauladhar, it's another five km from Triund to the snowline at Ilaqa. There is a *Forest Rest House* for overnight accommodation.

Orientation & Information

The Tourist Office is in the lower town close to the bus stand and the Dhauladhar Hotel. It's about 10 km from the lower part to McLeod Ganj – a 45-minute ride for Rs 1.75. Walking down, take the steep short cut round to the left of the monastery by the Dalai Lama's home, and down to the Cantonment by the library. It takes about 30 to 40 minutes to walk. There are lots of Tibetan handicrafts up in McLeod Ganj – small square Tibetan carpets for around Rs 100, bigger five-by-three (feet) carpets for Rs 750.

The Tibetan Medical Centre, just across from the Koko Nor Hotel, will be of interest to followers of alternative medicine.

Places to Stay

Dharamsala Dharamsala has two accommodation areas – the lower part of town and the upper part known as McLeod Ganj. In the lower part Dharamsala's

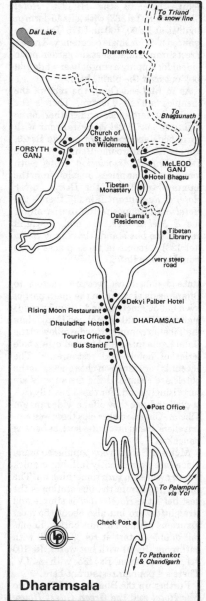

Dharamsala

deluxe hotel is the HPTDC *Hotel Dhauladhar* (tel 363) with a Rs 15 dorm or doubles at Rs 90, 100 and 175. Prices are reduced 25% for single occupancy. There's a restaurant and a pleasant garden patio – ideal for sipping a sunset beer while you look out over the plains below.

As in McLeod Ganj, the pick of the cheapies are all Tibetan. There's the extremely laid-back and rather basic *Rising Moon Hotel & Restaurant* with dorm beds and rooms for around Rs 20, some with bathroom. Behind it is the *Tibet United Association Hotel* with rooms at similar prices. Just left from the fountain you'll find the *Dekyi Palber Hotel & Restaurant*. Finally there's the *Hotel Simla* opposite the tourist office, the *B Mehra* (tel 241) and, downhill beyond the bus stand, the *Sun & Snow* (tel 123) – rooms in these places range from Rs 30 to Rs 75.

McLeod Ganj Most western visitors to Dharamsala stay not in the main part of town but 500 metres (and 10 km by road) higher up the hill at McLeod Ganj. Here the Tibetan community who followed the Dalai Lama into exile have set up a whole series of hotels and restaurants. The accent is very much on cheapness but the hotels are clean and the restaurants are surprisingly good. For those heartily sick of dhal and rice they offer a wide range of Tibetan-Chinese dishes plus those western-travellers' menu favourites such as banana pancakes.

McLeod Ganj is very popular so many places are permanently full, but a quick wander will soon turn something up. The Bhagsu road from the bus station is the best bet – the *Hotel Tibet* is simple and straightforward but also about the most luxurious of the Tibetan hotels. Rooms (all doubles) start at Rs 20, Rs 40 with bathroom, Rs 60 with hot water, Rs 100 deluxe and even Rs 135 with a TV! There's a popular restaurant here.

Further up the Bhagsu road the *Koko Nor Hotel* and the *Green Guest House*

both have rooms at Rs 15 to Rs 20. The *Tibetan Himalaya Restaurant* has rooms a few rupees cheaper. At the *Namgyal Guest House* there are rooms for Rs 25, 30 and 35.

Away from the Bhagsu road is the very popular *Om Hotel*, just below the main street, with prices around Rs 20. On the main street the *Toepa Hotel* is also in the standard Rs 15 to Rs 20 price range.

For those determined to spend more, the Tourist Department has the *Hotel Bhagsu*, a couple of hundred metres out of town towards the monastery. There are dorm beds at Rs 15 and doubles at Rs 90, 125 and 175. At the other extreme, long-stay visitors can find accommodation out of town for just a few rupees a day.

Places to Eat

Dharamsala The *Rising Moon* is a friendly place with a long menu, good food, good music and amazingly slow service. There are various other small restaurants around town, or you can try the tourist bungalow restaurant in the *Hotel Dhauladhar*. As with accommodation, there's more choice of places to eat up at McLeod Ganj.

McLeod Ganj The *Om Restaurant* is one of the most popular places to eat with low prices, good food and and an easygoing atmosphere. *Hotel Tibet* also has a good, busy restaurant. Continuing up the Bhagsu road, the *Tibetan Himalaya Restaurant* has good pancakes and excellent Tibetan bread amongst other things. The *Green Restaurant* is also very popular. These are all good meeting places too.

There are a number of places along the main street from the bus stop. Right on the corner is *Sangey Passang*, a popular place for breakfast with good tea and superb brown bread at Rs 4 a loaf. Next door is *Tashi's Restaurant*, and a couple of doors down is the popular little *Café Shambhala* – eating is an important activity in Dharamsala!

Other places include the *Tibet Memory*

	distance	time	fare
Manali	253 km	12½ hrs	Rs 50-60
Kulu	214 km	10	Rs 45-55
Simla	317 km	10	Rs 54
Chandigarh	248 km	9	Rs 36-40
Pathankot	90 km	3½	Rs 14
Delhi	526 km	14	Rs 60-90
Jullundur	197 km	8	Rs 35

DALHOUSIE

Sprawling over and around five hills, Dalhousie was, in the British era, a sort of 'second string' hill station. A place where those who could not aspire to Simla retired to. Founded by Lord Dalhousie, the town has some pleasant walks. Today Dalhousie also has a busy population of Tibetan refugees – if you take the footpath from Subhash Chowk to Gandhi (GPO) Chowk you'll pass brightly painted pictures the Tibetans have carved into low relief on the rocks. There is a nice little Tibetan refugee handicrafts shop with carpets in some quite different designs (unusual animals like rabbits and elephants). It's by GPO Chowk. With its dense forest, old English houses and colourful Tibetans, Dalhousie can be a good place to spend some time.

About two km from GPO Chowk along Ajit Singh Rd, Panchpulla (five bridges) could be quite a pleasant spot but it's disfigured by the series of horrible concrete steps and seats built over the stream. Along the way there's a small, and easily missed, freshwater spring known as Satdhara. Kalatop is 8.5 km from the GPO and offers a fine view over the surrounding country. There's a *Forest Rest House* here. Lakhi Mandi, 15 km out and at around 3000 metres, has stupendous mountain views.

Orientation & Information

The Tourist Office (tel 36) is by the bus stand but Dalhousie is very scattered. Most shops are clustered around GPO Chowk, while the 'town' – if Dalhousie can be spoken of as such a thing – is crowded down the hillside close to Subhash Chowk. The houses almost stand on top of one another.

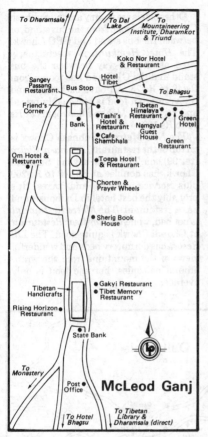

Restaurant and *Friend's Corner*, which is good for a drink either downstairs or up on the roof. Overall, food in McLeod Ganj is a pleasant change from the India norm.

Getting There

If you're taking an early-morning bus it's probably an idea to spend the night down in the lower town – all the buses start from there. There are about four buses a day to Simla and Delhi, just one or two to other destinations. Approximate distances, times and fares from Dharamsala are:

Places to Stay & Eat

Dalhousie has plenty of hotels, although a fair number of them have a run-down, left-by-the-Raj feel to them. Close to the bus stand, the old *Mount View Hotel* which burned down in 1985 is being replaced. Rooms will cost Rs 100 in season. A little up the hill there's the tourist bungalow, now known as the *Hotel Geetanjali*, with doubles at Rs 75.

Just below the bus stand the *Youth Hostel* (a sign points the way) has dorm beds at Rs 15, or if you're a student or YHA member just Rs 6. Up above the Mount View there's the *Grand View Hotel* (tel 23) with rooms at Rs 110/180 including meals. The *Dalhousie Club* has rooms from Rs 40 and also a self-contained cottage. All these places, but particularly the Youth Hostel, have fine views of the mountains in the distance. There are also the *Glory* and *Lall's*, two real cheapies, close to the bus stand.

Other hotels are mainly around Subhash Chowk, up the road from the bus stand, or between the bus stand and GPO Chowk. The *Hotel Hemkunt* is spectacularly sited about half-way between the bus stand and the GPO and has rooms from Rs 40 to Rs 75. All have bathrooms and the vegetarian food is reasonably priced and very good. *Mehar's* has rooms at Rs 30 to Rs 100.

The *New Metro* at Subhash Chowk is on top of the restaurant. *Aroma-n-Claire* (tel 99), on The Mall beyond Subhash Chowk, has doubles at Rs 140 to Rs 200 plus service charges and taxes. It's probably the best hotel in Dalhousie and has a restaurant. The *Metro Restaurant* is not bad, while the *Amritsar Restaurant* at Chandi Chowk is quite good. The *Lill Resort* has dormitory beds and wonderful views of the mountains from the wrap-around balconies, but the food is only average.

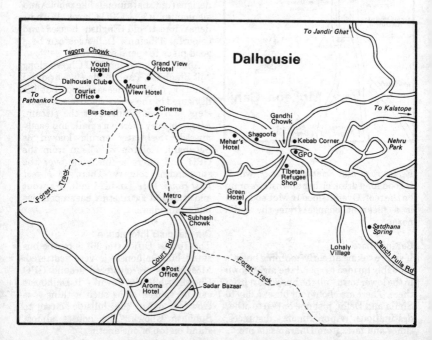

Getting There

Pathankot, 80 km away, is the usual departure point for buses to Dalhousie. The trip takes about four hours and costs Rs 14 to Rs 17 depending on the bus company. Jammu-Pathankot buses cost Rs 10 and take three hours.

From Pathankot on to Dharamsala costs Rs 14; there are some straight-through buses from Dalhousie to Dharamsala, but although the 'short route' is much more direct on the map it is a bad road and the trip very time-consuming. The 8.30 am bus arrives around 5 pm! Only 30 km is unsurfaced.

KHAJJIAR

This grassy 'marg' is 22 km from Dalhousie. Over a km long and nearly a km wide, it is ringed by pine trees with a lake in the middle. There's a golf course here and a golden-domed temple.

Places to Stay

The tourist bungalow, *Hotel Devdar*, has dorm beds at Rs 15 and doubles at Rs 50 to Rs 100. Other alternatives are the *Youth Hostel* with dorm beds at Rs 10 and the *PWD Rest House*.

Getting There

You can walk there in a day, or there are buses run by the Tourist Office and much cheaper regular buses for Rs 6 one way.

CHAMBA

Situated 56 km from Dalhousie, on beyond Khajjiar, Chamba is at 926 metres – quite a bit lower than Dalhousie so it's warmer in the summer. Perched on a ledge, high above the River Ravi, it has often been compared to a mediaeval Italian village and is famed for its many temples. Three of these carved and engraved temples are dedicated to Shiva and three to Vishnu.

Chamba also has the Bhuri Singh Museum with an interesting collection relating to the art and culture of this region – particularly the miniature paintings of the Basohli and Kangra schools. The Rang Mahal palace in the upper part of town had been badly fire damaged. Some of its murals are now in the museum.

Chamba has a grassy promenade known as the *chaugan* – it's only 75 metres wide and less than a km long. The village is a busy local trading centre for villagers from the surrounding hills and each year is the site for the Minjar festival in August, with a colourful procession and busy crowds of Gaddi Churachi, Bhatti and Gujjar people. An image of Lord Raghuvira leads the procession and other gods and goddesses follow in palanquins.

Chamba is the centre of the Gaddis, traditional shepherds who move their flocks up to the high alpine pastures during the summer and descend to Kangra, Mandi and Bilaspur in the winter. The Gaddis are found only on the high range which divides Chamba from Kangra.

Places to Stay

The *Akhand Chandi* (tel 171) on College Rd has rooms at Rs 35 to Rs 40 for singles, Rs 55 for doubles, and there's a restaurant. The HPTDC has two tourist bungalows – the *Hotel Champak* with doubles at Rs 30 to Rs 50, dorm beds at Rs 10; and the *Hotel Iravati* at Rs 75, 100 and 150 for doubles. The *Janta Hotel* is fairly cheap. Meals are available in the *Ravi View Café*.

Getting There

Taxis and jeeps can be hired in Dalhousie but they're expensive. The local bus is Rs 10 and takes two hours, or you can walk there in two days, resting overnight in Khajjiar. From Chamba trekkers can make an interesting, but hard-going, trek through Bharmour and Triund to Dharamsala. Or via Tisa you can trek all the way into Lahaul or Kashmir.

TREKS FROM CHAMBA

There are a number of interesting treks from Chamba, both short out-and-back treks and longer treks to places like Dharamsala. Shorter treks include the eight-km walk to Sarol, 24 km to Bandal or 40-km trek to Chhatrari. The temple of Devi Adi Shakti here is dedicated to the goddess of primaeval energy. Chhatrari is on the route to Brahmaur.

Brahmaur (Brahmpura)

Vehicles can cover the whole 65 km from Chamba to Brahmaur, although the last 16 km from Kharamukh requires four-wheel drive. Buses run the first distance. Also known as Shivbhumi, this is the heart of the Gaddi's land. There are some very old temples grouped in a compound known as the *chaurasi* in Brahmaur, and accommodation is available in a *Forest Rest House*.

From Brahmaur it is about 80 km to Dharamsala and takes about six days to walk:

Day 1	Brahmaur-Chanota	22 km
Day 2	Chanota-Kuarsi	13 km
Day 3	Kuarsi-Chatta	13 km
Day 4	Chatta-Lakagot	10 km
Day 5	Lakagot-Triund	6 km
Day 6	Triund-Dharamsala	13 km

The Chatta to Lakagot sector crosses the 4300-metre Indrahas Pass with fine views over the Kangra Valley.

From Brahmaur you can make the 35-km trek to Manimahesh Lake at 3950 metres. This important pilgrimage spot is at the base of the 5575-metre Manimahesh Kailash. Thousands flock here on the 15th day after Janamashtami, which falls in August or September each year.

Pangi Valley

Kilar, 167 km north-east of Chamba, is in the deep and narrow gorge of the Chenab River. Here you are in the high Himalaya, in the scenic but lightly populated Pangi Valley, between the Pangi and Zanskar ranges. From Kilar you can trek north-west to Kishtwar in Jammu & Kashmir, or turn east about half-way to Kishtwar and cross the Umasi La Pass into the Zanskar Valley, or trek south-east to Keylong and Manali.

THE KULU VALLEY

The fertile Kulu Valley rises northward from Mandi at 760 metres to the Rohtang Pass at 3915 metres, the gateway to Lahaul & Spiti. In the south the valley is little wider than a precipitous gorge, with the Beas River (pronounced Bee-Ahs) sometimes a sheer 300 metres below the narrow road. Further up the valley widens and its main part is 80 km long, though rarely more than a couple of km wide. Here there are stone fruit and apple orchards, rice paddies and wheat fields along the valley floor and lower slopes, and deodar forests higher up the slopes, with snow-crowned rocky peaks towering behind. The main towns, Kulu and Manali, are in this fertile section of the valley.

The light-complexioned people are friendly, devout, hard working and relatively prosperous. The men wear the distinctive Kulu cap, a pillbox with a flap around the back in which they may stick flowers. The women wear lots of silver jewellery and long garments of homespun wool secured with great silver pins; they are rarely without a large conical-shaped basket on their backs, filled with fodder, firewood or even a goat kid.

Other people of the valley are the nomads (Gaddis) who take their flocks of black sheep and white goats up to the mountain pastures in the early summer and retreat before the winter snows. You don't really know what wool smells like until you've travelled in an over-crowded bus of rain-soaked villagers. The valley also has many Tibetan refugees, some running restaurants and hotels in Manali, but many others in camps near the rivers, prayer flags fluttering. The Tibetans are great traders – you'll find them in all the bazaars – but many work in road gangs, whole families toiling together.

Himachal Pradesh Top: Children in Malana, Kulu Valley (HF)
Left: Hotel signs at McLeod Ganj, Dharamsala (HF)
Right: Bringing the crops in, Kulu Valley (HF)

Jammu & Kashmir Top: Kashmiri children on the Pahalgam-Aru walk (TW)
Bottom: A 'supermarket' shikara on Dal Lake in Kashmir (TW)

KULU (population 10,000)

At an altitude of 1200 metres Kulu is the district headquarters but it is not the main tourist centre; that honour goes to Manali. Nevertheless there are a number of interesting things to see around Kulu and some fine walks to be made. The town, which sprawls on the western bank of the Beas, is dominated by the grassy maidans at the southern side of town. They're the site for Kulu's fairs and festivals, in particular the colourful Dussehra festival, from which the Kulu Valley gained the name 'valley of the gods'.

Dussehra Festival

The Dussehra Festival, in October after the monsoons, is celebrated all over India but most particularly in Kulu. The festival starts on the 10th day of the rising moon, known as 'Vijay Dashmi', and continues for seven days. Dussehra celebrates Rama's victory over the demon king Ravana but in Kulu the festival does not include the burning of Ravana and his brothers, as in other places around India.

Kulu's festival is a great gathering of the gods from temples all around the valley. Approximately 200 gods are brought from their temples down to Kulu to pay homage to Raghunathji from the temple in Raghunathpura in Kulu. The festival cannot commence until the powerful goddess Hadimba, patron deity of the Kulu rajas, arrives from Manali. Like the other gods she is pulled in her own temple car or *rath*, and Hadimba likes speed so she has to be pulled as fast as possible. She not only arrives before all the other gods but also leaves before them. Another curiosity is that the Jamlu god from Manali comes to the festival but does not take part – this god stays on the opposite side of the river from the Dhalpur maidan.

The Raghunathji chariot is brought down, decked with garlands and surrounded by the other important gods.

Priests and the descendants of Kulu's rajas circle the *rath* before the car is pulled to the other side of the maidan. There is great competition to aid in pulling the car since this is a very auspicious thing to do. The procession with the cars and bands takes place on the evening of the first day of the festival. During the following days and nights of the festival there are dances, music, a market and festivities far into the night. On the penultimate day the gods assemble for the 'Devta darbar' with Raghunathji, and on the final day the temple car is taken to the riverbank where a small heap of grass is burnt to symbolise Ravana's destruction. Raghunathji is carried back to his main temple in a wooden palanquin.

Orientation & Information

The Tourist Information Office (tel 7) is by the maidan at the southern side of town. There's a bus and taxi stand here, and all the HPTDC accommodation units and several of the hotels are around the maidan, but the main bus station is in the northern area of town.

Temples

Some of the main temples in and around Kulu include:

Raghunathji Temple About a km from Dhalpur in Raghunathpura (or Sultanpur), the temple of the principal god is actually not very interesting. It is only open from 5 pm.

Jagannathi Devi Temple In the village of Bhekhli, three km from Kulu, it's a stiff climb but from the temple there are fine views over the town. Take the path off the main road to Akhara bazaar after crossing the Sarawai bridge.

Vaishno Devi Temple This small cave has an image of the goddess Vaishno and is four km along the Kulu-Manali road.

Bijli Mahadev Temple A jeepable road links Kulu with Bijli Mahadev, eight km away. Across the river, high on a projecting bluff, the temple is surmounted by a 20-metre-high rod said to attract blessings in the form of lightning. At least once a year the image of Shiva in the temple is supposed to be shattered by lightning, then miraculously repaired by the temple *pujari*.

Bajaura On the main road, 15 km south of Kulu, the famous temple of Basheshar Mahadev has fine stone carvings and sculptures. There are large image slabs facing north, west and south. There is a *PWD Rest House* in Bajaura.

Places to Stay

Only a little south of the maidan, but a short walk off the main road, the HPTDC tourist bungalow has been officially renamed the *Hotel Sarvari* (tel 33). It's a well-run place with doubles at Rs 100 and Rs 150 and dorm beds at Rs 15, although they don't seem very keen on people using the dorm beds.

The Tourist Office is right beside the maidan, opposite the bus halt. Beside it is the generally full *Rest House* and between the two are *'Aluminium Huts'* – comfortable enough at Rs 30 for a double but you can do better elsewhere.

Right behind the Tourist Office is the excellent *Bijleshwar Hotel*. This friendly and well-run place has doubles with own bathroom from Rs 40. Up the road behind the Maidan, the *Hotel Daulat* (tel 358) has very plain doubles with bath for Rs 60. Right beside the Maidan, also on this side, is the new *Hotel Rohtang* with rooms from Rs 30 to Rs 80.

Across the other side of the maidan, towards the river, are the cheap and basic *Sa Ba Guest House* and *Fancy Guest House*. There are other rock-bottom places at the Manali end of town, by the main bus stand, such as the *Kulu Valley Lodge* or the *Central Hotel*.

Finally, the *Ashok Travellers' Lodge* (tel 79) is to the left of the road just as you enter town from the south. It has six rooms with singles at Rs 200, doubles at Rs 250 to Rs 300. In the off-season they're Rs 100 and Rs 150 to Rs 200 respectively.

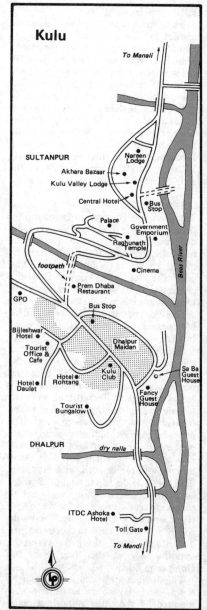

Kulu

Places to Eat

The *Tourist Bungalow* has the usual sort of dining hall. By the Tourist Office there's the *Tourist Department Monal Café* with good light meals and snacks, but sometimes painfully slow service. Just downhill from the main street is the *Prem Dhaba*.

Getting There

Air There is an airport at Bhuntar, 10 km south of Kulu, and Vayudoot fly Delhi-Chandigarh-Kulu twice weekly. The fare is Rs 500 from Delhi.

Bus & Taxi There are direct buses to Kulu from Dharamsala, Simla (235 km), Chandigarh (270 km) or Delhi (512 km). Kulu-Chandigarh buses do not go via Simla. All these direct buses continue to Manali, 42 km further north.

A direct bus from Delhi is supposed to take 15 hours but probably takes a good bit more. Regular buses cost Rs 57, but there are various classes right up to the HPTDC super-deluxe bus which costs nearly Rs 250. Chandigarh-Kulu takes about 12 hours and costs Rs 45. Plenty of taxis make the trip up from the plains, but count on around Rs 750 or more for Simla or Chandigarh to Kulu or Manali. A Kulu-Manali taxi would cost about Rs 150; it's Rs 6.50 by bus.

AROUND KULU

You can make some interesting excursions from Kulu to the adjoining valleys which run into the Kulu Valley. See also the Treks from Manali section.

Parvati Valley

The Parvati Valley runs off north-east from Bhuntar, which is south of Kulu. You can travel up the valley by bus. Manikaran is built near sulphur hot springs and it's interesting to watch the locals cook their food in the pools of hot water at the Sikh temple. There are also hot baths, separate for men and women, at the temple and, of course, free accom-

modation. Hot water is nice to have in Manikaran because the valley is so steep-sided that not much sun gets through.

There are a lot of French and Italian freaks in the area; they've been in Manikaran so long 'it's hard to tell them from the locals. Unfortunately there is much friction between freaks and locals although the locals are friendly and helpful'. There's great trekking and wonderful scenery here.

Places to Stay Rooms in shops or houses are easily available if you ask around. The *Phoda Family House*, near the bridge, is an excellent place where quite a few travellers stay. There are big, clean rooms with rope beds for Rs 15 and less. And there's a private sulphur rock bath indoors. You can get food and expensive, though beautiful, wild bee honey.

In the local chai shops try *kihr*, a delicious rice dessert made with milk, sugar, fresh coconut and sultanas. It's said that Shiva sat and meditated for 2000 years at Kihr Ganga, a 30-km walk from Manikaran.

Getting There Buses from Kulu to Bhuntar take 1½ hours and cost about Rs 4. Bhuntar to Manikaran is another 1½ hours for about the same price.

Sainj Valley

The area from Aut to Sainj is not as beautiful as the other valleys but it has a charm of its own. Plus it's very untouristed so the locals love visitors. There is no accommodation as such, but rooms are easily available if you ask around.

Getting There A bus from Bhuntar to Aut takes an hour and costs Rs 3.

KULU TO MANALI

There are a number of interesting things to see along the 42 km between Kulu and Manali. There are actually two Kulu-Manali roads. The direct road runs along the west bank of the Beas, while the much rougher and more winding east bank road is not so regularly used, but does take you via Naggar with its delightful *Rest House*.

Raison

Only eight km from Kulu there's a camping place on the grassy meadow beside the river. It's a good base for treks in the vicinity. There are 12 *Tourist Huts* at the site with doubles at Rs 40 that can be booked through the Kulu Tourist Office.

Katrain

At about the mid-point on the Kulu-Manali road, this is the widest point in the Kulu Valley and is overlooked by the 3325-metre Baragarh peak. Two km up the road on the left side is a trout hatchery.

Places to Stay There's a small *Rest House* and a pleasant HPTDC tourist bungalow known as the *Hotel Apple Blossom* with doubles at Rs 50, cottages at Rs 80 to Rs 150 and a larger three-bedroom cottage at Rs 275. It's an interesting alternative to staying in Kulu or Manali. There's also the very expensive riverside *Span Resort* (tel 40), which costs Rs 450/640 for singles/doubles with all meals.

Naggar

High above Katrain, on the east bank of the river, is Naggar with its superb castle hotel. Transport to the castle is a little problematical but the effort is worthwhile, for it is a stunning place to look around or stay at. At one time Naggar was the capital of the Kulu Valley and the castle was the Raja's headquarters. Around 1660 Sultanpur, now known as Kulu, became the new capital. The quaint old fort is built around a courtyard with verandahs right round the outside and absolutely stupendous views over the valley. It feels an eon away from any of the hassles India can dish up! Inside the courtyard is a small temple containing a

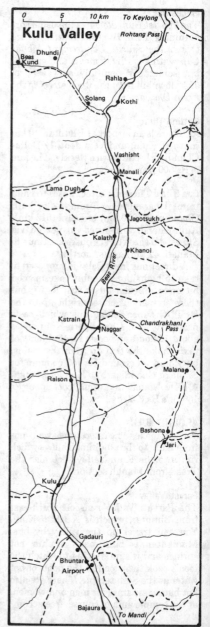

slab of stone with an intriguing legend about how it was carried there by wild bees.

There are a number of interesting temples around the castle. The grey sandstone Shiva temple of Gauri Shankar is at the foot of the small bazaar below the castle and dates from the 11th or 12th century. Almost opposite the front of the castle is the curious little Chatar Bhuj temple to Vishnu. Higher up the hill is the pagoda-like Tripura Sundri Devi Temple and higher still, on the ridge above Naggar, the Murlidhar Krishna temple.

Also up the hill above the castle is the Roerich Gallery, a fine old house displaying the artwork of both Professor Nicholas Roerich (who died in 1947) and his son. Its location is delightful and the views over the valley are very fine.

Places to Stay The HPTDC *Castle Hotel* has just six double rooms at Rs 60 plus a larger family suite for Rs 90. It's deservedly popular and often booked out; the Kulu Tourist Office can make reservations but plan ahead. There's also a *Forest Rest House* in Naggar.

Kulu-Manali Transport

Buses run regularly along the main road for Rs 6.50; the trip takes under two hours. There are only one or two buses daily on the east side of the river and the trip can take a long time, up to two hours from Manali to Naggar alone. Add another 1½ hours from Naggar to Kulu. The combined fare is not much different than the direct one, though.

Cars can get to Naggar by crossing the river at Patlikuhl near Katrain – the bridge is very narrow. Or you can get off the Kulu-Manali bus there and walk up. It's six km up to the castle by road but much less on foot, although the path is very steep.

MANALI (population 2500)

Manali, at the top end of the Kulu Valley, is the main resort in the valley. It's

beautifully situated and there are many pleasant walks around the town as well as a large number of hotels and restaurants. It's also very much a 'scene' – at the height of the tourist season it's packed out with Indian and western tourists. Smaller villages around Manali have semi-permanent 'hippy' populations. The nearby country and villages are truly beautiful and not to be missed.

Orientation & Information

Manali has one main street where you'll find the bus stop and most of the restaurants. The Tourist Office (tel 25) is further down the street towards the river and opposite the taxi stand. Hotels are scattered all over town, some of them within easy walking distance of the bus stop, some of them, like the Tourist Bungalow, a good long stretch uphill. It stays cold in Manali until surprisingly late in the season; there may still be snow on the ground in late March.

Warning Manali is famous for its marijuana, which is not only esteemed by connoisseurs, but also grows wild all around. However, there have been a number of police busts on the more popular cheap hotels so smokers should beware. In fact, recently the police have become a damn nuisance over drugs in all respects. On leaving Manali while researching this 3rd edition I was stopped on the edge of town by the police, and my bag (but not me) was comprehensively searched. We've also had reports of local dope sellers turning in the people they just sold stuff to.

Hadimba Devi Temple

The temple of the goddess Hadimba, who plays such a major part in Kulu's annual festival, is a sombre, wooden temple in a clearing in the dense forest about 2½ km from the Tourist Office. It's a pleasant stroll up to the temple, which was built in 1553. Also known as the Dhungri Temple, it's the site of a major festival in May of each year.

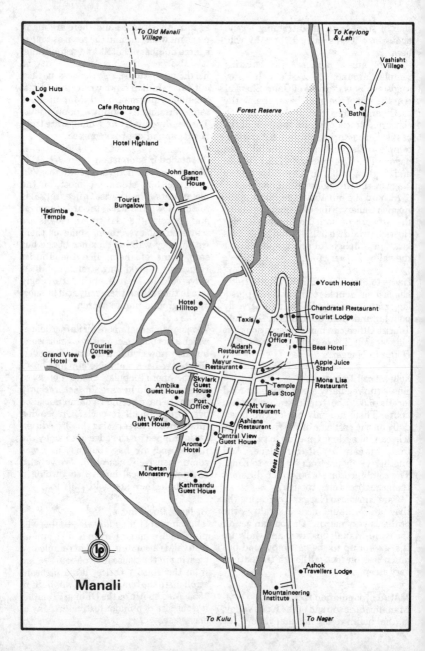

To Old Manali Village

To Keylong & Leh

Vashisht Village

Log Huts

Cafe Rohtang

Forest Reserve

Baths

Hotel Highland

John Banon Guest House

Tourist Bungalow

Hadimba Temple

Youth Hostel

Hotel Hilltop

Chandratal Restaurant
Tourist Lodge

Taxis

Tourist Office

Grand View Hotel

Tourist Cottage

Adarsh Restaurant

Beas Hotel

Mayur Restaurant

Apple Juice Stand

Skylark Guest House

Temple
Bus Stop

Mona Lisa Restaurant

Ambika Guest House

Post Office

Mt View Restaurant

Mt View Guest House

Ashiana Restaurant

Central View Guest House

Aroma Hotel

Beas River

Tibetan Monastery

Kathmandu Guest House

Ashok Travellers Lodge

Manali

Mountaineering Institute

To Kulu

To Nagar

Vashisht

Vashisht is an extremely picturesque little place, clinging to the steep hillside about three km out of Manali. On foot the distance is a bit shorter since you can follow paths up the hillside, while cars have to wind up the road. It's worth a wander round to admire the solid architecture and colourful people.

On the way up to the village you'll come upon the Vashisht Hot Baths, where a natural sulphur spring is piped into a modern bath-house. They're open from 7 am to 1 pm, 2 to 4 pm and 6 to 10 pm. Cost for a 20-minute soak is Rs 5 for the ordinary baths (plus Rs 1 per extra person) or Rs 10 for the larger family (plus Rs 2.50 per extra person). If you've suffered a long, rough bus trip up to Manali there's no better way to soak away the strain. There are some local public hot baths further up from the the commercial ones.

Old Manali Village

The current town of Manali is actually a new creation which has superseded the old village, a couple of km away. Follow the trail off the road out of town, cross the cascading Manalsu stream over a very picturesque bridge, and then climb up to this interesting little village.

Around the Town

Manali is basically a place to get out and walk around, but there are a few sites of interest in the town itself. The colourful, pleasant new Tibetan Monastery has a carpet-making operation; you can buy carpets and other Tibetan handicrafts here.

The Tourist Office will arrange a fishing licence if you want to try your luck with the Beas River trout – you'll need your own gear though.

Tours

In season there are daily bus tours to the Rohtang Pass (Rs 60) and Naggar Castle (Rs 35).

Places to Stay

Manali Prices in Manali are very variable. In May-June they go sky high, in July-August they drop down a bit and again in September-October. In December-January-February, when there are no tourists at all, the prices are very low. At that time people come down from the hills and can get rooms for Rs 100 to Rs 150 a month which, at the height of the season, can cost that much for a few days! Those same rooms go up to Rs 15 a day in March-April, then Rs 40 at peak times, even Rs 60 at peak-peaks. When the costs go up Manali's resident traveller population tends to head out to the villages around Manali.

Even at the height of the season it's possible to rent a house for Rs 100 to Rs 150 a month, but conditions are likely to be a little primitive. There may be a stove but you'll need your own cooking utensils, and you may have a long walk to get water. In the pits of the off season many places close completely.

The *Youth Hostel* is just outside the town, across the river on the road to Vashisht and the Rohtang Pass. Dorm beds are Rs 5.

Back in town are a number of places run by the HPTDC. They can all be reserved through the tourism development officer, phone 25. The tourist bungalow, now officially renamed the *Manalsu Hotel*, is up the hill a little from the town; it's totally covered in ivy and quite a picture. Doubles cost Rs 90 to Rs 150. There are also *Tourist Cottages* and *Log Huts* – these are self contained, with their own kitchens and living rooms and modern facilities. Nightly costs range from Rs 250 right up to Rs 850 for the flashier Log Huts.

The riverside *Tourist Lodge* is much simpler, with bare rooms with four beds costing Rs 60 plus additional charges for bedding. There's also the *Hotel Beas*, right beside the Beas River, with singles at Rs 50, doubles at Rs 75 to Rs 125. Finally there's a four-room *Tourist Inn* at

Rs 75 to Rs 100. All this HPTDC accommodation tends to be fairly heavily booked, so plan ahead.

The ITDC have an *Ashok Travellers' Lodge* (tel 31) in Manali, a little out of town on the Naggar road. There are just 10 rooms with singles at Rs 200 (Rs 100 off season) and doubles at Rs 250 to Rs 300 (Rs 150 to Rs 200). The season starts on 1 April. The doubles are really suites with a sitting room and fine views of the snow-capped peaks around Manali.

In the private-hotel sector your best bet is simply to wander around and have a look at a few, bearing in mind that prices are likely to be variable, depending on when you're there and how many rooms happen to be vacant. Some names to start with include the *Skylark Guest House* (rooms Rs 50 to Rs 75), *Kathmandu Guest House* (behind the gompa, Rs 40 to Rs 60), *Sunflower Hotel* (similarly priced), *Mount View Guest House* (Rs 50 to Rs 100, a pleasant place), *John Banon Guest House* (tel 35, more expensive at around Rs 200 including meals) and so on. Travellers have also recommended the *Capital Hotel*, the *Shivalik Hotel* just behind the Civil Hospital, the pleasant *Rising Star Hotel* and *Meadows Hotel*. The Tourist Office can supply a more-or-less complete list of Manali's 40 or so hotels and guest houses, together with their official prices.

Around Manali Vashisht, the picturesque little village just above the hot baths, is a centre for Manali's longer-term western residents. There are several places to stay and eat although it's much more active in the summer season. There are other villages around Manali with summer populations of westerners – you just have to ask around and talk to people; don't expect to find something on the first day.

Places to Eat
Manali is remarkably well endowed with places to eat. On the main street the *Adarsh Restaurant* has good food and, in winter, it's pleasantly warm from the stove in the middle of the room. Just off the main street the smaller *Mayur Restaurant* also has a stove and a similar menu. It's particularly popular for breakfast.

Right beside the bus station is the popular little *Monalisa Restaurant*, which appears to close down in the off season. There are quite a few other places around Manali – like the *Mount View Restaurant*, just down from the bus stop, for excellent Chinese-Tibetan food and good music to eat it by.

The cavernous *Chandratal Restaurant* is run by the HPTDC with the standard tourist department menu. Up the hill overlooking the river, the HPTDC's *Café Rohtang* has fine views. Between the Tourist Office and the bus stop there's a little place with delicious and cold bottled apple juice. Smaller places seem to come and go in Manali – *Peter & Patricia's* had home-made jam, peanut butter and muesli. The *Blue Dragon* is a small café near the bus stand.

Getting There
Chandigarh is the usual departure point for buses to Manali if you're coming up from Delhi. Chandigarh-Manali is 312 km, takes about 14 hours by bus (nine by car) and costs Rs 50. Mandi-Manali is 5½ hours for Rs 19. There are also direct buses from Simla (247 km) for Rs 50 and from Dharamsala (253 km) for a similar fare. It's a long trip to Manali from wherever you start! From Kulu there are frequent buses for Rs 6.50.

In season the HPTDC runs super-deluxe buses from Simla (Rs 100), Chandigarh (Rs 125) and Delhi (Rs 250), but even the fastest buses take 15 hours to Delhi. You can fly to Kulu from Delhi or Chandigarh; see the Kulu section for details.

AROUND MANALI

Jagatsukh

About 12 km north of Naggar and six km south of Manali on the east bank road, Jagatsukh was another former capital of Kulu State until it was supplanted by Naggar. There are some very old temples in the village, particularly the shikhara-style Shiva temple. Shooru village, nearby, has the old and historically interesting Devi Sharvali temple.

Other Places

Arjun Gufa, with a legendary cave, is near the village of Prini, five km from Manali. A cold-water spring, named the Nehru Kund after former Prime Minister Nehru, is six km from Manali on the Keylong road. The Solang Valley is a bit north-west of Manali, but before Kothi. The glacier nearest Manali is here, only 13 km from town. You can get here by taking a bus to Palchan village, and then following the jeep track.

Kothi is a pretty little village, 12 km from Manali on the Keylong road. Its *Rest House* is a popular resting place for trekkers heading for the Rohtang Pass. It's surrounded by glaciers and mountains, two old tea stalls and nothing else. Doubles have attached bathroom, two big beds, carpets and a balcony. The food is good and it's quiet. There are very fine views from Kothi, and the Beas River flows through a very deep and narrow gorge at this point. The Rahla Falls, 16 km away, are another popular excursion.

The Rohtang Pass to Lahaul is 51 km from Manali and is a favourite day excursion or trekking trip apart from its role as the gateway into Lahaul. The view of mountains from the pass crest is very spectacular. In early summer and late autumn the pass can be subject to strong winds and snow blizzards in the afternoon – so try to cross it early.

TREKS FROM MANALI

There are many treks from Manali, either round trip or further afield.

Malana Valley

It is less than 30 km from Katrain, on the Kulu-Manali road, across the Chandrak-hani Pass to the interesting Malana Valley. The pass is at less than 3600 metres and is open from March to December. Malana can also be reached from the Parvati Valley – either from Manikaran over the 3150-metre Rashoi Pass or from Jari. Jari is connected with the Kulu Valley by a jeepable road and is only 12 km from Malana.

There are about 500 people in Malana and they speak a peculiar dialect with strong Tibetan elements. The 6001-metre peak of Deo Tibba overlooks Malana and from the top of the Chandrakhani Pass you can see snow-capped peaks on the border of Spiti to the east. Starting from Naggar, it is possible to climb up to the pass summit and return to Naggar on the same day – but it is fairly hard going.

Local legends relate that when Jamlu, the main deity of Malana, first came there he bore a casket containing all the other Kulu gods. At the top of the pass he opened the casket and the breeze carried the gods to their present homes, all over the valley.

At the time of the Dussehra festival in Kulu, Jamlu plays a special part. He is a very powerful god with something of the demon in him. He does not have a temple image so, unlike the other Kulu gods, has no temple car to be carried in. Nor does he openly show his allegiance to Raghunathji, the paramount Kulu god, like the other Kulu gods. At the time of the festival Jamlu goes down to Kulu but stays on the east side of the river, from where he watches the proceedings. Every few years a major festival is held for Jamlu in the month of Bhadon. In the temple there is a silver elephant with a gold figure on its back which is said to have been a gift from Emperor Akbar.

It takes three days to trek from Naggar to Malana, spend a day there, then return to Naggar or continue to Jari. A seven-day trek Manali to Malana could be:

Day 1	Manali-Rumsu	2060 m	24 km
Day 2	Rumsu-Chandrakhani	3650 m	8 km
Day 3	Chandrakhani-Malana	2100 m	7 km
Day 4	Malana-Kasol	1580 m	8 km
Day 5	Kasol-Jari	1560 m	15 km
Day 6	Jari-Bhuntar	900 m	12 km
Day 7	Bhuntar-Manali	by bus	

The trek can be extended by continuing from Jari along the east bank of the Beas via Bijli Mahadev, with its famous temple, and Naggar to Manali.

Deo Tibba Trek

This is an easy trek east of Manali to the base of 6000-metre Deo Tibba. The trek offers fine views and pleasant walking through forests and alpine meadows. From Manali you start via Jagatsukh to Khanol and Chhika (not the Chhika north-east of Manali on the way to the Hamta Pass). Seri is at the base of Deo Tibba and from here you can make an excursion to Lake Chandratal.

Day 1	Manali-Khanol	8 km
Day 2	Khanol-Chhika	6 km
Day 3	Chhika-Seri	5 km
Day 4	Seri-Bhanara	14 km
Day 5	Bhanara-Manali	

Chandratal

This circular trek from Manali over the Hamta, Chandratal and Baralacha La passes is one of the finest in Himachal Pradesh and takes 11 days to complete. From Manali you start at Jagatsukh, on the east bank road to Kulu. At the village of Prini you turn north-east and climb up to Chhika – a steep climb at first but later it becomes easier over grassy downs and pleasant meadows.

The next day involves a long and wearisome climb over the 4270-metre Hamta Pass, then a quick descent to Chhatru on the Chandra River. The pass is generally open from June to September, although it may be open longer. There are fine views of Deo Tibba (6001 metres) and Indrasan (6221 metres) from the pass.

Two days' walk takes you through Chhota Dara to Batal, where the route branches off north-east to Spiti through the Kunzam Pass. There are magnificent views of the Bara Shigri glacier from here.

Succeeding days take you north over the Chandratal (lake of the moon) Pass, the Likhim Gongma (upper) and Likhim Yongma (lower), and the Topko Yongma before you reach the Keylong-Leh road at the Baralacha la Pass. Three more days of walking bring you to Keylong, where you can bus back to Manali. It may be possible to get a bus earlier and shorten the time to Keylong.

Day 1	Manali-Chhika	2960 m	21 km
Day 2	Chhika-Chhatru	3360 m	16 km
Day 3	Chhatru-Chhota Dara	3740 m	16 km
Day 4	Chhota Dara-Batal	3960 m	16 km
Day 5	Batal-Chandratal	4270 m	18 km
Day 6	Chandratal-Likhim Yongma	4320 m	12 km
Day 7	Likhim Yongma-Topko Gongma	4640 m	11 km
Day 8	Topko Gongma-Baralacha la	4885 m	10 km
Day 9	Baralacha la-Patsio	3820 m	19 km
Day 10	Patsio-Jispa	3320 m	14 km
Day 11	Jispa-Keylong	3340 m	21 km

Parvati Valley

The Parvati Valley is now accessible by bus from Kulu or Bhuntar (Rs 8 from Kulu). The last part of the Malana Valley trek descends the Parvati Valley to its junction with the Kulu Valley. An interesting alternative is to ascend the Parvati Valley to its upper reaches; it is much wilder and more rugged than the Kulu Valley. From Bhuntar, near the junction of the Beas and Parvati rivers, you can visit the Adibrahma temple in Khokhan, about a km from Bhuntar, or the pagoda-shaped temple of Triyugi Narain in Diar village. The first day's walk takes you to Jari, on a hillside high above the Parvati River and near where the Malana River joins the Parvati.

It's a short trek to Kasol with its pleasantly sited *Tourist Hut* (doubles Rs 25) and *Forest Rest House*. Good trout fishing here. Manikaran is a very short walk but the river is wild at this point. Manikaran's famous hot spring, at close to boiling temperature, is near the river as you enter the village. There are several guest houses in Manikaran. Be sure not to miss the evening worship accompanied by harmonium, tablas and singing.

It's a long walk, rough and stony at first, to Pulga, where again there is a very pleasant *Forest Rest House*. The pretty little village is 300 metres above the river and is the usual end point of this trek, although hardy and well-equipped trekkers could continue further up the Parvati River and cross the Pin Parvati Pass into Spiti. Khirganga, just 10 km upstream from Pulga, has more hot springs. Or you could explore the Tos Nullah, which joins the Parvati River from the north-east, just upstream from Pulga.

Day 1	Bhuntar-Jari	15 km
Day 2	Jari-Kasol	8 km
Day 3	Kasol-Manikaran	3 km
Day 4	Manikaran-Pulga	16 km

Seraj Valley to Narkanda

The Seraj Valley branches off south-east from the southern end of the Kulu Valley and makes an interesting alternative route between the Kulu Valley and Simla. Aut, on the main road between Kulu and Manali, is the starting point; and Larji, at the junction of the Sainj and Tirthan rivers, is the first stop. There's a *PWD Rest House* here and good fishing is available during March, April and October – when the Sainj River runs clear.

In the lower reaches of the Tirthan Valley is Banjar, with an interesting group of temples. Continuing south you reach Shoja, where there is another *PWD Rest House* with a scenic setting. From here you can make excursions to the old ruined fort of Raghupur Gahr where there

is a beautiful view; even Simla can be seen on a clear day. Another interesting day trip from Shoja is to the beautiful flower-strewn meadow of Dughu Thatch.

From Shoja you cross the 3135-metre Jalori Pass. The view of the surrounding mountains from the pass crest is stunning. Khanag, at 2500 metres, is on the other side of the pass and has a *PWD Rest House*. Ani, again with a *PWD Rest House*, is the next stop and from here you can either continue straight on to the main highway where buses run to Narkanda and Simla, or turn east to Nirmand with its temple of Devi Ambika. There is a bus service between Ani and Luhri, on the north side of the Sutlej River.

Day 1	Aut-Larji	5 km
Day 2	Larji-Banjar	20 km
Day 3	Banjar-Shoja	13 km
Day 4	Shoja-Khanag	10 km
Day 5	Khanag-Ani	20 km
Day 6	Ani-Luhri	15 km

As an alternative to this route, you can branch off at Banjar and follow the Tirthan River to Narkanda. Goshaini is the first day's walk from Banjar, but you can get that far by bus. It's then a gentle climb to Bathad where there is a *PWD Rest House*, followed by a very hard climb to the Bashleo Pass at 3250 metres, 13 km on. A steep descent takes you to Sarahan, only three km further.

There is another beautifully situated *Rest House* here. From here it is two easy, pleasant walks to Arsu (another *PWD Rest House*) and Rampur on the main road.

Day 3	Banjar-Goshaini	13 km
Day 4	Goshaini-Bathad	16 km
Day 5	Bathad-Sarahan	16 km
Day 6	Sarahan-Arsu	13 km
Day 7	Arsu-Rampur	13 km

Solang Valley

There are a number of treks from Manali to the Solang Valley looping back to

Manali, either from the north or the south. A seven-day trek takes you to Beas Kund, the source of the Beas River, and across the remains of dying glaciers. The first day takes you to Solang Nullah, where there is a mountain hut with rooms for 80 people. There are ski-runs here in the winter.

The second day's trek continues to Dhundi, where you can see Deo Tibba and Indrasan from this alpine plateau and admire the many alpine flowers. The third day takes you to Beas Kund and back, and the next day continues to Shagara Dugh with a good chance of seeing red bears along the way. On the fifth day you reach Marrhi over a small 4000-metre pass with views to the Kulu Valley and Rohtang Pass. Finally, on Day 6 you continue down the Keylong-Manali road to Kothi, via the Rahla waterfall. On the last day you return to Manali.

Day 1	Manali- Solang Nullah	2480 m	11 km
Day 2	Solang Nullah- Dhundi	2840 m	8 km
Day 3	Dhundi-Beas Kund & back	3540 m	10 km
Day 4	Dhundi- Shagara Dugh	3600 m	8 km
Day 5	Shagara Dugh- Marrhi	3380 m	10 km
Day 6	Marrhi-Kothi	2500 m	6 km
Day 7	Kothi-Manali	13 km	

Manali Pass Treks

These two treks continue on from the Solang Valley trek but loop back to Manali from the south. They are both difficult treks involving long, hard ascents over rugged terrain. The first alternative continues from Beas Kund over the Tentu Pass (an arduous and tiring climb) to Phulangot through an uninhabited region. You then cross the Manali Pass to Rani Sui and go via Bhogi Thatch to Kalath, a little south of Manali on the Kulu-Manali road.

Day 3	Dhundi- Beas Kund	3540 m	6 km
Day 4	Beas Kund-Tentu Pass	4996 m	4 km
Day 5	Tentu Pass- camping ground	3856 m	10 km
Day 6	camping ground- Phulangot	4000 m	6 km
Day 7	Phulangot- Manali Pass	4988 m	6 km
Day 8	Manali Pass- Rani Sui	4200 m	8 km
Day 9	Rani Sui- Bhogi Thatch	2800 m	6 km
Day 10	Bhogi Thatch- Kalath	1800 m	12 km

The second alternative is to join the Manalsu Nullah from the Manali Pass and follow this straight back to Manali – up to Day 8 this trek is the same as the alternative one.

An easy trek, which includes the last two days of the alternative one, involves going to Rani Sui via Lama Dugh. You leave Manali via the Hadimba Temple and climb through pleasant country to the camp site at Lama Dugh. On the second day you cross the Thanpri Tibba ridge to Rani Sui, and then Day 3 and Day 4 are as Day 9 and Day 10 above.

Day 1	Manali- Lama Dugh	3380 m	6 km
Day 2	Lama Dugh- Rani Sui	4200 m	5 km

LAHAUL & SPITI

Only since 1977 have visitors been permitted to cross the Rohtang Pass to Keylong in Lahaul. Just 117 km from Manali, this is a Tibetan region, quite unlike the Kulu Valley. The Rohtang Pass has the same 'gateway' nature as the Zoji La Pass between Kashmir and Ladakh. The region is bounded by Ladakh to the north, Kulu to the south and Tibet to the east. All of Spiti and a large chunk of Lahaul is off-limits to visitors. You cannot continue up the jeep road from Keylong to Leh in Ladakh, but you can make the long and difficult trek from Keylong to Padum in the Zanskar valley and from there into Ladakh. See the Lonely Planet guides *Kashmir, Ladakh & Zanskar* or *Trekking in the Indian Himalaya* for information on treks in this region.

Climate

As in Ladakh, little rain gets over the high Himalayan barrier so Lahaul & Spiti are dry and, for the most part, barren. The air is sharp and clear and the warm summer days are followed by cold, crisp nights. Beware of the burning power of the sun in this region – you can get burnt very quickly even on cool days. The heavy winter snow from September to May closes the passes except for a few months of each year.

Culture

The people of Lahaul & Spiti follow a Tibetan form of Tantric Buddhism with a panoply of demons, saints and followers. The monasteries, known as *gompas*, are colourful places where the monks or lamas lead lives ordered by complicated regulations and rituals. There are many similarities between these people and the Ladakhis, further north. The people of Spiti are almost all Buddhists of Tibetan stock, but Lahaul is split roughly 50:50 between Buddhists and Hindus.

Rohtang Pass

The 3915-metre Rohtang Pass is the only access into Lahaul and is open only from June to September each year, although trekkers can cross the pass a little before it opens for vehicles. During the short season it's open, there are regular buses from Manali to Keylong. The Tourist Office operates a daily Rs 60 bus up to the pass, mainly for tourists to 'see the snow'. It's a very spectacular trip over the pass.

Keylong

Keylong is the main town in the Lahaul & Spiti region; there are a number of interesting monasteries within easy reach of this oasis-like town. The old Kharding Monastery, formerly the capital of Lahaul, overlooks Keylong, only 3.5 km away. Other monasteries include Shashur (three km), Tayal (six km) and Guru Ghantal (11 km).

Ten minutes' walk from the bus stand past the Tibetan village, the Tibetan Centre for Performing Arts presents a video on Tibet several times a week in season.

Places to Stay & Eat The *HPTDC Tourist Bungalow* has just three doubles at Rs 50, but during the summer season they set up tents which cost Rs 30. There is also a *PWD Rest House*. The *Lamayuru* serves up good food and music in a pleasant atmosphere, although the Rs 25 rooms are dark and dirty.

Other Places

Gondhla, with its eight-storey castle of the Thakur of Gondhla and the historically significant gompa, is a short distance before Keylong on the Manali-Keylong road. You can trek back to Gondhla from Keylong, cutting across the loop the road makes. Between Gondhla and Keylong is Tandi, where the Chandrabagha or Chenab River meets the road.

Following the Chenab Valley to the north-west towards Kilar (see treks from Chamba) will bring you to Triloknath with its six-armed white-marble image of Avalokitesvara. Close by is the village of Udaipur, with a finely carved wooden temple from the 10th or 11th century which is dedicated to Mrikula Devi.

Spiti

The 4500-metre Kunzam Pass connects the Lahaul and Spiti valleys. Eventually a road will be completed from Kaza, the principal Spiti village, south-east through Samdoh to meet the Hindustan-Tibet road (see Kinnaur). There are few settlements in this barren, high region. Kaza (or Kaja) is the main village. Slightly north-west of it is Kibar (or Kyipur), which at 4205 metres is reputed to be the highest village in the world. Tabo Kye and Dhankhar are two of the most important gompas.

Getting There
Although the pass may be open by mid-May, a safer date is mid-June. The bus trip takes eight hours and costs Rs 30. It's 475 km from Manali to Leh via Keylong, but you need special permission to use this road.

KINNAUR
Most of this region, in the valley of the Sutlej River extending up towards the Tibetan border, is off limits without permission from the Ministry of Foreign Affairs in New Delhi. Without a permit you can only go as far as the Wangtu Bridge just beyond Nachar.

Rampur
Beyond Narkanda, 140 km from Simla, Rampur is the gateway to the region. It's the site for a major trade fair in the second week of November each year, and was once a major centre for trade between India and Tibet. There are direct buses from Simla to Rampur, which has a *PWD Rest House*.

Sarahan
The last village in the district before entering Kinnaur, Sarahan is a beautiful little place with the interesting Bhimkali temple which shows a curious blend of Hindu and Buddhist architecture.

Nachar
Situated on the old Hindustan-Tibet road, this picturesque village is four km

from the Wangtu Bridge, beyond which you need a permit to continue. As in Sarahan, the village is on the old road which has been replaced by the nearby new Hindustan-Tibet road. There's a *Rest House* in the orchards.

Tapri & Choltu
Only 15 km further up the valley from Nachar, three roads meet at this scenic spot. One is the main road continuing up the valley to Kalpa. The second is the old road, also continuing to Kalpa via Rogi. The third is a small road which crosses the river through Choltu and Kilba to the Sangla Valley. Choltu has a pleasant *Rest House*.

Sangla
The main village in the Sangla Valley is 18 km from Karcham, on the new Hindustan-Tibet road, and can be reached by jeep or on foot. It's a good base for trekking and there's a *Rest House*.

Kalpa
The main town in Kinnaur is close to the foot of 6050-metre-high Kinnaur Khailash. This is the legendary winter home of Lord Shiva; during the winter the god is said to retire to his Himalayan home here and indulge his passion for hashish. In the month of Magha – January-February – the gods of Kinnaur supposedly meet here for an annual conference with Lord Shiva.

Kalpa has a *Rest House* and from here you can continue on the northern side of the river to Puh and Namgia, close to the Tibetan border. Only 14 km from Kalpa, the tiny village of Pangli has a small *Rest House* and a fine view of Kinnaur Khailash. Rarang, eight km further on, is another centre for trade to Tibet.

Jammu & Kashmir

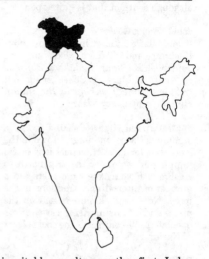

Population: 5 million
Area: 222,236 square km
Capital: Srinagar
Main languages: Kashmiri, Dogri

The state of Jammu & Kashmir, J&K for short, is a region of widely varying people and geography. In the south Jammu is a transition zone from the Indian plains to the Himalaya. Correctly the rest of the state is Kashmir but in practice this title is reserved for the beautiful Vale of Kashmir, a large Himalayan valley in the north of the state. Here the people are predominantly Muslim and in many ways look towards Pakistan and central Asia rather than towards India.

Finally, to the north-east is the remote Tibetan plateau region known as Ladakh. Only recently opened to foreign tourists, Ladakh is primarily Buddhist and Tibetan in its culture and a very clear contrast to the rest of Kashmir, indeed to the rest of India. Sandwiched between the Kashmir and Ladakh regions is a long narrow valley known as Zanskar. This valley is even more isolated than Ladakh and has still been visited by comparatively few westerners, although this will change as the new jeep road into the valley is extended and improved.

Jammu & Kashmir has always been a centre of conflict for independent India. When India and Pakistan became independent there was much controversy over whether the region should go to one country or the other. The population was predominantly Muslim but J&K was not a part of 'British India', it was a 'princely state' and as such the ruler had to decide which way his state would move – to Muslim Pakistan or Hindu India. As *Freedom at Midnight* relates, the indecisive Maharaja only made his decision when a Pakistani-prompted invasion was already crossing his borders and the inevitable result was the first Indo-Pakistan conflict. Since that first collision Kashmir has remained a flashpoint for relations between the two countries. The region is now divided approximately two-thirds to India, one-third to Pakistan, but both countries claim all of it. Furthermore, Kashmir's role as a sensitive border zone applies not only to Pakistan. In 1962 the Chinese invaded Ladakh, prompting India to rapidly reassess their position in this remote and isolated region.

For visitors J&K is one of India's most popular states. Kashmir is simply beautiful and a spell on a houseboat on Dal Lake is one of India's real treats. Kashmir also offers some delightful trekking opportunities and unsurpassed scenery. Ladakh, on the other hand, offers a chance to study a region which, in today's world, is probably even more Tibetan than Tibet. It's one of the most other-worldly parts of India. No special permits are required to visit Kashmir or Ladakh today, but your movements are restricted in that you are not allowed to approach within a certain distance of the border. In Ladakh this means you are not allowed more than a mile north of the Srinagar-Leh road, although south of that is quite open.

Lonely Planet Guides

If you'd like a lot more information about Kashmir and Ladakh, look for our guidebook *Kashmir, Ladakh & Zanskar* by Rolf & Margret Schettler or our trekking guide *Trekking in the Indian Himalaya* by Garry Weare.

JAMMU (population 160,000)

Jammu is the second largest town in the state, but for most travellers it is just a jumping-off point for the trip north to Kashmir. If you have time there are a number of interesting attractions in the town. Note that Jammu is still on the plains and in the summer is a sweltering, uncomfortable contrast to the cool heights of Kashmir.

Orientation & Information

Jammu is actually two towns – the old town sits on a hilltop overlooking the river. Here you'll find most of the hotels and the Tourist Reception Centre where the Tourist Office is located and from where upper-class buses depart for Kashmir. Down beside the hill is the station for buses to other parts of north India and for the lower-class buses to Srinagar. Finally, several km away across the river is the new town of Jammu Tawi where the railway station is located.

Things to See

The Raghunath Temple is in the centre of the city, only a short stroll from the Tourist Reception Centre. This large temple complex was built in 1835 but is not especially interesting, although it makes a good sunset silhouette. Also centrally located, the Rambireswar Temple, dedicated to Lord Shiva, dates from 1883. Situated in the Gandhi Bhavan, by the New Secretariat, the Dogra Art Gallery has an important

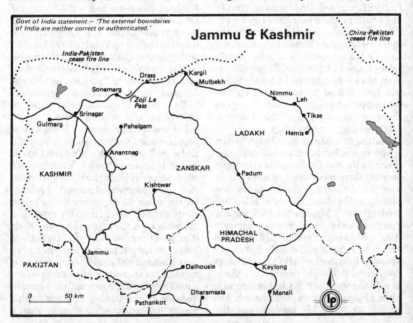

Govt of India statement – 'The external boundaries of India are neither correct or authenticated.'

Jammu & Kashmir

India-Pakistan cease fire line

China-Pakistan cease fire line

Drass · Kargil
Sonamarg · Mulbekh
Zoji La Pass · Nimmu · Leh
Srinagar · Tikse
Gulmarg · Pahalgam
LADAKH · Hemis
Anantnag
KASHMIR · ZANSKAR
Padum
Kishtwar
HIMACHAL PRADESH
Jammu
PAKISTAN · Dalhousie · Keylong
0   50 km
Dharamsala · Manali
Pathankot

LP

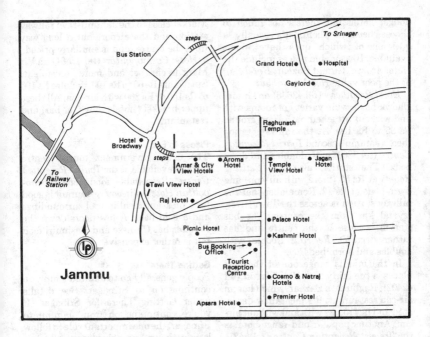

collection of miniature paintings including many from the locally renowned Basohli and Kangra schools. The gallery is open from 7.30 am to 1 pm in summer and from 11 am to 5 pm in winter but closed on Mondays. Admission is free.

On the northern outskirts of town, just off the Srinagar road, is the Amar Mahal Palace, a curious example of French architecture. The palace museum has a family portrait gallery and another important collection of paintings.

Places to Stay

If you're en route to Srinagar and arrive in Jammu by train (as most people do) then you have two choices. The first is not to overnight in Jammu but to take one of the buses which wait at the railway station for arriving trains and go straight to Srinagar. These buses stop overnight at Banihal, below the Banihal Tunnel, and continue on to Srinagar the following day.

Accommodation in Banihal is generally in the *Tourist Lodge* and is very basic.

The second choice is to stay overnight in Jammu and take a bus to Srinagar the first thing next day. Since they start earlier in the day, these buses complete the journey to Srinagar in one day. If you decide to stay overnight then it's important to first find yourself a room and then book a ticket on the bus. Don't hang about, as competition for both can be fierce during the tourist season. If you're coming down from Srinagar it's even more necessary to rush to find a room, as you arrive late in the day when spare rooms may be at a premium.

At the bottom of the market the popular *Tawi View Hotel* (tel 47301), Maheshi Gate is the best of the bunch with doubles with bath for Rs 35. Another simple but clean place is the *Hotel Kashmir*, Vir Marg, with bathless doubles at a similar price. There are many other budget hotels but there's not much to choose between them; it's usually a question of which ones have rooms available. Reasonable places include the *Hotel Aroma*, Gumat Bazaar; *Hotel Raj*; or the poor value *Hotel Aryabhat*.

Hotel Broadway (tel 43636) on Gumat Chowk has a wide variety of rooms with and without attached bath from around Rs 35 to Rs 100. At the railway station there's Jammu's second *Tourist Reception Centre* (tel 8803) with doubles and dorm beds. The station also has *Retiring Rooms* at Rs 50 (more with air-con) and dorm beds at Rs 12. Remember that the railway station is across the Tawi River, several km from the centre. The bus station is close to the centre and has rather decrepit *Retiring Rooms* with doubles and dorm beds.

In the middle range one of the best places is the fairly new *Hotel Jagan* (tel 42402), Raghunath Bazaar, which has an air-con restaurant. It's pleasantly decorated and has rooms with and without air-con. Another popular mid-range hotel is the *Tourist Reception Centre* (tel 5421) on Vir Marg. All the rooms have attached bathrooms and prices vary from Rs 60 to Rs 125 but the dormitory is grim. There is also a restaurant.

Across Vir Marg from the Tourist Reception Centre the much improved *Hotel Premier* (tel 43234) is one of the best places around the centre with rooms at Rs 75/100 or with air-con for Rs 135/175. Also on Vir Marg the *Natraj Hotel* (tel 7450) has rooms with attached bath at Rs 45/90. Down the road from the Raghunath Temple are a number of bottom and middle-bracket hotels. Other middle-bracket hotels include the hotels *Gagan, Amar* and *City View* (tel 46120), all in Gumat Bazaar.

At the top end of the market is the *Hotel Jammu Ashok* (tel 46154, 42084) on the outskirts of town to the north, close to the Amar Mahal Palace. Rooms are Rs 120/175 or Rs 265/350 with air-con. *Hotel Asia Jammu Tawi* (tel 6373-5) is in Nehru Market close to the Jammu Tawi railway station and the airport but a long way from the centre, and is similarly priced.

Hotel Cosmopolitan (tel 47561) on Vir Marg is cheaper and more convenient. Singles are Rs 60 to Rs 100, doubles Rs 100 to Rs 150 or Rs 200 with air-con. All these upper-bracket hotels have a bar and restaurant.

Places to Eat

The usual government tourist centre menu is available at the *Tourist Reception Centre*. Reasonable food. The *Cosmopolitan Hotel's* air-con restaurant is good for a pleasant meal in cool surroundings and a cold beer. A few doors down the *Premier* has Chinese and Kashmiri food but is rather expensive.

Getting There

People generally go to Jammu simply to continue on to Srinagar. See details under Getting There for Srinagar. If you're continuing on from Jammu to Srinagar, the one important rule to follow is to get your bus ticket as soon as you arrive. See the Places to Stay section above for information on the 'head straight through' or 'overnight in Jammu' decision.

Southbound there are frequent buses from Jammu to Amritsar (Rs 18), Pathankot (Rs 10, three hours) and other cities. Pathankot is the jumping-off point for Dharamsala, Dalhousie and the other Himachal Pradesh hill stations.

Getting Around

Jammu has metered taxis, auto-rickshaws, a minibus service and a tempo service between a number of points. From the railway station to the bus station costs Rs 1 by the new minibuses. The same trip by auto-rickshaw would be Rs 5 to Rs 7. It's only a short distance from the Tourist Reception Centre in the town centre to the bus station, say Rs 2 or Rs 3 by auto-rickshaw.

JAMMU-SRINAGAR

Although most people simply head straight through from Jammu to Srinagar, there are a number of places of interest between the two centres. Some can also be reached using Jammu as a base. Prior to the completion of the Jawarhar Tunnel into the Kashmir Valley, the trip from Jammu took two days with an overnight stop at Batote.

Akhnoor

The Chenab River meets the plains here, 32 km north-west of Jammu. This used to be the route to Srinagar in the Moghul era. Jehangir, who died en route to Kashmir, was temporarily buried at Chingas.

Basohli

Situated fairly close to Dalhousie, which is across the border in Himachal Pradesh, this is the birthplace of the Pahari miniature painting style.

Billawar, Sukrala, Babor & Permandal

All these places have ruined and uncompleted temples of some interest.

Surinsar & Mansar Lakes

East of Jammu, these lakes are picturesque and the scene for an annual festival at Mansar.

Vaishno Devi

This important cave temple is dedicated to the three mother goddesses of Hinduism. Thousands of pilgrims visit the cave each year after making a steep 12-km climb from the roadhead at Katra or a shorter and easier climb from a new road.

Riasi

Near this town, 80 km beyond Katra, is the ruined fort of General Zorawar Singh, renowned for his clashes with the Chinese over Ladakh. Nearby is a gurdwara with some interesting old frescoes and another important cave temple.

Ramnagar

The 'palace of colours' has many beautiful Pahari-style wall paintings. Buses run here from Jammu or Udhampur. Krimchi, 10 km from Udhampur, has Hindu temples with fine carving and sculpture.

Kud

This is a popular lunch stop on the Jammu-Srinagar route at 1738 metres. It's also popular in its own right as a hill resort and has a *Tourist Bungalow*. There's a well-known mountain spring, Swamai Ki Bauli, 1.5 km from the road.

Batote

Only 12 km further on, and connected to Patnitop and Kud by a number of footpaths, this hill resort at 1560 metres was the overnight stop between Jammu and Srinagar before the tunnel was opened. There is a *Tourist Bungalow*,

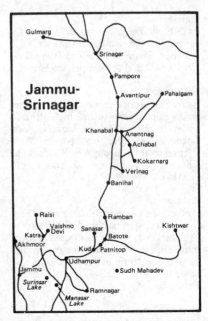

tourist huts and several private hotels. As in Kud, there is a spring close to the village – Amrit Chasma is only 2.5 km away.

Patnitop

At 2024 metres this popular hill station has many pleasant walks. Patnitop is intended to be the nucleus of tourist developments in this area. There are tourist huts, a *Rest House* and a *Youth Hostel*.

Sudh Mahadev

Many pilgrims visit the Shiva temple here during the annual July-August Asad Purnima festival which features three days of music, singing and dancing. Five km from Sudh Mahadev is Man Talai, where some archaeological discoveries have been made. An eight-km walking or jeep track leads to Sudh Mahadev from Kud or Patnitop.

Sanasar

At 2079 metres, this beautiful valley is a centre for the Gujjar shepherds each summer. There is a *Tourist Bungalow*, tourist huts and several private hotels.

Bhadarwah

Every two years a procession of pilgrims walks from this beautiful high-altitude valley to the 4400-metre-high Kaplash Lake. A week later the three-day Mela Patt festival takes place in Bhadarwah. There is a rest house in this scenic location.

Kishtwar

Well off the Jammu-Srinagar road there is a trekking route from Kishtwar to Srinagar. You can also trek from Kishtwar into Zanskar. There are many waterfalls around Kishtwar, and 19 km from the town is the pilgrimage site of Sarthal Devi.

Jawarhar Tunnel

During the winter months Srinagar was often completely cut off from the rest of India before this tunnel was completed. The 2500-metre-long tunnel is 200 km from Jammu and 93 km from Srinagar and has two separate passages. It's rather rough and damp inside. From Banihal, 17 km before the tunnel, you are already entering the Kashmiri region and people speak Kashmiri as well as Dogri. As soon as you emerge from the tunnel you are in the green, lush Vale of Kashmir. If you take a late bus from Jammu for Srinagar you will probably overnight at Banihal and stay in the rather primitive *Tourist Lodge*.

KASHMIR

This is one of the most beautiful regions of India. The Moghul rulers of India were always happy to retreat from the heat of the plains to the cool green heights of Kashmir, and indeed Jehangir's last words, when he died en route to the 'happy valley', was a simple request for 'only Kashmir'. The Moghuls developed the art of their formal garden style to its greatest heights in Kashmir and some of their gardens are beautifully kept even to this day.

One of Kashmir's greatest attractions is undoubtedly the Dal Lake houseboats. During the Raj period Kashmir's ruler would not permit the British (who were as fond of Kashmir's cool climate as the Moghuls) to own land here. So they adopted the superbly British solution of building houseboats – each one a little bit of England, afloat on Dal Lake. A visit to Kashmir, it is so often said, is not complete until you have stayed on a houseboat.

Of course Srinagar, Dal Lake and houseboats are not all there is to Kashmir. Around the edges of the valley are Kashmir's delightful hill stations. Places like Pahalgam and Gulmarg are pleasant in their own right and also good bases for trekking trips.

SRINAGAR (population 450,000)

The capital of Kashmir stands on Dal Lake and the Jhelum River, and is the transport hub for the valley as well as the jumping-off point for trips to Ladakh. Srinagar is a crowded, colourful city with a distinctly central Asian flavour. Indeed the people look different from those in the rest of India; and when you head south from Srinagar it is always referred to as 'returning to India'.

Orientation & Information

Srinagar is initially a little confusing since Dal Lake, which is so much a part of the city, is such a strange lake. It's actually three lakes, separated by dykes or 'floating gardens', and at times it's hard to tell where lake ends and land begins. On the lake there are houseboats that are definitely firmly attached to the bottom. And houses that look like they could float away. Most of the houseboats are at the southern end of the lake, although you will also find them on the Jhelum River and north on Nagin Lake.

The Jhelum River makes a loop around the main part of town, and a canal connecting the river with Dal Lake converts that part of town into an island. Along the south of this 'island' is the Bund, a popular walk. Here you will find the GPO and the handicrafts centre. The large Tourist Reception Centre is just north of the Bund and here the Tourist Office, Indian Airlines and the J&K Road Transport Corporation are located together with accommodation units and a rather poor restaurant. The Kashmir Tourist Office has had a poor reputation but they claim it is now much improved.

There are many restaurants, shops, travel agents and hotels in the island part of town. The more modern part of Srinagar stretches away south of the Jhelum while the older parts of town are north and north-west of here. The Boulevard, running alongside Dal Lake, is an important address in Srinagar.

Dal Lake

Much of Dal Lake is a maze of intricate waterways rather than a simple sheet of open water. The lake is divided into Gagribal, Lokut Dal and Bod Dal by a series of causeways. Dal Gate, at the city end of the lake, controls the flow of the lake water into the Jhelum River canal. Within the lake are two islands which are popular picnic spots. Silver Island (Sona Lank) is at the north end of the lake while Gold Island (Rupa Lank) is to the south. Both are also known as Char Chinar because they each have four chinar trees on them. There's a third island, Nehru Park, at the end of the main stretch of the lakeside Boulevard, but it is a miserable affair. North of here a long causeway juts out into the lake towards Kotar Khana, the 'house of pigeons', which was once a royal summer house.

The waters of Dal Lake are amazingly clear, considering what must be poured into them from the houseboats. Whether you're just lazing on your houseboat balcony watching the shikaras glide by, or visiting the Moghul gardens around the lake, there's plenty to see and do. A shikara circuit of the lake is a sybaritic experience not to be missed. A leisurely cruise around will take all day, including visits to the Moghul gardens, and cost about Rs 60. There's hardly a more leisurely and pleasurable way of getting into the swing of Srinagar. If your budget is tight you can circuit the lake yourself by bicycle. It's also possible to ride right across the lake on the central causeway.

Jhelum River & Bridges

The Jhelum flows from Verinag, 80 km south of Srinagar, to the Wular Lake to the north. It's wide, swift-flowing, muddy and picturesque as it sweeps through Srinagar. The river is famed for its nine old bridges, but new bridges have popped up between them. There are interesting mosques and other buildings near it; a stroll or bicycle ride through the narrow lanes near the river is rewarding.

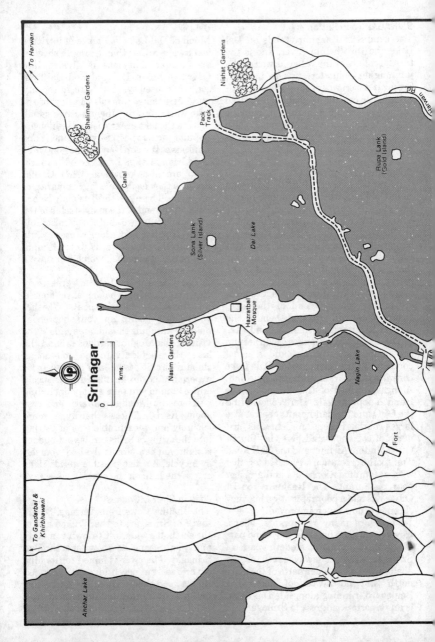

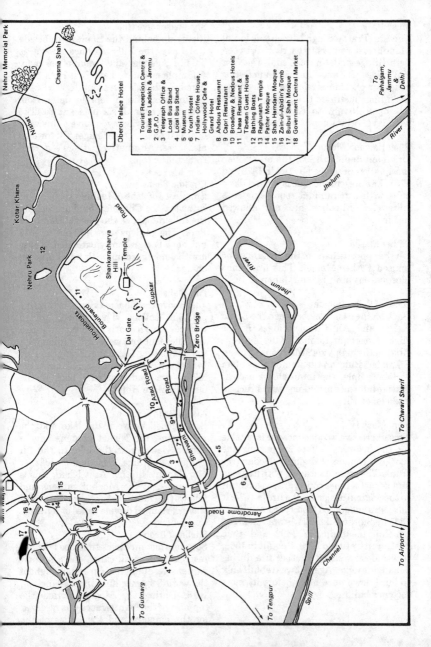

1 Tourist Reception Centre &
  Buses to Ladakh & Jammu
2 G.P.O.
3 Telegraph Office &
  Local Bus Stand
4 Local Bus Stand
5 Museum
6 Youth Hostel
7 Indian Coffee House,
  Hollywood Cafe &
  Grand Hotel
8 Andous Restaurant
9 Capri Restaurant
10 Broadway & Nedous Hotels
11 Lhasa Restaurant &
   Tibetan Guest House
12 Bathing Boats
13 Raghunath Temple
14 Pather Mosque
15 Shah Hamdan Mosque
16 Zain-ul-Abidin's Tomb
17 Bulbul Shah Mosque
18 Government Central Market

Museum

The Shri Pratap Singh Museum is in Lal Mandi, just south of the river between Zero Bridge and Amira Kadal, the first 'old' bridge. The museum has an interesting collection of exhibits relevant to Kashmir, including illustrated titles from Harwan. It's open 10 am to 5 pm, closed on Mondays. Admission is free.

Shah Hamdan Mosque

Originally built in 1395, the all-wooden mosque was destroyed by fire in 1479 and 1731. The present mosque is shaped like a cube with a pyramidal roof rising to a spire. Non-Muslims are not allowed inside.

Pather Masjid

On the opposite bank of the Jhelum is the unused Pather Masjid. This fine stone mosque was built by Nur Jahan in 1623.

Tomb of Zain-ul-Abidin

Back on the east bank between the Zaina Kadal and Ali Kadal bridges is the slightly decrepit tomb of King Zain-ul-Abidin, the highly regarded son of Sultan Sikander. Built on the foundations of an earlier temple, the tomb shows a clear Persian influence in its domed construction and glazed tiles.

Jami Masjid

This impressive wooden mosque is notable for the 300-plus pillars supporting the roof, each made of a single deodar tree trunk. The present mosque, with its green and peaceful inner courtyard, was rebuilt to the original design after a fire in 1674. It has had a chequered history: First built in 1385 by Sultan Sikander, it was enlarged by Zain-ul-Abidin in 1402 and then destroyed by fire in 1479. Rebuilt in 1503, it was destroyed by another fire during Jehangir's reign. Again it was rebuilt only to burn down once more before its most recent rebuilding.

Shankaracharya Hill

Rising up behind the Boulevard, beside Dal Lake, the hill was once known as Takht-i-Sulaiman, the Throne of Solomon. A temple is said to have first been built here by Ashoka's son around 200 BC, but the present Hindu temple dates from Jehangir's time. It's a pleasant stroll to the top, from where you have a fine view over Dal Lake – the Srinagar TV tower is also here. Alternatively there's a road right to the top.

Chasma Shahi

Smallest of the Moghul gardens at Srinagar, the Chasma Shahi are well up the hillside, above the Nehru Memorial Park. The gardens were laid out in 1632 but have been recently extended. These are the only gardens with an admission charge.

Pari Mahal

Just above the Chasma Shahi is this fine old Sufi college. The ruined, arched terraces have recently been turned into a very pleasant and well-kept garden with fine views over Dal Lake. From the Pari Mahal you can descend straight down the hill to the road that runs back to the Oberoi Palace Hotel.

Nishat Bagh

Sandwiched between the lake and the mountains, the Nishat gardens have a superb view across the lake to the Pir Panjal mountains. Designed in 1633 by Nur Jahan's brother Asaf Khan, this is the largest of the Moghul gardens and follows the traditional pattern of a central channel running down a series of terraces.

Shalimar Bagh

Set some distance back from the lake but reached by a small canal, the Shalimar gardens were built for Nur Jahan, 'light of the world', by her husband Jehangir in 1616. During the Moghul period the topmost of the four terraces was reserved for the emperor and the ladies of the court. During the May to October tourist season a nightly *son et lumière* (sound and light show) is put on in these beautiful gardens. The English performance is at 9 pm and tickets cost Rs 3 or Rs 7.50.

Hazratbal Mosque

This shiny new mosque is on the north-west shore of Dal Lake. The mosque enshrines a hair of the prophet, but to non-believers it will be most interesting simply for its stunningly beautiful setting on the shores of the lake with the snow-capped peaks as a backdrop.

Nasim Bagh

Just beyond the mosque, these gardens were built by Akbar in 1586. Today this oldest Moghul garden is used by an engineering college and is not maintained as a garden.

Nagin Lake

The 'jewel in the ring' is held to be the most beautiful of the Dal lakes and is ringed by trees. There are a number of houseboats on this quieter, cleaner lake. Ideal if you want to get away from it all.

Hari Parbat Fort

Clearly visible on top of the Sharika hill, to the west of Dal Lake, this fort was originally built between 1592 and 1598 during the rule of Akbar but most of the present construction dates from the 18th century. Visits are only possible with written permission from the director of tourism, so for most visitors the fort will remain just a pleasant backdrop. At the southern gate there is a shrine to the sixth Sikh Guru.

Pandrathan Temple

This small but beautifully proportioned Shiva temple dates from 900 AD and is in the military cantonment area on the Jammu road out of Srinagar.

Harwan

At the northern end of Dal Lake, archaeologists have discovered an unusual ornamented brick pavement near Harwan. Examples of these bricks can be seen in the Srinagar museum. The water supply for Srinagar is pumped from here and piped along the causeway across the lake.

Places to Stay

Although houseboats are a prime attraction of a stay in Srinagar, there are also plenty of hotels in all price categories. The tourist centre would like to handle all the houseboat booking but there is no reason why you shouldn't just go out to the lake and look around for yourself. Booking through the tourist centre only means you get less choice in the matter and pay a higher price. Srinagar is, however, notorious for its houseboat touts. They'll grab you at the airport, hassle you as you walk through town, even try to snare you right back in Jammu! Even at the height of the season it's wise to treat tales of 'every houseboat is full, better take mine right now' with healthy scepticism. Don't consider any houseboat until you've actually been out and looked at it for yourself. It may sound terrific on paper but turn out to be a miserable dump overdue for downgrading to a lower category. Or a fine place in a terrible location.

Houseboats There is no greater escape from the noise and hassle of Srinagar, a typically noisy Asian city, than the superbly relaxing houseboats. As soon as you get out on the lake traffic, pollution and hassles fade away. Basically most houseboats are the same. There's a small verandah at one end where you can sit and watch the world pass by. Behind this is a living room, usually furnished in British '30s style. Then there is a dining room and beyond that two or three bedrooms, each with attached bathroom. Officially houseboats come in five categories, each with an officially approved price for singles/doubles with and without meals.

	with meals	lodging only
deluxe or 5-star	Rs 265/390	Rs 180/270
A class	Rs 180/265	Rs 110/170
B class	Rs 120/205	Rs 75/120
C class	Rs 80/140	Rs 35/ 50
D class or 'donga boat'	Rs 55/ 75	Rs 55*

*for whole boat

In practice these 'official prices' are a bit meaningless. For a start there is a wide variance between boats – some are 5-star and others **5-STAR**! A good C class boat can be better than a poor A class boat. Also, most houseboats are managed in groups of three or more. You can be sure the food is not going to differ materially from the best boat in the group to the worst. Plus, of course, there is competition. With so many houseboats (there are hundreds of them) a little negotiation is inevitable.

To find a houseboat, go down to the shikara ghats along the lakeside and announce that you want one. Either there will be somebody there with a boat available or you can hire a kid with a shikara to paddle you around the boats to ask. Generally you can get away with paying at least the price level for the category below each boat – for an A class boat pay B class prices. If you decide to miss a meal, say lunch, each day that can generally be negotiated into a lower price. Check if shikara trips to shore are included; they should be. This is Kashmir so pin down as many details as possible. Check what breakfast is going to be, for example – exactly how many eggs? Check if they'll supply a bucket of hot water for washing each morning – Kashmir can be chilly.

It's virtually impossible to recommend a particular boat; there are so many, they all only have a few rooms and there are so many variable factors. A pleasant shikara man – who runs you back and forth between boat and shore, makes tea, supplies hot water and so on – can make a nondescript boat into a pleasant one. A pleasant boat can be ruined by a poor cook. Or simply having some pleasant fellow houseboaters to chat with in the evening can make all the difference. Even on the best boats the food can get rather monotonous but there are plenty of 'supermarket' boats cruising by if you need soft drinks, chocolate, toilet paper, hashish or any other of life's necessities.

A peaceful life out on the lake depends, to some extent, on avoiding the attentions of the salesmen who continually paddle by. If you don't want to spend your whole time going through everything from woodcarvings to carpets, embroidery to papier mâché, it's necessary to be very firm and decisive with these people. You can always retreat from the houseboat verandah to the more secluded roof, but why should you have to? Equally important is the attitude of the houseboat owners who rake off a handy little commission from everything that gets sold on their houseboat. On some houseboats you may actually find that the service, food or general attitude take a disastrous dip if you don't spend, spend, spend. The only answer to this policy is to move to a better houseboat, where the owners have more respect for their guests' comfort.

Places to Stay – bottom end

There are cheap hotels scattered all around Srinagar, although those in the Lal Chowk area tend to be noisy. The best bargains in cheap hotels are actually to be found on Dal Lake. Scattered amongst the houseboats are a number of small hotels on (semi) dry land. They're cheap and quiet, but prices are very variable, depending on demand. Real cheapies can go as low as Rs 15 per person, but if the weather is inclement some of these 'on the lake' hotels are flooded out.

Check the *Latif Guest House* or the *Hotel Sundowna* – the latter is fairly spartan but quite OK and has good food.

Right next door there's the *Hotel Savoy* with rooms from Rs 40 to Rs 75. Again the food is good. A little up-market from these places – and further up the channel towards Dal Gate – is *Hotel Heavan Canal*.

On solid ground, but still cheap, there's the popular *Tibetan Guest House* on Gagribal Rd, parallel to the Boulevard. *Zero Inn* (tel 77904), by Zero Bridge, is also reasonably quiet but rather more expensive with rooms for around Rs 60 a double. Kashmir is not a cheap place for accommodation by Indian standards. Across the Residency Rd from Ahdoo's the conveniently situated *Grand Hotel* has good doubles with bathroom for around Rs 50 with negotiation.

The J&K tourist department operates four accommodation units in Srinagar. At the *Tourist Reception Centre* there are a variety of rooms at Rs 80, 90 and 100. Dorm beds are Rs 10 for the first three days, Rs 15 for subsequent days. They have two hotels but both are in noisy Lal Chowk – at the *Lalla Rukh* (tel 72378) doubles are Rs 80, at the *Budshah* rooms are Rs 70/90. Finally there are the comparatively luxurious *Chasma Shahi Huts* near the Chasma Shahi gardens which cost from Rs 200 to Rs 350 in season. They come complete with kitchens and cooking equipment, but you really need your own transport to get out to them.

The *Srinagar Youth Hostel* is across the river from the town centre, near the museum. Nightly charges are Rs 8 and reservations must be made through the Education Department. Just beyond the Nagin Lake causeway, only a short distance before the Hazratbal Mosque, there's a campsite, a good place if you have your own vehicle.

Places to Stay – top end

The *Oberoi Palace* (tel 71241-2) is the ex-palace of the Maharaja of Kashmir and is Srinagar's top establishment. It's several km around the Boulevard from Dal Gate and singles/doubles are Rs 510/650 or Rs 695/925 with all meals. The actual building is rather uninspired, particularly if you've seen the sumptuous palace hotels of Rajasthan, but the gardens in front provide superb views over the lake.

Up at Chasma Shahi the new *Hotel Centaur Lake View* (tel 77601) has rooms at Rs 500/575 and is the largest hotel in Srinagar. There are a number of hotels along the Boulevard beside the lake such as *Hotel Boulevard* (tel 77089) with rooms at Rs 150/225 or *Hotel Mazda* (tel 72842) at Rs 100/150. The new and well-kept *Hotel Parimahal* (tel 71235-6) has rooms at Rs 180 to Rs 275 for singles, Rs 250 to Rs 335 for doubles.

The modern and centrally located *Broadway Hotel* (tel 71211-2) on Maulana Azad Rd (Hotel Rd) has rooms at Rs 400/520, a swimming pool and an excellent restaurant. Next door is the rather run down and decrepit-looking *Nedou's Hotel* (tel 73015-6), also on Hotel Rd. Rooms are Rs 225/275. On Residency Rd the *Hotel Sabena* (tel 78046) has singles for Rs 120 to Rs 130, doubles for Rs 160 to Rs 225. *Hotel Pomposh* (tel 75601-2) on the same road costs Rs 150/180.

Places to Eat

Because so many people eat on board their houseboats, Srinagar is not a very exciting place for eating out. The *Oberoi Palace Hotel* does a very superior buffet dinner and at lunch-time you can dine, or simply have a snack, on their sweeping lawn. The *Broadway* also has a slightly cheaper buffet in their pleasantly carpet-decorated restaurant. Food here (on the non-buffet nights) is reasonably priced and you can sample possibly the best kahwa tea in Srinagar – an expensive treat.

Ahdoo's, which fronts onto the Bund and backs onto Residency Rd, has been said to have some of the best Kashmiri food in Srinagar but generally fails to live up to its reputation. Most dishes are under Rs 15. Across the road the *Grand* has similar food, a more limited menu but lower prices. Others in this area include the *Capri Bar & Restaurant* and the *Premier*. Towards the GPO on Residency Rd the *Mughal Darbar* is reportedly very good.

Just off the Boulevard, the Tibetan-run *Lhasa Restaurant* with its 'candle-lit garden' does good Chinese-Tibetan food; this friendly place is very popular with travellers. Further back towards Dal Gate, on the Boulevard, there's the *Shamyana* with good vegetarian food and reasonable prices. The *Punjab Hotel & Restaurant*, on Lal Chowk opposite the Palladium Cinema, has cheap, tasty food plus more expensive tandoori dishes. Near Dal Gate the *Glocken Bakery* has good fresh brown bread and other baked goodies.

Right in the central area the *Indian Coffee House* is a good place for a coffee and a chat, though the food line is limited: good vegetable cutlets and so-so masala dosas. Across the road the *Hollywood Café* has much, much better food than its plain appearance would suggest. Seekh kebab or kanti roast make an excellent lunch, and their French fries are superb by any standards. Plus good cakes or snacks at other times of day.

Ice cream is not bad at *Dimples*, either in the centre (opposite the Hollywood) or by Zero Bridge. The latter is known as the *Little Hut* and has good milkshakes. There's a good selection of Indian sweets at *Shakti Sweets*, also by the Hollywood. The café at the *Tourist Reception Centre* is terrible but you can get early-morning snacks from the stalls which set up opposite the TRC for the early bus departures.

Getting There

Air Indian Airlines fly to Srinagar from New Delhi (Rs 672), Chandigarh (Rs 572), Amritsar (Rs 389) and Jammu (Rs 224), and there are flights from Srinagar to Leh and back. Flights are much more frequent during the summer tourist season. Flight time from Delhi on the direct flights is about an hour and 10 minutes. As usual in India, you should book your flights as early as possible.

In Srinagar the Indian Airlines office (tel 73538 & 73270) is at the Tourist Reception Centre and is open from 10 am to 5 pm. It's also at the Tourist Reception Centre in Jammu (tel 42735 & 47577).

Rail & Bus It's 880 km from Delhi to Srinagar, although almost everybody coming up from Delhi or other Indian cities by land will come through Jammu (591 km by road from Delhi), from where the buses run daily to Srinagar. By train there are about four services a day from Delhi or New Delhi to Jammu Tawi, across the river from Jammu. The 724-km trip takes nine to 13 hours, usually overnight, and costs Rs 59 in 2nd class, Rs 244 in 1st. There are also direct buses from Delhi (about Rs 200, 30 hours), but people making the trip by road will most probably be coming via Chandigarh or the Himachal Pradesh hill stations.

Buses leave Jammu early in the morning (between 6.30 and 7 am) for the 10 to 12-hour trip to Srinagar in the Kashmir Valley. Bus fares are Rs 34 (B class), Rs 45 (A class), Rs 65 (deluxe) and Rs 90 (super deluxe). B class buses seat two and three, A class two and two, deluxe two and two in individual seats with headrests. Between 11 am and 12 noon more buses depart from the Jammu Tawi railway station – take these if you don't want to overnight in Jammu. They stop for the night at Banihal on the way to Srinagar.

Although there are many buses (a veritable armada leaves Jammu each morning), you should book a seat as soon as you arrive in Jammu. Book in advance from Srinagar as well; the day before departure all seats may be sold out. In Jammu the A class and deluxe buses go from the town and the railway station, the B class buses go only from the bus station. There are also taxis operating between the two cities at about Rs 200 per seat or Rs 800 for the whole taxi.

For information about booking trains from Jammu while in Srinagar, enquire at the railways office in the Tourist Reception Centre or at N D Radha Kishen & Sons (tel 2146), Railway Out Agency, Badshah Chowk, Srinagar. Bus bookings are made at the Tourist Reception Centre (tel 2698). Allow plenty of time as the booking system is archaic.

Getting Around

There is a wide choice of transport available either on the lake or out and around it, plus a variety of tours. The tour buses are generally much more comfortable than the usual run of overcrowded local buses and, since many of them offer one-way fares, they can be used for getting out to hill stations in the valley.

Airport From Srinagar airport, which is about 13 km out of the city, there's an airport bus to the Tourist Reception Centre in Srinagar which costs Rs 5. By taxi it costs about Rs 40.

Shikaras These are the graceful, long boats which crowd the Srinagar lakes. They're used for getting back and forth from the houseboats or for longer tours. Officially there is a standard fare for every trip around the lake and these are prominently posted at the main landings (ghats); in practice the fares can be quite variable. To be shuttled across to your houseboat should cost Rs 2 in a covered ('full spring seats') shikara, but the kids who are always out for a little money will happily paddle you across for 50 paise or less in a basic, open shikara. Late at night, particularly if it is raining, the tables are turned and getting back to your houseboat at a reasonable price may require a little ingenuity! If you hire a shikara by the day or for a longer trip, count on about Rs 8 or Rs 9 per hour.

Try paddling a shikara yourself some-

time – it's nowhere near as easy as it looks. You'll spend lots of time going round in circles. If your houseboat hasn't got one to spare some children passing by will find you a boat for Rs 4 or Rs 5 per day.

Bus The Jammu & Kashmir Road Transport Corporation buses go from the Tourist Reception Centre, while private buses operate from a variety of stands in Srinagar. Certain major long-distance routes are reserved for the J&K buses (Jammu, Leh, etc), but others are open for competition and there will be a great number of buses operating.

Taxi & Auto-rickshaw There are stands for these at the Tourist Reception Centre and other strategic locations in town. Srinagar's taxi-wallahs are extremely reluctant to use their meters so you'll have to bargain hard. Count on about Rs 6 for a taxi from the Tourist Reception Centre to Dal Gate, Rs 4 by auto-rickshaw. For longer trips the official fares are all posted by the stands.

Tours The J&K Road Transport Corporation operates a number of daily tours from the Tourist Reception Centre. Private bus companies, particularly the KMDA (Kashmir Motor Drivers' Association) also have several tours. The J&K RTC tours are:

	round trip	one way
Pahalgam	Rs 45	Rs 26
Daksum, Kokarnag & Achabal	Rs 45	Rs 27
Gulmarg	Rs 45	Rs 26
Yusmarg	Rs 38	Rs 22
Wular Lake	Rs 38	Rs 24
Sonamarg	Rs 43	Rs 24
Srinagar, Moghul Gardens	Rs 18	-

Bicycle Seeing Srinigar by bicycle is a surprisingly pleasant way of getting around – economical too. You can hire bikes for Rs 8 per day from bicycle shops. There are several along the Boulevard close to Dal Gate. Pleasant trips to be made include:

Round Dal Lake – an all-day trip going by the Moghul gardens. It's particularly pleasant around the north of the lake where the villages are still relatively untouched.
Across the Lake – you can ride across the lake on the causeway, a nice trip since there are no traffic problems with vehicles and there is plenty of opportunity to observe lake life without being in a boat.
Nagin Lake – you can ride out to the Hazratbal Mosque via Nagin Lake and then make a complete loop around the lake on the way back. This trip can easily be combined with a trip along the Jhelum, taking in the various mosques close to the river. The streets here are very narrow so vehicles keep away and bike riding is pleasant.

Things to Buy
Kashmir is famous for its many handicrafts, and selling them is an activity pursued with amazing energy. You can visit workshops to see many of them being made. Popular buys include carpets, papier mâché articles, leather and furs, woodcarvings, shawls and embroidery, honey, tailor-made clothing, pleasantly coarse-knitted sweaters and cardigans,

that expensive spice saffron and many other items. There are a whole string of Government Handicraft Emporiums scattered around Srinagar, but the main one is housed in the fine old British Residency building by the Bund. The flashiest shops are along the Boulevard by Dal Lake. The Bund also has some interesting shops, including *Suffering Moses* with high-quality goods. Shikaras patrol Dal Lake like sharks, loaded down with goodies.

KASHMIR VALLEY
When lazing around on your houseboat begins to pall, it's time to head off around the valley. There are a number of interesting places in the Kashmir Valley for day trips from Srinagar as well as several popular hill stations which serve as good bases for short or long treks into the surrounding mountains. Pahalgam and Gulmarg are the two main Kashmiri hill resorts.

SRINAGAR-PAHALGAM
The route to Pahalgam passes through some interesting places including, if you take the bus tour to Pahalgam, enough Moghul gardens to leave you thoroughly saturated. Only 16 km out of Srinagar is Pampore, centre of Kashmir's saffron industry. Saffron is highly prized for its flavouring and colouring properties and is consequently rather expensive. Sangram, 35 km out, is a centre for production of (would you believe) cricket bats. They're lined up by the road in their thousands.

At Avantipur are two ruined Hindu temples built between 855 and 883 AD. The Avantiswami Temple, the larger of the two, is dedicated to Vishnu and still has some fine relief sculptures and columns of an almost Grecian appearance. The smaller temple to Shiva is about a km before the main temple but also close to the main road. At Anantnag the road forks, the Pahalgam road turning north from here.

Just beyond the Pahalgam turn-off is Achabal, a Moghul garden laid out in

1620 by Shah Jahan's daughter Jahanara. This carefully designed garden was said to be a favourite retreat of Nur Jahan. Kokarnag, further on, is certain to give you garden overload but is famous for its rose gardens. Back on the Pahalgam route Mattan has a fish-filled spring which is an important pilgrimage spot. Above Mattan on a plateau is the huge ruined temple of Martland.

Not actually on or even close to the Pahalgam route is Verinag in the extreme south of the Kashmir Valley. The spring here is said to be the actual source of the Jhelum River. Jehangir built an octagonal stone basin at the spring in 1612 and Shah Jahan laid out a garden around it in 1620.

PAHALGAM

Pahalgam is about 95 km from Srinagar and at 2130 metres the night-time temperatures here are warmer than in Gulmarg, which is higher up. The beautiful Lidder River flows right through the town, which is at the junction of the Sheshnag and Lidder rivers and surrounded by soaring, fir-covered mountains with snow-capped peaks rising behind them. This is an ideal base for short day treks or for the longer treks to Kolahoi Glacier or Amarnath Cave – see Treks in Kashmir. Pahalgam is also famous for its many shepherds. They're a common sight, driving their flocks of sheep along the paths all around town.

Information

The rather useless Tourist Office is just around the corner from the bus halt. Fishing permits have to be obtained in Srinagar but trekking supplies can be bought here.

Pahalgam Walks

Mamaleswara Only a km or so downstream and on the opposite bank of the Lidder, this small Shiva temple with its square stone tank is thought to date back at least to the 12th century.

Baisaran There are excellent views over the town and the Lidder Valley from this meadow, five km from Pahalgam. A further 11 km takes you to the Tulian Lake at 3353 metres. It is ice covered for much of the year.

Aru The pleasant little village of Aru makes a very interesting day walk, following the Lidder River for 11 km upstream. Unfortunately the main track also takes cars. This is actually the first stage of the Kolahoi Glacier trek.

Places to Stay

There are many hotels along the main street of Pahalgam, including the expensive *Pahalgam Hotel* (tel 26) which costs Rs 450/600 including all meals; or the

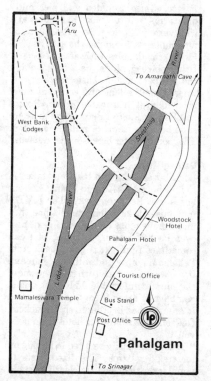

equally pricey *Woodstock* (tel 27) at Rs 500/650 and the *Mount View Hotel* (tel 21) at Rs 350/400 on the same basis.

There is also a *Government Tourist Bungalow* with dorm beds for Rs 8, rooms for Rs 30 to Rs 60 and huts for Rs 60 to Rs 225. During the summer season the tourist office operates several tent sites with ready set up and furnished tents. The *Dar Camp* has been particularly recommended. Just outside of Pahalgam on the Amarnath route the *Yog Niketan* ashram is an interesting place to stay and take yoga and meditation courses.

Most budget travellers head across the river to one of the lodges on the other bank. These include the popular *Aksa Lodge* with rooms from Rs 50, dorm beds and fine views from the garden. *Brown Palace* is also secluded and pleasantly quiet; this well-run place has rooms at a wide variety of prices, from Rs 20 to Rs 50 for doubles with common bath to Rs 60 to Rs 110 for doubles with attached bath. Other places include the *Windrush* and the cheaper and more basic *Bente's Hotel* where there's a long and varied menu of good food at reasonable prices. Rooms cost Rs 10 to Rs 35 at Bente's and there are superb views from its hillside location. The 'boiled' water here is rather dubious.

Getting There

Local buses cost about Rs 10 and take 2½ to four hours. J&K Road Transport tour buses cost Rs 26 one way. The KMDA tour buses take a long time since they make many stops on the way. Taxis cost over Rs 250 return, although you can sometimes find a taxi going back from Pahalgam empty and willing to bargain. If you want to get a return ticket on one of the more comfortable J&K tour buses, you have to catch them when they come in around noon in order to obtain tickets. Get someone from your hotel to do it for you.

Ponies can easily be hired in Pahalgam for trekking trips. The fixed costs to popular destinations are clearly posted.

GULMARG

The large meadow of Gulmarg is 52 km from Srinagar at 2730 metres. The name means 'meadow of flowers' and in spring it's just that. This is also an excellent trekking base and in winter it's India's premier skiing resort. The skiing equipment available is a bit primitive and limited but the costs are very low and the area would also be wonderful for ski-touring.

Gulmarg can get pretty cold at times, even compared to Pahalgam. Come prepared with plenty of warm clothes.

Information

The Tourist Office is the green/blue building complex with three patches of new wooden roof in the valley bottom about a half km beyond the golf course.

Gulmarg Walks

Outer Circular Walk A circular road, 11 km in length, runs right round Gulmarg through pleasant pine forests with excellent views over the Kashmir Valley. Nanga Parbat is visible to the north and Haramukh and Sunset Peak to the south-east.

Khilanmarg This smaller valley is about a six-km walk from the Gulmarg bus stop and car park. The meadow, carpeted with flowers in the spring, is the site for Gulmarg's winter ski-runs and offers a fine view of the surrounding peaks and over the Kashmir Valley. During the early spring, as the snow melts, it can be a very muddy hour's climb up the hill.

Alpather Beyond Khilanmarg, 13 km from Gulmarg at the foot of the 4511-metre Apharwat peak, this lake is frozen until mid-June, and even later in the year you can see lumps of ice floating in its cold waters. The walk from Gulmarg follows a well-graded pony track over the 3810-metre Apharwat Ridge, separating the lake from Khilanmarg, and proceeds up the valley to the lake at 3843 metres.

Ningle Nallah Flowing from the melting snow and ice on Apharwat Peak and Alpather Lake, this pretty mountain

Jammu & Kashmir Top: Crossing the Himalaya on the flight from Srinagar to Leh (TW)
Left: Shy monks in Tikse monastery (TW)
Right: Tikse monastery in Ladakh (TW)

Uttar Pradesh Top: Sunset at the Taj Mahal, Agra (PC)
Bottom: Keeping the Taj grass short with a two-bullock-two-man lawnmower,
Agra (TW)

stream is 10 km from Gulmarg. The stream continues down into the valley below and joins the Jhelum River near Sopore. The walking path crosses the Ningle Nallah by a bridge and continues on to the Lienmarg, another grassy meadow and a good spot for camping.

Ferozpore Nallah Reached from the Tangmarg road, or from the outer circular walk, this mountain stream meets the Bahan River at a popular picnic spot known as 'waters meet'. The stream is reputed to be particularly good for trout fishing; it's about five km from Gulmarg. You can continue on from here to Tosamaidan, a three-day, 50-km walk to one of Kashmir's most beautiful margs.

Ziarat of Baba Reshi This Muslim shrine is on the slopes below Gulmarg and can be reached from either Gulmarg or Tangmarg. The Ziarat, or tomb, is of a well-known Muslim saint who died here in 1480. Before renouncing worldly ways he was a courtier of the Kashmir king Zain-ul-Abidin.

Places to Stay

Tourists Hotel (tel 53) is a remarkably baroque and weathered fantasy in wood, like something out of *Lord of the Rings* although it's rather dirty and grubby inside. Rooms cost Rs 25 to Rs 60, supposedly all with attached bath and hot water – well perhaps in the early morning and late afternoon anyway. It's right outside the horse-and-pony stand. The *City View* has doubles at Rs 30, a friendly manager and fine food.

The popular *Gulmarg Inn* has doubles with bath for Rs 80. Other middle-priced places include the *Yamberzal Tourist Inn* opposite the bus stand.

Hotel Highland Park (tel 30, 91) is Rs 415/580 for singles/doubles including all meals. All rooms have attached bath and hot and cold running water. There's a beautiful lounge/bar with colonial trophies; and the restaurant offers English, Chinese, Indian and Kashmiri dishes, both vegetarian and non-vegetarian. This fine

establishment is worth a visit for a cup of tea or coffee in the beautiful gardens (or even a beer in a crested silver tankard!). Other more expensive places include the *Woodland Hotel* (tel 60) and *Nedou's Hotel* (tel 23), both at Rs 275/375. Special deals are available in winter if you come here for skiing.

Getting There

There are a variety of buses running from Srinagar to Gulmarg, many of them on day tours. On a day tour you have only a few hours at the hill resort, just long enough for one of the shorter day walks. J&K tour buses cost Rs 26 one way, ordinary buses are around Rs 10.

At one time the road from Srinagar only ran as far as Tangmarg, seven km in distance or 500 metres in altitude below Gulmarg. The last stretch then had to be completed on foot or by pony. A road has now been completed over the last stretch, although some buses still terminate at Tangmarg. The winding road from Tangmarg is 13 km in length, nearly twice as far as the more direct pony track. A riding pony costs about Rs 14 from Tangmarg up to Gulmarg. Riding or pack ponies can also be hired from Gulmarg to other sites around the valley. Rates are prominently posted at the car park.

SOUTH OF SRINAGAR

Interesting places in the south-west of the valley include Yusmarg, reputed to have the best spring flowers in Kashmir, and a good base for treks further afield. Chari Sharif is on the road to Yusmarg and has the shrine or Ziarat of Kashmir's patron saint. Aharbal was a popular resting place for the Moghul emperors when they made the long trip north from Delhi.

SINDH VALLEY

This is a scenic area north of Srinagar through which the road to Ladakh passes. The Zoji La pass marks the boundary from the Sindh Valley into Ladakh. From Srinagar you pass the Dachigam wildlife reserve, once a royal game park. You need a signed permit from the Srinagar Tourist Office to enter the reserve. Anchar Lake is close to Srinagar but rarely visited and has a wide variety of water birds. There is a Moghul garden built by Nur Jahan at Manasbal Lake. Wular Lake is possibly the largest freshwater lake in Asia and the Jhelum River flows into it.

Sonamarg, at 2740 metres, is the last major point in Kashmir and an excellent base for trekking. Its name means 'meadow of gold', which could derive from the spring flowers or from the strategic trading position it once enjoyed. There are *Tourist Huts*, a *Rest House* and some small hotels here. The tiny village of Baltal is the last place in Kashmir, right at the foot of the Zoji La.

When conditions are favourable you can walk to the Amarnath Cave from here. The Zoji La is the watershed between Kashmir and Ladakh – on one side you have the green, lush scenery of Kashmir while on the other side everything is barren and dry.

TREKS IN KASHMIR

There are various treks both within Kashmir and from Kashmir to Ladakh or Zanskar. The short Pahalgam-Kolahoi Glacier trek is particularly popular and the Pahalgam-Amarnath Cave trek is well known not only for the natural scenery, but for the great religious festival that takes place here. Porters are not used in Kashmir anywhere near as much as in Nepal; ponies carry the gear. Although trekking companies are not as widespread as in Nepal they are starting to pop up. Summit Treks and Choomti Trekkers, both in Srinagar, have been recommended.

Pahalgam-Kolahoi Glacier

This short trek takes only four days Pahalgam to Pahalgam, but it can be extended before returning to Pahalgam or continued up into the Sindh Valley. The first day from Pahalgam takes you to Aru

along the bank of the Lidder River. This is also a very popular day trek from Pahalgam since Aru is a pretty little village. The second day's walk takes you to Lidderwat, where there is a very pleasant campsite where the stream from the glacier meets the stream from Tarsar Lake and a Government Rest House. There is also the friendly *Paradise Guest House* here. Doubles are Rs 20 or you can sleep on the 'dormitory' floor for Rs 5. The people who run it cope admirably with large groups of hungry trekkers.

On the third day you trek up to the lake and back to Lidderwat. The glacier, climbing from 3400 metres to 4000 metres, descends from the 5485-metre Kolahoi mountain. On Day 4 you can either walk straight back to Pahalgam in one day or the trek can be extended another day by walking Lidderwat-Tarsar Lake-Lidderwat. You can shorten the trek by going straight from Pahalgam to Lidderwat in one day, quite an easy walk.

Instead of returning to Pahalgam, three days' further trek will take you to Kulan near Sonamarg in the Sindh Valley. It's only 16 km from Kulan to Sonamarg, which you can walk or travel by bus.

Day 1	Pahalgam-Aru	12 km
Day 2	Aru-Lidderwat	12 km
Day 3	Lidderwat-glacier-Lidderwat	13 km
Day 4	Lidderwat-Pahalgam	24 km
or		
Day 4	Lidderwat-Sekiwas	10 km
Day 5	Sekiwas-Khemsar	11 km
Day 6	Khemsar-Kulan	10 km

Pahalgam-Amarnath Cave

At the full moon in the month of July-August, thousands of Hindu pilgrims make the *yatra* to the Shri Amarnath Cave when a natural ice lingam, the symbol of Lord Shiva, reaches its greatest size. Although at the time of the yatra it's less a trek than a long queue, the spirit of this immense pilgrimage is amazing. The

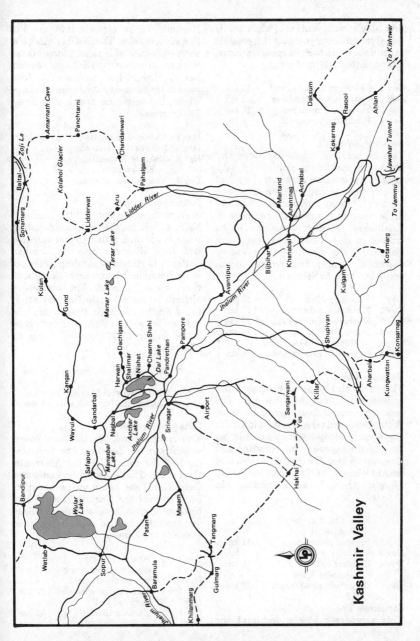

Kashmir Valley

first day's walk out of Pahalgam is jeepable and from Amarnath it is possible to continue north to Baltal near Srinagar, although that is a hard trek.

Day 1	Pahalgam-Chandanwari	13 km
Day 2	Chandanwari-Sheshnag	12 km
Day 3	Sheshnag-Panchtarni	11 km
Day 4	Panchtarni-Amarnath	8 km

Sonamarg-Wangat

This 81-km trek takes five days and reaches a maximum altitude of 4191 metres. It starts from Sonamarg (reached by bus from Srinagar), then climbs to Nichinai, crosses a mountain chain and drops down to the pleasant campsite at Krishansar. Another pass has to be crossed on Days 3 and 4 when you reach Gangabal Lake. From here it's a steep descent to Wangat, from where you can easily bus back to Srinagar.

Day 1	Sonamarg-Nichinai	15 km
Day 2	Nichinai-Krishansar	13 km
Day 3	Krishansar-Dubta Pani	17 km
Day 4	Dubta Pani-Gangabal Lake	17 km
Day 5	Gangabal Lake-Wangat	19 km

Gangabal Trek

This trek also goes to Gangabal but approaches it from the other side. The trek commences from Errin, north of Wular Lake, and takes five days in all. On Day 4 you need ropes and ice-axes to cross the glacier between the Kundsar and Gangabal lakes. The final day's trek also ends at Wangat. At Narannag, just before Wangat, there is an interesting old temple.

Day 1	Errin-Chuntimula-Poshpathri	11 km
Day 2	Poshpathri-Sarbaal	11 km
Day 3	Sarbaal-Kundsar Lake	9 km
Day 4	Kundsar Lake-Gangabal Lake	11 km
Day 5	Gangabal Lake-Wangat	19 km

Konsarnag Trek

This short trek in the south of the Kashmir Valley ascends into the Pir Panjal mountains. The first day's trek is a short walk only taking about three hours. With an early start from Srinagar you can bus to Aharbal and complete the first walk in the same day. Konsarnag Lake is a beautiful deep-blue stretch of water at 3700 metres.

Day 1	Aharbal-Kungwattan	9 km
Day 2	Kungwattan-Mahinag	
Day 3	Mahinag-Konsarnag-Kungwattan	
Day 4	Kungwattan-Aharbal	

Daksum-Kishtwar

Starting from the south of the Kashmir Valley at Daksum, this trek is an interesting route to Jammu, although you can also trek from Kishtwar into the Zanskar Valley or to Himachal Pradesh. Daksum is 100 km from Srinagar and takes about three hours by road. The maximum altitude is reached on the first day's trek to the Sinthan Pass. On the last day it is only a short walk to Dadpath from where buses depart at 10 am and 4 pm to Kishtwar.

Day 1	Daksum-Sinthan Pass	16 km
Day 2	Sinthan Pass-Chatru	8 km
Day 3	Chatru-Mughal Maidan	9 km
Day 4	Mughal Maidan-Dadpath	8 km

Pahalgam-Pannikar

This is a hard trek into the Suru Valley which leads to Zanskar. The first two days of the trek follow the Amarnath Cave route. The following days cross the Gulol Gali Pass, climb to the Lonvilad Gali, go over the Chalong Glacier and continue down to Pannikar. From Pannikar you can take the road north to Kargil or east into the Zanskar Valley.

Day 1 & 2	Amarnath Cave	
Day 3	Sheshnag-Rangmarg	8 km
Day 4	Rangmarg-Hampet	6 km
Day 5 & 6	Hampet-Lonvilad Gali	22 km
Day 7	Lonvilad Gali	
Day 8	Chalong Glacier-Pannikar	15 km

LADAKH

'Little Tibet', 'the moonland' and 'the last Shangri La' are names that have been applied to Ladakh, all with a bit of truth. Ladakh is a miniature version of Tibet – it is situated geographically in Tibet, which is a high-altitude plateau north of the Himalaya. The people are Tibetan in their culture and religion and there are many Tibetan refugees. The Himalaya are a very effective barrier to rain – few clouds creep across their awesome height and as a result Ladakh is barren beyond belief. Only where rivers running from far-away glaciers or melting snow carry water to habitation do you find plant life – hence the moonland label, since Ladakh is as dry as the Sahara.

Finally, Ladakh could well be a last Shangri La. Only in the mid-70s was it opened to outside visitors. Its strategic isolation is matched by its physical isolation – only from June to September is the road into Ladakh from Kashmir not covered by snow and only since 1979 has there been an airline flight into Ladakh. That flight is one of the most spectacular in the world.

If you're in Kashmir don't fail to make the trip to Ladakh. It's an other-worldly place – strange gompas perched on soaring hilltops, shattered-looking landscapes splashed with small but brilliant patches of green, ancient palaces clinging to sheer rock walls. But most of all there are the delightful Ladakhis – friendly as only Tibetan people can be and immensely colourful.

General Advice

A sleeping bag is very useful in Ladakh even if you're not trekking or camping. The nights can get very cold and visiting many of the gompas by public transport will require an overnight stop. Be prepared for dramatic temperature changes and for the extreme burning power of the sun in Ladakh's thin air (Leh is at 3500 metres). A cloud across the sun will change the air temperature from T-shirt to sweater level in seconds. Without a hat and/or sunscreen you'll have sunburn and a peeling nose in hours.

Acclimatise to Ladakh's altitude slowly – don't go scrambling up mountainsides as soon as you arrive. A spell in Kashmir is good half-way acclimatisation, but people who fly straight from Delhi to Ladakh may feel very uncomfortable for a few days. Note that outside Leh it is not easy to change money and that in the tourist season there is often a severe shortage of small change. One very important word to learn for Ladakh is the all-purpose and frequently used greeting 'Jullay'. Finally, remember that this is a sensitive border region disputed by India, Pakistan and China. You are not allowed more than a mile north of the Srinagar-Leh road.

Religion

At Kargil, on the Srinagar-Leh road, the Islamic influence dies out and you are in a Buddhist region. The people follow Tibetan Tantric Buddhism with much emphasis on magic and demons. All around Ladakh are gompas, the Buddhist monasteries. They're fascinating to visit, although they have become very commercially-minded since Ladakh's tourist boom commenced. There's a good side to this though. Prior to tourism the gompas were gradually becoming more and more neglected. Today many of them are being refurbished and repaired with the profits from visiting westerners! The monks are happy to have visitors wander around the gompas, sit in on the ceremonies, try the appalling taste of butter tea (bring your own cup) and take photographs.

SRINAGAR-LEH

It's 434 km from the Vale of Kashmir to Ladakh and the road is surfaced most of the way. It follows the Indus River for much of the distance. Buses run along this road daily during the summer season (see Getting There for Leh) and take two days with an overnight stop at Kargil. Sonamarg is the last major place in

Kashmir, shortly before you climb up over the Zoji La pass (3529 metres) and enter the Ladakh region.

Zoji La

This is one of the few unsurfaced stretches on the route. It's also the first pass to snow over in winter and the last to be cleared in summer. It is not, however, the highest pass along the route. The other passes get less snow because they are across the Himalaya and in the mountain rain shadow.

Drass

This is the first village after the pass and the place from where road crews work to clear the road up to the pass for the start of the summer season. In winter Drass is noted for its heavy snowfalls and extreme cold.

Kargil

Once an important trading post, Kargil is now simply an overnight halt on the way to Leh or the point where you turn south for the Zanskar Valley. The people of Kargil are chiefly Muslim and noted for their extreme orthodoxy. Already you are in a region where irrigation is vitally important.

Places to Stay & Eat *Suru View*, behind the bus station, has rooms from Rs 50 and is habitable. Cheaper hotels include the reasonable *Argalia* with doubles at Rs 20; the town's generator is uncomfortably close by but fortunately it shuts down at 11 pm. Down towards the river the *Crown Hotel* has basic and 'just about clean' doubles for Rs 30. The *International Hotel* is slightly better with doubles with bath for Rs 40. Or there's the *Hotel Greenlands*, behind the bus stand on the way to the Suru View, where clean doubles are Rs 50. Other cheapies include the dirt-cheap and rather dirty *Yak Tail*.

The *State Tourist Bungalow* near the river is simple, clean and adequate. It's about a half km from the main street. There are two *Tourist Bungalows* with most rooms around Rs 30; the one up the hill from the main street is good. In addition, Kargil has a circuit house and a pleasantly located *PWD Rest House*. There is also accommodation of some form or other at Drass, Mulbekh, Bodh Kharbu, Lamayuru, Khalsi, Nurla, Saspul and Nimmu.

Doubles are Rs 100 at the *Hotel D'Zojila*, 2.5 km from the town. A km from the centre of Kargil, the *Welcomgroup Highlands* (tel 41) has rooms with all meals for Rs 400/550. It's an indication of how much more 'civilised' this area is becoming that there should be a hotel like this here!

Food in Kargil tends to be mediocre and expensive, but the *Light Restaurant* on the main road has good food and is run by friendly folk. The *Babu Chinese Restaurant* is much more expensive than equivalents in Leh.

Shergol

Between Kargil and Shergol you cross the dividing line between the Muslim and Buddhist areas. The small village of Shergol has a tiny gompa perched halfway up the eastern slope of the mountain.

Mulbekh

There are two gompas on the hillside above the village of Mulbekh. As in other villages, it is wise to enquire if the gompa is open before making the ascent. If not, somebody from the village may have keys and will accompany you to the gompas. Just beyond Mulbekh is a huge Chamba statue, an image of a future Buddha, cut into the rock face beside the road. It's one of the most interesting stops along the road to Leh. Those with time to spare can make a short trek from Mulbekh to the village of Gel.

Lamayuru

From Mulbekh the road crosses the 3718-metre Namika La, passes through the

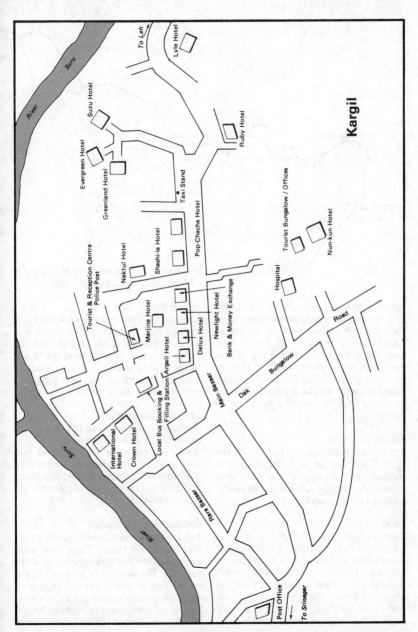

Kargil

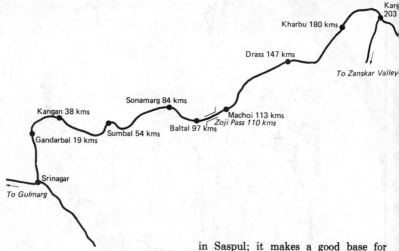

large military encampment of Bodh Kharbu and then crosses the 4094-metre Fatu La, the highest pass on the route. Lamayuru is the first of the typical Ladakhi gompas perched on a hilltop with its village at the foot of the hill. In its heyday the gompa had five buildings and as many as 400 monks, but today there is only one building, tended by 20 or 30 monks.

Rizong

On beyond Khalsi, and a few km off the road, is the nunnery of Julichen and the monastery of Rizong. If you stay here overnight men must stay in the monastery, women in the nunnery.

Alchi

Just beyond Saspul, this gompa is unusual in that it is built on lowland, not perched on a hilltop. It is noted for its massive Buddha statues and lavish woodcarvings and artwork. There are many *chortens* around the village. A hotel here has basic rooms and a small dorm. There's also a pleasant little hotel

in Saspul; it makes a good base for visiting Rizong, Alchi and Lekir.

Lekir & Basgo

Shortly after Saspul a steep road turns off to the Lekir Gompa, which also has a monastery school. Closer to Leh there is a badly damaged fort at Basgo and the Basgo Gompa with interesting Buddha figures, although its wall paintings have suffered much water damage.

LEH (population 8500)

Centuries ago this was an important stop on the old caravan silk route from China. Today it's merely a military base and tourist centre, but wandering the winding back streets of the town is still fascinating. It's about 10 km north-east of the Indus in a fertile side valley.

Orientation & Information

Leh is small enough to make finding your way around very easy. There's one main street with the Leh Palace rising up at the end of it. The bus station and jeep halt is on the airport side of town. The airport, with its steeply sloping runway, is several km out of town near the Spitok Gompa. There's a Tourist Office and Indian

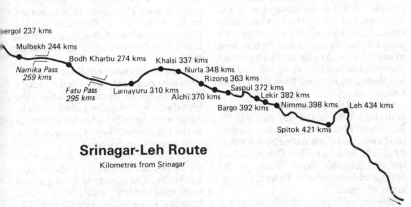

Srinagar-Leh Route

Kilometres from Srinagar

ergol 237 kms
Mulbekh 244 kms
Namika Pass 259 kms
Bodh Kharbu 274 kms
Fatu Pass 295 kms
Lamayuru 310 kms
Khalsi 337 kms
Nurla 348 kms
Rizong 363 kms
Alchi 370 kms
Saspul 372 kms
Lekir 382 kms
Bargo 392 kms
Nimmu 398 kms
Leh 434 kms
Spitok 421 kms
To Manali

Airlines office and a noisy power generator in the middle of town; fortunately it shuts down at 11 pm. The Ecological Development Group has a solar demonstration house and a fantastic library on Ladakh.

Leh Palace

Looking for all the world like a miniature version of the Potala in Lhasa, Tibet, the palace was also built in the 16th century. It is now deserted and badly damaged, a legacy of Ladakh's wars with Kashmir in the last century.

The main reason for making the climb up to the palace is for the superb views from the roof. The Zanskar mountains, across the Indus River, look close enough to touch. The palace is still the property of the Ladakhi royal family, although they now reside at nearby Stok. Try to get a monk to unlock the preserved, but now unused, central prayer room – dusty, spooky, with huge faces looming out of the dark. It's open 6 to 9 am and after 5 pm.

Leh Gompa

High above the palace and also overlooking the ruins of the older palace, the Red Gompa was built in 1430. It contains a fine three-storey-high seated Buddha image. It's open 7 to 9 am and 5 to 7 pm. The gompa above is in a very ruined condition but the views down on Leh are superb.

Sankar Gompa

It's an easy stroll to the Sankar Gompa, a couple of km up the valley from the town centre. This interesting little gompa is only open from 7 to 10 am and from 5 to 7 pm. There's a Rs 10 entry fee. The gompa has electric lighting so an evening visit is worthwhile. Upstairs is an impressive representation of Avalokitesvara complete with 1000 arms and 1000 heads.

Places to Stay

There are an amazing number of hotels and guest houses in Ladakh, many of which are only open during the tourist season. Prices are very variable – soaring in the peak season, plummeting at other times. The cheaper guest houses are generally just rooms rented out in private homes.

Down in the rock-bottom bracket, doubles can be found under Rs 30 (less in the off season) and dorm beds at Rs 5. Bed bugs are sometimes provided at no extra cost, so take care. The *Palace View Kidar Hotel*, close to the polo ground, is a very popular rock-bottom choice, as is the *New Antelope Guest House* on the main street. The *Manzor Guest House* is a pleasant family-run guest house with rooms from Rs 10 to Rs 25. The *Two Star Guest House* nearby is also good; both are 100 metres up the road from the Tsemo-Lah.

Down past the Dreamland, on the edge of the barley fields, the very pleasant *Ti-Sei Guest House* has a pretty garden, good views and clean rooms from Rs 25 to Rs 45. The food's good too. Others include the *Old Ladakh Guest House* or the *Moonland Guest House*. There are many, many cheapies.

Moving up in price, the *Dreamland* is very popular and close to the centre with rooms for around Rs 50. The *Kahyull Hotel* has rooms with attached bathroom and is well away from the noisy generator – Rs 50/75 in season. The *Khangri Hotel* is a good place with rooms from Rs 100 but is uncomfortably close to the generator. A number of Leh's middle-range hotels have pleasant gardens.

Leh's top-bracket hotels generally quote rates inclusive of all meals. They include the *Shambala Hotel*, which is rather a long way out of town. The *Kang-Lha-Chhen* and the *Hotel Lha-Ri-Mo* both have rooms from around Rs 400 and are fairly central. *Hotel Indus* is out of town on the Hemis road.

Places to Eat

The centrally located *Dreamland Hotel* has good food at reasonable prices. The Tibetan specialities and noodle dishes are a pleasant change from rice and more rice. They also make nice jasmine tea and it's a fine place for breakfast. Just across the road and up the stairs, the *Om Restaurant* is very good even if the service is sometimes very slow. The *Tibetan Restaurant* has excellent and cheap food and highly entertaining staff.

The *Khangri Restaurant*, almost next door to the Dreamland, is also pretty good; or there's the *Snow Lion* across the road. Or try *Hotel Pamposh* on Lal Chowk for good tea, coffee, curd and fresh bread. The *Ecology Centre* has interesting food.

Some of the other small cafés around town are remarkably insanitary looking – a sure ticket to stomach troubles. For breakfast buy freshly baked central-Asian-style bread from the little bakeries in the back streets by the mosque. Ideal with honey from Srinagar.

Try the locally made beer, *chang*, while you're in Leh, and at least sample the butter tea. The variety of locally grown vegetables and fruit is limited. It's worth bringing a few menu brighteners, like bars of chocolate or cans of apple juice, from Srinagar.

Getting There

Air Indian Airlines only started flying to Leh in 1979, but now there are flights from both Srinagar (Rs 334) and Chandigarh (Rs 477). The flight from Srinagar is very short (half an hour) and extremely spectacular (you cross right over the Himalaya), but also very problematic. Flights can only be made into Leh in the morning and only when weather conditions are good. If it's possible that the conditions could deteriorate after arrival and the aircraft could not leave, the flight will be cancelled. End result is a lot of cancellations, a lot of flights that actually leave Srinagar but are not able to land at Leh (since conditions can change very rapidly) and a lot of frustrated passengers. At difficult times of the year, such as when the season is about to start but the road is still closed, the flights can be heavily overbooked. The answer is to book well ahead but be prepared for disappointment. If you're unable to get on a flight from Srinagar ask your houseboat owner for help – every Kashmiri has 'connections'.

Road The road should be open from the

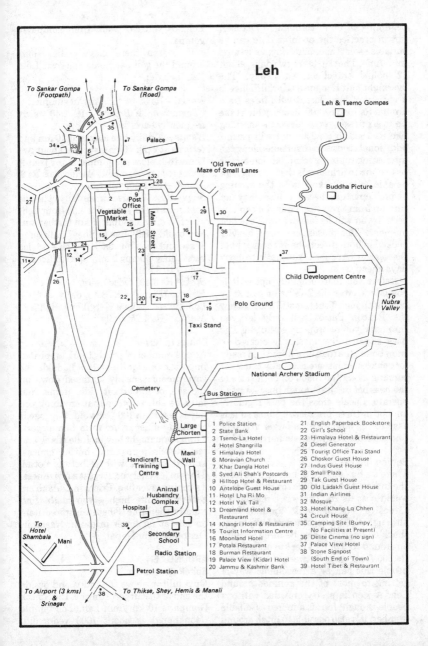

Leh

To Sankar Gompa (Footpath)

To Sankar Gompa (Road)

Leh & Tsemo Gompas

Palace

'Old Town' Maze of Small Lanes

Buddha Picture

Post Office

Vegetable Market

Main Street

Child Development Centre

To Nubra Valley

Polo Ground

Taxi Stand

National Archery Stadium

Cemetery

Bus Station

Large Chorten

Mani Wall

Handicraft Training Centre

Animal Husbandry Complex

Hospital

Secondary School

Radio Station

To Hotel Shambala

Mani

Petrol Station

To Airport (3 kms) & Srinagar

To Thikse, Shey, Hemis & Manali

1 Police Station
2 State Bank
3 Tsemo-La Hotel
4 Hotel Shangrilla
5 Himalaya Hotel
6 Moravian Church
7 Khar Dangla Hotel
8 Syed Ali Shah's Postcards
9 Hilltop Hotel & Restaurant
10 Antelope Guest House
11 Hotel Lha Ri Mo
12 Hotel Yak Tail
13 Dreamland Hotel & Restaurant
14 Khangri Hotel & Restaurant
15 Tourist Information Centre
16 Moonland Hotel
17 Potala Restaurant
18 Burman Restaurant
19 Palace View (Kidar) Hotel
20 Jammu & Kashmir Bank

21 English Paperback Bookstore
22 Girl's School
23 Himalaya Hotel & Restaurant
24 Diesel Generator
25 Tourist Office Taxi Stand
26 Choskor Guest House
27 Indus Guest House
28 Small Plaza
29 Tak Guest House
30 Old Ladakh Guest House
31 Indian Airlines
32 Mosque
33 Hotel Khang-Lo Chhen
34 Circuit House
35 Camping Site (Bumpy, No Facilities at Present)
36 Delite Cinema (no sign)
37 Palace View Hotel
38 Stone Signpost (South End of Town)
39 Hotel Tibet & Restaurant

beginning of June through to October, but in practice the opening date can be variable – sometimes mid-May, sometimes mid-June. The trip takes two days, about 12 hours' travel on each day. The overnight halt is made at Kargil. There is a variety of bus classes with fares from around Rs 70 to Rs 100. Jeeps, which take up to six passengers, will cost something like Rs 1800 to Rs 2400 but will permit additional stops and diversions along the interesting route. A complication on the return trip to Srinagar is that you may not be able to buy tickets until the evening before departure, because buses may not turn up from Srinagar. Thus you can't be certain you will be leaving until the last moment. The buses are very heavily booked in both directions at the height of the season (August). You have to book days ahead.

Before the road officially opens it is possible to cross the Zoji La on foot or by pony, although if there is still a lot of snow the Beacon Patrol will only let you through if you're properly equipped. The pass is generally physically cleared of snow before the road is repaired and ready for vehicles, and there is usually transport running along the roads on both sides of the pass before the through buses start to operate. Locals cross the pass regularly on foot in these pre-season times so it is easy to tag along with a larger group or find a guide. But it can be hard work!

Getting Around

There's a bus service to Leh airport from the Indian Airlines office for Rs 2. A jeep would cost Rs 25. There is a reasonably extensive bus network around Leh, although the buses are decidedly ram-shackle. Jeeps can also be hired – count on around Rs 3 or Rs 4 per km or Rs 250 to Rs 300 for a day. Between a half dozen people this can be a reasonable way of getting to most of the gompas around Leh. A jeep is pretty crowded with six people though; four is a more reasonable number. It's also possible to hitch around

Leh, or you can walk from gompa to gompa.

In season there may be bus tours around the gompas. Some bus costs from Leh include:

Kargil – Rs 35 to 45, daily in summer.
Choglamsar & Bridge – Rs 1.40, fairly frequently each day.
Hemis – A daily bus leaves at 10 am and returns at 2 pm. This gives you about two hours to explore the gompa; many people prefer to stay overnight. Each way is Rs 8.
Spitok – Rs 1.40, twice daily.
Shey – Rs 2.50, three times daily. The bus continues on to *Tikse* (Rs 3.50 from Leh) which is only a couple of km further out. You could easily bus to Shey, walk on to Tikse and then bus back to Leh – or vice versa. Shey Gompa is only open (officially) from 7 to 9 am.
Stok – Rs 3.40, twice daily.
Phyang (Fiang) – Rs 3.40, daily.
Lamayuru – take a Kargil bus, Rs 17.
Matho – Rs 4.25, daily.

Things to Buy

After a number of greedy tourists spirited important antiquities out of Ladakh, the government sensibly clamped down on the sale of important older items. You must be able to prove that anything you buy is less than 100 years old. Baggage is checked on departure from Leh airport. Things you might buy include chang and tea vessels, cups and butter churns, knitted carpets with Tibetan motifs, Tibetan jewellery or, for just a few rupees, a simple prayer flag. Prices in Ladakh are generally quite high – you might find exactly the same Tibetan-inspired item on sale at far lower prices in Kashmir, Dharamsala or Nepal.

AROUND LEH
Spitok Gompa

On a hilltop above the Indus and beside the end of the airport runway, the Spitok Gompa is 10 km from Leh. The temple (Gonkhang) is about 1000 years old.

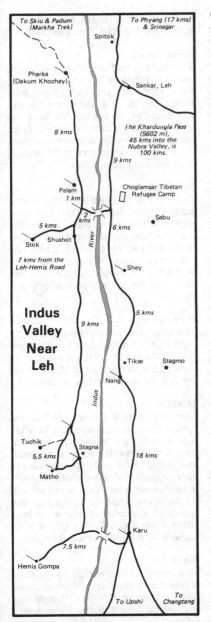

To Skiu & Padum (Markha Trek)

To Phyang (17 kms) & Srinagar

Spitok

Pharka (Dakum Khochey)

Sankar, Leh

8 kms

The Khardungla Pass (5602 m), 45 kms into the Nubra Valley, is 100 kms.

9 kms

Palam 1 km

Choglamsar Tibetan Refugee Camp

2 kms

Sabu

5 kms

River

6 kms

Stok

Shushot

7 kms from the Leh-Hemis Road

Shey

Indus Valley Near Leh

9 kms

5 kms

Tikse

Stagmo

Nang

Indus

Tuchik

Stagna

18 kms

5.5 kms

Matho

Karu

7.5 kms

Hemis Gompa

To Upshi

To Changtang

There are fine views over the Indus from the gompa. Entry fee is Rs 13.

Phyang

About 16 km from Leh, on the road back towards Srinagar, the gompa has 50 monks and the entry fee is Rs 10. There is an interesting little village below the gompa.

Beacon Highway

You are not allowed to visit the Nubra Valley without special permission, but if you could, it would involve taking what is probably the highest road in the world. It crosses a pass at 5606 metres! The road is only open in September and October – it takes the whole summer for the snow and ice to melt for that brief time.

Choglamsar

The Tibetan refugee camp here has become an important centre for the study of Tibetan literature and history and Buddhist philosophy. Don't indulge the kids who demand 'bon-bons' – it turns them into beggars. Nearby a bridge crosses the Indus to Stok and a rougher road along the other bank of the river to Hemis.

Shey

This was the old summer palace of the kings of Ladakh and was built about 550 years ago. It's now in ruins but the palace gompa has a 12-metre-high seated Buddha image. Entry fee is Rs 5 and the gompa is open 7 to 9 am and 5 to 6 pm. At other times ask for the monk Tashi in the village below; he will know where to find the key.

Tikse Gompa

The Tikse Gompa is visible from Shey and is about 17 km from Leh. Its new-found tourist wealth is being put to good use in extensive restoration work. The monastery is very picturesque and superbly sited on a hilltop overlooking the village and the Indus. Beside the car park is the small Zan-La Temple. The gompa has an important collection of Tibetan-style books in its library and some excellent artwork. This is an excellent place to watch the religious ceremonies either around 6.30 am or noon. They are preceded by long mournful sounds from horns on the roof. Entry fee is Rs 10.

Places to Stay You can get good doubles at the *Shalzang Chamba Hotel* for Rs 20. There are no dorm beds or singles here.

Hemis Gompa
One of the largest and most important gompas in Ladakh, Hemis is 45 km from Leh on the other side of the Indus. It's easy to get there by car or jeep, but on public transport you will have to spend the night at the monastery as it is not easy to bus out there, walk the six km up from the river to the gompa, see it, walk back down and get back in one day. The Hemis Gompa is famous for its Hemis Festival, which usually falls in the second half of June or in early July. This is one of the largest and most spectacular of the gompa festivals and at one time was virtually the only one which took place in the summer tourist season. The business-minded monks at some other gompas are now switching their festivals to more lucrative dates. The festival takes two days and features elaborate mask dances and crowds of eager spectators.

The gompa has an excellent library, particularly well-preserved wall paintings and good Buddha figures. Entry is Rs 10.

If instead of turning right at Karu to climb up to Hemis you had turned left, you would have reached the Chemre Gompa, five km off the road, and the Trak Tok Gompa, 10 km further on. Both lie in the restricted zone but tourists are allowed to visit them.

Places to Stay There's a *Tourist Hotel* with rather dirty dorm beds for Rs 10. You'll find cheaper and much cleaner rooms in local homes. The *Parachute Restaurant*, next to the bus stand, has good food.

Matho Gompa
The left bank road on the Indus is not in as good condition as the more used right bank road, but you can return from Hemis on it and there are several interesting places to visit. Matho is five km from Stagna, in a side valley. In an important festival the monks are possessed by spirits and go into a trance. Stagna, on the road, has a gompa too.

Stok Palace
Close to the Choglamsar bridge a road turns off the left bank road to the palace of Stok. The last king of Ladakh died in 1974 but his widow, the Rani of Stok, still lives in this 200-year-old palace. It is expected that her eldest son will become king when he reaches an auspicious age. You can enter only the museum here, which costs Rs 20.

Pharka Gompa
This small cave gompa is almost directly opposite the Spitok Gompa on the Stok side of the Indus. You can reach it by crossing the Choglamsar bridge, but the last few km must be made on foot.

ZANSKAR
The long, narrow Zanskar Valley was opened even more recently than Ladakh. A jeep road is gradually being extended from Kargil towards Padum, the capital, and this will eventually open Zanskar to more outside influence. Meanwhile it remains an area for trekkers, and some of the treks are definitely hard going. You can make a number of interesting ones either down the valley or out of it to Ladakh, Kashmir or Himachal Pradesh.

Padum
The 'capital' of Zanskar has a population of less than a thousand, of whom about 300 are Sunnite Muslims. Padum now has several hotels, a few shops and a

Tourist Office! A wider variety of supplies is also becoming available here. A number of interesting shorter treks can be made from Padum.

Zangla & Karsha Gompa

This is an interesting four-day trek around Padum. The first day takes you to Thonde on the riverbank with a monastery high above it. Since horses cannot cross the rope bridge from Padum, this is the first place on this side of the river where they can be hired for treks further afield to places like Lamayuru. The second day takes you from Thonde to Zangla, where the king of Zanskar has his castle. On day three you backtrack towards Thonde, cross the river and continue to Karsha, the most important gompa in Zanskar. On the final day you can cross the river directly by ferry or continue down to the wooden Tungri Bridge and double back to Padum.

Tungri & Zongkhul Gompa

This four-day trek around Padum takes you to the Sani and Zongkhul Gompas by following the route up towards the Muni La, then cutting across to the base of the Umasi La.

TREKS IN LADAKH & ZANSKAR

Trekking in Ladakh and Zanskar can be hard going and you should be equipped for every eventuality. Srinagar is the best place to purchase stores, but you will not find trekking gear like you do in Kathmandu in Nepal. Treks into Zanskar are principally down the valley from the north (from Kargil) or up the valley from the south (from Manali in Himachal Pradesh). Remember to take your garbage out with you; many areas are already becoming fouled with western trash.

Drass-Sanku

This is a short three-day trek into the Suru Valley joining the Kargil-Padum road at Sanku. It's simply an alternative route to the road down from Kargil.

Kargil-Padum

The seven-day trek to Padum from Kargil on the Srinagar-Ladakh road can be shortened by four days if you can get a ride all the way from Kargil to the Pensi La. When all bridges are complete the route will be open from early June to late October. The first day's travel is mainly on a surfaced road by bus as far as Sanku. Beyond Parkutse you pass close to Kun and Nun. The Rangdum Gompa is the first gompa reached in Zanskar; the road is still reasonably good to this point. Beyond the gompa you have to cross the 4401-metre Pensi La into Zanskar proper. On the last day's walk from Phe to Padum you cross the river and pass by the Sani Gompa, one of the most important in Zanskar.

Day 1	Kargil-Namsuru
Day 2	Namsuru-Pannikar-Parkutse
Day 3	Parkutse-Parkachik-Yuldo-Rangdum Gompa
Day 4	Rangdum Gompa-Pensi La
Day 5	Pensi La-Abran
Day 6	Abran-Phe
Day 7	Phe-Padum

Manali-Padum

This 10-day trek can be very hard going at its southern end. You first have to bus across the Rothang Pass from Manali to Keylong and on to Darcha where the trek starts. On the second day you cross the Baralacha La, a double pass where even the lower side is higher than Europe's highest mountain and twice the height of Australia's highest.

At the end of Day 6 you continue north to Padum or turn back south and cross the Shingo La back to Darcha in two days. You are not, however, allowed to take the alternative route if you're heading north. On Day 7 you make a detour to the spectacular Phuctal Gompa. Continuing all the way north to Kargil on this route would take, with a few days for shorter treks around Padum, something like 20 days.

Day 1	Darcha-Mane Bar
Day 2	Mane Bar-Sarai Kilang
Day 3	Sarai Kilang-Debni
Day 4	Debni-Chumik Marpo
Day 5	Chumik Marpo-Shingsan
Day 6	Shingsan-Kargiakh-Purni
Day 7	Purni-Phuctal Gompa
Day 8	Phuctal Gompa-Katge Lato
Day 9	Katge Lato-Reru
Day 10	Reru-Padum

Padum-Lamayuru

There are a number of alternatives for this trek from Padum into Ladakh, intersecting the road at Lamayuru, about half-way from Kargil to Leh. The trek starts out from Padum to Thonde, as on the short trek to the Zangla and Karsha gompas. On Day 3 the difficult ascent to the 4500-metre Shingo La pass has to be made, but on Day 4 the Nerag La, at 4900 metres, is even more difficult and a local guide is a necessity. Photosar is a small village from where it is only two days' walk to Lamayuru. There is an alternative route, taking a day longer, from Photosar. The alternative route from Padum starts out on the opposite side of the Zanskar River and takes you to the Linghsot Gompa before joining up with the first route at Day 5.

Day 1	Padum-Thonde
Day 2	Thonde-Honia
Day 3	Honia-Shingo La-Kharmapu
Day 4	Kharmapu-Nerag La
Day 5	Nerag La-Nerag
Day 6	Nerag-Yulching-Shingo La-Photosar
Day 7	Photosar-Shirshi La-Hanupatta
Day 8	Hanupatta-Wanla-Shill-Prikiti La-Lamayuru

or

Day 1	Padum-Pishu
Day 2-4	Pishu-Linghsot Gompa
Day 5	Linghsot Gompa-Yulching

Padum-Kishtwar

This trek into the southern part of Kashmir is not especially difficult although it crosses the 5234-metre Umasi La, which can only be done in fine weather. You cannot use horses on this route but must take porters. On the second day you reach the Zongkhul Gompa, which can also be visited on a short trek from Padum. Day 3 is a long climb and long descent over the snow-covered Umasi La. On Day 4 your Zanskari porters will not continue further and you must hire local porters or a pony. The last few days are hard work with many ascents and descents but the road from Kishtwar, already extending to Galar, is gradually being lengthened.

Day 1	Padum-Ating
Day 2	Ating-Ratrat
Day 3	Ratrat-Umasi La-Bhuswas
Day 4	Bhuswas-Matsel
Day 5	Matsel-Atholi
Day 6	Atholi-Shasho
Day 7	Shasho-Galar-Kishtwar

Other Treks

Padum-Nimmu follows the Padum-Lamayuru route for most of its length, then turns off eastwards to join the Srinagar-Leh road at Nimmu. Padum-Leh by the Markha Valley is a hard but rewarding trek which goes via Zangla before turning east over the Charcha La and the Ruberung La to the Markha Gompa, and eventually reaching Hemis near Leh. This trek can only be made in late August. Earlier than that the rivers which must be crossed are too high from melting snow and after that it's too cold. You can trek from Padum to the Phuctal Gompa by an alternative route to that described in Manali-Padum, but the trail is poor and very little used.

Uttar Pradesh

Population: 98 million
Area: 294,413 square km
Capital: Lucknow
Main language: Hindi

In terms of population Uttar Pradesh is the largest state in India. In terms of variety and of problems, it's also India larger than life. This is one of the great historical and religious centres of India. The Ganges River, which forms the backbone of Uttar Pradesh, is the holy river of Hinduism and there are a number of towns along the river of great importance for pilgrimages – in particular Rishikesh and Hardwar, where the river emerges from the Himalaya and starts across the plains; and Varanasi, the most holy city of all. Buddhism also has its great shrine in the state, for it was at Sarnath, just outside Varanasi, that the Buddha first preached his message of the middle way.

Over 2000 years ago the state was part of Ashoka's great Buddhist empire. More recently it was part of the Moghul empire, and for some years Agra was its capital. Today, of course, Agra is famed for that most perfect of Moghul masterpieces, the Taj Mahal. More recently still, it was in Uttar Pradesh that the Mutiny broke out in 1857 (at Meerut) and some of its most dramatic (Lucknow) and unfortunate (Kanpur) events took place. More recently Uttar Pradesh has produced five of six prime ministers since independence in 1947 – Nehru, Indira Gandhi, Rajiv Gandhi, Lal Bahadur Shastri and Charan Singh.

Geographically and socially the state has great variations. Most of it consists of the vast Ganges plain, an area of awesome flatness which suffers dramatic floods during the monsoon. The people of this region are predominantly backward farming peasants who scratch a bare existence from the overcrowded land. The north-west corner of the state is a part of the soaring Himalaya, with excellent treks, beautiful scenery and some of India's highest mountains. It's a state of strong contrasts.

MATHURA (population 150,000)

On the Delhi-Agra road, 57 km north of Agra, Mathura is a site of great age. According to legends this is where Lord Krishna was born 3500 years ago. Today Mathura is an important pilgrimage place for followers of this popular incarnation of Vishnu. There are many places in and around Mathura connected with the Krishna legend.

Mathura, or Muttra as it has also been known, is mentioned by Ptolemy and by the Chinese visitors Fa Hian (in India 401-410 AD) and the later Hiuen Tsang (634 AD). By that time the population of the 20 Buddhist monasteries (for this was a great Buddhist centre) had dropped from 3000 to 2000. By the time Mahmud of Ghazni arrived on his rape, burn, pillage trip from Afghanistan in 1017 Buddhism had totally disappeared.

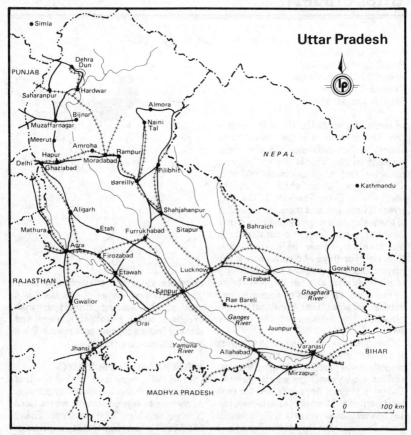

Uttar Pradesh

Sikandar Lodi did further damage to the shrines of Mathura in 1500, but the town rebounded during the tolerant reigns of Akbar and Jehangir, only for fanatical Aurangzeb to do another demolition job. He destroyed the Kesava Deo temple, which had been built on the site of one of the most important Buddhist monasteries, and built a mosque in its place.

Things to See

The Jami Masjid was built in 1661 by Aurangzeb's governor, Abd-in-Nabir Khan, on the site of the Kesava Deo temple. This is the place where Lord Krishna is supposed to have been born in prison. At one time the foundations of the old temple were still visible behind the mosque, but they have now been covered over with modern buildings. The modern Kesava temple has been rebuilt behind the Katra.

The 300-metre-wide Yamuna River, which flows through Mathura, is lined with bathing ghats and is full of large turtles. On the banks of the river the Sati Burj is a four-storey tower built in 1570 to commemorate the sati of the builder's mother. Aurangzeb knocked down the upper storeys, which have been rebuilt.

The ruined Kans Qila fort on the riverbank was built by Raja Man Singh of Amber; Jai Singh of Jaipur built one of his observatories here, but it has since disappeared. Vishram Ghat is the most important bathing ghat where Lord Krishna is said to have rested after killing a tyrant king. Mathura is so full of Krishna reminders (even the Hare Krishnas have their Indian HQ near here) that you can even see the Potara-Kund, near the Katra Kesava, where baby Krishna's nappies (diapers to Americans) are supposed to have been washed.

The Government Museum in Dampier Nagar has sculptures, terracotta work, coins and bronze objects dating from the 5th century AD. The standing Buddha image, found in excavations at Mathura, is particularly renowned. The museum is open daily except Mondays from 10.30 am to 4.30 pm from 1 July to 15 April, and 7.30 am to 12.30 pm the rest of the year. Admission is free. In the city, the Dwarkadheesh Temple is a modern Krishna temple while the Gita Mandir, also modern, is on the Mathura-Vrindaban road.

Around Mathura

Mahaban, 11 km south-east of Mathura, is another place from the Krishna legend. The Palace of Nanda, Krishna's foster-father, is said to contain his actual cradle. Gokul, a few km away, is where Krishna was secretly raised. Hordes of pilgrims flock here during his birthday festival each July-August.

At Goverdhan, 26 km from Mathura, Lord Krishna is said to have protected the inhabitants from Indra's wrath (in the form of rain) by holding the hilltops over them for seven days, neatly balanced on top of his finger. Krishna's favourite *gopi* (milkmaid) is said to have come from Barsana, 47 km from Mathura.

Vrindaban, 10 km north of Mathura, is the place where Krishna sported with his milkmaids and stole their clothes while they were bathing in the river. No wonder

he's so popular. The large Red Temple or Gobind Deo (Divine Cowherd, in other words Krishna) was built in 1590 and is one of the most advanced Hindu temples in the north of India. It has a vaulted ceiling, in contrast to the utilitarian ceilings found in most temples. Other temples in Vrindaban include Gopi Nath, Jugal Kishor (1027), Radha Ballabh (1626) and Madan Mohan.

One traveller wrote to suggest an interesting day trip to the village of Terauli about 20 km away, to find two local child-gurus – 'a bloody fascinating day'. You could hire a bike in Mathura or Vrindaban and ride there, he suggested.

Places to Stay

Mathura has a number of fairly basic hotels and many dharamsalas. The *Agra Hotel* (tel 3318) on Bengali Ghat has rooms from around Rs 30. The *Kwality Hotel* (tel 3379), near the bus stand, is similarly priced. There's a state *Tourist Bungalow* with rooms from Rs 25 to Rs 35. On Junction Rd on the way to the station the *Braj Lodge* is a good place with rooms at Rs 30/45; the manager, Captain Mahesh, is exceptionally helpful.

There are *Railway Retiring Rooms* at the Mathura Junction station with rooms for just Rs 8. The *Kisan Bhavan*, near the museum, has dirt-cheap rooms. There's an *Iskon Guest House* for Krishna freaks at Vrindaban, where the Hare Krishna movement has its HQ. 'A very nice hotel, if you don't mind 24-hour chanting'. Singles are Rs 35 for a very comfortable room with attached bathroom.

Getting There

Mathura is on the Delhi-Agra road and railway routes. It's 57 km north of Agra, 141 km south of Delhi. By rail the fare from Delhi is Rs 16 in 2nd class, Rs 65 in 1st.

AGRA (population 700,000)

At the time of the Moghuls, in the 16th and 17th centuries, Agra was the capital of India, and its superb monuments date from that era. Agra has a magnificent fort and the building which many people have visited India solely to see – the Taj Mahal. Situated on the banks of the Yamuna River, with its crowded alleys and predatory rickshaw riders, Agra is much like any other north Indian city once you're away from these imposing reminders of Moghul splendour. It's possible to day-trip to Agra from Delhi (there's an excellent train service making this eminently practicable), but Agra is worth more than a day, particularly if you intend to visit (as you certainly should) the deserted city of Fatehpur Sikri. In any case the Taj deserves more than a single visit if you're going to appreciate how its appearance changes under different lights.

Agra became the capital of Sikandar Lodi in 1501 but was soon passed on to the Moghuls, and both Babur and Humayun made some early Moghul constructions here. It was under Akbar that Agra first aspired to its heights of magnificence. From 1570 to 1585 he ruled from nearby Fatehpur Sikri. When he abandoned that city he moved to Lahore (now in Pakistan) but returned to Agra in 1599 and remained there until his death in 1605. Jehangir, with his passion for Kashmir, did not spend a great deal of time in the city; Shah Jahan is the name inevitably connected with Agra. He built the Jami Masjid, most of the palace buildings inside the Agra Fort and, of course, the Taj Mahal. Between 1638 and 1650 he built the Red Fort and Jami Masjid in Delhi and would probably have moved the capital there had he not been deposed and imprisoned by his son, Aurangzeb, in 1658. Aurangzeb did transfer the capital there.

In 1761 Agra fell to the Jats, who did much damage to the city and its monuments, even going so far as to pillage the Taj Mahal. In turn it was taken by the Marathas in 1770 and passed through several more changes before the British took control in 1803. There was much fighting around the fort during the Mutiny in 1857.

Orientation & Information

Agra is on the west bank of the Yamuna River, 204 km south of Delhi. The old part of the town is north of the fort where the Kinari Bazaar, the main market place, is located in a narrow street. The cantonment area to the south is the modern part of town, known as Sadar Bazaar. Here you will find the Government of India Tourist Office (tel 72377) at 191 The Mall. It's open 9 am to 5 pm weekdays, 9 am to 1 pm Saturday, closed Sunday. The GPO and poste restante is also on The Mall. In this area you will find handicraft shops, dry cleaners, restaurants and many moderately priced hotels. The Modern Book Depot on The Mall has a good selection. Deluxe buses for Delhi and Jaipur operate from here.

There are some lower-priced hotels and the Tourist Bungalow near the Raja Mandi railway station, but this area is rather inconveniently located. It's far from the Taj and the main hotel and restaurant area. The 'tourist class' hotels are mainly in the spacious areas of Taj Ganj, south of the Taj itself. Immediately south of the Taj is a tightly packed area of narrow alleys where you can find some popular rock-bottom hotels. It's a pleasant walk along the riverside between the Taj and the Red Fort.

Agra's main railway station is Agra Cantonment; trains from New Delhi arrive here. The main bus station for cities in Rajasthan and for Fatehpur Sikri is Idgah. The Fort Bus Station has buses going to Mathura. Indian Airlines (tel 73434) is in the Hotel Clarks Shiraz. Agra airport is seven km out of town.

Taj Mahal

If there's a building which represents a country – like the Eiffel Tower for France, the Sydney Opera House for Australia – then it has to be the Taj Mahal for India.

The Taj Mahal

This most famous Moghul monument was constructed by Emperor Shah Jahan in memory of his wife Mumtaz Mahal, the 'lady of the Taj'. It has been described as the most extravagant monument ever built for love, for the emperor was heartbroken when Mumtaz, to whom he had been married for 17 years, died in 1629 in childbirth, after producing 14 children.

Construction of the Taj commenced in 1632 and was not completed until 1653. Workers were recruited not only from all over India but also from Central Asia, and in total 20,000 people worked on the building. Experts were even brought from as far away as Europe – the Frenchman Austin of Bordeaux and the Italian Veroneo of Venice had a hand in its decoration. The main architect was Isa Khan, who came from Shiraz in Iran.

The most unusual story about the Taj is that there might well have been two of them. Shah Jahan, it is said, had intended to build a second Taj as his own tomb in black marble, a negative image of the white Taj of Mumtaz Mahal. Before he could embark on this second masterpiece

Aurangzeb deposed his father. Shah Jahan spent the rest of his life in the Agra Fort, looking out along the river to the final resting place of his favourite wife.

The Taj Mahal stands on a raised marble platform with tall white minarets at each corner of the platform. They are just for decoration; nobody is called to prayer from them. The central structure has four small domes surrounding the huge, bulbous, central dome. The tombs of Mumtaz Mahal and Shah Jahan are in a basement room. Above them in the main chamber are false tombs, a common practice in Indian mausoleums of this type. Light is admitted into the central chamber by finely cut marble screens. The echo in this high chamber, under the soaring marble dome, is superb and there is always somebody there to demonstrate it.

Although the Taj is amazingly graceful from almost any angle, it's the close-up detail which is really astounding. Semi-precious stones are inlaid into the marble in beautiful patterns and with superb craftsmanship in a process known as *pietra dura*. The precision and care which went into the Taj Mahal's design and construction is just as impressive whether you view it from across the river or from arm's length.

The building, which stands beside the Yamuna River, is in a large formal garden. Twin red sandstone mosques frame the building when viewed from the river. You enter the Taj grounds through a high red sandstone gateway inscribed with verses from the Koran in Arabic. Paths lead to the Taj, divided by a long watercourse in which the Taj is beautifully reflected – if it's filled with water! As is so often repeated, the Taj is worth more than a single visit. It's one building under the light of dawn, another at sunset. Still another under moonlight. Full moons bring people flocking to Agra in their thousands.

Admission is Rs 2 except on Fridays when it is free. Fridays also tend to be impossibly crowded and noisy, not very conducive to calm enjoyment of this most serene of buildings. Opening hours are normally from sunrise to 10 pm, but due to the unrest in the Punjab it has recently been opening later and closing earlier. Under normal circumstances, on full-moon nights and the four nights around the full moon it stays open until midnight. A bus from Sadar to the Taj is less than Rs 1.

A final sad note about the Taj – scientists fear that after centuries of undiminished glory the modern world may finally be shortening its life. Industrial pollution, particularly a proposed chemical plant, could cause irreparable damage to the marble before the turn of the century. Not that man hasn't damaged it in the past – in 1764 silver doors at the entrance were ripped off and carted away and raiders have also made off with the gold sheets that once lined the subterranean vault.

Agra Fort

Construction of the massive Agra Fort commenced with Emperor Akbar in 1565 and additions were made through to the time of his grandson, Shah Jahan. While in Akbar's time the fort was principally a military structure, by the time of Shah Jahan the emphasis had shifted and the fort had become partially a palace. A visit to the fort is an Agra 'must' since so many of the events which led to the construction of the Taj took place here.

There are many fascinating buildings inside the massive 20-metre walls which stretch for 2.5 km, surrounded by a moat over 10 metres wide. The fort is on the banks of the Yamuna River and only the Amar Singh Gate to the south is open. Inside, the fort is really a city within the city. It is open from sunrise to sunset and admission is Rs 2 except on Fridays when it is free. There's an entertaining sound & light show. Some of the important buildings within the fort include:

Moti Masjid The 'Pearl Mosque' was built by Shah Jahan between 1646 and 1653. The marble mosque is considered to be perfectly proportioned and a Persian inscription inside the building compares it to a perfect pearl. The mosque's courtyard is surrounded by arcaded cloisters and a marble tank stands in the centre.

Diwan-i-Am The 'Hall of Public Audiences' was also built by Shah Jahan and replaces an earlier wooden structure. Shah Jahan's predecessors had a hand in the hall's construction, but the throne room, with its typical inlaid marble work, is indisputably from Shah Jahan. Here he sat to meet officials or listen to petitioners. Beside the Diwan-i-Am is the small Nagina Masjid or 'Gem Mosque' and the 'ladies' bazaar' where merchants came to display and sell goods to the ladies of the Moghul court.

Diwan-i-Khas The 'Hall of Private Audiences' was also built by Shah Jahan, in 1636-37. Here the emperor would meet important dignitaries or foreign ambas-

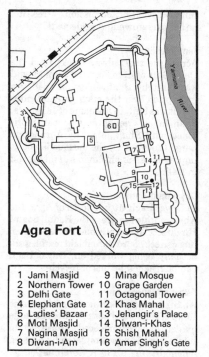

Agra Fort

1 Jami Masjid	9 Mina Mosque
2 Northern Tower	10 Grape Garden
3 Delhi Gate	11 Octagonal Tower
4 Elephant Gate	12 Khas Mahal
5 Ladies' Bazaar	13 Jehangir's Palace
6 Moti Masjid	14 Diwan-i-Khas
7 Nagina Masjid	15 Shish Mahal
8 Diwan-i-Am	16 Amar Singh's Gate

sadors. The hall consists of two rooms connected by three arches. The famous 'peacock throne' was kept here before being moved to Delhi by Aurangzeb. It was later carried off to Iran and its remains are now in Tehran.

Octagonal Tower The Musamman Burj or Octagonal Tower stands close to the Diwan-i-Khas and the small, private Mina Masjid. Also known as the Saman Burj, this tower was built by Shah Jahan for Mumtaz Mahal and is another of his finely designed and executed buildings. It was here, with its views along the Yamuna to the Taj, that Shah Jahan died in 1666, after seven years' imprisonment. Unfortunately the tower has been much damaged over the years.

Jehangir's Palace Akbar is believed to have built this palace, the largest private residence in the fort, for his son. This was one of the first constructions demonstrating the fort's changing emphasis from military to luxurious. The palace is also interesting for its blend of Hindu and central Asian architectural styles – a contrast to the unique Moghul style which had developed by the time of Shah Jahan.

Other Shah Jahan's Khas Mahal is a beautiful white marble structure used as a private palace. The rooms underneath it were intended as a cool retreat in the summer heat. The Shish Mahal or 'Mirror Palace' was supposed to have been the harem dressing room and its walls are inlaid with tiny mirrors. The Anguri Bagh or 'Grape Garden' probably never had any grapevines but was simply a small, formal Moghul garden. It stood in front of the Khas Mahal. The Delhi Gate and Hathi Pol or 'Elephant Gate' are now closed.

In front of the Jehangir Palace is the Hauz-i-Jehangri, a huge 'bath' carved out of a single block of stone – by whom and for what purpose is a subject of conjecture. The Amar Singh Gate takes its name from a Maharaja of Jodhpur who was killed beside the gate, along with his followers, after a brawl in the Diwan-i-Am in 1644! Justice tended to be summary in those days; there is a shaft leading down to the river into which those who made themselves unpopular with the great Moghuls could be hurled without further to-do.

Itmad-ud-daulah

There are a number of interesting sights on the opposite bank of the Yamuna and north of the fort. You cross the river on a narrow two-level bridge carrying pedestrians, bicycles, rickshaws and bullock carts. The first place of interest is the Itmad-ud-daulah – the tomb of Mirza Ghiyas Beg. This Persian gentleman's beautiful daughter married Emperor Jehangir and became known as Nur

Jahan, the 'light of the world'. In turn her daughter was Mumtaz Mahal, the lady of the Taj. The tomb was constructed by Nur Jahan between 1622 and 1628 and is very similar to the tomb she constructed for her husband, Jehangir, near Lahore in Pakistan.

The tomb is of particular interest since many of its design elements foreshadow the Taj, construction of which commenced only a few years later. The Itmad-ud-daulah was the first Moghul structure totally constructed of marble and the first to make extensive use of *pietra dura*, the inlay work of marble so much a part of the Taj. The mausoleum is small and squat compared to the soaring Taj, but the smaller, more human scale somehow makes it more attractive, and the beautifully patterned surface of the tomb is superb. Extremely fine marble lattice-work passages admit light to the interior. It's well worth a visit. The Itmad-ud-daulah is open sunrise to sunset and admission is Rs 2, free on Fridays.

China-ka-Rauza

The 'china tomb' is a km north of the Itmad-ud-daulah. The squat, square tomb, surmounted by a single huge dome, was constructed in his own life-time by Afzal Khan, who died in Lahore in 1639. He was a high official in the court of Shah Jahan. The exterior was covered in brightly coloured enamelled tiles and the whole building clearly displayed its Persian influence. Today it is much decayed and neglected, and the remaining tilework only hints at the building's former glory.

Ram Bagh

Laid out in 1528 by Emperor Babur, first of the Moghuls, this is the earliest Moghul garden. It is said that Babur was temporarily buried here before being permanently interred at Kabul in Afghanistan. The Ram Bagh is two to three km further north of the China-ka-Rauza on the riverside and is open from sunrise to sunset; admission is free. It's rather overgrown and neglected.

Jami Masjid

Across the the railway tracks from the Delhi Gate of Agra Fort, the Jami Masjid was built by Shah Jahan in 1648. An inscription over the main gate indicates that it was built in the name of Jahanara, Shah Jahan's daughter, who was imprisoned with Shah Jahan by Aurangzeb. Large though it is, the mosque is not as impressive as Shah Jahan's Jami Masjid in Delhi.

Dayal Bagh Temple

In Dayal Bagh, 10 km north of Agra, the white marble temple of the Radah Soami Hindu sect is currently under construction. You can see *pietra dura* inlaid marblework actually being worked on. Dayal Bagh can be reached by bus or bicycle.

Akbar's Mausoleum

At Sikandra, 10 km north of Agra, the tomb of Akbar lies in the centre of a large garden. Akbar commenced its construction himself but it was completed by his son, Jehangir, in 1613. A combination of Muslim and Hindu architectural styles, the building, with three-storey minarets at each corner, is built of red sandstone inlaid with white marble polygonal patterns. Four red sandstone gates lead to the tomb complex. One is Muslim, one Hindu, one Christian, one Akbar's patent mixture. Like Humayun's Tomb in New Delhi, it is an interesting place to study the gradual evolution in design that culminated in the Taj Mahal. Akbar's Mausoleum is open from sunrise to sunset and entry is Rs 2, except on Fridays when it is free.

Sikandra is named after Sultan Sikandar Lodi, the Delhi ruler who was in power from 1488 to 1517, immediately preceding the rise of Moghul power on the sub-continent. The Baradi Palace, in the mausoleum gardens, was built by Sikandar Lodi. Across the road from the mausoleum is the Delhi Gate. Between Sikandra and Agra are several tombs and two *kos minars* 'milestones'.

Getting There It's a fair way out to Sikandra; count on Rs 25 to Rs 40 for the return trip in an auto-rickshaw.

Other

The Kinari Bazaar or old market place is a fascinating area to wander around. It's in the old part of Agra, near the fort, and the narrow alleys of the market start near the Jami Masjid.

Women beckon to single men from upstairs balconies of the Malka Bazaar in the old city.

Tours

The ITDC operate Agra tours from Delhi for around Rs 225 for a day tour including breakfast. The tours include Fatehpur Sikri as well as the main sights in Agra itself. If your time is very limited these tours may be worth considering.

If you're day-tripping from Delhi to Agra, Agra tours commence from the railway station and tickets are sold on the Taj Express from Delhi. This tour lasts from 10.40 am to 6.30 pm and covers the Taj, the fort and Fatehpur Sikri; it costs Rs 35. Passengers are picked up half an hour earlier at the Tourist Office, 191 The Mall. At the Cantonment Station tickets can be bought near the Platform 1 enquiry window.

There are also tours just to Fatehpur Sikri, lasting from 10.40 am to 2 pm and costing Rs 22. Or there's an afternoon tour to the Itmad-ud-Daulah, Dayal Bagh and Sikandra from 2.30 to 5.45 pm which costs Rs 20.

Places to Stay – bottom end

The Sadar area, close to the Cantonment Railway Station, the Tourist Office and the GPO and only a Rs 2 or Rs 3 rickshaw ride from the Taj, is a good place for reasonably cheap accommodation. There are also many good restaurants in this

same vicinity. Taj Rd is the hub of the Sadar area, parallel to The Mall. Next to Sadar is an area called Baluganj which has some popular budget hotels. If you're after rock-bottom prices then head for the maze of small streets immediately to the south of the Taj.

The very popular *Tourist Rest House* (tel 64961) is opposite the office of the District Board and is conveniently close to the GPO and Tourist Office. It is run by two helpful brothers who will even make train reservations for you. This pleasant though slightly dog-eared hotel has a variety of rooms with and without attached bathroom. With bath, singles/doubles are about Rs 30/40 and there are dorm beds for Rs 7. Rooms with hot water are Rs 50. The rooms are around a small garden area; the verandah is a good place to meet others. Rickshaws are unwilling to take you there as they don't get a commission; and beware of the much inferior 'New Tourist Rest House' just a stone's throw away. The 'new' is very small and it's purely a rip-off from the original.

Hotel Khanna (tel 66634) is at 19 Ajmer Rd, not far from the Tourist Rest House. Rooms in this clean and pleasant hotel include singles with bath at Rs 60 or doubles at Rs 80, 100 and 120. There's a pleasant courtyard but the rooms at the front are probably a bit noisy. *Hotel Ajay International* (tel 64427) is at 1 Daresi, near the Fort Railway Station, and has rooms from Rs 20.

There are plenty of other cheap hotels around Agra. The *Jaggi Hotel* (tel 72370) on The Mall is a very straightforward place with singles for Rs 30, doubles for Rs 45 to Rs 60 with bath. *Hotel Akbar Inn* at 21 The Mall may also be worth checking – there's a pleasant garden but the food is somewhat expensive. *Hotel Jai Hind* (tel 73502) is on Naulakha Rd, a small street off Taj Rd, the main street of Sadar. Rooms cost from Rs 25 in this well-run and friendly place.

The late *Major Bakshi's Guest House* (tel 76828) at 33/83 Ajmer Rd is still

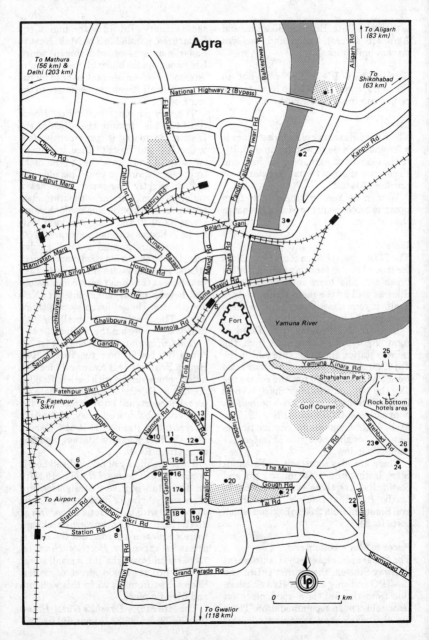

Agra

To Mathura
(56 km) &
Delhi (203 km)

To Aligarh
(83 km)

To Shikohabad
(63 km)

Balkeshwar Rd

Aligarh Rd

Kanpur Rd

National Highway 2 (Bypass)

Karbala Rd

Church Rd

Lala Lajput Marg

Chhili Int Rd

Nehru Rd

Pandit Kalicharan Tiwari Rd

Ramratan Marg

Kinari Bazaar

Hospital Rd

Bhagat Singh Marg

Capt Naresh Rd

Panchkulyan Marg

Sayyed Ali Nabi Marg

Ghalibpura Rd

Mantola Rd

M Gandhi Rd

Belan Gani

P Mandir Rd

Chhata Rd

Jama Masjid Rd

Fort

Yamuna River

Fatehpur Sikri Rd

To Fatehpur
Sikri

Ajmer Rd

Chhipi Tola Rd

General Cariappa Rd

Yamuna Kinara Rd

Shahjahan Park

Golf Course

Rock bottom
hotels area

Namner Rd

Kachahari Rd

Taj Rd

Fatehbad Rd

To Airport

Station Rd

Fatehpur Sikri Rd

Mahatma Gandhi Rd

Gwalior Rd

The Mall

Gough Rd

Taj Rd

Minto Rd

Station Rd

Prithvi Raj Rd

Grand Parade Rd

Shamsabad Rd

To Gwalior
(118 km)

0   1 km

• 1
• 2
3 •
• 4
5
• 25
13 •
23 •
26 •
• 10
11 •
12 •
24 •
• 6
15 •
• 14
9 •
16 •
• 20
17 •
• 21
22 •
18 •
• 19
8 •
7 •

lp

1	Ram Bagh
2	Chini ka Rauza
3	Itmad-ud-Daulah's Tomb
4	Tourist Bungalow
5	Agra Fort Railway Station
6	Idgah Bus Station
7	Agra Cantonment Railway Station
8	Grand Hotel
9	Agra Caterers
10	Lauries Hotel
11	Major Bakshi's
12	Khanna Hotel
13	Tourist Rest House
14	Agra Ashok Hotel
15	GPO
16	Tourist Office
17	Zorba the Buddha
18	Kwality Restaurant
19	Jaggi Hotel
20	Telegraph Office
21	Hotel Clarks Shiraz & Indian Airlines
22	Highway Inn
23	Galaxy Hotel
24	Mayur Tourist Complex
25	Taj Mahal
26	Mughal Sheraton Hotel

operating and has rooms with bath for Rs 75/100 and a couple of bathless doubles for Rs 50. There is a more expensive Colonel Bakshi's Guest House near the airport. *Colonel Duggal's Guest House* at 155 Pertabpura (near the GPO and Tourist Office) has doubles for Rs 60 and has been highly recommended. Away from the Sadar area towards the Taj the *Agra Hotel* (tel 72330) is on General Cariappa Rd and has rooms from Rs 35 to Rs 70 or from Rs 125 with air-con. It's 'the only hotel with a view of the Taj', the staff are friendly and the food can be good.

Camping facilities are available in Agra at several places, including the *Hotel Grand, Hotel Lauries* and *Mayur Tourist Complex*. Agra's *Tourist Bungalow* (tel 72123) is in the Raja Mandi area, a long way from anywhere, but it does have a garden and doubles cost Rs 40 to Rs 75. There are *Retiring Rooms* at the Cantonment and the Agra Fort Railway Station.

A labyrinth of winding, narrow streets runs back from the Taj. Follow the road straight back from the main entrance and you'll find the *Hotel Shah Jahan* with singles from Rs 15, doubles from Rs 20 to Rs 50 and a dormitory for Rs 5. It's reasonably clean and habitable and has an amazing menu of questionable food.

Continue into the maze, and by the tonga stand (ask) you'll find the *Hotel Mumtaz Mahal*. Again it's a reasonable place considering the rock-bottom prices. Continuing along Chowk Kagjiyan from the square by the Shah Jahan, you soon come to the relatively new *Shanti Lodge* with rooms from Rs 15 to Rs 50 – good value for this well-kept place. There are several other similarly cheap places in the area like the *India Guest House*, the *Gulshan Lodge* near South Gate and the *New Taj Hotel*.

Places to Stay – middle
In the same area as the more expensive hotels is the *Mayur Tourist Complex* (tel 64771) on Fatehabad Rd. The rooms are individual cottages at Rs 100/120, Rs 115/145, Rs 140/190 depending on facilities. There's a fair amount of flaking paint and general decay but it's reasonably priced and in a pleasant garden.

Near the Cantonment Railway Station the reasonably modern *Hotel Grand* (tel 74014) has singles at Rs 75, doubles from Rs 95 to Rs 150. There's a nice garden out front. *Hotel Lauries* (tel 77047) on Mahatma Gandhi Rd charges Rs 65/110 for old-fashioned and musty but reasonable rooms. There's a 'disgusting looking but surprisingly pleasant' mineral-water pool. This place is still used by overland groups.

Hotel Jaiwal (tel 64171) is also very centrally located in the Sadar area and is one of the better hotels in this price range – rooms with air-con are Rs 95/140. *Hotel Amar* (tel 65696) on Fatehabad Rd has rooms at Rs 100/140 up to Rs 145/200 with air-con and is quite a good place.

Out towards the airport, several km

from the town centre, is *Colonel Bakshi's Guest House* (tel 61292) at 5 Lakshman Nagar. He's the son of the late Major Bakshi whose guest house is in the Sadar area. Very pleasant rooms in this new, well-equipped and spotlessly clean home are Rs 150/200. The food is excellent, all rooms have attached bathrooms and in summer there's air-cooling, with possibly an additional charge. If you book ahead they'll arrange to collect you from the station or the airport.

Places to Stay – top end

Agra's tourist-class hotels are generally in the open area south of the Taj. *Hotel Mughal Sheraton* (tel 64701, 64729) on Fatehabad Rd has elegant, fort-like architecture and offers everything from camel or elephant rides to an in-house astrologer who will tell your fortune for Rs 50. There are 200 rooms with singles/doubles ranging from Rs 650/800.

The older *Hotel Clarks Shiraz* (tel 72421) is a long-standing Agra landmark. It too is fully air-conditioned and has a swimming pool; the Indian Airlines office is located here. Singles/doubles cost Rs 450/550. It is one of the better expensive Agra hotels.

South-east of the Taj, the *Hotel Mumtaz* (tel 64771) on Fatehabad Rd is a smaller hotel with 40 rooms, all air-con. Singles/doubles are Rs 200/280. On the same road the *Hotel Galaxy Ashok* (tel 64171) has rooms at Rs 300/375. There's an ITDC *Hotel Agra Ashok* under construction by The Mall. Rooms will be Rs 625/725.

Places to Eat

The deluxe hotels have excellent food – for a major splurge *Clarks Shiraz* is worth considering; their lunchtime buffet is Rs 65, snacks around Rs 15. At the *Mughal Sheraton* the buffet is Rs 85.

In the Sadar area the *Kwality Restaurant* on the Taj Rd is air-con and excellent. *Prakash Restaurant*, across the street, can also be good: 'The best-

tasting Indian food we had in India', wrote two New Zealanders. Opposite the Kwality in a modern shopping block, the *Brijwasi Sweet House* is very clean and helpful and all the sweets are named and priced. Further along from the Kwality is the Chinese *Chung Wah*.

On a tighter budget *Hotel Jai Hind* is good and *Hotel Jaggi*, also in the Sadar area, is all right. *Laxmi Vilas* is a good place for south Indian food in this same area. *Khaja Peeja* is a popular vegetarian place near the GPO and Tourist Office.

The *Plaza Restaurant* at Namner, round the corner from the Tourist Rest House, has good, cheap vegetarian food. At E/13 Shopping Arcade, off Gopi Chand Shivhare Rd which runs between The Mall and Taj Rd in Sadar, is *Zorba the Buddha*, another Rajneesh restaurant. The food is excellent and the desserts are delicious.

In the rock-bottom hotel area immediately south of the Taj is *Joney's Place*, which several travellers have written to recommend. It's as basic (and unhygienic looking) as you could ask for, but the food is said to be good – although service can be painfully slow. The *ITDC Cafeteria & Restaurant* just outside the Taj entrance is good for both Indian and western food. At the east gate the *Relax Restaurant* does fine real coffee and desserts.

Agra has a local speciality, the ultra-sweet candied melon called *petha*.

Entertainment

When you tire of the Taj there are various non-sightseeing possibilities in Agra. Non-residents can use the swimming pool at Clarks for Rs 25 or the pool at Lauries for Rs 15. The *Hotel Galaxy* pool can also be used. There is a cinema in the Baluganj area of the city which shows English-language movies every evening. *Hotel Maurya Sheraton* has a programme of Indian folk dancing almost every evening. It costs Rs 20 for half an hour from 6.30 pm.

Getting There

Air Agra is on the popular tourist daily flight route Delhi-Agra-Khajuraho-Varanasi-Kathmandu and return. It's only a 30-minute flight from Delhi to Agra. Fares from Agra are Delhi Rs 192, Khajuraho Rs 331, Varanasi Rs 499. Vayudoot fly Delhi-Agra-Jaipur and return three times a week.

Rail Agra is on the main Delhi-Bombay broad-gauge railway line, so there are plenty of trains coming through. There is a daily express train from Delhi to Agra known as the Taj Express which costs Rs 27 in 2nd class, Rs 63 in 1st. The Taj Express departs New Delhi Railway Station at 7 am daily and arrives in Agra three hours later. The return train departs Agra at 7 pm and arrives in Delhi at 10 pm – ideal for a day trip to Agra. Avoid the slow passenger trains at all costs. Take great care at New Delhi station; pickpockets, muggers and others are very aware that this is a popular tourist train and they work overtime at parting unwary visitors from their goods.

Guided tours of Agra and Fatehpur Sikri depart from the railway station as soon as the train arrives. Lucknow is about nine hours away by train. If you're heading north towards the Himalaya there are trains through Agra which continue straight through Delhi, saving you stopping and getting more tickets.

Bus Most regular buses leave from the Idgah Bus Station. Regular buses between Delhi and Agra operate about every hour and cost Rs 22 to Rs 24. Deluxe buses cost Rs 33. The trip takes about five hours. There's a daily ITDC deluxe bus between Agra and Jaipur which leaves at 7 am, takes five hours and costs Rs 45. There's an early-morning bus to Khajuraho, which is a long way from Agra but this is one of the better jumping-off points.

Getting Around

Agra is very spread out so walking is really not on – even if you could. It's virtually impossible to walk because Agra's hordes of rickshaw-wallahs pursue would-be pedestrians with unbelievable energy and persuasive ability. Beware of rickshaw men who take you from A to B via a few marble shops, jewellery shops and so on. Just great when you want to catch a train, but it can also work out very expensive!

A simple solution to Agra's transport problem is to hire a rickshaw for the day. You can easily negotiate an all-in daily rate (Rs 20 to Rs 30) for which your rickshaw-wallah will not only take you everywhere, he'll wait outside while you sightsee or even have a meal. Agra is so touristy that many of them speak fine English and, like western cabbies, are great sources of amusing information – like how much they can screw out of fat-cat tourists for a little pedal down to the Taj and back to the air-conditioning. Otherwise Rs 3 to Rs 5 will take you from pretty well anywhere in Agra to anywhere else.

If, however, you really don't want to be pedalled around, Agra is sufficiently traffic free to make pedalling yourself an easy proposition. There are plenty of bicycle-hire places around, such as the petrol station near the Tourist Rest House. They can be rented for Rs 5 a day.

Things to Buy

Agra is well known for leather goods, jewellery and marble items, inlaid like the *pietra dura* work on the Taj. The Sadar area and around the Taj itself are the main tourist shop areas, although the prices here are likely to be more expensive. Around Pratapur there are many jewellery shops, but precious stones are cheaper in Jaipur.

Beware of rickshaw-wallahs taking you to shops – they'll inevitably be raking off a commission at your expense. Beware too of 'marble' that turns out to be alabaster. Alabaster will scratch, marble will not. Agra's shopkeepers are unbelievably smooth talking and persuasive. There are *no* government craft shops apart from the state government emporiums. Don't believe people who tell you otherwise.

Agra, along with Jaipur and Varanasi, is one of the truly notorious places in India for buy-and-sell scams. If you believe any stories about buying here to sell at a profit there, you'll simply be proving (once again) that old adage about separating fools from their money! Precious stones are a favourite for this game. They'll tell you that you can sell stones in Australia, Europe or the US for several times the purchase price, and will even give you the (often imaginary!) addresses of dealers who will buy them. In actual fact the stones you buy will be worth only a fraction of what you pay.

FATEHPUR SIKRI

Between 1570 and 1586, during the reign of Emperor Akbar, the capital of the Moghul empire was situated here, 40 km west of Agra. Then, as suddenly and dramatically as this new city had been built, it was abandoned. Today it's a perfectly preserved Moghul city at the height of the empire's splendour. And an attraction no visitor to Agra should miss.

The legend relates that Akbar was without a male heir and made a pilgrimage to this spot to see the saint Shaikh Salim Chisti. The saint foretold the birth of Akbar's son, later Emperor Jehangir, and in gratitude Akbar named his son Salim. Furthermore, Akbar transferred his capital to Sikri and built a new and splendid city. Later, however, the city was abandoned due, it is said, to difficulties with the water supply.

Akbar was known to be very tolerant towards other religions although he was Muslim, and he spent much time discussing and studying them in Fatehpur Sikri. He also developed a new religion called 'Deen Ilahi' which attempted to synthesise elements from all the major religions. Akbar's famous courtiers, such

as Bibal, Raja Todarmal and Abu Fazal, had their houses near his palace in the city.

Orientation & Information

The deserted city lies along the top of a ridge while the modern village, with its bus stand and railway station, is down on the southern side. Fatehpur Sikri is open from sunrise to sunset and entry is Rs 1, free on Fridays. The Jami Masjid is outside the city enclosure.

As Fatehpur Sikri is one of the most perfectly preserved 'ghost towns' imaginable, you may well decide it is worthwhile spending a few rupees to hire a guide. When you arrive, look for 'Shahi Darwaza', not 'Buland Darwaza'. Shahi Darwaza is the official entrance to the fort where licensed guides are available. On the other hand, at the Buland Darwaza, the gateway to the mosque and shrine, unlicensed guides will try to lure you into hiring them. The mosque and shrine are not inside the city walls; you have to go there separately.

Jami Masjid or Dargah Mosque

Fatehpur Sikri's mosque is said to be a copy of the mosque at Mecca and is a very beautiful building containing elements of Persian and Hindu design. The main entrance is through the 54-metre-high Buland Darwaza, the Gate of Victory, constructed to commemorate Akbar's victory in south India. The impressive gateway is reached by an equally impressive flight of steps. An inscription inside the archway includes the useful thought that 'The world is a bridge, pass over it but build no house upon it. He who hopes for an hour may hope for eternity'. Just outside the gateway is a deep well, and when there is a sufficient number of tourists assembled local daredevils leap from the top of the entrance into the water.

Inside the mosque is the tomb or dargah of Shaikh Salim Chisti, surrounded by marble lattice screens. Just as Akbar

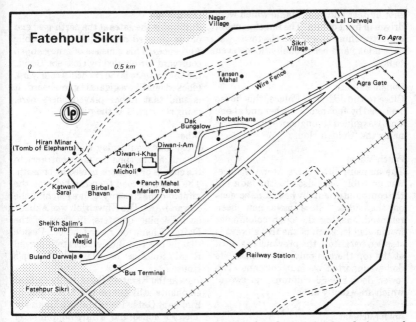

came to the saint four centuries ago, looking for a son, so do childless women visit his tomb today. The saint's grandson, Islam Khan, also has his tomb within the mosque. Abul Fazl and Faizi, adviser and poet to Akbar, had their homes just outside the mosque.

Palace of Jodh Bai
North-east of the mosque is this palace named after Jehangir's wife, although it was probably used more by Akbar's wife, who was a Hindu. Here again the architecture is a blend of styles with Hindu columns and Muslim cupolas. The 'Palace of the Winds' is a projecting room with walls made entirely of stone latticework. The ladies of the court probably sat in here to keep a quiet eye on events below.

Birbal Bhavan
Built either by or for Raja Birbal, Akbar's favourite courtier, this small palace is

extremely elegant in its design and execution. Victor Hugo, the Victorian-era French author, commented that it was either a very small palace or a very large jewellery box. Birbal, who was a Hindu and noted for his wit and wisdom, unfortunately proved to be a hopeless soldier and lost his life, and most of his army, near Peshawar in 1586. Enormous stables adjoin the Jodh Bai Palace, with nearly 200 enclosures for horses and camels. Some stone rings for the halters are still in place.

Karawan Sarai & Hiran Minar
The Karawan Sarai or 'caravanserai' was a large courtyard surrounded by the hostels used by visiting merchants. The Hiran Minar or 'Deer Minaret', which is actually outside the fort grounds, is said to have been erected over the grave of Akbar's favourite elephant. Stone elephant tusks protrude from the 21-metre-high tower from which Akbar is said to have

shot at deer and other game which were driven in front of him. The flat expanse of land stretching away from the tower was once a lake and occasionally floods even today.

Miriam's House

Close to the Jodh Bai Palace, this house was used by Jehangir's mother and at one time was gilded throughout – giving it the name the 'Golden House'.

Panch Mahal

The amusing little 'Five Storey Palace' was probably once used by the ladies of the court and originally had stone screens on the sides. These have now been removed, making the open colonnades inside visible. Each of the five storeys is stepped back from the previous one until at the top there is only a tiny kiosk, its dome supported by four columns. The lower floor has 56 columns, no two of which are exactly alike.

Ankh Michauli

The name of this building translates as something like 'hide and seek', and the emperor is supposed to have amused himself by playing that game with ladies of the harem! The building was more probably used for storing records, although it has some curious struts with stone monsters carved into them. By one corner is a small canopied enclosure where Akbar's Hindu guru may have sat to instruct him.

Diwan-i-Khas

The exterior of the Hall of Private Audiences is plain but its interior design is unique. A stone column in the centre of the building supports a flat-topped 'throne'. From the four corners of the room stone bridges lead across to this throne, and it is thought that Akbar sat in the middle while his four principal ministers sat at the four corners.

Diwan-i-Am

Just inside the gates at the north-east end of the deserted city is the Hall of Public Audiences. This consists of a large open courtyard surrounded by cloisters. Beside the Diwan-i-Am is the Pachchisi courtyard, blocked out like a gigantic gameboard. It is said that Akbar played chess here, using slave girls as the pieces.

Other

Musicians would play from the Norbat Khana, at one time the main entrance to the city, as processions passed by beneath. The entrance road then ran between the mint and the treasury before reaching the Diwan-i-Am. The Khwabgah was Akbar's own sleeping quarters, in front of the Daftar Khana or record office. Beside that is the tiny but elaborately carved Rumi Sultana or 'Turkish Queen's House'.

Near the Karawan Sarai, badly defaced elephants still guard the Hathi Pol or Elephant Gate. There is also a Hakim or doctor's house and a fine *hammam* or Turkish bath beside it. Outside the Dargah Mosque are the remains of the small stone-cutters' mosque. Shaikh Salim Chisti's cave was supposedly at this site and the mosque predates Akbar's imperial city.

Places to Stay

Although most people day trip from Agra, you can stay at the *Archaeological Survey Rest House* for only about Rs 10. It's great value; book it at the Archaeological Survey of India, 22 The Mall, Agra. You get great value food in the hotel across the road from the bus station.

Getting There

The tour buses only stop for an hour or so at Fatehpur Sikri. If you want to spend longer it is worth taking a regular bus from the Idgah Bus Station for about Rs 5. The trip takes a bit over an hour. Along the way you pass milestones, known as kos minars, about every three km.

Uttar Pradesh Top: Bathing ghats on the Ganges at Varanasi (PC)
Left: Sikh Pilgrims en route to the Valley of the Flowers (LH)
Right: The Great Imambara in Lucknow (TW)

Bihar Top: Buddhist monks under the Bo tree, Bodhgaya (TW)
Bottom: Spiral staircase up the Golgumbaz, Patna (TW)

There's a train service but it's very slow. Along the road you'll often see dancing bears; the villagers dance their trained bears out into the road to block your way while they demand money!

You can spend a day in Fatehpur Sikri and continue on to Bharatpur in the evening. The bus station restaurant will let you lock up your bags in their garage, but firmly agree on the price beforehand or they may try overcharging you when you return.

DELHI TO KANPUR
Aligarh (population 280,000)
Formerly known as Koil, this was the site of an important fort as far back as 1194. During the upheavals following the death of Aurangzeb and the collapse of the Moghul empire the region was scrapped over by the Afghans, Jats, Marathas and Rohillas – first one coming out on top, then another. In 1776 the fort's name was changed to Aligarh (the high fort) but in 1803, despite French support for the then-ruler Scindia, it fell to the British. The fort is three km north of the town and its present form dates from 1524. The ancient City of Koil has traces of Buddhist and Hindu temples of great antiquity.

Aligarh is best known today for the Aligarh Muslim University where the 'seeds of Pakistan were sown'. Muslim students come here not only from all over India but from all over the Islamic world.

Sankasya
Sankasya is reached via Farrukhabad and Pakhna, from where it is 11 km. There is an Ashokan elephant capital here. A mound, topped by a ruined stupa, marks the spot where Buddha descended from heaven to earth after preaching to his mother.

Kanauj
Only a few dismal ruins indicate that this was once a mighty Hindu city, which quickly fell into disrepair after Mahmud

of Ghazni's raids. This was where Humayun was defeated by Sher Shah in 1540, forcing him to temporarily flee India.

Etawah
This town rose to some importance during the Moghul period, only to go through the usual series of rapid changes during the turmoil that followed the Moghuls. The Jami Masjid shows similiarities to the mosques of Jaunpur and there are bathing ghats on the riverbank, below the ruined fort.

Bareilly (population 360,000)
Former capital of the region known as Rohilkand, Bareilly came under British control when the Rohillas, an Afghan tribe, became too involved with the Marathas and the Nawab of Oudh.

Rampur (population 180,000)
In this former Rohilla state capital the State Library has an important collection of old manuscripts and is housed in a fine building in the old fort. There is a large Jami Masjid nearby and interesting bazaars around the walls of the palace. The library contains a good collection of old miniatures, some of great importance, but these are normally only on view for scholars.

KANPUR (population 1,400,000)
Sometimes called 'the Manchester of India', this important industrial town attracts very few tourists, although it is not a great distance south of Lucknow. During the 1857 Mutiny some of the more tragic events took place here, at that time known as Cawnpore. Sir Hugh Wheeler defended a part of the Cantonment for most of the month of June, but with supplies virtually exhausted and having suffered considerable losses he surrendered only to have his party massacred. All Souls Memorial Church, built in 1875, has some rather moving reminders of the tragic events. It's two km from the

station. Kanpur has a large and modern zoo.

Places to Stay

A Rs 2 to Rs 3 rickshaw ride (two km) from the station, the *Hotel Parivar* (tel 53978) at 26/84 Birhana Rd, Karachi Khana, is behind the Navrang Cinema. Rooms range from Rs 21 for bathless singles to Rs 35 for doubles. It's clean and well kept. Nearby at 24/54 is the much more expensive *Hotel Saurabh* (tel 61725) with air-con rooms at Rs 200/250. The recently renovated *Hotel Berkeley* at Civil Lines is pleasantly situated in its own grounds and has rooms at Rs 80/120.

Other possibilities include the *Hotel Ganges* (tel 62432-5) at 51/50 Nayanganj, only a half km from the railway station, with rooms from Rs 25 to Rs 75, more with air-con. A similar distance from the centre is the small *Yatrik Hotel* (tel 67143) at 65/58A Circular Rd. Rooms here range from Rs 40 to Rs 120 with air-cooling, from Rs 120 to Rs 160 with air-con. Finally the large and all air-con *Hotel Meghdoot* (tel 51141) at 17/3B The Mall is inconveniently far out and has rooms from Rs 275 to Rs 400.

Getting There

Kanpur can be reached daily by air from Delhi (Rs 398). It's on the main Delhi-Calcutta railway line; some express trains take less than five hours Delhi-Kanpur. From Delhi the fare is Rs 42 in 2nd class, Rs 167 in 1st for the 435-km trip. From Calcutta it's 1007 km costing Rs 77 in 2nd class, Rs 313 in 1st.

LUCKNOW (population 1,100,000)

The capital of Uttar Pradesh, Lucknow rose to prominence as the capital of the Nawabs of Oudh. These rulers controlled a region of north-central India for about a century after the decline of the Mogul empire, and most of the interesting monuments in Lucknow date from this period from the mid-18th century. The Nawabs were:

Sa'adat Khan Burhan-ul-mulk	1724-1739
Safdar Jang	1739-1753
Shuja-ud-daula	1753-1775
Asaf-ud-daula	1775-1797
Sa'adat Ali Khan	1798-1814
Ghazi-ud-din Haidar	1814-1827
Nasir-ud-din Haidar	1827-1837
Muhammad Ali Shah	1837-1842
Amjad Ali Shah	1842-1847
Wajid Ali Shah	1847-1856

It was not until Asaf-ud-daula that the capital of Oudh was moved to Lucknow. Safdar Jang lived and ruled from Delhi and his tomb is a familiar landmark near the Safdarjang airport. After Sa'adat Ali Khan the rest of the Oudh Nawabs were a uniformly hopeless lot. Wajid Ali Shah was so extravagant and indolent that to this day his name is regarded by many in India as synonymous with lavishness. In 1856 the British, as was their wont, pensioned him off for incompetence and exiled him to Calcutta for the rest of his life. This was one of the sparks that lit the Indian Mutiny. Lucknow became the scene for some of the most dramatic events of the Mutiny, as the British residents held out in the Residency for 87 harrowing days, only to be besieged again for a further two months after being relieved.

The Nawabs were Shi'ite Muslims, and Lucknow remains the principal Indian Shi'ite city – unlike other major Muslim cities in India like Delhi and Agra, where the Muslims are mainly Sunnite. Shi'ites predominate in Iran (the Ayatollah is a Shi'ite), but in most other Islamic nations the Sunnites form the majority. Lucknow is a good place to see the Shi'ite Muharram celebrations. The activity can get very hectic as penitents scourge themselves with whips; keep a low profile.

Orientation & Information

Lucknow is rather spread out and there is quite a distance between the various places of interest. The town is interesting but sadly neglected by tourists, although the huge mausoleums of the Nawabs were jerry built and have generally deteriorated badly.

The historic monuments are mainly in the north-eastern part of the old city around the chowk area, about six km from the Tourist Bungalow. The main shopping area, with its narrow alleys, is Aminabad, while the modern area with wide avenues and large shops is the fashionable Hazratganj. The major bus stations, for Gorakhpur and Varanasi buses, are in Kaiserbagh. The main railway station, in the south of the city, is called Charbagh.

The Tourist Office is at the Tourist Bungalow (Hotel Gomti) in Hazratganj. There's also a Government of India Tourist Office upstairs at the back of Janpath Market, which is on Mahatma Gandhi Marg in Hazratganj.

Ram Advani's bookshop, next to the Mayfair Cinema on Hazrat Ganj, is excellent. In winter there are often excellent classical music performances and dances at the Rabindralaya auditorium in a garden down Vidhan Sabha Marg towards the new city from Charbagh Station.

Great Imambara

The Bara or Great Imambara was built in 1784 by Asaf-ud-Daula as a famine-relief project. The central hall of the Imambara is 50 metres long and 15 metres high, one of the largest vaulted galleries in the world. Beneath it are many underground passages which have now been blocked up. An external stairway leads to an upper floor laid out as an amazing labyrinth known as the *bhulbhulaiya* (entry Rs 2.50). From the top there's a fine view over the city and the Aurangzeb Mosque.

There is a mosque with two tall minarets in the courtyard of the Imambara but non-Muslims are not allowed to enter it. To the right of this, in a row of cloisters, is a 'bottomless' well. The Imambara is open from 6 am to 5 pm.

Rumi (Roomi) Darwaza

Beside the Bara Imambara and also built by Asaf-ud-Daula, this huge and finely designed *darwaza* or gate is a replica of one in Istanbul. 'Rumi' refers to Rome, the term Muslims used to apply to Istanbul when it was still Byzantium and the capital of the eastern Roman Empire.

Husainabad Imambara

Also known as the *Chhota* or 'small' Imambara, this was built by Muhammad Ali Shah in 1837 to serve as his own mausoleum. Thousands of labourers worked on the project as famine relief. The large courtyard encloses a raised rectangular tank with small imitations of the Taj Mahal on each side. One of them is the tomb of Muhammad Ali Shah's daughter, the other that of her husband. The main building of the Imambara is topped with numerous domes (the main one is golden) and minarets, while inside are the tombs of Ali Shah and his mother. Paying Rs 2 to the guide will permit you to see the Nawab's silver-covered throne.

The watchtower opposite the Imambara is known as Satkhanda or the 'seven-storey tower', but it actually has four storeys since construction was abandoned at that level when Ali Shah died in 1840. The Imambara is open from 6 am to 5 pm and is a little beyond the Great Imambara and the Rumi Darwaza.

Husainabad Trust, Lucknow

3 22 S

Labyrinth Pass 59

Rs. 2-50 Per Head

Note—Please get the ticket checked at labyrinth

नोट कृपया टिकट को भूलभुलैया के प्रवेश द्वार पर checked

suर

Clock Tower

Opposite the Husainabad Imambara is the 67-metre-high clock tower and the Husainabad Tank. The clock tower was built between 1880 and 1887.

Picture Gallery

Also facing the Husainabad Tank is a *baradari* or summer house, built by Ali Shah. Now restored, it houses portraits of the various Nawabs of Oudh. It is open from 8 am to 5 pm and admission is Rs 1.

Jami Masjid

West of the Husainabad Imambara is the great Jami Masjid mosque with its two minarets and three domes. Construction was commenced by Muhammad Ali Shah but completed after his death. This is one of the few mosques in India not open to non-Muslims.

Residency

Built in 1800 for the British Resident, this extensive building was to become the stage for the most dramatic events of the 1857 Mutiny (or War of Independence in India) – the Sieges of Lucknow. The British inhabitants of Lucknow all took refuge in the Residency with the outbreak of the Mutiny. The commander, Sir Henry Lawrence, expected to be able to hold out for as long as 15 days before relief arrived. It was 87 days later that a small force under Sir Henry Havelock broke through the besiegers to the remaining half-starved defenders. The story was still not over, for once Havelock and his troops were within the Residency the siege recommenced and continued from 25 September to 17 November, when Sir Colin Campbell broke through to the Residency for the second time.

Today the Residency is maintained in exactly the condition it was in at the time of the final relief. The shattered walls are still scarred by cannon shots and the cemetery at the nearby ruined church has the graves of 2000 men, women and children, including that of Sir Henry Lawrence, who died during the first siege. The area around the Residency is maintained as well-kept lawns and gardens, but at the time of the siege the surrounding buildings were only separated from the Residency by narrow streets and lanes. The besiegers frequently attempted to dig tunnels into the Residency.

From 1857 right up to the day India became independent in 1947 a Union Jack was flown night and day from one of the Residency's towers. Times have changed: today there is a Martyr's Memorial to the martyrs of India's independence struggle directly opposite the Residency. It was opened in 1957, the 100th anniversary of the Mutiny. There are no set opening hours for the Residency, but the 'model room', where a very tatty model of the positions during the siege is on display, is only open from 9 am to 5.30 pm. Admission is Rs 0.50 to the garden, Rs 1 to the model room, except on Fridays when it is free.

Lakshman Tila

This high ground on the right bank of the River Gumti was the original site of the town which became known as Lucknow in the 15th century. Aurangzeb's Mosque now stands on this site.

Shah Najaf Imambara

Close to the Tourist Bungalow, this mausoleum takes its name from Najaf, the town 190 km south-west of Baghdad in Iraq where Hazrat Ali, the Shi'ite Muslim leader, is buried. The Imambara is the tomb of Ghazi-ud-din Haidar Khan, who died in 1827. His wives are also buried here. This was the scene for desperate fighting in November 1857 during the second relief of Lucknow. The domed exterior is comparatively plain, but inside are chandeliers and it's said that at one time the dome was covered with gold. The building is used to store *tazia*, elaborate creations of wood, bamboo and silver paper which are carried through the streets at Muharram. They are usually models of the Kerbala in Iraq. Many precious items from the mausoleum were looted following the mutiny. The Imambara is open from 6 am to 5 pm.

Martiniere School

Outside the town is this strange school built by the Frenchman Major-General Claude Martin. Taken prisoner at Pondicherry in 1761, he joined the East India Company's army, then in 1776 entered service with the Nawab of Oudh, while at the same time maintaining his East India Company connections. He quickly made a very substantial fortune from his dual occupations of soldier and businessman, and started to build a palatial home which he named Constantia.

Martin designed much of the building himself, and his architectural abilities were (to say the least) a little mixed – Gothic gargoyles were piled merrily atop Corinthian columns to produce a finished product which a British Marquess sarcastically pronounced took its ideas from a wedding cake. Martin died in 1800, before his stately home could be completed, but left the money and directions that it should become a school. The building could definitely do with a coat of paint but Martin keeps watch from his tomb in the basement.

'Kim', the boy hero of Kipling's story of the same name, went to this school and there are similar establishments, also financed from Martin's fortune, in Calcutta and Lyons, France. The building is two km from the Tourist Bungalow and is fronted by an artificial lake (now dried up) with a 38-metre-high column in its centre. The school is still run like a very British private school – the boys sing hymns in chapel every morning even though, a teacher reported with almost a tinge of regret, 'very few of them are Christians'.

Other

Near Hotel Clarks Avadh and the Kaiserbagh, with the palace of the last Nawab, are the stone tombs of Sa'adat Ali and his wife. There is also a summer house in this very well-kept garden. There are two museums, both closed on Mondays, and a children's museum. The Archaeological Museum is on the Kaiserbagh. The State Museum (open 10.30 am to 4.30 pm) is in the Banarsi Bagh. The zoo, founded in 1921, is also here and has a large collection of snakes. It is open from 5 am to 7 pm.

Sikandarbagh, scene of pitched battles in November 1857, is now the home of the National Botanical Research Institute. The gardens are open from 6 am to 5 pm. General Havelock, who led the first relief of Lucknow, has his grave and memorial in the Almbagh. Nadan Mahal is the tomb of the first governor of Oudh appointed by Akbar. It is one of the earliest buildings in Lucknow, dating from around 1600. Other buildings nearby include the small Sola Khamba pavilion and the tomb of Ibrahim Chisti.

Places to Stay – bottom end

The big state government *Tourist Bungalow* (tel 34282) at 6 Sapru Marg in Hazratganj has officially been renamed *Hotel Gomti*. Rooms, all doubles with attached bathroom, cost from Rs 60 up to Rs 200 for the more expensive ones in the new wing with air-con. The rooms are well furnished, if slightly run down, and there's also a Rs 15 dorm. The Gomti is 4½ km from the railway station; get there on a No 4 bus, or take a cycle-rickshaw for about Rs 6. The tourist office is here also.

The popular *Hotel Capoore* (tel 43958) is on Mahatma Gandhi Marg, also in Hazratganj, and costs from Rs 40/75. *Hotel Elora* (tel 31307) is at 3 Lalbagh, about midway between the Kaiserbagh bus station and the Tourist Bungalow. Rooms start from Rs 65/120 and there are extra costs for air-cooling or air-con. The

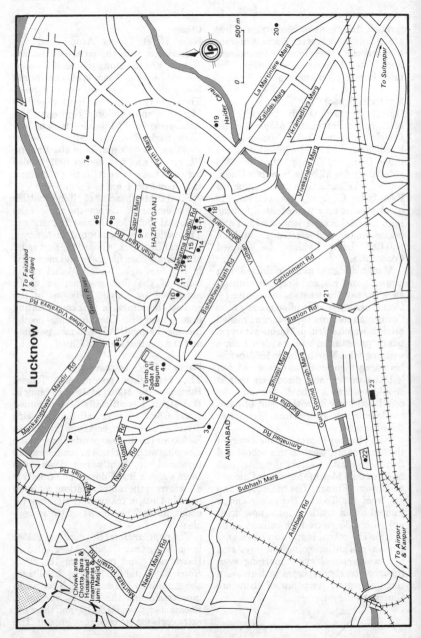

Lucknow

1	Residency
2	Kaiserbagh Bus Station
3	Hotel Gulmarg
4	Kaiserbagh
5	Hotel Clarks Avadh
6	Shah Najaf Imambara
7	Botanical Gardens
8	Carlton Hotel
9	Hotel Gomti
	(Tourist Bungalow) &
	State Tourist Office
10	Hotel Elora
11	Kwality Restaurant
12	Royal Cafe
13	Hotel Capoor's
14	Government of India
	Tourist Office
15	Janpath Market
16	Jone Hing Restaurant
17	Chaudhary's Place
18	GPO
19	Zoo & Museum
20	La Martiniere School
21	Hotel Kohinoor
22	Charbagh Bus Station
23	Railway Station

rooms are tiny but it's clean and friendly and does excellent food.

Other cheaper hotels include the *Avadh Lodge* (tel 43821) at 1 Ram Mohan Rai Marg near the botanical gardens; and the *Plaza Hotel*, just off Hewett Rd (Shivaji Marg) two km from the railway station. There are *Railway Retiring Rooms* from both the Northern and North-Eastern Railways at the Charbagh Station with rooms from Rs 50 and dorms.

Places to Stay – top end
Hotel Clarks Avadh (tel 40130-31) at 8 Mahatma Gandhi Marg is Lucknow's best hotel – its only real 'international' standard hotel in fact. It has everything from central air-conditioning to restaurants and a 24-hour coffee shop. The food here is surprisingly good. Singles/doubles cost Rs 500/550.

In the Hazratganj area near the Tourist Bungalow is the old-fashioned-looking *Hotel Carlton* (tel 44021-24) on Shah Najaf Rd. There are wonderful gardens

around the hotel, and rooms cost Rs 225/300 with air-con. *Hotel Kohinoor* (tel 33849, 43892), at 6 Station Rd near the railway station, is all air-con and costs Rs 250/300.

Places to Eat
There's a restaurant in the Tourist Bungalow with the usual sort of menu. The restaurant at the *Hotel Carlton* is said to be good; dinner costs Rs 50.

There are a number of restaurants along Mahatma Gandhi Marg in Hazratganj, including a *Kwality*. A bit further along is the *Royal Café* in the Hotel Capoore and then the Chinese *Jone Hing* restaurant and *Chaudhary's Sweet House*, which is very popular for Indian sweets and the snacks known as *chat*.

Other good restaurants include *Seem* in Lalbagh and the excellent-value *Maduvan Restaurant* on Hewett Rd (Shivaji Marg).

Lucknow has some fine Mughlai food specialities. *Kulfi* and *faluda* are popular desserts, a kind of ice cream with sweet noodles. There are several places in Aminabad that serve it. The sweet orange-coloured rice dish *zarda* is also popular. The huge paper-thin *rumali roti* chapattis are served in many small Muslim restaurants in the old city. They arrive folded up and should be eaten with a goat or lamb curry like *bhuna ghosht* or *roghan josh*. In the hot months of May and June Lucknow has some of the world's finest mangoes, particularly the wonderful *dashhari* mangoes grown in the village of Malihabad, west of the city.

Getting There
Air There are lots of air connections to Lucknow – two daily Delhi-Lucknow flights, a daily Delhi-Lucknow-Allahabad-Varanasi or Delhi-Lucknow-Gorakhpur connection, a daily Delhi-Lucknow-Patna-Ranchi-Calcutta flight and a four-times-a-week Bombay-Varanasi-Lucknow flight. Some fares include Delhi Rs 398, Varanasi Rs 248, Patna Rs 410. The Indian Airlines office (tel 44030, 48081) is at Hotel Clarks Avadh. Amausi Airport is 15 km out of Lucknow.

Rail By express train Lucknow is four hours from Varanasi, nine hours from Agra and only seven hours from Delhi if you travel on the Gomti Express. The Varanasi-Lucknow fare is Rs 33 in 2nd class, Rs 128 in 1st for the 324-km trip.

There is only a narrow-gauge line between Lucknow and Gorakhpur, for the Nepal border, so this trip takes eight hours by train. Both the narrow-gauge North-Eastern Railway lines and the broad-gauge Northern Railway lines run through the main railway station.

For Northern Railway enquiries ring 51234 or 51333. First-class bookings are made on 51833, 2nd class on 51488. North-Eastern Railway enquiries are made on 51433 and all reservations are made on 51383.

Bus Charbagh bus station, by the railway station, can be phoned on 50988. The Kaiserbagh bus station number is 42503. Buses to Delhi, Agra, Allahabad, Varanasi, Kanpur (Rs 8), Gorakhpur (six hours, Rs 33 to Rs 34) and so on all operate from Kaiserbagh.

To Nepal From the border at Sunauli, where you enter Nepal to Pokhara, it is a 12-hour, Rs 42 bus ride to Lucknow.

Getting Around

Local transport is not very frequent but a tempo will take you from the GPO to chowk, near the Great Imambara, for about Rs 1. There are also buses from chowk to the railway station. Or you could take a rickshaw from Hazratganj to Aminabad and then a bus to chowk. The two Imambaras and the Jami Masjid are all around the chowk area, while Shah Najaf is in Hazratganj and the Residency is about midway between the two. A cycle-rickshaw for a day's sightseeing will cost Rs 30 to Rs 40. A tonga tour of the historic areas of Lucknow is a quintessential Lucknow experience.

Things to Buy

Lucknow is famed for its hand-woven embroidery known as *chikan*. It's made into saris for women and kurtas for men. Prices are lower in Aminabad but you have to bargain. The traditional north Indian perfume known as *itar* has been made and sold by the firm of Muhammad Ali-Ashraf Ali since the time of the Nawabs; you can buy it in Aminabad. It's a very powerful perfume.

ALLAHABAD (population 600,000)

The city of Allahabad is 135 km west of Varanasi at the confluence of two of India's most important rivers – the Ganges and the Yamuna (Jumna). This meeting point of the rivers, the *sangam*, naturally has great sin-washing powers and is an important pilgrimage site. It is even more holy since the invisible Saraswati River is supposed to join the Ganges and the Yamuna at this point.

Allahabad also has an historic fort built by Akbar which overlooks the confluence of the rivers and contains an Ashoka pillar. The Nehru family home, Anand Bhawan, is in Allahabad and is open for inspection. Not many western visitors pause in this city, but it can be an interesting and worthwhile stop. Built on a very ancient site, it was known in Aryan times as Prayag, and Brahma himself is said to have performed a sacrifice here.

The Chinese pilgrim, Hiuen Tsang, described visiting the city in 634 AD and it acquired its present name in 1584, under Akbar. Later Allahabad was taken by the Marathas, sacked by the Pathans and finally ceded to the British in 1801 by the Nawab of Oudh. It was in Allahabad that the East India Company officially handed over control of India to the British government in 1858, following the Mutiny.

Orientation & Information

Allahabad is less congested and more modern than its sister city, touristy Varanasi. Civil Lines, with its modern shopping centre, has broad, tree-lined avenues and the main bus station. The older part of town is near the Yamuna River. See the Getting There section for information about the three railway stations in Allahabad.

The Tourist Office (tel 52722) is at the Tourist Bungalow on Mahatma Gandhi Rd. It's one of the most disinterested, off-hand and uninspired tourist offices you could ask for.

Sangam

The confluence of the rivers is the scene for a great annual bathing festival which takes place between mid-January and mid-February of each year. The festival, known as Magh Mela, lasts from 15 days to a month and attracts thousands of pilgrims who come for a dip in the holy rivers. Every 12th year the Magh Mela is known as the Kumbh Mela and the thousands grow to over a million pilgrims!

A huge temporary township springs up on the vacant land on the Allahabad side of the river and elaborate precautions have to be taken for the pilgrims' safety – in the early '50s, 350 people were killed in a stampede to the water. The Kumbh Mela alternates between Nasik, Ujjain and Hardwar every three years and will next return to Allahabad in 1989. At the confluence, the Ganges is about two km wide – it's a shallower, muddier river than the clearer, deeper, green Yamuna. Boats out on to the river are a bit of a tourist trap – right by the confluence you should be able to get a boat for about Rs 5; from further upriver from Saraswati Ghat you might pay, say, Rs 20.

The Fort

Built by Akbar in 1583, the fort, which stands at the confluence on the Yamuna side, has massive walls and pillars and three magnificent gateways flanked by high towers. It is made from huge bricks and is at its most impressive when viewed from the river. Apart from one Moghul

building there are no old constructions remaining within the fort – which is just as well, since foreigners aren't allowed inside. Officially passes can be obtained from the Security Officer (tel 51370), but it appears you're simply told 'No'.

Ashoka Pillar Unfortunately you're not allowed to see the Ashoka pillar in front of the gateway inside the fort. The 10.6-metre-high polished sandstone shaft dates from 232 BC; it was found lying on the ground in the fort in 1837 and was set up at its present location. Inscribed on the column are Ashoka's edicts and a later inscription eulogising the victories of Samudragupta (326-375 AD). This is the only record of the events in this Gupta ruler's life. There is also a later inscription by Jehangir.

The Undying Tree A small door in the east wall of the fort, near the river, leads to the 'undying banyan tree' – one place in the fort you are allowed to visit. This tree is mentioned by Hiuen Tsang, who tells of pilgrims sacrificing their lives by leaping to their deaths from it in order to seek salvation. Also known as Akshai Veta, the tree is actually in a curious basement and the only sign of it is the bunches of leaves tied haphazardly in place.

Anand Bhawan

The Nehru family home was donated to the Indian government by Indira Gandhi in 1970; it's in the eastern part of town, near the Ganges. The exhibits in the house show how this well-off family became involved in the struggle for Indian independence and later produced four generations of astute politicians – Motilal Nehru, Jawaharlal Nehru, Indira Gandhi and now Rajiv Gandhi.

The two-storey mansion has a large garden and contains many personal items connected with the life of three generations of the Nehru family. Opening hours are 10 am to 5 pm, closed Mondays. There's a charge for going upstairs in the building.

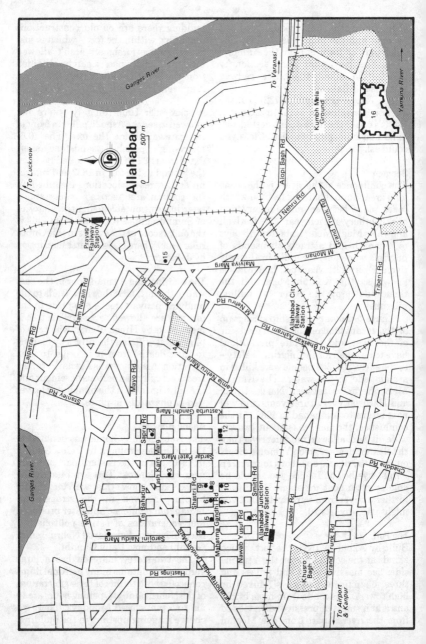

Allahabad

0   500 m

To Lucknow

Ganges River

To Varanasi

Yamuna River

Kumbh Mela Ground

16

Prayag Railway Station

•15

Alopi Bagh Rd

J Nehru Rd

Grand Trunk Rd

M Mohan

Malviya Marg

Tanna Garh Rd

M Nehru Rd

Allahabad City Railway Station

Kul Bhaskar Ashram Rd

Triben Rd

Ram Narain Rd

Lajpatrai Rd

Mayo Rd

Stanley Rd

Kamla Nehru Marg

14•

Kasturba Gandhi Marg

Chaddha Rd

Sapru Rd

•2

Sardar Patel Marg

•12
•11

Lash Kant Marg

Tej Bahadur

Shastri Rd

•3

Mahatma Gandhi Rd

Smith Rd

9• •8
•6 •10
5• •7

Leader Rd

Sarojini Naidu Marg

•4

Nawab Yusuf Rd

13•

Allahabad Junction Railway Station

Muir Rd

Ganges River

Hastings Rd

Khusro Bagh

Grand Trunk Rd

To Airport & Kanpur

1	YMCA
2	Allahabad Regency Hotel
3	Hotel Yatrik
4	GPO
5	Hotel Harsh
6	Kwality Restaurant
7	Tandoor Restaurant
8	El Chico Restaurant
9	Lucky Sweet Mart
10	Samrat Hotel
11	Tourist Office & Tourist Bungalow
12	Bus Stand
13	Royal Hotel
14	Museum
15	Anand Bhawan
16	Fort

Some of the exhibits would be of much more interest if they were labelled in English as well as Hindi.

Khusru Bagh

This peaceful garden, close to the railway station, contains the tomb of Prince Khusru, son of Jehangir, who was executed by his own father. Nearby is the unoccupied tomb intended for his sister and the tomb of his Rajput mother who was said to have poisoned herself in despair at Khusru's opposition to his father.

Allahabad Museum

Located on Kamla Nehru Rd, the museum has a fine collection of Rajasthani miniatures and terracotta figures. There are also an extensive Nehru collection and paintings by Roerich (see the Kulu Valley, Himachal Pradesh). Oddities include a gun used to kill somebody, now mounted on a revolving turntable and surrounded by plastic roses in a glass case. The museum is open 11 am to 4.30 pm and closed Mondays; admission is Rs 0.20. To the north of Alfred Park is the Municipal Museum and opposite that is a lovely Children's Park.

Other

The Bharadwaja Ashram is mentioned in the *Ramayana* and the Allahabad University now occupies its site. The Nag Basuki Temple on the banks of the Ganges and the subterranean Patalpuri Temple are other important shrines.

Places to Stay – bottom end

Most hotels are in Civil Lines, north of the railway line. Near the railway station at 24 South Rd, the *Royal Hotel* (tel 2520) is a big, spacious, fusty but fine old place. Rooms cost Rs 50 or Rs 70 for singles, Rs 70 or Rs 100 for doubles.

The *Tourist Bungalow* (tel 53640) is at 35 Mahatma Gandhi Marg and is probably the best place to stay in Allahabad. Rooms cost Rs 40 in the old wing, Rs 50 in the new wing or Rs 75 with air cooling. Dorm beds are Rs 15. It's about a Rs 2 to Rs 3 rickshaw ride from the main railway station.

Across the lines in the older part of town, the *Raj Hotel* at 6 Johnston Ganj has rooms at Rs 20/30 or with bath at Rs 30/35. In the rock-bottom bracket, the *Central Hotel*, near the clock tower in the centre of the old part of town, has rooms down to Rs 30 or less.

There are many other hotels around town, including several along Dr Katiu Rd, running south-east from the Allahabad Junction Station. The *Continental Hotel* (tel 4231, 4052) has rooms at Rs 25 single, Rs 45, 50 and 60 for doubles. There are *Railway Retiring Rooms* (tel 2278) at the station with doubles at Rs 30 and also dorm beds.

Places to Stay – top end

There's nothing very top end in Allahabad. The small *Harsh Hotel* (tel 3075) is at 14 Mahatma Gandhi Marg and has rooms for Rs 75/100 or deluxe rooms for Rs 100/125. It's a straightforward old place with big but very bare rooms although it is centrally located. Near the junction of Mahatma Gandhi Marg and Sardar Patel Marg, the *Hotel Samrat* (tel 4854) has rooms with singles at Rs 100,140, 160 or 200, doubles at Rs 150, 200, 240 and 250.It's a typical modern Indian hotel.

Hotel Yatrik (tel 4320) on Sardar Patel Marg has 38 rooms at Rs 100/150 or Rs 160/240 with air-con. It's certainly not very flashy; the lobby is furnished with folding garden furniture! The new *Hotel Allahabad Regency* (tel 3043) has just 13 rooms at Rs 180/220 or Rs 220/250 plus taxes. There's a very pleasant garden.

Places to Eat

You can get meals in the *Tourist Bungalow*, or there are a number of other places to eat along Mahatma Gandhi Marg. They include *El Chico Restaurant*, a *Kwality* and opposite that the *Tandoor*, which has the considerable virtue of staying open reasonably late at night. They're all in that darkened, gloomy style found in so many 'proper' Indian restaurants.

Just off Mahatma Gandhi Marg on Sardar Patel Marg, the *Lucky Sweet Mart* has good Indian sweets. There are also many restaurants in the crowded streets of the old town on the other side of the railway tracks, plus many small dhaba places close to the station along Dr Katiu Rd. Next to the Raj Hotel in the older part of town, the *Ginza Restaurant* has a typical non-vegetarian menu but the food is said to be very good.

Getting There

Allahabad is a good place from which to travel to Khajuraho. If you spend the night here you can catch a morning train to Satna, where buses go to Khajuraho. Alternatively you can take a bus to Satna (eight hours) and another from there to Khajuraho (three hours).

Air Allahabad is on the three-times-weekly Delhi-Lucknow-Allahabad-Varanasi route. Fares are Rs 551 from Delhi, Rs 179 from Lucknow and Rs 157 from Varanasi.

Rail There are three railway stations – the main one is Allahabad Junction in the central part of the city, just south of the Civil Lines area. Most trains for Varanasi, however, go from the city station, about three km away. Coming from Kanpur or Lucknow, you stop first at the Prayag station.

Allahabad is on the main Delhi-Calcutta railway route and takes about 10 hours from Delhi or three hours from Varanasi. From Delhi it's 627 km at a fare of Rs 54 in 2nd class, Rs 218 in 1st. Varanasi trains depart several times a day and the 137-km trip costs Rs 16 in 2nd class, Rs 64 in 1st.

Backpackers should beware of drug searches at Allahabad station. We warned you about them in the last edition; they're still going on.

Getting Around

If you arrive at Allahabad Junction station, the main entrance to the station faces towards the old city; you have to cross over the lines to the back entrance for Civil Lines. Allahabad has plenty of cycle and auto-rickshaws.

AROUND ALLAHABAD
Bhita

On the opposite side of the Yamuna, 18 km south-west of Allahabad, are the excavated remains of this fortified city. Archaeological digs in 1910-11 revealed successive layers dating from the Gupta period (320-455 AD) back to the Mauryan period (321-184 BC) and even earlier. There is a museum with stone and metal seals, coins from various kingdoms of the time, terracotta statues and figures and various utensils and personal possessions.

Garwha

The ruined temples in this walled enclosure are about 50 km from Allahabad. Garwha is eight km from Shankargarh and the final three km has to be completed on foot. The major temple has 16 beautifully carved stone pillars, and inscriptions reveal that the temples date back to the Gupta period at the very least. Some of the better sculptures from Garwha are now in the State Museum in Lucknow.

Kausambi

This ancient Buddhist centre is 63 km from Allahabad and used to be known as Kosam. At one time this was the capital of King Udaya, a contemporary of the Buddha. There's a huge fortress measuring over six km around near the village, and the broken remains of an Ashoka pillar, minus any pre-Gupta period inscriptions, can be seen inside the fort. A bus runs to the fort at Kausambi.

LUCKNOW TO VARANASI
Bahraich & Saheth-Maheth

The nephew of that scourge of India, Mahmud of Ghazni, was killed in Bahraich in 1033. There is a shrine to him about three km from the town. At Saheth-Maheth the Buddha performed the miracle of sitting on a thousand-petalled lotus and multiplying himself a million times. The town is also known as Sravasti and can be reached from Gorakhpur on the Naugarh-Gonda loop line. Gainjohwa is the nearest station and there are ruins and a few modern Buddhist temples.

Faizabad (population 120,000)

This was once the capital of Oudh but rapidly declined after the death of Bahu Begum. Her mausoleum is said to be the finest of its type in Uttar Pradesh. Her husband, who preceded her as ruler, also has a fine mausoleum. There are pleasant gardens in Guptar Park, where the temple from which Rama is supposed to have disappeared stands. Faizabad has a very spiritual feeling to it and the station has good food.

Ayodhya

Only six km from Faizabad, Ayodhya is the home town of *Ramayana* hero Ram Chandra. There are numerous picturesque temples and ghats, since the town is on the Gogra (Ghaghara) River. This was also a great Buddhist centre at one time and, as usual, Hiuen Tsang dropped by to list how many monasteries there were and how many monks in residence.

Places to Stay The rather primitive *New Saket Hotel* is near the station and has rooms at Rs 25/35 and a dormitory for Rs 10. They do vegetarian meals for Rs 5.

Jaunpur (population 85,000)

Founded by Feroz Shah Tughlaq in 1360, this town later became the capital of the independent Muslim Sharqui kingdom. Eventually it fell to Sikandar Lodi and then the Moghuls. Prior to the arrival of the Muslims it had a great number of Hindu, Buddhist and Jain temples, shrines and monasteries. Many of these have been utilised by the Muslims to construct Jaunpur's architecturally unique mosques.

The more important mosques include the 1408 Atala Masjid, built on the site of a Hindu temple dedicated to Atala Devi. The massively constructed Jami Masjid was built between 1438 and 1478 during the Sharqui period. There are a half dozen other interesting mosques – the Jaunpur mosques are notable for their use of Jain and Hindu building materials, for their two-storey arcades and large gateways, and for their unusual minarets. The tombs of the Sharqui sultans are north of the Jami Masjid. Other important constructions include Feroz Shah's 1360 fort and the stone Akbari Bridge built between 1564 and 1568.

Places to Stay Jaunpur has some cheap hotels and the *Marwari Dharamsala*, near the fort, where you can get a private room for just a few rupees.

Getting There Buses and taxis are available from Varanasi, 58 km away.

Chunar

The fort here overlooks the Ganges and was captured by Humayun in 1537, but was taken by Sher Shah soon after and not recovered by the Moghuls until 1575, when Akbar took it. Chunar is 37 km from Varanasi and can be reached by bus.

GORAKHPUR (population 250,000)

This is a town travellers on their way to Kathmandu or Pokhara from Delhi or Varanasi usually pass through. Gorakhpur is in the centre of a rich agricultural area which has nevertheless remained very backward. The famous temple of Gorkahnath is here, as is the Geeta Press, which specialises in publishing Hindu religious literature. In April, noted one visitor, 'Gorakhpur is covered solidly in flies'.

Places to Stay

Near the bus and railway stations, the *Modern Hotel* has excellent and clean rooms with bath for Rs 30, 40 or 55. Try not to be steered into a more expensive room because the cheaper ones are 'full'. The *Standard Hotel*, opposite the railway station, is a clean and comfortable place with Rs 40 doubles. There are excellent *Railway Retiring Rooms* from Rs 22 for a fine single with desk, table, chairs and towels.

In the city centre, known as the Golghar area, the *Hotel York* has rooms from Rs 30. It's another good place to stay. The *Vivek Hotel* is a nice place, 'like a rambling old English house and very friendly', with rooms from Rs 40. The cheaper *Gupta Tourist Lodge*, opposite the railway station, has rooms from Rs 25.

Getting There

The railway station has a foreigners' booking office! Buses for Nautanwa near the Nepalese border start from the bus station near the railway station. It's a three to four-hour trip for Rs 16, departing from near the Standard Hotel. At Nautanwa you can charter a rickshaw to take you through customs and on to Bhairawa, six km away and on the Nepalese side of the border. There are also buses for Pokhara from Sunauli, only a couple of hundred metres over the border.

Varanasi buses depart from a bus station a Rs 2 rickshaw ride away. Varanasi is five or six hours away and the fare is Rs 27.

KUSHINAGAR

The town of Kasia (Kushinagar), 55 km east of Gorakhpur, is supposed to be the site of Buddha's death and cremation. There are a number of Buddhist buildings of various ages and also large seated and reclining Buddha figures. A local bus to Kasia from Gorakhpur takes a couple of hours.

Places to Stay

There's a small ITDC *Traveller's Lodge* (tel 38) in Kushinagar.

TO LUMBINI

Lumbini is the birthplace of Buddha and also close to the 'backdoor' entrance into Nepal for Pokhara. All those going to Lumbini, even pilgrims just crossing the border for a few hours, require a Nepali visa. This can be obtained at the border checkpoint for Rs 60 Nepalese.

Buses run from the Naugarh station on the Gonda-Gorakhpur loop line as far as the border at Kakarhwa, where you take a rickshaw (Rs 5) for the last few km to Lumbini. There is a checkpoint in Naugarh (on the Indian side) where you must report before proceeding in either direction. Naugarh has a *Mahabodhi Society Rest House* where you can stay for a donation.

An alternative way to visit Lumbini is to cross the border into Nepal at Sunauli, stay overnight at Bhairawa and take a bus from there to Lumbini.

VARANASI (population 650,000)

Varanasi, the 'eternal city', is one of the most important pilgrimage sites in India and also a major tourist attraction. Situated on the banks of the sacred Ganges, Varanasi has been a centre of learning and civilisation for over 2000 years. It was at Sarnath only 10 km away that the Buddha first preached his message of enlightenment, 25 centuries ago. Later the city became a great Hindu centre, but was looted a number of times by Muslim invaders from the 11th century on. These destructive visits climaxed with that of the Moghul emperor Aurangzeb, who destroyed almost all of the temples and converted the most famous one into a mosque.

Varanasi has also been known as Kashi and Benares, but its present name is a restoration of an ancient name meaning the city between two rivers – the Varauana and Asi. For the pious Hindu the city has always had a special place. Besides being a pilgrimage centre, it is considered an especially auspicious place to die, ensuring an instant routing to heaven. To this day Varanasi is a centre of learning, especially for Sanskrit scholars, and students flock here from all over India. Ironically it is in the centre of one of the most backward areas of India – a largely agrarian, rural and over-populated area that has developed little since independence.

On the other hand Varanasi has become a symbol of the Hindu renaissance and has a special role in the development of Hindi – the national language of India. The well-known novelist Prem Chand and the literary figure Bharatendu Harischand have played their parts in this development. Tulsi Das, the famous poet who wrote the Hindi version of the *Ramayana* known as the *Ram Charit Manas*, also lived many years in this city.

Orientation

The old city of Varanasi is situated along the west bank of the Ganges and extends back from the riverbank ghats in a winding collection of narrow alleys. They're too narrow for anything but walking, and tall houses overhang the picturesque, though hardly clean, lanes. It's a fascinating area to wander around. The town extends from Raj Ghat, near the bridge, to Asi Ghat, near the university.

Areas known as Chowk, Lahurabir and Godaulia are situated just outside the old city area along the river.

One of the best ways to get oriented in Varanasi is to remember the positions of the ghats, particularly important ones like Dasaswamedh Ghat. The big 'international hotels' and the national tourist office are in the Cantonment area north of the Varanasi Junction railway station. The broad, tree-lined avenues of the Cantonment are a great contrast to the crowds of people, bicycles and rickshaws in the old part of town.

Information

The Indian Airlines Office (tel 64146, 66116) is in the Mint House Motel, opposite Nadesar Palace in the Cantonment. Railway reservations at the Varanasi Junction (Cantonment) Station are made by phoning 64920. The bus station is also

Cop — DIRECTING TRAFFIC, VARANASI

close to the Cantonment.

The state Tourist Office is in the Tourist Bungalow and there's a helpful smaller office in the railway station. The Government of India Tourist Office (tel 64189) is at 15B The Mall in the Cantonment. The Varanasi GPO is a good place to send parcels from, as there are tailors' stalls for wrapping and sealing right outside. There's a good bookshop outside the Tourist Bungalow and Nandi, the bookshop in the Varanasi Hotel, is also good. The *Pioneer* is an informative local English-language newspaper. *Banaras: City of Light* by Diana Eck (Princeton University Press) is a good guide to the city, with information on each ghat and temple and a good introduction to Hinduism.

If you're staying in Varanasi in one of the cheaper hotels and could do with a swim, several of the hotels in the Cantonment area permit the use of their pools for a charge of Rs 20 to Rs 40. They include Hotel Clarks Varanasi, Hotel Varanasi Ashok and Hotel Taj Ganges. If you're interested in studying yoga, pay a visit to the Malaviya Bhawan at the university. They offer courses in yoga and also in Hindu philosophy.

The Ghats

Varanasi's principal attraction is the long string of bathing ghats which line the west bank of the Ganges. Ghats are the steps which lead down to the river, from which pilgrims make their sin-cleansing dip in the river and on which, at the two 'burning ghats', bodies are cremated. The best time to visit the ghats is at dawn when pilgrims make their early-morning dip, the city is coming alive, the light is magical and Varanasi is an amazingly exotic place.

There are over 100 ghats in all, of which Dasaswamedh Ghat is probably the most convenient starting point. A trip from there to Manikarnika Ghat makes an interesting short introduction to the river and will cost around Rs 7 an hour (easy

bargaining) if you hire a boat. There are plenty of boatmen by the river waiting for tourists to appear.

Look out for the people on the ghats – the women bathing discreetly in their saris, the young men going through contortionist yoga exercises, the Brahmin priests offering blessings (for a price) and the ever-present beggars giving others an opportunity to do their karma some good. Look for the lingams which mark each ghat, for Varanasi is the city of Shiva. Look for the buildings and temples around the ghats, often tilting precariously or in some cases actually sliding down into the river. Each monsoon causes great damage to the riverbank buildings of Varanasi. Look for the burning ghats where bodies are cremated after making their final journey to the holy Ganges swathed in white cloth and carried on a bamboo stretcher – or even the roof of a taxi. Manikarnika and the less-used Harischandra Ghat are the main burning ghats. Don't try taking photos at these ghats at any time (particularly when cremations are taking place) unless you're feeling suicidal.

The Asi Ghat, the furthest upstream, is one of the five special ghats which pilgrims are supposed to bathe from in order and on the same day. The order is Asi, Dasaswamedh, Barnasangam, Panchganga and finally Manikarnika. Much of the Tulsi Ghat has fallen down towards the river. The Bachraj Ghat is Jain and there are three riverbank Jain temples. Many of the ghats are owned by Maharajas or other princely rulers – such as the very fine Shivala or Kali Ghat owned by the Maharaja of Varanasi. The Dandi Ghat is the ghat of ascetics known as Dandi Panths, and near that is the very popular Hanuman Ghat.

The Harischandra or Smashan Ghat is a secondary burning ghat. Bodies are cremated by outcastes known as *chandal*. Above the Kedar Ghat is a shrine popular with Bengalis and south Indians. Mansarowar Ghat was built by Man

Singh of Amber and named after the Tibetan lake at the foot of Mt Kailash, Shiva's Himalayan home. Someswar or 'Lord of the Moon' Ghat is said to be able to heal diseases. The Munshi Ghat is very picturesque, while Ahalya Bai's Ghat is named after the Maratha woman ruler of Indore.

The Dasaswamedh Ghat's name indicates that Brahma sacrificed (medh), 10 (das), horses (aswa) here. It's one of the most important ghats and conveniently central. Note its statues and the shrine of Sitala, goddess of smallpox. Raja Man Singh's Man Mandir Ghat was built in 1600 but has been poorly restored in the last century. The northern corner of the ghat has a fine stone balcony. Raja Jai Singh of Jaipur also erected one of his unusual observatories on this ghat in 1710. It is not as fine as the Jai Singh observatories in Delhi or Jaipur, but its setting is unique.

The Mir Ghat leads to the Nepalese Temple with its erotic sculptures. Between here and the Jalsain Ghat, the Golden Temple stands back from the river. The Jalsain Ghat, where cremations are made, virtually adjoins one of the most sacred of the ghats, the Manikarnika Ghat. Above the steps is a tank known as the Manikarnika Well; Parvati is said to have dropped her earring here and Shiva dug the tank out to recover it, filling the depression with his sweat! The Charandpaduka, a slab of stone between the well and the ghat, bears footprints made by Vishnu. Privileged VIPs are allowed to be cremated at the Charandpaduka. There is also a temple to Ganesh on the ghat.

Dattatreya Ghat bears the footprint of the Brahmin saint of that name in a small temple nearby. Scindia's Ghat was originally built in 1830 but was so huge and magnificent that it collapsed into the river and had to be rebuilt. The Ram Ghat was built by the Raja of Jaipur. As its name indicates, five rivers are supposed to meet at the Panchganga Ghat. Above the ghat is Aurangzeb's smaller mosque,

also known as the Alamgir Mosque, built over a Vishnu temple. The Gai Ghat has a figure of a cow made of stone upon it. The Trilochan Ghat has two turrets emerging from the river, and water between them is especially holy. Raj Ghat was the ferry pier until the road and rail bridge was completed here.

Golden Temple

Dedicated to Vishveswara (Vishwanath), Shiva as Lord of the Universe, the Golden Temple is across the road from its original position. Aurangzeb destroyed the original temple and built a mosque over it – traces of the earlier 1600 temple can be seen behind his mosque. The present temple was built in 1776 by Ahalya Bai of Indore and the gold plating (three-quarters of a tonne of it!) on the towers was provided by Maharaja Ranjit Singh of Lahore. Next to the temple is the Gyan Kupor well, the 'well of knowledge'. Much esteemed by the faithful, this well is said to contain the Shiva lingam removed from the original temple and hidden to protect it from Aurangzeb. Non-Hindus are not allowed into the temple but can view it from upstairs in a house across the street – soldiers sit downstairs. Near the temple, which is interesting to visit in the evening, are narrow alleys filled with an incredible number of shops.

Great Mosque of Aurangzeb

Constructed using columns from the Biseswar Temple razed by Aurangzeb, his great mosque has minarets towering 71 metres above the Ganges. Armed guards protect the mosque, as the Indian government wants to ensure there are no problems between Hindus and Muslims.

Durga Temple

The Durga Temple is commonly known as the Monkey Temple due to the many monkeys that have made it their home. It was built in the 18th century by a Bengali Maharani and is stained red with ochre. The small temple is built in north Indian

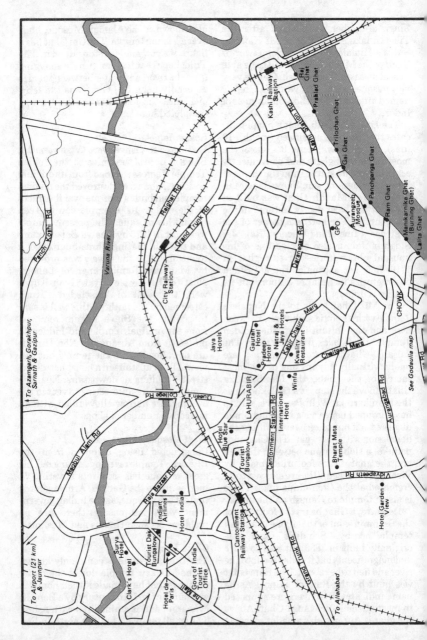

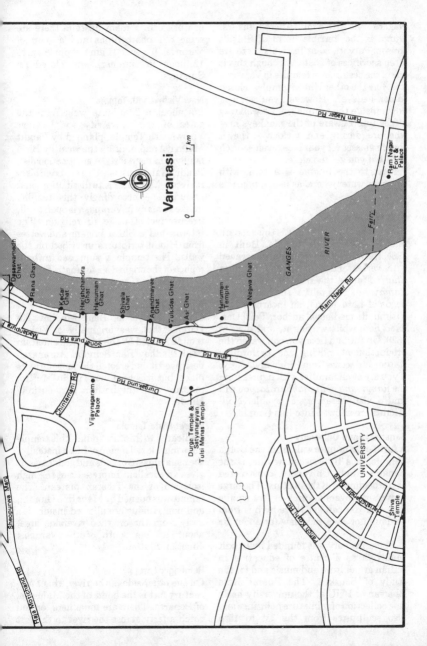

Varanasi

0   1 km

Ram Nagar Rd

Ram Nagar
Fort & Palace

Ferry

GANGES
RIVER

Dasaswamedh
Ghat

Rana Ghat
Kedar Ghat
Harishchandra Ghat
Hanuman Ghat
Shivala Ghat
Anandmayee Ghat
Tulsidas Ghat
Asi Ghat

Hanuman
Temple

Negwa Ghat

Madanpura

Sonarpura Rd

Asi Rd

Lanka Rd

Ram Nagar Rd

Chintamani Rd

Durgakund Rd

Vijaynagaram
Palace

Durga Temple &
Satyanarayan
Tulsi Manas Temple

UNIVERSITY

Banaras Rd

DT Hulex Rd

Shiva
Temple

Sheopurwa Marg

Raja Motichand Rd

Nagara style with a multi-tiered shikara. Durga is the 'terrible' form of Shiva's consort Parvati, so at festivals there are often sacrifices of goats. Although this is one of the best-known temples in Varanasi, it is, like the other Hindu temples, closed to non-believers. However, you can look down inside the temple from a walkway at the top. Beware of the monkeys here who are daring and vicious – they'll snatch glasses off your face, even scratch or bite if you get too close.

Next to the temple is a tank with stagnant water where, as usual, pilgrims bathe.

Tulsi Manas Temple

Next to the Durga Temple is this modern marble shikara-style temple. Built in 1964, the walls of the temple are engraved with verses and scenes from the *Ram Charit Manas*, the Hindi version of the *Ramayana*. This tells of the history and deeds of Lord Rama, an incarnation of Vishnu. Its mediaeval author, Tulsi Das, lived here while writing it, and died in 1623. On the 2nd floor you can watch the production of moving and performing statues and scenes from Hindu mythology. If you are at all familiar with figures from the *Ramayana* or *Mahabharata*, you will find a visit here very enjoyable. Non-Hindus are allowed into this temple.

Benares Hindu University

A further 20-minute walk from the Durga Temple, or a Rs 1 rickshaw ride, is the Benares Hindu University, constructed at the beginning of the century. The large university covers an area of five square km, and you can get there by bus from Godaulia or by a rickshaw for about Rs 3.

The university was founded by Pandit Malaviya as a centre of education in Indian art, culture and music and for the study of Sanskrit. The Bharat Kala Bhawan or BHU at the university has a fine collection of miniature paintings and also sculptures from the 1st to 15th

centuries. In a room upstairs there are some old photographs and a map of Varanasi. It's open 11 am to 4 pm (8 am to 12 noon in summer) and closed on Sundays.

New Vishwanath Temple

It's about a 30-minute walk from the gates of the university to the new Vishwanath Temple, planned by Pandit Malaviya and built by the wealthy Birla family of industrialists. A great nationalist, Pandit Malaviya wished to see Hinduism revived without its caste distinctions and prejudices – accordingly this temple, unlike so many in Varanasi, is open to all, irrespective of caste or religion. The interior has a Shiva lingam and verses from Hindu scriptures inscribed on the walls. The temple is supposed to be a replica of the original Vishwanath Temple, destroyed by Aurangzeb.

Alamgir Mosque

Locally known as Beni Madhav Ka Darera, this was originally a Vishnu temple erected by the Maratha chieftain Beni Madhav Rao Scindia. Aurangzeb destroyed it and erected the mosque in its place, but it is a curious Hindu-Muslim mixture with the bottom part entirely Hindu.

Bharat Mata Temple

Dedicated to 'Mother India', this temple has a marble relief map of India instead of the usual images of gods and goddesses. It gives an excellent impression of the high isolation of the Tibetan plateau. The temple was opened by Mahatma Gandhi, and non-Hindus are allowed inside. It's away from the crowded riverside area, about 1.5 km south of the Varanasi Junction Station.

Ramnagar Fort

On the other side of the river, this 17th-century fort is the home of the Maharaja of Benares. There are tours here, or you catch a ferry across the river to the fort with its interesting museum. The museum contains old silver and brocade palanquins for the ladies of the court, elephant howdahs made of silver, old brocades, a replica of the royal bed and an armoury of swords and old guns. The fort is open from 10 am to 12 noon and 1 to 5 pm; entry to the museum costs Rs 1.

Tours

Varanasi tours cost Rs 20 each for morning or afternoon tours or Rs 30 for both. They start from the Tourist Bungalow or the major hotels in the Cantonment area in the morning (and afternoon?) and from the Government of India Tourist Office on The Mall in the afternoon. Telephone 63233 for booking details.

The morning tour leaves at 6 am and takes you down the Ganges by the ghats, around the various temples and out to the university. The morning tour finishes at 12.15 pm and the afternoon tour commences at 2 pm and runs to 5.55 pm – definitely a full day. The afternoon tour takes you out to Sarnath and to the Ramnagar Fort – if there's time! In summer all times are half an hour earlier.

The Varanasi tours don't get unquestioned recommendations:

The bus arrived late and there were more people than could fit in . . . . we couldn't all get on the boat so had to take a second boat, for which they tried to charge extra . . . . we were marched through various temples without any explanation . . . arrived at the university to see the miniature paintings an hour before it opened . . . . the breakfast stop never happened . . . . we abandoned the afternoon tour and did it ourselves. As we were leaving the museum at the Ramnagar Fort the tour bus turned up, just before closing time!

Places to Stay – bottom end

For shoestring travellers there are three important areas for accommodation – the spacious Cantonment area (north of the railway tracks), the newer part of the city (south of the railway tracks) and the

crowded, confused but colourful old city area (by the river). The old city places are the cheapest you'll find, but staying close to the river has the advantage of being cooler during the hot season. Wherever you stay in Varanasi, remember that trishaw-wallahs are often reluctant to take you to places where they won't get a commission – be wary of tales that a lodge is 'closed up', 'full up' or 'burnt down'. Places by the river may even be 'flooded'!

Railway & Bus Station Area The *Tourist Bungalow* (tel 63186) is only a five-minute walk from the station and has dorm beds at Rs 10, singles at Rs 20 and Rs 30, doubles at Rs 40 and Rs 55. The more expensive rooms have attached bathrooms. In summer there's an extra Rs 10 charge for air-cooling. There's a pleasant grassy garden but the staff have a well-earned reputation for being less than helpful. Food in the restaurant is nothing special and the service can be very slow.

There are several hotels around the Tourist Bungalow. The best of them is the *Hotel Amar* (tel 64044), which charges Rs 20 for singles, Rs 45 for a double with bath. The rooms are clean, the service good and the showers often fully functioning! *Hotel Relax* has bathless singles at Rs 20, doubles at Rs 25 to Rs 35. There are a few other hotels in the same area, like the 'scruffy but cheap' *Hotel Diwan*. They all do good business when the Tourist Bungalow is full.

The well-run *Hotel Blue Star* is only half a km from the station; continue down the road from the Tourist Bungalow. Dorm beds are Rs 8, rooms without bath are Rs 20/25, a double with bath is Rs 35. Hot showers are free.

Half-way between the station and the ghats, the *Venus Hotel* and the *Garden View Hotel* (tel 63026) on Vidyapeth Rd are both cheap and have been recommended by travellers. The Garden View has singles at Rs 20 to Rs 25, doubles at Rs 30 to Rs 45. Beware of booking things through this hotel, however. They're very keen on big commissions, tours that go via the silk factories and so on. There are *Railway Retiring Rooms* at the Varanasi Junction Station.

Cantonment Area In the Cantonment area, on the other side of the station, hotels are mainly at the top of the price scale but *Hotel India* (tel 42161) is a good, comfortable and reasonably clean place. It's at 59 Patel Nagar, just behind the station and close to the Indian Airlines office. There's a garden, and rooms cost Rs 50/75, but this is another place not popular with touts and commission-seeking rickshaw riders. *Hotel Surya* is just behind the big *Hotel Clarks Varanasi* but is much cheaper at Rs 50/70 for good rooms with attached bathroom.

The *Tourist Dak Bungalow* (tel 56461) on The Mall is very popular with over-landers and has camping facilities. Singles/doubles cost Rs 45/75, and there's a Rs 20 dorm. If you're camping with your own vehicle it's Rs 8 per person. There's a beautiful garden here, ideal for relaxing, and the food is not bad.

City Centre – Godaulia & Lahurabir Area Godaulia is the place near the Dasaswamedh Ghat where auto-rickshaws, cycle-rickshaws and tempos stop. On the left side of the street between Godaulia and the ghats is the *Hotel Ganges*, a big place with rooms at Rs 35/50. On the other side of the street is the *Central Hotel* (tel 62776) – an old hotel with rooms that are OK but not that great.

In Godaulia itself the *Hotel KVM* (tel 63749) is now overpriced and nothing special at all. It's certainly not a travellers' place. Singles start from Rs 20, a double with bath is Rs 45. Prices go up to Rs 90 but they're mainly at the lower end. The *Binod Hotel*, also in Godaulia, is newish but grubby with rooms at Rs 25/30.

Hotels in Lahurabir, between the station and Godaulia, are mainly in the middle-price bracket. There are some

cheaper ones such as the *Ajay Hotel* (tel 54507), where singles are Rs 35, 45 and 60, doubles Rs 45, 60 and 75. The *International Hotel* (tel 67140) is in this same price bracket.

Old City & Ghats Area This is the place to look for rock-bottom hotels. The streets here are very narrow; you have to abandon even cycle-rickshaws and make your way down the convoluted alleys on foot. Near the river and the Golden Temple, the popular *Yogi Lodge* (tel 53986) is one of the best budget hotels in India. This fine old house has has been converted into a hotel, and there are dorm beds for Rs 7 (usually six beds to a dorm) and doubles for Rs 20 to Rs 25 (same price for single occupancy). It's clean and well maintained. Good, reasonably priced western and Indian food is available in the restaurant/common room on the ground floor. This friendly and busy place has that special atmosphere that makes it very popular with travellers, and is likely to be full unless you get there early in the day.

The *Golden Lodge*, just opposite, is a reasonable standby with rooms at just Rs 10/20, but it's nowhere near the same standard as the Yogi Lodge. *Trimurti Guest House* (tel 56084) at 35/12 Saraswati Phatak is a newer building with dorm beds at Rs 10 and doubles at Rs 25 or Rs 30 with bath. Given the low prices, rooms here are good value. Close to Dasaswamedh Ghat Rd *Sri Venkateshwar Lodge* is a well-kept place with rooms at Rs 12/24 up to Rs 39 for a triple with bath.

Further back from the river, *Om House Lodge*, in the Bansphatak area of the old city, is extremely cheap with dorm beds at Rs 3, singles at Rs 8 to Rs 10, doubles at Rs 15. It's popular with travellers on the cheap, and the owner gives yoga lessons. You have to wander down a winding maze of lanes to find it, but it's pleasantly quiet.

Tandon House Lodge, right on the river at Gaighat, is close to the GPO from

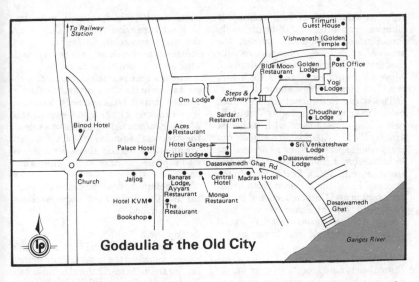

Godaulia & the Old City

Maidagin and is somewhat difficult to find. There are excellent views of the river from the courtyard. Near the Dasaswamedh Ghat, the friendly *Shiva Lodge* is another possibility. *Hotel Maharaja* near Dasaswamedh Rd is good value and reasonably clean and quiet. On the other side of the main road *Krishna Lodge* is above a sitar and tabla shop. Rooms cost from around Rs 20 and there are good views from the roof.

Places to Stay – top end

Varanasi's major 'tourist class' hotels are all in the new Cantonment area near the railway station. The somewhat Victorian *Hotel Clarks Varanasi* (tel 42401) is the oldest, dating back to the British era. Air-conditioned singles/doubles are Rs 350/450 and there is a swimming pool, shops and other facilities.

Hotel Varanasi Ashok (tel 52251) is fairly new and centrally air-conditioned, although somewhat smaller in size, and has rooms at Rs 325/450. *Hotel de Paris* (tel 56461-2, 56218) is also on The Mall and has singles/doubles from Rs 175/250 or slightly less without air-con. It's a wonderful old-style place in large grounds. The newer *Hotel Taj Ganges* (tel 42480) costs Rs 450/550.

There are several good medium-priced places in Lahurabir, between the station and Godaulia. The relatively new *Pradeep Hotel* (tel 66363) at Jagatganj has rooms at Rs 60/80, Rs 80/110 with air-cooling and Rs 150/200 with air-con. It's conveniently situated, well run and friendly. Also in Lahurabir, the *Gautam Hotel* (tel 52816) at Ramkatora has singles/doubles at Rs 75/120 or Rs 120/175 with air-con. It's conveniently located and has nice rooms, good service and wonderful food.

Hotel Diamond (tel 56561) is close to the centre at Bhelupura and has rooms at Rs 110/150 or Rs 160/210 with air-con. This is a good place if you're looking for a medium-priced hotel, although the service is somewhat haphazard. Their restaurant, however, is excellent.

Places to Eat

Tourist Bungalow & Lahurabir Areas Food at the *Tourist Bungalow* is overpriced but there are excellent places to eat close by. The *Chinese Mandarin Restaurant*, right outside it, does very reasonable Chinese food although it is distinctly Indo-Chinese. Round the corner, the small *Most Welcome* prepares excellent food and the manager is a real salesman. Most dishes are Rs 10 to Rs 15; a very complete meal will cost about Rs 25.

The *Winfa Restaurant* in Lahurabir, behind the cinema, is possibly Varanasi's best Chinese restaurant with dishes at around Rs 15. There is also a good but reasonably expensive *Kwality Restaurant* in Lahurabir, a *Kwality Snack Bar* and the vegetarian *Tulasi Restaurant*. In the Pradeep Hotel the *Poonam Restaurant* does Indian and Chinese food and is said to be good. *Basant Behar* has very good sweets. *Abhinanda* has remarkably good pizzas – good spices, fresh tomatoes.

Cantonment Area The *Tourist Dak Bungalow* is noted for its western breakfast, which includes porridge, eggs and toast with butter. Varanasi's railway station restaurant also has a good reputation for all types of food. Their breakfasts are particularly good, as is their 'pot tea'. If you want to dine in style in the Cantonment, *Hotel Clarks Varanasi* does continental breakfasts for Rs 35 or a buffet lunch for Rs 60.

Godaulia & the Old City The excellent *Aces Restaurant* has a pleasant courtyard and is great for a breakfast outside on a sunny morning. In the evening this popular and excellent value place is often packed out with travellers. The drab-looking place called *The Restaurant* is reputed to be the local meeting place for politicians. It's about 200 metres south of the main square, opposite the KVM Hotel, and has excellent Bengali food and a 'racy Bengali intellectual atmosphere'.

There are several places along the road from Godaulia to the ghats. On the right side of the street is *Ayyars Café*, under the Banares Lodge, with good masala dosa and other light meals. On the left side the *Sardar Restaurant* is also

popular with low-budget travellers looking for good vegetarian food. Try *Jaljog*, by the main square in Godaulia, for an Indian-style breakfast of pooris and vegetables known as *kachauri*.

There are many small restaurants with good thalis in the alleys between Godaulia and the ghats in Dasaswamedh. Varanasi is well known for its excellent sweets, and *Madhur Jalpan Grih*, on the same side of the street as the cinema in Godaulia, is an excellent place to try them. Varanasi is also supposed to have very high-quality pan.

In Bhelupura, near the Lalita Cinema, the *Sindhi Restaurant* does excellent vegetarian food.

Getting There

Air Varanasi is on several Indian Airlines routes, including the popular daily tourist service Delhi-Agra-Khajuraho-Varanasi-Kathmandu. Fares are Delhi Rs 638, Agra Rs 499, Khajuraho Rs 331. There are also connections with Allahabad (Rs 157), Bhubaneswar (Rs 602), Calcutta (Rs 602), Gorakhpur (Rs 159), Lucknow (Rs 248) and other cities.

Rail There are not a great number of trains running directly between Delhi and Varanasi or between Calcutta and Varanasi, although most Delhi-Calcutta trains do pass through Moghulserai, 10 km south of Varanasi, about 20 minutes by bus. Express trains between Delhi and Varanasi take 13 to 16 hours for the 764-km trip and cost Rs 62 in 2nd class, Rs 253 in 1st. From Calcutta the 678-km trip takes about 12 hours and costs Rs 57 in 2nd class, Rs 233 in 1st.

The Upper India Express is a direct Delhi-Varanasi train. It leaves Delhi at 8 pm and arrives in Varanasi at around 1 pm the next day. This is also a good train in the opposite direction, as it departs Varanasi around 6.30 pm and reaches New Delhi at 10 am. Patna and Allahabad are respectively about six and three hours away by train.

If you're travelling from Varanasi to Kashmir or Himachal Pradesh, you can avoid going through Delhi by taking the three-times-weekly overnight Himgiri Express. This originates in Howrah (Calcutta), runs through Lucknow and terminates at Jammu Tawi, so you can be well on your way to Srinagar by the evening. If you want to get to the Himachal Pradesh hill stations it also stops at Chakki Bank, the little-known alternative station for Pathankot, a couple of hours before Jammu Tawi. From there it's a Rs 4 rickshaw ride to the main Pathankot train and bus stations.

Varanasi has three railway stations – Kashi, City and Varanasi Junction. The Varanasi Junction Station used to be known as the Cantonment Station.

Bus The bus station is next to the main railway station. If you are heading for Nepal the bus may be better than rail since there are only metre-gauge trains from here to the border. Buses leave almost hourly to Gorakhpur, five hours away. A tourist bus operates from there to Sunauli on the Nepal border in eight hours. There are also direct Varanasi-Sunauli buses for about Rs 40 or deluxe buses for Rs 60.

There is a daily tourist bus service to Khajuraho which costs Rs 120 including lunch and tea. Leaving at 7 am, you arrive at 9 pm; you can enquire at the Tourist Bungalow. There is also a three-times-weekly Varanasi-Sunauli-Kathmandu or Pokhara bus which costs Rs 150, including spartan overnight accommodation at the border where you change buses. The bus leaves Varanasi at 7 am, stops at Sunauli for the night at 5 pm, and departs the next morning for Kathmandu or Pokhara at 8.15 or 8.30 am, with arrival at 4 pm and 3 pm respectively. You can also travel straight through, arriving in Kathmandu at 4 am, for Rs 140. Cost to Lumbini, just across the border in Nepal, is Rs 90 and takes about 16 hours.

Alternatively, you can simply travel to the border for Rs 60 and take another bus from the border to Kathmandu for the Nepalese rupee equivalent of about Indian Rs 30. This is not only much cheaper but you get a much better choice of bus within Nepal.

Getting Around
Airport The airline bus costs Rs 20 for the trip between the airport and the airline office in the Cantonment area. Babatpur Airport is a lengthy 22 km out of the city. Taxis are expensive, towards Rs 100 on average.

Bus Godaulia (also spelt Godowlia and Gadaulia) is the mid-town bus stop, just an easy walk from the ghats. It's a very useful city landmark. Lanka is the bus stop closest to Benares Hindu University. Between the railway station and Godaulia a bus costs less than a rupee, but unless you can get on at the starting point Varanasi buses tend to be very crowded.

Rickshaw & Bicycle Rickshaws are still comparatively cheap in Varanasi. Between the railway station and Godaulia, near Dasaswamedh Ghat, is about Rs 4. An auto-rickshaw would cost about Rs 8. You can hire a rickshaw for the whole day for Rs 20. There are a number of places to rent bicycles around Lanka – all-day rates are about Rs 5, although the Aces Restaurant in Godaulia rents new bikes for Rs 10 a day.

Things to Buy
Varanasi is famous all over India for silk brocades and beautiful Benares saris. However, there are lots of rip-off merchants and commission men at work. Invitations to 'come to my home for tea' will inevitably mean to somebody's silk showroom, where you will be pressured into buying things. There is a market near the GPO called Golghar where the makers of silk brocades sell directly to the shops in the area. You can get cheaper silk brocade in this area compared to in the

big stores, but you must be careful about the quality. The big shops selling silk brocades are all in the Chowk area of the old city.

The same care is necessary with sitars – yes, Ravi Shankar does live here (or nearby), but don't believe that every sitar maker is his personal friend!

SARNATH

Only 10 km away from Varanasi, that most holy of Hindu cities, is Sarnath, one of the major Buddhist centres. Having achieved enlightenment at Bodhgaya, the Buddha came to Sarnath to preach his message of the middle way to final nirvana. Later Ashoka, the great Buddhist emperor, erected magnificent stupas and other buildings here. Sarnath was at its peak when those indefatigable Chinese travellers Fa Hian and Hiuen Tsang visited the site. In 640 AD, when the latter made his call, Sarnath had 1500 priests, a stupa nearly 100 metres high, Ashoka's mighty stone pillar and many other wonders.

Soon after, Buddhism went into decline, and by the time the destructive Muslim invasions of India had commenced Sarnath was little more than a shell. The invaders destroyed and desecrated the buildings; even Akbar built a monument to his father, Humayun, over one stupa, and time did the rest. It was not until 1836 when British archaeologists commenced excavations that Sarnath regained some of its past glory. The city was known as the 'deer park'.

Dhamekh Stupa

Believed to date from around 500 AD, this stupa was probably rebuilt a number of times over earlier constructions. The geometrical and floral patterns on the stupa are typical of the Gupta period, but excavations have revealed brickwork from the Mauryan period around 200 BC.

Dharmarajika Stupa

This large stupa has been comprehensively excavated by 19th-century treasure seekers. Near it is the building known as the 'main shrine' where Ashoka is said to have meditated.

Ashoka Pillar

Standing in front of the main shrine are the remains of Ashoka's Pillar. At one time this stood over 20 metres high, but today the capital has been removed and can be seen in the Sarnath museum. An edict issued by Ashoka is engraved on the remaining portion of the column. The capital is the Ashokan symbol of four back-to-back lions which has now been adopted as the state symbol of modern India. On the lower portion of the column are representations of a lion, elephant, horse and bull. The lion is supposed to represent bravery, the elephant symbolises the dream Buddha's mother had before his birth, and the horse recalls that Buddha left his home on horseback in search of enlightenment.

Museum

Sarnath's excellent Archaeological Museum has the capital from the Ashokan pillar together with many other relics found on the site. These include many figures and sculptures from the various periods of Sarnath – Mauryan, Kushana, Gupta and later. Among them are the earliest Buddha image found at Sarnath, Buddha figures in various positions dating back to the 5th and 6th centuries and many images of Hindu gods such as Saraswati, Ganesh and Vishnu from the 9th to 12th centuries. The museum is open 10 am to 5 pm daily, except Fridays when it is closed. Entry is Rs 0.50.

Other

The modern Maha Bodhi Society temple known as the Mulgandha Kuti-Vihar has a series of frescoes by a Japanese artist in the interior. A Bo tree growing here is a

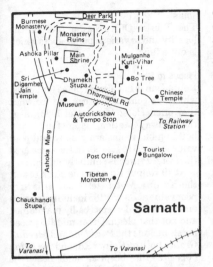

Sarnath

transplant from the tree in Anuradhapura in Sri Lanka, which in turn is said to be an offspring of the original tree under which the Buddha attained enlightenment. The brick remnants of the monastery or *vihara* can still be seen, and amongst the mango trees you can see a deer park off to one side.

Places to Stay
Sarnath has a *Tourist Bungalow* (tel 8485) with rooms at Rs 30 or dorm beds at Rs 8.

Getting There
You can visit Sarnath on a tour from Varanasi or get there by bus from Varanasi station for Rs 1.25. Six-seater tempos run to and from Godaulia and cost Rs 4 per person. An auto-rickshaw from Varanasi will cost about Rs 10 or Rs 25 return, with a reasonable waiting period at Sarnath.

NORTH FROM DELHI
Meerut (population 400,000) Only 67 km north-east of Delhi, this was the place where the 1857 Mutiny first broke out.

There's little to remember that event by today, although the cemetery near St John's Church has the grave of Sir Ochterlony, whose monument dominates the Maidan in Calcutta. The Suraj Khund is the most interesting Hindu temple in Meerut and there's a Moghul mausoleum, the Shahpir, near the old Shahpir Gate.

Meerut is a green revolution boomtown and the new-found wealth, indicated by the many well-stocked stores, has led to inter-communal tensions which sometimes turn into violence. The Nauchandi Mela is a huge month-long fair which takes place in the south-east of the city before the Hindu new year, which usually falls in April. Traditional *nautanki* dramas are a feature.

Meerut has some adequate hotels and restaurants. *Gajak*, a sweet made from crude sugar and sesame, is a local treat.

Saharanpur (population 250,000) Situated 178 km north of Delhi, the large botanical gardens here, known as the Company Bagh, are over 150 years old.

NORTHERN UTTAR PRADESH
The northern part of Uttar Pradesh, a rough rectangle bordered by Himachal Pradesh to the north-west and China to the north-east, is an area of hills, mountains and lakes. There are a number of popular hill stations, such as Naina Tal and Almora, and many trekking routes – most of them little known and even less used. Important pilgrimage centres include Hardwar and Rishikesh, where the holy Ganges leaves the Himalayas and joins the plains for its long trip to the sea.

Toll Taxes
If you're travelling up to the Uttar Pradesh hill stations (Naini Tal, Almora, Ranikhet, Mussoorie), somebody will jump on the bus just as you approach the towns to charge you a Rs 1 or Rs 2 toll tax. In Himachal Pradesh these toll taxes are included in the bus fare.

DEHRA DUN (population 250,000)

Also spelt Dehra Doon, this is the gateway to places in the Garwhal Himal such as Badrinath and Joshimath. Dehra Dun is in the centre of a forest area and has a forest research institute. The town is situated in an inter-montane valley in the Siwaliks, the southernmost and lowest of the Himalayan ranges. The high range just to the north contains the hill station Mussoorie, 22 km away.

Orientation & Information

The Tourist Office (tel 3217) is close to the bus stands and the railway station. The clock tower is the 'hub' of the town and most of the hotels are on the road from the railway station to the tower. There are two main bus stations – the one nearer the railway station is for buses to the hills, and the one nearer the clock tower is for other destinations.

Things to See

Dehra Dun is of very little interest in itself, although the Forestry Research Institute is the biggest of its kind in India and has a botanical garden. The institute's library was rather chaotic, reported a visitor: 'A far better source of information is a small publisher/bookshop on the road back to town; he had all the Research Institute's publications, along with a weird and wonderful collection that included all eight volumes of *The Fish in the British Museum*'. Dehra Dun is also the site for the 'Doon School', India's most exclusive private school (Rajiv went there).

Popular picnic spots, with their distance from the town, include: Sahastradhara (14 km) with natural sulphur springs; Takeshwar Temple (six km), a Shiva temple; the 'robbers cave' just beyond Anarwala village (seven km); Laxman Sidh, another temple, on the Dehra Dun-Rishikesh road; and Tapovan (six km) is two km off the Dehra Dun-Raipur road and has an ashram (six km), two km off the Dehra Dun-Raipur road.

Tours

The Tourist Office has a tour of the locality and to various picnic spots which is quite fun.

Places to Stay

Dehra Dun is not a great place for hotels, which are generally overpriced for what they offer. *Hotel Meedo* (tel 7088), near the railway station, is a fairly new building but rooms are grubby and poor value at Rs 80 to Rs 100. In the same area the *Hotel Prince* is similarly priced.

At 19 Rajpur Rd near the clock tower, the *Kwality Motel* (tel 27001-2) is very poor value at Rs 160/185 including service and taxes. It's decrepit, badly maintained and not that clean. Other middle-priced hotels include the *President* and *Meedo's Grand*, both on Rajpur Rd; and the *Relax* opposite the hospital and near the railway station. The Relax is OK and the staff are friendly but it can be noisy.

Dehra Dun's top-end hotel is *Hotel Madhuban* (tel 24094-97), much further out at 97 Rajpur Rd. Rooms, all with air-con, are Rs 400/475 plus service and taxes. They've also got separate cottages with kitchens.

Places to Eat

Vaishno Restaurant, opposite the Jain dharamsala near the station, has a bargain thali which includes the dessert known as *khir*. There are good Indian dishes at *Moti Mahal* on Rajpur Rd and a *Kwality Restaurant* on the same road.

Right by the clock tower, *Bengali Sweet Market* has a wide selection of Indian sweets. Nearby *Kumar Sweets* has an excellent selection including their speciality, *kesar ka halwa*. There are some good small restaurants on Pattan Bazaar near the Mussoorie Bus Stand.

Getting There

Vayudoot have daily (twice daily on some days) flights from and to Delhi; the fare is Rs 282. Dehra Dun is also connected with major north Indian cities by rail, and a deluxe bus service operates between Delhi and Dehra Dun. The trip takes about six hours. The Delhi-Hardwar-Dehra Dun 320-km train trip costs Rs 33 in 2nd class, Rs 127 in 1st. The overnight service departs Delhi at 10.30 pm and arrives Dehra Dun at 9 am.

By bus Dehra Dun-Hardwar is 54 km and takes about 1½ hours. It's a similar distance and time from Rishikesh at a fare of Rs 7. Continuing on to Simla is a long, weary all-day trip.

MUSSOORIE (population 20,000)

At an altitude of 2000 metres and 35 km beyond Dehra Dun, Mussoorie is a popular hill resort in the hot weather. It's on a horseshoe-shaped hill where much fruit is grown. There is a ropeway (Rs 4, enjoyable in the early morning) up to Gun Hill and Municipal Gardens to the west of the town. Mall Rd connects the two important bazaars – Kulri and Library.

The Rs 15 tour to Kempy Falls is good. Many of the walks around Mussoorie offer great views.

Places to Stay & Eat

There are hotels in Kulri and Library bazaars and along Camelback Rd. Prices in Mussoorie vary with the season. The *YWCA* is an old building with wide verandahs in a hectare of garden surrounded by shady trees. Rooms are Rs 50/90 (less in the off season); there are also dorm beds at Rs 25 plus larger rooms with kitchens. Food here is not very good. There are many other cheaper places to stay, including the *Apsar Hotel* in Kulri Bazaar, the *Snow View Hotel* in Library Bazaar, the *Deep Hotel* on The Mall and the *Mountain View Hotel*. There's a *Tourist Bungalow* on The Mall with dorm beds at Rs 15. The *Hotel Peak View* (tel 2652) has good rooms.

Hotel Priya, just off The Mall, has very

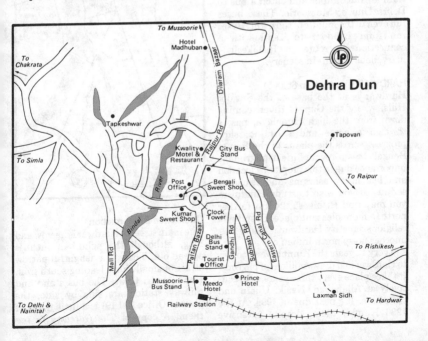

Dehra Dun

comfortable rooms. At the top of the price scale, the *Savoy Hotel* (tel 2510) has all-inclusive prices from Rs 500/750 for singles/doubles. *Hotel Gabriel* (tel 2201) at Roselynn Estate on The Mall has rooms from Rs 350/425. There are many other middle to top-end hotels in Mussoorie, particularly along The Mall.

Hotel Neelam has three restaurants – vegetarian, non-vegetarian and Chinese – all excellent and reasonably priced. *Alka* in Kulri Bazaar does great pizzas. There are also some good Tibetan places such as the *Rice Bowl*.

Getting There
Frequent buses operate between the railhead at Dehra Dun and Mussoorie. There is a road from Mussoorie to Simla direct, but foreigners are not allowed to take it without a permit. Travelling to Mussoorie from the west or north (ie Jammu), it is best to get off the express train at Saharanpur and catch a bus to Dehra Dun or Mussoorie. These buses run even in the middle of the night. Buses run from Landour to Tehri with a connection en route to Rishikesh – marvellous mountain scenery.

HARDWAR (population 85,000)
Hardwar is at the base of the Siwalik Hills, where the Ganges River, coming down from the high Himalaya, passes through a gorge and starts its slow progress across the plains to the Bay of Bengal. It is a town of great pilgrimage importance due to this propitious location and has many ashrams and itinerant sadhus. If you wish to study Hinduism you may find Rishikesh, 24 km further north, a more pleasant place. Despite its religious sanctity Hardwar is really just another noisy north Indian city.

Every 12 years the Kumbh Mela comes to Hardwar and draws millions of pilgrims. It takes place every three years, consecutively at Allahabad, Nasik, Ujjain and then here. It's next due in 1998. At the 1986 Kumbh Mela, despite extensive safety precautions, 50 people were killed in one stampede to the river, and dozens were drowned when they lost their footing in the swift flowing river.

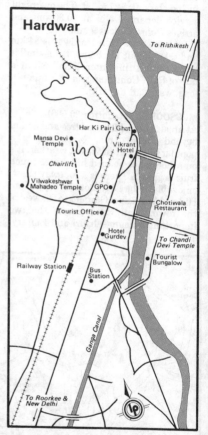

Orientation & Information
The main street of Hardwar is narrow and long, although the suburban area is spread out. There is a delightful narrow street of small shops leading south from Har-ki-pauri Ghat. The bus stand and railway station are side by side; the Tourist Office (tel 19) is a little north of them. A copy of *The Gateway to the*

Gods, Hardwar, Rishikesh & Kankhal
provides Rs 5 of guaranteed amusement.

Things to See

Although Hardwar is a very old town mentioned by the Chinese scholar-traveller Hiuen Tsang, its many temples are of comparatively recent origin and of little architectural interest. They do have many idols and illustrated scenes from the Hindu epics. Har-ki-pairi is the most important bathing ghat, as it is supposed to be at the precise spot where the Ganges leaves the mountains and enters the plains. Consequently the river's power to wash away sins at this spot is superlative. There is a footprint of Vishnu in a stone at this ghat.

The Daksha Mahadev Temple, four km downstream, is Hardwar's most important temple. According to legend, Daksha was the father of Sati, Shiva's first wife. Daksha performed a sacrifice here but neglected to invite Shiva, and Sati was so angry at this disrespect to her husband that she managed to spontaneously self-immolate! There are some fine but decaying old townhouses on the way to the temple – look for the coloured paintings on the outside.

Other temples and buildings of lesser interest include the Sapt Rishi Ashram, where the Ganges divides into several smaller streams; and the Parmath Ashram, six km towards Rishikesh, with fine images of the goddess Durga. The Mansa Devi Temple overlooks the Tourist Office and can be reached by a chairlift (Rs 6), while Beauty Point, in the same direction, offers fine views over the town. Chandi Devi and a number of other temples are reached by a three-km walk to the east.

'Hardwar is a far nicer place to visit than Varanasi', reported one traveller. 'There aren't the 'no entry' signs on the temples or the hard-sell salesmen. It's smaller and easier to get around, more beautiful'. Another added, 'Walking along the river is so relaxing'.

Places to Stay

Hardwar and Rishikesh are so close that it is easy to stay in the latter and day trip to Hardwar. If you want to stay in Hardwar, the *Tourist Bungalow* (tel 379) has doubles for Rs 60 or Rs 80 with air cooling and there's a Rs 10 dorm. It's pleasantly situated by the river but a little distance from the main part of town on the opposite side.

There are *Railway Retiring Rooms* with rooms and dorms as well as lots of hotels around town, particularly along the station road or near the river. On Station Rd, between the railway station and the Tourist Office, is the fairly modern *Hotel Gurudev* with rooms at Rs 60/100. Near the river, *Hotel Vikrant* is a reasonable sort of place with rooms at Rs 33, 44 and 55, but beware of the monkeys which will sneak into your room if you leave the door unlocked. They will also steal clothes left outside to dry.

Places to Eat

Chotiwala, across the road from the Tourist Office, does good value full thalis. *Hotel Gurudev* has a good restaurant.

Getting There

Hardwar is 222 km from Delhi, 52 km from Dehra Dun and 24 km from Rishikesh. There are direct buses from all these places. Dehra Dun-Hardwar is about Rs 7, more expensive from Dehra Dun due to the tax. The 54-km trip takes about 1½ hours. By train it is 14 hours from Lucknow or seven hours from Delhi. There's an overnight train service from Delhi, leaving at 10.30 pm, arriving at Hardwar at 6.30 am and continuing on to Dehra Dun. It's an excellent, hassle-free and comfortable train service. Fare for the 268-km trip is Rs 27 in 2nd class, Rs 110 in 1st.

RISHIKESH (population 22,000)

Surrounded by hills on three sides, Rishikesh is a quieter and more easygoing place than Hardwar, although at an altitude of 356 metres it is only 63 metres higher. Like Hardwar, there are many ashrams and sadhus and this is an excellent place to study Hinduism.

Back in the '60s Rishikesh gained instant, and fleeting, fame as the place where the Beatles came to be with their guru, the Maharishi Mahesh Yogi. Rishikesh is also the jumping-off point for treks to Himalayan pilgrimage centres like Badrinath, Kedarnath and Gangotri.

Orientation & Information

The Tourist Office (tel 209) is on Railway Station Rd. The bus stand is close by on Agarwal Rd.

Things to See

The most interesting ghats and temples in Rishikesh are across the river on the left (east) bank but are connected by a free launch system. The Lakshman Jhula suspension bridge is further upstream. Interesting temples include the Parmarth Temple with many images from Hindu mythology. The Lakshman Temple is by the bridge, three km from the town centre. Neel Khanth Mahadev is 12 km further on – fine views on the way up to the temple at 1700 metres.

Meditation

Studying Hinduism has, naturally, become somewhat commercialised at Rishikesh. The Divine Life Society, founded by Swami Shivanand, is an authentic place. It's on the Tourist Bungalow side of the river. You can stay there for short-term study or for longer three-month courses. Or simply drop by for the evening lecture at 'Satsanga'. At Ved Niketan an Indian sadhu gives lectures in English to those interested. And, of course, there's the Maharishi Mahesh Yogi's Transcendental Meditation Centre.

Places to Stay

The popular and pleasantly situated Tourist Bungalow (tel 372) is about three km from the bus and railway stations and has rooms at Rs 25 or rather awkward deluxe rooms at Rs 45. It has a dining hall and a pleasant garden for relaxing in.

Other hotels include the Hotel Menka (tel 285), right across from the bus stand, with rooms at Rs 30/40; and the Janta Tourist Lodge on Dehra Dun Rd. There are various other hotels around town and, as at Hardwar, many dharamsalas offering free accommodation to pilgrims.

The Inderlok Hotel (tel 555-56) on Railway Station Rd in the town centre has rooms at Rs 65/75 or with air-con at Rs 150/200. It has a good restaurant.

Getting There

There is a branch railway line from Hardwar up to Rishikesh and regular direct buses. The 24-km trip takes less than an hour by bus for about Rs 5. To Dehra Dun takes about two hours and costs Rs 7.

CORBETT NATIONAL PARK

On the banks of the Ram Ganga River in the foothills of the Himalaya, this park is famous for its wide variety of wildlife. The park is particularly renowned for its tigers but also has elephants, several types of deer including sambars, and panthers. The river has crocodiles and there is much birdlife. The park was established in 1935 and later renamed after Jim Corbett, who spent many years in this area and wrote the book The Man-Eaters of Kumaon.

Dhikala is the main accommodation centre in the park, 51 km from Ramnagar, the nearest railhead to the park. Ramnagar is connected with train with Moradabad and by bus with Delhi and Lucknow. Most tours into the park are operated from Dhikala, although there are also three-day package tours operated from New Delhi. Entry to the park costs Rs 30 (Rs 1 for students) for three days, then Rs 6 per day. That's for foreigners; it's only Rs 8 for Indians. The park is open from December to May but avoid the crowded weekends.

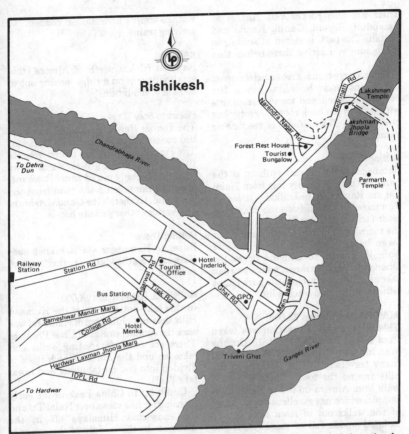

Rishikesh

The park is comparatively cool and at sunrise and sunset you can go out on elephant-back for Rs 12.50 for about two hours. The elephant rides are not to be missed; you search the elephant grass and the edge of the sal forest for an hour or more. As well as spotted and hog deer, wild boar, monitor lizards, jackals and many birds there is a good chance of seeing a tiger. There are crocodiles in the river; monkeys, sambar and other deer species in the woods; and wild elephants elsewhere in the park. Corbett is also a bird-watcher's paradise. During the day you can swim in the river or sit in one of the observation posts to watch for animals. Interesting films on wildlife and expeditions are shown in the evenings, free of charge.

Places to Stay

At Dhikala there are *Cabins* and *New and Old Forest Rest Houses* at Rs 100 per day. There are also *Tourist Hutments* (Rs 40), *Swiss Cottage Tents* (Rs 10), *Loghuts* (Rs 6 per person) and camping facilities (Rs 3 per person). One large restaurant caters for all the accommodation facilities. The meals are set price (Rs 10) but the food is good and it's eat-all-you-want.

There are also *Forest Rest Houses* at Sarapduli, Bijrani, Gairal, Kanda and Sultan. The park is closed at sunset, so make sure you arrive there before that time.

Ramnagar, which is a crossroads between the plains and the hills, has a few overpriced hotels and many restaurants with beds in the back rooms – grotty but cheap. The *Tiger Hotel* is reasonable value.

Getting There

Ramnagar is the nearest railhead to the park; or there is a daily bus from Naini Tal via Ramnagar to Dhikala. It leaves Ramnagar in the mid-afternoon and the return trip departures from Dhikala is in the morning. The trip should take six or seven hours. There are also buses just from Ramnagar to Dhikala or to the Dhangadri park entrance, where you can take an afternoon bus into the park HQ at Dhikala or try and hitch a lift.

ALMORA (population 23,000)

This picturesque hill station was taken from Nepal following the 1815 Gurkha War. It's at an altitude of 1650 metres and many travellers live in cottages in the hills around the town. There is a good walk from Almora up to the Kasar Devi temple, which has excellent views. Some of the walks out of town take you to isolated woods full of monkeys, if you walk far enough.

Places to Stay

There are a number of hotels as well as the popular *Tourist Cottage* (tel 12) with rooms from Rs 15 to Rs 25. The *Neelkanth Hotel* (tel 32) has rooms from Rs 20 to Rs 40. At the state government-operated *Tourist Bungalow* (tel 250) doubles are Rs 50, deluxe doubles Rs 75; there's a Rs 20 dorm.

Getting There

The nearest railhead to Almora and all the eastern Garwhal hill stations is Kathgodam, where buses connect to arriving trains.

KAUSANI

Situated 53 km north of Almora, this small village is on a ridge looking out to 300 km of mountains!

Places to Stay

The *Tourist Bungalow* (tel 26) has four-bed rooms at Rs 100 and a Rs 20 dorm. The *Pine View Hotel* has rooms from Rs 10 to Rs 25. There are excellent views from the similarly priced *Hotel Prashant*, about 10 minutes up the road from the bus stand. Or there's the *Gandhi Ashram* and various other private hotels.

Getting There

Buses to Ramnagar via Ranikhet pass Kausani. Kathgodam is the nearest railhead.

NAINI TAL (population 28,000)

In this lake-dotted area of the Kumaon Hills the pretty hill town of Naini Tal was once the summer capital of Uttar Pradesh. There are many interesting walks and lakes around the town – which itself is divided into two parts, upper and lower lake (Tal).

Climb up to China Peak in the early morning for fine views over Naini Tal and the snow-clad Himalaya off in the distance. In the middle of the summer season Naini Tal is packed full of local tourists and spoilt children and the prices go up.

Places to Stay & Eat

The *Youth Hostel* has dorm beds for Rs 6 but it's at the west end of the town, about three km from the bus stand. It's a 40-minute uphill walk in a lovely, peaceful location. They also have double rooms.

Hotel Coronation (tel 2649), opposite the Naini Tal Club in the old colonial part of town, is very basic with rooms from Rs 25. On the other side of town, which is less 'rich tourist', *Saidar Bhawan* and the

Punjab Hotel (tel 2545) are two more fairly basic places. They overlook the lake and are also in the Rs 20 to Rs 40 price range. The *Prashant* is a pleasant hotel with good food in its restaurant and doubles at Rs 50.

The *Evelyn Hotel* (tel 2457) has spacious doubles with bath, hot water and a separate sitting room for Rs 60 even at the height of the season. Terrific views from the top-floor rooms, a good restaurant and friendly management.

There are a great many other hotels plus expensive places like the *Grand Hotel* (tel 2406) on The Mall with doubles at Rs 170. Or the *Royal Hotel* (tel 2007) with doubles at Rs 220, and the similarly priced *Swiss Hotel* (tel 2603, both on The Mall.

The *Sharma Vaishnow Restaurant* in the Malli Tal Bazaar offers all-you-can-eat vegetarian meals for around Rs 5.

Getting There

Kathgodam is the nearest railway station. Almora is 68 km away by road, Ranikhet 59 km and there are bus services to these and other northern Uttar Pradesh towns.

RANIKHET

North of Naini Tal and only a short distance west of Almora, this hill station offers excellent views of the snow-capped Himalaya. Only eight km away, Chaubattia is famous for its fruits. There's a tourist office by the bus stand in Ranikhet.

Places to Stay

The *Moon Hotel & Restaurant* (tel 58) has rooms at Rs 50/75. There are many other hotels both cheaper and more expensive, including the *Tourist Bungalow* (tel 97) with rooms at Rs 75 and dorm beds at Rs 20.

Getting There

As with the other northern hill stations, Kathgodam is the nearest railhead.

TREKKING IN THE GARWHAL HIMAL

Although the Garwhal Himal is little known as a trekking region, it boasts a number of famous peaks, including Trisul and India's highest mountain, Nanda Devi. Or at least it was the highest until Sikkim (and thus Kanchenjunga) was absorbed into India. There are also many important pilgrimage sites, such as Badrinath and Kedarnath or Gaumukh, the actual source of the Ganges. The trekking routes pass through rich, green forests and cross beautiful meadows carpeted with flowers in summer. Glistening glaciers complement the soaring Himalayan peaks and there are many excellent state government-operated *Tourist Bungalows* along the routes to simplify the question of shelter.

The best times to trek in the Garwhal Himal are May-June and September-October. Some places, like the Valley of Flowers and the high-altitude *bugyals* (meadows), are at their best during the July-August rainy period. The Mountaineering Division, located at the Tourist Bungalow in Rishikesh, can provide more information on trekking in the Garwhal Himal; or check the Lonely Planet guide *Trekking in the Indian Himalaya*. Although high altitude trekking is difficult in the winter due to snow the hill country itself is still very pleasant.

Actually the term Garwhal Himal is something of a misnomer. There is only Garwhal (the Himal is an incorrect addition). Garwhal and Kumaon are neighbouring cultural provinces known under the combined name of Uttar-akhand.

Kedarnath

Like Badrinath, this is a Hindu pilgrimage spot of great importance. The temple of Lord Kedar (Shiva) is surrounded by snow-capped peaks, but although the shrine is said to date back to the 8th century, very little is known about it.

To get to Kedarnath you can either make the short, direct trek from Sonprayag,

205 km from Rishikesh, or you can follow the longer and more arduous yatra route from Gangotri. Along the way you pass through beautiful scenery and see many colourful mountain villages. The trek starts from Mala, 20 km beyond Uttarkashi towards Lanka and Gangotri.

Day 1	Mala-Belak Khal	15 km
Day 2	Belak Khal-Budakedar	14 km
Day 3	Budakedar-Ghuttu	16 km
Day 4	Ghuttu-Panwali Khanta	12 km
Day 5	Panwali Khanta-Maggu	8 km
Day 6	Maggu-Sonprayag	9 km
Day 7	Sonprayag-Kedarnath	20 km*
Day 8	Kedarnath-Sonprayag	20 km*

*the first six km of Sonprayag-Kedarnath can be made by taxi.

Gangotri & Gaumukh

This trek to the source of the holy Ganges can be made from either Mussoorie or Rishikesh. Lanka, reached via Uttarkashi-Bukhi-Dabrani, is the end of the vehicle road. It's 212 km from Mussoorie to Lanka, 247 km from Rishikesh. The tiny village of Gangotri stands at 3140 metres. The temple of the goddess Ganga is on the right bank of the Bhagirathi River, which eventually becomes the holy Ganges. Gaumukh is the actual source of the river, at the base of the Bhagirathi peaks.

At 4225 metres, the Gangotri Glacier is nearly 24 km long and two to four km wide. The glacier ends at Gaumukh, where the Bhagirathi River finally appears. The glacier has gradually retreated over the centuries, but during the Vedic era it is supposed to have reached down to Gangotri. Beyond Gaumukh places like Nandanvan and Tapovan are great pilgrimage centres where sadhus often retreat to meditate in remote caves.

Day 1	Lanka-Gangotri	11 km
Day 2	Gangotri-Chirbasa	12 km
Day 3	Chirbasa-Gaumukh	7 km
Day 4	Gaumukh-Chirbasa	7 km
Day 5	Chirbasa-Gangotri	12 km
Day 6	Gangotri-Lanka	11 km

Nanda Devi Sanctuary

Some of the most outstanding peaks in the central Himalaya are clustered between the glaciers of Gangotri and Milan. Nanda Devi with its camel-humped summit is the most important peak at 7818 metres. The Nanda Devi Sanctuary is surrounded by almost 70 white peaks, like some sort of natural fortress. The sanctuary has a perimeter of nearly 120 km and an area of 640 square km. It's dotted with meadows and waterfalls and is the base camp and starting point for mountaineering assaults on Nanda Devi.

The seven-day trek from Lata, the roadhead 15 km from Joshimath, to Tilchaunni is at times difficult and tedious but the scenic grandeur you walk through will often compensate for weary bodies and frayed nerves. The first six km from Lata to Lata Kharak is a tiring uphill struggle of 1524 metres, but one is well rewarded by glorious views of Ronti, Nanda Ghunti and Bethartoli across the Rishi Ganga. The broad, open grassy ridge of Lata Kharak is covered with flowers in the summer but is always windy and cold. From here there are fine views of the northern face of Bethartoli Himal and the Trisul massif to the south. Another long uphill trek crosses the 4253-metre Dharansi Pass and takes you to Dharansi. On approaching the pass you get your first glimpse of Dunagiri (7068 metres), and immediately after crossing it Nanda Devi can be seen.

From Dharansi the trail winds its way across the Malatuni Pass (4238 metres), where the western face of Hanuman (6076 metres) can be seen; it then descends almost 750 metres through grass and snow slopes and dense forest to a stream. After crossing the stream you finally arrive at the hospitable meadows of Dibrugheta, where a camp can be made by the river. In summer the grass is carpeted with flowers. From here to Deodi the track rises steeply at first, then makes a long traverse across several ridges before you cross a bridge over the

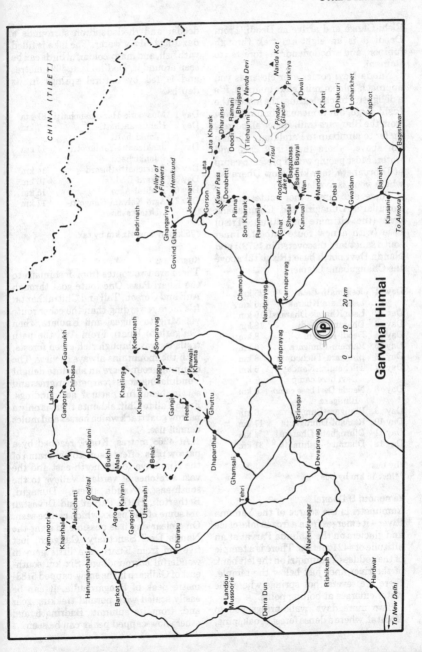

Garwhal Himal

Rishi Ganga and arrive at Deodi. From Deodi it is an eight-km trek through juniper and rhododendron forests to Ramani.

Nanda Devi comes ever closer as you approach Tilchaunni ('slate quarry'). It's a delightful birch clearing, the last on the Rishi gorge, but it means climbing *down* from the Bhujgara trail. Hence all porters prefer to climb up to Patalkhan, about a km above, where there is a cave and water. Most people would prefer to camp at Dibrugheta, four km below Dharansi, where wood is available.

There are three other routes in the sanctuary: Dunagiri and Changabang base (the ultimate mountain); Trisul base (with a new route into the inner south sanctuary discovered in 1979); and Nanda Devi north base (Rishi Tal above the Changabang Glacier).

Day 1	Joshimath-Lata	25 km*
	Lata-Lata Kharak	6 km
Day 2	Lata Kharak-Dharansi	10 km
Day 3	Dharansi-Deodi	13 km
Day 4	Deodi-Ramani	8 km
Day 5	Ramani-Bhujgara	6 km
Day 6	Bhujgara-Tilchaunni	8 km
Day 7	Tilchaunni-Nanda Devi base camp	5 km
Day 8	Nanda Devi base camp-Bhujgara	6 km
Day 9	Bhujgara-Ramani	6 km
Day 10	Ramani-Dibrugheta	17 km
Day 11	Dibrugheta-Dharansi	4 km
Day 12	Dharansi-Joshimath	31 km**

*by bus
**last 15 km by bus

Yamunotri & Dodital

Yamunotri is the source of the Yamuna River – it emerges from a frozen lake of ice and glaciers on the Kalinda Parvat at an altitude of 4421 metres. There is a temple of the goddess Yamunotri on the left bank of the river and, just below the temple, there are several hot springs where the water emerges at boiling point.

Two more days' walk brings you to Dodital, where a dense forest of oak, pine,

deodar and rhododendron surrounds a dazzling body of water. The lake is filled with fish, and many colourful birds can be seen around it. Dodital is at 4024 metres and is fed by natural springs in its depths.

Day 1	Mussoorie-Hanumanchatti	81 km*
Day 2	Hanumanchatti-Jankichatti	7 km
Day 3	Jankichatti-Yamunotri-Jankichatti	14 km
Day 4	Jankichatti-Basard	14 km
Day 5	Basard-Dodital	16 km
Day 6	Dodital-Agro	15 km
Day 7	Agro-Kalyani-Gangotri-Uttarkashi	17 km

*75 km by bus, six km by taxi

Kuari Pass

There are two routes from Joshimath to the Kuari Pass. One route goes through Auli and Gorson, Tali and Chitrakhanta. It's more rewarding than the other route via Mrig to Tugasi and Khulara, then Gailgarh to Kuari. From Auli the path trails its way through rich green forests, with the mountains always in view. The camping grounds are an absolute delight – undulating slopes, carpeted in grass and set in beautiful natural surroundings. From Tali to Chitrakhanta there is only a narrow goat track which horses and mules cannot use.

At 4268 metres, Kuari, reached by a narrow pass, offers a superb panorama of the Himalaya to the north-east and the vast stretches of verdant valleys to the south-east. Nanda Devi, Dunagiri, Bethartoli, Hathi Parvat and Devastan are some of the peaks which can be seen. On a clear day it is possible to sight the Nanda Devi Sanctuary. Gailgarh, just five km from Kuari, is a little gem in wonderful surroundings. Six km south-east of Gailgarh is the snow-capped 5183-metre peak of Pangarchulia. It can be easily scaled with normal trekking gear and, from its summit, Badrinath and other snow-capped peaks can be seen.

Delisera, six km east of Gailgarh, is a little hamlet at 3354 metres. In the local dialect *sera* means 'the rice fields', and the terraced slopes around here date back countless years. In late June the entire land is a tapestry of flowers. Bore Kund, six km north-east of Gailgarh, is a lovely lake reputed to be very deep.

Day 1	Joshimath-Gorson	15 km*
Day 2	Gorson-Chitrakhanta	9 km
Day 3	Chitrakhanta-Kuari	8 km
Day 4	Kuari-Donabetti	7 km
Day 5	Donabetti-Panna	8 km
Day 6	Panna-Son Kharak	14 km
Day 7	Son Kharak-Rammani	6 km
Day 8	Rammani-Ghat	14 km
	Ghat-Nandprayag	29 km**

*first eight km by taxi
**by taxi

Khatling Glacier

The first four days of this trek follow the yatra route to Kedarnath, before the trail branches off north-east to the glacier. It then retraces the route to Ghuttu and continues south-west to Ghamsali, where buses run to Tehri and Rishikesh. The Khatling Glacier is a lateral glacier from the centre of which the Bhilangana River emerges. The rich pasturelands here make ideal camping sites – the summer rains make the flat land on the glacial moraines into excellent pastures. The glaciers are associated with the giant hanging glaciers of Ratangian, Jogin and Phating. Around Katling Glacier are the snow-capped peaks of the Jogin ground (6466 metres), spectacular Sphetic Prishtwan (6905 metres), Kirti Stambh (6402 metres) and Barte Kanta (6579 metres).

The yatra route is tiring with its constant ascents and descents, but colourful. There are many rippling streams to be crossed by improvised log bridges. Gangi, the last village before the glacier, is still very much cut off from the outside world. The people here are so isolated that they have been forced to frequently intermarry within their own community and as a result many are sterile.

Day 1-3	as Kedarnath Trek	
Day 4	Ghuttu-Reeh	10 km
Day 5	Reeh-Gangi	10 km
Day 6	Gangi-Khansoli	15 km
Day 7	Khansoli-Khatling	11 km
Day 8	Khatling-Naumuthi	9 km
Day 9	Naumuthi-Kalyani	12 km
Day 10	Kalyani-Reeh	15 km
Day 11	Reeh-Dhapardhar	15 km
Day 12	Dhapardhar-Gamsali	25 km
	Gamsali-Tehri	31 km*
Day 13	Tehri-Rishikesh	72 km*

*by bus

The Khatling Glacier trek can also be made from the Kedarnath side. In that case the first three days of the trek are like Days 6, 5 and 4 of the Kedarnath Trek. On Day 3 you reach Ghuttu and then the route is the same as from the Gangotri side.

Valley of Flowers & Hemkund

The beautiful 'Valley of Flowers' and the holy Hemkund lake can be reached in one short trek from Govind Ghat. In addition, you can visit the pilgrimage centre of Badrinath, now accessible by road, on the same trip. From Rishikesh it is 252 km by bus to Joshimath and a further 44 km to Badrinath. You then have to backtrack 30 km to Govind Ghat for the start of the trek.

Badrinath Surrounded by snow-capped peaks, Badrinath has been a Hindu pilgrimage centre since time immemorial. There are many temples, ashrams and dharamsalas here. The most important temple, on the left bank of the Alakananda, shows clear Buddhist influence in its architecture, indicating that in an earlier period this must also have been a Buddhist centre.

The mountaineer Frank Smythe is believed to be the discoverer of the Valley of Flowers. Between mid-June and mid-September the valley is an enchanting sight with a bewildering variety of flowers fluttering in the gentle breezes. As a backdrop snow-clad mountains stand in bold relief against the skyline. The valley is nearly 10 km long and two km wide, and is divided by the Pushpawati stream, into which several tiny streams and waterfalls merge. The huge Ghoradhungi mountain blocks one end of the valley.

From the valley you can backtrack to Ghangariya, then follow the Laxma Ganga to the lake of Hemkund. In the Sikh holy book, the *Garanth Sahib*, the Sikh Guru Govind Singh recounts that in a previous life he had meditated on the shores of a lake surrounded by seven snow-capped mountains. Hemkund Sahib, Sikh pilgrims have decided, is that holy lake. From Govind Ghat it is a gentle incline to the Valley of Flowers, but the trek from the pretty hamlet of Ghangariya to Hemkund is rather steep.

Day 1	Govind Ghat-Ghangariya	14 km
Day 2	Ghangariya-Valley of Flowers	6 km
Day 3	Valley of Flowers-Ghangariya-Hemkund-Ghangariya	16 km

Roopkund Lake

At an altitude of 4778 metres, below the 7122-metre-high Trisul massif, Roopkund Lake is sometimes referred to as the 'mystery lake' because of skeletons of humans and horses found here. Every 12 years thousands of devout pilgrims make an arduous trek when following the Raj Jay Yatra from Nauti village, near Karanprayag. The pilgrims are said to be led by a mysterious four-horned ram which takes them from there through Roopkund to the Shrine of Nanda Devi, where it disappears. A golden idol of the goddess Nanda Devi is carried by the pilgrims in a silver palanquin.

The trek commences from Gwaldom, accessible by bus from Rishikesh. It passes through delightful alpine pasture-land and snow fields and offers magnificent views of peaks in the Garwhal Himal, such as Trisul and Nanda Ghunti.

Day 1	Rishikesh-Gwaldom	240 km*
Day 2	Gwaldom-Debal	10 km
Day 3	Debal-Mandoli	15 km
Day 4	Mandoli-Wan	14 km
Day 5	Wan-Badni Bugyal	8 km
Day 6	Badni Bugyal-Baggubasa	8 km
Day 7	Baggubasa-Roopkund-Baggubasa	8 km
Day 8	Baggubasa-Wan	16 km
Day 9	Wan-Kannual	9 km
Day 10	Kannual-Sheetal	9 km
Day 11	Sheetal-Ghat	14 km
	Ghat-Nandprayag	30 km**
Day 12	Nandprayag-Rishikesh	192 km*

*by bus
**by taxi

Pindari Glacier

The magnificent Pindari Glacier is the most easily accessible in the region. It owes its existence to the snow sliding down from Nanda Khat and other lofty peaks. The glacier, three km long and nearly half a km wide, is at an altitude of 3353 metres. Close to it is an undulating meadow, and to the east a moraine projects into the glacier.

The trek offers views of the soaring peaks all the way and passes through pine forests, glades of ferns and wildflowers, and tumbling waterfalls. From mid-May to mid-June there are many wildflowers, while from mid-September to mid-October the air is exceptionally clear and it has not yet got too cold. From Rishikesh buses now go to Song, only a km or so before Loharkhet. You can stay in Bharari, between Kapkot and Loharkhet, and catch the one daily bus (around 2 pm) for the hair-raising ride to Song. Or if you can get a jeep you can leave Bharari earlier in the day.

The first couple of days from Song through Loharkhet and up to the Dhakuri Pass is a long, hard, uphill slog. A km or two over the pass is the Dhakuri Dak

Bungalow. Nonetheless this a fine walk with wonderful scenery. There is an excellent view of the glacier from Purkiya, where some trekkers stop. On the return trek you can travel by road from Bajnath to Almora and Naini Tal rather than return to Rishikesh.

There are excellent PWD Bungalows at Kapkot, Loharkhet, Dhakuri, Khati, Dwali and Purkiya. Foreigners are charged Rs 30 for a huge suite but they tend to fill up relatively early in the day. Khati is the only place with supplies after Bharari. The small *Himalayan Hotel* (with a restaurant) is also here.

Day 1	Rishikesh-Gwaldom	240 km*
Day 2	Gwaldom-Kapkot-Bharari	80 km*
Day 3	Bharari-Song-Loharkhet	12 km**
Day 4	Loharkhet-Khati	18 km
Day 5	Khati-Purkiya	16 km
Day 6	Purkiya-Pindari	7 km
Day 7	Pindari-Khati	21 km
Day 8	Khati-Loharkhet	18 km
Day 9	Loharkhet-Bajnath	47 km*
Day 10	Bajnath-Kausani-Almora	71 km*

*by bus
**mostly by bus

Tony's Notebook

Weird Scenes

India is full of weird scenes, I'm on my way from Varanasi station in a rickshaw when we pass a guy walking along wearing an orange sarong, bare-chested with bangles on his arms and ankles and barefoot. He looks a bit like an Indian version of George Harrison when the Beatles just started, but obviously he's on some sort of yagna. He carries a long whip. Behind him walks a woman (his wife) clutching a drum in one arm, a small baby and drumstick in the other.

They stop, she beats the drum and he whirls the whip and flogs himself. The whip cracks and he turns, to his audience, to show more blood streaming down his already bloody chest and arm. He repeats the process twice more and then walks away to repeat it again a little further down the road. His wife passes the offering bowl around and then hurries after him. Why he was engaged in this particularly gruesome yagna I have no idea but it was sufficiently unusual for my rickshaw-wallah to stop and gawp. Nobody had so much as given a second glance to the dead body I saw floating by the bathing ghats that morning.

Form Filling

Introducing visas gave the form makers another line to add to the forms you're supposed to (but don't) fill out at every place you stop. Now, like most travellers I find my passport number, place and date of issue as familiar as my first name, but my visa number (and its place and date of issue) is another matter. But these forms have no purpose or relevance; they're just the Indian equivalent of junk mail, a way of consuming paper. So I lied. Every night I wrote down a different number. Good numbers, numbers with dashes and obliques, but wrong numbers. And since I couldn't remember the date of issue either I thought I might as well go the whole hog, so I issued my visa in different places each night. One day Bangkok, the next Hong Kong. This soon became quite addictive and I started inventing other parts of the form. Soon I was arriving in India before my visa had been issued, issuing my visa before the passport was issued, moving further afield to Rio de Janiero, Timbuktu. Nothing ever happened; the Indian civil service hasn't collapsed as far as I know.

Bihar

Population: 62 million
Area: 173,876 square km
Capital: Patna
Main language: Hindi

The northern state of Bihar is one of the most backward and depressed in India. Its tightly-packed population scratches a bare living from rice growing. For visitors Bihar is usually little more than a place to be crossed, with perhaps a pause in Patna if they are heading for Nepal by land. Yet 25 centuries ago this was the capital of the greatest empire in India, for Ashoka ruled his kingdom from Pataliputra, where Patna is today.

Furthermore Bihar was a great religious centre for Jains, Hindus and, most important, Buddhists. It was at Bodhgaya that the Buddha sat under the Bo tree and attained enlightenment, and a descendant of that original tree still flourishes there today. Nearby Nalanda was a world-famous university for the study of Buddhism in the 5th century AD, while Rajgir was associated with both the Buddha and the Jain apostle Mahavira.

PATNA (population 550,000)

For many centuries Patna, the ancient name for which was Pataliputra, was the capital of a huge empire which ruled a large part of ancient India. Today this surprisingly pleasant city is the capital of Bihar. The city sprawls along the southern bank of the Ganges, which at this point is very wide; between Varanasi and Patna three major tributaries join the Ganges, and the river triples in width.

Orientation & Information

The city stretches for 15 km along the south bank of the Ganges. The main railway station, airline offices and airport are all at the western end of the town, while the older and more traditional parts

of Patna are to the east. The 'hub' of the new Patna is at Gandhi Maidan. The main market area is Ashok Raj Path, which starts from Gandhi Maidan. Two important roads near the railway station, Frazer Rd and Exhibition Rd, have officially had their names changed to M Haque Path and Braj Kishore Path respectively, but in actual fact there is no indication whatsoever of a change. On the other hand Gardiner Rd does appear to have been renamed Beer Chand Patel Marg.

The state Tourist Office is on Frazer Rd but is of little use. The small counter on the railway station platform is much more helpful. There's a Government of India Tourist Office at the Tourist Bungalow. There are a couple of reasonable small bookshops on Frazer Rd. Non-residents can use the Welcomgroup Hotel's pool for Rs 10.

Golghar

Overlooking the maidan, the huge, beehive-shaped Golghar was built in 1786 as a granary to store surpluses against possible famines. It stands about 25 metres high

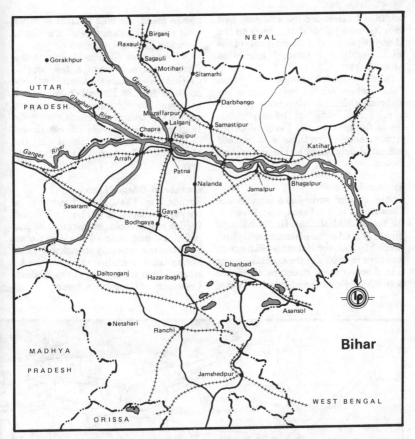

Bihar

and steps wind around the outside to the top, where you have a fine view over the town and the Ganges. Inside there is a superb echo. The Golghar was built by Captain John Garstin at the instigation of the British administrator, Warren Hastings, following a terrible famine in 1770, but it has scarcely been used since that time.

Patna City Museum

The excellent, albeit somewhat dog-eared, museum contains metal and stone sculptures dating back to the Maurya (3rd century BC) and Gupta periods, terracotta figures and archaeological finds from sites in Bihar such as Nalanda. There are also original Chinese and Tibetan scrolls and paintings. The museum is open 10.30 am to 4.30 pm, closed on Mondays.

Kumrahar

Pataliputra, Ashoka's capital in the 3rd century BC, has been excavated at the small village of Kumrahar, south of Patna. It was earlier the capital of Chandragupta (321-297 BC) and Bindusara (297-274 BC) before Ashoka ruled here between 274 and 237 BC. The main points of interest are the assembly hall with its large pillars dating back to the Mauryan period, and the remnants of the brick Buddhist monastery known as Anand Bihar.

North-west of Kumrahar is Bhikna Pahari, where Ashoka built a retreat for his brother Mahinda. Kumrahar is six km from central Patna but the excavations are fairly esoteric and likely to be an attraction only for those with a keen interest in archaeology and India's ancient history.

Har Mandir

At the eastern end of the city, in the Chowk area of old Patna, stands one of the holiest Sikh shrines. Built by Ranjit Singh, it marks the place where Govind Singh, the 10th and last of the Sikh gurus, was born in 1660. On the bottom floor of this dome-shaped structure there are holy Sikh scriptures and an exhibition of photos about the Sikh religion together with personal belongings of the Guru, including his shoes and cradle.

A tempo from Gandhi Maidan to the Chowk area only costs a few rupees. Celebrations to mark the Guru's birthday are held here in December-January of each year. Not only must you go barefoot within the temple precincts, but your head must be covered. They loan out cloths at the entrance. Shops near the Har Mandir sell attractive painted wooden toys.

Khudabaksh Oriental Library

Founded in 1900, this library has a renowned collection of rare Arabic and Persian manuscripts, Moghul and Rajput paintings, and oddities like the Koran inscribed in a book only an inch wide. The library also contains the only books rescued from the sacking of the Moorish University of Cordoba in Spain.

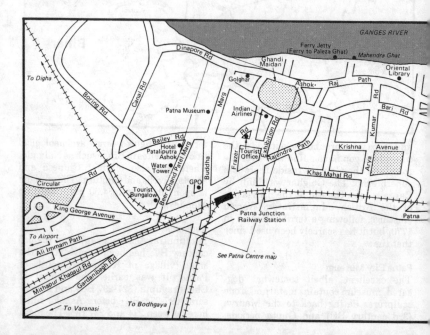

Other

Gulzarbagh, to the east of the city, was the site of the East India Company's opium warehouse. Today the building, if you can find it, houses a Bihar government printing works. Ask for the Barkipor bus stand from the Patna City Railway Station.

The Sher Shahi, built by the Afghan ruler Sher Shah in 1545, is the oldest mosque in Patna and a heavy, domed structure. Other mosques include the squat Pathar ki Masjid and the riverbank Madrassa. Jalan's Quila houses a collection of antiques. A km west of the Har Mandir is the very overgrown and decayed old cemetery, which may still bear some reminders of the British days. On Beer Chand Patel Marg, a little north of the Tourist Bungalow, there's a wonderful old water tower with brick walls two metres thick. It withstood the major 1934 earthquake and is still in use today.

Tours

Tours are only run if there are 20 passengers wanting to go – an unlikely occurrence.

Places to Stay – bottom end

Most visitors to Patna pause for just a day on their way to Kathmandu, and there are a number of reasonable hotels in the area from the railway station to Gandhi Maidan. Rooms are variable at the *Hotel Rajasthan* (tel 25102) on Frazer Rd, so look before you say OK. Rooms, all with bathroom, start from Rs 40/60. Deluxe rooms are Rs 90, rooms with air-con Rs 140. The hotel is pretty good value and has a good restaurant.

Just round the corner before the Rajasthan on Dak Bungalow Rd, the *Rajdhani Hotel* and the *Dai Ichi Hotel* across the road from it are both reasonably priced. On the next block over from Frazer Rd the *Ruby Hotel* is a reasonable

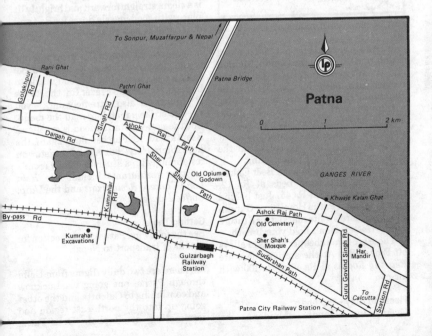

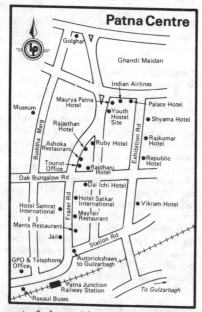

Patna Centre

Golghar

Ghandi Maidan

Indian Airlines

Museum

Maurya Patna Hotel

Youth Hostel Site

Palace Hotel

Shyama Hotel

Rajasthan Hotel

Buddha Marg

Ashoka Restaurant

Ruby Hotel

Exhibition Rd

Rajkumar Hotel

Tourist Office

Rajdhani Hotel

Republic Hotel

Dak Bungalow Rd

Dai Ichi Hotel

Frazer Rd

Hotel Satkar International

Vikram Hotel

Hotel Samrat International

Mayfair Restaurant

Manta Restaurant

Station Rd

Jail

GPO & Telephone Office

Autorickshaws to Gulzarbagh

Patna Junction Railway Station

To Gulzarbagh

Raxaul Buses

sort of place with rooms at just Rs 30/40.

There are several cheaper hotels along Exhibition Rd. From the Gandhi Maidan end the *Shyama Hotel* (tel 32539) has rooms with bath for Rs 25/40. The *Rajkumar Hotel* is a fairly new building with rooms with bathroom at Rs 35/55. Finally, the somewhat shabby *Vikram Hotel* (tel 26894) has singles/doubles at Rs 25/45 (Rs 5 more for carpet on the floor!) or Rs 40/70 with air-cooling.

The *Tourist Bungalow* on Beer Chand Patel Marg has dorm beds at Rs 12, doubles with bath at Rs 45. Just behind the big Maurya Patna Hotel, near Gandhi Maidan, there's a site marked for a future *Youth Hostel*. Don't hold your breath.

There are some cheaper hotels in alleys off Frazer Rd. At the station there are *Retiring Rooms* at Rs 45 or Rs 100 with air-con.

Places to Stay – top end
Overlooking Gandhi Maidan, the

Welcomgroup Maurya Patna (tel 22001-65) is Patna's top hotel. All rooms are air-con, and the usual mod-cons are available, including a pool. Singles cost Rs 400 to Rs 475, doubles Rs 500 to Rs 550. *Hotel Pataliputra Ashok* (tel 26270) at Beer Chand Patel Path has air-con rooms at Rs 300/400.

There are several newish medium-priced hotels along Frazer Rd from the station. The *Samrat International* (tel 31841) has rooms at Rs 160/225. Across the road from it is the *Satkar International* (tel 25771-8) with rooms at Rs 160/240. Over on Exhibition Rd in Lawly's Building, the *Hotel Republic* (tel 22021-4) is an older place with rooms at Rs 100/175 or with air-con at Rs 150/225.

Places to Eat
Patna has plenty of places to eat; again, many of them are found along Frazer Rd from the station. The *Mayfair Restaurant* is a clean, straightforward and brightly lit place with good masala dosas for Rs 4 and other snacks as well as 30-odd ice cream flavours.

Close by, the *Manta Restaurant* is one of the gloomy variety of more expensive Indian restaurants but the food is said to be good. Further up Frazer Rd, the *Ashok Restaurant* is also extremely dark – you need to strike a match to read the menu, but the non-vegetarian food is excellent. Beers are Rs 18. Further along again, the *Rajasthan Hotel* has a good vegetarian restaurant, with a separate 'family room'.

Other restaurants include the *Hsin Long Chinese Restaurant* and the *Udipi Coffee House*.

Getting There
See the following Patna-Nepal section for details of transport to Nepal.

Air There are two daily flights from Delhi through Patna, one going via Lucknow and continuing to Calcutta and the other going up into the north-east region and terminating at Imphal. Delhi-Patna costs Rs 751, Calcutta-Patna Rs 441, Lucknow-Patna Rs 410.

Rail There are several express and mail trains daily between Delhi and Patna taking 16 to 20 hours. The distance is almost exactly 1000 km. The Delhi-Patna fare is Rs 76 in 2nd class, Rs 312 in 1st. The 533-km trip Calcutta-Patna takes about eight to 10 hours and costs Rs 47 in 2nd class, Rs 193 in 1st. If the Patna-Calcutta train is full you can take a train to Dhanbad and change to a Calcutta train there. You can also catch trains for Bhubaneswar in Orissa from here.

If you're heading up to Darjeeling or the north-east region, the fast Assam Mail passes through Patna at a horrible hour of the night. Take an earlier evening train to Barauni, spend the night there (Rs 10 dorm or Rs 25 double in the *Retiring Rooms*) and then catch the Assam Mail when it comes through at around 7 am.

Bus Until the completion of the Gandhi Bridge over the Ganges in 1982, you had to cross the river by ferry. Now transport to the Nepal border or to places in north Bihar is much easier and quicker.

The main bus station is just west of the Patna Junction Railway Station, opposite the GPO and Hardinge Park. Buses go from here to Muzaffarpur and Raxaul on the Nepalese border. A bus to Siliguri for Darjeeling costs Rs 55; the trip takes at least 12 hours even on the fastest night bus. Some buses on this trip are very overcrowded – Ranjit Travel is one to beware of.

Getting Around

Airport The Indian Airlines bus is Rs 10 and you have to get to the Indian Airlines office to start with. The airport is so close to town you can get there on a cycle-rickshaw for Rs 8 to Rs 10.

Local Transport Shared auto-rickshaws shuttle back and forth between the main

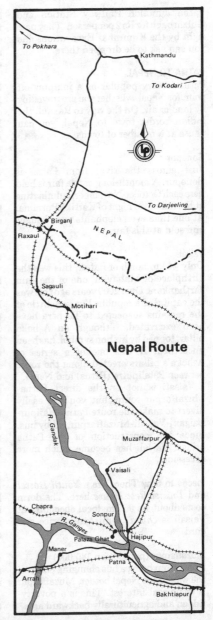

Patna Junction Railway Station and Gulzarbagh for Rs 2 per person. They pass right by the Kumrahar Excavations and you can ask to be dropped there.

PATNA TO NEPAL

Patna is very popular as a jumping-off point for Nepal, whether you are travelling by land or air. On the way to Raxaul, the Indian border town to Nepal, you can pause at a number of towns.

Sonepur

Just across the river from Patna is Sonepur. A month-long cattle fair is held here each October-November, culminating at the full moon night of Kartika Purnima. At one time even elephants were bought and sold at this fair.

Vaisali

Only 44 km north of Patna, this was the birthplace of Mahavira, one of the Jain Tirthankars. Over 2000 years ago this was the capital of a republic but very little of the remains suspected to lie here have been excavated, although an Ashoka pillar, topped by his lion symbol, has been unearthed. It was one of a series of Ashoka's pillars erected along the route between Pataliputra (Patna) and Nepal.

Vaisali is not on the direct Patna-Muzaffarpur route, but you can easily divert to make the route Patna-Hajipur-Laiganj-Vaisali-Muzaffarpur, all by bus. Since the construction of the Patna bridge, Vaisali has become much more accessible.

Places to Stay There are a *Youth Hostel* and *Tourist Rest House* here. The dorm costs about Rs 5. The local speciality at Vaisali is *chura*, a mixture of rice and curd.

Muzaffarpur (population 140,000)

Apart from being a bus changing point on the way to the Nepal border, Muzaffarpur is of no real interest. This is a poverty-ridden and agriculturally backward area.

Places to Stay *Hotel Deepak* has reasonable food and very spartan rooms. *Hotel Elite*, only a couple of hundred metres from the railway station on Saraiya Gunj, is more expensive.

Motihari & Raxaul

North of Muzaffarpur the area becomes even more backward and depressed. Motihari, where George Orwell was born, is a small provincial town which is also the district headquarters. Raxaul is right on the border and is virtually a twin town with Birganj, just across the border in Nepal. The border is open at night.

Places to Stay *Hotel Kaveri* in Raxaul costs Rs 20 per night for a single. The slightly more expensive *Hotel Taj* is also a reasonable place to stop if you don't want to cross the border and stay in Birganj.

Patna-Nepal Routes

Air Indian Airlines have a twice-weekly Patna-Kathmandu flight which costs US$41 (although this may soon increase). Compared to flying directly from Delhi to Kathmandu, you can make a considerable saving by travelling Delhi-Patna by land and flying Patna-Kathmandu. Even flying Delhi-Patna and Patna-Kathmandu is somewhat cheaper than flying direct.

Land Since the bridge over the Ganges was completed it makes little sense to take a train to the Nepal border; buses are now much faster. From the main Patna bus station buses cost Rs 30 for the six-hour trip to Raxaul, from where it costs about Rs 10 for a rickshaw across the border and Rs 55 on to Kathmandu. You can also get tickets all the way through to Kathmandu for Rs 125 including the border rickshaw, accommodation and breakfast before the 7 am departure for Kathmandu the next day. Night buses to Kathmandu go straight through from Patna, arrive at 5 am and cost Rs 100.

Some trains from Delhi go all the way to Muzaffarpur via Patna. They all take a

long time to reach Muzaffarpur, so it's better to get off in Patna and take a bus from there to the Nepalese border.

PATNA TO VARANASI
Sasaram

At the junction of the Grand Trunk Rd with the road to Patna there are some fine Muslim tombs in this town, particularly that of the Afghan ruler Sher Shah who died in 1545. The dome of his tomb, visible from the railway line, rises 46 metres above the water level of the surrounding tank. The tomb of his father and the unfinished tomb of his son are also in Sasaram.

There are more Muslim tombs at Maner. At Dehri, 17 km from Sasaram, the railway and the Grand Trunk Rd cross the River Son on a three-km bridge. The hill fort of Rohtas is 38 km from here.

PATNA TO GAYA
Nalanda

This was a great Buddhist centre over 1000 years ago until the monastery, school and library were sacked and burnt by Muslims. When Hieun Tsang, the Chinese scholar and traveller, stayed here for five years in the early 7th century

AD there were 10,000 monks and students in residence.

The remains are still extensive and include the Great Stupa with steps, terraces and a few still-intact votive stupas around it. An archaeological museum houses sculpture and other remains found on the site and an international centre for the study of Buddhism was established here in 1951. There are Burmese, Japanese and Jain rest houses at Nalanda. Buses connect Nalanda with Rajgir, Gaya and Patna; the latter is 90 km away.

Rajgir

Little remains of the Buddhist ruins at Rajgir, 19 km south of Nalanda towards Gaya. The first Buddhist council was held here after the Buddha attained nirvana. During the Buddha's life Rajgir was the capital of this part of India and he spent 12 years here. Buy one of the local guidebooks to the sites – they're only Rs 1 to 3. There is a Japanese stupa on a nearby hill, and three km away there are some overpopulated hot sulphur springs. There's a Tourist Information Office at Rajgir Kund.

Places to Stay The *Tourist Bungalow Number 2* (tel 39) is convenient and has a Rs 10 dormitory. The *Tourist Bungalow Number 1* (tel 26) has Rs 30 doubles as well as a dorm. There's also a *Rest House* and *Youth Hostel* in Rajgir. The Burmese Temple has a coffee house within the grounds which specialises in south Indian food and is also a good place to stay. It's clean, popular and handy for the Tourist Bungalow.

Triptee's Hotel has rooms from Rs 30. There are a number of cheaper hotels such as the *Anand Hotel* or the *Hill View Hotel*.

Pawapuri

The Jain Thirtankar, Mahavira, attained nirvana here, 25 km from Nalanda. It is an important Jain pilgrimage spot.

GAYA (population 200,000)

Just as nearby Bodhgaya is a major centre for Buddhist pilgrims so is Gaya a centre for Hindu pilgrims. Gaya is second only to Varanasi in its sanctity and pilgrims believe that offering *pindas* (funeral cakes) here will free their ancestors from bondage to the earth. They must also perform a lengthy circuit of the holy places around Gaya. Gaya is about 100 km south of Patna.

Vishnupad Temple

In the crowded central part of the old town the sikhara-style temple was constructed in 1787 by Queen Ahalya Bai of Indore. The temple is situated on the banks of the Falgu River, but although you can view its exterior and the picturesque bathing ghats, non-Hindus are not allowed into the temple interior. During the monsoon the river carries a great deal of water but it dries up completely during the winter. You can see cremations taking place on the river banks.

A 30-metre high octagonal tower surmounts the temple. Inside, the 40-cm long 'footprint' of Vishnu is imprinted in solid rock and surrounded by a silver-plated basin.

Other

A temple of the Sun God stands north of the Vishnupad temple. A flight of 1000 stone steps leads to the top of the Brahmajuni Hill, a km south-west. There is a good view over Gaya from the top of the hill. At the base of the hill is the Akshyabat or immortal banyan tree, which pilgrims visit to complete the cycle of rituals for their ancestors that they commenced in Varanasi. Gaya has a museum, but it is usually closed.

Situated 20 km north of Gaya, the Barabar caves are very ancient, dating back to 200 BC. Two of the caves have inscriptions from Ashoka himself. These are the 'Marabar' caves of E M Forster's *A Passage to India*.

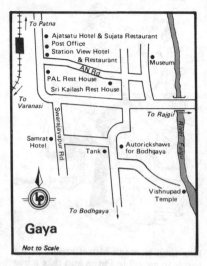

Gaya

Not to Scale

Places to Stay & Eat

There are *Railway Retiring Rooms* at Gaya station with a Rs 30 dorm and singles/doubles at Rs 60/100. There are a few other places to stay around the station – most of them spartan but OK for a short pause. The new *Ajatsatru Hotel* (tel 1514) is on Station Rd, just across the street from the station. There are good singles/doubles at Rs 40/55 and the *Sujata Restaurant* is pretty good.

The *Pal Rest House* has doubles with bathroom for Rs 25. At the *Station View Hotel & Restaurant* you can get very good meals very cheaply. The station Tourist Office may try to steer you into the *Sri Kailash Rest House* (tel 383) on Fateh Bahadur Siwala Rd. It's pretty basic with rooms from Rs 20. Further from the station the *Samrat Hotel* is OK although rather isolated. A rickshaw from the station will be about Rs 2, rooms are Rs 40/50 with bath. From there you can walk to the Bodhgaya auto-rickshaw stand.

Getting There

It takes eight to 10 hours by train for the 458 km trip from Calcutta (Rs 43 in 2nd, Rs 171 in 1st) or 3 ½ to six hours for the 220 km trip from Varanasi (Rs 25 2nd, Rs 94 1st). At Varanasi it's 'pandemonium boarding and they all bloody well got off at Moghulserai!' Patna to Gaya takes three to five hours by a slower train, they tend to run late on this short trip.

Getting Around

A rickshaw from the station through the narrow alleys to the Vishnupad temple will cost about Rs 2.

BODHGAYA

There are four holy places associated with the Buddha – Lumbini, in Nepal, where he was born; Sarnath, near Varanasi, where he first preached his message; Kushinagar, near Gorakhpur, where he died; and Bodhgaya where he attained enlightenment. A Bo tree growing at Bodhgaya is said to be a direct descendant of the original tree under which the Buddha sat, meditated and achieved enlightenment.

Buddhists from all over the world flock to Bodhgaya, along with many westerners who come here to learn about Buddhism or meditation. Bodhgaya is small and quiet but, if you are not planning a longer study stay, a day is quite sufficient to see everything. Apart from the stupa and various monasteries Bodhgaya is just a grubby little dump with an enormous population of flies.

Bodhi Tree

The sacred Bo tree growing here is said to be a direct descendant of the original tree under which the Buddha sat. Although that tree has died a sapling from the original tree was carried to Sri Lanka by Mahinda, the Emperor Ashoka's son, when he brought Buddhism to that island. That tree now flourishes at Anuradhapura in Sri Lanka, and in turn a sapling from that tree was carried back to Bodhgaya where it grows today. A red sandstone slab under the tree is said to be the Vajrasan, or diamond throne, on which the Buddha sat.

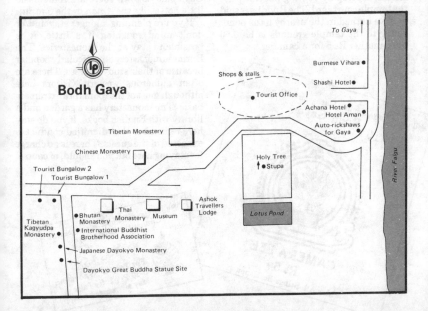

Mahabodhi Temple

A pyramidal spire 50 metres high tops the Mahabodhi temple, inside of which is a large gilded image of the Buddha. You enter the temple courtyard through the east gateway with a typical Buddhist *torana* gateway. The temple is said to stand on the site of a temple originally erected by Ashoka in the 3rd century BC. Although the current temple was restored in 1882 and earlier in the 11th century, it is said to be basically the same as one standing here in the 7th century, or even earlier. The Chinese pilgrim, Hiuen Tsang, describes visiting this earlier temple in 635 AD.

The stone railing around the temple, parts of which still stand, was originally thought to date from Ashoka but is now considered to be from the Sunga period around 184-172 BC. The carved and sculptured railing has been restored although parts of it now stand in the museum in Calcutta and in the Victoria & Albert Museum in London. Stone stupas, erected by visiting pilgrims, dot the temple courtyard. The Buddha is said to have bathed in the nearby lotus pond. Entry to the temple grounds is Rs 0.50 plus another Rs 5 for a camera.

Monasteries

The Tibetan monastery has an interesting wheel of law, while the Japanese monastery has a very beautiful image of the Buddha brought from Japan. There is also a Burmese monastery; the Burmese attempted a restoration of the Mahabodhi in 1306-09. The Thai monastery looks very much like the colourful *wats* you see throughout Thailand. Since Hindus regard the Buddha as an incarnation of Vishnu, Bodhgaya is also sacred to Hindu pilgrims. There's a small museum beside the Ashok Travellers' Lodge.

Places to Stay

The *Ashok Travellers' Lodge* (tel 25) has singles/doubles at Rs 150/175 including breakfast. Prices are lower in the April to September off-season. It's the best place available and all rooms have bathrooms. The charges go up during the tourist season. There's are also two *Tourist Bungalows* (No 1 and No 2) with rooms and a hostel-style dormitory. On the Gaya side of town there are some basic little hotels like the *Aman* or the *Shashi*.

If you're planning a longer stay and/or don't mind roughing it a little, it is possible to stay at the monasteries. The Burmese monastery is particularly popular because of their study courses. There are often numerous western visitors here although most of the rooms are extremely basic. The monastery has a garden and a library with English books. If you do stay here remember that dignified conduct is expected of the guests. There is no charge for staying here but you should, of course,

Buddha Gaya Temple Management Committee
No 13134 **Bodh Gaya**

CAMERA FEE
Rs.5/-
May All Beings Be Happy

Buddhagaya Temple Management Committee, BodhGaya
No. 21158
For Temple Renovation
0-50 P. (Fifty Paise)
May all beings be happy

make a donation. Unfortunately some western visitors have abused the monastery's hospitality by smoking or in other ways breaking the rules.

The Japanese monastery is also clean and comfortable but during the tourist season it can be packed with Japanese tour groups. Your stay there is limited to three days and, unhappily, some western visitors have made themselves unpopular here too.

You can also stay in the Tibetan restaurant tents behind the Tibetan temple or you can rent rooms in the village. Simple vegetarian meals are available at the *Kalpna Hotel* near the Mahabodhi Temple for just a few rupees. There are numerous other small restaurants and food stalls around, many of them of dubious cleanliness.

Getting There

Bodhgaya is 13 km from Gaya and auto-rickshaws shuttle back and forth. They start from the Kacheri in the city centre at Gaya, about a Rs 2 rickshaw ride from the station. The auto-rickshaws on this trip are phenomenally over-loaded. They put three on each side on benches in the back, one squeezed between them at the front, another standing up at the very back, then the driver up front sits on a plank with two people see-sawing on each side of him. A total of 13 people (plus children, goods, etc) on a vehicle intended for three! The fare is Rs 2, they depart as soon as they're full.

Buses depart less frequently. If you arrive in Gaya after dark you're advised to spend the night there rather than try to get to Bodhgaya.

SOUTHERN BIHAR

Parasnath

Just inside the Bihar state boundary from Bengal, and only a little north of the Grand Trunk Road, this is the major Jain pilgrimage centre in the east of India. Like so many other pilgrimage centres it's perched on top of a steep hill reached by a stiff climb on foot. The 24 temples, representing the Jain Tirthankars, stand at 1366 metres altitude. Parasnath, the 23rd Tirthankar, achieved nirvana at this spot, 100 years after his birth in Varanasi.

Hazaribagh

South of Gaya the hill resort of Hazaribagh is in the Damodar Valley. There's a wildlife sanctuary here and accommodation is available in a *Tourist Lodge* or a *Forest Rest House*. Hazaribagh is a quiet little place 67 km from the railway junction at Hazaribagh Road.

Ranchi

At the other end of the Damodar Valley, 93 km away, is Bihar's other hill resort. Ranchi is nearly as quiet as smaller Hazaribagh. At the foot of Ranchi Hill is an artificial lake flanked by two temples. Ranchi is particularly noted for its mental asylum, probably the best known one on the sub-continent.

Jagannathpur village, 10 km south-west, has the Jagannath Temple, a smaller copy of the great Jagannath Temple at Puri, and celebrates its own, smaller, festival of the cars. See the Orissa section for more details of this great festival. The high Hundru Falls are 43 km north-east of Ranchi; there are other falls in the area. The isolated but beautiful resort of Neterahat is 150 km away, close to the border with Madhya Pradesh.

Places to Stay The *Hotel Yuvraj* (tel 23430) in Doranda has rooms from Rs 60 to Rs 120 or from Rs 120 to Rs 250 with air-con. Other hotels include the new *Monarch Hotel* (tel 20440) which has good doubles with bath at Rs 75 and also a good restaurant. The *Hotel Akashdeep* or the *Palace Hotel* in Kadru are cheaper.

Getting There There are through buses to Ranchi from Raxaul, Patna and Gaya. A through bus to Puri takes 15 hours. Ranchi also has good rail connections.

Calcutta

Population: 9.5 million
Main language: Bengali

Calcutta is the capital of West Bengal

Calcutta is the largest city in India and is probably ahead of London as the largest city in the British Commonwealth. It's an often ugly and desperate place that to many people sums up the worst of India, yet it's also one of the country's more fascinating centres and has some scenes of rare beauty. At the beginning of this century Calcutta was the capital of British India but, unlike Delhi, it is not an ancient city with a long history and many impressive relics of its past. In fact Calcutta is really a British invention dating back only 300 years.

In 1686 the British abandoned Hooghly, their trading post 38 km up the Hooghly River from present-day Calcutta, and moved down river to three small villages – Sutanati, Govindpur and Kalikata. Calcutta takes its name from the last of those three tiny settlements. Job Charnock, an English merchant who later married a Brahmin's widow whom he dissuaded from becoming a sati, was the leader of the British merchants who made this move. At first the post was not a great success and was abandoned on a number of occasions, but in 1696 a fort was laid out near present-day BBD Bag (Dalhousie Square) and in 1698 Aurangzeb's grandson gave the British official permission to occupy the villages.

Calcutta then grew steadily until 1756, when Suraj-ud-daula, the Nawab of Murshidabad, attacked the town. Most of the British inhabitants escaped, but those captured were packed into an underground cellar where, during the night, most of them suffocated in what became known as 'the black hole of Calcutta'. Early in 1757 the British,

under Clive, retook Calcutta and made peace with the Nawab. Later the same year, however, Suraj-ud-daula sided with the French and in the Battle of Plassey, a turning point in British-Indian history, was killed. A much stronger fort was built in Calcutta and the town became the capital of British India. Much of Calcutta's most enduring development took place between 1780 and 1820. Later in the 19th century, however, Bengal became a spark point in the struggle for Indian independence, and this was a major reason for the decision to transfer the capital to New Delhi in 1911. Loss of political power did not alter Calcutta's economic control, and the city continued to prosper until after WW II.

Partition affected Calcutta more than any other major Indian city. Bengal and the Punjab were the two areas of India which were mixed in their Hindu-Muslim populations and positioned so that the dividing line would have to be drawn through them. The result in Bengal was that Calcutta, the jute-producing and export centre of India, became a city without a hinterland; while across the border in East Pakistan (Bangladesh today), the jute (a plant fibre used in making sacking and mats) was grown without anywhere to process or export it. Furthermore, West Bengal and Calcutta were disrupted by tens of thousands of refugees fleeing from East Bengal, although fortunately without the communal violence and bloodshed that partition brought to the Punjab.

The massive influx of refugees, combined with India's own post-war population explosion, led to Calcutta becoming an international urban horror story. The mere name was enough to conjure up visions of squalor, starvation, disease and death. The work of Mother Teresa's Calcutta mission also focused worldwide attention on Calcutta's festering problems. In 1971 the India-Pakistan conflict and the creation of Bangladesh led to another flood of refugees, and Calcutta's already chaotic condition further deteriorated. Economically it suffered further setbacks; the port has been silting up, making navigation from Calcutta down to the sea steadily more difficult and limiting the size of ships which can use the port. The Farakka Barrage, 250 km north of Calcutta, is designed to improve the river flow through Calcutta, but has been a subject of considerable dispute between India and Bangladesh since it will also affect the flow of the Ganges through the latter country.

Furthermore, Calcutta has been plagued by chronic labour unrest and resulting declines in productivity. The situation is summed up in the city's hopeless power-generation system. Electrical power in Calcutta has become such an on-again, off-again condition that virtually every hotel, restaurant, shop or small business has to have some sort of stand-by power generator or battery lighting system. The workers are blamed, the technicians are blamed, the power plants are blamed, the coal miners are blamed, even Indian railways are blamed for not delivering the coal on time, but it's widely pointed out

that Bombay certainly doesn't suffer the frequency and extent of power cuts that are a way of life in Calcutta. The Marxist government of West Bengal has come in for much criticism for the chaos currently existing in Calcutta but, it is also pointed out, their seeming neglect and misman-agement of the city is combined with a considerable improvement in the rural situation. Threats of flood or famine in the countryside no longer send hordes of refugees streaming into the city as in the past.

Despite all these problems Calcutta is a city with a soul, and one which many residents are inordinately fond of. The Bengalis, so ready to raise arms against the British in the struggle for indepen-dence, are also the poets and artists of India. The contrast between the Bombay and Calcutta movie industries more or less sums it up. While Bombay, the Hollywood of India, churns out movies of amazing tinsel banality, the smaller number of movie-makers in Calcutta make non-commercial gems that stand up to anything produced for sophisticated western movie-goers. The soul shows in other ways too; amongst the squalor and confusion the city has places and times of sheer magic – flower sellers beside the misty, ethereal Hooghly River; the majestic sweep of the Maidan; the arrogant bulk of the Victoria Memorial; the superb collec-tion exhibited in the Indian Museum – they're all part of this amazing city.

Orientation

Calcutta sprawls north-south along the Hooghly River, which divides it from Howrah on the west bank. If you arrive from anywhere west of Calcutta by rail, you come into the immense Howrah station and have to cross the Hooghly Bridge into Calcutta proper. Some of Calcutta's worst slums sprawl behind the station on the Howrah side.

For visitors, the more relevant parts of Calcutta are south of the bridge in the areas around BBD Bag and Chowringhee.

BBD Bag, as Dalhousie Square has been renamed, is the site of the GPO, the international telephone office and the West Bengal Tourist Office, and is close to the American Express Office and various railway booking offices. South of BBD Bag is the open expanse of the Maidan along the river, and away from the river is the area known as Chowringhee. Most of the cheap and middle-range hotels (and some of the upper-bracket ones) are concentrated in Chowringhee together with many of the airline offices, restaurants, travel agencies and the Indian Museum. At the southern end of Chowringhee you'll find the Government of India Tourist Office on Shakespeare Sarani, and nearby the Birla Planetarium and Victoria Memorial.

There are a number of landmarks in Calcutta and a couple of important streets to remember. The Ochterlony Monument at the northern end of the Maidan is one of the most visible – it's a tall column rising from the flat expanse of the Maidan. Sudder St runs off Chowringhee and is the core of the Calcutta travellers' scene. Most of the popular cheap hotels are along Sudder St so it is well known to any taxi or rickshaw-wallah, and the airport bus runs right by it. Furthermore, the Indian Museum is on the corner of Sudder St and Chowringhee. Further down Chowringhee, which runs alongside the Maidan all the way, is Park St with a great number of more expensive restaurants and the Thai International office – an important address for people heading on to South-East Asia. On again is Shakespeare Sarani.

Street Names As in many Indian cities, getting around Calcutta is slightly confused by the habit of renaming city streets, particularly those with Raj-era connotations. As usual this renaming has been done in a half-hearted fashion; many streets still have the old names up, some maps show old names, others show new ones, taxi-wallahs inevitably only know the old names. It's going to be a long time before Chowringhee Rd becomes Jawaharlal Nehru Rd!

Other renamed roads include Ballyganj Store Rd (now Gurusday Rd), Bowbazar St (Bepin Behary Ganguly), Buckland Rd (Bankim Ch Rd), Harrington St (Ho Chi Minh Sarani!), Harrison Rd (Mahatma Gandhi Rd), Kyd St (Dr M Ishaque Rd), Lansdowne Rd (Sarat Bose Rd), Lower Chitpur Rd (Rabindra Sarani), Lower Circular Rd (Acharya Jagadish Bose Rd), Machuabazar St (Madan Mohan St & Keshab Sen St), Mirzapore St (Suryya Sen St), Theatre Rd (Shakespeare Sarani), Wellesley St (Rafi Ahmed Kidwai Rd) and Wellington St (Nirmal Chunder St). I've always been amused at how the street the US consulate is on was renamed Ho Chi Minh Sarani!

Information

Offices The large Calcutta GPO is on BBD Bag (Dalhousie Square) and has an efficient poste restante and a philatelic bureau for stamp collectors. The Telephone Bhawan is also on BBD Bag, while the Central Telegraph Office is at 8 Red Cross Place. International phone calls can be made with often amazing ease from the telegraph office. The Foreigners' Registration Office (tel 44301) is at 237 Acharya J C Bose Rd. American Express is nearby at 21 Old Court House (tel 236281). Tax exemption certificates are available from Room 11, 4th floor, Income Tax Building, Bentinck St.

The Government of India Tourist Office (tel 441402, 443521) is at 4 Shakespeare Sarani. The West Bengal Tourist Bureau is at 3/2 BBD Bag (tel 238271) – the opposite side to the post office. Both the state and national tourist offices have counters at the airport.

Culture Calcutta is famous for its culture – film, poetry, art and dance all have their devotees here. There are dances on at the Oberoi Grand Hotel every night at 7 pm, Rs 15 or Rs 12 with a student card.

Sometimes the audience is extremely small. At Rabindra Sadan on Cathedral Rd (tel 449936) a dance-drama performance, Bengali poetry reading or similar event takes place on most nights.

Books & Bookshops Geoffrey Moorhouse's classic 1971 study *Calcutta* is available as a Penguin paperback. More recently Dominique Lapierre's *City of Joy* is a weighty Arthur Hailey-style novel throwing together every fact, figure and anecdote possible about Calcutta, with a thin storyline to tie them together.

The Cambridge Book & Stationery Company at 20D Park St is a good small bookshop. Further down Park St towards Chowringhee the Oxford Book Shop is larger, but much of their stock is either very specialised or very old. Upstairs at 56D Free School St, the Bookmark has a good general selection of books. There are quite a few secondhand bookshops along Free School St, and Booklands at that end of Sudder St.

Airlines Most airline offices are located around Chowringhee. Notable exceptions are Indian Airlines on Chittaranjan Avenue and Burma Airways just north of the Maidan tram terminus.

Aeroflot
    58 Chowringhee (tel 449831)
Air India
    50 Chowringhee (tel 442356)
Bangladesh Biman
    1 Park St (tel 212863)
British Airways
    41 Chowringhee (tel 248181)
Burma Airways
    8/2 Esplanade East (tel 231624)
Indian Airlines
    39 Chittaranjan Avenue (tel 263390)
Royal Nepal Airlines
    41 Chowringhee (tel 243949)
Thai International
    18G Park St (tel 249696)
Vayudoot
    53F Chowringhee (tel 447062)

If you're looking for cheap airline tickets,

various places advertise their services around Sudder St. Pan Asian Tours, a tiny office on the 2nd floor at 20 Mirza Ghalib St (Free School St), seem to know what they're on about. One traveller wrote to commend their 'friendly and efficient service'. P Roy in the Salvation Army Hostel also deals in discounted tickets.

Consulates Some of the useful addresses in Calcutta include:

Bangladesh
    9 Circus Ave (tel 444458)
Bhutan
    48 Tivoli Court, Pramothesh Barua Sarani (tel 441301)
West Germany
    1 Hastings Park Rd (tel 459141)
Nepal
    19 Sterndale Rd (tel 452024)
Netherlands
    18A Brabourne Rd (tel 262160)
Thailand
    18B Mandeville Gardens (tel 460836)
UK
    1 Ho Chi Minh Sarani (tel 445171)
USA
    5/1 Ho Chi Minh Sarani (tel 443611)

There is no Burmese consulate in Calcutta even though Calcutta is the main gateway for flights to Rangoon. Burma Airways cannot issue visas; the nearest cities with Burmese diplomatic representation are Kathmandu, Dhaka or New Delhi. The Thai consulate closes at noon and is somewhat difficult to find. A No 102 bus will get you close to it.

Botanical Garden
On the west bank of the Hooghly, south of Howrah, are the extensive Botanical Gardens. They stretch for over a km along the riverfront and occupy 109 hectares. The gardens were originally founded in 1786 and initially administered by Colonel Kyd. It was from these gardens that the tea now grown in Assam and Darjeeling was first developed. Prime attraction in the gardens is the 200-year-old banyan,

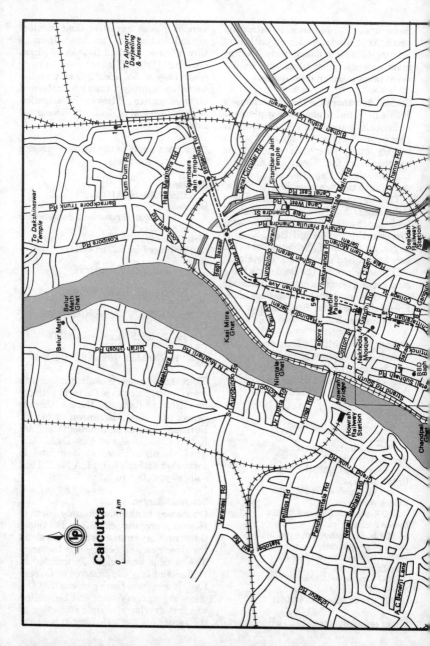

Calcutta

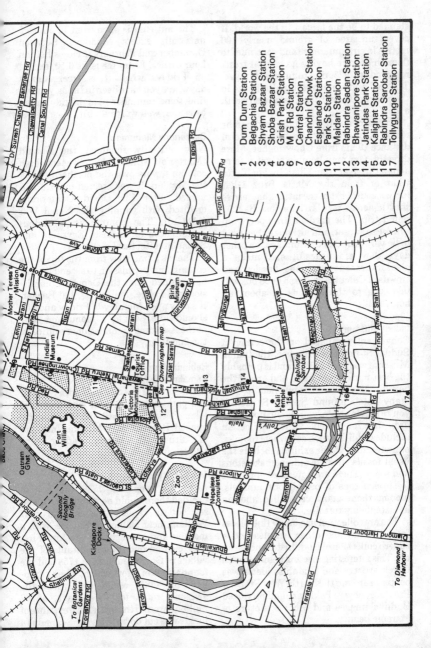

1 Dum Dum Station
2 Belgachia Station
3 Shyam Bazaar Station
4 Shoba Bazaar Station
5 Girish Park Station
6 M G Rd Station
7 Central Station
8 Chandni Chowk Station
9 Esplanade Station
10 Park St Station
11 Maidan Station
12 Rabindra Sadan Station
13 Bhawanipore Station
14 Jatindas Park Station
15 Kalighat Station
16 Rabindra Sarobar Station
17 Tollygunge Station

claimed to be the largest in the world. It covers an area of ground nearly 400 metres in circumference and continues to flourish despite having its central trunk removed in 1925, due to fungus damage. The cool and tropical tall palm house in the centre of the gardens is also well worth a visit.

The gardens are at Sibpur and can be reached by crossing the bridge – total distance 19 km from Chowringhee. More directly, you may be able to get a ferry across the river from Chandpal or Takta Ghat or from the Matia Bruz Ghat further south. From the latter ghat ferries shuttle across regularly for just Rs 0.50 round trip! The gardens are open from sunrise to sunset, and although they tend to be very crowded on Sundays, on other days they are peaceful and make a pleasant escape from the hassles and crowds of Calcutta. A No 55 or 56 bus will take you to the gardens in about an hour.

Indian Museum

Conveniently situated on the corner of Sudder St and Chowringhee, the Indian Museum was built in 1875 and is probably the best museum in India and one of the best in Asia. It's so convenient to the many hotels around Sudder St that if you're staying there you should not fail to drop in. Its widely varied collection includes oddities such as a whole roomful of meteorites. Other exhibits include the usual fossils, stuffed animals, skeletons and so on. There are a number of unique fossil skeletons of pre-historic animals, among them giant crocodiles and an amazingly big tortoise.

The art collection has many fine pieces from Orissan and other temples and a superb collection of Buddhist Gandharan art. This interesting meeting point between Greek artistry and Buddhist ideals was centered around the North-West Frontier Province, now in Pakistan, and produced Buddha images and other sculpture of extreme beauty.

The museum is open from 10 am to 5 pm daily except Mondays. Between December and February it closes half an hour earlier. Entry fee is Rs 0.50, except on Fridays when it is free. Almost anywhere you have been in India, you will find some reminder of it in the Indian Museum, well worth a visit.

Ochterlony Monument

Now officially renamed the Shahid (Martyr's) Minar, this 48-metre-high column towers over the northern end of the Maidan. It was erected in 1828 and named after Sir David Ochterlony, credited with winning the Nepal War (1814-16). The column is a curious combination of Turkish, Egyptian and Syrian architectural elements.

There's a fine view from the top of the column, but permission to ascend it must be obtained from the Deputy Commissioner of Police, Police HQ, Lal Bazaar. It's only open Monday to Friday and you should simply ask for a 'monument pass' at the Assistant Commissioner's office on the 2nd floor.

Rabindra Sarobar & Ramakrishna Mission

In the south of the city Rabindra Sarobar is a park and picnic spot with a central lake. Beside the park is the recently opened Ramakrishna Mission Institute of Culture with a library, reading rooms and lecture halls.

Maidan & Fort William

After the events of 1756 the British decided there would be no repetition and set out to replace the original Fort William, near Dalhousie Square, with a massive and impregnable new fort. First they cleared out the inhabitants of the village of Govindpur and in 1758 laid the foundations of a fort which, when completed in 1781, would cost them the awesome total, for those days, of £2 million. Around the fort a huge expanse of jungle was cut down to give the cannons a clear line of fire but, as usual, the fort has never fired a shot in anger. You can walk around the fort's massive walls with deep fortifications and trenches fronting them, but visitors are only allowed inside with special permission since the fort is still in use today.

The area cleared around Fort William became the Maidan, the 'lungs' of modern Calcutta. This huge green expanse stretches three km north to south and is over a km wide. It is bounded by Strand Rd along the river to the west and by Chowringhee Rd, lined with shops, hotels and eating places, to the east. The stream known as Tolly's Nulla forms its southern boundary, and here you will find a racecourse and the Victoria Memorial. In the north-west corner is Eden Gardens, while Raj Bhavan overlooks it from the north.

Within the gardens are cricket and football fields, tennis courts, ponds and trees. Cows graze, political discussions are held, people stroll across the grounds or come for early-morning yoga sessions. And of course the place is used, like any area of open land in India, as a public toilet.

Eden Gardens

In the north-west corner of the Maidan are the small and pleasantly laid out Eden Gardens. A tiny Burmese pagoda was brought here from Prome in Burma in 1856; it's set in a small lake and is extraordinarily picturesque. The gardens were named after the sister of Lord Auckland, the former governor general. The Calcutta cricket grounds, where international test matches are held, are also within the gardens.

Across from the gardens is a pleasant walk along the banks of the Hooghly. Ferries run across the river from several ghats and there are plenty of boatmen around offering to take you out on the water for half an hour.

Victoria Memorial

At the southern end of the Maidan stands the most solid reminder of British Calcutta, in fact probably the most solid reminder of the Raj to be found in India. The Victoria Memorial is a huge white-marble museum, a strange combination of classical European architecture with Moghul influences or, as some have put it, an unhappy British attempt to build a better Taj Mahal. The idea behind the memorial was conceived by Lord Curzon, the money for its construction was raised from 'voluntary contributions by the princes and peoples of India', the Prince of Wales (later King George V) laid the foundation stone in 1906 and it was opened by another Prince of Wales (later the Duke of Windsor) in 1921.

Whether you're interested in the British Raj period or not, the memorial is an attraction not to be missed. It tells the story of the empire in India at its peak, just when it was about to embark on its downhill slide. The imposing statue of Queen Victoria, at her bulky and least-amused best, fronts the memorial and sets the mood for all the displays inside.

Inside you'll find portraits, statues and busts of almost all the main participants in British-Indian history. Scenes from military conflicts and events of the mutiny are illustrated. There are some superb watercolours of Indian landscapes and buildings made by travelling Victorian artists. A Calcutta exhibit includes many early pictures of the city and a model of Fort William. Of course there are many fine Indian and Persian miniatures and rare manuscripts and books. Queen Victoria appears again inside, much younger and slimmer than her statue outside. There's also a piano she played as a young girl and other memorabilia. A huge painting depicts King Edward VII entering Jaipur in a regal procession in 1876. French guns captured at the Battle of Plassey are on exhibit, and so is the black stone throne of the Nawab whom Clive defeated in that battle. To top it all there is a good view over the Maidan from the balcony above the entrance.

The booklet *A Brief Guide to the Victoria Memorial* is available in the building. The memorial is open from 10 am to 3.30 pm in winter, an hour later in summer, but closed on Mondays. Entry costs Rs 1.

St Paul's Cathedral

Built between 1839 and 1847, St Paul's Cathedral is one of the most important churches in India. It stands just to the east of the Victoria Memorial at the southern end of the Maidan. The steeple fell during an earthquake in 1897, and following further damage in a 1934 quake was redesigned and rebuilt.

Birla Planetarium

This planetarium, near the Tourist Office, is one of the largest in the world and well worth the Rs 5 admission. There are programmes in English several times daily; consult the daily papers.

Kali Temple

Also known as Kalighat, this temple is believed to be about 200 years old and to be the actual temple from which Kalikata (anglicised to Calcutta) takes its name. According to legend, when Shiva's wife's corpse was cut up one of her fingers fell here. Since then it has been an important pilgrimage site. The temple is about two km directly south of St Paul's Cathedral.

Zoo

South of the Maidan, Calcutta's 16-hectare zoo was opened in 1876. Some of the animals are displayed in near natural conditions. The zoo is open from sunrise to sunset and admission is Rs 1. Just south of the zoo on Alipore Rd are the pleasant and quiet horticultural gardens. They're open 6 to 10 am and 2 to 5 pm except on Mondays; admission is Rs 0.50.

Howrah Bridge

Until 1943 the Hooghly was crossed by a pontoon bridge which had to be opened to let river traffic through. There was considerable opposition to construction of a bridge due to fears that it would affect the river currents and cause silting problems. This problem was eventually avoided by building a bridge that crosses the river in a single 450-metre span with no piers at all within the river. The cantilevered bridge is similar in size to the Sydney Harbour Bridge and, if anything, even uglier! It carries a flow of traffic which Sydney could never dream of – it's intriguing to stand at one end of the bridge at morning rush hour and watch the procession of double-decker buses come across. They heel over like yachts due to the weight of passengers hanging onto the sides. In between are countless rickshaws, lumbering bullock carts, hordes of bicycles and even the odd car. The bridge is also known as Rabindra Setu.

The bridge is usually horribly congested and some years ago an additional bridge was planned a couple of km downriver. Construction was commenced but the funds ran out at a very early stage and the site remained untouched for a number of years. In the early '80s the plans were revived and construction recommenced, but once again funds have dried up.

Dalhousie Square – BBD Bag

When Calcutta was the centre of administration for British India this was the centre of power. On the north side of the square stands the huge 'Writers Building' which dates from 1880. In those days clerical workers were known as 'writers' and the East India Company's 'writers' have been replaced by modern-day ones employed by the West Bengal state government. That's where all the quintuplicate forms, carbon copies and red ink come from. Also on Dalhousie Square is a rather more useful place – the Calcutta GPO – and on the other side of the square is the West Bengal Tourist Development Corporation's office.

Until it was abandoned in 1757, the original Fort William used to stand where the post office now does. It stretched from there down to the river, which has also changed its course since that time. Brass markers indicate where the fort walls used to be by the post office. Calcutta's famous black hole actually stood at the north-east corner of the post office, but since independence all indications of its position have been removed. The black hole was actually a tiny guardroom in the fort and 146 people were forced into it on that fateful night when the city fell to Suraj-ud-daula. Next morning only 23 were still alive.

St John's Church

A little south of Dalhousie Square is the Church of St John, which dates from 1787. The graveyard here has a number of interesting monuments, including the octagonal mausoleum of Job Charnock, founder of Calcutta, who died in 1692.

Admiral Watson, who supported Clive in retaking Calcutta from Suraj-ud-daula, is also buried here.

Other British Buildings

The Victoria Memorial is the most imposing reminder of the British presence in Calcutta, but the city's commercial wealth resulted in quite a few other interesting buildings. Raj Bhavan, the old British Government House, is now occupied by the governor of West Bengal and entry is restricted. The Marquess Wellesley built it between 1799 and 1805, modelling it on Lord Curzon's home, Kedleston Hall, in Derbyshire, England which was only completed a couple of years before. Raj Bhavan stands at the north end of the Maidan and contains many rare works of art and other interesting items, including Tipu Sultan's throne.

Next to it is the Doric-style Town Hall, and next to that the High Court, which was copied from the Staadhaus at Ypres and completed in 1872. It has a tower 55 metres high. Just south of the zoo in

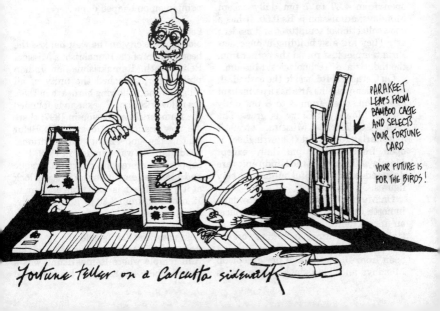

PARAKEET LEAPS FROM BAMBOO CAGE AND SELECTS YOUR FORTUNE CARD.

YOUR FUTURE IS FOR THE BIRDS!

Fortune teller on a Calcutta sidewalk

Alipur is the National Library, the biggest in India, which is housed in Belvedere House, the former residence of the lieutenant governor of Bengal.

South Park St Cemetery is being restored and shows the high price paid by the early settlers from England. There are marvellous tombs and inscriptions at this peaceful site.

Other Museums

Calcutta has a number of other interesting museums apart from the magnificent Indian Museum and the Victoria Memorial. In Calcutta University the Asutosh Museum has a collection of art objects with emphasis on Bengali folk art. Admission is free and it is open from 10.30 am to 4.30 pm on weekdays, 10.30 am to 3 pm on Saturdays.

At 19A Gurusday Rd is the Birla Industrial & Technological Museum, open from 10 am to 5 pm daily. Admission is free except on Sundays. Those philanthropic (and very wealthy) Birlas have also provided the Birla Academy of Art & Culture at 109-109 Southern Avenue, open from 4.30 to 7 pm daily except Mondays; admission is Rs 0.50. It has a good collection of sculptures and modern art. They are also building a huge new Birla temple, just round the corner from the Industrial & Technological Museum.

On Cathedral Rd beside the cathedral, the Academy of Fine Arts has a permanent exhibition, open from 3 to 8 pm daily except Mondays. Entry is free. The Nehru Children's Museum at 94/1 Jawaharlal Nehru Rd (Chowringhee) is open from 1 to 8 pm daily except Mondays. Tales from the Hindu epics are depicted with beautiful miniature clay figures.

On Muktaram Babu St, a narrow lane in north Calcutta, is the Marble Palace, an incongruous one-man collection of statues and paintings, including works of Rubens and Sir Joshua Reynolds. It's open from 10 am to 4.30 pm except on Mondays and Thursdays, and entry is free with a permit from the Government of India Tourist Office. Nearby is the rambling old Tagore House, a centre for Indian dance, drama, music and other arts. This was where Rabindranath Tagore, India's greatest poet, was born and later died. It's just off Rabindra Sarani.

Sitambara Jain Temple

In the north-east of the city, this temple was built in 1867 and dedicated to Sheetalnathji, the 10th of the 24 Jain Tirthankars. The temple is an ornate mass of mirrors, coloured stones and glass mosaics and overlooks a garden. It is open from 6 am to 12 noon and 3 to 7 pm daily.

Nakhoda Mosque

North of BBD Bag is Calcutta's principal Muslim place of worship. The huge Nakhoda Mosque is said to be able to accommodate 10,000 people and was modelled on Akbar's tomb at Sikandra near Agra. The red sandstone mosque has two 46-metre-high minarets and a brightly painted onion-shaped dome.

Belur Math

North of the city on the west bank is the headquarters of the Ramakrishna Mission, Belur Math. Ramakrishna, an Indian philosopher, preached the unity of all religions and, following his death in 1886, his follower Swami Vivekananda founded the Ramakrishna Mission in 1897; there are now branches all over India. Belur Math, the movement's international headquarters, was founded in 1899. It is supposed to represent a church, a mosque and a temple, depending on how you look at it. Belur Math is open from 6.30 am to 12 noon and from 3.30 to 7.30 pm daily. Admission is free.

Dakshineshwar Kali Temple

Across the river from Belur Math is this Kali temple where Ramakrishna was a priest when he reached his spiritual vision of the unity of all religions. The Kali temple was built in 1847.

Barrackpore

There is a memorial to Gandhi called Gandhi Ghat at this point, 25 km north of Calcutta on the banks of the Hooghly.

Serampore

Across the river from Barrackpore, 25 km from Calcutta, this was a Danish centre until the Danish holdings in India were transferred to the East India Company in 1845. The old Danish Church and cemetery still stand. The missionaries Ward, Marshman and Carey operated from here in the early 1800s. Mahesh, three km from Serampore, has a large and very old Jagannath temple. In June-July of each year the Mahesh Yatra car festival takes place here, second in size only to the great car festival of Jagannath at Puri in Orissa.

Tours

The India Tourism Development Corporation (tel 443124) at 4 Shakespeare Sarani and the West Bengal Tourist Bureau (tel 238271) at 3/2 BBD Bag both have daily tours of Calcutta except on Sundays. The morning tour from 8 am to 12.30 pm costs Rs 21 and takes in the area around BBD Bag in the city, including Eden Gardens, Raj Bhavan, the Jain temple plus the sights further out like Belur Math, the Dakshineshwar Temple and the Botanical Gardens.

The afternoon tour operates from 1.30 to 5.15 pm and costs the same, but you can get a combined ticket for Rs 26 if you take both tours on the same day. The afternoon tour covers the Indian Museum, Victoria Memorial and the Zoo.

The morning tour is better value since it covers the sights further out. Instead of taking the afternoon tour you could easily get around yourself and have more time. On Saturdays, Sundays and public holidays you can only take the full-day tour; no half-day tickets are sold. In any

case the number of half-day tickets is restricted. Tourist offices often cancel tours on short notice – check the day before if the tour will be operating.

Places to Stay – bottom end

Sudder St, running off Chowringhee beside the Indian Museum, is Calcutta's cheap accommodation centre. At 2 Sudder St the popular *Salvation Army Red Shield Guest House* (tel 242895) has dorm beds at Rs 13, singles/doubles at Rs 32/36 or Rs 40/50 with bath. The place is clean and well kept although the water supply is decidedly erratic; it's a real drag to arrive after a hot, sweaty train trip to find there'll be no water available for hours to come.

Down Sudder St a bit, Stuart Lane turns off to the right and here you'll find two of Calcutta's most popular budget establishments, with similar standards. The *Modern Lodge* (tel 244960) is at No 1, the very popular *Hotel Paragon* at No 2. The Paragon has dorm beds at Rs 10, singles/doubles at Rs 25/30, bigger upstairs doubles at Rs 35 and doubles with bath at Rs 50. There's a pleasant courtyard upstairs but the ground-floor rooms are rather gloomy. The Modern Lodge is very similar in price, with four to six-bed dorms at Rs 8 to Rs 10 a bed, singles/doubles at Rs 25/35. They're OK – the rooms have a fan, the toilets are clean, and the food is reasonable. The rooftop area is a popular meeting place in the evening, and tea and soft drinks are available. The manager is a good person to see about airline tickets and student cards.

The *Tourist Inn* (tel 243732) at 4/1 Sudder St has singles/doubles for Rs 35/70 but it's not as good as the Modern or the Paragon – although they do offer free yoga lessons by Chowbey Baba! Other cheap Sudder St hotels are the *Shilton Hotel* at 5A with rooms for Rs 55/80, and the *Hotel Diplomat* at 10 with rooms for Rs 60/70. There are more cheap hotels around Sudder St, but many are strictly

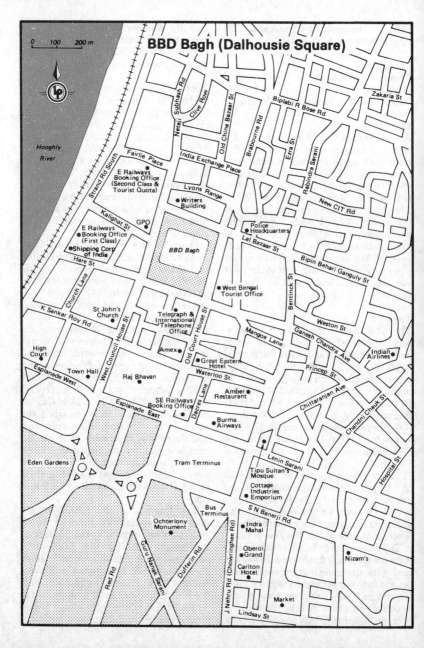

BBD Bagh (Dalhousie Square)

0 100 200 m

Hooghly River

Netaji Subhash Rd
Clive Row
Old China Bazaar St
Biplabi R Bose Rd
Zakaria St
Brabourne Rd
Ezra St
Rabindra Sarani
New CIT Rd

Fairlie Place
India Exchange Place
Strand Rd South
E Railways Booking Office (Second Class & Tourist Quota)
Lyons Range
Writers Building
Kalighat St
GPO
BBD Bagh
Police Headquarters
Lal Bazaar St
E Railways Booking Office (First Class)
Shipping Corp of India
Bipin Behari Ganguly St
Hare St
West Bengal Tourist Office
Bentinck St
Church Lane
St John's Church
Weston St
K Sankar Roy Rd
Telegraph & International Telephone Office
Old Court House St
Mangoe Lane
Ganesh Chandra Ave
High Court
West Council House St
Amex
Great Eastern Hotel
Princep St
Indian Airlines
Esplanade West
Town Hall
Waterloo St
Raj Bhavan
Decres Lane
Amber Restaurant
Chittaranjan Ave
Esplanade East
SE Railways Booking Office
Burma Airways
Chandni Chauk St
Eden Gardens
Tram Terminus
Lenin Sarani
Tipu Sultan's Mosque
Hospital St
Cottage Industries Emporium
S N Banerji Rd
Bus Terminus
Ochterlony Monument
Indra Mahal
Red Rd
Guru Nanak Sarani
Dufferin Rd
J Nehru Rd (Chowringhee Rd)
Oberoi Grand
Carlton Hotel
Nizam's
Market
Lindsay St

for emergency use only. 'Avoid them like the plague, you stand a good chance of getting it', reported one traveller.

There are a number of places which are up a notch, in price at least. At 6/2/3 Sudder St, opposite Stuart Lane, the *Astoria Hotel* (tel 241359, 242613) has rooms from Rs 60 up to Rs 150. More expensive rooms with attached bathroom go up to Rs 200 for a double with air-con, including 'bed tea' and breakfast. Or there's the *Capital Guest House* (tel 213844) at 11B Chowringhee Lane.

Round at 2 Chowringhee Place the *Carlton Hotel* (tel 233009 & 238853) is excellent value at Rs 99/165 including all meals. 'Excellent food', reported one traveller. 'The worst meal we ever had in India', reported another. There's a small sitting area here.

Calcutta has a collection of Ys. The *YMCA* (tel 233504) is at 25 Chowringhee – a big, gloomy building but a good place to stay. Including dinner and breakfast, rooms are Rs 140/170. All have attached bath and the breakfast features two eggs, porridge or cornflakes, toast and butter, tea and a banana. They also have rooms for three, four or five people at Rs 70 per person. On the mezzanine floor there are simpler rooms at Rs 30 per person without dinner. There's an additional Rs 10 per person temporary membership charge on the first night only. They've got some excellent full-size snooker and billiard tables in the lounge! If you're discreet it's possible to use them without being a resident.

There is a second, similarly priced *YMCA* (tel 240260) at 42 Surendra Nath Banerjee Rd. The *YWCA* (tel 240260) is also similarly priced at 1 Middleton Row – women only here. Shared rooms are Rs 50, singles are Rs 60, doubles with bath Rs 150. Breakfast is included and there's a good restaurant next door. 'It's fun to stay at the YWCA', reported one visitor.

The *Youth Hostel* (tel 672869) is at 10 J B Ananda Dutta Lane in Howrah. It's small and homely; take a No 52 or 58 bus from Howrah Station to Shamasri Cinema or a No 63 to Khirertala. Dorm beds are Rs 10, breakfast Rs 5.

If you're transitting Calcutta by air there are *Airport Rest Rooms* (tel 572611) at the airport. Check at the reservations desk in the terminal. Dorm beds are Rs 15, singles Rs 30 to Rs 45 or Rs 75 with air-con, doubles Rs 40 to Rs 70 or Rs 100 with air-con. Finally, Howrah and Sealdah stations have *Railway Retiring Rooms*. Both stations have singles and doubles. Howrah also has dorm beds, Sealdah also has air-con doubles.

Places to Stay – middle

It's said often enough that 'getting there is half the fun'. Well, at the *Fairlawn Hotel* (tel 244460 & 241835) at 13A Sudder St, staying there is half the fun. It's a piece of Calcutta that definitely should not be missed because here the Raj doesn't just live, it's simply never ended. The terribly English couple who still run it nearly 40 years after independence look like they've been time-warped from Brighton in the '50s and their establishment is spotless, packed with memorabilia and a positive delight.

The bearer bears your gear upstairs on his head, meal times are announced with a gong (and a hissed 'Sahib, Memsahib, dinner is ready' if you dare to be late) and in mid-afternoon there's tea and biscuits. In fact you don't really stay here so much as play your part in an on-going theatre performance. At Rs 280/400 for an air-con room with all meals, it's an experience not to be missed. There are also some non-air-con doubles at Rs 360. Major plus points at the Fairlawn are the open lounge areas and the garden area with tables and chairs. The land on which the hotel stands was originally purchased by Europeans way back in 1781. The main building was completed in 1803 as a gentleman's residence; not until this century did it become a guest house, run by two English spinsters. The parents of the present owner took over in 1936.

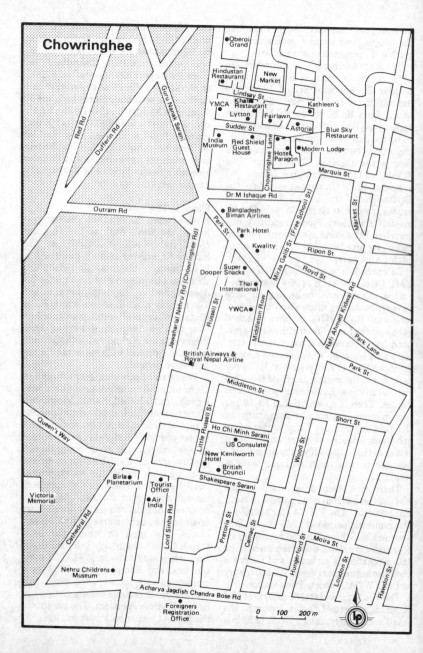

Chowringhee

Oberoi Grand
Hindustan Restaurant
New Market
Lindsay St
Khalsa Restaurant
YMCA
Lytton
Fairlawn
Kathleen's
Sudder St
Astoria
Blue Sky Restaurant
India Museum
Red Shield Guest House
Chowringhee Lane
Hotel Paragon
Modern Lodge
Marquis St
Market St
Dr M Ishaque Rd
Bangladesh Biman Airlines
Park Hotel
Park St
Kwality
Mirza Galib St (Free School St)
Ripon St
Royd St
Super Dooper Snacks
Thai International
Russell St
YWCA
Middleton Row
Rafi Ahmed Kidwai Rd
Park Lane
Park St
British Airways & Royal Nepal Airline
Middleton St
Short St
Ho Chi Minh Sarani
Little Russell St
US Consulate
New Kenilworth Hotel
British Council
Wood St
Shakespeare Sarani
Birla Planetarium
Tourist Office
Air India
Queen's Way
Cathedral Rd
Victoria Memorial
Pretoria St
Camac St
Hungerford St
Moira St
Loudon St
Nehru Childrens Museum
Acharya Jagdish Chandra Bose Rd
Rawdon St
Foreigners Registration Office

Red Rd
Dufferin Rd
Guru Nanak Sarani
Outram Rd
Jawaharlal Nehru Rd (Chowringhee Rd)
Lord Sinha Rd

0   100   200 m

Everything else pales into insignificance by comparison, but there are a few other places such as the *Lytton Hotel* (tel 232760 and other numbers) at 14 Sudder St. The Lytton has been almost completely rebuilt in the past couple of years; it's now an all-new centrally air-conditioned hotel, although some old rooms remain. The new rooms are Rs 330/400 for singles/doubles (room only), the old rooms Rs 150/200.

There are several guest houses just off Lindsay St in a multi-storey building. The *Gujarat Lodge* has rooms at Rs 90/150 with bath and some bathless doubles at Rs 90. The *Lindsay Guest House* (tel 248639) charges Rs 110/130 for rooms with bath, Rs 180/240 with air-con.

Places to Stay – top end

Out at the airport the *ITDC Airport Ashok* (tel 440933 & 575111) is modern and convenient for passengers in transit. Singles/doubles (all air-con) are Rs 600/700.

Most of the other hotels are centrally located. At 15 Chowringhee the *Oberoi Grand* (tel 230181) is pretty plain externally but pleasantly grand inside. In fact, in that central courtyard with the swimming pool and the palm trees it's hard to think Calcutta can be so close by! Rooms cost from Rs 950/1050 plus 20%. The *Park Hotel* (tel 248301) at 17 Park St is a more modern hotel at Rs 600/700 plus 20%.

Other more expensive hotels include the classic old *Great Eastern Hotel* (tel 232311) at 1-3 Old Court House St. Once again it's back to the Raj era in this large 200-room hotel; costs are Rs 375/475 with air-con, Rs 250 for a single without air-con. 'Fun to stay at and nice breakfasts', wrote one couple. The 212-room *Hotel Hindustan International* (tel 442394) is at 235/1 Acharya J C Bose Rd and costs from Rs 500 to Rs 600 for singles, Rs 600 to Rs 700 for doubles. The *Hotel Rutt Deen* (tel 443884) is at 212B Loudon St and has singles for Rs 350 to Rs 400, doubles for Rs 430 to Rs 450.

The *New Kenilworth Hotel* (tel 441422 & half a dozen other numbers) at 1 & 2 Little Russell St, just a stone's throw from the tourist office, has recently been extensively renovated and upgraded. Singles/doubles are Rs 405/505 plus 20%.

Places to Eat

Less Expensive Finding good food at reasonable prices is no problem in the Chowringhee/Sudder St area. Everyone seems to have their own favourite, but some of the best include the *Taj Continental*, a good and cheap place opposite the entrance to Stuart Lane. The popular *Blue Sky*, half-way down Sudder St on the same side as the Salvation Army, has excellent porridge, sandwiches, fruit juices and 'the finest curd in India' according to one traveller. They've also got a sign proclaiming, in large letters, 'No Dope'!

The Sikh-run *Khalsa Restaurant*, across from the Salvation Army Hostel and down the street a few doors, has been popular with travellers for many years. Turn right from Sudder St on Free School St and you soon come to the *Moghul Durbar*, which is clean and has flowers on the tables, free newspapers to read and food served out with real speed. Plus big signs reassuring Hindu customers that they do not serve beef! *Café 48* is another possibility.

Kathleen's Restaurant & Bakery at 12 Free School St (left from Sudder St) is a classier place with very good Indian and western food (about Rs 60 for a meal for two). They do good tandoori food; most main courses are Rs 15 to Rs 18. There are fantastic baked items in the confectionery level downstairs; check the amazing children's birthday cakes. You'll also find cakes and baked goods in *Flury's* on Park St. In the New Market on Lindsay St are some superb cake shops including *Nahoum*, a third-generation Jewish bakery in F row. 'An interesting old guy', wrote one traveller.

On Free School St, between Sudder St and Park St, the *How Hua* has good Chinese food. Most dishes are Rs 10 to Rs 15. They've even got northern Chinese dishes such as *jiaozi*, a bit like Tibetan *mo-mo*. Another reader found 'the best Chinese food in India' at the *Embassy Chinese Restaurant*, on Chowringhee across from the large cathedral near the Victoria Memorial.

In amongst the predominantly expensive restaurants along Park St are some cheaper places. *Super Dooper Snacks* is cheap and quick and has Kwality ice cream at Rs 4 to Rs 6, thalis for Rs 15 and other snacks. At 21 Park St the *Health Food Centre* has all sorts of health foods to take away, including wholemeal bread, brownies, halva, yoghurt, pizza slices, muesli and delicious (though rather expensive) bottled apple juice from Bhutan.

If you like south Indian food – and who doesn't? – then just off Chowringhee on Lindsay St the *Hindustan Restaurant* (upstairs) has excellent vegetarian food, although the prices have risen dramatically since the last edition – thalis are Rs 17, masala dosas Rs 5. In the same area *Nizam's*, across the street and around the corner from the Minerva Cinema, is popular among Calcuttans for mutton and chicken rolls, kebabs and Muslim food. Over towards BBD Bag the *Super Snack Bar* at 5 Old Court House St opposite American Express has the usual selection of Indian snack meals.

The Bengali sweet tooth is legendary and *Indra Mahal* is a great place to try Bengali sweets. It's on Chowringhee just up from the Grand Hotel; they also serve *chat* and other snacks. A local speciality in Calcutta is *moghul paratha*, but curiously it's all but impossible to find real Bengali food in Calcutta unless you dine at a Bengali's home.

More Expensive There are a number of places along Park St; in fact it's virtually solid restaurants along part of the street.

There's a good *Kwality* at 17 Park St, beside the Park Hotel. On that side of the street there are half a dozen other places, some with un-Calcutta names like *Blue Fox* and *Moulin Rouge*! The *Tandoor* has a reasonably swish upstairs room with reasonably good food and fairly reasonable prices. On the other side of the road there's a *Magnolia* for ice cream, *Gupta* for thalis, *Silver Grill* and *Flury's* for quick (but expensive) snacks and takeaways.

Amber at 11 Waterloo St, behind the Great Eastern Hotel, occupies three floors and is one of Calcutta's better restaurants for Indian and western food. It's so popular that you may have to book a table or be prepared to wait.

At the *Fairlawn Hotel* on Sudder St food is English style, but surprisingly good. If you're staying there, all meals are included in the room cost. If you're not, and would like to experience that old-style service, meals can be arranged. Breakfast is Rs 32, lunch or dinner Rs 37.

Getting There

Air Calcutta is connected by air with all the major centres and in particular is the jumping-off point for flights to the north-east region, to Darjeeling and to Port Blair in the Andaman Islands. Some fares include: Madras Rs 1202, flights daily; Bombay Rs 1372, flights twice daily; Delhi Rs 1007, two direct flights and a multi-stopper daily; Bhubaneswar Rs 365; Varanasi Rs 602; Patna Rs 444; Bagdogra (for Darjeeling) Rs 421; Gauhati Rs 398; Port Blair (Andaman Islands) Rs 1114.

Calcutta's Indian Airlines office is now fully computerised, but amusingly somebody forgot to put a cooling fan in the computer terminals so each one has a large floor fan standing behind it!

Calcutta is a good place for competitive air fares to South-East Asia and there are also flights to Kathmandu. Official fares are Dhaka Rs 346, Bangkok Rs 2131, Kathmandu US$96. You can find Thai

International tickets to Bangkok, including a Rangoon stopover for Rs 1600. Bangladesh Biman also offer competitive fares to Rangoon and Bangkok via Dhaka. If you have to overnight in Dhaka, make sure Biman give you concrete proof that they are going to provide accommodation – as they should. Other airlines out of Calcutta include Burma Airways to Rangoon and Bangkok or Royal Nepal Airlines to Kathmandu.

Rail Calcutta has two major railway stations. Howrah on the west bank of the Hooghly handles most trains into the city, but if you're going north to Darjeeling or the north-east region then the trains will be from Sealdah Station on the east side. Beware of pickpockets and other people of similar inclination at Howrah. The Eastern Railway Book Office (tel 224356) is at 6 Fairlie Place for 2nd-class and tourist-quota bookings. For 1st class it's at 14 Strand Rd. The South-Eastern Railway Booking Office (tel 235569) is at Esplanade Mansions. There's a Foreign Tourist Quota Office at Fairlie Place which is good for booking trains.

To Delhi, trains take from 17 hours for the 1441-km trip, which costs approximately Rs 99 in 2nd class, Rs 408 in 1st. To Varanasi the 678-km trip takes from 12 hours and costs Rs 57 in 2nd class, Rs 233 in 1st. For Darjeeling the 566-km trip takes about 12 hours from Calcutta (Sealdah Station) to New Jalpaiguri or Siliguri, where you take a bus or the toy train up to the hill station. Fare from Calcutta to New Jalpaiguri is Rs 49 in 2nd class, Rs 201 in 1st.

It's a long way from Calcutta to Bombay, a 1968-km trip taking 36 hours even on the fast mail train. Fares are Rs 124 in 2nd class, Rs 515 in 1st. The trip to Madras is nearly as long – 33 hours to cover 1662 km at a cost of about Rs 109 in 2nd class, Rs 453 in 1st. During and soon after the monsoon the railway line can be cut off by the Godavari or the Krishna rivers in north Andhra Pradesh. If this is the case the Calcutta-Madras service will make a loop inland and the trip will take rather longer. The normal service runs down the coast all the way, passing through Bhubaneswar in Orissa en route.

Bus The bus services from Calcutta are not as good an alternative as they are from a number of other Indian cities. It's generally better to travel from Calcutta by rail, although there are several useful routes to other towns in West Bengal. Buses depart from the bus stand area at the north end of the Maidan, near Chowringhee.

Ship See the Andaman & Nicobar Islands section for details on the shipping services from Calcutta.

Getting Around
Airport An airport bus costing Rs 13 runs by the Indian Airlines office and down Chowringhee past Sudder St on the way in. On the way out it only departs from the IA office. A taxi costs Rs 40 to Rs 50, so between four that is as cheap as the bus, and since so many people leave India from Calcutta on the same (Thai International) flights it is easy to get a group together for a taxi.

There is a public minibus from BBD Bag to the airport for about Rs 2. If your endurance knows no limits you can get to the airport from Howrah Station in a No 11A and then a No 30B bus, or from the Esplanade Bus Terminal in a No S10 bus for just Rs 1. Incidentally, Calcutta's airport takes its name, Dum Dum Airport, from the fact that this was the site of the Dum Dum Barracks, where the explosive dum dum bullet, banned after the Boer War, was once made.

Bus Calcutta's bus system is absolutely hopelessly crowded. It's an edifying sight to watch the double deckers come across Howrah Bridge during the rush hour. Fares are Rs 0.50 to Rs 1.30. Take a No 5 or 6 between Howrah Station and Sudder St and ask for the Indian Museum. There is a secondary private minibus service, rather faster and slightly more expensive, with fares from Rs 0.75 to Rs 2. You need to be a midget to ride in these buses though. Beware of pickpockets in any Calcutta public transport.

Trams Calcutta has a public tram service but the trams are like sardine tins. Take a No 12A from Howrah to the Indian Museum. Standard fares are Rs 0.35 in the front, Rs 0.30 in the back. On Sunday it is possible to buy a ticket from the terminus for Rs 1. They're quiet – well, quiet by Calcutta standards – on that day.

Underground Calcutta's underground railway system is being built at minimum cost and in maximum time almost totally by hand. The soggy soil makes digging holes by hand no fun at all, and after each monsoon it takes half the time to the next monsoon simply to drain out what has already been dug. Nevertheless, after many delays the first stretch along Chowringhee is now open, but only Monday to Friday from 9 to 11 am and 3 to 8 pm. The standard fare is Rs 1. Eventually the Metro Railway will run from Tollygunge Station in the south to Dum Dum Station in the north.

Taxi Calcutta's taxi drivers are renowned not only for their passion for strikes, which in turn causes the buses to be even worse than usual, but also for their belligerent refusal to use the meters. If they did use them, the fares were meter plus 40% in '86. If they won't use the meter it's certainly worth arguing about the price, but there's no room for optimists. Sudder St to Howrah Station, for example, should cost no more than Rs 20.

Rickshaw Calcutta is the last holdout of the man-powered rickshaw. The rickshaw-wallahs would not accept the new-fangled bicycle rickshaws when they were intro-

duced elsewhere in India. After all, who could afford a bicycle? You may find it morally impossible to have a man trotting around pulling you in a carriage, but they are useful for carting heavy baggage. And Calcutta's citizens are quite happy to use them. You only find these rickshaws in central Calcutta, though. Across the river in Howrah or in other Calcutta suburbs cycle-rickshaws are available.

Bicycle The Blue Sky restaurant on Sudder St rents bicycles at Rs 2 an hour or Rs 10 per day.

Things to Buy

Calcutta has the usual government emporiums and quite a good Central Cottage Industries Emporium at 7 Chowringhee. There are numerous interesting shops along Chowringhee selling everything from carpets to handicrafts. The shops along the entrance arcade to the Grand Hotel are particularly interesting. There is also an amazing variety of pavement dealers; at night lurid (for India) condom peddlers appear along Chowringhee and Park St.

New Market, formerly Hogg Market, is Calcutta's premier shopping bargain despite part of it being burnt out in late '85. Here you can find a little of almost everything, and it is always worth an hour or so wandering around. A particular bargain, if you're flying straight home from Calcutta, is caneware. Ridiculously cheap compared to prices in the west and, of course, very light if rather bulky.

The market is a place to sell as well as buy, so long as those 'Singapore goodies' are not recorded in your passport. Whisky, cigarettes, watches, Sony Walkmans and cameras are in great demand. You can also change money for a slightly better rate than the bank. If nobody approaches you, the uniformed porters can direct you.

Down Sudder St, a tola (about 12 gm) of the best 'dreaded resin' should cost less than Rs 100.

West Bengal

Population: 49 million
Area: 87,853 square km
Capital: Calcutta
Main language: Bengali

At the time of partition Bengal was split into East and West Bengal. East Bengal became the eastern wing of Pakistan and later, with the disintegration of that country, Bangladesh. West Bengal became a state of India with its largest city, Calcutta, as its capital. The state is long and narrow, running from the delta of the Ganges River system at the Bay of Bengal in the south to the heights of the Himalaya at Darjeeling in the north.

There is not a great deal of interest in the state apart from these two extremes – Calcutta, all noise, confusion and squalor at one end; and Darjeeling, serene and peaceful, at the other. Nevertheless the intrepid traveller will find a number of places to consider visiting, either south of Calcutta on the Bay of Bengal or north along the route to Darjeeling.

PERMITS

Before you can visit Darjeeling, Kalimpong or Sikkim, special permits are required. Only in the case of Darjeeling are certain exceptions made to this rule (see below). All these places are in what the Indian government refers to as 'sensitive border regions' and the rationale behind the permit requirements is to keep track of who goes there. Anyone having the slightest familiarity with Indian bureaucracy will know what a farce this is. As far as Darjeeling and Kalimpong are concerned it's merely a formality, but it keeps plenty of people employed pushing pens and wielding rubber stamps. With Sikkim, obtaining a permit is more involved and you must plan ahead.

Darjeeling

The only exception to the permit rule is if you travel by air from Calcutta to Bagdogra (the nearest airport to Darjeeling), return the same way, and do not stay in Darjeeling more than 15 days from the date of arrival at Bagdogra. If you do this you can have your passport endorsed at Bagdogra airport checkpost for a visit to Darjeeling.

If you intend to go there by bus or train then you must obtain a permit. You can get these from any of the following places:

Indian Embassies, Consulates and High Commissions outside India.
Ministry of Home Affairs, Government of India, North Block, New Delhi.
Home Political Department, 1st floor, Block 2, Writers' Building, BBD Bagh, Calcutta.
Any Foreigners' Registration Office in India. In Delhi the office is in Hans Bhavan; in Calcutta it's at 237 Acharya J C Bose Rd.

There is one form to complete, no

photographs are required and the permit is issued free of charge within 24 hours in India. If you apply outside India then three photographs are needed. Permits allow for a stay of 15 days, which *may* be extendable in Darjeeling at the Foreigners' Registration Office, Laden La Rd (tel 2261). If extensions are being granted no photographs are required, no fee is charged and they are issued while you wait. On first application you are given what you ask for, so always ask for the maximum – ie 15 days.

If you're planning on trekking to Sandakphu and/or Phalut, a separate special permit is required – again obtainable from the Foreigners' Registration Office in Darjeeling. If you flew into Bagdogra airport then you are exempt from this requirement on condition that you report your intentions to the Darjeeling office 24 hours before leaving.

In the last edition we mentioned two travellers who arrived at New Jalpaiguri without a permit and managed to talk their way into one. This trip I met a traveller who did a lot of talking but didn't manage to get one. He thought it might have been because the permit inspector's superior was there, but I think it's unwise to go all the way there in the hope that you can bluff your way through. I got my permit at the Foreigners' Registration Office in New Delhi, and despite the seeming chaos of the office it took me less than an hour to obtain it. At New Jalpaiguri there are two inspectors waiting for every train, although on my train I was the only foreigner disembarking! I got my Kalimpong permit in Darjeeling and it took minutes – I should have put a stopwatch on them because as I left they asked if they'd managed it in under five minutes.

Tony Wheeler

Kalimpong

A permit for Darjeeling does not automatically entitle you to visit Kalimpong. To go there you must obtain a separate endorsement on your Darjeeling permit. Ask for it at the same time you apply for the Darjeeling permit, or get one from the Foreigners' Registration Office in Darjee-

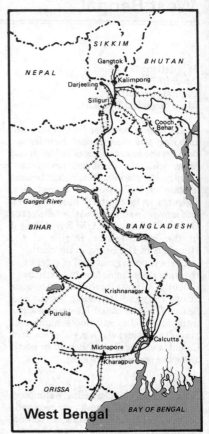

West Bengal

ling. A three-day visit is normally allowed. If you want longer, get authorisation before you go.

Sikkim

There are no exceptions to the permit requirements for Sikkim regardless of your mode of transport. You need to apply at least six weeks in advance of your proposed visit, either to an Indian Embassy/Consulate/High Commission outside India or to the Deputy Secretary, Ministry of Home Affairs (F-1), North Block, New Delhi 110001. Reportedly it's much faster to apply from abroad than to the New Delhi office in person! There are three forms to complete, three photographs are required and you have to state the exact days on which you want to visit. No fee is charged for the permit.

If you apply via an Embassy/Consulate/High Commission, you will receive a letter some four to six weeks after you applied which states that 'the Government of India has no objection to your visit' and that you can pick up your permit from the Deputy Commissioner's Office, Darjeeling (at the junction of Cutchery Rd and Cart Rd next to the Loreto Convent). The initial permitted length of stay varies between two and four days but is extendable in Gangtok at the Foreigners' Regional Registration Office. Extensions are a mere formality and issued on the spot – just tell them where you want to go and how much time you require. No photographs are required and no fee charged for extensions. Your permit will be collected on leaving Sikkim at the Rangpo checkpost.

Recently permits have been changed and now only allow foreigners to go to Gangtok, Rumtek and Phodang. Pemayangtse can only be visited if you are travelling in a group with a liaison officer, so that means when making a trek to Dzongri, after you have got permission from the Indian Mountaineering Federation in New Delhi. Nobody in Sikkim seems to know why this change was made, since Pemayangtse was open to individual foreign tourists for some years.

SOUTH OF CALCUTTA
Down the Hooghly
The Hooghly River is a very difficult river to navigate due to the constantly shifting shoals and sandbanks. Hooghly River pilots have to continuously stay in touch with the river to keep track of the frequent changes in its course. When the Hooghly Bridge was constructed it was feared that it would cause severe alterations to the river's flow patterns. The tide rises and falls 3.5 metres at Calcutta and there is a bore, which reaches two metres in height, at the time of the rising tide. Because of the navigational difficulties and the silting up which the Hooghly is experiencing, Calcutta is losing its importance as a port.

Falta, 43 km downriver, was the site of a Dutch factory. The British retreated here in 1756 when Calcutta was captured by Suraj-ud-daula. It was also from here that Clive recaptured Calcutta. Just

DLIP-62-X

OFFICE OF THE FOREIGNERS REGIONAL REGISTRATION OFFICER, HANS BHAWAN, NEW DELHI

Special Permit No... *31/ S&W 1D21 A56*

[Under paragraph 5 of the Foreigners (Restricted Area) Order, 1963]

Registration No... ...dated... ...

1. Mr./Mrs./Miss. *ANTHONY TAN WHEELER* holder of Passport No... *B 266163.*
dated. *18-4-85* ... *Cambridge* ... National residing at... *Imperial Hotel*
... *N Delhi* ...

is hereby permitted to enter the restricted area for purpose of... *Tourism* ...

at... *Darjeeling* ... from *18-12-86* ... to *29-12-86*

2. He/She/They shall while residing in the said area, comply with the conditions specified below.

3. Mr./Mrs./Miss. *ANTHONY TAN WHEELERS*
shall not remain in the said area after the... *29-12-86* ... unless he/she/they has/have obtained the prior permission of the District Magistrate concerned.

Applications for any extension of the period of this permit must be made at least seven days before its expiry date.

Foreigners Regional Registration Officer, New Delhi *7.12.86*

... No... .../For. dated the... ...

below Falta the Damodar joins the Hooghly. The Rupnarain also joins the Hooghly and a little up this river is Tamluk, an important Buddhist centre over 1000 years ago. The James & Mary Shoal, the most dangerous on the Hooghly, is just above the point where the Rupnarain River enters. It takes its name from a ship which was wrecked here in 1694.

Diamond Harbour

A resort 51 km south of Calcutta by road, Diamond Harbour is at the point where the Hooghly turns south and flows into the open sea. Launches run from here to Sagar Island.

Places to Stay Accommodation in the *Sagarika Tourist Lodge* can be booked through the West Bengal Tourism Corporation in Calcutta.

Haldia

The new port of Haldia is 96 km south of Calcutta, on the west bank of the Hooghly. The port was constructed to try to regain the shipping lost from Calcutta due to the port's silting problems. There are regular buses between Calcutta and Haldia.

Sagar Island

At the mouth of the Hooghly, this island is considered the point where the Ganges joins the sea, and a great three-day bathing festival takes place here early each January. A lighthouse marks the south-west tip of the island but navigation is still difficult for a further 65 km south.

Digha

Close to the border with Orissa, 185 km south-east of Calcutta on the Bay of Bengal, Digha is a beach resort with a six-km-long beach. There are daily buses between Calcutta and Digha operated by the CSTC. The trip takes about six hours and buses depart from 7 am. The Chandaneshwar Shiva temple is just

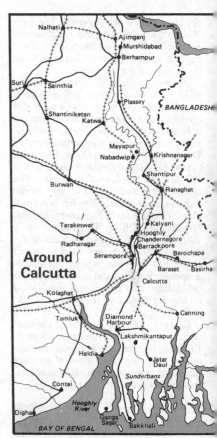

Around Calcutta

across the border in Orissa, eight km from Digha.

Places to Stay There is a *Tourist Lodge* (tel Digha 54-55) with rooms from Rs 25/50 and reasonably priced meals. Digha has a wide range of other accommodation, including new and old *Tourist Cottages* and a *Youth Hostel* with dorm beds at Rs 6. *Hotel Sea Hawk* (tel Digha 35) has rooms from Rs 25 up to Rs 105, even more with air-con. There's also a Rs 15 dorm. These can all be booked through the West Bengal Tourist Development Corporation in Calcutta (tel 235917). Digha also has a number of private hotels and boarding houses.

Bakkhali

Also known as Fraserganj, this is another beach resort, 132 km from Calcutta and on the east side of the Hooghly. Accommodation here can again be reserved through the West Bengal Tourist Corporation. From here you can get boats to the small island of Jambu Dwip to the southwest.

Sunderbans

Spreading across the border into Bangladesh, the Sunderbans is the forest at the delta where the Ganges meets the sea. Royal Bengal tigers can still be seen here, particularly on Lothian Island and Chamta Block. There are many other animals, including deer, wild boar, monkeys, snakes and crocodiles.

NORTH OF CALCUTTA

Chandernagore

This was another of the French enclaves in India which were handed over at the same time as Pondicherry in 1951. On the banks of the Hooghly, 39 km north of Calcutta, are several buildings dating from the French era. The first French settlers arrived here in 1673 and the place later became an important trading post, although it was taken by the British during conflicts with the French.

Hooghly

This historic town is 41 km north of Calcutta and very close to two other interesting sites – Chinsura and Bandel. Hooghly was an important trading port long before Calcutta rose to prominence. In 1537 the Portuguese set up a factory here; prior to that time Satgaon, 10 km further north, had been the main port of Bengal but was abandoned due to the river silting up. There are still a few traces of Satgaon's former grandeur, including a ruined mosque.

The Portuguese were kicked out of

Hooghly in 1632 by Shah Jahan, after a lengthy siege, but were allowed to return a year later. The British East India Company also established a factory here in 1651. The Imambara, built in 1836, with its gateway flanked by lofty minarets, is the main sight in the city. Across the road is an older Imambara, dating from 1776-77.

Chinsura

Only a km or so south of Hooghly, Chinsura was exchanged by the Dutch for the British-held Indonesian island of Sumatra in 1825. The Dutch Church is octagonal and dates from 1678. There is a Dutch cemetery with many old tombs a km to the west.

Bandel

A couple of km north of Hooghly, Bandel is 43 km north of Calcutta. A Portuguese church and monastery was built here in 1599 but destroyed by Shah Jahan in 1640. It was later rebuilt.

Getting There Get off the train at Naihati and take the hourly shuttle service across the river.

Bansberia

A further four km north of Bandel, Bansberia has the Vasudev temple with interesting terracotta wall carvings and the Hanseswari Temple.

Jairambati & Kamarpukur

Ramakrishna was born in Kamarpukur, 143 km north-west of Calcutta, and there is a Ramakrishna Mission Ashram here. Ramakrishna was a 19th-century Hindu saint who did much to rejuvenate Hinduism when it was going through a period of decline during the British rule. Jairambati, five km away, is another important point for Ramakrishna devotees.

Shantiniketan

Near Bolpur, the Vivabharati University

is located here. The brilliant and prolific poet, writer and nationalist Rabindranath Tagore (1861-1941) founded a school here in 1901. It later developed into a university with emphasis on man's relation with nature – many classes are conducted in the open air. Tagore went on to win the Nobel Prize in 1913 and is credited with introducing India's historical and cultural greatness to the modern world. Despite his work for India's independence, he was knighted by the British.

Places to Stay There are a small *University Guest House* and *Railway Retiring Rooms* at Bolpur station.

Nabadwip & Mayapur

Nabadwip is an ancient centre of Sanskrit culture, 114 km north of Calcutta. There are many temples here and across the river at Mayapur; both are important pilgrimage centres and Mayapur is a centre for the Iskon (Hare Krishna) movement.

Plassey

In 1757 Clive defeated Suraj-ud-daula and his French supporters here, a turning point in British influence in India. Plassey is 172 km north of Calcutta.

Murshidabad (population 18,000)

This was once an important trading town between inland India and the port of Calcutta, 221 km south. Today it's a quiet town in central Bengal, a chance to see typical rural Bengali life. It was also once the home of Suraj-ud-daula, the local sultan who put Calcutta's British residents into that infamous 'black hole'. A year later the British defeated his forces at Plassey and nominated a more reliable successor.

They built him a large Italian-style palace, the Nizamat Kila, which was completed in 1837 and still stands beside the Bhagirathi River (closed Fridays). Cross the river in a small boat to see Suraj's tomb at Khusbagh, the 'Garden of Happiness', where the Nawabs are buried. Opposite it is the Moti Jhil or 'Pearl Lake', a fine place to view the sunsets. There are a number of other interesting buildings and ruins, and this is a notable silk-producing area.

Places to Stay Near the palace in Murshidabad is the cheap *Hotel Historical*. If it's full you can sleep on the roof. Meals are also cheap. The *Tourist Lodge* in Berhampore is cleaner and more reliable, but it's 12 km away by bus. Rooms can be booked through the West Bengal Tourism Corporation in Calcutta and there is also a dorm.

Getting There There are half a dozen trains daily from Sealdah Station in Calcutta and the trip takes six hours.

English Bazaar (population 70,000)

Near this town, north of the Ganges on the route to Darjeeling, are the interesting remains of several ancient Bengali capital cities.

Gaur

Seven km south of English Bazaar, this was the capital of Bengal in the pre-Muslim days. The large city stood at the junction of the Ganges and Mahananda rivers and was once extensively fortified. There are still many remains of the fortifications, mosques and towers as well as a footprint of the prophet – what on earth was he doing here?

Old Malda

At the junction of the Kalindri and Mahananda rivers, this was once an important port for the former Muslim capital of Pandua. An English factory was established here in 1656 but moved to English Bazaar in 1771.

Pandua

Gaur once alternated with Pandua as the seat of power. Many of Pandua's now ruined buildings were constructed from material taken from Gaur, which accounts for its strange blend of architectural styles. Pandua is 11 km from Old Malda and 18 km from English Bazaar.

SILIGURI & NEW JALPAIGURI

This crowded, sprawling, noisy place is the jumping-off point for visits to Darjeeling, Kalimpong or Sikkim. Siliguri is a real boom town as the major trade centre for the north-east, Darjeeling, Sikkim and the east of Nepal, so it's packed with trucks and buses and not a pleasant place to stay for a moment more than necessary. New Jalpaiguri, the main railway junction, is a couple of km south of Siliguri.

Orientation & Information

Siliguri is very confusing at first, especially if you arrive at night. New Jalpaiguri is the main railway junction, nothing more. The distance is about five km from there to Siliguri Town station and another three or four km on to Siliguri Junction station. You can catch the toy train to Darjeeling from any of these three stations. Siliguri is essentially just one north-south main road. There's a tourist information counter at the New Jalpaiguri station.

Places to Stay

If you arrive in Siliguri too late to continue straight on to Darjeeling, there are numerous places to stay. There are good *Retiring Rooms* at Rs 20 a double at New Jalpaiguri station but they're often full. Dorm beds are Rs 10.

Just past the Siliguri Town station and to the left is the *Rajasthan Guest House* (tel 21815), with singles/doubles with bathroom at Rs 50/90 including bed tea. There are some bathless doubles for Rs 70. It's a fairly modern hotel, fine for overnighting.

Continuing along Hill Cart Rd, there is a string of places including, just before the river and opposite the bus stand, the

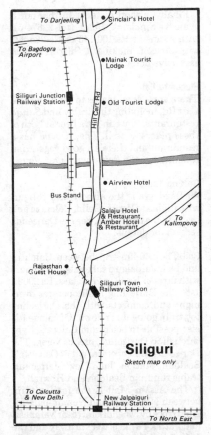

Airview Hotel. It's a typical big Indian hotel with lots of rooms – most of them very grubby and dirty. Singles cost from Rs 17, doubles Rs 35 or Rs 45.

Just north of the Airview you cross a river, and the old *Tourist Lodge* is on the right, just before the Siliguri Junction station. Here dorm beds cost Rs 18, doubles Rs 35, 45 or 50. Further along is the larger and newer *Mainak Tourist Lodge* (tel 20986), also run by the West Bengal Tourism Development Corporation. Rooms are Rs 75/110. With air-con they're Rs 130/170; deluxe rooms are Rs 175/240.

Finally, a short distance further north again is *Sinclair's Hotel* (tel 22674-5), with rooms at Rs 100/145 or Rs 225/325 with air-con, making it Siliguri's most expensive hotel.

Places to Eat

There are several places to eat along Hill Cart Rd, including the *Amber* and *Saluja* restaurants. You can get a beer at both of these places as well. The *Airview* has a restaurant and there's a good vegetarian restaurant at the *Rajasthan Guest House*.

Getting There

Air Bagdogra is the airport near Siliguri with flights to Patna, Delhi, Calcutta and towns in the north-east. See the Darjeeling section for details.

Rail The 566-km trip between Calcutta and New Jalpaiguri takes about 13 hours with fares of Rs 48 in 2nd class, Rs 200 in 1st. The Darjeeling Mail operates overnight and connects with the Darjeeling toy train going up or down. Of course it's also possible to book from Calcutta right through to Darjeeling, or vice versa. The Darjeeling Mail operates out of Calcutta's Sealdah station but New Jalpaiguri trains run from Sealdah and Howrah.

The Assam Mail is the fastest train between New Delhi and New Jalpaiguri. It also goes by Moghulserai (near Varanasi) and Patna. Patna is 634 km away and the 13½-hour trip costs Rs 55 in 2nd class, Rs 221 in 1st. Moghulserai is 847 km away and the trip takes 17 hours with fares of Rs 67 in 2nd class, Rs 276 in 1st.

See the Darjeeling section for details on the toy train.

Bus The overnight 'Rocket' bus service between Calcutta and Siliguri costs Rs 76. Buses can be booked in Darjeeling, in Calcutta at the North Bengal State Transport Corporation (tel 231854) at Esplanade Bus Stand, or in Siliguri at the Bus Stand (tel 20531). This bus is faster than the train and has fairly comfortable

seats. The company also runs buses from Siliguri to Patna (Rs 65) and vice versa.

Buses to Darjeeling are much faster than the toy train; the fare is Rs 11. A taxi would cost Rs 30 to Rs 40 per person. Buses also run to Kalimpong (Rs 11.50), Gangtok and other places in India. The cost is Rs 100 for the Siliguri-Kathmandu bus service, which starts with a jeep to the Nepal border, from where you catch the bus.

Getting Around

A cycle-rickshaw from New Jalpaiguri station to Siliguri Town will cost about Rs 4; to Siliguri Junction would be Rs 7 or Rs 8.

DARJEELING (population 50,000)

Straddling a ridge at 2123 metres and surrounded by tea plantations on all sides, Darjeeling has been a very popular hill station since the British established it as a rest-and-recreation centre for its troops in the mid-1800s. These days people come here to escape from the heat, humidity and hassle of the north Indian plain, and some indication of its popularity can be gleaned from the fact that there are about 60 hotels recognised by the West Bengal Tourist Development Corporation, apart from scores of others which don't come up to its requirements. Here you will find yourself surrounded by mountain people from all over the eastern Himalaya who have come here to work, to trade or – in the case of the Tibetans – as refugees.

Outside of the monsoon season (June-September) the views over the mountains to the snowy peaks of Kanchenjunga and down to the swollen rivers in the valley bottoms are magnificent. Darjeeling is a fascinating place where you can see Buddhist monasteries, visit a tea plantation and see how it's processed, go for a ride on the chairlift (if it's operating), spend days hunting for bargains in colourful markets and handicraft shops, or go trekking to high-altitude spots near the border with Sikkim. Like most places in the Himalaya, half the fun is in getting there and Darjeeling has the unique attraction of the famous 'toy train'. This miniature train loops and switchbacks its way up the steep mountainsides from New Jalpaiguri to Darjeeling.

History

Until the beginning of the 18th century the whole of the area between the present borders of Sikkim and the plains of Bengal, including Darjeeling and Kalimpong, belonged to the Rajas of Sikkim. In 1706 they lost Kalimpong to the Bhutanese, and control of the remainder was wrested from them by the Gurkhas who invaded Sikkim in 1780, following consolidation of the latter's rule in Nepal.

These annexations by the Gurkhas, however, brought them into conflict with the British East India Company. A series of wars were fought between the two parties, eventually leading to the defeat of the Gurkhas and the ceding of all the land they had taken from the Sikkimese to the East India Company. Part of this territory was restored to the Rajas of Sikkim and the country's sovereignty guaranteed by the British in return for British control over any disputes which arose with neighbouring states.

One such dispute in 1828 led to the despatch of two British officers to this area, and it was during their fact-finding tour that they spent some time at Darjeeling (then called Dorje Ling = 'Place of Thunderbolts'). The officers were quick to appreciate Darjeeling's value as a site for a sanatorium and hill station and as the key to a pass into Nepal and Tibet. The officers' observations were reported to the authorities in Calcutta and a pretext was eventually found to pressure the Raja into granting the site to the British in return for an annual stipend of Rs 3000 (raised to Rs 6000 in 1846).

This transfer, however, rankled with the Tibetans who regarded Sikkim as a vassal state, and Darjeeling's rapid development as a trading centre and tea-growing area in a key position along the trade route leading from Sikkim to the plains of India began to make a considerable impact on the fortunes of the lamas and leading merchants of Sikkim. Tensions arose and in 1849 two British travellers, Sir Joseph Hooker and Dr Campbell, who were visiting Sikkim with the permission of the Raja and the British government, were arrested. Various demands were made as a condition of their release, but the Sikkimese eventually released both prisoners unconditionally about a month later.

In reprisal for the arrests, however, the British annexed the whole of the land between the present borders of Sikkim and the Bengal plains and withdrew the annual Rs 6000 stipend from the Raja. The latter was restored to his son, raised to Rs 9000 in 1868 and raised again to Rs 12,000 in 1874. The annexations brought about a significant change in Darjeeling's status. Previously it had been an enclave within Sikkimese territory and to reach it the British had to pass through a country ruled by an independent Raja. After the takeover, Darjeeling became continuous with British territory further south and Sikkim was cut off from access to the plains except through British territory. This was eventually to lead to the invasion of Sikkim by the Tibetans and the British military expedition to Lhasa.

When the British first arrived in Darjeeling it was almost completely under forest and virtually uninhabited, though it had once been a sizeable village before the wars with Bhutan and Nepal. Development was rapid and by 1840 a road had been constructed, numerous houses and a sanatorium built and a hotel opened. By 1857 it had a population of some 10,000.

Most of the increase in the population was accounted for by the recruitment of labourers from Nepal, who were brought in to work the tea plantations established in the early 1840s by the British following the smuggling of tea seeds from China. Even today, the vast majority of people speak Nepali as a first language and the name Darjeeling continues to be synonymous with tea.

People

Although the Buddhists, with their monasteries at Ghoom and Darjeeling, are perhaps the most conspicuous religious group, they constitute only a minority of the population – about 14%. The majority of the inhabitants profess Hinduism, reflecting their origins in the northern Indian states and Nepal. Christians and Muslims comprise little more than 3% each of the district's total population, though there are numerous churches scattered around Darjeeling.

Orientation

Darjeeling is draped over a west-facing ridge, spilling down the hillside in a complicated series of interconnecting roads and flights of steps. Along Cart Rd, the main road through the lower part of the town, are the railway station and the bus and taxi stand. The most important route connecting this road with Chowrasta at the top of the ridge is Laden La Rd/ Nehru Rd. The Youth Hostel is further back up the ridge, virtually at the high point.

Along these two roads are a fair number of budget hotels and cheap restaurants, the GPO, the bus terminals for Sikkim and Kathmandu, the Foreigners' Registration Office, the State Bank of India, curio shops, photographic supply shops and the Tourist Office. At the Chowrasta end of Nehru Rd and on Gandhi Rd above Laden La Rd are many of the mid-range hotels and restaurants. The bulk of the top-range hotels are clustered around Observatory Hill beyond Chowrasta. There are others along Dr Zakir Hussain Rd and A J C Bose Rd.

1	Ropeway (Chairlift)
2	Himalayan Mountaineering Institute Zoo
3	Happy Valley Tea Estate
4	Tibetan Refugee Centre
5	Raj Bhavan
6	Maple Tourist Lodge
7	Deputy Commissioner's Office
8	Darjeeling Tourist Lodge & Gymkhana Club
9	Youth Hostel
10	Ghoom Monastery
11	Monastery
12	Tiger Hill
13	New Elgin Hotel
14	Windamere Hotel
15	Chowrasta Restaurant
16	Bellevue Hotel, Tourist Office & Indian Airlines
17	Snow Lion Restaurant
18	Buses to Kalimpong & Siliguri
19	Market
20	Taxi Stand
21	Keventer's Snack Bar
22	Dekevas Restaurant
23	New Dish Restaurant
24	Grindlay's Bank
25	Foreigner's Registration Office
26	Shabnan Restaurant
27	State Bank of India
28	Himalayan Restaurant
29	Buses to Gangtok (Sikkim Nationalised Transport)
30	GPO
31	Prestige Hotel
32	Timber Lodge & Washington Restaurant
33	Tara Hotel
34	Tibetan Restaurants
35	Hotel Pagoda
36	Shamrock Hotel
37	Hotels Kadambari & Nirvana
38	Railway Station & Tourist Reception Centre

Information

Offices The Tourist Office (tel 2050) is in the Bellevue Hotel, Chowrasta. (The address is officially 1 Nehru Rd.) Very little literature is available except their Rs 1 map of Darjeeling and their trekking leaflet – not very good. The people are helpful and well informed though. Indian Airlines (tel 2355) is in the same building.

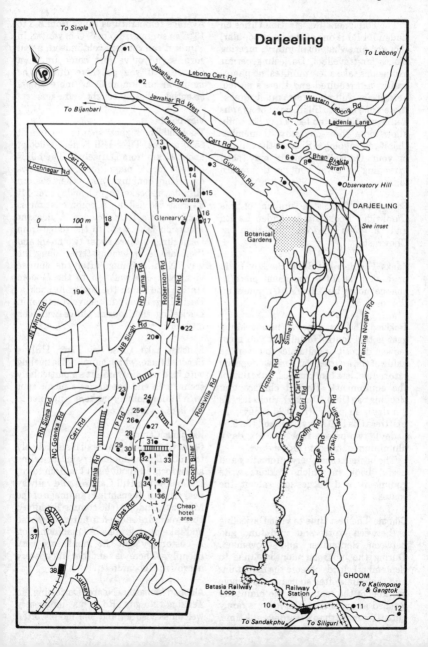

Darjeeling

To Singla
To Lebong
Jawahar Rd
Lebong Cart Rd
Jawahar Rd West
To Bijanbari
Western Lebong Rd
Ladenia Lane
Pamphawati
Cart Rd
Gurunmi Rd
Bhan Bhakta Sarani
Lochnagar Rd
Cart Rd
Observatory Hill
Chowrasta
Gleneary's
DARJEELING
See inset
Botanical Gardens
HD Lama Rd
Robertson Rd
Nehru Rd
NB Singh Rd
RN Mitra Rd
Sinha Rd
Victoria Rd
Tenzing Norgay Rd
Cart Rd
DB Giri Rd
Gandhi Rd
RN Sinha Rd
NC Goenka Rd
Cart Rd
I P Rd
Ladenia Rd
Rockville Rd
Cooch Bihar Rd
AJC Bose Rd
Dr Zakir Hassain Rd
Cheap hotel area
SM Das Rd
BK Gonaba Rd
Batasia Railway Loop
Railway Station
GHOOM
To Kalimpong & Gangtok
To Sandakphu
To Siliguri

The Foreigners' Registration Office on Laden La Rd is one of the most popular, though somewhat involuntary, meeting places for travellers. Darjeeling permit extensions take a few minutes, no photographs are required and there's no fee. Permits for Kalimpong are equally quick; there's one form to fill in, no photographs and again there's no fee. They normally allow for a three-day stay. Remember that if you're going to Sikkim, the validity of your Darjeeling permit may need extending to cover you for the return journey.

Bookshops There's a branch of the Cambridge Bookshop on Laden La Rd and a good Oxford Bookshop at Chowrasta.

Banks The decrepit State Bank of India on Laden La Rd is the usual place to change money but there's a Grindlays up the road.

Trekking The best place to hire trekking gear is the Youth Hostel, but you must leave a deposit or valuables to cover the value of the articles you borrow (deposits returnable, less hire charges, on return of the equipment). Typical charges are: sleeping bag (Rs 4.50 a day), rucksack (Rs 2 a day), air pillow (Rs 0.25 a day), air mattress (Rs 1.50 a day), bed roll (Rs 2.50 a day), two-person tent (Rs 6 a day), aluminium camp cot (Rs 4 a day).

The hostel keeps a very interesting and useful book in which trekkers write comments and suggestions about the routes.

Climate The best time to visit Darjeeling is between April and mid-June and between September and November. During the monsoon months (June to September) clouds obscure the mountains and the rain is often so heavy that whole sections of the road from the plains are washed away, though the town is rarely cut off for more than a few days at a time.

Average temperatures range from 8.5 to 15°C in summer, 1.5 to 6°C in winter. In winter it can get very cold indeed, a real surprise if you've just come up from Calcutta. If you go there during the monsoon an umbrella is more-or-less essential – cheaply bought in the market.

Viewpoints
Tiger Hill The highest spot in the area at 2590 metres, Tiger Hill is near Ghoom, about 11 km from Darjeeling. The hill is famous for its magnificent dawn views over Kanchenjunga and other eastern Himalayan peaks. On a clear day even Mt Everest is visible. Accommodation is available at a Tourist Lodge. A pleasant excursion is to walk to the lodge from Darjeeling; it takes about two hours and there are several monasteries along the way. Next morning, after the sunrise view, you can walk on to the Ghoom station and catch the toy train back to Darjeeling. If you can't leave your gear in Darjeeling the Tourist Office will look after it for you.

Senchal Lake Close to Tiger Hill is Senchal Lake, which supplies Darjeeling with its domestic water. It's a particularly scenic area and popular as a picnic spot with Indian holiday-makers. Entrance to the lake costs Rs 0.50.

Religious Centres
Ghoom Buddhist Monastery This is probably the most famous monastery in Darjeeling and is located about eight km from town, just below the Hill Cart Rd and railway near Ghoom. It enshrines an image of the Maitreya Buddha (the coming Buddha). Foreigners are allowed to enter the shrine and take photographs. A small donation is customary and the monks are very friendly. There is another monastery nearby in Ghoom itself.

Aloobari Monastery Nearer Darjeeling, on Tenzing Norgay Rd, this monastery welcomes visitors and the monks often sell Tibetan and Sikkimese handicrafts and religious objects (usually hand bells). If the monastery is closed you can get the keys from the cottage next door.

Dhirdham Temple The most conspicuous Hindu temple in Darjeeling, this is just below the railway station and is built along the lines of the famous Pashupatinath Temple in Kathmandu.

Museums, Parks & Gardens
Himalayan Mountaineering Institute Entered through the zoo, on Jawahar Rd West about two km from the town, the institute is the only one of its kind and exists to train mountaineers. It also has a museum containing an interesting collection of historic mountaineering equipment, specimens of Himalayan flora and fauna (though not one of the Abominable Snowman!) and a relief model of the Himalaya.

The institute is open from 9 am to 1 pm and 2 to 4.30 pm. The entrance fee is Rs 0.50.

Zoological Park Adjacent to the Mountaineering Institute, the park has a collection of high-altitude fauna including the Siberian tiger, Himalayan black bear, deer, panda and a bird collection. Most of the animals are housed in miserable and squalid conditions. The entrance fee is Rs 1 and hours are 8 am to 4 pm.

Botanical Gardens Below the bus and taxi stand near the market, these gardens contain a representative collection of Himalayan plants, flowers and orchids. The hot-houses are well worth a visit. The gardens are open between 6 am and 5 pm; entrance is free.

Handicraft Centres
Tibetan Refugee Self-Help Centre The centre was established in October 1959 to help rehabilitate Tibetan refugees who fled from Tibet with the Dalai Lama following the Chinese invasion. Religious

importance is attached to this place, as the 13th Dalai Lama (the present is the 14th) stayed here during his visit to India in 1919-22. The centre produces superb carpets, woollens, woodcarvings and leatherwork, and has various Tibetan curios for sale (coins, banknotes, jewellery, etc).

You can wander at leisure through the workshops and watch the work in progress. The weaving and dyeing shops and the woodcarving shop are particularly interesting and the people who work there very friendly. Their prices, however, are on a par with those in the curio shops of Chowrasta and Nehru Rd. It's an interesting place to visit apart from the workshops, and the views are magnificent.

Curio Shops The majority of these are on Chowrasta and along Nehru Rd. All things Himalayan are sold here – *thankas*, brass statues, religious objects, jewellery, woodcarvings, woven fabrics, carpets, etc – but if you're looking for bargains you have to shop judiciously and be prepared to spend plenty of time looking. Thankas in particular are nowhere near the quality which was usual 10 years ago. They may look impressive at first sight, but on closer inspection you will find that little care has been taken over the finer detail. The brocade surroundings (said to originate from China) are often of much finer quality.

If you're looking for bronze statues, the real goodies are kept under the counter and cost in multiples of US$100! You have to indicate that you are not interested in the mass-produced stuff on display before they get the better ones out.

Woodcarvings tend to be excellent value for money. Most of the shops accept international credit cards. There is also a market off the Cart Rd next to the bus and taxi stands. Here you can find excellent and relatively cheap patterned woollen sweaters. If you need an umbrella these can be bought here for around Rs 15.

Made out of bamboo, they are collectors' items themselves!

Bengal 'Manjusha' Emporium Located on the Cart Rd about two km from town on the way to Ghoom and opposite the Ava Art Gallery, this emporium sells Himalayan handicrafts, silk and handloomed products from West Bengal. It's open on all working days from 8 am to 5 pm.

Tea Plantations

Tea is, of course, Darjeeling's most famous export. From its 78 gardens 10.5 million kg are produced annually – 2% of India's total. It employs over 46,000 people in the area. The most convenient garden to visit is the Happy Valley Tea Estate only two km from the centre of town, where tea is still produced by the 'orthodox' method as opposed to the 'Curling, Tearing and Crushing' (CTC) method adopted on the plains. The process is a fascinating one to observe and you should set aside a half day to visit the estate. It's open daily from 8 am to 12 noon and between 1 and 4.30 pm except on Mondays and Sunday afternoons.

After picking, the fresh green leaves are placed 15 to 25 cm deep in a 'withering trough' where the moisture content is reduced from 70 to 80% down to 30 to 40% using high-velocity fans. When this is complete the withered leaves are rolled and pressed to break the cell walls and express their juices onto the surface of the leaves. Normally two rollings at different pressures are undertaken, and in between rolls the leaves are sifted to separate the coarse from the fine. Next the leaves, coated with their juices, are allowed to ferment on racks in a high-humidity room, a process which develops their characteristic aroma and flavour. This fermentation must be controlled carefully since either over or under-fermentation will ruin the tea.

The process is stopped by passing the fermenting leaves through a dry air chamber at 115-120°C on a conveyer belt to further reduce the moisture content to around 2 to 3%. The last process is the sorting of the tea into grades. In their order of value they are: Golden Flowery Orange Pekoe (unbroken leaves), Golden Broken Orange Pekoe, Orange Fannings and Dust (the latter three consisting of broken leaves).

In the last few years modern agricultural practices have been brought to the tea estates to maintain and improve their viability. They were one of the first agricultural enterprises to use clonal plants in their replanting schemes, though very little of this has been done and most of the tea trees are at least 100 years old and nearing the end of their useful or even natural lives. Although Darjeeling produces some of the world's finest tea, the ageing plants and deteriorating soil causes grave concern. Tea is not only a major export item but also provides much employment in the area.

The Passenger Ropeway

At North Point, about three km from town, this was the first passenger ropeway to be constructed in India. It is five km long and connects Darjeeling with Singla Bazaar on the Little Ranjit River at the bottom of the valley. This is a superb excursion, though not one for vertigo sufferers. The return fare is Rs 15, but at present only part of the ropeway is operating so it's of limited interest.

Other Activities

Beware of the pony wallahs who congregate in Chowrasta. They'll come along with you as a guide and at the end you'll find you're paying for a second pony and for their guiding time! Usual charge is around Rs 10 an hour, but make sure of the price first.

The video craze has hit India everywhere, particularly Darjeeling and some other hill stations. Lots of places have set themselves up as mini-cinemas; a blackboard outside indicates what they're showing. Often it's western films that would have had trouble getting by the censor in the old days.

A British traveller wrote of the joys of a visit to the Darjeeling Gymkhana Club:

This majestic ghost of the Raj offers snooker, badminton, rollerskating, table tennis, tennis and squash, and membership is Rs 5 per day or

Rs 25 for a week. The building is a grand reminder of how the Brits enjoyed themselves in Darjeeling, with magnificently wood-panelled foyer and stairs and an old ballroom and auditorium on the ground floor redolent of former glories. Streamers hang dusty in the ballroom – from Christmas in the 1980s or 1920s? The place has not been cleaned, it seems, since the British Army officers' wives' social club spring clean in 1935!

We played snooker for an afternoon – good tables, fine old cues and rests. We had a keen snooker-wallah re-spot the balls, hand us the rest, score and encourage us with frequent 'nice shot, sirs'. More out of respect for our citizenship than our snooker prowess. Afterwards you may retire to the members' bar for a tipple after your sporting exertions.

Matt Simmonds, UK

Tours

Various tours are booked through the Tourist Office. A trip to Tiger Hill to catch the sunrise costs Rs 18. A half-day local sightseeing tour is the same price. There is a round-trip tour to Murik for Rs 38, but this is a restricted area for foreigners despite its Tourist Lodge. Tours are also operated to Kalimpong and Gangtok.

Places to Stay

There are a great number of places to stay in Darjeeling; those that follow are only a limited selection. Prices vary widely with the season; as far as possible those listed are for high season. In the low season middle-range places costing Rs 250 might drop to Rs 100, bottom-end places costing towards Rs 100 can drop to Rs 25 to Rs 40.

Places to Stay – bottom end

The *Youth Hostel* (tel 2290), above Dr Zakir Hussain Rd (tel 2290) right on the top of the ridge, is very popular with trekkers and other budget travellers although it's a 10-minute walk from the centre. From the railway station simply walk straight up the hill – it'll take you 15 minutes with a pack that first time! There are two rooms (Rs 25) and dormi-

tories (Rs 6 members, Rs 8 non-members). Couples can't get a room together because the manager 'doesn't want to have to ask people if they are married'! The hostel is clean and well-maintained, the manager is friendly, meals can be provided, there are cooking facilities and the rooftop view of the mountains is excellent. The hostel also rents trekking gear and keeps an informative book of trekkers' comments and suggestions.

Hotel Kadambari is down below the road near the railway station and has concrete box rooms with attached 'bathroom' (buckets of hot water delivered). Rooms are Rs 45 to Rs 50, and it's clean and run by very friendly staff. The lounge and dining room on the top floor offer excellent views across the valley. Next door the *Hotel Nirvana* is similar in quality, facilities and price and again run by friendly people.

Just beyond the post office is a cluster of cheap hotels either on Laden La Rd or on the alleys and steps running off it. Take the stone steps uphill just beyond the post office and turn right to the *Timber Lodge*. It's popular with people on a very tight budget and the manager is friendly, although the rooms are definitely on the decrepit side of rustic.

Shamrock Hotel is 100 metres further along the dirt track from the Timber Lodge. The upstairs rooms are more expensive than the downstairs ones, but this Tibetan-run place is very friendly and well kept and there is a fire at night. *Hotel Pagoda* (tel 2143) is right next door and similarly priced.

If you continued up the stone steps rather than turned off to the Timber Lodge, you'd soon come to the *Hotel Prestige*, which is not very prestigious at all but does have very small rooms with attached bathrooms and hot water. They are pretty good value at Rs 75 to Rs 90 in season. There are also cheap places along Gandi Rd such as *Puri Villa* (the Springburn Hotel) at No 70, although rooms may cost Rs 100 or more in season.

Numerous other places can be found in the vicinity.

Nabins Lodge is a small guest house just below the Youth Hostel, between Zakir Hussain Rd and A J C Bose Rd. The rooms are a bit spartan and can be cold because the guest house is on the shadowed side of the hill, but it's good value. There's another good hostel alternative just two doors up at 52 Dr Zakir Hussain Rd. If the hostel is full the warden will suggest good alternatives in the vicinity.

The West Bengal tourist department has two tourist lodges in Darjeeling plus the one at Tiger Hill. The *Maple Tourist Bungalow* is their cheaper Darjeeling one. In season singles are Rs 75, doubles Rs 90 to Rs 120. The rooms are simple but they do have hot water and there are fine views towards the Happy Valley tea estate. Out of season prices go down to Rs 30/40.

At Tiger Hill near Ghoom you can stay at the *Tourist Lodge* to watch the sunrise over Kanchenjunga next morning. Including dinner, a dorm bed costs Rs 21 or a double Rs 65. Advance booking is advisable – either ring the lodge direct (tel 2813) or contact the Tourist Office.

At the lower end of the middle-price range the *Tara Hotel* has unexceptional rooms from Rs 100 to Rs 150 in season. It's at 125 Gandhi Rd, beside the steps which run up to Gandhi Rd from Laden La Rd by the post office. Another middle-priced place is the *Swiss Hotel* (tel 2265), also on Gandhi Rd.

Places to Stay – top end

Just beyond Chowrasta on the slopes of Observatory Hill, the *Windamere Hotel* (tel 2841) on Bhanu Sarani (The Mall) is a wonderfully eccentric old Raj-era place. Including all meals, rooms are Rs 396 single, Rs 566 double.

Hotel Bellevue (tel 2129) overlooks the square at Chowrasta; there's always plenty to see from the rooms. You can even see Kanchenjunga right from your room if it's clear. In season prices are Rs 150/300, rather lower in the off season when you can get a single for Rs 90. It's a friendly, well-run place, possibly worth a splurge.

At the *Central Hotel* (tel 2033), centrally located on Robertson Rd, rooms are Rs 200/300. In the off season the hot water is a long way short of reliable, but the staff are helpful and the food is very good. Including all meals, rooms at the *New Elgin Hotel* (tel 2182) on H D Lama Rd are Rs 285/425. Rooms have fireplaces and they'll even put a hot water bottle in your bed at night. At the top of the Darjeeling price scale there's *Sinclair's Hotel* (tel 2930), 18/1 Gandhi Rd, where singles are Rs 400 to Rs 450, doubles Rs 620 to Rs 675, again including all meals. It's advertised as the only hotel in Darjeeling with central heating!

The *Tourist Lodge* (tel 2611-3), Bhanu Sarani (The Mall) is on the slopes of Observatory Hill, just beyond the Windamere Hotel, and is managed by the West Bengal Tourist Department. Including breakfast and dinner, singles are around Rs 160 to Rs 300, doubles Rs 225 to Rs 325. Prices are lower in the off season. It's not a particularly inviting building but many people stay here.

A little downhill from Chowrasta along Nehru Rd, the *Darjeeling Club* (formerly the *Tea Planters' Club*) is another Raj leftover. In season singles/doubles are Rs 300/500 including three meals and morning and afternoon tea. There's a billiard room, a musty library, fires in the bedrooms and lots of pleasant sitting areas. It's all run with considerable old-fashioned style and children are welcome.

Places to Eat

There are numerous cheap restaurants, a number of them Tibetan-run, including the very popular *Himalaya Restaurant* on Laden La Rd opposite the State Bank of India. Meals cost under Rs 10 at this small place. A little further uphill towards Chowrasta, the *Shabnam Restaurant* (also known as the 'Grub Pub') is another popular little travellers' centre. Service can be slow but the food is good – try the Tibetan bread. Both these places are good for breakfast.

A short diversion downhill from Laden La Rd will bring you to the *New Dish Restaurant*, a straightforward place with the usual non-vegetarian Indian menu and quite good food. Their sizzling chicken really sizzles, but talk about tough!

Continue up Laden La Rd, and at the junction with Nehru Rd and Robertson Rd is *Keventer's Snack Bar*, upstairs above the shop. It's a good place for breakfast – they've got ham, bacon, sausages, cheese, and other unusual delicacies from their own farm. Across the road – on Nehru Rd overlooking the small square – is the *Dekevas Restaurant*. It's a neat, clean, shiny little place with great pizzas for Rs 10 to Rs 20 (ideal for a quick Indian escape) and other food in the same price bracket.

Continue uphill again and you soon come to *Glenary's*, an excellent place with surprisingly reasonable prices and a definite ghost-of-the-Raj air to it. There's a bakery shop underneath it. Across the road, and right behind the Bellevue Hotel on Chowrasta, is the *Snow Lion Restaurant* with more expensive but very good Chinese and Tibetan food.

On Chowrasta itself the *Chowrasta Restaurant* is an open-air restaurant with south Indian vegetarian food. Retreating back downhill, there are several cheap restaurants and Indian sweet shops in the cheap hotel area around the GPO. They include the *Washington Restaurant, Beni's, Lhasa Restaurant, Penang Restaurant* (how on earth did that name get here?) and others.

Moving up-market, the new Valentino Hotel has the very pleasant *New Embassy Chinese Restaurant* with an extensive menu. If you're staying at the Youth Hostel and don't want to make the trek into town, the *Ratna Restaurant* and the *Little Corner Restaurant* are two good

little places nearby. Finally, if you simply want to be put off food altogether, check the meat market directly behind the Kalimpong Motor Syndicate at the Cart Rd Motor Stand – it's enough to turn anybody vegetarian!

Getting There
Kurseong is the usual mid-trip halting place between Siliguri on the plains and Darjeeling. If you want to overnight there, the *Tourist Lodge* (tel 409) has doubles for Rs 100; or there is the much cheaper *Jeet Hotel*.

Air The nearest airport to Darjeeling is at Bagdogra down on the plains near Siliguri, about 90 km from Darjeeling. From Bagdogra you can get to Darjeeling either by rail or road. There are daily flights by Indian Airlines between Calcutta and Bagdogra. The fares is Rs 421 and the journey takes 55 minutes. There's also a daily flight from New Delhi to Bagdogra via Patna, and a direct New Delhi flight most days of the week. Fares to or from Badogra are New Delhi Rs 1119 and Patna Rs 386.

Indian Airline offices in the Darjeeling area are at Siliguri (tel 21201), Kalimpong (tel 241), Darjeeling (tel 2355) and Bagdogra Airport (tel 20366).

If you fly into *and* out of Bagdogra then you are exempted from the permit requirements for Darjeeling. On arrival at Bagdogra your passport will automatically be endorsed for a 15-day visit to Darjeeling. Flying into and out of Bagdogra does not exempt you from the permit requirements for Sikkim.

Rail See the Siliguri section for rail details to or from Calcutta and other centres. You can make reservations at the Darjeeling station for trains out of New Jalpaiguri. Although a bus or taxi is the fastest means of getting from New Jalpaiguri or Siliguri up to Darjeeling, the most interesting way of doing this last stage of the journey is to take the 'toy train', even though this will add at least three hours to the journey.

Toy Train The journey to Darjeeling from New Jalpaiguri or Siliguri on the famous miniature railway is a superb experience which shouldn't be missed, even though it does take much longer than the buses.

Officially there are two or three departures in either direction daily, but in practice there can be more and the departures from New Jalpaiguri don't necessarily follow the official timetable (though they usually do from Darjeeling). Fares are Rs 12 in 2nd class, Rs 75 in 1st. The journey takes seven hours and you stop en route long enough to grab something to eat. If you can't face the whole trip, you can simply make the short excursion between Ghoom and Darjeeling. If you walk up to Tiger Hill, near Ghoom, to watch the Himalayan dawn, you can then ride the toy train back.

Until the late 1800s, all supplies for Darjeeling and all exports from the town had to be transported by bullock cart along the Siliguri road. This road, which is still known as the Hill Cart Rd, was so called because its gradient is such that even bullock carts could climb it. Naturally, this form of transportation was slow and expensive. Rice which sold in Siliguri for Rs 98 a ton fetched Rs 240 a ton by the time it reached Darjeeling.

The idea of a railway to Darjeeling was put forward by Franklin Prestage, an agent working for the Eastern Bengal Railway, in 1870. The scheme was accepted and construction begun in 1879. It was completed in 1881, and in 1885 a further km extension was added to take the line into the market area (now in disuse). Later on, in 1914, it was further extended south towards Kishanganj close to the Nepalese border to cope with the transport of jute and, in 1915, from Siliguri to 15 km beyond Sevok on the way to Kalimpong. The cost of the original section to Darjeeling was Rs 1,700,000 including rolling stock.

The whole line is an ingenious feat of engineering and includes four complete loops and five switchbacks, some of which were added after the initial construction had been completed to ease the line's gradient at certain points. One of the most important additions was the Batasia loop on the final descent into Darjeeling. Altogether, there are 132 unmanned level crossings!

Bus Most of the buses from Darjeeling depart from the Bazaar Bus Stand (Cart Rd). Most jeeps and taxis depart from the Motor Stand, Robertson Rd/Laden La Rd. There are many different companies operating buses, jeeps and taxis. Buses to Calcutta, Kathmandu and other points further afield generally go through Siliguri; see that section for further details.

New Jalpaiguri/Siliguri There are numerous buses, jeeps and taxis in either direction daily between 6 am and 10 pm. The journey takes 3½ to four hours by bus (sometimes less) and costs from Rs 11 from Siliguri, slightly more from New Jalpaiguri. A taxi will cost Rs 30 to Rs 40.

Bagdogra There is a bus to connect with flights from Bagdogra. The fare is Rs 30 and the trip takes about 3½ hours.

Kalimpong Land-Rovers, taxis and buses make this three-hour trip regularly. The Land-Rovers cost Rs 20 and are so much more convenient than the buses that they're worth the extra expense. Land-Rovers and buses go from the Bazar Motor Stand, taxis from the Robertson Rd/Laden La taxi stand. Your permit for Kalimpong will be checked by the military at Teesta bridge. The road as far as Teesta is rough in parts, but from there to Kalimpong it's in good shape.

Gangtok If you don't want to go by taxi or jeep, there is only one bus line to Gangtok. This is run by Sikkim Nationalised Transport (SNT), which has its Darjeeling office in the first building below the GPO on Laden La Rd (it's unmarked). There is one minibus daily in either direction, and as there are few seats available, early booking is essential. The bus departs at 8 am, takes seven hours and costs Rs 35. Your permit will be inspected before you cross the bridge at Rangpo, and at Rangpo itself you will have to visit the police station to fill in the visitors' book. On the way out your permit will be collected at Rangpo.

Other Places Deluxe buses are available to Calcutta (Rs 98), Patna (Rs 81), Gauhati (Rs 108), Shillong (Rs 140), Silchar (Rs 200) and Agartala (Rs 248).

Kathmandu Several companies operate buses between Darjeeling and Kathmandu. You might start from Darjeeling at 7.30 am, arrive at the border (Kakarbitta) around 5 pm, drive through the night and arrive Kathmandu around 7 am the next morning. There are also some services which overnight in Kakarbitta and travel to Kathmandu by day. Fares vary with the company, with the bus and with day and night services, but are typically around Rs 115 to Rs 125.

With some services you take a bus to Siliguri and a jeep from there to the border, and then catch the Kathmandu bus. Hotels are available at the border town, but these days most buses travel overnight. There is no Nepalese consulate in Darjeeling; the nearest one is in Calcutta, but seven-day visas are available at the border and can be extended in Kathmandu.

It's just as easy to make the three stages (Darjeeling-Siliguri, Siliguri-border, border-Kathmandu) yourself. Not only does it cost much less, you get a choice of buses from the border and you have the option of overnighting there or along the way.

Avalanches can sometimes delay the bus. A traveller's experience of the Darjeeling-Kathmandu trip during the monsoon:

. . . . took us three days to do the trip due to the landslides and bridges being destroyed. Got some incredible shots of us wading through thigh-deep water in swirling, full-flowing rivers to get across and hopefully find another bus to the next disaster. Never again!

TREKS IN THE DARJEELING REGION

The best months to trek in this region are April, May, October and November. There may be occasional showers during April and May but, in a way, this is the best time to go as many shrubs are in flower, particularly the rhododendrons. There may be occasional rains during the first half of October if the monsoon is prolonged. November is generally dry and visibility excellent during the first half of December, though it's usually cold by then. After the middle of December there are occasional snowfalls.

In planning what clothes to take with you, bear in mind that you will be passing through valley bottoms as low as 300 metres and over mountain ridges as high as 4000 metres, so you'll need clothing for low, tropical climates and high mountain passes. No matter what time of year you go, it's a good idea to take a light raincoat which can be folded up and put inside your rucksack since the weather may be unpredictable, particularly at high altitudes.

Trek 1

Darjeeling – Rimbik – Raman – Phalut – Sandakphu – Rimbik – Bijanbari – Darjeeling

This is currently one of the most popular treks and is documented by numerous travellers in the Youth Hostel's trekking book. It offers fine mountain views and avoids too much climbing, and some food is available along the route.

Buses now run as far as Rimbik from Darjeeling; the trip takes five hours and costs Rs 12. Chetak, Monokamana and the Government of West Bengal all operate buses there. From Rimbik it's a half-hour walk to the very popular *Shiva Pradhan Hotel* which charges Rs 8 for a bed, another Rs 8 for dinner. Other accommodation is available in Rimbik as well, and if you need supplies there is a small bazaar.

From Rimbik you can walk to Raman in four hours. The trek starts level, then drops steeply for a km to Shirikhola River. After crossing the river the trail is more or less level for nine km to Raman, where there is a Youth Hostel.

It's three km from Raman to the Raman River, which is crossed by a bridge. The walk takes you through dense forests of rhododendrons, silver firs, chestnuts, oaks, magnolias and hemlocks. From the river there's a steep ascent along a forest bridle path for the remaining 11 km to Phalut. The day's walk takes six to seven hours. At Phalut there's a Dak Bungalow and on a clear day you can see both Kanchenjunga and Everest. Nepal, Sikkim and West Bengal meet at this point.

The third day of the trek starts with a steep zig-zag descent from Phalut. The next 13 km are fairly level before the final steep ascent to Sandakphu. The day's walk again takes six to seven hours. There is another Dak Bungalow at Sandakphu and the views are similar to Phalut. Kanchenjunga is only 144 km from here as the crow flies. Day four takes you back to Rimbik, but rather than bus back from there to Darjeeling you can continue to Jhepi and bus back via Bijanbari. The next day's walk begins with a fairly steep descent over about eight km to the bridge across the Lodoma River. After this the path levels out and passes through cultivated land until it reaches Jhepi Bungalow, 17 km from Rimbik. From Jhepi the road climbs some 150 metres over two km to a spur on which Kaijali sits, and then drops down to Bijanbari six km further on. You can either take a jeep from here to Darjeeling 36 km away, or walk there via Pulbazar and Singtam.

The bus from Jhepi to Bijanbari is irregular; you may have to walk. If the only hotel/restaurant in 'town' is full you can stay for free at the government *Haryana Bhawan* – very basic but nobody complains. The key (no one lives there) can be borrowed from the shop on the corner diagonally opposite the hotel/restaurant in the main street. A bus back to Darjeeling from Bijanbari costs Rs 15.

Trek 2

Darjeeling – Manaybhanjang – Tonglu – Sandakphu – Phalut and return (118 km to Sandakphu and 160 km to Phalut return)

This is another good trek with excellent views of Kanchenjunga and Everest. The route passes through superb tropical countryside.

On the first day, either walk or take a jeep or taxi to Manaybhanjang, 26 km from Darjeeling. The first day's walk to Tonglu is a fairly steep climb of 11 km via a succession of zig-zags all the way up to the bungalow. Tonglu looks directly on Darjeeling and commands an excellent view of Kanchenjunga.

The next day's walk to Sandakphu covers 22 km and initially passes through bamboo thickets with many ascents and descents until Kalapokhri is reached. About five hours should be allowed for this part of the trek. The last part up to Sandakphu bungalow involves a steep climb and should take about three hours. The mountain views from here are excellent. You can either continue on to Phalut from Sandakphu or return to Darjeeling. This last stage to Phalut and back is as on Trek 1.

It's possible to return to Manaybhanjang from Phalut in one day if you start out early enough (allow about eight hours of continuous walking), or you can return in two days at a more leisurely pace by breaking the journey at Tonglu.

Due to disrepair of the accommodation at Tonglu, most people now turn west from Meghma and walk the extra five km to Javbari in Nepal – no problems about the border.

Trek 3

Darjeeling – Manaybhanjang – Tonglu – Sandakphu – Phalut – Raman – Rimbik – Jhepi – Darjeeling via Bijanbari (153 km in total)

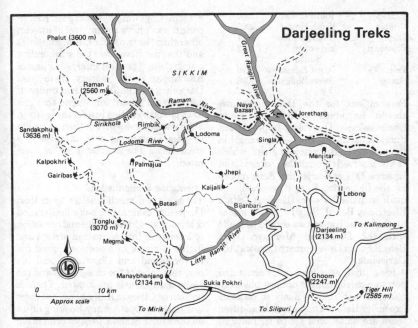

Darjeeling Treks

The first part of this trek up to Phalut follows the same route as in Trek 2. The second part from Phalut through Rimbik to Bijanbari is the same as Trek 1.

Trek 4

Darjeeling – Manaybhanjang – Tonglu – Sandakphu – Phalut – Raman – Rimbik – Palmajua – Batasi – Manaybhanjang – Darjeeling (178 km in total)

This trek initially follows the same route as Trek 3 as far as Rimbik. From Rimbik to Palmajua is about 14 km with views of Kanchenjunga all the way. A further 11 km takes you to Batasi along a track which ascends steadily to Deorali and then descends, gradually at first and steeply towards the end, to Batasi. The next day's walk takes you over the final 14 km to Manaybhanjang, where you can either take a jeep or walk to Darjeeling.

Places to Stay

There are an adequate number of bunga-lows and Youth Hostels along the trekking routes though, if possible, advance reservations should be made for the bungalows before you leave Darjeeling. This isn't necessary with the Youth Hostels. The bungalows are fairly well furnished and have cooking equipment, sheets and blankets. Firewood can be bought from the chowkidar. The Youth Hostels provide, as you might expect, somewhat more basic accommodation and usually only have mattresses and blankets, though some do have basic cooking equipment. Bungalows and Youth Hostels are located in the following places:

place	accommodation	meters
Manaybhan-jang	Youth Hostel	2134
Jorepokhri	Dak Bungalow	2256
Tonglu	Dak Bungalow	3070
Sandakphu	Youth Hostel	3636
	Dak Bungalow	
Phalut	Dak Bungalow	3600

Raman	Youth Hostel	2560
Rimbik	Youth Hostel	2286
Jhepi	Dak Bungalow	1624
Bijanbari	Inspection Bungalow	762
Palmajua	Forest Bungalow	2210
Batasi	Forest Bungalow	2098

Reservations for the Dak Bungalows should be made with the Deputy Commissioner, Darjeeling Improvement Fund Department, Darjeeling, except in the case of the Bungalow at Jhepi, which can be reserved through the District Land Revenue Officer, Darjeeling. Reservations for the Inspection Bungalows should be made with the Divisional Engineer, State Electricity Board, Siliguri. Reservations for the Forest Bungalows should be made with the Divisional Manager, West Bengal Forest Development Corporation, Darjeeling.

Rice, dhal, eggs, chicken, onions and potatoes can be bought at most places en route, though they're likely to be more expensive than in Darjeeling. In addition there are small chai shops en route at Sandakphu, Meghma, Garibas, Rimbik, Jhepi, Lodoma and Bijanbari. If you would be happy with this kind of diet then you need carry no food with you. If not, then take your own supplies from Darjeeling.

Before you go on any of these treks you're advised to browse through the Darjeeling Youth Hostel's book in which trekkers write their comments about the routes.

KALIMPONG

Kalimpong is a quiet little bazaar town set amongst the rolling foothills and deep valleys of the Himalaya at an altitude of 1250 metres. It was once part of the lands belonging to the Rajas of Sikkim until the beginning of the 18th century, when it was taken from them by the Bhutanese. In the 19th century it passed into the hands of the British and thus became part of West Bengal.

Though its name conjures up images of a fascinating Himalayan outpost, Kalimpong doesn't have a great deal of interest other than the two Buddhist monasteries and the fine views over the surrounding countryside. The most interesting part of Kalimpong is the journey there from Darjeeling via the Teesta River bridge. If you have no permit for Sikkim then the town is worth visiting just for the journey, but if you do have a permit then you could by-pass Kalimpong without missing a great deal. The market here is over-rated.

Orientation & Information

Though it's a much smaller town than Darjeeling, Kalimpong has a similar kind of lay-out, straddling a ridge and consisting of a series of interconnected streets and flights of steps. Life centres around the Motor Stand and Chowrasta, and it's here that most of the cheap cafés and the really cheap hotels are located. There is no Tourist Office in Kalimpong, but there is a Railway Out-Agency Booking office on the Motor Stand where you can make reservations.

Monasteries

The Tharpa Choling Monastery belongs to the Yellow Hat sect (Geluk-pa) of Tibetan Buddhism founded in Tibet in the 14th century and to which the Dalai Lama belongs. The monastery was founded in 1937, though it looks like it has been on the decline for centuries.

Lower down the hill, the Thongsa Gompa or Bhutanese Monastery is the oldest monastery in the area and was founded in 1692. Unlike the Tharpa Choling Monastery, it obviously has some enthusiastic benefactors as it has been repainted and restored and looks very prosperous.

Flower Nurseries

Kalimpong is an important orchid-growing area and flowers are exported from here to many cities in northern India. The Sri Ganesh Moni Pradhan Nursery, the

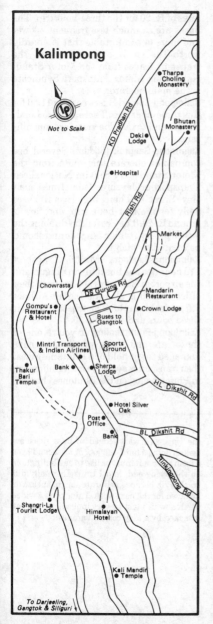

Kalimpong

Not to Scale

Tharpa Choling Monastery

Bhutan Monastery

Deki Lodge

Hospital

KD Pradhan Rd

Rishi Rd

Market

Chowrasta

DS Gurung Rd

Mandarin Restaurant

Gompu's Restaurant & Hotel

Crown Lodge

Buses to Gangtok

Mintri Transport & Indian Airlines

Sports Ground

Bank

Sherpa Lodge

Thakur Bari Temple

HL Dikshit Rd

Hotel Silver Oak

Post Office

Bank

BL Dikshit Rd

Rinkingpong Rd

Shangri-La Tourist Lodge

Himalayan Hotel

Kali Mandir Temple

To Darjeeling, Gangtok & Siliguri

Standard Nursery and the Sri L B Pradhan Nursery are among the most important in the area.

The Market

The market is over-rated and not worth a special journey to Kalimpong. There's nothing for sale that you can't find in either Darjeeling or Gangtok.

Places to Stay – bottom end

The majority of the really cheap places on the far side of the Motor Stand look like the ceiling would fall on your head if you raised your voice and can't really be recommended. They're certainly cheap, but before you try them, ask at *Gompu's Hotel & Restaurant* on Chowrasta. They have a few rooms above the restaurant with good views of the street life outside. Singles/doubles are Rs 25/40. The *Venus Hotel*, right by the Motor Stand, is rock bottom in price but reasonably habitable.

The *Crown Lodge* is a few metres down a side street off Ongden Rd and visible from the Motor Stand. The rooms are clean, pleasantly furnished and have a fan and attached bathrooms. They also have amazingly immaculate electrical wiring! Singles/doubles are Rs 44/88. *Sherpa Lodge*, overlooking the playing field, is also fairly good and has rooms at Rs 20/40.

Deki Lodge is away from the centre towards the Tharpa Choling Monastery. Run by a Tibetan woman, it's a simple but clean place with rooms with common bathroom facilities for Rs 15/30. Finally, the popular *Shangri La Tourist Lodge* (tel 230) is just off the Darjeeling road on the Darjeeling side of town. Doubles are Rs 50 and there's a Rs 11 dormitory.

Places to Stay – top end

The rustic old *Himalayan Hotel* (tel 248) is on the right-hand side up the hill just past the post office. The former home of a British Tibet trader named David MacDonnel who wrote *20 Years in Tibet* and *Land of the Lamas*, it's expensive at

Rs 80/170 plus 10% but is an interesting place to stay. Meals are available; dinner costs Rs 25. There's not even running water here, but they bring you drinking water and a bucket of hot water when you want to wash.

The modern new *Hotel Silver Oaks* (tel 296) is between the town centre and the post office and has rooms at Rs 285/390 including meals.

Places to Eat
Gompu's Restaurant, Chowrasta is a pleasant restaurant with friendly staff. They serve Tibetan, Indian and Chinese food and western breakfasts (omelettes, toast and so on). Good food but 'stick to the Chinese dishes', recommended one traveller.

The *Usha Restaurant* is a tiny and very friendly chai shop between the Crown Lodge and the Motor Stand, with simple food. The *Mandarin Restaurant* on the Motor Stand does Chinese food. There are plenty of other cafés along Main Rd.

Getting There
Kalimpong-Darjeeling There are frequent Land-Rovers in either direction with fares of Rs 20 for the three-hour trip. The buses are so much less frequent, slower and more uncomfortable that it's hardly worth the small cost saving. All the transport leaves from the Motor Stand. Kalimpong Motor Transport Syndicate is the main operator.

Kalimpong-Siliguri Buses cost Rs 11.50 for this three-hour trip. There are also Land-Rovers and taxis. The views are magnificent.

Kalimpong-Gangtok (Sikkim) Several bus companies operate this route from the Motor Stand – try Sikkim Nationalised Transport or Jayshree (sometimes spelt 'Joy Shree'). There are several buses daily for the four-hour trip, and fare is around Rs 20. They're fond of dubbing the buses 'luxury', which is a joke and should be treated as such.

Kalimpong-Bagdogra Mintri Transport Ltd operates one bus daily to Siliguri and the airport at Bagdogra at 8 am from their office (which is also the Indian Airlines office) on Main Rd. The trip takes about three hours and costs Rs 30.

Kalimpong-Phuntsholing If you're one of those rare and lucky people who have managed to get hold of a Bhutanese visa, then transport is available from Kalimpong to Phuntsholing on the Bhutanese border.

Tony's Notebook

Beware of Cows
You walk by cows a dozen times a day in India. In Varanasi you can make that 100 times a day. Once I'd got used to their presence in places where cows would hardly be expected in the west, I hardly gave them a second thought. Until one day in Varanasi one of them suddenly wheeled its head round and jabbed me in the ribs with its horn. I couldn't get out of the way, as I was wedged in by a rickshaw wallah doing a hard-sell job. For a second I got a flash of what it must be like to be a bullfighter on the losing end, and I think I actually did crack a rib because it hurt to laugh, sneeze or lie down for the next week. I give cows a wider berth now; it must be very inauspicious to get attacked by a holy cow in Varanasi.

Calcutta Top: The Howrah Bridge over the Hooghly River, Calcutta (TW)
Bottom: Billboards along Chowringhee, Calcutta (TW)

West Bengal Top: The Toy Train to Darjeeling (MC)
Bottom: The Bhutan Gompa in Kalimpong (TW)

Sikkim

Population: 250,000
Area: 7214 square km
Capital: Gangtok
Main language: Nepali

Until fairly recently Sikkim ('New House') was an independent kingdom, though in treaty relations with the Indian government which allowed the latter to control Sikkim's foreign affairs and defence. In 1975, however, following a period of political crises and riots in the capital, Gangtok, India annexed the country and Sikkim became the 22nd Indian state. The move was far from universally popular at the time, though tensions have now cooled and the central government has been spending relatively large amounts of money to subsidise road building, electrification, water supply, and agricultural and industrial development. India's motivation for much of this activity was undoubtedly its fear of Chinese military designs in the Himalayan region, and even today you'll see a lot of military activity going on along the route from Darjeeling to Gangtok.

For many years, Sikkim was regarded as one of the last Himalayan 'Shangri Las' because of its remoteness, spectacular mountain terrain, varied flora and fauna and ancient Buddhist monasteries. It was never easy to get to, and even now a special permit must be obtained from the central government before a visit can be made. This requirement will probably continue for the foreseeable future, but it's becoming more and more a formality as tourism is promoted. Foreign visitors are now permitted to trek up into the remote Dzongri region of western Sikkim but further permission is needed from Delhi and, for the present at least, much of eastern Sikkim along the Tibetan border remains out of bounds.

History

The country was originally peopled by the Lepchas, a tribal people thought to have migrated from the hills of Assam around the 13th century. The Lepchas were forest foragers and small-patch cultivators who worshipped nature spirits and were a pacific people in temperament. They still make up some 18% of the total population of Sikkim, though their ability to lead their traditional life style has been severely limited due to immigration from Tibet and, more recently, from Nepal.

The Tibetans started to emigrate into Sikkim during the 15th and 16th centuries due to religious strife between the various Lamaist sects at that time. In Tibet itself the Yellow Hat sect – the Geluk-pa, to which the Dalai Lama belongs – gradually gained the upper hand whereas in Sikkim the Red Hat sect – Nyingma-pa – remained in control and was, until the country became a part of India, the official state religion. Though the Lepchas originally retreated to the more remote regions in the face of the waves of Tibetan immigrants, a blood brotherhood was eventually engineered between their leader, Thekong Tek, and the Bhutias leader, Khye-Bumsa, and the heavy hand of spiritual and temporal authority was imposed on the anarchistic Lepchas. The union generated a good deal of suspicion between the two groups, particularly when the Lepchas were persuaded to bring all their literature and totems to a ceremony, where they were destroyed by the Tibetans. Having imposed control over the Lepchas, the Dalai Lama in Lhasa appointed Penchoo Namgyal as the first king of Sikkim in 1641. At this time the country included the whole of the area bounded by the present state plus a part of eastern Nepal, the Chumbi Valley (Tibet), the Ha Valley (Bhutan) and the Terai foothills from the present border down to the plains of India, including Darjeeling and Kalimpong.

Between 1717 and 1734, during the reign of the fourth king, a series of wars was fought with the Bhutanese which resulted in the loss of much territory in the southern foothills including Kalimpong, then a very important bazaar town on the trade route leading from Tibet to India. More territory was lost after 1780 following the Gurkha invasion from Nepal, though the invaders were eventually checked by a Chinese army with Bhutanese and Lepcha assistance. Unable to advance into Tibet, the Gurkhas turned south and came into conflict with the British East India Company. A series of wars was fought between the two parties, ending in the treaty of 1817 whereby the borders of Nepal were delineated, and the Gurkhas ceded to the British all the Sikkimese territory they had taken. A substantial part of this territory was returned to the Raja of Sikkim in return for control by the British of all disputes between Sikkim and its neighbours. The country thus became a buffer state between Nepal, Tibet and Bhutan.

In 1835, the British, seeking a hill station as a rest-and-recreation centre for its troops and officials, persuaded and pressured the Raja into ceding the Darjeeling area in return for an annual stipend. The Tibetans objected to this transfer of territory as they continued to regard Sikkim as a vassal state, and Darjeeling's rapid growth as a trade centre began to make a considerable impact on the fortunes of the leading lamas and merchants of Sikkim. Tensions rose and in 1849 a high-ranking British official and a botanist, who were exploring the Lachen region with the permission both of the Sikkimese Raja and the British government, were arrested. Following threats of intervention, the two prisoners were unconditionally released a month later, but the British annexed the whole of the area between the present Sikkimese border and the Indian plains and withdrew the Raja's stipend (the latter was eventually restored to his son).

Further British interference in the affairs of this area led to the declaration of a protectorate over Sikkim in 1861 and the delineation of its borders. The Tibetans, however, continued to regard all these actions as illegal and in 1886 invaded Sikkim to reassert their authority. They were thrown back by the British, and a military expedition was sent to Lhasa in 1888 as a punitive measure. The powers of the Sikkim Raja were further reduced, and high-handed treatment by the British officials prompted him to flee to Lhasa in 1892, though he was eventually persuaded to return.

Keen to develop the area, the British encouraged immigration from Nepal, as they had done in Darjeeling, and a considerable amount of land was brought under rice and cardamom cultivation. As a result of this influx of labour, which was still going on right up until the 1960s, the Nepalese constitute some 75% of the population of Sikkim. The subject became a heated topic of discussion in the late '60s and the Raja was constrained to prohibit further immigration. Further steps were taken to placate those of non-

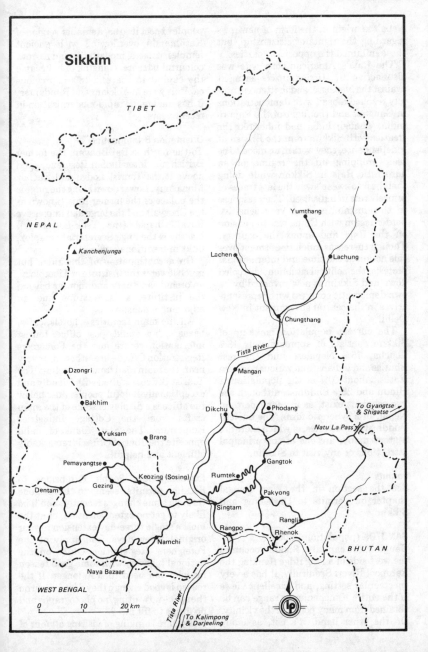

Sikkim

TIBET

NEPAL

▲ Kanchenjunga

Yumthang

Lachen ●

● Lachung

Chungthang

Tista River

● Dzongri

● Bakhim

● Yuksam

● Brang

Pemayangtse ●

Keozing (Sosing)

Dentam

Gezing

Namchi

Naya Bazaar

WEST BENGAL

0   10   20 km

Mangan

Dikchu

● Phodang

To Gyangtse
& Shigatse

Natu La Pass

Rumtek ●

Gangtok

Pakyong

Singtam

Rangli

Rangpo

Rhenok

BHUTAN

Tista River

To Kalimpong
& Darjeeling

Nepalese origin in the form of new laws regarding the rights of citizenship, but these inflamed the opposition parties.

The Raja's American-born wife was also active in stirring up resentment against the Nepalese, and matters eventually reached a head with demonstrations in Gangtok and the flight of the Raja to India. Though India had inherited the treaties with Sikkim from the British at independence, they were in no mood to be seen propping up the regime of an autocratic Raja in Sikkim while doing their best to sweep away the last traces of princely rule in India itself. Their response to this instability in a very sensitive border region with China was to pension off the Raja and annex the country. Though there was much resentment over this action at the time and international protests, the political situation has cooled down and Sikkim is now governed by its own democratic congress with representatives in the central government in New Delhi.

The current population make-up of Sikkim consists of approximately 18% Lepcha, 75% Nepalese and the rest Bhutias and Indians from various northern states. About 60% of the population is Hindu and 28% Buddhist, although the two religions exist, as in many parts of Nepal, in a syncretic form. The ancient Buddhist monasteries, of which there are a great many, are one of the principal attractions of any visit to Sikkim.

Permits
See the section in the West Bengal chapter on permits to Darjeeling and Sikkim.

GANGTOK (population 14,000)
Gangtok, the capital of Sikkim, occupies the west side of a long ridge flanking the Ranipool River. Scenically, it has a very spectacular setting, and excellent views of the entire Kanchenjunga range can be obtained from many points in the vicinity. On the other hand, it's not, as many

people expect it to be, a smaller version of Kathmandu overflowing with ancient temples, palaces, monasteries and narrow, colourful bazaars. Gangtok only became the capital in the mid-1800s; previous capitals were at Yoksam and Rabdantse. It has undergone rapid modernisation in recent years.

Orientation & Information
To the north is Raj Bhavan, the former British and later Indian Residency, and above it the Tourist Lodge and Enchey Monastery. Lower down along the ridge is the palace of the former Raja (known as the Chogyal) and the large and impressive Royal Chapel (the Tsuk-La-Khang). Nearby is the huge Secretariat complex, built in traditional style.

On a continuation of this ridge but much lower is the Institute of Tibetology, an orchid sanctuary and, not far beyond the institute, a large stupa and an adjoining monastery.

All the main facilities – hotels, cafés, bazaars, bus stand, post office, tourist information centre and the Foreigners Registration Office – are either on, or very near, the main road from Darjeeling. The Tourist Office is staffed with friendly and exceptionally helpful people. Just below the office is a display of some of the main crafts from the Cottage Industries Emporium. The State Bank of India opposite the Tourist Office is remarkably efficient and helpful.

Extending Your Permit Extensions to Sikkim permits seem to have gone through some changes recently. You'll be likely to get no extension at all, or at the most a single three-day extension to your original seven days. You apply at the Foreigners' Registration Office on the national highway with some good reason for why you need to stay longer. If the reason is good enough they do it for you on the spot – no waiting, no photographs and no forms to fill in.

If you're thinking of visiting all four of

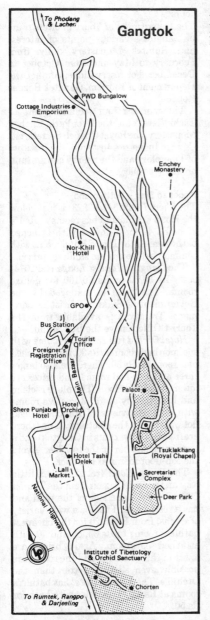

Gangtok

To Phodang & Lacher,

PWD Bungalow

Cottage Industries Emporium

Enchey Monastery

Nor-Khill Hotel

GPO

Bus Station

Tourist Office

Foreigner's Registration Office

Main Bazaar

Palace

Shere Punjab Hotel

Hotel Orchid

Tsuklakhang (Royal Chapel)

Hotel Tashi Delek

Lall Market

Secretariat Complex

Deer Park

National Highway

Institute of Tibetology & Orchid Sanctuary

Chorten

To Rumtek, Rangpo & Darjeeling

the most famous monasteries in Sikkim – Rumtek, Pemayangtse, Tashiding and Phodang – you'll need *at least* one week and probably longer because the bus schedules prevent you from returning on the same day. If you're travelling to places in Sikkim away from Gangtok, it's wise to bring some food and, more important, drink with you.

Tsuk-La-Khang

The Royal Chapel is the principal place of worship and assembly of the Buddhists and the repository of a large collection of scriptures. It's a beautiful and impressive building; its interior is covered with murals, and lavishly decorated altars hold images of the Buddha, Bodhisattvas and Tantric deities. There are also a great many fine woodcarvings. It's not always open to visitors, particularly in the off season, and no photography is allowed inside.

The chapel is the site for important festivals like the mid-September one to the god of Kanchenjunga, and the New Year celebration when the famous Black Hat dance demonstrates the triumph of good over evil.

Namgyalk Institute of Tibetology

Established in 1958 and built in traditional style, this unique institute promotes research on the language and traditions of Tibet as well as on Mahayana Buddhism. It has one of the world's largest collection of books and rare manuscripts on the subject of Mahayana Buddhism, plus many religious works of art and a collection of astonishingly beautiful and incredibly finely executed silk-embroidered *thankas*. The director of the institute is a very friendly man who will spend time showing you around if you care to approach him. The institute is open 10 am to 4 pm, Monday to Saturday, and there is no entrance fee.

Orchid Sanctuary

Surrounding the institute and itself

enclosed by a peaceful forest is the Orchid Sanctuary, where many of the 454 species of orchid found in Sikkim can be seen. The best times to visit are April-May, July-August and October-November.

Chorten & Monastery

About a km beyond the institute stands a huge white chorten with a gold apex visible from many points in Gangtok. Next to it is a monastery for young lamas with a shrine containing huge images of Guru Padmasambhava, the Indian teacher of Buddhism in Tibet, and his manifestation, Guru Snang-Sid Zilzon.

Institute of Cottage Industries

High up on the main road above the town, the Cottage Industries Emporium specialises in producing hand-woven carpets, blankets, shawls, Lepcha weaves, patterned decorative paper and 'Choktse' tables, exquisitely carved in relief. It's open 9 am to 12.30 pm and 1 to 3.30 pm daily, except Sundays and every second Saturday. In addition to the shop there is a smaller display of craftwork on the ground floor of the Tourist Office.

Deer Park

This popular viewpoint is on the edge of the ridge next to the Secretariat building. In it, as you might expect, are deer and a replica of the Buddha image at Sarnath in India.

Enchey Monastery

Next to the Tourist Lodge, about three km from the centre of town, the 200-year-old Enchey Monastery is well worth a visit, particularly if you're in Gangtok when religious dances are performed in December.

Lall Market

If you've been to markets in Kathmandu or Darjeeling, this one will come as a disappointment as it has none of their colour, magic or range of products.

Tours

The Department of Tourism offers tours of Gangtok's various points of interest and Rumtek Monastery daily from February to May and from October to December. For reservations, contact the Department of Tourism, Gangtok Bazaar (tel 664).

The morning tour includes visits to Tashi View Point, the Deer Park, Enchey Monastery, the Royal Chapel, Secretariat, Cottage Industries Institute, the Institute of Tibetology and the nearby chorten and orchid sanctuary.

Places to Stay – bottom end

The *Shere Punjab* (tel 2823) is just below the Hotel Orchid and has rooms at Rs 15/25 or Rs 40 for a double with attached bathroom. At the *Doma Hotel* rooms with common bathrooms are similarly priced.

The *Gangtok Tourist Lodge* (tel 2074) costs Rs 30/50 or Rs 60/100 for deluxe rooms. The hotel is managed by the Government of Sikkim Tourist Department. Transport is available from the Tourist Office above the Bus Stand.

Hotel Orchid (tel 2381) has rooms with common bathroom for Rs 30, with attached bathroom for Rs 50. There are also larger three and four-bed rooms, and prices are lower in the off season. The place is clean and has friendly staff, attractive rooms with excellent views of Kanchenjunga, hot water when the electricity is on (there are frequent power cuts in Gangtok) and a restaurant and bar on the top floor. Avoid the top-floor rooms at the back.

The *Green Hotel* (tel 2254) is a little way up the main bazaar from the Tourist Office on the same side of the road and has a restaurant. There is a wide variety of rooms, from Rs 15/20 for the cheapest bathless rooms to Rs 30, 50 and 70 with attached bathroom. Again prices are lower in the off season and the rooms are possibly even slightly better than the Orchid's. The *Karma Hotel* has bathless rooms at Rs 15/35, doubles with bath for Rs 50.

Hotel Kanchen View (tel 2086) has dorm beds and also rooms from Rs 25 to Rs 50. Other hotels include the *Deeki Hotel* (tel 2301), the rock-bottom *Leden La Hotel* and the *Holiday Inn* (no relation to the chain).

If you can get in, the *PWD Bungalow* is high up on the National Highway beyond the Cottage Industries Emporium. There are only two double-bed rooms available at Rs 12 per person; book with the Executive Engineer, CPWD North, Sikkim Highway, Gangtok.

Places to Stay – top end
There are a surprising number of more expensive hotels in Gangtok. The centrally located *Nor-Khill Hotel* (tel 2386) has rooms at Rs 275/400 including all meals. *Hotel Tashi Delek* (tel 2038) is similarly priced with rooms at Rs 150/200 or with all meals at Rs 275/450. *Hotel Ashok Mayur* (tel 2558) is in that same price bracket, with rooms at Rs 175/225 or with all meals at Rs 275/400.

The Tibetan-run *Hotel Tibet* (tel 2523) on Stadium Rd has rooms at Rs 95/125 up to Rs 150/175 so it's really middle priced. Travellers have written to recommend it ('Best hot water in India', wrote one happy visitor) and the staff are friendly and helpful.

Places to Eat
Most restaurants are attached to the hotels, such as the Hotel Tibet's excellent *Snow Lion Restaurant*. The *Hotel Orchid's* restaurant is also popular with good chicken curry, vegetables, fried dhal and so on. In the Orchid's bar beer is cheap, a tot of Sikkimese spirit even cheaper. The *Green Hotel's* restaurant also has very good food, although not quite up to the standard of the Orchid.

The excellent *Blue Sheep Restaurant* is in the Tourist Office complex and has good food. The *Tashi Delek* has a restaurant where you can sit outside, pleasant in summer.

Other than this, there are a number of simple vegetarian cafés around the bus stand and along the main bazaar where you can obtain basic food at very low prices. About half a km uphill from the bus stand on the National Highway, where a road branches off to the stadium and Nor-Khill Hotel, there is a café which serves snacks and tea or coffee.

Try *thungba* from a chang shop in the market – a large bamboo mug full of millet to which you add hot water to get fresh chang.

Getting There
There is no airport or rail connection to Sikkim. You can get there via Darjeeling or Kalimpong, or directly from Siliguri on the plains. Sikkim Nationalised Transport (SNT) is the main bus operator to Gangtok but their buses are almost always hopelessly over-crowded.

Siliguri The trip to or from Gangtok takes about five hours; there are a half dozen or so buses a day and the fare is Rs 20 to Rs 25. Apart from SNT, buses are also operated by North Bengal Services, Apsara and other companies.

Bagdogra SNT have a daily bus connecting with flights from Bagdogra airport. The journey takes five hours.

Darjeeling SNT and North Bengal Services have buses on this route; the journey takes six or seven hours and costs Rs 35. SNT use what is probably its best minibus for this trip. The service is heavily booked so plan well in advance. If the bus is booked out you can always go via Kalimpong, as there are more buses operating Gangtok-Kalimpong and there are frequent Land-Rovers Kalimpong-Darjeeling. The road house at Rangpo, on the West Bengal-Sikkim border, is the only place you can get food between Sikkim and Darjeeling. The service is impossibly slow so perhaps it's better to bring some food with you.

Kalimpong SNT, Jayshree and Sangam operate on this route. The journey takes about four hours and costs Rs 20.

AROUND GANGTOK
Rumtek Monastery

Rumtek is visible from Gangtok on the other side of the Ranipool Valley at about the same elevation, yet it's 24 km away by road. The monastery is the seat of the Gyalwa Karmapa, the head of the Kagyu-pa sect of Tibetan Buddhism. The sect was founded in the 11th century by Lama Marpa, the disciple of the Indian guru Naropa. It later split into several sub-sects, of which the most important are Druk-pa, Kagyu-pa and Karma-pa. The teachings of the sect are orally transmitted to the disciples.

The main monastery here is a recent structure, built by the Gyalwa Karmapa strictly according to the traditional designs of his monastery in Tibet. Visitors are welcome and there's no objection to you sitting in on the prayer and chanting sessions. They'll even bring you a cup of salted butter tea when it's served to the monks. Mural work is still being done; if you're interested in Tibetan religious painting then Rumtek is a must.

If you follow the tarmac road beyond Rumtek for two or three km, off to the left through a gate is another interesting, but smaller, monastery which was restored in 1983. Opposite it is an old and run-down monastery with leather prayer wheels.

Places to Stay The *Kunga Delak Hotel & Restaurant* is off the square in front of the monastery and has rooms for Rs 15. It's dirty, there's no water (although the rooms have attached bathrooms!) and the bus will probably arrive too late in the evening to get any food. *Hotel Sangay* is 100 metres down the motor road from the monastery. It's basic but clean and blankets and candles are provided (there's no electricity most of the time). Beautifully quiet and peaceful, the Sangay is run by friendly people. The price of the rooms is negotiable but should be around Rs 10 per bed. Just below the lodge is a small chai shop which serves eggs and fresh bread in the morning, chow-chow in the evening.

Getting There There's a daily bus from Gangtok in the late afternoon for Rs 5, returning from Rumtek early the next morning. This means you have to spend at least two nights at Rumtek. The journey takes about two hours. Jeeps and Ambassador taxis are available. Count on around Rs 200 return per car. The return journey takes half a day.

Pemayangtse & Tashiding Monasteries

Pemayangtse Monastery, at a height of 2085 metres, is the second oldest monastery in Sikkim and belongs to the Nyingma-pa sect. This Tantric sect was established by the Indian teacher, Padmasambhava, in the 8th century. All of its monasteries are characterised by a prominent image of this teacher, together with two female consorts. The followers of the sect wear red caps and this monastery is the head of all others in Sikkim.

Pemayangtse is about six km from the bus terminus at Gezing, but Tashiding is a full-day hike up a ridge from Pemayangtse. The hike starts with a 1½-hour all-uphill walk to Tashiding village. The monastery itself is further up the hill near the summit but hidden by pine trees. Sangacholing monastery is also in the vicinity.

At present it appears that permits to visit Pemayangtse are very restricted.

Places to Stay For accommodation there is a choice of at least four basic lodges at Gezing for around Rs 15 a room – any number of people can share a room. Food of the rice, dhal and eggs variety is available.

If you want something slightly better, there is the *PWD Rest House* about two km up the hill from Gezing towards Pemayangtse. It's excellent value but prior booking is necessary from the CPWD in Gangtok between 9.30 am and 4.30 pm. The chowkidar cooks excellent meals for a further charge.

At Tashiding there is a *Forestry Department Bungalow* but you must

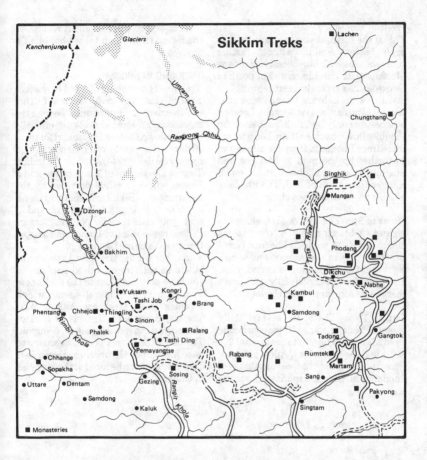

Sikkim Treks

Kanchenjunga ▲ Glaciers

Umram Chhu

Rangyong Chhu

Lachen

Chungthang

Chockhurang Chhu

Dzongri

Bakhim

Singhik

Mangan

Tista River

Phodang

Dikchu

Nabhe

Yuksam   Kongri
Tashi Job
Chhejo Thingling   Brang
Phentang   Sinom

Kambul

Samdong

Phalek

Ralang

Tadong

Gangtok

Tashi Ding
Chhange   Pemayangtse
Sopakha

Rabang

Rumtek

Martam

Uttare Dentam   Gezing Sosing

Rimbi Khola

Rangit Khola

Sang

Pakyong

Samdong

Kaluk

Singtam

■ Monasteries

bring your own blankets and sheets. To stay here you need authorisation from the Tourist Office in Gangtok or the Forestry Department in Gezing. The monastery is some 15 minutes' walk from the village. Good meals are available in the village chai shop, and if you eat there you'll have the whole village for company!

If you're looking for luxury accommodation, the *Pemayangtse Tourist Lodge* (tel 73) has rooms around Rs 200 to Rs 300 including all meals. For reservations contact the Tourist Office in Gangtok.

Getting There Between Gangtok and Gezing (sometimes spelt Geyshing) there's one bus daily in either direction leaving in the morning. The journey takes about seven to eight hours and costs Rs 30. Pemayangtse is about six km from Gezing but basic accommodation is available in Gezing if the bus is late. It's clear that a trip to Pemayangtse will take at least three days, so make sure your permit covers you for this period.

As with Rumtek, you can hire a car or jeep for the round trip for around Rs 700 to Rs 800 depending on the route taken.

Phodang Monastery

This is the furthest you are permitted to go in eastern Sikkim without further entanglement with bureaucracy. Phodang Monastery at Thumlong, 40 km north of Gangtok, has recently been rebuilt, but just above it is Labrang Gompa where the original construction is still intact. Labrang is accessible only by bridle path and you should allow about half an hour to get there from Phodang. If you're allowed to go further up the road to Mangan and Singhik, a clear, unobstructed view of Kanchenjunga can be had. The Phodang Monastery is sometimes closed.

Places to Stay The *Yak & Yeti*, along the highway to Mangan, has big, clean rooms for around Rs 15 per bed. The food here – rice, dhal, vegetables, momos and so on – is excellent and so is the *chang* and *raksi*. The people are very friendly and don't charge you any more than the locals.

Getting There There are several daily buses to Phodang, some of them continuing on to Mangan. The trip takes around 2½ hours and the fare is Rs 7. Allow plenty of time if you want to see anything of Phodang and the other monasteries in the area.

A car or jeep will cost about Rs 250 for the return trip, which takes about half a day.

TREKKING IN SIKKIM

Trekking is now being allowed in western Sikkim, but you may need a further endorsement on your permit. Though the regulations are somewhat elastic, officially you're allowed to trek to Dzongri for up to 10 days so long as: 1) you're accompanied by a travel agent recognised by the Indian Tourist Development Corporation and a liaison officer or guide provided by the government of Sikkim; 2) that you travel by air from Calcutta to Bagdogra; and 3) that you either walk Nayan Bazaar-Pemayangtse-Yoksum-Dzongri or Rangpo-Gangtok-Yaksum-Dzongri.

In other words, you have little choice but to go with an organised tour unless you have political clout in the Sikkimese bureaucracy. The travel agents which organise these treks are Yak & Yeti Travels, Snow Lion Travels or Sikkim Himalayan Adventure, all in Gangtok. The best time to trek is mid-February to late May and October to December. Trekking gear can be hired at the agencies in Gangtok.

North-East Frontier

state	capital	area (sq km)	population
Assam	Gauhati	79,500	19,200,000
Manipur	Imphal	22,300	1,400,000
Meghalaya	Shillong	22,400	1,300,000
Nagaland	Kohima	16,500	700,000
Tripura	Agartala	10,400	2,000,000
Arunachal Pradesh	Itanagar	83,600	500,000
Mizoram	Aizawi	21,000	400,000

The north-east region is the most varied and at the same time the least-visited part of India. Prior to independence the whole region was known as Assam Province, but it was finally split into five separate states and two Union Territories – Mizoram and Arunachal Pradesh. In many ways the north-east is unlike the rest of India. It is the country's chief tribal area, with a great number of tribes who speak many different languages and dialects – in Arunachal Pradesh alone over 50 distinct languages are spoken! These tribal people have many similarities to the hill tribes across the sweep of the country at the eastern end of the Himalaya, which extends from India through Burma and Thailand into Laos. Also, the north-east has a high percentage of Christians, particularly in the more isolated areas where the population is predominantly hill tribespeople.

For a number of reasons India has always been touchy about the north-east, and a visit to the region is a tricky proposition. For a start the north-east is a sensitive border zone where India meets Bhutan, China, Burma and Bangladesh. Equally important, the region is physically remote from the main Indian land mass – only the narrow Siliguri corridor connects it to the rest of India, and prior to independence the usual route to Assam would have been through Bangladesh. Today, going far into the north-east by train involves a long journey by metre-gauge rail. Roads have been dramatically improved but there are still very few of them compared to the rest of India. The Indian government has been sensitive about visitors and in the past only permitted them to go to Assam and Meghalaya; the other five regions, all bordering with China or Burma, were for all practical purposes off-limits. Even a visit to Assam and Meghalaya required a special permit, although this was readily available, at least for certain distinct tourist attractions.

Then in the early '80s the north-east was the scene for a whole series of riots, strikes, violence and terrorism, and for a time it was completely off-limits to outsiders. There were a number of reasons for this unrest, including a feeling of neglect by the central government – poor transport links and lack of infrastructure development were the main complaints. This feeling became increasingly strong with the rising price of oil since Assam has a substantial part of India's small, but important, oil reserves. Very little of this oil wealth found its way back to improve Assam's industrial

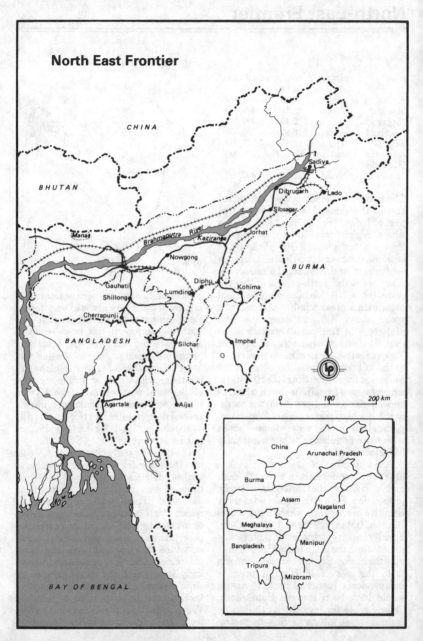

development, and the whole region remains overwhelmingly agricultural.

Neglect may have been a minor issue, but the number-one complaint was about 'foreigners'. The cycle of events in Bangladesh, just to the south-east of the region, combined with that tightly packed country's undiminished birth rate, pushed thousands of Bengalis over the lightly policed borders into the north-east region. This influx of 'foreigners' resulted, in some cases, in the indigenous population actually becoming outnumbered. Demands that 'foreigners' be repatriated were a major part of the unrest. Of course, such a wholesale repatriation was an impossibility, particularly since many of these Bengali 'foreigners' had been resident in the region for generations – legally or not.

In 1983 the unrest led to wholesale massacres in some villages, but more recently things seem to have quietened down, not to mention being pushed off the front page by the greater unrest in the Punjab. The door to the north-east may be gently opening again.

Permits

Normally permits are required for the two accessible states of the region – Assam and Meghalaya. You can approach these states by looping north of Bangladesh through the Siliguri corridor, or by air.

Assam Permits for Assam actually only permit you to visit Gauhati (the capital) and the game reserves at Manas and Kaziranga. Permits can be applied for at India consular offices overseas. In India they are issued by the Foreigners' Registration Office, Hans Bhavan (near Tilak Bridge), Bahadur Shah, Zafar Marg, New Delhi 110002; or by the Trade Adviser, Government of Assam, 8 Russel St, Calcutta 700071.

Normally the permit allows a maximum stay of 15 days, but this could be extended in Assam. If you fly to Gauhati and follow a specified route to Kaziranga and back,

you are allowed to visit Assam without a permit. For places in Assam apart from Gauhati, Manas and Kaziranga permission must be requested from the Home Ministry, Government of India, North Block, New Delhi at least six weeks in advance. In Calcutta you must apply to the Trade Adviser 'sufficiently in advance'.

Meghalaya The Meghalaya Information Centre in Calcutta is next to the Assam office at 9 Russel St; they issue permits with equal ease for a seven-day visit. Shillong, the capital of Meghalaya, is approached via Gauhati or through Bangladesh. As in Assam, permits are usually extendable after you arrive.

Assam

The largest and most easily accessible of the north-east states, Assam is a major tea-producing area (60% of India's tea comes from here) and also produces a large proportion of India's oil. The main attractions for the visitor are the Manas and Kaziranga wildlife reserves, which are home for India's rare one-horned rhinoceros.

GAUHATI (population 140,000)

Capital of the state, Gauhati is on the banks of the Brahmaputra River. It has many ancient Hindu temples but its main importance is as a gateway to the north-east and a jumping-off point for the wildlife reserves.

Information

The Tourist Office (tel 24475) is on Station Rd.

Temples

Umananda Temple is a Shiva temple on Peacock Island in the middle of the river. There's a pleasant ferry across the river. The Navagrah Temple is the Temple of

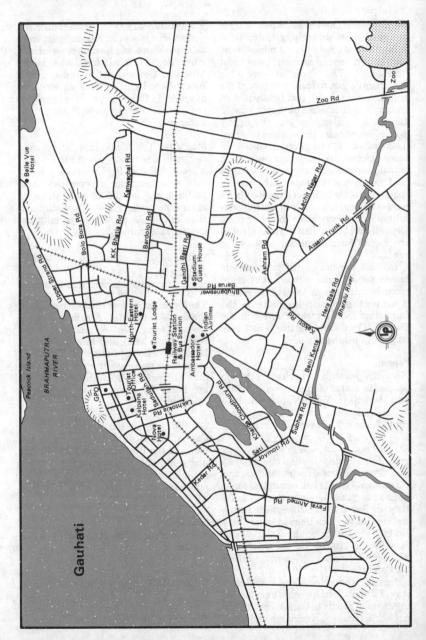

the Nine Planets. In ancient times this was a centre for the study of astrology. It is on Chitrachal Hill, near the city.

Gauhati's best-known temple is the Kamakshya on Nilachal Hill, 10 km from the city. It attracts pilgrims from all over India, especially during the Ambuchi festival in August. The temple is the centre for Shakti (energy) worship and Tantric Hinduism due to the fact that when Shiva was sorrowfully carrying away his first wife's (Sati's) corpse her *yoni* fell here! The temple was rebuilt in 1665 after being destroyed by Muslim invaders. In the centre of Gauhati the Janardhan Temple has an image of the Buddha, indicating how Buddhism was assimilated back into Hinduism.

Other

The Assam State Zoo has tigers, lions, panthers and, of course, Assam's famous rhinos – plus African two-horned ones for comparison purposes. There is an Assam State Museum with exhibits pertaining to Assam and its history, as well as the Assam Government Cottage Industries Museum.

Tours

There are government-operated tours to Kaziranga and Manas.

Places to Stay

Cheaper hotels include the *Hotel Alka* (tel 31767) at Pt M S Rd in Fancy Bazaar with rooms at Rs 36 for singles, Rs 50 to Rs 75 for doubles. Other cheapies include the similarly priced *Hotel Ambassador* (tel 25587) and the *Happy Lodge* (tel 23409), both in Paltan Bazaar. Middle-range hotels include the *Hotel Nova* (tel 23258) in Fancy Bazaar and the *Hotel North-Eastern* (tel 25314) on G N Bordoloi Rd.

There's a government *Tourist Bungalow* (tel 24475) on Station Rd and *Railway Retiring Rooms* (tel 26688) with very cheap doubles, triples and dormitory accommodation.

At the top of the Gauhati price scale the *Hotel Belle Vue* (tel 28291-2) on Mahatma Gandhi Rd has rooms with and without air-con from around Rs 100 to Rs 250. It's 'a bit spartan but satisfactory'. *Hotel Nandan* (tel 31281) on G S Rd is in the same upper price range and also has rooms with and without air-con.

Air Fares

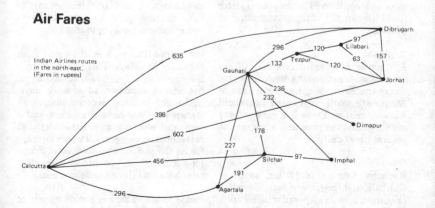

Indian Airlines routes in the north-east. (Fares in rupees)

Getting There

Air See the chart for details of air routes to the north-east – these mainly run from Calcutta. Vayudoot also operate some services in the north-east and may be taking over some of these routes from Indian Airlines.

Rail & Bus There are buses and a number of train services, but a change from broad-gauge to narrow-gauge is necessary to continue to Gauhati.

From Calcutta it's 991 km to Gauhati and the trip takes about 24 hours with fares of Rs 76 in 2nd class, Rs 309 in 1st. It's about 19 hours to Dibrugarh, 1552 km from Calcutta, with fares of Rs 104 in 2nd class, Rs 430 in 1st. New Delhi is 2050 km and nearly 40 hours away, even on the fastest train, the Assam Mail. There are a number of services from Lucknow, 1400 km away.

AROUND GAUHATI

Hajo

On the north bank of the Brahmaputra, 24 km from Gauhati, Hajo is an important pilgrimage centre for Buddhists and Muslims. Some Buddhists believe that it was here the Buddha attained nirvana, and they flock to the Hayagriba Madhab temple. For Muslims the Pao Mecca mosque is considered to have one-quarter *(pao)* the sanctity of the great mosque at Mecca.

Sualkashi

Also across the river from Gauhati, 20 km away, this is a famous silk-weaving centre where the Endi, Muga and Pat silks of Assam are made in a small household weaving centre. There is a regular ferry service across the river and a bus service several times daily.

Other

Basistha Ashram is 12 km south of Gauhati, and the *rishi* or sage, Basistha, once lived here. It's a popular picnic spot. The beautiful natural lagoon at Chandubi

is 64 km from Gauhati. Darranga, 80 km away on the Bhutan border, is a great winter trading area for the Bhutias mountain folk. Barpeta, with a monastery and the shrine of a Vaishnavaite reformer, is 145 km north-west of Gauhati.

WILDLIFE PARKS

Assam is famous for its rare one-horned Great Indian Rhinoceros – when Marco Polo saw it he thought he had found the legendary unicorn! Kaziranga and Manas are the two well-known parks in Assam. There are smaller parks at Orang and Sonai.

Kaziranga

North-east of Gauhati, Kaziranga Wildlife Reserve is on the banks of the Brahmaputra River and is famous as the last major home of 'Rhinoceros Unicornis'. The 430-square-km park is thought to have a rhino population approaching 1000, although in 1904 they were on the verge of extinction. The park became a game sanctuary in 1926, and by 1966 the numbers had risen to about 400.

The park also has wild buffalo, deer, elephants, tigers, bears and a wide variety of water birds including pelicans, which breed here. One of the standard ways of observing the wildlife is from elephant-back, and the rhinos are said to have become quite used to elephants toting camera-packing tourists.

Information The park is at its best from February to May. There is a Tourist Information Centre (tel 23) at Kaziranga, but you're supposed to give 10 days' notice for booking accommodation or transport. They have a minibus and a jeep and also organise those elephant rides into the long grass. There's an entry fee for the park and an additional charge for a still camera, plus higher charges for telephoto lens (!) or movie cameras.

Places to Stay There is a wide variety of accommodation around the park, including

Forest Inspection Bungalows at Beguri (no bedding or mosquito nets), Arimarh (no electricity) and Kohora. Or there is a *Soil Conservation Inspection Bungalow*, a very cheap *PWD Inspection Bungalow* at Kaziranga and two *Tourist Bungalows*. At the top of the price scale there's the *Kaziranga Forest Lodge* with rooms with and without air-con and prices from around Rs 100 to Rs 200.

Getting There There are flights from Calcutta to Jorhat, 84 km from the park. By rail Furketing is the most convenient station, 72 km away; from here buses run to Kaziranga. Gauhati is 233 km away on Highway 37. There are state transport buses from Gauhati.

Jorhat

A little beyond Kaziranga, this is the gateway to the north-eastern part of Assam. Sibsagar, 55 km away, has the huge Jay Sagar tank and many temples in the environs; it was the old capital of the Ahom kingdom. There's a small *Tourist Bungalow* by the tank.

Manas

In the foothills of the Himalaya, north-west of Gauhati, Manas Wildlife Sanctuary is on the border with Bhutan. Three rivers run through the sanctuary, which has a wide variety of bird and animal life. The rare pygmy hog and the golden langur (monkey) are amongst the notable animals here, although you may also see rhinos.

Information Manas is best between January and March; there is excellent fishing in November-December. Mothangiri is the main town in the park but the Tourist Information Centre (tel 49) is at Barpeta Road. Park entry charges and camera charges are the same as in Kaziranga. Boats can be hired for excursions or fishing trips on the Manas River.

Places to Stay *Manas Tourist Lodge* has rooms in the Upper Bungalow and the

Lower Bungalow from around Rs 15 per bed up to Rs 50 or more per room. You can camp if you have a tent. The *Forest Bungalow* is cheaper and includes bedding and mosquito nets but no electricity. There is a *Rest House* at the Barpeta Road Tourist Centre.

Getting There Gauhati, 176 km away, has the nearest airport. Barpeta Road, 40 km from Mothangiri, is the nearest railway station. Transport from here to Mothangiri must be arranged in advance.

Meghalaya

Created in 1971, this state is the home for Khasia, Jantia and Garo tribespeople. The hill station of Shillong is the state capital while Cherrapunji, 58 km away, is said to be the wettest place on earth with an average annual rainfall of 1150 cm, nearly 40 feet! In one year 2300 cm (75 feet) of rain fell. It's no wonder Meghalaya means 'abode of clouds'.

Other places of interest around the state include Jakrem with its hot springs, Kayllang Rock at Mairang, Mawjymbuin Cave at Mawsynram and Umiam Lake. Recently Mawsynram had an annual rainfall total that even surpassed the record at Cherrapunji.

SHILLONG (population 173,000)
This pleasant hill station, standing at 1496 metres, is renowned for its climate and breathtaking views; it's even had the label 'Scotland of the East' applied to it! Around town you can pass the time observing the tiny red-light district behind the Delhi Hotel, as there's not a lot to do apart from pass through. The people around Shillong, the Khasias, are matrilineal, passing down property and wealth through the female rather than the male line.

The State Museum covers the flora, fauna, culture and anthropology of the state. The town has a number of parks and gardens and a Botanic Garden and Botanical Museum beside the central Ward Lake. Crinoline Waterfalls are near Lady Hydari Park, and there are various other waterfalls around Shillong. The town takes its name from 1960-metre-high Shillong Peak, from which there are fine views. It's 10 km from the centre.

Information

Police Bazaar has a Government of Meghalaya Tourist Office (tel 6054) and a Government of India Tourist Office on G S Rd. The GPO is also on G S Rd.

Tours

There are morning tours of the city area, and day tours to Cherrapunji and the hot springs at Jakrem.

Places to Stay & Eat

There's a good *Tourist Bungalow* near the polo grounds with rooms and dormitory accommodation. There are many other middle-priced hotels around, and cheap accommodation can be found in the Police Bazaar near the Tourist Office. Good food at the *Lhasa Restaurant*; there are several other restaurants around town.

Hotel Pinewood Ashok (tel 23116, 23765) is Shillong's premier hotel (and Ashok's worst, said a visitor), with rooms from Rs 150 to Rs 200. The disgruntled visitor reported that it was damp and mouse infested.

Getting There

A good road runs the 100 km from Gauhati in Assam to Shillong. Cherrapunji is 58 km south of Shillong; if it's not raining the views from here over Bangladesh are superb. Permission is required from the commissioner of police to visit the area, but it's given readily. Coming from Bangladesh, you cross the border (if it's open) at Dawki, from where it's a 1½-km walk to the town, and then a 3½-hour trip to Shillong.

Other States & Territories

The other north-eastern regions are generally hard to get permission to visit even at the best of times. All of them border either with China or Burma. The following information is for interest only.

Transport in the Region

The only railway to these states and territories terminates at Ledo, but the roads have been much improved of late. Indian Airlines operate a comprehensive service to the region from Calcutta, but Vayudoot may be taking over some of the services.

ARUNACHAL PRADESH

The furthest north-east of the regions, this was known as the North-East Frontier Agency under the British. Arunachal Pradesh borders with Bhutan, China and Burma and is a mountainous, remote and predominantly tribal area. The old 'Stillwell Road' used to run from Ledo in the south of Arunachal Pradesh to Myitkyinya in the north-east of Burma. Built in 1944 by General 'Vinegar Joe' Stillwell, it must rate as one of the most expensive roads in the world. The 430 km cost US$137 million way back then, and after just a few months' use has hardly been used since. All road routes into Burma are closed.

NAGALAND

South of Arunahal Pradesh and north of Manipur, the remote and hilly state of Nagaland is bordered by Burma. Kohima, the capital of Nagaland, was the furthest point Japanese troops advanced into India during WW II.

MANIPUR

South of Nagaland and north of Mizoram, Manipur also borders with Burma. The state is inhabited by over two dozen different tribes, many of them Christians. It is famous for its Manipuri dances and handloomed textiles. Imphal (population 110,000), the capital, is surrounded by wooded hills and lakes and has the golden Shri Govindaji temple. During WW II a road was built from Imphal to Tamu on the Burma border but, as with the Stillwell road further north, this route into Burma is also closed.

MIZORAM

This finger-like extension in the extreme south-east of the region pokes down between Burma and Bangladesh. The name means hill people's land – Mizo (man of the hill) and ram (land). It's a picturesque place where the population is both predominantly tribal and overwhelmingly Christian.

TRIPURA

The tiny state of Tripura is almost totally surrounded by Bangladesh. It's a wooded and lush region with many beautiful waterfalls. Agartala is the capital; near it is the lake palace of Nirmahal. Here, too, the population is largely tribal.

Tony's Notebook

Women

Compared to some Asian countries the attitude towards women in India is relatively liberal and they enjoy considerable personal freedom. Nevertheless a girl is considered a much less desirable child than a boy and studies show that literacy is much lower, malnutrition and infant mortality much higher amongst female children than male.

Furthermore, 'bride burning' is still a much-discussed national scandal – if you don't like your new wife you simply burn her to death. Actually it isn't even a question of not liking her, bride-burning cases usually revolve around the wife not providing as much dowry as the husband (or his family) had their hearts set on.

The male/female imbalance has been steadily growing to the point where there are now 1200 males born for every 1000 females and it's likely to get worse if stories in the Indian press can be believed. Amniocentesis is a technique in which fluid is drawn from the womb of a pregnant woman; it's used in the west to test for possible pre-natal defects when the woman is in a high-risk category – such as those having children at a 'late' age for child-bearing. Apart from indicating possible defects, amniocentesis also indicates, with considerable accuracy, the sex of the foetus.

The inference in India is that women have amniocentesis simply to find what sex their baby would be – and then abort it if it's a girl. A newspaper article stated that in Bombay a survey of women having amniocentesis revealed that 8000 of them were carrying girls and 7999 of the 8000 then had abortions. The sole exception, the paper explained, was Jewish!

Noise

In one way bus travel in India has taken a terrible step backwards in the past few years. The reason? Video buses. This horrible invention combines VCRs, TV sets, Hindi movies and Indian buses into a form of purgatory even Dante couldn't have dreamed up. It doesn't take long in India to realise that popular music is the Indian equivalent of Chinese water torture or having the soles of your feet beaten by the police in South America. It isn't that the music is bad (bad to western ears, but not that bad), it's the unalterable practice of always playing it at top volume, at levels way beyond the capacity of the speakers, at levels that result in nothing but ear-shattering, nerve-twisting distortion. Get the picture? Now put that noise inside a bus, put yourself into the bus, shut the doors, turn the volume up and suffer!

Rajasthan

Population: 29 million
Area: 342,214 square km
Capital: Jaipur
Main languages: Rajasthani & Hindi

Rajasthan, the 'Land of the Kings', is India at its exotic and colourful best. This is the home of the Rajputs, a group of warrior clans who have controlled this part of India for 1000 years with a code of chivalry and honour akin to that of the mediaeval European knights. The Rajputs were never a united force, like the Marathas of central India; when they were not warring against outsiders they were generally squabbling amongst themselves. Thus they were never a real opposition to the Moghuls, but their bravery and sense of honour were unparalleled.

The Rajput warriors would fight on against all odds and, when no hope was left, the women and children would commit suicide by marching into a funeral pyre in a ritual known as *jauhar*. Meanwhile the men would don the saffron robes of rejoicing worn at weddings and ride forth to certain death. Over and over this grim tale would unfold as stronger forces attacked the Rajputs. In Chittorgarh's long history, three times the women consigned themselves to the flames while the men rode out to their martyrdom. It's hardly surprising that Akbar persuaded Rajputs to lead his army or that Aurangzeb clashed unsuccessfully with them.

Under the British, Rajasthan continued as a collection of princely states named Rajputana, each with its own Maharaja. Independent India combined them with Ajmer to make Rajasthan. Huge, often battle-scarred forts dominate almost every town in Rajasthan. They're a clear reminder of the state's warlike past. And what forts they are, with battlements, turrets, massive walls and inside palaces of amazing luxury and whimsical charm. They're redolent of that impossibly romantic Rajput sense of honour and bravery above all.

Rajasthan's exotic atmosphere extends to far more than just splendid forts, for the Rajasthanis themselves are a brilliant splash of colour. The men top their outfit with a huge, pastel-coloured turban and almost without exception sport fierce 'soup strainer' moustaches. The bright, mirrored skirts of the women are equally colourful. They are complemented with chunky jewellery worn from head to toe – Rajasthani jewellery is a favourite purchase for visitors to the state.

Rajasthan is a somewhat dry and inhospitable place, but geographically it's very varied. A line drawn south-west to north-east divides the state into the hilly and rugged south-east region and the barren north-east Thar Desert, which extends across the border into Pakistan. Apart from historic cities, colourful people and superb scenery, Rajasthan has some popular travellers' centres – peaceful Pushkar with its holy lake, and

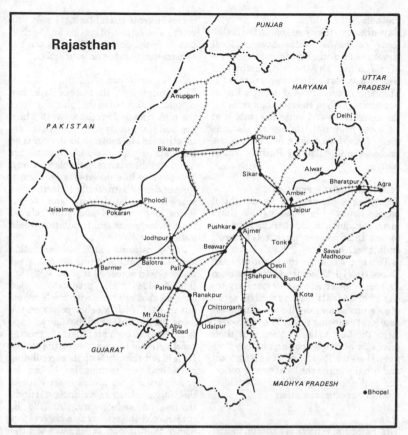

Rajasthan

PUNJAB

HARYANA

UTTAR
PRADESH

PAKISTAN

Anupgarh

Delhi

Churu

Bikaner

Sikar

Alwar

Bharatpur

Agra

Amber

Pholodi

Jaipur

Jaisalmer

Pokaran

Pushkar

Ajmer

Jodhpur

Beawar

Tonk

Sawai
Madhopur

Barmer

Balotra

Pali

Deoli

Shahpura

Bundi

Palna

Ranakpur

Kota

Chittorgarh

Mt Abu

Abu
Road

Udaipur

GUJARAT

MADHYA PRADESH

Bhopal

the exotic desert city of Jaisalmer, like some fantasy from *The Thousand & One Nights*. It's a fascinating state.

Art & Architecture

Rajasthan has a school of miniature painting, derived from the Moghul style but with some clear differences – in particular, the palace and hunting scenes are complemented by religious themes, particularly relating to the Krishna legends. This art carried through to the elegant palaces the Rajputs built. Many of them are liberally covered with colourful frescoes.

Most of Rajasthan's early architecture was damaged or destroyed by the first waves of Muslim invasions. Fragments remaining from that period include the Adhai-din-ka-jhonpra mosque in Ajmer, which is basically a converted Hindu temple of great elegance, and the ruined temples at Osian, near Jodhpur. There are many buildings from the 10th to 15th century, including the superb Jain temples at Ranakpur, Mt Abu and Jaisalmer. Most of the great forts date, in their present form, from the Moghul period.

Festivals

Rajasthan has the usual Indian festivals – some celebrated with especial local fervour – and a number of special festivals of its own. The harvest festival of Gangaur is particularly important, as is Teej, at the end of August or beginning of September. When the monsoon rains fill the many lakes and tanks the state is at its most beautiful. Rajasthan also has many fairs, best known of which is the immense and colourful Pushkar cattle fair.

Palaces & Tourist Bungalows

Rajasthan is famous for its delightful palace hotels – in these harder times many of Rajasthan's Maharajas have had to turn their palaces into hotels to make ends meet.

Two of the best are the beautiful Lake Palace Hotel in Udaipur and the Rambagh Palace in Jaipur. At a rather more day-to-day level the state has an excellent series of government-operated Tourist Bungalows in almost every big town. They were very often the best value in town, but their prices are no longer the bargain they once were. However, they often have a restaurant and usually house the local tourist office. For real shoestringers they often offer dormitory accommodation.

Trains

The 'Palace on Wheels' is a special tourist train service which operates weekly tours of Rajasthan, departing from Delhi. The carriages used to belong to various Maharajas. The cost includes tours, entry fees, accommodation on the train plus all meals. The cost depends on the berth but ranges around a hefty US$150 a day.

Buses

Rajasthan has an extensive and reasonably good bus system. If you're taking a bus from a major bus stand it's worth buying a ticket from the ticket office rather than on board the bus. It guarantees (or at least comes closer to guaranteeing) a seat, and you're also certain of getting on the right bus since the ticket clerk writes the bus registration number on your ticket.

JAIPUR (population 650,000)

The capital city of the state of Rajasthan is popularly known as the 'pink city' from the pink-coloured sandstone with which the buildings in its old, walled city are constructed. In contrast to the cities on the Ganges plain, Jaipur's avenues are broad and there is a remarkable harmony. The town is in a desert-like landscape, surrounded by barren hills. Rajasthan is a sparsely populated state and Jaipur seems less crowded and more relaxed than its large size and population would indicate.

Jaipur owes its name, its foundation and its careful planning to the great warrior-astronomer Maharaja Jai Singh II (1699-1744). His predecessors had enjoyed good relations with the Moghuls but in 1727, with Moghul power on the wane, Jai Singh decided the time was ripe to move down from his hillside fortress at nearby Amber to a new site on the plains. He laid out the city with its surrounding walls and six rectangular blocks by principles of town planning set forth in the *Shilpa-Shastra*, an ancient Hindu treatise on architecture. In 1728 he constructed the remarkable observatory which is still one of Jaipur's central attractions.

Orientation & Information

The walled 'pink city' is in the north-east of Jaipur, while the new parts are the spread to the south and west. The main shopping centre in the old city is Johari Bazaar or the jeweller's market. Unlike other shopping centres in narrow alleys in India and Asia, this one is broad and open.

Mirza Ismail Rd (M I Rd) is the main street of the new part of Jaipur and the modern shopping centre. Most of the hotels and restaurants frequented by budget travellers are around the railway station and bus stand to the south-west. A small enclave across from the GPO on M I Rd has become a popular centre for travellers on a really tight budget. There are many souvenir shops and cheap restaurants here.

Jaipur's tourist attractions are mainly concentrated in the old city. There are state Tourist Offices in the bus and railway stations, while the Government of India Tourist Office is in the Rajasthan State Hotel. The State Bank of India has a very quick and efficient foreign exchange counter on the 1st floor of its branch in M I Rd at the Sanganeri Gate. It's open six days a week too. Jaipur has some night branches open later than usual hours. The Rambagh Palace Hotel has a good bookshop.

Jaipur's elephant festival takes place 14-15 March in 1987, 2-3 March in '88, 20-21 March in '89.

Old City

The old city is encircled by a crenellated wall with seven gates – the major gates are Chandpol, Sanganeri and Ajmeri. The broad (over 30 metres wide) avenues of the pink city divide it up into neat rectangles. It's an extremely colourful city – in the evening light the pink and orange buildings have a magical glow which the brightly clothed Rajasthanis complement. The strange-looking camel-drawn carts are part of the passing scene in Jaipur, and black-faced monkeys peer out from some of the buildings. The Iswari Minar Swarga Sul, the 'minaret piercing heaven', near the Tripolia Gate, was built to overlook the city.

Palace of the Winds

Built in 1799, the Hawa Mahal or Palace of the Winds is Jaipur's central landmark, although it is actually little more than a facade. The five-storey building looks out over the main street of the old city. Its pink sandstone windows are semi-octagonal in shape and delicately honey-combed. It was originally built to enable ladies of the royal household to watch the everyday life and processions of the city. You can climb to the top of the Hawa Mahal and get an excellent view over the city. The palace was originally built by Maharaja Sawaj Pratap Singh and is part of the City Palace complex.

Entrance to the Hawa Mahal is from the rear of the building and is a little difficult to find. Hours are 9 am to 4.30 pm. It's worth spending Rs 1 to enjoy the views of the snake charmers and camels down below: 'We always found the camel carts amusing; very rarely did we see them actually pulling anything on those silly little carts'.

City Palace

In the heart of the old city the City Palace occupies a large area divided into a series of courtyards, gardens and buildings. The outer wall was built by Jai Singh but other additions are much later, some right up to the start of this century. Today the palace is a blend of Rajasthani and Moghul architecture. The former Maharaja still lives in part of the palace.

The centre of the palace is the seven-storey Chandra Mahal with fine views over the gardens and the city. The ground and 1st floor of the Chandra Mahal form the Maharaja Sawai Man Singh II Museum. The apartments are maintained in luxurious order and the museum has an extensive collection of art, carpets, enamel-ware and old weapons. The paintings include miniatures of the Rajasthani, Moghul and Persian schools. The armoury has a collection of guns and swords dating back to the 15th century plus many of the ingenious and tricky weapons for which the warrior Rajputs were famous. The textile section contains dresses and costumes of the former Maharajas and Maharanis of Jaipur.

Other points of interest in the palace include the Diwan-i-Am or Hall of Public Audiences with its intricate decorations and manuscripts in Persian and Sanskrit, and the Diwan-i-Khas or Hall of Private Audiences with a marble-paved gallery. There is also a clock tower and the newer Mubarak Mahal.

Outside the buildings you can see a large silver vessel which a former Maharaja used to take drinking water with him to England. Being a devout Hindu, he could not drink the English water! The palace and museum are open daily except on holidays and entry is Rs 6 (Rs 3 for students). Hours are 9.30 am to 4.45 pm.

Observatory

Across from the City Palace is the observatory or Jantar Mantar which Jai Singh began in 1728. Jai Singh's passion for astronomy was even more notable than his prowess as a warrior, and before commencing construction he sent scholars abroad to study foreign observatories. Of the five he built, the Jaipur observatory is the largest and the best preserved – it was restored in 1901. The others are in Delhi (the oldest, dating from 1724), Varanasi and Ujjain. There was one in Muttra, but it has now disappeared.

At first glance the observatory appears to be just a curious collection of sculptures, but in fact each construction has a specific purpose, such as measuring the positions of stars, altitudes and azimuths, or calculating eclipses. The most striking instrument is the sundial, with its 30-metre-high gnomon. This casts a shadow which moves up to four metres an hour! It's very accurate, but on Jaipur local time! Admission to the observatory is Rs 1, free on Mondays; hours are 9 am to 5 pm.

Central Museum

Situated in the Ram Niwas Gardens, south of the old city, the museum is housed in the architecturally impressive Albert Hall. The upper floor contains portraits of the Jaipur Maharajas and many other miniatures and works of art. The ground floor has a collection of costumes and woodwork from different parts of Rajasthan and a description of the people and life in the rural areas of the state. The collection, which started in 1833, is also notable for its brassware, jewellery and pottery. Entry to the museum is Rs 1, free on Mondays. It is open every day except Friday from 10 am to 5 pm.

Other

The Ram Niwas Gardens also has a zoo with birds, animals and a crocodile breeding farm. Jaipur has a Modern Art Gallery in the 'theatre' near the zoo. 'They unlock it specially and it is quite interesting'. By phoning 62227 you can visit the Kripal Kumbh at B-18/A Shiv Marg, where Jaipur's famous blue pottery is made. The Hotel Rambagh Palace puts on an hour-long cultural programme of Rajasthani folk dances in the evening. Admission is Rs 30 but the standards of dancing are not high.

Finally, if you see only one Hindi movie the whole time you're in India, make it at the Raj Mandir. This opulent, grandiose and extremely well-kept cinema is a Jaipur tourist attraction in its own right. Tickets cost Rs 4 to Rs 8 but it's always full, despite its immense size. They don't build them like this in the west anymore.

For a change of pace try kite flying in the park. There are numerous kite shops in the old town, but buy lots of kites (Rs 1 to Rs 2 each) because you'll most likely destroy five before getting the hang of it. There will be lots of kids more than willing to show you how it's done.

Adam Ciayman, USA

Tours

The Rajasthan Tourist Office operates a daily Rs 15 tour which starts from the Teej Tourist Bungalow (tel 74260) or the Railway Station (tel 69714). The tour lasts from 8 am to 1 pm or from 1.30 to 6.30 pm and visits the Hawa Mahal, the City Palace, the observatory and Amber. A similar tour is operated in the mornings by the ITDC from the Rajasthan State

Hotel (tel 65451). The state office also have an all-day tour from 9 am to 6 pm costing Rs 30.

The tours are especially good value if your time in Jaipur is limited, particularly if it's in the summer when travelling is exhausting. 'Our guide even translated all the Hindi jokes cracked by the (otherwise entirely) Hindi-speaking tour group', wrote one traveller. Alternatively, you can get around the city on your own by bicycle or rickshaw, and you can take a bus out to Amber Fort.

Places to Stay – bottom end

Finding accommodation in Jaipur is somewhat complicated by the local rickshaw-wallahs who act as hotel touts. That is, they skim off a commission for taking you to certain hotels – which naturally gets added onto your bill. If you want to go to a place which doesn't pay a commission, or doesn't pay a good enough one, they may make great efforts to take you elsewhere. Your requested hotel may suddenly be 'closed' or 'full', or may have mysteriously become a terrible place to stay.

The *Jaipur Inn* (tel 66057) in Bani Park is one of Jaipur's most popular places to stay for budget travellers. It's clean, well run, helpful and friendly and good food is available – Rs 15 for a good evening meal. A dorm bed costs Rs 15, or there are doubles from Rs 35 to Rs 50 with common bathroom, doubles with attached bathroom for Rs 75. You can also camp here (Rs 10) and it's a good meeting place.

The state government has the budget-priced *Swagatam Tourist Bungalow* with doubles (no singles), all with attached bathroom, for Rs 40, deluxe doubles for Rs 50 and rooms with four beds for Rs 60. There's also a Rs 12 dorm. The bungalow is conveniently close to the railway station.

Down an alley across from the GPO and a little down from the Kwality Restaurant is a small group of very cheap places. Most popular of these is the *Ever*

ONE OF THE MULTITUDE OF INDIAN TAILORS AND APPRENTICES.

Green Guest House where dorm beds cost Rs 8, singles/doubles Rs 15/20. It's very basic (you may have to insist that you get clean sheets) but very popular with travellers, although the management is not always the friendliest. There's a pleasant little garden and the food is good. Other places in this same area, like the *Ever Happy Guest House*, are distinctly grottier and much less popular. There are also several places to eat here; the sign to the *Milky Way Café* is the easiest way to find the alley for these places.

Continuing down M I Rd, you come to the *Tourist's Hotel* (tel 64133), nicely priced at Rs 25/35. The rooms have

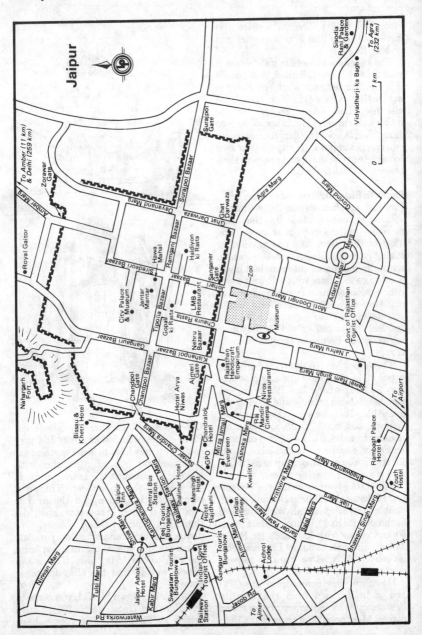

Jaipur

verandahs overlooking the pleasant garden, but it's a shame they're so grubby and badly kept. Round the corner from the Teej Tourist Bungalow towards the bus station is the *Hotel Assam* (tel 68474), with rooms at Rs 25/35 or rooms with bath at Rs 35/50. It's clean and OK, but try to get an outside room.

Near the railway station *Hotel Rajdhani* (tel 61276) has rooms at Rs 25/40 or with attached bathroom at Rs 60/80. Back off Station Rd, *Hotel Chandraloak* (tel 77301) is for emergencies only; rooms cost from Rs 30 to Rs 120 but are primitive. Several travellers have recommended the *Hotel Rose* (tel 77422) at B6 Shopping Centre, Subhash Nagar Bani Park, but I thought it was a very, very long way out from the centre. Rooms are Rs 20/25 or Rs 50/75 with bath and there's a basement dormitory at Rs 8.

Finally there's the 60-bed *Youth Hostel* (tel 67576), inconveniently far out from the centre of things. There are so many alternatives in Jaipur that few people are likely to venture out here, but dorm beds are Rs 12 (Rs 9 with YHA card), singles/doubles Rs 20/35 (Rs 10/25 with YHA card). They do a thali dinner for Rs 14. There are *Railway Retiring Rooms* at the station with singles (Rs 15), doubles (Rs 30) and dormitory accommodation (Rs 6).

Places to Stay – middle

Apart from the Swagatam Tourist Bungalow there are two others. The *Gangaur Tourist Bungalow* (tel 60231) is on M I Rd and has rooms at Rs 70 to Rs 90 for singles, Rs 90 to Rs 115 for doubles. With air-con, singles are Rs 140, doubles Rs 175.

The *Teej Tourist Bungalow* (tel 74206) in Bani Park costs Rs 30/40 for rooms without bath, Rs 60/75 with bath, Rs 75/100 with air-cooling, Rs 100/125 with air-con. There's also a Rs 12 dorm.

Hotel Arya Niwas (tel 73456), behind the Amber Cinema on Sansar Chandra Marg and near the GPO, is a relatively new and very popular hotel. This well-run place has singles for Rs 60 to Rs 100, doubles from Rs 70 to Rs 120. All rooms have attached bathroom; the main differences are the size of the room. Its small vegetarian restaurant does good food (including thalis for Rs 15) and there's a verandah and garden area out front. After we'd finished researching this edition we had one irate complaint about standards at the Arya Niwas although it seemed absolutely fine when I was there.

Khasa Kothi (tel 75151) (it used to be the Rajasthan State Hotel) is by the roundabout up Station Rd from the station. It's the site for the Government of India Tourist Office and has 41 rooms at Rs 140/185 and very spacious grounds.

There are a couple of smaller palace hotels near Chandpol Gate. *Hotel Bissau Palace* (tel 74191) has a wonderful lounge and library, a garden and swimming pool (not always filled), and rooms which are a little worn at the edges but just fine. Costs are very moderate at Rs 99 for a single, Rs 140 to Rs 180 for a double, Rs 250 for a suite. This is an interesting place with real charm. A little beyond it is the *Khetri House Hotel* (tel 69183), which doesn't have the whimsical palace feel of its neighbour but does have enormous rooms for Rs 99/180, some simpler doubles for Rs 120 and a huge suite for Rs 220.

Hotel Imperial (tel 78651), in the main shopping centre midway between the railway station and the City Palace, has rooms at Rs 60/90 or deluxe rooms at Rs 90/120. It's good value and the rooms are pretty well kept.

There is a string of new medium-priced hotels near the bus station. *Hotel Shalimar* (tel 61187) on Banasthali Marg is fairly typical with rooms at Rs 70 to Rs 90 for singles, Rs 90 to Rs 110 for doubles. With air-con and TV, rooms are Rs 170/200. On Sansar Chandra Marg, near the Arya Niwas Hotel, *Hotel Mangal* (tel 61332) is another modern hotel with rooms at Rs 70/90, Rs 100/120 with air cooling, Rs 150/170 with air-con.

Places To Stay – top end

Jaipur is a major tourist centre conveniently close to Delhi, so it has a wide variety of hotels in all categories. The *Rambagh Palace* (tel 75141) on Bhawani Sangh Marg was the palace of the Maharajas of Jaipur after the City Palace. Situated to the south of the town, it is a charming old building, fully air-conditioned with a luxurious indoor swimming pool. Singles/doubles cost Rs 550/600. The Polo Bar is one of the hotel's main attractions. Polo is still a big deal in Jaipur; the previous Maharaja died while playing! The *Rajmahal Palace Hotel* (tel 61257-9) is a lesser palace hotel with huge and palatial rooms at Rs 475/550. There's a pleasant garden and swimming pool.

The modern *Welcomhotel Mansingh* (tel 78771) is on Sansar Chandra Rd, close to the railway and bus stations. It is a part of the Welcomhotel group, looks like a huge red sandstone palace and costs Rs 500/600.

Hotel Jaipur Ashok (tel 75171) is also centrally located in Bani Park. Part of the ITDC chain, it costs Rs 350/450, and like others in the chain is on the downhill path to complete disaster! *Hotel Clarks Amer* (tel 82216) is on Jawahar Lal Nehru Marg, an uncomfortably long way from the town, and costs Rs 450/550.

Places to Eat

In Johari Bazaar near the centre of the old city, *LMB* is well known for its excellent vegetarian food. It also has amazingly pristine '50s 'hip' decor, definitely worth seeing. Main courses are Rs 10 to Rs 20. A dessert speciality is LMB kulfi – including dry fruits, saffron and cottage cheese for Rs 11.50. A complete meal will cost Rs 40 to Rs 50 per person. Out front there's a snack counter that does good snacks and excellent ice cream and has a wide range of Indian sweets. LMB stands for Laxmi Mishthan Bhandar.

On M I Rd *Niro's* is one of Jaipur's best and most expensive restaurants – pleasant decor, soft music, chicken specialties and a cost of about Rs 45 per person for a meal. Main courses are typically Rs 16 to Rs 30, or Rs 20 to Rs 40 for tandoori dishes. Desserts are Rs 10 to Rs 12, ice cream Rs 6.50 to Rs 10. The menu has the usual non-veg blend of Indian, Chinese and continental dishes. Surprisingly, it's not one of those dark and gloomy up-market Indian restaurants. At least at lunchtime. Also on M I Rd there's a *Kwality*, closed on Tuesdays.

Still on M I Rd and on the same side as the GPO, opposite the Tourist's Hotel, is the *Chandraloak Restaurant*. It's hard to find because there's no sign in English, but if you venture upstairs next to the Canara Bank you'll find this bargain-priced vegetarian place where thalis cost just Rs 7. Closer to the GPO but on the opposite side of the road is *Handi*, a small, open-courtyard place with a relaxed atmosphere and good kebabs and tandoori food. If you're staying in the small, ultra-cheap accommodation enclave around the Ever Green Guest House, the small *Restaurant Bambino* is popular – it bills itself as 'a haven in the desert'.

At the other end of the price scale you can eat in fine style at the *Rambagh Palace Hotel*, but the food is tilted strongly towards the bland tastes of international tourists.

You can't stay at the *Circuit House*, in the entranceway to the *Kasha Kothi* hotel and the Government of India Tourist Office, but it is a great place for breakfast. For less than Rs 10 you get cornflakes, toast, eggs and coffee or tea – excellent value.

Some of the new medium-priced hotels have good restaurants – try the *Rituraj* vegetarian restaurant upstairs in the Hotel Mangal on Sansar Chandra Marg. Or try the *Vaishali Restaurant* in the Chandragupta Hotel on Station Rd, next to the bus station. Jaipur has a number of good Chinese restaurants. In the Ram Niwas gardens there are open-air restaurants with good masala dosas and other south Indian food.

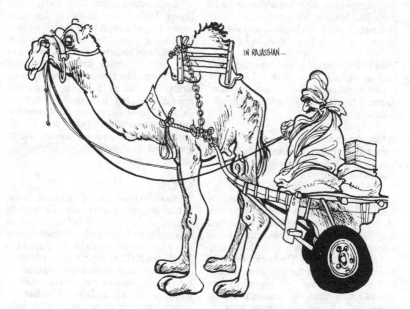

IN RAJASTHAN...

Getting There

Air There are two direct flights daily from Delhi to Jaipur continuing (with a multitude of stops) to Bombay (and vice versa). Fares to or from Jaipur are Delhi (Rs 236), Bombay (Rs 853), Jodhpur (Rs 296), Udaipur (Rs 307) and Ahmedabad (Rs 227). The Indian Airlines office (tel 72940 or 74500) is on Ajmer Rd. Vayudoot also fly through Jaipur to Jodhpur, Jaisalmer and Bikaner; their office is at the Gangaur Tourist Bungalow.

Rail The train services from Jaipur are generally not as fast as buses because they are on metre gauge. The Pink City Express leaves old Delhi Railway Station at 6 am and reaches Jaipur at 11 am. The Jaipur-Delhi service leaves at 5 pm and arrives at 10.20 pm. Fares for the 308-km trip are Rs 31.50 in 2nd class, Rs 124 in 1st. A late evening train leaves Delhi and arrives in Jaipur around dawn. All Jaipur trains leave from the old Delhi station.

The Chetak Express continues through Jaipur to Ajmer and Udaipur. There is now a 'superfast' train from Jaipur to Agra which only takes five hours; it leaves Jaipur at 5.45 am. A daily train to Jodhpur arrives there just over seven hours later.

Bus From Delhi, deluxe buses operated by the Rajasthan State Transport take five hours to Jaipur. The 306-km trip costs Rs 50 or Rs 55 for deluxe buses, Rs 35 to Rs 40 for the slower regular ones. A deluxe Agra bus departs from the Khasa Kothi and the Hotel Jaipur Ashok at 4 pm, takes 4½ hours and costs Rs 45. A regular bus to Agra costs Rs 34.

Buses run very regularly to Ajmer; the 2½-hour trip costs Rs 17.50 to Rs 24.50. Bharatpur takes 4½ hours and costs Rs 23. Alwar is also 4½ hours away and costs Rs 19. Jodhpur takes seven hours and costs Rs 44 to Rs 62. Jaisalmer takes 14 hours (one bus daily) and costs Rs 77.

Bikaner takes seven hours and costs Rs 47 to Rs 50. Udaipur takes nine to 10 hours and costs Rs 55 to Rs 85. Barmer takes 14 hours (one bus daily) and costs Rs 75.

Tours ITDC operate a one-day conducted tour to Jaipur from Delhi. The tours depart from the hotels Janpath, Ashok or Akbar or from the ITDC office in L Block, Connaught Place.

Getting Around
Airport The airport is 15 km out of town. The airport bus costs Rs 15. A taxi will cost about Rs 60.

Local Transport Jaipur has taxis (unmetered), auto-rickshaws and a city bus service which also operates out to Amber. A cycle-rickshaw from the station to the Jaipur Inn will cost Rs 2, from the station to Johari Bazaar Rs 5. Cycle-rickshaws in Jaipur are notorious for their commission-gathering activities – an especially low fare to a hotel from the station probably means he's planning on an especially big commission at your expense. They're also avid shop visitors, again to rake in commissions.

It is possible to share 'four seaters' or 'six seaters' – larger auto-rickshaw-like devices which go from the station to the main gates of the city (ie Sanganeri – Rampol) for Rs 1 or Rs 1.50. You can hire bicycles from near the railway station, and the city bus service is quite useful and cheap.

Things to Buy
Jaipur is well known for precious stones which seem cheaper here than anywhere else in India. It is even better known for semi-precious stones. For precious stones find a narrow alley called Haldion ka rasta off Johari Bazaar (near the Hawa Mahal). For semi-precious stones there's another alley on the opposite side of the street called the Gopalji ka rasta. There are many shops here which offer bargain prices.

Shops around the City Palace and Hawa Mahal are likely to be more expensive, although they do have many interesting items, including miniatures and clothes. Marble statues, jewellery and textile prints are other Jaipur specialties. The Rajasthan Government Emporium in M I Rd is reasonably priced, and has a branch in Amber. Jaipur's salespeople are hard working and very persuasive; take care. This is another place where many unwary visitors get talked into buying things for resale at jacked-up prices.

AMBER
Situated on the Jaipur-Delhi road, 11 km out of Jaipur, Amber was the ancient capital of Jaipur state before the move was made to Jaipur. The fortress-palace was constructed from 1592 by Raja Man Singh, the Rajput commander of Akbar's army. It was later extended and completed by the Jai Singhs before the shift to Jaipur on the plains below. The fort is a superb example of Rajput architecture, stunningly situated on a hillside overlooking a lake which reflects its terraces and ramparts.

From the road you can climb up to the fort in 10 minutes, but it's a popular activity to ride up on elephant-back – at a hefty cost of Rs 65 one way. That's per elephant, not per person; an elephant can carry up to four people. A quick ride around the palace courtyard costs about Rs 5. Within the palace you can get cold drinks, should the climb be a hot one.

An imposing stairway leads to the Diwan-i-Am or Hall of Public Audiences with a double row of columns and latticed galleries above. Steps to the right lead to the small Kali temple. There is also the white-marble Sila Devi Temple.

The Maharaja's apartments are on the higher terrace – you enter through a gateway decorated with mosaics and sculptures. The Jai Mandir or Hall of Victory is noted for its inlaid panels and glittering mirror ceiling. Opposite the Jai

Mandir is the Sukh Niwas or Hall of Pleasure with an ivory inlaid sandalwood door, and a channel running right through the room which at one time carried cooling water. From the Jas Mandir you can enjoy the fine views from the palace ramparts over the lake below.

Amber palace is open from 9 am to 4.30 pm and entry costs Rs 6 (Rs 3 for students).

Getting There
A bus to Amber from the Hawa Mahal in Jaipur costs about Rs 1 and the trip takes half an hour. Buses depart every few minutes. A taxi would cost Rs 60 to Rs 70.

AROUND JAIPUR
There are several other attractions around Jaipur, including several on the road between Jaipur and Amber. Jaipur tours usually stop at some of these sites on the way to or from Amber.

Gaitor
The cenotaphs of the royal family are at Gaitor, 6.5 km from Jaipur on the road to Amber. The white marble cenotaph of Maharaja Jai Singh II is the most impressive and is decorated with carved peacocks. Next to it is the cenotaph of his son. Opposite the cenotaphs is the Jal Mahal water palace in the middle of a lake and reached by a causeway. Or at least it was in the middle of a lake; the water is now all but squeezed out by the infamous weed, water-hyacinth. There is another Royal Gaitor just outside the city walls.

Galta
If you leave the city by the Surya Gate it's a 2.5-km climb to the temple of the Sun God at Galta, 100 metres above the city to the east and with fine views over the surrounding plain. A deep temple-filled gorge stands behind the temple.

Tiger Fort
The Nahargarh Fort looks out over the city from a sheer ridge 6.5 km away. It's reached by a jeepable road from Amber through the hills. You can get there by rickshaw too, but the actual top is at the end of 1½ km of zigzag path. The views fully justify the effort and the entry fee. There's a small and all-but-deserted restaurant on the top. The fort was initially built in 1734 and extended in 1868.

Jaigarh Fort
The imposing Jaigarh Fort, built by Jai Singh in 1726, was only opened to the public in mid-83. It's walking distance from Amber and there's a fine view over the plains from the *Diwa Burj* watchtower. The fort, with its water reservoirs, residential areas, puppet theatre and the cannon *Jaya Vana* is open from 9 am to 4.30 pm. Entry is Rs 6.

Sisodia Rani Palace & Gardens
Eight km from the city on the Agra road, this palace was built for the second wife of Maharaja Jai Singh, the Sisodia princess. The outer walls are illustrated with murals of hunting scenes and the Krishna legend. The palace is surrounded by terraced gardens.

Vidyadhar's Garden
Nestled in a narrow valley, this beautiful garden was built in honour of Jai Singh's chief architect and town planner.

Sanganer
Situated 16 km south of Jaipur, this small town is entered through the ruins of two *tripolias* or triple gateways. The town has a ruined palace and a group of Jain temples with fine carvings. Entry to the temples is restricted. The town is noted for hand-made paper and block printing.

Balaji
The Hindu exorcism temple of Balaji is about 1½ km off the Jaipur-Agra road,

about 1½ hours by bus from Bharatpur. The exorcisms are sometimes of a very violent kind and those being exorcised don't hesitate to discuss their experiences. There are two morning buses from the bus terminal in Delhi for Balaji.

BHARATPUR

This small town is best known for its bird sanctuary – a must if you are interested in bird watching. Bharatpur also has an 18th-century fort with a small museum. It is 55 km from Agra and 180 km from Delhi via Mathura. Bring your repellent; there are plenty of mosquitoes.

Bird Sanctuary

No less than 328 kinds of birds have been sighted at the sanctuary, 117 of which are migrants which come from as far away as Siberia or China. It takes about a week to fly from Siberia to India! The sanctuary was the duck-shooting preserve of the Maharajas of Bharatpur when this was a princely state. Shooting has not been permitted since 1964, and today there are 80 types of ducks in the sanctuary.

October to February is the best time to visit the sanctuary because there are many migratory birds to be seen. There is an entry fee per car or bus plus charges for photography or for taking boats onto the waters. The sanctuary covers 29 square km of low-lying marshland. Entrance to the park costs Rs 10 for foreigners, and a boat with guide will cost about Rs 20 an hour – 'well worth it to have a closer look at the birds'. The Tourist Bungalow does a dawn minibus tour at Rs 15, as long as enough seats are sold.

Two travellers reported that 'even for those with no interest in ornithology, Bharatpur is a must. See the sun rise over the lakes and the enormous Siberian cranes weighing down the branches of the tiny trees'. The sanctuary is now known as the Keoladeo National Park.

Lohagarh Fort

The 'Iron Fort' was built in the early 18th century and took its name from its supposedly impregnable defences. Maharaja Suraj Mal, the fort's constructor and founder of Bharatpur, built two towers within the ramparts, the Jawahar Burj and Fateh Burj, to commemorate his victories over the Moghuls and the British. The fort is open from 9 am to 5 pm daily and admission is free. The museum is closed Fridays; it has sculptures, inscriptions and works of art from the region.

Places to Stay

There is an ITDC-operated *Ashok Bharatpur Forest Lodge* (tel 2260) two to three km into the sanctuary. Singles/doubles cost from Rs 150/225 or Rs 265/340 with air-con. You have to pay the Rs 10 sanctuary entry fee to get to it, so if you arrive late one day ask that it be dated for the following day.

The cheaper *Saras Tourist Bungalow* (tel 2169) is on the Agra road just 200 metres from the sanctuary entrance. Rooms are Rs 60/80, with air-cooling Rs 90/115 or with air-con Rs 120/150. There are hot showers and a Rs 15 dormitory. The rooms are excellent and the restaurant food is very good too, but not everybody seems to think the staff are too wonderful! At both places prices are lower in the off season.

A cycle-rickshaw from town will cost Rs 3 to Rs 5 to the Tourist Bungalow, which is some distance out. If you're told it's full, a little polite persistence may well solve the problem. Near the bus station the *Tourist Lodge* has rooms from Rs 15 for a single, but the food is not good value. In the town, a km from the park, the *Govind Niwas Guest* (tel 3347) has rooms from Rs 100, all with attached bath and balconies. The *Kohinoor Hotel* is near the main intersection and has rooms from Rs 15 and good food.

Getting There

It is only three hours by train from Delhi to Bharatpur. The town is on the Agra-

Rajasthan Top: Fruit sellers outside the bus station, Jaipur (TW)
Bottom: Palace of the Winds, Jaipur (TW)

Rajasthan Top: City Palace, Udaipur (TW)
Left: Wall painting, Udaipur Palace (PC)
Right: Doorman, Rambagh Palace Hotel, Jaipur (TW)

Jaipur road, just two hours by bus from Agra or an hour from Fatehpur Sikri – buses cost about Rs 4. The Agra and Fatehpur Sikri buses run right by the front door of the Tourist Bungalow and will stop if you ask. By bus it's 4½ hours from Jaipur and the fare is Rs 23. 'The Rajasthan bus company seem to select their most decrepit bus for this run; beware of holes in the floor almost big enough to fall through. Our bus had no starter motor or seat back cushions', wrote one visitor. Travel time and fare from Delhi are similar.

Getting Around

There are tongas and cycle-rickshaws for getting around the town, and the Rajasthan Tourist Office has a minibus (see the tourist officer in the Tourist Bungalow). You can hire bicycles for Rs 6 a day, a good way to make a dawn visit to the sanctuary, although you'll have to hire your bike the night before. Cycle-rickshaws are also a good way to explore the sanctuary; some of the riders are very helpful and it's much quieter than a minibus.

DEEG

This small town, 35 km from Bharatpur or Mathura, contains the summer palace of the Maharaja of Bharatpur. Built two centuries ago, it seems like a 'modest' palace for a 'modest' Maharaja but in 1762 the Maharaja of Bharatpur had the temerity to attack the Red Fort! Some of the booty he carried off included an entire marble building which can still be seen. The palace is open from 8 am to noon and 1 to 7 pm, and admission is free. Deeg has other palaces and gardens laid out with foundations in the Moghul style.

Places to Stay

The *Deeg Dak Bungalow* (tel 18) costs Rs 6/10.

SARISKA WILDLIFE SANCTUARY

Situated 107 km from Jaipur and 200 km from Delhi, the sanctuary is in a valley surrounded by barren mountains. It covers 480 square km and has blue bulls, sambhar, spotted deer, wild boar and, above all, tigers. The sanctuary can be visited year-round, except during July/August when the animals move to higher ground.

The best time to see the wildlife is in the evening or at night; night outings are arranged at a rather steep cost of Rs 40 per person. 'You see mainly deer during the two-hour tour', reported a visitor, 'most of them fleeing in panic at the approach, at tremendous speed, of a lurching minibus full of screaming tourists with a man halfway out of the cab waving a spotlight and shouting excitedly'.

A cheaper game run can be had for only a rupee by taking the daily bus to the Kaligati ranger post. Nilgai, spotted deer, sambhar, wild boar and other animals can be seen on the way. At Kaligati there is a 'watch tower' – a pill-box affair beside a waterhole which is an excellent hide from which to watch and photograph animals. You can stay over-night for Rs 20 (Rs 10 for Indians), but take a sleeping bag, food and drink – mattresses are provided. If you don't want rats for company it would pay to block up the windows at night!

Entry to the park costs Rs 10 for foreigners, only Rs 2 for Indians.

Places to Stay

The *Tiger Den Tourist Bungalow* at the sanctuary is very good but rather expensive with rooms from Rs 60 to Rs 160. It also has a Rs 10 dormitory. There is a cheaper *Forest Rest House* and the much more expensive *Hotel Sariska Palace* where rooms cost Rs 300 to Rs 500. This former Maharaja's hunting lodge is worth visiting for a drink.

Getting There

Sariska is 35 km from Alwar, which is a convenient town for getting to the sanctuary. There are direct buses to Alwar from Delhi (170 km) and Jaipur (146 km).

ALWAR

The huge fort stands 300 metres above the city. It was seized from the Moghuls by Maharaja Pratap Singh in 1775. Alwar also has a city palace, the Vinay Vilas Mahal, and the Government Museum which is closed on Fridays.

Places to Stay

The *Lake Castle Tourist Bungalow* (tel 3764) is at Siliserh, some distance from Alwar, and has rooms at Rs 60 to Rs 100. There is a variety of cheaper hotels, including the *Alka Hotel* (tel 2796) and the *Ashoka Hotel* (tel 2027) plus *Railway Retiring Rooms*.

AJMER (population 280,000)

South of Jaipur, Ajmer is a green oasis on the shore of the Ana Sagar Lake and hemmed in by barren hills. Ajmer always had great strategic importance and in its time was sacked by Mahmud of Ghanzi on one of his periodic forays from Afghanistan. Later it became a favourite residence of the great Moghuls. Sir Thomas Roe met with Jehangir in Ajmer in 1616 – one of the first contacts between the Moghuls and the British.

Later the city was taken by the Scindias, then handed over to the British in 1818 – it was thus one of the few places in Rajasthan controlled directly by the British rather than being part of a 'princely state'. Ajmer is a major pilgrimage place for Muslims during the fast of Ramadan. Today it is an easygoing and interesting town, although for most travellers it is just a stepping-stone to nearby Pushkar.

Orientation & Information

The Tourist Office is in the Tourist Bungalow (tel 20430). The bus stand is on the Jaipur side of town and close to the Tourist Bungalow, while the railway station, and most of the other hotels, are on the other side of town. The lake is more-or-less between the two, but slightly to the north.

Ana Sagar Lake

This artificial lake was created in the 12th century by damming the River Luni. On its bank is a fine park, the Dault Bagh, with a series of marble pavilions erected by Shah Jahan in 1637. It's a popular site for an evening stroll. Because the lake tends to dry up if the monsoon is poor, the city's water supply is taken from Foy Sagar Lake, five km further up the valley. There are good views from the hill beside the Dault Bagh.

Dargah

In the old part of town, at the foot of a barren hill, this is one of India's most important places of pilgrimage for Muslims. The Dargah is the tomb of a Sufi saint who came to Ajmer in 1192. Construction of the shrine was completed by Humayun and the gate added by the Nizam of Hyderabad. Akbar used to make the pilgrimage to the Dargah from Agra once a year.

As you enter the courtyard, removing your shoes at the gateway, there is a mosque constructed by Akbar on the right. The large iron cauldrons are for offerings customarily shared amongst families connected with the shrine's upkeep. In an inner court there is another mosque built by Shah Jahan. Constructed of white marble, it has 11 arches and a Persian inscription running the full length of the building.

The saint's tomb is in the centre of the second court with a marble dome; inside, the actual tomb is surrounded by a silver platform. The shrine doors have horseshoes nailed on them, offerings from successful horse dealers! Beware of 'guides' hassling for donations around the Dargah with the standard fake donation books, all donations over Rs 50!

Adhai-din-ka-jhonpra

Continue on beyond the Darah and, on the very outskirts of town, you'll come to the ruins of this mosque which, according to legend, was built in 2½ days – as its

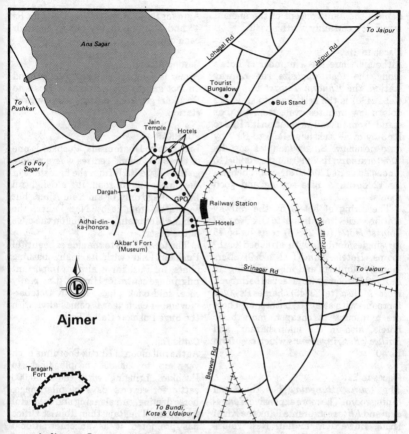

name indicates. It was originally a Jain college built in 1153, but in 1192 Muhammad Ghori took Ajmer and converted it into a mosque by adding a seven-arched wall in front of the pillared hall.

Although the mosque is now much damaged, it is a particularly fine piece of architecture – the pillars are all different and the arched 'screen', with its damaged minarets, is noteworthy. If you continue beyond the mosque for three km you'll reach, after a steep 1½-hour climb, the Taragarh or Star Fort with an excellent view over the city.

Akbar's Palace

Back in the city near the railway station, this imposing fort was built by Akbar in 1570 and today houses the Ajmer museum. The collection has some fine sculpture and a rather poor collection of Moghul and Rajput armour. The museum is closed on Fridays and there's a small admission fee.

Nasiyan Temple

The 'Red Temple' is a Jain temple built in the last century with a double-storey hall containing gilt wooden figures from Jain mythology. The series of large models depicts the Jain concept of the ancient world. It's certainly worth a visit.

Places to Stay

Although there are a number of hotels along the road opposite the railway station, the *Khadim Tourist Bungalow* (tel 20490) is the best place to stay. It's only a few minutes' walk from the bus stand; from the railway station it's Rs 2 to Rs 3 by cycle-rickshaw, Rs 5 to Rs 7 by auto-rickshaw. Singles/doubles cost Rs 40/50 ordinary, Rs 70/90 deluxe, Rs 90/115 air cooled or Rs 120/150 air-con. There's a Rs 12 dorm. A nice setting and good rooms.

The string of hotels by the railway station varies from dismal to OK. *Nagpal Tourist Hotel* (tel 21603) costs Rs 55/75 for singles/doubles with attached bathrooms. *Hotel Anand* (tel 20090) offers 'homely comforts and modern living' in its Rs 40/60 rooms with attached bathroom; *Hotel Malwa* (tel 23343) charges Rs 30/55 for rooms with attached bathroom. There are a number of cheaper, more basic hotels, also in the main bazaar, and *Railway Retiring Rooms* which cost from Rs 40.

Places to Eat

The *Tourist Bungalow* has the usual dining room. The more expensive *Honeydew* and *Elite* restaurants flank the KEM (King Edward Memorial) Rest House near the railway station.

Getting There

There are buses every half-hour from Jaipur to Ajmer. Some go straight through non-stop. The trip costs Rs 17.50 to Rs 24.50. The 138-km trip takes 2½ hours. The Pink City express train takes a similar amount of time.

From Ajmer you can continue on to Jodhpur (198 km, 4½ hours, Rs 34), Udaipur (302 km via Chittorgarh, Rs 40), Chittorgarh (190 km, Rs 21 to Rs 25), Kota (200 km via Bundi, Rs 27) and Bikaner (Rs 36). There's a daily bus to

Agra for Rs 46, a bus to New Delhi for Rs 47 and also one luxury bus to Jodhpur each day.

Getting Around

Ajmer is compact enough to get around on foot and by cycle-rickshaw. Buses to Pushkar go from outside the railway station.

PUSHKAR

Like Goa or Dharamsala, Pushkar is one of those travellers' centres where people go for a little R&R from the hardships of life on the Indian road. It's a delightful little village only 11 km from Ajmer but separated from it by Nag Pahar, the 'Snake Mountain', and right on the edge of the desert.

The town clings to the side of beautiful Pushkar Lake with its many bathing ghats, for Pushkar is also an important pilgrimage centre for Hindus. It's a really nice, laid-back place, but in October-November each year it comes alive with the huge Pushkar Cattle Fair.

Cattle Fair

At the full moon of Kartik Poornima each year up to 200,000 people flock to Pushkar, bringing with them 50,000 cattle for several days of pilgrimage, horse dealing, camel racing and colourful festivities. The Rajasthan Tourist Office has promoted it as an international attraction by adding Rajasthan dance programmes and other cultural events, and by putting up a huge tent city for foreign visitors. It's one of India's biggest and most colourful festivals. Future dates:

1987	2-6 November
1988	20-23 November
1989	10-13 November

Temples & Lake

Pushkar is packed with temples, although many were destroyed by Aurangzeb. The most famous is what is said to be the only temple to Brahma in India. It's marked by a red spire and over the entrance gateway is the *hans* or goose symbol of Brahma, who is said to have personally chosen Pushkar as its site. The Rangji temple is also important.

Numerous ghats run down to the lake, and pilgrims are constantly bathing in the lake's holy waters. Don't photograph the bathers, and approach the lake with a little reverence. The pilgrims are touchy, and tossing a cigarette end in the lake would probably get you an instant one-way ticket out of your current cycle of existence. As a change from the lakeside you can make the one-hour trek up to the hilltop temple overlooking the lake. Do it early in the morning; the view is very fine.

Places to Stay

There's a severe accommodation shortage at Pushkar and hotels are often full, especially the nicer places. The *Sarovar Tourist Bungalow* (tel 40) is on the side of the lake opposite the Brahma Temple. Part of it is an exotic-looking old palace once owned by the Maharaja of Jaipur. Despite a recent extension which completely fails to match the fine old part, getting a room here is still difficult. Dorm beds are Rs 12, bathless singles Rs 15, better rooms Rs 25/30 or with bath Rs 40/50. Some recent visitors have complained about neglect and declining standards.

The *Pushkar Hotel* has a wonderful lawn ending right by the lakeside. This proximity to the lake has caused some local difficulties; the hotel permits no non-vegetarian food to enter its area. Rooms start from Rs 15 to Rs 25, deluxe rooms are Rs 50/60 and there's a dorm. It's often full up.

The *Peacock Holiday Resort* has a spacious and shady courtyard that's pleasantly quiet except for the birds. Very basic singles cost from Rs 10; rooms with bath are Rs 25 single, Rs 35 double, Rs 40 with fan.

There are plenty of small hotels and guest houses around town like the *Krishna Hotel* (tel 43) which costs Rs 15/20 or Rs 30 for a room with bath – it's a friendly little place with a pleasant garden. Halfway around the lake at the Pushkar bazaar the *Natraj Guest House* is just Rs 10/15. Or there's the *Gopal Rest House* and a host of others.

During the Cattle Fair, which attracts several thousand foreign visitors, the tourist office erects a tent city with beds for about 1000 people. Costs run from Rs 30 in a dormitory tent up to as much as Rs 450 in a deluxe tent with meals. Prices everywhere skyrocket at this time of year.

Places to Eat

There are plenty of small food stalls and cafés all over town, but take care where you eat. A lot of people get sick in Pushkar.

The *Sunset Café* by the Tourist Bungalow and right by the water is popular, but the food is indifferent and the service terribly slow. It's run like an Indian version of Fawlty Towers and the standards of hygiene are very low. The fruit juices are good, but they too take a long time to come.

In the middle of Pushkar, by the bazaar, the *Rooftop Restaurant* is in the same building as the Natraj Guest House and is very popular in the evenings. The menu features Russian caviar on toast (Rs 300), smoked Scottish salmon (Rs 450) and other extremely unlikely delicacies! The real menu is all less than Rs 10.

Right at the end of the lakeside road, by the Brahma temple, the *RS Restaurant* is said to be good and safe – a sign out front announces that they boil all the water for 30 minutes. *Shri Venkatesh* at the start of the main street is friendly and cheap.

Getting There

Buses run frequently from Ajmer, outside the railway station, for Rs 2.25. They also go, less frequently, from the bus stand and then end up at the other side of Pushkar. It's a spectacular climb up and over the hills, but the bus is likely to be too crowded to offer much of a view.

You can continue straight on from Pushkar to Jodhpur without having to backtrack to Ajmer, but this bus via Merta can take eight hours. It's much faster to go to Ajmer and take the 4½-hour express bus.

Things to Buy
Like any good freak centre Pushkar has lots of travellers' clothes tailors. During the Cattle Fair there are many artisans selling locally made jewellery and other items.

KISHANGARH
Noted for its school of painting which is still produced today, this small town is 27 km from Ajmer.

KOTA (population 240,000)
Kota was the capital of an independent state of the same name, which was integrated into Rajasthan after independence. Today Kota is the industrial centre of Rajasthan (mainly chemicals), due principally to the hydro-electric power plants on the Chambal River. There is also an atomic power plant near Kota.

Orientation & Information
The Tourist Office is at the Chambal Tourist Bungalow. Kota is strung out along the east bank of the Chambal River. The railway station is well to the north; the Tourist Bungalow and bus stand are in the middle; and Chambal Gardens, the fort and the Kota Barrage are to the south.

Fort
Kota Fort has two museums. The government museum (open 10 am to 5 pm, daily except Friday) is only of mild interest, but the Rao Madho Singh Museum (open

11 am to 5 pm, daily except Friday) is superb. It is entered by a gateway topped by rampant elephants like the ones at the fort at Bundi. Inside you'll find exhibits of weapons, clothing and more fine murals like those at nearby Bundi. Until 1572 Kota was part of the state of Bundi.

Chambal Gardens
The gardens south of the fort at Amar Niwas are popular for picnics and have a pond well stocked with garwhal crocodiles. The pond also has some flamingoes, which appear remarkably unbothered by their companions. At Bhitariya Kund, upstream from Chambal Gardens, there is a popular swimming spot in the surprisingly clear waters of the Chambal River.

The Kota Barrage acts as a control over the river's waters and feeds an irrigation canal system. It's also used to cross the river when the 'Irish' bridge from Bundi is flooded. A little upstream from Kota the Chambal runs through a spectacular gorge.

Jag Mandir
Near the Tourist Bungalow, this large tank has a building on a small island in the centre. Beside the Tourist Bungalow is a curious collection of somewhat neglected but imposingly large royal tombs.

Close to Kota
There are a number of interesting sites around Kota. At Baroli, 40 km from Kota on the way to Pratap Sagar, is one of the oldest temple complexes in Rajasthan. Many sculptures from these 9th-century temples are displayed in the Kota government museum. The Pratap Sagar Dam is the Chambal's second dam.

At Jhaira Patan, 60 km from Kota on the Jhalawar road, are the ruins of an old Surya or sun temple. Ramgarh, 64 km from Kota on a jeepable road, has some notable temples. Only eight km out of Kota there's a bridge built by Colonel

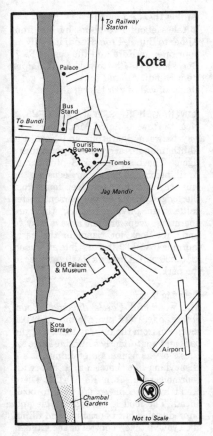

Kota

right up to Rs 170 for a double with air-con. There are *Railway Retiring Rooms* at the station.

The *Brij Raj Bhawan Palace Hotel* (tel 3071) is mainly used by Kota's not-too-frequent tourist groups. The palace is not particularly special although lots of hunting pictures decorate the walls, including one of the local Maharaja hunting moose in Canada.

Getting There

Kota is connected by buses to Bundi, Ajmer, Chittorgah (six hours), Udaipur and other centres in Rajasthan. If you're heading into Madhya Pradesh, a through bus to Gwalior takes 10 to 12 hours. Kota is a junction town on the Bombay-Delhi broad-gauge line and you can fly to Kota with Vayudoot.

Getting Around

Around town there are cycle and auto-rickshaws, buses and tempos. The tempos run a regular service between the railway station, bus stand and main part of town.

BUNDI (population 35,000)

Bundi is a picturesque little town well off the beaten tourist track, 142 km to the south-east of Ajmer and only 39 km west of Kota. The town is beautifully sited in a narrow valley, brooded over by the gloomy Taragarh Fort. The road into Bundi comes in along the other side of the valley so you have a good view over the town and across to the fort as you arrive.

A word of warning – Bundi is almost too unspoilt. So few tourists pass through that most things are kept under lock and key. If you want to see the famous palace murals, you must either make enquiries beforehand to ensure the keys are there, or else be prepared to 'persuade' the chowkidar to let you into whatever is open.

Tod, a notable British 'Political Agent' of the Raj days, and the author of the *Annals & Antiquities of Rajasthan*.

Places to Stay

The pleasant *Chambal Tourist Bungalow* (tel 26527) is conveniently close to the bus stand. There are singles/doubles at Rs 45/ 60, Rs 70/90 and Rs 100/125 with air-con. Dorm beds are Rs 8.

There are several other hotels in Kota, including the *Payal Hotel* (tel 5401) at Nayapura and the *Navrang Hotel* (tel 3294) at Civil Lines with rooms from Rs 30

Orientation

The bus station is at the Kota, eastern end of town. Since accommodation is limited you can best see Bundi by stopping, looking around and then continuing on rather than planning to stay overnight. Simply walk into the town and you'll see the Taragarh Fort and palace up the hill on your right. The town is surrounded by a walled fortification with four gateways.

Taragarh Fort

The Star Fort was built in 1372 and is reached by a steep road up the hillside to its enormous gateway, topped by rampant elephants. Inside the palace is the Chitrashala or picture gallery covered with murals of hunting, historical and religious scenes painted in Bundi style. There's a fine view over Bundi from the fort ramparts. Directly below are the Ratan Daulat or horse stables.

Naval Sagar

Also visible from the fort is the square artificial lake of Naval Sagar. In the centre is a temple to Varuna, the Aryan god of water.

Other

Bundi's other attractions are all out of town and difficult to reach without transport. The modern palace with its beautiful artificial tank and gardens is several km out of town on the Ajmer side at Phool Sagar. Shikar Burj is a small hunting lodge and picnic spot near Bundi. Cenotaphs of Bundi's rulers are near here at Khshar Bagh. Another small palace, the Sukh Niwas, is located at the Jait Sagar tank.

Places to Stay

Bundi's accommodation is of the 'government officials only tourists not welcome' variety. There's a *Circuit House* (Rs 20) and a much less luxurious *Dak Bungalow* near the bus stand.

Getting There & Around

It takes about five hours by bus from Ajmer to Bundi. From Bundi it's only an hour or so to Kota and the cost is Rs 7. Buses also go to Chittorgarh and Udaipur from Bundi. Around town, you've got a choice of walking or taking a tonga.

RANTHAMBHOR – SAWAI MADHOPUR

Near the town of Sawai Madhopur, midway between Bharatpur and Kota, the Ranthambhor reserve is the place to see tigers. The best time is September to April, before the monsoon. Jeeps are the only way into the park. Jeep tours from the lodge cost Rs 50 per person, better value than private jeeps *if* they are operating. Jeeps are not always easy to find. You look for tigers in the early morning (6 to 9.30 am) and late afternoon (3 to 5.30 pm). There's a Rs 10 entry fee to the park.

Places to Stay

The wonderful *Castle Jhoomar Baori Forest Lodge* (tel Sawai Madhopur 620) is seven km from the railway station at the park and was formerly a hunting lodge for guests of the Maharaja of Jaipur. It's a Disneyland-like hotel on a hill with enormous rooms from Rs 100/125. There aren't many rooms so it's wise to book ahead. The food is 'unimaginative and unpredictable but nourishing and filling once you've taken control of the kitchen and the cook!'

The Maharaja of Jaipur's *Hunting Lodge* is three km from the railway station and rooms are often available. Book through the City Palace at Jaipur. *Jogi Mahal* is a small lodge on the edge of a water-lily-covered lake (with crocodiles?), overlooked by an old fort on a rocky hill. A 'magical' place although lacking electricity and certain other basic necessities! Rooms are Rs 75 and you must bring your own food. It's about 15 km from the railway station.

Getting There

Sawai Madhopur is on the main Delhi-Bombay railway line. You can get on or off at Bharatpur and Kota too. From the railway station it's a one-hour tonga ride (Rs 20) the 12 km to the tourist lodge at Ranthambhor.

CHITTORGARH (population 30,000)

The hilltop fortress of Chittorgarh sums up the whole romantic, doomed ideal of Rajput chivalry. Three times in its long history Chittor was sacked by a stronger enemy, and on each occasion the end came in textbook Rajput fashion. The men donned the saffron wedding robes of martyrdom and rode out from the fort to certain death. Meanwhile the women built a huge funeral pyre and marched into the flames in the form of ritual suicide known as *jauhar*.

Chittor's first defeat took place in 1303 when Ala-ud-din Khilji, the Pathan king of Delhi, besieged the fort in order to capture the beautiful Padmini who was married to Bhim Singh, uncle of the Rana. When defeat was inevitable the Rajput noblewomen, including Padmini, committed jauhar and Bhim Singh led the orange-clad noblemen out to their deaths.

In 1535 it was Bahadur Shah, the Sultan of Gujarat, who besieged the fort and once again it was jauhar for the women and the orange robes for the men. It is said that 13,000 Rajput women and 32,000 Rajput warriors died.

It was only 33 years later, in 1568, that the final 'Sack of Chittor' took place, and on this occasion it was the Moghul emperor Akbar who took the town. Once again the fort was defended heroically, but once again the odds were overwhelming and the women performed jauhar, the fort gates were flung open and 8000 orange-robed warriors rode out to their deaths. Maharana Udai Singh fled to Udaipur and re-established his capital there. In 1616 Jehangir returned Chittor to the Rajputs, but they did not move the capital back from Udaipur.

Today the fort of Chittor is a virtually deserted ruin, but impressive reminders of its heyday still stand and perhaps you can catch a whiff of the romantic heroism in the air.

Orientation

The fort stands on a 280-hectare site on top of a 180-metre-high hill, which rises abruptly from the surrounding plain. Until 1568 the town of Chittor was also on the hilltop, within the fort walls, but today the modern town, known as Lower Town, sprawls to the west of the hill. A river separates it from the bus stand, railway line and modern part of the town.

Information

The Tourist Office (tel 9) is in the Janta Tourist Rest House near the railway station. It's open 8 am to 12 noon and 3 to 6 pm.

The Fort

Bhim, one of the Pandava heroes of the *Mahabharata*, is credited with the fort's original construction. All of Chittor's attractions are within the fort. A zigzag ascent over a km long leads through seven gateways to the main gate on the western side, the Ram Pol.

On the ascent you pass two *chhatris*, memorials marking spots where Jaimal and Kalla, heroes of the 1568 siege, fell during the struggle against Akbar. Another chhatri, further up the hill, marks the spot where Patta fell. The main gate on the eastern side of the fort is the Suraj Pol. Within the fort there is a circular road around the ruins and a deer park at the southern end.

Palace of Rana Kumbha

Entering the fort and turning right, you come almost immediately to the ruins of this palace. It contains elephant and horse stables and a Shiva temple. One of the jauhars is said to have taken place in a

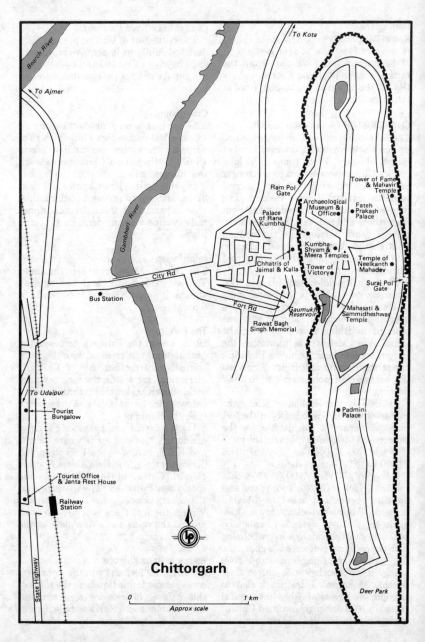

To Kota

To Ajmer

Beach River

Gambheri River

Tower of Fame
& Mahavir
Temple

Ram Pol
Gate

Archaeological
Museum &
Office

Fateh
Prakash
Palace

Palace
of Rana
Kumbha

Kumbha-
Shyam &
Meera Temples

Temple of
Neelkanth
Mahadev

City Rd

Chhatris of
Jaimal & Kalla

Tower of
Victory

Suraj Pol
Gate

Bus Station

Fort Rd

Gaumukh
Reservoir

Mahasati &
Sammidheshwar
Temple

Rawat Bagh
Singh Memorial

To Udaipur

Tourist
Bungalow

Padmini
Palace

Tourist Office
& Janta Rest House

Railway
Station

State Highway

Chittorgarh

0   1 km
Approx scale

Deer Park

vaulted cellar. Across from the palace is the archaeological office and museum, and the treasury building or Nau Lakha Bhandar.

Fateh Prakash Palace
Just beyond the Rana Kumbha Palace, this much more modern palace (Maharana Fateh Singh died in 1930) houses an interesting museum with statues found in various buildings in the fort.

Tower of Victory
Continuing anti-clockwise around the fort, you come to the Tower of Victory or Jaya Stambh. Erected by Rana Kumbha to commemorate his victory over Mahmud Khilji of Malwa in 1440, the tower was constructed between 1458 and 1468. It rises 37 metres in nine storeys and, for Rs 0.50, you can climb the broad stairs to the top. Watch your head on the low bits.

Hindu sculptures adorn the outside of the tower, but the dome was damaged by lightning and repaired during the last century. Close to the tower is the Mahasati, an area where the *ranas* were cremated during Chittorgarh's period as the Mewar capital. There are many *sati* stones here. The Sammidheshwar Temple stands in the same area.

Gaumukh Reservoir
Walk down beyond the temple, and at the very edge of the cliff is this deep tank. A spring feeds the tank from a carved cow's mouth in the cliffside – from which the reservoir got its name. The opening here leads to the cave in which Padmini and her compatriots are supposed to have committed jauhar.

Padmini's Palace
Continuing south you come to Padmini's Palace, beside a large pool with a pavilion in its centre. Legends relate that Padmini stood in this pavilion and that Ala-ud-din was permitted to see her reflection in a mirror in the palace. This glimpse was the spark that convinced him to destroy Chittor in order to possess her.

The bronze gates in this pavilion were carried off by Akbar and can now be seen in the fort at Agra. Continuing round the circular road, you pass the deer park, the Bhimlat Tank, the Suraj Pol Gate and the Neelkanth Mahadev Jain temple, and reach the Tower of Fame.

Tower of Fame
Chittor's other famous tower, the Kirti Stambha or Tower of Fame, is older (probably built around the 12th century) and smaller (22 metres high), than the Tower of Victory. Built by a Jain merchant, it is dedicated to Adinath, first Jain Tirthankar, and is decorated with nude figures of the various Tirthankars – thus indicating that it is a Digambara or 'sky clad' monument. A narrow stairway leads through the seven storeys to the top.

Other Buildings
Close to the Fateh Prakash Museum is the Meera Temple, built in the ornate Indo-Aryan style during the reign of Rana Kumbha, and associated with the mystic-poetess Meerabai. The larger temple in this same compound is the Kumbha Shyam Temple or Temple of Vriji. The Jain (but Hindu-influenced) Singa Chowri Temple is nearby.

Across from Padmini's Palace is the Kalika Mata Temple, an 8th-century Surya or Sun God temple, which was later converted to a temple to the goddess Kali. At the northern tip of the fort is another gate, the Lokhota Bari, while at the southern end is a small opening from which criminals and traitors were hurled into the abyss.

Tours
There is a daily Rs 12 tour which takes in all the main sites at the fort. The tour operates from the Tourist Office and Tourist Bungalow from 8 to 11.30 am and from 3 to 6.30 pm. In summer the morning tour is half an hour earlier, the afternoon tour half an hour later.

Places to Stay & Eat

Accommodation possibilities in Chittor are limited. The *Panna Tourist Bungalow* (tel 273) is close to the railway station and the Udaipur road. It's a fairly modern building with rooms at Rs 30/40, Rs 45/60 for deluxe rooms, Rs 75/90 with air cooling, Rs 100/125 with air-con. There's also a Rs 12 dormitory.

Closer to the railway station is the *Janta Tourist Rest House* (Janta Avas Grah) (tel 9) where the Tourist Office is located. Spartan doubles at Rs 20 or Rs 30 with bath. Also close to the railway station is the very basic and not so special *Hotel Sanvaria* where rooms cost Rs 15/30. There are other similar hotels and *Railway Retiring Rooms* at Rs 25 or Rs 50 with air-con.

The *Tourist Bungalow* has a dining-hall breakfast for Rs 16, thalis for Rs 12, a vegetarian lunch or dinner for Rs 26. There are various small restaurants and a refreshment room at the station. The *Janta Rest House* has a restaurant but it doesn't look too good.

Getting There

Chittor is on the main bus and rail routes. It's 182 km from Ajmer or 112 km from Udaipur by road. Bus fare to Udaipur is Rs 15 to Rs 16; the trip takes three hours and along the way you can see fields of pink and white opium poppies growing (quite legally) by the roadside. Bundi (156 km) costs Rs 20 to Rs 22 by express bus, Ajmer Rs 25.

Getting Around

It's six km from the railway station to the fort, and the fort itself sprawls quite a bit – so if you're not taking a tour you'll need transport. There are tongas or unmetered auto-rickshaws for hire, or you can rent a bicycle.

AROUND CHITTORGARH
Menal

On the Bundi-Chittorgarh road, 48 km from Bundi, Menal is a complex of Shiva temples built during the Gupta period. Bijolia, 16 km from Menal, was once a group of 100 temples but today only three are left standing. One has a huge figure of Ganesh. A diversion between Menal and Bijolia takes you to Mandalgarh, the third fort of Mewar built by Rana Kumbha – the others are the great fort of Chittorgarh and the fort at Kumbhalgarh.

Nagri

One of the oldest towns in Rajasthan, Nagri is 14 km north of Chittor. Hindu and Buddhist remains from the Mauryan to the Gupta period have been found here.

Bhilwara

Between Chittor and Ajmer, this small industrial city is of no interest except for one of those weird pieces of dislocated reality that India throws at you from time to time. A man asked a local industrialist for a lakh (100,000 rupees) donation to build a temple with. No, replied the factory owner. Then I'll stand on one leg outside your factory until you change your mind, replied the would-be temple builder. As you pass through Bhilwara on the main road, you'll see a traffic island in the middle of the road with a tree and a shrine. And under the tree stands the man, on one leg, as he has done since 1970! He has a sort of swing at chest height to lean against to sleep and, as has anybody in India engaged on a great but hopeless quest, he has a band of followers to tend to his needs. He does change legs from time to time.

UDAIPUR (population 225,000)

The lake city of Udaipur is a cool oasis in the dry heart of Rajasthan. It's probably the most romantic city in a state where every city has some romantic or exotic tale to tell.

Udaipur has several palaces, two of which should not be missed. The Lake Palace, now converted into a luxury hotel, is simply delightful – if you can afford to stay there don't miss the opportunity. If you can't afford to stay, consider a meal and at least a look around. The huge City Palace on the lake side has been converted into a museum and is well worth a visit. Udaipur also has gardens, fountains, museums and temples, and there are a number of interesting excursions around town.

The Maharana of Udaipur is the highest ranking of the Rajput rulers and head of the 'Solar' Rajput clan. Udaipur is also known as the 'City of Sunrise' and the Maharana's standard bears an image of the sun. The city was founded in 1567 by Maharana Udai Singh, following the third sack of Chittor.

Orientation & Information

The old city, bounded by the remains of a city wall, sprawls away on the east side of Lake Pichola. The railway station and bus station are both just outside the city wall to the south-east. The Tourist Office (tel 3509) and the Tourist Bungalow are also outside the city walls, to the north-east and only a km or so from the bus stand. Tourist Office hours are 10 am to 5 pm Monday to Saturday.

There are also tourist information counters at the railway station and airport. The GPO is directly north of the old city, behind the movie theatre at Chetak Circle, but the poste restante is at the post office at the junction of Hospital Rd and the road north from Delhi Gate, near the Tourist Bungalow.

Pichola Lake

The beautiful Pichola Lake was enlarged by Maharana Udai Singh after he founded the city. He built a masonry dam known as the Badi Pol, and the lake now stretches four km in length by three km wide. The City Palace extends a considerable distance along the east bank of the lake, while south of the palace a pleasant garden runs down to the lake. North of the palace it is very interesting to wander along the lake, where there are some beautiful scenes of bathing and dhobi ghats. Out in the lake are two islands – Jagniwas and Jag Mandir. You can take a Rs 40 sunset barge tour complete with musicians from the Lake Palace Hotel.

Islands

Jagniwas is the Lake Palace island, about 1.5 hectares in size. The palace was built by Maharana Jagat Singh II in 1754 and covers the whole island. Today it has been converted into a luxury hotel with courtyards, fountains, gardens and a swimming pool. It's a delightful place, and even if you can only dream of staying there, it's worth the trip out to have a look around. A launch crosses to the island from Bhansi Ghat, just south of the Palace Museum, but casual visitors are discouraged unless you're planning to dine. Or say you are.

The other island palace, Jag Mandir, may also eventually become a hotel. It was commenced by Maharana Karan Singh, but takes its name from Maharana Jagat Singh (1628-1652), who made a number of additions to it. It is said that the Moghul emperor Shah Jahan derived some of his ideas for the Taj Mahal from this palace after he stayed here in 1623-24, while leading a revolt against his father, Jehangir. The view across the lake from the southern end, with the city and its great palace rising up behind the island palaces, is a scene of rare beauty. A couple of the cheap hotels (see Places to Stay below) have absolutely superb views across the lake.

City Palace & Museum

The huge City Palace towering over the lake is the largest palace complex in Rajasthan. The palace is actually a conglomeration of buildings added by various maharanas, but it manages to retain a surprising uniformity of design. It was originally commenced by Maharana Udai Singh, the city's founder. The palace is surmounted by balconies, towers and cupolas, and there are fine views over

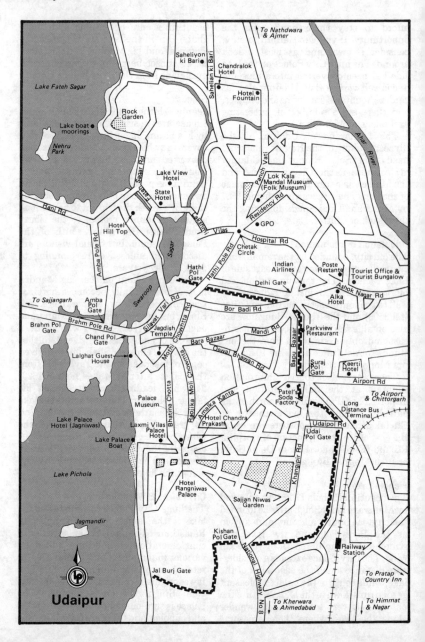

Udaipur

the lake and the city from the upper terraces.

The palace is entered from the northern end through the Bari Pol of 1600 and the triple Tripolia Gate of 1725 with its eight carved marble arches. It was once a custom for Maharanas to be weighed under the gate and their weight in gold or silver to be distributed to the populace.

The main part of the palace is now preserved as a museum with a large and varied, although somewhat run down, collection. The museum includes the Mor Chowk with its beautiful mosaics of peacocks, the favourite Rajasthani bird. The Manak or Ruby Mahal has glass and porcelain figures. Krishna Vilas has a remarkable collection of miniatures. In the Bari Mahal there is a fine central garden. More paintings can be seen in the Zanana Mahal. The Moti Mahal has beautiful mirror work, the Chini Mahal is covered in ornamented tiles. Other exhibits even include the princely Rolls-Royces.

The City Palace Museum is entered through the Ganesh Deori to the Rai Angam or Royal Courtyard. The museum is open from 9.30 am to 4 pm; entry is Rs 3 plus Rs 3 for a camera. There's also a government museum within the palace complex. Exhibits include a stuffed kangaroo and Siamese-twin deers.

Jagdish Temple

Only 150 metres north of the entrance to the City Palace, this fine Indo-Aryan temple was built by Maharana Jagat Singh in 1651 and enshrines a black stone image of Vishnu as Jagannath, Lord of the Universe. A brass image of the Garuda is in a shrine in front of the temple, and the steps up to the temple are flanked by elephants.

Lake Fateh Sagar

North of Lake Pichola, this lake was originally built in 1678 by Maharana Jai Singh, but heavy rains destroyed the dam and it was reconstructed by Maharana Fateh Singh. A pleasant lakeside drive winds along the east bank of the lake and a number of hills and parks overlook it. Nehru Park is a popular garden island with a restaurant in the middle of the lake. You can get to it by a boat service from the bottom of Moti Magri Hill (Rs 2).

Pratap Samak

Atop the Moti Magri or 'Pearl Hill' overlooking Fateh Sagar Lake is a statue of Rajput hero Maharana Pratap, who frequently defied the Moghuls, astride his charger Chetak. A visitor commented that his growth in popularity since independence owes much to the fact that he was a Hindu and the Moghuls Muslim! He added that the regard paid to his horse contrasts strongly with the ill-treatment received by tonga ponies below the hill. The path to the top goes through elegant gardens, including a Japanese rock garden. The park is open from 9 am to 6 pm and admission is Rs 1.

Bhartiya Lok Kala Museum

This small museum and foundation for the preservation of folk arts has an interesting collection, including dresses, dolls, masks, musical instruments, paintings and – the high point of the exhibits – puppets. There are regular puppet shows in the museum. Opening hours are 9 am to 6 pm and admission is Rs 2.

Saheliyon ki Bari

In the north of the city, the 'Garden of the Maids of Honour' is a small ornamental garden with fountains, kiosks, marble elephants and a delightful lotus pool. It's open 9 am to 6 pm. Entry is Rs 0.50. It costs Rs 2 to have the fountains turned on, Rs 5 to bring your camera in with you.

Ahar Museum

East of Udaipur are the remains of an ancient city with a small museum and the cenotaphs of the Maharanas of Mewar.

Other

Patel or Sukhadia Circle is north of the

city – in the centre is a huge fountain, illuminated at night. Sajjan Niwas Gardens have pleasant lawns, a zoo and a children's train ride (if it's operating). Beside it is the Rose Garden or Gulab Bagh. Don't confuse the Nehru Park opposite Bapu Bazaar with the island park of the same name in Lake Fateh Sagar. The city park has some strange topiary work, a giant cement teapot, and children's slides incorporating an elephant and a camel.

On the far range of mountains, visible from the city, the gleaming white palace used to be the Maharaja's Monsoon Palace. It's now deserted and the views from the top are incomparable. Round trip is about three hours.

Tours

A daily tour starts at the Tourist Bungalow from 8 am to 1 pm each day. It costs Rs 15 and takes in all the main city sights. A Rs 35 afternoon tour from 2 to 7 pm goes out to Eklingi, Haldighati and Nathdwara.

Places to Stay – bottom end

The *Keerti Hotel* (tel 3639) on Sarsvati Marg is very popular with travellers. It's a short stroll out from the Suraj Pol Gate. There are rooms at all sorts of prices, from Rs 10 for the smallest single up to Rs 35 for the biggest double. All rooms have bathrooms and there's also a Rs 5 dormitory. It's popular, straightforward, crowded and cheap. Don't confuse the Keerti with the nearby 'Keerti Tourist Hotal', so named to cash in on the Keerti's popularity. The impostor is across the road and a bit closer to the gate.

Behind the Keerti on College Rd, the *Ghunghru Guest House* is a reasonable overflow place with rooms at Rs 20 and Rs 25 and a pleasant garden.

Right beside the lake, close to the City Palace and behind the Jagdish Temple, is the excellent *Lalghat Guest House*. Simple rooms, all with common bathroom facilities, are Rs 15/25 for singles/doubles. It's worth the price for the view alone

because the front terrace overlooks the lake. There's a pleasant roof for sunbathing. One of the rooms with bath is right at the front overlooking the lake and costs Rs 75. They do food here and there's a pleasant courtyard.

The nearby *Badi Haveli* is back from the lake and close to the Jagdish Temple, but the view from the roof is, if anything, even better – both these places have five-star views! The Badi Haveli is a nice old building with rooms at Rs 20, 30 and 40. It's pleasant enough but not to the same standard as Lalghat. In the same area on City Palace Rd, the *Hotel Mona Lisa* has rooms at Rs 30/50 with bath. It's OK, nothing special but a reasonable place to fall back on. *Hotel Natural* by Rang Sagar Lake has clean rooms at Rs 20/30. The *Lake View Hotel* (tel 23640) has rooms at Rs 35 to Rs 40, some of them facing the lake.

Continue back down from this crowded and interesting old city area by the lake, and there are several good places along Lake Palace Rd by the Sajjan Niwas Gardens. The *Rang Niwas Palace Hotel* (tel 23891) is a relaxed, pleasant place, built around a green courtyard. Rooms start at Rs 40 without bath, Rs 50 and Rs 75 with bathroom. There are some family rooms at Rs 150 with a double and single room and a huge bathroom. The rooms are fine, the garden is a great place to lounge around in and prices are lower in the off season. Beware of service charges, however. You'll get 10% added onto your room bill, and restaurant charges (food is relatively expensive) are hiked up by 10% for service and 6% for tax.

A little further along Lake Palace Rd is the *Chandra Prakash Hotel* (tel 28109), with rooms at Rs 40 with common bath, Rs 60 with bath, Rs 80 for larger rooms, Rs 130 for a room with air cooling and everything. There's a garden out front. This is another well-run, good-value place.

Across the road from the Chandra Prakash and the Rang Niwas hotels is

Hotel Ratnadeep (tel 24730), with rooms at Rs 25/30 with bath, Rs 35/40 with hot water as well. They even have some Rs 100 super-deluxe 'honeymoon' rooms complete with bathtub and TV! Good value. Close to the bus station (but not right on that busy road), the *Hotel Shalimar* (tel 26807) is run by the same people and is similarly priced.

The *Kajri Tourist Bungalow* (tel 23509), at the traffic circle on Ashoka Rd, is conveniently situated but it's not one of the better tourist bungalows in Rajasthan. The Tourist Office is here and there is a restaurant. It has a Rs 12 dormitory, singles/doubles at Rs 30/40, deluxe rooms Rs 70/90, rooms with air cooling Rs 90/115, rooms with air-con Rs 120/150. There are some larger family rooms at Rs 50 to Rs 80.

Near the bus stand is a string of hotels, all with low prices and most of them offering reasonable accommodation, useful for emergencies if the above places should be full. The *Apsara Hotel* (tel 23400) and the *Sonika Hotel* (tel 25353) are on City Station Rd. *Hotel Raj* (tel 28262) is in this same area and has rooms at Rs 20. The *Alka Hotel* (tel 23611) is on Shastri Circle across from the Tourist Bungalow and has rooms from Rs 20/35 with common bathroom or Rs 35/50 to Rs 60/85 with bathroom. The rooms look into a central courtyard and the place is big, well kept and pretty good value. Udaipur also has *Railway Retiring Rooms* with rooms and a dormitory.

Finally, there's one interesting place just outside Udaipur. The *Pratap Country Inn* is operated by the same people who manage the Keerti, so go there first and they'll arrange transport out there for you. It's at Titadha village, about seven to eight km out of the city. City buses run there every hour for about a rupee; you can even ride out on a bicycle. They have tents and rooms at prices from as low as Rs 10 to Rs 20 to as high as Rs 50 to Rs 100, as well as a Rs 6 dormitory. There's a swimming pool, free horse riding, camels,

slightly expensive food, beautiful surroundings and a very laid-back atmosphere, but it's straightforward and fairly primitive. If you come out here expecting any luxuries you'll be disappointed.

Places to Stay – top end

Udaipur's top hotel is one of the most delightful in India. It's the luxurious *Lake Palace Hotel* (tel 23241-45), in the middle of Pichola Lake. Singles are Rs 525, doubles Rs 600 to Rs 850, suites up to Rs 2500, and it's the very image of what a Maharaja's palace should be like, with the additional touch of its own little island.

On the lake shore, close to the Lake Palace landing, is the ultra-luxurious *Shivniwas Palace* (tel 23262) with 14 rooms at Rs 500 and 16 suites from Rs 1500 to Rs 3000. 'Prior approval' is needed before you can stay in one of the 'Royal Suites'. It's heavily booked, as is the Lake Palace. If you want to stay in these hotels you have to plan ahead.

Between Pichola and Fateh Sagar lakes are two upper-notch hotels side by side. The ITDC-operated *Laxmi Vilas Palace Hotel* (tel 24411) has rooms at Rs 375/460 with air-con, Rs 190/245 without. Right beside it is the *Hotel Anand Bhawan* (tel 23257) with rooms at Rs 125/165 or at Rs 150/190 with air-con – big rooms with big bathtubs!

A number of hotels span the top to bottom bracket. *Hotel Hilltop* (tel 23708) really is at the top of a hill, overlooking Fateh Sagar from 5 Amba Mata Marg. Rooms are Rs 225/300 with air-con, Rs 150/225 without. The food and service are good and there are fine views over the lake. A little further around the lake, the *Lake End Hotel* (tel 23841) is a good medium-priced hotel. Rooms are Rs 55 to Rs 80 for singles, Rs 85 to Rs 150 for doubles. With air-cooling they're Rs 140/200, with air-con Rs 175/250.

Near the Saheliyon ki Bari gardens *Hotel Chandralok* (tel 24598) on Saheliyon ki Bari Marg is a neat and tidy place with rooms at Rs 125/175. Also at this quiet northern end of town, *Hotel Fountain* (tel 26646) on Sukhadia Circle is a new hotel with singles at Rs 110, 150 and 250; and doubles at Rs 160, 210 and 250. There's a good lawn area out front.

The *Shikarbadi Hotel* (tel 3200) is about three km out of town on the Ahmedabad Rd and has singles/doubles at Rs 325/450. It's a small but pleasant hotel set in beautiful grounds with swimming pool, lawns and a small lake. It has a deer park and a stud farm – horse and elephant rides are available. The food here is excellent.

Places to Eat

Udaipur is not over-endowed with good places to eat. The *Tourist Bungalow* has a restaurant with the usual menu and variable results – sometimes the food is surprisingly good, sometimes it is not. There are a number of places by Chetak Circle, including a *Kwality* and *Berry's Restaurant* which is rather good. A cold-drinks place here does fruit juice and ice cream.

Opposite Nehru Park (the city's park, not the one in the middle of the lake) and close to the Bank of Baroda is the *Parkview Restaurant*. It might well have a view if it wasn't one of those blackened-window, gloomy-interior Indian places. The food is pretty good, though with the usual non-vegetarian menu.

Patel's Soda Factory near the Suraj Pol gate is a clean and friendly spot for a cold drink; the fruit juices (orange Rs 4) are terrific. They got an autographed picture of Roger Moore from the filming of the James Bond 007 epic *Octopussy* in Udaipur in late '82, but they haven't got any sign in English script. It looks like a cold-drinks place though. There are several cheap vegetarian places around Suraj Pol Gate but no signs in our script.

If you venture across the waters to the *Lake Palace Hotel*, their excellent buffet dinner is Rs 85. Ordering a la carte would typically cost Rs 100 to Rs 140 per person plus drinks, but non-residents are only allowed to have the buffet! A beer will set you back Rs 35.

Getting There

Air There's a daily multi-stop flight Delhi-Bombay via Udaipur and vice versa. Three days a week there's also a direct Delhi-Udaipur flight. Fares to or from Udaipur include Delhi Rs 514, Jaipur Rs 307, Jodhpur Rs 228, Aurangabad Rs 557 and Bombay Rs 616. The direct flight between Udaipur and Aurangabad can save an awful lot of bus or train time. The Indian Airlines office (tel 23952) is at Delhi Gate.

Rail The daily Chetak Express between Delhi and Udaipur takes nearly 21 hours. Fares for the 739-km trip are Rs 61 in 2nd class, Rs 250 in 1st. The train goes via Jaipur and Ajmer. There is also a daily express between Udaipur and Ahmedabad taking nine to 10 hours.

Bus There are frequent buses from Udaipur to other regional centres such as Ahmedabad, Mt Abu, Ajmer, Jodhpur (a gruelling eight to 10 hours, Rs 40 to Rs 52), Bundi-Kota, Jaipur and Chittorgarh (approximately hourly, three-hour trip, Rs 14 to Rs 15). There are daily luxury buses to Ahmedabad (eight hours, Rs 50) and Jaipur (nine hours, Rs 80).

There are now two routes to Mt Abu – a 180-km route via Gogunda and Pindwara, or a 320-km route via Eklingi, Nathdwara, Sadri and Bali. Some buses go all the way to Mt Abu, while some stop at Abu Road (the railhead for Mt Abu). A daily luxury bus takes five hours and costs Rs 55; the regular bus is Rs 28.

Getting Around

Airport The airport is 25 km from the city, a long way so a taxi will cost you about Rs 75. There's no airport bus, although you could walk out to the main road (half a km) and get a regular bus into the city.

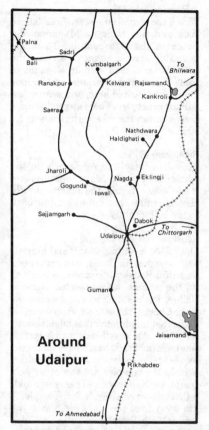

Around Udaipur

Local Transport There's a reasonably OK city bus service. Taxis and auto-rickshaws are unmetered so you have to bargain hard. Udaipur is small enough and vehicle traffic slow enough to make getting around on a bicycle quite enjoyable. You can hire bicycles all over town for around Rs 4 to Rs 5 per day.

Things to Buy
Udaipur has countless small shops and many interesting local crafts. Along Lake Palace Rd and around the Jagdish Temple are particularly good shopping areas.

AROUND UDAIPUR
Eklingi (22 km)
This interesting little village with a number of ancient temples is only a short bus ride north of Udaipur. In the village itself is a Shiva temple originally built in 734 AD, although its present form dates from the rule of Maharana Raimal, who ruled from 1473 to 1509. The walled complex includes an elaborately pillared hall under a large pyramidal roof. There is a four-faced Shiva image of black marble. The temple is open rather odd hours – 5 to 7 am, 10 am to 1 pm, 5 to 7 pm.

At Nagada, about a km off the road and a km before Eklingi, there are three old temples. The Jain temple of Adbudji is fairly well ruined, but its architecture is interesting and it's very old. Nearby is the Sas Bahu or 'Mother and Daughter-in-Law' group. It's quite a little complex, with some very fine and intricate architecture and carvings, including some erotic figures.

Getting There You can get out to these temples most conveniently by hiring a bicycle in Eklingi itself. There are buses from Udaipur to Eklingi every half hour to an hour, although one visitor wrote that the buses weren't that frequent and they couldn't find a bicycle to hire, so the round trip ended up taking a whole day. There is a small Rs 10 guest house in the village.

Haldighati (40 km)
This is where Maharana Pratap valiantly defied the superior Moghul forces of Akbar in 1576. The site is a battlefield and the only thing to see is the chhatri to his horse, Chetak, a few km away. There's a *Rest House* here – clean, with good food and a lovely setting.

Nathdwara (48 km)
The important 18th-century Vishnu temple of Sri Nathji stands here. It's a popular pilgrimage site, but non-Hindus

are not allowed inside. The black stone Vishnu image was brought here from Mathura in 1669 to protect it from Aurangzeb's destructive impulses. According to legend, when an attempt was later made to move the image, the getaway vehicle, a wagon, sank into the ground up to the axles – indicating that the image preferred to stay where it was! The *Gokul Tourist Bungalow* has rooms from Rs 40 to Rs 80 and a dormitory.

Kankroli & Rajsamand Lake (65 km)

At Kankroli, Dwarkadhish (an incarnation of Vishnu) is similar to the temple at Nathdwara and, like that temple, is open at extremely erratic hours. Nearby is a lake created by the dam constructed by Maharana Raj Singh in 1660. There are many ornamental arches and *chhatris* along the huge bund. Raj Singh tangled with Aurangzeb on a number of occasions.

Kumbhalgarh Fort (84 km)

The most important fort in the Mewar region after Chittorgarh, this was built by Maharana Kumbha in the 15th century. The seven great gates of the Badal Mahal lead to the Cloud Palace. The fort, with its many temples and palaces, was renovated in the last century. There's a game reserve here; March to June are the best months to see animals due to the scarcity of waterholes at that time. There are lots of animals including antelope, panther and bear, and it's a good area for walking. You can go through the sanctuary to Ranakpur, and there's a PWD Rest House in Kumbhalgarh. The reserve is 80 km from Udaipur on a good road and then 30 km on a jeepable road (outside of the monsoon).

Jagat (58 km)

The 10th-century Ambika Mata Temple here is not as good as some tourist literature would indicate. It is not in very special condition.

Jaisamand Lake (48 km)

This is the second largest artificial lake in Asia and was built by Maharana Jai Singh in the 17th century. There are beautiful marble *chhatris* around the embankment, each with an elephant in front. The summer palaces of Udaipur queens are located here, and nearby is a wildlife sanctuary. There's a good *Tourist Bungalow* on the lake with rooms at Rs 40/50.

Rikhabdeo (65 km)

This Jain temple to Adinath is on the Ahmedabad road. Major offerings are made every day in the architecturally elegant temple, parts of which date back to the 14th century.

Ranakpur (98 km)

One of the most important, and biggest, Jain temples in India, the extremely beautiful Ranakpur complex is situated in the remote and peaceful Aravalli Valley. The main temple in the complex is the Chaumukha or 'Four-Faced' temple, dedicated to Adinath. This huge, beautifully crafted and well-kept marble temple was built in 1439. It has 29 halls supported by 1444 pillars, no two of which are alike. Within the complex are two other Jain temples to Neminath and Parasnath and, a little distance away, a Sun Temple. A km away from the main complex is the Amba Mata Temple.

The temple is open to non-Jains from noon to 5 pm.

Places to Stay Ranakpur has the *Shilpi Tourist Bungalow* with rooms at Rs 25/30 and Rs 40/50 and a particularly good dormitory at Rs 12. There is also a dharamsala within the complex where you can stay for a donation. If you arrive at a meal time you can get a good thali in the dining hall just inside the main entrance to the complex on your left, again for a donation. Staying overnight at Ranakpur breaks up the long trip between Udaipur and Jodhpur.

Getting There Ranakpur is 39 km from Palna (or Falna) Junction on the Ajmer-Mt Abu rail and road routes. From Udaipur there are half a dozen buses a day to Ranakpur, and you can continue on from here to Jodhpur or Mt Abu on the same day – but the trip to Ranakpur can be a real time-consuming bore. It can take five to six hours, an average of well under 20 kph! There's a daily bus from Mt Abu which terminates at Sadri, only seven km from Ranakpur. The fare is Rs 28.

Ghanerao

About a km out of this attractive small town is the *Ghanerao Royal Castle*, a small castle/palace with six well-kept rooms at Rs 150/200. Ghanerao can make a good base for exploring the various attractions around Udaipur, and the castle's helpful owners arrange a trek from Ghanerao to Kumbhalgarh with an overnight stay at their hunting lodge, Bagha ka Bagh, en route.

MT ABU (population 12,000)

Rajasthan's only hill station spreads out along a 1200-metre-high plateau in the south of the state. It's a pleasant hot-season retreat from the plains, but you won't find many western travellers here – visitors are predominantly Indians, including many honeymooners. Mt Abu is a popular hill station for Gujarat as well as for Rajasthan and its pace is easygoing and relaxed. There is more than simply lower temperatures to attract visitors up here – Mt Abu has a number of important temples, particularly the superb Dilwara group of Jain temples.

Orientation & Information

Mt Abu stretches along a plateau about 22 km long by six km wide. It is 27 km from Abu Road, the railway station for Mt Abu. The main part of the town extends along the road in from Abu Road, down to Nakki Lake. Coming in by bus, you pass first the Tourist Bungalow, up a hill to your right, then a string of hotels,

before you arrive at the bus stand, opposite which is the Tourist Office (tel 51). The office is open 8 to 11 am and 4 to 8 pm.

Continuing from here you pass more hotels and restaurants, the small market to your right, and eventually arrive at the lakefront. The GPO is on Raj Bhavan Rd, opposite the art gallery and museum. Several banks and the Hotel Hill Tone will change money.

Mt Abu has 'the only mountaineering school in the whole of India', reported a rock-climbing visitor, 'but everything about the school was archaic and dangerous. I'm glad the climbs we did were easy, as these guys appear to have no idea about safety'.

Nakki Lake

Virtually in the centre of Mt Abu, the small lake takes its name from the legend that it was scooped out by a god, using only his nails or *nakk*. It's a short and easy stroll around the lake – look for the strange rock formations around it. Best known is Toad Rock, which looks just like a toad about to hop into the lake. Others, like Nun Rock, Nandi Rock or Camel Rock, require rather more imagination. You can hire boats and row (or be rowed) out on the lake. The 14th-century Raghunath Temple stands beside the lake.

Viewpoints

There are various viewpoints around the town, best known of which is Sunset Point. Hordes stroll out here every evening to catch the setting sun and there are food stalls and all the usual entertainments. Other popular points include Honeymoon Point, with a view of the Crags, Robert's Spur and the sunset.

Museum & Art Gallery

The small museum is not very interesting and maintenance leaves a lot to be desired. There are some items from archaeological excavations which date from the 8th to 12th centuries, plus Jain bronzes, carvings, brasswork and local textiles. The term 'art gallery' is really a joke since they only have a half dozen pictures. The museum is on Raj Bhavan Rd and is open from 10 am to 4.30 pm daily, except Fridays. Admission is free. There is also a Rajasthan Emporium further back towards the market.

Adhar Devi Temple

Three km out of the town, there are 200 steep steps to climb to this Durga temple in a natural cleft in the rock. You have to stoop down to get through the low entrance into the temple. There are good views over Mt Abu from up here.

Dilwara Temples (5 km)

These Jain temples are Mt Abu's main attraction and amongst the finest examples of Jain architecture in India. The complex includes two temples where the art of carving marble has been carried to unsurpassed heights. The older of these temples is the Vimal Vasahi, dedicated to the first Tirthankar, Adinath, and built in 1031. The central shrine has an image of Adinath, while around the courtyard

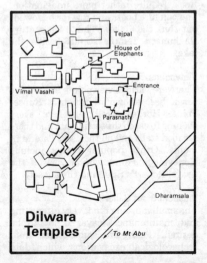

Dilwara Temples

are 52 identical cells, each with a Buddha-like cross-legged image. The entrance to the courtyard is formed by 48 elegantly carved pillars. In front of the temple stands the 'House of Elephants' with figures of elephants marching in procession to the temple entrance.

The later Tejpal temple is dedicated to Neminath, the 22nd Tirthankar, and was built in 1230 by the brothers Tejpal and Vastupal. Like Vimal, they were ministers in the government of the ruler of Gujarat. Although the Tejpal temple is important as an extremely old and complete example of a Jain temple, its most notable feature is the fantastic intricacy and delicacy of the marble carving. In places the carving is so fine that the marble becomes almost transparent. In particular, the lotus flower which hangs from the centre of the dome is an incredible piece of work. It's difficult to believe that this huge lace-like filigree actually started as a solid block of marble. The temple employs several full-time stone carvers to maintain and restore the work.

There are three other temples in the enclosure but they all pale beside the Tejpal and Vimal Vasahi. The complex is open from 12 noon to 6 pm and there is a Rs 5 camera change. Note that no leather at all is permitted in the complex – apart from removing shoes or sandals, you must take off belts and even camera cases if they are leather. You can stroll out to Dilwara in less than an hour from the town, or take a taxi for about Rs 10.

Achalgarh (11 km)

The Shiva temple of Achaleshwar Mahandeva has a number of interesting features, including a toe of Shiva, a brass Nandi and, where the Shiva lingam would normally be, a deep hole said to extend all the way to the underworld. Outside, by the car park, is a tank beside which are three stone buffaloes and the figure of a king shooting them with a bow and arrows. A legend states that the tank was once filled with ghee, but demons in the form of buffaloes came down and drank each night – until the king shot them. A path leads up the hillside to a group of colourful Jain temples with fine views out over the plains.

Guru Shikhar (15 km)
At the end of the plateau is 1721-metre Guru Shikhar, the highest point in Rajasthan. There is a road almost up to the summit. At the top is the Atri Rishi Temple, and good views all around.

Gaumukh Temple (8 km)
Down on the Abu Road side of Mt Abu a small stream flows from the mouth of a marble cow, giving the shrine its name. There is also a marble figure of the bull Nandi, Shiva's vehicle. The tank here, Agni Kund, is said to be the site for the sacrificial fire made by the sage Vasishta from which four of the great Rajput clans were born. An image of Vasishta is flanked by figures of Rama and Krishna.

Tours
There are daily tours from the bus stand costing Rs 15. They run from 8.30 am to 1.30 pm and 1.30 to 7.30 pm and visit the Dilwara Temples, Achalgarh, Guru Shikhar, Adhar Devi and other places. In the high season they tend to be heavily booked, so plan ahead.

Places to Stay – bottom end
The excellent *Hotel Lake View* (tel 240) overlooks picturesque Nakki Lake with superb views from the rooftop. Rooms all have fans and attached bathrooms – there are only a couple of singles at about Rs 40; the others are doubles at about Rs 60. Rates probably drop by half in the off season.

The straightforward and fairly clean *Ambika Guest House* is opposite the polo ground and has reasonably spacious rooms with fan and bathroom around Rs 30/50 in season. The pleasant *Tourist Guest House* (tel 160), at the foot of the driveway to the Tourist Bungalow, is

another popular low-budget place. Built around a pleasant courtyard, this clean, well-run place has doubles with bath and mosquito nets which cost only Rs 40 in the off season. In season they can easily rocket to Rs 100 or Rs 120.

Back from the bus stand, and up a steepish path, the *Shikar Tourist Bungalow* (tel 69) is the biggest place in Mt Abu with about 100 rooms. Rooms vary widely in price and also from the high season to low season. Off-season singles/doubles start from Rs 30/40, in-season rooms start at Rs 50/75. With air-con, prices are Rs 60/75 off season, Rs 120/150 in season. There's also a Rs 8 dorm. The Shikar has a bar and a rather poor restaurant.

The *Youth Hostel* is central and has dorm beds at Rs 12, but it's not good value (lots of beds in each dorm) unless you are really stuck, which at the height of the season can happen, especially if you arrive at night.

Places to Stay – top end
The *Navjivan Hotel* (tel 53) has rooms with attached bathroom at Rs 50/80 and is a pleasant and clean place. In the same building and run by the same people, the *Samrat International Hotel* (tel 73 & 53) is somewhat more expensive with prices in season of Rs 160/200 or Rs 260 for a deluxe double. Prices halve in the off season. They claim to have 'super facilities with starlike comfort'!

Across the street from these two hotels is the new *Hotel Maharaja* (tel 61) directly facing the polo ground. In season doubles are Rs 150, out of season they're Rs 105, but the management is not particularly friendly or helpful.

If you can get in, the whimsically delightful *Bikaner Palace* (tel 21 & 33) is a worthwhile treat – this former summer residence of the Maharaja of Bikaner is usually heavily booked in season. The very amiable and helpful manager is the son-in-law of the Maharaja. There are 24 elegantly decorated rooms with separate sleeping and living areas at Rs 175/225,

1	Hotel Bikaner Palace	9	Hotel Saraswati
2	Art Gallery & State Museum	10	Abu Restaurant
3	Rajasthan Emporium	11	Tourist Office
4	Market	12	Bus Station
5	MK Cold Drinks	13	Hotel Hill Tone
6	Jaipur House Hotel	14	Tourist Guest House
7	Youth Hostel	15	Tourist Bungalow
8	Nina Sheeba Restaurant		

Mt Abu

and four magnificent suites at Rs 260/350. Prices do not change with the seasons. The hotel is in a beautiful location near the Dilwara Temples and has well laid-out gardens, a private lake, two tennis courts and pony rides by arrangement.

If you want a familiar and homely atmosphere, the very small *Mount Hotel* (tel 55) is 10 minutes' walk from the Main Bazaar. The manager is very helpful and the immaculate rooms cost Rs 130/175, again with no increase in season. The centrally located *Hotel Hill Tone* (tel 137) has singles/doubles at Rs 230/290 and an intriguing sign outside announcing that

they have honeymoon suites: 'cave and bamboo type'! It's nothing special but they do change money at a fairly good rate.

Places to Eat

Apart from some of the hotels, the best eating places in Mt Abu are a trio of restaurants on the main road opposite the polo ground and near the Navjivan Hotel. The *Veena Restaurant* has excellent Gujarati thalis with plenty of refills for just Rs 8. Their 'super masala dosas' are equally good. Next door is the *Ambika Restaurant*, which specialises in south

Indian food and also does a fine masala dosa. Finally there's the *Sagar Restaurant*, with a wide choice of vegetarian and non-vegetarian food. At all three you can sit outside.

Café Madras has south Indian snacks plus good ice cream. There are also lots of small food stalls around. At the corner of the road down to the lake, *MK Cold Drinks* has excellent ice cream and does thalis. The *Bharti Restaurant*, across the road, does Gujarati thalis too. From here down to the lake there are a number of small snack places, including a *Havmor Icecream*. This is a popular place for an evening stroll. On the lake itself there's a large concrete 'boat' restaurant, the *Sarovar Café*; it's OK for a cup of tea or coffee but nothing much else is available.

Watch out for Mt Abu's own soft drink, the ginger Rim Zim. It tastes absolutely appalling.

In the Samrat International Hotel the *Aangan* has Gujarati thalis at Rs 12. At the *Taksha Shila* you can get Punjabi or western food. The *Hotel Maharaja* restaurant features Gujarati, Punjabi and south Indian food. The *Handi Restaurant* at the Hotel Hill Tone has Indian and western cuisine and will prepare picnic lunches.

The dining hall at the wonderful *Bikaner Palace* is as superb as the rest of this fine hotel. Dinner, at around Rs 150 for two including drinks, is a worthwhile splurge.

Getting There
Rail The fastest trains take less than four hours between Abu Road and Ahmedabad – a 187-km metre-gauge journey. Fares are Rs 22.50 in 2nd class, Rs 83 in 1st. There are also direct trains from Abu Road to Delhi, Jodhpur and Agra. For Bhuj and Kutch in Gujarat you must change trains at Palanpur.

Bus Abu Road, the railhead for Mt Abu, is a small place with the bus station right by the railway station. From 6 am there are

regular buses making the 27-km climb up to Mt Abu. It takes about an hour and costs Rs 3.50. A jeep costs Rs 5 per person, a taxi about Rs 70. There's a toll gate as you enter Mt Abu where passengers are charged Rs 3.

There's an extensive bus schedule from Mt Abu, and to many destinations you will find it faster and more convenient to go straight there by bus rather than going down to Abu Road and waiting for a train. Buses to Ahmedabad, for example, take about seven hours and cost Rs 25. To Udaipur takes seven hours, depending on the route taken, and costs from Rs 28. Luxury buses do the trip to Udaipur in four hours for Rs 55.

Coming to Mt Abu, note that some buses go all the way there, while some terminate at Abu Road.

Getting Around
There are buses from the bus stand to the various sites in Mt Abu, but it takes a little planning to get out and back without too much hanging around. Some buses go just to Dilwara, others out to Achalgarh, so it's a matter of deciding which to go to first, depending on the schedule. It takes about 40 minutes to Achalgarh for Rs 2; to Dilwara is Rs 1.

There are plenty of taxis with posted fares to anywhere you care to mention. Mt Abu's unique form of transport is large 'baby prams' in which you can sit and be wheeled around! They're all seemingly operated by 'Abu Enterprises', but are mainly used by parents to transport their children.

Things to Buy
The Rajasthan Emporium is on Raj Bhavan Rd but there are also quite a few shops on the road down to the lakefront. Jewellery shops have a good selection. As in most of India, jewellery is usually sold by weight.

ABU ROAD
This is the rail junction for Mt Abu.

Places to Stay
In the main market area the *Bhagwati Guest House* is only five minutes from the train and bus stations. It has bathless singles at Rs 15 or doubles with bath for Rs 25 as well as dorm beds for Rs 10. It's OK for one night and there are other simple places around. The station has *Railway Retiring Rooms*.

Getting There
Bus fares from Abu Road include Jodhpur Rs 35.50, Ajmer Rs 46.50 and Jaipur Rs 65.50. For Ahmedabad or Udaipur it's more convenient to catch a direct bus from Mt Abu.

JODHPUR (population 400,000)
The largest city in Rajasthan after Jaipur, Jodhpur stands at the edge of the Thar Desert. The massive fort, topping a sheer rocky hill which rises right in the middle of the town, totally dominates the city. Jodhpur was founded in 1459 by Rao Jodha, a chief of the Rajput clan known as the Rathores. His descendants ruled not only Jodhpur, but also other Rajput princely states. The Rathore kingdom was once known as Marwar, the 'Land of Death'.

The old city of Jodhpur is surrounded by a wall 10 km long, which was built about a century after the city was founded. From the fort you can clearly see where the old city ends and the new begins. The old city is a fascinating jumble of winding streets of great interest to wander around. Eight gates lead out from the walled city. It's one of the more interesting cities in India and, yes, it was from here that those baggy/tight horse-riding trousers, jodhpurs, took their name. Today you're more likely to see them actually worn in Saurashtra in Gujarat than here.

Orientation & Information
The Tourist Office, railway stations and bus stand are all outside the old city. High Court Rd runs from the Raika Bagh railway station, directly across from the bus stand, round by the Umaid Gardens, the Tourist Bungalow and Tourist Office, and round beside the city wall towards the main station and the GPO. Most trains from the east stop at the Raika Bagh station before the main station – quite handy if you want to stay at the Ghoomar Tourist Bungalow.

The GPO is right by the main station. The Tourist Office (tel 21900) is at the Tourist Bungalow and is open Monday to Saturday 8 am to 12 noon and 3 to 6 pm. You can use the subterranean swimming pool at the Umaid Bhawan Palace Hotel (tel 22316) for a fee.

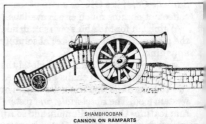

SHAMBHOOBAN
CANNON ON RAMPARTS
MEHRANGARH MUSEUM FORT, JODHPUR.

Meherangarh Fort
The 'Majestic Fort' is just that. Sprawled across the 125-metre-high hill, this is the most impressive and formidable fort in fort-studded Rajasthan. A winding road leads up to the entrance from the city below. The first gate is still scarred by cannon balls – indicating that this was a fort that earned its keep. The gates include the Jayapol, built by Maharaja Man Singh in 1806 following his victory over the armies of Jaipur and Bikaner, and the Fatehpol or Victory Gate, erected by Maharaja Ajit Singh in 1907 to commemorate his defeat of the Moghuls. The final gate is the Lahapol or Iron Gate, beside which there are 15 handprints, the sati marks of widows of Maharaja Man Singh who threw themselves upon his funeral pyre in 1843.

Inside the fort, which is still run by the Maharaja of Jodhpur, there is a whole series of courtyards and palaces. The palace apartments have evocative names like the Moti Mahal or Pearl Palace, the Sukh Mahal or Pleasure Palace, the Phool Mahal or Flower Palace. They house a fantastic collection of the trappings of Indian royalty. There's an amazing collection of elephant howdahs, used when the Maharajas rode on elephant-back in glittering processions through their capitals. Miniature paintings of a variety of schools hang on the walls. There's a superb collection of folk music instruments and the inevitable Rajput armoury, palanquins, furniture and costumes. One room even has a collection of often humorous baby cradles! The palace apartments are beautifully decorated and painted and have delicately carved latticework windows of red sandstone.

At the southern end of the fort there's a collection of old cannons on the ramparts, looking out over the sheer drop down to the old town below. There's no guard rail and you can clearly hear voices and shouts carrying up from the houses far below – it's magical. Note the many blue houses – painted that colour to distinguish them as belonging to Brahmins. The Chamunda Temple, to Durga, stands at this end of the fort.

The fort is open from 9 am to 5 pm and admission is Rs 10 (Rs 4 for Indians). There's an additional Rs 10 charge to use a camera – Rs 15 for a flash and Rs 25 for a movie camera. A couple of musicians usually stand near the entrance and strike up a merry Rajasthani number to herald your arrival – it helps set the mood for a visit to this superb fort.

Jaswant Thanda

Part way down from the fort, just off the fort road, is this white marble memorial to Maharaja Jaswant Singh II. The cenotaph was built in 1899, and the royal crematorium and three later cenotaphs nearby. Inside is a collection of portraits of the various Jodhpur rulers.

Near this turn-off, about 200 metres down that winding road from the fort, an interesting old chap provides a 'water service' for weary travellers. If you've just ridden a bicycle up that long and winding road you may well feel like stopping for a rest and a chat with him – he speaks fluent English and is full of local knowledge and wisdom.

Clock Tower & Markets

The clock tower is a popular landmark in the old city. The colourful Sardar Market is close to the tower, and narrow alleys lead from here to bazaars for textiles, silver and handicrafts. See the note in Places to Eat about Makhania Lassi in the café in the gateway to the market.

Umaid Gardens & Museums

The Tourist Bungalow is on the edge of this garden on High Court Rd. The Government Museum is within the gardens and has a unique and amusing collection. Scarcely a thing has been added (or maintained) since the British departed; consequently it's a frozen-in-time Raj-era display.

There are lots of badly moth-eaten stuffed animals, including a number of almost featherless desert birds in two glass cases, each with a thorn bush. Some of them have toppled off their perches and lie stiffly on the ground with their feet pointing at the ceiling! The military section includes cumbersome wooden biplane models and an extraordinary brass battleship. The museum is open from 10 am to 4.30 pm and admission is Rs 0.60.

The gardens also contain a zoo and a library.

Umaid Bhawan Palace

Maharaja Umaid Singh, who died in 1947, lived at first in the Raika Bagh Palace, but in 1928 commenced construction of the Umaid Bhawan Palace on the outskirts of town. Constructed of marble and red sandstone, this immense palace was designed by the president of the British Royal Institute of Architects and not completed until 1943. It is also known as the Chhittar Palace because of the local Chhittar sandstone used.

Probably the most surprising thing about this grandiose palace is that it was built so near independence. Surely the Maharaja, or even more to the point his British advisers, could see that the upheavals of independence were just around the corner and that Maharajas, princely states and the grand extravagances would all soon be a thing of the past? Some say it was built as a sort of royal job-creation programme!

Today most of the palace has been turned into a hotel, but it's a gloomy, sepulchral place – devoid of that zany, whimsical charm that the Udaipur and Jaipur palaces have in such abundance. Even the basement swimming pool is a dark, clinical sort of place. The present Maharaja still has quite a circle of fiercely protective servants and retainers who not only closely guard the Maharaja but also his Mercedes – number plate 'Rajasthan 1'. The palace is open 9 am to 5 pm and admission is Rs 3.

Tours

If there are tours operating, they will start from the Tourist Bungalow. Cost will probably be around Rs 15 and they will cover the Umaid Bhawan Palace, Meherangarh Fort, Jaswant Thanda, Mandore Gardens and the museum.

Places to Stay – bottom end

Jodhpur's attractions can all be seen in a day so many people arrive in the morning, leave their gear at the Tourist Bungalow, and then depart on the overnight train for Jaisalmer. The popular *Ghoomar Tourist Bungalow* (tel 21900) is on High Court Rd by the Umaid Gardens. Costs are from Rs 40/50 for singles/doubles, Rs 70/90 for deluxe rooms, Rs 90/115 with air cooling,

Rs 120/150 with air-con. Dorm beds are Rs 10. The rooms in the new wing are quite good. The Tourist Office and the Indian Airlines desk are located here.

At the main railway station there are very clean *Railway Retiring Rooms* (tel 22741) costing Rs 25/50. There is a string of cheaper hotels near the station with rooms in the Rs 15 to Rs 25 bracket. Best of them is probably the *Adarsh Niwas Hotel* (tel 23936), which also has a very good restaurant. Rooms start at Rs 17 for the plainest bathless singles, and go up to Rs 50, 60 and 70 with bath. Others include the *Chanderlok*, the well-kept and pleasant *Galaxy* (tel 20796), the *Agarwal Lodge* (tel 20837), the *Charli Bikaner* (tel 23985), the *Alpana Hotel* (tel 24504) and the *Shanti Bhawan Lodge* (tel 21689).

The *Arun Hotel* (tel 20238) is at Sojati Gate and is 'good, clean and handy' with singles at Rs 20 to Rs 30, doubles at Rs 30 to Rs 50 and a dorm at Rs 10. Some of the rooms are windowless boxes and the hotel's own business card insists that it's an 'excellent, mediocre hotel'! An Australian visitor recounted how he left his money belt with all his valuables under the pillow of his bed when he checked out, but got it back complete and untouched three days later.

Near Jalori Gate, 10 minutes' walk from the railway station, the *New Tourist Hotel* is a straightforward little place with rooms at Rs 20, 30 or 40. There's a quiet courtyard and you can leave gear here if you're only staying for the day in Jodhpur. To get there, walk straight out from the station (past the Kalinga Restaurant), turn left at the temple and right opposite the Gandhi Hospital, then continue straight till the road forks (you can see the electrical transformer straight ahead). The road turns right but the hotel is just to the left. An auto-rickshaw will be Rs 3 to the train station, Rs 4 to Rs 5 to the bus station.

Places to Stay – top end

The *Umaid Bhawan Palace Hotel* (tel

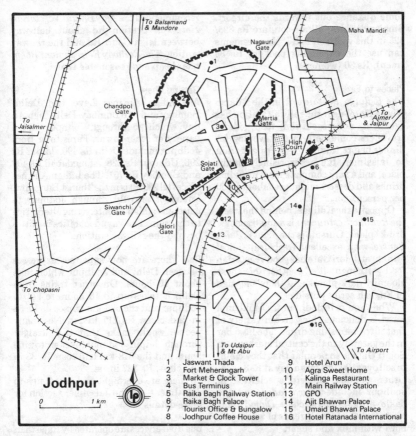

Jodhpur

0   1 km

1	Jaswant Thada	9	Hotel Arun
2	Fort Meherangarh	10	Agra Sweet Home
3	Market & Clock Tower	11	Kalinga Restaurant
4	Bus Terminus	12	Main Railway Station
5	Raika Bagh Railway Station	13	GPO
6	Raika Bagh Palace	14	Ajit Bhawan Palace
7	Tourist Office & Bungalow	15	Umaid Bhawan Palace
8	Jodhpur Coffee House	16	Hotel Ratanada International

22316), 'where you can live like a Maharaja' is Jodhpur's premier hotel. There are just 55 rooms but it has all the palatial luxuries, from a theatre to squash and tennis courts, an underground swimming pool and a bar. Singles/doubles cost Rs 450/550. The huge suites are Rs 700 to Rs 1250. There are fine views across to the fort from the terrace.

The *Ajit Bhawan Palace* (tel 20409) on Airport Rd is a delightful place, great for a small splurge. Most of the rooms are actually separate cottages, each in its own very whimsical style. Plus there are lots of princely trappings around the

place – polo and hunting photographs, a couple of old cars parked in the odd corner including a delectable old MG-TC. These palaces are really frozen in time – the late '40s, when India became independent. The 20 separate cottages (they call them pavilions) are good value at Rs 165/265. The food is reported to be good and there's folk entertainment over dinner in the courtyard. In fact it's rather like being a guest in a stately home, and the Maharaja is even likely to check that you're comfortable.

Hotel Ratanada International (tel 25911) is a new place on Residency Rd, some distance out towards the airport. Singles/doubles, all air-con, are Rs 325/425 in this well-run hotel. Non-residents can use the swimming pool for Rs 35 (men), Rs 30 (women)!

Places to Eat

The *Kalinga Restaurant* in the Adarsh Niwas Hotel near the railway station has excellent non-vegetarian food. Many travellers come here in the evening for dinner before taking the overnight train to Jaisalmer. It's a surprisingly bright place, and a very complete meal including drinks and dessert might cost about Rs 50 per person.

Opposite the Kalinga, behind the trees, the *Renuka Restaurant* is a small snacks/drinks place. Outside is the *Fruit & Juice Centre* with excellent fresh fruit juice. *Pankaj* at Jalori Gate has good vegetarian food although it's another of those gloomily dark places and there's no sign in English script outside.

While you're in Jodhpur try Makhania Lassi, a delicious thick cream variety of that ultra-refreshing drink. The lassi bar in the gateway to the central market near Sojati Gate is so popular that they claim to sell over 1000 glasses a day at Rs 3 each. Other popular dessert specialties in Jodhpur include *mawa ladoo* and the baklava-like *mawa kachori. Dhood fini* is a cereal dish of fine threads of wheat in a bowl with milk and sugar.

Agra Sweet Home, directly opposite Sojati Gate, is also said to have good lassi but it's not very hygienic looking. Round the corner *Dimples Snack Bar* has a variety of snacks; 'Try the Bombay Special Butter Pav Bihaji' (whatever that may be), wrote a traveller. A short distance down the road towards the Tourist Bungalow, the *Coffee House* has cheap masala dosas, but very little else. The restaurant at the *Tourist Bungalow* is not bad, especially for breakfast.

The *Vama Restaurant* at Ratanada Bazaar on the road to the airport is said to have good non-veg food. Travellers have

recommended the *Ajay Bharat Vegetarian Hotel* on Station Rd about half-way between High Court Rd and the railway station. The *Railway Refreshment Room* has cheap and reasonable thalis.

Getting There

Air Indian Airlines have two Delhi-Bombay and two Bombay-Delhi flights a day which go through Jodhpur and a variety of other towns. Fares to or from Jodhpur include Delhi Rs 490, Jaipur Rs 296, Udaipur Rs 228, Ahmedabad Rs 400 and Bombay Rs 751. The Indian Airlines office (tel 20909) is in the Tourist Bungalow. Vayudoot also fly through Jodhpur to Jaisalmer; this is an interesting alternative to the train. The Vayudoot office is a little beyond the railway station.

Rail There are now superfast expresses between Delhi and Jodhpur which take about 10 hours. On other trains from Delhi it takes up to 16 hours to get to Jodhpur and the 626-km trip costs Rs 54 in 2nd class, Rs 217 in 1st. Not many people would make that trip straight through. Jaipur-Jodhpur takes six to nine hours and the 318-km trip costs Rs 33 in 2nd class, Rs 127 in 1st.

There are overnight and day trains to Jaisalmer – see the Jaisalmer section for more details.

Bus Bus services are operated by Rajasthan State Roadways from the bus stand at Raika Bagh to other major centres in Rajasthan. Some road distances from Jodhpur include Barmer 220 km, Bikaner 240 km, Jaipur 340 km, Jaisalmer 290 km, Mt Abu 264 km, Ranakpur 175 km, Udaipur 275 km.

There are daily buses to Jaisalmer; the trip takes seven to 10 hours and costs Rs 35 to Rs 43 depending on the bus. Udaipur takes eight to 10 hours, much faster than the train, and costs from Rs 40 up to Rs 52 for the deluxe bus. Bikaner is six hours across the desert for Rs 31. Buses to Ajmer go hourly, take 4½ hours and cost Rs 28.

Jodhpur-Mt Abu takes about 10 hours and costs Rs 35 but there are no direct buses. All the way to Ahmedabad is Rs 55. The overnight bus from Jaipur is a hard, uncomfortable trip.

Getting Around

Airport The airport is only five km out from the centre – less than Rs 10 in an auto-rickshaw, Rs 20 to Rs 30 in a taxi.

Local Transport Jodhpur has unmetered taxis and metered (but not very metered) auto-rickshaws as well as tongas. You'd have difficulty getting through the narrow lanes of the old city in anything wider than an auto-rickshaw. Jodhpur is a good place to explore by bicycle; you can even ride up that winding road to the fort. There are a number of bicycle-hire places along the road straight in front of the railway station, by the Kalinga Restaurant. Rates are the usual Rs 0.50 an hour, Rs 5 per day.

There are regular city buses to places around Jodhpur like Mandore, Balsamand and Mahamandir.

Things to Buy

The usual Rajasthani handicrafts are available in Jodhpur, but this is a good place to look for antiques. There are many little shops in the convoluted streets of the old town but Abani Handicrafts, next door to the Tourist Bungalow, has a large and varied collection. They also have a branch in the Palace Hotel. Zinc water bottles are a good buy in Jodhpur; they're covered in felt which you can soak so the evaporation keeps the water cool.

AROUND JODHPUR

Mahamandir (2 km)

The 'Great Temple' is a small walled town north-east of the city. It is built around a 100-pillared Shiva temple but is not of great interest.

Balsamand Lake & Palace (7 km)

Originally constructed in 1159, this lake

and garden is to the north of the city. A palace, built in 1936, stands by the lakeside and this is a popular excursion spot. The gardens are open 8 am to 6 pm and entry is Rs 1. The larger Pratap Sagar Lake and Kailana Lake (where there is also a garden), west of Jodhpur, provide the city's water supply.

Mandore (9 km)

Further north, this was the capital of Marwar prior to the foundation of Jodhpur. Today it is a popular local attraction due to its extensive gardens with high rock terraces. The gardens also contain the cenotaphs of Jodhpur rulers, including Maharaja Jaswant Singh and, largest and finest of all, the soaring temple-shaped memorial to Maharaja Ajit Singh.

The 'Hall of Heroes' contains 15 figures carved out of a rock wall. The brightly painted figures represent Hindu deities or local heroes on horseback. The Shrine of 33 Crore (330 million) Gods has painted figures of gods, spirits and divinities. There are regular buses to Mandore from Jodhpur.

Other

Sardar Samand Lake is a wildlife centre 55 km from Jodhpur. The route passes through a number of colourful villages and there is a summer palace of the Maharaja here – accommodation can be arranged. Dhawa or Doli is another wildlife sanctuary with many antelope, 45 km from Jodhpur on the road to Barmer.

Osian is an ancient Thar Desert town, 58 km out. The ruins of 16 Jain and Brahmanical temples from the 8th to 11th centuries stand here and the town is inhabited by hundreds of peacocks. The architecturally interesting temples are in a beautiful area of small hills and sand dunes. There are a half dozen buses a day from Jodhpur; the trip takes two hours and costs Rs 7.50.

At Soyala, 74 km out on the Nagaur road, there is an interesting Shiva temple.

Nagaur is 135 km from Jodhpur and has an historic fort and palace – it's an interesting site in an otherwise dull stretch of desert.

JAISALMER (population 20,000)

Remote Jaisalmer is one of Rajasthan's, indeed India's, most exotic and unusual towns. Travellers who make the effort to get here are never disappointed in this mediaeval-looking place, something right out of tales of the Arabian Nights. A 'living museum' and the 'golden city' are just two descriptions which have been applied to the desert outpost.

Centuries ago its strategic position on the camel train routes between India and central Asia brought great wealth to Jaisalmer. The merchants and townspeople built magnificent houses and mansions – all exquisitely carved from a golden-yellow sandstone. From the humblest shop to the palace and the temples in the fort, the whole town glows in the same golden colour. Even today new buildings must be designed to blend in with the old.

The rise of shipping trade and the port of Bombay pushed Jaisalmer into decline. Partition, and the cutting off of the trade routes through to Pakistan after WW II, seemingly sealed the town's fate, and water shortages could have pronounced the death sentence. But the '65 and '71 Indo-Pakistan wars revealed Jaisalmer's strategic importance, paved roads and a railway linked it to the rest of Rajasthan, and even electricity finally reached out to the remote town. Today military bases are the pillar of the town's economy but increasing numbers of travellers are waking up to the fascination of this exotic place.

Orientation & Information

Finding your way around Jaisalmer is not really necessary – it's a place you simply wander around and get lost in. Within the old city walls the streets are a tangled maze but it's small enough not to matter. You simply head off in what seems like the right direction and eventually you'll get there. The old city is completely surrounded by a lofty fort wall and, within this, a hill rises with more fortified walls. The Jain temples and the old palace are on this hilltop.

The central market area is directly below the hill, while the bank, the new palace and several other shops and offices are near the Amar Sagar Gate to the west. Continue outside the walled city in this direction and you'll soon come to the Tourist Bungalow, where the Tourist Office is also located. The Tourist Office is open Monday to Saturday, 8 am to 12 noon and 3 to 6 pm. The Fort View Hotel also has plenty of tourist information. The bus station and railway station are outside the city walls on the other side.

Havelis

The beautiful mansions built by Jaisalmer's wealthy merchants are known as *havelis*, and several of these fine sandstone buildings are still in beautiful condition. Patwon ki Haveli is the most elaborate and magnificent of all the Jaisalmer havelis. It stands in a narrow lane and one of its apartments is painted with beautiful murals. You can go inside it and there is a fine view from the roof.

Salim Singh ki Haveli was built about 300 years ago and is still partially lived in. Salim Singh was the prime minister when Jaisalmer was the capital of a princely state, and his mansion has a beautifully arched roof with superb carved brackets in the form of peacocks. The mansion is just below the hill and, it is said, once had two additional wooden storeys in an attempt to make it as high as the Maharaja's palace. The Maharaja had the upper storeys torn down!

The late 19th-century Nathmal ki Haveli was also a prime minister's house. The left and right wings of the building were carved by brothers and are very similar, but not identical. Yellow sandstone elephants guard the building, and the front door alone is a beautiful work of art.

Gadi Sagar Tank

This tank, south of the city walls, was once the water supply of the city and there are many small temples and shrines around it. In winter a wide variety of water birds flock here. The beautiful arched gateway across the road down to the tank is said to have been built by a famous prostitute. When she offered to pay to have this gateway constructed, the Maharaja refused permission since he would have to pass under it on going down to the tank, and that, he felt, would be unseemly. While he was away she built the gate – and added a Krishna temple so that the king could not tear it down.

Fort

Built in 1156 by Rawal Jaisal, the fort crowns the 80-metre-high Trikuta hill. About a quarter of the old city's population resides within the fort walls, which have 99 bastions around the circumference. There is a very fine view over the old city from the fort walls. Jaisalmer's seven-storey palace stands just within the first gate of the fort. There are carved balconies and cupolas and the Satiyon ki Sidhiyan where women became satis.

Jain Temples

This group of fine Jain temples was built in the 12th to 15th centuries within the fort walls. They are beautifully carved and dedicated to Rikhabdevji and Sambhavanthji. The Gyan Bhandar, a library containing some extremely old manuscripts, is within the temple complex. The temples are only open in the morning until 12 noon; the library is only open from 10 to 11 am. There are also Shiva and Ganesh temples within the fort.

A stroll around the outer fort ramparts at sunset offers fine views over the old city. Carry a handful of stones to ward off the snarling curs that threaten your progress periodically. And be warned that the entire outer rampart is popular as a public toilet. The ledge makes a convenient squatting place and you can watch the activity below while you defecate! You're likely to come face to arse with a bare bottom at any corner.

Outside the Walls

Outside the town walls the Jawahar Niwas, opposite the Tourist Bungalow, is a splendid guest house for private guests of the Maharaja. It even features a grand billiard room, alas unused! At the road intersection is a war memorial from the '71 Indo-Pak conflict. Almost every military man involved, or at least those of officer rank, manages to get a mention in an exceedingly long and tedious inscription.

Festivals

The annual Desert Festival is supposed to have camel races and dances, folk music, desert ballads and puppeteers, but it seems to have quickly become a purely commercial tourist trap. Future dates are 11-13 February in '87, 31 January-2 February in '88 and 18-20 February in '89. At the full-moon night of Purnima a sound-and-light drama is performed at Sam.

Places to Stay – bottom end

There is quite a travelling community in Jaisalmer these days, and many cheap hotels have sprung up to cater for them. Almost all of them offer very similar spartan standards, although some are distinctly better kept than others.

Near the Amar Sagar Gate the *Swastika Guest House* is the best kept of the lot. Rooms here are Rs 20 to Rs 30 for singles, Rs 40 for doubles or with bath Rs 50/60. There's a Rs 10 dorm. They provide free tea on arrival.

Very close to the entrance to the fort, the *Fort View Hotel* has fine views of the fort from the roof – but not the best views in town! This is a very popular place, in part because of its live-wire manager.

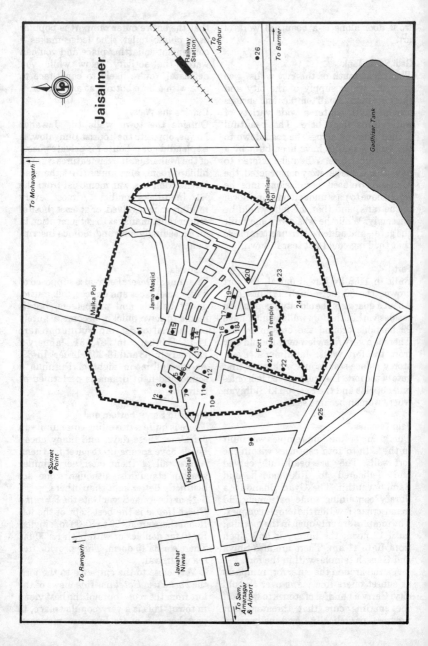

He's talkative and a real character as well as a mine of information on everything about Jaisalmer. Many people book camel safaris through him; he seems to have lots of satisfied customers. Simple rooms are Rs 20, rooms with bath are Rs 30 or upstairs Rs 40, 50 and 60.

Down the road around the east side of the fort, the *Hotel Desert* is a very simple place but it has a pleasant sitting area in the middle and people staying there seem to really like it. Rooms are just Rs 10/15 and there are even camels parked right outside. A little beyond it is the *Tourist Hotel* with singles at Rs 15, doubles with bath at Rs 20 and more expensive rooms at Rs 25/40.

Right back in the centre of the old town, other places include the extremely basic *Sunil Bhatia Rest House* with rooms at Rs 15/20. The *Rama Guest House* is even more rock bottom but it does have fantastic fort views from the roof – you can 'see both sunrise and sunset from the roof'. Rooms are Rs 15/20; you can sleep on the rooftop for Rs 5. The *Golden Rest* has rooms with bathroom at Rs 20 and an open courtyard. Right up in the fort with rooms at Rs 10/20 and a dorm at Rs 7, the *Deepak Rest House* is also extremely rock bottom. *Rang Niwas* and *Laxmi Niwas* are other places actually inside the fort.

The relatively new *New Tourist Hotel* has rooms with bath at Rs 30, 40 and 50, or you can sleep on the roof for Rs 5. Near the Amar Sagar Gate the *Hotel Pleasure* is another very basic, but friendly and helpful, place with rooms from Rs 20. There are many others to choose from, but these bottom-end cheapies are generally every bit as as basic as their prices would indicate. In the desert air, sleeping on the rooftop can be very pleasant. Local musicians sometimes visit the lodges, stay overnight and can be persuaded to do an encore the next morning, on the flat roof.

Places to Stay – top end

Jaisalmer's 'top end' places are more middle than top. The *Moomal Tourist Bungalow* (tel 92) is just outside the city walls to the west. It's very close to the bus halt, but quite a distance from the railway station, on the other side of the walled town. Singles/doubles cost Rs 40/50, deluxe rooms Rs 70/90, air-cooled rooms Rs 100/125, rooms with air-con Rs 120/150. There's also a Rs 12 dormitory. It's a modern building with a restaurant and a bar and is quite comfortable, although V S Naipaul tore into it in *India – A Wounded Civilisation*. They've recently added some small thatched-roof bungalows outside.

Also outside the city walls, *Hotel*

1	Nariyan Niwas		14	Rama
2	Hotel Pleasure		15	Patwon ki Haveli
3	Swastika Hotel		16	8 July Restaurant
4	Purohit		17	Hotel Fort View
5	Gaylord Restaurant		18	Post Office
6	Safina Restaurant		19	New Tourist Hotel
7	State Bank of India		20	Salim Singh ki Haveli
8	Tourist Bungalow		21	Deepak Restaurant
9	Post Office		22	Jaisal Castle Hotel
10	Badal Wilas		23	Hotel Desert
11	Sunray		24	Tourist Hotel
12	Golden Restaurant		25	Hotel Neeraj
13	Nathmal ki Haveli		26	Central Bus Stand

Neeraj is a newer place built around a central courtyard with rooms with bath at Rs 50/80. It's pleasant but, like the Tourist Bungalow, rather featureless.

Back in the old city the delightful *Jaisal Castle Hotel* (tel 62) is right on the ramparts of the fort, by the Jain temples. The hotel is in a traditional old Jaisalmer house with large rooms, all with attached bath for Rs 100/125. Sunsets from the roof of the hotel are superb, and the hotel is 'out of this world', according to one visitor. It can get chilly at night in winter; the wind whistles through the rooms. One catch is you have a long walk up to the hotel, tough work if you're toting much baggage. The food here is not very good.

Finally, up the lane by the Gaylord Restaurant (across from the State Bank of India) the *Narayan Niwas Palace* (tel 108) is Jaisalmer's most expensive hotel with rooms at Rs 200/250. You might even get the room Princess Anne had when she visited Jaisalmer. There's a good restaurant here and entertainment some evenings.

Places to Eat

There are a number of cold-drink and food places around the market area and near the Golden Rest as well as some good special lassi places. Overall, though, the dining-out possibilities in Jaisalmer are very limited. Standards seem to rise and fall rapidly – this year's best restaurant may be well down the list next year. The small (and basic) *Gaylord Restaurant* is across from the State Bank of India and has friendly sparrows; it must be doing something right as it has been here longer than most eating places. On the same square is the *Purohit Restaurant* with, at present at least, very good vegetarian food.

The *Safina Restaurant* also seems to be fairly popular, and *Durga's* is said to be good. Others include the *Kalpana Restaurant* next to the State Bank and the *City Heart Restaurant* where the 'constant retching, heaving and spitting noises from the kitchen would put anyone off their food!'

For a while the *8th of July Restaurant*, just outside the fort walls near the post office, got rave reviews. It certainly has a good-looking menu. There are lots of other small hole-in-the-wall places, or you could try the *Tourist Bungalow* or the more expensive *Narayan Niwas Palace*.

Getting There

Jaisalmer is 295 km from Jodhpur via Pokaran, Dechu and Balesar or 330 km from Bikaner via Pokaran and Phalodi.

Air You can now fly Jodhpur-Jaisalmer three times a week with Vayudoot. The interesting flight takes an hour and costs Rs 282.

Rail The 295-km trip Jodhpur-Jaisalmer by day or night train in each direction takes about 10 hours. Fares are Rs 30.50 in 2nd class, Rs 119 in 1st. In Jaisalmer, the reservations office is open only from 10 am to 1 pm, 2 to 4 pm and in the chaotic period just before departure.

The train journey from Jodhpur, at least by day, can be rather gruelling due to dust and the coal smuts, which swirl in and turn your hair to wire! Still, fleeting glimpses of gazelles, or the still rarer bustard, compensate. At night it can get very cold out in the desert. If you haven't got a sleeping bag, reserve one of the limited number of bedrolls. At Pokaran, which until 1968 was the rail terminus, the train goes into reverse – the engine is switched from front to rear for the leg out to Jaisalmer.

If you're going through from Jaisalmer to Jaipur, the connection at Jodhpur misses often enough that it might be worth considering not buying a through ticket in case you have to change to a bus at Jodhpur.

Bus Buses from Jodhpur take 10 hours and cost Rs 38. The same buses continue to Jaipur at a cost of Rs 84. Barmer is a five-hour trip costing Rs 21. To Bikaner takes about 8½ hours and costs Rs 47; the early-morning bus is the fastest one.

Getting Around

Vayudoot have a bus to the airport for Rs 15. There's no terminal; you just wait for the aircraft beside the runway. A share-taxi between Jaisalmer railway station and the town should be about Rs 2 to Rs 3 per person.

Unmetered taxis and jeeps are available, Rs 12 to Rs 15 from the railway station to the Tourist Bungalow. Around the city the tourist office's jeep can be hired for sightseeing for Rs 30 for up to 10 km locally, Rs 2 a km for more than 10 km out of the city. You can also hire bicycles in Jaisalmer and ride out to nearby places. See the section below on camel safaris for details on hiring camels.

Things to Buy

Jaisalmer is famous for embroidery, Rajasthani mirror work, rugs, blankets, old stonework and antiques. At Kadi Bundar, north of the city, tie dye and other fabrics are made.

AROUND JAISALMER

There are some fascinating places in the area around Jaisalmer, although it soon fades out into a barren sand-duned desert which stretches across the lonely border into Pakistan. Apart from the very popular camel safaris, the Hotel Fort View also organises taxi tours out to the sand dunes, covering Bada Bagh, Amar Sagar, Lodruva, Mool Sagar, the Sam sand dunes and other places of interest. Costs vary from Rs 20 to Rs 30 person.

Camel Safaris

The most interesting way of exploring the desert around Jaisalmer is on a camel safari. These typically cost Rs 50 to Rs 60 per day including three meals. Although you can take short camel trips – day trips or even half day – you really need four days to get out to the sand dunes and to get to grips with camel travel. The camels are all independently owned; there are *no* hotels or agents owning camels so these people are just middlemen. Camel safaris are a very big deal in Jaisalmer and it is absolutely no problem at all to join one. Asking around is the best way to do so; Mr Vyas at the Fort View Hotel seems an excellent middleman and people generally seem pleased with the service he provides. Several hotels have camels virtually parked out front, so they should be good too. Mahendra Tours and the Narayan Niwas Hotel organise safaris, although the latter are much more expensive. Some hotels will be less than happy if you don't book a safari through them; you may have to move elsewhere when you come back!

The usual tours take four days and three nights in a circuit around Jaisalmer via Mool Sagar, the Sam sand dunes and back via Lodruva, passing through Hindu, Muslim, Rajput, tribal and abandoned villages. October to February is the best time for the camel safaris. The agents usually have books with tourists' comments on their trips, well worth reading. Check what you're getting in terms of food, blankets and sights before signing up.

You may experience stiff muscles and saddlesore behinds from the unaccustomed rocking motion, so take a cushion perhaps, and certainly bring tangerines as the desert is very parching. An individual water bottle is a good idea too – you can hang it off the front saddle prong; sunburn cream and a head-cloth (Arab style) are also advisable. Normally the tourist sits in front with feet in stirrups with a camelman/boy behind, perched on top of a large fodder bag. The reins are fastened to the camel's nose peg and they are easily steered. At resting points the camels are completely unsaddled and then hobbled. They limp away to browse on nearby shrubs while the camelmen brew sweet chai or prepare basic food – rice, chappatis and the inevitable dhal. The whole crew rests in the shade of thorn trees by a tank or well.

It's a great way to see the desert, which is surprisingly well-populated and sprinkled with ruins. You constantly come across tiny fields of millet, girls picking berries or boys herding flocks of sheep or goats. The latter are always fitted with tinkling neckbells and in the desert silence it sounds like beautiful music. Camping out at night in the Sam sand dunes, huddling around a tiny fire beneath the stars and listening to the camelmen's yarns can be quite romantic. You may hear tales of their other source of income apart from tourists – smuggling trips over the border into Pakistan!

Anatomically, the camels are interesting. They have strange calloused pads on knees and chest, appallingly bad breath and an uncomfortable-looking sitting position with back legs tucked under. Nevertheless, 'you can rapidly get fond of them,' reported two visitors. Not if you're 'on a female pursued by several amorous males', reported another. 'Two days, preferably to the west of Jaisalmer, would be interesting and quite long enough', was another comment. Your camelman will probably expect a tip or gift in addition to the money paid to the tour agent.

Amar Sagar

North-west of Jaisalmer, this used to be a very pleasant formal garden but it has now fallen into ruins. The lake here dries up several months into the dry season. A beautifully carved Jain temple is being painstakingly restored by craftspeople brought in from Agra. Commenced in the late '70s, this monumental task is expected to take many years.

Lodruva (15 km)

Further out beyond Amar Sagar are the deserted ruins of this ancient capital. The Jain temples, which were rebuilt in the late '70s, are the only reminders of the magnificence of the city at its peak. The temples have ornate, carved arches at the entrance and a Kalputra, the 'divine-tree', within. In the temple, there's a hole from which a snake is said to come every evening to drink an offering of milk. Only the 'lucky' can see it. At the same time that they rebuilt the temples, Jain benefactors had the road out from Jaisalmer sealed, but immediately beyond Lodruva it deteriorates into a desert track.

Mool Sagar (9 km)

Directly west of Jaisalmer, this is another pleasant small garden and tank. Continuing in this direction you reach the Sam sand dunes, about 40 km from the town. This is the nearest point to Jaisalmer for the real Sahara-like desert.

Khuri

Khuri is a village about 40 km south-west of Jaisalmer, out in the desert. It's a delightfully peaceful places with houses of mud and straw decorated like the patterns on Persian carpets, but this is a touchy area near the Pakistan border.

Bada Bagh & Cenotaphs

North of the town, Bada Bagh is a fertile oasis with a huge old dam. Much of

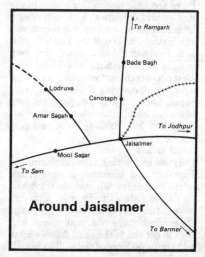

Around Jaisalmer

Jaisalmer's vegetables and fruit is grown here and carried into the town by colourfully dressed women each day. Above the gardens are royal cenotaphs with beautifully carved ceilings and equestrian statues of the former rulers. This is a popular place to come in the early evening to watch the setting sun turn Jaisalmer a beautiful, golden brown.

Other

Three km off the road to Barmer, at a point 14 km from Jaisalmer, the 180-million-year-old fossils of trees can be seen. A desert national park has been established in the Thar Desert near Sam village and a separate park permission is required to enter it.

POKARAN

The junction where the Jaisalmer-Bikaner and Jaisalmer-Jodhpur roads split is the site for another magnificent Rajasthan fortress. The yellow sandstone fort rises from the yellow desert sands and shelters a tangle of narrow streets with balconied houses decorated with parrots, elephants and Rajasthan's inevitable peacocks. The usually quiet town springs to life at its annual cattle fair. It must also have sprung to life in May 1974 when a nuclear explosion took place nearby!

BARMER

This desert town is a centre for wood-carving, carpets, embroidery, block printing and other handicrafts. Barmer is 153 km from Jaisalmer and 220 km from Jodhpur. At Kiradu, 35 km west of Barmer, there are 11th-century Kathiawar-style temples with Gupta elements in their design.

Barmer could conceivably become much more interesting to travellers in the future, as India and Pakistan seem to be moving (slowly) towards re-opening the road and rail links between Barmer and Hyderabad in the Sind region of Pakistan. This would not only make a very interesting route from Rajasthan through to Karachi, but would save the long trip north to the touchy Punjab region where the only current India-Pakistan border crossing is situated.

BIKANER (population 200,000)

This desert town in the north of the state was founded in 1488 by Rao Bikaji, a descendant of the founder of Jodhpur, Jodhaji. Like many other Rajasthan cities, it is surrounded by a high, battlemented wall, and like Jaisalmer, its smaller sister to the south, it was once an important staging post on the great caravan trade routes. The city is chiefly interesting for its superb large fort, but it is also noted for the fine camels bred here. There is a government camel breeding farm near the city. The Gang Canal, built between 1925 and 1927, has irrigated a great area of previously arid land around Bikaner.

Orientation & Information

The old city is encircled by a seven-km-long city wall with five entrance gates, built in the 18th century. The fort and palace, built of Bikaner's same reddish-pink sandstone, is outside the city walls. The GPO is at the collectorate; the city post office is inside Kot Gate. The Tourist Office is in Junagarh Fort and is open 10 am to 5 pm, closed on Sundays.

Junagarh Fort

Constructed between 1588 and 1593 by Raja Rai Singh, a general in the Moghul emperor Akbar's army, the fort has a 986-metre-long wall with 37 bastions and two entrances. The Suraj Pol or Sun Gate is the main entrance to the fort. The palaces within the fort are at the southern side – they're a picturesque ensemble of courtyards, balconies, kiosks, towers and windows.

Among the places of interest are the Chandra Mahal or Moon Palace with paintings, mirrors and carved marble panels. The Phool Mahal or Flower Palace is also decorated with glass and

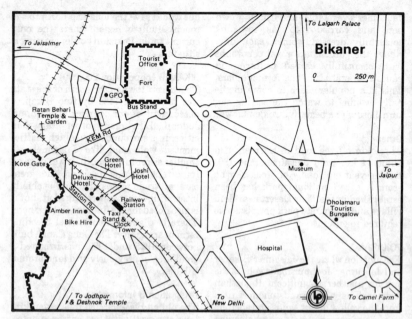

mirrors. The Karn Mahal was built to commemorate a notable victory over the Moghul Aurangzeb. Other palaces include the Rang Mahal, Bijai Mahal and Anup Mahal. The contents include not only the usual Rajput weapon collection but also the decaying pieces of a couple of old WW I biplanes! The Durga Niwas is a beautifully painted courtyard while the Ganga Niwas, another large courtyard, has a finely carved red sandstone front. Har Mandir is the royal temple, dedicated to Lord Shiva.

The fort is open from 10 am to 4.30 pm and it's closed on Fridays. The admission fee of Rs 4 (plus Rs 10 for a camera) includes a Hindi-speaking guide. 'Stay with him and he'll try to speak some English!' There are a museum, library of Persian and Sanskrit manuscripts and armoury in a corner of the fort.

Lalgarh Palace

The 'Red Fort' was built by Maharaja Ganga Singh (1881-1942) in memory of his father Maharaja Lal Singh. The Bikaner royal family still lives in part of the palace, which is made of red sandstone and has beautiful latticework. There is a collection of old photographs and the usual exhibition of half of India's wildlife, shot and stuffed. The Shri Sadul Museum to the glory of the Maharajas is open 10 am to 5 pm, closed Wednesdays.

Ganga Golden Jubilee Museum

This small museum near the Tourist Bungalow contains pre-Harappan, Gupta and Kushan pieces and a wide collection of weapons, terracottas, pottery and paintings – particularly miniatures of the Bikaner school. It is open from 10 am to 5 pm but closed on Fridays.

Places to Stay

The pleasantly quiet *Dhola-Maru Tourist Bungalow* (tel 5002) is on Pooran Singh Circle and has singles/doubles from Rs 60/75 or with air-con for Rs 100/125. It's

Bikaner, Rajasthan

A SIDEWALK HOT MILK VENDOR ON A GRAND SCALE. HOT MILK, SUGAR & CURD MIXED UP WITH A FLOURISH FOR 75 PAISA (9¢) A GLASSFULL. ENTERTAINMENT FREE.

rather a long way out from the town centre and the fort, Rs 4 to Rs 5 by autorickshaw or a long but pleasant stroll.

There is a string of low-priced hotels near the station on Station Rd, like the *Deluxe Hotel* (tel 192) with rooms with bath at Rs 20/25. The *Green Hotel* (tel 296) has rooms at Rs 18 or with bath at Rs 25. Near the railway crossing on Station Rd, the *Sankhla Rest House* (tel 3949) has rooms from Rs 12 to Rs 25. Others include the *Delight Hotel* and the *Roopan Hotel* (tel 373). There are also *Railway Retiring Rooms* at the station.

In the same station area is the slightly up-market *Joshi Hotel* with rooms at Rs 65/85. Bikaner's sole top-end hotel is the *Lalgarh Palace Hotel* (tel 3263), which

costs Rs 345/500 including meals and is some distance out from the centre.

Places to Eat

Chhotu Motu Joshi Restaurant is just down from the Green Hotel towards the station and has good and cheap vegetarian food, icy cold lassi and lots of Indian sweets. The *Green Hotel* and the *Deluxe Hotel* both have similar small, clean restaurants with snacks and drinks. Their cold lassis are Rs 3.

Across the road from these hotels are a number of open-air places like *Krishna, Laxmi* and *Ganesh* where you can get cheap vegetarian food or, for Rs 1.50 a bowl, great curd. The more expensive *Amber Restaurant* is on Station Rd.

Getting There

Air Vayudoot fly Delhi-Jaipur-Bikaner three times a week. Jaipur-Bikaner takes just over an hour and costs Rs 325.

Rail There are day and night trains from Delhi to Bikaner and the 468-km trip takes 11 to 12 hours. Fares are Rs 43 in 2nd class, Rs 176 in 1st. There is a daily overnight train to and from Jodhpur; the 277-km trip takes eight hours and costs Rs 29 in 2nd class, Rs 114 in 1st. The 379-km trip between Jaipur and Bikaner takes 10 to 11 hours, and again there is an overnight train with fares of Rs 37 in 2nd class, Rs 147 in 1st.

An alternative way of travelling Jaisalmer-Bikaner is to take the Jodhpur-bound night train as far as Phalodi, arriving there at 1.30 am and taking the connecting bus at 2 am. This gets to Bikaner around 6 am. Continuing on from Bikaner to Amritsar by rail can be hard work.

Bus On the edge of the Thar Desert, Bikaner is connected by road with the rest of Rajasthan. There is a national highway to Jaipur (320 km) and to Jaisalmer (330 km). The bus from Jaisalmer takes a weary eight to nine hours and costs Rs 47. It's a desert crossing with the usual interminable stops for no discernible reasons. Jodhpur is 240 km away and costs Rs 28.50 or Rs 33.50 by express bus.

Getting Around

Auto-rickshaws are unmetered. Bikaner also has tongas. There are lots of bicycle-hire places along Station Rd, across from the railway station.

AROUND BIKANER

Bhand Sagar Temple (5 km)

The 16th-century Jain temple to the 23rd Tirthankar, Parasvanath, is the most important of the complex, but others include the Chintamani Temple of 1505 and the Adinath Temple. There is a fine view of the city wall and surrounding countryside from the park behind the temple.

Devi Kund (8 km)

This is the site of the royal *chhatris* or cenotaphs of many of the Bika dynasty rulers. The white marble *chhatri* of Maharaja Surat Singh is among the most imposing.

Camel Breeding Farm (10 km)

This government-managed camel breeding station is probably unique in Asia. There are hundreds of camels here and rides are available. It's a great sight at sunset as the camels come back from grazing. The British army had a camel corps drawn from Bikaner during WW I.

Gajner Wildlife Sanctuary (32 km)

A number of animals can be seen in this reserve on the Jaisalmer road. In winter imperial sand grouse migrate here. The old royal summer palace stands on the bank of the lake and is sometimes used as a hotel.

Karni Mata Temple (33 km)

At Deshnok on the Jodhpur road, this temple is dedicated to the mystic Karni Mata. The huge silver gates to the temple and the marble carvings were donated by Maharaja Ganga Singh and a golden umbrella tops the temple, but the main interest here is the rats. The temple is infested with holy rats, which are fed and cared for in the belief that they will reincarnate as mystics or holy men. As you stroll around the temple rats play leapfrog over your *bare* feet.

You can get to the temple by the hourly bus from Bikaner for about Rs 4, or you can hire a taxi or jeep from in front of the railway station for about Rs 90 for the round trip. There's a Rs 5 camera fee at the temple.

Tony's Notebook

Buying a Ticket

At least once on each trip to India it seems guaranteed that I will have to suffer some operation of such mind-boggling and bewildering obtuseness that Kafka himself would be impressed. This time it was Vayudoot Airlines. I wanted to fly from Jodhpur to Jaisalmer so I strolled into the Vayudoot office in Jaipur to buy a ticket.

Me: A Jodhpur-Jaisalmer ticket please.
Him: A Jaipur-Jaisalmer ticket?
Me: No, not a Jaipur-Jaisalmer ticket, a Jodhpur-Jaisalmer ticket.
Him: But this is Jaipur.
Me: Yes, I know we are in Jaipur, but I do not want to fly from here, I want to fly from Jodhpur.
Him: The flight leaves Jaipur at 6.35 am.
Me: Fine, but I don't want to fly from Jaipur, I want to fly from Jodhpur.

Unbelievably this went on for a further 15 minutes and was eventually resolved only when I got a timetable and drew boxes around the sector I wanted to fly and put Xs through the Jaipur-Jodhpur sector. We finally worked all this out, but then they wouldn't take travellers' cheques or credit cards, and I didn't have enough cash on me. So I went out and found a bank, changed money, came back to the Vayudoot office.

He then wrote the ticket – Jaipur-Jodhpur-Jaisalmer. We ran through our recent conversation all over again, I drew more pictures of planes taking off from Jaipur without me on board. Me patiently waiting in Jodhpur and getting on the plane when it arrived there, happily flying off to Jaisalmer. Finally the light dawned, the ticket was written and I paid

for it. He sat and calculated numbers for several minutes and then announced:

Him: You have to pay another Rs 28 because I have added up the fares wrong.
Me: Added up? Added up what fares?
Him: The Jaipur-Jodhpur and Jodhpur-Jaisalmer fares.
Me: But I'm not flying Jaipur-Jodhpur, I'm only flying Jodhpur-Jaisalmer.
Him: So?

For the third time we had to run through the whole routine again to convince him that irrespective of the fact that we were sitting in Jaipur, there was no reason I should pay to fly to Jodhpur if I wasn't flying to Jodhpur. That the air fare from Jodhpur to Jaisalmer was the same whether you bought the ticket in Jaipur or Jodhpur. That Jodhpur-Jaisalmer did not include Jaipur-Jodhpur if .... Oh, my head. In all, issuing this simple ticket took over two hours, including my half-hour at the bank changing money which I didn't need to change because I had enough cash for the correct fare in the first place!

A Useful Sign

The turnoff to the Pratap Country Inn outside Udaipur is signposted and about 100 metres up a dusty track there's a large old metal gate leading to the inn. I rode my bicycle several hundred metres further up the track before I realised I had missed the entrance, and backtracked. Typical, I thought; why the hell didn't they put the name on it? Half an hour later I opened the gate to find, on the other side, a small boy with a tin of black paint having just painted 'Pratap' and busily misspelling 'Cohntry'.

Gujarat

Population: 29 million
Area: 195,984 square km
Capital: Gandhinagar
Main language: Gujarati

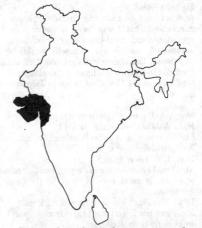

The west coast state of Gujarat is not one of India's busiest destinations. Although it is quite easy to slot Gujarat in between Bombay and the cities of Rajasthan, few people pause to explore this interesting state. Yet Gujarat has a long and varied history and a great number of interesting places to visit. If you want to go right beyond history into the realms of legend, then the Temple of Somnath was actually there to witness the creation of the universe! And along the south coast are the sites where many of the great events in Lord Krishna's life took place.

On more firm historic footing, Lothal was the site of a Harappan or Indus Valley Civilisation city over 4000 years ago. The main sites from this very ancient culture are now in Pakistan, but it is thought Lothal may have survived the great cities of the Sind by as much as 500 years. Gujarat also played host to the great Buddhist emperor Ashoka, and one of his rock edicts is near Junagadh.

Later Gujarat was to suffer Muslim incursions from Mahmud of Ghazni on through the Moghuls and was to be a battlefield between the Moghuls and the Marathas. It was an early contact point with the west, and at Surat the first British commercial outpost was established. The Portuguese enclaves of Daman and Diu survived within the borders of Gujarat right up to 1961. More recently Gujarat had a close tie with the life of the father of modern India, Mahatma Gandhi. It was in Gujarat that the Mahatma was born and spent his early years and it was to Ahmedabad, the great city of Gujarat, that he returned to wage his long struggle with the British for independence.

Gujarat has always been a centre for the Jains, and some of its most interesting sights are Jain temple centres like those at Palitana and Girnar. The Jains are an influential and energetic group, and as a result Gujarat is one of the wealthier states of India with a number of important industries, particularly textiles. Apart from the Jain temples, other major attractions of Gujarat include the last Asian lions in the Gir Forest and the fascinating Indo-Saracenic architecture of Ahmedabad.

Geographically, Gujarat can be divided into three areas. The mainland region includes the major cities of Ahmedabad, Surat and Baroda. The Gulf of Cambay divides the mainland strip from the flat, often barren, plain of the Kathiawar Peninsula, also known as Saurashtra. This was never incorporated into British India, but survived as more than 200 princely states right up to independence. In 1956 they were all amalgamated into the state of Bombay, but in 1960 this was in turn split, on linguistic grounds, into Maharashtra and Gujarat. Finally, the Gulf of Kutch divides Saurashtra from

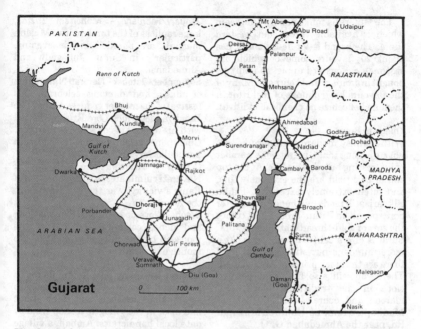

Gujarat 0   100 km

Kutch, which is virtually an island cut off from the rest of Gujarat to the east and Pakistan to the north, by the low-lying 'Ranns' of Kutch.

Though much less touristed than neighbouring Rajasthan, Gujarat has provided a surprisingly large proportion of India's emigrants, particularly to the UK and USA. More than half of the 100,000 Indians in the New York area are Gujaratis; there the name Patel, a popular Gujarati surname, has become commonly identified as Indian.

Gujarati Food

The strict Jain vegetarianism has contributed to Gujarat's distinct regional cuisine. Throughout the state you'll find the Gujarati variation of the thali – it's the traditional all-you-can-eat vegetarian meal with an even greater variety of dishes than usual. But with the drawback, if you're not sweet-toothed, that it can be overpoweringly sweet.

Popular dishes include *kadhi*, a savoury curry of yoghurt and fried puffs, flavoured with spices and finely chopped vegetables. *Undhyoo* is a winter specialty of potatoes, sweet potatoes, broad beans and aubergines roasted in an earthenware pot which is buried upside down (*undhyoo*) under a fire. In Surat there's a local variation on this which is more spicy and curry hot. *Sev ganthia* is a crunchy fried chickpea-flour snack, which you buy from *farsan* stalls.

In winter, in Surat, you can try *paunk*, a curious combination of roasted cereals; or *jowar*, garlic chutney and sugar. Then there's *khaman dhokla*, a salty, steamed chickpea-flour cake. Or *doodhpak*, a thick, sweetened, milk-based dessert with nuts. *Srikhand* is a dessert made from yoghurt spiced with saffron, cardamom, nuts and candied fruit. *Gharis* are a rich sweet made of milk, clarified butter and dried fruits. In summer *am rasis* is a popular mango-juice drink.

The Gujaratis make superb ice-cream which is available throughout western India. The brand is *Va-de-lal* and it has about 20 flavours some of which are seasonal, eg 'custard apple' can only be bought in January and February. Many of the flavours have chunks of real fruit in them and of course no chemical additives.

Things to Buy

With its busy modern textile works, it's not surprising that Gujarat has a number of interesting buys in this line. At the top end of this field are the extremely fine, and often extremely expensive, Patola silk saris still made by a handful of master craftspeople in Patan. From Surat comes the *zari* or gold-thread embroidery work. Surat is also a centre for silk saris. At a more mundane but still beautiful level there are the block prints of Ahmedabad. There you will also find hand-painted cloth in the traditional black, red, maroon and ochre. Look for them at Madhupura Rani-no-Hajiro on Mirzapur Rd, near the Ahmedabad GPO.

Jamnagar is famous for its tie-dye work, which you'll find in bazaar shops in Jamnagar and other centres in Saurashtra. Brightly coloured peasant embroideries and beadwork are also found in Saurashtra, along with woollen shawls, blankets and rugs, while brass-covered wooden chests are manufactured in Bhavnagar. In Kutch embroidered stuffed toys are made. Finally, in Ahmedabad there are antique shops with wooden carvings such as window frames, shutters or doorways from old houses. In Ahmedabad you'll find most Gujarati handicrafts displayed at Handloom House or Gujari, both on Ashram Rd.

Festivals & Fairs

Gujarat has a busy calendar of events. Some of the main ones include:

January – Mankar Sankranti An end-of-winter festival celebrated with kite-flying contests.

January/February – Muharram *Tazias*, large replicas of the tombs of two Muslim martyrs, are paraded in the evening, particularly in Surat, Junagadh and Ahmedabad.

September/October – Navarati Nine nights of music and dancing celebrate this festival of the mother goddess Amba. The Dandiya Ras, which Lord Krishna danced with his milkmaids or *gopis*, is featured. Champaner celebrates this festival with particular fervour.

October – Dussehra The 10th day of Navarati culminates in the celebration of Rama's victory over the evil Ravana in the *Ramayana*.

October/November – Sharad Purnima Song and dance celebrate the end of the monsoon on the full-moon night of the month of Sharad.

Gujarat has many fairs in temple towns and small villages. They're a chance to see religious festivals and celebrations and also, in the villages, a shop window onto local handicrafts. Ambaji, a village 177 km north of Ahmedabad, celebrates four major festivals in the year. At the Bhavnath Fair, at the foot of Mt Girnar in the month of Magha (January/February), you have a fine chance to hear local folk music and see folk dances.

The tribal Adivasi people have a major festival at Dangs near Surat – it's known as the Dangs Durbar. Lord Krishna's birthday or Janmashtamia falls in August and his temple at Dwarka is the place to be. Along the coast at Porbandar the Madhavrai Fair is held in the month of Chaitra (March/April) and celebrates Lord Krishna's elopement with Rukmini. In the same month there is a major festival at the foot of Pavagadh Hill by Champaner, near Baroda. Mahakali is the goddess it honours. Somnath has a large fair at the full moon of Kartika Purnima in November/December. Lord Shiva, the three-eyed one or Trinetreshwar, has an important festival in his honour in Bhadrapada (August/September) in

Ternetar village – a chance to see colourful local tribal costumes.

AHMEDABAD (population 1,750,000)

The principal city of Gujarat, Ahmedabad is also one of the major industrial cities of India. It has been called the 'Manchester of the East' due to its many textile industries. Today it is destined to be the earth station for India's satellite TV project, but it's also a rather noisy and polluted city. Over the centuries Ahmedabad has had a number of periods of grandeur followed by decline. It was originally founded in 1411 by Ahmed Shah and in the 1600s was thought to be one of the finest cities in India. In 1615 Sir Thomas Roe, the noted English ambassador, judged it to be 'a goodly city, as large as London', but in the 1700s it went through a period of decline. Its industrial strength once again raised the city up, and from 1915 it became famous as the site for Gandhi's ashram and the place where he launched his famous march to break the Salt Law.

Today this comparatively little-visited city has a number of attractions for travellers. Gandhi's ashram at Sabarmati can be visited and there is a small museum. In the city there are some of the finest examples of Islamic architecture in India and a number of other interesting buildings both religious and secular. Ahmedabad is one of the best places to study the blend of Hindu and Islamic architectural styles known as the Indo-Saracenic. The new capital of Gujarat, Gandhinagar, is 23 km from Ahmedabad. Visitors in the hot season should bear in mind the Moghul emperor Jehangir's derisive title for Ahmedabad: Gardabad, 'the city of dust'.

In recent years Ahmedabad has been the centre for violent communal outbursts, mainly between Muslims and Hindus. There is fear that the city will eventually be divided into areas strictly segregated on religious grounds.

Orientation

The city sprawls across the Sabarmati River. Two main roads run back from the river to the railway station, about a km away. They are Relief Rd (Tilak Rd) and Gandhi Rd. The city walls are now virtually all demolished but some of the gates remain. The airport is off to the north-east of the city. The Gandhi Ashram is on the west bank of the Sabarmati River, to the north of the city.

Information

The state Tourist Office is across the river from the centre, just off Sri R C Rd. Hours are 10.30 am to 1.30 pm and 2 to 5.30 pm. They're late starters even by Indian standards. On Ashram Rd just before the Tourist Office is Gujari, the Gujarat state crafts emporium. Across the road is Handloom House. Indian Airlines is close to the Nehru Bridge, behind and across the road from the Sidi Saiyad Mosque.

The British Library is opposite the Sidi Saiyad Mosque and has air-conditioning, a drinking fountain and spotless toilets! The Victoria Gardens beside M G Rd are pleasant and 'almost quiet'.

Bhadra & Teen Darwaza

The ancient citadel, the Bhadra, was built by Ahmed Shah in 1411 and later named after the goddess Bhadra, an incarnation of Kali. It is now used for government offices and is of no particular interest. There is a post office in the former Palace of Azam Khan within the citadel. In front of the citadel stands the triple gateway or Teen Darwaza, from which sultans would watch processions from the palace to the Jami Masjid.

Jami Masjid

The Friday Mosque is beside Gandhi Rd, a short distance down from Teen Darwaza. This large mosque was built in 1424 by Ahmed Shah, the city's founder. There are 260 columns supporting the roof with its 15 cupolas, but in the great earthquake of 1819 the two 'shaking' minarets lost half their height and another tremor in 1957 completed the demolition. In this early Ahmedabad mosque much of the building was made from items salvaged from demolished Hindu and Jain temples. It is said that a large black slab by the main arch is actually the base of a Jain idol, buried upside down for the Muslim faithful to tread on!

Tombs of Ahmed Shah & His Queens

The Tomb of Ahmed Shah stands just outside the east gate of the Jami Masjid. His son and grandson, who did not long survive him, also have their cenotaphs in this tomb, with its perforated stone windows. Women are not allowed into the central chamber. Across the street is the tomb of his queens on a raised platform – it's now really a market and in very poor shape compared to Ahmed Shah's tomb.

Sidi Saiyad's Mosque

This small mosque once formed part of the city wall; it is close to the river end of Relief Rd. Constructed by Sidi Saiyad, a slave of Ahmed Shah, it is noted for its beautiful carved stone windows in which the branches of a tree are intricately intertwined to form the complete window.

Ahmed Shah's Mosque

Dating from 1414, this was one of the earliest mosques in the city, rebuilt from a ransacked Hindu temple. It is located in the south-west of the Bhadra. The front of the mosque is now a garden.

Rani Rupmati's Mosque

A little north of the centre, this mosque was built between 1430 and 1440 and named after the Sultan's Hindu wife. The minarets were partially brought down by the disastrous earthquake of 1819. Note how the dome is elevated to allow light in around its base. The mosque, as with so many of Ahmedabad's early ones, displays elements of Hindu and Islamic design.

1	Mata Bhawani's Well
2	Dada Hari's Well
3	Hathee Singh Temple
4	Tourist Office
5	Hotel Karnavati
6	Cama Hotel
7	Ritz & Ambassador Hotels
8	Hotel Capital
9	Rani Rupmati Mosque
10	Indian Airlines
11	Roopalee Cream Station
12	Gulmarg & Esquire Hotels
13	Siddi Saiyad Mosque
14	Local Bus Terminal
15	Mehul, Capri, Metropole & Plaza Hotels & Kwality Restaurant
16	GPO
17	Hotel Kingsway
18	Fruit Juice Stand
19	Chetna Restaurant
20	Swami Temple
21	Hotel Moti Mahal
22	Havmor Ice Cream Bar
23	Hotel Ashiana
24	Gandhi Cold Drinks Bar
25	Balwas Hotel
26	Paramount Restaurant
27	Azam Khan's Mosque
28	Bhadra
29	Hotel Neelam & Restaurant
30	Teen Darwaza
31	Jami Masjid & Market
32	Hotel Payall
33	Shaking Minarets
34	Rama Sipri Mosque
35	Long Distance Bus Station

Rani Sipri's Mosque

A little south-east of the centre, this small mosque was built in 1514 and is also known as the Masjid-e-Nagira or 'jewel of a mosque' due to its extremely graceful and well-executed design. Its slender, delicate minarets are again a blend of Hindu and Islamic styles. The mosque is said to have been built by a wife of Sultan Mehmood Begada after he executed their son for some minor misdemeanour.

Sidi Bashir Mosque – shaking minarets

Just south of the railway station, outside

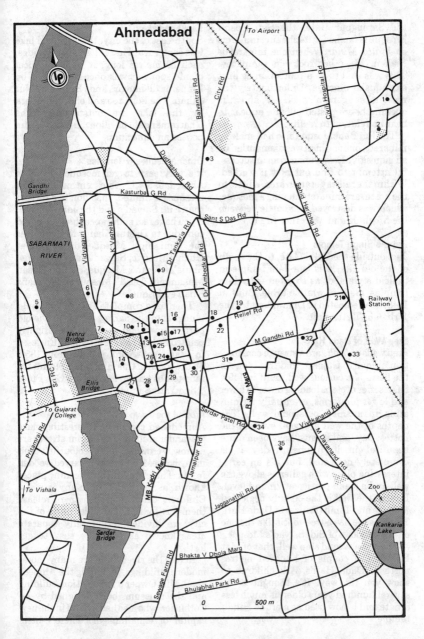

the Sarangpur Gate, the Sidi Bashir Mosque is famed for its shaking minarets or *Jhulta Minar*. When one minaret is shaken, the other rocks in sympathy. This was said to be a protection against earthquake damage. Unfortunately the mosque is generally closed and the opening hours posted outside appear to bear no relation to reality.

The Raj Babi Mosque also had shaking minarets, one of which was dismantled by an inquisitive Englishman in an unsuccessful attempt to find out how it worked. Within the railway station area, a little to the north, are minarets lacking a mosque, which was destroyed in a battle between the Moghuls and Marathas in 1753.

Hathee Singh Temple

Just outside the Delhi Gate, to the north of the old city, this is a Jain temple in typical style and, as so often with Jain temples, made of white marble. Built in 1848, it is dedicated to Dharamanath, the 15th Jain Tirthankar.

Step Well of Dada Hari

Step wells or *baolis* are a strange construction unique to Gujarat, and this is one of the best. The curious well, built in 1499, has a series of steps leading down to lower and lower platforms, eventually terminating in a small octagonal well. The depths of the well are cool, even on the hottest day, and it must have been quite beautiful in its prime. Today it is completely neglected, but it's an eerie, interesting place with galleries above the well and a small portico at ground level. Behind the well is the equally neglected Mosque and Tomb (Rauza) of Dada Hari. The mosque has a tree-motif like the one on the windows of Sidi Saiyad's Mosque.

There is a second step well, that of Mat Bhawani, a couple of hundred metres north of Dada Hari's. Ask children to show you the way. It's thought to be several hundred years older, is much less ornate and is now used as a crude Hindu temple.

Kankaria Lake

South-east of the city, this artificial lake was constructed in 1451 and has 34 sides, each 60 metres long. It is now a local picnic spot but was once frequented by Emperor Jehangir and Empress Nur Jahan. The huge zoo and children's park by the lake are outstanding. The Ghattamendal pavilion in the centre houses an aquarium.

Other Mosques & Temples

It's very easy to get mosque-ed out in Ahmedabad. If your enthusiasm for mosques is limited, then don't go further than Sidi Saiyad's and the Jami Masjid. If you have real endurance then you could continue to Dastur Khan's Mosque near the Rani Sipri Mosque, or to Haibat Khan's Mosque, Saiyad Alam's Mosque, Shuja'at Khan's Mosque, Shaikh Hasan Muhammed Chisti's Mosque and Muhafiz Khan's Mosque.

Then for a complete change you could plunge into the narrow streets of the old part of town and seek out the brightly painted Swami Narayan Temple. Enclosed in a large courtyard, it dates from 1850. To the south of this Hindu temple are the nine tombs known as the Nau Gaz Pir or 'Nine Yard Saints'.

Around the Town

Ahmedabad can be an interesting place to wander around. The bazaar streets are narrow, crowded and colourful, and many houses have ornately carved wooden fronts. There are Jain bird-feeding places known as *parabdis* in many streets. Children catch pigeons, then release them just for fun. The older parts of the city are divided into totally separate areas known as *pols*. It's easy to get lost!

Across the river there are many more-modern buildings, including the Ahmedabad Mill Owner's Association building and the museum, both designed by Le Corbusier, who also had a hand in the new capital of Gandhinagar. There's little evidence of the British period in Ahmedabad, unlike in so many large cities. The chief landmarks of the era are the tall smokestacks that ring this industrial city. On the sandy bed of the Sabarmati River traditional block-printed fabrics are still stretched out to dry, despite the 70-plus large textile mills. The river dries up to a mere trickle in the hot season.

Other places of interest in and around the town include the ruined tomb of Darya Khan (1453) north-west of the Hathee Singh Temple. It has a particularly large dome. Near it is the Chhota Shahi Bagh and across the railway line is the Shahi Bagh. Ladies of the harem used to live in the chhota (small) garden. In Saraspur, east of the railway line, the Temple of Chintaman is a Jain temple originally constructed in 1638, but converted by Aurangzeb into a mosque.

Museums

Ahmedabad has a number of museums. The Calico Museum of Textiles (tel 5100) has a display of antique and modern textiles including rare tapestries, wall hangings and costumes. Also on display are old weaving machines. The museum is in Sarabhai House in the Shahi Bagh gardens. It is open 10 am to 12.30 pm and 2.30 to 5 pm but closed on Wednesdays. Admission is free and it has 'great antique fabrics and is the best laid out museum I've seen', said one traveller. An interesting little museum shop sells cards, books and reproductions of some of the pieces.

The N C Mehta Museum of Miniatures (tel 78369) at Sanskar Kendra, Paldi has an excellent exhibit of the various schools of Indian miniature paintings. It is open 9 to 11 am and 4 to 7 pm, daily except Mondays. The building was designed by Le Corbusier.

The Shreyas Folk Museum has exhibits of the folk arts and crafts of Gujarat. There's also the National Institute of Design, the Tribal Research & Training Institute Museum and a Philatelic Museum. The Institute of Indology on the

university campus (tel 78295) has an important collection of illustrated manuscripts and miniatures and one of the finest collections relating to Jainism in India. It is open afternoons only from around 3 pm.

Sabarmati Ashram

Situated six km from the centre of town, on the west bank of the Sabarmati River, this was Gandhi's headquarters during his long struggle for Indian independence. His ashram was founded in 1918 and still makes handicrafts, handmade paper and spinning wheels. Gandhi's spartan living quarters are preserved as a small museum and there is a pictorial exhibit of the major events in his life.

The ashram is open from 8.30 am to 6.30 pm (to 7 pm April to September). Admission is free. On Sunday, Tuesday, Thursday and Friday evenings there is a *son et lumière* show in English at 8.15 pm, with a small admission fee. An autorickshaw from the city-centre side of Nehru Bridge to the ashram at Sabarmati will cost around Rs 4. Bus Nos 81, 82, 83 or 84 will get you there for Rs 1.

Tours

Tours operate from the Lal Darwaza bus stand each day at 8 am and 2.30 pm. They cost Rs 12. The Tourism Corporation of Gujarat have longer (four or five days) tours around north Gujarat, south Gujarat and Saurashtra. They cost Rs 450 to Rs 700.

Places to Stay – bottom end

Cheap hotels are scattered although they are mainly around the centre. There's nothing very special or any great bargains to be found. Right behind the big Capri Hotel and the Kwality Restaurant on Relief Rd is the *Plaza Hotel* where singles/doubles with attached bathroom are Rs 34/68. They'll win no awards for their cleaning abilities and the toilets are filthy. Close by, in a small alley off Relief Rd, is the *Metropole Hotel* which is a bit better (ie habitable) but not knockout and much more expensive at Rs 79/99. Nearby the *Hotel Mehul* costs Rs 65 for a double with bathroom. It's cleaner, rooms have balconies and it's probably the pick of this bunch.

Hotel Ashiana is also central. Doubles cost Rs 35 without bath, Rs 45 with. It's very basic but an acceptable and reasonably clean place at which to stay. The new and clean *Alita Guest House* is only a minute from the GPO and has rooms at Rs 35/40. Behind the Bhadra citadel, right next to the Ahmed Khan Mosque, is the *Hotel Natraj* with singles/doubles at Rs 32/55. The modern building is close to the centre but fairly quiet. It is also near the Lal Darwaza bus station.

For emergencies more than anything, there's the *Alankar Hotel* at Kapasia Bazaar near the railway station. There are many other hotels (like the more expensive *Hotel Moti Mahal* at Rs 103/122) close to the railway station. The *Railway Retiring Rooms* charge Rs 28/56 or Rs 63/106 with air-con and has a Rs 15 dorm. *Hotel Gulmarg* and *Hotel Esquire* are both in Lal Darwaza, near the river end of Relief Rd. Both are relatively expensive, and the Gulmarg is rather drear.

If you don't mind being out of town a bit, the modern *Gandhi Ashram* is close to the river. It has just nine rooms (so it's wise to book ahead), each with attached bath and balcony. Singles/doubles are Rs 75/100 plus 10%. Phone 86 7652 or contact the tourist office (tel 44 9683).

Places to Stay – top end

The *Cama Hotel* (tel 25281-85) is on Khanpur Rd, centrally located and pleasantly situated overlooking the river. Singles/ doubles with air-con are Rs 460/505 plus 20%. It's got a pretty good restaurant where breakfast costs Rs 21 or Rs 29; this is probably the best top-end place in Ahmedabad. Nearby is the new *Rivera Hotel* (tel 24201) with rooms at Rs 250/325.

Close to the Cama Hotel and the river, the *Ritz Hotel* (tel 24373-75) is pleasantly secluded in a large garden well back from the road. Singles/doubles at this older hotel are Rs 210/255 plus 20% with air-con. There is a handful of non-air-con rooms at around Rs 100. Almost next door to it is the modern *Hotel Ambassador* (tel 392244) with rooms from Rs 100/150 or with air-con for Rs 150/200 plus 20%.

Moving away from the river, the *Hotel Capri* (tel 24643-4) is on Relief Rd, almost next door to the Kwality Restaurant. Singles/doubles cost Rs 110/150 without air-con, Rs 160/200 with it, plus 15% in both cases. The Capri is rather tatty, grubby and run-down looking and the front rooms are very noisy from the street. Right across the road is the *Hotel Balwas* (tel 395535), a well-kept new place with simple rooms at a variety of prices. Singles/doubles are Rs 85/120 or Rs 130/160 with air-con. It's better value than the Capri. The restaurant here is said to be good.

Hotel Kingsway (tel 26221-5) near the Relief Cinema on GPO Rd has rooms at Rs 100/140 or from Rs 150/190 with air-con. Or there's the big and relatively quiet *Hotel Capital* (tel 24633) at Chandanwadi, Mirzapur where rooms cost Rs 44/69, Rs 91/134 with bath or from Rs 167/206 with air-con. There's a wide variety of rooms here, and although the basic cheapies are certainly very basic they look clean enough.

Across the river the centrally air-conditioned *Hotel Karnavati* (tel 402161) is on Ashram Rd and has singles/doubles at Rs 360/390. On the same road the *Hotel Nataraj* (tel 448747) has rooms at Rs 405/485. *Hotel Siddhartha Palace* (tel 66505) at Dafnala Shahibagh has rooms at Rs 125/150 or with air-con at Rs 175/200. Once again these places add 20% service and tax to the bill.

Places to Eat

A number of hotels, like the *Cama Hotel*, have pleasant dining rooms, often with air-con, a near necessity in the hot weather. On Relief Rd there's a *Kwality Restaurant* with an extensive English-Chinese-Indian menu, but in 1986 it was on an extended long-term strike! The Capri Hotel's *Gold Coin* restaurant comes complete with mirrors and a spiral staircase.

Across the road there's a *Havmor* ice cream parlour and another further down Relief Rd. Apart from good quality ice cream, you can also get snacks and cold flavoured milk. There are a number of clean milk bars where you can get bottles of (curiously) flavoured milk. On the corner of Relief Rd and Dr Ambedkar Rd, across from the second Havmor, there's a large open-air fruit juice stand serving up superb fruit juices. Another good place for drinks, ice cream and snacks is the *Roopalee Cream Station* near Indian Airlines and the Roopalee Cinema.

Very close to the Teen Darwaza Gate is the tiny *Gandhi Cold Drinks Bar* with more good ice cream (Rs 2 to Rs 4) and cold drinks. Near Teen Darwaza the *Neelam Hotel* and the *Paramount* are both good for western food – 'the best in the city'. The Paramount is much less expensive than the somewhat pretentious Neelam, where you can easily spend Rs 60 for a meal. Over the river and opposite Gujarat College, the *Collegian Restaurant* is popular with college students. The food is mainly Punjabi with lots of variety, and reasonably priced too.

Ahmedabad is, of course, a good place to sample a Gujarati thali; see the Gujarat food section. One of the best thali specialists in Ahmedabad is the *Chetna Restaurant* on Relief Rd where the all-you-can-eat thali costs Rs 14. It can be a little hard to locate since the sign is not in Roman script, but it almost adjoins the Krishna Cinema (well, their sign is not in our script either) and is directly across the road from the Oriental Building. It's so popular that you may have to queue to get in, and a special waiter is provided to ply the waiting customers with water. 'We ate all we could', reported one gourmand, 'and had to lie down in a park to recover'.

Hotel Payall at Khadia Char Rasta is even more anonymous and charges Rs 15 for their standard Gujarati thali plus Rs 5 for dessert. There's a sort of waiting room before the main restaurant. One traveller recommended 'the little hole-in-the-wall *Vepari Hotel* between Teen Darwaza and Manek Chowk'. It's back from the street along a narrow lane, up flights of stairs, and it's crowded so you always have to wait 15 minutes for a table. 'The thalis are great and it's also a good place for a real taste of old Ahmedabad and its bustle and energy'.

Finally, for an interesting night out in Ahmedabad try *Vishala*, a rural complex evoking the atmosphere of a Gujarat village. It's on the southern edge of town and you dine in Indian style, seated on the floor while watching puppet shows and local dancing. It's peaceful, friendly and very well done. The cost is Rs 28 for lunch from 11 am to 1 pm, Rs 35 for dinner from 7 to 11 pm.

Getting There

Air Indian Airlines have two daily flights Bombay-Ahmedabad and Ahmedabad-Bombay and a daily Delhi-Jaipur-Jodhpur-Ahmedabad-Bombay (and reverse) flight. Plus there's a Madras-Bangalore-Ahmedabad flight three times a week. Fares to or from Ahmedabad include Bombay Rs 410, Delhi Rs 695, Jodhpur Rs 400 and Bangalore Rs 1143.

Rail Ahmedabad is not on the main broadgauge line between Delhi and Bombay, although there is a broad-gauge line running south to Bombay and a metregauge line running north to Delhi via the major towns of Rajasthan. Delhi-Ahmedabad is 938 km and takes around 24 hours except for the three-times-weekly Ashram Express and the twice-weekly Sarvodaya Express, which only take 17 or 18 hours. The latter train takes the broad-gauge line from Delhi via Kota and Ratlam to Baroda, then turns north to Ahmedabad. Fares between Delhi and Ahmedabad are Rs 73 in 2nd class, Rs 297 in 1st.

There are plenty of daily trains between Ahmedabad and Bombay. The 492-km trip takes 10 to 15 hours, with the fastest mail trains making the trip in around nine hours. Fares are Rs 45 in 2nd class, Rs 181 in 1st. The Delhi trains taking the metre-gauge line north will get you to Abu Road in about five hours (186 km), to Ajmer in 12 hours (491 km), and to Jaipur in 15 hours (626 km).

Bus There are plenty of buses both around Gujarat and to neighbouring states. If you're heading north into Rajasthan, the direct bus to Mt Abu (seven hours, Rs 28) will probably be faster than a train to Abu Road and a bus from there. A bus to Udaipur will take about six hours, to Bombay about 11 hours.

Getting Around

Airport An airport bus from Lal Darwaza goes at flight times and a half dozen other times a day and costs Rs 6 or Rs 7. It costs Rs 0.80. An auto-rickshaw will cost about Rs 20 to Rs 25, a taxi about Rs 50.

Local Transport There are the usual buses and taxis around Ahmedabad and hordes of reckless auto-rickshaw drivers. In Ahmedabad's frantic traffic conditions, venturing out in an auto-rickshaw is a nerve-shattering experience. On the plus side the auto-rickshaw wallahs use their meters 100% and without argument. The meters may be well away from the correct fare, but they do use them. The bus stand is known universally as Lal Darwaza. The routes, destinations and fares are all written in Gujarati.

AROUND AHMEDABAD
Sarkhej

Only eight km out of Ahmedabad, the suburb of Sarkhej is noted for its elegant group of buildings. The architecture here is interesting in that the style is almost purely Hindu, with little evidence of the Saracenic influence felt so strongly in Ahmedabad. The buildings include the Mausoleum of Azam and Mu'azzam, built in 1457. These brothers were responsible for Sarkhej's architecture.

As you enter Sarkhej you pass the Mausoleum of Mahmud Begara and, beside the tank and connected to his tomb, that of his queen, Rajabai (1460). Also by the tank is the tomb of Ahmad Khattu Gaj Buksh, a renowned Muslim saint and spiritual adviser of Ahmed Shah. The saint is said to have died in 1445 at the age of 111. Next to this is the fine mosque – 'the perfection of elegant simplicity'. Like the other buildings, it is notable for the complete absence of arches, a distinct feature of Muslim architecture. Also around the tank is the palace with pavilions and a harem. The Dutch established a factory in Sarkhej in 1620 for the indigo grown here.

CHAI
AH CHAI
AH CHAI
CHAI
HAI

A1 (TEA) VENDOR AT ANY RAILWAY STATION

Batwa

South-east of Ahmedabad, the suburb of Batwa has tombs of a noted Muslim saint (himself the son of another saint) and the saint's son. Batwa also has an important mosque.

Adalaj Vav

Situated 19 km north of Ahmedabad, this is one of the finest of the Gujarati step wells or *baolis*. Built by Queen Rudabai in 1499, it provided a cool and secluded retreat during the hot summer months. Buses run here regularly and cost about Rs 3.

Cambay

The old sea port of Ahmedabad is to the south-west, at the northern end of the Gulf of Cambay. At the height of Muslim power in Gujarat the entire region was known as Cambay, and when the first ambassadors arrived from England in 1583 they bore letters from Queen Elizabeth addressed to Akbar, the 'King of Cambay'. The Dutch and Portuguese had established factories in the port before the British arrived, but the rise of Surat eclipsed Cambay and when its port silted up the city's decline was inevitable.

Nal Sarovar

From November to February this 116-square-km lake is home for vast flocks of indigenous and migratory birds. Particularly early in the morning and in the evening you may see ducks, geese, pelicans and flamingoes. There is a *Holiday Home* with accommodation near the lake; it has to be booked through the tourist office in Ahmedabad.

Lothal

About 80 km south of Ahmedabad, towards Bhavnagar, this site is of great interest to archaeologists. The city which stood here 4500 years ago was clearly closely related to the Indus Valley cities of Moenjodaro and Harappa – both in Pakistan. It has the same neatly laid out street pattern, the same carefully assembled brickwork and the same scientific drainage system.

The name Lothal actually means 'mound of the dead' in Gujarati, just as Moenjodaro does in Sindhi. At its peak, this was probably one of the most important ports on the sub-continent and trade was possibly carried on with the civilisations of Mesopotamia, Egypt and Persia.

Places to Stay Cheap accommodation is available at the *Tourist Centre*.

Getting There Lothal is a day trip from Ahmedabad. You can reach it by rail, disembarking at Bhurkhi on the Ahmedabad-Bhavnagar railway line, from where you can walk or take a bus. Or you can bus straight there from Ahmedabad.

Modhera

The ruined Sun Temple of Modhera was built by King Bhimdev I (1026-27) and bears some relationship to the later, and far better known, Sun Temple of Konarak in the state of Orissa. Like that temple, it was designed so that the sun shone on the image of Surya, the Sun God, at dawn at the time of the equinoxes. The main hall and shrine are reached through a pillared porch. The exterior of this fine temple is intricately and delicately carved. As at Somnath, it was Mahmud of Ghazni who did the ruining. The temple is open 8 am to 6 pm daily.

Places to Stay There is a *PWD Rest House* with singles for Rs 15.

Getting There Modhera is 106 km north-west of Ahmedabad. There are buses direct to Modhera, or you can take the train to Mehsana, where buses make the 40-km trip to Modhera.

Unjha

A little north of Mehsana, the station for visits to the Modhera Temple, the town of Unjha is interesting for the marriage customs of the Kadwakanbis who live in this region. Marriages occur only once every 11 years, and on that day every unmarried girl over 40 days old must be wed – if no husband can be found a proxy wedding takes place and the bride

immediately becomes a 'widow'. She later remarries when a suitable husband shows up.

Further north again is Sidhpur with the very fragmented ruins of an ancient temple. This region was an important centre for growing opium poppies.

Patan

About 120 km north-west of Ahmedabad, this was an ancient Hindu capital before being sacked by Mahmud of Ghazni in 1024. Now a pale shadow of its former glory, it still has over 100 Jain temples and is a centre for the manufacture of beautifully designed Patola silk saris. There's another step well here.

Getting There Patan is 25 km north-west of the Mehsana railway station, which also serves as a jumping-off point for Modhera.

GANDHINAGAR (population 25,000)

The old state of Bombay was split into Maharashtra and Gujarat in 1960 and a new capital was planned for the state of Gujarat. Situated on the west bank of the Sabarmati, 32 km north-east of Ahmedabad, Gandhinagar is named after Mahatma Gandhi, who was born in Gujarat. It is India's second planned city, after Chandigarh, and like that city is laid out into numbered sectors. Construction of the city commenced in 1965 and the secretariat was moved there in 1970.

Places to Stay

Gandhinagar has an excellent *Youth Hostel* in sector 16, and in sector 11 there is the *Panthik Ashram* government rest house. Other rest houses and guest houses are located at Pethapur and opposite Sachivalaya. The Tourist Information Centre (tel 2211/479-82) is also at Sachivalaya but is a 'dead loss'.

Getting There

Buses from Ahmedabad cost about Rs 2.

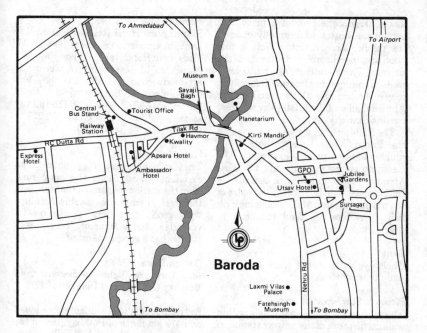

Baroda

BARODA (Vadodara) (population 500,000)
Baroda was the capital of the princely
Gaekwad state prior to independence.
Today it is a pleasant, medium-sized city
with some interesting museums and art
galleries and a fine park. A good place for
a short pause.

Orientation & Information
The railway station, bus stand and a
cluster of cheaper hotels are all off to one
side of the city. The tourist office is in a
small, upstairs room across from the
station to the left. A road runs straight
out from the station, across the river by
the Sayaji Bagh and into the main part of
town.

Sayaji Bagh & Baroda Museum
This extensive park is a popular spot for
an evening stroll and also has a small zoo.
A mini-railway encircles the park. Within
the park is the Baroda Museum & Art

Gallery, open 9.30 am to 4.45 pm daily
except Saturday, when it opens at 10 am.
The museum has a varied collection,
while the gallery has Moghul miniatures
and a collection of European masters.
Also within the park grounds is the
relatively new planetarium, where there
is an English-language performance each
evening.

Maharajah Fateh Singh Museum
A little south of the centre, this royal art
collection includes European works by
Raphael, Titian and Murillo and exhibits
of Graeco-Roman, Chinese and Japanese
art as well as Indian exhibits. The
museum is in the palace grounds and is
open 9 am to 12 noon and 3 to 6 pm from
July to March, 4 to 7 pm April to June. It
is closed on Mondays.

Other
The flamboyant Lakshmi Vilas Palace

has a large collection of armour and sculptures, but is not normally open to the public. The Naulakhi Well, a fine *baoli* or step well, is 50 metres north of the palace. These interesting multi-level wells are unique to Gujarat. Others you may visit are the Dada Hari well in Ahmedabad and the Adalaj Vav well just outside that city.

The Railway Staff College now occupies the Pratap Vilas Palace; there are a number of other palaces in the city. The Gaekwad rulers' family vault, the Kirti Mandir, is decorated with murals by Indian artist Nandial Bose. The centre of town is built around a lake swarming with fish – vendors sell food to throw to them.

Tours

Check with the tourist office about the daily tours of Baroda.

Places to Stay – bottom end

There are a lot of cheaper hotels within walking distance of the railway station. If you head straight out from the station and take the second road right, you'll find the *Laxmi Lodge* where rooms cost from Rs 50. The pleasant and well-kept *Apsara* is Rs 60 for small but comfortable doubles with attached bathroom. Across the road and a little further down is the big *Ambassador* with rooms from Rs 60. Finally, right down on the corner is the similarly priced *Chandan Mahal*. There are other cheap hotels along this road (like the *Baroda Guest House*), but they're not so good.

On Race Course Rd the *Green Hotel* (tel 63111) has rooms at Rs 32/64 with attached bath. The *Municipal Corporation Guest House*, or Pravashi Gruh, is directly opposite the railway station and has rooms from around Rs 30. It's conveniently situated but rather drab and grey. There are also *Railway Retiring Rooms*. The new *Motel Suren* has small rooms from Rs 50.

Places to Stay – top end

The *Express Hotel* (tel 67051-4) on R C Dutt Rd has air-con rooms at Rs 345/405. The *Utsav Hotel* (tel 51415) on Professor Manekrao Rd, near the centre, is centrally air-conditioned and also has the Tana Restaurant. At Sayajigunj the *Hotel Surya* (tel 66592) is close to the railway station and has rooms at Rs 150/225 or with air-con for Rs 250/300.

Places to Eat

The *Ambassador Hotel* is popular for its excellent thalis. Along the main road from the station towards the gardens and the river, there's a reasonable *Kwality*, with good lunch-time snacks on its verandah, and a *Havmor*. The railway station has a good restaurant.

Getting There

Air There are flights to Baroda from Bombay (Rs 342) and Delhi (Rs 772).

Rail Baroda is 112 km south of Ahmedabad and 419 km north of Bombay. It's on the main Bombay-Ahmedabad railway line so there are plenty of trains running through, or you can go by bus. Rail fare to Bombay is Rs 41 in 2nd class, Rs 161 in 1st. To Ahmedabad it is Rs 12 in 2nd class, Rs 57 in 1st.

Between Baroda and Ahmedabad you pass through Anand, a small town noted for its dairy production. At the station hordes of sellers besiege passing trains selling bottles of *cold* milk.

BROACH (Bharuch) (population 100,000)

This very old town was mentioned in historical records nearly 2000 years ago. In the 1600s English and Dutch factories were established here. The fort overlooks the wide Narbada (or Narmada) River from its hilltop location; at its base is the Jami Masjid, which was constructed from a Jain temple. On the riverbank, outside the city to the east, is the Temple of Bhrigu Rishi, from which the city took its name of Bhrigukachba, later shortened to Bharuch.

Near Broach the town of Suklatirtha has a *Holiday Home*. The nearby island of Kabirwad, in the river, has a gigantic banyan tree which covers a hectare.

AROUND BARODA
Champaner

North-east of Baroda, 47 km along the main broad-gauge railway line to Delhi, Champaner was taken by Sultan Mahmud Begara in 1484. The Jami Masjid in this city is one of the finest mosques in Gujarat and is similar in style to the Jami Masjid of Ahmedabad. The hill of Pavagadh, with its ruined fort, rises beside Champaner, in three stages. In 1553 the Moghuls, led by Humayun himself, scaled the fort walls with the use of iron spikes driven into the rocks, and took the fort and its city. Parts of the massive fort walls still stand.

Two important festivals are held here each year. The name Pavagadh means 'quarter of a hill' and is said to indicate that the hill is actually a chunk of the Himalayan mountainside which the monkey god Hanuman carted off to Lanka in an episode of the *Ramayana*.

Places to Stay Champaner has a *Holiday Home* with singles, doubles and dormitories.

Dabhoi Fort

The 13th-century fort of Dabhoi is 29 km south-east of Baroda. It is a fine example of Hindu military architecture and noted for the design of its four gateways – particularly the Hira or Diamond Gate.

Dakor

Equidistant from Baroda and Ahmedabad, the temple of Ranchodrai in this town is sacred to Lord Krishna and is a major centre for the Sharad Purnima festival in October or November.

SURAT (population 500,000)

Standing on the banks of the River Tapti,

this was once one of the major ports and trading towns of western India. Two hundred years ago it had a bigger population than it does today and was far more important than Bombay. In the 12th century Parsis first settled in Surat; they had earlier been centred 100 km south in Sanjan, where they had fled from Persia five centuries before. In 1573 the city fell to Akbar after a prolonged siege, and became an important Moghul trading port and also the departure point for Muslim pilgrims bound for Mecca.

Surat soon became a wealthy city and in 1612 the British established a trading factory there, followed by the Dutch in 1616 and the French in 1664. Portuguese power on the west coast had been severely curtailed by a crushing naval defeat at the hands of the British settlement in India. In 1664 Moghul power and prestige suffered a severe blow when the Maratha leader Shivaji sacked the town. In a classic display of British stiff upper lip, Sir George Oxenden sent a message to Shivaji from the strongly defended English Factory, saying that he should 'save the labour of his servants running to and fro on messages and come himself with all his army'. Perhaps Shivaji took him seriously because the English Factory was not attacked.

Although the English Factory later transferred its 'presidency' to Bombay, Surat continued to prosper and in 1720 a dock was built followed by two British shipyards. In 1759, by which time Moghul power was long past its prime, the British virtually took full control over the city's ruler and by 1800 the city was in British hands. Today Surat is no longer of any importance as a port, but it is an important manufacturing town with a major textile industry.

Orientation

An eight-km-long wall encircled Surat on its land side, while the Tapti River forms the other side. Until the sack of the city by Shivaji the walls were made of mud, but

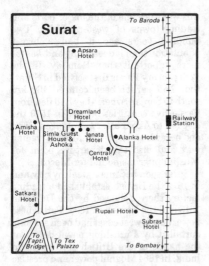

Surat

To Baroda

Apsara Hotel

Dreamland Hotel

Railway Station

Amisha Hotel

Simla Guest House & Ashoka

Janata Hotel

Alanka Hotel

Central Hotel

Satkara Hotel

Rupali Hotel

Subras Hotel

To Tapti Bridge

To Tex Palazzo

To Bombay

they were then reconstructed in brick. The railway station, with many cheaper hotels in its immediate vicinity, is connected to the old fort beside the river by one of Surat's few wide roads.

Castle

Built in 1546, the castle is beside the Tapti Bridge on the riverbank. It is of no great interest today since most of it is given over to offices, but there is a good view over the city and river from the bastions. Ask for the Tapti Bridge if you want to get to it.

Factories

Without a guide you would have difficulty finding the remains of the factories, and in any case there is little to indicate their former importance. They are near the IP Mission High School. The English Factory is about midway from the castle to the Kataragama Gate out of the old city. Standing close to the river, the Portuguese Factory, French Lodge and Persian Factory were close by. From the riverbank you can see the Tapti Bridge to your left, and across the river to your right you'll see

the mosque-studded suburb of Rander. There's a small temple to Hanuman by the river.

Cemeteries

Just beyond the Kataragama Gate, to the right of the main road, is the now very run down, overrun and neglected English Cemetery. Many of the tombstones are for children under five years of age. As you enter the cemetery the huge mausoleum to the right is that of Sir George Oxenden, who died in 1669. The structure is actually a tomb within a tomb since his brother was buried here 10 years earlier, and a larger mausoleum was constructed over that tomb. Another large tomb next to it is said to be that of Gerald Aungier, the next president of the English Factory. Like any scrap of waste ground in India, the English Cemetery has become a public toilet and the imposing mausoleums are in a sorry state.

Back-track towards the city, and about half a km after the Kataragama Gate, and 100 or so metres off the road to the left (to the right if you are coming from the centre), is the Dutch Cemetery. The mausoleum of Baron Adriaan van Reede, who died in 1691, is a massive structure and at one time was decorated with frescoes and woodcarvings. Note the inscription on the wall where 'Souratta' rates capital letters while lesser 'bombai' is in lower case. Adjoining the Dutch Cemetery is the Armenian Cemetery.

Other

Surat has a number of mosques and Jain, Hindu and Parsi temples. Cotton, silk and the manufacture of bangles are important industries in Surat. The nearby town of Rander, five km across the Hope Bridge, was built on the site of a very ancient Hindu city after it had been taken by the Muslims in 1225. Swally (Suvali) was the old port for Surat, situated 19 km to the west. It was off Swally, in 1615, that Portuguese colonial aspirations in India were ended by the British navy.

Places to Stay

There are lots of hotels near the railway station but no standouts. They're all within reasonable walking distance. In the rock-bottom bracket the *Subras* has dorm beds and cell-like rooms from Rs 20 with common bath, from Rs 25 with attached bath. The *Rupali* next door is a grubby little place with a cheap dorm and rooms from around Rs 20.

With rooms from around Rs 40, the *Central* is slightly higher class, as is the pleasant enough *Hotel Dreamland*. Close by are two cheaper and more basic hotels which are fair value and reasonably clean – the *Hotel Ashoka* and the *Simla Guest House*. A bit further down is the *Hotel Anishna*, with a wide variety of rooms with and without bathroom and air-con. The *Satkara* would be better value if it was better kept – it's on the 6th floor and rooms are reasonable. Surat bottom-end hotels offer no real bargains.

Surat's numero uno hotel is a km or two away from the railway station on top of the textile market. The *Tex Palazzo Hotel* (tel 23301-10) is on Ring Rd and has rooms with and without air-con from around Rs 125 and up.

Places to Eat

The *Tex Palazzo Hotel* boasts India's first revolving restaurant, and as with so many revolving restaurants around the world the food takes a distant second place to the view. At least it's not outrageously expensive, but the splendours of Surat unfold below you through windows nearly as grubby and dirty as those on the average Indian bus!

Back at ground level you can get a good Gujarati thali in the same hotel. You pay a similar price in the good air-con restaurant upstairs in the otherwise rather grotty *Subras Hotel* near the railway station. Downstairs the thalis are cheaper but you pay extra for second helpings.

mongoose

AROUND SURAT

There are a number of beaches near Surat. Only 16 km out, Dumas is a popular health resort. Hajira is 28 km from the city, Ubhrat is 42 km out, while Tithal is 108 km away and only five km from Valsad on the Bombay-Baroda rail line.

Navsari, 29 km south of Surat, has been a headquarters for the Parsi community since the earliest days of their settlement in India. Udvada, only 10 km north of Vapi, the station for Daman, has the oldest Parsi sacred fire in India. It is said that the fire was brought from Persia to Diu, on the opposite coast of the Gulf of Cambay, in 700 AD. Sanjan, in the extreme south of the state, is the small port where they first landed. A pillar marks the spot.

DAMAN

Right in the south of Gujarat, the tiny enclave of Daman was, along with Diu, taken from the Portuguese at the same time as Goa. It is still officially governed from Goa along with Diu. Its main function in Gujarat seems to be as a place to get a drink, since Gujarat is completely 'dry'. The streets of Daman are lined with bars selling 'Finest Scotch Whisky – Made in India'!

The Portuguese seized Daman, which totals 56 square km in area, in 1531 and were officially ceded the region by Bahadur Shah of Gujarat in 1559. There is still some Portuguese flavour to the town, with its fine old fort and a number of churches and other imposing Portuguese buildings. The town is split in two by the Damao Ganga River. The northern part of the town, with the hotels, restaurants, bars and so on, is known as Nani Daman ('little' Daman); the southern part, with government buildings and churches enclosed within an imposing wall, is known as Moti Daman ('big' Daman).

Although Daman is, like Goa, beside the sea, its beaches bear no relation to those glowing, golden stretches further south. Daman's beaches are grey, drab, dirty and dismal – quite apart from their function as the local toilet.

Churches

The Se Cathedral in the Moti Daman fort dates from the 1600s and is totally Iberian. It's less impressive than the Church of Our Lady of the Rosary with its cool, damp floor with ancient Portuguese tombstones set into it. The altar is a masterpiece of intricately-carved gold-painted wood. Light filters through the dusty windows, illuminating wooden panels painted with scenes of the apostles and Christ.

Other

The remnants of an old bastion in the fort was once the stronghold of an Ethiopian mercenary who held off the Portuguese for

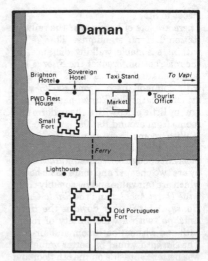

the Sultan of Gujarat for some time. Near the river on the Nani Daman side is an interesting Jain temple. If you enquire in the temple office a white-robed caretaker will show you around. The walls inside are completely covered with glassed-over 18th century murals depicting the life of Mahavira, who lived around 500 BC.

Places to Stay & Eat

The *PWD Rest House* is very well kept and a great bargain, but is often full up. Right across the road, the *Brighton Hotel* is a reasonable second best although it too is often full. A little further back up the road from the beach, the *Sovereign Hotel* is big and well kept with rooms at a variety of prices from Rs 30 and up. Some of them are rather cubical, but there is a popular upstairs restaurant – a good place for a beer on the verandah.

Back beyond the taxi stand, the *Hotel Tourist* is a dump to avoid – a newish building but totally neglected and miserable. Daman has lots of bars but not a great variety of places to eat. The more expensive *Hotel Gurukripa* (tel 446-7) on Seaface Rd has rooms at Rs 50/75 or with air-con at Rs 110/130. You can rent houses on the Moti Daman side.

Daman is noted for *papri*, boiled and salted sweetpeas served wrapped in newspaper in February. Crabs and lobsters are in season in October. *Tari* palm wine is a popular drink, you buy it in earthenware pots.

Getting There & Around

Vapi Station, on the main railway line, is the jumping-off point for Daman. Vapi is about 170 km from Bombay and 90 km from Surat. Take care; not all trains stop at Vapi so be very certain yours will be halting there or you'll sail straight by. Sometimes the train slows down enough that you can jump off anyway.

From Vapi it's 10 or so km into Daman and there are plenty of share-taxis for a couple of rupees per person. Or buses at less than Rs 1. You can easily rent bicycles in the Nani Daman bazaar.

SAPUTARA

In the south-east corner of the state, this cool hill resort stands at 1000 metres and is a popular base for excursions to Mahal Bardipara Forest Wildlife Sanctuary 60 km away or to the Gira waterfalls 52 km distant. Saputara means 'abode of serpents' and there is a sacred snake image on the banks of the River Sarpagana.

Places to Stay

Saputara has a variety of *Holiday Homes* and *Tourist Bungalows*.

SAURASHTRA

The often bleak plains of the Kathiawar Peninsula are inhabited by colourful and friendly, but reserved, people. The country people are distinctively dressed, with the men in white turbans, laced-across smocks (short-waisted and long-sleeved) and jodhpurs (baggy seat and drainpipe legs). They often sport golden ear-studs. The women are nearly as colourful as in Rajasthan but wear a distinctive embroidered backless halter-top.

Although pretty much off the main tourist routes, Saurashtra is a pleasant area to travel around and there is an extensive network of metre-gauge railway lines to make that travel much easier, although the trains are very slow. Most people travel by bus – there are limited-stop deluxe buses. A severe cyclone in late '82 caused extensive damage and more than 600 deaths in the Veraval, Amreh, Bhavnagar region.

The peninsula took its name from the Kathi tribespeople who used to roam the area stealing whatever was not locked into the many village forts or *kots* at night. You may notice, around Kathiawar, long lines of memorial stones known as *palias* – men are usually shown riding on large horses while women ride on wheels, which shows that they were in carriages.

BHAVNAGAR (population 250,000)

Founded as a port in 1723, Bhavnagar is still an important trading post for the cotton goods manufactured in Gujarat. The Gandhi Smitri is a library, small museum, gallery and memorial to the founder of India. Bhavnagar also has Gaurishankar Lake, a popular picnic spot, and Takhteshwar Temple with fine views from its hilltop location. The Bhavnagar lock gate keeps ships afloat during low tides in the city's port.

Places to Stay

Basic hotels include the *Evergreen Guest House* (tel 4605), the *Kashmir Hotel* near the Pathik Ashram and *Geeta Lodging & Boarding* (tel 3985). The *Pathik Ashram* has rooms around Rs 20 and there are *Railway Retiring Rooms*.

The *Natraj Guest House*, Nirmalnagar, Diamond Market is a 10-minute walk from the bus station and has rooms from Rs 20 and a dorm. It's a good place although it doesn't (or didn't) have a sign, but everyone knows the diamond market, and once there, it's easy. Yes, there really are lots of little shops that sell diamonds. Why in Bhavnagar? Their first-ever western guest, who wrote to tell us about this hotel, says his photograph was going up in the reception area! Next door is the *Hotel Embassy* which also has a good, cheap restaurant.

Bhavnagar has two better hotels, both with air-con rooms. They are the *Apollo Hotel* (tel 29551) opposite the Central Bus Stand and the *Hotel Takte-Khurshid* (tel 6881) on Waghawadi Rd, near Takhteshwara. The Apollo has rooms at Rs 105/115 or with air-con at Rs 150/175.

Places to Eat

There's nowhere much to eat around the bus station apart from the expensive Apollo. Take an auto-rickshaw (Rs 2 or Rs 3) to the *Nataraj Restaurant*, which has good food and a two-page menu of ice cream goodies! Outside, the *Vadilal Ice Cream* sign is more prominent than *Nataraj*. Tell rickshaw wallahs it's opposite Ganga Devi.

There's a *Havmor Restaurant* diagonally across from the main covered food market and on the edge of the extensive shopping area. The *Mahavir Lodge* near the station has good thalis.

Getting There

Bhavnagar is 244 km by road from Ahmedabad or about 270 km by rail. The rail trip takes about seven hours and costs Rs 27 in 2nd class, Rs 110 in 1st. There are also buses connecting Bhavnagar with Ahmedabad and other centres in the region. There's a daily Indian Airlines flight connection with Bombay which costs Rs 307. Vayudoot fly between Surat and Bhavnagar.

PALITANA

Situated 56 km from Bhavnagar, the town of Palitana is merely a gateway to Shatrunjaya, the 'place of victory'. From the town you have a two-km walk, ascending 600 metres to the hilltop where, over a period of 900 years, 863 temples have been constructed. The hilltop is dedicated entirely to the gods; at dusk even the priests depart from the temples and leave them deserted.

Almost all the temples are Jain, and this hill, one of their holiest pilgrimage places, is another indication of the merit Jains believe is derived from constructing temples. The hilltops are bounded by sturdy walls and the temples are grouped into nine enclosures or *tunks* – each with a central major temple and many minor ones clustered around. Some of the earliest temples were built here in the 11th century, but in the 14th and 15th centuries those spoilsport Muslims knocked them down, so the current temples date from the 1500s to the present.

The hilltop affords a very fine view in all directions; on a clear day you can see the Gulf of Cambay beyond Bhavnagar. The most notable of the temples is that to Shri Adishwara, the first Jain Tirthankar. Note the frieze of dragons around the temple. Adjacent to this temple is the Muslim shrine of Angar Pir. Women wanting children make offerings of miniature cradles at this shrine.

Built in 1618 by a wealthy Jain merchant, the Chaumukh or 'four faced' shrine has images of Adinath facing out in the four cardinal directions. Other important temples are those to Kumar Pal, Sampriti Raj and Vimal Shah. The marble temples are so thick on the hill summit that it looks like some giant, glistening white wedding cake from a distance. The temples are open from 7 am to 7 pm. Temple jewels are shown at 9 am to 3 pm. Image washing is at 9.45 am, puja at 10.45 am.

If you're taking a camera up the hill you'll need a photography permit – ask about it at your hotel. You will only be asked for the permit at the main entrance, which you get to by taking the left-hand fork as you near the top. If you enter the complex by taking the right-hand fork there's no one there to ask for the permit.

A horse cart to the base of the hill costs Rs 3 per person or Rs 5 if you're by

Rajasthan Top: Intricately carved dome of the temple at Ranakpur (TW)
Left: Fort entrance at Bundi (TW)
Right: Sati hand prints at the fort gate, Jodhpur (TW)

Gujarat Top: Ferry at Daman (TW)
          Left Jain temples on the hilltop at Palitana (GC)
          Right: Padlock salesman with stall, Ahmedabad (TW)

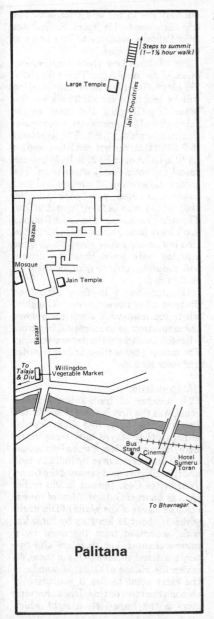

Palitana

(Map labels: Steps to summit (1–1½ hour walk); Large Temple; Jain Choultries; Bazaar; Mosque; Jain Temple; Bazaar; To Talaja & Diu; Willingdon Vegetable Market; Bus Stand; Cinema; Hotel Sumeru Toran; To Bhavnagar)

yourself. The walk is not strenuous although it's time consuming. For Rs 40 round trip (one way up Rs 30) you can take a *dooli* swing chair!

Valabhipur

North of Palitana, this ancient city was once the capital of this part of India. Extensive ruins have been located and archaeological finds are exhibited in a museum, but there's little to see apart from scattered stones.

Places to Stay

Palitana has scores of *choultries* (pilgrims' rest houses), but unless you're a Jain it's unlikely any of them will allow you to stay. *Hotel Sumeru Toran* (tel 227) on Station Rd is a Gujarat Tourism enterprise which offers excellent accommodation at reasonable prices. Rooms with attached bathroom and balcony are Rs 60/75 or with air-con Rs 100/160. There are several dormitories at Rs 15.

The new *Hotel Shravak* (tel 328) is opposite the bus station and has rooms at Rs 34/65 or with air-con Rs 88/121. There are rather crowded dormitories with beds at Rs 10 but no lockers, so the Sumeru Toran dorms are better. Several travellers have highly recommended this new hotel. The manager of the Sumeru Toran, whom we said was very good in the last edition of this book, apparently now manages the Shravak.

Places to Eat

The *Sumeru Toran* and *Shravak* have excellent restaurants with full Gujarati thalis for Rs 11 (Sumeru) or Rs 7 (Shravak) and also Punjabi food. Down the alley towards the cinema beside the Shravak is a wildly busy 24-hour snack place with puris, sabzi, curd, roasted peppers and *ganthia* – varieties of fried dough.

Getting There

If you're coming from the north there are plenty of state transport buses from

Bhavnagar. They cost Rs 5 and take half an hour to 45 minutes (or more), but it's advisable to buy a seat reservation ticket for Rs 1 as they tend to be very crowded. Pay your fare on the bus. There are also trains between Bhavnagar and Palitana; they take about two hours.

From Ahmedabad, express trains make the trip in nine to 11 hours with a change at Sihor shortly before Palitana. Express buses take four hours, ordinary ones 5½ and the fare is Rs 17. Bhavnagar is the nearest airport, with flights there from Bombay.

Between Palitana and Diu, which is the route most travellers take, the route is Palitana-Talaja-Mahuva-Una-Diu. If you're going in that direction then it's advisable to travel early in the day (before 10 am). As soon as the heat gets up local people behave as though there were a pack of lepers advancing down the main street intent on mischief. Even buses in Kerala are like a vicarage tea party in comparison!

The first part of the journey isn't too trying even if you set off late. If you're interested in Jain temples, Talaja also has hill-top monuments though they're nowhere near as extensive as those at Palitana. Most of the buses which come through Talaja, however, originate elsewhere (usually at Bhavnagar, Mahuva or Una) and they are always full to bursting when they arrive. Despite the obvious impossibility of getting anyone else on, a good percentage of those who have been waiting do achieve this feat. Including Geoff, who then spent 2½ hours hanging from a roof rail with a pack on his back and a shoulder bag in one hand being jostled like crazy every time the bus stopped (which was frequently) because nobody could get past him.

Palitana-Talaja has frequent buses which take one hour along the rough road. Take the 7 am bus if you're heading for Diu. Talaja-Mahuva (pronounced 'Mauwa') has fairly regular buses through the morning and early afternoon but very few in the late afternoon. The trip takes one to 1½ hours. Some buses from Palitana continue to Una and you won't have to change.

For Mahuva-Una there are frequent buses all day until 5 pm. They take about 3½ hours. Total bus fares Palitana-Una will be less than Rs 20. There are few buses Una-Ghoghla, but most people take a shared auto-rickshaw, motorcycle-rickshaw or pickup truck. The locals pay Rs 2.50 for this trip, but you'll be asked for Rs 10 to Rs 15, even Rs 25 to Rs 50 in some cases! Tell them firmly where to go! The journey takes about 20 minutes and your passport or even your pack may be checked as you cross from Gujarat to Diu. The auto-rickshaws and so on for Ghoghla don't leave from outside the bus stand in Una but from another street about three minutes' walk away. Rickshaw drivers will, naturally, offer to take you there for Rs 2 to Rs 3.

Ghoghla-Diu is by ferry. You'll be dropped off at the entrance to Ghoghla, where you must walk about a km down the main street to the ferries. They cross when full throughout the day and evening. The crossing takes three or four minutes and costs Rs 0.30.

DIU (population 30,500)

Diu, another of India's undiscovered gems, was the first landing point for the Parsis when they fled from Persia, although they stayed only three years. Like Daman and Goa, it was a Portuguese colony until taken over by India in 1961 and it is still governed as part of the Union Territory of Goa, Daman & Diu rather than as a part of Gujarat. Most of the ex-colony consists of the island of Diu itself, which is about 11 km long by three km wide, separated from the coast by a narrow channel, but there are also two tiny mainland enclaves. One of these, on which the village of Ghoghla stands, is the entry point to Diu if you come in through the town of Una. Diu's crowning glory is the huge fort, a sight which

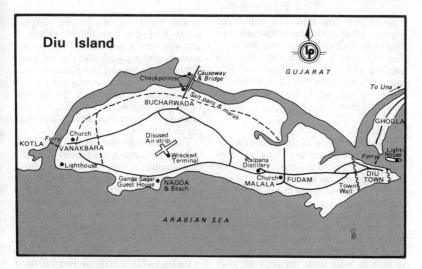

rewards all the trials and tribulations of getting here on public transport.

These days its hard to understand why the Portuguese should have been interested in capturing and fortifying such an apparently unimportant and isolated outpost, but in the 14th to 16th centuries Diu was an important trading post and naval base from which the Ottoman Turks controlled the shipping routes in the northern part of the Arabian Sea.

After an unsuccessful attempt to take the island in 1531, during which the Sultan of Gujarat was assisted by the Turkish navy, the Portuguese finally secured control in 1534 by taking advantage of a quarrel between the Sultan and the Moghul emperor, Humayan. He had sent an army into the Sultan's territory in search of Mirza Zamal, who had made an attempt on the emperor's life. Not wanting to fight on two fronts, the Sultan concluded a treaty with the Portuguese which allowed them to stay in Diu in return for providing 500 infantry men for service with the Sultan. The treaty was soon cast to the wind and although both Bahadurshah, the Sultan of Gujarat, and his nephew, Sultan Mahmad III, attempted

to contest the issue, a peace treaty was eventually signed in 1539 in which the island of Diu and the mainland enclave of Ghoghla were ceded to the Portuguese. Soon after this treaty was signed the Portuguese began constructing their fortress.

The northern side of the island, facing Gujarat, is tidal marsh and salt-pans while the southern coast alternates between limestone cliffs, rocky coves and sandy beaches, the best of which is at Nagoa. The somewhat windswept and arid island is riddled with quarries where the Portuguese removed vast quantities of limestone to construct huge monuments and buildings. The rocky or sandy interior reaches a maximum height of just 29 metres, so agriculture is limited although there are extensive stands of coconut and other palms. Branching palms (Hyphaene species) are very much a feature of the island and were originally introduced from Africa by the Portuguese.

The Indian government appears to have an official policy of playing down the Portuguese era. Seven Rajput soldiers (six of them Singhs) and a few civilians were killed in Operation Vijay, which ended Portuguese rule. The Indian Air Force bombed the airstrip terminal, near Nagoa, and it has still not been repaired! The old church in Diu Fort was also bombed and is now a roofless ruin. It's said the Portuguese blew up Government House to prevent it from falling into 'enemy' hands.

Information

The Tourist Office is open Monday to Friday from 9.30 am to 1.15 pm and 2 to 5.45 pm. It's got all the bus, train and air travel information and is a nice place to sit and read the *Times of India*. The State Bank of Saurashtra is the most efficient place in town for changing travellers' cheques. The main post office opens remarkably early for India. There's another post office at Ghoghla, about a 10-minute walk from the jetty on your left. Manesh Medical Store is the only pharmacy in town; there's a doctor in the same building.

Diu Town

The main industry of the island would have to be fishing, followed by booze and salt! A distillery at Malala produces rum from mainland-grown sugar cane. The town boasts quite a few bars, where visitors from the 'dry' mainland can enjoy a beer (or stronger IMFL – 'Indian Made Foreign Liquor'). The town is sandwiched between the massive fort to the east and a huge city wall to the west. An old gateway in the wall has some nice carvings of lions, angels and a priest, while just inside the gate is a miniature chapel with an icon, dating to 1702. Diu Town has two churches – St Paul's and St Francis of Assisi. It's said there are only 15 Christian families left on the whole island!

The town is a maze of meandering and often leafy lanes. Many of the houses are well ornamented and brightly painted, a legacy of the Portuguese era. The main 'town square' is on the northern shore and all the buses operate from it. The post office and banks (three of them) are nearby, along with Goa Travels, customs, a few bars and the Tourist Office. A gateway with a bell leads off the square down to the ferry quay. Diu also has a tiny but beautiful bazaar. In a pleasant small park on the esplanade between Baron's Inn and the police station, the Marwar Memorial, topped by a griffin, commemorates the liberation of the island from the Portuguese.

The massive Portuguese fort, constructed in 1547, must have been virtually impregnable in the past with its double moat – one tidal – but sea erosion and neglect are leading to its slow, inevitable collapse. Piles of cannon balls litter the place and the ramparts have a superb array of cannons, many old and in good condition. One dates from 1624, built by Don Diego de Silva Conde de Porta Legre in the reign of Don Philippe, Rex d'Espana – all legible. The cannons have all been catalogued by the Archaeological Survey of India and bear ASI numbers, but someone cemented out many of the old inscriptions – an unforgiveable act of vandalism! Diu urgently deserves a museum, but it's hardly probable given the lack of official imagination here.

Other Villages

There are a number of interesting villages on the island:

Fudam has a huge abandoned church, Our Lady of Remedies. A large old carved wooden altar with Madonna and child remains inside but the vestry has become a manger, full of straw!

Vanakbara at the extreme west has another church (Our Lady of Mercy), a fort, a lighthouse and a post office. A sailing ferry runs from here across to Kotla village on the mainland. You can get a bus from Kotla to Kodinar.

Bucharwada is the village on the northern side, not far from the mainland. There is a checkpoint either side of the bridge, where vehicle drivers have to sign a book.

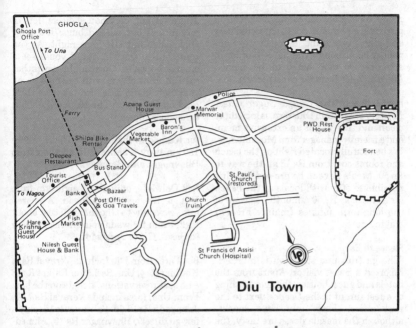

Diu Town

Nagoa has a beautiful palm-fringed beach, safe for swimming. As at Goa, Sunday is 'zoo day' when the locals come to watch the westerners on the beach, who watch the locals, who . . . .

Places to Stay
Diu Town There's a *PWD Rest House* towards the fort which is clean, quiet, well run and incredible value at Rs 10 a double, but it's usually full. Meals, other than breakfast, have to be ordered in advance. Lunch is a thali; good fish and prawn dishes are available on request. Alternatively, the *Nilesh Guest House* has doubles at Rs 30 or bigger doubles (really triples) with attached bath for Rs 50. It's OK but lacks atmosphere, has a noisy bar and a mediocre restaurant.

The *Hare Krishna Guest House* is better value with rooms at Rs 20 to Rs 30, all with common bath but very neat and clean. It's between the fish market and the Tourist Office, and the manager is

extremely friendly and helpful and speaks excellent English. The popular restaurant here does fried fish, rice and salad for Rs 10, but it's only open to residents and you must order in advance.

If you want to reward yourself for perseverance in getting here, *Baron's Inn* is a fine old Portuguese villa on the Old Fort Rd, halfway between the ferry quay and the PWD Rest House. It's right by the sea, overlooking the channel between Diu town and Ghoghla. The friendly management are keen to retain the ambience of the place. Spacious rooms with fan and attached bathroom cost from Rs 90. Good meals, Indian or seafood, can be provided on request – fried fish, dhal/chips and roti, for example.

Next to Baron's Inn, the *Apana Guest House* is a new place in a very beautiful setting. Doubles are Rs 40 or Rs 75 with attached bathroom. There are no singles but you can ask for a reduction if you're alone or there's a Rs 15 dorm. Some of the rooms have great sea views. The rooftop terrace is a popular spot to sip a cold beer and the restaurant is open to non-residents, although you have to order in advance. A new hotel to be named *Mocambique* is under construction.

Nagoa Beach The *Ganga Sagar Guest House*, 7½ km from Diu town, is incredibly clean and tidy. It has an extensive menu and a friendly manager from Mozambique. It's beautifully located right on the beach and rooms cost from Rs 15 all the way to Rs 50. Meals have to be pre-ordered. It's possible to stay with locals at the beach for as little as Rs 50 a month – beware of the long-term junkies (mainly French) staying here.

Places to Eat
'The gastronomic situation is murder!' reported a Swiss visitor. Apart from the hotels and guest houses, the nearest thing to a restaurant is the *Deepee* next to the post office. They only have snacks, although the masala dosas are tasty, the ice cream is good and they have sodas. The *Saraswati Hotel* is a good chai shop almost opposite Goa Travels. It's a foreigners' hangout in the morning and serves excellent sweets and other goodies.

Getting There
See the Palitana section for transport details from Bhavnagar and Palitana to Diu. From Diu town ferries sail or are poled across to Ghoghla, a large village on a sandspit opposite, from where frequent buses (about a half dozen a day) run into the nearby town of Una for Rs 2.50. There are also 'motorcycle buses' – an Enfield motorcycle with a trailer. The ferries struggle against a strong current but they operate until late at night.

If, en route to Diu, you get into Mahuva after 5 pm at night, you'll have to stay there overnight as there will be no connecting bus to Una. You can try the *Rupam Guest House*, where hardboard-partitioned cubicles cost from Rs 15.

There's a fan, common showers, lots of mosquitoes but no bed bugs. It's a bit Dickensian but OK for a night. As you come out of the bus stand you'll see a cinema opposite. Go straight down that road in front of you with the cinema on your right-hand side and take the third road on the right. The Rupam is about three doors down.

Air Keshod is the nearest airport, about 150 km away. There are flights there from Bhavnagar and Bombay.

Rail Delwada, only about eight km from Diu, is the nearest railhead. A shared auto-rickshaw to Ghoghla will cost about Rs 2. From Delwada you can take a train to Sasan Gir or Junagadh.

Bus Fares from Diu include Veraval Rs 9, Kodinar Rs 4, Una Rs 2.50 or Rajkot Rs 18 – no seat reservations, tickets on the bus. From Una, fares include Veraval Rs 7.60, Junagadh Rs 13.60, Palitana Rs 15 (only a few go direct), Bhavnagar Rs 15, Ahmedabad Rs 29.

Goa Travels operate a daily 'luxury' bus between Diu and Bombay via Bhavnagar, Anand and Vapi (for Daman). The trip takes 20-plus hours and costs Rs 120. The Bombay agent is Hirup Travel Service (tel 358186, 359856), Prabhakar Sadan, ground floor, Khetwadi Back Rd, 12th Line, Bombay 400004. In Daman the agent is Satish General Stores, Nani Daman.

Ferry There are rumours of a hydrofoil commencing operations between Jafarabad (near Una, connected by bus) and Bombay. This would take only 6½ hours.

Getting Around
No rickshaws or tongas exist on the island, but you can hire bicycles from Shilpa Cycle Store on the main square or Kishma Cycle Store near the fishmarket and State Bank of Saurashtra. Costs vary from Rs 5 to Rs 7 per day. There are two

local bus services – Diu-Nagoa three times daily for Rs 0.75 or Diu-Bucharwada-Vanakbara 16 times daily for Rs 1.

JUNAGADH (population 100,000)

Few travellers make the trip out to Junagadh, but it's an interesting town in itself and is situated right at the base of the temple-studded Girnar Hill. Junagadh is also the jumping-off point for visits to the Gir Forest, last home of the Asian lion.

The city takes its name from the fort which enclosed the old city. The Ashokan edicts dating from 250 BC near the town indicate the great antiquity of this site. At the time of partition the Nawab of Junagadh opted to take his tiny state into Pakistan, but the inhabitants were predominantly Hindu and the Nawab soon found himself in exile.

Information

The Tourist Office is near the Durbar Hall museum and is open 11.30 am to 5 pm on working days. The tourist officer is well informed and helpful, and they have a large map of Gujarat on the wall and some terrible postcards for sale. There's an excellent map of Junagadh on the wall behind the counter in the GPO.

'We changed money at the Bank of India', wrote one visitor. 'It only took 90 minutes'. The Bank of Saurashtra is also good! You can find out more about the city in the booklet *Junagadh & Girnar* by S H Desai. The kiosk inside the long-distance bus station is about the only place in town to get English-language newspapers.

Uparkot

The old fort, from which the city derived its name, stands on the eastern side of Junagadh. It is very old and has been rebuilt and extended many times in its history. In places the walls are 20 metres high and the fort is entered by an ornate triple gateway. It's said that the fort was once besieged, unsuccessfully, for a full 12 years; in all it was besieged 16 times! It is also said that the fort was completely abandoned from the 7th to 10th centuries and was rediscovered, completely swamped by jungle. The top of the old fort forms a plateau area covered in lantana. Paths follow the points of interest.

Inside the fort is a mosque, the Jami Masjid, built from a demolished Hindu temple. Other points of interest include the Tomb of Nuri Shah and two fine wells known as the Adi Chadi and the Naughan. The Adi Chadi was named after two slave girls who fetched water from it. The Naughan is reached by a magnificent circular staircase. Cut into the hillside close to the mosque are some very old Buddhist caves thought to be more than 1500 years old. The double-storey cave has six pillars with very fine carvings. There are other caves in Junagadh, including some thought to date back to the time of Ashoka. The soft rock on which Junagadh is built encouraged the construction of caves and wells.

Apart from the amazing wells and caves, another point of interest is the colossal five-metre-long cannon called *Nilam*. It was cast in Egypt in 1531 and left behind by a Turkish admiral, who was assisting the Sultan of Gujarat against the Portuguese at Diu in 1538.

Maqbara

The mausoleums of the Nawabs of Junagadh feature silver doors and intricate architecture, including minarets with spiralling stairways. The keys can be obtained from the adjacent mosque. The Maqbara badly needs maintenance work.

Durbar Hall Museum

In the Durbar Hall and Sileh Khana of the palace, the usual weapons and armour from the Nawabs are displayed along with their collection of silver chains and chandeliers, settees and thrones, howdahs and palanquins, a few cushions and gowns. There's a portrait gallery of the Nawabs and local petty princes, including photos of the last Nawab with his various beloved dogs. It's open 9.30 to 11.45 am and 3 to 5.30 pm.

Other

Junagadh's zoo in the Sakar Bagh has Gir lions, should you be unable to visit the Gir Forest. It's surprisingly good with well-kept lions, tigers and leopards as main attractions. The garden also has a fine local museum with paintings, manuscripts, archaeological finds and various other exhibits including a natural history section. The museum is open daily except on Wednesdays and second and fourth Saturdays each month. The Sakar Bagh are at 3 ½ km on the Rajkot road. A No 1, 2 or 6 bus will get you there, or you can walk there by the old Majevadi Gate on your right.

Junagadh has a number of other lovely gardens. Narsi Mehta, a Gujarati 'poet-saint', has a shrine in the city.

Ashoka Edicts

On the way to the Girnar Hill temples you pass a huge boulder on which Emperor Ashoka inscribed 14 edicts around 250 BC. His inscription is in the Pali script. Later inscriptions were added in Sanskrit around 150 AD by Rudradama and 450 AD by Skandagupta, the last emperor of the Mauryas. The 14 edicts are moral lectures while the other inscriptions mainly refer to recurring floods destroying the embankments of nearby Sudershan Lake, which no longer exists. The boulder is actually housed in a small roadside building, on the right if you're heading towards Girnar.

Girnar Hill

It's a 600-metre ascent up 10,000 stone steps to the 1118-metre-high summit of Girnar. The steps are well built and maintained and were constructed between 1889 and 1908 from the proceeds of a lottery! The start of the climb is a km or two beyond the sacred Damodar Kund in a scrubby teak forest. There are frequent refreshment stalls on the ascent, which takes two hours. You'll see monkeys by the path and eagles soaring by. At the summit, sadhus may lecture you on the virtues of reading the *Gita* and practising yoga! It's best to make the climb early in the morning, preferably at dawn.

Like Palitana, the temple-topped hill is of great significance to the Jains. The sacred tank of Damodar Kund marks the start of the climb to the temples. The path ascends through a wood to the marble temples near the summit. Five of them are Jain temples, including the largest and oldest – the 12th-century temple of Neminath, the 22nd Jain Tirthankar. There is a large black image of Neminath in the central shrine and many smaller images around the temple.

Nearby is the triple temple of Mallinath, the 19th Tirthankar, which was erected by two brothers in 1177. During festivals this temple is a favourite gathering place for sadhus. A great fair is held here during the Kartika Purnima festival in November or December. On top of the peak is the temple of Amba Mata, where newly-weds are supposed to worship at the shrine of the goddess in order to ensure a happy marriage.

A local bus No 3 or 4 from the stand opposite the GPO will take you to Girnar Taleti at the base of the hill. Buses run about hourly, cost Rs 0.50 and go by the Ashoka edicts.

Places to Stay

Junagadh has *Railway Retiring Rooms* with clean and neat rooms at Rs 10/18 and dorm beds for Rs 9. There are a number of rather basic hotels such as the clean and well-run *Sharda Lodge* where rooms are Rs 15/25 and dorm beds Rs 8. Or try the *Lake Guest House* or the *Capital Guest House* next door, both at Rs 12/24.

Several places are clustered around Kalwa Chowk, one of the two main squares in Junagadh. The *Murlidhar Guest House* has rooms at Rs 18/28 and the *Murlidhar Lodge* is an annexe across

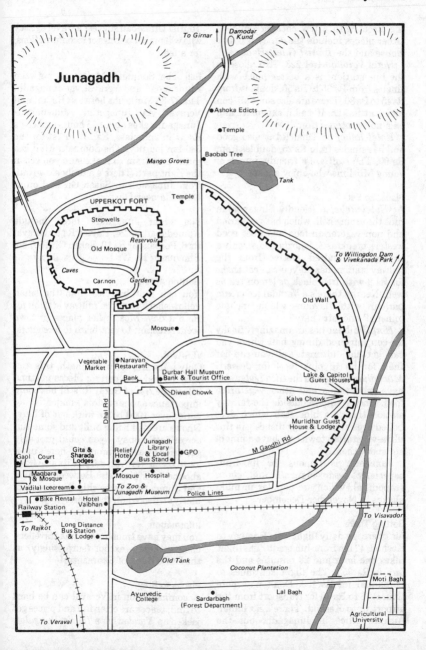

Junagadh

To Girnar
Damodar Kund

Ashoka Edicts

Temple

Baobab Tree

Mango Groves

Tank

UPPERKOT FORT

Temple

Stepwells

Reservoir

Old Mosque

Caves

Cannon

Garden

To Willingdon Dam & Vivekanada Park

Old Wall

Mosque

Narayan Restaurant

Vegetable Market

Bank

Durbar Hall Museum
Bank & Tourist Office

Diwan Chowk

Lake & Capitol Guest Houses

Kalva Chowk

Dhal Rd

Murlidhar Guest House & Lodge

Gita & Sharada Lodges

Relief Hotel

Junagadh Library & Local Bus Stand

GPO

M Gandhi Rd

Court

Gaol

Maqbara & Mosque

Mosque

Hospital

Vadilal Icecream

To Zoo & Junagadh Museum

Police Lines

Bike Rental

Hotel Vaibhan

Railway Station

To Rajkot

Long Distance Bus Station & Lodge

To Visavador

To Veraval

Old Tank

Coconut Plantation

Moti Bagh

Ayurvedic College

Sardarbagh (Forest Department)

Lal Bagh

Agricultural University

the street with a few cheaper doubles. Other places include the *Jai Shri Guest House* and the *Tourist Guest House*.

Hotel Vaibhav (tel 223, 716), close to the bus station, is a better place with singles from Rs 35 to Rs 50, doubles from Rs 45 to Rs 80. There are also some air-con rooms at Rs 125. It's a bit expensive and on a noisy intersection.

Hotel Relief on Dhal Rd is also good and has singles from Rs 25, doubles from Rs 60. The staff are a friendly bunch of young Muslims who enjoy a joke.

Places to Eat

At *Hotel Relief* a friendly Singaporean runs the dining hall, which has vegetarian and non-vegetarian food and does good western breakfasts. *Sharda Lodge*, only a couple of hundred metres from the railway station, has all-you-can-eat thalis for Rs 9 with free black or lemon tea as well. Nearby there's a Vadidal ice cream parlour with flavours which include 'pinepal' and 'stro bary'.

Hotel Vaibhav has an amazingly flashy air-con mirrored dining hall where you can get the 'ultimate' all-you-can-eat thali for Rs 15 plus Rs 4 for dessert. *Murlidhar Lodge* and the *Gita Lodge* also have good thalis and other vegetarian food. On the square outside the railway station there's a blue stall which does boiled eggs and other egg dishes – in this ultra-vegetarian town eggs have a hint of sin about them!

Junagadh is famous for its fruit, especially *kesar* mangoes and *chiku* (sapodilla), which are popular in milkshakes in November-December.

Getting There

Air There is a daily flight from Bombay to Keshod, 47 km from Junagadh. The flight takes one hour and 20 minutes and the fare is Rs 353. The flight continues to Porbandar for Rs 109. Don't pay more than Rs 5 to Rs 10 for transport from the airport in to Keshod. There's no Indian Airlines office in Junagadh, but the Tourist Office can suggest a travel agency who will make bookings or reconfirmations, for a fee.

Rail The Somnath Mail runs between Ahmedabad and Veraval via Junagadh. The 37-38 Mail runs between Rajkot and Veraval via Junagadh. Ahmedabad-Junagadh takes about 13 hours and costs Rs 37 in 2nd class, Rs 147 in 1st for the 380-km journey. The Somnath Mail is a multi-part train so make sure you get in the right part. There's a daily slow train from Junagadh to Sasan Gir and on to Delwada near Diu.

Bus From Junagadh, fares include Ahmedabad Rs 24, Rajkot Rs 9, Veraval Rs 8, Porbandar Rs 10, Sasan Gir Rs 6.50, Bhavnagar Rs 17.

Getting Around

You can rent bicycles from the small yellow shack near the railway station for Rs 6 a day. Most other places in town seem reluctant to rent bikes to foreigners!

VERAVAL

Only a few km from Somnath, this was once the major seaport for Mecca pilgrims before the rise of Surat. It still has some importance as one of India's major fishing ports; over 1000 boats work out of here. Dhows are still being built and some run across to Bombay – you could probably get a ride by asking around. There's not a lot to see in Veraval, despite its size. Pigs abound in the streets. Between Veraval and Somnath, a large ship lies (spectacularly) wrecked on the shore.

Information

You may have trouble changing travellers' cheques here – except (surprisingly) at the State Bank of Saurashtra!

Places to Stay

Accommodation in Veraval can be hard to find; places are often full and prices get jacked up. Veraval has a *Tourist Bungalow*

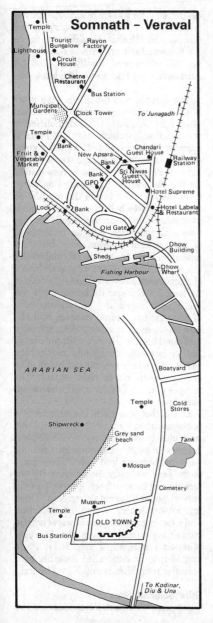

Somnath – Veraval

and a *Circuit House* near the lighthouse – fine views of the sunset over the sea. The Tourist Bungalow is quiet and has rooms from Rs 40. Meals have to be ordered in advance.

The *Satkar Hotel* (tel 120) near the bus stand is clean and well maintained. They have all sorts of rooms, from dorm beds at 15 through regular rooms from Rs 25 up to rooms with air-con from Rs 130. Their prices may rise when there's an accommodation squeeze. There are *Railway Retiring Rooms* at the station, close by is the *Chandrani Guest House* while a little further away is the *Sri Niwas Guest House* and the *Hotel Supreme*.

In Somnath about half-way between the bus stand and the temple, about 100 metres north of the road, the *Sri Somnath Temple Trust* has a vast guest house. There are 100 double rooms, a bit dingy but not very old and good value at Rs 12. The signs for the guest house are only in Hindi and Gujarati but you can ask directions.

Places to Eat

There's not much choice in eating places in Veraval. *Hotel Satkar*, near the bus station, does good Gujarati thalis with plenty of refills for Rs 18. *Hotel La'Bela* is actually a restaurant which does (hot) thalis. The *New Apsara*, not far from the station, does vegetarian thalis and dosas downstairs and non-vegetarian (including local fish) upstairs, but it's fairly basic. Street stalls all over town sell drinking coconuts.

Getting There

Air The nearest airport is Keshod, but there is no Indian Airlines office in Veraval. Somnath Travels (tel 162) in Satta Bazaar will obtain tickets for a fee. The Bombay-Keshod fare is Rs 353. Keshod-Porbandar costs Rs 109. There is a good road to Keshod and the bus takes only an hour for Rs 6.

Rail It's about 13 hours from Ahmedabad

to Veraval. Fares for the 459-km trip are Rs 43 in 2nd class, Rs 171 in 1st. There's also a slow train which goes to Delwada, near Diu and just south of Una.

Bus From the bus station buses run to Diu daily via Kodinar for Rs 8. Buses also go along the coast road to Porbandar via Chorvad and Mangrol. Bhavnagar is nine hours away; the trip costs Rs 25.

Getting Around

An auto-rickshaw to Somnath, six km away, costs about Rs 10. There are municipal and local buses to Somnath – Rs 1 to Rs 1.50.

AROUND VERAVAL

Chorvad

On the coast, 70 km from Junagadh and just 20 km from Veraval, Chorvad is a popular beach resort. This was the site of the summer palace of the Junagadh Nawabs and has now been converted into a guest house.

Somnath

The Temple of Somnath, at Somnath Patan near Veraval and about 80 km from Junagadh, has had an extremely chequered history. Its earliest history fades into legend; it is said to have been originally built by Somraj, the Moon God himself, out of gold, only to be rebuilt by Rawana in silver, then by Krishna in wood, then by Bhimdev in stone. What is more certain is that a description of the temple by Al Biruni, an Arab traveller, was so glowing that it prompted a visit in 1024 by a most unwelcome tourist – Mahmud of Ghazni. At that time the temple was so wealthy that it had 300 musicians, 500 dancing girls and even 300 barbers simply to shave the heads of visiting pilgrims.

Mahmud of Ghazni, who was to gain quite a reputation for his raids on the riches of India from his Afghan kingdom, descended on Somnath and after a two-day battle took the town and temple and, having carted off its fabulous wealth,

destroyed it for good measure. He started a tradition of Muslims destroying the temple and Hindus rebuilding it, for in the following centuries it was razed again in 1297, 1394 and finally in 1706 by Aurangzeb, that notorious Moghul spoil-sport.

The temple was rebuilt in 1169 after Mahmud's visit, again in 1325 and soon after 1394. After the 1706 demolition it was not finally rebuilt until 1950 and is currently being extended. Outside, opposite the entrance, is a large statue of S V Patel (1875-1950), who was responsible for the restoration. There are fine views from the 2nd floor inside the temple, as well as a photo collection with English commentary on the archaeological excavations and restoration of the seven temples.

The current temple was built to traditional patterns on the original site by the sea. It is one of the 12 sacred Shiva shrines known as Jyotorlingas, but despite its long history and its holiness it's not really very interesting. Hardly anything of the original temple remains and the new one is an unimaginative monstrosity and dead boring. There's a simple dining hall in the temple compound, north of the main gate, where you can get lunch. The grey sand beach is right outside the temple and it's OK for a swim although there's no shade.

Down the lane from the temple is a museum, open 9 am to 12 noon and 3 to 6 pm, closed Wednesdays and holidays. Admission is 20 paise plus 20 paise for each photograph you take. They don't count very seriously. Remains of the old temple can be seen here, a jumble of old carved stones littering a courtyard. There are pottery shards, a seashell collection and a (strange) glass case of water bottles containing samples from the Danube, Nile, St Lawrence, Tigris, River Plate and Murray in Australia! Together with seawater from Hobart and New Zealand.

Other Somnath Sites

The town of Somnath Patan is entered by

the Junagadh Gate from Veraval. This very ancient triple gate was the one through which Mahmud finally broke to take the town. Close to the second gate is an old mosque dating from Mahmud's time. The Jami Masjid, reached through the town's picturesque bazaar, was constructed using parts of a Hindu temple and has interesting Bo tree carvings at the four corners. It is now a museum with a collection from many of these temples.

About a km before the Junagadh Gate, coming from Veraval, is the finely carved Mai Puri which was once a Temple of the Sun. This Hindu temple was converted into a mosque during Mahmud's time and there are thousands of tombs and *palias* around it. Close by are two old tombs and on the shore is the Bhidiyo Pagoda, which probably dates from the 14th century.

To the east of the town is the Bhalka Tirth, where Lord Krishna was mistaken for a deer (he was sleeping in a deerskin) and wounded by an arrow. The legendary spot is at the confluence of three rivers. You get to it through the small Sangam (confluence gate), which is simply known as the Nana (small gate). North of this sacred spot is the Temple of the Sun or Suraj Mandir which Mahmud also had a go at knocking down. This very old temple probably dates from the same time as the original Somnath Temple. Around the walls is a frieze of lions with elephant trunks. Back inside the small gate is a temple which Ahalya Bai of Indore built as a replacement for the Somnath Temple. Below this a subterranean temple with a domed roof can be reached via the steps.

Sasan Gir Forest

The last home of the Asian lion is 54 km from Junagadh via Keshod. There are less than 200 lions left. The sanctuary covers 1400 square km and the best time to visit this dry scrubland is between October and June. Apart from the lions there are also bears, hyenas, foxes and a number of species of deer and antelope. The deer include the largest Indian antelope (the *nilgai*), the graceful *chinkara* gazelle, the *chousingha* and the barking deer. You may also see parrots, peacocks and monkeys. The tourist office in Junagadh will have details about visiting the park – you need a jeep. You can wait in Sasan in the early morning for a group to form; the jeep, if one is available, will cost about Rs 100 to Rs 150 and will carry up to eight people. On Fridays (or is it Sundays?) the rangers round the lions up for visitors!

Places to Stay The State Forest Department has a *Guest House*, very spaciously laid out in a garden. Chalets with bathroom cost about Rs 30 per person and meals are available. There's also the modern, two-storey *Sasangir Forest Lodge* (tel 21) operated by ITDC. This costs Rs 150/225 or Rs 225/300 with air-con. Prices are lower in the off season.

Getting There It's around a two to 2½-hour trip on a very crowded bus from Junagadh at a fare of Rs 7.50. To or from Veraval takes a little under two hours by bus for Rs 4. There is also a daily slow train direct from Junagadh to Sasan Gir which takes 2½ hours and costs just Rs 6. The train continues on to Delwada near Diu. The railway station is only 10 minutes' walk from the Forest Lodge.

Tulsi Shyam

In the Gir Forest, 165 km from Junagadh, there is a scenic hot spring together with a temple to Bhim and a *Holiday Home*.

JAMNAGAR (population 350,000)

The princely state of Jamnagar was ruled by the Jadeja Rajputs prior to independence. The city is built around a lake with an island in the middle reached by a bridge. On this island, the Lakhota Fort is a museum with a good collection of sculptures and archaeological finds from surrounding villages – particularly Ghumli in the Bardo Hills to the south.

Also on the island, the Kotha Bastion has an old well from which water can be drawn by blowing into a small hole in the floor. Jamnagar has two local ports, Rosi and Bedi. The town also has a long history of pearl fishing and there is a local variety of tie dyeing.

Places to Stay
There are a number of hotels along Station Rd and also the *Lal Bungalow*.

Getting There
There are direct trains from Ahmedabad 308 km away, via Rajkot, and from Mehsena. The fare from Ahmedabad is Rs 31.50 in 2nd class, Rs 124 in 1st. There is a daily flight from Bombay to Jamnagar, continuing to Bhuj. The fare from Bombay is Rs 456, on to Bhuj is Rs 120.

DWARKA
On the extreme western tip of the Kathiawar Peninsula, Dwarka is one of the four holiest Hindu pilgrimage sites and is closely connected to the Krishna legend. It was here that Krishna set up his capital after his flight from Mathura. Dwarkanath, the name of the temple, is a title of Lord Krishna.

The temple is only open to Hindus (you can sign a form and go in, one visitor reported), but the exterior, with its tall five-storey spire supported by 60 columns, is far more interesting than the interior. Archaeological excavations have revealed five earlier cities at the site, all now submerged. Dwarka is the site for an important festival at Janmashtami which falls in August or September.

Island of Bet
A little north of Dwarka you can ferry across from Okha to the island of Bet, where Vishnu is said to have slain a demon. There are modern Krishna temples on the island. There are other important religious sites around Dwarka.

Places to Stay
Dwarka has *Railway Retiring Rooms*, a *Rest House* and a number of small hotels.

Getting There
Dwarka is 145 km from Jamnagar and connected by rail.

PORBANDAR
On the south coast, about mid-way between Veraval and Dwarka, Porbandar is today chiefly noted as the birthplace of Mahatma Gandhi. In ancient times the city was known as Sudamapuri after Sudama, a compatriot of Krishna, and at one time there was a flourishing trade from here to the Persian Gulf and Africa. The Africa connection seems apparent in the number of Indianised blacks around, called Siddis, who form a virtually separate caste of Harijans.

Porbandar has several large cement and chemical factories and a textile mill. A massive breakwater was constructed recently to shelter a deep-water wharf and fishing harbour. Dhows are still being constructed here. Fish drying is an important activity and lends a certain 'aroma' to the town!

Swimming is not recommended near the Tourist Bungalow. The beach, called Chowpatty, is used as a local toilet and there is a factory drain outlet by the Hazur Palace. Swimming is said to be OK a few km down the coast towards Veraval.

Kirti Mandir
As in so many places in India, there is a collection of Gandhian memorabilia in the Kirti Mandir, his birthplace. A swastika on the floor in a small room marks the actual spot! There is also a collection of photographs, *some* of which have English captions, and a small bookshop.

Planetarium
Across the muddy creek, spanned by the

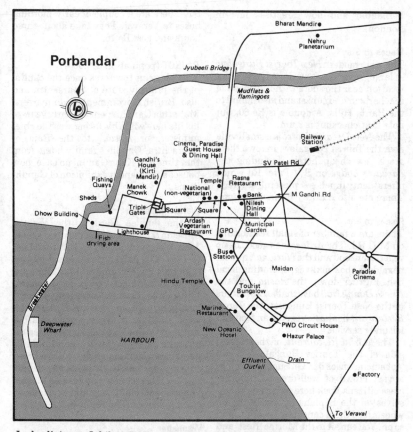

Porbandar

Jynbeeli (once Jubilee) Bridge, are the Nehru Planetarium and the Bharat Mandir (Hall of India). Flocks of flamingoes are an unexpected sight along the creek. The planetarium has afternoon sessions in Gujarati. Men and women enter from the verandah by separate doors, whose panels celebrate Indian 'non-alignment' – on one side showing Shastri with Kosygin and the other Nehru with JFK! The projection equipment is a little antiquated and stars chase one another across the domed roof to the sound of whirring machinery.

Bharat Mandir

Opposite the planetarium, in a charming irrigated garden, is the large Bharat Mandir hall. Inside there's a huge relief map of India on the floor. The pillars of the building have brilliantly painted bas-reliefs of over 100 legendary persons from Hindu epics and religious figures. The verandah has six distorting mirrors, popular with kids.

Hazur Palace

Near the shore, this massive and forlorn-looking building has been deserted by the present Maharana. He has also deserted

Porbandar and now practises law in London!

Places to Stay

There is a modern *New Tourist Bungalow* – large, spacious and in a very quiet location near the shore with fine views of sea, harbour and sunset and also inland to the Barda Hills. A double is Rs 60, but note that checkout is 9 am.

The *New Oceanic Hotel* is a small villa near the Tourist Bungalow. In town there are a few cheap hotels, including the *Paradise Lodge* on S V Patel Rd which offers 'denty lunches & piecefull staying'. There are also *Railway Retiring Rooms*.

Places to Eat

There are a number of small restaurants on M G Rd. The *Ardash* has good, basic vegetarian food and the *National*, almost next door, has non-veg, including local fish. Further down, the *Rasna* and the *Nilesh Dining Hall* have thalis. Downstairs in the New Tourist Bungalow the *Toran Restaurant* has basic vegetarian food and leisurely service.

The *Marine Restaurant*, on the seaward side of the Tourist Bungalow, is an 'ephemeral' snack bar. On Sunday evenings a vast crowd of well-dressed, middle-class citizens flock here to parade themselves on the Esplanade, and stalls on wheels feed them cane juice, peanuts and so on. You can sit in the Marine 'Rest' and enjoy excellent samosas or ice cream.

Getting There

Air There's a daily flight from Bombay to Porbandar via Keshod. The fare from Bombay is Rs 421.

Rail Porbandar is the terminus of a rail line; the main services are the Kirti Express to and from Rajkot (6½ hours) and the 45/46 Express to and from Ahmedabad (473 km, 14 hours). Fares from Ahmedabad are Rs 43 in 2nd class, Rs 145 in 1st.

Bus There are a couple of early-morning buses to Veraval. They take about three hours and cost Rs 15.

RAJKOT (population 350,000)

This pleasant town was once the capital of the princely state of Saurashtra and also British government headquarters. Mahatma Gandhi spent the early years of his life here while his father was the chief minister, or *Diwan*, to the Raja of Saurashtra. Gandhi's family home from that time, the Kaba Gandhi no Delo, now houses a permanent exhibition of Gandhi items.

Watson Museum

In the Jubilee Gardens the Watson Museum & Library commemorates Colonel John Watson, Political Agent from 1886 to 1889. The entrance is flanked by two imperial lions and among the exhibits are copies of artefacts from Moenjodaro, 13th-century carvings, silverware, natural history exhibits and textiles. Perhaps the most startling piece is a huge marble statue of Queen Victoria; she is seated on a throne and is decidedly 'not amused', perhaps with reason as she wears a brass crown and thumblessly holds an orb and sceptre. This section also has two plaster Venuses and many splendid portraits of colonial heroes. The Raj lives!

Wankaner

Situated about 50 km from Rajkot, the Royal Palace of Wankaner is now, like so many Indian palaces, a hotel and holiday resort. The regal palace has a swimming pool, museum and game reserve, not to mention the Maharana's collection of vintage cars. Reservations must be made in advance if you wish to stay; it's mainly used for groups. From here, those who can afford it can make excursions to the Little Rann of Kutch or to the palace and monuments of Halvad.

Wadhwan (Surendranagar)

On the route to Rajkot from Ahmedabad,

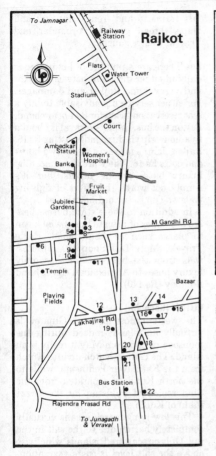

1	Watson Museum
2	Information Centre
3	Library
4	Telegraph Office
5	Cemetery
6	GPO
7	Bank
8	Gandhi School & Statue
9	Havmor Restaurant
10	Galaxy Hotel
11	Bhabha Guest House
12	Taj Restaurant
13	Library
14	Rainbow Restaurant
15	Vishram Restaurant
16	Hotel Intimate
17	Anand Guest House
18	Jyoti Guest House
19	Angels Hotel
20	Sindh Punjab Restaurant
21	Ashok Guest House & Municipal Office
22	Ruby & Jeel Hotels

this town has the very old temple of Ranik Devi, who became involved in a dispute between local rulers Sidh Raja (who planned to marry her) and Rao Khengar (who carried her off and did marry her). When Sidh Raja defeated Rao Khengar she chose sati over dishonour and Sidh Raja built the temple as a memorial to her.

Places to Stay – bottom end

On the road which leads into the heart of the bazaar area – Lakhajiraj Rd – are a number of hotels. At the upper end of this group is the *Hotel Intimate* which offers 'laxurious living' with doubles from Rs 75 up to Rs 125 with air-con. More or less opposite is the *Himaliya Guest House* which offers budget accommodation with attached bath at Rs 20/40. The entrance to this place is hard to find – it's right inside the shopping complex. Others places you could try are the *Jyoti Guest House* or the *Anand Guest House* behind the Hotel Intimate.

Around the back of the bus station on Kanak Rd are several mid-range hotels. The *Ruby Hotel* (tel 31722-3) is probably the best with rooms from Rs 50 up towards Rs 200 with air-con. All the rooms have attached bathrooms and there's a restaurant. There are also a number of rock-bottom places on this same road. *Hotel Jeel* has window-less rooms from Rs 25, more for rooms with window and for deluxe rooms. All the rooms have attached bathrooms and the friendly manager speaks English. Opposite the bus stand are two branches of the *Ashok Guest House*, where you can find typical Indian guest house accommodation with attached shower and toilet from Rs 20/40.

Places to Stay – top end

Rajkot's most expensive hotel is the *Galaxy Hotel* (tel 31781-7) on Jawahar Rd. It has singles/doubles for Rs 55-85/80-115 or with air-con for Rs 140-180/180-220. All rooms have attached bath and some have large balconies.

Angel's Hotel (tel 22026, 32016), Dhebar Chowk, is of a similar standard and slightly cheaper. The management are friendly and speak good English. Indian Airlines have their office on the ground floor, and one of Rajkot's best restaurants is in the basement. It might also interest you to know that there's 'pentry service round the clock'. Other more expensive hotels include the *Hotel Tulsi* (tel 33991-3) on Kanta St and Vikas Gruh Rd, *Hotel Jayson* (tel 26170) on S V P (Canal) Rd and *Hotel Mohit International* (tel 33338) on Sir Harilal Gosaliya Marg.

Places to Eat

The *Havmor* is a better-class restaurant with Indian, Chinese and western food. It's near the Galaxy Hotel. Also nearby, but in the other direction, is the vegetarian-only *Taj Restaurant*. The *Sindh Punjab* in the Municipal Office is a cheaper place for vegetarian and non-vegetarian food.

Try the basement restaurant at *Angel's Hotel* for a really good Gujarati thali. The *Bhabha Dining Hall* at the Bhabha Guest House on Panchnath Rd also does superb thalis.

Getting There

Air There are daily direct flights between Bombay and Rajkot; the fare is Rs 398. Indian Airlines have a bus service to the airport.

Rail The overnight (broad gauge) Saurashtra Express connects Rajkot with Ahmedabad 246 km away – fares are Rs 26 in 2nd class, Rs 101 in 1st. There are other fast trains to and from Jamnagar and Hapa (broad gauge), Porbandar and Veraval (metre gauge).

Bus There are a number of luxury buses daily in either direction between Rajkot and Veraval and Rajkot and Jamnagar. For either service it's advisable to buy a seat reservation ticket for Rs 1 beforehand. Pay on the bus. Rajkot-Veraval is about a five-hour trip via Junagadh costing Rs 18. Rajkot-Jamnagar takes about two hours and costs Rs 16. There are three morning luxury buses among others, but it's simply not worth the effort of fighting your way on to the ordinary buses.

In addition to these state buses there are a number of private buses which run to places such as Ahmedabad. Eagle Travels, Moti Tati Shop (10 minutes' walk from the bus station), has daily luxury buses to Ahmedabad (Rs 75) and Bombay (Rs 140).

KUTCH (Kachchh)

The western-most part of Gujarat is virtually an island; indeed during the monsoon period from May it really is an island. The Gulf of Kutch divides Kutch from the Kathiawar Peninsula, while to the north Kutch is separated from the Sind region of Pakistan by the Great Rann of Kutch.

This low-lying marsh area is virtually completely barren due to the salt in the soil. Only on scattered 'islands' which rise above the salt level is there vegetation. During the dry season the Rann is a vast expanse of hard, dried mud. Then, with the start of the monsoon in May, it's flooded by sea water, then flooded deeper again by the fresh water from rivers as they fill up. Kutch is also separated from the rest of Gujarat to the east by the Little Rann of Kutch.

The Gulf of Kutch is a breeding ground for flamingoes and pelicans during the winter. In the Little Rann of Kutch the rare Indian wild ass roams. Because of their isolation the people of Kutch have maintained their local customs and traditions.

BHUJ (population 50,000)

The major town of Kutch, Bhuj is an old walled city – until very recently the city gates were still locked each night from dusk to dawn! It's one of those places which leaps right out of the pages of Rudyard Kipling. It's the Jaisalmer of Gujarat, a walled city surrounding a lake and enclosing an extremely colourful and lively bazaar.

You can lose yourself for hours in the maze of streets and alleyways of this town. There are walls within walls, crenellated gateways, old palaces with intricately carved wooden pavilions, Hindu temples decorated with that gaudy, gay abandon which only tribal people seem capable of, equally colourful tribespeople and camels pulling huge cartfuls of produce into the various markets. In short, never a dull moment. All this is right next to one of the largest Indian Air Force bases in the country, with aircraft taking off on average every 20 minutes.

Bhuj is like a lot of India was before the tourist invasion. You can expect to get stared at by just about everyone because they don't get many westerners. On the other hand, because people remain largely unaffected by what goes on outside the area, you're much more likely to come across that disarming hospitality which was once the hallmark of rural India. Where else would someone offer you a lift on their bicycle?

Information

The State Bank of India on Station Rd near the Indian Airlines office changes money with amazing speed. If you go to the main post office, the postmaster may well offer you a cup of tea or coffee while you conduct your business!

Palace & Museum

The Kutch Museum was originally known as the Fergusson Museum. Built in 1877, it's the oldest museum in Gujarat and has an excellent collection. The well-maintained exhibits include a picture gallery, an anthropological section, archaeological finds, textiles, weapons, musical instruments, a shipping section and, of course, stuffed animals. The museum is open daily except Wednesdays from 9 to 11.30 am and 3 to 5.30 pm. There's no English sign outside the museum but it's near the impressive Mahadev Gate beside the lake.

Rao Pragmalji's Palace is an ornate marble building; parts of it are now used for government offices but it's still picturesque and of great charm. The palace has a wonderful inlaid wood and ivory door which has been coveted by the British Museum for a number of years. The correspondence relating to the British attempt to 'borrow' this priceless object some years ago, is solemnly set out next to the door. Next to the old palace climb the clocktower and get a good view of the town and the Rann of Kutch marshes toward the Pakistan border.

Other

A huge old wall stretches around the hills overlooking the city – the view is best from near the railway station. Unfortunately you cannot explore as it's all a restricted military area. The dilapidated Maharao Palace is to the north of the lake and is noted for its quaint pillars. Stone statues flank the entrance but inside many statues are now headless and deteriorating.

The colourful and richly decorated Swaminarayan Temple is near the bazaar and also beside the lake.

Around Bhuj

The city is connected by road with the old port of Mandvi to the south-west and by road and rail to the new port of Kandala. It is intended that Kandala should substitute for Karachi as a port for this area. There is a boat service from

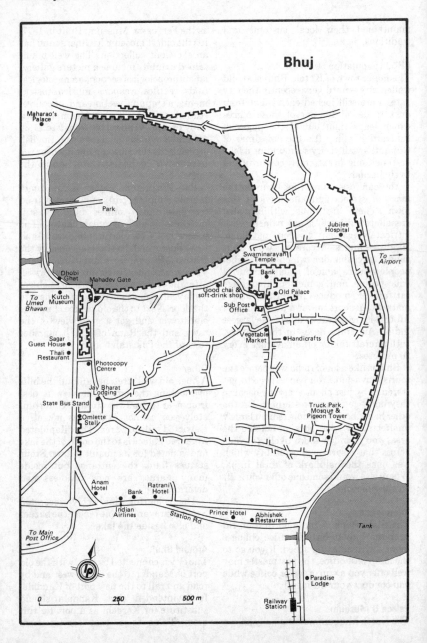

Bhuj

Maharao's Palace

Park

Jubilee Hospital

To Airport

Swaminarayan Temple

Bank

Dhobi Ghat

Mahadev Gate

Good chai & soft-drink shop

Old Palace

To Umed Bhavan

Kutch Museum

Sub Post Office

Sagar Guest House

Vegetable Market

Handicrafts

Thali Restaurant

Photocopy Centre

Jay Bharat Lodging

State Bus Stand

Truck Park, Mosque & Pigeon Tower

Omlette Stall

Anam Hotel

Bank

Ratrani Hotel

Indian Airlines

Prince Hotel

Abhishek Restaurant

Station Rd

Tank

To Main Post Office

Paradise Lodge

0   250   500 m

Railway Station

Kandala to Navlakhi, which is on the Kathiawar Peninsula and connected to Morvi and Wankaner by rail.

Gandhidham, near Kandala, is a new town established to take refugees from the Sind, following partition. About 150 km north-east of Bhuj, the remains of Indus Valley Civilisation fortifications have been discovered.

Places to Stay – bottom end

Hotel Ratrani (tel 1607) on Station Rd between the Hotel Prince and Hotel Anam is a good budget hotel with rooms from Rs 20/30, all with attached bathroom and fan. The manager can be surly but the rest of the staff are very friendly and there's an air-con restaurant serving Gujarati thalis for Rs 12 and good Punjabi food.

Near the bus station, the clean and neat *Sagar Guest House* has rooms with attached bathroom at Rs 20/30 and an excellent laundry service. On the upper floor there's a Rs 6 dormitory. *Hotel Ambassador* is near the main post office and has a Rs 10 dorm or rooms at Rs 15/25. There are other even cheaper places such as the *Umed Bhavan* (the Government Rest House) which costs Rs 12 per bed and comes complete with imbecilic staff.

The very run down *Paradise Lodging & Boarding* is notable for having the house rules painted right on the outside walls. Including warnings that: 'If passengers conduct any doubtful movement should be found they should rusticate from the lodge' and the dire threat that there must be 'no chitcheting with servents!'

Peter Russenberger, Switzerland

Places to Stay – top end

Bhuj's most expensive hotel is the *Hotel Park View* (tel 344) on Hospital Rd, Camp Corner, which has air-con rooms with attached bath, an air-con dining hall and other facilities.

Closer to the old city are two somewhat less expensive hotels which are perfectly adequate for most people's requirements. *Hotel Prince* (tel 1095, 1370, 1371), Station Rd, is a very pleasant, well-maintained place with friendly and helpful staff. Rooms with attached bath and hot water cost from Rs 60/90, with air-con Rs 110/150. There's a restaurant with very good vegetarian and non-vegetarian food but no Gujarati thalis!

Hotel Anam (tel 1390-3, 1397), also on Station Rd, is of similar standard and has equally pleasant staff. Rooms cost Rs 40/60 or Rs 100/140 with air-con. The hotel restaurant is open daily except Sundays and has Gujarati thalis for Rs 14 plus Rs 3 for dessert.

Places to Eat

Apart from the hotel restaurants mentioned above, the *Grand Punjab Hotel* does good Punjabi food. The *Omlet Centre* is a blue shack near the bus terminal and does indeed do excellent omelettes and toast. Very close to the Hotel Prince, the *Abhishek Restaurant* is good for drinks and south Indian snacks. To the left of the Sagar Guest House is a restaurant with filling thalis for Rs 7.

Getting There

Air Indian Airlines have daily flights from Bombay to Bhuj via Jamnagar. Fares are Rs 534 from Bombay, Rs 120 from Jamnagar.

Rail There is a daily rail connection with Ahmedabad, 310 km away, but some trains take a much longer route via Palanpur. Fares are Rs 31.50 in 2nd class, Rs 124 in 1st. There are also trains between Bhuj and Kandala Port. A fast way of getting to Bhuj from Bombay is to take the daily super-fast express from Bombay to Gandhidham, broad gauge all the way via Ahmedabad. From Gandhidham to Bhuj takes about two hours but there are also plenty of buses available.

Bus Buses run to other centres in Gujarat,

including Ahmedabad Rs 32, Rajkot Rs 20, Kandala Port Rs 7. You can also take taxis between Bhuj and Rajkot. These depart from near the state bus stand and cost about Rs 30 per seat. N K Travels at the north end of the bus station have an overnight deluxe bus to Ahmedabad for Rs 60. It's a long two days of bus travel north from Bhuj through Barmer to Jaisalmer in Rajasthan.

Getting Around

Airport The airport is only four km out and taxis and auto-rickshaws appear to charge the same. The fare should be only about Rs 6, but Rs 10 to Rs 12 is the normal quote – although some drivers ask much more. It's worth waiting for a driver who will accept a reasonable fare.

If you're flying out of Bhuj the airport security check takes offence at cameras. They'll tell you that they are 'prohibited' and should have gone into the hold in your baggage. They don't appreciate it if you point out that the notices say 'photography prohibited' not 'cameras prohibited'. Just apologise and say it won't happen again!

Local Transport When you're not just wandering around the bazaars there are plenty of auto-rickshaws which will get you from A to B – they'll go anywhere, including down some of the narrowest streets in the bazaar.

Things to Buy

Ramnik K Shah, Gopiani St, Shroff Bazaar is a very friendly person, speaks English and is involved in the import/export trade. His crafts shop is on the map. For the renowned Kutchi embroideries you must go out to the villages and deal directly with the villagers.

Tony's Notebook

Retiring Rooms

Railway retiring rooms at stations are generally excellent and at many stations a real effort is made to attract people. Sometimes it isn't. I was on my way from Patna to Darjeeling. Rather than catch the Assam Mail out of Patna at 3.30 am I decided to travel 3½ hours down the line in the evening, spend the night at a station and catch the Assam Mail when it came through around 7 am.

I duly got off at Bairini at 9.30 pm, wandered around until I found the retiring rooms and then spent a good half hour trying to track down who was responsible for them. One of the problems with retiring rooms is that they're usually looked after by somebody who is tied up with the trains while they're in the station. Eventually I ascertained it was the ticket collector, so I had a cup of tea in the restaurant and waited until my train departed. Unfortunately when he finally showed up he was a new ticket collector and didn't know how to allocate retiring rooms. We had to wait for the other ticket collector.

He eventually showed up around 11 pm and then thought about it for a bit. Forms were produced for me to fill in. I filled them in and then we all waited some more. Did I want a room (Rs 25) or a bed (Rs 10)? A room. How about a bed? I'd prefer a room. A bed was cheaper? I didn't care. I had nothing against dorm beds but if a room was available I wanted a room. By this time I was beginning to wonder why I hadn't just left the station and gone to a hotel an hour ago. We sat and waited. This is a favourite way of resolving anything in India – you wait until the problem goes away. Finally it was announced that I couldn't have a room because a room was a double and I was a single. By this time I was getting a little stubborn about it so I announced I'd pay for a double. Please give me Rs 10 he announced. No, I want to pay Rs 25 for a room I said. We waited some more. By this time there were seven of us in the ticket collector's office – all thinking, waiting, considering. Eventually at 11.30 we had waited long enough. I got my room.

Madhya Pradesh

Population: 46 million
Area: 442,841 square km
Capital: Bhopal
Main language: Hindi

The large state of Madhya Pradesh is the geographical heartland of India. Most of the state is a high plateau and in summer it can be very dry and hot. The size and geographical isolation of Madhya Pradesh, historically known as Malwa, kept it relatively immune from outside invaders, but virtually all phases of Indian history have left their mark on it. There are still many pre-Aryan Gond and Bhil tribal people in the state, but Madhya Pradesh is overwhelmingly Indo-Aryan with the majority of the people speaking Hindi and following Hinduism.

The state's history goes back to the time of Ashoka, the great Buddhist emperor whose Mauryan empire was powerful in Malwa. At Sanchi you can see the Buddhist centre founded by Ashoka, the most important reminder of him in India today. The Mauryans were followed by the Sungas, and the Sungas by the Guptas before the Huns swept across the state. Around 1000 years ago the Parmaras ruled in south-west Madhya Pradesh – they're chiefly remembered for Raja Bhoj, who gave his name to the city of Bhopal and also ruled over Indore and Mandu.

Between 950 and 1050 AD the Chandellas constructed the fantastic series of temples at Khajuraho, in the north-east of the state. Today Khajuraho is one of India's main attractions. Between the 12th and 16th century the region saw continuing struggles between Hindu and Muslim rulers or invaders. Often the fortified city of Mandu in the south-west was the scene for these battles, but finally the power of the Moghuls overcame Hindu resistance and controlled the region, only to fall to

the rise of the Marathas who, in turn, were to fall to the advance of British power.

Two of Madhya Pradesh's attractions are remote and isolated – Khajuraho is off to the north-east, a long way from anywhere and most easily visited by travelling between Agra and Varanasi. Jabalpur, with its marble rocks, is in the south-east of the state and can be reached if you are travelling between the west of India and Calcutta, or Orissa on the east coast.

Most of the state's other attractions are on, or close to, the main Delhi-Bombay rail line. From Agra, just outside the state to the north, you can head south through Gwalior, with its magnificent fort, Sanchi, Bhopal, Ujjain, Indore and Mandu. From there you can head east to Gujarat or south to the Ajanta and Ellora caves in Maharashtra.

GWALIOR (population 450,000)
In the extreme north-west of Madhya Pradesh, only a few hours from Agra by train or road, Gwalior is famous for its very old and very large fort. Within the

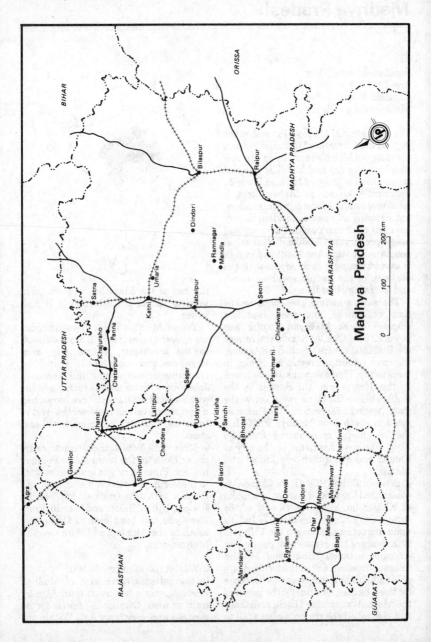

fort walls are a number of interesting temples and ruined palaces. The dramatic and colourful history of the great fort certainly goes back over 1000 years.

Gwalior's legendary beginning stems from a meeting between Suraj Sen and the hermit Gwalipa, who lived on the hilltop where the fort stands. The hermit cured Suraj Sen of leprosy with a drink of water from the Suraj Kund, which still remains in the fort. Then he gave him a new name, Suhan Pal, and said his descendants would remain in power so long as they kept the name Pal. His next 83 descendants did just that, but number 84 changed his name to Tej Karan and, you guessed it, goodbye kingdom.

What is more certain is that in 1398 the Tomar dynasty came to power in Gwalior and, over the next several centuries, Gwalior fort was a scene of continual intrigue and clashes with neighbouring powers. Man Singh, who came to power in 1486, was the greatest of these Tomar rulers but in 1516, after earlier repelling an assault by Sikandar Lodi of Delhi in 1505, the fort was besieged by Ibrahim Lodi. The siege had no sooner started than Man Singh died, but his son held out for a year before finally capitulating. Later the Moghuls, under Babur, took the fort and held it, despite an assault by Man Singh's grandson during the time of Akbar, until the Marathas took it in 1754.

For the next 50 years the fort changed hands on several occasions, including being taken twice by the British. It finally passed into the hands of the Scindias, although behind the scenes the British retained control. At the time of the Indian Mutiny in 1857 the Maharaja remained loyal to the British but his troops didn't, and in mid-1858 the fort was the scene for some of the final, and most dramatic, events of the mutiny. It was near here that the British finally defeated Tantia Topi and it was in the final assault on the fort that the Rani of Jhansi was killed. See Jhansi for more details on this heroine of the mutiny. There is a memorial to her in Gwalior.

The area around Gwalior, particularly between Agra and Gwalior, was well known until recent years for the dacoits who terrorised travellers and villagers. They were especially concentrated in the valleys along the Chambal River, which forms the boundary between Rajasthan and Madhya Pradesh. In that area you still see many men walking along the roads carrying rifles.

Orientation & Information

The Tourist Office is in the Tansen Hotel, about a half km west of the railway station. Old Gwalior town is off to the north of the fort which, topping the long hill to the north of the newer part of the town, totally dominates the area. The newer town is known as Lashkar and stands to the south-west of the fort. The railway station and the modern town are to the south-east. There are regular tempos running along the main route from the railway station to Lashkar.

Fort

You can approach the fort from the south-west or the north-east. The north-east path, starting from the Archaeological Museum, follows a wide, winding slope to the doors of the Man Singh Palace. The south-west entrance is a long, gradual ascent by road, passing cliff-face Jain sculptures. The climb can be sweaty work in the hot season. A taxi or auto-rickshaw up the south-west road is probably the easiest way in. You can then walk down from the palace to the museum when you've looked around the fort. No refreshments are available in the fort – come prepared in summer.

The fort hill rises 100 metres above the town and is about three km in length. Its width varies from nearly a km to less than 200 metres. The fort walls, which continue around almost the entire hilltop, are 10 metres high and imposingly solid. Beneath the walls, the hill face is a sheer drop away to the plains. On a clear day the view from the fort walls is superb; the crowded streets of the older part of the town, known as Lashkar, are off to the south-west, while the more modern spacious part of the town lies to the south-east. Old Gwalior itself clings to the northern and north-eastern end of the fort hill. The view extends far out over the surrounding plains.

There are a number of things to see in and around the fort, although most of the enclosed area is simply open space and fields.

Archaeological Museum The museum is within the Gujari Mahal palace, at the start of the north-east ascent to the fort. The palace was built in the 15th century by Man Singh for his favourite queen, Mrignayani. The building is now rather deteriorated but the museum has a collection of Hindu and Jain sculptures and copies of the Bagh Caves frescoes. The museum is open 10 am to 5 pm daily, closed on Mondays.

North-East Entrance There is a whole series of gates as you ascend the path to the Man Singh palace. At one time the path had steps in it but it has now been smoothed into one long ascent, though still more suitable for feet than wheels. The first of the six gates is the Alamgiri Gate, dating from 1660. It was named after Aurangzeb, who took the title of governor of Alamgiri in this region. The second gate dates from the same period as the Gujari Mahal and is known as the Badalgarh, after Badal Singh, Man Singh's uncle, or as the Hindola Gate after a swing or *hindol* which used to stand here. The third gate, the Bansur or archer's gate, has disappeared.

The interesting fourth gate was built in the 1400s and named after the elephant-headed god, Ganesh. There is a small pigeon house or Kabutar Khana here and a small four-pillared Hindu temple to the hermit Gwalipa, after whom the fort and

town were named. Next you pass a Vishnu shrine dating from 876 AD known as Chatarbhujmandir, shrine of the four-armed. A tomb nearby is that of a nobleman killed in an assault on this gate in 1518. From here a series of steps lead to rock-cut Jain sculptures at the north-east of the fort. They are not of the same size, quality and importance as the sculptures on the south-west side. There are other Hindu sculptures along this same face.

The Hathiya Paur, or Elephant Gate, forms the entrance to the palace. Within the palace was the final gate, the Hawa Gate, but this has also been removed.

Man Singh Palace The palace, or Man Mandir, which forms the entrance to the fort is a delightfully whimsical building, also known as the Chit Mandir or Painted Palace because of the tiled and painted decorations of ducks, elephants and peacocks. Painted blue, with hints of green and gold, it still looks very good today. The palace was built by Man Singh between 1486 and 1516 and repaired in 1881. It has four storeys, two of them underground and all of them now deserted. The subterranean ones are cool, even in the summer heat, and were used as prison cells during the Moghul period. The east face of the fort, with its six towers topped by domed cupolas, stands over the fort entrance path.

The museum in the palace is open from 8 am to 5 pm, Tuesday to Sunday.

Other Palaces There are a number of other palaces clustered within the fort walls at the northern end. None of them are as interesting or as well preserved as the Man Singh Palace. The Karan Palace or Kirti Mandir is a long, narrow, two-storey palace on the western side. At the northern end are the Jahangiri and Shah Jahan palaces with a very large and deep tank. The Jauhar Tank, north-west of the palaces, was named after the *jauhar*, or ritual Rajput suicide, that took place here in 1232.

Sasbahu Temples The 'mother-in-law' and 'daughter-in-law' temples stand close to the eastern wall about mid-way along that side of the fort. The two temples are similar in style and date from the 9th to 11th centuries. The larger temple has an ornately carved base and figures of Vishnu over the entrances. Four huge pillars carry the heavy roof.

Teli-ka-mandir On the opposite side of the fort, beyond the Suraj Kund tank, this temple probably dates from the 9th century and has a peculiar plan and design. The roof is Dravidian while the decorations – the whole temple is covered with sculptures – are Indo-Aryan. A Garuda tops the 10-metre-high doorway. This is the highest structure in the fort.

South-West Entrance The long ascent on the south-west side climbs up through a ravine to the fort gate. Along the rock faces flanking this road are a large number of Jain sculptures, some impressively big. Originally cut into the cliff faces in the mid-1400s, they were mutilated by the forces of Babur in 1527 but were later repaired.

The images are in five main groups and are numbered. In the Arwahi group, image 20 is a 17-metre-high standing image of Adinath, while 22 is a 10-metre-high seated figure of Nemnath, the 22nd Jain Tirthankar. The south-eastern group is the most important and covers nearly a km of the cliff face with more than 20 images.

Jai Vilas Palace

Located in the 'new town', which actually dates from 1809, this was the palace of the Scindia family. Although the current Maharaja still lives in the palace, a large part of it is used as a museum. It's full of the erratic sort of items Hollywood Maharajas are supposed to collect – like Belgian cut-glass furniture, including a rocking chair. Or what looks like half the tiger population of India, all shot, stuffed

and moth-eaten. Then there's a little room full of erotica, including a life-sized marble statue of Leda having her way with a swan. But the *pièce-de-résistance* is a model railway that carried brandy and cigars around the dining table after dinner.

It's a long way from the palace entrance around the part still in use to the museum section. If you go there by auto-rickshaw, get it to drop you off at the museum, not at the palace entrance. The museum is open daily except Mondays from 10 am to 5 pm, admission Rs 5.

The palace is in Lashkar, which took its name 'camp' from the camp which Daulat Rao Scindia set up here in 1809, when he took control of Gwalior. The Moti Mahal Palace is also in Lashkar and there is another museum.

Old Town

The old town of Gwalior lies to the north and north-east of the fort hill. The 1661 Jami Masjid mosque is a fine old building, constructed of sandstone quarried from the fort hill. Muhammed Ghaus, a Muslim saint who played a key role in Babur's acquisition of the fort, has his fine, large tomb on the eastern side of the town. It has hexagonal towers at its four corners, and a dome which was once covered with glazed blue tiles. It's a very good example of early Moghul architecture. Close to the large tomb is the smaller Tomb of Tansen, a singer much admired by Akbar. Chewing the leaves of the tamarind tree near his grave is supposed to do wonders for your voice.

Places to Stay – bottom end

There's nothing much close to the railway station, but only a minute or so from there (turn left) is the very (very) basic *Hotel Ashok* with accommodation at Rs 15 per person. Straight across the road there's the rather better, but at Rs 40/50 for singles/doubles rather more expensive, *Hotel India* (tel 24983). Both are noisy but there are plenty of eating places around. The station has *Railway Retiring Rooms*, but a female traveller suggested that the 2nd-class ladies' waiting room is almost as comfortable and free – so long as you can manage the mosquitoes and the constant comings and goings.

About a half km from the station, accessible by walking or by auto-rickshaw for a couple of rupees, is the state government's *Tansen Hotel* (tel 215688) at 6 Gandhi Rd. It's comfortable and has reasonably well-kept rooms with attached bathrooms for Rs 70/90 or Rs 175/225 with air-con. Camping in the garden is possible and the food is good and reasonably priced. It's a popular place with foreign visitors.

None of Gwalior's accommodation is concentrated in one area – there's nothing much around the bus station in Lashkar either. *Hotel Gujri Mahal* (tel 23492-93) on High Court Lane has rooms at Rs 40/60 or with air-con at Rs 125/150. The rooms are reasonable, the food is very good, and all-in-all it's a pleasant hotel. On M L B Rd in Lashkar the *Regal Hotel* has rooms with (Rs 120/150) and without (Rs 60/90) air-con but we've had well-documented complaints about concealed peepholes in the bathrooms!

Hotel Hemsons at Phalke Bazaar is one of the few places in Lashkar. Very basic rooms cost from Rs 15. The bathrooms are primitive but, according to a visitor, 'they seemed delighted to serve a foreigner; maybe I was one of their first'.

Places to Stay – top end
Gwalior's top-end hotel is the *Welcomgroup Usha Kiran Palace* (tel 22049 & 23453) at Jayendraganj, Lashkar. It's right behind the Jai Vilas Palace. The 25 rooms are all air-con or air-cooled and singles/doubles are Rs 250/400.

Hotel Vivek Continental (tel 23624) is centrally located in Topi Bazaar and has rooms at Rs 70/100 or with air-con for Rs 100/150. Other more expensive hotels include the *Hotel President* (tel 24673) and the *Hotel Safari* (tel 24638).

Places to Eat
There's the usual selection of places to eat, including a *Kwality* and a *Wengier's Restaurant*, both between the station and Lashkar. The Kwality has air-conditioning of Arctic intensity.

Getting There
Air There is a daily flight from Delhi through Gwalior to Bhopal, Indore and Bombay and the reverse. Fares include Delhi Rs 283, Bombay Rs 896, Bhopal Rs 342 and Indore Rs 490.

Rail Gwalior is on the main Delhi-Bombay rail line, 317 km from Delhi, 118 km from Agra and 1225 km from Bombay. From Delhi the express or mail trains take about six hours to Gwalior, and the fare is Rs 33 in 2nd class, Rs 126 in 1st. It's only two hours between Agra and Gwalior and the fares are Rs 15 in 2nd class, Rs 59 in 1st. The fast Taj Express from Delhi continues on to Gwalior from Agra three times a week.

Bus There are regular bus services from Gwalior to Delhi, Agra, Ujjain, Indore, Bhopal, Jabalpur and Khajuraho, as well as to nearby centres like Shivpuri.

Getting Around
There are taxis, rickshaws, auto-rickshaws and tempos. Auto-rickshaw drivers in Gwalior will not use their meters – arrange the fare before you depart. Tempos run regular services around the city; from the railway station to Bada, the main square in Lashkar, is about Rs 1.

AROUND GWALIOR
Shivpuri
The old summer capital of Shivpuri is 117 km south-west of Gwalior or 51 km east of Jhansi. The road runs through a national park where you sometimes see animals on the road. Near Shivpuri there's a pleasant lake with gardens around the perimeter. The road from Gwalior passes through Narwar, with its large old fort.

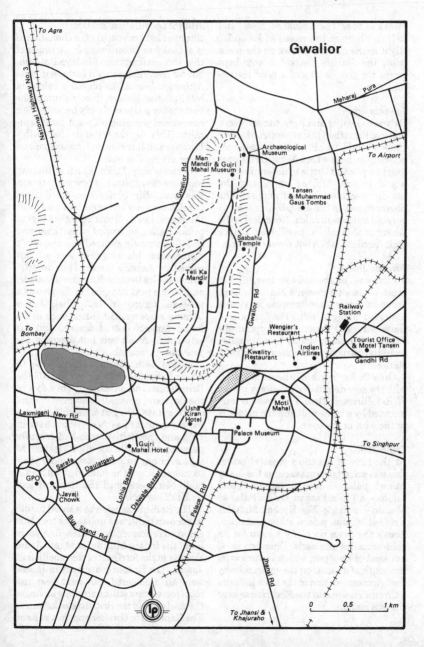

Gwalior

To Agra

National Highway No. 3

Maharaj Pura

To Airport

Gwalior Rd

Archaeological Museum

Man Mandir & Gujri Mahal Museum

Tansen & Muhammad Gaus Tombs

Sasbahu Temple

Teli Ka Mandir

Gwalior Rd

Railway Station

Wengier's Restaurant

To Bombay

Tourist Office & Motel Tansen

Kwality Restaurant

Indian Airlines

Gandhi Rd

Moti Mahal

Laxmiganj New Rd

Usha Kiran Hotel

Palace Museum

To Singhpur

Gujri Mahal Hotel

Sarafa

Daulatganj

GPO

Jayaji Chowk

Lohia Bazaar

Dalwala Bazaar

Palace Rd

Bus Stand Rd

Jhansi Rd

To Jhansi & Khajuraho

0   0.5   1 km

Places to Stay The *Chinkara Motel* (tel 297) in Shivpuri has rooms at Rs 50/75. Right in the middle of town on the main road, the *Harish Lodge* has well-kept rooms for just Rs 25 and a good restaurant.

Towards Agra

Between Gwalior and Agra, actually on a finger of Rajasthan that separates Madhya Pradesh and Uttar Pradesh at this point, is Dholpur, near where Aurangzeb's sons fought a pitched battle to determine who would succeed him as emperor of the rapidly declining Moghul empire. The Shergarh fort in the old Dholpur state is very old but now in ruins. Near Bari is the Khanpur Mahal, a pavilioned palace built for Shah Jahan but never occupied.

Towards Jhansi

To the east of the railway line, 61 km south of Gwalior towards Jhansi, a large group of white Jain temples is visible scattered along a hill. They're one of those strange, dream-like apparitions that so often seem simply to materialise in India. Sonagir is the nearest railway station.

Only 26 km north of Jhansi is Datia, with the now-deserted seven-storey palace of Raj Birsingh Deo. The town is surrounded by a stone wall and the palace is to the west of the town.

CHANDERI

At the time of Mandu's greatest power this was an important place, as the many ruined palaces, *sarais*, mosques and tombs – all in a Pathan style similar to Mandu – indicate. The Koshak Mahal is a ruined Muslim palace, still maintained. Today the town is chiefly known for its gold brocades and saris. Chanderi is 33 km west of Lalitpur, which in turn is 90 km south of Jhansi, on the main railway line. Accommodation in the town includes a *Circuit House* and the *Rest House* near the bus stand.

JHANSI (population 225,000)

Situated 101 km south of Gwalior, Jhansi is actually in Uttar Pradesh – a finger of that state extends into Madhya Pradesh, but for convenience we'll include it here. Although Jhansi has played a colourful role in Indian history, most visitors to the town today go there simply because it's a convenient jumping-off point for Khajuraho. This is the closest the Delhi-Bombay rail line runs to Khajuraho, and there are regular buses.

Orchha, only 11 km south of Jhansi, was once the capital of a powerful state in this area. Bir Singh Deo ruled from Orchha between 1605 and 1627 and built the Jhansi fort. A favourite of the Moghul prince Salim, he feuded with Akbar and in 1602 narrowly escaped the emperor's displeasure; his kingdom was all but ruined by Akbar's forces. Then in 1605 Prince Salim became Emperor Jehangir, and for the next 22 years Bir Singh was a powerful figure. In 1627 Shah Jahan became emperor, Bir Singh once again found himself out of favour, and his attempt to revolt was put down by 13-year-old Aurangzeb.

In the 18th century Jhansi rose to power, eclipsing Orchha, but in 1803 the British East India Company got a foot in the door and gradually assumed control over the state. The last of a string of none-too-competent rajas died without a son in 1853 and the British, who had recently passed a neat little law allowing them to take over any princely state under their patronage when the ruler died without a male heir, pensioned the Rani off and took full control.

The Rani of Jhansi, who wanted to rule in her own right, was unhappy about this enforced retirement and when, four years later, the Indian Mutiny burst into flame she was in the forefront of the rebellion at Jhansi. The British contingent in Jhansi were all massacred, but next year the rebel forces were still quarrelling amongst themselves and the British retook Jhansi. The Rani fled to Gwalior and, in a valiant last stand, she rode out against the British, disguised as a man, and was killed. She has since become a heroine of the Indian independence movement, a sort of Joan of Arc of central India.

The Jhansi fort, now much modernised, still offers excellent views from its ramparts. The British ceded the fort to the Maharaja of Scindia in 1858, then exchanged it for Gwalior in 1866.

Places to Stay

There are dorm beds in the *Railway Retiring Rooms* and a handful of low-priced places close to the station. Turn left out of the station and head straight a few hundred metres to half a km. The *Central Hotel* and *Hotel Sipri* are both close to the junction and have rooms for Rs 20 to Rs 30. The Central is simple but clean and pleasant, with a friendly manager and reasonable food. Rooms on the roof have good views and there are lots of clean showers. *Hotel Ashok*, near the Natraj Cinema, is a little more expensive.

The *Jhansi Hotel* on Shastri Marg has rooms at a variety of prices from Rs 80 to around Rs 200, some with attached bath, some without. There's good food at the *Railway Station*.

Getting There

Jhansi is on the main Delhi-Agra-Bhopal-Bombay railway line and is a jumping-off point for Khajuraho. Buses to Khajuraho leave early in the morning and cost about Rs 25.

ORCHHA

The former capital of this region is now just a village, but the old fort on an island in the Betwa River still stands and contains Bir Singh Deo's fine palace (the Raja Mahal) and another palace built for, but never used by, Jehangir (the Jehangir Mahal). The palaces are of impressive size and there are pleasant views of the countryside from their upper levels. For a small admission fee an attendant with door keys takes visitors through the palace to see the murals and other points of interest. Orchha is another of those undiscovered Indian gems, a good place for rambling around, tripping over the ruins.

The immense seven-storey Chatturbhuj Temple and the Lakshmi Narayan Temple are architecturally unusual. The booklet *A Study of Orchha*, available from Madhya Pradesh State Tourism, makes interesting reading.

Places to Stay

There's a state tourist department guest house, the *Hotel Sheesh Mahal*, in a wing of the Jehangir Mahal. Rooms are Rs 50/70; deluxe rooms are Rs 80/110.

SANCHI

Beside the main railway line, 68 km north of Bhopal, a hill rises from the plain. It's topped by some of the oldest and most interesting Buddhist structures in India. Although this site had no direct connection with the life of Buddha himself, it was the great Emperor Ashoka who built the first stupas here in the 3rd century BC, and a great number of stupas and other religious structures were added over the succeeding centuries.

Then, with the decline of Buddhism, the site decayed and was eventually completely forgotten. In 1818 a British officer rediscovered the site, but in the years that followed amateur archaeologists and greedy treasure hunters did immense damage to Sanchi before a proper restoration was first commenced in 1881. Finally, between 1912 and 1919, the structures were carefully repaired and restored to their present condition by Sir John Marshall.

Orientation & Information

Sanchi itself is little more than a tiny village at the foot of the hill. You must pay admission to enter the site. At the small museum you can get a copy of the guidebook *Sanchi*, published by the Archaeological Survey of India.

The Great Stupa

Stupa 1, as it is listed on the site, is the main structure on the hill. Originally constructed by Ashoka in the 3rd century BC, it was later enlarged and the original brick stupa enclosed within a stone one. In its present form it stands 16 metres high and 37 metres in diameter. A railing encircles the stupa and there are four entrances through magnificently carved gateways or *toranas*. These toranas are the finest works of art at Sanchi and amongst the finest examples of Buddhist art in India.

Toranas The four gateways were erected around 35 BC and had all fallen down at the time of the stupa's restoration. The scenes carved onto the pillars and their triple architraves are mainly tales from the *jatakas* – the episodes of the Buddha's various lives. At this stage in Buddhist art the Buddha was never represented directly. His presence was always alluded to through symbols such as the Bo tree, the wheel of law or his footprint. Even a stupa is itself a symbol of the Buddha.

Go round the stupa clockwise, as one should around all Buddhist monuments:

Northern Gateway The north gateway, topped by an unfortunately broken wheel of law, is the best-preserved of the gateways. It shows many scenes from the Buddha's life, both in his last incarnation and in earlier lives. Scenes include a monkey offering a bowl of honey to the Buddha, whose presence is indicated by a Bo tree. In another panel he ascends a road into the air (again represented by a Bo tree) in the 'miracle of Sravasti'. This is just one of several miraculous feats he performs on the north gateway – all of which leave his spectators stunned. Elephants, facing in four directions, support the architraves above the columns, while horses with riders and more elephants fill the gaps between the architraves.

Eastern Gateway This gateway includes scenes of the Buddha's entry to *nirvana* on a pillar. Across the front of the middle architrave is the 'great departure', where the Buddha (symbolised by a riderless horse) renounces the sensual life and sets out to find enlightenment. Maya's dream of an elephant standing on the moon, which she had when she conceived the Buddha, is also shown on one of the columns. The figure of a *yakshi* maiden, hanging out from one of the architraves, is one of the best-known images of Sanchi.

Southern Gateway The oldest of the gateways, this includes scenes of the Buddha's birth and also events from Ashoka's life as a Buddhist. As on the western gateway, the tale of the Chhaddanta Jataka features on this gateway.

Western Gateway The western gateway, with the architraves supported by dwarves, has some of the most interesting scenes. The rear face of one of the pillars shows the Buddha undergoing the temptation of Mara, while demons flee and angels cheer his resistance. Mara also tempts on the back of the lowest architrave. The top front architrave shows the Buddha in seven different incarnations, but since he could not, at the time, be represented directly, he appears three times as a stupa and four times as a tree. His six incarnations prior to the seventh, Gautama Buddha, are known as the Manushi Buddhas.

The colourful events of the Chhaddanta Jataka are related on the front face of the bottom architrave. In this tale the Buddha, in a lower incarnation, took the form of a six-tusked elephant, but one of his two wives became jealous; she managed to reincarnate as a queen and then arranged to have the six-tusked elephant hunted and killed. The sight of his tusks, sawn off by the hunter, was sufficient for the queen to die of remorse! Pot-bellied dwarves support the architraves on this gateway.

Madhya Pradesh Top: Athletic positions temple sculpture, Khajuraho (TW)
Left: Champa Baoli building in Royal Enclave, Mandu (TW)
Right: Taj-ul-Masjid, Bhopal (TW)

Orissa Top: Dhauli Peace Pagoda, near Bhubaneswar (TW)
Left: Sculptures on the Temple of the Sun, Konarak (TW)
Right: Strange three-part fishermen's boat, Puri (TW)

Pillars Scattered around the site are a number of pillars or the remains of pillars. The most important is pillar 10, which was erected by Ashoka and stands close to the south entrance to the great stupa. Only the base of this beautifully proportioned and executed shaft now stands, but the fine capital can be seen in the museum. The three back-to-back lions, which once topped the column, are an excellent example of the Graeco-Buddhist art of that era at its finest. They now form the state emblem of India and can be seen on every bank note.

Pillars 25 and 35, both dating from the 5th century AD, are not as fine as the earlier Ashoka pillar. Pillar 35, also broken, stands close to the north gateway of the great stupa; again, the capital figure is in the museum.

Other Stupas

There are many other stupas on the hill, some of them tiny votive ones less than a metre high. They date from the 3rd century AD. Eight of them were built by Ashoka but only three of them remain, including the great stupa. Stupa 2, one of the most interesting of the lesser stupas, is half-way down the hill to the west. If you come up from the town by the main route you can walk back down via stupa 2. There are no gateways to this stupa, but the 'medallions' which decorate the surrounding wall are of great interest. Their design and execution is almost childlike, but full of energy and imagination. Flowers, animals and people, some of them mythological creatures, are found all around the stupa.

Stupa 3 stands north-east of the main stupa and is similar in design, though smaller in size, to the great stupa itself. It has only one gateway and is thought to have been constructed soon after the completion of the great stupa. Stupa 3 once contained relics of two important disciples of the Buddha. They were removed and taken to London in 1853 but returned to Sanchi in 1953. Stupa 2, down

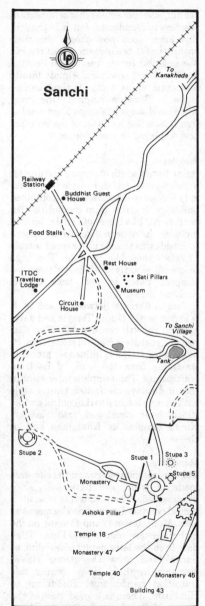

the hill, also contained relics of important teachers of Buddhism, but it is thought this lower spot was chosen for their enshrinement because the top of the hill was reserved for shrines to the Buddha and his direct disciples. Almost totally destroyed, stupa 4 stands right behind stupa 3. Between stupa 1 (the great stupa) and stupa 3 is stupa 5, unusual in that it once had an image of the Buddha, now displayed in the museum.

Temples

Immediately south of stupa 1 is stupa 18, a *chaitya* hall which in style is remarkably similar to classical Greek-columned buildings. It dates from around the 7th century AD but traces of earlier, wooden buildings have been discovered beneath it. Beside this temple is the small temple 17, also Greek-like in style. The large temple 40, slightly south-east of these two temples, dates in part back to the Ashokan period.

Temple 6 stands between 40 and 18. It is known as the Gupta Temple and dates back to the 4th century AD. The flat-roofed structure is made of stone slabs. It, too, shows a Greek influence, probably stemming from the work of Bactrian craftspeople. This temple is interesting in that it displays the Indian temple style with a porch leading to the central shrine, which later developed into classical Hindu temples at Khajuraho and in Orissa.

Monasteries

The earliest monasteries on the site were made of wood and have long since disappeared. The usual plan is of a central courtyard surrounded by monastic cells. Monasteries 47 and 45 stand on the higher, eastern edge of the hilltop. They date from the later period of building at Sanchi and show the strong Hindu elements in their design during this transition period from Buddhism to Hinduism. There is a good view of the village of Sanchi and away to Bhilsa

(Vidisha) from this side of the hill. Monastery 51 is part-way down the hill on the western side toward stupa 2.

Other Buildings

The modern *vihara* (monastery) on the hill was constructed to house the returned relics from stupa 3. The design is a poor shadow of the former artistry of Sanchi. Close to monastery 51 is the 'great bowl' in which food and offerings were placed for distribution to the monks. It was carved out of a huge boulder. The Sanchi guidebook describes all these buildings, and many others, in much greater detail.

Places to Stay & Eat

Best value for money in Sanchi is probably (and surprisingly) the *Railway Retiring Rooms*. There are just two of them but they're big, spacious, spotlessly clean (in fact the whole Sanchi station is most un-Indian like - clean, prim and proper). Crowning touch is the toilets though - you've got a western and Asian toilet side by side! Almost beside the station is the *Buddhist Guest House*, which is rather more spartan and has rooms and dorm beds. Supposedly you should make reservations in advance, but in practice you can just drop in.

Continue on to the main road and turn right 250 metres to the *Ashok Traveller's Lodge* (tel 23), where rooms are available at Rs 75/100 or with air-con at Rs 175/225. There's a restaurant and a pleasant lounge. If you crossed the main road towards the hill you'd come to the Gothic-looking *Rest House* on the left just before the museum. It has only two rooms and is mainly intended for government workers. There's also the very pleasant-looking *Circuit House* (tel 22) on the right, but again it's usually unavailable.

To eat you've got a choice of the *Traveller's Lodge*, where the food is bland and expensive, or the cluster of food stalls on the main road - most of them remarkably insanitary looking.

Getting There

Rail Sanchi is on the main Delhi-Bombay railway line only 68 km north of Bhopal. Note that certain mail and express trains do not stop at Sanchi. First-class passengers who have travelled a minimum distance to Sanchi can request that the train be halted for them. It is necessary to arrange this in advance.

Bus Buses run from Bhopal to Sanchi. The 69-km route takes three hours and the 47-km route takes 2¼ hours. Fares are Rs 6 to Rs 10. You can get everywhere in Sanchi on foot.

AROUND SANCHI

In the immediate vicinity of Sanchi there are a number of other Buddhist sites, although none are of the scale or in the state of preservation of Sanchi itself. Sonari, 10 km south-west of Sanchi, has eight stupas, two of them important. At Satdhara, west of Sanchi on the bank of the Beas River, there are two stupas, one 30 metres in diameter. Another eight km south-east is Andher, where there are three small but well-preserved stupas. These stupas were all discovered in 1851, after the discovery of Sanchi itself.

Other places of interest around Sanchi include:

Vidisha (Bhilsa or Besnagar)

Vidisha was an important town in Ashoka's time; his wife came from here. Today the city is known as Besnagar, and Bhilsa railway station has an important collection of antiques discovered in the area. The Khamb Baba pillar is one of the more interesting attractions. It was erected by Heliodorus, a Greek ambassador to the city from Taxila (now in Pakistan). The pillar celebrates his conversion to Hinduism and is dedicated to Vishnu. Also in town is the Bija Mandal, a mosque built from the remains of Hindu temples.

Udayigiri

The Gupta caves here date from 320 to

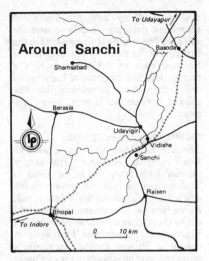

606 AD; two of them are Jain, the other 18 Hindu. In cave 5 there is a superb image of Vishnu in his boar incarnation. Cave 7 was cut out for King Chandragupta II's personal use. The caves are seven km west of Vidisha.

Raisen

On the road to Bhopal, 23 km south of Sanchi, the huge and colourful hilltop fort has temples, cannons, three palaces, 40 wells and a large tank. This Malwa fort was built around 1200 AD, but was later dependent to Mandu. Raisen declared its independence at one time, but was conquered by Bahadur Shah.

Gyaraspur

There are tanks, temples and a fort at this town, 51 km north-east of Sanchi. The town's name is derived from the big fair which used to be held here in the 11th month, Gyaras.

Udaypur

Reached through Basoda and Gyaraspur, Udaypur is 90 km north of Sanchi. The large Neelkantheswara Temple is thought to have been built in 1059 AD. It's profusely and very finely carved with four prominent decorated bands around the *shikara*. The temple is aligned so that the first rays of the morning sun shine on the Shiva lingam in the sanctum. It's a particularly fine example of Indo-Aryan architecture and is reached via the railway station at Bareth, seven km away.

BHOPAL (population 425,000)

The capital of Madhya Pradesh takes its name from its legendary 11th-century founder Raja Bhoj. He is supposed to have created the lakes around which the city is built by constructing a dam or *pal*. Hence Bho-pal. The present city was laid out by the Afghan chief Dost Mohammed Khan. Dost Mohammed had been in charge of Bhopal during Aurangzeb's reign, but took advantage of the confusion following his death in 1707 to carve out his own small kingdom.

Today, however, Bhopal is world famous for the Union Carbide disaster in December 1984. Poisonous gas escaped from a plant here and the deadly cloud killed over 1000 people in the world's worst industrial disaster. Responsibility for the catastrophe is still being kicked back and forth but few people who have travelled for any time in India would be that surprised by the litany of carelessness and neglect that led to the gas leak.

Orientation & Information

The Tourist Office (tel 3400) is at 5 Hamidia Rd close to the railway station. It's open from 11 am to 5.30 pm daily. The bus station is a little further down the same road. The older part of town is north of the twin lakes while the newer part, where you'll also find the Youth Hostel, is to the south of the lakes. The GPO is near Hamidia Hospital.

Taj-ul-Masjid

Commenced by Shah Jahan Begum, but never really completed, the Taj-ul-Masjid is one of the largest mosques in India, if not the largest. It's a huge pink mosque with two massive white-domed minarets and three white domes over the main building.

Other Mosques

The Jama Masjid was built in 1837 by Qudsia Begum and is surrounded by the bazaar. It has very squat, short minarets. The Moti Masjid was built by Qudsia Begum's daughter, Sikander Jahan Begum, in 1860. Similar in style to the Jama Masjid in Delhi, it is a smaller mosque with two dark-red minarets crowned by golden spikes.

The Lakes

The larger Upper Lake covers six square km and a bridge separates it from the Lower Lake. You can rent boats to get out on the lakes, which are very picturesque when they reflect lights from surrounding houses at night.

Other

From Shamla or Idgah hills you get a very fine view over the city and the lakes. The minarets of the city's mosques can be seen, towering over the lesser buildings. On Arera Hill, south of Lower Lake, there's a modern Lakshmi Narayan Temple and a temple museum. It's open from 8 am to 12 noon and from 2 to 6 pm daily; admission is free. There's also an Archaeological Museum near Tagore Bhavan – open 10 am to 5 pm daily, admission free. Bhopal has a surprisingly good museum of modern art on Lake View Rd on the south side of Upper Lake. It is divided into sections on urban and rural arts. There are parks and gardens around Lower Lake.

Tours

The State Tourism Development Corporation has a number of tours in and around Bhopal. There are tours of the city, Sanchi, Udayigiri, Kerwan Dam and Islamnagar. Bookings can be made through the Tourist Office on Hamidia Rd.

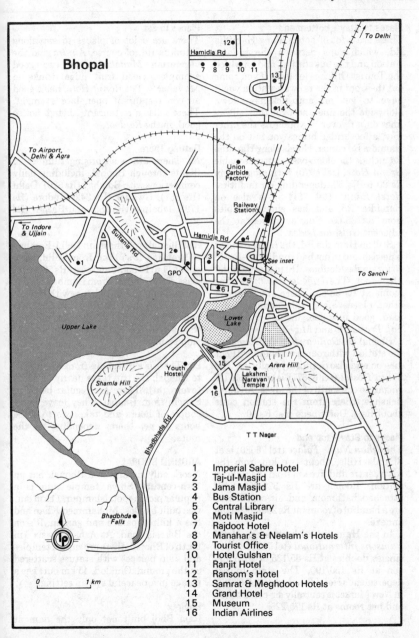

Bhopal

Hamidia Rd

To Delhi

To Airport, Delhi & Agra

Union Carbide Factory

Railway Station

To Indore & Ujjain

Suntania Rd

Hamidia Rd

GPO

See inset

To Sanchi

Lower Lake

Upper Lake

Youth Hostel

Arera Hill

Lakshmi Narayan Temple

Shamla Hill

Bhadbhda Rd

T T Nagar

Bhadbhda Falls

0   1 km

1   Imperial Sabre Hotel
2   Taj-ul-Masjid
3   Jama Masjid
4   Bus Station
5   Central Library
6   Moti Masjid
7   Rajdoot Hotel
8   Manahar's & Neelam's Hotels
9   Tourist Office
10   Hotel Gulshan
11   Ranjit Hotel
12   Ransom's Hotel
13   Samrat & Meghdoot Hotels
14   Grand Hotel
15   Museum
16   Indian Airlines

Places to Stay – bottom end

There are a lot of hotels along Hamidia Rd, which runs between the railway station and the bus station, and on which the Tourist Office is located. If you come out the front of the railway station you'll have to get an auto-rickshaw down alongside the line and over the railway lines on a flyover. If you cross the other way, a footbridge brings you out on the Hamidia Rd corner. Hotels along Hamidia Rd include the older, basic, but reasonable *Grand Hotel* (tel 4070) with rooms from Rs 20 to Rs 60, depending on facilities. *Hotel Ranjit* (tel 7511-5) is also on Hamidia Rd and has singles/doubles from Rs 35/60. Similar prices at the adjacent *Gulshan Lodge*.

Still on Hamidia Rd, the *Hotel Samrat* is newish and in not bad condition – Rs 30/45 for singles/doubles. Ditto for the *Hotel Meghdoot*. The *Pagoda* (tel 73949) has rooms at Rs 35/55. There are plenty of other places along this popular hotel road; good new ones include the hotels *Taj, President* and *Maywi*.

Bhopal has *Railway Retiring Rooms* at the station with rooms with and without air-con and also dormitory facilities. The *Youth Hostel* (tel 63671) is in North TT Nagar, to the south of the lakes. An auto-rickshaw there from the station costs about Rs 4. Dorm beds cost Rs 10.

Places to Stay – top end

The *Jehan Numa Palace* (tel 76080) is at Shamla Hills, about two km from the town centre and five km from the railway station. Rooms are Rs 320/360 with attached bathroom and air-con. There are a handful of rooms at Rs 250/300 in the annexe.

In the Hamidia Rd hotel strip, *Hotel Ramsons International* (tel 72298-9) has singles/doubles at Rs 85/135 or with air-con at Rs 150/190. The state tourist department's *Hotel Panchanan* (tel 63047) in New Market is centrally air-conditioned and has rooms at Rs 175/225.

Places to Eat

There are a lot of places to eat along Hamidia Rd, of course. *Anjura* and the vegetarian *Manohar's* are two good examples. Good fruit juice drinks in *Manohar's*. The *Ranjit Hotel* has a good air-con restaurant open late at night. There's also a restaurant, though not so good, in the *Rajdoot*.

Getting There

Air There are a surprising number of flights through Bhopal, including daily connections with Bombay (Rs 620), Delhi (Rs 551), Gwalior (Rs 342), Indore (Rs 179), Jabalpur (Rs 283) and Raipur (Rs 503).

Rail Bhopal is on the main Delhi-Bombay railway line. It's 705 km from Delhi, takes about 11 to 13 hours and costs Rs 58 in 2nd class, Rs 237 in 1st. From Bombay it's 837 km and takes 13 to 16 hours with fares of Rs 67 in 2nd class, Rs 275 in 1st. Sanchi is only 68 km north of Bhopal, but note the warning in the Sanchi section on non-stop trains.

Bus There is a direct bus from Khajuraho to Bhopal; the trip takes nearly 12 hours (overnight). There are regular buses to Sanchi from Bhopal. They leave every couple of hours and take two to three hours to get there, depending on the route.

AROUND BHOPAL

Neori, only six km from Bhopal, has an 11th-century Shiva temple and is a popular picnic spot. Islampur, 11 km out, was built by Dost Mohammed Khan and has a hilltop palace and garden. It's on the Berasia road. At Ashapuri, six km north of Bhopal, there are ruined temples and Jain palaces with statues scattered on the ground. Chiklod, 45 km out, has a palace in a peaceful sylvan setting.

Bhojpur

Raja Bhoj built not only the dam at

Bhopal but also a dam here, which created a massive lake. Hoshang Shah, the ruler of Mandu, destroyed it. A massive but never completed Shiva temple dating from the 11th century overlooks the lake. Bhojpur is 28 km from Bhopal.

Ginnorgarh Fort

This hilltop fort is 61 km from Bhopal and reached its peak in the 13th century during the reign of Udayavarman. It's famous for its parrots.

Bhimbetka

Neolithic caves and cave paintings discovered in this village, 40 km from Bhopal, are some of the earliest traces of man in India.

UJJAIN (population 225,000)

Only 80 km from Indore, on the right bank of the River Sipra, Ujjain is a very holy city for Hindus. It is also the site for the triennial Kumbh Mela, which comes to Ujjain every 12 years – next time in 1992.

The city has a long and distinguished history. It was an important city in the kingdom ruled by Ashoka's father, when it was known as Avanti. Later it was so attractive to Chandragupta II (380-414 AD), one of the Gupta kings, that for a long period he ruled from here rather than his actual capital, Pataliputra. His court supported the 'nine gems' of Hindu literature, including the important poet Kalidasa.

Later Ujjain became a centre for much turmoil, and although it was for a time capital of the Malwa region, it passed between the Rajputs and Moghuls before eventually falling to the Scindias of Gwalior.

Temples

Mahakala Temple, later restored by the Scindias, was destroyed by Altamish of Delhi in 1235. An ancient gateway known as the Chaubis Khanba Ghaj is said to

date from the original temple. It stands near the palace of Maharaja Scindia. The riverside temples and ghats are west of here.

Other temples include the small Bridh Kaleshwar, south of the Mahakala. The marble-spired Gopal Mandir was built by Jai Singh of Jaipur, but is so buried in the bazaar that it's easy to miss. The Temple of Nine Planets is on the Indore road where two other rivers join the Sipra.

Other

Out of the city (which was once bounded by a stone wall) to the south-west is the Jantar Mantar – another of those strange observatories constructed by Maharaja Jai Singh. This is in poor condition and not as impressive as the Jantar Mantars of Jaipur or New Delhi.

Eight km north of the town is the water palace of the Mandu Sultans. Known as Kaliadah, it stands on an island in the Sipra River. River water is diverted over stone screens in the palace, and the bridge to the island uses carvings from the sun temple which once stood on the island.

Places to Stay

The *Shipra Motel* (tel 4862) on University Rd has singles/doubles at Rs 50/60. There are also *Railway Retiring Rooms* and a variety of hotels opposite the railway station such as the *Hotel China* (Rs 25/30, OK), but avoid the bed-bugged although slightly cheaper *Hotel Vikram*.

INDORE (population 600,000)

Indore is not in itself of great interest, but it does make a good jumping-off point for visiting Mandu. It's an affluent-looking town and a major textile-producing centre, with plenty of new houses and flats. The rivers Khan and Sarasvati run through the town. From 1733 Indore was ruled by the Holkar dynasty who were firm supporters of the British, even at the time of the mutiny.

Orientation & Information

The older part of town is on the western side, the newer part on the east. The railway line forms a rough north-south dividing line, while Mahatma Gandhi Rd bisects the town in an east-west direction. The railway and bus stations are close together but separated by a complicated flyover system. Curiously, there seem to be as many pigs congregating in the bus and train stations as the ever-present cows. Rupayana, by the Central Hotel, is a reasonably good bookshop.

The Tourist Office (tel 38888), where you can find out about tours to Mandu, is on R N Tagore Marg behind the R N Tagore Natya Griha.

Palaces

In the old part of town the multi-storey gateway of the Rajwada or 'old palace' looks out onto the main square in the crowded streets of the Kajuri Bazaar. It's now given over to government offices, while the 'new palace' has become a hospital. The bazaar streets are busy and picturesque with deep verandahs onto the road. The Manik Bagh, to the south of the city, and the Lal Bagh, to the south-west, also have palaces. Daly College, a public school for the sons of Maharajas, is worth seeing – it's more like a palace than a school.

Kanch Madir

On Sunday St (Jawahar Rd), close to the Rajwada, is the Kanch Mandir or Seth Hukanchand Temple. This Jain temple is very plain externally, but inside is completely mirrored with pictures of sinners being tortured in the after-life as light relief.

Museum

Near the GPO, the museum has a car park which was a 'battlefield in the Independence War of 1857'. It specialises in sculptures and coins excavated in the Malwa region. In particular, there are over 700 pieces from Mandsaur. It has the biggest collection of antiques in Madhya Pradesh. Admission is free; it's closed on Mondays.

Chhatris

The *chhatris* or memorial tombs of the region's former rulers are now neglected and forgotten. They stand in the Chhatri Bagh on the banks of the River Khan. The cenotaph of Malhar Rao Holkar I, founder of the Holkar dynasty, is the most impressive.

Tours

There are a number of conducted tours from Indore, including tours to Mandu, Omkareshwar and Ujjain.

Places to Stay – bottom end

The railway station and the Sarwate Bus Station are only a few minutes' walk apart, and there's a reasonable selection of places directly opposite the bus station on Nasia Rd. There are *Retiring Rooms* in the bus station from Rs 25.

The *Janta Hotel* (tel 37695 & 36691), across from the bus station, is OK – fairly clean, fans, rooms from Rs 15 to Rs 40, the more expensive ones with attached bathrooms. Flanking it on one side is the *Standard Lodge* (tel 37370 & 36889) with rooms at slightly higher prices. The *Ganesh Hind Lodge* on Chhoti Gwaltoli Rd is friendly and clean and has Rs 25 doubles with common bathroom.

On the other side is the newish *Hotel Ashok* (tel 37391-5), rather more expensive with rooms from Rs 40. It's pleasant, clean and well kept though the front rooms are a little noisy, due to the bus station. *Hotel Neelam* (tel 37161 & 37274) at 33/2 Chhoti Gwaltoli is also close to the railway and bus stations – rooms cost from Rs 20 or from Rs 30 with attached bathroom.

Places to Stay – top end

A little further away from the bus/train centres on Mahatma Gandhi Rd, there are a number of more expensive places to

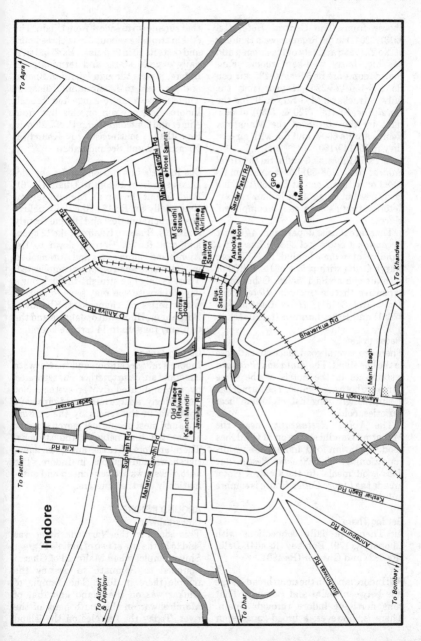

Indore

To Agra

New Dewas Rd

Mahatma Gandhi Rd

Hotel Samrat

M Gandhi Statue

Indiane Airlines

Sardar Patel Rd

GPO

Museum

Railway Station

Ashoka & Janata Hotel

D Ahilya Rd

Bus Station

Central Bazar

Bhavarkua Rd

To Khandwa

Manik Bagh

Manikbagh Rd

Sadar Bazaar

Old Palace (Rajwada)

Kanch Mandir

Jawahar Rd

Subhash Rd

Mahatma Gandhi Rd

Kila Rd

To Ratlam

Keshar Bagh Rd

To Airport & Depalpur

Annapurna Rd

Sukhniwas Rd

To Dhar

To Bombay

choose from. The *Central Hotel* (tel 32131, 32041) in the Rampurawala Building at No 27 is attractively old fashioned and has big, fairly well-kept rooms. Fan-cooled rooms are Rs 60-90/90-135, air-con Rs 125-150/175-225. If you cross the railway tracks on M G Rd you'll find the *Hotel Sheeba* (tel 7720 & 7750) at 562, right by the statue of the Mahatma. Rooms are Rs 60/80 and up; with air-con they're Rs 140/160.

At 18/5 Mahatma Gandhi Rd the *Hotel Samrat* (tel 30758-59) has rooms from Rs 60/80 or with air-con at Rs 150/175. It's fairly new but is one of the Indian 'rapidly deteriorating as soon as it's completed' places.

The state tourist department's *Tourist Reception Centre* (tel 38888) has just a handful of rooms behind R N Tagore Natya Griha with prices of Rs 75/100 or with air-con at Rs 175/225. Other more expensive hotels include *Hotel Shri Maya* (tel 34151), *Hotel Central* (tel 32041) and *Hotel Lantern* (tel 30371).

Places to Eat

There are several good places to eat close to the bus stand. The *Janta* and *Standard* restaurants in the hotels of the same name are both good value. The former has a surprisingly long list of Indian beer varieties, cold.

The *Volga Restaurant*, near the Mahatma Gandhi statue on M G Rd, has good vegetarian food and aggressive air-conditioning. The *Sheeba Restaurant* does good meals. In the Central Hotel arcade the *Indore Coffee House* is sombre but restful.

Getting There

Air There are daily connections with Bhopal (Rs 179), Bombay (Rs 464), Delhi (Rs 682) and Gwalior (Rs 490).

Rail Indore is not on the main broad-gauge line between Delhi and Bombay. That runs north of Indore through Ujjain. There is, however, a broad-gauge spur

that runs down to Indore from Ujjain. The 80-km trip takes about 2½ to three hours and costs Rs 10 in 2nd class, Rs 45 in 1st. A daily express starts and terminates in Indore; it runs through Ujjain to Bhopal and then east to Jabalpur and Bilaspur. There is also a metre-gauge line through Indore. Services run on this line from Ajmer and Chittorgarh, north of Indore in Rajasthan, south-east to Khandwa, Nizamabad and Secunderabad.

Bus Indore's bus station can be chaotic. Buses run from Indore to Ujjain (Rs 6), Bagh (about the same), Mandu (several times daily for Rs 12 – the daily deluxe bus is much superior) and Bhopal (hourly for Rs 20). Buses to Udaipur take 12 hours and cost Rs 50. Getting down to the Ajanta and Ellora caves and Aurangabad in Maharashtra can be rather complicated. There is only one straight-through bus a day; otherwise you may have to make a whole series of changes at Khandwa, Burhanpur, Bhusawal or Jalgaon and the trip may take up to 14 terrible hours.

Getting Around

Indore's railway station and the Sarwate bus stand are close together, but separated by a complicated flyover system. Not surprisingly, a large number of gaps have appeared in the fences by the railway lines and most people just march straight across the line between the stations. There are lots of taxis, auto-rickshaws, rickshaws and tempos in Indore. The auto-rickshaws are very cheap and automatically use their meters.

AROUND INDORE
Omkareshwar

This island in the Narmada River was said to be the site of two of India's 12 great Shiva temples when Mahmud of Ghazni marched to Somnath to destroy the temple there in 1024. The Temple of Omkar was on the island and that of Manileshwar on the south bank of the river. Today the temples on the island

and the nearby riverbanks have been damaged by Muslims or time, but there are still some very fine buildings to be seen. The island temples are dedicated to Shiva; on the riverbanks are ones to Vishnu as well as Jain temples.

Getting There Omkareshwar Road is on the railway line 60 km from Khandwa. Omkareshwar is 10 km from here. Day tours are operated to Omkareshwar from Indore, 80 km away.

Maheshwar

The *chhatri* of Ahalya Bai, who died in 1795, is located here. She was the widow of Malhar Rao Holkar's son (see Indore), and after his death she ruled with great ability. She also has a cenotaph in the Chhatri Bagh in Indore. Maheshwar is 100 km from Indore on the banks of the Narmada River.

Dhar

Founded by Raja Bhoj, the legendary founder of Bhopal and Mandu, this was the capital of Malwa until Mandu rose to power. There are good views from the ramparts of Dhar's well-preserved fort. Dhar also has the large stone Bhojashala Mosque with ancient Sanskrit inscriptions, and the adjoining tomb of the Muslim saint Kamal Maula.

MANDU

The extensive and now mainly deserted hilltop fort of Mandu is one of the most interesting sights in central India. There is accommodation in Mandu, or you can make a day trip from Indore if your time is short. Mandu is on an isolated outcrop separated from the tableland to the north by a deep and wide valley, over which a natural causeway runs to the main city gate. To the south of Mandu the land drops steeply away to the plain far below and the view is superb. Deep ravines cut into the sides of the 20-square-km plateau occupied by the fort.

History

Mandu, known as the 'city of joy', has had a chequered and varied history. Founded as a fortress and retreat in the 10th century by Raja Bhoj (see Bhopal), it was conquered by the Muslim rulers of Delhi in 1304. When the Mongols invaded and took Delhi in 1401, the Afghan Dilawar Khan, governor of Malwa, set up his own little kingdom and Mandu embarked on its golden age. Even after it was added to the Moghul empire by Akbar it retained a considerable degree of independence, until the declining Moghuls lost control of it to the Marathas. The capital of Malwa was then shifted back to Dhar, and Mandu became a ghost town. For a ghost town it's remarkably grandiose and impressive, and worth a day's inspection at the very least. Mandu has one of the best collections of Afghan architecture to be seen in India.

Although Dilawar Khan first established Mandu as an independent kingdom, it was his son, Hoshang Shah, who shifted the capital from Dhar to Mandu and raised it to its greatest splendour. Warlike as he was, Hoshang's rule from 1405 was marked by the construction of the Delhi Gate, the Jami Masjid, his own fine tomb and the extensive and complex fortifications.

Hoshang's son ruled for only a year before being poisoned by Mahmud Shah, who became king himself and ruled for 33 years. During his reign Mandu was in frequent and often bitter dispute with neighbouring powers. There are few architectural remains of his reign because his most imposing structures, such as his own tomb, were poorly designed and built, and soon collapsed. Nevertheless his constant war-making raised Mandu to great importance and prosperity.

In 1469 Mahmud Shah's son, Ghiyas-ud-Din, ascended the throne and spent the next 31 years devoting himself to women and song – if not wine, for he was reputed to be teetotal. His son, Nasir-ud-Din, became so fed up with waiting for over-indulgence to finish off his father that he poisoned him in 1500, when he was 80 years old. The son lived only another 10 years before dying, some say of guilt. In turn his son, Mahmud, had an unhappy reign during which his underlings, like Gada Shah and Darya Khan, often had more influence than he did. Finally, in 1526, Bahadur Shah of Gujarat conquered Mandu.

In 1534 Humayun, the Moghul, defeated Bahadur Shah, but as soon as Humayun turned his back an officer of the former dynasty took over. Several more changes of fortune eventually led to Baz Bahadur taking power in 1554; his chief pursuits were not conquest or building, like his predecessors, but music. In 1561 he fled from Mandu rather than face Akbar's advancing troops, and Mandu's period of independence ended. Although the Moghuls maintained the fort for a time and even added some new minor buildings, its period of grandeur was over.

Orientation & Information

The buildings of Mandu can be divided into three groups. When you enter through the Delhi Gate at the north, a road branches off to the west almost immediately. This leads to the group of buildings known as the Royal Enclave. If you continue straight on from the entrance you'll pass the Tourist Bungalow and come to the tiny village which is all that Mandu is today. The buildings here are known as the village group. Continuing on, you'll eventually reach the Rewa Kund group at the extreme south of the fort. You can get a copy of the Archaeological Survey of India's excellent guidebook *Mandu* from the Taveli Mahal in the Royal Enclave. There are many other buildings in Mandu apart from those described below.

Royal Enclave Buildings

Jahaz Mahal The 'Ship Palace' is probably the most famous building in Mandu. It really is ship-like, being far longer (110 metres) than it is wide (15 metres), and the illusion is completed by the two lakes that flank it to the east and west. It was built by Ghiyas-ud-Din, son of Mahmud Shah. Ghiyas had become thoroughly fed up with his father's warring ways and decided to dedicate himself to more pleasurable pursuits. The Jahaz Mahal is his magnificent harem. At the northern end of the 'ship' is a beautifully tiered bath where one can easily imagine the ladies of the harem lolling around seductively.

Hindola Mahal Just north of Ghiyas' stately pleasure dome, this church-like hall is known as the 'swing palace' because the inward slope of the walls is supposed to create the impression that the walls are swaying. 'Supposed to', anyway. A wide, sloping ramp in the northern end of the building is said to exist so the ruler could be conveyed upstairs by elephant. The building is massively constructed, quite strong enough to handle the odd elephant.

Champa Baoli To the west of the first two Royal Enclave buildings is this interesting building on the north shore of the lake. Its subterranean levels featured cool wells and baths and it was obviously a popular hot-weather retreat. Several other buildings in the enclave include the 'house and shop' of Gada Shah and the 1405 Mosque of Dilawar Khan, one of the earliest Muslim buildings in Mandu. Just south of the Jahaz Mahal is the Taveli Mahal, used as a rest house.

Village Group Buildings

Jami Masjid The huge, 1454 mosque dominates the village of Mandu. It is claimed to be the finest and largest example of Afghan architecture in India. Construction was commenced by Hoshang Shah, who patterned it on the great mosque in Damascus, Syria. The mosque features an 80-metre-square courtyard.

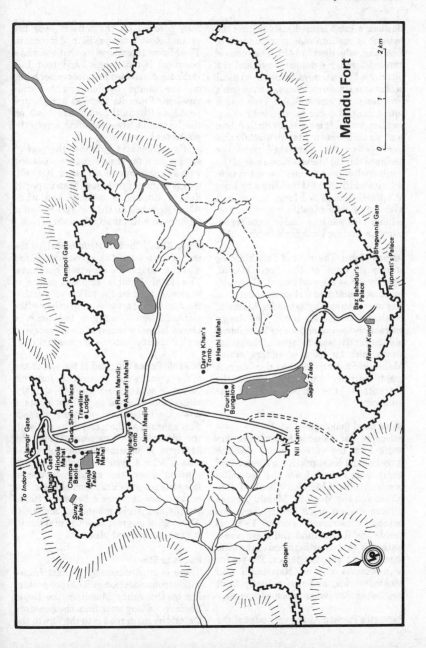

Mandu Fort

2 km

1

0

To Indore

Alamgir Gate

Rampol Gate

Bhangi Gate

Hindola Mahal

Champa Baoli

Gada Shah's Palace

Travellers' Lodge

Ram Mandir

Ashrafi Mahal

Jahaz Mahal

Munja Talao

Suraj Talao

Jami Masjid

Hughang's Tomb

Darya Khan's Tomb

Hathi Mahal

Tourist Bungalow

Sagar Talao

Nil Kanth

Songarh

Bhagwania Gate

Rupmati's Palace

Baz Bahadur's Palace

Rewa Kund

Hoshang's Tomb Immediately behind the mosque is the imposing marble tomb of Hoshang, who died in 1435. The tomb is entered through a domed porch and the interior is lit by stone *jali* screens – typical of the clear Hindu influence on the tomb's fine design. It has a double arch and a squat, central dome surrounded by four smaller domes. It is said that Shah Jahan sent his architects to Mandu to study this tomb before they embarked upon the design of the Taj Mahal. To one side of the tomb enclosure is a long, low colonnade with its width divided into three by rows of pillars. Behind is a long, narrow hall with a typically Muslim barrel-vaulted ceiling. This was intended as a shelter for pilgrims visiting Hoshang's tomb.

Ashrafi-Mahal The ruin of this building stands in front of the Jami Masjid, directly across the road from it. Originally built as a *madrasa* (religious college), it was later extended by its builder, Mahmud Shah, to become his tomb. The design was simply too pretentious for its builders' abilities and it later collapsed. The seven-storey, circular tower of victory, which Mahmud Shah erected, has also fallen. A great stairway still leads up to the entrance to the empty shell of the building.

Rewa Kund Buildings

Palace of Baz Bahadur About three km south from the village group, past the large Sagar Talao tank, is the Rewa Kund group. Baz Bahadur was the last independent ruler of Mandu. When he fell to Akbar and the Moghuls, Mandu became a mere shadow of its former glory. His palace, constructed around 1509, is beside the Rewa Kund and there was a water-lift at the northern end of the tank to supply water to the palace. The palace is a curious mix of Rajasthani and Moghul styles, and was actually built well before Baz Bahadur came to power.

Rupmati's Pavilion At the very edge of the fort, perched on the hillside over the plains below, is the pavilion of Rupmati. The Malwa legends relate that she was a beautiful Hindu singer, and that Baz Bahadur persuaded her to leave her home on the plains by building her this pavilion. From its terraces and domed pavilions Rupmati could gaze down on the Narmada River, winding across the plains far below.

It's a romantic building, the perfect setting for a fairytale romance – but one with an unhappy ending. Akbar, it is said, was prompted to conquer Mandu partly due to Rupmati's beauty. And when Akbar marched on the fort Baz Bahadur fled, leaving Rupmati to poison herself.

Darya Khan's Tomb & Hathi Mahal To the east of the road, between the Rewa Kund and the village, are these two buildings. The Hathi Mahal or 'elephant palace' is so named because the pillars supporting the dome are of massive proportions – like elephant legs. Nearby is the tomb of Darya Khan, which was once decorated with intricate patterns of mosaic tiles.

Nilkanth Palace Situated at the end of one of the ravines which cuts into the fort, this palace is actually below the level of the hilltop and reached by a flight of steps down the hillside. At one time it was a Shiva shrine, as the name – the god with the blue throat – suggests. Under the Moghuls it became a pleasant water palace with a typical Moghul cascade running down the middle. It was a favourite place for Emperor Jehangir, but today it has once again become a Shiva temple and a playground for monkeys. Although of no great architectural merit, it's very pretty and pleasant.

Places to Stay

There is an *Archaeological Rest House* with accommodation at Rs 20 per person. It's by the Jahaz Mahal in the Royal Enclave – a long walk from the bus stop. Or, on the main road into the fort to the village group, there's the *Travellers' Lodge* (tel 21) with rooms for Rs 70/90 or with air-con at Rs 175/225. There are also rates including all meals.

Rooms at the *Tourist Bungalow* (tel 35) can be booked through the Tourist Office in Indore. Four-bed rooms cost Rs 15 per person, or there are deluxe rooms at Rs 50/75, but again it's a long walk from the bus stop. At the same location, *Tourist Huts* cost Rs 75/100; deluxe ones are Rs 100/120. There are several small eating places in the village and a *dharamsala* (less than Rs 10) near the bus stop, but it's not very good value.

Getting There

There are buses from Bhopal, Mhow, Ujjain, Dhar and Indore to Mandu. From Indore buses depart several times daily; the 115-km trip costs Rs 12 and takes about four hours. There are also regular tours from Indore to Mandu.

Getting Around

Be prepared for lots of walking if you haven't come on a tour. It's OK, this is a fine area for walking and pleasantly unpopulated.

BAGH CAVES

The Bagh Caves are seven km from the village of Bagh and three km off the main road. Bagh is about 50 km west of Mandu, on the road between Indore and Baroda in Gujarat. The Buddhist caves date from 400 to 700 AD and are all in very bad shape. Cave-ins, smoke and water damage have reduced them to such poor condition that restoration work is barely worthwhile. Compared to the caves of Ajanta or Ellora, the Bagh Caves are hardly worth the not-inconsiderable effort of getting to them.

In the Archaeological Museum in Gwalior you can see reproductions of the wall paintings from Cave 4, known as Rang Mahal or the Painted Hall, when they were in much better condition than today.

There is a *PWD Dak Bungalow* at the caves.

KHAJURAHO

The temples of Khajuraho are one of India's major attractions – close behind the Taj and up there with Varanasi, Jaipur and Delhi. The temples, of course, are superb examples of Indo-Aryan architecture, but it's the decorations with which they are so liberally embellished that has made Khajuraho so famous. Around the temples are bands of exceedingly fine and artistic stonework. The sculptors have shown many aspects of Indian life 1000 years ago – gods and goddesses, warriors and musicians, animals real and mythological. But two elements appear over and over again and in greater detail than anything else – women and sex. Stone figures of *apsaras* or 'celestial maidens' appear on every temple. They pout and pose for all the world like Playboy models posing for the camera. In between are the *mithuna* couples (or even some larger groups on some of the temples) running through a whole Kama Sutra of positions and possibilities. Some obviously require amazing athletic contortions, some just look like good fun!

These temples were built during the Chandella period, a dynasty which survived for five centuries before falling to the onslaught of Islam. Khajuraho's temples almost all date from one century-long burst of creative genius from 950 to 1050 AD. Almost as intriguing as the sheer beauty and size of the temples themselves is the question of why and how they were built here. Khajuraho is a long way from anywhere and was probably just as far off the beaten track 1000 years ago as it is today. There is nothing of great interest or beauty to recommend it as a building site, there is no great population centre here and during the hot season Khajuraho is very hot, dry, dusty and uncomfortable.

Having chosen such a strange site, how did the Chandellas manage to recruit the labour to turn their awesome dreams into stone? To build so many temples of such monumental size in just 100 years must have required a huge amount of manpower. Whatever their reasons, we can be thankful they built Khajuraho where they did, because its very remoteness must have helped preserve it from the desecration Muslim invaders were only too ready to inflict on 'idolatrous' temples elsewhere in India.

Orientation & Information

The modern village of Khajuraho is a cluster of hotels, restaurants, shops and stalls around the bus station. A little north there are three government-run hotels. By the bus stand are the museum, Tourist Office (tel 47) and post office. The temples are in three groups. By the modern part of Khajuraho is the western group, most of its temples in a well-kept enclosure; it includes the largest and most important temples.

A km or so east of the bus stand is the old village of Khajuraho; around it are the temples of the eastern group. Finally, the two southern groups of temples are further south. Small images of the gods can be bought from the shops in Khajuraho – plus lots of postcards.

Terminology

The Khajuraho temples follow a fairly consistent design pattern pretty well unique to Khajuraho. Understanding the architectural conventions and some of the terms will help you enjoy the temples more. Basically they all follow a five-part or three-part plan.

You enter the temples through an entrance porch, known as the *ardhamandapa*. Behind this is the hall or *mandapa*. This leads into the main hall or *mahamandapa*, supported with pillars and with a corridor around it. A vestibule or *antarala* then leads into the *garbhagriha*, the inner sanctum where the image of the god to which the temple is dedicated is displayed. An enclosed corridor, the *pradakshina*, runs around

this sanctum. The simpler three-part temples delete part 2 (the *mandapa*) and part 5 (the *pradakshina*), but otherwise follow the same plan as the five-part temples.

Externally the temples consist of successive waves of higher and higher towers culminating in the soaring *sikhara*, which tops the sanctum. While the lower towers, over the *mandapa* or *mahamandapa*, may be pyramid-shaped, the *sikhara* is taller and curvilinear. The ornate, even baroque, design of all these vertical elements is balanced by an equally ornate horizontal element from the bands of sculptures that run around the temples. Although the sculptures are superbly developed in their own right, they are also a carefully integrated part of the overall design – not some tacked-on afterthought.

The interiors of the temples are as ornate as the exteriors. The whole temple sits upon a high terrace, known as the *adisthana*. Unlike temples in most other parts of India, these had no enclosing wall but often had four smaller shrines at the corners of the terrace; many of them have disappeared today. The finely carved entrance gate to the temple is a *torana*. The lesser towers around the main sikhara are known as *urusringas*.

The temples are almost all aligned east-west, with the entrance facing east. Some of the earliest temples were made of granite, or granite and sandstone, but all the ones from the classic period of Khajuraho's history are made completely of sandstone. At that time there was no mortar, so the blocks were fitted together. The sculptures and statues play such an important part in the total design that many have their own terminology:

apsara – heavenly nymph, beautiful dancing woman.
salabhanjika – woman figure with tree, which together act as supporting brackets in the inner chambers of the temple. Apsaras also perform this function.

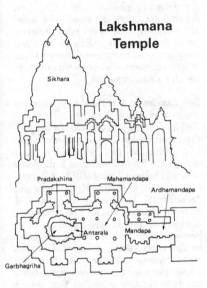

Lakshmana Temple

Sikhara

Pradakshina　Mahamandapa

Ardhamandapa

Antarala　Mandapa

Garbhagriha

surasundari – when a surasundari is dancing she is an apsara. Otherwise she attends the gods and goddesses by carrying flowers, water, ornaments, mirrors or other offerings. She also engages in everyday activities like washing her hair, applying make-up, taking a thorn out of her foot, fondling herself, playing with pets and babies, writing letters, playing musical instruments or posing seductively.

nayika – it's really impossible to tell a nayika from a surasundari, since the only difference is that the surasundari is supposed to be a heavenly creature while a nayika is human.

mithuna – Khajuraho's most famous image, the sensuously carved, erotic figures which adorn so many of the temples. They're reputed to have been shocking people from Victorian archaeologists to blue-rinse tourists, but no one is really certain about their purpose.

Some say they represent the sexual side of the path to final deliverance, others that the sculptors were trying to include all of life in the temples. Whatever the reason, they're certainly an important part of Khajuraho.

sardula – a mythical beast, part lion, part some other animal or even man. Sardulas usually carry armed men on their backs, and can be seen on many of the temples. They all look like lions but the faces are often different. They may be demons or *asuras*.

Western Group

The western group of temples is the most conveniently situated to the tourist part of Khajuraho, and also has the most interesting temples. Most of them are contained within a fenced enclosure, which is very well maintained as a park. The enclosure is open from sunrise to sunset and the admission fee covers you for multiple entries for one day. It also permits entry to the archaeological museum across the road, so don't lose your ticket. Admission is free on Fridays. The enclosure temples are described below in a clockwise direction.

Lakshmana The large Lakshmana Temple is dedicated to Vishnu, although in design it is similar to the Kandariya Mahadev and Vishvanath temples. It is one of the earliest of the western enclosure temples, dating from around 930 to 950 AD, but also one of the best preserved since it has not only the full five-part floor plan, but retains its four subsidiary shrines. Around the temple are two – rather than the usual three – bands of sculpture; the lower one has some fine figures of *apsaras* and some erotic scenes.

On the subsidiary shrine at the south-west corner you can make out an architect working with his students – it is thought this may be the temple's designer, including himself in the grand plan. Around the base of the temple is a continuous frieze with scenes of battles, hunting and processions. The first metre or two of the frieze consists of a highly energetic orgy, including one gentleman proving that a horse can be man's best friend, while a stunned group of women look aside in shock.

Lakshmi & Varah Facing the large Lakshmana Temple are these two small shrines. The Varah Temple, dedicated to Vishnu's boar incarnation or Varah Avatar, actually faces the Matangesvara Temple which is outside the enclosure. Inside this small, open shrine is a huge, solid and intricately carved figure of the boar.

Kandariya Mahadev The first of the temples on a common base – at the back of the western enclosure – is the one temple to see in Khajuraho above all others. The Kandariya Mahadev is not only the largest of the temples, it is also artistically and architecturally the most perfect. Built between 1025 and 1050, it represents Chandella art at its most finely developed. Although the four subsidiary shrines which once stood around the main temple have long disappeared, the central shrine is in superb condition and shows the typical five-part design of Khajuraho temples.

The main spire soars 31 metres high and the temple is lavishly carved. The English archaeologist Cunningham counted 226 statues inside the temple and a further 646 outside – 872 in total with most of them nearly a metre in height. The statues are carved around the temple in three bands and include gods, goddesses, beautiful women, musicians and, of course, some of the famed erotic groups. The *mithuna* on the Kandariya Mahadev include some of the most energetic eroticism to be seen at Khajuraho. In the sexual Olympics there would definitely be some gold-medal winners here.

Mahadeva This small and mainly ruined

temple stands on the same base as the Kandariya Mahadev and the Devi Jagadamba. Although small and insignificant compared to its mighty neighbours, it houses one of Khajuraho's best sculptures – a fine figure of a person (man or woman, observers have been unable to decide), caressing a lion.

Devi Jagadamba The third temple on the common platform is slightly older than the Kandariya Mahadev and of a simpler, three-part design. It was probably originally dedicated to Vishnu, but later changed to Parvati and then Kali. Some students believe it may still be a Parvati temple and that the Kali image (or Jagadamba) is actually an image of Parvati, painted black. The sculptures around the temple are again in three bands. Many of the two lower band images are of Vishnu with *sardulas* in the inner recesses. But on the third and uppermost band the *mithuna* again come out to play, and some feel that this is Khajuraho's most erotic temple.

Chitragupta The fourth temple at the back of the western enclosure does not share the common platform with the other three. Similar in design to the Devi Jagadamba, this temple is probably slightly later and is unique, at Khajuraho, in being dedicated to Surya, the Sun God. The temple has obviously been much restored and is not in as good condition as other temples. Nevertheless it has some very fine sculptures that include processions, dancing girls, elephant fights and hunting scenes. In the inner sanctum Surya can be seen driving his chariot and seven horses, while on the central niche in the south facade you can see an 11-headed statue of Vishnu. The central head is that of Vishnu himself; the 10 others are of his incarnations.

Parvati Continuing around the enclosure, you come to the Parvati temple on your right. The name is probably incorrect

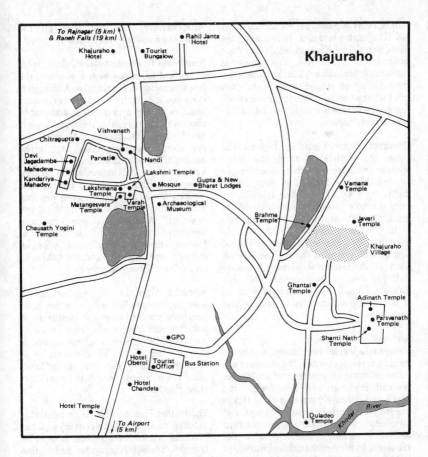

Khajuraho

To Rajnagar (5 km)
& Raneh Falls (19 km)

Khajuraho Hotel

Tourist Bungalow

Rahil Janta Hotel

Chitragupta

Vishvanath

Parvati

Nandi

Devi Jagadamba

Mahadeva

Kandariya-Mahadev

Lakshmi Temple

Lakshmana Temple

Mosque

Gupta & New Bharat Lodges

Matangesvara Temple

Varah Temple

Archaeological Museum

Chausath Yogini Temple

Vamana Temple

Brahma Temple

Javari Temple

Khajuraho Village

Ghantai Temple

Adinath Temple

Parsvanath Temple

Shanti Nath Temple

GPO

Hotel Oberoi

Tourist Office

Bus Station

Hotel Chandela

Hotel Temple

Duladeo Temple

Khodar River

To Airport (5 km)

since this small and not so interesting temple was originally dedicated to Vishnu and now has an image of Ganga riding on the back of a crocodile.

Vishvanath Temple & Nandi Believed to have been built in 1002, this temple has the complete five-part design of the larger Kandariya Mahadev temple, but two of its four subsidiary shrines still stand. That it is a Shiva shrine is made very clear by the large image of his vehicle, the bull Nandi, which faces the temple from the other end of the common platform.

Steps lead up to this high terrace, flanked by lions on the northern side and elephants on the southern side. The sculptures around the temple include the usual Khajuraho scenes, but the sculptures of women are particularly notable here. They write letters, fondle a baby, play music and, perhaps more so than at any other temple, languish in provocative poses.

Matangesvara Temple Standing next to the Lakshmana Temple, this temple is not within the fenced enclosure because it is still in everyday use, unlike all the other old Khajuraho temples. It is one of the older temples at Khajuraho, dating from around 900 to 925 AD. The temple is rather simpler in floor plan than the later, more highly developed temples and does not have the same profusion of carvings. Inside the shrine is a highly polished 2.5-metre-high lingam.

Chausath Yogini Standing beyond the tank, some distance from the other western group temples, this ruined temple is probably the oldest at Khajuraho, dating from 900 AD or earlier. It is also the only temple constructed entirely of granite and the only one not aligned east-west. Chausath means 64 – the temple once had 64 cells for figures of the 64 yoginis who attended the goddess Kali. A 65th cell sheltered Kali herself. A further half km west is the Lalguan Mahadev Temple, a small, ruined shrine dedicated to Shiva and constructed of granite and sandstone.

Archaeological Museum

Close to the western enclosure, across the road from the post office, the museum has a fine collection of statues and sculptures rescued from around Khajuraho. It's small and definitely worth a visit. Hours are 9 am to 5 pm daily except Fridays, and admission is included in the western enclosure entrance fee. Opposite the museum, in the Archaeological Survey of India's compound beside the Matangesvara Temple, there are many more rescued sculptures – but it's off limits.

Eastern Group

The eastern group of temples can be subdivided into two groups. The first is made up of the interesting Jain temples in the walled enclosure. The other four temples are scattered through the small village of Khajuraho. The easiest way to see these temples is to take a rickshaw out to the Jain enclosure, and then walk back to your hotel through Khajuraho village.

Alternatively, you can visit all the temples en route to the southern group.

Parsvanath The largest of the Jain temples in the walled enclosure is also one of the finest temples at Khajuraho. Although it does not approach the western enclosure temples in size, and does not attempt to compete in the sexual activity stakes, it is notable for the exceptional skill and precision of its construction, and for the beauty of its sculptures. Some of the best-known figures at Khajuraho can be seen here, including the classic figures of a woman removing a thorn from her foot and another of a woman applying eye make-up. Although it was originally dedicated to Adinath, an image of Parsvanath was substituted about a century ago and the temple takes its name from this newer image.

Adinatha Adjacent to the Parsvanath Temple, the smaller Adinatha has been partially restored over the centuries. It has fine carvings on its three bands of sculptures and, like the Parsvanath, is very similar to the Hindu temples of Khajuraho. Only the image in the inner sanctum indicates that it is Jain rather than Hindu.

Santinatha This temple is a relatively modern one built about a century ago, but it contains many components from older temples around Khajuraho and a fine collection of Jain sculpture. The Jain compound also contains a small museum.

Ghantai Walking back from the eastern Jain temple group towards Khajuraho village, you come to this small, ruined Jain temple. Only its pillared shell remains, but it is interesting for the delicate columns with their bell and chain decoration and for the figure of a Jain goddess astride a Garuda which marks the entrance.

Javari Walk through the village, a typical

small Indian settlement, to this temple. Dating from around 1075 to 1100 AD, it is dedicated to Vishnu, and is a particularly fine example of Khajuraho architecture on a small scale. The exterior has more of Khajuraho's delightful women.

Vamana About 200 metres north, this temple is dedicated to Vamana, the dwarf incarnation of Vishnu. Slightly older than the Javari Temple, the Vamana Temple stands out in a field all by itself. It's notable for the relatively simple design of its *shikara*. The bands of sculpture around the temples are, as usual, very fine with numerous 'celestial maidens' adopting interesting poses.

Brahma Turning back towards the modern village, you pass this granite and sandstone temple, one of the oldest at Khajuraho. It was actually dedicated to Vishnu and the definition of it as a Brahma temple is incorrect. Taking the road directly from the modern village to the Jain enclosure, you pass a temple to Hanuman with a large image of the monkey god.

Southern Group

There are only two temples in the southern group, one of which is several km south of the river.

Duladeo A dirt track runs to this isolated temple, about a km south of the Jain enclosure. This is the latest temple at Khajuraho, and experts say that at this time the skill of Khajuraho's temple builders had passed its peak and that the sculptures are more 'wooden' and 'stereotyped' than on the earlier temples. Nevertheless, it's a fine and graceful temple with figures of women in a variety of pin-up poses and a number of *mithuna*.

Chaturbhuja South of the river, about three km from the village and a healthy hike down a dirt road, this ruined temple has a fine three-metre-high image of Vishnu.

Tours

There are a number of walking tours around the western group of temples. Sometimes the Archaeological Survey of India in Khajuraho provides cheap tours by competent guides. Licensed private guides cost Rs 25 for a half day.

Places to Stay – bottom end

The *Rahil (Janata Hotel)* (tel 62) run by the state government is fairly close to the Khajuraho Hotel. Singles/doubles are Rs 50/70, with hot showers. In the dormitory beds are Rs 12 each. A less-than-enthusiastic traveller complained that it is 'not new, clean or comfortable', and that not only did she get 'apathetic (barely existent) service', but her 'toothpaste was eaten by rats'!

The *Tourist Bungalow* (tel 64) has rooms at Rs 50/75 or four-bed rooms at Rs 100; air-con doubles are Rs 140. The Rahil and the Tourist Bungalow both have parking places so they're good for people with vehicles. Also run by the state tourist department, the *Tourist Village* (tel 62) has rooms at Rs 50/75.

There is a cluster of cheap hotels, some of them reasonable, with rooms from around Rs 20 or Rs 25. Try the *New Bharat Lodge* (tel 82), popular with travellers, or the *Jain Lodge* (tel 52). Doubles in those two cost Rs 40 to Rs 50. Others include the *Gupta Lodge* and the *Laxmi Lodge*, which has recently been repainted; every room has the warning 'Check Out Time 12 Noon'.

Hotel Sunset View (tel 77) has doubles with bath for just Rs 40 in the low season and is very clean and modern. Rooms face in to a courtyard in this pleasant hotel, but don't buy jewellery from its crafts shop! It's on the main road from the airport, just before the town.

Places to Stay – top end

The state tourist department's *Hotel Payal* (tel 76) has spacious rooms at Rs 100/120 or with air-con at Rs 175/225. It's clean, well kept and everything seems to work. The hotel's restaurant is very good too.

Hotel Chandela (tel 54) is south of the modern village, towards the airport. It's the number-one hotel at Khajuraho and its 102 rooms are all air-con, costing Rs 545/715 for singles/doubles. You can use the Chandela's swimming pool, if you are not a guest there, for Rs 20.

Hotel Khajuraho Ashok (tel 24, 42), a short walk north of the modern village, is somewhat cheaper at Rs 170/225 or Rs 355/440 with air-con. Both have restaurants; but at the Khajuraho Ashok 'the staff hang around like vultures waiting for tips' and this is yet another Ashok hotel getting a decisive thumbs-down from visitors. The relatively new *Jass Oberoi* (tel 65, 85-7), on By Pass Rd, has rooms at Rs 450/650 plus a swimming pool, air con and other mod cons.

Places to Eat

Opposite the entrance to the western enclosure, *Raja's Café* is run by a Swiss woman. It's a popular gathering spot under the large shady tree in the restaurant's courtyard. They also operate a free book-swap system. The *New Bharat Lodge* does good thalis and other food plus really good tea – if you're heartily sick of the usual over-milky, over-sweet tea in India. *Gupta Restaurant* has reasonable food.

Getting There

Getting to Khajuraho can be a major pain. It is really on the way from nowhere to nowhere, and is not near any railway station. Although many travellers slot in between Varanasi and Agra, it involves a lot of travelling to cover not particularly great distances. If you can afford to fly, then do; you'll save a lot of time.

Air Indian Airlines have a daily flight which operates Delhi-Agra-Khajuraho-Varanasi-Kathmandu, then returns by the same route to Delhi. It's probably the most popular tourist flight in India and

can often be booked solid for days by tour groups. Delhi-Khajuraho costs Rs 468, Agra-Khajuraho Rs 331 and Varanasi-Khajuraho Rs 331.

Rail & Bus From the west there are bus services from Agra (391 km, 12 hours), Gwalior (280 km) and Jhansi (175 km). Jhansi is the nearest approach to Khajuraho on the main Delhi-Bombay rail line, and there are half a dozen buses a day on the Jhansi-Khajuraho route. This is the most popular route to Khajuraho by public bus. It's a five or six-hour trip costing Rs 20. 'All the hours were hell', commented one unhappy bus traveller!

There is no direct route to Varanasi from Khajuraho. Satna, 120 km from Khajuraho, is the nearest railhead for visitors from Varanasi, Calcutta or Bombay. It's on the Bombay-Allahabad line. From Varanasi it takes six to nine hours to Satna on the faster express services. The 322-km trip costs Rs 33 in 2nd class, Rs 127 in 1st.

Once there, it's about two km to the local bus station. On a straight through bus it takes about four hours to Khajuraho at a fare of Rs 14. So an early-morning start from Varanasi should get you to Khajuraho by evening. The four-times-weekly Ganga-Kaveri Express departs Varanasi at 7 am and arrives Satna at 1.15 pm. Buses depart Satna for Khajuraho at 3.30 pm and also at 6.45 am.

In Satna the *Park Hotel* (tel 2646) has clean rooms from Rs 30 and is 1½ km from the railway station. Directly opposite the stand is the *India Hotel*, which is not so clean but rather cheaper – maybe OK for one night. *Hotel Natraj* is also marginally cheaper. The state tourist department's *Tourist Motel* (tel 2941) has rooms at Rs 75/100 or with air-con at Rs 175/225; their *Tourist Bungalow* has rooms at Rs 40. Or you can sleep in the 1st-class waiting room.

There are two direct night buses from Khajuraho to Bhopal, good for moving on to Sanchi. It's an 11-hour trip for Rs 44.

Another alternative from Khajuraho to Varanasi is to take a bus to Mahoba (hourly, four hours, Rs 10) and a train from there, but it's a rather slow passenger train. Harpalpur is 99 km from Khajuraho, closer than Satna. Buses make the four-hour trip twice daily for Rs 12. There are also buses from Khajuraho to Jabalpur (10 hours) and Indore (16 hours).

Getting Around

The airport bus into town costs Rs 8 but a taxi only costs Rs 20. The western temples are all for viewing on foot. To the eastern or southern group, take a rickshaw. You can go out to the Jain enclosure and walk back from there, or for Rs 4 or Rs 5 make a round trip to Duladeo. All the rickshaw-wallahs have 'fixed rates' to any temple or group of temples you care to name, but it's for show. The rates are round trip for two people. Bicycles can be hired in Khajuraho for Rs 5 a day.

AROUND KHAJURAHO

'Masochists', suggested one writer, 'might enjoy the four-hour, 63-km bus trip from Khajuraho to Mahoba where there is an under-used 12-room *Tourist Bungalow* with singles at Rs 25. A trip out to the ruined Surya temple five km from Mahoba is a worthwhile excursion'. Another suggestion was a jeep trip to 'an amazing, undiscovered fort called Kalinjer. On the way you cross the lovely Ken River, itself worth a visit and a picnic. It is about half an hour by bus from Khajuraho, and there is even a *Dak Bungalow* nearby'. Another traveller recommended a trip (23 km, hard going on a bicycle) to a river with a huge waterfall and good swimming – perhaps it's the same place.

The people who run the Raja Café in Khajuraho are opening a *Tree Top Restaurant*, complete with accommodation, about 45 km from Khajuraho. En route you can visit the Panna Safari Park, 30 km from Khajuraho and, a little further on, the famous Panna diamond mines, Pandwa Falls and Rajgarh Palace.

JABALPUR (population 550,000)

Almost due south of Khajuraho and due east of Bhopal, the large town of Jabalpur, the second largest town in the state, is principally famous today for the gorge of the Narmada River known as the Marble Rocks. A century ago Jabalpur was the centre for the long British effort to suppress the practice of 'Thuggee'. The practitioners of this strange activity were known as 'Thugs', from which the word comes. They engaged in ritual murders, strangling their victims with a silken cord, in order to please the goddess Kali.

In 1829 Colonel Sleeman was appointed to wipe out this bizarre activity and the 'School of Industry', where at one time suspected Thugs were interned, can still be seen in Jabalpur. Today it is used as a boys' reform school. It took the best part of 50 years to totally wipe out the Thugs. Between Satna and Jabalpur the town of Sleemanabad is named after him. There's even a temple with an eternal flame burning to his memory. Jabalpur also has the Rani Durgavati Museum.

Information

At the station there is a Tourist Office (tel 2211).

Marble Rocks

Known locally as Bhera Ghat, the marble rocks are white limestone cliffs rising 30 metres above the water of the Narmada River. The gleaming rocks have a magical effect, especially by moonlight. If you wait for a group to form it will cost just a few rupees to boat up the gorge. The water falls down the Dhuandhar or 'smoke cascade' at the top of the gorge, and on the trip down the gorge you can see the Hathi-ka-paon or 'elephant's foot', a group of curiously shaped rocks, the ledge known as 'monkey's leap' and an inscription cut by Madho Rao Peshwa.

It's about 24 km to the marble rocks. You can take a bus or, if you're feeling fit, cycle out and back in a day. The road is fairly flat, and there are plenty of stalls to stop at along the way. You can buy cheap marble carvings there.

Madan Mahal & Chausath Yogini Temple

This ancient Gond fortress is on the route to the marble rocks, perched on top of a huge boulder. The Gonds, who worshipped snakes, lived in this region even before the Aryans arrived, and maintained their independence right up until the arrival of Akbar.

Above the lower end of the gorge, a flight of over 100 stone steps leads to the Chausath Yogini or Madanpur Temple. The circular temple has damaged images of the 64 yoginis, or attendants of the goddess Kali.

Places to Stay

The *Raja Gokuldass Dharamsala*, near the railway station, is very good and dirt cheap. *Rajhans Hotel* at Naudera Bridge has rooms from Rs 20. Also at Naudera Bridge, the *Sawhney Hotel* is marginally more expensive. There are numerous other hotels around the station area.

At the top end of the scale there's *Jackson's Hotel* (tel 21320) in Civil Lines. Rooms are Rs 45/60; with air-con they are Rs 100/125. The Tourist Department's *Tourist Motel* (tel 38) has just four rooms at Rs 50/75. It used to be known as the Marble Rocks Inn and actually overlooks the gorge. At Wright Town the *Ashok Hotel* (tel 22267) has rooms for Rs 70/90; doubles with air-con are Rs 175.

Getting There

There are twice-daily flights between Jabalpur and Bhopal (Rs 283) and daily to Raipur (Rs 283).

There are buses to Jabalpur from Allahabad, Khajuraho, Varanasi, Bhopal and other main centres. Jabalpur is on the Bombay-Allahabad-Calcutta railway line. It's 1183 km from Calcutta, 369 km from Allahabad and 990 km from Bombay.

OTHER PLACES – East & South-East
Pachmarhi

At an altitude of 1100 metres, this is Madhya Pradesh's hill station. It's near Itarsi on the Bombay-Jabalpur-Allahabad railway line. There are fine views out over the surrounding red sandstone hills and some interesting walks.

Places to Stay The Tourist Department has a variety of accommodation at Pachmarhi. The *Satpura Retreat* (tel 97) on Mahadeo Rd has rooms at Rs 90/110, while in the *Holiday Homes* (tel 99) near the bus stand there are rooms from Rs 25. The more expensive Holiday Homes have cooking facilities. There are various other state government bungalows and huts.

Bandhavgarh National Park

In the Vindhyan Mountain Range in central Madhya Pradesh, there is a wide variety of wildlife in this national park although you'd have to be lucky to see a tiger. If you want to explore by elephant it costs Rs 20 an hour – for the whole elephant. Umaria, on the Katni-Bilaspur rail line, is the nearest railhead. It's also accessible from Satna on the Bombay-Allahabad rail line.

Places to Stay *White Tiger Forest Lodge* in the park has rooms at Rs 50/75. The manager is friendly and the food good although not dirt cheap. Accommodation can be booked in advance in Bhopal or Jabalpur.

Mandla & Ramnagar

On the route to Nagpur in Maharashtra, 100 km south of Jabalpur, is the fort of Mandla, in a loop of the Narmada River so that the river protects it on three sides and a ditch on the fourth. Built in the late 1600s, the fort is now subsiding into the jungle although some of the towers still stand. About 15 km away is Ramnagar with a ruined three-storey palace overlooking the Narmada. The palace, and then the fort, were both built by Gond kings, retreating south before the advance of Moghul power. Near Mandla is a stretch of the Narmada where many temples dot the riverbank.

Kanha National Park

There are rest houses and watchtowers in this park, 77 km from Mandla and 173 km from Jabalpur.

Places to Stay There is a variety of accommodation possibilities, including the *Kisli Youth Hostel* with dorm beds at Rs 10; *Forest Bungalows, Forest Lodges* and *Tourist Huts* at Rs 25; and *Log Huts* with rooms at Rs 75/100.

Bilaspur & Raipur

There are larger towns in the east of the state on the Bombay-Calcutta railway line. Ratanpur, 25 km north of Bilaspur, was the capital of the old kingdom of Chattisgarh, the 'kingdom of 36 forts'.

Places to Stay Raipur has a state government *Tourist Motel* (tel 28063) on Durg Rd with rooms at Rs 50/75.

OTHER PLACES – North-West
Indore/Ujjain-Chittorgarh

The railway line passes through Ratlam, capital of a former princely state whose ruler died in one of those tragically heroic Rajput battles against the might of the Moghuls. At Mandsaur, north of Ratlam, a number of interesting archaeological finds were made in a field three km from the town. Some others are displayed in the museum at Indore. Two 14-metre-high sandstone pillars are on the site, and an inscription commemorates the victory of a Malwa king over the Huns in 528 AD. In the fort are some fine pieces from the Gupta period.

Tony's Notebook

Newspapers

Indian newspapers are generally very bland. They simply report events in a very straightforward manner with little comment or interpretation. But sometimes this deadpan style makes the news seem all the more remarkable:

'Student killed in exam clash', reported the paper. Armed police had been brought in to prevent cheating, students 'demanding the right to cheat' had started to hurl stones, the police opened fire and a student had died. Wait a minute, you ask yourself – armed police to prevent cheating? Demanding the right to cheat? Well, in some states cheating at school exams has become so common that students whose parents don't have the clout or the bribe money to get advance previews of the exams have demanded the right to cheat by bringing in crib sheets, books or whatever to the exams.

Self-immolation is a popular way of death in India. Many people cook with kerosene stoves, so soaking yourself in kerosene and lighting the match is the Indian housewife's equivalent of putting your head in the gas oven. Of course it's an equally popular way of getting rid of her if the dowry hasn't come up to expectation. It's also a popular form of protest, but the newspaper report of six students who tried to self-immolate themselves as a protest against the college authorities' refusal to postpone their exams for 10 days was remarkable. Would six young men really decide to die in such a painful manner simply because the exams were 10 days earlier than they wanted?

Orissa

Population: 24 million
Area: 155,842 square km
Capital: Bhubaneswar
Main language: Oriya

The State of Orissa lies along the eastern seaboard of India, south of Bengal. Its main attractions are the temple towns of Puri and Bhubaneswar and the great Sun Temple at Konarak. These three sites make a convenient and compact little triangle, and Bhubaneswar is on the main Calcutta-Madras railway route. The state is predominantly rural, with fertile green plains along the coast rising up to the hills of the Eastern Ghats.

Orissa's hazy past comes into focus with the reign of Kalinga. In 260 BC he was defeated by Ashoka, the great Indian emperor, but the bloody battle left such a bitter taste with Ashoka that he converted to Buddhism and spread that gentle religion far and wide. Buddhism soon declined in Orissa, however, and Jainism held sway until Buddhism reasserted itself in the 2nd century AD. By the 7th century AD Hinduism had, in turn, supplanted Buddhism and Orissa's golden age was in full swing.

Under the Kesari and Ganga kings the Orissan culture flourished and countless temples from that classical period still stand today. The Orissans managed to defy the Muslim rulers in Delhi until the region finally fell to the Moghuls during the 16th century. Many of Bhubaneswar's temples were destroyed at that time. Today Orissa is tapping the hydroelectric potential of its many rivers, and fledgling industries are being started, but the state is still a region of green fields and small villages.

Temple Architecture

Orissan temples, whether it is the mighty Lingaraj in Bhubaneswar, the Jagannath

in Puri, the Sun Temple at Konarak, or the many smaller temples, all follow a similar pattern. Basically there are two structures – the *jagamohan* or entrance porch, and the *duel* where the image of the temple deity is kept and above which the temple tower rises. The design is complicated in larger temples by the addition of one or more entrance halls in front of the jagamohan. These are the *bhoga-mandapa* or 'hall of offering' and the *nata-mandir* or 'dancing hall'.

Lingaraja Temple

The whole structure may be enclosed by an outer wall and within the enclosure there may be smaller subsidiary temples and shrines. The most notable aspects of the temple design are the soaring tower and the intricate carvings that cover every surface. These may be figures of gods, men and women, plants and trees, flowers, animals and every other aspect of everyday life, but to many visitors it is the erotic carvings which create the greatest interest. They reach their artistic and explicit peak at Konarak, where the close-up detail is every bit as interesting as the temple's sheer size.

Things to Buy

Orissan handicrafts include the appliqué work of Pipli and the filigree jewellery of Cuttack. In Sambalpur, tie-dye fabrics are produced and there is a variety of Orissan handloomed fabrics. At Puri you can buy strange little carved wooden replicas of Lord Jagannath and his brother and sister. At Balasore lacquered children's toys are manufactured.

Tribal People

Orissa has no less than 62 distinct tribal groups of aboriginal people who date from prior to the Aryan invasion of India. They live mainly in the hilly area of central Orissa. Amongst the better-known tribes are the Kondhs, who still practise colourful ceremonies, although animal sacrifices have now been substituted for the human ones which the British took so much trouble to stop – particularly around Russelkonda (Bhanjanagar).

The Bondas, known as the 'naked people', are renowned for their wild ways and for the dormitories where young men and women are encouraged to meet for night-time fun and frolics. Other major tribes are the Juangs, the Santals, the Parajas, the colourful and primitive Godabas, and the Koyas.

BHUBANESWAR (population 125,000)

The capital of Orissa is known as the temple town due to its many temples in the extravagant Orissan architectural style. At one time the Bindusagar tank had over 7000 temples around it. Today there are about 500, but most of these are

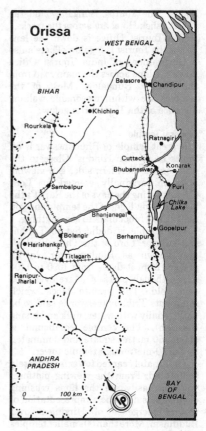

decayed fragments. Perhaps a dozen are of real interest, including the great Lingaraj Temple, one of the most important temples in India. The Puri temples are in a variety of Orissan styles and date from the 8th to the 13th century AD.

Orientation & Information

Bhubaneswar is a sprawling town divided into old and new parts – the railway line forms the approximate dividing line. The bus stop and the Indian Airlines office are both in the new town, as are most of the hotels. The Tourist Bungalow and the ITDC Ashok Hotel are across the tracks.

The Tourist Office is down the lane beside the Tourist Bungalow. There's also a Government of India Tourist Office down the lane across the main road from the Tourist Bungalow. Most of the temples are within reasonable walking distance of the Tourist Bungalow.

Lingaraj Temple

The great temple of Bhubaneswar is off limits to all non-Hindus. Close to the wall, on the northern side, is a viewing platform, originally erected for Lord Curzon during the days of the Raj. It's the best view you'll get of the temple and you really need binoculars to see anything.

The temple is dedicated to Tribhuvaneswar or 'Lord of the Three Worlds', also known as Bhubaneswar. In its present form it dates from 1090 to 1104 AD, although parts of it are over 1400 years old. The granite block which represents Tribhuvaneswar is said to be bathed daily with water, milk and bhang (hashish). The temple compound is about 150 metres square and dominated by the 40-metre-high temple tower.

The ornately carved tower is intricately sculptured. From the viewing platform you can easily see the lions crushing elephants, said to be a representation of the re-emergence of Hinduism over Buddhism. More than 50 smaller temples and shrines crowd the enclosure. In the north-east corner a smaller temple to Parvati is of particular interest.

Bindusagar

The 'Ocean Drop' tank just north of the great temple is said to contain water from every holy stream, pool and tank in India. Consequently, when it comes to washing away sin this is the tank which washes whitest. There are a number of temples and shrines scattered around the tank, several of them with towers in imitation of the ones at the Lingaraj Temple. In the centre of the tank is a water pavilion where, once a year, the Lingaraj Temple's deity is brought to be ritually bathed.

Siddharanya

Close to the main Bhubaneswar-Puri road, on the same side as the Lingaraj Temple, the 'Grove of the Perfect Beings' is a cluster of about 20 smaller temples, including some of the most important in Bhubaneswar. Right by the road the small, 11-metre-high Mukteswar Temple is finely detailed with some excellent carving, but unfortunately much of it is defaced. The dwarves are particularly nice. The Mukteswar features an arched *torana*, a gateway showing clear Buddhist influence.

Also by the road, across the path from the Mukteswar, the Kedareswar is one of the older temples at Bhubaneswar and has a small tank. Close to the Mukteswar is Siddeswar Temple, an interesting old temple with a fine standing Ganesh figure. If you follow the path from these temples towards the Lingaraj you soon come to the Prashurameswar on your right. It's the best preserved of the early (7th century AD) temples and has interesting bas-reliefs of elephant and horse processions. All its fine carvings are vigorous and alive.

If you work up a thirst while temple hunting, the shop beside the cinema near the junction has cold, cheap soft drinks.

Raj Rani

Across the road and about 100 metres to the right, the Raj Rani stands alone in a green field. It's one of the latest of the Bhubaneswar temples and particularly finely sited. Statues of nymphs, embracing couples, elephants and lions fill the niches and decorate the pillars.

Brahmeswar

About a km east of the main road, the Brahmeswar Temple stands in a courtyard flanked by four smaller structures. It's notable for its very finely detailed sculptures with erotic and sometimes amusing

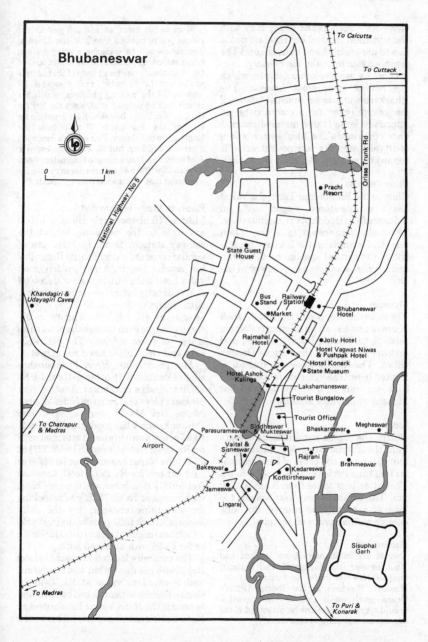

Bhubaneswar

To Calcutta

To Cuttack

0   1km

National Highway No 5

Orissa Trunk Rd

Prachi Resort

State Guest House

Khandagiri & Udayagiri Caves

Bus Stand

Railway Station

Market

Bhubaneswar Hotel

Rajmahal Hotel

Jolly Hotel

Hotel Vagwat Niwas & Pushpak Hotel

Hotel Konark

State Museum

Hotel Ashok Kalinga

Lakshamaneswar

Tourist Bungalow

Tourist Office

Parasurameswar

Siddheswar & Mukteswar

Bhaskareswar

Megheswar

To Chatrapur & Madras

Airport

Vaital & Sisneswar

Rajrani

Brahmeswar

Bakeswar

Kedareswar

Kotitirtheswar

Jameswar

Lingaraj

Sisuphal Garh

To Madras

To Puri & Konarak

elements – such as the young lady with the surprised look on her face, no doubt due to her lover's hand in her pants! The temple dates from the 9th century.

Close by are two other temples which are not of such great interest. The Bhaskareswar has an unusual 'stepped' design in order to accommodate an unusually large (three-metre) lingam it once contained. The Megheswar is in a courtyard and its shrine entrance is topped by a figure. Beside it is a tank.

Other Temples

Close to the Bindusagar Tank, the Vaital has a double-storey 'wagon roof', an influence from Buddhist cave architecture. The Lakshamaneswar is a very plain temple. Dating from the 7th century, it is one of the earliest specimens of Orissan architecture and acts as a gateway to the city.

Museum

The museum is opposite the Hotel Ashok Kalinga and has an interesting collection relating to Orissan history, culture and architecture and to the various Orissan tribes. The Tribal Research Bureau is located here. The museum is open 10 am to 1 pm and 2 to 4 pm daily except Mondays and entry is Rs 0.25.

Tours

During the season various tours operate from the Tourist Bungalow, including a tour of temples and caves of Bhubaneswar for Rs 24 or a Puri-Konarak tour for Rs 33. The latter tour takes from 9 am to 6.30 pm. The Bhubaneswar tour 'spends too long at a zoo/nature reserve, not long enough at the caves and temples'.

Discrimination

Two of the main attractions in Puri and Bhubaneswar (the Jagannath and Lingaraj temples) are 'off limits' to foreigners (non-Hindus). Nowhere in the Tourist Office's Orissa brochures is this ban mentioned – should tourist attractions be promoted if the tourists are not allowed into them?

More to the point, should you pay for the places you're banned from? At the Lingaraj Temple there'll be someone waiting for you near the viewing platform to ask for not one but two donations – one for upkeep of that temple you're not fit to enter, and a second for 'upkeep' of the viewing platform, which has clearly had no upkeep at all since the British built it. You'll also be asked for a donation for viewing the Jagannath Temple from the Raghunandan Library. Fair enough, since it's a private building, but Rs 1 is quite enough. Just because all the names in the visitors' book have Rs 25 written after them doesn't mean for a moment that that's what they've 'donated'!

Places to Stay – bottom end

Most of Bhubaneswar's cheaper hotels are close to the museum, behind the railway station. Some of them are of similar standard to the Tourist Bungalow but much cheaper. A particularly good value hotel is the *Bhubaneswar Hotel* (tel 51977) directly behind the railway station, with singles/doubles at Rs 35/55 or with air-con at Rs 100/125. There's a 5% service charge even though the hotel rules state 'No room service'. The big, well-kept and clean place has a restaurant.

Also good value, *Hotel Pushpak* has singles/doubles with attached bath for Rs 35/50 and has a restaurant. Another very pleasant place to stay is the *Hotel Vagwat Niwas* (tel 54481), very close to the Pushpak, which has good, clean singles at Rs 25 or rooms with fan and attached bath for Rs 30/45. *Hotel Gajapati* (tel 52371) at 77 Budha Nagar has rooms at Rs 35/40 or with air-con for Rs 120. *Hotel Anarkali* (tel 54031) is another station-area hotel with rooms at Rs 60/75. If you're looking for something cheaper, try the *Jolly Lodge*, Cuttack Rd, opposite the Pushpak, which has small but clean rooms for Rs 20, or for Rs 25 with attached bath.

The centrally located *Rajmahal Hotel* (tel 52448) has its own bar and restaurant and is excellent value at Rs 30/40 for singles/doubles with attached bath. Round behind it the *Hotel Venus* has doubles at Rs 50 but it's nothing special. There are a lot of other small cheap lodges along the main road between the Rajmahal and the expensive Hotel Konark. They include the *Gajapali Hotel, Samita Lodge* and *Ratna Lodge*.

The Government of Orissa has an *Inspection Bungalow* on Old Station Bazaar, Satyanagar. The railway station has *Retiring Rooms* (tel 52233), as does the bus station. At the railway station, per-person cost is Rs 7 in the dorm, Rs 15 in a room or Rs 30 with air-con. Out at the Udayagiri-Khandagiri hills there's a very run-down building claiming to be the *Khandagiri Youth Hostel*.

Places to Stay – top end
Prices in the state government-run Tourist Bungalows have increased so dramatically that they are now top-end rather than middle or bottom-end places. They are all similarly priced throughout Orissa and offer very similar standards. They're well kept, all rooms have attached bathrooms, and there's a reasonably priced restaurant. In Bhubaneswar the still popular *Panthnivas Tourist Bungalow* (tel 54515) is conveniently near the many temples. Rooms with attached bath are Rs 100 or Rs 150 with air-con. There are also a couple of four-bed rooms which can be used as dormitories at a very pricey Rs 30 per bed.

Nearby is the *Hotel Ashok Kalinga* (tel 53318), opposite the museum. It's modern, centrally air-conditioned, has a good restaurant and bar, and has recently been considerably expanded and had a swimming pool added. Singles/doubles cost Rs 350/425 in the new block. There are some cheaper non-air-con rooms at Rs 140/190. Continue across the railway line towards the centre of town, where *Hotel Konark* (tel 53330, 54330-1) is centrally air-conditioned. All rooms have attached bath, and there's a restaurant, bar, swimming pool and bookshop. Singles cost Rs 375 to Rs 415, doubles Rs 475 to Rs 515.

Hotel Prachi Bhubaneswar (tel 52521)

at 6 Janpath is some distance from the centre but good value at Rs 100/150 or Rs 225/325 for rooms with air-con. It also has a swimming pool. *Hotel Swosti* (tel 54179) at 103 Janpath has rooms at Rs 250/325, all with air-con. Some distance out of town at Nayapalli, the new *Oberoi Bhubaneswar* (tel 54216) has rooms at Rs 400.

Places to Eat
The *Tourist Bungalow* has a reasonably priced, if monotonous, dining hall. Amongst the eating places in town you could try the *South Indian Hotel*, behind the Rajmahal Hotel and under the Venus Lodge, for a thali. The restaurant at the *Hotel Pushpak* offers reasonable and inexpensive food but the service is agonisingly slow.

The *Ashok Kalinga* is an excellent place for an escape to air-con comfort and good food – say Rs 60 to Rs 70 per person for a complete meal. They have a nice bar with free peanuts or other snacks.

Getting There
Air There are daily flights Delhi-Varanasi-Raipur-Bhubaneswar (and reverse) and Calcutta-Bhubaneswar (and reverse). Four times a week the Calcutta flight continues to Hyderabad. Fares include Calcutta Rs 365, Delhi Rs 1119, Hyderabad Rs 830 and Varanasi Rs 602.

Rail Bhubaneswar is 437 km from Calcutta and 1226 km from Madras. Since it is on the main Calcutta-Madras railway line there are plenty of trains to Bhubaneswar as well as the trains terminating at Puri. The crack Coromandel Express departs Calcutta at 4 pm and arrives in Bhubaneswar just over seven hours later. Other trains are rather slower; the Madras Mail leaves at 8 pm and takes eight hours. Other trains can take as long as 10 hours. Fares are Rs 42 in 2nd class, Rs 168 in 1st.

From Madras the Coromandel Express takes about 20 hours, the Howrah Mail about 24 hours and other trains 30 or more hours. Fares from Madras are Rs 88 in 2nd class, Rs 362 in 1st. Trains terminating in Puri take 1½ hours to two hours longer from Calcutta or Madras.

There are one or two trains a day from Delhi to Bhubaneswar and Puri and they take 34 to 44 hours. Delhi-Bhubaneswar is 2074 km and the fares are Rs 129 in 2nd class, Rs 537 in 1st.

Bus There are frequent private buses from Bhubaneswar to Puri. The trip takes 1½ to two hours and costs Rs 6. It's a similar amount of time and Rs 6.40 to Konarak. See Konarak for Puri-Konarak information. If it is not possible to get a direct bus to Konarak, any Puri bus will go through Pipli, where the Konarak road branches off.

Getting Around
Airport The airport is very close to the town. A taxi costs Rs 25 but you could also get a rickshaw for Rs 10 – rather uphill from the town, though.

Local Transport From the Tourist Bungalow a rickshaw to town or the Lingaraj Temple would be Rs 2 to Rs 3. If you plan on staying at one of the hotels along Cuttack Rd, at the back of the station, it isn't worth getting a rickshaw all the way round there – simply cross the railway tracks at the southern end of the station and walk through. It's much quicker.

AROUND BHUBANESWAR
There are two interesting sites close to Bhubaneswar, both dating from the Buddhist period.

Udayagiri & Khandagiri Caves
About five km out of Bhubaneswar, these two hills flanking the road on each side are riddled with caves. On the right of the road, Udayagiri or Sunrise Hill has the most interesting caves, scattered at various levels up the hill. All are numbered. At the base of the hill, round to the right,

is the two-storey Rani ka Naur or Queen's Palace Cave (1). Both levels have eight entrances and the cave is extensively carved.

Return to the road via the Chota Hathi Gumpha (3), with its carvings of elephants coming out from behind a tree. The Jaya Vijaya Cave (5) is again double-storeyed and a Bo tree is carved in the central compartment. Back at the entrance, ascend the hill to cave 9, the Swargapuri; and 14, the Hathi Gumpha or 'Elephant Cave'. The latter is plain but an inscription relates in 117 lines the exploits of its builder, King Kharaveli of Kalinga, who ruled from 168 to 153 BC.

Circle round the hill to the right, to the Ganesh Gumpha (10), which is almost directly above the Rani ka Naur. The carvings here tell the same tale as in the lower-level cave but are better drawn. The cave is only single-storey. Retrace your steps to cave 14, then on to the Pavana Gumpha 'Cave of Purification' and the small Sarpa Gumpha or 'Serpent Cave', the tiny door to which is surmounted by a three-headed cobra.

Only 15 or so metres from this is the Bagh Gumpha (12) or Tiger Cave, entered through the mouth of the beast. The hill is topped by the foundations of some long-gone building. The oldest of these various caves date back to the 2nd century BC. Some are of Jain origin.

Across the road, Kandagiri Hill is not so interesting, apart from the fine view back over Bhubaneswar from its summit. You can see the airport, the tower of the Lingaraj Temple rising behind it, and further away the Dhauli Stupa. The steep path divides about a third of the way up the hill. The right path goes to the Ananta Cave (3) with carved figures of athletes, women, elephants and geese carrying flowers. The right path leads to a series of Jain temples. At the top of the hill is an 18th-century Jain temple.

Getting There Only a few buses go specifically to the caves, but there are

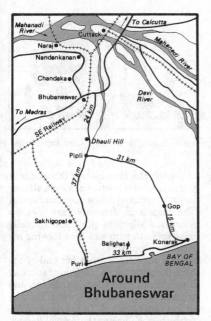

Around Bhubaneswar

plenty going by the nearby road junction. It's about a rupee from town, or by rickshaw you can get there for about Rs 10.

Dhauli Edicts

About eight km south of Bhubaneswar, to the right of the Puri road, King Ashoka carved his famous edicts into a rock five metres by three metres. The great Buddhist emperor related the horrors he experienced in the Kalinga wars, which he won, and his subsequent conversion to Buddhism. These 13 inscriptions are still remarkably clear after over 2000 years. The rock is at the base of the small rocky hill. The adjacent larger hillock is topped by a shiny new Peace Pagoda. You can get to the place where you turn off the main road on any Puri or Konarak bus for Rs 1.

Other

The only partly excavated ruins at Sisupal Garh are thought to be the remains of an Ashokan city. At Nandankanan, 30 km from Bhubaneswar, there is a garden divided into a wildlife sanctuary, botanical garden and lake. You can rent boats on the lake.

PURI (population 75,000)

On the coast, 61 km from Bhubaneswar, Puri is one of the four holiest cities in India. The city revolves around the great Jagannath Temple and its famous Rath Yatra or Car Festival. It is thought that Puri was the hiding place for the Buddha tooth of Kandy before it was spirited away to Sri Lanka. There are similarities between the Rath Yatra and the annual Kandy procession.

Orientation & Information

There is only one wide road in Puri, the Baradand or Grand Road which runs from Jagannath Temple to the Gundicha Mandir. Buses stop along this road. Most of the hotels are along the seafront but there are two distinct beach areas – Indians to the west, travellers to the east. The Tourist Office is on Station Rd and there's a counter (open longer hours) at the station.

Jagannath Temple

The temple of Jagannath, 'Lord of the Universe', is not open to non-Hindus, but amongst Hindus its considerable popularity is partially due to the lack of caste distinctions – all are welcome before Jagannath. Non-believers can look down into the temple from the roof of the Raghunandan Library, opposite the main entrance to the temple. You'll be asked for a donation.

The temple enclosure is nearly square, measuring almost 200 metres on each side. The walls of the enclosure are six metres high. Inside, a second wall encloses the actual temple. The conical tower of the temple is 58 metres high and is topped by the flag and wheel of Vishnu. It is visible from far out of Puri. The temple was built in its present form in 1198. In front of the main entrance is a beautiful pillar, topped by an image of the Garuda, which originally stood in front of the temple at Konarak. The main entrance is known as the Lion Gate from the two stone lions guarding the entrance.

In the central Jagmohan, pilgrims to the temple can see the images of Lord Jagannath, his brother Balbhadra and sister Subhadra. Although non-believers are not, of course, able to see them, the many shop stalls along the road outside the temple all sell small wooden replicas. The curious images are carved from tree trunks, in a child-like caricature of a human face. The brothers have arms but the smaller Subhadra does not. All three are garlanded and dressed for ceremonies and the various seasons. The temple employs 6000 men to perform the temple functions and the complicated rituals involved in caring for the gods. It has been estimated that in all, 20,000 people are dependent on Jagannath, and the god's immediate attendants are divided into 36 orders and 97 classes!

Rath Yatra or Car Festival
One of India's greatest annual events takes place in Puri each June or July when the fantastic festival of the cars sets forth from the Jagannath Temple. It commemorates the journey of Krishna from Gokul to Mathura. The images of Jagannath, his brother and his sister are brought out from the temple and dragged in huge 'cars', known as *raths*, down the wide Baradand to the Gundicha Mandir or 'Garden House' over a km away.

The main car of Jagannath stands 14 metres high, over 10 metres square and rides on 16 wheels, each over two metres in diameter. It is from these colossal cars that our word 'juggernaut' is derived and, in centuries past, devotees were known to have thrown themselves beneath the wheels of the juggernaut in order to die in the god's sight. To haul the cars takes over 4000 professional car-pullers, all employees

Balabhadra, Subhadra & Lord Jagannath

of the temple. Hundreds of thousands of pilgrims (and tourists) flock from all over India to witness this stupendous scene. The huge and unwieldy cars take an enormous effort to pull, are virtually impossible to turn and once moving are nearly unstoppable.

Once they reach the other end of the road the gods take a week-long summer break, then are reloaded onto the cars and trucked back to the Jagannath Temple, in a virtual repeat of the previous week's procession. Following the festival the cars are broken up and used to make religious relics. New cars are constructed each year. At intervals of eight, 11 or 19 years or combinations of those numbers, depending on various astrological occurrences, the gods themselves are also disposed of and new images made. In the last century and a half there have been new images in 1863, 1893, 1931, 1950, 1969 and 1977.

Gundicha Mandir
The Garden House, in which the images of the gods reside for seven days each year, is off-limits to non-believers. The walls enclose a garden in which the temple is built. Puri has a number of other temples, but these too are forbidden to non-Hindus.

The Beach
Puri has a fine stretch of white sand from which Indian pilgrims bathe in their customary, fully attired manner. Orissan fishermen, wearing conical straw hats,

guide bathers out through the surf. You can hire your own lifeguard for Rs 4 a morning or afternoon, but their main function is to guard people's clothes. They're unlikely to be much help should trouble arise, as an elderly English traveller reported: 'I called out to my husband – There's going to be a rescue! – when to our amazement the lifeguards turned back having done only 10 yards and the swimmer (or non-swimmer?) disappeared for good. Too late for anyone else to go by then – the victim was a young man of 19'. This, it turned out, was far from the only recent drowning and the 'lifeguards' have no equipment or real ability.

Further east you come to the travellers' beach, in front of the cluster of popular budget hotels like the Z Hotel and the Shankar International. Beyond this is the local fishing village. The fishermen's crude boats are quite unusual – they're made of solid tree trunks and are enormously heavy. Flotation is purely from the bulk of the wood. They're made in two or three pieces, split longitudinally and bound together. When they're not in use they're untied and the pieces laid out on the beach, presumably to dry out? There are an enormous number of them, and since each one uses so much wood entire forests must have fallen to construct this fishing fleet. The other thing on the beach in enormous quantity is shit.

Tours

Now that the Puri-Konarak road is complete, more tours operate out of Puri. Daily except Monday a tour operates to Konarak, Pipli, Dhauli, Bhubaneswar and the Udayagiri and Khandagiri hills. It departs at 6.30 am, returns at 6.30 pm and costs Rs 35 or Rs 50 in an air-con bus. Three days a week there is a Rs 50 tour to Chilka Lake.

Places to Stay – bottom end

Almost all the accommodation in Puri is along the seafront. Most of the budget hotels popular with travellers are at the east end of the beach towards the fishing village, along or off Chakra Tirath Rd. In the centre are most of the mid-range and top-end hotels, while at the west end is a mixture of mid-range and budget hotels – the latter catering mainly to Indian pilgrims.

Near the Tourist Bungalow the pleasant *Sea Side Inn* (tel 2531) has doubles with bath for Rs 66. The big and modern *Youth Hostel* (tel 424) has separate dormitory accommodation for men and women at Rs 8 per bed, Rs 5 if you're a YHA member. Some of the dorms have only two or three beds but others are larger. The hostel has its own restaurant, which does good thalis. Checkout time is 12 noon and there's a 10 pm curfew.

A number of popular budget hotels are clustered together a little further west. The very popular *Z* (Zed you Americans!) *Hotel* is an old, rambling, well-maintained building with large, airy rooms, many of them facing the sea. The management is friendly and easygoing, there's a 'terrific ocean view' and it's 'quiet and pleasant and has good seafood'. Singles are Rs 25, doubles Rs 40 or Rs 60 depending on whether they share a bathroom with one other room or have attached bath. You can also get a dorm bed for Rs 15; the beds are in an open area on the top floor.

The *Sea Foam* is fairly small with a friendly, intimate atmosphere, western music and clean communal showers and toilets. Singles are Rs 20, doubles Rs 40 or Rs 45. The rooms have a fan and mosquito net. The food is indifferent, so although most people eat breakfast here they take lunch and dinner out at one of the nearby restaurants. Towards the beach from the Sea Foam is the popular *Shankar International*. A number of new rooms, all facing the sea with verandah and attached bath, have recently been added to this hotel where singles/doubles are Rs 40/60. There's a good restaurant.

Other possibilities include *Hotel Casuarina*, between the Shankar and the

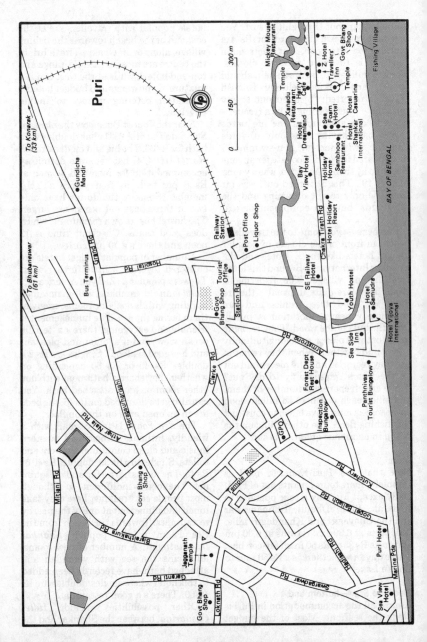

Puri

To Konarak
(33 km)

To Bhubaneswar
(61 km)

BAY OF BENGAL

Fishing Village

Gundicha Mandir

Bus Terminus

Railway Station

Post Office

Liquor Shop

Grand Rd

Hospital Rd

Govt Bhang Shop

Tourist Office

Station Rd

SE Railway Hotel

Chakra Tirath Rd

Hotel Holiday Resort

Youth Hostel

Hotel Samudra

Hotel Vijova International

Sea Side Inn

Grand Rd

Armtron Rd

Clarke Rd

Heranampathu Rd

Forest Dept Rest House

Inspection Bungalow

GPO

Panthnivas Tourist Bungalow

Kutchery Rd

Temple Rd

Gopal Ballab Rd

Mittani Rd

Govt Bhang Shop

Biraktkura Rd

Hejiram Rd

Puri Hotel

Marine Pde

Garanti Rd

Jagganath Temple

Swargdwar Rd

Loknath Rd

Govt Bhang Shop

Sea View Hotel

Mickey Mouse Restaurant

Govt Bhang Shop

Z Hotel

Travellers' Inn

Xanadu Temple

Harry's Cafe

Hotel Dreamland

Sea Foam Hotel

Hotel Casuarina

Bay View Hotel

Sambhoo Restaurant

Hotel Shanker International

Holiday Home

Hotel Temple

0   150   300 m

Sea Foam, or the *Travellers' Inn* beside the Z Hotel. The *Bay View Hotel* is a quiet and very pleasant place with rooms from Rs 20 to Rs 50 and a nice verandah area for sitting out on. Across the road is the *Holiday Home*. There are several very cheap lodges, like the *Sri Balajee*, further down the beach road in the fishing village. At the station, *Railway Retiring Rooms* cost Rs 12 per person and there's a Rs 7 dormitory.

At the pilgrims' beach, about a km west, there are numerous hotels along Marine Parade. Most of them only offer all-inclusive rates and are patronised almost 100% by Indian pilgrims. The *Sea View Hotel* (tel 117) advertises on its cards as commanding a 'Full View of Refreshing Sea – Rubberised Coir Mattress Beds – Attached Baths & Homely Living' (all true!). Full board is Rs 60 per person per day depending on the room. It's excellent value and includes bed tea (6 am), breakfast (7 to 8 am), lunch (12 noon to 1 pm), tiffin (4 to 5 pm) and dinner (8.30 to 9.30 pm). The only disadvantage is that checkout time is *6.30 am*!

Alternatively the big *Puri Hotel* (tel 2114) has rooms from Rs 30 to Rs 35 for singles, Rs 50 to Rs 70 for doubles. There are also air-con rooms from Rs 90 to Rs 150. Rates inclusive of meals are available and there's a 10% service charge on top.

Places to Stay – top end

First of the hotels at the east end of the beach is the *Panthnivas Tourist Bungalow* (tel 562), with doubles with attached bathroom and fan at Rs 80, 90 and 100. It's well kept, well located and, as usual, has a dining hall. There are several new hotels along the beach from the Tourist Bungalow. *Hotel Vijoya International* (tel 2701-2) has rooms at Rs 200/250 or with air-con at Rs 250/300. The adjacent *Hotel Samudra* (tel 2705) is right on the beach; each room has a balcony and looks out on the sea. Rooms are Rs 90/120 or with air-con Rs 140/190.

A little back from the beach on the main road is the delightfully 'olde worlde' *South-Eastern Railway Hotel* (tel 62), with air-con singles/doubles including all meals at Rs 310/435. Non-air-con singles are Rs 185 to Rs 230, doubles Rs 320 to Rs 340, again with all meals. It has a pleasant lounge, bar, dining hall and an immaculate stretch of lawn. Non-residents can eat here; lunch or dinner costs Rs 55 and the food is good. Further along the road the *Hotel Holiday Resort* (tel 2440) was under construction in 1986. The ITDC are also building a new hotel at Puri, the *Nilacha Ashok*, while at the west end of the beach is the *Hotel Prachi Puri* (tel 2638) with rooms at Rs 200/300.

Places to Eat

Although Puri is nowhere near as 'developed' as the other popular travellers' beaches, you can still get excellent seafood in pleasant and congenial surroundings at the *Xanadu* or the *Sambhoo Restaurant*. Both offer lobsters, prawns, fish, chips and a range of salads as well as a variety of sweets. Most dishes cost Rs 3 (fish curry) to Rs 7 (prawn curry), although naturally you pay more for a lobster (Rs 30) or a whole fish. Across the road from the Z Hotel is the very popular (even if they do get the orders confused) *Mickey Mouse Restaurant*. Great name for Puri! The Shankar's *Om Restaurant* does good seafood and great chips.

If you're looking for a cup of tea and/or a snack at other times of the day, the best chai shop in Puri is two doors up the hill from the Xanadu, on the roadside. It's run by a very friendly, older man and his young son. There are a number of other small cafés down at this end of the beach. In the old town there are countless vegetarian places like the *Jagannath South Indian Restaurant* on Grand Rd. Down the road beside the Puri Hotel there's even a Chinese restaurant, the *Cung Wah*.

Getting There

All trains into and out of Puri pass through Bhubaneswar, the Orissa state capital. If you want to travel between these two places the buses are faster and more convenient than the trains, and only marginally more expensive. By train it's about two hours for Rs 5 in 2nd class. Buses, which run every half hour throughout the day, take about 1½ hours and cost Rs 6.

If you're going to Madras, avoid the Tirupathi Express which originates in Puri but doesn't terminate in Madras and involves you in a lot of unnecessary hassle at that end. Go to Bhubaneswar first and take a more convenient train from there. There are one or two trains to Delhi every day from Puri. The Puri Railway Booking Office is open daily from 9 am to 1 pm and 1.30 to 4.30 pm. There's a city booking office on Grand Rd just opposite the town police station. It has its own berth quota (2nd class only), but this might be worthwhile in the pilgrim season when trains to Madras and Calcutta are often booked out five to 10 days ahead.

There are State Transport buses to Calcutta daily at 6.15 am and 4.45 pm. A number of private buses also go to Calcutta, most of them departing around 6.30 pm.

See Konarak for Puri-Konarak transportation details. Puri doesn't really have a bus station – just a stretch of street where buses depart and arrive. It can be chaotic.

Getting Around

A rickshaw from Puri bus stand to the hotels along the beach is around Rs 4. There are lots of rickshaws in Puri.

Things to Buy

Puri is one of those delightfully eccentric Indian towns where the use of ganja and bhang is not only legal, the government very thoughtfully provides for smokers' requisites in the form of shops selling high-quality weed at very reasonable prices. Should you be unfortunate enough to be suffering from Delhi Belly, they do a nice medicinal line in opium. There are several of these shops, one of them close to the railway station and another just beyond the Z Hotel.

You'll come across quite a few craftspeople/salesmen offering fabric, bead and bamboo work. Some of it is well worth a second look. Prices are negotiable, as always with this sort of thing. There are also plenty of people trying to sell snake and animal skins in such numbers that one dreads to think what is happening to the wildlife in the Orissan forests.

KONARAK

Situated on the coast, 64 km from Bhubaneswar and only about 30 km north of Puri, the site consists of little more than the mighty temple and a handful of shops, stalls and places to stay. The Temple of the Sun was constructed at some time in the 13th century, but remarkably little is known about its early history. It is thought to have been built by an Orissan king to celebrate a military victory. It has been in ruins for centuries but until the early 1900s was simply an interesting ruin of impressive size.

Then in 1904 debris and sand were cleared from around the temple base and the sheer magnitude of its architect's imagination was revealed. The entire temple was conceived as a chariot for the Sun God, Surya. Around the base of the temple are 24 gigantic carved-stone wheels. Seven mighty horses haul at the temple and the immense structure is covered with carvings, sculptures, figures and bas-reliefs. It is not known if the construction of the temple was ever completed. If the tower was completed it

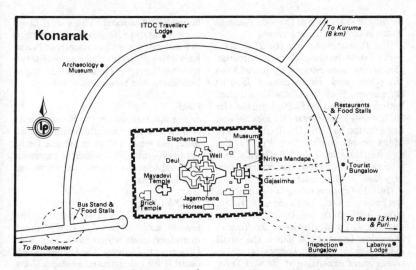

would have soared to 70 metres and archaeologists wonder if the sandy foundations could have supported such a structure. Part of the tower was still standing in 1837 but by 1869 had collapsed, and today the temple's interior has been filled in to support the ruins.

The main entrance, from the Tourist Bungalow side, is guarded by two stone lions crushing elephants. Steps ascend to the main entrance, flanked by straining horses. The entrance porch or *jagamohan* still stands, but the *duel* behind it has collapsed. The three images of Surya, the Sun God, still stand and are designed to catch the sun at dawn, noon and sunset. Between the main steps up to the *jagamohan* and the enclosure entrance is an intricately carved 'dancing hall' or *nata-mandir*. To the north is a group of elephants and to the south a group of rearing horses, trampling down men.

Around the base of the temple and up the walls and roof is a continuous procession of carvings. Many are in the erotic style for which Konarak, like Khajuraho, is famous. These erotic images of entwined couples, or solitary exhibitionists, can be minute images on the spoke of a temple wheel or life-size figures higher up the walls.

Outside the temple enclosure is a museum (open 10 am to 5 pm, closed Fridays) containing many sculptures and carvings found during the temple excavation. The sea is a couple of km from the temple; you can walk there or hire a cycle-rickshaw. The temple was once known as the Black Temple by sailors, in contrast to the whitewashed temples of Puri. It was said to contain a great mass of iron which would draw unwary ships to the shore.

Places to Stay

Now that there is a direct, sealed road along the coast between Puri and Konarak there's no real need to stay here. If you take an early-morning bus from Puri and a late bus back (or on to Bhubaneswar) in the afternoon then you're going to get all the time in the world to have a look at the temple. Of course there are always people who disagree with anything; we've had letters recommending staying in Konarak and visiting Puri from there! The sunsets, the superb beach and, of course, the temple, could encourage long stays. Sunbathing or swimming at this very pleasant beach is likely to draw a crowd.

The *Tourist Bungalow* (tel 21 & 31) is very close to the temple's main entrance. Rooms are more reasonably priced than the Puri and Bhubaneswar Tourist Bungalows. Here doubles with attached bathroom and fan are Rs 50, dorm beds Rs 15. It's well kept, pleasantly located and has a dining hall and the Tourist Office. Many people coming from Puri for the day use the dining hall for meals, but although the food is OK the service can be very slow. A thali costs Rs 7.50.

Only 100 metres towards the beach is the *Labanya Lodge* with rooms at Rs 25, rooms with bath at Rs 35, or rooms upstairs at Rs 50. Between the Tourist Bungalow and the bus halt is the small ITDC *Ashok Tourist Lodge* (tel 23) – rather more expensive at Rs 65/100 for pleasant singles/doubles. It has dining facilities. Finally the flashy new *Inspection Bungalow* has doubles at Rs 50 but you must book ahead in Puri or Bhubaneswar. Around the bus halt there's a collection of extremely basic little 'boarding & lodging' huts.

There is a string of small restaurants along the road near the Tourist Bungalow. You can get very basic Indian food at a couple of the shacks down at the beach.

Getting There

Puri-Konarak There is now a direct route the 33 km along the coast between Puri and Konarak and the trip only takes an hour. Prior to the opening of that road you had to go back towards Bhubaneswar to Pipli, then double back to the coast – total distance 85 km. Now there is plenty of transport running along the coast, although they don't really run on any schedule. The standard fare is Rs 4 and sometimes, but not always, the buses can be incredibly crowded. Coming back from Konarak is no problem – simply flag down any bus/minibus/jeep at any point along the road.

Konarak-Bhubaneswar There are buses fairly regularly to Bhubaneswar, including at least one express bus, usually at 10 am. Fare is Rs 6.40 and can take as little as two hours on the express tourist bus, as long as four hours on a stop-go local service.

PIPLI

At the junction, where the Konarak road branches from the Bhubaneswar-Puri road, this small village is notable for its appliqué craft. The colourful materials are used to make temple umbrellas and wall hangings.

CHILKA LAKE

South of Puri, Chilka Lake is dotted with islands and is noted for the many migratory birds which flock here each December to January. The shallow lake is about 70 km in length and averages 15 km wide. It is separated from the sea only by a narrow sand bar. The railway line and the main road run along the inland edge of the lake. Rambha at the lake is 130 km from Bhubaneswar. There is another Ashokan rock edict at Jangada.

Places to Stay

There are *Tourist Bungalows* at Rambha at the southern end of the lake, and at Barkul six km north of the railway station of Balugaon and 32 km north of Rambha. The *Barkhul Tourist Bungalow* is very small with just two rooms.

GOPALPUR-ON-SEA

This popular but decaying little beach resort is 18 km from Berhampur, where there is a railway station. There are regular buses between Berhampur and Gopalpur. From here you can make excursions to the hot springs at Taptapani, 45 km away.

Places to Stay

At the top end there is the 21-room *Oberoi Palm Beach Hotel* with rooms from Rs 435/580 including meals; at the other end of the scale there is a 16-bed *Youth Hostel*

(Rs 8) and a selection of local hotels. *Hotel Sea Breeze* has doubles for Rs 50 to Rs 60 while the *Hotel Holiday Home* is marginally more expensive and the *Wroxham House Tourist Lodge* is cheaper.

The *Motel Mermaid* on Beach Rd is flashy, clean, modern and right on the beach. Rooms are Rs 80/100, although with bargaining you can get a fine room for around Rs 50. The food is good too and the beers are very cold.

CUTTACK (population 200,000)

Only 35 km north of Bhubaneswar, this riverine city was the capital of Orissa until the new city was constructed at Bhubaneswar. Only a gateway and the moat remain of the 14th-century Barabati Fort. The stone revetment on the Kathjuri River, which protects the city from seasonal floods, dates from the 11th century.

Places to Stay

Hotel Ashoka (tel 21942) on Ice Factory Rd has rooms at Rs 60/80 or with air-con at Rs 100/120. *Hotel Orienta* (tel 24249) in Buxi Bazaar has rooms at Rs 60/90 or with air-con at Rs 90/120. *Hotel Anand* (tel 21936) on Canal Bank Rd is a little cheaper. There are a number of other small hotels, but if you wish to visit Cuttack it is probably easier to day-trip from Bhubaneswar.

BALASORE & CHANDIPUR

Balasore is the first major town on the railway line from Calcutta in north Orissa. It was once an important trading centre with Dutch, Danish, English and French factories. It was, in 1634, the first British East India Company factory in Bengal. Remina, eight km away, has the Gopinath Temple, an important pilgrimage centre. Chandipur, 16 km away on the coast, is a beach resort where the beach extends six km at low tide! There are buses twice a day from Balasore.

Places to Stay

There are a few small hotels in Balasore such as the *Hotel Sagarika* or the *Hotel Moonlight*. The Municipal Tourist Bungalow, known as *Deepak Lodging*, is new, very pleasant and reasonably priced. Walk from the station to the main road, turn left and it's on the right-hand side, two blocks from the corner and across the street from the cinema. In Chandipur there is a *Tourist Bungalow*.

OTHER PLACES

In the north of Orissa, about 200 km inland from the coast, Khiching was once an ancient capital and has a number of interesting temples, temple ruins and a small museum. Further inland is the important industrial city of Rourkela with a major steel plant. North-east of Cuttack, about 100 km from Bhubaneswar, there are Buddhist relics and ruins at the three hilltop complexes of Ratnagiri, Lalitgiri and Udayagiri. The Ratnagiri site has the most interesting ruins. At Lalitgiri craftspeople make replicas of stone sculptures.

In the extreme west of the state, the twin villages of Ranipur-Jharial are 30 km from Titlagarh and are noted for the extensive collection of temples on an outcrop of rock. They include a circular 64-yogini temple, similar to the one at Khajuraho. Harishankar, near Bolangir in the west, has a number of temples and a waterfall. The Similipal National Park is in the north-east of the state, near Khiching. The Ushakothi Wildlife Sanctuary is in the north-west. In the south-west of the state is Gupteswar Cave; this is the region of the Bonda tribespeople. A little north-west of Cuttack is the Shiva temple of Kapilas.

Bombay

Population: 10 million
Main languages: Hindi & Marathi

Bombay is the capital of Maharashtra

Bombay is the economic powerhouse of India. It's the fastest-moving, most affluent, most industrialised city in India. It also has India's busiest airport for international arrivals and departures and India's busiest port, handling nearly 50% of the country's total foreign trade. It's the stronghold of free enterprise in India, a major manufacturing centre for everything from cars and bicycles to pharmaceuticals and petrochemicals. It's the centre for India's important textile industry as well as the financial centre and an important base for overseas companies. Nariman Point is rapidly becoming a mini-Manhattan with India's tallest buildings. Yet once upon a time Bombay was nothing more than a group of low-lying, swampy and malarial mud flats passed on to the British by its Portuguese occupiers as a wedding dowry!

When the Portuguese arrived on the scene Bombay consisted of seven islands occupied by simple fisherfolk known as Kolis. In 1534 the seven islands, from Colaba in the south to Mahim in the north, were ceded to Portugal by the Sultan of Gujarat in the Treaty of Bassein. The Portuguese did little with them and the major island of the group, Mumbadevi, was part of the wedding dowry when Catherine of Braganza married England's Charles II in 1661. In 1665 the British government took possession of all seven islands and in 1668 leased them to the East India Company for an annual £10 in gold.

Soon after the British takeover Bombay started to develop as an important trading port. One of the first signs of this was the arrival of the Parsis, who settled

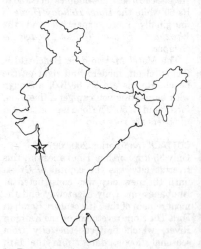

in Bombay in 1670 and built their first Tower of Silence in 1675. In 1687 the presidency of the East India Company was transferred from Surat to Bombay and by 1708 it had become the trading headquarters for the whole west coast of India.

Although Bombay grew steadily for the next century, it was around the middle of the 1800s that its most dynamic development took place. The first railway was laid out of Bombay in 1854, and one of the effects of the Mutiny of 1857 was to further improve the city's image as a 'safe' place, far from the insurrections of the north. Then the American Civil War provided Bombay's young cotton and textile industries with an enormous boost as supplies of cotton from the US dried up. In 1862 a major land-reclamation project joined the original seven islands into a single land mass and a year later the governor, Sir Bartle Frere, dismantled the old fort walls, sparking a major building boom.

During this century Bombay has further extended its position as the major commercial, industrial, financial and trading centre of India. Its role as an economic magnet, the Indian city with streets paved with gold, has also contributed to enormous slum problems and overcrowding. Coming in from the airport to the centre, particularly if you take the back road, is one hell of an introduction to urban India at its very worst. Nevertheless it's an active, alive city, full of interest in its own right and yet also an ideal gateway to the states around it.

Orientation

Bombay is an island, connected by bridges with the mainland. Low, swampy areas indicate where it was once divided into several islands. The principal part of the city is concentrated at the southern end of the island; the northern end is comparatively lightly populated. The airport, Santa Cruz, is 26 km to the north. There are three main railway stations in the city centre. Churchgate and Victoria Terminus are conveniently central, but Bombay Central is some distance out.

Orientation in Bombay is relatively simple. The southern promontory is Colaba Causeway and the northern end of this peninsula is known as Colaba. Most of the cheap hotels and restaurants, together with a number of Bombay's top-notch establishments, are located here. Bombay's two main landmarks – the Gateway of India and the Taj Mahal Hotel – are at Colaba.

Directly north of Colaba is the area known as Bombay Fort, since the old fort was once here. Most of the impressive buildings from Bombay's golden period during the last 40 years of the last century are located here, together with the GPO, offices, banks, Tourist Office and two main railway stations. To the west of the fort is Back Bay, around which sweeps Marine Drive. The southern end of this drive is marked by Nariman Point. This is the modern business centre of Bombay, with more international-class hotels, skyscrapers, airline offices (including Indian Airlines and Air India) and banks.

The other end of the drive is Malabar Hill, a classy residential area.

Bombay (now officially Mumbai) has had lots of official name changes which everyone completely ignores. Colaba Causeway is not known as Shahid Bhagat Singh Marg, Wodehouse Rd is not known as N Parekh Marg. Wellingdon Circle is not known as Dr S P Mukherjee Chowk; in fact it's usually known as Regal after the cinema there. Veer Nariman Rd is sometimes called that; the rest of the time it's still Churchgate St. Victoria Terminus is always VT.

Information

The Government of India Tourist Office (tel 293144) is at 123 Maharashi Karve Rd, Churchgate, directly across from the Churchgate Station. It's open from 8.30 am to 5.30 pm weekdays and every other Saturday, and 8.30 am to 1.30 pm Saturdays and public holidays. It's closed on Sundays. They also have a counter at the airport and in the Taj Inter-Continental Hotel. The main office has a comprehensive leaflet and brochure collection and can be quite helpful.

There is a Maharashtra Tourism Development Corporation Office (tel 296241) at CDO Hutments, Madame Cama Rd. They offer city and suburban tours of Bombay and operate long-distance buses to Mahabeleshwar, Aurangabad and Panaji.

The GPO, with its efficient poste restante service, is an imposing building on Nagar Chowk near Victoria Terminus Station. You can also get mail sent to the Government of India Tourist Office. The American Express office (tel 269421) is on Dadabhoy Naoroji Rd. The banking facilities at the airport are relatively fast and efficient. There's a good pharmacy in the Taj Mahal Hotel as well as many wonderful and expensive crafts shops.

Bookshops Nalanda bookshop in the Taj Hotel is excellent. Other good bookshops are Strand, just off Sir P M Rd (parallel to Churchgate behind Horniman Circle and

Flora Fountain), and Bookpoint, in the Ballard Estate. *City of Gold, the Biography of Bombay* is a good book to read about the city. An indication of Bombay's relative affluence and fast-moving nature is that the city even has its own fortnightly 'what's on' magazine, *Bombay*.

Travel Agencies For discounted tickets, agents worth trying include Space Travels (tel 257773), 4th floor, Nanabhai Mansions, opposite India Bank, Sir P M Rd; or Travel Corner Ltd, Marine Drive, near the Ambassador Hotel. Transway International (tel 310395) at 12 Cawasji Patel Rd, Parker Building, has also been recommended as quick, efficient and reasonably priced. Curiously enough, despite the great number of airlines flying through Bombay it is not as good a centre for cheap tickets as New Delhi.

Airlines If you're staying in the Colaba area of Bombay and want to make bookings/reservations with either Air India or Indian Airlines, you don't have to go all the way to Nariman Point. There's an Air India office in the Taj Mahal Hotel. Many airline offices can be found in the big Air India building on Nariman Point. The airport buses depart from here, and there are a number of shops and fast money-changers in the building.

Some of the airlines with offices in Bombay include:

Aeroflot
    87 Stadium House, Veer Nariman Rd (tel 221682, 221743)
Air France
    Taj Mahal Hotel, Apollo Bunder (tel 245021)
Air India
    Air India Building, Nariman Point (tel 2024142, 2023747)
Air Lanka
    Mittal Towers, Nariman Point (tel 223299, 234142)
Alitalia
    Industrial Assurance Building, Veer Nariman Rd (tel 220613, 222112, 222144)

Bangladesh Biman
    Airlines Hotel, 199 J Tata Rd (tel 221339, 220676)
British Airways
    Vulcan Insurance Building, Veer Nariman Rd (tel 220888)
Cathay Pacific
    Taj Mahal Hotel, Apollo Bunder (tel 2023366)
Czechoslovak Airlines
    308/309 Raheja Chambers, 213 Nariman Point (tel 220736, 220765)
Egypt Air
    Oriental House, 7 J Tata Rd (tel 221415)
Garuda Indonesian Airways
    5 Raheja Centre, Nariman Point (tel 243075, 243725)
Gulf Air
    Air India Building, Nariman Point (tel 2021441, 2021626)
Indian Airlines
    Air India Building, Nariman Point (tel 2023031)
Japan Air Lines
    No 2 Raheja Centre, Nariman Point (tel 233348, 233136)
Kenya Airways
    Airlines Hotel, 199 J Tata Rd (tel 220015, 220064)
Kuwait Airlines
    86 Veer Nariman Rd (tel 298351)
LOT (Polish Airways)
    Maker Arcade, Cuffe Parade (tel 211440)
Lufthansa
    Express Towers, Nariman Point (tel 2023430)
PIA
    Hotel Oberoi Towers, Nariman Point (tel 2021372, 2021598)
Pan American
    Taj Mahal Hotel, Apollo Bunder (tel 2023366, 2029221)
Qantas
    Oberoi Towers, Nariman Point (tel 2029297)
Singapore Airlines
    Air India Building, Nariman Point (tel 2023365)
Swissair
    Maker Chambers, 220 Nariman Point (tel 222402, 222559)
Thai International
    World Trade Centre, Cuffe Parade (tel 219191, 215207)

Consulates Due to Bombay's importance as a business centre, many countries maintain consulates or embassies in Bombay as well as in the capital, New Delhi. They include:

Australia
    Maker Towers, E Block, Cuffe Parade (tel 211071)
West Germany
    Hoechst House, Nariman Point (tel 232422)
Netherlands
    16 M Karve Rd (tel 296840)
UK
    Mercantile Bank Building, Mahatma Gandhi Rd (tel 274874)
USA
    Lincoln House, Bhulabhai Desai Rd (tel 8223611)

The honorary Irish consul can be found in the Royal Bombay Yacht Club by India Gate!

Movies

Quickly, what are the biggest film-producing city and country in the world? Hollywood and the USA? Wrong twice – Bombay and India! The Indians turn out 500 to 600 full-length feature films a year and, of these, nearly half get made in Bombay. Calcutta makes some arty, intellectual films; Madras some family comedies or musicals; but for extravaganzas, action dramas, the 'starcast' A features, it's Bombay all the way.

A visit to the film studios in Bombay is easy to arrange – just tell the Tourist Office you'd like to see a film being made and they'll fix it all up for you. It's a real education, as we found when we turned up at Famous Film Studios. For a start the film production company and the studios are totally separate. Bombay has about 12 studios and far more film-makers. When they want to make a film they simply hire the studio by the day. Nor are Indian films made one at a time as in the west. A big star could be involved in a number of films simultaneously – shooting a day on one, a week on another, a morning on a third. This involves phenomenal scheduling problems and also means that Indian films generally take a long time to make.

A glance at Indian film posters or film magazines gives you the impression that Indian movie actors are a band of escapees from weight-watchers. Well, there's no glamour in being thin in India. Every beggar in the street is skinny; it's the well-padded look which appeals. It's amusing to see how this works on western films shown in India – familiar European and American film stars become remarkably rotund when they're repainted for the Indian posters.

Our image of these chubby, smug actors was quickly shattered when we were asked into the dressing room to meet the star of the film we went to see. He was friendly, very open about the problems involved in making films in India – and not a kilo overweight! Life for a lot of Indians is not all that much fun and illiteracy is still widespread. Bombay film-makers are not trying to produce something for a sophisticated and intellectual audience. It's pure, straightforward, down-to-earth entertainment. Escapism and nothing more.

Indian films are always a bit of everything – drama, action, suspense, music, dancing, romance – all mixed together into one extravagant blend. They've even got a name for them – 'masala films', since masala is the all-purpose word for spices, something you add to make it tasty.

Within their commercial constraints Indian movie-makers often do a surprisingly good job, particularly the cameramen and technicians, who manage to produce reasonable standard films from hopelessly outdated equipment. Apart from the restrictions on importing new equipment, a large slice of the proceeds goes to the Indian government. Film admission prices may be only Rs 3, 4 or 5, but the government gulps down about 75% of that figure. To make an Indian movie and earn money out of it, you really have to know what you're about.

Tony Wheeler

Gateway of India

In the days when most visitors came to India by sea and when Bombay was India's principal port, this was indeed the 'gateway' to India. Today it's merely Bombay's principal landmark. The gateway was conceived following the visit of King George V in 1911 and officially opened in 1924. Architecturally it is a conventional Arch of Triumph, with elements in its design derived from the Muslim styles of 16th-century Gujarat. It is built of yellow basalt and stands on the Apollo Bunder, a popular Bombay meeting place in the evenings. The Taj Mahal Inter-Continental Hotel overlooks the Apollo Bunder and launches run from here across to Elephanta Island. Close to the gateway are statues of Swami Vivekananda and of the Maratha leader, Shivaji, astride his horse.

Colaba Causeway

The streets behind the Taj Mahal Hotel are the travellers' centre of Bombay. Here you will find most of the cheap hotels and restaurants. Colaba Causeway, now renamed Shahid Bhagat Singh Rd, extends to the end of the Colaba promontory, the southern end of Bombay Island. Sassoon Dock is always interesting to visit around dawn, when the fishing boats come in and unload their catch in a colourful scene of intense activity. There's an old lighthouse at the end of the promontory, although the actual lighthouse used today is further south still on a rocky island.

St John's Church

The Afghan Church was built in 1857 and is dedicated to the soldiers who fell in the Sind campaign of 1838 and the First Afghan War of 1843.

Prince of Wales Museum

Beside the Wellingdon Circle, close to the Colaba Causeway hotel enclave, the Prince of Wales Museum was built to commemorate King George V's first visit to India in 1905, while he was still Prince of Wales. The first part of this interesting museum was opened in 1914. It was designed in the Indo-Saracenic style and has sections for art and paintings, archaeology and natural history. Among the more interesting items is a very fine collection of miniature paintings, images and bas-reliefs from the Elephanta Caves and Buddha images.

The museum is open from 10.15 am to 5.30 to 6.30 pm depending on the time of year. It is closed on Mondays and entry is Rs 2 (children Rs 1), except on Tuesdays when it is free.

Jehangir Art Gallery

Within the compound of the museum stands Bombay's principal art gallery. There are often special exhibitions of modern Indian art here. The gallery also has public phones, public toilets and a good snack bar so it's a useful place. It opens at 10.30 am.

University & High Court

Along K B Patel Marg, overlooking Cross Maidan, there are a number of imposing public buildings erected during Bombay's period of great growth under the British. The university is in Gothic 14th to 15th-century style and dominated by the 80-metre Rajabai Tower. This impressive clock tower rises above the university library, and if you can obtain permission to ascend it (extremely difficult) there is a fine view from the top. Statues of Justice and Mercy top the huge High Court building beyond the university. It was built in Early English style and completed in 1878.

Flora Fountain

This is the business centre of Bombay, around which many of the major banks and business offices are centred. Now officially renamed Hutatma Chowk, it was erected in honour of Sir Bartle Frere, who was governor of Bombay from 1862 to 1867, when Bombay experienced its most dramatic growth due to the worldwide cotton shortage caused by the American Civil War. Close to the fountain is the Cathedral of St Thomas, begun by Gerald Aungier in 1672 and finally formally opened in 1718. There are several interesting memorials inside the cathedral, which has had a series of additions and alterations over the years.

Horniman Circle

Several interesting old Bombay buildings

stand close to Horniman Circle. If you're walking from the GPO back to Colaba some time, it's worth pausing to have a glance at some of these buildings. The old Mint was completed in 1829 and has an Ionic facade. It was built on land reclaimed in 1823 and adjoins the Town Hall. Behind the Town Hall stand the remains of the old Bombay Castle.

Opened in 1833, the Town Hall still houses the library of the Royal Asiatic Society. Ascend the imposing steps at the front of the Town Hall and have a short wander inside. You'll see statues of a number of the government officials and wealthy benefactors of Bombay's golden period, including Sir Bartle Frere and Sir Jamsetjee Jeejeebhoy. Continuing on, you pass the Old Customs House built in 1720. The old Bombay dockyards stand behind the building.

Marine Drive

Now officially renamed Netaji Subhash Rd, Marine Drive is built on land reclaimed in 1920. It runs along the shoreline of Back Bay, starting at Nariman Point and sweeping around by Chowpatty Beach and up to Malabar Hill. The road is backed with high residential buildings and this is one of Bombay's most popular promenades.

Taraporewella Aquarium

Constructed in 1951, the aquarium on Marine Drive is one of the best in India and has both freshwater and saltwater fish. It's open from 11 am to 8 pm, closed Mondays, and admission is Rs 1. Also along Marine Drive, before the aquarium, is a series of cricket pitches where in summer there always seems to be games underway.

Chowpatty Beach

Bombay's famous beach attracts few bathers and even fewer sunbathers – neither activity has much of a following in India, and in any case the water is none too healthy. Chowpatty has plenty of other activities though. It's one of those typical Indian slices of life where anything and everything can happen, and does. Sand-castle sculptors make elaborate figures in the sand, contortionists go through equally elaborate contortions and family groups stroll around. In between there are kiosks selling Bombay's popular snack, *bhelpuri*, and *kulfi* ice cream.

Chowpatty Beach is also the scene for the annual Ganesh Chaturthi festival, during which large images of the elephant-headed god are immersed in the sea.

Mani Bhuvan

At 19 Laburnum Rd, near August Kranti Maidan, is the building where Mahatma Gandhi stayed on his visits to Bombay between 1917 and 1934. Today it has a pictorial exhibit of incidents in Gandhi's life and contains a library of books by or about the Mahatma. It is open from 9.30 am to 6 pm.

Malabar Hill

At the end of Back Bay, Marine Drive climbs up to Malabar Hill. This is an expensive residential area, for not only is it a little cooler than the sea-level parts of the city, but there are fine views over Back Bay and Chowpatty Beach to the town. At the end of the promontory is Raj Bhavan, the old British government headquarters.

Close by is the temple of Walkeswar, the 'sand lord', an important Hindu pilgrimage site. According to the *Ramayana*, Rama rested here on his way from Ayodya to Lanka to rescue Sita. He constructed a lingam of sand at the site. The original temple was built about 1000 years ago but was reconstructed in 1715.

Jain Temple

This marble temple was built in 1904 and is dedicated to the first Jain Tirthankar, Adinath. It's typical of modern Jain temples in its gaudy, mirrored style. The

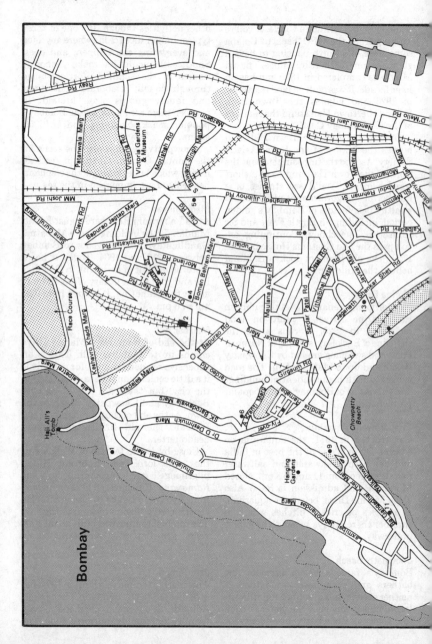

Bombay

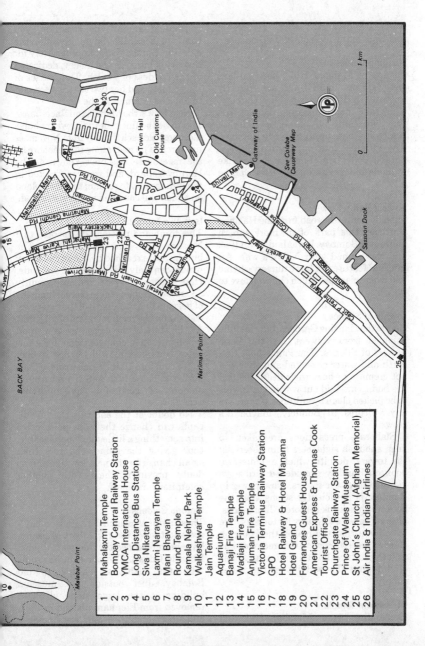

BACK BAY

Malabar Point

Nariman Point

Sassoon Dock

See Colaba Causeway Map

Gateway of India

Town Hall

Old Customs House

Marine Drive

Netaji Subhash Rd

Maharshi Karve Marg

Mahatma Gandhi Rd

Mangalika Marg

Soman Rd

Thackersey Marg

Nariman Rd

Wacha Rd

Mint Rd

Medows Careton

Shahid Bhagat Singh Rd

Capt Prakash Marg

N Parekh Marg

Colaba Causeway

Shivaji Marg

Nazroll Rd

1 km

0

1   Mahalaxmi Temple
2   Bombay Central Railway Station
3   YMCA International House
4   Long Distance Bus Station
5   Siva Niketan
6   Laxmi Narayan Temple
7   Mani Bhavan
8   Round Temple
9   Kamala Nehru Park
10 Walkeshwar Temple
11 Jain Temple
12 Aquarium
13 Banaji Fire Temple
14 Wadiaji Fire Temple
15 Anjuman Fire Temple
16 Victoria Terminus Railway Station
17 GPO
18 Hotel Railway & Hotel Manama
19 Hotel Grand
20 Fernandes Guest House
21 American Express & Thomas Cook
22 Tourist Office
23 Churchgate Railway Station
24 Prince of Wales Museum
25 St John's Church (Afghan Memorial)
26 Air India & Indian Airlines

walls are decorated with pictures of incidents in the lives of the Tirthankars.

Hanging Gardens

On top of Malabar Hill, these gardens were laid out in 1881 and are correctly known as the Pherozeshah Mehta Gardens. They take their name from the fact that they are built on top of a series of reservoirs that supply water to Bombay. The formally laid out gardens have a notable collection of hedges shaped like animals and there are good views over the city.

Kamala Nehru Park

Directly across the road from the Hanging Gardens, this park offers more superb views over Bombay. It was laid out in 1952 and was named after Nehru's wife. An unusual feature is a large nursery-rhyme 'old woman's shoe' which children love to play in.

Towers of Silence

Beside the Hanging Gardens, but carefully shielded from viewers, are the Parsi Towers of Silence. The Parsis hold fire, earth and water as sacred and thus will not cremate or bury their dead. Instead the bodies are laid out within the towers to be picked clean by vultures. If there are any vultures in Bombay, maybe it's crows.

Elaborate precautions are taken to keep ghoulish sightseers from observing the towers, despite which a *Time-Life* book on Bombay provided a bird's-eye view of one of the towers. Parsi power in Bombay is sufficiently strong that the book was black-ink censored. Tour guides, always fond of a tall story for tourists, like to tell you that the reason the Hanging Garden reservoirs were covered over was that the vultures had an unpleasant habit of dropping the odd bit in the water supply.

Mahalaxmi Temple

Descending from Malabar Hill and continuing around the coastline, you come to the Mahalaxmi Temple, the oldest in Bombay and, appropriately for this city of business and money, dedicated to the goddess of wealth. The images of the goddess and her two sisters were said to have been found in the sea.

Near here is the Mahalaxmi Racecourse, said to be the finest in India, where horse races are held each Sunday from November to March. The road along the seashore by the racecourse was once known as the Hornby Vellard, and was constructed in the 18th century to reclaim the swampland on which the course is now constructed.

Haji Ali's Tomb

This tomb and mosque are devoted to a Muslim saint who drowned here. The buildings are reached by a long causeway which can only be crossed at low tide. Here a scene of typical Indian ingenuity and resourcefulness takes place. Hundreds of beggars line the length of the causeway waiting for the regular stream of pilgrims. At the start of the causeway is a small group of money-changers who, for a few paise commission, will change a one-rupee coin into 100 one-paise coins. Thus a pilgrim can do his soul the maximum amount of good for the minimum expenditure.

No doubt at the ebb tide the mendicants can change their one-paise coins into something a little more manageable, thus giving the money-changers their small change for the next low tide and no doubt providing them with another commission rake-off.

Victoria Gardens

These gardens, which contain Bombay's zoo and the Victoria & Albert Museum, have been renamed the Veermata Jijabai Bhonsle Udyan. The museum has some interesting exhibits relating to old Bombay. Just outside the museum building is the large stone elephant removed from Elephanta Island in 1864, and after which the island was named.

The museum is open from 10 am to 6 pm, the zoo from sunrise to sunset. Both are closed on Wednesday and charge Rs 0.20 admission.

Other

The Nehru Planetarium is on Dr Annie Besant Rd at Worli near the Haji Ali Tomb. There are shows in English at 3 and 6 pm daily except on Mondays, when it closed. Admission is Rs 5.

Falkland St is the centre for Bombay's notorious red-light district known as 'the cages'. The ladies stand behind metal-barred doors, hence the name. A No 130 bus from the museum passes through this fascinating area.

Colaba, Colaba, the foreign itinerant's Bombay, it has more strange, surreal people than anywhere else in India. What are they doing here? Why Bombay? Outside the Rex/Stiffles, which now has its very sign translated into Arabic, Arab women squat on the pavement, wearing those strange mini-masks which make them look like some sort of trained hawk. In the Leopold Café it's a mix of Indian, African, Arab, Europeans of varied nationalities and strange purposes. There are fresh-faced young travellers, others looking worn and hardened by drugs and the road. Meanwhile over at the Taj hotel money drips. The people in the lobby, chatting in the shops, wandering off to the bars and restaurants, positively gleam with that shiny glow of money. Do they set the room rates to equate with India's per capita GNP? A night in the Taj must come close to the average peasant's annual income. At my hotel the lift door slides open to reveal two men totally filling the compartment from side to side and top to bottom. It's Gustav the Horrible and Dick the Bruiser, or two people with similar names. They're in Bombay for a wrestling bout. Ah Colaba, Colaba is weird.

Tours

There are numerous tours of Bombay but they tend to be more expensive than in most Indian cities. Daily city tours are operated by the ITDC, the Travel Corporation of India and the Maharashtra Tourist Development Council. Morning tours generally last 9 am to 1 or 2 pm and cost Rs 35 with the ITDC or Rs 40 with the MTDC. Afternoon tours last from 1.45 or 2 pm to 6 or 7 pm and cost Rs 30, 35 or 40.

The MTDC also have an all-day suburban tour which operates from 10 am to 6 pm and costs Rs 65. This goes to the Kanheri Caves, Juhu Beach and other places. Launch services and tours to Elephanta leave regularly from Apollo Bunder and can be booked at the kiosk there. The round trip takes four hours. The ITDC and the MTDC have some tours further afield, such as four-day tours to Aurangabad and the Ajanta and Ellora caves. Check at the Tourist Office for details.

Places to Stay

Bombay is India's most expensive city for accommodation, so if your funds are limited you should plan on spending as little time as possible here. Not only that, but it's a magnet for Middle East and Gulf Arabs who come here for holidays, shopping expeditions and business. They invariably bring with them their entire harem. Not all of these visitors are super-rich oil sheikhs who can afford to stay in the Taj Mahal Inter-Continental, so the pressure for accommodation – even at the bottom end of the market – is intense.

Because of this, there is no guarantee that you will be able to find a room in the price range you expected to pay and, at least for the first night, you may well have to settle for something considerably more expensive. As though that were not enough, the standard of accommodation you get at the bottom end of the market is often poor.

The only way to give yourself a fighting chance, not only for a room, but for something half-way decent, is to arrange to get into Bombay as soon as possible after dawn. Luckily, most international flights into Bombay arrive in the early morning. The same is true of the ferry from Panaji (Goa) to Bombay.

It's also a distinct advantage to be part

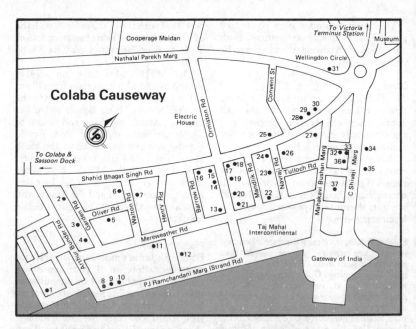

1	Hotel Fariyas	20	Rex & Stiffles Hotel
2	Hotel Ascot	21	Hotel Diplomat
3	Godwin Hotel	22	Carlton Hotel
4	Garden Hotel	23	Laxmi Vilas
5	Bentley's Hotel	24	Leopold Restaurant
6	Cowie's Guest House	25	Olympic Coffee House
7	Oliver Guest House	26	Apollo Restaurant
8	Shelley's Guest House	27	Café Mondegar
9	Strand Hotel	28	Delhi Durbar
10	Sea Palace Hotel	29	Canteena
11	Whalley's Guest House	30	Hotel Majestic (restaurant)
12	Hotel Prosser	31	Woodside Pizza
13	Salvation Army Red Shield Hostel	32	Suba Guest House
14	Dipti's Pure Drinks	33	Naval & Military Restaurant
15	Ananda Punjabi	34	Cottage Industries Emporium
16	Kamat Hotel (restaurant)	35	Mandarin & Hong Kong Restaurant
17	Café Apsara	36	Nanking Restaurant
18	Food Inn	37	Royal Bombay Yacht Club
19	Moti Hotel International		

of a small group (impromptu or otherwise), since if the first place you try is full, then one or two of you can look after the baggage, while the rest fan out in search of somewhere else. If you should be unlucky

enough not to find anything in the price range that you can afford on the first day, try making a booking for the following day.

The Tourist Office or the desk at the

airport can sometimes be helpful in finding an empty room, but in Bombay even budget accommodation is expensive.

Places to Stay – bottom end

Colaba The majority of the budget hotels are to be found in the Colaba area directly behind that useful landmark, the Taj Mahal Inter-Continental. Best known are the *Rex* and *Stiffles* (tel 231518, 230960), 8 Ormiston Rd; it's here that many travellers start their search for a room. The Rex is on floors 3 and 4, the Stiffles on 1 and 2. A great deal has been said and written over the years about the standard of accommodation at these two places – some of it good, most of it bad.

Given the standards of Bombay, these places aren't bad although every square cm of space has been converted into rooms, so some are cramped and window-less while others have weird and wonderful ways of entering them. Also, you must get there early in the morning if you want any chance of finding a room. The management is pleasant and gear left in your room is secure. Singles cost Rs 45 to Rs 93, doubles Rs 90 to Rs 180; the more expensive rooms have air-con.

Across the road on the corner of the street is another old favourite, the *Salvation Army Red Shield Hostel* (tel 241824), 30 Mereweather Rd. Full board here costs Rs 50 in the dormitory, although there are also rooms. Safe-deposit lockers can be hired for a returnable deposit of Rs 50 plus Rs 1 per day. Checkout time is 9 am and you need to be there early in the morning in order to be well up the line when 9 am rolls round. Some say that there's usually more room for women than men. The hostel provides good entertainment, reported a visitor:

A bizarre cast of travelers is always available to occupy your leisure time. A young British chap who insists he is from Italy will explain the secrets of the Bible. He is the first to have 'decoded' the Bible, using a base-one numbering system.

Another cheapie in the Colaba area is the *Carlton Hotel* (tel 230642), 12 Mereweather Rd, an interesting old place with singles at Rs 50, doubles at Rs 90 to Rs 100 with common bathrooms. There are some cheaper doubles without windows. Not everybody is impressed, however. 'The grottiest place I saw in *all* of India', wrote one traveller. 'Basic but clean', wrote another!

Others include *Hotel Prosser* (tel 241715), corner of Henry Rd and P J Ramchandani Marg, which has rooms with shared bath and hot and cold water for Rs 90/100. *Whalley's Guest House* (tel 234206), Mereweather Rd, is a plain place with rooms with common bath for Rs 77/145 including breakfast. As at the other cheapies, check if your room has a window.

Opposite Cowie's Guest House on Walton Rd, the *Oliver Guest House* is cheap, clean and unfriendly at Rs 70 to Rs 80 for rooms with common bathrooms. Another place you might like to try is the *Moti Hotel International* (tel 225714), 10 Ormiston Rd, right next door to the Rex and Stiffles. Doubles with attached bath and air-con cost Rs 150 to Rs 175 but they also have doubles with common bath and air-con for Rs 100.

There's a whole collection of small hotels on various floors along Arthur Bunder Rd. They include the neat and clean *Seashore Hotel, Janata Guest House, Imperial Guest House, India Guest House, Hotel Mukund, Gateway Guest House, Gulf Hotel* and *Hotel Al-Hijaz*. Many of them look like they ought to be cheap, but don't let appearances fool you. Even though most offer only airless, windowless, hardboard-partitioned boxes for rooms, prices can vary from as little as Rs 45 for a single to as much as Rs 200 for a double with bath, air-con and *window*. Have a look at them if you're stuck, but remember that prices and standards vary considerably.

Elsewhere Away from the Colaba area,

one of the most popular places – deservedly so – is the 3rd-floor *Lawrence Hotel* (tel 243618), Ashok Kumar Lane (sign-posted as Rope Walk Lane) off K Dubash Marg at the back of the Prince of Wales Museum. It's often full since it only has nine rooms, but it's excellent value with singles/doubles with common bathroom at Rs 50/90. Some of the rooms have balconies.

There are a number of cheapies on P D'Mello Rd at the eastern end of the GPO/Victoria Terminus Station. The *Railway Hotel* (tel 351028), 249 P D'Mello Rd, has rooms from Rs 50 to Rs 130. It's definitely for those who don't care too much about windows and hardboard partitioning. At 239 the *Rupam Hotel* (tel 267103/4) is slightly more expensive, with rooms from Rs 70 to Rs 150. The management are friendly and it's clean despite being somewhat run down.

At 221-225 P D'Mello Rd the *Hotel Manama* (tel 263860) has recently been upgraded and modernised and has rooms at Rs 100 or Rs 120 with common bathroom, Rs 140 with attached bath. The *City Lodge*, directly across from the station and GPO and above a tailor shop, is good for a short stop and has clean doubles for Rs 80.

Between here and Colaba in Ballard Estate, *Fernandes Guest House* (tel 260554) in the Balmer Lawrie Building at 5 J N Heredia Marg is very similar to the Lawrence Hotel (see above). There are just seven rooms – one single at Rs 50, the rest doubles at Rs 80.

The Ys Like other Indian cities, Bombay has its share of YMCAs and YWCAs. Although very good value for money, they're invariably full. The most popular is the *YWCA International Guest House* (tel 2020445), 18 Madame Cama Rd, which takes both men and women, and offers bed and breakfast for Rs 71/139 plus Rs 10 membership charges (valid for one month). It's generally booked out three months in advance.

The *YMCA International Guest House* (tel 891191) is at 18 YMCA Rd near Central Railway Station. This is a rather long way from downtown Bombay and the popular Colaba area. The rooms are pleasant and well kept and cost Rs 115/210 or with attached bathroom Rs 124/240. There's also a Rs 40 per person transient membership charge, valid up to 90 days.

Other For men only there is excellent dormitory accommodation for Rs 15 or rooms for three people at Rs 20 per person at *Siva Niketan* (tel 372395) on J Jijibhoy Rd, which is also in the north part of the city near Central Station.

There are no purpose-built Youth Hostels as such in Bombay, but during university/college vacations you may be able to find cheap accommodation at *Bhavan's College* (tel 572192), Versova Rd, Bhavan's Camp, Andheri; *University Hostel* (tel 472425), L A Kidwai Rd; or *Podar College of Commerce Hostel* (tel 472414), 193 Sion Koliwada Estate.

Finally, both Bombay Central and Victoria Terminus have *Railway Retiring Rooms*. At Victoria Terminus dorm beds cost Rs 35, doubles Rs 100.

Places to Stay – middle
Many of the middle-bracket hotels – along with the Taj Inter-Continental and most of the cheapies – are in the Colaba area. The other main group is clustered along Marine Drive (Netaji Subhash Rd) between Madame Cama Rd and Veer Nariman Rd, and along Veer Nariman Rd itself. The ones in Colaba tend to be less expensive than those on Marine Drive.

Colaba Three popular places in the Colaba area can be found along Garden Rd. The *Ascot Hotel* (tel 240020), 38 Garden Rd, has air-con singles/doubles with attached bath for Rs 324/370 including breakfast. There are also a number of rooms with common bathrooms for Rs 224/240. A few doors down, the *Godwin*

Hotel (tel 241226), 41 Garden Rd, offers accommodation of a similar standard for Rs 332/433. The *Garden Hotel* (tel 240895) at 42 Garden Rd has air-con singles/doubles with attached bath for Rs 250/300 plus tax as well as two very ritzy deluxe rooms at Rs 450. This hotel also has its own bar and restaurant.

Cowie's Guest House (tel 240232), Walton Rd, offers full board and lodging for Rs 125/200 with attached bath, or Rs 150/230 with air-con and attached bath. *Hotel Diplomat* (tel 231661), at 24 Mereweather Rd on the corner of Ormiston Rd, is a relatively new place with its own bar and restaurant. Singles/doubles are Rs 336/421, an extra bed costs Rs 56. Like many other Bombay hotels, it's poor value and the rooms are not very clean.

Still in the Colaba area, but less expensive, are a number of hotels along the waterfront. The *Sea Palace Hotel* (tel 241828), 26 P J Ramchandani Marg (Strand Rd), is a large building with reasonable air-con singles/doubles with attached bath for Rs 225/370 including tax and service. The hotel has its own restaurant. Next door is the *Strand Hotel* (tel 241624), which has singles/doubles for Rs 120/150 or with air-con for Rs 200/ 220. Bathrooms are shared between two rooms. It's very worn looking and not special value. At the end of the same block is *Shelly's Hotel* (tel 240229), 30 P J Ramchandani Marg, which offers air-con rooms for Rs 210/250.

Back from the harbourfront, *Bentley's Hotel* (tel 241733), 17 Oliver Rd, has singles for Rs 75, doubles for Rs 120 to Rs 165. Add on Rs 45 for air-con. Over on Shivaji Marg, the road running back from the Gateway of India, the *Suba Guest House* has rooms at Rs 100, at Rs 200 with air-con, at Rs 270 with air-con and attached bathroom.

Hotel Apollo (tel 230223), on M Bhushan Marg (Landsdowne Rd) behind the Regal Cinema, has its own bar and restaurant. Rooms range from Rs 185 to Rs 275 or with air-con from Rs 235 to Rs 325.

Marine Drive Moving to the Marine Drive (Netaji Subhash Rd) area, you can try the *Sea Green Hotel* (tel 222294) at number 145, where rooms are Rs 150/250 or with air-con Rs 211/315. Next to it is the *Sea Green South Hotel* (tel 221662), where prices are virtually identical. These charges include taxes and breakfast. Both popular hotels are often full up.

On the corner of Marine Drive and D Rd, the clean and simple *Norman's Guest House* (tel 294234) has a few singles at Rs 150, doubles at Rs 170 or Rs 180 with bath. The *Bentley Hotel* on the other corner has rooms at Rs 95/120; some of them are very small.

Nearby is the *Chateau Windsor Guest House* (tel 293376), 86 Veer Nariman Rd, which has a wide variety of rooms both with and without air-con and attached bathrooms, and varying widely in size. Some of the windowless little boxes are poor value but singles and doubles go all the way from Rs 175 to Rs 290, on up to over Rs 500 for very large rooms. The lift has a sign announcing that 'servants may only use the lift if accompanied by children'.

In this same area is the *Astoria Hotel* (tel 299121), 4 Jamshedji Tata Rd, with rooms at Rs 322/368 including breakfast. Some travellers have recommended *Hotel Hiramani* (tel 4134502) on Dr Babasaheb Ambedkar Rd, Lalbaug – reasonably close to Marine Drive – with rooms from Rs 225.

Places to Stay – top end

Hotels in this category will usually have a 10% service charge and 7% state 'luxury' tax tagged on top of the room charge – as do some of the middle-range places.

Bombay has the hotel reputed to be the best in India. It certainly has an air of glamour. Most of Bombay's cheap hotels cluster right behind it, and the hotel has a comfortable air-conditioned lounge and one of the best bookshops in the city, so you'll find a fair number of backpackers around it too! The *Taj Mahal Hotel* is an elegant turn-of-the-century building on Apollo Bunder near the Gateway of India. More recently the *Taj Inter-Continental* was added to it, so it is now known as the *Taj Mahal Hotel & Taj Inter-Continental* (tel 243366). There are 650 rooms with singles/doubles at Rs 995/1100. The affluence in the Taj is amazing; this is one place in India where you see BMWs and Mercedes parked outside and where people look rich!

On Nariman Point, and in an equally high price range, the *Hotel Oberoi-Towers* (tel 234343) has singles/doubles at Rs 1095/1195 plus a variety of restaurants, bars, coffee bars and a swimming pool.

The rather out-of-the-way *Hotel President* (tel 4950808) is at 90 Cuffe Parade, about half-way down the Colaba Causeway. Rooms here are Rs 630 to Rs 735 for singles, Rs 735 to Rs 840 for doubles. Or you could try the *Hotel Fariyas* (tel 242680) at 25 Off Arthur Bunder Rd in Colaba, where rooms are Rs 580/700.

The *Welcomgroup Searock* (tel 6425421) at Land's End, Bandra has 405 rooms at Rs 675/785 for singles/doubles. Centrally located on Jamshedji Tata Rd in Church-gate, the *Ambassador Hotel* (tel 291131) is topped by a revolving restaurant and has rooms at Rs 575/675. On the same road the *Ritz Hotel* (tel 220141) has rooms at Rs 435/545. Ballard Estate is to the east side of Bombay, between Colaba and the GPO. In this central but relatively quiet area you'll find the *Grand Hotel* (tel 268211) at 17 Sprott Rd with rooms at Rs 315/365.

Places to Stay – Airport & Juhu

There are a number of hotels out by the airport and a lot of them along Juhu Beach. They're mainly at the more expensive end of the market, and unless you have some compelling reason to be out by the airport there's little reason to stay there. It's hard to think of any compelling reason to stay at Juhu Beach.

Airport Right outside the domestic terminal (Terminal 1) is the *Centaur Hotel* (tel 612660), a large circular hotel with conference facilities, all the usual amenities of a five-star hotel including a swimming pool, and rooms from Rs 750.

There are several other hotels very close by, either beside the Centaur or just across the road. They're all air-con and offer good but expensive standards. *Hotel Airport Plaza* (tel 6123390) is Rs 405/485 and has a swimming pool. *Hotel Airport International* (tel 6122891) has rooms at Rs 350/400.

The helpful and friendly *Avion Hotel* (tel 6123902), across the main road, is Rs 314/385. *Hotel Aircraft International* (tel 6123667) is beside the Avion and has rooms at Rs 250/290. The comfortable and well-kept *Hotel Jal* (tel 6123820) is on the other side of the Avion and costs Rs 275/350. The *Sabena Restaurant* next door has good food and a varied selection of beers. On Nehru Rd the *Hotel Transit* (tel 6129325) is Rs 330/450.

If you're looking for something cheaper, *Retiring Rooms* at the domestic airport are Rs 75 per person. In Vile Parle ('Veelay Parlay') the *Ramakrishna* (tel 6146664) has singles at Rs 150, doubles at Rs 200 to Rs 250. The international terminal is a couple of km away and hotels are under construction there, including the five-star *Leela Penta*.

Juhu Beach Hotels at Juhu are generally at the expensive end of the price range. Don't even consider swimming at Juhu – one look at the untreated sewage which slithers sluggishly out to sea from the vast slum encampments from Dadar to Juhu will convince you.

Cheaper hotels (for Juhu) include the *Kings Hotel* (tel 579141), 5 Juhu Tara Rd, which provides air-con rooms for Rs 215/270. On the beach road the *Sea Side Hotel* (tel 621972) has similarly priced rooms, but back on Juhu Tara Rd the *South End Hotel* (tel 6125213) is somewhat cheaper.

Other places to try at the cheaper end of the market are the *Sea View Hotel* and the *Purnima Guest House* (tel 541215). There's even a Krishna Consciousness hotel, the *Iskcon-Ashram* (tel 626860) with doubles at Rs 190 to Rs 240.

Right at the top is the *Holiday Inn* (tel 571425-35), Balraj Sahani Marg, which has air-con singles/doubles for Rs 700/800, a swimming pool and other facilities. The *Palm Grove Hotel* (tel 624622) is another five-star hotel with rooms at Rs 500/600. The *Sun-n-Sand Hotel* (tel 571481) has a variety of rooms from Rs 400 to Rs 700.

Hotel Ajanta (tel 6124890) is a little cheaper at Rs 300/400. At the *Hotel Horizon* (tel 571411) there's a variety of rooms from Rs 300 to Rs 575. The pleasant *Hotel In Phom* (tel 576850) has rooms at Rs 275.

Places to Eat

The accommodation shortage certainly doesn't spill over into restaurants. Bombay probably has the best selection of restaurants of any major Indian city. As in other cities, a meal in a better-class restaurant can be one of India's bargains. A foray into the more expensive places is a worthwhile investment, even for back-packers.

Less Expensive There are plenty of places to eat around Colaba. *Dipti's Pure Drinks*, near the Rex and Stiffles, is popular for its wonderful fruit juices (Rs 4 to Rs 7), fruit salads and ice cream (Rs 6 to Rs 7). The high prices don't put people off this tiny establishment, although one traveller reported that 'the society consists of European junkies nodding into their lassi. Oh, and they ask you for money, too. Lexington Avenue in Harlem is worth a special trip if you like this sort of thing'.

Round the corner on Nawroji Furounji Rd, *Laxmi Vilas* has excellent vegetarian thalis for Rs 6, lassi for Rs 3.50. On Wodehouse Rd (alias the extension of Colaba Causeway alias Shahid Bhagat Singh Rd) the *Ananda Punjabi* is more expensive but tasty, say Rs 30 to Rs 40 for two. A couple of doors down, the *Kamat Hotel* has vegetarian food such as thalis for Rs 7 and Rs 13; it's air-con upstairs.

The *Apsara Restaurant* is a popular newer place with good Indian and Chinese food and lots of travellers. Nearby, the *Food Inn* is also new, popular and very clean and shiny looking although their tea is 'in the face of some stiff competition, the worst in Bombay'.

The *Leopold Restaurant* is a very popular place, not only for breakfast, lunch and dinner, but for hanging around and enjoying a cold beer. And not only for travellers; indeed some good Muslim Gulf Arabs seem to spend all day and night here! The Leopold has a very pleasant, unhurried, olde worlde atmosphere. The service is fast, the food pretty good, the place fairly hygienic and the prices reasonable even if the bottom of the menu does apologise because 'we are not pure vegetarian'. Still, you'll never be short of someone to chat with. Round the corner from the Leopold, *Alps* offers delicious 'sizzler' meals and cheap beer.

Café Mondegar, a pleasant coffee bar in the next block towards Wellingdon Circle, is very similar. Across the road, the *Hotel Majestic* is a big vegetarian plate-meal specialist. Directly across from the Leopold, the *Olympic Coffee House* is a traditional old coffee bar with wonderful decor.

The *Samovar*, in the Jehangir Art Gallery, is a good place for a cold drink or a quick snack. The *Naval & Military Restaurant*, a couple of doors up from the Nanking, has good snacks at low prices. At the top of Garden Rd, next to the garage, the *Edward VIII Restaurant* is a well-kept little place with good fruit juices.

Colaba is renowned for fine prawns and seafood. You can get fish and chips in a few places, including right beside the Marine Drive aquarium! *Bhelpuri* is a

Bombay speciality – a tasty snack of crisp noodles, spiced vegetables and other mysterious ingredients for a rupee or less. It's available from stalls all over town, but particularly on Chowpatty Beach. There are several restaurants along the beach road.

There are several places if you want a meal, a snack or just a drink while you read the mail you've just picked up from the GPO. *Kohinoor* is virtually directly opposite the GPO. Or there's the *New Empire Restaurant*, on the corner of Nagar Chowk (Murzbar Rd), opposite the main entrance to Victoria Terminus Railway Station. Go round the corner from the New Empire, and next to the Sterling Cinema *Waikiki* is a kind of snack bar. It specialises in *panbhaji* – a Bombay speciality which is a tasty, hot mixture of different vegetables. At 204 D Naoroji Rd, from the GPO and Victoria Terminus back towards Colaba, the small *Swidha* restaurant in the National Insurance Building has excellent vegetarian food although it's crowded at lunch. Bombay also has its own string of fast-food places called *Open House*, but they're mainly away from the centre.

More Expensive The Taj Mahal Hotel has a whole range of restaurants and snack bars, including the *Harbour Bar* where a beer for just Rs 23 almost seems a bargain. The *Rendezvous* on the rooftop caters for western tastes and has fine views. The *Shamiana* coffee bar has light meals – breakfast is Rs 27 to Rs 40 and not all that good. The *Tanjore* is probably the best place for a splash-out meal – traditional Indian food (most dishes Rs 40 to Rs 70) accompanied by sitar music and classical Indian dancing. They have thalis for no less than Rs 51. There's also a 'wonderful pastry shop' here.

There are several restaurants along K Dubash Marg, just across from the Jehangir Art Gallery and Prince of Wales Museum. The *Copper Chimney* has a typical 'non-veg' menu while the *Chinese Home* has good Chinese food. There's a second *Copper Chimney* at Worli. The *Delhi Durbar* on Falkland St is reputed to have excellent curries, but you're advised to take a taxi there.

In Colaba the *Delhi Darbar* doesn't serve alcohol but it does have a wide-ranging menu. This would be a good place to try the Parsi dish *dhaansak* – vegetable dhaansak is Rs 17.50. They have very good milkshakes and ice cream (try the pista kulfi). There are branches of *Kwality* at Worli and Kemps Corner. Good ice cream desserts.

Bombay has a particularly good selection of Chinese restaurants. Some say the *Nanking*, on Shivaji Marg in Colaba, has the best Chinese food in India. Directly across the road, the *Mandarin* is marginally more expensive. The adjacent *Hong Kong* does excellent Szechuan food – 'the best Chinese food we've ever found anywhere', reported a Canadian traveller. The *Kabab Corner* in the Hotel Nataraj on Marine Drive has excellent food and a sitar player.

There are a number of restaurants along Veer Nariman Rd off Marine Drive, such as the vegetarian *Purohit Hotel* where thalis cost from Rs 17 to Rs 29 and lassis Rs 5. It's relatively expensive and not as good as the prices would indicate. Others along this road include *Berrys* and *Gaylord* for non-vegetarian food or *Kamling* and *Chopsticks* for Chinese.

Daba Lunches

Mr Bombay Business-Wallah sets off from home, boards his train or bus and heads into the city every morning – just like his office-worker counterpart in Australia, England or America. Just like many of his overseas office-wallah brothers, he'd like to take his lunch with him and eat in the office. But an Indian lunch isn't as simple as a couple of sandwiches and an apple. A cut lunch could never satisfy an Indian – there has to be curry and rice and parathas and spices and a lot of things that take a lot of time to prepare and would hardly slip into a brown paper bag in the briefcase.

Naturally there's a supremely complex, yet smoothly working, Indian solution to this problem – it's called the daba lunch system. After he's left for work, his wife – or more likely the cook or bearer – sets to and fixes his lunch. When it's all prepared it's packed into a metal bucket about 15 cm in diameter and about 30 cm high. On the lid there's a mysterious colour-coded notation. The container is then carried down to a street corner pick-up point where it meets up with lots of other little lunch buckets and heads towards their city office destination. From the pick-up point they're conveyed to the nearest train station where they're transported to the appropriate city station.

In the city they're broken down to their separate destinations, and between 11 and 12 in the morning thousands upon thousands of individually coded lunches pour out of Victoria Terminus, Churchgate, Bombay Central and other stations. On the heads of porters, carried in carts, slung from long poles, tied on bicycle handlebars, those lunch buckets then scatter out across the city. Most of the daba-wallahs involved in this long chain of events are illiterate, but by some miracle of Indian efficiency, when Mr Business-Wallah opens his office door at lunchtime there will be his lunch by the door. Every day, without fail, they never lose a lunch.

Getting There

Air There is a very extensive network of flights operating into and out of Bombay's Santa Cruz airport. The domestic terminal is now separate and some distance away from the international terminal. Bombay is the main international gateway to India, with far more flights than New Delhi, Calcutta or Madras. It also has the busiest domestic network of flights.

Between Delhi and Bombay there are frequent daily flights, including a number of direct Airbus connections. There are a couple of daily flights to and from Calcutta and Madras, and connections with numerous other cities in India. Examples of fares include Ahmedabad Rs 410, Aurangabad Rs 296, Bangalore Rs 772, Calcutta Rs 1372, Cochin Rs 938, Dabolim (Goa) Rs 398, Delhi Rs 1007, Hyderabad Rs 638, Madras Rs 950, Pune Rs 157, Trivandrum Rs 1086 and Udaipur Rs 616.

Rail Two railway systems operate out of Bombay. Central Railways handles services to the east and south, plus a few trains to the north. The booking office (tel 264321) at Victoria Terminus has a vast and bewildering collection of different ticket windows on two floors. It takes time to locate the right window for the train you want, so don't go there in a hurry.

The best thing to do is go to the tourist kiosk in the main concourse first – that's the one on the right-hand side as you enter from the GPO – since it's here that the tourist quota is held. The booking offices are open daily from 9 am to 1 pm and 2 to 4.30 pm.

The other system out of Bombay is Western Railways, which has services to the north from Churchgate and Central stations. Bookings in 1st class can be made at Churchgate (tel 291952) between 9 am and 4 pm; or at the booking office, next to the Government of India Tourist Office opposite Churchgate, between 8 am and 8 pm. It's closed for lunch between 1.45 and 2.15 pm. This is also where they hold the tourist quota for 1st and 2nd classes. With the exception of the tourist quota, 2nd class has to be booked from Central Station (tel 395757) between 9 am and 4 pm.

There are a number of Central trains that do not depart from either Central or Churchgate but from Dadar Station, further north of Central. These trains include the Dadar-Madras Express, the fastest train to Madras.

From Bombay it is 1588 km and 17 hours to Delhi, and the fare is Rs 104 in 2nd class, Rs 433 in 1st. The Rajdhani Express is the fastest train; it's a special one-class train which costs Rs 320 in the air-con chair car, Rs 1056 in an air-con sleeper. Fares include tea, dinner, coffee and breakfast on board.

Bombay-Calcutta is a lengthy 1968-km trip taking 36 hours and costing Rs 125 in 2nd class, Rs 516 in 1st. As with Delhi there's a special new express, 2nd class and 2nd class air-con only, which does the

Bombay-Calcutta trip in 29 hours. Bombay-Madras is 1279 km and takes from 26 hours at a cost of Rs 90 in 2nd class, Rs 376 in 1st.

Bus Long-distance buses depart from the State Transport Terminal opposite Bombay Central Station. The state bus companies of Maharashtra, Gujarat, Karnataka and Madhya Pradesh all have offices here and bookings can be made (tel 374272 or 376622) between 8 am and 11 pm. Some travel times and approximate costs include:

Aurangabad	11 hours	Rs 51	(Rs 77*)
Bangalore	25 hours	Rs 151	(Rs 182*)
Indore	16 hours	Rs 75	(Rs 113*)
Surat	9 hours	Rs 36	
Hyderabad	16 hours	Rs 100	
Mangalore	25 hours	Rs 147	(Rs 178*)
Nasik	5 hours	Rs 25	
Panaji (Goa)	17 hours	Rs 86	(Rs 106*)
Pune (Poona)	5 hours	Rs 20	

*deluxe buses

Boat See Goa for more details on the popular Moghul Lines Bombay-Goa ferry, a very pleasant alternative to taking a bus or train. Departures are every day except Tuesday, but the service is suspended during the monsoon between June and September. Cabins cost Rs 220, 235, 260 and 300. Upper-deck class is Rs 72, lower-deck class is Rs 48. Ferry bookings can only be made at the jetty. The ferry is very heavily booked at Christmas time.

Arriving from Goa in Bombay, ignore the taxi drivers offering to take you to Colaba for Rs 50, continue 100 metres, turn left to the bus stop on the left with English numbers on it. Bus No 43 will get you to Colaba for less than Rs 1. Several buses run down D'Mello too.

Getting Around

Airport The airport bus service operates between Air India/Indian Airlines headquarters at Nariman Point and Terminals 1

(Domestic) and 2 (International). The journey from Nariman Point to Terminal 1 takes about 40 minutes and costs Rs 20. To Terminal 2, it takes about an hour and costs Rs 25. From Nariman Point departures are around 4 am to 2 am, airport to city from around 2 am to 11 pm.

Tickets for the buses are bought either on the buses themselves, at Air India/Indian Airlines headquarters or at the Terminals. Buses between the terminals depart every 15 minutes and cost Rs 10.

For those die-hards determined to get there on the el cheapo regardless of inconvenience, it is possible to get from the International Terminal to central Bombay for less than Rs 15. First take the airport bus from the International to the Domestic Terminal, then an ordinary bus to Vile Parle (number 321) or Santa Cruz, followed by a suburban train to Churchgate. If you're carrying more than a toothbrush, avoid doing anything as defiant as this in rush-hours.

A taxi to the domestic airport on the meter will cost about Rs 65 from Colaba, Rs 60 from Churchgate, Rd 40 from Dadar, Rs 30 from Juhu. It's a bit further to the international airport. During rush hours you won't find anyone who's prepared to use the meter, so expect to pay more. From the airport there is a police-operated taxi booth where you pay a set fare and are then assigned to a taxi. You give the driver your slip and there's no further fuss. You do, however, pay a bit more than the meter fare (plus adjustment card) – the official domestic airport-to-Colaba fare is Rs 80. An alternative is to walk down the line of taxis until you get to one far enough back that he will be willing to take less to go now rather than wait to get to the front of the line. Or stroll out to the main road.

Rail Bombay has an extensive system of electric trains, and it's virtually the only place in India where it's worth taking trains for intra-city travel. But *avoid* rush hours.

The main suburban route of interest to travellers is Churchgate-Bombay Central-Dadar, with many other stops in between. There's a train every 10 to 15 minutes in either direction between 4.30 am and 10.30 pm. The fare between Churchgate and Central is Rs 1 in 2nd class and Rs 13 in 1st.

A taxi over the same distance would cost you about Rs 15 to Rs 20 on the meter. If you arrive at Bombay Central on the main railway system, your ticket covers you for the journey from there to the more convenient Churchgate station.

Bus Bombay has probably the best public transport system of any major Indian city. There are lots of well-kept double-decker buses with fares ranging from Rs 0.50. They tend to be crowded, especially during rush hours, and Bombay's pickpockets are notoriously adept. Take care. The buses are operated by BEST (Bombay Electric Supply & Transport) and have separate route maps for their extensive city and suburban services. From the Victoria Terminus Railway Station take a No 1, 6 Ltd, 7 Ltd, 103 or 124 to 'Electric House', a useful landmark in Colaba. From Bombay Central take a No 70 or a 124. Ltd means 'limited stops'.

Taxi Bombay has a large fleet of metered taxis so you won't have any trouble finding one. As usual, the meters are out of date, so you pay according to a fare conversion card which all drivers carry, regardless of how reluctant they are to pull them out when they'd prefer to tell you the first figure that comes into their head. At last count the metered flagfall was Rs 1 but the adjustment was meter times four!

You probably won't have any difficulties about drivers re-setting the meters from dawn until late evening, but between midnight and dawn they're reluctant to take you anywhere on the meter so you'll have to negotiate a price.

Things to Buy

Bombay has a number of intriguing markets and some feel it's much better for shopping than Delhi. Chor Bazaar is Bombay's thieves' market. It's off Grant Rd (Maulana Shaukatali Rd) and here you'll find a phenomenal collection of 'antiques', jewellery, wooden items, leather and general bric-a-brac. Mutton St has a particularly interesting collection of shops for miscellaneous 'junk'. Shops are generally open from 10 am but are closed on Fridays.

Crawford Market, officially renamed Mahatma Phule Market, is the centre for flowers, fruit, vegetables, meat and fish in Bombay. This is the place to look for Bombay's two famous fish – the pomfret and the 'Bombay duck'. The market building was constructed in 1867 and is one of the most colourful and photogenic places in Bombay. Nearby is Javeri Bazaar, the jewellery centre off Mumbadevi Rd. There is some fantastic stuff here, especially silver belts and old statues and charms. Nearby is the brass bazaar on Kalbadevi Rd.

There are all sorts of places selling handicrafts, artefacts, antiques and art around the Colaba area. Shops in the Taj Hotel specialise in high quality – and high prices. Check the Jehangir Gallery by the Prince of Wales Museum too. If you're buying miniatures, only trust people 'who bring out a magnifying glass, without being asked, for you to inspect the paintings with'. The evening stalls along S B Singh Rd in Colaba are good places to buy things, as are Kheedi House and the Rajasthan Emporium at 286 and 230 D Naoroji Rd respectively. You can find some real bargains in the Khadi Village Industries Emporium.

AROUND BOMBAY
Elephanta Island

The island of Elephanta is about 10 km north-east from Apollo Bunder and is Bombay's major tourist attraction due to the four rock-cut temples on the island.

They are thought to have been cut out between 450 and 750 AD, and at that time the island was known as Gharapuri, the 'fortress city'. When the Portuguese arrived they renamed it Elephanta after the large stone elephant near the landing place. This figure collapsed in 1814 and the remaining pieces were removed to the Victoria Gardens in Bombay in 1864 and reassembled in 1912.

Unfortunately the Portuguese took their traditional disdain for other religions to its usual lengths at Elephanta, and did considerable damage to the sculptures. Although some people feel that Elephanta is not as impressive as the rock-cut temples of Ellora, the size, beauty and power of the sculptures are unexcelled.

The caves are reached by a stairway up the hillside from the landing place. Palanquins are available for anybody in need of being carried up. There is one main cave with a number of large sculptured panels, all relating to Shiva, and a separate lingam shrine.

The most interesting of the panels includes one of Trimurti, or the three-headed Shiva, where he also takes the role of Brahma, the creator, and Vishnu, the preserver. In other panels Shiva appears as Arddhanariswar, where he unites both sexes in one body – one side of the sculpture is male, one side female.

There are figures of Shiva and his wife Parvati and of their marriage. In another panel Shiva dances the Tandava, the dance that shakes the world. Parvati and their son, Ganesh, look on a little astonished. One of the best panels is that of Rawana shaking Kailasa. The demon king of Lanka decided to carry Shiva and his companions off by the simple expedient of removing their Himalayan home, the mountain Kailasa. Parvati became panic-stricken at his energetic attempts to jerk the mountain free, but Shiva calmly pushed the mountain back down with one toe, trapping Rawana beneath it for 10,000 years.

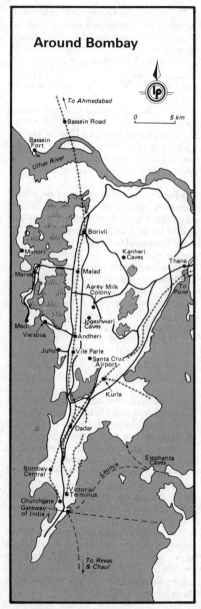

Around Bombay

To Ahmedabad

Bassein Road

0   5 km

Bassein Fort

Ulhas River

Borivli

Manori

Kanheri Caves

Thana

Marve

Malad

To Pune

Aarey Milk Colony

Jogeshwari Caves

Madh

Versova

Andheri

Juhu

Vile Parle

Santa Cruz Airport

Kurla

Dadar

Elephanta Caves

Bombay Central

Launch

Victoria Terminus

Churchgate

Gateway of India

To Revas & Chaul

Getting There Launches leave regularly from Apollo Bunder by the Gateway of India. The economy boats cost Rs 16 (children Rs 10), deluxe ones Rs 30 (children Rs 20), more with air-con. The more expensive trips include a guide. A good guide, and there are some excellent ones, can considerably increase your enjoyment and understanding – even, as one tubby little gentleman with glasses does, show you how Shiva danced the Tandava. During the monsoon, boats may not run if the water is too rough. Elephanta gets very crowded on weekends. Harbour cruises, costing Rs 5, also operate from the Gateway of India.

Juhu

Close to Bombay's international airport, Santa Cruz, Juhu is 18 km north of the city centre. It's the nearest beach to the city and has quite a collection of upper-notch hotels, but it's no place for a pleasant swim. On weekdays it is fairly quiet, but on weekends there are donkeys, camels, dancing monkeys, acrobats and every other type of Indian beach entertainment. From Santa Cruz station you can get there on a No 182, 231 or 253 bus.

Aarey Milk Colony

Fresh milk is produced at this model milk-production centre. It's notable also for its hilltop viewpoint with a fine view over the island. There's an entry fee and not much to see.

Krishnagiri Upavan National Park

Reached via the Borivli station, the national park contains the Kanheri Caves and lakes Vihar, Tulsi and Powari, which act as reservoirs for much of Bombay's water supply.

At the entrance to the park there's a huge outdoor movie lot, including a fort frontage partly constructed from old oil drums. Also near the park entrance is, believe it or not, a Lion Safari Park. It's open from 9 am to 5 pm daily except Mondays (Tuesdays if Monday is a public holiday) and trips are made through the park in a 'safari vehicle'.

Kanheri Caves

Within the national park, about 42 km from Bombay, 109 caves line the side of a rocky ravine. The caves are Buddhist and date from around the 2nd to 9th century AD. Although there are so many of them, most are little more than holes in the rock and only a handful are of real interest. The most important is cave 3, the 'Great Chaitya Cave', which has a long colonnade of pillars around the *dagoba* at the back of the cave. Further up the ravine are some good views out to the sea.

Kanheri can be visited on the regular suburban tours, or you can take a train to Borivli station and then a taxi the 10 km or so to the caves. On Sundays and holidays there is a bus service from the station to the caves.

Other Beaches

Bombay's best-known beach, Juhu, is too close to the city and not sanitary enough for a pleasant swim, but there are more remote beaches on the island. Marve and Manori beaches are near each other, about 40 km out of the city. You can get to them via the station at Malad, 32 km out. Marve, unfortunately, has also become dirty and the water unhealthy. There's an interesting fishing village and an old Portuguese church nearby.

A nice place to stay near the village of Manori is the *Manoribel Hotel* (tel 241707), which has double rooms with attached bath from Rs 100. Or there's the friendly *Hotel Dominica* with rooms at Rs 100 to Rs 150. To get there, take the suburban electric train to Malad, then a bus to Marve ferry, cross on the ferry and walk to the Manoribel. The walk to the beach is a km and a bit from where the ferry stops at Manori. Aksa Beach, reached by bus No 272 or by an auto-rickshaw from Malad, is OK. It's probably the best beach close to Bombay.

Other beaches around Bombay include Madh, 45 km out and also reached via Malad. Versova is 29 km from the city, reached via Andheri station, but is very dirty too. Getting to Uran involves a 74-km trip, the last 10 km by sea. Launches leave from the New Ferry Wharf.

Montpezir & Jogeshvari Caves

There are a few Hindu caves, one of which was converted into a Portuguese church, at Montpezir near Borivli. The Jogeshvari Caves are near the Andheri station.

Bassein

Just across the river which separates the mainland from Bombay island is Bassein, a Portuguese fortified city from 1534 to 1739. The Portuguese took Bassein at the same time as Daman, further north in Gujarat. They built a fort containing a city of such pomp and splendour that it came to be known as the 'Court of the North'. Only the Hidalgos or aristocracy were permitted to live within the fort walls, and by the end of the 17th century there were 300 Portuguese and 400 Indian-Christian families here, with a cathedral, five convents and 13 churches.

Then in 1739 the Marathas besieged the city, and the Portuguese surrendered after three months of appalling losses. Today the city walls are still standing and you'll see the ruins of some of the churches and the Cathedral of St Joseph.

Bassein is 11 km from the Bassein Road (Vasai Road in Marathi) railway station. Sopara, near Bassein Road, is thought to be the Biblical Ophir. About an hour by bus from the station are the Vajreshwari hot springs.

Chaul

South of Bombay, this was another Portuguese settlement, although not as important as Bassein. They took it in 1522 and lost it to the Marathas at the same time as Bassein. There are a few remains and old ruined churches within the Portuguese fortifications. Looking across to the Portuguese fort from the other side of the river is the hilltop Muslim Korlai Fort.

Ferries run to Revas from the New Ferry Wharf, a 1½-hour trip. From there you've got a 30-km bus trip to Chaul. It's possible to continue on from here by road to Mahabaleshwar, or to join the Bombay-Pune road.

Maharashtra

Population: 56 million
Area: 307,762 square km
Capital: Bombay
Main language: Marathi

The state of Maharashtra is one of the largest in India, both in terms of population and in area. Its booming capital, Bombay, makes it not only one of the most important states economically, but also a major arrival point for overseas visitors. From Bombay you can head off into India in a number of directions, but most travellers will either be going south to Goa through Pune (Poona), with its famous ashram, or north-east to the amazing cave temples of Ajanta and Ellora. Most of the state stands on the high Deccan Plateau. Historically this was the main centre for the Maratha empire which defied the Moghuls for so long, and which under the fearless rule of Shivaji carved out a large part of central India as their own domain.

Cave Architecture

The rock-cut caves in Maharashtra have several distinct design elements. The Buddhist caves, which are generally the older ones, are either *chaityas* (temples) or *viharas* (monasteries). Chaityas are usually deep and narrow with a stupa at the end of the cave. There may be a row of columns down both sides of the cave and around the stupa.

The *viharas* are usually not as deep and narrow as the *chaitya* caves. They were normally intended as living and sleeping quarters for the monks and often have rows of cells along both sides. In the back there is a small shrine room, usually containing an image of the Buddha. At Ajanta, the cliff face into which the caves are cut is very steep and there is often a small verandah or entrance porch in front of the main cave. At Ellora the rock face is

more sloping and the verandah or porch element generally becomes a separate courtyard.

The cave temples reach their peak of complexity and design in the Hindu caves at Ellora, in particular the magnificent Kailasa temple. Here they are hardly caves any longer, for the whole enclosure is open to the sky. In design they are much like other temples of that era – except that instead of being built up from the bottom they were cut down from the top. They are an imitation of conventional architecture of that period.

Though the caves are notable for their sculptures and paintings, the famous Ajanta 'frescoes' are not, technically speaking, frescoes at all. A fresco is a painting done on a wet surface which absorbs the colour. The Ajanta paintings are more correctly tempera since they were painted on a dry surface. The rough-hewn rock walls were coated with a cm-thick layer of clay and cow-dung mixed with rice husks. A final coat of lime was then applied to produce the high gloss polished surface on which the artist painted.

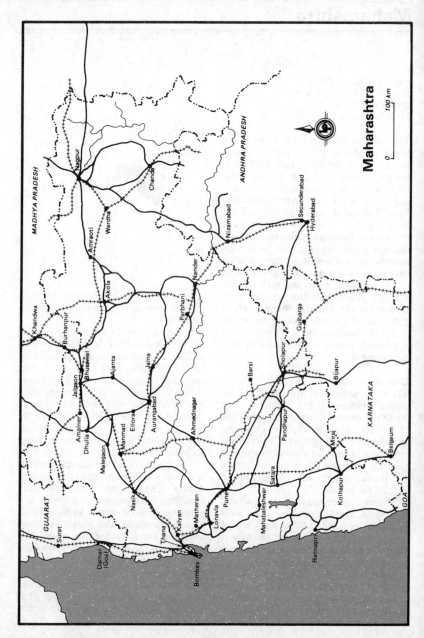

MATHERAN

The nearest hill station to Bombay, Matheran is 171 km from the city via Neral on the Bombay-Pune railway line. The name means 'jungle topped' or 'wooded head', which is just what it is – an undulating hilltop cloaked in shady trees. It's the abundance of shade as much as the 700 to 800-metre altitude which makes Matheran a slightly cooler place than Bombay. Matheran became a popular hill station during the days of the Raj; Hugh Malet is credited with its discovery in 1850.

Getting to Matheran is half the fun; from Neral you take a tiny narrow-gauge toy train up the 21-km route to the hill. It's a choice of train or walk; there are no motor vehicles in Matheran and the trekking route is an 11-km climb. The train twists, turns and winds on its steep, two-hour ascent. Food and drink vendors cling to the outside and at one point you pass through 'one kiss tunnel'.

Matheran sprawls north-south along the hilltop. Many km of walking tracks lead to the viewpoints that ring the station; at many of them the ground drops sheer to the plains far, far below. On a clear day the view can be fantastic and even in the hazy air of the pre-monsoon dry season the eerie views of surrounding hills are very fine.

From Porcupine, Monkey or Hart points on the north-west of the hill you can see the lights of Bombay on a clear night. Porcupine is also a good place for catching the sunset, but Panorama Point, at the extreme north, is said to have the finest views. The western side, from Porcupine to Louisa Point, is known as Cathedral Rocks, and Neral can be seen far below, straddling the Central Railway line. At the south, near One Tree Hill, a trail down to the valley below is known as Shivaji's Ladder, so called because the Maratha leader is said to have used it.

Places to Stay

The *Laxmi Hotel* has rooms with attached bathroom from Rs 45. *Khan's Cosmopolitan Hotel* (tel 40) is even cheaper and also close to the centre but rather primitive. For the real economisers there is dormitory accommodation at the *Holiday Camp* (the train stops at the camp, a km or two before Matheran) or at *Maneklal Terrace*, two km south of the railway station. Or try the *Holiday Resort* with rooms at Rs 50, and *Scott Bungalow* with rooms big enough for five at Rs 75. he *Giririhar Hotel* has peaceful, spacious gardens and doubles with balcony for Rs 50.

In the middle range the *Alexander Guest House* (tel 51) has doubles from Rs 120 to Rs 170. The *Silvan Guest House* (tel 74) has rooms at Rs 150/230 or room-only accommodation at Rs 100. The *Divadkar Lodging & Boarding House* (tel 23) is almost directly opposite the railway station and has rooms at Rs 150 per person. These places have attached bathrooms and small verandahs with chairs and tables. At many places in Matheran prices may be negotiable midweek, but at the weekend they tend to be full up.

Most of the more expensive places provide boarding and lodging only – you must take all your meals at the guest houses. They include the *Lord's Central House* (tel 28) (also called just Central Hotel) and the *Regal Hotel* (tel 43, 87), which costs Rs 350 for a double including all meals. The *Royal Hotel* (tel 47, 75) costs Rs 200 for a double. The *Rugby Hotel* (tel 91-2) has rooms at Rs 110 to Rs 150 per person or air-con doubles at Rs 425.

Places to Eat

Away from the hotels and guest houses there is a string of snack-style eating places in the town centre. Good fruit juices at the *Kwality Fruit Juice House*. Matheran is famed for its honey and for *chikki* – a toffee-like confection made of gur sugar and nuts. Chikki is sold at many shops in Matheran.

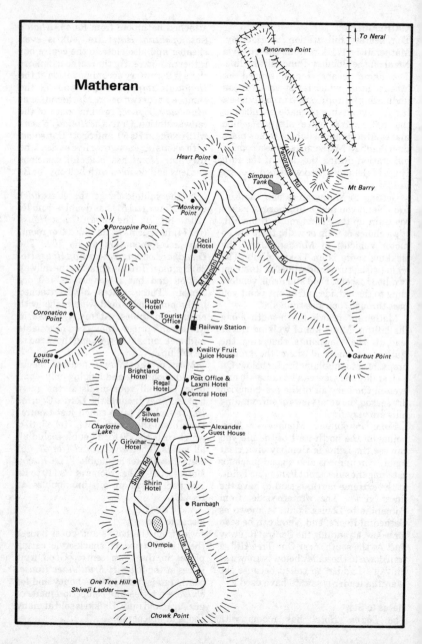

Matheran

To Neral

Panorama Point

Panorama Rd

Heart Point

Simpson Tank

Mt Barry

Monkey Point

Cecil Hotel

M Gandhi Rd

Garbut Rd

Porcupine Point

Marlet Rd

Rugby Hotel

Coronation Point

Tourist Office

Railway Station

Louisa Point

Kwality Fruit Juice House

Garbut Point

Brightland Hotel

Post Office & Laxmi Hotel

Regal Hotel

Central Hotel

Silvan Hotel

Charlotte Lake

Alexander Guest House

Girivihar Hotel

Shivaji Rd

Shirin Hotel

Rambagh

Little Chowk Rd

Olympia

One Tree Hill

Shivaji Ladder

Chowk Point

There are many monkeys in Matheran; watch out for them if you buy bananas in the market!

Getting There

From Bombay, the Pune expresses or the Karjat local trains will take you to Neral, where the toy train runs up to Matheran. It's about two hours from Bombay to Neral and two hours again up to Matheran. The Matheran train generally connects with the Pune expresses. Fare from Bombay is Rs 18 in 2nd class, Rs 107 in 1st – the Matheran toy train has pink curtains on the 1st-class carriage!

Trains depart from Matheran for Neral three or four times daily, or you can take a share-taxi for Rs 22. There's a Rs 4 'capitation tax' on each arrival at Matheran; you pay it as you leave the station. During the monsoon the Neral-Matheran train service is suspended.

Getting Around

In Matheran itself the only transport is rickshaws – one man pulls, two push (or hold it back on the descents). If your gear is too heavy to carry very far, and you're staying a long way from the station, you may want to use one to get your bags to the hotel. Ponies can also be hired for riding on the many trails that wind around Matheran.

KARLA & BHAJA CAVES

Situated 126 km south-east of Bombay on the main rail line to Pune, Lonavla (sometimes spelt Lonavala) is the place from which to visit the Karla and Bhaja caves. If, however, your interest in archaeological sites is such that you intend to spend more than a day exploring the caves, then it would be more convenient to stay either at the Government Holiday Camp near the Malavli railway station, or at the Karla Hotel, since there's little of interest in Lonavla itself. The Karla Cave is about 12 km from Lonavla, about 1½ km off the main road. The Bhaja Caves are about three km off the main road. If you plan on walking to the latter, take a train to Malavli first.

The Tourist Office at Lonavla Station is completely useless.

Karla Cave

It's a steep half-km climb up the hillside to Karla Cave. The cave temple is Hinayana Buddhist and was completed around 80 BC. One of the best-preserved of its type in India, it dates from the time when this style of temple was at its height in terms of design purity.

A beautifully carved 'Sun Window' filters the light in towards the small stupa at the inner end of the deep, narrow cave. Unfortunately an ugly little modern temple has been erected just outside the cave entrance. Inside, the pillars are topped by two kneeling elephants and two seated figures with their arms over each other on the elephants. Generally the figures are male and female, but sometimes they are two women. The roof of the cave is ribbed with teak beams said to be original; at Ajanta and Ellora the wooden beams that may once have been there are now gone. On the sides of the vestibule are carved elephant heads which once had real ivory tusks.

Other carvings can also be seen along the sides. A pillar topped by four back-to-back lions, an image usually associated with Ashoka, stands outside the cave. It may be older than the cave itself.

There are some small monastery or *vihara* caves at Karla, further round the hillside. Some of these have been converted into Hindu shrines.

If possible, avoid going to the Karla Cave at weekends or on public holidays, when it is invaded by the transistor radio and picnic mobs from Bombay. The noise and mess which they create isn't going to do anything for your appreciation of this beautiful site. Bhaja is too far from the main road for this to happen on the same scale, but it does get its fair share too.

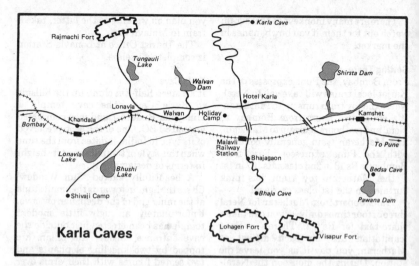

Karla Caves

Bhaja Caves

It's a fairly rough route from the main road to the 18 Bhaja Caves. They're in a lusher, greener setting than the Karla Cave's dry hillside, and are thought to date from around 200 BC. Cave 12, a *chaitya* cave similar in style to the Karla Cave, is the most important. South of this is a strange group of 14 stupas, five inside and nine outside the cave. The last cave on the south side has some fine sculptures.

Other

Further along the line, six km south-east of Kamshet station, are the Bedsa Caves. They are thought to be newer than the better-executed Karla Cave. At one time the roof of the main cave was probably painted. There are a number of old forts in the vicinity, including the hilltop Lohagen Fort, six km from Malavli, which was taken twice by Shivaji, and lost again on each occasion. Above the Bhaja Caves is Visapur Fort.

Khandala, before Lonavla, is picturesquely situated overlooking a ravine. In the wet season there is a fine waterfall near the head of the ravine.

Places to Stay & Eat

Lonavla Like Khandala and Mahabaleshwar, Lonavla is regarded as a kind of hill station by people from Bombay so there's quite a range of accommodation here. It's a compact town and there are several places close to the bus and railway stations.

Hotel Girikunj (tel 2529) has rooms with own bathroom from Rs 55 as well as a vegetarian restaurant. *Hotel Purohit* (tel 2695) is similar in standard although there are also some rather cheaper rooms without attached bath. *Pitale Boarding & Lodging* (tel 2657) is similar again; doubles with attached bath are Rs 50. The Pitale is a charming old stone and wood colonial-style bungalow encircled by a verandah, and has a restaurant and bar.

At the cheaper end of the market is the friendly *Hotel Chandralok* (tel 2294) with rooms at Rs 45 and a vegetarian restaurant. The *Dinesh Hotel* (tel 2561) is a little more expensive. The *Janata Hotel* (tel 2689), opposite the Girikunj, is cheaper but somewhat drab. If you don't mind dormitory accommodation, try the

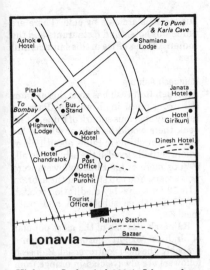

To Pune & Karla Cave

Ashok Hotel

Shamiana Lodge

Pitale

To Bombay

Bus Stand

Janata Hotel

Highway Lodge

Adarsh Hotel

Hotel Girikunj

Hotel Chandralok

Post Office

Dinesh Hotel

Hotel Purohit

Tourist Office

Railway Station

Lonavla

Bazaar

Area

Highway Lodge (tel 2321). It's run by a nice old Persian man.

There are a number of other places out along the main road to the Karla Cave. They include the *Shamian Lodge* and the *Maharaja Inn*, as well as the *Hotel Filmstar* near Walvan Lake.

At the top of the market are the *Adarsh Hotel* (tel 2353) close to the bus station, the *Fariyas Holiday Resort* (tel 2701-5) with rooms at Rs 415/525, and *Biji's Ingleside Inn* (tel 2638) at Rs 320/350.

There are several eating places along the Bombay-Pune road through Lonavla and others across the railway tracks in the main part of this small town.

Khandala Khandala is the station before Lonavla and can be used as an alternative jumping-off point for the caves. *Hotel Mount View* (tel 746) on Khandala Rd is reasonably cheap. The *Khandala Hotel* (tel 239) and *Hotel on the Rocks* (tel 690) are at the luxurious end of Khandala's scale. Right at the top there's *Hotel Dukes Retreat* (tel 2189) with rooms with bathroom from Rs 300 to Rs 350.

Karla The most convenient location for a

cave visit is the government-operated *Holiday Camp* (tel 30) just off the Bombay-Pune road near the caves. There are two types of accommodation blocks from Rs 35 per day plus a couple of dormitories. From the Holiday Camp you can get to both the Karla and Bhaja caves relatively easily, but during the monsoon you can't get to the camp from the Malavli railway station because a river blocks the way. At that time you must leave the train at Lonavla and bus to the camp. Food is available there.

You can also find similarly priced rooms at the *Karla Hotel* at the junction where the road to Karla turns off from the main road. They're not as pleasant as those at the Holiday Camp.

Getting There

It's possible to see the Karla and Bhaja caves comfortably in a day from either Bombay or Pune, so long as you're prepared to hire an auto-rickshaw in Lonavla to take you there and back. There is a choice of both trains and buses to Lonavla from either of the cities, but you can give up the idea of a bus *from* Lonavla to Bombay or Pune because they invariably turn up full, and if anyone does get off you can be sure that someone else has booked that seat in advance.

Bombay-Lonavla takes about three hours, and various trains run through Lonavla from Bombay in the morning, in the opposite direction in the afternoon. Fares for the 128-km trip are Rs 16 in 2nd class, Rs 61 in 1st.

From Pune long-distance express trains as well as commuter shuttles run the 64 km to Lonavla. The expresses take about one to 1½ hours, the commuter trains about two hours.

Getting Around

In theory there are local buses about a dozen times a day between Lonavla and Karla and to the Rajmachi Fort. Unfortunately the timetable seems to be imaginary; the buses arrive full and leave even fuller, everybody fights like crazy to get on and you never know which buses are going where because there are no signs. If you're determined to go by bus, practise saying 'Karla zanarkhai?' – Marathi for 'is this going to Karla' – since no one speaks English.

You can save a lot of time and frustration by hiring an auto-rickshaw. The prices are fairly standard: Lonavla-Karla Rs 15, Lonavla-Karla-Lonavla Rs 40 including waiting time, Lonavla-Karla-Bhaja-Lonavla Rs 50 to Rs 60 including waiting time at both sites. It would, of course, be cheaper to stay at the Holiday Camp overnight and walk to the caves.

PUNE (Poona) (population 950,000)

Shivaji, the great Maratha leader, was raised in Pune, which was granted to his grandfather in 1599. Later it became the capital of the Peshwas, but in 1817 went to the British, under whom it became the capital of the region during the monsoon. It has a rather more pleasant climate at that time than muggy Bombay.

Although Pune has a number of points of interest and can be conveniently visited if you're heading from Bombay to Aurangabad (for Ajanta and Ellora) or to Goa, its major attraction for western visitors was the Shree Rajneesh Ashram. The ashram became so well known that it was even included on the city bus tour, where, in a superb reversal of roles, Indians flocked to view westerners. With the Bhagwan on the run, however, the Pune ashram is a mere shadow of its former self.

Orientation & Information

There's a Tourist Information Counter at the railway station where tours can be booked and some information is available. The Regional Tourist Office is in Central Buildings but is not of great use. Manney's on Arsenal Rd is a good bookshop.

The city is at the confluence of the Mutha and Mula rivers. The railway and

bus stations are side by side. There are numerous hotels and restaurants and the Indian Airlines office in this same central area.

Rajneesh Ashram

Although Rajneesh has gone, his ashram still continues in Koregaon Park, a relatively spacious suburb of Pune. At its peak there would be 3000 or 4000 of his followers at a time in Pune, about 1000 of whom actually lived at the ashram. In all, 90% or more of his Pune followers were westerners. You can still visit the ashram – Rs 12 for a one-day meditation course, Rs 25 for three substantial and tasty meals.

Rajneesh was one of the most popular of India's 'export gurus' and, quite probably, the most controversial. Rajneesh followers are always clad in orange from head to toe and wear a picture of their guru on a wooden bead chain around their neck. Rajneesh's approach to the guru business caused controversy from the start; it's a curious blend of Indian mysticism and Californian pop-psychology. You don't just meditate – you do 'dynamic meditation'. Hyped-up tales of tantric sexual rites have also fuelled the controversy, and tabloid papers in the west are always happy to run a headline with 'Sex Guru' in it.

Raja Kelkar Museum

This interesting museum is one of Pune's real delights. The exhibits are the personal collection of Shri Dinkar Kelkar, a smiling old man in a white dhoti whom visitors will often see wandering around the building. There's actually far more to his zany collection than is actually on show. The museum building is simply too small and exhibits have to be rotated.

Amongst the items you might see are Peshwa and other miniatures, a coat of armour made of fish scales, a bizarre collection of musical instruments, carved doors and windows, hookah pipes, strange locks, oil lamps and a superb collection of

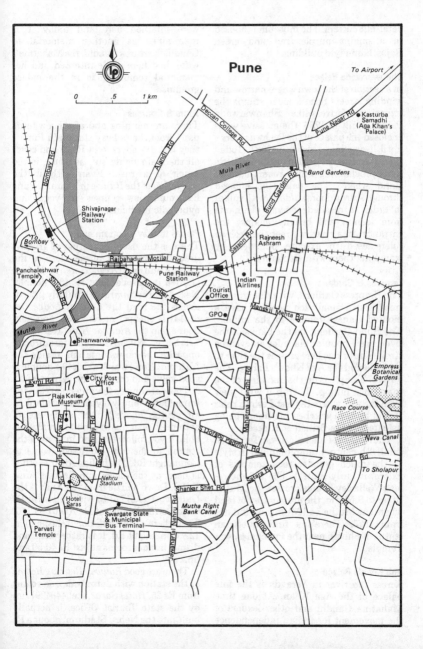

Pune

0   .5   1 km

To Airport

Kasturba
Samadhi
(Aga Khan's
Palace)

Deccan College Rd

Pune Nagar Rd

Alandi Rd

Mula River

Bund Gardens

Bund Garden Rd

Bombay Rd

Shivajinagar
Railway
Station

Sasson Rd

Rajneesh
Ashram

To
Bombay

Raibahadur Motilal Rd

Panchaleshwar
Temple

Shivaji Rd

Dr BR Ambedkar Rd

Pune Railway
Station

Tourist
Office

Indian
Airlines

Manekji Mehta Rd

GPO

Mutha River

Shanwarwada

Empress
Botanical
Gardens

City Post
Office

Laxmi Rd

Race Course

Raja Kelkar
Museum

Sanas Rd

Shivaji Rd

Bhandar Rd

Nava Canal

Mahatma Gandhi Rd

Tilak Rd

Jungle Fair Roa Rd

S Dorabji Padmal Rd

Sholapur Rd

To Sholapur

Nehru
Stadium

Shankar Shet Rd

Satara Rd

Wanowri Rd

Hotel
Saras

Jawaharlal Nehru Rd

Mutha Right
Bank Canal

Katraj no Rd

Swargate State
& Municipal
Bus Terminal

Parvati
Temple

betel-nut cutters. The museum is housed in a quaint purple, red and green Rajasthani-style building.

Shanwarwada Palace

In a section of the town where narrow and winding streets form a maze stands the imposing, fortress-like Shanwarwada Palace. Built in 1736, the massive walls enclosed the palace of the Peshwa rulers – until it was burnt down in 1827. Today there is a pleasant garden inside and little signs proclaiming which rooms used to stand where. The palace is entered through sturdy doors studded with spikes in order to dissuade enemy elephants from leaning too heavily against the entrance! In a nearby street the Peshwa rulers used to execute offenders by trampling them with elephants.

Temples & Gardens

The Empress Gardens, with fine tropical trees and a small zoo nearby, have a moated Ganesh temple in the middle. The Bund Gardens, on the banks of the river, are a popular place for an evening stroll. The bridge here crosses the river to Yeravda and the Aga Khan's Palace. The Parvati Temple is on the outskirts of the town on a hilltop. There's a good view from the top, where the last Peshwa ruler is said to have watched his troops being defeated by the British at Kirkee.

The rock-cut Panchaleshwar Temple, a small 8th-century temple similar in style to the much grander rock temples of Ellora, is fairly central. The 150-metre-long Wellesley Bridge crosses the Mutha River to Sangam, the promontory of land where the Mutha and Mula join. It dates from 1875. There's a fine equestrian statue of Shivaji near the Panchaleshwar Temple.

Aga Khan's Palace

Across the river in Yeravda is the fine palace of the Aga Khan. At one time Mahatma Gandhi and other leaders of the movement for Indian independence were interned here and today it is maintained as another memorial to Gandhi. Kasturba Gandhi, the Mahatma's wife, died here while interned and her memorial tomb stands in the palace grounds.

Tours & Courses

There are morning and afternoon tours daily from the railway station in Pune – they last 3½ hours, cost Rs 25 and cover all the main sights but, as usual, in too much of a rush. Even without the attraction of the Rajneesh Ashram, Pune has numerous courses in yoga and ayurvedic medicine.

Places to Stay – bottom end

There is the usual collection of grubby, drab and/or dismal places close to the railway station. *Green Hotel* in Wilson Garden is reasonable at Rs 40 a double. Next door the *Samrat* is similarly priced, across the road the *Central Lodge* (tel 61414) is cheaper at Rs 25/35, and next door again the *Alankar Hotel* (tel 63505-7) is better. Wilson Gardens start directly opposite the railway station, beside the *National Hotel* which at Rs 40 a double is good value and the staff are very helpful.

There are quite a few other places in the immediate vicinity if you draw a blank at all of the above – but some are of extremely poor quality, quite uninhabitable. If you follow the road in front of the station to the left you'll soon come to Connaught Rd. The Indian Airlines office is here, at the bigger and flashier Amir Hotel. Down a little from the Amir is the *Gulmohr* (tel 61773-5) with singles at Rs 60 to Rs 75, doubles at Rs 100 to Rs 110. Then there's the *Shalimar* (tel 65990) at 12A Connaught Rd. It is rather drab and dismal but has rooms at just Rs 40/50 and up.

There are good *Railway Retiring Rooms* at the station with dorm beds and rooms from Rs 25. *Hotel Saras*, (tel 448499) run by the state Tourist Office, is actually built into the Nehru Stadium, about a Rs

5 or Rs 6 auto-rickshaw ride from the railway station but very close to the Swargate Bus Station. It's quite pleasant.

Places to Stay – top end
Hotel Amir (tel 61841) is very close to the railway station at 15 Connaught Rd. This is one of the best places in Pune, with air-con rooms at Rs 225/300 and non-air-con at Rs 150/200. It has the usual mod cons, a vegetarian restaurant and a good (and fairly reasonably priced) snack bar, if you're in need of something non-Indian.

The *Blue Diamond* (tel 63775) is in Koregaon Park. Rooms here are from Rs 525/650 for air-con singles/doubles, and again it's all mod cons including a swimming pool, restaurants and coffee bar.

Places to Eat
The food scene is pretty good in Pune. The *Amir* and *Blue Diamond* have more expensive restaurants, but there are several good cheap places right in front of the station to the left. *Neelam Restaurant* is pleasant and the *Hotel Madhura* (only a very small sign in English but it's in the big Hotel Metro building) has excellent thalis, good lassi and super-cool drinks. A couple of doors further down there's the *Savera Restaurant*, also with good food.

On Mah Gan Rd *Spicers Health Foods* has brown bread, peanut butter, tofu and other rarities. There's good Indian food at *Vaishali* and *Amrapali* on Ferguson College Rd. *Darshan* at 759 Prabhat Rd, Deccan Gymkhana has fruit juices, milkshakes and an unusual menu of Indian and western light meals. At 96B on the same road *Suvarna Rekha Lodge* has, according to one visitor, 'superb thalis – don't let the decor discourage you'.

The ground-floor restaurant at the *Ashiwad Hotel* is good, clean and efficient. For an upmarket evening try the *Coffee House Restaurant* on Arsenal Rd.

Getting There
Air There are daily flights between Pune and Bombay (Rs 157), Delhi (Rs 1133), Bangalore (Rs 731) and less frequently Hyderabad (Rs 491).

Rail Pune is 192 km from Bombay. Trains take four or five hours and cost Rs 22.50 in 2nd class, Rs 83 in 1st.

Bus There are daily regular and air-con buses between Bombay and Pune and also long-distance share-taxis. From Pune the taxis operate from the Pune taxi stand in front of the railway station. Buses run from Pune to Mahabaleshwar, Panaji (Goa) and Aurangabad (via Ahmednagar). Pune-Aurangabad takes about six hours.

Pune has three bus stations:

Railway Bus Stand – points south including Goa – Belgaum, Panaji, Kolhapur, Mahabaleshwar, Ratnagiri, Panchgani, Satara and Sholapur.
Shivaji Nagar Bus Stand – points north and north-east – Ahmednagar, Amravati, Aurangabad, Belgaum, Dehu, Jalgaon, Lonavla, Murud, Nanded and Nasik.
Swargate Bus Stand – Baneshwar, Bhorgar, Daund, Khodakwasla, Morgaon, Purandar, Saswad, Shivapur and Simhagad.

Getting Around
There are lots of taxis and auto-rickshaws. From the railway station to the Swargate Bus Stand or the Saras Hotel costs about Rs 5 to Rs 6, to the Shivaji Nagar Bus Stand is about Rs 5. Pune is packed with bicycles and lots of places rent them.

AROUND PUNE
Simhagad, the 'lion fort', is 25 km south-west of Pune and was the scene of another of Shivaji's daring exploits. The fortress stands on top of a sheer-sided hill at 1270 metres altitude. In 1670 Shivaji's general, Tanaji Malusre, led a force of men who scaled the steep hillside in the dark and defeated the unprepared forces of Bijapur.

Legends about this dramatic attack relate that the Maratha forces used trained lizards to carry ropes up the hillside! There are monuments at the spot where Tanaji died, and also at the place where he lost his left hand before his death. Purandar is another old fortress 27 km south-east of Pune, further by road.

MAHABALESHWAR

This popular hill station was the summer capital of the Bombay presidency during the days of the Raj. At an altitude of 1372 metres, Mahabaleshwar has pleasant walks and good lookouts (the sea, 30 km away, is visible on a clear day), and the area has interesting historical connections with Shivaji. Mahabaleshwar was founded in 1828 by Sir John Malcolm.

Elphinstone Point, Babington Point, Bombay Point, Kate's Point and a number of other lookouts around the wooded plateau offer fine views over the plains below. Arthur's Seat, 12 km out, looks over the coastal strip between the ghats and the sea known as the Konkan, a sheer drop of 600 metres. There are pleasant waterfalls such as Chinaman's Waterfall (2½ km out), Dhobi Waterfall (three km) and Lingmala Waterfalls (six km).

Venna Lake, within Mahabaleshwar, has boating and fishing facilities. In the village of Old Mahabelshwar there are three old temples. The Krishnabai or Panchganga ('Five Streams') Temple is said to contain five streams, including the Krishna River.

Pratapgarh Fort

Built in 1656, this fort is about 24 km and 500 steps from Mahabaleshwar. It's connected with one of the more notable feats in Shivaji's dramatic life. Outnumbered by the forces of Bijapur, Shivaji arranged to meet with the opposing General Afzal Khan. Neither was supposed to carry any weapon or wear armour; but neither, it turned out, could be trusted.

When they met, Afzal Khan pulled out a dagger and stabbed Shivaji, but the Maratha leader had worn a shirt of mail under his white robe and concealed in his left hand was a deadly set of 'tiger claws'. This nasty weapon consisted of a series of rings to which long, sharpened, metal claws were attached. Shivaji drove these claws into Khan and disemboweled him. Today a tomb marks where their encounter took place and a tower was erected over the Khan's head. There is a statue of Shivaji in the ruined fort. There is another Shivaji fort at Raigarh, 80 km from Mahabaleshwar.

Places to Stay

There are a lot of hotels at Mahabaleshwar. The *Ripon Hotel* (tel 257) has rooms at Rs 60, the *Bharat Hotel* (tel 233) at around Rs 40. There is a state government-operated *Holiday Camp* (tel 318) with a variety of rooms and dorm facilities. Reservations can be made through the Maharashtra Tourism Development Corporation (tel 234522-482) at Express Towers, Nariman Point, Bombay.

More expensive hotels, with tariffs over Rs 100, include the *Dreamland Hotel* (tel 228), *Regal Hotel* (tel 317), *Dina Hotel* (tel 246) and *Fredrick Hotel* (tel 240). These more expensive places generally quote all-inclusive prices in the Rs 120 to Rs 250 per person range.

There are tourist information centres at the bus stand (tel 271) and at the Holiday Camp (tel 318).

Getting There

Pune is the normal departure point for Mahabaleshwar and is also the nearest railhead. Mahabaleshwar is 120 km from Pune, via Panchgani which is 19 km before it. From Pune the ordinary bus fare is Rs 15. There are also state transport deluxe buses and taxis. From Bombay it's 286 km via Pune or 259 km via Mahad.

PANCHGANI

'Five Hills' is just 19 km from Mahabaleshwar and, at 1334 metres, just 38 metres lower. It's a popular hill station but overshadowed by better-known Mahabaleshwar. On the way up to Panchgani you pass through Wai, a site which featured in the *Mahabharata*.

Places to Stay
As in Mahabaleshwar, there are various hotels, from the expensive *Amir Hotel* (tel 211, 346) on down. Here, too, there is a *Holiday Camp* with rooms and a dorm.

SATARA
On the main road from Pune to Belgaum and then Goa, but 15 km off the railway line from Satara Road, this town houses a number of relics of the Maratha leader Shivaji. A building near the new palace contains his sword, the coat he wore when he met Afzal Khan and the *waghnakh* or 'tiger's claws' with which he killed him. The Shivaji Maharaj Museum is opposite the bus station.

The Fort of Wasota stands on the south of the town – it has had a colourful and bloody history, including being captured from the Marathas in 1699 by the forces of Aurangzeb, only to be recaptured in 1705 by means of a Brahmin who befriended the defenders, then let in the Marathas.

OTHER PLACES IN THE SOUTH
Kolhapur
With a population of nearly 300,000, this was once the capital of an important Maratha state. The old palace contains some interesting items, including a collection of swords. One of Kolhapur's Maharajas died in Florence, Italy, and was cremated on the banks of the Arno where his *chhatri* (cenotaph) now stands.

Ratnagiri
Ratnagiri, on the coast 130 km west, was the place where Thibaw, the last Burmese king, was interned by the British from 1886 until his death in 1916.

Panhala & Pawangarh
These are interesting hill stations. At Panhala there is a fort with a long and convoluted history; it was originally the stronghold of Raja Bhoj II in 1192. The Pawala Caves are nearby, plus a couple of Buddhist cave temples.

Sholapur
If you have an hour or two to kill in Sholapur (changing buses or trains on your way to or from Bijapur), check out the superlatively decorated municipal offices. *Hotel Rajdhani* near the railway station is a reasonable place to stay.

AHMEDNAGAR (population 130,000)
On the road between Pune (82 km away) and Aurangabad, Ahmednagar has had a colourful history. It was here that the Emperor Aurangzeb died in 1707, aged 97. The town's imposing fort was erected in 1550, and at one time Nehru was imprisoned here by the British.

Places to Stay
There are various hotels, including the *Ashoka Tourist Hotel* and the *Hotel Sablok*. The Ashoka (tel 3607-8) is at Kings Gate, about a km from the centre, and has rooms with and without air-con.

NASIK (population 200,000)
This interesting little town with its picturesque bathing ghats makes a good stopover on the way from Bombay to Aurangabad. The town is actually about eight km north-west of the station, which is 187 km from Bombay. Nasik stands on the Godavari River, one of the holiest rivers of the Deccan. Like Ujjain, this is the site for the triennial Kumbh Mela which comes here every 12 years. The riverbanks are lined with steps above which stand temples and shrines. Although there are no particularly notable temples in Nasik, the Sundar Narayan Temple, to the west of the city, is worth seeing.

Other points of interest in Nasik include the Sita Gupha Cave from which Sita was supposed to have been carried off to the island of Lanka by the evil king Rawana, according to the *Ramayana*. Near the cave, in its grove of large banyan trees, is the fine house of the Panchavati family. Also nearby is the temple of Kala Rama or 'black Rama', in a 96-arched enclosure. The Kapaleswar Temple upstream is said to be the oldest in the town.

Kumbh Mela

Aeons ago the gods and demons, who were constantly at odds, fought a great battle for a *kumbh* or pitcher, drinking the contents of which would ensure immortality. They had combined forces to raise the pitcher from the bottom of the ocean, but once it was safely in their hands Vishnu grabbed it and ran. After a struggle lasting 12 days the gods eventually defeated the demons and drank the nectar – it's a favourite scene in illustrations of Hindu mythology. During the fight for the pitcher's possession four drops of nectar spilt on the earth – at Allahabad, Hardwar, Nasik and Ujjain. Thus each holds its own Kumbh Mela over a 12-year (for a god's day is a human's year) span – the *mela* span. The *mela* is held each three years, rotating between the four cities.

Pandu Lena

About eight km south-west of Nasik, close to the Bombay road, are these 21 Hinayana Buddhist caves. They date from around the 1st century BC to the 2nd AD. The most interesting caves are 3, 10 and 18. Cave 3 is a large *vihara* with some interesting sculptures. Cave 10 is also a *vihara* and almost identical in design to cave 3, although it is much older and finer in its details. It is thought to be nearly as old as the Karla Cave. Cave 18 is a *chaitya* cave thought to date from the same time as the Karla Cave. It too is well-sculpted and its elaborate facade is particularly noteworthy. Cave 20 is another large *vihara*. The other caves are not of great interest.

Trimbak

The source of the Godavari River is here, 33 km from Nasik. From this source high on a steep hill, the river virtually dribbles into a bathing tank reputed to perform the usual washing duties upon one's sins. From this tiny start the Godavari eventually flows down to the Bay of Bengal, clear across India.

Places to Stay

Singles/doubles are Rs 65/70, more with air-con at the *Hotel Siddhartha* (tel 73228) on the Nasik-Pune road.

On Trimbak Rd, two km from the centre, the *Green View Hotel* (tel 72231-4) is more expensive at Rs 70/110 or Rs 95/150 with air-con. *Hotel Samrat* (tel 77211) near the Central Bus Station is similarly priced. There are many other places to stay in Nasik, including a *Tourist Bungalow*.

On the highway between Nasik and Indore at Dhule, the *Hotel Dina* on Sakri Rd has rooms at Rs 50/75.

AURANGABAD (population 175,000)

It's easy to think of Aurangabad simply as a place to stay when visiting the cave temples of Ajanta and Ellora. In fact Aurangabad has a number of attractions in its own right and could easily stand on its own were it not so overshadowed by the famous caves. The city is named after Aurangzeb, but earlier in its history it was known as Khadke.

Orientation & Information

The railway station, Tourist Office and a variety of cheaper hotels and restaurants are clustered at the south of the town. There's a fairly open gap from here to the more crowded and older part of the town to the north, where you'll also find the bus station. In comparison to other Deccan towns Aurangabad is remarkably uncrowded and quiet.

The more expensive hotels are between the old town and the railway station or on the road out to the airport. There is a not

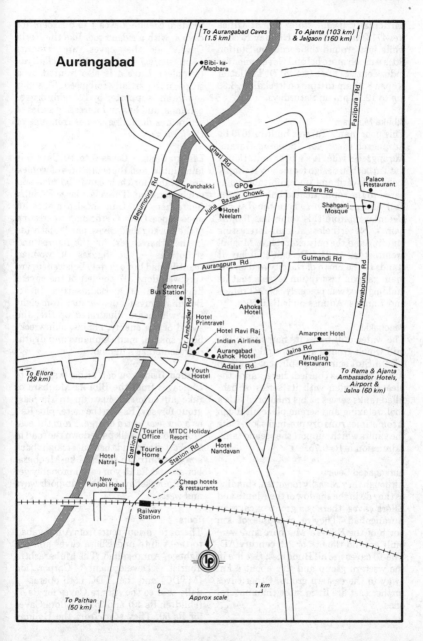

Aurangabad

To Aurangabad Caves (1.5 km)

To Ajanta (103 km) & Jalgaon (160 km)

Fazilpura Rd

Bibi-ka-Maqbara

Ghati Rd

Begumpura Rd

Panchakki

GPO

Juna Bazaar Chowk

Hotel Neelam

Safara Rd

Palace Restaurant

Shahganj Mosque

Aurangpura Rd

Gulmandi Rd

Nawabpura Rd

Central Bus Station

Dr Ambedkar Rd

Ashoka Hotel

Hotel Printravel

Hotel Ravi Raj

Indian Airlines

Aurangabad Ashok Hotel

Amarpreet Hotel

Jaina Rd

Mingling Restaurant

Adalat Rd

To Rama & Ajanta Ambassador Hotels, Airport & Jalna (60 km)

Youth Hostel

To Ellora (29 km)

Station Rd

Tourist Office

MTDC Holiday Resort

Tourist Home

Hotel Natraj

New Punjabi Hotel

Station Rd

Hotel Nandavan

Cheap hotels & restaurants

Railway Station

0   1 km

Approx scale

To Paithan (50 km)

particularly useful state Tourist Office (tel 4713) in the MTDC Holiday Resort, while just around the corner on Station Rd is a much more helpful Government of India Tourist Office (tel 4817). The latter is open 8.30 am to 6 pm on weekdays, 8.30 am to 12.30 pm on Saturdays.

Bibi-ka-Maqbara

This poor man's Taj was built in 1679 by Aurangzeb's son for Rabia-ud-Darani, Aurangzeb's wife. It's a poor imitation of the Taj both in design (somehow it simply looks awkward and uncomfortable compared to the sophisticated balance of the Taj) and execution (where the Taj has gleaming marble this tomb has flaking paint). Nevertheless it's an interesting building and the only example of Moghul architecture on the Deccan Plateau. It stands to the north of the city and on the main gate an inscription reveals that its building cost was precisely 665,283 rupees and 7 annas. Admission is Rs 0.50.

Panchakki

The water mill takes its name from the mill which ground grain for pilgrims. In 1624 a Sufi saint and spiritual guide to Aurangzeb was buried here, and the pleasant garden with its series of fish-filled tanks serves as his memorial. It's a cool, relaxing and serene place although it sometimes runs dry pre-monsoon. Note the vaults which support the second tank. Admission is Rs 0.75.

Aurangabad Caves

Although they're easily forgotten, standing as they do in the shadow of the Ajanta and Ellora caves, there is a group of caves in Aurangabad. They're a couple of km north of the Bibi-ka-Maqbara and were built around the 6th or 7th century AD. The 10 caves are all Buddhist; five are in the western group and five about a km away in the eastern group. Other caves further east are little more than natural ones.

Western Group - Caves 1 to 5 Except for cave 4, with a ridged roof like the Karla Cave, all the caves are *viharas* (monasteries) rather than *chaityas* (temples). Cave 4 is also fronted by a stupa, now partially collapsed. Cave 3 is square and supported by 12 highly ornate columns, and has an interesting series of sculptures depicting scenes from one of the *jatakas*.

Eastern Group - Caves 6 to 10 Cave 6 is fairly intact and the sculptures of women are notable for their exotic hairdos and ornamentation. There is a large Buddha figure here but Ganesh also makes an appearance. Cave 7 is the most interesting of the Aurangabad caves, particularly (as in the other caves) for the figures and sculptures - the figures of women, scantily clad but ornately bejewelled, are very well done. To the left of the cave a huge figure of a Bodhisattva (near-Buddha) prays for deliverance from eight fears which are illustrated as fire, the sword of the enemy, chains, shipwreck, lions, snakes, mad elephants and death, represented as a demon.

Getting There You can either walk up to the caves from the Bibi-ka-Maqbara or take an auto-rickshaw up to the east group for, say, Rs 4 on the meter plus Rs 3 as a one-way extra charge. From the east group you can walk back down the road to the west group and then cut straight back across country to the Bibi-ka-Maqbara. For around Rs 15 you could probably get an auto-rickshaw to take you both ways and wait.

Tours

There are various tours from Aurangabad to the Ajanta and Ellora caves and the sights of Aurangabad. The Maharashtra Tourist Development Corporation (MTDC) and the ITDC both operate a daily tour to the Ajanta Caves for Rs 65 (children Rs 40) and to the Ellora Caves for Rs 50. They start from the Holiday

Resort and the Government of India Tourist Office respectively, but also pick up from the major hotels.

The Ellora tour includes Daulatabad and the attractions in Aurangabad itself (but not the Aurangabad Caves), so it saves a lot of travelling and waiting time compared to doing it yourself. On the other hand it's quite a distance to the Ajanta Caves, and many people prefer to stay near the caves rather than day-trip from Aurangabad. If you're thoroughly fed up with local buses, it's worth enquiring about the tour bus to or from the caves – much faster than the stop-start-stop-start local bus service.

As well as the MTDC and ITDC tours the state transport system also runs daily tours which start from the railway station. At Rs 16.50 for Ellora and Rs 38 for Ajanta, they are much cheaper than the other tours and from all reports they're quite OK.

Places to Stay – bottom end

Most of Aurangabad's cheaper hotels are close to the railway station. The notable exception is the excellent *Youth Hostel* mid-way between the railway station and the main part of town. The 40 dorm beds cost Rs 10 each (Rs 6 for YHA members) and the place is spotlessly clean. It has hot and cold water, and breakfast and evening meals are available. There's also one family room for three people.

A hundred metres or so from the station is the *MTDC Holiday Resort*, where you'll also find the state government Tourist Office. There are several wings in this large accommodation complex with rooms at Rs 60/80 with bathroom and mosquito nets. Equivalent 'Indian-style' doubles are Rs 60 and there are a couple of air-con doubles at Rs 120. There are also rooms for three (Rs 45) or four (Rs 45) without attached bathrooms. It may be possible to use these dormitory-style for Rs 15 per person. The Holiday Resort is a long way short of helpful – check-out time is 8 am and they positively will not look

after baggage for you, even if you're going on one of their tours during the day and then departing Aurangabad that night. Even if you're departing on their own bus service to Bombay!

There are lots of other possibilities in the station area. Between the Holiday Resort and the station there is a string of very cheap and basic places like *Ashoka Lodging, Ambika Lodge* or the *Ashoka Tourist Hotel*. Continue straight on beside the railway tracks for a short distance and you'll come to the *New Punjabi Hotel*, with rooms which are a bit grubby but reasonably good value at Rs 30 or Rs 40 with bathroom.

There are a couple of similar standard hotels along the road from the station to the Youth Hostel. *Hotel Natraj* is a simple but acceptable place with rooms with bath at Rs 30/40. Next comes the *Tourist's Home* at Rs 30/35, just before the Government of India Tourist Office. It's marginally the best of this threesome.

Over towards the old part of town, between the bus station and post office and near the Panchakki water mill, *Hotel Neelam* (tel 4561-2) is a newer-looking building with rooms with bath at Rs 40/45. It's again similar in standard to the previous three hotels. There are other hotels in the old part of town, like the rock-bottom *Ashoka Hotel*. Close to the Youth Hostel the medium-priced *Printravel Hotel* (tel 2707) has old-fashioned rooms at Rs 50/90 with mosquito nets and huge baths in the bathrooms.

Places to Stay – middle

There are also a number of medium-priced hotels like the *Hotel Ravi Raj* (tel 3939) between Indian Airlines and the Youth Hostel. Rooms are Rs 125/175 or Rs 200/250 with air-con. Out towards the airport, but not as far as the two most expensive places, the *Hotel Amarpreet* (tel 4615) is a new place with rooms at Rs 150/200 or Rs 200/250 with air-con. Finally, on Station Rd *Hotel Nandavan* (tel 3311-3) is much cheaper but its standards are only a notch above bottom end. Rooms are Rs 85/125 or Rs 185 for an air-con double.

Places to Stay – top end
There are two 'international-standard' hotels a couple of km out of town towards the airport. The *Welcomgroup Rama International* (tel 8455-9) has all mod cons from air-con, restaurants and swimming pool to tennis courts, and costs from Rs 400/500 for singles/doubles. The *Ajanta Ambassador* (tel 8211-5) is virtually beside it in Chikalthana and is similarly equipped. Rooms cost from Rs 375/475 and reportedly this hotel is very good – 'the service perfect, the restaurant offering a wide choice of high-quality dishes'.

The *Aurangabad Ashok* (tel 4520-9) is more centrally located on Dr Rajendra Prasad Marg beside the Indian Airlines office and costs Rs 210/265 or Rs 290/345 for rooms with air-con.

Places to Eat
There is a string of rock-bottom eating places along Station Rd near the railway station – none of them standouts although the *Prem Popular Punjab* must set a record for the number of switches on the panel above the cashier. The *Holiday Resort* has a dining hall which serves the usual state government menu – when it's open. The *New Punjabi Hotel* has an air-con vegetarian and non-vegetarian restaurant in the basement.

Further along Station Rd at the Nandavan Hotel, the *Radhika Restaurant* has vegetarian food and the *Rathi Snack Bar* is also here. Or opposite the Amarpreet Hotel on the airport road, the *Mingling Restaurant* has good Chinese food; most dishes are Rs 20. In the centre of the old town at Shahganj opposite the Shahganj Mosque, the *Palace Restaurant* is a typical Muslim restaurant with so-so biryanis and other dishes. Finally, the *Rama International* has a good Rs 60 buffet, including entertainment.

Getting There
The cave groups at Ajanta and Ellora are off the railway lines and are usually approached from either Aurangabad (Ellora 30 km, Ajanta 106 km) or from Jalgaon (Ajanta 59 km). Jalgaon is on the main broad-gauge line from Bombay to Allahabad, but Aurangabad is off the main line and getting there requires a change to metre-gauge line at Manmad. On the other hand Aurangabad is the access point from Pune (by road) or Hyderabad (by rail). Plus it has the airport.

Air There's a daily flight connection Bombay-Aurangabad-Udaipur-Jodhpur-Jaipur-Delhi and the reverse – it's another popular tourist-route flight. Fares to or from Aurangabad are Bombay Rs 296, Delhi Rs 858 and Udaipur Rs 557.

Rail Jalgaon is 420 km from Bombay; the trip takes about eight hours by rail and costs Rs 41 in 2nd class, Rs 161 in 1st. From Jalgaon there are frequent buses to Ajanta and Aurangabad. By rail direct to Aurangabad you change trains at Manmad, 261 km from Bombay, for the 113-km trip to Aurangabad. Travelling time is about eight hours, plus the time changing trains. The cost is Rs 36 in 2nd class, Rs 145 in 1st. From Hyderabad (Secunderabad), which is on the same metre-gauge line as Manmad, the distance is 510 km, takes 12 hours and costs Rs 46 in 2nd class, Rs 186 1st.

Bus There are bus connections to and from Aurangabad, in particular if you're coming north from Pune or south from Nagpur and Madhya Pradesh. Fares to Aurangabad include Pune Rs 31, Nasik Rs 30, Indore Rs 50. There's a daily superdeluxe MTDC bus to Bombay which departs Aurangabad at 8.30 pm and arrives in Bombay next morning at 7.30 am. The fare is Rs 112. Other overnight buses are cheaper.

Getting Around

Airport An auto-rickshaw to or from the airport costs Rs 15. The Aurangabad auto-rickshaw wallahs all use their meters and in '86 this was one of the few places in India where the meters were actually set correctly!

To the Caves Aurangabad is a good base for visiting either the Ellora or Ajanta caves. Unless you're planning on doing a day-tour from Aurangabad to Ajanta, you'll probably find it more convenient to actually stay at Ajanta. Bus fares from Aurangabad are Rs 4 to Ellora (every half hour), Rs 15 to Ajanta, Rs 22 to Jalgaon. Ajanta-Jalgaon is Rs 10.

Most of the Ajanta accommodation is actually at Fardapur, about five km from the caves – Rs 1.50 or so by the reasonably frequent buses. You can negotiate round-trip rates to the caves by taxi – say Rs 180 for Ellora, Rs 525 for Ajanta.

AURANGABAD TO ELLORA
Daulatabad

Between Aurangabad and the Ellora Caves is the magnificent hilltop fortress of Daulatabad. The fort is surrounded by five km of sturdy wall, while the central bastion tops a 200-metre-high hill. In the 14th century the slightly nutty Mohammed Tughlaq, Sultan of Delhi, conceived the crazy plan of not only building himself a new capital, but marching the entire population of Delhi 1100 km south to populate it. His unhappy subjects proceeded to drop dead like flies on this forced march, and 17 years later he turned round and marched them all back to Delhi. The fort remained.

It's worth making the climb to the top for the superb views over the surrounding country. Along the way you'll pass through a complicated series of defences, including multiple doorways so that elephants could not charge them, and spike-studded doors just in case they did. A magnificent tower of victory built in 1435, the Chand Minar, soars 60 metres

high. The Qutb Minar in Delhi, five metres higher, is the only loftier victory tower in India. On the other side of the entrance path is a mosque built from the remains of a Jain temple.

Higher up is the blue-tiled Chini Mahal palace where the last king of Golconda was imprisoned for 13 years until his death. Finally you climb the central fort to a huge six-metre cannon, cast from five different metals and engraved with Aurangzeb's name. The final ascent to the top goes through a pitch-black, spiralling tunnel down which the fort's defenders could hurl burning coals at any invaders. Of course, your guide may tell you, the fort was once successfully conquered despite these elaborate precautions – by the simple expedient of bribing the guard at the gate.

The hill on which the fort stands was originally known as Devagiri, the 'hill of the gods', but Mohammed Tughlaq renamed it Daulatabad, the 'city of fortune'.

Rauza

Also known as Khuldabad, the 'heavenly abode', this walled town is only three km from Ellora. It is the Karbala or holy shrine of Deccan Muslims. A number of historical figures are buried here, including Aurangzeb, the last great Moghul emperor. Aurangzeb built the battlemented wall around the town, which was once an important centre although today it is little more than a sleepy village.

The emperor's final resting place is a simple affair of bare earth in a courtyard of the Alamgir Dargah at the centre of the city. Aurangzeb's pious austerity extended even to his own tomb, for he stipulated that his mausoleum should be paid for with money he earned himself by copying out the Koran. Within the building there is also supposed to be a robe worn by the Prophet Mohammed; it is only shown to the faithful once each year. Another shrine across the road from the Alamgir

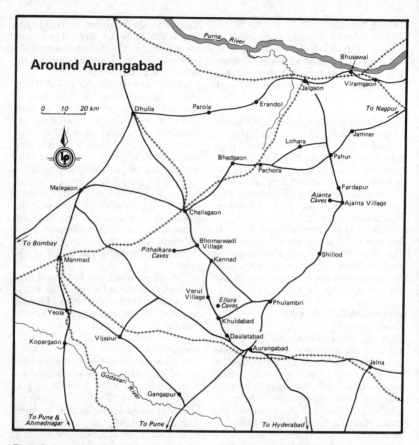

Around Aurangabad

0   10   20 km

Dargah is said to contain hairs of the Prophet's beard and lumps of silver from a tree of solid silver, which miraculously grew here after a saint's death.

Guidebooks

At many sites in India you can buy excellent, locally produced guidebooks very cheaply which will help give you a deeper appreciation of what you are seeing. The caves of Ajanta and Ellora are no exception, and both *Aurangabad, Daulatabad, Ellora & Ajanta* by Professor Dr S Siddiqui and *Ajanta, Ellora & Aurangabad Caves – an Appreciation* by T V Pathy are worthwhile investments. The former has good black-and-white pictures, which help in the identification of the actual sculpture or painting being described. The latter guide has more examples of the delightful way Indians have with English. The author describes a statue as being a 'semi-nude dryad with a slender waist, pouting lips and abundant mammalian equipment . . . .' What a fine way of saying she had big boobs.

ELLORA CAVES

The caves of Ellora are about 30 km from Aurangabad. Whereas the Ajanta Caves are noted for their paintings, here the sculpture is remarkable. Chronologically the Ellora Caves start where the Ajanta

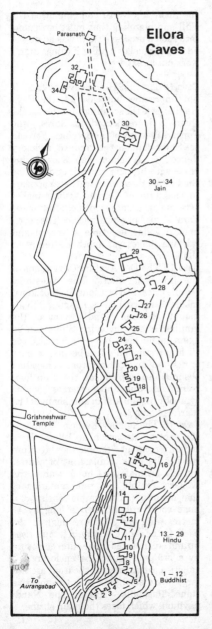

Ellora Caves

Parasnath

32
34

30

30 – 34
Jain

29

28

27
26
25

24
23
21
20
19
18
17

Grishneshwar
Temple

16
15
14

12

11
10
9
8
7
6
5

13 – 29
Hindu

1 – 12
Buddhist

1 2 3

To
Aurangabad

Caves finish – it's thought that the builders of Ajanta moved to Ellora when they suddenly ceased construction at their earlier site. The Ellora Caves are not all Buddhist like those of Ajanta – the earliest are, but during this time Buddhism was declining in India and a later series of Hindu and Jain cave temples was added.

In all there are 34 caves at Ellora: 12 Buddhist, 17 Hindu and five Jain. Although the temples are numbered consecutively, from 1 at the southern end to 34 at the northern end, and although the various religious groups do not overlap, the caves are not arranged chronologically. It is thought that construction of the Hindu caves commenced before the Buddhist caves were completed, for example. Roughly, the Buddhist caves are thought to date from around 600 to 800 AD, the Hindu caves to around 900 AD. The Jain caves were not commenced until about 800 AD and were completed by 1000 AD.

The caves are cut into a hillside running north-south. Because the hill slopes down rather than drops steeply, as at Ajanta, many of them have elaborate entrance halls to the main shrines. From south to north, the caves stretch two km.

Buddhist Caves
Apart from cave 10, all the Buddhist caves are *viharas* (monasteries) rather than *chaityas* (temples). They are not as architecturally ambitious as the Hindu caves, although 11 and 12 show signs of attempting to compete with the complex Hindu designs. The Buddhist caves chart the period of Buddhism's division and decline in India.

Caves 1 to 4 These are all *vihara* caves. Cave 2, with its ornate pillars and figures of the Buddha, is quite interesting. Caves 3 and 4 are earlier, simpler and less well preserved.
Cave 5 This is the biggest *vihara* cave. The rows of stone benches indicate it may have been an assembly or dining hall.

Caves 6 to 8 In cave 6 there is a large seated Buddha in the shrine room, but this ornate *vihara* also has a standing figure thought to be either the Hindu goddess of learning, Saraswati, or her Buddhist equivalent, Mahamayuri. Caves 7 and 8 are not so interesting.

Cave 10 The Viswakarma or Carpenter's Cave is the only *chaitya* cave in the Buddhist group. It takes its name from the ribs carved into the roof, in imitation of wooden beams. The temple is entered by steps to a courtyard, followed by further steps to the main temple. A finely carved horseshoe window lets light in and a huge seated-Buddha figure fronts the nine-metre-high stupa.

Cave 11 The Do Thal 'two-storey' Cave is also entered by a courtyard. Curiously, it actually has three storeys but the third was not discovered until 1876. Construction of the middle floor was never completed.

Cave 12 The Tin Thal 'three-storey' Cave also has three storeys and is entered through a courtyard. It contains a very large seated Buddha and a number of other figures. The walls are carved with relief pictures, as in the Hindu caves.

Hindu Caves

The Hindu caves are the most dramatic and impressive of the Ellora cave temples. In size, design and energy they are in a totally different league from the Buddhist or Jain caves. If calm contemplation describes the Buddhist caves, then dynamic energy is the description for the Hindu caves. The sheer size of the Kailasa Temple (cave 16) is overwhelming. It covers twice the area of the Parthenon in Athens and is 1½ times as high. Remember that this whole, gigantic structure was cut out of solid rock! It has been estimated that carving out the Kailasa entailed removing 200,000 tons of rock!

All these temples were cut from the top down, so that it was never necessary to use any scaffolding – their builders started with the roof and moved down to

the floor. It's worth contemplating the skill and planning that must have gone into such a process – there was no way of adding a panel or a pillar if things didn't work out as expected.

Cave 14 The first Hindu cave, cave 13, is not impressive but cave 14, the Rava Kakhai, sets the scene for the others. Like them it is dedicated to Shiva, who appears in many of the carvings. You can see Shiva dancing the *tandava*, a victory dance over the demon Mahisa, or playing chess with his wife Parvati, or defeating the buffalo demon. Parvati also appears in the form of Durga. Vishnu makes several appearances too, including one as Varaha, his boar incarnation. The seven 'mother goddesses' can also be seen, and Rawana makes yet another attempt to shake Kailasa.

Cave 15 The Das Avatara Cave is one of the finest at Ellora. The two-storey temple is reached by a long flight of steps. Inside there is a modern image of Shiva's mount, the bull Nandi. Many of the familiar scenes involving Shiva can be again found here, but you can also see Vishnu resting on a five-hooded serpent or rescuing an elephant from a crocodile. Vishnu also appears as the man-lion, Narsimha, while Shiva emerges from his symbolic lingam and in another panel he marries Parvati.

Cave 16 The mighty Kailasa Temple is the central attraction at Ellora. Here Indian rock-cut temple architecture reaches its peak. Kailasa is, of course, Shiva's Himalayan home, and the Kailasa Temple is a representation of that mountain. The temple consists of a huge courtyard, 81 metres long by 47 metres wide and 33 metres high at the back. In the centre, the main temple rises up and is connected to the outer enclosure by a bridge. Around the enclosure are galleries, while towards the front are two large stone elephants with two massive stone 'flagstaffs' flanking the Nandi pavilion, which faces the main shrine.

As in the previous two caves, there is a variety of dramatic and finely carved panels, the most impressive being the image of Rawana shaking Kailasa. In the *Ramayana* the demon king Rawana flaunted his strength by lifting up Shiva's mountain home. Unimpressed, Lord Shiva simply put his foot down on the top and pressed the mountain and the upstart Rawana back into place. Vishnu also appears along one gallery as Narsimha once again – in this legend he defeats a demon, who could not be killed by man or beast by the simple expedient of becoming a man-lion, neither man nor beast.

Other Caves The other Hindu caves pall beside the majesty of the Kailasa, but several of them are worth at least some study. Cave 21, known as the Rameswara, has a number of interesting interpretations of scenes also depicted in the earlier temples. Shiva once again marries Parvati and plays dice with her, and the goddesses Ganga and Yamuna appear again. The figure of Ganga, standing on her crocodile or *makara*, is particularly notable.

The very large cave 29, the Dumar Lena, is similar in design to the Elephanta Cave at Bombay. It is thought to be a transitional model as the designers moved from the simpler hollowed-out caves towards the fully developed temples exemplified by the Kailasa.

Jain Caves

The Jain caves mark the final phase of Ellora. They do not have the drama and high-voltage energy of the best Hindu temples nor are they as ambitious in size, but they balance this with their exceptional detail work. There are only five Jain temples, several hundred metres north of the last Hindu temple.

Cave 30 The Chota Kailasa or 'little Kailasa' is a poor imitation of the great Kailasa Temple and was never completed. It stands by itself some distance from the other Jain temples, which are clustered closely together.

Cave 32 The Indra Sabha or 'Assembly Hall of Indra' is the finest of the Jain temples. The ground-floor plan is similar to the Kailasa, but the upstairs area, reached by a stairway, is as ornate and richly decorated as downstairs is plain. There are images of the Jain *tirthankars* Parasnath and Gomatesvara, the latter surrounded by vegetation and wildlife. Inside the shrine is a seated figure of Mahavira, the 24th and last *tirthankar*, and founder of the Jain religion. Traces of paintings can still be seen on the roof of the temple.

Other Caves Cave 31 is really an extension of 32. Cave 33, the Jagannath Sabha, is similar in plan to 32 and has some particularly well-preserved sculptures. The final temple, the small cave 34, also has interesting sculptures. On the hilltop over the Jain temples a five-metre-high image of Parasnath looks down on Ellora. An enclosure was built around it a couple of hundred years ago.

Grishneshwar

Close to the Ellora Caves in the village of Verul, this 18th-century Shiva temple is one of the 12 Shiva *jyotorlingas* in India.

Places to Stay

Although most people tend to stay in Aurangabad, there is some accommodation available at the caves. The relatively expensive *Hotel Kailasa* is very close to the caves and has rooms from Rs 60 – or with attached bath. The restaurant attached to the hotel is cheaper than the other government restaurant here, which is of course intended for tour groups.

AJANTA CAVES

The caves of Ajanta pre-date those of Ellora, so if you want to see the caves in chronological order you should visit here first. Although the Ellora Caves are easily visited using Aurangabad as a base, it's much easier to stay near the Ajanta Caves rather than make a day trip to them. Unlike the Ellora Caves, which are Buddhist, Hindu and Jain, the Ajanta Caves are all Buddhist and, whereas at Ellora the caves are masterpieces of sculpture, at Ajanta it's the magnificent paintings for which the caves are famous.

After their abandonment with the move to Ellora and the decline of Buddhism, the Ajanta Caves were gradually forgotten and their rediscovery was dramatic. In 1819 a British hunting party stumbled upon them, and their remote beauty was soon unveiled. Their isolation had contributed to the fine state of preservation in which some of the paintings remain to this day. The caves are cut into the steep face of a deep rock gorge. There are 29 caves in a curve of the gorge, and there is a good viewpoint from across the ravine. They date from around 200 BC to 650 AD and do not follow the chronological order that the Ellora Caves generally do; the oldest are mainly in the middle and the newer ones are to each end.

The cave paintings initially suffered some deterioration after their rediscovery, and some heavy-handed restoration also caused damage. Between 1920 and 1922 two Italian art experts conducted a meticulous restoration process and the paintings have been carefully preserved since that time. Many of the caves are dark, and without a light the paintings are hard to see – it's worth paying for a lighting ticket which will ensure that the cave guards turn the lights on for you. Or you could try tagging along with a tour party, although normally the doors are shut after each party enters a cave.

Five of the caves are *chaityas* or temples while the other 24 are *viharas* or monasteries. Caves 8, 9, 10, 12 and 13 are the older Hinayana caves, while the others are Mahayana. In the simpler, more austere Hinayana school the Buddha was never represented directly – his presence was always alluded to by a symbol such as the footprint or wheel of law. The Ajanta paintings are not,

Tour guide & freak · AJANTA CAVES · MARVELLING AT THE NATURAL WONDERS...

strictly speaking, frescoes but tempera paintings – a difference purely of technique. Although the Ajanta paintings are particularly notable, there are also many interesting sculptures here.

Cave 1 This *vihara* cave is one of the most recent and also most fully developed of the Ajanta Caves. A verandah at the front leads to a large square hall with elaborate carvings and paintings and a huge Buddha statue. Cave 1 is notable both for its sculpture and its paintings. Amongst the interesting sculptures is one of four deer sharing a common head. There are many paintings of women, some remarkably similar to the paintings at Sigiriya in

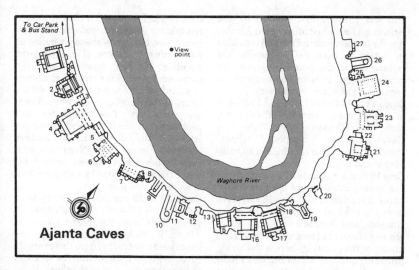

To Car Park & Bus Stand

●View point

Waghore River

Ajanta Caves

Sri Lanka. Notable paintings include those of the 'black princess' and the 'dying princess'. Other paintings include scenes of the *jatakas* (events from the Buddha's previous lives), and portraits of the Bodhisattvas (near-Buddhas), Padmapani (holding a lotus flower) and Vajrapani.

Cave 2 Also a more recent *vihara* cave, this one has important paintings too, although some are unfortunately damaged. As well as murals, there are paintings on the ceiling. Scenes include a number of *jatakas* and events connected with the Buddha's birth, including his mother's dream of the six-tusked elephant which heralded the Buddha's conception.

Cave 4 This is the largest *vihara* cave at Ajanta and is supported by 28 pillars. Although it was never completed, the cave has some fine sculptures, including scenes of people fleeing from the 'eight great dangers' to the protection of the Buddha's disciple Avalokitesvara. One of the great dangers is an angry-looking elephant in pursuit of a man and woman. Caves 3, 5 and 8 were never completed.

Cave 6 This is the only two-storey cave at Ajanta, but parts of the lower storey have

collapsed. Inside is a seated figure of the Buddha with an intricately carved door to the shrine. Upstairs the hall is surrounded by cells with fine paintings on the doorways.

Cave 7 & 8 This cave is of unusual design in that the verandah does not lead into a hall with cells down the sides and a shrine room at the rear. Here there are porches before the verandah, which leads directly to the four cells and the elaborately sculpted shrine. Cave 8 is used solely for the generating equipment which lights the caves.

Cave 9 This is a *chaitya* cave and one of the earliest at Ajanta. Although it dates from the Hinayana period, two Buddha figures flanking the entrance door were probably later Mahayana additions. Similarly, the paintings inside, which are not in excellent condition, show signs of being refurbished at some time in the past. Columns run down both sides of the cave and around the three-metre-high *dagoba* at the far end. At the front there is a horseshoe-shaped window above the entrance, and the vaulted roof has traces of wooden ribs.

Cave 10 is thought to be the oldest cave

and was the one first spotted by the British soldiers who rediscovered Ajanta. It is the largest *chaitya* cave and is similar in design to cave 9. The facade has collapsed and the paintings inside are rather damaged, in some cases by graffitists soon after the caves' rediscovery.

Caves 11 to 14 Caves 11, 12 and 13 are not of great interest – they are all relatively early, either Hinayana or early Mahayana. Cave 14 is an incompleted *vihara*, standing above cave 13, which is an early Mahayana *vihara*.

Cave 16 Some of Ajanta's finest paintings can be seen in this, one of the later *vihara* caves. It is thought that cave 16 may have been the original entrance to the entire complex, and there is a very fine view of the river from the front of the cave. Best known of the paintings here is the 'dying princess'. Sundari, wife of Buddha's half-brother Nanda, is said to have expired at the hard news that her husband was renouncing the material life (and her) in order to become a monk. This is one of the finest paintings at Ajanta. Nanda features in several other paintings, including his conversion by Buddha.

Cave 17 This is the cave with the finest paintings at Ajanta. Not only are they in the best condition, they are also the greatest in number and variety. They include beautiful women flying overhead on the roof while carved dwarfs support the pillars. A popular scene shows a woman, surrounded by attendants, applying make-up. In another there is a royal procession, while in another a couple engage in a little private love-making. The Buddha returns from his enlightenment to his own home to beg from his wife and astonished son in another panel. A detailed panel tells the story of Prince Simhala's expedition to Ceylon. With his 500 companions he is shipwrecked on an island where ogresses appear as beautiful women, only to seize and devour their victims. Simhala escapes on a flying horse and returns to conquer the island.

Cave 19 The facade of this *chaitya* cave is remarkably detailed and includes an impressive horseshoe-shaped window as its dominant feature. Two very fine standing Buddha figures flank the entrance. Inside this excellent specimen of a *chaitya* cave is a tall *dagoba* with a figure of the Buddha on the front. There are also some fine sculptures and paintings, but one of the most important is outside the cave to the west, where there is an image of the Naga king with seven cobra hoods arrayed around his head. His wife, hooded by a single cobra, is seated beside him.

Caves 20 to 25 are either incomplete or not of great interest, although cave 24 would have been the largest *vihara* at Ajanta, if finished. You can see how the caves were constructed from this example – long galleries were cut into the rock and then broken across to each other.

Cave 26 The fourth *chaitya* cave's facade has fallen and almost all trace of its paintings have disappeared. Nevertheless there are some very fine sculptures remaining. On the left wall is a huge figure of the 'reclining Buddha', lying back as he prepares to enter Nirvana. Other scenes include a lengthy depiction of the Buddha's temptation by Mara. In one scene Mara attacks the Buddha with demons, and then his beautiful daughters tempt him with more sensual delights. The Buddha's resistance is too strong however, and the final scene shows a glum and dejected-looking Mara having failed to deflect the Buddha from the straight and narrow.

Caves 27 to 29 Cave 27 is virtually a *vihara* connected to the cave 26 *chaitya*. There's a great pond in a box canyon 200 metres upstream from the cave. Caves 28 and 29 are higher up the cliff face and relatively hard to get to.

Places to Stay & Eat

There is a *Forestry Rest House* right by the caves, but it only has two rooms and isn't much good. You can't get in until late afternoon either. There is, however, a new *State Travellers Lodge* by the cave entrance.

Most people stay at Fardapur, five km from the caves, where there is an excellent *MTDC Holiday Resort* run by the state government. Rooms along the pleasant verandah cost from Rs 45; they are supposed to be cheaper in the June to September off-season. All rooms have attached bathrooms and there is a restaurant at one end.

Right behind the Holiday Resort, the *Fardapur Travellers' Bungalow* has cheaper rooms with and without attached bathroom but may be closed now. There's no sign or name; just follow the path next to the Holiday Resort. The small village of Fardapur, set back from the road, is worth wandering around. You can get simple truck-stop food from the stalls along the road through Fardapur.

Getting There

It's Rs 15 from Aurangabad to Ajanta. The caves are a couple of km off the main road from Aurangabad to Jalgaon, and Fardapur is a little further down the main road towards Jalgaon. There are regular buses between Fardapur and the Ajanta Caves, costing around a rupee – the fare seems to vary with every bus! On from Ajanta (or Fardapur), buses go to Edalbad and on from there to Indore, 10 hours in all. Some go direct.

There's a 'cloak room' at the Ajanta Caves where you can leave gear, so that it is possible to arrive on a morning bus from Jalgaon, look around the caves, and continue to Aurangabad in the evening. Or vice versa.

NAGPUR (population 950,000)

Situated on the River Nag, from which the town takes its name, Nagpur is the orange-growing capital of India. This was once the capital of the central province, but was later incorporated into Maharashtra. Long ago it was a centre for the aboriginal Gond tribes who remained in power until the early 18th century. Many Gonds still live in this region. Later it went through a series of changes before eventually falling to the British.

Ramtek

About 40 km north-east of Nagpur, Ramtek has a number of picturesque 600-year-old temples surmounting the 'Hill of Rama'. In summer this is one of the hottest places in India. The old British cantonment of Kemtee is nearby and a memorial to the Sanskrit dramatist Kalidas is just along the road from the *Tourist Bungalow*, which has a spectacular view of the town.

Wardha & Sevagram

About 80 km south-west of Nagpur, near Wardha station, is Sevagram, the 'Village of Service', where Gandhi established his ashram in 1933. For the 15 years from then until India achieved independence, this was in some ways the alternative capital of India.

The Centre of Science for Villages (Magan Sangrahalaya) is a museum intended to explain and develop Gandhi's ideals of village-level economics. The huts of his ashram are still preserved in Sevagram and there is a photo exhibit of events in the Mahatma's life at Mahadev Bhawan, beside the Sevagram hospital. Only three km from Sevagram is the ashram of Vinoba Bhave, Gandhi's follower who walked throughout India persuading rich landlords to hand over tracts of land for redistribution to the landless and poor.

Places to Stay

There are all sorts of hotels in Nagpur. Among the centrally located cheaper places is the *Hotel Shyam* (tel 24073) on Pandit Malviya Rd, with rooms at Rs 45/65. *Hotel Blue Diamond* (tel 47461-9) at 113 Dosar Square Central Avenue has cheaper rooms at Rs 25 to Rs 75 and more expensive air-con rooms at Rs 100/125.

Other more expensive places include

the *Hotel Upvan* (tel 34704-5), 65 Mount Rd, with rooms with air-cooling at Rs 100/150 or with air-con at Rs 150/200. There are numerous other middle-priced hotels, including the overpriced *Mount Hotel*.

JALGAON & OTHER PLACES

At Jalgaon, for those en route to the caves, the *Morako* and the friendly *Tourist Hotel* are lower middle-range places. The *Tourist Hotel* a km from the railway station has rooms at Rs 40/70 and a popular non-vegetarian restaurant. The *PWD Rest House*, just behind the Tourist Hotel, has rooms from Rs 50 and is much better. *Railway Retiring Rooms* at Jalgaon are good value at Rs 30.

Between Jalgaon and Nagpur you can try the new *Maharaja Guest House* at Amraoti or the *Hotel Dreamland* at Akola – the latter has rooms at Rs 30/60 and is already on the downhill path to Indian hotel oblivion. Amraoti has the biggest cotton market in India and the old Amba temple near the walled city. The town has a famous sports college with old-fashioned wrestling pits.

Tony's Notebook

The Rules

Things are done by the book in India – rules are not lightly broken. A traveller wrote that when he booked into a hotel he was offered a standard room or a deluxe one. Deluxe meant it had hot water. He opted for the hot water only to discover that due to a water shortage there was no water at all, hot or cold. This did not mean he would be charged the cold-water price. He had a hot-water room and if there had been any water it would have been hot!

Somebody else I met told me of making an urgent long-distance phone call and paying the extra fee for 'instant' connection. The call took 26 hours to get through but he still got charged for instant connection. In his case 26 hours was instantly.

Keeping Your Cool

Sometimes India can simply be too much for anyone to take. This has been called culture shock enough times, and in a way that is what it is. Remember that habits and practices which annoy or even revolt you – the continuous hawking and spitting, the practice of making every wall a public urinal – are probably matched by some western habits that an Asian would find just as incomprehensible. Westerners blithely walk into houses without pausing to take their shoes off, they sit on toilet seats, they carry dirty handkerchiefs in their pockets.

The habit of fixedly staring at you is one you just have to get used to. It's simply unembarrassed interest and there is nothing you can do about it. Staring right back is not going to change anything.

Summon up as much understanding as you can, but sometimes pushing and shoving, cutting into queues, continuously trying to get you to do something you don't want to, the inevitable rip-offs, all become too much and even the most easygoing travellers lose their temper. Treat these things as part of life, practise staying more relaxed next time, but if they start to happen too often perhaps it's time you took a break from India. After all, that's what Nepal and Sri Lanka are there for, aren't they?

Goa

Population: 1 million*
Area: 3813 square km*
Main languages: Marathi, Konkan &
Gujarati

*including Daman & Diu

The small former Portuguese enclave of
Goa is still one of India's most touristically important places. It combines old
Portuguese architecture with a Portuguese
flavour to the lifestyle which somehow
manages to exist even 25 years after India
took Goa over. Most important to many
travellers, there are the superb beaches
and the 'traveller scene' which so many of
them offer. Officially Goa is governed
with two other Portuguese coastal enclaves,
Daman and Diu, which were taken over
at the same time. The latter two are both
in the state of Gujarat and are covered in
the Gujarat section of this book.

Goa has a long history stretching back
to the 3rd century BC, when it formed
part of the Mauryan empire. It was later
ruled by the Satavahanas of Kolhapur at
the beginning of the Christian era and
eventually passed to the Chalukyans of
Badami, who controlled it from 580 to 750
AD. Over the next few centuries it was
ruled successively by the Shilharas, the
Kadambas and the Chalukyans of Kalyani.
The Kadambas are credited with constructing the first settlement on the site of
Old Goa in the middle of the 11th
century, when it was called Thorlem
Gorem.

Goa fell to the Muslims for the first
time in 1312, but they were forced to
evacuate it in 1370 by Harihara I of the
Vijayanagar empire whose capital was
at Hampi in Karnataka state. The
Vijayanagar rulers held on to Goa for
nearly 100 years, during which its
harbours were important landing places
for Arabian horses on their way to Hampi

to strengthen the Vijayanagar cavalry. In
1469, however, Goa was reconquered, this
time by the Bahmani Sultans of Gulbarga.
When this dynasty broke up, the area
passed to the Adil Shahis of Bijapur, who
made Goa Velhaa their second capital.
The present Secretariat building in
Panaji is the former palace of Adil Shah,
later taken over by the Portuguese
Viceroys as their official residence.

The Portuguese arrived in Goa in 1510
under the command of Alfonso de
Albuquerque after having been unable to
secure a base on the Malabar coast
further south. This was due to opposition
from the Zamorin of Calicut and stiff
competition from the Turks who, at that
time, controlled the trade routes across
the Indian Ocean. Blessed as it was by
natural harbours and wide rivers, Goa
was the ideal base for the seafaring
Portuguese, bent on their quest for
control of the spice route from the east
and the spread of Christianity. For a
while their control was limited to a small
area around Old Goa, but by the middle of
the 16th century it had expanded to
include Bardez and Salcete.

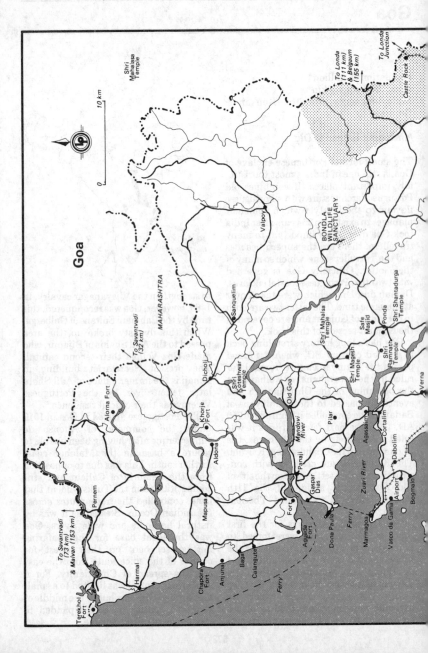

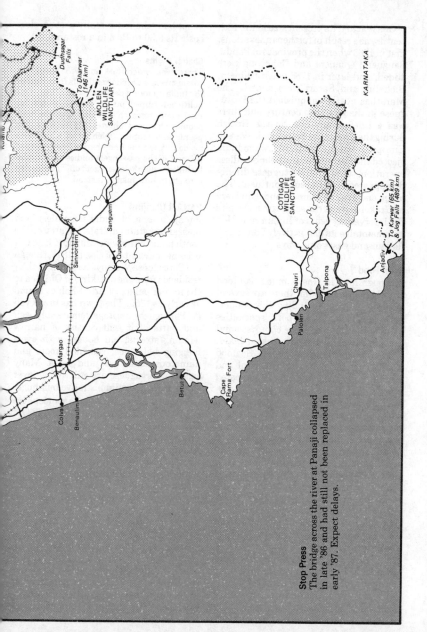

Stop Press

The bridge across the river at Panaji collapsed in late '86 and had still not been replaced in early '87. Expect delays.

Goa reached its present size in the 18th century as a result of further annexations, first in 1763 when the provinces of Ponda, Sanguem, Quepem and Canacona were added, and later in 1788 when Pednem, Bicholim and Satari were added. The Marathas nearly vanquished the Portuguese in the late 18th century and there was a brief occupation by the British during the time of the Napoleonic Wars in Europe. It was not until 1961, when India ejected the Portuguese in a near bloodless operation, that the Portuguese finally disappeared from the sub-continent. The other enclaves of Daman and Diu were also taken over at the same time. Despite the intervening years of Indian rule, Goa still maintains its distinctively Portuguese flavour and easygoing ways.

Goan Food

Although food in Goa is much like food anywhere else in India, there are several local specialties, including the popular pork *vindaloo*. Other pork specialties include the Goan sausage *chourisso* and the pig's-liver dish known as *sarpotel*. *Xacuti* is a chicken or meat dish. Seafood of all types is, of course, plentiful and fresh. *Bangra* is Goan mackerel, prepared in a variety of delicious ways.

There are the usual travellers' menu items at the beach restaurants. Bread is surprisingly good, a real treat after the oversweet Indian imitations of western bread. *Sanna* are rice 'cupcakes' soaked in palm toddy before cooking. There are a variety of special Christmas sweets called *dodol, bebinca* and so on. *Moira kela* are cooking plantains (bananas) from Moira village in Bardez. They were probably introduced from Africa and are sold in Panaji at a shop on the corner of the Hotel Venite street.

Although the ready availability (and low price) of alcohol contrasts with some other parts of India, the Goans brew their local *feni* spirits, made from coconut or cashews. They also produce reasonably palatable wines these days. The dry white is not bad; the red is really port. A glass costs Rs 3.50 to Rs 5 in a restaurant.

Charter Flights

There was much fuss in 1985 about the commencement of charter flights from Europe to India, more specifically to Goa. One politician zipped off to Europe where his meticulous research revealed that the only people who used charter flights were 'old people and hippies'! Neither of which Goa needed. When the first charter finally turned up most of the passengers (oldies and hippies included) didn't even get off, continuing through to Kathmandu instead.

PANAJI (Panjim)

Panaji is one of India's smallest and pleasantest state capitals. Located on the south bank of the wide Mandovi River, it became the capital of Goa in 1843, though the Portuguese Viceroys had shifted their residence from the outskirts of Old Goa to the former palace of Adil Shah at Panaji as early as 1759. The town has preserved its Portuguese heritage remarkably well and parts of it still consist of narrow winding streets, old houses with overhanging balconies, red-tiled roofs and numerous small bars and cafés. Many signs in Portuguese are still visible over shops, cafés and administrative buildings.

People are friendly and the atmosphere is easygoing. The main attraction is Old Goa, nine km east of Panaji and the former capital founded by Alfonso de Albuquerque in 1510, but Panaji is well worth a visit for its own sake apart from its services and facilities.

Panaji's main attractions are the narrow winding streets, small cafés and bars, and occasional old stone buildings dating from the 16th and 17th centuries. Its 'sights' are few, but among those worth visiting are the old Church of the Immaculate Conception (on the hillside at one end of the Municipal Gardens) and the Mahalaxmi Temple. If you're staying in Panaji rather than on the beaches of Goa, then the nearest beach is at Miramar, three km along the road to Dona Paula.

Bombay &   Top: Entrance to the Bhaja Caves (GC)
Maharashtra   Left: Unloading the fish at dawn, Sassoon Dock, Bombay (TW)
              Right: Buddha statue in Ajanta cave temple (TW)

Goa Top: Colva Beach, Goa (TW)
Left: Sunset at Colva Beach, Goa (TW)
Right: The Goa ferry from Bombay, docked in Panaji (TW)

Orientation & Information

The town has a wide range of hotels, many excellent restaurants, old churches and monuments. It is well served by transport facilities connecting it to the rest of India.

The Tourist Office is in the Tourist Home (a kind of Youth Hostel with dorm-type accommodation) in a new complex between the bus stand and Ourem Creek – turn left when you get to the bridge which leads into town (it's signposted).

Post Office The poste restante at the GPO is pretty efficient. They give you the whole pile to sort through yourself and will willingly check other pigeon holes if expected letters are not arriving.

Airlines Indian Airlines (tel 3822) is at Dempo Building, D Bandodkar Marg, on the riverfront, and it's computerised. Air India is at the Fidalgo Hotel on 18th June Rd. Georgeson (tel 2150) opposite the GPO (1st floor) is a travel agent which seems to be reasonably reliable and efficient. The sign may still announce MGM Travel. There's a branch office at Calangute Beach. If you have to reconfirm international flights, check if Air India will do it first; travel agent charges can be heavy.

Tax Clearance If you've stayed in India so long that you need a Tax Clearance Certificate before you depart, then the Taxation Department is in the Shanta Building at the end of 18th June Rd. Vasco de Silva Ferreirra, a solicitor who has an office on the 1st floor next to the New Punjab Restaurant opposite the Municipal Park, will do the necessary.

Other The hotels Mandovi and Fidalgo both have good bookshops. *Inside Goa* by Manshar Mulgastion with illustrations by Mario Miranda is excellent, though somewhat expensive. The dreaded weed is readily available in Goa (it's usually from Kerala). Travellers who've come

from Kashmir or the Kulu Valley may offer you resin but the quality varies. Test before buying, and remember that like everywhere else in India the police are getting much fiercer about dope.

Tours

Tours of Goa are offered both by the Tourist Office and by private agencies. Apart from tours to the temples and churches of Goa and the excursion to Bondla Forest, the tours aren't very good because they attempt to pack too much into a short day so you end up seeing very little. Also, much attention is focused on 'seeing the hippies on the beach'.

The north Goa tour visits Panaji, Arvalem Falls, Datta Mandir, Mayem Lake, Mapusa, Vagator, Anjuna, Calangute and Aguada Fort. The south Goa tours take in Miramar, Dona Paula, Pilar, Marmagoa, Vasco da Gama, Colva, Margao, Shanta Durga Temple, Ramnath Temple, Mangesh Temple and Old Goa. The tours cost Rs 35 and depart at 9 am daily. The beach tour is Rs 15, a river cruise is Rs 25 and a pilgrim tour is Rs 15.

Places to Stay

Whenever there is a religious festival in Goa – especially the festival of St Francis Xavier (several days on either side of 3 December) – it can be difficult to find accommodation in Panaji, even in the small, inexpensive lodges. There is no accommodation at Old Goa.

Places to Stay – bottom end

Most of the budget hotels in Panaji are very definitely at the dim and dusty end of 'basic'. Don't expect too much wherever you decide to stay.

Probably the best of the bunch is the *Republica Hotel* (tel 2638), Jose Falca Rd at the back of the Secretariat block. It's an old place with fine views over the Mandovi River. Rooms here with common bath cost Rs 20 to Rs 25 a single, and Rs 30 to Rs 35 a double with fan. The showers

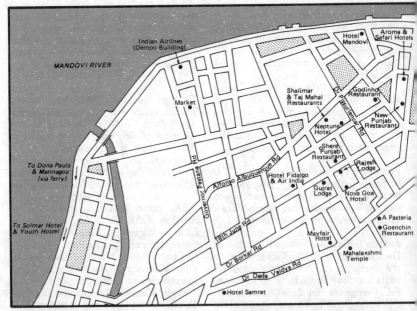

and toilets are kept clean, but if there's a water shortage you'll have to make do with a cup and bucket – the same goes for all the budget hotels. The staff are friendly. If possible, try to get one of the rooms overlooking the river – the others are a bit dingy.

If the Republic is full, try the *Hotel Palace* next door. If you can get one of the two double rooms with balconies that overlook the street, you're in luck; most of the others are dismal, hardboard-partitioned cells. Singles/doubles are Rs 15/30 but only a couple of rooms have attached bath; most have shared baths and toilets.

Up the road from the Republica and at the back of the Tourist Hostel is the *Mandovi Pearl Guest House*. This is an old house with large, spacious rooms, plenty of mosquitoes and no nets, but it's run by a very friendly and easygoing proprietor and is popular with travellers. Singles/doubles are Rs 50/80 and it's often full, so if you want to stay here, arrive early.

Hotel Sona (tel 4426), Rua de Ourem, has singles at Rs 55 to Rs 65, doubles at Rs 65 to Rs 75 plus some more expensive front rooms and triples. All have attached bathrooms. The hotel has its own restaurant and bar. Beside the Municipal Gardens, two doors from the Aroma Hotel, the small *Safari Hotel* has rooms at Rs 25/35. The *Panjim Inn* is an old merchant house of the early 1700s still owned by the same family. It's a five-minute walk from the cathedral and has large rooms with shower at Rs 60 and lots of character.

There are some rock-bottom places worth trying, like *Kiran Boarding & Lodging* opposite the Bombay steamer jetty, where singles are Rs 30, doubles Rs 40 to Rs 45 at the height of the season. *Glemar Lodge*, Rebelo Building, D Antao de Noronha Rd, is around the corner from the Aroma Hotel. The rooms are dingy, but it's secure and the staff are friendly.

There is a whole collection of cheap hotels in the old, narrow streets behind

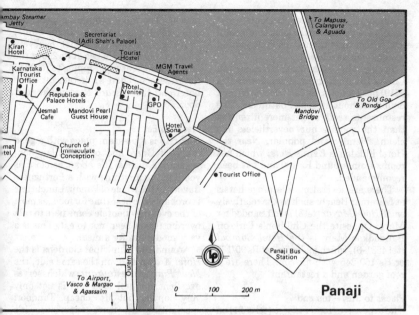

the GPO. They include the *Hotel Venite, Elite Lodge, Goa Tourist Lodge, De-lux Lodge, Everest Lodge* and *Orav's Guest House*.

There are two excellent places with dormitory-style accommodation. The *Tourist Home* is in a complex which includes the Tourist Office by the riverside between the bus station and town centre. It's very popular with westerners and Indians alike, and costs Rs 10 per bed per night. There is a restaurant and bar.

Out at Miramar Beach the *Youth Hostel* (tel 5433) has dorm beds for Rs 8 (Rs 10 for non-members) and a solitary double room with attached bath for Rs 50. Officially the hostel is closed between 1 and 4 pm, but they're not strict about it. The hostel has a superb location right next to the beach. Its only drawback is the distance from the centre of town, but regular buses will get you there within five minutes.

Also at the beach, *Hotel Solmar* (tel 4555-6) on Avenida Gaspar Dias has

rooms at Rs 40/50 or Rs 75 for a double with air-con. Or there's the rustic *Belvila Lodge* on the main road opposite the turn-off for the Youth Hostel.

Places to Stay – middle

The *Tourist Hostel* (tel 2303) is the bargain among the mid-range hotels. The only trouble is that it's often booked solid for up to eight weeks in advance! It's clean, cheap and semi-western in style, and on the ground floor there's a whole complex of shops selling photographic supplies, postcards and souvenirs. Rooms cost Rs 50/60, Rs 80/90 or with air-con Rs 120 to Rs 150. All have attached bathrooms and there is a pleasant open-air restaurant on the 1st floor with good food.

The *Mayfair Hotel* (tel 5952, 5772) on Dr Dada Vaidya Rd is a pleasant place and good value with rooms at Rs 120 or with air-conditioning at Rs 150 at the height of the season. Prices drop to as little as Rs 60 for a single without air-con in the off season. All rooms have attached bathrooms, some have balconies and there's a restaurant with Goan, continental and Indian vegetarian and non-vegetarian food as well as a bar.

Facing the Municipal Gardens on Cunha Rivara Rd, the *Hotel Aroma* (tel 3519) has rooms at Rs 75/100 or Rs 85 for a double without attached bathroom. The restaurants seem to get more attention than the rooms, but nevertheless it's clean, friendly and popular. Near the Hotel Fidalgo is *Keni's Hotel* which has rooms from around Rs 100 and has been recommended.

There are several middle-range hotels at Miramar Beach, such as the relatively small *Hotel Mayur* (tel 3174) off Bandodkar Marg. Opposite the Children's Park off Bandodkar Marg is the *Hotel Campal* (tel 4531-6), which has rooms at Rs 90/175 or Rs 150/245 with air-con. There are a roof garden and a restaurant.

Places to Stay – top end

The expensive *Hotel Fidalgo* (tel 3321) on 18th June has rooms at Rs 325/425 plus a bookshop, restaurant, bar, swimming pool, central air-conditioning and hordes of spoilt brats rampaging around. The new *Hotel Nova Goa* (tel 4575-80) is on Dr Atmaram Borkar Rd and has singles from Rs 150 to Rs 300, doubles from Rs 200 to Rs 350. The hotel is centrally air-conditioned and has a restaurant and snack bar.

Other hotels in the upper end of this bracket include the *Hotel Mandovi* (tel 4481-5), Bandodkar Marg overlooking the Mandovi River, which has singles at Rs 150 to Rs 180, doubles at Rs 280 to Rs 340. All the rooms are air-conditioned and have attached bathrooms. The hotel has a roof garden, two restaurants – Indian, Chinese, western – a bar, money-changing facilities and a good bookshop.

Out at Vainguinim Beach, Dona Paula, the *Welcomgroup Cidade de Goa* (tel 3301) has rooms at Rs 600 at the height of the season. They fall to Rs 450/500 in the shoulder season, Rs 300/350 in the off

season. There's a swimming pool and other mod cons. Also at Dona Paula, *Prainha Cottages* (tel 4004) has very pleasant rooms by the sea at Rs 200 at the height of the season, dropping to Rs 90 in the off season. There's a restaurant at the hotel and the *Pescaro Restaurant* next door.

Places to Eat

Godinho is a pleasant place with a good range of Goan and other Indian non-vegetarian dishes. It's about as close as you'll get to anything with a Portuguese flavour in the whole of Panaji. Lunchtime is probably the best time for food, as most of the evening clientele come here to talk over bottles of beer, not to eat. This is a very good place for a meal.

Around the Municipal Gardens is the *Hotel Aroma* and, on the same side, the *New Punjab Restaurant* which serves excellent Punjabi food and is not only very popular but also cheap. Tandoori specialities are more expensive. It's closed on Saturdays. At the top of the gardens is the vegetarian *Kamat Hotel*, while just off the gardens at the other end the *Jesmal Café* has excellent milkshakes (particularly mango). Next to the residency the *Casa Juka* sandwich bar does good cold milkshakes and lassi.

Upstairs at the Tourist Hostel is the *Chit Chat Restaurant* with its pleasant open-air verandah. It's a good place for breakfast and they have excellent lassi. *Hotel Venite* is in the narrow streets behind the GPO. This is a beautiful old place on the 1st floor with polished wood floor, balconies overlooking the street and bags of atmosphere. It has a limited but colourful menu and is a great place to sit and have a drink. It's open for breakfast despite its sign. 'The menu', reported one visitor, 'is authentically Portuguese but translated into English. Re-translated into Portuguese you find some of the best-prepared Portuguese food I've ever had.' Try the cabbage-based vegetable soup, the fish which is done like grilled Portuguese sardines and the superb Portuguese-style cream caramel. Another traveller reported that it is no longer that clean.

Other good restaurants include the *Shere Punjab Restaurant* on 18th June Rd, and the *Shalimar* and *Taj Mahal* restaurants next to each other on Alfonso de Albuquerque Rd. The former is non-vegetarian and the latter vegetarian. The *Goenchin* is an excellent but expensive new Chinese restaurant just off Dr Dada Vaidya R. The *A Pasteria* cake shop is on the corner.

Finally, some locals say that *O'Coquiero* has the best food in Goa. It's several km north of Panaji at the junction where the Mapusa and Calangute roads split. An auto-rickshaw will cost about Rs 15 or a bus 40p. Prices at the restaurant are not excessive and they have an all-you-can-eat Rs 40 buffet. It gained some notoriety in 1986 when international serial-murderer Charles Sobhraj, who had escaped from prison in New Delhi, was captured here.

Getting There

Air Indian Airlines have two flights a day most days of the week from Bombay to Goa. The fare is Rs 398. There are also flights most days of the week to and from Bangalore (Rs 456), Delhi (Rs 1318), Cochin (Rs 597) and Trivandrum (Rs 731).

Rail The railhead in Goa is at Vasco da Gama (it actually continues on to Marmagoa but very few of the main trains start from there). See the Getting Around section for details of getting to Vasco from Panaji. The other main station in Goa is at Margao. Seats and sleepers on the trains can be booked at Vasco, Margao or the South Central Out-Agency Booking Office at counter 5 at the Panaji bus station. It's open 10 am to 1 pm and 2 to 5.30 pm except Sundays.

Apart from the main trains from Vasco and Margao, some local trains ply between Kolamb (another Goan town further up the line) and Marmagoa, but they're of little interest to travellers.

Trains to Bangalore take from 20 to 25 hours depending on the one you take. There are some through carriages from Margao, so you do not have to change trains at Londa. Fares for the 689-km trip are Rs 58 in 2nd class, Rs 234 in 1st. To Bombay takes 21 to 25 hours and involves a change of train at Miraj. Fare for the 788-km trip is Rs 65 in 2nd class, Rs 262 in 1st.

Getting to New Delhi from Goa involves several changes of train, usually at Miraj and Bombay. Total journey time is about 48 hours and the fare for the 2400-km trip is about Rs 145 in 2nd class, Rs 600 in 1st.

Bus Several private companies offer 'super luxury' buses to places like Bombay and Bangalore. Most of them depart at night, but even if the roughness of the roads didn't prevent you from sleeping, the videos probably would. There are offices in Panaji, Mapusa and Margao. The 16-hour trip to Bombay costs Rs 100 to Rs 130 or even Rs 150 depending on the company.

Slightly cheaper buses are operated by the Karnataka State Road Transport Corporation, the Maharashtra State Road Transport Corporation and Goa's own bus company, Kadamba Transport Company.

Buses go to Londa (where you can get a direct railway carriage to Mysore every day), Hubli (a railway junction on the main Bombay-Bangalore line, where you can also get trains to Gadag for both Bijapur/Badami and Hospet/Hampi) and Belgaum. A bus to Hubli takes seven hours and costs Rs 22.50. From Hubli to Hospet is Rs 18 and another 4½ hours. There are daily buses to Mysore for Rs 76, 88 or 92; they take 16 hours. Mangalore is an 11-hour trip for Rs 66. Other buses include Pune for Rs 54, 69 or 80 and Bangalore for Rs 102 or Rs 110.

Ferry The Goa-Bombay ferry service operates daily except Tuesdays from Bombay and Wednesdays from Panaji. Departures are at 10 am, although from Panaji the departure time may be affected by the tides. The trip takes 22 hours but the service is suspended during the monsoon and at other times when the weather is very rough. The steamer is a far pleasanter way of getting to or from Bombay than the train, and highly recommended by many travellers. If you're travelling in deck class at peak times of year, make sure you get to the quay about an hour before departure, because when the gates are opened it's the usual panic. If you're right at the back, and therefore one of the last on, you'll have a very limited choice of places to sleep. An alternative is to buy a deck cloth and get a porter to rush on board and use it to claim a patch of deck for you.

Fares are as follows: Owner's Cabin (two-berth cabin, shower and toilet) Rs 600 for two; Deluxe A (four-berth cabin, shower and toilet) Rs 260; Deluxe B (four-berth cabin) Rs 235; 1st class (20-berth cabin) Rs 220; upper deck (deck space for 290) Rs 72; lower deck (deck space for 700) Rs 48. Bedding is available for hire in both deck classes for Rs 15. In theory, there's nothing to stop you paying for lower deck and then going to sleep in upper deck. The front and back of the upper deck are classified as lower deck so they're good places for lower-deck ticket holders to head for. Lunch and dinner are available on board – fairly good food at reasonable prices (vegetarian and non-vegetarian).

The booking office in Panaji is V S Dempo & Co (tel 3842), opposite the steamer jetty. You can book any number of days ahead for 1st class and above, but only six days ahead for deck class. Advance bookings can be made daily except Wednesdays from 10 am to 12.30 pm (cabin classes only), and from 2.30 to 5 pm (cabin and deck classes). If you want a ticket on the day of sailing, these go on sale at 8 am. Cabin classes are usually booked out several weeks in advance. In Bombay you book tickets at the wharf.

Getting Around

Airport Indian Airlines operate buses from their office in Panaji to Dabolim Airport near Vasco da Gama in time for flights; the fare is Rs 15. A taxi costs Rs 60 to Rs 80.

Bus If you've done much travelling by Indian bus, you're in for a pleasant surprise in Goa. Most of the buses here are privately owned, and they're pretty good as far as maintenance and standards of comfort go. There's not the same mad scramble for seats there is in other states, and people will make room for you instead of trying to squeeze you out. There is no timetable, but services to most places in Goa are frequent. The conductors holler out their destinations and buses go when approximately full. Some of the more popular routes include:

Panaji-Vasco da Gama/Marmagoa There are two ways of getting there. You can either go via the ferry from Dona Paula to Marmagoa or by road via Agassaim and Cortalim. Unless you know there will be a ferry waiting for you on arrival at Dona Paula, the route via Agassaim and Cortalim is the quicker of the two. Either way it will cost about Rs 3 to Rs 4 and take about one hour – the exact cost depends on the sort of bus you take.

Panaji-Margao You can get to Margao either via Agassaim/Cortalim or Ponda. The former is the more direct route and will take about 1½ hours. It's Rs 3 to Rs 4 depending on what type of bus you take. Via Ponda it will take about an hour longer and cost a little more.

Panaji-Old Goa To get here you can take one of the frequent buses going straight to Old Goa or any bus going to Ponda. The journey costs Rs 1 and takes 20 to 30 minutes.

Panaji-Calangute There is a frequent service thoughout the day and evening.

The journey takes about 35 to 45 minutes and costs Rs 1.30.

Panaji-Mapusa Buses cost Rs 1 and take about 25 minutes. Frequent service. There are also three buses daily direct to Chapora Village via Mapusa. Mapusa is pronounced 'Mapsa', and this is what the conductors shout.

Local Ferries One of the joys of travelling around Goa are the ferries across the many rivers in this small state. Almost without exception they are combined passenger/car ferries. The main ferries are:

Dona Paula-Marmagoa This ferry runs between September and May only. There are regular crossings but they are somewhat infrequent, and at certain times of the day you could find yourself waiting about two hours. The crossing takes 30 to 45 minutes and costs Rs 1.20. Buses wait on either side for the arrival of boats. This is a passenger ferry only, but it's the best way of getting from Panaji to Vasco da Gama.

Old Goa-Piedade Ferries every 30 minutes.

Other Other ferries include: Aldona-Corjuem; Colvale-Macasana; Pomburpa-Chorao; Ribander-Chorao; Siolim-Chopdem and St Estevam-Tonca. There are also launches from the central jetty in Panaji to Aldona (once daily), Britona (twice daily), Naroa (twice daily) and Verem.

Bicycle It's easy to hire bicycles (Rs 5 to Rs 6) at most of the major Goan towns or beaches. You can also hire motorcycles (if you've ever wanted to try a Rajdoot) from around Rs 50 or Rs 60.

OLD GOA (Goa Velha)

Even before the arrival of the Portuguese, Old Goa was a thriving and prosperous city and the second capital of the Adil Shahi dynasty of Bijapur. At that time it was surrounded by fort walls, towers and a moat, and contained many temples and mosques as well as the large palace of Adil Shah. Today none of these structures remain except a fragment of the gateway to the palace. What there is dates from the Portuguese period.

Under the Portuguese the city grew rapidly in size and splendour, eventually coming to rival Lisbon itself, despite an epidemic in 1543 which wiped out a large percentage of the population. Many huge churches, monasteries and convents were erected by the various religious orders which came to Goa under royal mandates, the Franciscans being the first to arrive. Old Goa's splendour was short-lived, however, since by the end of the 16th century Portuguese supremacy on the seas had been replaced by that of the British, Dutch and French. The city's decline was accelerated by the activities of the Inquisition and a devastating epidemic which struck the population in 1635. Indeed had not the Portuguese been in treaty relations with the British it is probable that Goa would either have passed to the Dutch or been absorbed into British India.

The city muddled on into the early 19th century as the administrative capital of Portugal's eastern empire (Goa, Daman and Diu in India, Timor in Indonesia, and Macau in China) but, following the transfer of the seat of power to Panaji in 1843 and repressive religious orders in 1835, the city was deserted. Today it's a small village surrounded by the huge churches and convents built during its heyday, and which attract visitors from many parts of the world. Some of them remain in active use, though others have become museums maintained by the Archaeological Survey of India – a maintenance very necessary since unless the lime plaster which protects the laterite structure is renewed frequently, the monsoons soon reduce such buildings to ruin.

Information

The Archaeological Survey of India

publishes *Old Goa* by S Rajagopalan (New Delhi 1975), an excellent booklet about the monuments. It's available from the Archaeological Museum at Old Goa.

Se Cathedral

The largest of the churches at Old Goa, Se Cathedral was begun in 1562 during the reign of King Dom Sebastiao (1557-78) and substantially completed by 1619, though the altars were not finished until 1652. The cathedral was built for the Dominicans and paid for by the Royal Treasury out of the proceeds of the sale of the Crown's property.

Architecturally, the building is Portuguese-Gothic in style with a Tuscan exterior and Corinthian interior. There were originally two towers, one on either side of the facade, but the one on the southern side collapsed in 1776. The existing tower houses a famous bell, one of the largest in Goa and often referred to as the 'Golden Bell' on account of its rich sound. The main altar is dedicated to St Catherine of Alexandria, and old paintings on either side of it depict scenes from her life and martyrdom.

Convent & Church of St Francis of Assisi

This is probably one of the most interesting buildings in Old Goa. It contains gilded, carved woodwork, old murals depicting scenes from the life of St Francis, and a floor substantially made of carved gravestones – complete with family coats of arms dating back to the early 1500s. The church's humble beginnings were made by eight Franciscan friars who arrived here in 1517 and constructed a small chapel consisting of three altars and a choir. This was later pulled down and the present building was constructed on the same spot in 1661.

The convent at the back of this church is now the Archaeological Museum. It houses many portraits of the Portuguese Viceroys – most of them inexpertly touched up – fragments of sculpture from

Hindu temple sites in Goa which show Chalukyan and Hoysala influences, stone Vetal images from the animist cult which flourished in this part of India centuries ago, and a model of a Portuguese caravelle minus the rigging (surely someone could get it together to do the rigging?!).

Professed House & Basilica of Bom Jesus

The Basilica of Bom Jesus is famous throughout the Roman Catholic world since it contains the tomb and mortal remains of St Francis Xavier who, in 1541, was given the task of spreading Christianity among the subjects of the Portuguese colonies in the east. A former pupil of St Ignatius Loyola, the founder of the Jesuit Order, St Francis Xavier made missionary voyages in the east that became a legend and, considering the state of communications at the time, that are nothing short of miraculous.

Arriving in Goa in 1542, St Francis Xavier spent the next few years spreading the Christian faith along the Malabar and Coromandel coasts, until news reached him that Christianity had begun to make inroads in the Molucca Islands (now Maluku in Indonesia). Wishing to make sure that the converts properly comprehended their new faith, he set out on a voyage to those islands, returning to Goa in 1548. He stayed in Goa only a short time, however, and soon embarked on a voyage to Japan where he sought permission to teach Christianity from the King of Yamaguchi. Though permission was granted, Francis made little headway due to the opposition of the Bonzes. Disappointed, he boarded a ship bound for Goa but got off at Sancian Island just off the coast of China. There he fell ill and died in December 1552 at the age of 46.

His body was buried on Sancian, but subsequently taken to Melaka (Malacca) and placed in the Church of Our Lady of the Mount. Four months later Francis' successor had the grave opened in order to pay his respects and, finding that the body was still fresh and life-like, had it sent to Goa in 1554. It was first kept in St Paul's College but transferred to the Professed House in 1613. After canonisation the body was removed to the Basilica of Bom Jesus. The body is exposed to public view once every 10 years (1994 is the next occasion) on the anniversary of St Francis' death; but is no longer whole, having been through some weird and wonderful mutilations at the hands of relic seekers, both lay and ecclesiastical.

While in Melaka, the body was kept in too small a grave, which resulted in the neck being broken. One of the toes was bitten off in 1554 by a Portuguese woman who wanted a relic of the saint. In 1615 part of the right hand was cut off and sent to Rome where it is venerated in the Church of Gesu, and in 1619 the remaining part of the hand was removed and sent to the Jesuits in Japan. Portions of the intestines have been removed from time to time and distributed to various places.

As well as the 10-year cycle of expositions, a festival is held in Old Goa every year on the anniversary of the saint's death (3 December), at which time the normally sleepy little village becomes a mad-house of pot and pan stalls, food and beer tents, trinket sellers, balloons, firecrackers, buses from all over Goa and even further afield, and thousands of pilgrims, many of whom doss down in the cloisters of the Basilica. When Mass is said there isn't a square cm of space left in the church. It's like a sardine tin!

Apart from the richly gilded altars, the interior of the church is remarkable for its simplicity, and this is the only church which is not plastered on the outside. It was commenced in 1594 and completed in 1605. The centre of interest inside the church is, of course, the tomb of St Francis, the construction of which was underwritten by the Duke of Tuscany and executed by Florentine sculptor Giovanni Batista Foggini. It took 10 years to build and was completed in 1698. The remains of the body are housed in a silver casket which at one time was covered in jewels.

On the walls surrounding it are murals depicting scenes from the saint's journeys, including one of his death on Sancian Island.

The Professed House, next door to the Basilica, is a two-storeyed laterite building covered with lime plaster which was completed in 1585 despite much opposition to the Jesuits. Part of the building burned down in 1663 but was rebuilt in 1783. There's a modern art gallery attached to the basilica.

Church of St Cajetan

Modelled on the original design of St Peter's Church in Rome, the Church of St Cajetan was built by Italian friars of the Order of Theatines, who were sent by Pope Urban III to preach Christianity in the kingdom of Golconda (near Hyderabad). The friars were not permitted to work in Golconda and so settled down at Goa in 1640. The construction of the church was begun in 1655. Historically, it's of much less interest than the other churches.

Church of St Augustine Ruins

All that is left of this church is the enormous 46-metre-high tower which served as a belfry and formed part of the facade of the church. What little is left of the other parts of the church is choked with creepers and weeds, and access is difficult. The church was constructed in 1602 by Augustinian friars who arrived in Goa in 1587.

It was abandoned in 1835 as a result of repressive policies followed by the Portuguese government, which resulted in the eviction of many religious orders from Goa. The church fell into neglect and the vault collapsed in 1842. Many years later, in 1931, the facade and half the tower fell down, followed by more parts in 1938.

Church & Convent of St Monica

This huge, three-storeyed laterite building was commenced in 1606 and completed in 1627, only to burn down nine years later.

Reconstruction started the following year, and it's from this time that the buildings date. Once known as the Royal Monastery on account of the royal patronage which it enjoyed, the building is now used by the Mater dei Institute as a nunnery which was inaugurated in 1964. Visitors are allowed inside if they are reasonably dressed. There are fading murals on the western inside walls.

Other Buildings

Other monuments of minor interest at Old Goa are the Viceroy's Arch, Gate of Adil Shah's Palace, Royal Chapel of St Anthony, Church of St John of God, Chapel of St Catherine, ruins of the Church of the Carmelites, and Church of Our Lady of the Mount.

Getting There

You need the best part of a day to wander around the churches and other monuments of Old Goa. 'An afternoon is quite enough', wrote a non-believer. 'I needed the best part of an hour and a half', said another. There are frequent buses to Old Goa from the bus stand at Panaji, but as all the buses from Panaji to Ponda also pass through Old Goa, you can use these buses too. Buses take 20 to 30 minutes and cost Rs 1. Whenever there is a festival at Old Goa (such as the Festival of St Francis Xavier at the end of November/beginning of December) boats ply between Panaji (from the Bombay Steamer Jetty) and Old Goa. This 45-minute trip is a very pleasant way of getting there.

MARGAO (Madgaon)

The capital of Salcete Province, Margao is the main population centre of southern Goa and a pleasant provincial town which still displays many reminders of its Portuguese past. In itself it's not of great interest to travellers, though the old Margao church is worth a visit and the covered market is the best of its kind in the whole of Goa. Its importance is as a service and transport centre for people

staying at Colva Beach. If you're planning on staying at Colva you must first head for Margao, which is connected to the rest of Goa and to the neighbouring states by bus, train and taxi.

If you're coming to Margao from outside Goa, the last bus to Colva Beach leaves at 8 pm. After that you will either have to hire a taxi (or motorcycle taxi) to get to Colva or stay overnight in Margao.

Orientation & Information

The Tourist Office is in the Secretariat building on the bottom side of the Municipal Gardens. The staff are friendly and helpful though, as elsewhere in India, they're limited in what they can offer because of lack of funds.

The poste restante is not in the GPO on the Municipal Gardens, but in a separate office about 300 metres away.

The covered market is a fascinating place to wander through, even if you don't want to buy anything. If you'll be staying at Colva for some time and renting a house, the other, smaller market behind the Secretariat building is excellent for pots, pans and other kitchen equipment. The taxi stand is behind the Secretariat building. Rau Raje Deshprabhu, Old Market, is an Indian Airlines agent.

Around Margao

There are some interesting places around Margao. About three km from the small village of Raia, which is on the road from Margao to the Borim bridge, is the Rachol Seminary and Church. The old church dates from the early 1600s and the seminary has interesting architecture, a decaying library and interesting paintings of Christian characters done in Indian styles. This is not a tourist site so you must ask about looking around.

To the east of the Margao-Cortalim road near the village of Nuvem is the Christ Ashram exorcism centre. Although it has been condemned by Catholic authorities the trappings are Catholic but the ambience definitely Hindu.

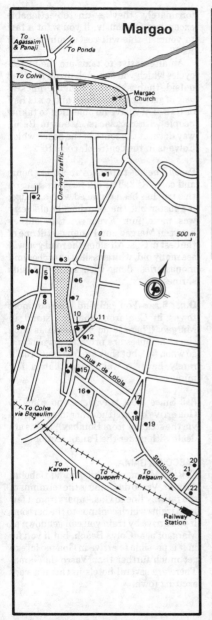

Margao

1	Hotel Metropole
2	Twiga Lodge
3	GPO
4	Poste Restante
5	Bus Stand
6	Mabai Hotel
7	Marliz
8	Bank
9	Goa Woodlands
10	Kandeel Restaurant & Bar & Kamat Hotel
11	Buses to Colva
12	La Marina
13	Tourist Office
14	Market
15	Rukrish Hotel
17	Paradise Bar & Restaurant
18	Centaur Lodging
19	Milan Kamat Hotel
20	Sangam Boarding
21	Vishranti Lodge
22	Hotel Sanrit

Places to Stay – bottom end

At the top of this bracket is the *Woodlands Hotel* (tel 3121), which has friendly staff, its own bar and restaurant and rooms at Rs 30/40 or rooms with air-con at Rs 80/90. It's good value.

Most of the other cheaper hotels are strung out along Station Rd between the central Municipal Park and the railway station. I'd nominate the friendly *Rukrish Hotel* as the best of the bunch. Here you can get a good, clean single with a small balcony overlooking the street for Rs 30 or doubles with attached bath for Rs 30 to Rs 50.

Other hotels of similar standard along Station Rd include the *Milan Kamat Hotel* (tel 2715) and the *Sanrit Hotel* (tel 3226-7) in front of the railway station. *Centaur Boarding & Lodging*, around the corner from the Sanrit, is in the same category. Across the other side of the railway tracks, close to the turn-off for Benaulim, is the *Hotel Annapurna*.

Near the market in the middle of town the *Tourist Hostel* has rooms at Rs 40/50. The *Twiga Lodge* is a pleasant place on the other side of town and well off the busy main streets.

Places to Stay – top end
The *Mabai Hotel* (tel 3653-5), conveniently located on the top side of the Municipal Gardens, has rooms at Rs 45/75 or rooms with air-con at Rs 75/115. The rooms are large, airy and pleasantly decorated and there's a restaurant, bar and roof garden.

Hotel Metropole (tel 3552-7) on Avenida Concessao is an ugly building a short walk from the centre. Rooms are Rs 100/135 or Rs 150/200 with air-con. There are two restaurants, a roof garden, bar, discotheque and bookshop.

Places to Eat
The partially air-con *Kandeel* is beside the Municipal Gardens and the friendly staff serve superb Goan-style food. Try the Goan fish, masala chicken and rice which come complete with chappati, papadum, salad and pickles. They also have ice-cold beers.

La Marina Café, a few metres from the Colva bus stand, is a very reasonable restaurant although they don't have everything their extensive menu promises. There is a bakery next door. Directly opposite the Tourist Office, the charming *Longuinhos* does ultra-hot curries ('recommended only for fire eaters') and good sweets and cakes.

For snacks and breakfasts, the *Marliz* on the top side of the Municipal Gardens is an extremely popular café and has been for many, many years. It's always crowded – and for very good reason, as its snacks are excellent. They include sandwiches, vegetarian and non-vegetarian pasties, cakes and coffee.

Getting There
Colva Beach Buses run to Colva via Benaulim on an approximately hourly basis. The first bus from Margao leaves at about 7.30 am and the last at 8 pm. The fare is Rs 1 and the journey takes 20 to 25 minutes. Taxi cost at least Rs 2 per person – they usually take six people, sometimes more. A few drivers demand Rs 10 or more, even when the taxi is shared, but

fortunately they're an objectionable exception. Obviously, if you want a taxi to yourself this will cost a minimum of Rs 12.

An alternative to taxis are the motorcycles which you can pick up on the road outside the bus stand. This is the quickest way of getting to the beach and costs Rs 7 or Rs 8. They have no objection to taking people with rucksacks. A bus to Betul, way down at the south of the beach which Colva is in the centre of, costs Rs 2.

Panaji The bus trip takes about 1½ hours and costs Rs 3. The old ferry crossing on this trip has been replaced with a bridge; it's faster but the ramshackle old ferry was more fun. Even so, the journey between Margao and Panaji is still one of the best in Goa. All along the road you will see many old, whitewashed churches and monasteries along with small roadside shrines.

Other Buses You can find buses to most towns in Goa from the bus stand in Margao. There is no timetable as such since the buses are privately owned and go when full, but they are frequent. You'll rarely have to wait more than a few minutes.

Rail Since most travellers who come to Goa arrive by rail (the other main route is via the steamer from Bombay), trains are dealt with under the Panaji section.

VASCO DA GAMA
Close to Marmagoa Harbour and Dabolim Airport, Vasco da Gama is the terminus of the railway line to Goa – apart from a few local trains which continue to the harbour. If you arrive by train you can get down at Margao, near Colva Beach, but if you fly in it is possible to arrive in Goa too late to get much further than Vasco da Gama. There are several hotels in this not very exciting town.

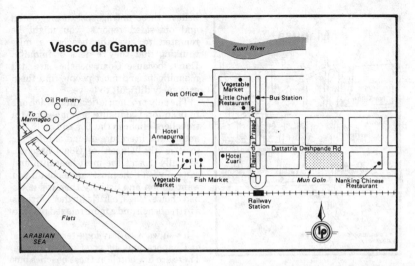

Places to Stay

The recently opened and centrally located *Tourist Hostel* (tel 3119) has rooms at Rs 40/50. The new and clean *Hotel Annapurna* (tel 3185) has doubles at Rs 55 and a good vegetarian restaurant. Otherwise there are a number of hotels with similar prices – the *Hotel Rebelo* (tel 2620) at Vadem has rooms with bath for Rs 30 to Rs 45 or with air-con for Rs 75 to Rs 125. *Lapaz Hotel* (tel 2121) on Swatentrya Path is rather more expensive and has rooms with air-con. *Hotel Zuari* (tel 127) is similarly priced. There are several cheaper local hotels.

Places to Eat

The *Nanking Chinese Restaurant*, three blocks from the railway station, is a friendly place with good food. The *Little Chef* is almost like a western fast-food place. The food at *Hotel Zuari* is excellent, if somewhat expensive.

MAPUSA

Mapusa (pronounced locally as 'Mapsa') is the main centre of population in the northern provinces of Goa and the main town for supplies if you are staying either at Anjuna or Chapora. If you're staying at Calangute or Baga, you have a choice of Panaji or Mapusa as a service centre. In itself, there's nothing to see in Mapusa, though the Friday market is perhaps worth a visit. You may, however, need to stay here overnight if you're catching a bus to Bombay the following day.

Places to Stay

There's no need to stay at Mapusa – accommodation at the nearby beaches of Anjuna, Vagator and Chapora is far preferable. If you have to stay here, *Hotel Bardez* (tel 2607) is the best place in town and has rooms at Rs 40/50 with attached bath.

The *Tourist Hostel* is a large, newly constructed place on the roundabout at the entrance to Mapusa and has singles for Rs 40, doubles for Rs 50 to Rs 60, plus larger family rooms. Otherwise there's the new *Satyahara Hotel* (tel 2849) with rooms at Rs 40/60, more with air-con or TV; and the cheap but rather grim *Janki Shankar Lodge* (tel 401).

Places to Eat

The *Tourist Hostel* has a large dining

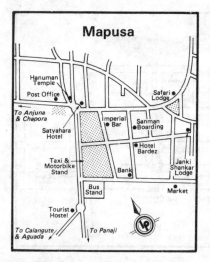

Mapusa

Hanuman Temple
Post Office
To Anjuna & Chapora
Satyahara Hotel
Taxi & Motorbike Stand
Tourist Hostel
To Calangute & Aguada
Imperial Bar
Bank
Bus Stand
To Panaji
Safari Lodge
Sanman Boarding
Hotel Bardez
Janki Shankar Lodge
Market

hall. The *Imperial Bar & Restaurant* serves good non-vegetarian food and cold beers. It's clean, easygoing and popular with local people.

Getting There

As at Panaji, there's no schedule, but bus services are frequent. Buses to Anjuna and Chapora can be very crowded – mostly with westerners staying on the beaches. Mapusa-Panaji takes about 25 minutes and costs Rs 1. There are also buses to Calangute, Anjuna and Chapora as well as to other population centres in northern Goa.

As an alternative to the buses you can take either a taxi or a motorcycle. A motorbike to Anjuna or Calangute will cost Rs 12 and take about 15 minutes. Taxis ask for considerably more.

BEACHES

Goa is justifiably famous for its beaches, and westerners have been flocking to them since the early '60s. They occasionally suffer from a bad press both in the western and Indian media, because of the real or imagined nefarious activities of a small minority of visitors. If you were to

believe these outrageously exaggerated and one-sided reports, you might be tempted to give the beaches a miss thinking that they're dens of iniquity. Don't, because Goan beaches are still magnificent and most people find them extremely difficult to leave.

The only problem is deciding which one to head for. Calangute became almost a travellers' cliche in the '60s and early '70s and tourist literature is fond of referring to it as the 'Queen' of Goa's beaches. Actually it isn't the most beautiful and certainly isn't the most serene, but if you want action and activity then it's not a bad choice. Baga, a little further north, is a better beach and a more relaxed place to stay.

If you want to stay long-term, Anjuna or Chapora may be good places to try. There are few hotels at these beaches but rented houses are scattered among the coconut plantations. Both beaches have retained their charm. This isn't Kuta Beach!

If any beach deserves the title of 'Queen' it is Colva, as this beach is without equal in India. It's nothing short of paradise, with 40 km of uninterrupted white sand fringed with coconut palms along the whole of its length and a warm, calm sea. Go a little way in either direction from Colva village and you will find the nearest thing to a deserted beach. The other main beaches at Aguada and Bagmalo are largely for the jet set and sport expensive five-star resorts.

It's wise to be at least a little security-conscious on the Goa beaches. Things do get stolen both on the beach and from rooms.

COLVA

Colva stretches sun-drenched, palm-fringed and virtually deserted for km after km. Fifteen years ago precious little disturbed its soft, white sands and warm, crystal-clear turquoise waters, except the local fishermen who pulled their catch in by hand each morning, and a few of the more intrepid hippies who had forsaken the obligatory drugs, sex and rock & roll of Calangute for the soothing tranquility of this corner of paradise. Since there were only two cottages for rent and one café (Vincy's), most people stayed either on the beach itself or in palm-leaf shelters, which they took over from departing travellers or constructed themselves.

Those days are gone forever, and even in the days of yore, the property speculators and developers had begun to sniff around in search of a fast rupee. Today, you can see the results of their efforts – air-conditioned resort complexes, serried ranks of tourist cottages, discotheques, trinket stalls and cold-drink places. You'll be lucky if you see a fisherman around the main area and, anyway, they all appear to have acquired motorised trawlers which stand anchored in a line offshore. Likewise, you won't come across anyone sleeping out on the beach these days or throwing up a palm-leaf shelter; the determination of the average Indian day-tripper to catch a glimpse of a scantily-dressed body (preferably female) put paid to all that.

It's only fair to point out that this development is concentrated in a relatively small area at the end of the road from Margao, and that it's simplicity itself to get away from it. Walk two km either side of here, and you'll get close to what it used to be like before the cement mixers began chugging away. When you're there, if you're tired of wearing clothes, take them off. Everyone else does.

It could be said we have only ourselves to blame for making the beach so popular in the first place, but Colva still has a long way to go before it gets as developed as Calangute, or a lot of other beaches I could think of around the world. It's still the best of the Goan beaches, and if you like a really quiet life you can always head further south to Benaulim or Betul.

Information

The nearest post office is in Colva village.

Letters can be sent poste restante there rather than to Margao if you like. At present there is no bank in the village, but the Hotel Silver Sands may be prepared to change travellers' cheques.

Places to Stay

The best deal – if you're going to stay here for a while – is to rent a house with a number of other people. If you're not already part of a large enough group, ask around in the cafés at Colva and Benaulim, or take a walk along the road which runs parallel to the beach from Colva village in both directions and ask every time you see a likely-looking place. It shouldn't take more than a few days. Obviously you get what you pay for, but prices vary from Rs 200 to Rs 400 per month. Between November and March competition is stiff, so get there before then if possible. There are very few places to rent on a long-term basis on the beach itself; most houses are a good 15 to 20 minutes' walk from the beach.

Colva For short-term accommodation there is a wide choice. At the cheaper end of the market are various places strung out along the beach, north of the main area. They're all much the same price of around Rs 25 or Rs 30 for rooms with shared bath and toilet and are perfectly adequate for most peoples' purposes. The *Lucky Star* has singles at Rs 15, doubles with shower at Rs 40.

The *Tourist Cottages* have recently been considerably extended, but although they look flashy they're reasonably priced. This is another of those Indian places that seem to look old and worn even before they finish building them. Singles/doubles with attached bathroom are Rs 65/80 and the dorm is a bargain at Rs 10.

The *Sea View Cottages* are in front of the expensive Silver Sands Hotel and have doubles with fan and attached bathroom for Rs 50. Next door the *Mar e Sol Hotel* is similar but in 1986 was in the middle of a prolonged strike. Further

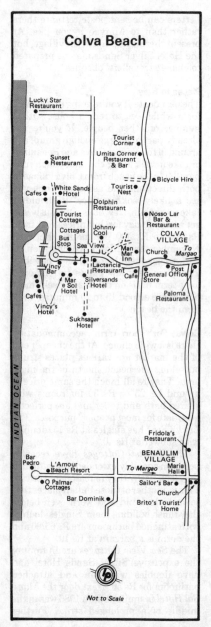

Colva Beach

Lucky Star
Restaurant

Tourist
Corner

Umita Corner
Restaurant
& Bar

Sunset
Restaurant

Bicycle Hire

White Sands
Hotel

Cafes

Tourist
Nest

Dolphin
Restaurant

Tourist
Cottage

Nosso Lar
Bar &
Restaurant

Cottages

Johnny
Cool

Bus
Stop

Sea View

COLVA
VILLAGE

Man
Mar Inn

Church

To
Margao

Vincy
Bar

Lactancia
Restaurant

Mar
e Sol
Hotel

Silversands
Hotel

Post
Office

Cafe

General Office
Store

Cafes

Paloma
Restaurant

Vincy's
Hotel

Sukhsagar
Hotel

INDIAN OCEAN

Fridola's
Restaurant

BENAULIM
VILLAGE

Bar
Pedro

L'Amour
Beach Resort

To Margao

Maria
Hall

O Palmar
Cottages

Sailor's Bar

Church

Bar Dominik

Brito's Tourist
Home

Not to Scale

back from the road is the *Sukhsagar Beach Resort* (tel 3888), where rooms with attached bathroom cost Rs 65/80 with fan cooling, Rs 145/160 with air-con. That's the season price; the cost is hiked up at the peak season, dropped down in the off season. In 1986 *Vincy's Hotel* was under construction behind the restaurant of the same name.

Back from the sea on the road which runs parallel to the beach is the rambling old *Tourist Nest*, built in traditional Goan style and very popular despite its distance from the beach. It has a range of different rooms from Rs 15 to Rs 25 with common bath, Rs 35 with attached bath.

The *Whitesands Hotel* (tel 3253) has 13 doubles and 13 suites, all with attached bath, all within 100 metres of the beach. Rooms are Rs 70 or Rs 80, suites Rs 100 or Rs 130. There's also a Rs 20 dorm and a good restaurant. Prices drop dramatically in the June to mid-September monsoon season.

At the top end of the market is the air-con *Hotel Silver Sands* (tel 3645-6), with 55 rooms and three suites. It has a bar, restaurant, coffee shop and other facilities. Singles/doubles are Rs 165/275 and they will provide free airport transport.

Benaulim If you hanker after the more tranquil aspects of Colva Beach, think instead of Benaulim Beach less than two km south of Colva. *L'Amour Beach Resort* has good rooms at Rs 45 and Rs 50 for a double with attached bathroom and fan. Most of the rooms are cottages which cost Rs 60 and are aligned so that they catch the sea breezes. Furthermore the staff are very friendly and helpful and the restaurant is terrific. Highly recommended.

More-or-less opposite are the *O Palmar Beach Cottages*, with rooms at Rs 45, again with fan and attached bathroom. If there's nobody around, enquire at *Pedro's Bar & Restaurant* by the beach. There are some places a 15-minute walk back from the beach at Benaulim village. *Brito's Tourist Home* is a large, clean new building with doubles with bath for Rs 30. Other places include *Palm Grove* next to Domnik's Bar, and *Caravan*. Rooms are typically Rs 20 to Rs 25. *Trinity High School*, 10 minutes from the crossroads, has a few rooms at Rs 15 but it's usually full.

Bogmalo North of Colva, nearly at the airport, is Bogmalo where the *Oberoi Bogmalo Beach* (tel 2191-2) has 118 rooms with prices of Rs 650/700 at the height of the season. At the depths of the off season prices drop to Rs 400/450. There's a swimming pool, water sports and all the other five-star facilities.

Places to Eat

If you're at the beach you naturally want to eat outside – it doesn't matter how good the food is if it's spoilt by having to eat it inside glass and concrete and away from the sight and sound of the very things which attracted you to Goa in the first place.

Colva At the Colva end of the beach the popular *Lucky Star* restaurant has good food and a good sound system – all within sight and sound of the beach. Another extremely popular place is the *Lactancia Restaurant*, next door to the Silver Sands Hotel, which has been a favourite meeting point for years and has good food, especially the fish. *Vincy's Bar* was Colva's original restaurant, but although it now occupies about three times its former space and still attracts a fair share of customers, it appears to have lapsed into a kind of middle-aged smugness and is a mere shadow of its old glory. The *Peacock Bar & Restaurant* at the Hotel Mar e Sol has really ice-cold beers and good food.

The *Dolphin*, part of the Whitesands Hotel, has good Goan and Portuguese food as well as seafood. The small open-air cafés on the beach are currently the major Colva attraction. Just choose the one with the best crowd; all have very similar travellers' menus with the familiar dishes from pancakes to fruit salad plus, of course, fish, prawns and the like. The *Paradise* and *Connie M* seem to be particularly popular in this group but each café seems to have just one single tape to play! A little further down the beach, *Franc's* is also popular.

Away from the beach, the *Umita Corner Restaurant & Bar* is popular with travellers who are renting in the area and has a pleasantly relaxed atmosphere even if it isn't on the beach. This is a popular place for breakfast. The nearby *Nosso Lar Bar & Restaurant* is an interesting old place with some Portuguese flavour, but try to order your food a day early. In the same area the popular *Tourist Nest* has its own restaurant, and the *Men Mar Inn* also attracts the crowds. Wonderful doughnuts are available at the kiosks by the roundabout; they arrive hot around 9.30 in the morning.

Benaulim Down at Benaulim, the *L'Amour Beach Resort* restaurant (Tona) has fish, prawns or calamari with chips or salad at Rs 8. Lobster costs Rs 35, a beer Rs 8 or Rs 9. The food here is some of the best at Goa, although the portions are small. *Pedro's Bar & Restaurant* on the beach at Benaulim has reasonable food if you can find somebody to order it from; the service is very erratic. On the beach, *Johnncy's* is very popular, especially for the occasional 'buffet & party nights'.

There are a number of places back from the beach at Benaulim village. The *Satkar Tea House, Seshaa Restaurant, Sailor's Bar & Restaurant, Mayrose Bar & Restaurant* and *Fridola's Restaurant* are all small snack bars or bars. Five minutes' walk towards Colva, *Precilia's Bar & Restaurant* is the local hot spot with cold beer and videos, some in English.

Getting There & Around

Buses run to Margao about every hour and take 25 minutes. The fare is Rs 1. The first bus from Colva departs around 7.30 am and the last one back leaves about 8 pm.

A share-taxi from Colva to Margao will cost you about Rs 2 – assuming the driver can find six to 10 people to pack into the taxi. If you're hiring one for yourself, expect to pay around Rs 12. If you like the wind through your hair, the easiest way to get between the two places is to take a motorcycle. The standard fare is about Rs 10.

Several places around Colva and Benaulim rent bicycles. The usual charge is Rs 10 a day. At low tide you can ride down the beach to the picturesque fishing port of Betul at the southern end. It's possible to get a boat across the estuary and then cycle back via Margao.

Johnncy's, the popular restaurant at Benaulim, organises a bus to Anjuna for the flea market each Wednesday. It costs Rs 20 return and saves a lot of messing around and changing buses.

CALANGUTE & BAGA

Until very recently, Calangute was the beach all self-respecting hippies headed for, especially around Christmas when all psychedelic hell broke loose and the beach was littered with more budding rock stars than most people have hot dinners. If you enjoyed taking part in those mass *pujas* with their endless half-baked discussions about 'when the revolution comes' and 'the vibes, man', then this was just the ticket. You could frolic around with not a stitch on, be ever so cool and liberated, and completely disregard the feelings of the local inhabitants. You could get totally out of your head every minute of the night and day on every conceivable variety of ganja from Timo to Tenochtitlan, exhibit the most bizarre behaviour, babble an endless stream of drivel and bore everybody shitless. Naturally, John Lennon or The Who were always about to turn up and give a free concert. Ah, Woodstock! Where did you go!

Calangute's heyday as the Mecca of all expatriate hippies has passed and the place has settled down to the more bourgeois pursuits of selling handicrafts, jewellery and woven fabrics to the tourists. It no longer provides the Indian press with a permanent shock-horror story about the decadent, drug-crazed (not to mention naked) fiends who were supposed to be rotting the moral fibre of Indian youth. Calangute isn't one of the best Goa beaches – there are hardly any swaying palms to grace the shoreline, much of the sand is contaminated with red soil and the beach drops pretty rapidly into the sea – but there's plenty going on and people who find Colva too quiet may find Calangute just the place.

Only two km north of Calangute is Baga, where the beach is better and there's a good choice of restaurants and accommodation. In between the two it's pleasantly quiet.

Orientation & Information

The Tourist Office and the post office are next to each other where the road forks to Baga and Calangute Beach. Across the road is a useful little tourist 'lending library' and second-hand bookshop. Halfway between these places and Calangute village is a branch of the State Bank of India where you can change travellers' cheques and cash. Once a week there's a soccer match between the western visitors and the local Calangute team – who usually win!

Close to the Tourist Office are two travel agents – MGM and Space Travels – which offer discount tickets to other parts of the world at rates similar to those you can get in Bombay. There's also a branch of Spaceways, who have a branch in Bombay and are associated with Tripsout Travel in New Delhi.

There are numerous stalls all the way from the crossroads to the beach selling genuine and reproduction Tibetan and Rajashtani crafts. Most of them are very well made and some of them stunningly beautiful, but they aren't cheap! Interesting jewellery, bangles and other ethnic trinkets (usually Tibetan, Kashmiri and Indian tribal in origin) are available.

Places to Stay

Prices and quality depend a lot on the season and thus on what is available. There are places to stay at Calangute, along the road from Calangute to Baga and at Baga.

Calangute There is a cluster of places south of the road down to the beach. The *Calangute Beach Guest House* is a modern place and looks more expensive than it is, although it's actually a bit grubby. In season, doubles cost Rs 40 or with bath Rs 70. Prices drop out of season. The rooms are spacious and clean, the beds have mosquito nets, the management is very friendly and there's a restaurant. There are several small guest houses nearby, all with similar prices and standards. The *International Guest House* and *Francisco's Sun Shine Guest House* both have rooms from Rs 20 to Rs 30, while the *Angela P Fernandes Guest House* has doubles with bath at Rs 45.

The *Souza Lobo Restaurant* has attractively constructed bamboo matting rooms for Rs 40. They're clean and a table fan is provided. Back from the Souza Lobo the *Hotel A'Canôa* has rooms at Rs 50/75, less in the off season.

The *Concha Hotel* has rooms at Rs 220/260 in season (less out of season) and is a fine middle-range place but is overshadowed by the excellent Varma's – see below. A little further back again is the *Coco Banana*, a pleasantly situated place with a nice verandah and doubles with bath for Rs 75. Just avoid the weekly disco night here.

The big, ugly *Tourist Hostel* on the beach has recently added some more attractive cottages and had a purely cosmetic facelift which manages to make it look much better. Rooms are Rs 65/80, and there's a dormitory where beds cost Rs 10. There's also a bar and restaurant.

Round behind the Tourist Hostel, *Meena's Lodge* has rooms at Rs 40 to 60 or with bath at Rs 90 to Rs 100, but it's terribly noisy (in fact so noisy that hotels close by complain) and they're so busy trying to pretend they're a disco that the hotel function gets neglected.

Next back from the beach is *Varma's Beach Resort* (tel 22 & 77), which must rate as one of the best-kept and most thoughtfully designed hotels in India. The rooms face a lush and well-kept garden and have attached bathrooms where everything works, as well as their own little verandahs with table and chairs. The whole thing is neat and clean as a pin. If you can afford Rs 200/250 a night (Rs 150/175 in the off season), this place is worth it.

There are various other places around Calangute, including the *Tourist Dormitory & Annapurna Restaurant* where dorm beds cost Rs 10 a night.

Calangute to Baga Along the road to Baga, apart from the regular hotels there are quite a few places that hang out a 'room available' sign whenever they have rooms. The *Oseas Tourist Home* is a quiet, shady place with rooms at Rs 25/50 or with bath at Rs 35/70. There's a restaurant and bar.

The *Sunshine Beach Resort* has big, airy rooms with attached bathroom for Rs 88. There are some smaller, cheaper rooms, and prices drop out of season. The rooms surround a large, shady courtyard and the place has a very relaxing atmosphere and a good restaurant too. In the bottom-end category, the *Saahil Hotel* is OK with rooms at Rs 30/40 or with bath at Rs 35/50. The *Estrela do Mar* is a pleasant and quietly secluded place on the beach side of the road with a nice garden and rooms with bath and fan for Rs 110/220.

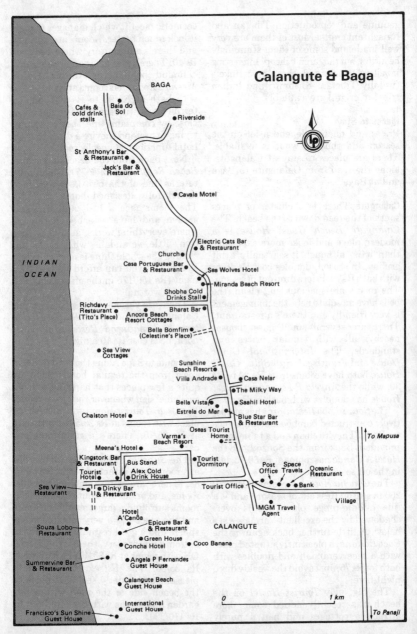

Calangute & Baga

BAGA

Cafes & cold drink stalls
Baia do Sol
Riverside

St Anthony's Bar & Restaurant
Jack's Bar & Restaurant

Cavala Motel

INDIAN OCEAN

Electric Cats Bar & Restaurant
Church
Casa Portuguese Bar & Restaurant
Sea Wolves Hotel
Miranda Beach Resort
Shobha Cold Drinks Stall

Richdavy Restaurant (Tito's Place)
Bharat Bar
Ancora Beach Resort Cottages
Bella Bomfim (Celestine's Place)

Sea View Cottages

Sunshine Beach Resort
Villa Andrade
Casa Nelar
The Milky Way
Saahil Hotel
Bella Vista
Estrela do Mar
Blue Star Bar & Restaurant

Chalston Hotel

Oseas Tourist Home

Varma's Beach Resort

To Mapusa

Meena's Hotel
Kingstork Bar & Restaurant
Tourist Hotel
Bus Stand
Alex Cold Drink House
Tourist Dormitory

Post Office
Space Travels
Oceanic Restaurant
Bank

Sea View Restaurant
Dinky Bar & Restaurant

Tourist Office
Village

MGM Travel Agent

Hotel A'Canôa
Epicure Bar & Restaurant
Green House
Coco Banana
CALANGUTE

Souza Lobo Restaurant
Concha Hotel

Summervine Bar & Restaurant
Angela P Fernandes Guest House

Calangute Beach Guest House

International Guest House

0   1 km

Francisco's Sun Shine Guest House

To Panaji

A little further on, just before you get to the turn-off to the beach, is *Vila Bomfim* (formerly Celestine's Place). This is an excellent place with large, airy rooms with fan at Rs 75 to Rs 100 (all Rs 100 at the height of the season). It's run by an exceptionally friendly family and most of the rooms have attached bathrooms except the two enormous front rooms, which would be spoilt by such additions.

Down the road to the beach, the *Ancora Beach Resort* has a somewhat grandiose name for what is essentially a few cottages and costs just Rs 50 for doubles. Right down by the beach, near the Richdavy Restaurant, the *Sea View Cottages* has pleasant rooms with bath, fan and verandah for Rs 100 – some are a bit cheaper. Back on the Baga road the *Cavala Motel* (tel 90) has inside rooms at Rs 100 or front rooms with verandah for Rs 110.

Baga As you come into Baga *Jack's Bar & Restaurant* is on the left-hand side. At the back is a row of clean and pleasantly decorated rooms from Rs 40 to Rs 60.

At the end of Baga the *Baia do Sol* is a modern hotel set in an attractive flower garden. Rooms cost Rs 200 to Rs 250, much less in the off season. Back from the beach by the river, the *Riverside* is a pleasant place with a number of Rs 90 cottages set in leafy surroundings. All the rooms have attached bath and the hotel has its own restaurant and bar. There are also a number of cheaper and much more basic Rs 40 single cottages across the river. They're reached by a most extraordinary bridge which has to be seen to be believed. Somebody was given an unlimited amount of concrete and told to construct the ugliest and most wasteful bridge they could. They managed to build a covered footbridge that could support a tank and survive a direct nuclear hit.

Places to Eat

There are any number of small restaurants all the way from Calangute village to the beach, especially around the bus stand, and a whole collection of them on the beach at Baga. There is not, however, much Indian food available – it's mainly international beach-resort food. The *Tourist Hotel* is one of the few places with real Indian food.

At Calangute the *Souza Lobo Restaurant* has a wonderful setting and is a perfect place to watch the sunset or relax in the afternoons. The food is superb – some say the best in Goa. The tiger prawns are a particular treat and Indian wine by the glass is Rs 3.50!

Behind the Tourist Hotel the *Alex Cold Drink House* is a popular little place, especially for breakfast. *King Stork*, in the Tourist Hotel grounds, also does good food. Across the road from the Tourist Hotel the long-running *Sea View Restaurant* still has reasonably good food, but the portions are tiny. Up towards the main road the *Oceanic Restaurant* has a pleasant upstairs open-air eating area.

Half-way from Calangute to Baga and near the beach, the *Richdavy Restaurant* (Tito's Place) has a pleasant setting and is popular with travellers. The prices are higher than elsewhere but the food is good. Fruit juices are Rs 7 to Rs 9, various fish dishes Rs 14 to Rs 25, prawns, chips and salad Rs 38, desserts Rs 5 to Rs 10.

Along the road to Baga there are several small bars or snack bars, but *Casa Portuguese* is a good place for a night out – a pleasant place with a nice setting although the food is not the best. At Baga, *St Anthony's* has the best food, including especially good desserts. The *Riverside* has good food too.

Entertainment

At Calangute the Saturday night disco at the *Coco Banana* is the high spot of the week's social activities! Between Calangute and Anjuna on Friday nights *Haystack* has a Rs 100 show which includes a buffet dinner, singing, Portuguese music and local folk dancing.

Getting There

There are frequent buses to Panaji and Mapusa from Calangute throughout the day. The fare is Rs 1.30 from Calangute to Panaji and the trip takes 35 to 45 minutes.

Getting Around

There are no regular buses between Calangute and Baga, but minibuses run between the two places. It's often easier to hitch or simply walk. Bikes can be hired in Calangute for Rs 6 a day, a great way to explore the area. This is the Goa centre for renting motorcycles and mopeds – they start from Rs 40 to Rs 50 a day.

AGUADA

South of Calangute, near the mouth of the Mandovi River, Aguada is Goa's jet-set beach. Its chief attraction is the 16th-century Portuguese Aguada Fort in which the main hotel is built.

Places to Stay

There are several hotels here, all very much at the top end. The *Fort Aguada Beach Resort* (tel 4401-11) is built within the ramparts of the old fort and has rooms or individual cottages at Rs 550 to Rs 650 for singles, Rs 650 to Rs 750 for doubles. The resort has a swimming pool, tennis courts, shops, boats and canoes to rent, and bicycles. They also have a number of villas known as the *Aguada Hermitage* costing Rs 1500 for one-bedroom units, Rs 2000 for two.

The *Taj Holiday Village* (tel 4415-5) is a slightly smaller resort a little to the north of the Fort Aguada, and has villas at Rs 400 to Rs 520 for singles, Rs 460 to Rs 580 for doubles. There are some slightly cheaper rooms without air-con. Again there are all sorts of entertainment and sporting facilities.

ANJUNA

If you want to know where everyone went when Calangute had been filmed, recorded, reported and talked about into the sand, this is the beach to head for. There's a weird and wonderful collection of overlanders, monks, defiant ex-hippies, gentle lunatics, 'orange' people, artists, craftspeople, seers, searchers and peripatetic expatriates who normally wouldn't be seen out of the organic confines of their health-food emporia in San Francisco or London.

There's no point in trying to define what Anjuna is or what it's like – it's many different things to many different people. The only way to find out is to stay here for a while and make some friends. Full moon is a particularly good time to be here; there's usually a mass party with psychedelics freely available. Unlike Calangute, the place has retained its charm. Nude bathing is *de rigeur* with the added satisfaction that you're unlikely to attract the voyeuristic attentions of any but the most intrepid holidaymaker.

Orientation & Information

There is a post office to which you can have mail sent poste restante. There is no bank.

Flea Market

The Wednesday flea market at Anjuna Beach is a major attraction for people from all the Goa beaches. It's a wonderful blend of Tibetan traders, rapacious and colourful Gujarati tribal women, blissed-out '60s-style hippies plus just about anybody else you might meet in India. Whatever you need, from a used paperback to read to a new *tanga* (G-string monokini) for the beach, you'll find it here. There's lots of good food, both Indian and western – many long-term western visitors seem to get out their favourite recipes from back home and cook up a batch of whatever it might be to sell at the flea market. It's quite a scene.

Places to Stay

It isn't easy to find a place to stay between November and March. Most of the

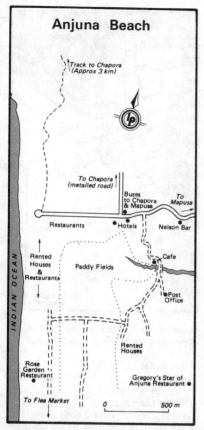

Anjuna Beach

Track to Chapora
(Approx 3 km)

To Chapora
(metalled road)

Buses
to Chapora
& Mapusa

To
Mapusa

Restaurants • Hotels • Nelson Bar

INDIAN OCEAN

Rented
Houses
& Restaurants

Paddy Fields

Cafe

Post
Office

Rented
Houses

Rose
Garden
Restaurant

Gregory's Star of
Anjuna Restaurant •

To Flea Market

0   500 m

available houses are rented on a long-term basis, often six months to a year, by people who come back again and again. There are only two or three hotels, which are located near the junction where the road from Chapora meets the road to the beach, but they're more-or-less permanently full. If you want to stay here you may initially have to make do with a very primitive shack or even sleep outside a restaurant, leaving your gear with the owner until you've made some friends or had a good scout around for a house. It's not a beach to head for if you're expecting immediate comforts in the shape of a

hotel. This beach is definitely for people with plenty of initiative. If you're only planning on staying a few days then it's not really worth coming here.

Places To Eat

There are any number of restaurants and cafés strung out along the road to the beach and all along the beachfront. Which one you choose as your favourite will depend largely on what sort of person you are and who you meet. The *Rose Garden Restaurant* has excellent seafood and cold beer, and is one of the more popular places. Back from the beach, and difficult to find so ask directions, *Gregory's Star of Anjuna* has a particularly good reputation – people come here from Calangute to eat. It's only open in the evenings and the food is strictly western.

Getting There

There are buses every one to two hours to Chapora and Mapusa from Panaji. They can be very crowded at certain times of the day. Plenty of motorcycles are available; they cost Rs 12 to Mapusa and take about 15 minutes.

CHAPORA

This is one of the most beautiful, interesting and unspoilt areas of Goa and a good deal more attractive than Anjuna either for a short or a long stay. Much of the inhabited area nestles under a canopy of dense coconut palms and the village is dominated by a rocky hill on top of which sits an old Portuguese fort. The fort is fairly well preserved and worth a visit, and the views from its ramparts are excellent. Secluded, sandy coves are to be found all the way around the northern side of this rocky outcrop, though the main beaches face west towards the Indian Ocean.

Many westerners stay here on a long-term basis but it's not a ghetto. The local people remain friendly and since the houses available for rent are widely scattered and there are many beaches and coves to choose from, it's rare to see more than 100 travellers together in one place.

Places to Stay

There are very few places where you can find instant accommodation in Chapora. This is one of the things which makes it such a pleasant place to stay, particularly as most people who do come here stay for a long time. However, you need somewhere to stay until you can find a house or room to rent.

At the top end of the market is the *Vagator Beach Resort* (tel Siolim 41), on the beach in its own palm-shaded grounds. It comprises a main block containing the restaurant (Indian and seafood), bar and reception area and two types of cottages. It's a friendly place and, as beach 'resorts' go in Goa, deserves top billing. Accommodation is in cottages with a variety of standards costing Rs 80, 120 or 156 for singles, Rs 130, 180 or 216 for doubles.

At the bottom end of the market you can find a room either at *Dr Lobo's* house – a very friendly family but the facilities are somewhat basic – or at the *Noble Nest Restaurant & Boarding*, opposite the church at the bottom of the track which leads to Dr Lobo's, where doubles are Rs 40.

Most people who stay in Chapora come on a long-term basis and find a house or room to rent. If you're particular about where you want to stay, this can take some time. It helps if you get here before most of the others – try September and October when there are only a few people about. On the other hand, it isn't particularly difficult to find somewhere to live – just make it your top priority and keep asking around in the stores and cafés. Wherever you decide to live, make sure you have a torch (flashlight) handy. There are no street lights, and finding your way along the paths through coconut palms late at night when there's no full moon is a devil of a job without a light! As at the other beaches, houses for rent cost

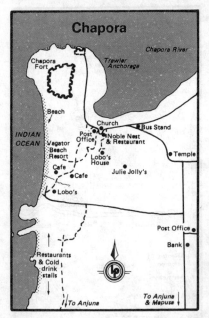

between Rs 150 to Rs 400 a month depending on their size and location.

Places To Eat

There are numerous restaurants along the main street of Chapora village, opposite the church, at the back of the Vagator Beach Resort and along the beach south of the road which leads to Vagator. Most are pleasant and serve good seafood, but *Lobo's* (not to be confused with Dr Lobo's house in the village) is exceptionally good and they have cold beers. It's a superb little restaurant, but turn up early as seating is limited. They're closed on Sundays. *Julie Jolly's* is currently extremely popular.

Getting There

There are frequent buses to Mapusa throughout the day for Rs 1 as well as direct buses to Panaji daily which follow the coast and do not go through Mapusa. The bus stand is near the road junction in

Chapora village. There are also motor-cycles here which will take you to Mapusa or Anjuna.

HARAMBOL

This may be the last of the Goan beaches, but in recent years it, too, has become much more popular. By the bus stop there is a chai shop and a few other tiny shops. A road takes you to the village by the sea where kids will offer you a room for around Rs 10 a day. All you get is bare walls and no beds, apart from those in an old hotel/house which is always full in any case. You can rent mattresses, cookers and all the rest from two shops at the village – obviously one comes here for at least a week. In the village there are 10 or so chai shops that serve 'westernised-Indian' food.

The seashore is beautiful, the village quiet and friendly – just a few hundred locals, mostly fishermen, and a couple of hundred western residents in the November to February high season. Over a rocky hill, 10 minutes' walk from the village beach, there's another beach with the last of the hippies, young people living in huts made of palm leaves on the slopes of a jungle valley with a river that makes an inland lake, just 20 metres from the sea. Some mutter that the lake is being polluted by people who come, stay two days, and use soap . . . .

Getting There

To get to Harambol, near Harmal on the maps, is a near three-hour bus journey from Mapusa.

OTHER ATTRACTIONS IN GOA
Bondla Wildlife Sanctuary

Up in the foothills of the Western Ghats, Bondla is being promoted by the Department of Tourism and is a good place to see sambar and wild boar among other things. It's the smallest of the Goan wildlife sanctuaries but the only one at present which has accommodation for those wishing to stay more than a day.

The larger sanctuaries are Molem Wildlife Sanctuary and Cotigao Wildlife Sanctuary.

You can get to Bondla by taking a bus to Ponda, followed by a taxi or tourist bus trip if they are being run. Accommodation in Bondla is available at the *Tourist Cottages*, which has rooms and a dormitory. They're very comfortable and meals are available, although you must book well in advance.

Temples

When the Portuguese arrived in Goa they destroyed every Hindu temple and Muslim mosque they could lay hands on, so temples in Goa are generally back from the coast and comparatively new although some date back as much as 400 years. The temples are direct descendants of the original temples destroyed by the Portuguese and their lamp towers are a distinctive Goan feature. Despite their earnest attempts to spread Roman Catholicism, only 38% of Goans today are Christian. In Ponda itself is the Safe Masjid mosque, built in 1560; for some reason the Portuguese neglected to knock it down.

Most of the Hindu temples of interest are close to Ponda, on the inland route between Panaji and Margao. The Shiva temple of Shri Mangesh is at Priol-Ponda Taluka, about 22 km from Panaji. The tiny temple with its white tower, a local landmark, is on top of a small hill. Only a km further down the road is Shri Mahalsa, a Vishnu temple.

About five km from Ponda are Shri Ramnath and Shri Mahalakshmi, and nearby is the Shri Shantadurga temple. Dedicated to Shantadurga, the goddess of peace, it has a strange, almost pagoda-like tower in the temple compound. To get to these temples, get off the bus about a km on the Old Goa side of Ponda and take the turn on your right if travelling towards Ponda, the turn on the left if travelling away.

Forts

There are quite a few old Portuguese forts dotted around Goa, most of them on the coast. Most of them are in a reasonable state of preservation and are worth a visit if you have the time. The one at Chapora is particularly recommended. The one at Terekhol has been converted into hotel accommodation.

Festivals

The Christian festivals in Goa take place on the following dates:

6 January
Feast of Three Kings at Reis Magos, Cansaulim and Chandor
2 February
Feast of Our Lady of Candelaria at Pomburpa
February/March
Carnival
Monday after 5th Sunday in Lent
Procession of the Franciscan Order at Old Goa
1st Sunday after Easter
Feast of Jesus of Nazareth at Siridao
16 days after Easter
Feast of Our Lady of Miracles at Mapusa
24 August
Festival of Novidades
1st fortnight of October
Fama de Menino Jesus at Colva
3rd Wednesday of November
Feast of Our Lady of the Rosary
3 December
Feast of St Francis Xavier at Old Goa

8 December
Feast of Our Lady of Immaculate Conception at Panaji and Margao
25 December
Christmas

Hindu festivals are harder to date because of the different calendar but they include:

January
Festival of Shantadurga Prasann at the small village of Fatorpa, south of Margao. There is a night time procession of chariots bearing the goddess and as many as 100,000 people flock to the festival.
The Shri Bodgeshwar *zatra* or temple festival takes place just south of Mapusa.
February
The three day *zatra* of Shri Mangesh takes place in the lavish temple of that name in the Ponda district.
In the old Fontainhas district of Panaji the Maruti *zatra* draws huge and colourful crowds. Maruti is another name for Hanuman.
March
In Goa the festival of Holi is called Shigmo. There's a parade in Panaji and numerous temple festivals around Goa. In the Procession of Umbrellas at Cuncolim, south of Margao, a solid silver image of Shantadurga is carried in procession over the hills to the original temple site wrecked by the Portuguese in 1580. The route taken is the same one by which the image was spirited away to safety outside the Portuguese borders. It's a colourful and dramatic event.

Karnataka

Population: 32 million
Area: 191,773 square km
Capital: Bangalore
Main language: Kannada

The state of Karnataka, formerly known as Mysore, is one of the more easygoing Indian states. It's a state of strong contrasts, with the modern, industrialised city of Bangalore at one extreme and expanses of rural farming areas at the other. Karnataka also has some of the most interesting historic architecture in India, and a varied and tumultuous history.

It was to Sravanabelagola in Karnataka that Chandragupta Maurya, India's first great emperor, retreated after he had renounced worldly ways and embraced Jainism. Later the mighty statue of Gomateshvara was erected at Sravanabelagola and it celebrated its 1000th anniversary in 1981. At Badami, in the north of the state, the Chalukyans built some of the earliest Hindu temples in India, 1500 years ago. All later south Indian temple architecture stems from the Chalukyan designs at Badami and the Pallavas at Kanchipuram and Mahabalipuram in Tamil Nadu.

Other important Indian dynasties, such as the Cholas and the Gangas, have played their part in Karnataka's history, but it was the Hoysalas, who ruled between the 11th and 14th centuries, who left the most vivid evidence of their presence. The beautiful Hoysala temples at Somnathpur, Belur and Halebid are gems of Indian architecture with intricate and detailed sculptures rivalling anything to be found at Khajuraho or Konorak.

In 1327 Hindu Halebid fell to the Muslim army of Mohammed bin Tughlaq and in the succeeding centuries Karnataka was held by first the followers of one religion, then the other. Founded in 1336, the Hindu kingdom of Vijayanagar, with its capital at Hampi, is one of the least visited and thus most surprising of India's ruined kingdoms. Vijayanagar reached its peak in the early 1550s, but in 1565 it fell to the Deccan Sultans and Bijapur became the most important city of the region. Today Bijapur is just a small city surrounded by an imposing wall and packed with an amazing collection of mosques and other reminders of its glorious past.

Finally, Hyder Ali took control in 1761 and the seat of power moved back south to Srirangapatnam near Mysore. His son, Tipu Sultan, with help from the French, further extended his father's kingdom and put the British in their place on more than one occasion before being defeated and killed in 1799.

The British installed a Hindu ruler when they brought the region under their control, and a series of enlightened and progressive rulers held power right through to independence. The Maharaja at that time was so popular that he became the first governor of the state.

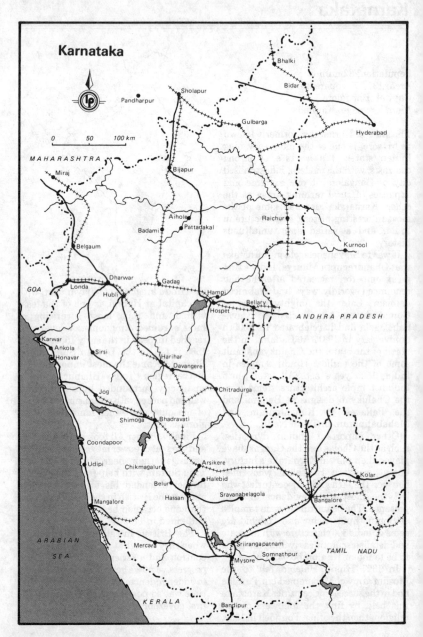

Karnataka

MAHARASHTRA

Pandharpur

Sholapur

Bhalki

Bidar

Gulbarga

Hyderabad

0   50   100 km

Miraj

Bijapur

Aihole

Badami   Pattadakal

Raichur

Kurnool

Belgaum

GOA

Dharwar   Gadag

Londa

Hubli

Hampi

Hospet

Bellary

ANDHRA PRADESH

Karwar

Ankola

Honavar

Sirsi

Harihar

Davangere

Jog

Chitradurga

Shimoga   Bhadravati

Coondapoor

Udipi

Chikmagalur

Arsikere

Belur

Halebid

Kolar

Hassan   Sravanabelagola

Bangalore

Mangalore

ARABIAN
SEA

Mercara

Sriirangapatnam

Somnathpur

TAMIL NADU

Mysore

KERALA

Bandipur

BANGALORE (population 2,900,000)
Though a modern, bustling city and an important industrial centre, Bangalore remains one of India's pleasantest cities. The central area is studded with beautifully laid out parks and gardens, wide tree-lined avenues, imposing buildings and lively bazaars. Situated 1000 metres above sea level and with a very pleasant climate, it's a city to which people from all over India and from abroad have come to look for work, business opportunities and higher education. The pace of life, like the intellectual and political climate, is brisk, and hardly a day goes by without some new controversy boiling over across the front pages of its daily newspapers or into the streets. Bangalore's important industries include machine tools, aircraft, electronics and computers.

Now the capital of Karnataka state, Bangalore was founded by Kempegowda in the early 16th century and became an important fortress city under Hyder Ali and Tipu Sultan two centuries later, though there are few remains from this period except for the Lalbagh Botanical Gardens. Bangalore is an excellent place to visit if you're looking for a wide range of hotels, restaurants, films and other cultural activities; otherwise its 'attractions' are definitely over-rated. The name means 'the town of beans'.

Orientation
Life in Bangalore revolves around Kempegowda Circle and bustles in the narrow, busy streets of Gandhi Nagar and Chickpet adjacent to the bus and railway stations. Here are the main shopping areas, restaurants, cinemas, bookshops and many of the mid-range hotels. It's a very popular area at lunchtime and in the evening, when the crowds spill over on to the roads, and long queues form outside the cinemas. Further to the west of Cubbon Park along Mahatma Gandhi Rd (five km from the railway station) are the more expensive hotels and restaurants plus various offices.

The budget-hotel area lies south of the railway station along Cottonpet Bhashyam Rd and around the City Market on Sri Narsimharaja Rd. This is the old part of the city with narrow, winding streets, an endless variety of small cottage industry services and manufacturing concerns, old temples, bullock carts and tea shops. Most government offices and museums are to be found either in or around Cubbon Park, while Bangalore's few remaining historical relics are all south of the City Market – some of them a considerable way to the south.

Brigade Rd is a busy central shopping area with cheap western-style clothing, plenty of cinemas and numerous interesting places to eat. Commercial Rd is another busy shopping area.

If you are in Bangalore for less than 24 hours, it may be more convenient to stay close to the station. For a longer stay, and if you don't mind spending a little more, the Mahatma Gandhi Rd area will be better. It's usually abbreviated to M G Rd and has good restaurants with Chinese, Indian and western food and a dozen cinemas showing only English movies. Bangalore is the most westernised city in India after Bombay, but is comparatively quiet and more relaxed.

Information
Tourist Offices The Government of India Tourist Office is at 48 Church St in the Mahatma Gandhi Rd area. They have a friendly staff and a lot of material to give away. In the same area Karnataka state has its own Tourist Information Centre (tel 572377) at 52 Shrungar Shopping Centre. The state Department of Tourism (tel 597139) is at 9 St Marks Rd. There are also tourist information kiosks at the airport and at the City Railway Station. Obviously, with so many different tourist offices there's a considerable amount of unnecessary duplication and stretching of resources.

At Badami House, Narsimharaja Square, there's yet another office which deals with reservations for the various tours operated by the Karnataka State Tourism Development Corporation (tel 74711).

Post Office There's no poste restante service at the new GPO at Cubbon Park. It's at the old GPO by the Bangalore International Hotel on Crescent Rd.

Other Offices The Railway Enquiry Offices are at the City Railway Station (tel 74173-4) and the Cantonment Railway Station (tel 27000). You can leave luggage at the railway station. For the KSRTC Bus Station Enquiry Office phone 73377. Indian Airlines (tel 79431) is at the CBAB Buildings, K G Rd. Air India (tel 77222, 76396) is at Unity Buildings, J C Rd. Thomas Cook (tel 51729) is on M G Rd.

Bookshops There are various book stalls on Brigade Rd, Residency Rd and Avenue Rd (west of Cubbon Park) but the best bookshops are all on M G Rd. Gangaram's Book Bureau is the best and next door is a branch of Higginbotham's. The Bangalore Tract & Book Society on the corner of St Marks and M G Rd is not bad, despite its unpromising name, mainly because it's an agent of Oxford University Press.

The British Library, near Oxford University Press at the Cubbon end of M G Rd, has lots of British newspapers and magazines and several good restaurants next door. The German Cultural Centre or Max Mueller Bhawan on M G Rd has a pleasant library and contains books in English as well as German, including ones on India.

Vidhana Soudha

This is one of Bangalore's – and indeed one of India's – most spectacular buildings. Built of granite in the neo-Dravidian style of architecture and located at the northern end of Cubbon Park, it houses both the Secretariat and the State Legislature. The cabinet room is famous for its massive door made of pure sandalwood. The building is floodlit on Sunday evenings and on public holidays. If you want to pay a visit, join the queue at the top of the main front entrance staircase at 5.30 to 6.30 pm.

Cubbon Park & the Museums

One of the main 'lungs' of the city, this beautiful shady park, full of flowering trees, covers an area of 120 hectares and was laid out in 1864. In it are the red Gothic building which houses the Public Library, the High Court, the Government Museum and the Technological & Industrial Museum.

The Government Museum, one of the oldest in India, was established in 1886 and houses sections on geology, art, numismatics and relics from Moenjodaro (one of the cradles of Indian civilisation, dating back 5000 years). 'I think the curator must have died 50 years ago and not been replaced', wrote a museum-goer. 'The caption on one stuffed fish stated that the flesh was somewhat insipid and eaten only by the lower classes of natives!' Admission costs Rs 0.20 and the museum is open daily except Wednesdays and public holidays from 8 am to 5 pm.

The Technological & Industrial Museum, also on Kasturba Rd adjacent to the Government Museum, is open daily except Mondays and public holidays between 10 am and 5 pm. Admission costs Rs 1. Its theme is the application of science and technology to industry and human welfare. It is full of happy children pressing the buttons of exhibits reflecting India's technological progress. However, it is nothing special and you can skip it if you are short of time.

Lalbagh Botanical Gardens

Again, this is a beautiful and popular park in the southern suburbs of Bangalore. It covers an area of 96 hectares and was laid out in the 18th century by Hyder Ali and his son Tipu Sultan. It contains many centuries-old trees (most of them labelled), lakes, lotus ponds, flower beds,

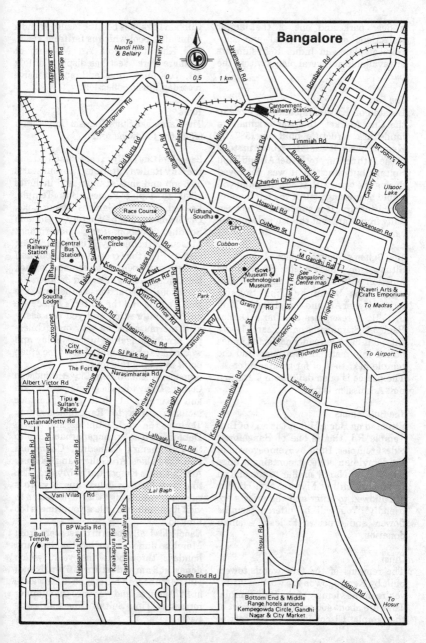

Bangalore

To Nandi Hills & Bellary

0   0.5   1 km

Margosa Rd
Sampige Rd
Bellary Rd
Javanehal Rd
Bosebank Rd

Cantonment Railway Station

Seshadripuram Rd
Old Buta Rd
Palace Rd
Kempju's Rd
Millers Rd
Cunningham Rd
Queen's Rd
Timmiah Rd
St John's Rd
Broadway Rd
Cavalry Rd

Chandni Chowk Rd

Race Course Rd
Vidhana Soudha
Hospital Rd
Ulsoor Lake
Dickenson Rd

Race Course
GPO
Cubbon St

City Railway Station
Central Bus Station
Kempegowda Circle
Seshadri Rd
Cubbon
Park
M Gandhi Rd

B Hashyam Rd
Kempegowda Rd
Palace Rd
Post Office Rd
Govt Museum & Technological Museum
See Bangalore Centre map
St Mark's Rd

Soudha Lodge
Balipet Subahdar Rd
Chickpet Rd
District Office Rd
Anjanappa Rd
Grant Rd
Lavelle St
Residency Rd
Brigade Rd
Kaveri Arts & Crafts Emporium
To Madras

Cottonpet
Nagartharpet Rd
Kasturba Rd
To Airport

City Market
SJ Park Rd
Richmond Rd
Langford Rd

The Fort
Narasimharaja Rd
Lalbagh Rd
Kengal Hanumanthiah Rd

Albert Victor Rd
Avenue Rd
Tipu Sultan's Palace
Jayachamaraja Rd

Puttannachetty Rd
Lalbagh
Fort Rd

Bull Temple Rd
Shankarmutt Rd
Hardinge Rd

Vani Vilas Rd
Lal Bagh

Bull Temple
BP Wadia Rd
Nagasandra Rd
Kanakapura Rd
Rashtreeya Vidyalaya Rd
Hosur Rd

South End Rd

Hosur Rd

To Hosur

Bottom End & Middle Range hotels around Kempegowda Circle, Gandhi Nagar & City Market a deer park and one of the largest collections of rare tropical and sub-tropical plants in India. Refreshments are available at several places within the park.

The Fort

Located on Krishnarajendra Rd close to the City Market, this was originally a mud-brick structure built in 1537 by Kempegowda. It was later rebuilt in stone in the 18th century by Hyder Ali and Tipu Sultan, but much of it was destroyed during the wars with the British and you would be missing little if you left it out of your itinerary. It is supposed to be open daily from 8 am, but this isn't always the case.

Tipu Sultan's Summer Palace

Situated on Albert Victor Rd near the junction with Krishnarajendra Rd, this palace was begun by Tipu Sultan's father, Hyder Ali, and completed by Tipu in 1791. It resembles the Daria Daulat Bagh at Srirangapatnam near Mysore City, but has been sadly neglected and is falling into disrepair. You may find the temple next to it of far greater interest. The palace is open daily from 6 am to 6 pm. Admission is free.

The Bull Temple

Situated on Bugle Hill at the end of Bull Temple Rd, this is one of Bangalore's oldest temples. Built by Kempegowda in the Dravidian style, it contains a huge monolith of Nandi similar to the one on Chamundi Hill at Mysore. Non-Hindus are allowed to enter and the priests are friendly. You will be offered jasmine flowers and expected to leave a small donation.

Other

The remains of the four watch towers built by Kempegowda are worth a visit if you're in the vicinity of the Bull Temple. They are about 400 metres to the west of the temple. Ulsoor Lake, to the east of Cubbon Park, has boating facilities and a swimming pool which is far from clean. The Karnataka Folk Art Museum at Kumara Park West has displays of folk art, costumes, toys and an extensive recorded music collection.

Tours

The Karnataka State Tourism Corporation offers the following tours:

Bangalore City Daily except Sundays from the City Railway Station. The tour starts at 8 am and ends at 2 pm and includes visits to Tipu's Palace, Bull Temple, Lalbagh Botanical Gardens, Ulsoor Lake, Government Soap Factory, Vidhana Soudha, Cubbon Park, Government Museum, Technology Museum and Art Gallery. The tour costs Rs 20. About half of the tour is spent at government-owned emporiums selling silks and handicrafts. Such tourist attractions as the park, the Bull Temple and the Sultan's Palace are not that interesting and you can easily visit the museums on your own. Unless you are in Bangalore just for a day and would like to rush things I don't see much point in taking this tour.

Srirangapatnam, Mysore City & Brindavan Gardens Daily tours beginning at 7.15 am and returning at 10.45 pm. The tour includes visits to Ranganathaswamy Temple, the Fort, Gumbaz and Daria Daulat Bagh at Srirangapatnam; and to St Philomena's Cathedral, Chamundi Hill, the Palace, Art Gallery and Cauvery Arts & Crafts Emporium at Mysore. The tour costs Rs 80 by deluxe bus. Mysore is such a pleasant city that it is better to visit it on your own unless your time is too limited.

Nandi Hills Daily tours in the season –from March to June – as well as Sundays and holidays throughout the year, which depart at 8 am and return at 6 pm. Nandi Hills is the nearest hill station to Bangalore at 1479 metres, and was once the summer retreat of Tipu Sultan. The tour costs Rs 35.

Karnataka Top: Dhobi ghats at Halebid (GC)
Left: Temple carvings on the Hoysala temple at Halebid (GC)
Right: Golgumbaz Mausoleum at Bijapur (GC)

Karnataka Top: Frieze on the Hoysala temple at Somnathpur, near Mysore (GC)
Left: Statue of Gomateshvara, Sravanabelagola (GC)
Right: Statue of demon, Chamundi Hill, Mysore (PR)

Hampi & Tungabhadra Dam This is a two-day tour, which departs on Fridays at 10 pm and returns to Bangalore at 9.30 pm on Sunday. It includes visits to Mantralaya (the village associated with the Hindu saint, Raghavendra Swami), Tungabhadra Dam and Hampi. Overnight accommodation is at the *T B Dam Hotel*. The tour costs Rs 200, including accommodation.

There is also a three-day tour to Srirangapatnam, Mysore, Ooty and the Bandipur Game Sanctuary, which costs Rs 300 including accommodation for two nights. A two-day tour to Tirupathi costs Rs 140. It's much more convenient to visit Tirupathi from Madras if you're heading that way.

These tours can be booked at any of the following places:

KSTDC, 10/4 Kasturba Rd, Queens Circle, Bangalore 1 (tel 578753, 578901)
KSTDC Booking Counter, Badami House, opposite Corporation Office, Bangalore (tel 74711)
KSTDC Information Counter, Public Utility Building, M G Rd, Bangalore 1 (tel 52377)
KSTDC Tourist Information Counter, City Railway Station, Bangalore 2 (tel 70068)

Places to Stay – bottom end
There are several budget hotels around the railway and bus station. The *Sudha Lodge*, Cottonpet Main Rd, is still one of the best and most pleasant of the cheapies, and used by many travellers. It's a no-frills and sometimes rather noisy place which offers rooms with their own cold-water showers and toilets for Rs 20/32. Right next to it is *Ganesh Lodge* where singles cost Rs 17, with bathroom Rs 20 and doubles Rs 26 to Rs 30. There is a restaurant in the hotel.

On the opposite side of the bus stand there are more hotels and lodges. *Sandhya Lodge* (tel 74064) is in an entirely new building and has clean singles/doubles for Rs 36/65. *Sudarshan Hotel* (tel 27709), diagonally opposite the elevated pedestrian walkway which goes through the Central Bus Station, has plenty of well-kept rooms at Rs 20/40 and the staff are friendly.

Next to Sudha Lodge the best among the cheapies is *Ramakrishna Lodge* (tel 73071), about 100 metres from Kempegowda Circle, where singles/doubles are Rs 30/50. It is somewhat run down but has a good and popular restaurant. *Hotel Tourist* (tel 72381), on Race Course Rd near the junction with Subahdar Rd, is often full, costs Rs 20/30 for singles/doubles and has long been popular. I remember staying there in 1966 when I first visited Bangalore. *Hotel Suprabhat* (tel 79466) has rooms for Rs 30/55 and is also good.

Hotel Laxmi (tel 74177) is at 11 First Cross off Gandhinagar and a block from Kempegowda Circle. It's a straightforward, clean place with rooms at Rs 50 to Rs 60 or with air-con at Rs 70 to Rs 80. At 10/1 Fifth Cross the *Hotel Santhash* (tel 28804) has rooms at Rs 35/60. Turn right off Gandhinagar and continue two blocks to a quiet plaza.

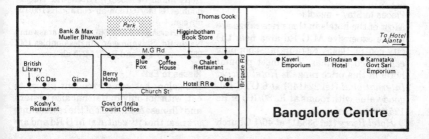

Bangalore Centre

Other cheapies are located around the City Market on Sri Narsimharaja Rd. They include the hotels *Bilal, Rainbow, Delhi Bhavan, Chandra Bihar, Natraj* and *Isaquia*. If you want to get there on foot from either the railway station or bus station, go down to Cottonpet Rd as far as the Kangeri Police Station (on the right-hand side), and then turn left. This is Police Rd, though there are no signs to tell you this. Continue down Police Rd for several hundred metres and you will find yourself outside City Market. It is 10 to 15 minutes' walk from the railway station. Also 10 minutes from the station, the *Swagath Hotel* at 75 Hospital Rd has big doubles for Rs 80 and excellent service.

The M G Rd area in the city centre has some inexpensive hotels. *Hotel Ajantha* (tel 53321) at 22A M G Rd has parking, and singles/doubles are Rs 40/70 – a bargain for its neighbourhood. It is often full unless you get there in the morning. *Hotel Brindavan* (tel 573271) at 40 M G Rd charges 30/65 for singles/doubles and is in the same area. At Trinity Circle on M G Rd the *Hotel Kamadhenu* (tel 54451) is a comparatively large hotel but with low prices.

Just north of the M G Rd area there is a *YMCA* (tel 24848) on Infantry Rd which has single rooms for Rs 20 but is only open to men. There's another *YMCA* (tel 555885) in a similar price range in the Bensontown area near Bangalore Cantonment Railway Station; it's open to all. There is also a *YWCA Guest House* in Infantry Rd but it seems to be permanently full with students.

Places to Stay – middle

Most of the hotels in this price range are in the expensive M G Rd area near the city centre, flashy restaurants, shopping centre and cinemas. The most popular hotel in this price range is *Hotel Luciya International* (tel 224148) at 6 OTC Rd, good value with rooms at Rs 80/100 or Rs 125/190 with air-con.

Hotel Berry (tel 53331) at 46/1 Church St is centrally located off M G Rd and costs Rs 70/130 or Rs 130/170 with air-con. The *New Victoria Hotel* (tel 570336) at 47-48 Residency Rd is also popular. *Hotel Nilgiris Nest* (tel 577501) in the same area at 171 Brigade Rd has singles at Rs 100 to Rs 120 or with air-con at Rs 130 to Rs 150. Doubles are Rs 140 or Rs 170 with air-con.

Places to Stay – top end

Hotel Westend (tel 29281) on Race Course Rd has a pleasant garden and a pool. Singles/doubles cost Rs 475/595. *Hotel Taj Residence* (tel 563566) on M G Rd has rooms from Rs 365 to Rs 425, all air-con. The new and spacious *Welcomgroup Windsor Manor* (tel 79431) at 25 Sankey Rd has rooms from Rs 525/625 and up.

The *ITDC Hotel Ashok* (tel 79411) at Kumara Krupa, close to the city centre, has all mod-cons from tennis courts, shops and a swimming pool to full air-conditioning. Singles/doubles cost from Rs 385/465. The *Bangalore International* (tel 26011) is at 2A-B Crescent Rd, High Grounds and is rather smaller than the large Hotel Ashok. Singles/doubles with air-con cost from Rs 190/285, without air-con from Rs 180/210. Another cheaper top-end hotel is the *Cauvery Continental* (tel 29350-9) at 11/37 Cunningham Rd. Rooms are Rs 150/175 and there are vegetarian and non-vegetarian restaurants as well as monkeys in the garden.

Other more expensive hotels in Bangalore include:

Hotel Rama (tel 53381), Levelle Rd, singles/doubles Rs 145/160 non-air-con and Rs 160/190 air-con.
Hotel Harsha (tel 565566), 11 Venkataswamy Naidu Rd, Shivajinagar, singles/doubles 150/225 non-air-con and Rs 225/275 air-con.

Places to Eat

Bangalore has some excellent places to eat, with not only Indian but also western and Chinese food. Most of the restaurants are near the city centre at M G Rd and are relatively expensive – say Rs 20 to Rs 40 for a meal. Restaurants near the station mainly offer only Indian food. In the Gandhi Nagar and Chickpet areas of Bangalore, it is impossible to walk more than a few metres without coming across a restaurant. Most of them offer the standard south Indian fare of dosa, idli, rice and vegetables and coffee, but they are clean and extremely cheap – a masala dosa and coffee costs on average Rs 3. There are several *Kamat Hotels* in the area, which offer a plate meal (thali) for Rs 5 with curry, fried vegetables, curd, pickles and rice.

If you would like more choice, *Hotel Blue Star* opposite the Tribhuvan Cinema in Gandhi Nagar, at the back of Kempegowda Circle, has an extensive menu (much of it unavailable) for both vegetarian and non-vegetarian food. The food is not always that well prepared but they even have fish & chips! *Aishwarya Restaurant*, 1st floor, Gupta Market, Kempegowda Rd has good non-vegetarian food and an attached bar. This is a good place for a night out; the food is excellent. Opposite the railway station, the *Kadamba Restaurant* has excellent food and cold beer.

In the M G Rd area the popular though expensive *Rice Bowl* has very good Cantonese Chinese food and is packed in the evening. This is a Chinese restaurant even visiting Hong-Kongers approve of. *Chalet* has excellent pizza (perhaps the best in south India) for Rs 17 as well as other Italian dishes. *Casa Piccola* in Kasturba Rd has good hamburgers, veggie-burgers, pizza and pasta. *KC Das*, near the British Council, is a well-known snack-and-sweet shop whose headquarters are in Calcutta. Try their famous *rasagoollas*. The *Village Restaurant*, past KC Das on St Marks Rd and roughly opposite the British Council, also has excellent sweets and curd.

Bangalore's *Kwality* on Brigade Rd has air-conditioning and very good food. *Charms* at 161 Brigade Rd has excellent although rather expensive food and the owner and son are indeed charming. *Koshy's* is slightly expensive and has good Indian and continental food. *Blue Heaven* in Church St has good Chinese food.

Getting There

Air Indian Airlines have flights at least twice daily connecting Bangalore with Bombay (Rs 772), Delhi (Rs 1594), Hyderabad (Rs 490) and Madras (Rs 283). There are also regular connections to Ahmedabad (Rs 1143), Calcutta (Rs 1385), Dabolim (Rs 456), Madurai (Rs 342), Mangalore (Rs 307), Pune (Rs 731) and other centres.

Rail Bangalore is connected by direct daily express trains with all the main cities in southern and central India and with New Delhi. But, as elsewhere in India where there is more than one express per day, you should be careful to choose the right train if speed is your priority, as journey times vary considerably from one express to the next. The fastest night express trains are often booked out days in advance so your choice may be limited. No tourist quota is available for sleeping berths at Bangalore Station. They do have an emergency quota but they are reluctant to release these to tourists – although one visitor reported getting one without difficulty. If you're stuck it's worth a try – contact the Station Superintendent on Platform 1.

The fastest express train to New Delhi (Karnataka Express) departs twice a week on Wednesdays and Sundays and takes 38 hours to make the 2444-km trip. The fare in 2nd class is Rs 147, in 1st class Rs 613. The Bangalore-Trivandrum Express leaves daily at 6.15 pm and costs Rs 67 in 2nd class, Rs 276 in 1st. The 851-km trip takes about 18 hours.

Various expresses operate between Bangalore and Bombay, some of which require a change of train at Miraj. The trip varies from 1129 to 1211 km depending on the route and takes 24 to 27 hours. Fares are about Rs 87 in 2nd class, Rs 358 in 1st.

There are several express services between Bangalore and Madras. The 358-km journey takes six to seven hours and the fare is Rs 35 in 2nd class, Rs 141 in 1st. From Bangalore to Hyderabad there is a daily express train at 5 pm and various other services. The 646-km trip takes about 18 hours with fares of Rs 62 in 2nd class, Rs 224 in 1st.

There are half a dozen daily trains to Mysore, some of them faster than others – three hours is about the average. Most people take the buses between these two cities.

Bus Bangalore's well-organised central bus station handles most local buses and is directly in front of the City Railway Station. You can get route maps of Bangalore and Karnataka express services from the station for Rs 2.50 each. There's a separate station for long-distance buses.

There are four buses daily to Bombay. Regular state buses cost Rs 150 and take 24 or more hours. Luxury video buses departing from near the railway station cost Rs 184. To Hospet there are regular daily buses plus a 'luxury' KSTDC bus. The 340-km journey takes nine hours.

The Madras run takes about nine hours and there are three buses daily. Ordinary buses cost Rs 34 and deluxe buses Rs 40. There are a dozen buses daily to Mangalore and the 357-km journey takes eight hours. There are very frequent and remarkably civilised buses to Mysore. The trip takes 3½ hours and costs around Rs 18. It passes by the 'Marabar Hills', as filmed in *Passage to India*.

Other important routes include Bijapur (four buses daily, 14 hours); Calicut (two buses daily); Ernakulam (three buses daily); Hassan (nine buses daily, 185 km); Ooty (two buses daily); Vellore (two buses daily); Puttapathy, Jog Falls and Goa (one bus daily to each).

All the regular buses are operated by the Karnataka State Road Transport Corporation. Andhra Pradesh State Road Transport Corporation and Tiruvalluvar Transport Corporation also run buses from Bangalore, and their offices are at counter 13 of the bus stand. The twice-daily APSRTC bus service to Hyderabad costs Rs 81. Tiruvalluvar Transport Corporation also run buses to Madras a dozen or so times daily. The fare is Rs 37 (super deluxe) and Rs 58 (air-con). The buses go via Chittore or Vellore and the latter route is cheaper. Tiruvalluvar also has two buses via Dindigul to Madurai with fares of Rs 42, and another two daily to Coimbatore for Rs 35.

In addition to the various state buses, numerous private companies offer buses between Bangalore and the other major cities in central and southern India. You'll find them all over the central area. Their prices are higher than the state service, but their buses are better and there's more leg room – important on long journeys.

The thing you need to watch out for is that recent Indian fad – 'video coaches'. We know you've travelled on these buses in other regions and found them pleasant enough, but this is India. By the time you've reached Bangalore, you'll be well aware of what Indians do with the volume control on any sound equipment! If you want to sleep (even in the back seats, far from the TV screen) then don't take a 'video coach' – the ones without video are also cheaper.

Getting Around

Airport If you take a taxi or auto-rickshaw from the airport be careful you don't get stuck with the parking fee, which a sign clearly states is the driver's responsibility. Since the airport is outside the city limits you'll probably have to agree on an over-the-meter fee.

Local Transport In Bangalore auto-rickshaws are not that good – the drivers often don't know where they're going. Beware of over-the-meter charges at night.

Things to Buy

The Cauvery Arts & Crafts Emporium (tel 51418), 23 Mahatma Gandhi Rd, like its sister establishment at Mysore, stocks a huge range of superb handcrafted tables, carvings (many of them in sandalwood), jewellery, ceramics, carpets and *agarbathis*. Few things are cheap as such, but this emporium stocks some of the best craftwork in India and they're good at packing and posting.

For silk saris the Government Emporium, next to the Symphony Theatre in the M G Rd area, sells good-quality non-creasable 'crepe' saris for Rs 600.

AROUND BANGALORE
Nandi Hills

This hill station 68 km from Bangalore was a popular summer retreat even in Tipu Sultan's days. Tipu's drop, a 600-metre-high cliff face, provides a good view over the surrounding country. There are two ancient temples here. Cheap accommodation is available through the Horticulture Department in Bangalore (tel 602231).

Kolar Gold Fields

The mines here, 100 km east of Bangalore, are the major gold producers for India and are said to have the deepest shafts in the world, reaching over 3000 metres below the surface. Visits can be arranged.

MYSORE (population 476,000)

Sandalwood City! Everywhere you go in this beautiful city you'll find yourself enveloped with the lingering aromas of sandalwood, jasmine, rose, musk, frangipani and a hundred others. Whenever you smell them again, you'll be reminded of this place. It's one of the major centres of incense manufacture in India, and scores of small, family-owned *agarbathi* (incense) factories are scattered all over town, their products exported all over the world.

Every one of the incense sticks is hand-made – usually by women and children – and a good worker can turn out at least 10,000 a day! They are made with thin slivers of bamboo, dyed red or green at one end, onto which is rolled a sandalwood putty base. The sticks are then dipped into small piles of powdered perfume and laid out to harden in the shade. You can see them being made if you visit the Government Sandalwood Oil Factory or enquire at any of the small firms you come across.

Mysore is also a crafts centre and there are numerous shops selling an incredible range of sandalwood, rosewood and teak carvings and furniture. Probably the most stunning display can be seen at the Cauvery Arts & Crafts Emporium in the centre of town. Their rosewood tables and elephants, intricately inlaid with ivory and other woods, are perhaps the best you will see anywhere in the world. Hardly anyone comes here and leaves empty-handed. It's impossible to visit the post office without seeing at least two or three travellers going through the motions of sending a package back home!

There are plenty of other reasons why you would not want to miss Mysore. Until independence, the city was the seat of the Maharajas of Mysore, a princely state covering about a third of present-day Karnataka, and their walled Indo-Saracenic palace in the centre of the city is a major attraction drawing visitors from all over the world. Just south of the city lies Chamundi Hill, topped by its important Shiva temple.

Outside of the city to the north-west lie the extensive ruins of the former capital of Mysore, the fortress city of Srirangapatnam, built by Hyder Ali and Tipu Sultan on an island in mid-Cauvery. Tipu Sultan fought the last of his battles with the British here in the closing years of the 18th century. But probably the biggest attraction outside the city is the beautiful temple of Somnathpur.

Mysore, at an altitude of 770 metres, is a travellers' Mecca and it's easy to see why. Apart from offering many attractions, it's a friendly, easygoing city with plenty of shade trees, well-maintained public buildings, clean streets and a good climate, yet it's small enough not to overwhelm (you can walk from one end to the other in 20 minutes).

Orientation

The railway station and local bus station are conveniently close to the city centre and only a few minutes' walk from all the main hotels and restaurants. The main shopping street is Sayaji Rao Rd, which runs from New Statue Square on the north side of the Maharaja's Palace, across Irwin Rd to the north of the city. The long-distance bus stand is two km from the railway station.

The budget hotels are mostly along Dhanvantri Rd and around Gandhi Square. The mid-range and top-end hotels are mostly to be found south of Government House along Nazarbad Rd and at the railway-station end of Jhansi Lakshmi Bai Rd.

Information

The Tourist Office (tel 23251) is in the Old Exhibition Building, Irwin Rd. Tourist literature is available if you ask for it, and they have a breakdown of all the information you're likely to need pinned to a number of boards.

Indian Airlines (tel 21486) is in the Hotel Mayura Hoysala on Jhansi Lakshmi Bai Rd. It's open from 10 am to 5.15 pm daily, but is closed for lunch 1.30 to 2.15 pm. Don't miss Mysore's eccentric evening newspaper the *Star of Mysore*.

Bookshops Two very good bookshops in Mysore are the Geetha Book House, New Statue Square (at the bottom of Sayaji Rao Rd), and the Ashok Book Centre, Dhanvantri Rd (near the junction with Sayaji Rao Rd). Both have plenty of Penguins and other English paperbacks.

Festivals During the 10-day Dussehra festival in early October each year accommodation prices can zoom to the sky – if you can even find a room. Mysore also has an active horse-race course, patronised by the Maharaja.

Wildlife Sanctuaries If you're planning a visit to the wildlife sanctuaries of Bandipur (80 km from Mysore) or Nagarhole (93 km from Mysore), it's advisable to book accommodation and transport in advance with the following people:

Bandipur Field Director, Project Tiger, Government House, Nazirbad, Mysore (tel 20901)
Nagarhole Assistant Conservator of Forests, Wildlife Preservation, Chamarajendra Circle, Vanivilas Rd, Mysore (tel 21159).
At present there are two travellers' bungalows at Nagarhole – *Kaveri* and *Gangothri*. Their costs are the same but *Kaveri* is the better of the two. There's also dormitory accommodation. Contact the range officer there, Mr Chinappa, if you want to go for a ride in their safari van (24-km ride for Rs 5 per person. If you have your own van the entrance fee is Rs 14).

Maharaja's Palace

The beautiful profile of this walled, Indo-Saracenic palace, the seat of the Maharajas of Mysore, dominates the city's skyline. It was built in 1911-12 at a cost of Rs 4.2 million to replace the former palace which burned down. Internally it reminds one of an Afghani waistcoat – an extravaganza of stained glass, mirrors, gilt and gaudy colours. There are also beautiful carved wooden doors and mosaic floors as well as a whole series of mediocre, though historically interesting, paintings depicting life in Mysore during the Edwardian Raj. Note the beautifully carved mahogany ceilings, solid silver doors, white marble floors and superb columned Durbar Hall. The palace even has its own Hindu temple inside the walls, complete with gopuram. On Sunday nights the palace is spectacularly illuminated.

The Maharaja's son is still in residence at the back of the palace. During the 10-day festival of Dussehra, held the first and second weeks of October each year, he leads one of India's most colourful processions. Richly caparisoned elephants, liveried retainers, cavalry, and the gaudy and flower-bedecked images of deities make their way through the streets to the sound of jazz and brass bands and the inevitable clouds of incense.

Depending on how many tourist coaches there are outside in the parking lot, the palace can sometimes rival the departure lounge of a major international airport. Check this out before you go in! Entry is from the south gate only and the palace is open daily from 10.30 am to 5.30 pm. Tickets cost Rs 2 and you must leave your shoes at the shoe deposit (there's a 10 paise charge for this). 'For once we forgot our scruples and used our status as foreigners to jump the three-hour queue', reported a visitor. Students are free if you ask and sign a form.

You can get permission to photograph the palace by contacting the Arch Unit near the shoe deposit during office hours. Booklets about the palace are on sale inside. Outside in the parking lot there's a permanent gaggle of snakeskin sellers and postcard vendors. The postcards are abysmal.

Chamundi Hill

You can spend a very pleasant half-day walking up the 1000-odd steps to the top of this hill, where the temple to Sri Chamundeswari stands 1062 metres above sea level. It's a fairly strenuous climb but there are plenty of trees on the way. The views over the surrounding countryside and Mysore City, even from half-way up, are superb. Three-quarters of the way up you come across the famous Nandi (Shiva's bull) carved out of solid rock and, at five metres high, one of the largest in India. It's always garlanded in flowers and constantly visited by bevies of pilgrims offering *prasad* to the priest in attendance there.

Sri Chamundeswari temple on the summit is a huge structure with a seven-storey gopuram 40 metres high which is visible from far away. Visiting hours (non-Hindus are allowed inside) are 9 am to 12 noon and 5 to 9 pm. The priests are quite enthusiastic to show you around.

If you don't walk up the hill or, having walked up, you don't want to walk back down again, there are buses approximately every half hour from the central bus station. The terminus on the hill is about 300 metres from the temple. Demand for buses can be very heavy on Sundays (I've seen 500 people waiting for a bus!). Refreshments, snacks and south Indian plate meals are available at cafés around the temple.

Though local guidebooks and tourist literature will tell you that the summit is 13 km from the city, this refers to the winding and switchbacked road only. Going via the steps it's about four km.

Devaraja Fruit & Vegetable Market

This market stretches almost the whole length of Sayaji Rao Rd from Dhanvantri Rd to New Statue Square and is one of the most colourful in India. It provides excellent subject material for photographers.

Cauvery Arts & Crafts Emporium

Even if you're not going to buy anything, this place is worth a visit – more details under Things to Buy.

Other

The Government Sandalwood Oil Factory, where sandalwood oil is distilled and incense sticks are made, used to be a really interesting place to visit but these days they tend to rush you round ('timed it at four minutes', reported a visitor) and quickly shepherd you into the sales office. Visiting hours are 9 to 11 am and 2 to 4 pm daily except Sundays and Thursdays.

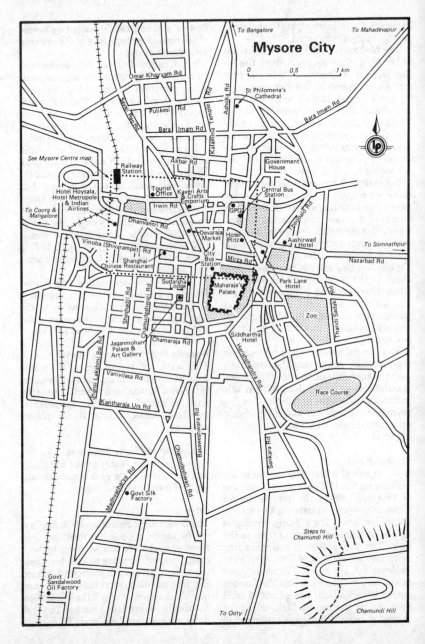

Mysore City

0   0.5   1 km

To Bangalore
To Mahadevapur
Omar Khayyam Rd
Pulikesi Rd
Bara Imam Rd
St Philomena's Cathedral
Bara Imam Rd
Sawai Ram Rd
Kalamma Temple Rd
Ashoka Rd
Akbar Rd
Government House
See Mysore Centre map
Railway Station
Tourist Office
Kaveri Arts & Crafts Emporium
Central Bus Station
Hotel Hoysala, Hotel Metropole & Indian Airlines
Irwin Rd
GPO
To Coorg & Mangalore
Dhanvantri Rd
Devaraja Market
Hotel Ritz
Theobald Rd
Aashirwad Hotel
To Somnathpur
Vinoba (Shivarampet) Rd
City Bus Station
Mirza Rd
Nazarbad Rd
Shanghai Chinese Restaurant
Sheshadri Rd
Chamudeshwari Rd
Park Lane Hotel
Sudarsha Lodge
Maharaja's Palace
Zoo
Thandi Sadak Rd
Jhansi Lakshmi Bai Rd
Chamaraja Rd
Siddhartha Hotel
Jaganmohan Palace & Art Gallery
Harishchandra Rd
Vanivilasa Rd
Sankara Rd
Kantharaja Urs Rd
Race Course
Basaveswara Rd
Madhvachrya Rd
Chamudeshwari Rd
Govt Silk Factory
Steps to Chamundi Hill
Govt Sandalwood Oil Factory
To Ooty
Chamundi Hill

Excellent sandalwood oil is on sale here and they also have some good incense.

The Government Silk Weaving Factory, where pure silk saris are made, is a short walk back down the road from the sandalwood factory. Hours are 7.30 to 11.30 am and 12.30 to 4.30 pm daily except Sundays.

Another place worth a visit is Sri Chamarajendra Art Gallery in Jaganmohan Palace. Not only does it display paintings, particularly by Ravi Varma, it has handicrafts, historical objects of interest and rare musical instruments. Visiting hours are 8 am to 5 pm daily and entry is Rs 1.50.

St Philomena's Cathedral is of interest if you want to see what the Christians got up to here in the last century. It's one of the largest churches in India, built in neo-Gothic style. Across the line from the railway station there's a small but fascinating railway museum with a Maharani's saloon carriage dating from around 1888 – complete with royal toilet.

Tours

There are a number of Tourist Office tours available from Mysore, including one to Mysore City, Somnathpur, Srirangapatnam, Brindavan Gardens and, in season, the Ranganathittu Bird Sanctuary. The daily tour starts at 7.30 am and finishes at 8.30 pm and costs Rs 30. This tour attempts to do too much in one day but if you're in a hurry . . . .

The tour to Belur, Halebid and Sravanabelagola visits the other two Hoysala temples and the Jain pilgrimage centre where the immense statue of Lord Gomateshvara stands. Tours on Fridays and Sundays between December and April start at 7.30 am and finish at 9 pm. The cost is Rs 60 but the buses sometimes break down and guides are not always provided, although they are supposed to be. A number of travellers have written to complain bitterly about this tour; a few have written to commend it!

There is also a daily tour to Ootacamund, the hill station in the Nilgiris. In season they start at 7 am and finish at 9 pm and cost Rs 50.

You can book these tours at numerous places, especially around Gandhi Square, or at:

Mysore Tourist Centre, 2 Jhansi Lakshmi Bai Rd
Tourist Office, Cauvery Arts & Crafts Emporium, Sayaji Rao Rd
Tourist Office, opposite Shalimar Hotel round the corner from the New Gayathri Bhavan Hotel, Dhanvantri Rd

Beware of the tour operators in the Dhanvantri Rd area, some of whom try to create the impression that they are part of the Tourist Office and then overcharge you on tours similar to those operated by the Tourist Office.

Places to Stay – bottom end

Virtually all the budget hotels are either along Dhanvantri Rd or around Gandhi Square. There are literally scores of them.

New Gayathri Bhavan (tel 21224) on Dhanvantri Rd is popular with budget travellers. Singles are Rs 20 or Rs 25 with attached bath, doubles from Rs 40. The rooms are secure and there's hot water in the mornings and evenings. The staff are pleasant and downstairs there's a 'meals' café.

The well-kept Agarwal Lodge (tel 22730), Dhanvantri Rd has rooms for Rs 25/40 with attached bathroom. The quality and facilities are the same as the Gayathri. On the same road, Hotel Indra Bhavan (tel 23933) has rooms with bathroom for Rs 25/35. Hotel Santiniwas on a side road off Dhanvantri Rd has clean singles/doubles for Rs 30/50. Naga Lodge (tel 26704) is at 155 Old Santhepet in an interesting godown area near the City Bus Station. It has good singles for Rs 30 and is becoming increasingly popular.

Over in the Gandhi Square area, check out the *Hotel Satkar*, opposite the Hotel Dasaprakesh. It only has a few rooms, but they're reasonably priced at Rs 25/50 with attached bath. Close by is the *Hotel Durbar* where rooms at Rs 25/50 are a little over-priced with common bath and it's rather noisy at night. The hotel has a rooftop restaurant and has recently moved up in the world – there's an armed guard at the door and coloured lights on the restaurant! On Ashoka Rd near Gandhi Square the *Balaji Lodge* has doubles at Rs 30 and very friendly management.

The *Park Lane Hotel* (tel 30400) is at 2720 Curzon Park Rd, next to the KEB Building on the top side of the palace and close to Gandhi Square. It's a good place with rooms for Rs 35/50, has a cosy atmosphere and is a popular meeting place. *Hotel Ritz* (tel 22668), on the Bangalore-Ooty road, has doubles for Rs 60. It's an older building with very pleasant staff, who display a remarkably sardonic sense of humour about the hotel's facilities. There's a restaurant with a good variety of cuisines and a bar.

The *Srikanth Hotel* (tel 22951), Gandhi Square, has clean rooms with attached bath for Rs 30 to Rs 70. Some rooms have balconies over the lively streets and you even get a paper under the door in the morning. *Hotel Anugraha* (tel 20581), Sayaji Rao Rd, is a popular place with travellers and Indians alike as it's right in the centre of the city, and very good value with rooms and attached bath from Rs 35. *Hotel Athithya* (tel 25466) on Dhanvantri Rd offers similar standards; the management is very pleasant and tries hard to please. There is a rooftop restaurant with vegetarian food.

Two popular new hotels in the Dhanvantri Rd area offer good value. The clean *Hotel Aashraya* (tel 27088) has rooms for Rs 30/60, friendly staff and a restaurant which serves snacks. *Hotel Chalukya* (tel 27374) has rooms with attached bath for Rs 35/66.

One very good budget hotel not in the Dhanvantri Rd or Gandhi Square areas is *Lakshmi Lodge* (tel 22316), Shivarampet (Vinoba Rd). This new place is clean and tidy with hot water, pleasant staff and rooms at Rs 25/40.

Outside Mysore City, accommodation is available at Somnathpur, Srirangapatnam and Brindavan Gardens. See Around Mysore.

Places to Stay – middle

In the Gandhi Square area, *Hotel Dasaprakesh* (tel 24444) is one of a chain of hotels through south India and is ideal for budget travellers. It is a huge place and has a variety of rooms ranging from Rs 40/60 or Rs 70/125 with air-con. They also have a good restaurant serving Indian food.

One of the better new hotels in Mysore is *Hotel Siddhartha* (tel 26869) at 73/1 Government Guest House Rd near the Central Bus Stand. It's clean and good value for Rs 50/80 or Rs 75/125 with air-con. *Hotel Mayura Hoysala* (tel 25349), Jhansi Lakshmi Bai Rd opposite the Hotel Metropole, is operated by the KSTDC and offers spacious, pleasantly decorated singles/doubles with attached bath for Rs 65/85. The tours operated by KSTDC start from this hotel.

Of similar standards is the *Hotel Aashirwad* (tel 23210), 3 Nazarbad Rd, which has an air-con bar and restaurant, money-changing facilities, laundry service and car-rental counter. Rooms cost Rs 45 to Rs 75 or with air-con Rs 75 to Rs 100. All have attached bathrooms and hot and cold running water. It's used mainly by Indian middle-class holiday-makers and businesspeople.

Places to Stay – top end

Mysore offers a rare opportunity to stay in an ex-Maharaja's palace, so if you can afford it try the *Lalithamahal Palace* (tel 23650), a huge, gleaming white structure on the eastern outskirts of town. Rooms cost Rs 395/505 (less without air-con),

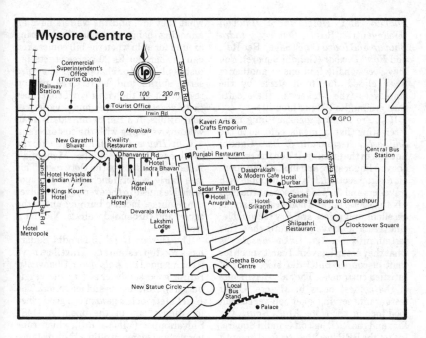

Mysore Centre

Commercial Superintendent's Office (Tourist Quota)

Railway Station

0 100 200 m

Tourist Office

Irwin Rd

Kaveri Arts & Crafts Emporium

GPO

Hospitals

New Gayathri Bhavar

Kwality Restaurant

Dhanvantri Rd

Punjabi Restaurant

Central Bus Station

Hotel Indra Bhavan

Hotel Hoysala & Indian Airlines

Kings Kourt Hotel

Agarwal Hotel

Aashraya Hotel

Dasaprakash & Modern Cafe

Hotel Durbar

Sadar Patel Rd

Hotel Anugraha

Hotel Srikanth

Gandhi Square

Buses to Somnathpur

Ashoka Rd

Devaraja Market

Lakshmi Lodge

Shilpashri Restaurant

Clocktower Square

Hotel Metropole

Jhansi Lakshmi Bai Rd

Geetha Book Centre

New Statue Circle

Local Bus Stand

Palace

although if you want the 'Viceroy Suite' you can shell out Rs 2000! The less expensive rooms are worth it for a night, even if you can't afford to stay longer, although the standards inside aren't as good as the external appearance would lead you to believe.

Hotel Rajendra Vilas Palace (tel 22050), at the top of Chamundi Hill, is similar and has rooms at Rs 200/300 and superb views over the city, particularly at night. You can drop in for a pot of coffee and biscuits in the sumptuous Canopy Restaurant for around Rs 10.

In Mysore itself, the *Hotel Metropole* (20681, 20871) at 5 Jhansi Lakshmi Bai Rd is tucked away in its own spacious and well-kept grounds. The service is erratic but this is where the colonials stay. Rooms are Rs 150/210 or with air-con Rs 200/260. There is a restaurant serving Indian, Chinese and western food, a bar, barbecue, money-changing facilities and

laundry service. *Hotel Highway* (tel 21117-9), New Bannimantap Extension-7, offers double rooms with attached bathroom for Rs 175 to Rs 250.

Hotel Kings Kourt (tel 25250) in the same area has rooms for Rs 120/150 or with air-con Rs 180/220. It also has a restaurant. *Hotel Dasaprakesh Paradise* (tel 26666, 25555) at 105 Yadavagiri has singles/doubles at Rs 160/200 and a good restaurant; it will eventually have a swimming pool.

Places to Eat

There are any number of reasonably good 'meals' restaurants where you can get standard south Indian vegetarian food for Rs 5. *Hotel Dasaprakesh* has a good vegetarian restaurant with meals for Rs 10. They also have an excellent ice cream parlour – try the date and walnut or fig and honey ice cream. Other vegetarian restaurants include the *New Gayathri*

Bhavan and *Hotel Indra Bhavan* (Dhanvantri Rd); *Bombay Indra Bhavan* and *Indra Café* (Sayaji Rao Rd); and *Hotel Durbar* (Gandhi Square). You may occasionally find one or another of these closed due to a strike by the employees (the workers in these cafés earn around Rs 100 per month!).

If you're looking for something more interesting than a 'meals' café, go to the *Shilpashri Restaurant & Bar*, Gandhi Square, in the evening. It's on the 1st floor above a liquor store and includes an open-air rooftop section. It's very popular with travellers and for good reason, as the food – both vegetarian and non-vegetarian – is excellent and prices are very reasonable. One ecstatic traveller wrote that this restaurant's *chicken tikka masala* 'is what they eat in heaven'. I can't vouch for that, of course, but I did meet a lot of satisfied customers. They also have some of the coldest beers in Mysore. Other restaurants serving good non-vegetarian food include the *Hotel Kings Kourt*, the *Ritz* and the *RRR* just off Gandhi Square. In fact the RRR has 'the best food in south India', according to one happy visitor. Thalis are Rs 8 but the waiters may hover around, waiting for a tip.

Similar to the Shilpashri, but considerably more expensive, is the *Punjabi Restaurant & Bombay Juice Centre*, Dhanvantri Rd near the junction with Sayaji Rao Rd. They serve excellent Punjabi food and you see a lot of people eating there, but a full meal is going to cost you more than your accommodation for the night. Likewise, the fruit juices are good but they're top dollar. *Paras Restaurant*, near the Indra Café in the Gandhi Square area, has excellent snacks and ice cream. Good drinks from the *Panir Soda Factory* on Vinoba Rd by New Statue Circle.

The *Kwality Restaurant* on Dhanvantri Rd serves both vegetarian and non-vegetarian food as well as 'Chinese' and tandoori specialities, but their vegetarian dishes all taste the same regardless of what they are, and the waiters have an annoying habit of obviously hovering around for a tip when the bill comes. You can eat here for Rs 20 (three vegetarian dishes plus nan or chappatis). They also serve spirits and beers. The rooftop restaurant at the *Athithya Lodge* does tasty vegetarian dishes and a variety of cold drinks. It's run by an elderly man who enjoys joking with the customers.

Gun House Imperial is close to the south-east corner of the Maharaja's Palace at the start of the Ooty road. This is a fairly select lunch-and-night spot with live music in the evenings plus silver candelabras, incense burning under the tables and turbanned waiters. Nice for a treat.

The *Durbar Hotel* in Gandhi Square has a rooftop restaurant. Travellers have recommended the *Kalpaka* on Dhanvantri Rd for good sandwiches (try the veggie burgers), fruit drinks and ice cream. The *Hotel Metropole's* garden is a good place for dinner out in the open. At 1487 Shivarampet (Vinoba Rd), which runs parallel to Dhanvantri Rd a little distance from the centre, the *Shanghai Chinese Restaurant* has been recommended by several travellers.

Finally, some places at top and bottom. The deluxe *Lalithamahal Palace Hotel* has an excellent evening buffet. The *Canopy* at the Rajendra Vilas Palace is also good. Or you can look for the street stalls selling steamed chick peas, pooris stuffed with potatoes, dhal and raw carrots, all for a rupee. The glass-sided carts marked 'Welcome' by the gray-and-yellow colonial building near New Statue are great.

Getting There

Air There are no Indian Airline flights to Mysore, but Vayudoot Airlines has recently introduced flights to Bangalore (Rs 130), Hyderabad (Rs 560) and Tirupathi (Rs 315).

Rail The enquiry office at Mysore station

is very good and rarely has more than two or three people in it. If you're trying to book sleeper tickets on trains from Mysore and you're told that the quota is full for the day you're hoping to leave, buy a ticket anyway and go to the Commercial Superintendent's Office, Irwin Rd – that's the entrance just before you cross the road and come to the Tourist Office. Find the office marked, 'Concession Orders Issued Here' – it's on your right as you enter – and ask for the 'Tourist Quota'. Have your ticket handy – you can't do this without a ticket for the journey – fill in a form, wait for five minutes, and you'll get that sleeper. The quota here has precedence over the official waiting list compiled at the station ticket office.

If you're heading for Bombay but don't want to go through Bangalore, there's a service through to Miraj from where you can take an express to Bombay; the whole trip takes about 36 hours. The 2700-km trip to Delhi costs Rs 160 in 2nd class, Rs 665 in 1st. It's 2170 km to Calcutta and the fare is Rs 134 in 2nd class, Rs 556 in 1st.

Bangalore There are a half dozen express trains daily on the 140-km trip to Bangalore. The trip usually takes around 3½ hours at a fare of Rs 16 in 2nd class, Rs 65 in 1st. There are also slower passenger trains to Bangalore or to Maddur which can be used to get to Srirangapatnam.

Arsikere There are three passenger trains daily to Arsikere via Hassan. If you plan on visiting the Hoysala temples of Belur and Halebid and the Jain centre of Sravanabelagola, and if you're going to use Hassan as a base, these are the trains to take. To Hassan the 130-km journey takes 4½ hours and costs Rs 16 in 2nd class, Rs 61 in 1st; only Rs 9 in 2nd class on an ordinary passenger train.

Chamarajanagar There are five passenger trains to Nanjangud daily and three passenger trains to Chamarajanagar daily, but they're of little use to travellers.

If you're heading for Bandipur it is more convenient to take a bus.

Goa There's a daily train from Mysore which includes a 2nd-class sleeping carriage as far as Londa Junction. Here you change and take another train to Margao/Vasco da Gama. The 700-km trip costs Rs 58 in 2nd class, Rs 235 in 1st.

You have to wait several hours at Londa for a connection, so an alternative is to take a bus on from there. There are buses to several centres in Goa, including half a dozen to Panaji via Ponda. The fare is Rs 10 and the journey takes about 3½ hours. There are also half a dozen buses to Margao and a couple to Mapusa.

To get to the bus station from Londa railway station, cross the tracks to your right and walk uphill until you reach the main street of Londa – it's essentially a one-street town. Turn left when you get to this street and keep going until you pass the bulk of the buildings. About 100 metres past that point, head up one of the paths on your right. The bus stand is just a patch of tarmac. You can't miss it.

Bus Local buses go from the City Bus Stand at New Statue Circle near Gandhi Square. The new Central Bus Stand handles inter-city buses and is north of the Hotel Ritz on the main road parallel to Ashoka Rd.

Somnathpur First get a bus from the Central Bus Stand (Gandhi Square) to the village of T Narisipur (tell the conductor you want to go to Somnathpur). This part of the journey costs Rs 3.75. At T Narisipur take another bus to Somnathpur. You'll have no trouble locating this bus, as all the local kids and the bus conductors will make sure you know when it arrives. These buses are frequent and this part of the journey costs Rs 1. A shorter alternative is to take a bus to Bannur (Rs 2.50) and change there for Somnathpur (Rs 1).

You can either return to Mysore via the same route or continue to Srirangapatnam.

There is a daily direct bus from Somnathpur to Srirangapatnam. If you want to go before or after this, take a bus from Somnathpur to Bannur and then another bus from there to Srirangapatnam (Rs 3.25). The buses from Bannur to Srirangapatnam can get incredibly crowded. The bus I was on had 202 people on board and I ended up with a child on my knee and two pails of milk in each hand!

Srirangapatnam There are plenty of buses all day and night from both bus stands. Some go only as far as Srirangapatnam; others pass through on their way to somewhere else. The fare is Rs 1.75. There's no problem getting back to Mysore along the same route. As an alternative to the bus it's also possible to get there by taking the Bangalore passenger train from Mysore station. If you want to visit Somnathpur from Srirangapatnam, use the route indicated above under Somnathpur in the reverse direction.

Other Places To Arsikere buses depart a dozen times daily. You can use Arsikere as a base from which to visit Belur, Halebid and Sravanabelagola, though Hassan is the more usual base. There are a couple of dozen buses daily to Hassan from various platforms for Rs 15.

To Bandipur, there are three buses daily. To Bangalore non-stop buses depart every 20 to 30 minutes from early morning to late evening; ordinary service with stops runs every 30 minutes. This very organised and comfortable bus service takes three to 3½ hours. To Bellary there's one bus daily and this is the one to take if you want to visit the Vijayanagar ruins at Hampi direct from Mysore.

There are two or three buses daily to Coimbatore, Cannanore, Nagarhole and Udipi. Half a dozen buses a day go to Calicut, and several of them continue to Ernakulam. This is an interesting trip through the Bandipur Sanctuary (watch for elephants) and over the Nilgiris. The Cochin-Mysore service also goes via Calicut; it takes about 13 hours.

Chikmagalur has a half dozen buses daily via Belur. Mangalore has a dozen buses daily. There are a half dozen buses daily to Ootacamund which you can take to get to the wildlife sanctuaries of Bandipur and Mudumalai. The trip takes five hours and costs Rs 20. A similar number of buses go to Sravanabelagola. Finally, there's a daily overnight service to Panaji in Goa.

Getting Around

Bus Local buses which you may find useful include Nos 1 and 1A (to the Sandalwood Oil Factory); and Nos 1A, 1AS, 1AF, 4 and 5 (to the Silk Weaving Factory). Bus No 150 goes to Brindavan Gardens. For buses to Chamundi Hill, go to the City Bus Stand at the eastern end of Gandhi Square and take No 101. They run approximately every 30 minutes and cost Rs 1.75.

Auto-rickshaw There are plenty of auto-rickshaws if you prefer this form of transport (Sayaji Rao Rd to the Sandalwood Oil Factory will cost Rs 5 to Rs 6). The drivers use the meters.

Things to Buy

Mysore is famous for carved sandalwood and ivory articles, inlay works, silk saris and incense *(agarbathi)*. The best place to see the whole range of what is available is the Cauvery Arts & Crafts Emporium on Sayaji Rao Rd. It's open daily except Thursdays from 10 am to 2 pm and 3.30 to 7.30 pm (Sundays from 10 am to 2 pm). They won't take credit cards, but they will take foreign currency or travellers' cheques and will arrange packing (they do a very good job) and export.

Few of the larger things are cheap by Indian standards (the smallest of the inlaid tables costs about US$100), but the place is worth a visit even if you're not going to buy anything. One traveller commented, however, that the selection was better and the prices comparable at the Cottage Industries Emporium in New

Delhi. There are many other crafts shops along Dhanvantri Rd with similar prices. Some of them specialise in ivory chess sets, but a 10-cm set can cost you US$1000 to US$1500! The best bargains are the carved sandalwood images of Indian deities. They retain their scent for years. There are always a number of street hawkers outside the Cauvery Emporium. They sometimes have interesting and cheap bangles, rings and old coins.

Happy Handicrafts on the Mysore-Bangalore road about 100 metres from New Statue Circle has also been recommended. For more straightforward purchases the Mohan Bhandar Department Store on Sayaji Rao Rd has everything from film to toilet paper, batteries to tinned food.

AROUND MYSORE
Srirangapatnam

Sixteen km from Mysore on the Bangalore road stand the ruins of Hyder Ali and Tipu Sultan's capital from which they ruled much of southern India during the 18th century. They were finally defeated by the British, allied with disgruntled local leaders and with the help of a traitor, in 1799. Tipu's defeat marked the real beginning of British territorial expansion in southern India.

There isn't a great deal left of Srirangapatnam, as the British did a good job of demolishing the place, but the extensive ramparts and battlements and some of the gates still stand and the dungeon where Tipu held prisoner a number of British officers has been preserved. Inside the walls there's also a mosque and the Sri Ranganathaswamy Temple, a popular place of pilgrimage with Hindus. Non-Hindus can go all the way inside except to the inner sanctum, where there is a black stone image of sleeping Vishnu. The population of the town inside the fort is about 20,000.

Across the other side of the road from Srirangapatnam stands the Daria Daulat Bagh, Tipu's summer palace, and the Gumbaz, Tipu's mausoleum. These are perhaps the most interesting parts of a visit to Srirangapatnam. The Daria Daulat Bagh stands in well-maintained ornamental gardens and is now a museum which houses some of Tipu's belongings as well as many ink drawings of him and his family and 'artists' impressions' of the last battle, executed by employees of the British East India Company. All around the internal walls of the ground floor are paintings depicting Tipu's campaigns against the British with French mercenary assistance. The Daria Daulat Bagh is open daily until 5 pm.

Places to Stay Contact the Assistant Engineer, PWD, Srirangapatnam for accommodation at the *Travellers Bungalow*, close to Sri Ranganathaswamy Temple.

Getting There There are scores of buses every day in either direction from the central bus station in Mysore. The fare is Rs 1.75.

Somnathpur

Built around 1260 AD during the heyday of the Hoysala kings, the Sri Channakeshara Temple is at Somnathpur, 45 km east of Mysore. It's one of the most beautiful and interesting buildings in the world. The walls of the star-shaped temple are literally covered with superb sculptures in stone depicting various scenes from the *Ramayana, Mahabharata, Bhagvadgita* and the life and times of the Hoysala kings. No two friezes are alike.

If you like this place then don't miss the other Hoysala temples at Belur and Halebid, north of Mysore. The temple is open daily from 9 am to 5 pm.

Information A useful booklet, *The Hoysalas* by P K Mishra, is on sale at the temple for Rs 6.

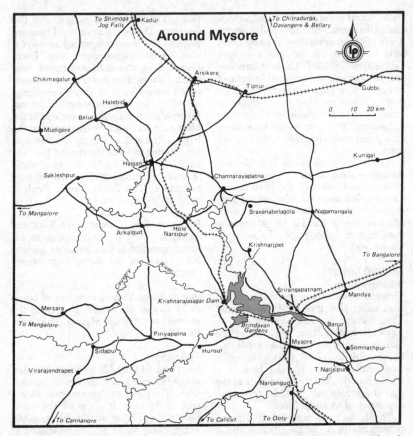

Around Mysore

To Shimoga / Jog Falls — Kadur
To Chitradurga, Davangere & Bellary
Chikmagalur
Arsikere
Tiptur
Gubbi
Halebid
Belur
Mudigere
Kunigal
Hassan
Sakleshpur
Channarayapatna
Nagamangala
To Mangalore
Sravanabelagola
Arkalgud
Hole Narsipur
Krishnarjpet
To Bangalore
Cauvery River
To Mangalore
Mercara
Krishnarajasagar Dam
Srirangapatnam
Mandya
Brindavan Gardens
Banur
Piriyapatna
Mysore
Somnathpur
Sidapur
Hunsur
T Narisipur
Virarajendrapet
Nanjangud
To Cannanore
To Calicut
To Ooty

0 10 20 km

Places to Stay Just outside the temple compound is a KSTDC *Tourist Home & Restaurant*. The pleasantly decorated rooms are great value from around Rs 40 with attached bathrooms and carpeted floors, yet they're rarely full. The restaurant serves excellent food.

Getting There See the Mysore section for details on how to get to Somnathpur by public transport.

Bandipur Wildlife Sanctuary

Eighty km south of Mysore on the Mysore-Ootacamund road, this wildlife sanctuary is part of a larger national park which also includes the neighbouring wildlife sanctuaries of Mudumalai in Tamil Nadu and Wynad in Kerala. The sanctuary is noted for its herds of bison, spotted deer, elephant, sambar, tiger and leopard. There are supposed to be two dozen tigers but they are rarely seen. The Forestry Department has jeeps and trucks available for hire and, as in Mudumalai, you can go on safari on elephant-back. Boats are available for use on the river. Motorised transport and accommodation in the sanctuary should be booked in advance.

For reservations contact the Field Director, Project Tiger, Government House Complex, Mysore (tel 20901). Food and accommodation at the park are very good. The best time to go is between October and May, although one traveller wrote of seeing elephant, bison, jungle fowl, peacocks, monkeys, mongoose, sambar and deer in February! If there is a drought, the park may not be worth visiting, as the animals migrate to the adjoining park at Mudumalai in Tamil Nadu for water. Entry is only possible from 6 to 9 am and 4.30 to 6 pm. There's no place to get food or drink in the park so bring it with you.

Places to Stay There are huge deluxe bungalows at the park with attached bathrooms, mosquito nets, hot water and a big lounge for Rs 25 per night plus a one-time charge of Rs 15. The caretaker (or somebody) will fix excellent meals. You can see chitral (spotted deer) right from your windows. Films are shown at the centre each night.

Getting There You can make a day trip to Bandipur by catching a bus at 5.30 am towards Ooty. You'll arrive at the Bandipur office two or three hours later and can take a jeep trip (Rs 125 for up to nine people) or hire an elephant and guide (Rs 40 for four persons). Doing both, you'll still be in time to catch the last bus back to Mysore around 5.30 pm. Jeeps are better than trucks, which tend to be crowded and noisy.

Ranganathittu Bird Sanctuary

The sanctuary is on one of three islands in the Cauvery River, three km from Srirangapatnam. If you're interested in birds this is a good place to visit at any time of year, though it's best between June and September. Access is by a motorable road, open all year. Boats are available for use on the river but there are no accommodation facilities.

Brindavan Gardens

These ornamental gardens are laid out below the Krishnarajasagar dam across the Cauvery River, 19 km from Mysore. They're popular for picnics and pleasant enough, but probably not worth a special trip to see although they are colourfully lit for two hours each night – 'cosmic kitsch' somebody described the lighting! Entry costs Rs 4 plus Rs 20 (!) if you have a camera. One of the tours operated by the KSTDC will bring you here.

Places to Stay There are three places to stay at the gardens. *Hotel Krishnarajasagar* (tel Mysore 20681) is an expensive western-style hotel with air-conditioning, restaurant and so on. Rooms cost from Rs 150 to Rs 250.

The KSTDC *Tourist Home* is similar to the one at Somnathpur and doubles with attached bathroom cost from Rs 40. Finally, there's a *Travellers' Bungalow* for which reservations are made with the executive engineer, Krishnarajasagar.

Shivasamudram

India's first hydro-electric power station was built here at the Cauvery River falls in 1902. Shivasamudram is 80 km east of Mysore, beyond Somnathpur. The twin falls known as Gaganachukki and Bharchukki drop nearly 100 metres in a series of cascades.

Hunsur

Outside of Hunsur, to the west of Mysore, is a Tibetan refugee settlement called Rabgayling – which means 'Good Progress Place' although nobody calls it that! There are 15 villages scattered over low, rolling hills in a grid pattern – lovely to see against the green cornfields. There are two monasteries, one of them a Tantric college, both involved in the village life.

The two carpet factories are glad to produce Tibetan carpets to your own design. Thankas are painted at the Tantric college. There's no commercial accommodation in the area although two small cafés serve momos, noodles and curd.

BELUR & HALEBID

The temples at Belur and Halebid, along with that at Somnathpur east of Mysore, are the cream of what remains of one of the most artistically exuberant periods of Hindu cultural development. The sculptural decoration on these superb temples even rivals the temples of Khajuraho and Konarak or the best of European Gothic art.

Amazing though they all are, the wealth of sculptural detail on the Hoysaleswara Temple at Halebid makes it easily the most outstanding example of Hoysala art. Every cm of the outside walls and much of the interior are covered with an endless variety of Hindu deities, sages, stylised animals and birds and friezes depicting the life and times of the Hoysala rulers. No two are alike. Scenes from war, hunting, agriculture, music and dancing and some very sensual sculptures explicitly portraying the après-temple activities of the dancing girls are represented here, together with a huge Nandi (Shiva's bull) and a monolithic Jain statue of Lord Gomateshvara.

The Hoysala temples are squat and low, more human in scale than the soaring temples found elsewhere in India. What they lack in size they make up in the sheer intricacy of their sculptures. They were carved from a soapstone which is relatively soft and easily cut when first quarried, but with age and exposure gradually hardens. The Hoysaleswara Temple at Halebid was constructed about 10 years after the temple at Belur, but despite 80 years' labour was never finally completed. There is also a smaller temple, the Kedareswara, at Halebid.

At Belur, the Channekeshava Temple is the only one at the three Hoysala sites still used as a functioning temple. Non-Hindus are allowed inside. In design it is very similar to the others but here much of the decoration has gone into the internal supporting pillars and lintels and larger, but still very delicately carved, images of deities and guardian beasts. As at Halebid, the external walls are covered in friezes. The other, lesser, Hoysala temples here are the Channigaraya and the Viranarayana.

The Hoysalas, who ruled this part of the Deccan between the 11th and 13th centuries, had their origins in the hill tribes of the Western Ghats and were for a long time feudatories of the Chalukyas. They did not become fully independent until about 1190 AD, though they first rose to prominence under their leader Tinayaditya (1047-78 AD), who took advantage of the waning power of the Gangas and Rashtrakutas. Under Bittiga (1110-52 AD), better known by his later name of Vishnuvardhana, they began to take off on a course of their own and it was during his reign that the temples of Belur and Halebid were built.

The times saw great religious upheaval, with the Jain faith being predominant due to the patronage of the Chalukyas and the Gangas; although tolerance of other sects was usually practised, religious persecution was not unknown. Bittiga's predecessors were Jains; he was a devout Jain himself in his earlier years and encouraged one of his generals, Gangaraja, to restore the Jain temples destroyed by the Shaivite Chola invaders from the south-east. Later in his reign he came under the influence of the famous saint, Ramanuja, who converted him to faith in Vishnu. As a result of this conversion he adopted the name of Vishnuvardhana and devoted himself to erecting temples honouring his new creed, but continued to show tolerance for other religious sects. Indeed, records show him making grants to Shaivite and Jain temples and going on pilgrimage to Sravanabelagola even after his conversion.

Vishnuvardhana's conversion was one of the main factors which led to a decline of Jainism, but it was not the only one. Corruption among the priesthood and the public defeat of the Jain texts by Ramanuja also undermined its influence, but it was by no means extinguished and at least one of Vishnuvardhana's wives and a daughter continued to practise that faith. Later Hoysala rulers also continued to patronise the religion. This normally easy co-existence between Shaivites, Vaishnavites and Jains explains why you will find images of all these various sects' gods, their consorts and associated companions in Hoysala temples.

The early temples of this dynasty closely followed the style of those of their Chalukyan overlords, but by Bittiga's time they had developed a distinctive style of their own. Typically, the temple is a relatively small star-shaped structure set on a platform to give it some height, with most of the attention devoted to sculptural embellishment.

It's quickly apparent from a study of these sculptures that the arts of music and dancing reached a high point in grace and perfection during their time. As with Kathakali dancing in Kerala, the arts were used to express religious fervour or the joy of a victory in battle, or simply to give domestic pleasure – but there the similarity ends, as it's obvious these were times of a relatively high degree of sexual freedom and prominent female participation in public affairs. Most Indian books which describe these temples and the ones at Khajuraho bend over backwards to play down the sensuality of these sculptures. Perhaps this embarrassment reflects the repressed attitudes of the average urban Indian today regarding all matters physical. Of course a century ago our Victorian ancestors were also slightly shocked by some Indian temples!

Both temples are open every day. A spotlight is available inside to enable you to see the sculptural work (it's quite dark otherwise), but if it's not already turned on you'll be charged Rs 2 for the privilege. Entry to Halebid is free, although as at Belur, it's customary to tip the shoe minder. This temple is now maintained

by the Archaeological Survey of India. There is a small museum adjacent to the temple but it's of little interest. It does, however, sell excellent postcards of the temple and the one at Belur for Rs 0.50. The attendant who works here will attempt to waylay you before you get to the museum and sell you the same postcards for Rs 1 each. Where else but India?!

Places to Stay

Though Halebid was once the capital city of the Hoysala rulers, it is now little more than a rural village. KSTDC *Tourist Cottages* adjoin the Halebid temple; rooms with bathroom cost from Rs 30. It's a very pleasant place with catering facilities; there is nowhere else to stay. A sign in the village centre indicates the temple as being 1.6 km away; someone can't measure since it's only 500 metres.

Belur is just a small town. There are KSTDC *Tourist Cottages* 200 metres from the temple at the same price as the Halebid Cottages, but they have no catering facilities (there are plenty of small cafés in the town). In addition to these there is a *Travellers' Bungalow* and two fairly basic hotels, the *New Hotel Gayatri* and the *Tourist Hotel*. Both have attached restaurants and are two minutes' walk from the bus stand.

Though it's obviously possible to stay in either place – and this would be a good idea if you wanted to spend a day at each temple – most people use Hassan as a base. Arsikere is another possibility. Accommodation and transport facilities at both of these places are covered later in this chapter.

SRAVANABELAGOLA (population 5000)

This is one of the oldest and most important Jain pilgrimage centres in India and site of the huge 17-metre-high statue of Lord Bahubali (Gomateshvara), said to be the world's tallest monolithic statue. It overlooks the small town of Sravanabelagola from the top of the rocky hill known as Indragiri and is visible even at a distance of 25 km. Its simplicity is in complete contrast to the complexity of the sculptural work at the temples of Belur and Halebid. The word 'Sravanabelagola' means 'the monk on the top of the hill'. It is a Digambara or 'sky-clad' Jain shrine.

Sravanabelagola has a long historical pedigree going back to the 3rd century BC when Chandragupta Maurya came here with his guru, Bhagwan Bhadrabahu Swami, after renouncing his kingdom. In the course of time Bhadrabahu's disciples spread his teachings all over the region and thus firmly established Jainism in the south. The religion found powerful patrons in the Gangas who ruled the southern part of what is now Karnataka between the 4th and 10th centuries, and it was during this time that Jainism reached the zenith of its influence. The statue of Lord Bahubali was created during the reign of the Ganga king Rachamalla. It was commissioned by a military commander in the service of Rachamalla and executed by the sculptor Aristanemi in 981 AD.

Legend has it that Bahubali was the youngest son of Jain Emperor Adi Thirthankara Vrishabha Deva, who ruled a kingdom in northern India and later became the first Jain saint. When Vrishabha Deva renounced his kingdom and retired to the forest to perform penance, a bitter struggle for succession broke out between his two sons, Bahubali and Bharatha. The battle culminated in a duel between the two brothers in which Bahubali emerged the victor, but in his moment of triumph he realised the futility of worldly success, gave his kingdom and all his worldly possessions to Bharatha, and retired to the forest to begin a 1000-year penance.

The statue is the subject of the spectacular Mahamastakabhisheka ceremony, which takes place once every 12 to 14 years when the small town of Sravanabelagola becomes a Mecca for thousands of pilgrims and tourists from all over India and abroad. The 1981 festival coincided with the 1000th anniversary of the erection of the statue and because of this attracted over one million people! Seven satellite towns had to be constructed to accommodate the extra people, and transport was diverted from all over the state. The climax of the Mahamastakabhisheka involves the anointing of Lord Bahubali's head with thousands of pots of coconut milk, yoghurt, ghee, bananas, jaggery, dates, almonds, poppy seeds, milk, gold coins, saffron and sandalwood from the top of a scaffolding erected for the purpose. There must be a lot of work for cleaners after this event!

The rest of the time, Sravanabelagola reverts to a quiet little country town which is a very pleasant place to stay for a few days. The people are friendly, the pace is unhurried and the place is full of cosy little chai shops.

In addition to the statue of Lord Bahubali – which to get to you have to climb 614 steps carved out of the sheer rock face of Indragiri Hill – there are several very interesting Jain *bastis* (temples) and *mathas* (monasteries) both in the town and on Chandragiri Hill, the smaller of the two hills between which Sravanabelagola nestles. Two of these – the Bhandari Basti and the Akkana Basti – are in the Hoysala style, and a third – the Chandragupta Basti – is believed to have been built by Emperor Ashoka the Great. The well-preserved paintings in one of the temples are like a 600-year-old comic strip of Jain stories.

Information

A Tourist Office run by the KSTDC is inconveniently situated two km from the shrine. There is, however, a small reception centre at the entrance to the hill. A contribution of Rs 1 is expected. Postcards of the statue of Lord Bahubali are on sale here for Rs 1. You can leave your belongings safely in the Tourist Office while you climb the hill. There's no charge for this but they're closed between 1 and 2.15 pm.

Places to Stay & Eat
The KSTDC *Tourist Home* is two km away, charges Rs 20/35 for singles/doubles and looks somewhat run down. A better place to stay just outside the temple complex is the *SP Guest House* (started by one of the richest men in India) which charges Rs 25 a double. The *Tourist Canteen* has good, cheap food.

The alternative is one of the pilgrims' rest houses, all of which are two to three km from the town itself. A room costs Rs 6. Most people use Hassan as a base.

Getting There
Belur and Halebid are only 16 km apart and can be seen in one day using public transport and starting from Hassan around 9 am. On returning to Hassan there's still time to catch the 6.30 pm bus to Sravanabelagola or a bus to Mysore, Bangalore or Arsikere. To visit Belur, Halebid and Sravanabelagola all in one day using public transport requires a very early start and a late finish.

If you don't have a lot of time at your disposal, and want to see them all in one day, the best thing to do is go on one of the tours organised by the KSTDC from Mysore. Make sure they have an English-speaking guide – they are supposed to, but don't always.

HASSAN
Hassan is probably the most convenient base from which to explore Belur, Halebid and Sravanabelagola. In itself it has little of interest – it's simply a place for accommodation and transport.

Information
The Tourist Office is friendly and helpful and has a good selection of leaflets on places of interest in the area. If you want to stay at the KSTDC Tourist Cottages at Belur or Halebid, book them here.

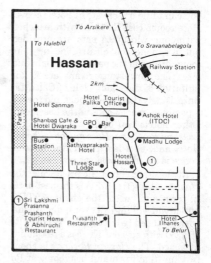

Places to Stay
Although there are quite a few hotels in Hassan, many of them appear to be semi-permanently full. An early check-in is advisable. The alternative is to check with the Tourist Office about the KSTDC *Tourist Cottages* at Belur and Halebid and, if there's room, to go there.

Hotel Palika (tel 7145) is an entirely new hotel and good value at Rs 30/50 for rooms with attached bathroom. Several travellers have written to commend this clean and well-kept hotel. *Hotel Sanman* has rooms with attached bath for Rs 20/35 and a restaurant that does thalis for Rs 4.

Hotel Dwaraka is a very popular hotel with rooms with common bathroom at Rs 12/20. It's basic but fills up rapidly and you're unlikely to get a room here later in the day. The *Sathyaprakash Hotel* (above the Shanbag Café) next door is of similar quality. *Prashanth Tourist Home* is a pleasant little place where rooms with attached bathroom cost Rs 15/25, but it's another popular hotel which fills up rapidly. Watch the steps on the way down to the street – they're hazardous!

Madhu Lodge is the place to come if

you can't find a room at the hotels above. Here rooms cost Rs 15/20 with attached bathroom. Mosquito nets are provided but it's none too clean. The upstairs rooms are by far the best and are light and airy. The downstairs rooms are a fair imitation of the Black Hole of Calcutta. Surprisingly there are no bugs and there's a passable 'meals' café in the basement. Other hotels you could try include *Sri Lakshmi Prasanna, Hassan Hotel, Ilhanes Hotel* and, as a last resort, the *Ashoka Lodge* is about as basic as you can get.

At the other end of the price scale, the *Hassan Ashok* (tel 8731) is the best hotel in town and one of the chain of ITDC hotels you will find all over India. Rooms with attached bath cost Rs 120/175 or Rs 250/350 with air-con. There is a restaurant attached. The *Hassan Regency* is about two km from town and has rooms at Rs 200/300.

Places to Eat

Although the name may have changed, *Shanbag Café* next to the bus stand is still a reasonable place to eat. For Rs 4 you'll get a huge plate of rice, chappatis, masala sauces, pickles, curd and as much mixed vegetables as you can eat. They serve excellent masala dosa and coffee. You can also get a vegetarian set meal in the *Madhu Lodge* for about the same price. The *Prashanth Restaurant* is a pleasant, cheap and clean vegetarian place.

For non-vegetarian food, a good choice is the *Three Star Lodge*. This is the only place open late – the manager says until 1.30 am. It's popular with Indian students and young men then – friendly staff and good teas. The best north Indian food is served at the *Abiruchi Restaurant* although it's a little expensive – a good meal costs Rs 10 to Rs 15.

On the city circle *Ruchi* does good fruit drinks and excellent ice cream and desserts. If you want a beer, there are several bars but you won't find a *cold* beer anywhere. Hassan has lots of shops with delicious baked goods.

Getting There

Rail There are several Hassan-to-Mysore passenger trains daily. The 119-km journey takes 4½ hours and costs Rs 8. There are also several Hassan-to-Arsikere passenger trains daily. There are no express trains.

The station at Hassan is about two km from the centre of town, so if you want a choice of hotels when you get there, hire an auto-rickshaw.

Bus If you're planning on visiting Belur and Halebid in one day, there's no need to return to Hassan after you've seen one of the places, as there are buses in either direction between Belur and Halebid. In addition to the bus services detailed below, there are at least 20 buses daily to Mysore and the same number to Bangalore.

Belur There are about 20 buses daily to Belur; the journey takes 1½ hours and costs Rs 3.75. Ignore the claim on the timetable about some of the buses being 'express', it's a figment of the imagination.

From Belur there are frequent buses to Halebid. Ask at the bus stand in Belur, but once the bus arrives don't hang about. There is always a mad rush. This bus takes about half an hour and costs Rs 1.50.

Halebid There are 10 buses daily to Halebid. The journey takes two hours and costs Rs 2.75. It's a dirt track most of the way, hence the two-hour journey.

If you went to Belur in the morning and Halebid in the early afternoon, there's a bus back to Hassan from Halebid at about 3.30 pm. Just hang around in the centre of the village – several chai shops.

Sravanabelagola There are three buses daily to Sravanabelagola and the 1½-hour journey costs Rs 5. Going back to Hassan, there is a bus at 3.30 pm. Late in the afternoon bus paranoia sets in and the usual chaos results.

If you miss the direct buses, you can

travel between Hassan and Sravana-belagola via Channarayapatna – there are frequent buses until late. Hassan-Channarayapatna takes 1½ hours and costs Rs 3.75. Channarayapatna-Sravana-belagola takes half an hour and costs Rs 1.25. There are also direct buses from Sravanabelagola to Mysore.

Arsikere Buses to Arsikere depart many times daily, though the exact times are hard to ascertain as the bus schedule is entirely in Kannada. The journey takes about 1¼ to 1¾ hours along a good road and costs Rs 4. You can continue from Arsikere to the Jog Falls in one long day's travel.

Goa It's 8½ hours to Hubli and another 5½ hours to Panaji at a total cost of about Rs 65.

ARSIKERE

Like Hassan, this is a convenient base from which to explore the temples of Belur and Halebid and the Jain centre of Sravanabelagola, but unlike Hassan it has a Hoysala temple of its own. Unfortunately, much of the temple has been defaced and vandalised, and many contemporary structures have been added so it's no longer very represent-ative. Arsikere is also a railway junction where express trains to Bangalore and Bombay (via Miraj) can be taken.

Places to Stay

Only fairly basic accommodation is available in Arsikere. The *Tourist Lodge* is on B H Rd, one minute from the bus stand and about five minutes from the station, and is probably the best of the hotels in Arsikere. Rooms cost from Rs 15. They are pleasantly decorated and have a fan; the attached bathrooms are clean, though decorated with amusing graffiti from aspiring Indian romantic poets who seem to have read too much Shelley. Coffee is brought round at about 7 am. The friendly management seem perplexed at the sight of a westerner in this backwater.

The *New Gayitri Lodge*, on B H Rd directly in front of you as you come to the end of the road leading from the station, has rooms from Rs 10. It's not as pleasant as the Tourist Lodge. *Janatha Hotel* is next door to the Gayitri Lodge and the same price, pretty basic. *Sri Raghavendra Lodge* is the first building on the left after leaving the railway station. It's a quiet, pleasant place which costs the same as the Gayitri and has a vegetarian café downstairs.

Places to Eat

Prasanna Hotel is probably the best of the vegetarian places. They serve standard 'meals' and tiffin. *Rathin Hotel* is next door to the Prasanna. Their 'meals' are OK, but they won't give you extra vegetables – a very unusual occurrence in southern India. *Hotel Majestic* is a Muslim non-vegetarian café which serves food at very reasonable prices. Open late – at least until 11.30 pm – for food and tea.

Getting There

Rail There is no sleeping-accommodation quota on the Bangalore-Miraj Mail at Arsikere. Arsikere-Bangalore is 156 km and the fare is Rs 19 in 2nd class, Rs 71 in 1st. If you're heading for Mysore there are several passenger trains daily. If you're trying to get from Arsikere to Hospet (for the Vijayanagar ruins at Hampi), take the passenger trains as far as Harihar and then a bus from there. The bus station at Harihar is just opposite the railway station.

Bus The bus schedule here is entirely in Kannada, which is bad news if you've just mastered the rudiments of Tamil or Hindi (or Malayalam or Telugu or ...), but there are plenty of buses. Just ask. People here are very friendly!

COORG & THE SOUTH-WEST

Until 1956, when it was included in Karnataka, Coorg was a mini-state in its

own right. A mountainous area, Coorg is in the south-west of Karnataka, bordering with Kerala.

Mercara (population 25,000)

The small town of Mercara is the capital of Coorg and stands 124 km west of Mysore. There is a fort here which has played an important part in Karnataka's tumultuous history, and there's also the Omareswara Temple. This region, where the Western Ghats start to tumble down towards the sea, is green, scenic and fertile and an important coffee-growing area. The view from the Raja's Seat is wonderful.

Places to Stay Mercara is a very pleasant hill station. A double room at the KSTDC *Tourist Lodge* costs Rs 35.

Nagarhole

This 18-square-km wildlife sanctuary is in the south-east of Coorg. Elephant rides are available in the early morning. The best time to visit is from October to May. Accommodation can be booked in Mysore; see the Mysore Information section.

MANGALORE (population 305,000)

The west coast railway line through Kerala crosses the border into Karnataka and terminates at this port. At one time Mangalore was a port of great importance and was the major seaport and ship-building centre of Hyder Ali's kingdom. Even today it is a major centre for the export of coffee and cashew nuts. The Sultan's Battery, the old lighthouse and nearby St Aloysius College Chapel are all worth seeing. There's a good view from Kadri Hill, and temples such as Shri Yogeshwar Math are nearby. There may still be a shipping service which makes its way, with many stops, along the coast between Mangalore and Bombay.

Places to Stay

Nirmal Lodge, near the bus stand, has rooms at Rs 20. The government *Tourist Home* at Kadri Hills, about three km away and just opposite the All India Radio Station, has rooms, also a dorm. There are *Railway Retiring Rooms* at the station.

At the other end of the scale there's the *Moti Mahal Hotel* (tel 22211) on Fahnir Rd with rooms at Rs 125/175 or with air-con at Rs 150/200. The *Summer Sands Beach Resort* (tel 6400) is at Ullal, five km from Mangalore, and has rooms at Rs 100/120 or with air-con at Rs 125/150.

The newish *Hotel Navaratna* (tel 27941) on K S Rao Rd has singles/doubles at Rs 50/80 or with air-con at Rs 100/125, but it looks like it may be subject to rapid deterioration due to lack of maintenance.

Places to Eat

Good vegetarian meals are served upstairs at the *Taj Mahal Restaurant* near the bus stand. *Navratna Restaurant* is also near the bus stand, another good place for a quick meal while waiting for a bus.

Getting There

Air Indian Airlines has daily flights to and from Bangalore (Rs 307) and twice daily to and from Bombay (Rs 662).

Rail The twice-weekly Bangalore-Mangalore fast passenger train takes about 16 hours for the 447-km trip. Fares are Rs 42 in 2nd class, Rs 168 in 1st. Trivandrum-Mangalore takes about 14 to 16 hours for the 635-km trip via Calicut, Ernakulam and Quilon. Fares are Rs 55 in 2nd class, Rs 221 in 1st.

Madras-Mangalore is a 900-km trip taking around 18 hours with fares of Rs 70 in 2nd class, Rs 288 in 1st. Direct trains between Delhi and Mangalore take 2½ days for the 3036-km trip. Fares are Rs 176 in 2nd class, Rs 734 in 1st.

Bus A Goa government bus (Kadamba) to Panaji leaves the main bus stand at 11.30 am, but beware – it leaves earlier if full. It takes nearly 10 hours at a fare of around Rs 65. This is a super-luxury bus and the trip is pretty reasonable. It would be possible to do the journey for less by taking an ordinary bus from Mangalore to Karwar, crossing by ferry and then taking another bus to Panaji – only for those desperate to save rupees. The trip will speed up when the bridge is completed at Karwar. Southern Travels have a slightly more expensive night bus.

To Hassan the Rs 20 minibuses are much faster than the regular buses.

AROUND MANGALORE
If you enjoyed Sravanabelagola there are several other famous Jain pilgrimage centres fairly close to Mangalore:

Dharmastala
A little south of the Mangalore-Belur road, about half-way between the two, there are a number of Jain *bastis* at Dharmastala, including the famous Manjunatha Temple. There is also a 14-metre-high statue of Lord Bahubali which was erected in 1973.

Venur
Mid-way between Mangalore and Dharmastala, 41 km from the latter, Venur has eight *bastis* and the ruins of a Mahadeva temple. An 11-metre-high statue of Lord Bahubali stands on the south bank of the Gurupur River, where it was installed in 1604.

Mudbidri
At this site 22 km from Venur there are 18 *bastis*, the oldest of which is the Chandranatha Temple with its 1000 richly carved pillars.

Karkala
A further 31 km north of Mudbidri are several important temples and a 13-metre-high statue of Lord Bahubali, which was completed in 1432.

JOG FALLS
Near the coast, 348 km north-west of Mysore at the terminus of the Birur railway line, Jog Falls are the highest in India. The Shiravati River drops 253 metres in four distinctly separate falls known as the Rani, the Rocket, the Raja and the Roarer. During the dry season the falls are less impressive and during the wet they may be totally obscured by mist. The best time to see them is just after the monsoon. The most exciting view seems to be from the top of the Raja, where you can see it fall over the Roarer! Even in the dry season the ever-changing fans of rainbows over the falls are superb.

To get to the falls take the road towards Sirsi, cross the bridge, turn left and take the second path on your left. Don't fall off the cliff! There's a swimming pool with diving platforms at the falls.

Places to Stay
There's the *Hotel Woodlands* (tel 22) or the Karnataka Government *Youth Hostel*, which has dormitory accommodation. There is also an electricity board *Guest House* and a Power Corporation *Guest House*, since there is a major hydro-electric power plant nearby.

If you're travelling north from Mangalore you can overnight at Hhonavar, where the *Krisna Lodge* is adequate at Rs 25 a double and the *Kamat Hotel* underneath it is a good place to eat.

UP THE COAST

There are a number of good beaches and interesting small ports along the coast from Mangalore to Goa. Ullal Beach is only five km from Mangalore itself.

Udipi

Further up the coast from Mangalore is Udipi, where the 13th-century Shri Krishna Temple is located. There's also a *Tourist Bungalow* here. Manipal, five km from Udipi, has a large college with many foreign students and a major hospital.

Malpe

Only five km from Udipi, Malpe has a good beach, swimming and fishing.

Maravanthe

There's another good beach here, nine km from Coondapur. Kollur, 30 km from Maravanthe, is a famous pilgrimage centre. Mookambika Temple was founded by Shankaracharya.

Ankola

There's a little-used beach at this small village. Near the highway are ruins of the walls of the fort of King Sarpamalika, also a temple. The Shri Venkatraman dates to the same period, about the 15th century. In an unmarked mud-brick garage near the temple are two giant wooden chariots, of a size to be pulled by elephants, carved every cm with scenes from the *Ramayana*. Near Ankola the village of Gokarna is an important pilgrimage place due to the Mahabaleshwara Temple.

... a realistic little town. The taxi drivers at the bus station indicated it by pointing the direction to lodging, rather than offering to take me there – does this suggest 'untouristed'? Two processions were proceeding through the incredibly crowded small mall on the night I arrived there. One was schlepping a god around, the other distributing bits of fire to the shops. The tinkers in the pot stands were beating on their pots with a better rhythm than the drummers in the procession.

Ray Spears, USA

Places to Stay & Eat *Jai Hind Lodge* is a 'dingy, wretched pit' but at Rs 10 for a single it's cheap. The toilets smell. *Azab's Cold Drinks* is nice. No restaurants to speak of, just meals places.

Karwar

Only a short distance south of Goa, 56 km north of Gokarna, Karwar has excellent beaches. You can make trips up the Kali River from Karwar and there's an *Inspection Bungalow* (tel 305) for accommodation. Between 1638 and 1752 there was an English factory involved in the pepper trade at Karwar.

Inland from Karwar

Near Yallapur on the Hubli-Karwar road are Magod Falls (*Tourist Home* nearby) and Lal Guli Falls.

OTHER PLACES IN CENTRAL KARNATAKA

Chitradurga

On the Bangalore-Hampi road Chitradurga has a famous fort of the Naik Pallegars (chieftains) of the 17th and 18th centuries. There's a cheap lodge opposite the bus maintenance depot.

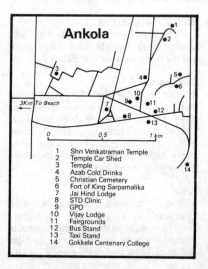

Ankola

1	Shri Venkatraman Temple
2	Temple Car Shed
3	Temple
4	Azab Cold Drinks
5	Christian Cemetery
6	Fort of King Sarpamalika
7	Jai Hind Lodge
8	STD Clinic
9	GPO
10	Vijay Lodge
11	Fairgrounds
12	Bus Stand
13	Taxi Stand
14	Gokkele Centenary College

Vijayanagar

Narahari Brindavana

Purandaradasara Mandapa
Old Stone Bridge

Vishnu Temple
Vittala Temple

King's Balance

Tungabhadra River

Rama Temple

Canal

Talarigattu Gate

Sule Bazar

To Kampli

Virupaksha Temple
Hemakuta Temple
Hampi Bazar
Achyutaraya Temple

Krishna Temple
Narasinha Colossus

Vishnu Temple
Malyavanta Raghunatha Temple

Chandikeswara Temple

Hanuman Temple

Lotus Mahal & Watch Tower

To Hampi Power House

Underground Temple
Elephant Stables

Ganesha Temple

Hazara Rama Temple
Palace Area

Mint

Queen's Bath

Siva Temple

Bhima's Gate

Virabhadra Temple

P W D Bungalow
Museum

Domed Gate

Pattabhirama Temple

Basavanna Temple

Kamalapura Village

To Hospet

Nagareswara Temple

0   0.5   1Km

Harihar

On the Bangalore-Hubli railway line, Harihar has a Hoysala temple dating from 1223 AD. Shri Harihareswara was later added to in 1268 by Soma, who built Somnathpur near Mysore. The image in the temple is of Harihar, half-Shiva, half-Vishnu. There is a *Travellers Bungalow*.

Sringeri

In the lush coffee-growing hills of Chikmagular, near Harihar, Sringeri is the southern seat of the orthodox Hindu hierarchy. The other three centres founded by Shankaracharya are Joshimath in the

Himalaya (north), Puri (east) and Dwarka (west). The very interesting Vidyashankar Temple has zodiac pillars and a huge paved courtyard. A beautifully clean second temple is dedicated to Sharada, the goddess of learning. The Tunga River flows past the old monastery in this charmingly unspoilt town.

Gadag

There are a number of interesting temples in this cotton-growing town south of Badami. The Shiva temple of Trimbakeswar (or Trikuteswar), the 'Lord of the

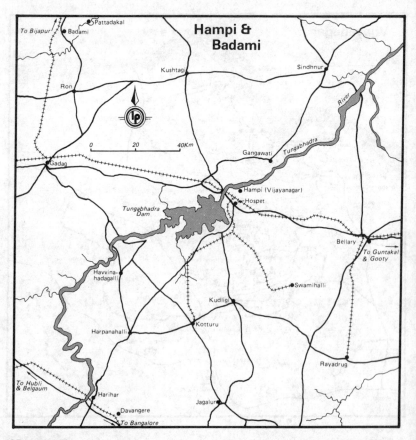

Three Peaks', is elaborately carved. In the back of the enclosure is the Temple of Saraswati, with a porch supported by extremely elegant pillars.

Lakkandi

Only 13 km south-east of Gadag, Lakkandi has several interesting temples, including the fine Kashi Vishwanath Temple, Nandeswar Temple and the partially ruined but very finely carved Iswara Temple. Near the latter temple, which is thought to have been built by the architect and sculptor of Halebid, is a fine *baoli* or well. Beyond this is a temple to

Manikeswar, another name for Krishna.

HAMPI (population 1500)

Hampi (Vijayanagar) was once the capital of one of the largest Hindu empires in Indian history. Founded by the Telugu princes Harihara and Bukka in 1336, it reached the height of its power under Krishnadevaraya (1509-29), when it controlled the whole of the peninsula south of the Krishna and Tungabhadra rivers, except for a string of commercial principalities along the Malabar coast. Comparable to Delhi in the 14th century, the city covered an area of 33 square km, was surrounded by seven concentric lines of fortification and was reputed to have had a population of about half a million. It maintained a mercenary army of over one million according to the Persian ambassador, Abdul Razak, which included Muslim mounted archers to defend itself from the Muslim states to the north.

Hampi's wealth was based on control of the spice trade to the south and the cotton industry of the south-east. Its busy bazaars, described by such European travellers as Nunez and Paes, were centres of international commerce. The religion was a hybrid of current Hinduism with the gods Vishnu and Shiva being lavishly worshipped in the orthodox manner though, as in the Hoysala kingdom, Jainism was also prominent. Brahmins were privileged, *sati* (the burning of widows on the funeral pyres of their husbands) was widely practised and temple prostitution was common. Brahmini inscriptions discovered on the site date the first settlement here back to the 1st century AD and suggest that there was a Buddhist centre nearby.

The empire came to a sudden end in 1565 after the disastrous battle of Talikota when the city was ransacked by the confederacy of Deccan Sultans (Bidar, Bijapur, Golkonda, Ahmadnagar and Berar), thus opening up southern India for conquest by the Muslims.

Hampi is set in a strange and beautiful landscape – hill country strewn with enormous, rounded boulders – with the Tungabhadra River running through the centre of it. It has a magic quality to it and the ruins are superb, though scattered over a large area. It is possible to see all the main sites in one day on foot if you start early, but a hired bicycle makes life a lot easier. Signposting on the site is somewhat inadequate and a lot of the land between the ruins is planted out with sugar cane and other crops. All the same, even where the trail is indistinct, there are plenty of cattle and goat tracks so you can't really get lost.

Information
There are good Archaeological Survey of India maps of the area in Hampi Bazaar, next to the Lotus Mahal in the palace area and outside the Archaeology Office at Kamalapuram. A publication entitled *Hampi* by Mitchell and Fritz describes the general layout of the ruins and is distributed by the Tourist Office in Hospet. A book on sale at the Malligi Guest House Book Store called the *Forgotten Valley* also provides good information.

Things to See
The most interesting sites include the Vittala Temple with its famous stone chariot, musical pillars and incredible sculptural work, supposed to be the highest achievement of Vijayanagar art. The Purandara Dasara Mandapa (the riverside temple) stands near a ruined stone bridge which used to span the Tungabhadra River. There are two markets, the Sule and Hampi bazaars – the latter is partially occupied by squatters, a surreal sight!

Other sites include the Achutaraya Temple, palace area with its Dasara Platform, Lotus Mahal, Queen's Bath and Watchtower. The Elephant Stables are supposed to be one of the largest in the world. Hazarama Temple or 'temple of 1000 Ramas' was formerly the royal house of worship and contains beautifully preserved carvings of the various incarnations of Vishnu and scenes from the *Ramayana*. The Virupaxa Temple complex is reputed to predate the founding of the Vijayanagar empire and is the only temple in the ruins still used for worship.

Excavation at Hampi started in 1976 by the Archaeological Survey of India in collaboration with the Karnataka state government, and is still continuing.

Places to Stay
If you'd prefer to stay near the ruins rather than in Hospet, the *Hampi Power*

Station Inspection Bungalow is three km from Kamalapuram. The chances are that you'll get in without prior reservation, but if you want to make sure contact the Superintending Engineer (tel 8272), HES, Tungabhadra Board, Tungabhadra Dam, Hospet. A pleasant, carpeted double with fan and a rather grubby bathroom costs just Rs 8. If you want a meal (veg or non-veg) you must order it before 5 pm as they go down to the village to buy the ingredients. Those at rock bottom have found spartan rooms at Virupaxa Temple for only Rs 5.

Places to Eat

There are several simple cafés in Kamalapuram where you could get a meal. Elsewhere there is a *Government Tourist Canteen* between Hazarama Temple and the palace site which has a *very* limited menu – omelettes are the only thing available – although they do have ice-cold beers. There is also the *Sri Sngameshwara Hotel*, a simple café in Hampi Bazaar, and a chai shop next to the Varaha Temple near Sule Bazaar – a very friendly little place. Fruit sellers usually hang around between the King's Balance and Vittala Temple.

Getting Around

Hampi is 13 km from Hospet, the town which most people use as a base. There are two main points of entry to the ruins – Hampi Bazaar and Kamalapuram -- and buses run frequently to these two points from Hospet. As an alternative to the buses you can hire a bicycle in Hospet, which definitely makes the going easier since there is no transport between the various sites. 'Not if you get five punctures', reported one unhappy bicyclist! If you're walking, expect to cover at least seven km just to see the main sites. It is possible to see most of the ruins in a day, though two days would allow a more leisurely pace.

HOSPET (population 114,000)

Most people who come to see the Vijayanagar ruins at Hampi use Hospet as a base. It's a fairly typical Karnataka country town with dusty roads, plenty of bullock carts, bicycles and dilapidated buses. There's an unobtrusive industrial area near Tungabhadra Dam.

For much of the year Hospet is not a particularly interesting place in itself, but because it has a large Muslim population it comes alive during the festival of Moharam. If you're here at this time don't miss the firewalkers, who walk barefoot across the red-hot embers of a fire that's been going all day and night. Virtually the whole town turns out to watch or take part and excitement gets to fever pitch around midnight. The preliminaries which go on all day appear to be a bewildering hybrid of Muslim and Hindu ritual and quite unlike any other Muslim festival I've ever seen.

Information

The Tourist Information Office, Station

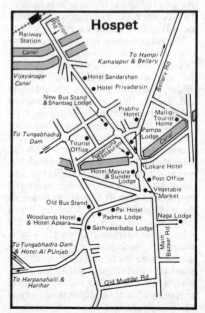

Rd, is run by friendly people with a good selection of information. Their duplicated handout on Hospet, Hampi and Tungabhadra is fairly comprehensive and they have a free map of the ruins and a book on the excavation work. They conduct tours on some days of the week if there are a sufficient number of interested tourists. The tour costs Rs 20 and includes Tungabhadra Dam, but make sure there is an English-speaking guide.

Places to Stay

Malligi Tourist Home (tel 8377), off Hampi Rd, is definitely the pleasantest hotel in town and, for the price, it's one of the better budget hotels in south India. Rooms – all with attached bathrooms, fan and mosquito nets – cost Rs 20/40 and there are larger rooms for three or four. The rooms are pleasantly decorated, there's running hot water between 6 and 10 am and the management is very friendly. They also have two air-con rooms. A rickshaw from the station costs about Rs 2.

Hotel Priyadarshini at V/45A Station Rd opened in 1986 and is slightly more expensive at Rs 27/48 or Rs 70/100 with air-con. They have a TV lounge. *Hotel Sandarshan* (tel 8574), Station Rd has singles/doubles with attached bathroom for Rs 18/35 and a vegetarian restaurant. It's convenient for the railway and bus station but the rooms are not as pleasant as the Malligi.

Hotel Mayura (tel 8418), Gandhi Chowk opposite the GPO, has rooms with and without attached bathroom from Rs 10 to Rs 25 and there's a vegetarian restaurant downstairs. *Lokare Lodge* (tel 8447), Station Rd, is a pleasant lodge with rooms at Rs 8 to Rs 10 or Rs 20 with attached bathroom. *Padma Lodge* (tel 8780) is opposite the old bus stand. The rooms have attached bathrooms and they're cheap but very basic; there's no hot water at any price. There is a good view from the roof though.

The *Shanbag Hotel*, New Bus Stand,

has rooms at Rs 15 or at Rs 25 with attached bathroom and also a dormitory. Then there are *Railway Retiring Rooms*, the *Pampa Lodge* on Station Rd, *Janatha Lodge* and *Naga Lodge* down a side street off the main bazaar. These places all have rooms from around Rs 10 to Rs 25.

If you want to stay near the ruins at Hampi it is possible to stay at Kamalapuram. There is also the *Tourist Home* near Tungabhadra Dam.

Places to Eat

For vegetarian set meals you can't beat those at the *Prabhu Hotel*, the restaurant at the Malligi Tourist Home. Their meals are excellent and a real bargain. The *Pai Hotel* near the Padma Lodge also does very good vegetarian set meals.

For non-vegetarian food try the *Nagarjuna Bar & Restaurant* at the junction of Gandhi Chowk and Station Rd. It has ice-cold beer and a wonderful visitors' book going back for years. If you like *plenty* of ginger in your food try the *Prabhu Hotel* on Hampi Rd – not to be confused with the other Prabhu Hotel at the Malligi. The *Am Ruth Cream Parlour* has excellent vegetarian snacks and milkshakes. It's to the right of the bus station, off the main road on a side street. Three km from Hospet the new *Hotel Al Punjab* serves good north Indian food.

Getting There

Rail The Hospet railway station has a healthy quota allotment for the express trains between Hubli and Bangalore and they are rarely booked up more than one day in advance. If you are heading to Hospet from Goa either by train or bus it is necessary to change at Hubli. Hospet to Hubli takes about 3½ hours; see the Hubli section for onward travel.

Bus There are 12 express buses daily on the 358-km trip to Bangalore from 7 am to 11.45 pm. There's also a luxury overnight KSTDC bus which costs Rs 55; regular buses take hours longer.

Heading for Goa there are two buses daily for the 3½-hour trip to Hubli. Hyderabad is 445 km away and there are two express buses daily. Badami is 170 km and there is one bus daily. There are two direct buses to Bijapur and the 190-km trip takes six hours.

It's five hours from Hospet to Bagalkot and another hour to Badami. Buses depart hourly to Bellary. Other services include Davanegere, Shimoga and Karwar.

Getting Around
The Hospet railway station is a 15-minute walk or Rs 1 to Rs 2 by rickshaw from the centre of town.

Buses run frequently to Hampi from the New Bus Stand and the trip takes about half an hour and costs Rs 1.75. The terminus is at Hampi Bazaar, but you can also get down at Kamalapuram and walk into the ruins from there or rent a bicycle. A taxi would cost Rs 100 for a round trip to Hampi but a share-taxi would only cost Rs 4 per person. Taxis from Kamalapuram to Hospet cost Rs 1.50 per person and go when they are full (they take four or five people).

Buses depart frequently from Hospet to Tungabhadra Dam. The buses have 'TB Dam' on the front. The 15-minute trip costs Rs 0.60. If you find yourself waiting a long time for a bus back to Hospet from the dam, walk down to the junction at the bottom. There are more frequent buses to and from there.

TUNGABHADRA DAM
If you've spent any time browsing through Indian tourist literature you'll know that the Indians love their dams and will go into the most breathless eulogies to put them on the tourist map and project their unsurpassed potential as 'picnic spots'. Possibly it comes from living in a country where famine was always just around the corner when there were no facilities to compensate for a failed monsoon. Whatever the reason, Tungabhadra gets the

same treatment, but if you've seen dams before this one isn't going to radically alter your appreciation of them. If you've already visited Hampi and have time to spare, then it's worth a visit as there's very little else of note in Hospet. Two Netherlanders (lots of dams and dykes there so they must have been appreciative) wrote that it was terrific!

The literature makes the dubious claim that the Tungabhadra is the largest masonry dam in the world. It is 2421 metres long and 49 metres high and has created a lake some 370 square km in area. Begun in 1945 and completed in 1953 at a cost of over one billion rupees, the dam is used to generate electricity and to irrigate Bellary and Raichur in Karnataka, and Cuddapa and Kurnool districts in Andhra Pradesh.

Places to Stay
Naturally, a *Tourist Home* has been built below the dam where tourists are encouraged to stay but it's very inconvenient for anything other than the dam. Rooms, all with attached bathroom, cost Rs 15 to Rs 40. A multi-star western-style hotel, the *Vaikunta Guest House*, overlooks the dam on the hilltop. There are frequent buses to the dam from the bus station in Hospet.

CHALUKYAN CAVES & TEMPLES
Set in beautiful countryside amongst red sandstone hills, rock-hewn 'tanks' (artificial lakes) and peaceful farmlands, these three small rural villages were once the capital cities of the Chalukyan empire which ruled much of the central Deccan between the 4th and 8th centuries AD. Here you can see some of the earliest and finest Dravidian temples and rock-cut caves with forms and sculptural work that provided inspiration for the later Hindu empires which rose and fell in the southern part of the peninsula before the arrival of the Muslims. Though principally promoters of the Vedic culture, the Chalukyans were tolerant of all sects, and

elements of Shaivism, Vaishnavism, Jainism and even Buddhism can be found in many of their temples, especially in the rock-cut caves at Badami.

Aihole

At Aihole, the capital between the 4th and 7th centuries, can be seen Hindu temple architecture in its embryonic stage from the earliest Ladkhan Temple to the later and more complex structures like the Kunligudi and Durgigudi temples. The Durgigudi is particularly interesting, probably unique in India, being circular in shape and surmounted by a primitive gopuram – those structures which typify the temples throughout Tamil Nadu. There are over 70 structures in and around this village which stand witness to the vigorous experimentation in temple architecture undertaken by the Chalukyans. Most are in a good state of preservation.

Badami

Badami, the later capital from about 540 until 757 AD when the Chalukyans were overthrown by the Rashtrakutas, is magnificently nestled in a canyon and is famous for its rock-cut temples. Cut into the cliff-face of the red sandstone hill and overlooking the picturesque tank of Agastyatirtha (itself constructed in the 5th century), these caves display the full range of religious sects which have grown up on Indian soil. There are five caves altogether, four of them artificial and one natural, all connected by flights of steps. Of the rock-cut temples, two are dedicated to Vishnu, one to Shiva and the fourth is a Jain temple. The natural cave is a Buddhist temple. Fragments of a fresco in the upper Vaishnavite temple show that the art of painting had reached the same stage of perfection as sculpture, and it's probable that most of the images in these caves are the originals.

The caves are only one of the many things to be seen at Badami. All over the sides and tops of the hills, which enclose the tank on three sides, are temples and fortifications, carvings and inscriptions dating not just from the Chalukyan period but from other times when its value as a fortress site has been appreciated. After it fell to the Rashtrakutas, Badami was occupied successively by the Chalukyans of Kalyan (a separate branch of the Western Chalukyans), the Kalachuryas, the Yadavas of Devagiri, the Vijayanagar empire, the Adil Shahi kings of Bijapur and the Marathas.

All these various rulers have left their mark at Badami, and there's even a Pallava inscription dating back to 642 AD when their king Narasimhavarman briefly overwhelmed the Chalukyans and occupied Badami for 13 years before being driven out again. Of these other monuments, some of the most beautiful are the two groups of lakeside temples (known as the Bhutanatha temples). Reflected in the water of the tank, they're a most enchanting sight and have the simplicity and freshness found in the very early Pallava temples at Mahabalipuram, south of Madras. The Archaeological Museum, on the north side of the tank, is also well worth a visit. It houses superb examples of sculpture collected locally, as well as the remarkable Lajja-Gauri images of a fertility cult which flourished in the area.

Badami is a small town; off the main street it's full of narrow, winding lanes, old houses, the occasional Chalukyan ruin and tiny squares. It's a pleasant place and people are friendly, but the street kids can be incredibly persistent in hassling you for pens and money. They'll follow you down the streets in packs chanting 'Ta, ta!', 'Ta, ta!' or 'One pen!', 'One pen!' Of course you get this elsewhere in India, in most places in fact, but it's the persistence with which they do it here that's surprising. Yet if you meet another traveller you'll be lucky; very few come this way.

Pattadakal

Pattadakal reached the height of its glory during the 7th and 8th centuries, when most of the temples here were built. It was not only the second capital of the Badami Chalukyans, but the place where all coronations took place. The most important monument here, the Lokeshwari or Virupaksha Temple, is a huge structure with sculptures that narrate episodes from the Hindu epics the *Ramayana* and *Mahabharata* as well as throw light on the social life of the early Chalukyans. The other main temple, Mallikarjuna, has sculptures which tell a different story – this time from the *Bhagvadgita*, the story of Lord Krishna. The old Jain temple with its two stone elephants, about a km from the centre, is also worth visiting.

Orientation & Information

Badami, Pattadakal and Aihole are fairly close to each other and can be visited from a single base – either Badami or Aihole, or Bagalkot if you want a better class of accommodation. There are no accommodation facilities at Pattadakal. Both Badami and Bagalkot are on the railway line which runs from Gadag to Bijapur. Local buses connect Badami, Pattadakal and Aihole, but you deserve a medal for tenacity and endurance if you can locate the right bus.

There are no charges for visiting the monuments or Archaeology Museum, but the attendants at the cave temples won't allow flash photography. The so-called Archaeological Office on the main road in Badami has a painted sketch map of the Badami-Pattadakal-Aihole area on the wall, but nothing else. It appears that the staff (when they're actually around) are paid simply to 'oversee' the attendants, who loaf about at the cave temples and museum. They have no information at all.

At the first cave temple you can buy a copy of *The Cave Temples of Badami* by A M Annigeri for Rs 4. If you'd like more detail about them or about the other monuments at Badami, it's worth buying though it's written in typically verbose Indian English and peppered with nonsense like 'This shows dwarfs dancing in different poses . . . . Some of them have interesting hair-styles . . . . They are also engaged in different activities . . . . Visitors forget themselves at the sight of these delightful dwarfs' and 'These dwarfs are very amusing and create laughter . . . . These arrest the attention of the visitors'.

Places to Stay

Badami There are only two places to stay in Badami (many places are called 'Something or Other Boarding' but, in fact, they have no rooms to let). The *KSTDC Tourist Bungalow & PWD Inspection Bungalow*, about a half km from the centre of town, is undoubtedly the best place to stay. Rooms with attached bathroom cost Rs 47/60.

Sri Mahakuteshwar Lodge, next to the bus stand, is run by a reincarnation of The Mekon (Dan Dare fans). Rooms are available with and without attached bathroom and range from around Rs 10 to Rs 40. The downstairs rooms are another determined attempt to re-create the Black Hole of Calcutta. All rooms have been painted in the most ugly and depressing combination of colours I've seen anywhere in India. Mosquito nets are provided, but since they don't reach the mattress, are useless. The locks they provide are a joke but by this time you should have acquired one of your own.

The *Travellers Bungalow* close to the railway station is very inconvenient for anything other than the trains. *Sri Laxmi Lodging* in the town centre has very good food and very variable rooms at Rs 12/20 – some are fine, some are filthy.

Aihole If you'd like to stay at Aihole, accommodation is available at the KSTDC *Tourist Bungalow*. Rooms with attached bathroom cost Rs 20 to Rs 40. It's of a

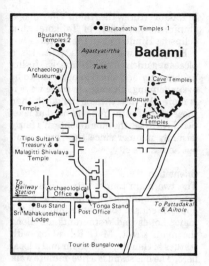

Badami

Bhutanatha Temples 1
Bhutanatha Temples 2
Agastyatirtha Tank
Archaeology Museum
Cave Temples
Temple
Mosque
Cave Temples
Tipu Sultan's Treasury & Malagitti Shivalaya Temple
To Railway Station
Archaeological Office
Bus Stand
Sri Mahakuteshwar Lodge
Tonga Stand
Post Office
To Pattadakal & Aihole
Tourist Bungalow

similar standard to the Tourist Bungalow at Badami but the food is poor.

Places to Eat

Probably the best place to eat in Badami is the *Hotel Sanman*, next to the Sri Mahakuteshwar Lodge. It has a la carte vegetarian and non-vegetarian meals, cold beers, other alcoholic drinks and loud music from current Indian films which the proprietor is loathe to turn down.

There are plenty of small cafés, especially around the tonga stand on the main road, but most of them serve only tiffin. If you want a vegetarian set meal go to either *Sri Veera Bhadreshwar Boarding* or *Sri Raghuvendra Bhavan*, opposite one another at the tonga stand; the latter has excellent masala dosas and not very friendly people. One of the friendliest tiffin places is the *Udaya Vilas* on the main road. Great vegetarian food at the *Laxmi Vilas Hotel*.

Getting There

Rail All the trains from Badami station are passenger trains; there are no express trains. The trains may be slow but the journeys I made on this line were the liveliest I had in India. Virtually the whole of the way from Gadag to Bijapur buskers boarded the train and entertained the passengers. Some of them were excellent, particularly two women (very unusual to see this in India) who sang Kannada folk songs in harmony to the accompaniment of a harmonium. Judging by the way people delved into their pockets for small change and quietly sang along with them, they must have been singing some very popular songs.

If you're heading for Bijapur you can take the train either for Bijapur or Sholapur. Similarly, if heading for Gadag you can take the train either for Gadag or Hubli. The journey from Badami to Bijapur takes 3½ hours and costs about Rs 8.

Bus To Bijapur there is one bus daily and the four-hour journey costs Rs 14. There are a dozen buses daily to Bagalkot. Buses also run to Hospet, Hubli, Bangalore and Gadag.

Getting Around

Rail Badami railway station is five km from the village itself and a tonga from outside the station will cost you Rs 2 to Rs 3. The locals pay less than a rupee but you need brown skin, black hair, brown eyes and fluency in Kannada to get it for that! Local buses also run between the station and village approximately hourly. It takes a whole day to see the cave temples, ruins and fortifications at Badami. You could see Pattadakal and Aihole on the following day if you start out as early as possible.

The nearest railway stations to Aihole are at Bagalkot (46 km) and Badami (51 km).

Bus Finding buses from Badami used to be chaotic but is now much improved. The trip to Aihole takes two hours and costs Rs 4. There are also Aihole-Bagalkot buses.

Bicycle It's convenient and pleasant to hire a bicycle to explore these places, but the round trip will involve cycling about 100 km. If you're not up to this then you'll need two days. The bicycle shop opposite the tonga stand on the main road in Badami hires bicycles for Rs 5 a day plus a deposit. I was asked for Rs 300 deposit, but managed to persuade them that my student card was a passport and left that.

BIJAPUR (population 120,000)

Bijapur is the Agra of the south, full of ruined and still-intact gems of 15th to 17th-century Muslim architecture – mosques, mausoleums, palaces and fortifications. Like Agra, it has its world-famous mausoleum, the Golgumbaz. This enormous structure with its vast hemispherical dome, said to be the world's second largest, dominates the landscape for miles around. The austere grace of the monuments in this city is in complete contrast to the sculptural extravaganza of the Chalukyan and Hoysala temples further south. The Ibrahim Roza mausoleum, in particular, is one of the most beautiful and finely proportioned Islamic monuments anywhere in the world.

Bijapur was the capital of the Adil Shahi kings (1489-1686), one of the five splinter states formed when the Bahmani Muslim kingdom broke up in 1482. The others, formed at roughly the same time, were Bidar, Golconda, Ahmednagar and Gulbarga. Like Bijapur, all these places have their own collection of monuments dating from this period, though the ones at Bijapur are definitely more numerous and generally in a better state of preservation. The rulers of these states spent their days fighting each other and the Hindus further south, with any spare resources being used to build palaces and tombs for themselves and to pay for entertainers at their courts. They did, however, occasionally act in consort and it was a confederacy of these states which

in 1565 overthrew the Hindu Vijayanagar empire at the battle of Talikota, thus eclipsing Hindu rule in the south.

Bijapur is well worth a visit. It's a pleasant garden city, still strongly Muslim in character and small enough not to be overwhelming, although in some ways it is more like the cities of the north than those of the south. You will need at least two days to see the monuments in a fairly leisurely manner since they are spread out across the city.

Orientation

The two main tourist attractions – the Golgumbaz and the Ibrahim Roza – are at opposite ends of the town. Almost all the major hotels and restaurants are along the main street, M G Rd, along with statues of Gandhi, Ambedkar and a local hero. The bus stand is a five-minute walk from this road along the citadel ruins.

Information

The Tourist Office is in Hotel Adilshahi. They have sketch maps of the city and verbose leaflets which don't tell you a great deal and take up lots of paper. If you want a guidebook to the city, pick up a copy of *Tourist Guide to Bijapur* by H Padmaraj, on sale at many stationers and bookshops.

The best place to change money is at the State Bank of India in the public offices in the Citadel. They have the current exchange rates and are fast. Avoid the banks in the old part of the city on the north side of Gandhi Rd (especially the Canara Bank). They'll keep you waiting all morning, tell you a lot of unadulterated garbage and then offer you a rate well below par.

Golgumbaz

The most famous and largest though not the most beautiful monument in Bijapur, the Golgumbaz is a simple building with four walls that enclose a majestic hall 1704 square metres in area, and are buttressed by octagonal seven-storied towers at each of the corners. This basic structure is capped by an enormous dome said to be the world's second largest (St Peter's in the Vatican City, Rome, has the largest). St Peter's dome diameter is 42 metres, St Paul's in London is 33 metres, the Golgumbaz is 38 metres. It was built in 1659.

Around the base of the dome at the top of the hall is a three-metre-wide gallery known as the 'whispering gallery', since the acoustics here are such that any sound made is repeated 10 times over (some guidebooks claim it's repeated 12 times over). Fortunately you won't have the chance to get embroiled in that controversy as the 'whispering gallery' is permanently full of kids running amok and screaming at the top of their voices. 'Bedlam gallery' would be a more appropriate name. Access to the gallery is via a narrow but, for most of the way, well-lit staircase up the left-hand tower. There's a notice on the wall just before you enter the gallery from outside the dome. It says, 'Silence please'.

The views over Bijapur from the base of the dome are superb. You can see virtually every other monument and almost the whole of the city walls from here. You can also ascend the south-east tower, the right tower as you enter from the south.

The Golgumbaz is the mausoleum of Mohammed Adil Shah (1626-56), two of his favourite wives (Rambha and Arusbib), one of his daughters and a grandson. Their caskets stand on a raised platform in the centre of the hall, though their actual graves are in the crypt, reached by the steps under the western door.

Hours are 6 am to 6 pm and entrance costs Rs 0.50 except on Fridays, when it's free. If you get there before 7 am you may actually be able to test the gallery acoustics too – the school groups don't start to arrive until then. Shoes have to be left at the entrance. An archaeological museum in the front opens at 10 am and is free.

Ibrahim Roza

The beautiful Ibrahim Roza was constructed at the height of Bijapur's prosperity by Ibrahim Adil Shah II (1580-1626) for his queen. Unlike the Golgumbaz, which is impressive only for its immensity, here the emphasis is on elegance and delicacy. Its minarets, which rise 24 metres from the ground, are said to have inspired those of the Taj Mahal. It's also one of the few monuments in Bijapur with substantial stone filigree and other sculpturally decorative work.

Buried here are Ibrahim Adil Shah, his queen Taj-Sultana, his daughter, two sons, and his mother Haji Badi Sahiba. There is no entrance charge, but shoes should be left on the steps up to the platform on which the mausoleum stands.

Jami-e-Masjid

This is another finely proportioned building with graceful arches, a fine dome and a large inner courtyard containing fountains and a reservoir. It's quite a large monument covering an area of 10,800 square metres and has room for 2250 worshippers. Spaces for them are marked out in black on the polished floor of the mosque. There's very little ornamentation here, the whole concept being one of simplicity. The flat roof is accessible by several flights of stairs. This mosque was constructed by Ali Adil Shah I (1557-80), who was also responsible for erecting the fortified city walls and Gagan Mahal, and for installing a public water system.

Asar Mahal

To the east of the citadel, the Asar Mahal was built by Mohammed Adil Shah about 1646 to serve as a Hall of Justice. The rooms on the upper storey are profusely decorated with fresco paintings, many of them using foliage and flower motifs, some portraying male and female figures in various poses. The latter have all been defaced. The building was also used to house two hairs from the Prophet's beard. The front of the building is graced with a square tank still fed by conduits from Begum Tank.

The Citadel

Surrounded by its own fortified walls and wide moat in the city centre, the citadel once contained the palaces, pleasure gardens and Durbar Hall of the Adil Shahi kings. Unfortunately, most of them are now in ruins although some superb fragments remain.

Of the important fragments, the Gagan Mahal probably gives the best impression of the scale on which things were built here. This monument was built by Ali Adil Shah I around 1561 to serve the dual purpose of a royal residence and a Durbar Hall. Essentially it's an enormous hall completely open to the north, so that an audience outside the hall had a full and unobstructed view of the proceedings on the raised platform inside. The hall was flanked by small chambers used to house the families of the royal household. Through suspended screens which enclosed

the projecting balconies overhanging the Durbar on all sides, the ladies of the harem were able to witness the proceedings below. Most of this has now been destroyed, but the immense arch which spanned the whole front of the Durbar still stands.

Nearby, the Sat Manzil, Muhammed Adil Shah's seven-storied palace, is now substantially in ruins and the remaining parts of it are used for public offices, but just across the road stands one of the most delicate pieces of architecture in Bijapur. This is the Jala Manzil or Jala Mandir, a water pavilion no doubt intended as a cool and pleasant place to relax in the days when it was surrounded by secluded courts and gardens within the palace precincts. Opposite the citadel on the other side of Station Rd are the graceful arches of Bara Kaman, the ruined mausoleum of Ali Roza.

Malik-e-Maidan

This huge cannon must be one of the largest mediaeval guns ever made. It

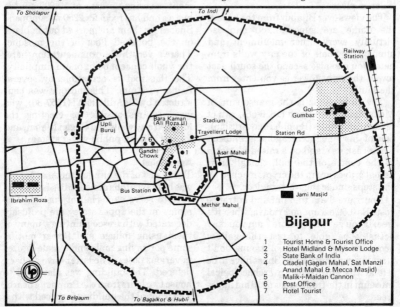

Bijapur

1	Tourist Home & Tourist Office
2	Hotel Midland & Mysore Lodge
3	State Bank of India
4	Citadel (Gagan Mahal, Sat Manzil Anand Mahal & Mecca Masjid)
5	Malik-i-Maidan Cannon
6	Post Office
7	Hotel Tourist

measures over four metres long and almost 1.5 metres in diameter, and is estimated to weigh 55 tonnes! It was cast in 1549 by Mohammad-bin-Hasan Rumi, a Turkish officer in the service of the king of Ahmednagar, from an alloy of copper, iron and tin. It was brought to Bijapur as a trophy of war and set up here with the help of 10 elephants, 400 oxen and hundreds of men. Its outer surface is polished dark green and adorned with inscriptions in Persian and Arabic, one of them attributed to the Moghul emperor Aurangzeb saying that he subdued this gun, the name of which means Monarch of the Plains.

Upli Buruj

This watchtower, 24 metres high and located on high ground near the western walls of the city, was built by Hyder Khan, a general in the service of Ali Adil Shah I and of Ibrahim II, in about 1584. The tower can be climbed by a flight of steps which winds around the outside of the building. The top commands a good view of the city and is well furnished with guns, powder chambers and water cisterns. The guns are much longer than the Malik-e-Maidan (nine metres and 8.5 metres respectively), but of much narrower bore – only 29 cm.

Other

There are a number of other monuments worth visiting in Bijapur, the most important being the Anand Mahal and the Mecca Masjid, both in the Citadel, and the Mehtar Mahal. The much-photographed Mehtar Mahal is typical of the architecture of Bijapur and has been richly decorated with sculptural work. It serves as an ornamental gateway leading to a small mosque.

Places to Stay

The former Ashok Travellers Lodge on Station Rd has become an annexe of the Hotel Adilshahi with rooms at Rs 60/90. It's pleasantly situated in a well-main-tained flower garden. Hotel Adilshahi itself is Bijapur's best place to stay, with rooms at Rs 35/50. The rooms are carpeted and have mosquito nets and attached bathrooms. Furthermore the staff are friendly and the Tourist Office is located here, though the food is nothing special. It's just off Station Rd at the entrance to the citadel and there's a quiet, pleasant courtyard ablaze with bougainvillea.

Hotel Samrat is a new one near the Golgumbaz and has rooms at Rs 35/50. If you're on a tight budget, Hotel Tourist on Gandhi Rd (a continuation of Station Rd) is good value. Rooms with attached bathroom cost Rs 18 to Rs 22 and there's a good vegetarian restaurant downstairs.

At the rock-bottom end of basic the Hotel Midland on Station Rd has a variety of rooms from Rs 10 to Rs 15 and a good vegetarian restaurant downstairs. 'My room had not been cleaned since the 1973 All India Convention of Carnivorous Bugs & Communicable Diseases took place there', commented a reluctant visitor. Other places with similarly basic bathless rooms include the much superior Mysore Lodge next door to the Midland on Station Rd; and the Krishna Lodge, an old stone house converted into a lodge which even has dorm beds for Rs 5.

At the other extreme Hotel Mayur Adil Shahi (tel 934) on Anandmahal Rd is centrally located and has rooms at Rs 70/140.

Places to Eat

Good vegetarian set meals (excellent curd) can be found in the restaurant attached to the Hotel Tourist – lunch or dinner costs Rs 5. The popular Swapna Hotel, on the 1st floor of the building next to the Tourist Hotel, has excellent non-vegetarian food. Their Rs 11 chicken biriyani is especially good.

Hotel Adilshahi has a restaurant which serves western-style breakfasts in the morning but their food is nothing special. It has been suggested that the MRF beer they feature here stands for 'Made Really Foul'.

Getting There

Rail Bijapur station has a healthy quota of sleeping berths allotted to it on all the main trains which pass through Sholapur and Gadag. These are rarely taken up more than one day in advance. The line from Bijapur to Gadag is a slow but entertaining ride as it's the permanent pitch of at least three lots of buskers.

Bijapur to Hubli takes as much as nine hours for the 243-km trip (it's usually late) and costs Rs 25 in 2nd class, Rs 99 in 1st.

Bus Buses run from Bijapur to Aurangabad (441 km, Rs 51), Badami (one goes via Kerur), Bangalore (630 km, half dozen daily, two of them express buses), Belgaum (dozen buses daily), Bidar, Gadag, Miraj and Pune. There's a daily express bus to Bombay; the 669-km trip takes 12 hours and costs Rs 60. A daily bus also runs to Vasco da Gama in Goa. The 412-km trip to Hyderabad takes 12 hours and costs Rs 48; there are two buses daily.

Use the Bagalkot bus as an alternate way of getting to Badami, Aihole and Pattadakal. There's a daily express bus to Bellary. You can use this bus to get to Hospet and the Vijayanagar ruins at Hampi, although there are also two direct buses daily (eight hours, Rs 37). Most of the dozen or so Hubli buses go via Jamkhandi but there is also a luxury bus via Belgaum. The trip to Sholapur takes two to three hours and there are a dozen buses daily.

Getting Around

The most convenient forms of local transport are auto-rickshaw and tonga (horse-drawn cart). From the railway station to Hotel Adilshahi will cost Rs 3 (local people pay less than a rupee). From the Hotel Adilshahi to Ibrahim Roza will cost about Rs 4 per person in a tonga (these take four or five people). Haggling

is a must. There's a surprisingly uncrowded local bus from the bus stand to the railway station via the Golgumbaz. The fare is only Rs 0.50 and it runs every 15 minutes.

HUBLI

Hubli is important to the traveller principally as a major railway junction on the routes from Bombay to Bangalore, Goa and north Karnataka. Other than this it's an industrial city and there's precious little to see. It's included since you may have to spend the night here on your way somewhere else. All the main services – hotels, restaurants, etc – are conveniently close to the railway station.

Places to Stay

The highly recommended *Hotel Ajanta* (tel 2216), Jaichamarajanaga, is a short distance off the main street and visible from the railway station. It's a huge place and you'll always be able to find accommodation here. Rooms have a fan and bathroom and cost Rs 20 to Rs 40. The rooms are pleasantly decorated and provided with mosquito nets, there is room service and the staff are friendly. On the ground floor there is a 'meals' café.

Modern Lodge is on the main street before you get to the Ajanta. This is a typical one-night-stand hotel with basic facilities. Rooms cost Rs 20 to Rs 30 and although they have a fan and attached bathroom you must provide your own sheets. There is a 'meals' café on the ground floor.

Further down the street from the Modern Lodge on the opposite side of the road is the *Udipi Hotel*, which offers similar accommodation to the Modern Lodge and has a ground-floor meals café.

Places to Eat

The *Kamat Hotel*, close to the Modern Lodge, offers fairly good plate meals at lunchtime and in the early evening. During the rest of the day coffee and tiffin are available. The *Bombay Restaurant* is next door to the Kamat and provides plate meals similar to those at the Kamat for the same price. There is an excellent juice bar/ice cream parlour opposite the Kamat Hotel.

Getting There

Hubli is a major rail junction on the Bombay-Bangalore route and for trains to Bijapur and Hospet. If you're heading for Goa (either Vasco da Gama or Margao) the 237 Hubli-Miraj 'Link Express' has a 2nd-class three-tier sleeping coach and another combined 1st class/2nd class two-tier sleeping coach attached to the train which goes all the way to Vasco, thus avoiding the need to change at Londa.

At Londa these coaches are detached from the 237 and added to the 206 Miraj-Vasco Express at about 3.30 am. There's a quota in the three-tier sleeper, the two-tier sleeper and for 1st class at Hubli station. The full quota is rarely taken up even on the day of departure, but booking closes at 4 pm. After that time you have to apply for reservations at the Ticket Collector's Office, but don't count on getting one at that time. There's also baksheesh flying around for these unbooked sleepers.

If you are changing trains at Londa, the restaurant at the station is very good.

BELGAUM (population 250,000)

In the north-west corner of the state and on the Bombay-Pune-Goa bus-and-rail route, Belgaum was a regional capital in the 12th and 13th centuries. Today there's an old town area and a more modern cantonment. 'Sunset Point' on the old racetrack road offers fine views.

Fort

The old oval-shaped stone fort is very near the bus terminus – it's of no real interest unless you like malarial moats, although Gandhi was locked up here once. Outside the fort gate to the left is the local cattle market, which is colourful and aromatic.

Mosques, Temples & Other Buildings

The Masjid-Sata Mosque dates from 1519. There are also two interesting Jain temples, one with an extremely intricate and complicated roof, while the other has some fine carvings of musicians. Belgaum's watchtower gives a nice panorama of the countryside.

Gokak Falls

A little north of Belgaum and eight km off the railway line from Gokak Rd are Gokak Falls, where the Ghataprabha River takes a 52-metre drop.

Places to Stay & Eat

Hotel Sheetal (tel 25483) in Khade Bazaar is clean, bright, efficient and very comfortable. Ordinary rooms are Rs 20/40, deluxe ones Rs 25/45. The bus station canteen has excellent and inexpensive snack foods. Belgaum also has lots of sweet shops.

THE NORTH-EAST

Bidar

This little-visited town in the extreme north-east corner of the state was the capital of the Bahmani kingdom from 1428 and later of the Barid Shahi dynasty. It's a pleasant town with a splendid old 15th-century fort containing the Ranjeenmahal, Chini Mahal and Turkish Mahal palaces. The impressive Khwaja Mahmud Gawan Madrasa and the tombs of the Bahmani and Barid kings are also worth seeing.

Places to Stay The KSTDC *Tourist Home* near the bus station has rooms from Rs 20 to Rs 30, or you can try the *Sri Venkateshwara Lodge* on the main street. The adjoining *Kalpana Hotel* has good food.

Gulbarga (population 160,000)

This town was the Bahmani capital from

1347 until its transfer to Bidar in 1428. Later the kingdom broke up into a number of small kingdoms – Bijapur, Bidar, Berar, Ahmednagar and Golconda. The last of these, Golconda, finally fell to Aurangzeb in 1687. Gulbarga's old fort is in a much deteriorated state, but has a number of interesting buildings inside.

The Jami Masjid, inside the fort, is reputed to have been built by a Moorish architect during the late 14th or early 15th century in imitation of the great mosque in Cordova, Spain. The mosque is unique in India, with a huge dome covering the whole area, four smaller ones at the corners, and 75 smaller still all the way around. The fort itself has 15 towers. Gulbarga also has a number of imposing tombs of Bahmani kings, a shrine to an important Muslim saint and the temple of Sharana Basaveshwara.

Places to Stay There are a number of hotels in the town and a KSTDC *Tourist Home*.

Raichur

The town of Raichur was part of the 13th-century Kakatiyas kingdom and then part of the Bahmani kingdom. It became the first capital of Bijapur when the Bahmani kingdom fragmented in 1489, and later came under the rule of Vijayanagar. The fort, with its impressive gate, has a citadel with a fine view from the top.

Places to Stay Raichur has *Inspection* and *Tourist Bungalows* as well as hotels such as the *Uma Hotel* near the railway station and the *Ashok Hotel* near the bus stand.

Tony's Notebook

Getting Things Done

You soon realise why better-off Indians have lots of servants. It's nothing to do with being lazy, it's simply that everything takes so long in India that if you did it all yourself you'd never have had the time to become better off in the first place. Travellers, too, find that a lot of their time is tied up in interminable queues or trying to find out when things depart or where a room is available. The answer is don't do it – get somebody to do it for you. In India labour is cheap; there'll always be some boy at the hotel who will happily stand in the line for hours to pick up your train ticket – all for a few rupees baksheesh.

Similarly those hotel touts who swoop out to meet new arrivals in any reasonable-sized town really do fill a need if every place in town is full. They'll know exactly where the last free room is and save you a lot of futile marching around. If you want something in India and you don't know where to get it, don't waste your time looking – announce loudly, 'I want to take a taxi to X tomorrow'. Nine chances out of 10 somebody at your hotel will have heard about the empty taxi going back to X and willing to take a passenger for half price. Get somebody else to do the leg work!

Trees

Deforestation is a major problem in many parts of Asia and critically so in India, where despite tree-planting projects and much talk the remaining forest cover is disappearing rapidly. You don't have to see missing forests to realise the pressure on trees in India – almost any tree will tell its story. It's a rare one that goes untouched. If a branch can be reached it will be wrenched off for firewood. Almost any tree you see seems to have half its branches lopped off, and the fact that so many continue to grow despite their stunted condition is a real tribute to the resilience of nature. Trees and India's crushing population just don't go together.

Hard Work

The old adage that 'many hands make light work' certainly gets its come-uppance in India. Every job has at least twice as many people doing it as are necessary, and inevitably the result is that it takes twice as long. Indian hotel employees always seem to be scurrying around cleaning things up, but as often as not that simply means sweeping everything under the bed.

Andhra Pradesh

Population: 53 million
Area: 276,754 square km
Capital: Hyderabad
Main language: Telegu

The large state of Andhra Pradesh was created by combining the old princely state of Hyderabad with the Telegu-speaking portions of the former state of Madras. Most of the state stands on the high Deccan Plateau, sloping down to the low-lying coastal region to the east where the mighty Godavari and Krishna rivers meet the Bay of Bengal in wide deltas.

Andhra Pradesh was once a major Buddhist centre and part of Ashoka's large empire until it broke apart. Traces of that early Buddhist influence can still be seen in several places. Later the Chalukyas held power in the 7th century but they in turn fell to the Chola kingdom of the south around the 10th century. In the 14th century Muslim power finally reached this far south, and for centuries the region was an arena for Hindu-Muslim power struggles. Finally it was taken over by a general of the Moghul emperor Aurangzeb in 1713. His successors, the Nizams of Hyderabad, ruled the state right down to independence.

The final Nizam of Hyderabad was reputed to be one of the richest men in the world, but Andhra Pradesh itself is one of the poorest and least developed states in India. New dams and irrigation projects are improving the barren, scrubby land of the plateau but much of the state remains economically backward. There is not a great deal of interest in Andhra Pradesh apart from the capital, Hyderabad. Visitors with a keen interest in architecture or archaeology may wish to visit some of the excavations or old temple sites.

HYDERABAD (population 2,500,000)
Like Bijapur further to the west in

neighbouring Karnataka state, Hyderabad is an important centre of Islamic culture and offers central India's counterpart to the Moghul splendours of the northern cities of Delhi, Agra and Fatehpur Sikri. Consisting of the twin cities of Hyderabad and Secunderabad, it is the capital of Andhra Pradesh state and famous as the former seat of the fabulously wealthy Nizams of Hyderabad. Here lively, crowded bazaars surround huge and impressive Islamic monuments dating from the 16th and 17th centuries. The city – India's fifth largest – was founded in 1590 by Mohammed Quli, the fourth of the Qutab Shahi kings. They ruled this part of the Deccan from 1512 until 1687, when the last of their line was defeated by the Moghul emperor Aurangzeb, following suspension of the annual tribute due to their nominal suzerain in Delhi.

Before the founding of Hyderabad, the Qutab Shahi kings ruled from the fortress city of Golconda, 11 km to the west. The extensive ruins of this fort, together with the nearby tombs of the Qutab Shahi kings, are the principal attractions of any visit to Hyderabad.

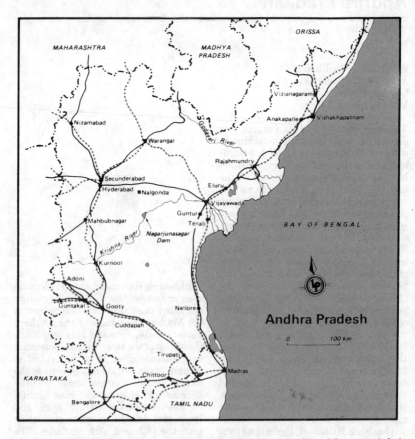

Following Aurangzeb's death in 1707, Moghul control over this part of India rapidly waned and the viceroys who had been installed to look after the interests of the empire broke away and established their own independent state, first taking the title of Subedar and later that of Nizam. These new rulers became embroiled in the rivalry between the French and British for control of India during the latter half of the 18th century as allies of the French, but after the defeat of the French and subsequent Maratha raids which seriously weakened their kingdom, they were forced to conclude a treaty with the British and relinquish most of their power.

When independence came to India in 1947, the Nizam toyed with the idea of declaring an independent state and went so far as to allow an Islamic extremist group to seize control. This, however, led to his downfall, as the Indian government, mindful of Hyderabad's Hindu majority of around 85% and unwilling to see the creation of an independent and possibly hostile state in the centre of the Deccan, used the insurrection as an excuse to occupy Hyderabad in 1948 and force its accession to the union. The dusty city retains much of its 19th-century atmosphere, unlike cities further south.

Orientation

The old city of Hyderabad itself straddles the River Musi, while to the north the Hussain Sagar lake effectively divides Hyderabad from its twin city Secunderabad. Most of the historical monuments, the bulk of the hotels and restaurants used by travellers, the city bus depot, Salar Jang Museum and the zoo are all in the old city. Most of the budget hotels are in the area known as Abids between the GPO and Hyderabad railway station. The more expensive hotels are, in general, clustered around the Secretariat building at the south end of Hussain Sagar.

The main road to Abids is Nehru Rd but is often referred to as Abids Rd. From the roundabout in front of the GPO, Nampally Station Rd (or Station Rd) runs straight up to Hyderabad Railway Station. Nampally High Rd goes across in front of the station.

The ruins of Golconda Fort and the tombs of the Qutab Shahi kings lie about 11 km to the west of the city. The newer city of Secunderabad is on the north side of Hussain Sagar and, if you are coming by train, you will get off at Secunderabad railway station (the main station). The YMCA, YWCA and Youth Hostel are all here, but few travellers stay in Secunderabad itself. To get to Hyderabad you will have to take a bus, auto-rickshaw or taxi (about 10 minutes' journey). Few trains pass through Hyderabad railway station.

Information

There are tourist information kiosks at both Secunderabad and Hyderabad railway stations but they're not very good. The state and national tourist offices are both in Himayatnagar on Himayatnagar Rd. The Government of India Tourist Office (tel 66877) is in the Sandozi Building; it's helpful and has a good supply of literature. A bit further down and on the other side of the road is the Andhra Pradesh Tourist Office (tel 223384-5) in the Lidcap Building. Along this same street you'll also find the Andra Pradesh State Tourism Development Corporation (tel 237360) in Diamond House, just before the Sandozi Building. The India Tourism Development Corporation (tel 220730) is in the Lidcap Building. These latter two organisations operate tours in Hyderabad and elsewhere in the state.

Air India (tel 222883) and Indian Airlines (tel 72051-3) are both in Saifabad near the Secretariat building. Hyderabad has an incredibly active bazaar.

Charminar

Standing in the heart of the old walled city, this huge triumphal arch was built by Mohammed Quli Qutab Shah in 1591 to commemorate the end of a plague in Hyderabad. It's surrounded on all sides by lively bazaars, and the views from the top are superb. An image of this building graces every packet of *Charminar* cigarettes, one of India's most popular brands. The monument is open every day from 9 am and entry costs Rs 0.50. No guides are necessary.

Mecca Masjid

Situated next to the Charminar, this is one of the largest mosques in the world and is said to accommodate up to 10,000 worshippers. Construction began during the reign of Mohammed Quli Qutab Shah in 1614 but was not finished until 1687, by which time the Moghul emperor Aurangzeb had annexed the Golconda kingdom. The colonnades and door arches are made out of single slabs of granite, which history records were quarried 11 km away and dragged to the site by a team of 1400 bullocks! The minarets were originally planned to have been much higher than they are, but the enormous cost of erecting the main part of the building apparently forced the ruler to settle for something less grand.

This very beautiful and impressive building is disfigured by huge awnings of chicken wire, erected to stop birds nesting in the ceiling and liming the floor. They still get in and the steel supports which have been carelessly cemented into the tiled and patterned floor to hold this netting are nothing short of vandalism.

To the left of the mosque is an enclosure containing the tombs of the Nizams.

Birla Mandir (Naubat Prahad) Temple

This stunningly beautiful modern Hindu temple, built out of white marble, graces the rocky hill which overlooks the south end of Hussain Sagar. It's a very popular Hindu pilgrimage centre but non-Hindus are allowed inside. There's no entry fee and the priests make no effort to press you for contributions. There are excellent views over the city from the summit, especially at sunset. The temple is open 4 to 9 pm on weekdays, 7 to 11 am and 3 to 9 pm on Saturdays and Sundays.

Nearby is the Birla Planetarium with presentations in English several times daily. Admission is Rs 5.

Salar Jang Museum

This is India's answer to the Victoria & Albert Museum in London. The collection was put together by Mir Yusaf Ali Khan (Salar Jang III), the prime minister of the Nizam. It contains 35,000 exhibits drawn from all corners of the world, including sculptures, woodcarvings, religious objects, Persian miniature paintings, illuminated manuscripts, armour and weaponry. You'll also see the swords, daggers and clothing of the Moghul emperors and of Tipu Sultan, as well as many other objects. All of this is housed in one of the ugliest buildings imaginable.

The museum is open daily except Fridays from 10 am to 5 pm, but avoid Sundays when it's bedlam. Entrance costs Rs 2 (Rs 1 if you have a student card). Bags and cameras must be deposited in the entrance hall.

Archaeological Museum

In the public gardens between Nampally High Rd and the branch railway line which leads to Hyderabad railway station, this museum has a small collection of archaeological finds from the area together with copies of the Ajanta frescoes. Other odds and ends include an Egyptian mummy and a superb temple cart just inside the entrance gate. Hours are daily except Mondays from 10 am to 5.30 pm. Entry is Rs 0.25.

The gardens also feature an aquarium in the Jawahar Bal Bhavan. It's open 10.30 am to 1 pm and 1.30 to 5.30 pm.

Golconda Fort & Tombs of Qutab Shahi Kings

You need at least half a day to explore these extensive ruins, so the Tourist Office bus tours, which bring you here for just one hour, are ridiculously short. That is only sufficient to quickly climb to the summit and, equally quickly, come back down again.

Though the bulk of the ruins date from the time of the Qutab Shahi kings (16th-17th centuries), the origins of the fort have been traced back to the earlier Hindu periods of Deccan history when the Yadavas and later the Kakatiyas

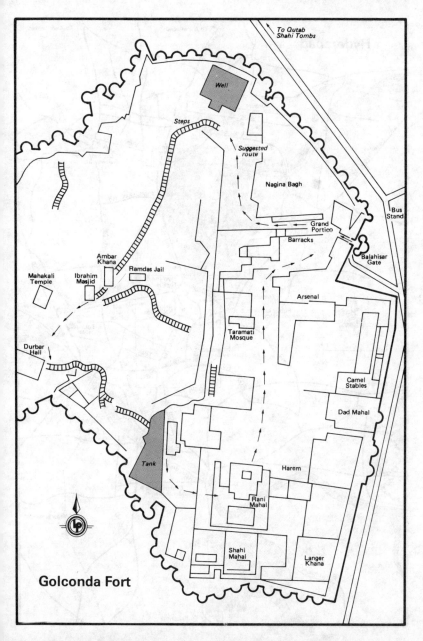

To Qutab Shahi Tombs

Well

Steps

Suggested route

Nagina Bagh

Grand Portico

Barracks

Bus Stand

Balahisar Gate

Ambar Khana

Ramdas Jail

Mahakali Temple

Ibrahim Masjid

Arsenal

Taramati Mosque

Durbar Hall

Camel Stables

Dad Mahal

Tank

Harem

Rani Mahal

Shahi Mahal

Langer Khana

Golconda Fort

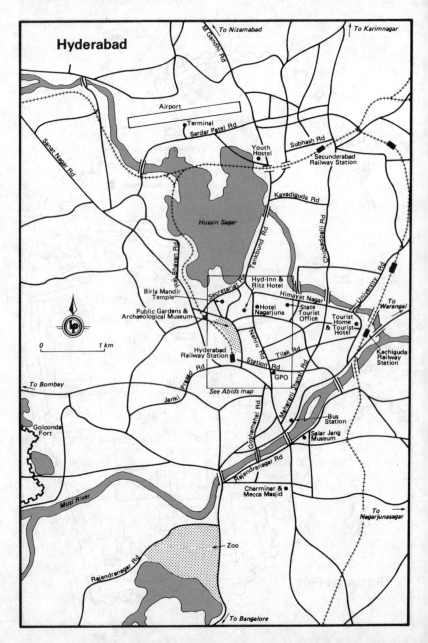

ruled this area of India. In 1512, Sultan Quli Qutab Shah, a Turkoman adventurer from Persia who had risen to be governor of Telangana under the Bahmani rulers, declared independence and made Golconda his capital.

It remained the capital until 1590, when the court was moved to the new city of Hyderabad, but subsequently came into its own again on two separate occasions in the 1600s when Moghul armies from Delhi were sent against the kingdom to enforce payment of tribute. Abul Hasan, the last of the Qutab Shahi kings, held out in the fort of Golconda against a Moghul army commanded by Emperor Aurangzeb for seven months before losing it by treachery in 1687. Following Aurangzeb's death early in the next century, his viceroys (later the Nizams) made Hyderabad their capital and abandoned Golconda.

The citadel itself is built on a granite hill 120 metres high and surrounded by battlemented ramparts constructed of large blocks of masonry, some of them weighing several tonnes. The massive gates are studded with large pointed iron spikes intended to prevent elephants from battering them and are further protected by a cordon wall to check direct attack. Outside of the citadel stands another battlemented rampart with a perimeter of 11 km. All of these walls are in an excellent state of preservation.

Unfortunately, many of the structures inside the citadel – the palaces and harem of the Qutab Shahi kings, assembly halls, arsenal, stables and barracks – have suffered a great deal from past sieges and the ravages of time, but enough remains to give a good impression of what the place must once have looked like. Restoration work is underway on the buildings around the Balahisar Gate (the main entrance) – even the wrought iron work is being replaced – but it will be many years before this is anywhere near completion.

One of the most remarkable features of this fort is its system of acoustics whereby the sound of hands clapped in the Grand Portico can be heard in the Durbar Hall at the very top of the hill – a fact not lost on tour guides (or their charges) who do their utmost competing with each other to make as much noise as possible! There is also supposed to be a 'secret' underground tunnel leading from the Durbar Hall to one of the palaces at the foot of the hill but, predictably, you are not allowed to investigate this.

The tombs of the Qutab Shahi kings lie about a km north of the outer perimeter wall of Golconda. These graceful structures are surrounded by landscaped gardens, and a number of them display beautifully carved stonework. Entrance to these tombs costs Rs 0.25 plus Rs 2 if you have a camera (Rs 10 for a movie camera). A small guidebook, *Guide to Golconda Fort & Qutab Shahi Tombs*, is on sale at both the tombs and the fort and is a good Rs 2 investment if you intend to spend the day here.

Service bus Nos 142 or 119 from Nampally High Rd opposite Hyderabad Railway Station will take you to the main fort entrance at Balahisar Gate. The 11-km trip takes about an hour and costs about Rs 2. An auto-rickshaw will cost about Rs 8 one way.

Nehru Zoological Park

One of the largest in India, the zoo is spread out over 120 hectares of landscaped gardens with the animals contained in large, open enclosures. They don't look any less bored than animals in zoos anywhere else in the world, but at least here an effort has been made, which is more than can be said for most other zoos in India.

The park is open from 9 am to 6 pm daily except Mondays. There's also a Lion Safari Park which you can go around in a minibus and a toy train for children. It's a very popular park with local people.

Other

Tourist literature on Hyderabad raves on about various 'lovely picnic spots', such as the lake of Osmansagar (Gandipet) from which the city receives its water supply, but take this with a pinch of salt. They're nothing special. Lovers of graffiti should make a point of visiting Osmania University, where every available square cm of stone and brickwork is plastered with political slogans. This is fairly common in many Indian cities, but here it's taken to extreme lengths!

Tours

Andhra Pradesh Travel & Tourism Development Corporation and the India Tourism Development Corporation both offer daily tours of the city. The tours usually start at 8 am, run to 6 or 6.30 pm and cost Rs 30. Additionally you usually have to pay your own entrance fees. There are also half-day tours for Rs 25. Visits are made to Osmania University, Birla Mandir, Qutab Shahi Tombs, Golconda Fort, Gandipet, Salar Jang Museum, Charminar, Mecca Masjid and the Zoological Gardens.

Unfortunately the time allowed for each sight is ludicrously short. Five and 10-minute stops are the order of the day and a lot of time is wasted on an inconsequential visit to Gandipet Lake. Even Golconda Fort only gets an hour and the tombs of the Qutab Shahi kings just over an hour. If there is anything to choose between them, then the ITDC tour would be the better of the two as the lunch break is in Abids, in the centre of Hyderabad, where there is a choice of restaurants. The state corporation tour halts at Gandipet where there is no choice and facilities are very limited.

Places to Stay – bottom end

Other than the Youth Hostel, YMCA and YWCA, the best cheap places are on Nampally High Rd, opposite Hyderabad railway station. There are others (very basic) around the Charminar.

The *Royal Lodge* is on Nampally High Rd near the junction with Station Rd. There are plenty of rooms in this huge place; singles cost Rs 30 to Rs 33, doubles Rs 50 to Rs 60 or Rs 65 to Rs 70 for deluxe rooms. The more expensive rooms have attached bathrooms. In this same enclave, around a courtyard, there are several other 'Royal' hotels. The *Royal Home, Royal Hotel, Neo Royal Hotel* and *Gee Royal Lodge*! Good grief. The *Royal Hotel* has singles from Rs 20 to Rs 30, doubles with shower at Rs 35. Across the road is the extremely basic *Asian Lodge* which has singles from Rs 15.

There are a number of good bottom to middle-bracket hotels in Abids along Station Rd, which runs between Hyderabad Railway Station and the GPO. Starting from the station end of the road, the *Hotel Imperial* (tel 225436) is right on the corner and has singles for Rs 30, doubles for Rs 40 to Rs 46. All rooms have attached bathrooms but the rooms on the roof are unbearably hot in summer. Their restaurant serves vegetarian and non-vegetarian food. The *Palace Hotel* (tel 52011) has singles/doubles at Rs 50/75 and a few more expensive air-con rooms.

A few doors down is the *Hotel Apsara* (tel 556105) with rooms with attached bath at Rs 45/60. It's a fairly large multi-storey place. Further down the road on the other side is the big *Sri Brindavan Hotel* (tel 220820) which has large, airy rooms with fan and attached bath for Rs 50/70. Avoid the noisy rooms over the main road at the front; most of the rooms are built around a quiet courtyard well off the road. The staff are friendly (but watch out for extra charges) and you even get a newspaper pushed under your door every morning. The Sri Brindavan also has a very good restaurant; see below.

Other budget hotels in the Abids area include the *Sri Anu Hotel* on Nehru Rd near the junction with Station Rd; and the *Metro Lodge* and *Everest Lodge*, both on Tilak Rd near the junction with Nehru Rd.

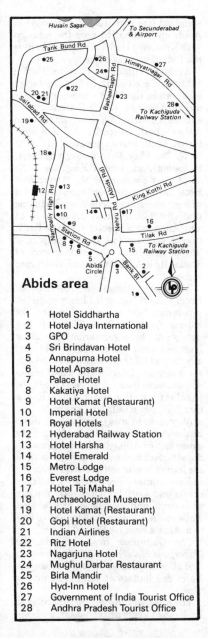

Husain Sagar

To Secunderabad & Airport

Tank Bund Rd

●25   ●26   Himayatnagar Rd   ●27

24●

20 21   ●22   ●23

Saifabad Rd   28●

To Kachiguda Railway Station

19●

18●

12●   ●13

●11   King Kothi Rd

●10   14●   ●17

●9   16

8 7 6   Station Rd   Tilak Rd

●4   To Kachiguda Railway Station

5   15

Abids Circle   3   Bank St   2

Abids area

1.

1   Hotel Siddhartha
2   Hotel Jaya International
3   GPO
4   Sri Brindavan Hotel
5   Annapurna Hotel
6   Hotel Apsara
7   Palace Hotel
8   Kakatiya Hotel
9   Hotel Kamat (Restaurant)
10   Imperial Hotel
11   Royal Hotels
12   Hyderabad Railway Station
13   Hotel Harsha
14   Hotel Emerald
15   Metro Lodge
16   Everest Lodge
17   Hotel Taj Mahal
18   Archaeological Museum
19   Hotel Kamat (Restaurant)
20   Gopi Hotel (Restaurant)
21   Indian Airlines
22   Ritz Hotel
23   Nagarjuna Hotel
24   Mughul Darbar Restaurant
25   Birla Mandir
26   Hyd-Inn Hotel
27   Government of India Tourist Office
28   Andhra Pradesh Tourist Office

Away from Abids the *Tourist Hotel* (tel 65691-7) is close to the Kachiguda Railway Station, which makes it convenient if you're heading for Guntakal, Bangalore or Madras by rail but otherwise out-of-the-way. Rooms cost Rs 30/40.

Even further from the central Abids area, the *Youth Hostel*, behind the Boat Club at the north-eastern end of Hussain Sagar, Secunderabad, offers the cheapest dormitory-type accommodation in town. There are 51 beds and the cost is Rs 5 per night if you have a YHA card, Rs 8 if you don't.

The *YMCA* (tel 57850) and *YWCA* are semi-permanently full with students. Only Secunderabad railway station (tel 70144/5) has *Railway Retiring Rooms*, but you would be lucky to get one since they have only one double room and one dormitory.

Places to Stay – middle

Close to the Ritz Hotel and the lake, the small and pleasant *Hyd-Inn* (tel 38481-5) on Lake Hill Rd, Basheer Bagh has rooms at Rs 75/110 or with air-con for Rs 100/ 175. According to one guest: 'It's a prize with its charmingly decorated rooms and excellent, well-maintained buildings'. Moving back towards Abids, the *Emerald Hotel* (tel 237835-6) is just off Abids Rd on Chirag Ali Lane and has rooms at Rs 90/ 120 or with air-con at Rs 125/175.

Back in the centre of Abids the *Annapurna Hotel* is on Station Rd in amongst the numerous bottom-end and middle-range hotels. Singles here are Rs 80 or with air-con Rs 125. Doubles are Rs 105 to Rs 115 or with air-con Rs 155 to Rs 185. There's also a good restaurant. Closer to the station on Station Rd, *Hotel Kakatiya* (tel 553767-70) has clean and well-kept rooms at Rs 65/90 or air-con doubles from Rs 125 to Rs 150.

Also in Abids, *Hotel Jaya International* (tel 223444) is just off to the left on Nehru Rd as you face the GPO. This very pleasant modern hotel has singles/doubles at Rs 70/90 or with air-con at Rs 110/140.

All rooms have attached bathrooms and the hotel has its own restaurant.

Still close to Abids on the corner of Nehru Rd and King Kothi Rd, the sprawling *Hotel Taj Mahal* (tel 221167) has singles at Rs 55 to Rs 75, doubles at Rs 85 to Rs 120. On the other side of the GPO *Hotel Siddhartha* (tel 557421) has singles from Rs 60 up to Rs 110 with air-con, doubles from Rs 80 to Rs 130 with air-con. On Nampally High Rd, a little north from the railway station, the modern *Hotel Harsha* (tel 236188) has singles from Rs 90 to Rs 110 or with air-con Rs 140. Doubles are Rs 120 to Rs 130 or with air-con Rs 175.

Places to Stay – top end

The small and well-kept old *Ritz Hotel* (tel 33571) is pleasantly situated on Hill Fort Rd, Basheer Bagh, between Nampally High Rd and Nehru Rd. It is one of Hyderabad's more expensive hotels. Rooms cost Rs 275/350 plus 16% for singles/doubles and there are all the usual mod cons, from air-conditioning to swimming pool to tennis courts.

The much larger *Welcomgroup Banjara* (tel 222222) is at Banjara Hills, overlooking the lake and 15 minutes from the railway terminal by car. Singles are Rs 545 to Rs 595, doubles Rs 645 to Rs 695, and again there are all the usual facilities and luxuries.

Other top-end hotels include the centrally located *Hotel Sampurna International* (tel 40165-6) on Mukram Jahi Rd, with rooms at Rs 250/300. *Hotel Deccan Continental* (tel 70981) on Minister Rd has rooms at Rs 235/315 but also cheaper rooms without air-con for Rs 120/180. *Hotel Nagarjuna* (tel 37201) is on Basheerbagh Rd, the extension of Nehru Rd from Abids. The hotel is centrally air-conditioned and rooms are Rs 130/150 or with air-con Rs 200/275.

Places to Eat

Good, cheap vegetarian meals can be found at any *Kamat Hotel*, where the standard fare costs Rs 5. There's one in Abids on Station Rd near the junction with Nampally High Rd and another near the Indian Airlines office.

At the Sri Brindavan Hotel on Station Rd there's good south Indian vegetarian food, while the hotel's more expensive air-con *Shalimar Bar & Restaurant* has excellent Indian, Chinese and western dishes – both vegetarian and non-vegetarian. Main courses are generally Rs 15 to Rs 20. They have a range of beers, including locally brewed Kingfisher at Rs 16. Across Station Rd the *Annapurna* Hotel has an air-con vegetarian restaurant where you can get good food, including thalis for Rs 9, 'Bombay' thalis for Rs 14 and 'Annapurna Special' thalis for Rs 27. Good ice cream too. In the complex of 'Royal' hotels at the station end of Station Rd in Abids, the *Laxmi Restaurant* is good.

The *Saphire Restaurant* in the *Emerald Hotel* just off Nehru Rd has 'wonderful' vegetarian food as well as snacks like masala dosas for Rs 4. There are any number of cheap vegetarian cafés along Nampally High Rd, Station Rd and around the GPO on Nehru Rd. Close to the Emerald Hotel several small places do good fresh fruit juices. Near the Royal Hotel at the station end of Station Rd the *Gop Milk Shop* sells lassi and curd.

As you head away from Abids down Basheerbagh Rd, the *Mughul Darbar* is a glossy fast-food place with snacks (masala dosas for Rs 2.50), ice cream from Rs 4 and the Indian idea of self-service. Beside the Indian Airlines office the *Gopi Hotel* does drinks and south Indian snacks. You can sit outside and look down on the road while you're having a thali for Rs 5 to Rs 7 or a masala dosa for Rs 3.50.

The *Gulmohar Restaurant* in the *Nagarjuna Hotel* has Indian and western food at slightly higher prices. The *Banjara Hotel* has buffets at lunch and dinner time.

The *Ruby Restaurant*, in the centre of Hyderabad's very active bazaar, is a large

Muslim restaurant where, if you are a woman, you may find yourself sitting in a room full of women, traditionally separated from the menfolk in the party!

Getting There
Air There are flights at least daily between Hyderabad and Bangalore (Rs 460), Bombay (Rs 640), Calcutta (Rs 1167), Delhi (Rs 1086) and Madras (Rs 503). Connections to other places, including Bhubaneswar, are less frequent.

Rail The main railway station is at Secunderabad. Hyderabad Railway Station is only a branch line, but if you're heading south to Guntakal, Bangalore or Madras and staying in Abids you can board the train at Kachiguda station instead of going all the way up to Secunderabad. As elsewhere, the fastest night express trains are booked up days in advance, so reserve your seat or sleeper as early as possible.

New Delhi-Secunderabad can take less than 24 hours on the Andhra Pradesh Express. The 1675-km trip costing Rs 110 in 2nd class, Rs 456 in 1st. It's 6½ hours for the 361-km trip on the Golconda Express between Hyderabad and Vijayawada (this train does go from Hyderabad). The fare is Rs 35 in 2nd class, Rs 141 in 1st. The quickest route from Calcutta is to take the Madras Mail from Howrah Station (daily) and change at Vijayawada. If you're coming from Nagpur, change at Kazipet – just west of Warangal.

Bombay-Secunderabad, a distance of 800 km, takes as little as 15 hours on the Minar Express; fares are Rs 65 in 2nd class, Rs 263 in 1st. Madras to Secunderabad is a 510-km trip taking about 15 hours. The fare is Rs 46 in 2nd class, Rs 185 in 1st. The 329-km trip to Bangalore takes 19 hours and costs Rs 32.50 in 2nd class, Rs 131 in 1st.

The line from Secunderabad to Aurangabad is metre gauge – the 517-km trip takes 12 hours at a cost of Rs 46 in 2nd class, Rs 189 in 1st. The express continues

through Aurangabad to Manmad, which is on the Bombay-Delhi line via Bhopal and Agra. The Secunderabad-Ajmer line is also metre gauge. This route goes through Khandwa, Mhow, Indore, Ratlam and Chittorgarh. All the way to Ajmer is a 1818-km trip, taking 39 hours at a cost of Rs 117 in 2nd class, Rs 490 in 1st.

Bus Deluxe buses connect Hyderabad with Bangalore (Rs 100), Bombay (Rs 120), Madras (Rs 120) or Tirupathi (Rs 90). There are also direct buses through to Aurangabad; the trip takes 16 hours.

Getting Around
Airport Hyderabad airport is surprisingly well appointed and less frantic than most other Indian airports. There is no airport bus, but an auto-rickshaw to or from Abids should cost about Rs 10 by the meter. Don't trust the auto-rickshaw wallahs at the airport; make sure the meter is switched on and starts at zero.

Local Transport There are buses, cycle-rickshaws, auto-rickshaws and taxis.

Bus Getting on any service bus in Hyderabad, other than at the terminus, is (as one traveller put it) 'like staging a banzai charge on Guadalcanal'. He wasn't exaggerating! Useful ones which you might be able to get on include: No 2 – Secunderabad Railway Station to Charminar & vice versa; No 7 – Secunderabad Railway Station to Afzalganj & vice versa (this is the one to catch if you're heading for Abids, as it goes down Tankbund Rd and Nehru Rd via the GPO); Nos 119 or 142 – Nampally High Rd (opposite Hyderabad Railway Station) to Golconda Fort & vice versa.

Auto-rickshaw is the cheapest alternative during the day. Unlike those in many other cities in India, the drivers here appear to need no prompting about use of meter. Some sample fares include the YHA to Abids Rs 6, Abids to the

Charminar Rs 4, Secunderabad to GPO Rs 7.

NAGARJUNAKONDA & NAGARJUNASAGAR

Nagarjunakonda, 150 km south-east of Hyderabad on the Krishna River, was once one of the largest and most important Buddhist centres in southern India, spanning a period from the 2nd century BC until the 3rd century AD. In those days known as Vijayapur, it takes its present name from Nagarjuna, one of the most revered of Buddhist monks and founder of the Madhyamika school, who governed the *sangha* for nearly 60 years around the turn of the 2nd century AD. The school he established attracted students from as far afield as Sri Lanka and China.

The site was discovered in 1926 and subsequent excavations, particularly in the '50s and '60s, have unearthed the remains of stupas, *viharas, chaityas* and *mandapas*, as well as some outstanding examples of white marble carvings and sculptures depicting the life of the Buddha. These have been moved to a museum on the site, following a decision to create Nagarjunasagar Dam which will eventually submerge the whole of this area. The dam is one of the largest masonry constructions in the world and India claims that it will create the world's third largest artificial lake.

The Nagarjunakonda panels lack the more elaborate sculptural features of those found further downriver at Amaravathi – 32 km north of Guntur – but are the best you will find in this part of India today. Amaravathi itself, once the capital of Andhra during the Buddhist period but now described in tourist literature as 'a squalid little village', contained over 20 monasteries with more than 1000 monks and had a huge marble stupa unrivalled elsewhere in the world.

Every cm of this stupa and the rail which surrounded it was richly carved and the whole decorated with lamps on festive occasions, but before you rush off to see it you should know that it was largely destroyed at the end of the 18th century by local people in their quest for building material. Marble is excellent raw material for a lime-kiln. The fragments which remained were spirited off to the Madras Museum and the British Museum in London during the 19th century.

Places to Stay

At Nagarjunasagar there is a choice of accommodation maintained by the Andhra Pradesh Travel & Tourism Development Corporation (tel Hyderabad 36252), which includes the *Soundarya Guest House, Project House, Sethu Sadan*, a number of separate cottages, and the *Konda Guest House* at Nagarjunakonda. They're all very reasonably priced and there's also a *Youth Hostel* with dormitory accommodation. Other accommodation can be arranged through the Executive Engineer, R&B Division, Nagarjunasagar Dam, Hill Colony.

Getting There

Bus Probably the easiest way to visit Nagarjunakonda and Nagarjunasagar is to take the deluxe tourist bus from Hyderabad organised by the India Tourism Development Corporation. It departs four days a week at 7.30 am, returns at 9.30 pm and costs Rs 80. The tour includes visits to the Nagarjunakonda Museum, Pylon (an engraved granite monolith from the Buddhist period), Nagarjunasagar Dam, and the working model of the dam.

Local sight-seeing tours of Nagarjunakonda and Nagarjunasagar are organised by the Tourist Department, Project House, Hill Colony, Nagarjunasagar.

If you'd prefer to make your own way there, regular buses connect Hyderabad, Vijayawada and Guntar with Nagarjunasagar. The nearest railway station is at Macherla – a branch line running west from Guntur and ending at Macherla. If coming from Hyderabad, head first for

Guntur. There are regular buses from Macherla to Nagarjunasagar.

Boat If you're not part of one of the local tours or those organised from Hyderabad, launches to Nagarjunakonda Museum, which is on an island in the lake, depart at 9.30 am and 1.30 pm.

WARANGAL (population 160,000)

This was once the capital of the Kakatiya kingdom, which ruled the greater part of present-day Andhra Pradesh from the latter half of the 12th century until the early 14th century, when it was conquered by the Tughlaqs of Delhi. The Hindu Kakatiyas were great builders and patrons of the arts, and it was during their reign that the Chalukyan style of temple architecture and decoration reached the pinnacle of its development.

If you have an interest in the various streams of Hindu temple development and have either visited or intend to visit the early Chalukyan sites at Badami, Aihole and Pattadakal in neighbouring Karnataka state, then an outing to Warangal would be worthwhile.

The Fort

Warangal's main attraction is the enormous deserted mud-brick fort, which has a terrific atmosphere and many interesting features, including carved stones from wrecked Chalukyan temples indiscriminately set in the massive stone walls. These walls form a distinct fortification almost a km inside the outer mud walls. The construction and defences of the gateways are very interesting. The fort was built by the Kakatiyas, who were responsible for the first fort at Golconda – also constructed from mud-brick but later converted to masonry by the Qutab Shahi kings.

Chalukyan Temples

The most notable remaining Chalukyan temples are the Thousand-Pillared Temple on the slopes of Hanamkonda Hill (one shrine of which is still in use), Bhadrakali

Temple on a hillock between Warangal and Hanamkonda, and Shambu Lingeswara or Swayambhu Temple (originally a Shiva temple). The Thousand-Pillared Temple is, however, much inferior to those found further south, and Bhadrakali Temple is not very interesting.

Ramappa Temple at Palampet, 77 km from Warangal, represents a combination of the Chalukyan and the later Hoysala styles. It's hard to get to but reputed to be one of the finest examples of Deccan architecture.

Places to Stay & Eat

Accommodation facilities are modest. A *Tourist Rest House* opposite the English College with rooms at Rs 25 and dorm beds at Rs 8. The *Vijaya Lodge* (tel 4142, 4345) on Station Rd is excellent value although there is no restaurant. Most of the hotels and lodges are on R N Tagore Rd and on Chowrasta. They include *Hotel Nataraj* (about a km from the railway station) and *Krishna Lodge* (both on R N Tagore Rd); and *Annapurna Lodge, Ganesh Lodge, Hotel Kohinoor, Ananda Lodge* and the *Venkatarama Lodge* (all on Chowrasta).

Hotel Ashoka has rooms at Rs 40 or with air-con for Rs 80. They do a good non-vegetarian breakfast (that means eggs, toast and jam). It's hard to find a reasonable non-vegetarian restaurant in Warangal so it's a good place. Good non-vegetarian meals can also be found at the *Kohinoor Hotel*. There are plenty of vegetarian restaurants in town.

Getting There

Air Vayudoot have a three-times weekly flight between Hyderabad and Warangal.

Rail The daily Kakatiya Express takes four hours from Hyderabad to Warangal, half an hour less from Secunderabad. The 152-km trip costs Rs 18 in 2nd class, Rs 70 in 1st. There are also good rail connections to Vijayawada, so you can visit Warangal quite easily if travelling that way. If you're coming from outside the state, Kazipet, a few km west of Warangal, is the most convenient point at which to alight. Regular buses connect Kazipet with Warangal.

Bus Regular buses connect Warangal with Hyderabad, Nizamabad and other major centres of population. Local buses connect Warangal with Kazipet and Hanamkonda.

The Andra Pradesh TDC have a weekly tour to Warangal for Rs 100.

TIRUPATHI & TIRUMALA

The town of Tirupathi and the 'holy hill' of Tirumala, 13 km away in the extreme south of Andhra Pradesh, are two of the most important pilgrimage centres in the whole of India on account of the temple of Sri Balaji at Tirumala. Balaji is the god whose picture you will find in the reception area of most lodges and restaurants in southern India. He's the one with his eyes covered up (since his gaze would scorch the world) and garlanded in so many flowers that the only part of him visible is his feet.

Amongst his attributes is the belief ('realisation' would be a better word as far as his devotees are concerned) that any wish made in front of the idol at Tirumala is granted. With a legend like that, pilgrims flock in from all over India and there are never less than 5000 here at any one time. Such numbers also ensure that the temple is one of the richest in India, though it's fair to say that a lot of its income is ploughed back into schemes to help the poor and into providing shelter for pilgrims on their way to Tirumala. It's considered auspicious to have your head shaved when visiting the temple, so if you see people with shaved heads in south India then you can be pretty sure they've recently been to Tirupathi – this applies to men, women and children.

In order to cope with this army of pilgrims, everything at Tirupathi and Tirumala is organised to keep them fed, sheltered and moving. Most of the hotels and lodges are in Tirupathi so a whole fleet of buses (known as the Tirumala Link Buses) constantly ferries pilgrims to and fro between Tirupathi and Tirumala. To get back down again you'll have to join the wire cages just like everyone else.

The temple is one of the few in India which will allow non-Hindus into the sanctum sanctorum, but before you can do this you must go to the 'Complaints Office' and sign a statement which says, 'I — am of the — religion and have reverence for Sri Balaji'. They will expect you to say you're a Christian and that Tamil Nadu Tourist Development Corporation is your sponsor. After that you pay Rs 25 for 'special darshan' and then you're allowed into the temple. Special darshan allows you to jump the queue ahead of all those who have paid only Rs 5 for ordinary darshan and who have to queue up – often for up to 12 hours – in the wire cages which ring the outer wall of the temple.

In some ways it's commercialism gone mad. There are a whole series of darshans which range from the simplest at Rs 5 up to ones costing thousands of rupees. A huge signpost outside the temple details what is available. Then there are the trinket stalls and the prasad stalls. The laddha prasad, round sweets made with chickpea flour and raisins, are delicious. And, lastly, the wig stalls. Having had your hair shaved off, you can now buy it back (or rather you can buy someone else's).

Places to Stay

Tirupathi is chock-a-block full of hotels and lodges so there's no problem finding somewhere to stay. The *Tourist Rest House* (tel 2794) has rooms at Rs 20/25 and Rs 25/30. *Bhima's Deluxe Hotel* (tel 2501-4) at 42 G-Car St has excellent doubles at Rs 90 – the marble continues from the lobby to the rooms and there are hot showers, comfortable beds and even phones in every room! You can see it from the walkway over the tracks at the railway station. Tirumala only has one hotel offering private rooms – most of the pilgrims stay in vast dormitories which ring the temple.

Getting There

Bus Unless you particularly want to stay in Tirupathi overnight, you can get there and back from Madras easily in one day so long as you make an early start. Tiruvalluvar have express buses from the Esplanade bus station at 9.30 am, 2.30 pm and 8.30 pm as well as many other ordinary buses (the latter are not particularly recommended as they take circuitous routes).

Andhra Pradesh state transport also have buses from the same depot 16 times daily, the first at 4.30 am and the last at 8 pm. Fares range from around Rs 15 to Rs 25 depending on the bus. Getting back to Madras is simplicity itself – just wait at the express bus terminal until a Madras bus arrives, and get on. They're very frequent. The journey takes 3½ to four hours.

Although it's easy to get there under your own steam, most people who visit Tirupathi do so on one of the tour buses operated by Tamil Nadu Tourist Development Corporation, Andhra Pradesh TDC or Karnataka TDC. If you're going to take one of these tours then Madras is the most convenient place to do it from, as the journey is only 3½ hours. Taking a tour bus works out about twice as expensive as doing it yourself, but if you're that keen to save $5 .... From Madras daily tour buses cost from around Rs 120 to Rs 150. From Hyderabad tours operate weekly and cost Rs 275.

Getting Around

Bus Tirumala Link Buses operate from the state bus stand next to the express bus stand and from the Sri Venkateshwara bus station near the tank in Tirupathi. They run from dawn till well past dusk. The fare is Rs 4.50 going up and Rs 3.50

coming down. Getting a bus back down can take some time.

SOUTH OF HYDERABAD

Other places south of Hyderabad include:

Kurnool (population 150,000)
Situated 240 km south of Hyderabad, Kurnool has fragments of its old fortress still standing and a number of mosques and mausoleums. Nearby Mallikarjuna Temple is an important Shiva shrine and a major pilgrimage centre.

Tadpatri

Fifty km south-east of the junction town of Gooty are the remains of two temples dating from around 1485, when they were built by the rulers of Vijayanagar. The riverbank Rameswaraswami Temple was never completed, but is more imposing than the Chintalarayaswami.

Kalahasti & Tiruttani

Kalahasti is another important pilgrimage centre, east of Tirupathi. Almost on the border with Tamil Nadu, 60 km south of Tirupathi, Tiruttani is a very old hilltop temple.

Konai Waterfalls

These waterfalls are 90 km north-west of Madras on the Madras-Uthukottai-Tirupathi road. Get down after Nagalapuram at Narayanawanam and walk two km to the quiet, lonely and unspoilt falls. October to January, after the monsoons, is the best time to go but avoid weekends or public holidays when people come in droves from Madras. Accommodation is available in a small cottage.

Puttaparthi

Prasanthi Nilayam or the Abode of Highest Peace, the ashram of Sri Sathya Sai Baba, is here, 150 km from Bangalore. His followers are predominantly Indian although he has many followers from the west. When he celebrated his 60th birthday in late 1985 400,000 people came to his ashram. It is large, spacious and beautiful and the accommodation and food are good – at least when the numbers aren't overwhelming. It does get very dry here in the hot season.

Getting There Puttaparthi is in Andhra Pradesh but is most easily reached from Bangalore by taking a train or bus to Dharmavaram or Anantapur, the nearest railway station.

EAST COAST

Although the main Calcutta-Madras railway line runs along the east coast of Andhra Pradesh, few travellers stop south of Orissa. During the monsoon the extensive deltas of the Godavari and Krishna rivers may flood, forcing the Calcutta-Madras trains to take an alternate route further inland through Raipur, Nagpur and Hyderabad.

Waltair & Visakhapatnam
(population 400,000)
These two towns have really merged into one and the local people do not observe any distinction between them. The northern residential area can be thought of as Waltair and the booming southern business and industrial area towards the docks as Visakhapatnam (abbreviated as Vizag). The railway station, roughly in the centre, is called Waltair Junction.

Waltair, a popular seaside resort, has rocks and pools as well as several km of sand. The beach must be one of the best in India, unused except by some Russians building a steel works. Simhachalam Hill, about 10 km north of Waltair, has an 11th-century Vishnu temple in fine Orissan style.

Places to Stay Vizag has plenty of hotels right up to five-star level. The excellent bus station has *Retiring Rooms*. Cheap hotels include the *Hotel Poorna* (tel 62344) on Main Rd with rooms from Rs 30. On the same road *Hotel Prasanth* (tel 65282) has rooms at Rs 25/35 and a

dormitory. *Hotel Apsara* (tel 64861) on Waltair Main Rd is more expensive with rooms from Rs 75 to Rs 175.

The *Ocean View* (tel 64828) is near the best (northern) end of the beach and is very comfortable, peaceful and friendly with doubles for Rs 100. The *Dolphin Hotel* (tel 64811-20) has rooms from Rs 150 to Rs 350. The *Sun-n-Sea Park Hotel* (tel 64333) on Beach Rd is even more expensive. Also on Beach Rd the *Palm Beach Hotel* (tel 63006-8) has singles at Rs 135 to Rs 175 and doubles at Rs 175 to Rs 200. *Silver Sands Inn* (tel 63683) at 2 Kirlampudi, Beach Rd has rooms at Rs 80/120 or with air-con at Rs 145/190.

Getting There Vizag is connected by broad-gauge railway line to Raipur and by Indian Airlines directly to Calcutta, Hyderabad and Madras. There's a new and well-organised bus station in Vizag, quite different from the usual bus station confusion. Good services run to and from Puri and Vijayawada.

Rajamundry (population 200,000)
A three-km-long railway and road bridge, the second longest in India, crosses the Godavari River at Rajamundry. This delta region of the Godavari is very flat, but 100 km inland, where the Deccan Plateau drops away to the delta, the scenery is very fine. Yanam, on the coast near Rajamundry, is another portion of the former French enclave of Pondicherry.

Vijayawada (population 380,000)
On the banks of the mighty Krishna River, only 149 km south of Rajamundry and the Godavari River, Vijayawada is the junction for the railway line to Warangal and Hyderabad. Two thousand years ago this was an important Buddhist area and there are interesting excavations upstream at Amaravathi (now much damaged) and Nagarjunakonda. See the Nagarjunakonda section for more information.

To reach Amaravathi you have to

continue south to Guntur, then turn back north, a distance of about 65 km. Kondapalli, only 20 km from Vijayawada, is renowned for the wonderful small toys which have been made here for many years. Only a few km from Vijayawada, but across the river, are the ancient Hindu cave temples of Undavalil. There is also a museum in Vijayawada itself. Masulipatam, 80 km from Vijayawada on the coast, once had English, Dutch and French factories and was the subject of violent dispute between the English and the French.

Places to Stay In Vijayawada the *Ashok*,

near the bus station, is very comfortable, with doubles with bath from Rs 55 and a helpful manager. *Sri Durga Bhavan* (tel 61251) is centrally located on Eluru Rd and has singles at Rs 15 to Rs 25, doubles at Rs 30 to Rs 40. At the same address and with the same phone number is the more expensive *Hotel Mamata* with rooms at Rs 60/100 or with air-con at Rs 100/130.

Hotel Manorama (tel 77221) on Bunder Rd has rooms at Rs 60/100 or Rs 100/135 with air-con. At the top of the price scale the *Hotel Kandhari International* (tel 61311) on Bunder Rd in Labbipet is very good, with air-con rooms at Rs 225/275.

Kerala

Population: 25 million
Area: 38,864 square km
Capital: Trivandrum
Main language: Malayalam

Kerala, the land of 'green magic', is a narrow, fertile coastal strip bordered by the Western Ghats on the south-west coast of India. These high mountains have sheltered Kerala from invaders from the rest of India, but at the same time Kerala has a very long history of contact with the outside world. In Cochin there is still a small community of descendants of Jewish settlers who fled from Palestine 2000 years ago. Kerala has also had Christians for as long as Christianity has been in Europe! The Portuguese were more than a little surprised to find Christianity already established along the Malabar coast when they arrived here 500 years ago. And more than a little annoyed that these Christians had never heard of the Pope.

Long before Vasco da Gama led the Portuguese to India, the coast had been known to the Phoenicians who came in search of spices, sandalwood and ivory. Kerala was not only a spice centre in its own right but a trans-shipment point from the Moluccas. The Biblical Ophir, visited by King Solomon, is thought to be at the site of the small village of Puvar, south of Trivandrum. The Arabs and Chinese also made their mark on Kerala, and fishermen use Chinese fishing nets to this day.

The present-day state of Kerala was created in 1956 from Travancore, Cochin and Malabar, which was formerly part of Madras State. Both Travancore and Cochin were princely states ruled by Maharajas, who paid considerable attention to providing basic services and education for their people, in contrast to some Maharajas in other parts of India who exploited and terrorized their subjects.

The people speak Malayalam, which hundreds of years ago was derived from Tamil. In 1957 Kerala became the first place in the world to freely elect a communist government. Although the communists are currently in power, they have not always held power since that initial election success. The princely state of Travancore had, however, carried out a far-sighted policy of land distribution over a century ago. Today Kerala has a more equitable distribution of land ownership than almost anywhere else in India, and this has resulted in unusually intensive cultivation and a much more even distribution of income than is found elsewhere in India. Although Kerala, predominantly agricultural and with little industry, is far from top of the per capita income scale in India, it has remarkably little real poverty. Many Keralites have also worked in the Gulf and are now returning with their earnings.

This distribution of wealth applies also to education and health. The literacy rate in Kerala is 70%, twice the all-India

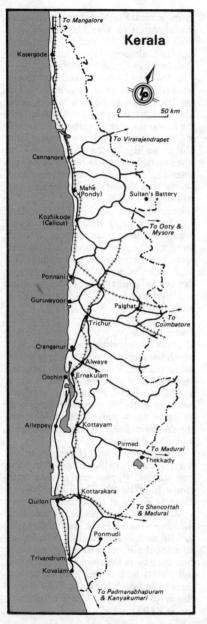

average, and is actually growing faster than in the rest of India despite the already high literacy level. Similarly, infant mortality in Kerala is relatively low and both these achievements have been made without spending a higher proportion of the state's income on education or health than other states.

For visitors Kerala offers one of the best beaches in India at Kovalam, a unique wildlife sanctuary at Periyar, an intriguing blend of cultures and some unusual ways of getting around. Perhaps more than anywhere else in India, getting there can be half the fun, particularly on the backwater trips along the coastal lagoons. Best of all Kerala has an easygoing, relaxed atmosphere unlike the bustle you find elsewhere in India.

Things to Buy

Good choices are Kathakali dance masks, sandalwood carvings, rush mats, hand-loomed cottons, and brass temple lamps and figurines. There are Kerala Cottage Industries Emporiums in Trivandrum, Cochin and Calicut.

Religions

Kerala has an amazing mixture of religions. About 24% of the population today is Christian, and Christianity has been established here longer than almost anywhere in the world. St Thomas the Apostle, 'doubting Thomas', is supposed to have landed on the Malabar coast in 52 AD near Cranganore, where a church with carved Hindu-style columns supposedly dates from the 4th century AD. Further south there is the 9th-century Syrian church of Vallia Palli. Kerala's Syrian Christians were here at least as early as 190 AD; a visitor at that time reported seeing a Hebrew copy of St Matthew. The main Christian area of Kerala is in the central part of the state around Cochin and Kottayam. Hindus form about half of the population of the state and are mainly concentrated in the southern part around Trivandrum.

Kerala's now-disappearing Jewish population also made a very early appearance on the sub-continent. The 'black Jews' are supposed to have fled here in 587 BC when Nebuchadnezzar occupied Jerusalem. Their descendants have now intermarried with the Hindu population, but there is still a small number of the later 'white Jews' in Cochin. Kerala also has a large Muslim population constituting 20%, mainly found in the northern part of the state near Calicut.

NORTH OF CALICUT

Mahe, 60 km north of Calicut, was a small French dependency made over to India at the same time as Pondicherry. Today Mahe's main function is to supply passing truck drivers with cheap Pondicherry beer. It's still part of the Union Territory of Pondicherry. Only eight km north of Mahe is Tellicherry, with some interesting houses and a fine bazaar. The English factory established here in 1683, to purchase pepper and cardamom, was set up by the Surat presidency and was the first permanent English factory on the Malabar coast. The East India Company had a fort here in 1708.

Directly east of here, in the Western Ghats, is Sultan's Battery, a fort built by Tipu Sultan. Cannanore, 88 km north of Calicut, was another port where Vasco da Gama dropped in. The Portuguese built their Fort St Angelo here in 1505, but it later passed to the Dutch and was eventually taken by the British.

CALICUT (Kozhikode)
population 360,000)
Vasco da Gama landed in India at Calicut in 1498. He was the first European to reach India via the sea route around the southern cape of Africa, and his arrival heralded the period of Portuguese supremacy in India. The history of Calicut after that time was certainly dramatic. The Portuguese attempted to conquer the town, a centre of Malabar power under the Zamorins or 'Lords of the Sea', but their attacks in 1509 and 1510 were both repulsed, although in the latter assault the town was virtually destroyed.

In 1513 the Zamorins and Portuguese reached an agreement which permitted the Portuguese to build a factory here. The British followed in 1616, but in 1766 the Zamorins were defeated and a period of local turmoil followed with Tipu Sultan adding to the damage in 1789 when he laid the whole region waste and destroyed the coconut, sandalwood and pepper tree plantations. British rule was established in 1792.

Despite its colourful past Calicut does not have a great deal to see. 'Auto-rickshaws use their meters without prompting – which proves no tourists come here', reported a rare visitor. The word 'calico' is derived from Calicut. You can see kalarippayat, the local martial art, performed at CVN Kalari, East Naddakavu.

Places to Stay
Cheaper hotels include the *Hotel Imperial*, which has pleasant doubles with attached bathroom from Rs 20. And fleas, reported one visitor. Good vegetarian food is available. *Hotel Foura* has excellent rooms from Rs 30, more with air-con. A couple of doors nearer to the bus station, the *Neelima Lodge* is new, presentable and a bit cheaper.

The *Western Tourist Home*, a couple of hundred metres to the left as you exit the bus station, is reasonably clean with rooms from Rs 20. There are *Railway Retiring Rooms* at the station.

More expensive places include the *Alakpuri Guest House* (tel 73361-6) on Jail Rd with singles/doubles from Rs 30/40 without air-con or Rs 75/125 with air-con. Nearby is the newish *Mogul Hotel* (tel 63624) with rooms from Rs 30. Or there's the *Beach Hotel* (tel 73851-53) on Beach Rd with rooms at Rs 60 or with air-con at Rs 90.

Hotel Maharani (tel 76161) is on Taluk Rd and has rooms from Rs 30 or with air-con from Rs 90. There is also a good *Tourist Bungalow* here. The *Kalpaka Tourist Home* (tel 76171-80) on Town Hall Rd has rooms from as little as Rs 20 to Rs 30 for singles, Rs 50 to Rs 70 for doubles, up to Rs 90 to Rs 100 for air-con doubles. The *Sea Queen Hotel* (tel 60201) on Beach Rd has rooms at Rs 50/75 or air-con rooms at Rs 100/125.

Places to Eat

Around the bus station there are several vegetarian and non-vegetarian restaurants. *Hotel Sagar* has not too special non-vegetarian food (including Chinese and tandoori) at tolerable prices.

Hotel Foura has a vegetarian restaurant, as does the *Hotel Shobra* next door, which has been voted Calicut's best vegetarian restaurant by the local Rotary Club. If you ask for 'toast-butter-jam' they'll do you a curious jam sandwich. *Hotel Sarovar*, to the right of the state bus stand, has non-vegetarian food.

Getting There

The bus trip to Calicut from Ooty or Mysore is hard work but spectacular as the bus climbs up and over the Western Ghats. From Mysore it's a painful 5½-hour trip with amazing views down to the sea from the top of the range.

TRICHUR

Situated 74 km north of Ernakulam, Trichur has the old temple of Guruvayur (Hindus only), a museum and a zoo with a notable collection of snakes. In April-May of each year the Pooram festival is one of the biggest in the south with fireworks and colourful processions, including brightly decorated elephants. The Kerala Kala Mandalam at Cheruthuruthy, north of Trichur, is an important centre for training Kathakali dancers.

Places to Stay

Trichur has a comfortable *Tourist Bungalow*. The *Jaya Lodge* has rooms from just Rs 15.

There are several more expensive places. *Hotel Elite International* (tel 21033) is on Chemboottil Lane and has rooms with attached bathroom at Rs 35/65 or with air-con at Rs 100/125. *Casino Hotel* on T B Rd is similarly priced.

COCHIN & ERNAKULAM

Cochin population 480,000
Ernakulam population 130,000

With its wealth of historical associations and beautiful setting on a cluster of islands and narrow peninsulas, Cochin is one of India's most interesting cities. It reflects the eclecticism of Kerala perfectly. Here you can see the oldest church in India, winding streets crammed with old houses constructed by the Portuguese 500 years ago, cantilevered Chinese fishing nets, a Jewish community with roots going back to 1000 AD and a 16th-century synagogue, a palace built by the Portuguese and given to the Raja of Cochin (later renovated by the Dutch, it contains perhaps the most beautiful murals in India), a performance of the world-famous Kathakali dance-drama and many other things.

This unlikely pastiche of mediaeval Portugal, Holland and an English country village grafted onto the tropical Malabar coast, which you find in the older parts of Fort Cochin and Mattancherry, contrasts wildly with the bright neon lights, dimly lit seamen's bars and big hotels of mainland Ernakulam. A strange contrast perhaps, but Port Cochin is one of India's largest ports and a major naval base. On any day of the year the misty silhouettes of huge merchant ships can be seen anchored off the point of Fort Cochin waiting their turn for a berth in the docks of Ernakulam or Willingdon Island. This man-made island was created with material dredged up when the harbour was deepened. It also provides a site for the airport. As you might expect in a major port, there's a lot of wheeler-dealing going on so don't be too surprised if, when staying in Ernakulam, you get approached with offers for things which are not easy to acquire in India such as cameras, watches, tape recorders and the like.

Orientation

Cochin consists of mainland Ernakulam; the islands of Willingdon, Bolgatty and Gundu in the harbour; Fort Cochin and Mattancherry on the southern peninsula; and Vypeen Island north of Fort Cochin. All these separate parts are connected by ferry. In addition there are bridges and a road connecting Ernakulam with Willingdon Island and the Fort Cochin/Mattancherry peninsula. The railway station, bus station, Tourist Reception Centre and the bulk of the hotels and restaurants are in Ernakulam.

Mahatma Gandhi Rd is the locale of most of the top-range hotels, while the road connecting the railway station to Mahatma Gandhi Rd and Shanmughan Rd on the waterfront has most of the mid-range hotels. Most of the budget hotels are on Press Club Rd and Canon Rd off Broadway, with a few just outside the railway station.

Almost all the historical sites are in Fort Cochin or Mattancherry, but hotel and restaurant facilities are very limited – there are only four budget-type hotels in this area. The GPO (including the poste restante) and Chinese fishing nets are also in Fort Cochin. On Willingdon Island is the airport and, at the tip of the island opposite Fort Cochin, the main Tourist Office and Cochin's top hotel, the Malabar.

One of the best hotel bargains in Cochin, the Bolgatty Palace Hotel is on Bolgatty Island. The Tourist Reception Centre, outside the shopping precinct where Shanmughan Rd meets Broadway in Ernakulam, operate a launch to the island. Vypeen Island is only of interest if you want to see the nearest surviving Portuguese fort, which is on the northern end at Pallipuram.

Information

The Tourist Reception Centre (tel 33234) on Shanmughan Rd in Ernakulam has friendly, helpful staff but not a lot of literature. They'll fix you up with accommodation at the Bolgatty Palace Hotel and with the conducted boat cruise around the harbour.

The Tourist Office headquarters is attached to the Malabar Hotel on Willingdon Island. This is the best tourist office in southern India; it's friendly, helpful and has a whole range of leaflets and maps. Indian Airlines are now in Durbar Hall Rd. Sita World Travel, next to the Air India office, are friendly and helpful. Ernakulam's poste restante is not very efficient; sort through letters yourself if possible.

You could use the Malabar Hotel's swimming pool for a fee, although prior to recent renovations it 'looked like it had been filled with green-pea soup.' Coconut products like bowls or placemats, teak bowls and coir (coconut fibre) items are good buys in Cochin. Current Books on Press Club Rd is a good bookshop.

Fort Cochin

St Francis Church This is the oldest church constructed by Europeans on Indian soil. Vasco da Gama, first European to reach India by sailing around Africa, died in Cochin in 1524 and was buried here for 14 years until his body was transferred to Lisbon in Portugal. His tombstone still stands. The church was built in 1503 by Portuguese Franciscan friars who accompanied the expedition led by Pedro Alvarez Cabral. The original structure was wood but it was rebuilt in stone about the middle of the 16th century – the earliest Portuguese inscription found in the church dates back to 1562. In 1663 it passed into the hands of the Protestant Dutch with their capture of Cochin, and they later restored it in 1779. After the

Andhra Pradesh Top: 'Vote bicycle!', election sign in Hyderabad (IW)
Right: Charminar triumphal arch, Hyderabad (TW)
Left: In Golconda Fort, near Hyderabad (TW)

Kerala Top: Backwater trip from Alleppey to Quilon (GC)
Bottom: Chinese fishing nets, Cochin (HF)

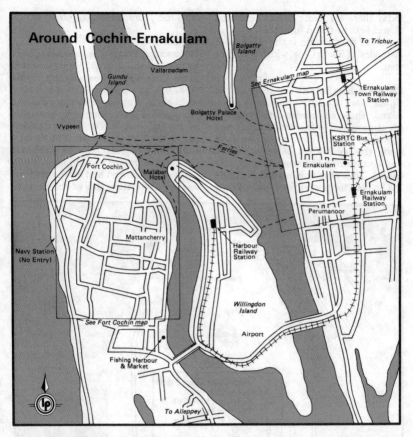

occupation of Cochin by the British in 1795 it became an Anglican church and is at present used by the Church of South India.

Christianity has a much longer history on the Malabar coast than this church. Tradition has it that St Thomas the Apostle landed here in AD 52, though there's no archaeological evidence to support this, and the first documentary evidence of churches in Kerala comes from the accounts of a Byzantine monk who travelled here in the 6th century. By the middle of the 9th century the Christian communities were playing an important part in the trade and commerce of this area and there are records of substantial gifts of property to the Church of Teresa (no longer in existence) during the reign of Sthanu Ravi (844-85).

These earlier Christian communities were all Syrian Orthodox and, until the 16th century when the Portuguese put a stop to the practice in their efforts to enforce the supremacy of Rome, all the Keralan bishops were brought from Persia and Mesopotamia. This suppression of the Syrian Church was only partially successful, however, and even today there are many Syrian Orthodox churches to be found in Kerala.

Also in Fort Cochin is the much later Cathedral of Santa Cruz, which is worth a visit.

Chinese Fishing Nets Strung out along the tip of Fort Cochin opposite Vypeen Island, these cantilevered fishing nets were introduced by traders from the court of Kublai Khan. You can also see them along the backwaters between Cochin and Kottayam and between Alleppey and Quilon. They're mainly used at high tide – 'a hell of a lot of work for a few piddling little fish', commented one observer.

Mattancherry

Mattancherry Palace The palace was built by the Portuguese in 1557 and presented to the Cochin Raja, Veera Kerala Varma (1537-61), as a gesture of good will (and probably as a means of securing trading privileges). It was substantially renovated by the Dutch after 1663, hence its other name, the 'Dutch' Palace. The double-storied quadrangular building surrounds a central courtyard containing a Hindu temple. The central hall on the 1st floor was the Coronation Hall of the Rajas of

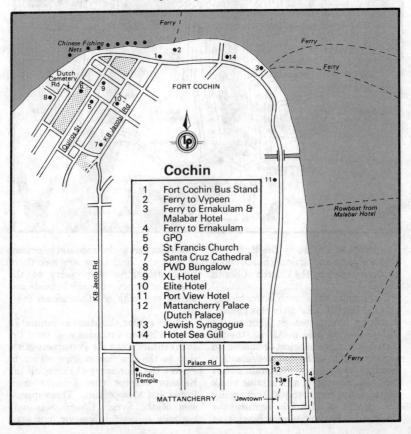

Cochin

1	Fort Cochin Bus Stand
2	Ferry to Vypeen
3	Ferry to Ernakulam & Malabar Hotel
4	Ferry to Ernakulam
5	GPO
6	St Francis Church
7	Santa Cruz Cathedral
8	PWD Bungalow
9	XL Hotel
10	Elite Hotel
11	Port View Hotel
12	Mattancherry Palace (Dutch Palace)
13	Jewish Synagogue
14	Hotel Sea Gull

Cochin; on display are dresses, turbans and palanquins belonging to these rulers.

The most important aspect of this palace, however, is the astonishing murals in the bed-chambers and other rooms, depicting scenes from the *Ramayana* and Puranic legends connected with Shiva, Vishnu, Krishna, Kumara and Durga. These are without doubt some of the most beautiful and extensive you will see anywhere in India. You can pick up pamphlet after pamphlet of Indian tourist literature containing breathless eulogies of the murals at Ajanta and Ellora but never see a mention of these, yet they are one of the wonders of India. There are similar murals at the Shiva temple in Ettumanur (a few km north off Kottayam).

The palace is open Monday to Saturday, 9 am to 1 pm and 2 to 5 pm; closed Sundays. Entrance is free but flash photography is prohibited (effectively precluding photography altogether), which is a great pity since there are no books or postcards for sale. The murals can be photographed quite well by holding your camera on the railing, wrote one visitor. There are three black-and-white photographs of the murals in the Archaeological Survey of India's booklet, *Monuments of Kerala* by H Sarkar (1978, Rs 3.25). Other books in which they're illustrated are *Cochin Murals* by V R Chitra & T N Srinivasan (Cochin, 1940), and *South Indian Paintings* by C Sivaramamurti (New Delhi, 1968).

The Jewish Synagogue Built in 1568, this is the oldest synagogue in the Commonwealth. It was preceded by an earlier one at Kochangadi, built in 1344, which has since disappeared, although a stone slab inscribed in Hebrew from this earlier building can be found on the inner surface of the wall which surrounds the present synagogue. The present building was destroyed by shelling during a Portuguese raid in 1662 and rebuilt two years later when the Dutch took over Cochin. It's an interesting little place with handpainted, willow-pattern floor tiles (no two alike) brought from Canton, China, in the mid-18th century by Ezekial Rahabi who had trading interests in that city. He was also responsible for the erection of the clock tower which surmounts the building.

The synagogue is open daily from 10 am to 12 noon and from 3 to 5 pm except Saturdays and Jewish holidays. Entrance is a hefty Rs 25. The synagogue guardian is very friendly, keen to tell you about the history of the place and the Jewish community here, and to talk about what's happening in the rest of the world. He speaks fluent English.

This unexpected and isolated Jewish community has roots going back to the time of St Thomas the Apostle's voyage to India in AD 52. Their first settlement was at Cranganore, north of Cochin. Like the Syrian Orthodox Christians, they became involved in the trade and commerce of the Malabar coast; preserved in the synagogue are a number of copper plates inscribed in an ancient script with the grant of the village of Anjuvannam (near Cranganore) and its revenue to Jewish merchant Joseph Rabban by King Bhaskara Ravi Varman I (962-1020). You may view these plates if you ask the synagogue guardian for permission.

The concessions given by Ravi Varman I included permission to use a palanquin and parasol – in those days the prerogative of rulers – and so, in effect, gave sanction for the creation of a tiny Jewish kingdom. On Rabban's death his sons fought amongst themselves for control of the 'kingdom' and this led to its break-up and the move to Mattancherry.

Quite a lot of research has been done on this community, and one particularly interesting study by an American professor of ethnomusicology found that the music of the Cochin Jews contained strong Babylonian influences and that their version of the 10 Commandments was almost identical with a Kurdish version housed in the Berlin Museum Archives.

Naturally, there's also been much local influence and many of the hymns are similar to ragas.

The area around the synagogue is known as Jewtown and is one of the centres of the spice trade in Cochin. Scores of small firms huddle together in old, dilapidated buildings and the air is filled with the pungent aromas of ginger, cardamom, cumin, turmeric and cloves. Many Jewish names are visible on business premises and houses, but the community has diminished rapidly since Indian independence and now numbers less than 50. At one time there may have been as many as 4000. Most of the young people have gone to Israel, and few people under 50 years of age remain. When they die the community will probably go the same way and the synagogue will become a museum. As a mark of its decline, there has been no rabbi within living memory so all the elders are qualified to perform religious ceremonies and marriages. There are many interesting curio shops on the street leading up to the synagogue.

There is another synagogue in Ernakulam at the junction of (predictably) Jews and Market Sts, but it appears to be unused. The 'head' of the Jews lives in Old Harbour House in Jewtown. He can be contacted if you are interested in seeing historic documents relating to the Jews of India.

Ernakulam
Kathakali Dancing The origins of India's most spectacular dance-drama go back around 400 to 500 years, when open-air performances were held in a temple courtyard or on the village green. There are over 100 different arrangements, all of them based on stories from the *Ramayana* and *Mahabharata*, those two epics of Indian mythology, and they were designed to continue well into the early hours of the morning. Since most visitors don't have the inclination to stay up all night, the centres which put on the dance in Ernakulam offer shortened versions lasting

about two hours. I personally felt this was too abbreviated.

Kathakali isn't simply another form of dancing, as it incorporates elements of yoga and ayurvedic (traditional Indian) medicine. All the props are fashioned out of natural materials – powdered minerals and the sap of certain trees for the bright facial make-up; the beaten bark of certain trees, dyed with fruits and spices, for wigs; coconut oil for mixing up the colours; burnt coconut oil for the black paint around the eyes; and eggplant flowers tucked under the eyelids to turn the whites of the eyes deep red. Usually you're welcome to see the make-up process before the dance, quite a show in its own right. The dancers are accompanied by two drummers and another musician, who plays finger cymbals. A school run by the government in northern Kerala near Palghat teaches Kathakali dancing.

Each of the three companies which put on performances kick off the evening with an explanation of the symbolism involved in the dance drama – the facial expressions, hand movements and ritualistic gestures. This is then followed by an actual dance drama lasting about one hour. 'Bring mosquito coils', suggested one visitor. The centres which offer Kathakali are:

The Cochin Cultural Centre (tel 37866), Durbar Hall Grounds, Durbar Hall Rd. Daily performances; entry Rs 15 with Rs 10 camera 'donation'. Advance booking not required. A beautiful little theatre in traditional style, on the Durbar Hall grounds next to Cochin Museum.

Art Kerala, Menon & Krishna Annexe, near junction of Chittoor and Church Landing Rds, opposite Devi Temple. Daily performances at 7 pm; entry Rs 15.

See India Foundation (tel 31871), Kalathiparambil Lane. Daily performances except Thursdays, 7 to 8.30 pm; entry Rs 25. Slightly more expensive but with better introductory lecture on Hinduism and explanation of gestures used in performance. No charge for photos.

Mr Devan near the station. Dance performances at his home, round the block from Central

Lodge, near Art Kerala. With amusing pre-show chat on dance history; Rs 28.

Cochin Museum The museum is housed in what was previously Durbar Hall on Durbar Hall Rd – an enormous building constructed in traditional Keralan style. It contains collections of 19th-century oil paintings, old coins, sculptures and Moghul paintings as well as exhibits from the Cochin royal family. Open daily except Mondays and public holidays from 9.30 am to 12 noon, and 3 to 5.30 pm. Entry is free.

Gundu Island
The smallest island in Cochin harbour is close to Vypeen Island. There is a coir factory here – the only building on the island – where attractive doormats are made out of coconut fibre. You come across their mats all over Cochin. The only way to get there is on the boat tour organised by the Kerala Tourist Development Corporation.

Tours
The Kerala Tourist Development Corporation offers two conducted boat cruises daily around Cochin harbour and includes visits to Willingdon Island, Mattancherry Palace, the Jewish Synagogue, Fort Cochin including St Francis Church and Bolgatty Island. The first tour is 9 am to 12.30 pm; the second 2 to 5.30 pm. The morning tour is better because the afternoon one leaves out Mattancherry Palace. Cost of this very worthwhile tour is Rs 15. The Tourist Department also arranges a two-day tour to Periyar Wildlife Sanctuary departing Saturday morning and costing Rs 75.

For reservations contact either the Tourist Reception Centre, Shanmughan Rd, Ernakulam (tel 33234); or the manager, Bolgatty Palace Hotel, Bolgatty Island (tel 35003). The tour starts and finishes at the boat jetty in front of the Sealord Hotel, Shanmughan Rd, Ernakulam. You can also board the boat at the Tourist Office Jetty, Willingdon Island, 20 minutes after the start of each tour from the Sealord boat jetty. They seem to put foreigners on the roof of the boat and crowd the locals below decks. Beware of ticket sellers at the Sealord jetty – their tickets are not for the government launch.

Places to Stay
If you want top-range hotels then you have a choice between Ernakulam and Willingdon Island. For mid-range hotels, the choice is between Ernakulam and Bolgatty Island plus a limited choice in Fort Cochin. If you want a budget hotel you can stay in Ernakulam, Bolgatty Island or Fort Cochin, although the choice is widest in Ernakulam.

Places to Stay – bottom end
If you want the sleepy, laid-back atmosphere of the old part of the city then head for Fort Cochin. There are only two places and they are very basic. If you want the beer, drugs and city action of an international port, stay in Ernakulam.

Fort Cochin The *Elite Hotel* (tel 257330), very close to St Francis Church, has rooms with common bathroom and toilet for Rs 9/18. It's an old building, so expect the floorboards to creak. The non-vegetarian café on the ground floor is excellent value and popular with local young people and students. Nearby is the *Princess Lodge* which is marginally more expensive. The *YWCA* is a few metres from the GPO, overlooking the green in front of St Francis Church. It's a very small place and often full but worth enquiring about if you're in the area.

Port View Lodge (tel 352140) is about half-way between Fort Cochin and Mattancherry and is one of the very few places in that area that can be classified as a budget hotel, although there are a few incredibly decrepit doss-houses along this road. It's an old place with beautifully carved stairways and bannisters, and although it has been allowed to go to seed it retains a lot of character and the views from the roof are excellent. However, I'd be reluctant to leave anything valuable 'locked up' in a room here (I can't substantiate that, it's just a feeling). Rooms cost from Rs 10 and some of them look like an Indian impression of an *Antony & Cleopatra* film set – all with common bathrooms and toilets.

Ernakulam Of the budget hotels in Ernakulam the *Basoto Lodge*, Press Club Rd, is one of the best. It's a small, simple, friendly place, popular with travellers, so get there early if you want a room. They cost from Rs 15; a double with attached bath is Rs 30. Other cheap places in the bottom-end category are near the station and include *Central Lodge* and *Apsara Tourist Home*.

The *Hakoba Hotel* on Shanmughan Rd is on the waterfront with excellent views over the harbour from the front rooms. Non-air-con rooms are Rs 25/35 and there are also five rooms with air-con. It is conveniently located and not too big, with a restaurant and bar and even a (not very reliable) lift. The *Broadway Lodge* (tel 38679) is centrally located and has rooms at Rs 20/30 with bath.

Another good place in this bracket is *Biju's Tourist Home* (tel 39881), Cannon Shed Rd, near the junction with Market Rd. It has good, spacious rooms with attached bath and hot and cold water at Rs 25/40, Rs 80 with air-con, plus friendly staff. 'Probably the best value place in the whole of our stay in India', wrote one entranced visitor. 'Lots of mosquitoes', said another.

Nearer the railway station is the *Piazza Lodge* (tel 37408), Kalathiparambu Rd, a new place with friendly staff and excellent value at Rs 20/30 with attached bath. Also good value in this area are the *Premier Tourist Home* with singles/doubles/triples for Rs 20/30/35, all with attached bath; and the *Ernakulam Tourist Bungalow* which costs Rs 17/29/42 or has air-con doubles for Rs 65.

Ninan's Tourist Lodge (tel 31235) is opposite the KSRTC bus station and has fairly clean rooms with shower and fan at Rs 18/36.

Places to Stay – middle

Bolgatty Island Although it's suffering from increasingly lazy and greedy staff, the *Bolgatty Palace Hotel* (tel 35003) on Bolgatty Island is still full of character. Formerly a palace built by the Dutch in 1744 and later a British Residency, it is now run by the Kerala Tourist Development Corporation as a hotel. It's set in six hectares of lush green lawns with a golf course, bar and restaurant which, depending on the writer, varies from 'good' to 'appalling'! The regular rooms are Rs 35/62 with attached bathroom but no air-conditioning, and are very often full. Air-con doubles cost Rs 150; you might get a Rs 10 discount if the power's off all day! There are also some new circular 'honeymoon cottages' with round beds and balconies overhanging the water. It's a shame this hotel seems to be on a downhill slide due to neglect.

For the ferry service to the island contact the Tourist Reception Centre, Shanmughan Rd, Ernakulam, or ring the hotel itself. Ferries to the island run on a definite schedule, but if you want to get across at any other time rowboats are available (price negotiable). There's also a regular ferry, every 20 minutes from 6 am to 10 pm, from the 'Bolgatty Ferry Station'. On the island turn left, walk to the hotel gate (uniformed guard) and cross the golf course. The ferry is Rs 0.20.

Fort Cochin *Hotel Sea Gull* (tel 28128) overlooks the harbour about half-way between the two ferry stops. The hotel has been created by converting a number of old houses/warehouses and is a great place to stay. It has a restaurant and bar. Doubles (there are no singles) are Rs 45 or Rs 90 with air-con. It's interesting to watch the ships come and go from the hotel restaurant.

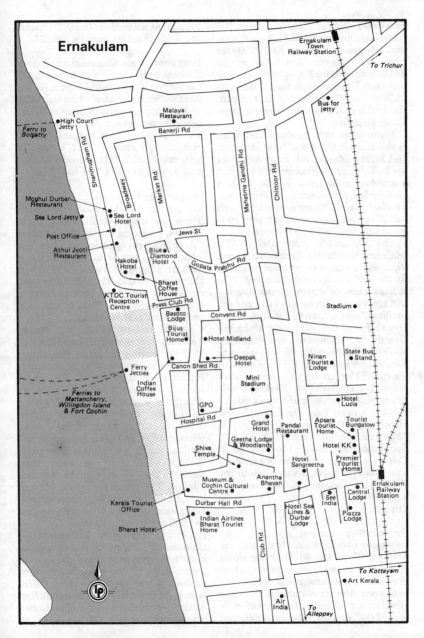

Ernakulam

Ernakulam Town Railway Station

To Trichur

Ferry to Bolgatty

High Court Jetty

Bus for jetty

Malaya Restaurant

Banerji Rd

Shanmugham Rd

Broadway

Market Rd

Mahatma Gandhi Rd

Chittoor Rd

Moghul Durbar Restaurant

Sea Lord Jetty

Post Office

Athul Jyoti Restaurant

Sea Lord Hotel

Jews St

Hakoba Hotel

Blue Diamond Hotel

Gopala Prabhu Rd

Bharat Coffee House

KTDC Tourist Reception Centre

Press Club Rd

Basoto Lodge

Convent Rd

Stadium

Bijus Tourist Home

Hotel Midland

Deepak Hotel

Ninan Tourist Lodge

State Bus Stand

Ferry Jetties

Canon Shed Rd

Mini Stadium

Indian Coffee House

Ferries to Mattancherry, Willingdon Island & Fort Cochin

GPO

Hospital Rd

Hotel Lucia

Grand Hotel

Geetha Lodge & Woodlands

Pandal Restaurant

Apsara Tourist Home

Tourist Bungalow

Hotel KK

Shiva Temple

Hotel Sangreetha

Premier Tourist Home

Ernakulam Railway Station

Museum & Cochin Cultural Centre

Anantha Bhavan

Kerala Tourist Office

Durbar Hall Rd

See India

Central Lodge

Indian Airlines Bharat Tourist Home

Hotel Sea Lines & Durbar Lodge

Piazza Lodge

Bharat Hotel

Club Rd

To Kottayam

Art Kerala

Air India

To Alleppey

Ernakulam *Bharat Tourist Hotel* (tel 33501) on Durbar Hall Rd is a good hotel and charges Rs 45/80 or Rs 110/200 for rooms with air-con. *Hotel Luciya* (tel 34433) on Stadium Rd, opposite the bus station in Ernakulam, is good value at Rs 25/50 or Rs 60/125 with air-con. It's clean, the food is good and you even get a paper under your door.

Some other very pleasant mid-range hotels include the *Hotel Blue Diamond* (tel 33221), Market Rd. Singles/doubles are Rs 30/58; air-con doubles with attached bathroom are Rs 100 to Rs 200. It has a roof garden, restaurant (vegetarian, non-vegetarian and Chinese food) and air-con bar. The rooms are nice, it's very good value and the staff are very friendly.

The *Woodlands Hotel* (tel 31372), Mahatma Gandhi Rd, Ernakulam is good value with rooms with attached bathroom for Rs 55/80 or with air-con for Rs 90/115. It has an air-con vegetarian restaurant – 'a direct connection between tips and the quality of service', wrote one visitor. The *Grand Hotel* (tel 33211) on Mahatma Gandhi Rd, Ernakulam, has singles for Rs 50 to Rs 70 or Rs 95 with air-con. Doubles are Rs 70 to Rs 100 or Rs 115 with air-con. There are only five non air-con rooms. It's a pleasant place with spacious rooms, superb service and a nice garden.

On the same road the *International Hotel* (tel 33911) has rooms for Rs 75 to Rs 130; with air-con, singles are Rs 100, doubles Rs 100 to Rs 140. The rather plush *Coq d'Or Restaurant* here is excellent. The *Gaanam Hotel* is very close to the Ernakulam Railway Station and has rooms at Rs 77/110 or with air-con at Rs 110/132.

Places to Stay – top end

Willingdon Island Cochin's best hotel, the *Malabar Hotel* (tel 6811) at the tip of Willingdon Island, has a superb location overlooking the harbour and is expected to be open after renovations in 1987. The Government of India Tourist Office is part of the complex. Also on Willingdon Island the *Casino Hotel* (tel 6821) has air-con singles/doubles from Rs 225/275.

Ernakulam On Shanmughan Rd in Ernakulam the *Sealord Hotel* (tel 32682) has air-con singles/doubles from Rs 140-200/180-250. *Hotel Abad Plaza* (tel 39720) on M G Rd has singles/doubles at Rs 130/180 or deluxe rooms at 200/280 – each with TV and video. This well-located and exceptionally well-kept hotel is centrally air-conditioned. It has a seafood restaurant and, as they put it, a 'fast-food joint'.

Places to Eat

Many hotels have their own restaurants. There are also several *Indian Coffee Houses*, including one at the bottom of Canon Shed Rd opposite the main ferry jetties, and another at the junction of Mahatma Gandhi Rd with the road from the railway station. They offer very good, cheap semi-western and Indian food and excellent real coffee. Popular with local people, they're always busy.

For a western escape the *Pandal Restaurant*, opposite the Grand Hotel on M G Rd, serves good pizza, hamburgers and banana splits as well as absolutely superb north Indian food. The pastry shop is often crowded, and although slightly expensive is worth it. It's not a bad-looking modern building either. *Mathura*, a km south of the Pandal Restaurant on M G Rd, has indoor and outdoor dining and a huge glass panel through which you can watch their tandoori chef at work in his spotless kitchen. The prices are reasonable and the food delicious. At both these remarkably good restaurants a complete meal for two will run Rs 60 to Rs 80.

Ranjim Vegetarian Restaurant on Chittoor Rd is part of the Sangeetha Hotel and has excellent food and a varied menu with an air-conditioned room upstairs if you need it. *Bharat Coffee House*, on Broadway next door to Indian Airlines, is similar to the Indian Coffee Houses with good, cheap, Indian vegetarian food and excellent coffee. *Arul Jyothi*, 50 metres from the Hakoba Hotel, has good masala dosas. At the top of Press Club Rd the *Broadway Restaurant* has good south Indian food and excellent coffee.

The *Woodlands Hotel*, M G Rd, has been recommended by a number of travellers. The *Jaya Restaurant* here serves good vegetarian food and several kinds of ice cream, and also has a special western menu. The *Grand Hotel* is well known for its seafood – try their special Rs 15 'Karemin fish' prawn dish.

Fish stuffed with grapes and baked cheese at the *Sealord Restaurant* on Shanmughan St is delicious. Numerous travellers have written to recommend this as a good place for a splurge; they even have *good* live western music! The *Mughal Durbar* is nearby with three floors (and classes) of dining available. On the 2nd floor of the *Abad Plaza* the *Regency Restaurant* is a classy but reasonably priced place with good Indian, Chinese and western food. The *Ceylon Bakehouse*, near the Tourist Office on Broadway, has good Chinese and Indian food. *Malang's Restaurant*, down a side road opposite the Thekkady road, has very good Chinese food.

There are many lively, dimly lit bars along Mahatma Gandhi Rd and Shanmughan Rd in Ernakulam if you're looking for light entertainment. Ageing western pop music is played non-stop and beers are the same price in all the bars – Rs 25 a large bottle.

In Fort Cochin the very popular *Elite Hotel*, near St Francis Church, is recommended for good non-vegetarian meals. The *Malay Restaurant*, near the Sangeetha Theatre, is a popular Chinese place with reasonable prices – say Rs 10 to Rs 15 for a full meal. *Hotel Seashells* also has an inexpensive restaurant and good fish dishes.

The *Bolgatty Palace* gets mixed reports for its food, although it does do great fish and chips and the airport restaurant is OK for snacks.

Getting There

Air Indian Airlines has three or four flights daily between Bombay and Cochin for Rs 938. There are also regular connections with Bangalore (Rs 353), Dabolim in Goa (Rs 597), Delhi (Rs 1757), Madras (Rs 606), Madurai (Rs 263) and Trivandrum (Rs 192).

Rail Ernakulam has two stations; Ernakulam Junction is more central than Ernakulam Town. Twice .a week the Karnataka-Kerala runs from New Delhi to Ernakulam. The 2833-km trip takes 43 hours and costs Rs 166 in 2nd class, Rs 695 in 1st. On the other days of the week it runs from Hazrat Nizamuddin (just outside New Delhi) to Cochin but is considerably slower.

The 201-km trip to Trivandrum takes four to five hours at a cost of Rs 23 in 2nd class, Rs 86 in 1st. Bangalore is a 629-km trip taking 14 hours and costing Rs 53 in 2nd class, Rs 218 in 1st on the Island Express. Bombay is 1841 km and 38 hours away and the Jayanti Janata Express only has 2nd class, which costs Rs 117. This train continues on right down to Trivandrum.

The Malabar Express makes a daily run from Mangalore to Trivandrum right along the Kerala coast through Calicut, Trichur, Ernakulam, Cochin, Kottayam and Quilon. Other trains also follow part of this coastal route. The Ernakulam-Kottayam daily service at 7 am and 5.30 pm and the Ernakulam-Quilon service at 11.30 am are local passenger trains which you might find useful.

Bus Buses depart from the KSRTC Bus Stand in Ernakulam. Since Ernakulam is almost in the middle of the state, obviously a lot of buses start in places north and south of here, but pass through Ernakulam en route. It's often possible to get a seat on these buses, but you cannot make advance reservations. You simply have to join the scrum when it turns up. Buy a priority ticket (Rs 0.50) and wave this in front of the conductor's nose when the bus arrives. In theory, if there are more passengers than seats and standing room allow, those with these tickets are taken on first.

Even with buses which start out of Ernakulam, it isn't always easy to make an advance reservation. Unless you read Malayalam, you're not going to be able to make head or tail of the timetable at the bus stand. Fortunately there is a way round this, and that is to buy the monthly booklet *Time Table (Travel Guide)*, published by Jaico. It costs Rs 1.50 and is available at the bus stand or at bookshops in the city. In it – in readable form – are the schedules, journey times and fares of all KSRTC bus routes, together with details of which buses it's possible to make advance reservations for. It also contains train and air schedules, and a list of the better hotels.

Going South Buses to Cape Comorin, 306 km away at the southern tip of India, cost Rs 36.

There are more than a dozen buses daily to Alleppey (62 km), including a couple of limited-stop buses. The fare is Rs 8 and the journey takes 1½ hours.

To Quilon (150 km) there is one express bus daily; the fare is Rs 18 and the journey takes 3½ hours. You can get to Quilon at other times of the day by taking a Trivandrum bus via Alleppey.

There are two routes to Trivandrum (221 km), one via Alleppey and the other via Kottayam. About 10 buses daily go via Alleppey, another half dozen via Kottayam. The fare is Rs 25 by fast passenger – 6½ hours – and Rs 27 by express – about five hours.

Going East There are several buses daily originating in Ernakulam for the 324-km trip to Madurai in Tamil Nadu. The fare is Rs 36.

There are about 10 buses daily to Kottayam (76 km). The fare is Rs 8 and the journey takes 2¼ hours. To Thekkady (Kumily) (192 km) there are only a few

buses daily via either Kottayam or, less frequently, Kattappana. The fare is Rs 23 and the journey takes 6¾ hours.

Going North Interstate Express buses originate in Ernakulam and make the 565-km trip to Bangalore in 15 hours at a cost of Rs 65.

A half dozen buses daily make the 317-km trip to Cannanore. Most of them are limited-stop and the fare for the 8½-hour trip is Rs 38.50.

There are also a half dozen buses daily to Kozhikode (Calicut). The 219-km trip takes 6½ hours and the fare is Rs 25.50. The 360-km trip to Palghat takes 4½ hours and costs Rs 18. There are four or five buses daily.

It takes 2¼ hours to make the 81-km trip to Trichur and the cost is Rs 10. There are a half dozen buses daily. From Trichur buses connect to Mysore, a further seven-hour trip costing Rs 35.

Getting Around

Ferry This is the main form of transport between the various parts of Cochin. If you're going to be making your own way around the sights of Cochin and Mattancherry (especially if you're staying in Ernakulam), then you need to think about the sequence you're going to do it in, since there are no ferries or convenient bus connections between Fort Cochin and Mattancherry. Also, there are two Fort Cochin ferry jetties and they too are not connected with each other (it's a 10 to 15-minute walk between the two). In some ways it's easier to get to the main part of Fort Cochin from Ernakulam by taking the ferry to Vypeen and then another ferry from there to Fort Cochin. There are no ferry connections between Fort Cochin and Willingdon Island; you have to hire a rowboat at about Rs 2 per person.

If you're taking the ferry from Ernakulam to Fort Cochin the boarding arrangements are ridiculously chaotic, the typical mass-hysteria trip. You often have to scramble across three boats to get to the ferry you want, and there are no indications as to which boat is going where. It's suggested you don't attempt this with a backpack! This is the only chaotic ferry – all the others are well organised. 'It helps being a woman', wrote one visitor, 'as the ladies' ticket queue never has so many people'.

Perumanoor-Willingdon Island 35 times daily in either direction. First ferry at 6 am and the last at 10 pm. Costs Rs 0.15 and takes 10 minutes. Not a very useful ferry since the jetty on Willingdon Island is a long way from the Tourist Office and Malabar Hotel, although there is a service to a jetty near the Tourist Office.

Ernakulam-Mattancherry Goes via Willingdon Island. This is the ferry to take if you want to go to the Tourist Office or to the Mattancherry Palace and the Jewish Synagogue. It operates 29 times daily in either direction. From Ernakulam the first ferry is at 6.30 am and the last at 9.40 pm. From Mattancherry the first ferry is at 6 am and the last at 9 pm. Costs Rs 0.65 and takes 20 minutes.

Ernakulam-Fort Cochin 18 times daily in either direction. From Ernakulam the first ferry is at 6.30 am and the last at 8.40 pm. From Fort Cochin the first ferry is at 6.50 am and the last at 9 pm. Costs Rs 0.65 and takes 10 to 15 minutes.

Ernakulam-Vypeen Island 40 times daily in either direction. From Ernakulam the first ferry is at 5.30 am and the last at 10.30 pm. From Vypeen the first ferry is at 6 am and the last at 10 pm. Costs Rs 0.65 and takes 15 minutes. Ferries also go from Ernakulam to Vallarpadan.

Mattancherry-Willingdon Island Willingdon Island is known as 'Terminus' on the timetable board at Mattancherry. Two ferries every hour (on the hour and the half hour as a rule). The first ferry is at 6 am and the last at 9 pm. Costs Rs 0.35 and takes five to 10 minutes. A small boat service also crosses directly between Mattancherry and Willingdon.

Fort Cochin-Vypeen Island Approximately every 10 minutes in either direction throughout the day and evening. Costs Rs 0.25 and takes three to four minutes. There is also a drive-on drive-off car ferry between these two points which operates 15 times daily in either direction.

Ernakulam-Varapoja If you can't take longer backwater trips such as Alleppey-Quilon, this could be a good substitute. Each way the trip takes two hours and costs just Rs 1.

Bus & Auto-rickshaw There are no convenient bus services between Fort Cochin and the Mattancherry Palace/Jewish Synagogue. Buses do run from Fort Cochin down K B Jacob Rd to South Mattancherry, but it's a 15-minute walk back to the palace from where you get off. If you're planning on walking between the two (a pleasant half-hour), you can go either along K B Jacob Rd and then Palace Rd or along the port-side road. It's probably best to take an auto-rickshaw, but none of the drivers are willing to use the meter so expect to pay at least Rs 3 (they won't take you unless you agree to the price asked).

In Ernakulam, auto-rickshaws are the most convenient form of transport and drivers use the meters. The trip from the bus station to the Tourist Reception Centre, Shanmughan Rd costs between Rs 3 and Rs 3.50. The buses are fairly good and cheap – minimum fare is Rs 0.50 for a long journey, such as Hotel Hakoba to the airport. An auto-rickshaw from Ernakulam to the airport will cost Rs 10.

If you have to get to Fort Cochin after the ferries stop running, the bus stand in Ernakulam is on M G Rd and Durbar Hall and the fare is Rs 1.40. Auto-rickshaws will try to charge Rs 50 but the buses run until at least 9.30 pm.

Taxi Taxis charge round-trip fares between the islands, even though you only go in one direction.

A taxi from Ernakulam to the airport costs Rs 20.

AROUND COCHIN

High in the Western Ghats, 137 km inland from Cochin, Munnar is a cool retreat amongst the tea plantations. Kaladi is 48 km north-east of Cochin and was the birthplace of the 8th-century philosopher and monotheist Shankara-charaya. Cranganore is only 35 km north of Cochin by ferry and 77 km north by road. There's a Portuguese fort and Hindu temples here plus the oldest mosque in India. St Thomas first set foot in India in 52 AD at nearby Kottapuram.

KOTTAYAM

There is a regular ferry service (more than 10 boats a day) through the lagoons from Alleppey to Kottayam – an interesting alternative to the Quilon backwater trip. This was a centre for the Syrian Christians of Kerala and there are several of their churches, including Cheria Palli and Vallia Palli, about five km north-west of the railway station. Today Kottayam is also a centre for Indian rubber production, and a good base for visits to the Periyar Wildlife Sanctuary. Its two-km-long main street is busy and colourful.

Idukki District

Kerala's best ganja is grown in the Idukki district, between Kumily and Mumar. Idukki, a town 100 km east of Cochin, is the main centre. The town has a good bank and small game and forest reserves. You can visit Idukki from Kumily, 2½ hours away by bus. One visitor's Kerala ganja report:

A policeman approached me and asked if I'd like to buy some grass. Why not? He led me off to a side road, disappeared for a few minutes and returned with the goods. When I asked if he had any papers too, he took me to the police station where all his colleagues were sitting outside, sat me down and proceeded to make a superb joint using a cigarette. Very friendly type.

Places to Stay

The *Anjali Hotel* (tel 3661-6) on K K Rd

THE NUTS ARE SOLD BY WEIGHT.

has singles/doubles at Rs 65/95 with air-con. At the *Hotel Ambassador* (tel 3755, 3293-4), also on K K Rd, prices are similar but there are some cheaper non air-con rooms. It's worn and decrepit and the bathrooms 'leave a lot to be desired' but the management are friendly and the Chinese-style food is OK.

Opposite the bus stand the *Anurag Lodge* is reasonably clean and acceptable at Rs 20/30. Kottayam also has a *Tourist Bungalow*. *Hotel Aida* (tel 3691-5) on M C Rd has rooms at Rs 40/70 or with air-con at Rs 60/90.

Getting There

Kottayam has two bus stations – a local one for town buses and a chaotic state one for longer-distance buses. As the boat jetty is at the bottom of a steep hill and over a km from the state bus stand, it's best to take an auto-rickshaw. Buses to Thekkady for the Periyar Wildlife Sanctuary go about every two hours and cost around Rs 14. Some go right through to Madurai, a tediously long six to seven-hour trip.

PERIYAR WILDLIFE SANCTUARY

This 800-square-km sanctuary in the Thekkady district on the border of Tamil

Nadu is one of the most important in India. In it you can see elephants, bison, antelope, sambar, wild boar, monkeys and, if you're very lucky, those elusive tigers. The park is centred around a large artificial lake, and there's a choice of private or KTDC accommodation. Unfortunately, you won't see much in the way of wildlife if that's how far you get, as there's too much human activity and traffic noise around the lodges. Indeed, at weekends they're inundated by day trippers and tourist coaches, and the only things you will hear are transistor radios and ape-like noises made by fellow human beings.

Elephants are the animals you're most likely to see, although as with any wildlife sanctuary it's quite possible to see nothing at all. They're worth checking for if the time of year is good.

If you don't have four or five days to spare, you'll have to take one of the launch trips down the lake. These are

good value as far as they go, and you'll probably see a variety of game, but it doesn't equal the experience of being alone in a small hut in the middle of the night engulfed by the noises of the jungle. 'As soon as a shy animal sticks its head up', reported one visitor, 'all aboard shout and scream until it goes again'.

It's advisable to bring warm clothes and waterproof clothing to Periyar. These cannot be hired when you get there. Kumily is the nearest place to buy supplies if you're going to stay in one of the forest rest houses/observation towers.

A traveller's report of a visit:

All we saw was a shadowy shape on a distant shore, which a nun said was a hyena (so naturally we took her word for it). Then we spotted a herd of elephants; I've become used to elephants painted with sacred symbols, tusks tipped with gold sheaths and bells, heads with gold plaques and embroidered brocade .... but these beasts were stark naked *and* they were doing peculiar things with their

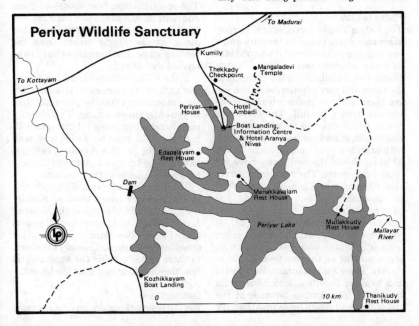

trunks to each others' bottoms! I don't mind naked people but elephants are a bit much. The only wildlife worth seeing is in the back creeks – the biggest tadpoles in the world with heads like golfballs!

D'Arcy Ryan, Australia

Orientation & Information

Periyar means the whole park; Thekkady is used to refer to the area where Aranya Nivas and Periyar House are located. Kumily is a separate village which is beginning to develop into quite a travellers' centre. These three place names tend to get used synonymously and confusingly.

Mangaladev Temple

It's an interesting excursion to this temple, 28 km from Kumily. The temple is just a few ruins but the views are magnificent. You can rent bicycles and ride there but it's uphill all the way (coast back). Alternatively, you can rent a jeep for about Rs 150, a three to four-hour trip with a lunch stop.

Places to Stay

The Kerala Tourist Development Corporation runs three places in the park and if you're going on a weekend it's a good idea to make advance reservations. *Periyar House* (tel Kumily 26) is the cheapest of the three and very popular, so unless you get there early or make advance reservations it may be full. There are two dorms which take 10 people each plus singles with shared bathrooms and doubles with attached bathrooms. Rooms are Rs 30 to Rs 50 and the bathrooms have hot (very hot!) water. The restaurant serves good vegetarian and non-vegetarian food at reasonable prices, considering you have no choice.

Aranya Nivas (tel Kumily 23) is considerably more expensive and offers ordinary, deluxe and VIP rooms with prices ranging all the way from Rs 100 to Rs 300. There's a restaurant, bar, postal and banking facilities, and handicrafts showroom. The Aranya Nivas is at the end of the road which leads into the park

from Kumily. Periyar House is about half a km back from there.

Lake Palace, the most expensive of the three, is on the lakeshore, a long way into the park. If you can afford it (doubles with full board are Rs 500), this is a delightful place to stay and you can actually see animals from your room. There are a restaurant, bar, postal and banking facilities and handicrafts showroom. To get to the Lake Palace you have to arrange to be at the Aranya Nivas launch jetty by 5 pm at the latest. The ferry costs Rs 10.

If possible you should try to book accommodation at Periyar in advance. This can be done at any Kerala Tourist Office. If you haven't done so, make sure you call at the Tourist Office in Kumily before catching a bus into the sanctuary. The man there will ring up and find out what rooms are available. There are also Forest Bungalows, but beware of being overcharged for being ferried to them. The special return boat comes at 9 am and costs Rs 30 regardless of the numbers. It's a long (two km) walk to the bungalow along narrow jungle tracks from the landing stage. The bungalows have to be booked well ahead.

If the KTDC places are all full or you can't afford the more expensive ones, try the *Ambadi* (tel 11) at the checkpost, just as you enter the sanctuary. This recently built hotel offers beautiful cottages with hot and cold running water and teak furniture for Rs 50 a double. They also have four-bed dorms. Indian and Chinese food are available in the evenings.

There's a good selection of cheap hotels in the pleasant small town of Kumily itself. Try the *Mini Lodge* or the *Kavitha Lodge*, which both have rooms at less than Rs 10. The *Impala* is a popular travellers' restaurant. The only drawback to these places outside the sanctuary is that they're a long way from the launch.

Getting There

Bus Although there are bus connections

between Kumily and Cochin, Idukki, Kottayam, Madurai, Quilon and Trivandrum, it's best to come in from Cochin, Kottayam or Madurai. Periyar is right on the main road from Madurai to Cochin; no detours are necessary. The bus from Quilon takes all day and may involve confusing changes in what seems like the middle of nowhere. The bus from Trivandrum takes even longer, and it will take you half the morning to find the right bus at the terminal.

For Kumily there are several buses daily from Cochin, Madurai, Trivandrum or Idukki and about 10 from Kottayam. The trip from Kottayam takes four or five hours and costs Rs 16 by express bus. There are plenty of connecting buses for the two-hour trip to Cochin, which costs Rs 10.

All the express buses and many of the others come down to the Aranya Nivas and Periyar House before leaving Kumily, so you can catch them there rather than go up to the bus stand in Kumily.

Getting Around

There are local buses between Kumily and Periyar House/Aranya Nivas about 15 times a day for Rs 1, but it's also possible to hitch. You can take an elephant from the park office to Periyar House.

Two launches operate on the lake. One is run by the Aranya Nivas on a charter basis (ie you must hire the whole launch), and the other is run by the Forest Department. The latter takes all comers and costs Rs 6 each, but it doesn't leave until it's full – this can take up to two hours. There are several departures every day.

OTHER SANCTUARIES

Thattekkad Bird Sanctuary is 20 km from Kothamangalam on the Ernakulam-Munnar road. The Parambikulam Wildlife Sanctuary stretches around the Parambikulam, Thunacadavu and Peruvaripallam dams – there are lots of

crocodiles in the dam reservoirs. Thunacadavu is the sanctuary headquarters and there are forest rest houses here and at other centres.

ALLEPPEY (population 175,000)

Like Quilon, this is a pleasant, easygoing market town surrounded by coconut-palm plantations and built around canals which service the coir industry of the backwaters. There's precious little to see in Alleppey; when I got there a bunch of medical students at St George's Lodge said to me, 'Why have you come here? There's nothing in Alleppey!'

While that may be true for most of the year, there is one event which you should not miss if you're anywhere in the vicinity on the second Saturday of August. This is the snakeboat races for the Nehru Cup. On this day scores of long, low-slung dugouts with high decorated sterns and up to 100 rowers compete for the cup watched by thousands of spectators on the banks. It's the biggest event of the year.

The other reason you might pass through here on any other day of the year is, of course, to make the backwater trip to Quilon (or, if you're coming from that place, to stay here overnight before heading further north). For full details on this unforgettable trip, refer to the section on Quilon.

Orientation & Information

The bus station and boat jetty are conveniently close to each other on the canal but some distance from the main hotels so, if you have a lot of baggage, it's worth taking an auto-rickshaw. If you don't want to do this, St George's Lodging – Alleppey's best bargain in hotels – is a good 15 minutes' walk from the boat jetty. There is no rail connection with Alleppey.

Things to See

The Hindu temple (see map) is worth a look, although as a non-Hindu you won't be allowed inside. It's a fine example of an elaborately carved wooden south Indian temple reminiscent of those in Nepal. Alleppey also has a lengthy beach.

Places to Stay – bottom end

St George's Lodging is magnificent value. It's spotlessly clean, pleasantly decorated and has curtained windows. The staff are very friendly and there's even a Gideon's Bible on the desk and a rose garden on the roof! Rooms are Rs 10/14 or Rs 14/30 with attached bathroom. There's nothing to compare with it in Alleppey.

Hotel Komala (tel 3631) near the boat jetty and the bus station has singles/doubles for Rs 30/40 or Rs 75/90 with air-con. It also has a good restaurant. It may not represent as good value as St George's, but it does have more facilities and is closer to the bus and boat stations. The *Municipal Rest House* opposite has doubles with bath for Rs 20.

Dhanalekshmi Lodge, diagonally opposite the Hindu temple, is an older building than St George's Lodging and not as well-maintained. *Raja Tourist Home* is probably the next best after St George's. Rooms here cost Rs 9 a single and Rs 15 a double, both with attached bathroom.

There are several other budget hotels opposite the boat jetty such as *Krishna Bhavan* and *Mahalakshmi Lodge*, but they look decidedly scruffy. Near the Komala Hotel the modern *Sheeba Lodge* has doubles for Rs 20. Close to the Medical College Hospital, two km from the boat jetty, the *Raiban Tourist Home* has rooms at Rs 30/50 with attached bath.

Out of town the *PWD Bungalow* is a very pleasant place to stay and cheap at Rs 7.50 per person, but you must add the cost of getting there by auto-rickshaw or taxi. Also, there are no restaurants nearby and meals at the PWD are expensive. Nevertheless, it's recommended by many travellers and is near the beach.

Places to Stay – top end

Up the price scale the very pleasant *Alleppey Prince Hotel* (tel 3752) on A S Rd has centrally air-con rooms from Rs 100/150 and a swimming pool. It's two km from the centre towards Cochin and has an excellent restaurant.

Places to Eat

The pleasant *Indian Coffee House* is quite a way from the centre, across the canal, opposite the hospital and near Hotel Ashoka. It's divided up into several rooms furnished with comfortable chairs and coir matting on the floor. The waiters display a touch of the Raj in their white uniforms, cummerbunds and frilly turbans. Prices are very reasonable and they serve cheap non-vegetarian food and excellent real coffee – of course. The café is popular with students and the local intelligentsia.

The *Komala Hotel*, on the other side of the canal bridge, has been recommended by one traveller as having 'the best food in south India'. 'We were not impressed', reported a later visitor! If you're looking for vegetarian plate meals (standard south Indian menu), there are a number of vegetarian restaurants near the Raja Tourist Home. *Dhanalaxmi Restaurant* is clean and has good vegetarian food, good quality curd and they will even boil water for you. The *Shree Durga Bhavan Restaurant* in the Udipi Hotel on Cullen Rd does great thalis.

The restaurant on the top floor of *St George's Lodging* gets mixed reports. Some say it is good; another traveller reported that 'half of the items on the menu are unavailable, the waiters are pretty clueless and the cashier is absurdly particular about the bills he accepts'.

Getting There

Bus The main express services are:

Going South There are eight to 10 buses daily to Quilon and 30-odd to Trivandrum.
Going North There are about 40 buses

daily to Ernakulam and the 1½ to two-hour trip costs Rs 8. If you are heading for Fort Cochin as opposed to Ernakulam, you can get off this bus just before the bridge which connects Cochin and Willingdon Island and take a local bus or autorickshaw from there into either Mattancherry or Fort Cochin. This will save you a lot of messing about with ferries when you get to Ernakulam.

There are also daily buses to Cannanore, Calicut (Kozhikode) and Palghat.

Boat See the Quilon section for details on the backwater trip.

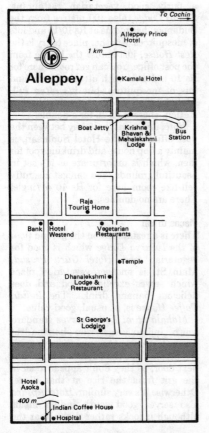

Boats to Kottayam cross Lake Vembanad, take 2½ hours and cost Rs 2.50. There are about 15 boats daily and it's a good short taste of the backwaters.

QUILON (population 140,000)
Buried amongst coconut palms and cashew tree plantations on the edge of Ashtamudi Lake, this small market town of old wooden houses with red-tiled roofs overhanging winding streets is perhaps the most typical of Keralan towns. If you're coming up from the south, it's also the gateway to the backwaters of Kerala. The trip by boat to Alleppey through these backwaters is a fascinating and unique experience.

Quilon has roots going back centuries. The Malayalam era is calculated from the founding of this town in the 9th century. Its history is interwoven with the rivalries between the Portuguese, Dutch and English for control of commodities grown in this part of the sub-continent and the trade routes across the Indian Ocean. Only three km from the centre of town at Thangasseri stand the ruins of a fort originally constructed by the Portuguese and later taken over by the Dutch. In Ashtamudi Lake are many Chinese fishing nets of the type more usually associated with Cochin, further north. The name Quilon is pronounced 'Kai-lon'.

Orientation & Information
Other than the Tourist Bungalow (not to be confused with the Travellers' Bungalow) which is a long way from the centre of town (Rs 10 auto-rickshaw ride), most hotels are in the central area between the clock tower and the post office. There is no Tourist Office in Quilon. The GPO is open until 8 pm from Monday to Saturday and until 6 pm on Sundays and public holidays.

Things to See
Apart from the miserable ruins of the Portuguese/Dutch fort at Thangasseri,

there are few 'sights' in Quilon. It's just a pleasant place to stroll around for a day or so and soak up the atmosphere of a Keralan market town. Most travellers come here to take the boat through the backwaters or, if coming from Alleppey, are en route to Trivandrum. As such it's an overnight stop.

Places to Stay

The most interesting place to stay is the *Tourist Bungalow* – a former British Residency converted to a hotel. The tourist literature is fond of telling you that 'Lord Curzon slept here'. It's a beautiful place overlooking the lake but rather a long way from town. Rooms cost Rs 15 per person but there are only eight of them, and although meals are available they're on the expensive side. On the surface, it seems a cheap place to stay, but you have to add on the cost of getting there by auto-rickshaw (about Rs 10 one way).

The best place to stay in the centre of Quilon itself is the large and pleasantly decorated *Hotel Karthika* (tel 3760, 3764), although some recent reports indicate that it's starting to suffer from lack of upkeep. It's excellent value at Rs 25/40 and there are more expensive air-con rooms. All rooms have their own bathroom and the hotel has a restaurant. 'This is yet another place', reported a windswept guest, 'with fans that either spin so fast they pin you up against the wall or they don't go at all'.

Hotel Seabea is a new hotel very conveniently located near the bus station and boat jetty. Singles/doubles cost Rs 40/75 non air-con and Rs 60/100.

Before the Karthika was constructed the *Hotel Sudarsan*, Parameswar Nagar between the post office and the boat jetty, used to be the best hotel in town, but it's been allowed to run down over the last few years and some rooms are decidedly tatty at the edges. Rooms with attached bath cost Rs 30 to Rs 35 for singles, Rs 45 to Rs 55 for doubles. The hotel has two restau-rants, one air-con, the other non-air-con, and its own bar. The food is reasonable but the service haphazard; room service is also very poor. Better than the Sudarsan is the *Iswarya Lodge*, another fairly new building, but quite a way from the centre of town. Rooms here cost Rs 20/40 with attached bath and there is a good restaurant on the ground floor.

If you're looking for something cheaper, try the *Sika Lodge/Hotel Apsara* (tel 7096) about 100 metres down the road, opposite the bridge across the river. It's reasonable value at Rs 18/30 with attached bath and fan. On the ground floor there is a fairly good vegetarian restaurant. *Samos Lodge*, also 100 metres from the Sudarsan, has rooms at Rs 10/15 and lots of mosquitoes. Another place to try is the *Rest House*, just across the bridge from the post office. You can get rooms here for Rs 15 a double with attached bath and lots of mosquitoes, but it's often full. *Mahalakshmi Lodge*, opposite the bus station, charges Rs 16 for a double.

Hotel de Orient, half-way between the post office and the Hotel Sudarsan, is mainly a flop house and drinking spot for men, which is unfortunate as it's set in beautiful grounds. You can get a scruffy cell-like room here for Rs 10 a single. There are no doubles.

Places to Eat

There is a restaurant on the ground floor of the *Iswarya Lodge* which is good for vegetarian food. *Hotel Guru Prasad*, Main St, is another vegetarian place which serves excellent food and does delicious banana drinks. The *Indian Coffee House* is, as usual, good value.

Mahalakshmi Lodge serves standard south Indian vegetarian banana-leaf meals. If you want to preserve your teeth it's better than the *Mysore Restaurant* next door, as they don't appear to sieve the grit from the rice at that place. Otherwise it's very similar. *Hotel Apsara* also serves good south Indian meals although it looks rather drab. Near the clock tower *Superabadham's* vegetarian food is superb value.

Although Quilon is supposed to be a cashew-growing centre they do not seem to be bargains in the town. The nuts cost Rs 10 for 100 grams, the same as you pay in Trivandrum. A good price is supposed to be Rs 8 for 100 grams.

Getting There

Rail Quilon is 156 km south of Cochin and takes three or four hours by train at a fare of Rs 19 in 2nd class, Rs 71 in 1st. The Madras-Cochin service continues on to Quilon, as does the Bombay-Cochin and the Mangalore-Trivandrum coastal service.

There are also trains between Quilon and Madras Egmore via Madurai (760 km, eight hours, Rs 62 in 2nd class, Rs 253 in 1st). The trip across the Western Ghats is a pure delight. Passenger trains between Quilon and Trivandrum are very slow in comparison to the buses (they take about three hours) but are also very cheap. From Quilon they depart several times daily.

Bus Many of the buses from Quilon bus station do not originate from there but are en route from somewhere else. To Trivandrum there are a couple of dozen buses daily and the two-hour trip costs Rs 9.

To Alleppey or Shencottah there are a half dozen buses daily, while to Ernakulam there are about 15. There are plenty of other buses going further up the coast and to intermediate towns.

There is daily service to Kumily (Periyar National Park) which takes eight hours and costs Rs 25. If you take this bus, you may have to change at Kottayam.

Backwater Trip by Boat This trip is one of the highlights of a visit to Kerala. It takes you across shallow, palm-fringed lakes studded with cantilevered Chinese fishing nets; goes along narrow shady canals where coir (coconut fibre), copra (dried coconut meat) and cashews are loaded onto dugouts; and calls at many small settlements along the way.

It's interesting to see how people live on narrow spits of land only a few metres wide, water all around, yet still manage to keep cows, pigs, chickens and ducks and cultivate small vegetable gardens. On the more open stretches of canal, you'll see dugouts with huge sails and prows carved into the shape of dragons. The sight of three or four of these sailing towards you in the late afternoon sun is one never to be forgotten. The boat crews are friendly and

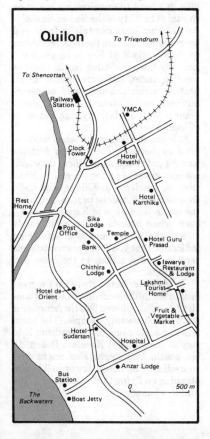

Quilon

To Trivandrum

To Shencottah

Railway Station

YMCA

Clock Tower

Hotel Revathi

Rest Home

Hotel Karthika

Sika Lodge

Post Office

Temple

Hotel Guru Prasad

Bank

Chithira Lodge

Iswarya Restaurant & Lodge

Lakshmi Tourist Home

Hotel de Orient

Fruit & Vegetable Market

Hotel Sudarsan

Hospital

Anzar Lodge

Bus Station

The Backwaters

Boat Jetty

0   500 m

will allow you to sit on the roof if you exchange a little conversation with them. It gets kind of hot up there, though. On some days during the winter season, almost half of the passengers in the boat could be western travellers. A decade earlier there were few if any.

There are two 10-minute 'chai stops' along the way where snacks and tea can be bought, but you may decide it's worth bringing some food with you. Beware of jacked-up prices for food and drink at these stops. There is usually a day and a night departure in each direction – Quilon-Alleppey and Alleppey-Quilon – although recently the morning departure from Alleppey has not always been operating. Although some travellers have reported that with a full moon the night trip can be interesting, you really want to do it by day. The trip takes approximately 8½ hours and costs only Rs 4.50 per person. If you're pushed for time you can take a bus from Ernakulam to Alleppey, make the trip to Quilon and get a bus back to Ernakulam all in the same day.

Some people find the whole trip from Quilon to Alleppey too long for comfort, but other, shorter boat trips are possible. They include Quilon-Kapapuzha twice daily and Quilon-Guhanandapuram a half dozen times daily. Or you can go to Changanacheeri from Quilon by train and from there to Alleppey by boat in about three hours. It's not necessary to book any of the boat trips ahead, although one traveller wrote of not being allowed on board because he didn't have a ticket in advance (?). There's usually (but not always) plenty of room and no problems with backpacks or other gear.

Getting Around

The transport facilities are at opposite ends of the town, three km apart, so if you arrive by rail and want to get to the bus station or the boat jetty you will need to take an auto-rickshaw (approximately Rs 4). The hills in Quilon are too steep for cycle-rickshaws. An auto-rickshaw from the station to the Hotel Sudarsan will be about Rs 3.

VARKALA

Only 19 km south of Quilon, 55 km north of Trivandrum, Varkala is a seaside resort with a mineral-water spring on the beach and the Janardhana Temple. At nearby Anjengo one of the earliest British East India Company trading posts was established in 1684.

TRIVANDRUM (population 513,000)

As you stroll around this friendly, relaxed city built over seven luxuriously forested hills, it's hard to imagine this is a state capital. The 'City of the Sacred Snake' is unlike other state capitals in India and has managed to retain the magic ambience so characteristic of Kerala in general – low sky-line, red-tiled roofs, narrow winding lanes, intimate corner cafés, beat-up municipal buses and necessary business accomplished in a friendly manner with a relatively high degree of efficiency.

At least, this is how it is when political tensions between the various factions haven't got to the stage where they spill out into violence on the streets. Political slogans, emblems and flags, especially those of the communist parties, dominate the urban landscape of Kerala. Luckily, even when there's violence, it rarely affects the visitor and is generally an indication that you'll be drawn into some very lively discussions in the cafés and restaurants.

On the other hand, there isn't a great deal to see in Trivandrum itself, and non-Hindus aren't allowed into the famous Sri Padmanabhaswamy Temple. The main reason people come to Trivandrum is to stay at magnificent Kovalam Beach, 16 km south. You might also might find yourself staying here a day or so if you're planning on flying to Sri Lanka or to the Maldive Islands.

Orientation

Trivandrum spreads over a large area but most of the services and places of interest are on or very close to Mahatma Gandhi Rd – the main road through the centre of the city from the zoological gardens to Sri Padmanabhaswamy Temple. The long-distance bus terminal, railway station and Tourist Reception Centre are all to be found within a few metres of each other, as are many of the budget hotels. The main market area is in Chalai Bazaar near the railway station.

The municipal bus stand is five minutes' walk from the railway station opposite Sri Padmanabhaswamy Temple. The post office in Trivandrum is a good half-hour walk from the railway station, so to get to it, as well as to the museum, art gallery and zoological gardens, you will need to take either an auto-rickshaw or taxi.

Information

There is a Tourist Office near the railway station and central bus station and another near the museums. From these offices you can book tours of Trivandrum and to Cape Comorin and Thekkady Wildlife Sanctuary.

Museum, Gallery & Zoo

These are all in the same area in the park at the north end of the city. They are open daily, except Monday and Wednesday mornings, between 8 am and 6 pm.

Museums Housed in an attractive building, the Napier Museum has a good collection of bronzes, historical and contemporary ornaments, temple carts, ivory carvings and life-size figures of Kathakali dancers in full regalia. Entrance is free. The Science & Industry Museum is not that interesting unless you are a high-school student in science.

Sri Chitra Art Gallery On display are paintings of the Rajput, Mughal and Tanjore schools together with works from China, Tibet, Japan and Bali. In addition, there are many modern Indian paintings, especially those of Ravi Varma. Entrance is Rs 2.

Zoological Gardens This is one of the best laid out zoos in Asia, set amongst woodland, lakes and well-maintained lawns. Some of the animal enclosures are still miserable, however. It includes a botanical garden with examples of almost every tropical tree. About a half km beyond the zoo, the ex-Maharaja's palace (palace is probably too grand a word for it) is now a state government building; you can see the conference room and banqueting/ballroom from the Maharaja's time and admire the fine view from the terrace. Rs 2 entrance fee.

Aquarium

The aquarium is quite a distance from the city centre near the airport and houses fish and many rare species of aquatic animals. It's open daily except Mondays between 9.30 am and 6 pm.

Padmanabhaswamy Temple

This temple, thought to be to the 'presiding deity' of Trivandrum, is dedicated to Vishnu. It was constructed in the Dravidian style by a Maharaja of Travancore in 1733. Unusually there are no beggars at the entrance to the temple. Only Hindus are allowed inside and even they have to wear a special *dhoti* which can be rented for Rs 1. There is a pool for the faithful to bathe in.

Padmanabhapuram Palace

Although actually in Tamil Nadu, this fine palace is easily visited from Trivandrum. See the Kanyakumari section in Tamil Nadu for more details. To get there you can either take a local bus from Trivandrum (or Kovalam Beach) or go on one of the tours organised by the Kerala Tourist Development Corporation. It's closed Mondays.

Tours

The Trivandrum city tour operates daily except Mondays at 8 am, returning at 7 pm. The tour costs Rs 35 per person and includes visits to Sri Padmanabhaswamy Temple (for Hindus only), museum, art gallery, aquarium, Kovalam Beach, zoo and Neyyar Dam. This tour is not worth taking unless your stay in Trivandrum is very short.

The daily Cape Comorin tour departs at 7.30 am and costs Rs 45. It includes visits to Padmanabhapuram Palace and Cape Comorin.

The Thekkady Wildlife Sanctuary tour to the sanctuary in the mountains of Kerala near the border with Tamil Nadu departs every Saturday at 6 am and returns the following day at 9 pm. The tour costs Rs 85 excluding board and lodging. If you're staying at Kovalam, you will miss the last bus back from Trivandrum. This must be one of the silliest tours in India, since there's no way you're going to have the time to see any wildlife at all – even if it were that easy!

Places to Stay – bottom end

There are many cheap lodging places along Station Rd (near the railway station and bus stand), but they're often full, many of them are very basic and this road is busy and noisy.

Nalanda Tourist Home has long been popular with budget travellers. It's on M G Rd on the right-hand side after you have crossed over the bridge over the railway. The building is modern, clean and convenient but somewhat noisy. Singles/doubles are Rs 20/30 and it's OK for just an overnight stay. *MGM Lodge* in the same area is even cheaper, with singles for as little as Rs 15, but it is very basic.

If you are staying in Trivandrum longer than a day you can look for a place further along M G Rd. *Onkar Lodge* (tel 65192) is between the bus station and the Secretariat, and doubles at Rs 25 are good value. Further from the bus and railway stations,

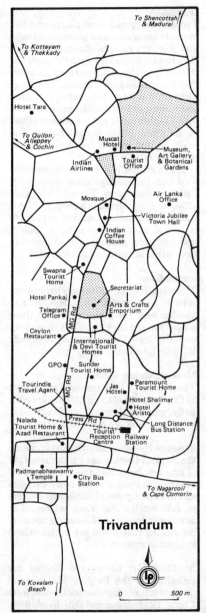

Trivandrum

To Shencottah & Madurai

To Kottayam & Thekkady

Hotel Tara

To Quilon, Alleppey & Cochin

Muscat Hotel

Indian Airlines

Tourist Office

Museum, Art Gallery & Botanical Gardens

Mosque

Air Lanka Office

Victoria Jubilee Town Hall

Indian Coffee House

Swapna Tourist Home

Secretariat

Hotel Pankaj

Arts & Crafts Emporium

Telegram Office

MG Rd

Ceylon Restaurant

International & Devi Tourist Homes

GPO

MG Rd

Sunder Tourist Home

Tourindia Travel Agent

Jas Hotel

Paramount Tourist Home

Hotel Shalimar

Hotel Aristo

Nalanda Tourist Home & Azad Restaurant

Press Rd

Tourist Reception Centre

Long Distance Bus Station

Railway Station

Padmanabhaswamy Temple

City Bus Station

To Nagarcoil & Cape Comorin

To Kovalam Beach

0   500 m

going up M G Rd, is the *International Tourist Home* in the United Bank of India Building on Press Rd. This is a pleasant, quiet and clean hotel where singles with attached bathroom cost Rs 15 – a bargain for what you get. Nearby on the same road is the cheaper but more basic *Devi Tourist Home*, which has a choice of small and spartan rooms for Rs 10.

There is also a *Youth Hostel* in the Veli area of Trivandrum with Rs 5 beds in an eight-bed dormitory.

Places to Stay – top end
Most people seeking five-star comfort head for the *Kovalam Ashok Beach Resort* at Kovalam Beach (a quarter of an hour away by taxi). Meanwhile, in Trivandrum itself the KTDC-run *Mascot Hotel* (tel 68990) is one of the best value hotels in its price category in southern India. It's near the museums in the northern part of the city and has rooms at Rs 65/95 or with air-con at Rs 115/150.

Hotel Pankaj (tel 66557) is a fine hotel conveniently situated opposite the Government Secretariat. It has two restaurants, one on the roof overlooking the city, with a choice of Mughlai, tandoori, Chinese and western cuisine. Singles are Rs 90 or Rs 120 to Rs 200 with air-con. Doubles are Rs 120 or Rs 160 to Rs 200 with air-con. Another hotel of a similar standard in the centre of town is the *Rajdhani* (tel 3353) at East Fort.

Hotel Luciya Continental (tel 73443) is a new top-end hotel at East Fort. Singles/doubles are Rs 125/190 or Rs 215/290 with air-con and in this category it's very good value. There are two good restaurants and the travel bureau here has been recommended.

Places to Eat
The best place for vegetarian food in Trivandrum is *Athul Jyoti* near the Secretariat, where a thali with nine different vegetables, dhals and curd is only Rs 6.

The *Khyber Restaurant* near the railway station has Chinese and western food but is somewhat expensive. The *India Coffee House* (north of Statue Rd and between the museum and the Secretariat) has very good masala dosas. The *Aradhana Restaurant* in the station area serves inexpensive vegetarian food.

The *Azad Restaurant* on M G Rd between the railway bridge and the temple is not as good as it used to be but may still be worth trying. The *Ceylon Restaurant* in the same area serves non-vegetarian food such as fish or meat curries and is popular with the locals.

On the expensive side, the restaurant in the Hotel Woodlands does food well. The *Jas Hotel* is good for a splurge meal or even a cold beer in air-con comfort. *New Agra Sweets* has good snacks and exceptionally fine lassi.

Getting There
Air Trivandrum is a popular place from which to fly to Colombo (Sri Lanka) and Male (Maldives). Fares are Rs 479 to Colombo, Rs 572 to Male, and you can pay in rupees so long as you have bank receipts showing you changed at least that much in a bank. There are two Indian Airlines flights a week to Male and two a week to Colombo plus two more flights to Colombo with Air Lanka. The Air Lanka office is in the Hospital Geetangali Building on Reserve Bank Rd.

One traveller reported that somebody at Trivandrum airport tried to charge him Rs 100 airport tax on his flight to Colombo because he was only transitting Sri Lanka and therefore it was not an 'adjacent country' Rs 50 flight. Another claimed that Trivandrum airport was the most chaotic he'd experienced in 20 years of travel and that checking in for the 45-minute flight to Colombo took over two hours!

Domestically there are flights to and from Bombay (Rs 1086), Cochin (Rs 192), Dabolim (Goa, Rs 731), Delhi (Rs 1924), Madras (Rs 569) and Trichy (Rs 296).

Rail Although buses are much faster than the trains, Kerala State Road Transport buses, like most others in southern India, make no concessions to comfort and the drivers are pretty reckless. If you like to keep your adrenalin levels down the trains are a pleasant alternative, so long as you're not going too far.

The trains through Trivandrum are the same as those right down the coast through Cochin/Ernakulam and Quilon. The same twice-weekly Karnataka/Kerala Express departs from New Delhi and arrives at Trivandrum 48 hours later. The 3054-km trip costs Rs 177 in 2nd class, Rs 737 in 1st. Madras-Trivandrum is a 921-km trip costing Rs 70 in 2nd class, Rs 291 in 1st. It takes 18 hours on the Trivandrum Mail.

The Mangalore-Trivandrum coastal route takes 11 hours from end to end on the Yercaud Express. Trivandrum-Quilon is just 65 km (Rs 9 in 2nd class, Rs 37 in 1st), Trivandrum-Ernakulam is 201 km (Rs 23 in 2nd, Rs 86 in 1st) and Trivandrum-Calicut is 414 km (Rs 40 in 2nd, Rs 160 in 1st).

Trivandrum-Bangalore takes 19 hours on the Island Express. Fares for the 950-km trip are Rs 72 in 2nd class, Rs 299 in 1st. From Bombay it's a lengthy 45 hours and the 2062-km trip costs Rs 129 in 2nd class, Rs 536 in 1st. To Mettuppalaiyam (for Ooty) is a 14-hour trip involving changes of train at Shoranur and Coimbatore – not a bad trip though. There is also a direct train from Trivandrum to Gauhati in Assam which takes about 72 hours; that's just about as long (in distance) a train ride as you could find in India.

Bus The bus station in Trivandrum opposite the railway station is total chaos. There is a timetable of sorts, but nothing in English. Even so, it's largely a fiction, and as there are no bays you have to join the scramble every time a bus arrives just in case it happens to be the one you want. It's the law of the jungle

each time a battered old bus comes to a screeching halt in a cloud of dust, but it does help if you buy a 'priority ticket' (Rs 0.50). In theory, this entitles you to a seat on the bus of your choice, so wave it above your head as you're fighting to get on. If the conductor sees it, he'll generally pull you on board, but don't count on that seat.

There are frequent buses to all the main cities in Kerala and to Kanyakumari. Long-distance buses are also available to Madras, Mysore and Bangalore, but it would be better to take a private bus company if you're going that far, as the State Transport buses are very tatty and often hopelessly overcrowded.

There are seven buses daily for Cape Comorin; the 2½-hour trip costs Rs 10. There are more frequent buses between Trivandrum and Nagercoil, from where it is easy to get buses to the Cape. Buses start at 7.30 am for Ernakulam/Cochin and pass through Quilon. The trip to Quilon, from where you can start the backwater trip, takes two hours. The daily bus to the Thekkady Wildlife Sanctuary takes eight hours.

Other destinations include Madurai for Rs 27 or Madras for Rs 80.

Getting Around
Airport The chaotic little airport is six km from the city centre. A No 14 local bus goes there for less than a rupee.

Local Transport The local state government buses are very crowded but there are also auto-rickshaws and taxis. For transport around the city itself, auto-rickshaws are probably your best bet. The drivers need no prompting about using the meters, and fares are cheap.

For Kovalam Beach, bus No 15 runs 25 times daily from the Fort Bus Depot. The first departs at 6.20 am and the last at 9 pm, but don't pay too much attention to the timetable at the bus stop! The journey takes about half an hour and although the bus starts out ridiculously overcrowded it rapidly thins out. A taxi from Trivandrum to Kovalam Beach will cost Rs 7 to Rs 8 per person – they leave when they have seven passengers. Sometimes it is possible to get the taxi for Rs 5 each.

KOVALAM

Kovalam, just south of Trivandrum, is not only one of India's best beaches – perhaps *the* best – but the favourite watering hole of travellers in the south of India. It consists of a number of small, palm-fringed bays separated by rocky headlands. There is good surf on most days, although unless you are a strong swimmer you should approach the water cautiously until you're familiar with the rip, as one or two people get drowned here every year.

There are plenty of cheap places to stay and a choice of simple restaurants, many of which stand right on the water's edge and most of which offer excellent seafood. If anything, the atmosphere at Kovalam is even more mellow than it is on the beaches of Goa, and many people who turn up here intending to stay for a few days find themselves staying considerably longer.

Back from the beach and on either side of the two main coves, life goes on as it always has. The local people continue to cultivate their rice, coconuts, bananas, pawpaws and vegetables; the fishermen still row their dugouts out to sea and pull the nets in by hand. The influx of westerners hasn't radically affected the lifestyles of the people who live at the back of the two main coves. What it has meant is that extra income can be earned by selling fruit and other produce to the sun-and-waves worshippers and that anyone who can is offering rooms for rent or doing something to make this possible. Otherwise the place is, as yet, relatively unspoiled.

It requires a little effort and time to get to Kovalam, and most people have given India a chance to seep into their veins by the time they arrive. This is one of the reasons why you get such an interesting collection of people on the beach.

Orientation & Information

The nearest post office is in Kovalam village. A bank will change travellers' cheques without fuss or form-filling at the Kovalam Ashok Beach Resort, although sometimes it can still take a long time. Suntan lotion, Nivea cream, pain-killers and other general store commodities can be bought from the chai stalls at the bus stop.

Kovalam is very spread out and finding a place at first can involve a long walk – especially if you're carrying all your gear. The paths through the coconut palms and around the back of the paddy field are difficult to negotiate at night without a full moon unless you're familiar with them. If you're not, and want to try Silent Valley or Sreevas House for an evening meal, go before dark. This also ensures that you eat before midnight at Silent Valley.

You can go round the lighthouse between 3 and 4.30 pm for Rs 0.25. As you walk east from the lighthouse there is another beach and a small fishing village with a mosque.

Places to Stay – bottom end

There is no shortage of places to stay at the bottom end of the market – the coconut groves between the road and the beach are littered with small lodges, houses for rent and blocks of recently constructed rooms. To a large extent you get what you pay for, though it is worth shopping around and not necessarily taking the first place you are offered. In general, the nearer you are to the beach, the more you pay. Similarly, the more people there are chasing rooms, the more you pay. These factors can increase prices by up to Rs 10.

If you're planning on staying for more than a few days – many do regardless of previous intentions – it's worth asking around for a house to rent. There are a *very few* pleasant houses available. Likewise, if you let the owner of the accommodation know that you're staying for several days and possibly longer, then the price of a room will drop, even though you may have to pay in advance.

Kovalam is a small, intimate place and most travellers quickly develop a liking for particular lodges and restaurants, which makes it difficult to single out particular ones for recommendation. Those near the road, between the bus stand and Trivandrum, tend to be brick buildings with large rooms and are quite reasonable for what you pay. The main disadvantage is the 50-metre descent to the beach, which takes 10 minutes and is difficult in the dark. *Hotel Raja* and *Hotel Palm Garden* are in this category and cost about Rs 50 a double. Places like *Moon Cottage* are the real cheapies.

Along the beach many of the lodges are simply thatched huts, some set up just for the tourist season and dismantled later. The average rate for a double with fan and attached bath is Rs 50. *Apsara Cottage* is in a new building with a patio and has a small centre court with lots of potted green plants and cane chairs. The roof is flat and can be reached by a stairway, if you like some privacy while tanning. They have doubles for Rs 40 or with bath for Rs 45. *My Dream Restaurant* has a block of reasonable rooms with shower on the lighthouse beach for Rs 25.

Sreevas Hotel is a popular meeting place run by a retired army sergeant who speaks good English; surprisingly few people in Kovalam do. *Jeevan House* has ordinary rooms with fans and charges Rs 40 a double. *Hotel Surye*, run by a police officer, has some rooms with fans and some without. Doubles cost Rs 30 and there is a small garden. Hotels *Holiday Home, Orion* and *Kavitha* are all close to each other at the far end of the beach and charge Rs 40 to Rs 50 for doubles with attached bath. Rooms at the Hotel Orion overlook the sea.

Places to Stay – middle

If you want to stay close to the road and away from the beach, *Hotel Raja* is good value for Rs 50 a double, especially compared to some of the similar places closer to the beach. *Hotel Palm Garden* is in a new building and has nice rooms which cost Rs 40 per single. *Hotel Blue Sea* charges Rs 75 for a double and has a nice garden. If you want to enjoy both beach and a garden during your stay in Kovalam, this is the place to be. It is actually a mansion built in a traditional style and has numerous kinds of rooms.

The best hotel to stay at in this price range is *Hotel Rockholm*. The location is superb – although not at the beach itself it commands a beautiful view. It has a small library, TV and good restaurant. Singles/doubles cost Rs 125/150 but are worth it if you can afford this price. Closer to the beach, *Sea Weed Hotel* is cheaper at Rs 75 for a double but still pleasant. *Sea Rock Lodge* has a new two-storey addition in front of the cheaper original rooms. The rooms are huge and have balconies overlooking the beach. Doubles are Rs 60 in the low season, Rs 175 to Rs 200 in the high season.

The KTDC *Hotel Samudhra* is a pleasant, modern building, nicely placed on the quiet side of the beach 15 minutes' walk north of the Kovalam Beach Resort. Rooms are Rs 50/75 or with air-con Rs 65/100 in the off season. After we criticised the service in the last edition they wrote to say it was now 'considerably good'.

Places to Stay – top end

The most luxurious place to stay is the *Kovalam Ashok Beach Resort* (tel 68010), on the headland just above the bus terminal. Studio rooms, double rooms and cottages are Rs 550 single and Rs 650 double. The hotel has every facility you would expect, including air-conditioning, swimming pool, bar, crafts shop and boats for hire. It's a beautiful place and obviously a lot of effort has been put into its design and construction. It has facilities

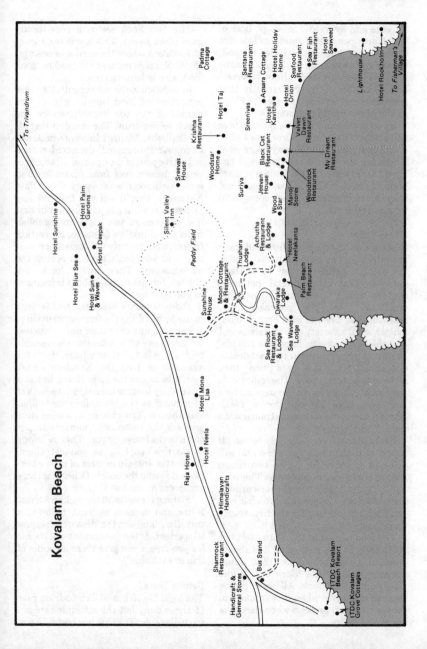

Kovalam Beach

To Trivandrum

Hotel Sunshine
Hotel Palm Gardens
Hotel Blue Sea
Hotel Deepak
Hotel Sun & Waves

Silent Valley Inn

Paddy Field

Sunshine House

Moon Cottage & Restaurant

Thushara Lodge

Dwaraka Lodge

Sea Rock Restaurant & Lodge

Sea Rock II Lodge

Hotel Mona Lisa

Hotel Neela

Raja Hotel

Himalayan Handicrafts

Shamrock Restaurant

Handicraft & General Stores

Bus Stand

ITDC Kovalam Grove Cottages

ITDC Kovalam Beach Resort

Padma Cottage

Hotel Tai

Krishna Restaurant

Woodstar Home

Sreevas House

Suriya

Achutha Restaurant & Lodge

Hotel Neelakanta

Palm Beach Restaurant

Santana Restaurant
Apsara Cottage
Hotel Holiday Home
Hotel Kavitha
Hotel Orion
Seafood Restaurant
Sea Fish Restaurant
Hotel Seaweed

Lighthouse

Hotel Rockholm

To Fisherman's Village

Sreenivas

Velvet Dawn Restaurant

Black Cat Restaurant
My Dream Restaurant
Jeevan House
Wood Star
Manoj Stores
Woodrock Restaurant

for yoga and ayurvedic massage, both of which are open to non-residents at a cost of Rs 40 per session. Facilities for golf, tennis, and swimming (Rs 30) can also be used by non-residents. We have, however, had a number of reports recently that standards and service here aren't as high as the prices would indicate.

If you're planning on a night out, a beer will cost you Rs 30 or so, three times what it will cost you virtually anywhere else! There are also Kathakali dances at the hotel three times a week. Unless you are planning to visit Cochin, you should not miss this performance, which costs Rs 20 for non-residents.

Places to Eat

Restaurants line the beachfront but there are others just as good scattered among the coconut palms. Almost all of them cater to that international palate – western-style breakfasts (porridge, omelettes, toast, jam, pancakes, etc), seafood (fish, prawns with French fries, lobster, etc), a variety of fruit salads and custard-based sweets. Everyone has his/her favourite but there isn't a great deal to choose between in quality or price – they all tend to be pretty good. The restaurants vary widely, however, in serving size, how long you have to wait for a meal, distractions in the meantime (music or no music) and lighting.

Some places have definitely bitten off much more than they can chew and will attempt to cater for up to two dozen customers on one primus stove. This isn't just a commendable case of over-enthusiasm; it's clearly impossible, which is why you'll still be waiting for the first course three hours after you ordered it.

The food is good at the *Shangri-la* but come early in the evening as it is always crowded. Others which are OK if things are going well include *Black Cat, Velvet Dawn* and *Woodstock*. All these places seem to rate raves when they manage to get the food out, protests when they take hours and hours.

The *Sea Rock* seems a consistently good place to eat. This is one restaurant at Kovalam where the service is prompt. *Rockholm* also manages to produce good food, ample helpings too.

In addition to the restaurants, there are a number of local women who do the rounds of the sun worshippers on the beach selling fruit. The familiar ring of, 'Hello, baba. Mango? Papaya? Banana? Coconut? Pineapple?' delivered with a seductive pout of the lips and a flashing of bright, brown eyes from under lowered eyelids will soon become part of your day. Naturally, they'll sell you fruit for any price you're willing to pay, so on your first few encounters you have to establish what you think is a fair price for certain fruits. After that they'll remember your face and you don't have to repeat the performance. They rarely have any change, but are reliable about bringing it to you later on.

Toddy (coconut beer) and *feni* (spirits made by distilling the fermented mash of either coconuts or cashew nuts – the two varieties taste quite different) are available from shops in Kovalam village. Beers are available at both the Kovalam Ashok Beach Resort or the Raja Hotel, but at a price likely to singe the hair on the back of your hand as you reach for your wallet. Buy them in Trivandrum at a wine store and ask the restaurant manager to put them in the fridge for you. They're happy to do this, so long as you eat there. Cigarettes are sold in most of the restaurants down on the beach. Otherwise there are stores at the bus stop.

'Fishing is easy from the rocks with just a line and mussels as bait', reported a traveller, 'and for the diehard cheapies it's perfect, as the restaurants will cook it for you free if you give them a couple of fish in exchange'!

Getting There

The local No 15 bus to Trivandrum runs 25 times daily but the schedules are not too believable. The first bus is at 6.15 am, the last at 10 pm. The depot is right outside the Kovalam Beach Hotel. It costs Rs 1.40. If you want to get to Kovalam from Trivandrum, there are plenty of taxis hanging around the bus stop there. They'll take you to the beach for Rs 7 to Rs 8 per person – Rs 5 if you're lucky. They leave when they have seven passengers.

There are also direct services to Ernakulam and Kanyakumari (Cape Comorin), which are a good way of avoiding the crush at Trivandrum. Cape Comorin is two hours away and there are four departures daily. To Thekkady in the Periyar Wildlife Sanctuary buses start at 7 pm. There are also direct buses to Quilon if you want to do the backwater trip.

Kovalam travel agents charge Rs 40 for flight reconfirmations but you can use the Ashok Resort phone for Rs 5. They will provide a taxi service to the airport if you have an early-morning flight, but it's expensive at about Rs 100.

Things to Buy

Apart from the fruit sellers there are men who come around selling *lungis*. It seems batik has arrived in Kovalam because there are some fine bargains to be picked up in this line, so have a look through what they've got. You may also come across a local artist who sells exquisite and subtly executed leaf paintings.

There is usually plenty of excellent ganja for sale – a *tola* (about 10 grams) should cost about Rs 8 to Rs 10. Most of it comes from the Idukki District in the mountains east of Cochin, though you may well be told that is comes from 'around Thekkady'.

LAKSHADWEEP

The 27 scattered Lakshadweep islands are 200 to 300 km off the Kerala coast and form a northern extension of the Maldives chain. Ten of the islands are inhabited. They are, in descending order of size, Minicoy, Androth, Kavaratti, Kadmat, Agathy, Ameni, Kalpeni, Kiltan, Chetlat and Bitral. The population of the islands is about 40,000, of which 93% are Muslim. The economy centres around copra production from coconuts.

Permits

Permission to visit the islands must be obtained from the Ministry of Home Affairs, Government of India, New Delhi. It takes four to six weeks to issue the permit, which must then be taken to the Secretary to the Administrator, Union Territory of Lakshadweep, Willingdon Island, Cochin for transport details and itinerary. Permits for conducted tours to the islands can be obtained directly from the administrator, but these only apply to certain islands, including uninhabited Bangaram and Suheli.

Places to Stay

There are 'family huts' at Rs 60 on Kavaratti and Kadmat islands and 'beach resorts' at Rs 25 per person at Kalpeni, Minicoy and Kavaratti. Kadmat also has a 'honeymoon resort' at Rs 60 for a double and a large *Youth Hostel* which costs Rs 10.

Getting There

The Shipping Corporation of India ships *MV Bharatseema* and *MV Amindivi* operate to the islands from Cochin three to five times a month. The trip takes about 18 hours and passengers should be prepared for rough seas. The *Bharatseema* is the more comfortable of the two ships – it even has air-con cabins. M/S Jairam & Sons on Willingdon Island sell tickets – deck class is Rs 160, bunk Rs 200, cabins Rs 320 to Rs 450.

Madras

Population: 3.5 million
Main language: Tamil

Madras is the capital of Tamil Nadu

Madras is India's fourth largest city and capital of Tamil Nadu state, but despite its size it is an example of how pleasant other Indian cities might be if they were not so overcrowded. Madrassis are not only zealous guardians of Tamil culture, which they regard as inherently superior to the hybridised cultures further north, they also appear to know the meaning of relaxation and efficiency with regard to public services – a remarkable combination, to be found only in isolated pockets elsewhere in India! Here it's possible to use public buses without undue discomfort and the urban commuter trains without a second thought. There are, it is true, slums and beggars but they are far less obtrusive and smaller in number. The city also has the advantage of a long beachfront on the Bay of Bengal, which ensures a good supply of refreshing sea air and provides a popular place to relax in the evening.

Madras was the site of the first important settlement of the East India Company – founded in 1639 on land given by the Raja of Chandragiri, the last representative of the Vijayanagar rulers of Hampi. A small fort was built in the settlement in 1644 and a town which subsequently became known as Georgetown, in the area of Fort St George, arose north of it. The settlement became independent of Banten in Java in 1683 and was granted its first municipal charter in 1688 by James II. It thus has the oldest Municipal Corporation in India, a fact which Tamil Nadu state governors are only too keen to point out at every available opportunity.

During the 18th and early 19th centuries, when the British and French rivalled for supremacy in India, the city's fortunes waxed and waned, being briefly occupied by the French on one occasion. It was also the base from which Clive set out on his military expeditions during the Wars of the Carnatic. During the 19th century it was the seat of the Madras presidency, one of the four divisions of British Imperial India.

Though the city has long been important for textile manufacture, a great deal of industrial expansion has taken place in recent years and its concerns now include car assembly plants, railway coach and truck works, engineering plants, cigarette factories, film studios and educational institutes. As a tourist attraction Madras is something of a non-event compared to the real marvels elsewhere in the state. The main reason travellers come here is to transact business (mail, money, tickets, visas) or to make a long-distance travel connection.

Orientation

The city may be conveniently divided into two parts. The older section is west of the dock area and north of Poonamallee High Rd. In these narrow, busy streets and bazaars are the offices of shipping and forwarding agents, some cheaper hotels and restaurants, other large office buildings, the GPO and American Express. Its main focal point is Parry's Corner/ Popham's Broadway, which runs alongside the High Court Buildings. The official name of this road is Netaji Subhash Bose Rd, but everyone knows it simply as Parry's Corner. Along this road are the municipal bus terminals and just off it, along Esplanade Rd, is the Tamil Nadu State Bus Stand and the Tiruvalluvar Bus Stand, the two long-distance bus terminals.

The other main part of the city is south of Poonamallee High Rd. Through it runs Madras' main road, Anna Salai, which is still generally known as Mount Rd. Along it are most of the airline offices, theatres, banks, bookshops, crafts centres, consulates, tourist offices and the bulk of the top-range hotels and restaurants.

Egmore and Central, Madras' two main railway stations, are close to Poonamallee High Rd. If you're arriving from anywhere other than Tamil Nadu or Kerala you'll come into Central Station. Egmore is the arrival point for most Tamil Nadu and Kerala trains.

Information

The Indian Government Tourist Office (tel 88685-6) is at 154 Anna Salai and is open daily except Sundays from 9 am to 6 pm. Holidays and every second Saturday it's only open 9 am to 1 pm. This Mount Rd Tourist Office is a good one; the staff are knowledgeable, friendly and helpful. A bus No 11 or 18 from Parry's Corner or Central Station will take you there.

Information counters at the domestic and international airport terminals are open daily from 9 am to 9 pm. The Tamil Nadu Government Tourist Office (tel 840752) is at 143 Anna Salai (Mount Rd). Various other state tourist departments have information centres in Madras.

The Automobile Association (tel 86121) is at 38A Anna Salai. Apart from route information, the organisation offers accommodation for members of any foreign automobile association, and car-parking facilities on the premises. *Hallo Madras* is a monthly tourist guide to the city with hotels, restaurants, tourist attractions, bus routes both local and further afield, and lots of addresses. It's available from newsstands.

Offices Immigration is at 9 Village Rd just off Nungambakkam Rd and before the junction with Sterling Rd – bus route No 10. Visa extensions can be obtained here and, if you're planning to visit the Andaman & Nicobar islands, you can arrange a permit from here – see the appropriate section.

Banks American Express is at Binny Ltd, 7 Armenian St (PO Box 66), but this office does not cash travellers' cheques and they may not even be able to replace them very quickly.

International banks include Bank of America (tel 82103) at 150B Anna Salai; First National City Bank (tel 810756) at 153 Anna Salai; and Grindlay's Bank (tel 87474) at 36D Anna Salai. The State Bank of India has an airport office open longer hours. Income tax clearance certificates are available from the Foreign Section, 121 Nungambakkam High Rd.

Bookshops Higginbothams at 814 Anna Salai has a good selection of books; or you could try the small but excellent bookshop in the Hotel Connemarra. The Kennedy Book Depot on Mount Rd near C-in-C Rd is also very good.

Airlines The Indian Airlines/Air India office is close to the Hotel Connemarra.

Air India
   19 Marshalls Rd, Egmore (tel 847799)
Air Lanka
   Hotel Connemarra Annexe, Binny's Rd (tel 87432)

Indian Airlines
  19 Marshalls Rd, Egmore (tel 847522, 848879)
Maldives Airways
  Crossworld Tours, 7 Rosy Towers, Nungambakkam High Rd (tel 471497)
MAS
  189 Anna Salai (tel 88970, 88525, 88675)
Singapore Airlines
  167 Anna Salai (tel 86156-8)

Shipping Agents
Binny & Co Ltd
  101/102 Armenian St (tel 26894)
Indo-Malaysian Shipping Agency
  103 Armenian St (tel 24525)
KPV Sheikh Mohammed Rowther & Co Ltd
  41 (or 202) Linghi Chetty St (tel 25756)

Consulates
West Germany
  22 Commander-in-Chief Rd (tel 82125)
Japan
  60 Spur Tank Rd, Chetput (tel 665594)
Malaysia
  23 Khader Nawaz Khan Rd (tel 473584)
Netherlands
  739 Anna Salai (tel 811566)
Sri Lanka
  9-D Nawab Habibullah Ave, Anderson Rd (tel 472270)
UK
  24 Anderson Rd (tel 473136)
USA
  Gemini Circle, 220 Anna Salai (tel 473040)

Fort St George & St Mary's Church
Built in 1653 by the British East India Company, but much altered from its original design, the fort presently houses the Secretariat and the Legislative Assembly. The Fort Museum, open 9 am to 5 pm but closed on Fridays, has a fascinating collection of memorabilia from the days of the East India Company and the British Raj, including a 'Clive's Corner'. A real curiosity is the tiny wooden 'Anstruther Cage' in which a rather tall British soldier was imprisoned in China from September 1839 to February 1840. Entrance to the museum is free. Nearby is the Banqueting Hall, built in 1802, around the walls of which hang

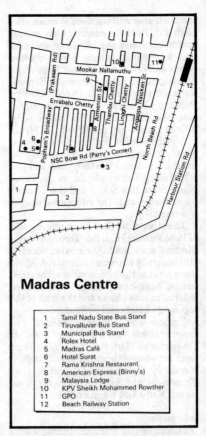

Madras Centre

1	Tamil Nadu State Bus Stand
2	Tiruvalluvar Bus Stand
3	Municipal Bus Stand
4	Rolex Hotel
5	Madras Café
6	Hotel Surat
7	Rama Krishna Restaurant
8	American Express (Binny's)
9	Malaysia Lodge
10	KPV Sheikh Mohammed Rowther
11	GPO
12	Beach Railway Station

many paintings of the governors of Fort St George and other high officials of the British regime.

St Mary's Church was built in 1678-80, the first English church in India. There are reminders here of Robert Clive, who was married in this church in 1753, and of Elihu Yale, the early governor of Madras who went on to found the famous university bearing his name in the US. North of the fort is the old 1844 lighthouse and the 1892 High Court, with its lighthouse tower superseding the earlier one.

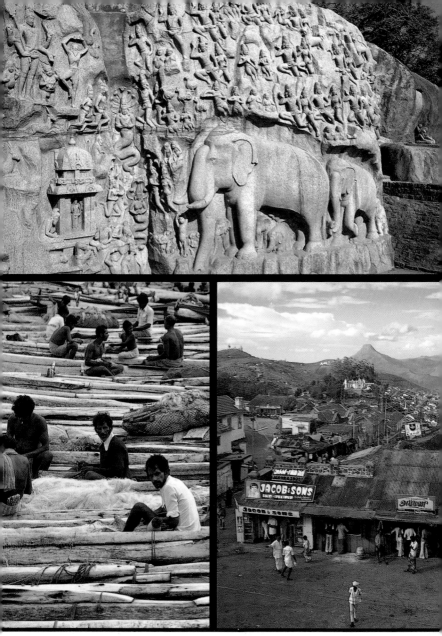

Tamil Nadu Top: Arjuna's penance, Mahabalipuram (TW)
            Left: Fishing boats on the beach, Kanyakumari (HF)
            Right: Kodaikanal (HF)

Tamil Nadu Top: Meenakshi Temple, Madurai (TW)
Left: Temple at Tirikkalikundram (TW)
Right: Visitors to the Five Rathas, Mahabalipuram (GC)

Government Museum & Art Gallery

On Pantheon Rd, near Egmore Station, the most interesting parts of this museum are the archaeological section and the bronze gallery. The latter has some excellent examples of Chola bronze workmanship. The museum and gallery are open daily except public holidays between 8 am and 5 pm. Entrance is Rs 0.50.

Kapaleeshwara Temple

Off Kutchery Rd, in the southern part of the city, this ancient Shiva temple has a typical Dravidian gopuram. It's worth a visit if your time is limited and you won't be visiting the more famous temple cities of Tamil Nadu. As with other functioning temples in this state, non-Hindus are only allowed into the outer courtyard.

San Thome Cathedral

Near Kapaleeshwara Temple at the southern end of South Beach Rd, close to the seafront, this Roman Catholic church is said to house the remains of St Thomas the Apostle. It was originally built in 1504 but was rebuilt in 1893.

Parathasarathy Temple

On Triplicane High Rd, the temple is dedicated to Lord Krishna. Built in the 8th century during the reign of the Pallavas, it was subsequently renovated by the Vijayanagar kings in the 16th century.

Marina & Aquarium

The sandy stretch of beach known as the Marina extends for 13 km, as far south as the San Thome Cathedral. The aquarium is on the seafront near the junction of Pycroft's Rd and South Beach Rd and is open daily between 2 and 8 pm except on Sundays and holidays, when it is open from 8 am. Entrance costs Rs 0.50 but it's a miserable place, 'worth giving a miss just to discourage its continued existence'.

Near the aquarium is the 'ice house'. This relic of the Raj era was used 150 years ago to store enormous blocks of ice cut from lakes in the northern USA and sent to India by sailboat. If you wanted a cold drink, that was how you got it in the days before refrigerators and air-conditioners. There was once a similar building in Calcutta. Watching the fishing boats come ashore in the evenings always provides an interesting hour. The fish are bartered to women on the spot.

Guindy Deer & Snake Parks

Close to Raj Bhavan at Guindy, on the southern outskirts of Madras, this is the only place in the world where it is still possible to see fairly large numbers of the fast-dwindling species of Indian antelope (black buck). It also has small numbers of spotted deer, civet cats, jackals, mongoose and various species of monkeys.

The reptile house is open daily between 9 am and 6 pm and entrance costs Rs 0.50. Probably the best way to get to Guindy is to take the urban commuter train from either Beach Railway Station, opposite the GPO, or from Egmore Station. There are also regular buses from central Madras (45 or 45B from Anna Salai).

Other

From the end of December through the second week of January, *Ramayana* dance performances take place in the dance school auditorium featured in the film *Phantom India*.

Tours

Both the India Tourism Development Corporation (ITDC) and Tamil Nadu Tourism Development Corporation (TNTDC) have tours of Madras, the nearby temple cities and further afield:

City Sightseeing Tour This includes visits to Fort St George, Madras Museum & Art Gallery, Valluvar Kottam, Gandhi Mandapam, Snake Park, Kapaleeshwara Temple and Marina Beach. The daily tours are fairly good value, start at 2 pm and end at 6 pm and cost Rs 25.

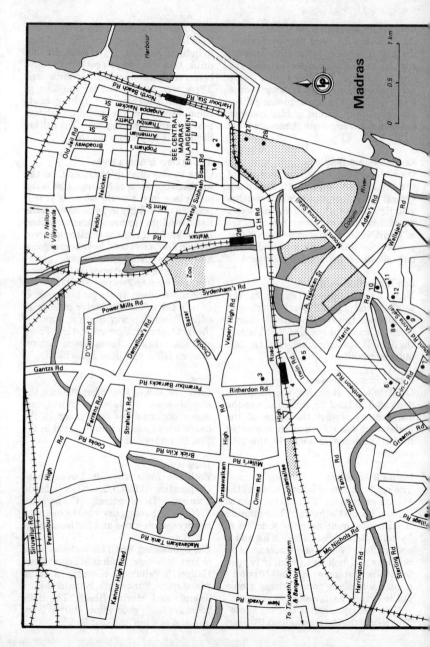

Madras

Harbour

North Beach Rd
Harbour Sta. Rd
Angappa Naicken St
Thambu Chetty St
Armenian St
Popham's
Broadway
Old Jail Rd
Naicken St
Peddu
Mint St
SEE CENTRAL MADRAS ENLARGEMENT
Netaji Subhash Bose Rd
G H Rd
Walltax Rd

To Nellore & Vijayawada

Zoo
Sydenham's Rd
Power Mills Rd
D'Castor Rd
Demellow's Rd
Choolai
Bazar Rd
Vepary High Rd
Gantzs Rd
Perambur Barracks Rd
Ritherdon Rd
High Rd
Irwin Rd
Road
Mount Rd and Anna Salai
Cooum River
Adam's Rd
Wallajah Rd
A. Naicken St
Harris Rd
Pantheon Rd
Com-C Rd
Greams Rd
(Anna Salai) Mount Rd

Ferens Rd
Cooks Rd
Strahan's Rd
Brick Kiln Rd
Miller's Rd
Ormes Rd
Purasawalkam
High Rd
Perambur
Siruvallur Rd
Madavakam Tank Rd
Kamur High Road
New Avadi Rd
Poonamallee
Spur Tank Rd
Mc Nichols Rd
Harrington Rd
Sterling Rd
Village Rd

To Tirupathi, Kanchipuram & Bangalore

0   0.5   1 km

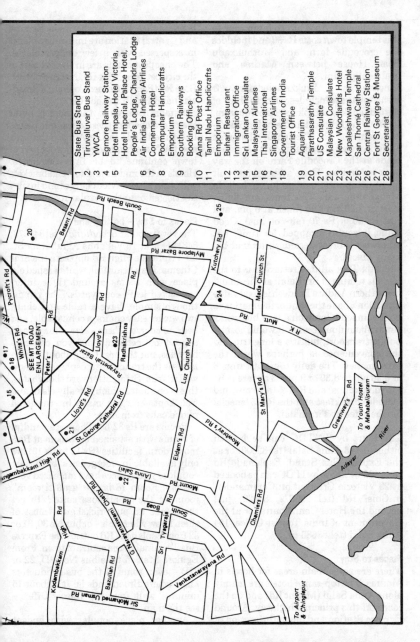

1 State Bus Stand
2 Tiruvalluvar Bus Stand
3 YWCA
4 Egmore Railway Station
5 Hotel Impala, Hotel Victoria, Hotel Imperial, Palace Hotel, People's Lodge, Chandra Lodge
6 Air India & Indian Airlines
7 Connemara Hotel
8 Poompuhar Handicrafts
9 Emporium
Southern Railways Booking Office
10 Anna Rd Post Office
11 Tamil Nadu Handicrafts Emporium
12 Buhari Restaurant
13 Immigration Office
14 Sri Lankan Consulate
15 Malaysian Airlines
16 Thai International
17 Singapore Airlines
18 Government of India Tourist Office
19 Aquarium
20 Parathasarathy Temple
21 US Consulate
22 Malaysian Consulate
23 New Woodlands Hotel
24 Kapaleeshwara Temple
25 San Thomé Cathedral
26 Central Railway Station
27 Fort St George & Museum
28 Secretariat

Mahabalipuram An 8 am to 5 pm tour to this temple town costs Rs 30 and includes the crocodile farm and Muthukkadu Boat House between Madras and Mahabalipuram.

Kanchipuram, Tirukkalikundram & Mahabalipuram Includes visits to three of the four ancient temples at Kanchipuram, the famous hilltop temple of Tirukkalikundram and the 7th-century Pallavan antiquities at Mahabalipuram. A stop is made at the Crocodile Farm on the way back to Madras. There's a breakfast halt in Kanchipuram and a lunch halt in Mahabalipuram. The tours are daily, start at 7.30 am and finish at 6 pm, and cost Rs 50 or Rs 70 (air-con bus). Good value if you're strapped for time, but otherwise a breathless dash around too many places.

Tirupathi This all-day return tour to the famous temple of Sri Balaji at Tirumalai in southern Andhra Pradesh is good value if you don't have the time or inclination to do it yourself. Going on a tour bus works out at about double what it would cost by public transport, but it's a long trip and the convenience is perhaps worth the extra money. The daily tours last from 6 or 6.30 am to 8.30 or 9 pm. The fare is Rs 115 (deluxe bus) and Rs 145 (air-con), and includes breakfast and the Rs 25 'special darshan' fee at Tirumalai.

The tours by TNTDC can be booked either at 143 Anna Salai (tel 88806) or at the Express Bus Stand, Esplanade Rd (tel 21835). Those by ITDC can be booked at 29 Victoria Crescent off Commander-in-Chief Rd (tel 890672, 88520) just beyond the Hotel Connemarra; or at the Government of India Tourist Office, 154 Anna Salai (tel 88685-6).

Places to Stay

There are three main areas for hotels in Madras. The top-range hotels are mainly along Anna Salai (Mount Rd) and on the roads off this principal highway. Around Egmore Station and along the section of

Poonamallee High Rd between Egmore and Central Station are mid-range places interspersed with a few budget places. The cheapest hotels are in the old part of the city between Mint Rd, Netaji Subhash Bose Rd (Parry's Corner/Popham's Broadway) and North Beach Rd.

Egmore Station is the most popular area for travellers these days, but places like Broadlands in the Anna Salai area and the Malaysia Lodge in the old part of town continue to be firm favourites. Hotels in the middle and top-end brackets will often have service charges and luxury tax tagged onto the regular room rate.

Places to Stay – bottom end

The very popular *Broadlands* (tel 845573, 848131) is at 16 Vallabha Agraharam St, off Triplicane High Rd opposite the Star Cinema. It's a beautiful, whitewashed old place with rooms around three interconnected leafy courtyards. The rooms, though simple, have a table and chair, two wicker easy chairs, a coffee table, and beds, of course. There's also a library and a good noticeboard, and you can hire bicycles, but the best thing about Broadlands is the tranquil atmosphere and how well it's run. Straightforward though it is, this is one hotel which is really clean and well kept. You can make international phone calls from here.

Rooms are Rs 32/63. There is a handful of rooms with attached bathroom at Rs 5 more; dorm facilities (Rs 12 to Rs 15) are only available in emergencies. In the last couple of years prices have increased very steeply. Room 18 is the 'graffiti room', room 44 the 'penthouse suite'. To get there take an auto-rickshaw – most of them know where it is – or bus No 30, 31 or 32 from Esplanade Rd outside the Express Bus Terminal in the centre of town. From Egmore Station take bus No 29D, 22 or 27B – even some of the bus conductors know where Broadlands is! It's about 15 minutes' walk from the Tourist Office – see the map.

Another place popular with budget

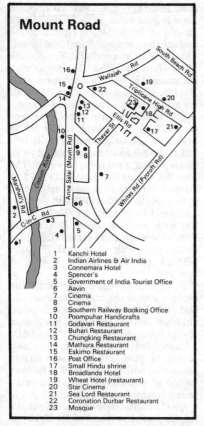

Mount Road

1 Kanchi Hotel
2 Indian Airlines & Air India
3 Connemara Hotel
4 Spencer's
5 Government of India Tourist Office
6 Aavin
7 Cinema
8 Cinema
9 Southern Railway Booking Office
10 Poompuhar Handicrafts
11 Godavari Restaurant
12 Buhari Restaurant
13 Chungking Restaurant
14 Mathura Restaurant
15 Eskimo Restaurant
16 Post Office
17 Small Hindu shrine
18 Broadlands Hotel
19 Wheat Hotel (restaurant)
20 Star Cinema
21 Sea Lord Restaurant
22 Coronation Durbar Restaurant
23 Mosque

travellers for years is the *Malaysia Lodge* (tel 27033), 44 Armenian St off Popham's Broadway, at the back of the GPO. Like the Rex and Stiffles in Bombay, much has been written and said about the Malaysia Lodge over the years – some of it good, most of it bad. It's undeniably extremely cheap and equally basic – 'In our four-bed room a rat used a bloke's head as a springboard to get to a banana lying on a table', wrote one impressed visitor. Rooms are Rs 16/22 or with attached bathroom Rs 18/26.

If you can't handle the Malaysia but want somewhere in the centre of town, try

the *Hotel Rolex* (tel 24236-9), 190 Netaji Subhash Chandra Bose Rd (Popham's Broadway). It has only one single at Rs 25, but doubles are a reasonable Rs 39 with attached bath. Get there early in the day, otherwise it could be full.

Away from the centre of town a cheap, popular place to stay is the *YWCA Guest House & Camping Ground* (tel 34945), 1086 Poonamallee High Rd, which takes both men and women and has its own restaurant with good food. Singles or doubles cost Rs 35 per person, rooms for four are Rs 30 per person. In addition there's a Rs 5 transient membership fee per head. The camping ground costs Rs 15 per person plus Rs 15 for a motorcycle, Rs 25 for a car. The rooms are clean and well kept and there's a big garden where you can sit and relax. It's right at the back of the Egmore Station. The *YMCA* at 24 West Cott Rd, Royapettah has rooms for members only.

Places further down Poonamallee High Rd towards Central Station are assaulted by horrendous noise and pollution from the road in front and the railway line behind. For major emergencies only, you could try *Everest Boarding & Lodging* (tel 30772-3), which has rooms from Rs 20/39. Or there's the *Hotel Devi* with singles at Rs 15 to Rs 20, doubles from Rs 32 to Rs 39. The more expensive rooms have attached bathrooms.

The hotels around Egmore Station are in the high-bottom to low-middle range. *Hotel Ramprasad* (tel 847875) at 22 Gandhi Irwin Rd has rooms with attached bath for Rs 55/75 or with air-con for Rs 90/120, and has its own air-con restaurant. Directly opposite the station the *Hotel Impala Continental* has rooms overlooking a quiet, leafy courtyard in what is otherwise a fairly noisy area. Unfortunately the rooms are far from well kept, although at Rs 25/45 they are quite cheap. After that, try the *Tourist Home* (tel 844079), 21 Gandhi Irwin Rd, which has friendly staff and rooms with bath at Rs 50 single, Rs 55 to Rs 100 double.

Two other places to try are the *People's Lodge*, Whannels Rd around the corner from the Imperial, which has singles/doubles with attached bath for Rs 50/75, and a gruff manager; or the *Hotel Majestic* (tel 842679), 20 Kennets Lane opposite the Hotel New Victoria, with rooms with bath for Rs 25/60. Both places are likely to be full later in the day.

World University Service Centre (tel 663991) is on Spur Tank Rd, west of Egmore Station and south of Poonamallee High Rd. International Student Card holders can stay in the dorm here for Rs 5 (Rs 7 otherwise). There are also rooms – cheaper if you're a teacher.

The *Youth Hostel* (tel 412882), Indiranagar, is on the southern outskirts of the city, 30 minutes by bus – Nos 19B, 19M, 19S, 21A, 21D, 23A – from Parry's Corner. Dormitory accommodation costs Rs 7 and no YHA card is necessary. Cooking and camping facilities are available, or you can have meals prepared for you. If you're arriving in Madras by air, take the commuter train into the city as far as Saidapet Station, and then take a bus to Adyar from there.

There's a big 50-bed dorm at the TTC bus stand; you have to have a bus ticket. There are also *Retiring Rooms* at the Central Railway Station (tel 32218) – Rs 50 a double, Rs 120 with air-con – and at the Egmore Station (tel 848533) – Rs 30/40 for singles/doubles.

Places to Stay – middle

Hotel Imperial (tel 847076), 14 Whannels Rd right in front of Egmore Station, is one of the better mid-range places. Singles/doubles are Rs 75/150 or with air-con Rs 150/200 plus 10%. The Imperial is an enormous place with many different buildings surrounding a garden and courtyards. It has three restaurants, a bar, nightclub, disco, bookshop and faulty plumbing.

Some other mid-range places are excellent value. *Hotel Kanchi* (tel 471100) is at 28 Commander-in-Chief Rd, just

down from the Connemarra. This modern hotel is good value at Rs 75/100 or with air-con at Rs 90/145. It's got a round rooftop (but non-revolving) restaurant. Close by at 69 Marshalls Rd, Egmore, the *Hotel Guru* (tel 87939) has rooms with bathroom at Rs 50/75 or with air-con at Rs 100/125. It's reasonably clean, the staff are helpful and it's conveniently located.

The relatively large *Hotel President* (tel 842211) on Edward Elliots Rd in Mylapore has air-con rooms at Rs 180/220. It also has a swimming pool but we've had reports of it not being very good. The *New Woodlands Hotel* (tel 473111), 72-75 Dr Radhakrishnan Rd, has singles at Rs 60 to Rs 90 (Rs 100 to Rs 125 with air-con), doubles at Rs 90 to Rs 120 (Rs 150 to Rs 200 with air-con). *Hotel Ranjith* (tel 470521) at 9 Nungambakkam High Rd is a clean place with rooms for Rs 75/120 or with air-con for Rs 120/150. Good food here too.

If you're searching for something at the cheaper end of the middle bracket, the best place to head for is Egmore Station, although some of the places are almost always full up. *Hotel Vaigai* (tel 844031), 3 Gandhi Irwin Rd, is a very good new place with pleasantly decorated double rooms with bathroom for Rs 85 to Rs 95 or Rs 180 with air-con. It has a reasonably priced vegetarian restaurant.

Hotel Atlantic (tel 810561), 2 Montieth Rd, Egmore, has rooms at Rs 75/125 or with air-con at Rs 100/150. Also in Egmore the *Hotel New Victoria* (tel 847738) at 3 Kennet Lane is slightly more expensive at Rs 105/185 or with air-con at Rs 125/215.

Although Poonamallee High Rd is horribly noisy close to Central Station, it's not at all bad a km or two further out. *Hotel Dasaprakash* (tel 661111) at 100 Poonamallee High Rd is a very pleasant hotel with lots of small garden courtyards. Rooms are Rs 70 to Rs 100 single or Rs 150 double and they're well kept and clean. With air-con rooms are Rs 110/175, but all the rooms are heavily booked. There's a dining hall and an ice cream parlour at the front. Right across the road at No 934 (yes the numbers make no sense), the modern *Hotel Blue Diamond* (tel 665981-5) has rooms at Rs 95/120 or with air-con at Rs 135/175.

Finally, if you're just passing through Madras by air, the *Airport Inn* (tel 433546) is just two km from the airport at 7 Govindaswamy St, Nanganallur, and has rooms at Rs 80/150 or Rs 140/175 with air-con. If you're in transit check first to determine if the airline provides free accommodation.

Places to Stay – top end

Probably Madras' best-known hotel is the old-fashioned but elegant *Hotel Connemarra* (tel 810051) on Binny's Rd, off C-in-C Rd, near the Tourist Office on Anna Salai. The air-con singles and doubles are becoming somewhat run down and cost Rs 450 and Rs 500 respectively. The swimming pool is often engaged for private functions and hence barred to guests. The Connemarra has an excellent bookshop and its buffet lunches are a popular budget traveller's splurge.

Hotel Taj Coromandel (tel 474849), 17 Nungambakkam High Rd, is probably Madras' most luxurious hotel with singles at Rs 550 to Rs 600, doubles at Rs 630 to Rs 700. It's a long way from the centre, but like the Connemarra does excellent buffet lunches. Others with similar price and quality are the *Welcomgroup Chola Sheraton* (tel 473347), 10 Cathedral Rd, with singles/doubles at Rs 600/650; and the *Welcomgroup Adyar Gate Hotel* (tel 452525), 132 T T K Rd some distance from the centre, with rooms for Rs 550/650.

More centrally located at 53 Montieth Rd, the *Hotel Sudarsan International* (tel 812061-8) has singles at Rs 350 to Rs 400, doubles at Rs 425 to Rs 475. The food is excellent and the service friendly and efficient, but the rooms and facilities are somewhat run down and tatty. *Hotel Savera* (tel 474700), 69 Dr Radhakrishnan Rd, Mylapore costs Rs 330/400.

Places to Eat

There are numerous vegetarian restaurants in Madras; this is the place for thalis! On the other hand it is not the place for a beer. You no longer need a 'liquor permit' to buy one, but in return you pay much higher prices – count on at least Rs 20 for a bottle in a restaurant or bar, Rs 13 to Rs 18 in a liquor store.

Egmore Station Along Gandhi Irwin Rd in front of Egmore Station are places like the *Rajabhavan* at the entrance to the Imperial Hotel with thalis for just Rs 4.50, or *Ram Prasad* at the Vaigai Hotel where they cost Rs 8. Also nearby is *Vega Vasanta Bhavan* with tasty thalis and fine lassi. Remember that in south India 'meals' means lunchtime; ask for 'tiffin' at other times. The *Matsya*, in the Udipi Home at the corner of Gandhi Irwin Rd and Harris Rd, has good masala dosas and air-conditioning – when they switch it on.

The restaurant at the *Hotel Imperial* on Gandhi Irwin Rd opposite Egmore Station provides chillingly cool air-con comfort, an extensive menu and somewhat indifferent food. Count on around Rs 40 for a meal. The bar is open until 10 pm. The *Hotel Dasaprakash's* dining hall at 100 Poonamallee High Rd does good thalis for Rs 11 to Rs 12.

Mount Rd – Anna Salai There are several good places to eat along Anna Salai close to the Broadlands Hotel. The *Godavari* although it is dark and gloomy has air-conditioning upstairs where they do excellent thalis. Downstairs it's brighter and they have snacks including dosas and excellent poories for Rs 2.

If you want to try upmarket vegetarian food, cross the road to the air-con and somewhat flashy *Mathura* on the 2nd floor, Tarapore Tower, Anna Salai – see map. You can have an excellent Madras thali for Rs 18, a Bombay thali for Rs 22 or a business lunch for Rs 10. A straight-forward masala dosa costs Rs 4.

Unfortunately the non-vegetarian *Buhari Hotel* at 3/17 Anna Salai has gone seriously downhill. The food is no longer so good and the waiters are so busy watching TV that the service is terrible. Nearby, on the corner of Wallajah Rd and Anna Salai, *Coronation Durbar* has good vegetarian food at reasonable prices. Also in this same area the *Chungking* is good for Chinese food. Or there's the huge and sprawling *Yadgar Hotel* across the road from the post office.

Two other places to try in the vicinity of Broadlands are the straightforward and budget-priced *Wheat Hotel* on Triplicane High Rd, and the *Sea Lord* at the junction with Pycrofts Rd.

Another good place to have a meal along Anna Salai – or preferably a cold drink and a snack as the meal prices are quite high – is the *Fiesta Restaurant* at the front of Spencer's Building, diagonally opposite the Tourist Office. You can either eat outdoors under the fans or inside with air-con, and they're open every day until 11 pm. If you decide on western food, try the 'lamburgers'.

Only a few doors down from the Tourist Office on Anna Salai, *Aavin* is a stand-up milk bar where you can get lassis (Rs 1.25), ice cream (from Rs 1.25) and excellent cold milk plain or flavoured (Rs 1). The *Connemarra Hotel* has a wonderful pastry shop, great for a treat. For a real treat head for the *Connemarra's* Rs 60 buffet. This is a long-running favourite and the restaurant here is very good – try the lobster.

Not far from the Mount Rd area the *New Woodlands Hotel* on Radhakrishnan Rd has great vegetarian thalis. They can't be beat for value or quality but remember to open your banana leaf or you'll wonder why the waiters are ignoring you!

Downtown In the old part of the town there are many vegetarian restaurants. Few shine out, although the *Madras Café* on Popham's Broadway does excellent

and cheap thalis. *Rama Krishna*, next door to the YMCA at Parry's Corner, looks good (although their lassis aren't) but the number of people it takes to provide 'self-service' is astounding even by Indian standards.

Getting There

Air Madras is an international arrival point for India as well as an important domestic airport. There are flights from Singapore (Singapore Airlines and Air India), Penang (MAS) and Colombo (Air Lanka and Indian Airlines).

There are frequent domestic connections between Madras and Bangalore Rs 283, Bombay Rs 950, Calcutta Rs 1202, Delhi Rs 1429 and Hyderabad Rs 503. There are connections to Cochin, Madurai, Tirupathi, Tiruchirappalli, Trivandrum and other towns. You can also fly from Madras to Port Blair in the Andaman Islands.

Rail If you're arriving from anywhere other than Tamil Nadu or Kerala you will come into Central Station. Most Tamil Nadu and Kerala trains, apart from the principal Kerala expresses and the Nilgiri Express from Ootacamund, come in to Egmore.

On the 2nd floor of the new building at Madras Central there is an Indrail office which can be immensely useful for foreign visitors. Like the equally wonderful railway tourist office in New Delhi Station, it handles all manner of tourist railway problems, not just Indrail enquiries and bookings. It's open from 10 am.

Apart from the two main railway stations, there is also a Southern Railway Booking Office on Mount Rd (tel 85642) which is open 10 am to 6 pm but can only reserve 2nd class. If you want tourist-quota sleeping berths it's best to check first with the Southern Railway booking office next to Central Station (tel 39101). The booking hours at Egmore and Central are 8.30 am to 1 pm and 1.30 to 4.30 pm for both classes.

The rail journey to Delhi is 2188 km in length, taking from 40 hours and costing Rs 135 in 2nd class, Rs 560 in 1st. Calcutta is 1662 km away and takes from 27 hours at a cost of Rs 109 in 2nd class, Rs 453 in 1st. The Coromandel Express is the fastest Calcutta train. Bombay trains take from 26 hours to cover the 1279 km at a cost of Rs 90 in 2nd class, Rs 376 in 1st. The Bombay, Calcutta and Delhi trains all depart from Madras Central Station.

There are daily trains from Central to Ernakulam/Cochin – a 700-km trip taking 12 hours and costing Rs 58 in 2nd class, Rs 235 in 1st. This train continues on to Quilon and Trivandrum. The daily Yercaud Express, also from Central, takes 10½ hours to make the 530-km trip to Mettuppalaiyam, from where you continue by the rack train up to Ooty. Fares are Rs 47 in 2nd class, Rs 191 in 1st.

Bangalore, 356 km away, is connected by frequent trains from Central. The fast Brindavan Express and Bangalore Mail take just seven hours at a fare of Rs 35 in 2nd class, Rs 141 in 1st. Also from Central the daily Hyderabad Express whisks you to Hyderabad, a 794-km journey, in 16 hours for Rs 65 in 2nd class, Rs 263 in 1st.

From Egmore there are a number of daily trains to Trichy – 337 km direct, eight hours, Rs 34 in 2nd class, Rs 134 in 1st. They continue on to Madurai – 492 km, 11 hours, Rs 45 in 2nd class, Rs 181 in 1st. The Vagai Express takes only eight hours; it's all 2nd class but comparatively luxurious. The fast overnight express to Rameswaram takes only 14 hours for the 656-km trip. Fares are Rs 56 in 2nd class, Rs 226 in 1st. There are also trains from Egmore to Pondicherry (a five-hour, 200-km trip costing Rs 22 in 2nd class, Rs 86 in 1st), Chidambaram and Tanjore.

Bus Both the Tamil Nadu State Transport and the privately run Tiruvalluvar Transport Corporation have their terminals off Esplanade Rd. The schedule at the State Transport depot is entirely in Tamil (as elsewhere in the state) except for the Mahabalipuram buses. This does not present any real difficulties since an army of young boys attach themselves to every foreigner who enters the terminal and for 10 to 20 paise (though, naturally, they try for more) find you your bus. Services to most large towns in the state are frequent. The Tiruvalluvar schedule is in English and is also listed in *Madras Today*. Buses include:

Mahabalipuram There are frequent State Transport buses (Nos 19A, 19C and 68) to Mahabalipuram from around 6 am to 8 pm. The 2½-hour journey costs Rs 5.70 or Rs 6.70 depending on whether the bus takes the shorter coast route or goes via Chingleput.

Bangalore KSRTC buses also operate on this route via Kanchipuram and Vellore. The trip takes eight or nine hours and fares range from Rs 40 up to Rs 60 for buses with air-con.

Madurai This trip takes 12 hours and costs Rs 38 to Rs 47. There are other buses bound for Shenkottah, Nagercoil and Trivandrum which pass through Madurai.

Pondicherry This trip takes about four hours and costs Rs 14.

Tanjore The journey takes about 8½ hours and costs Rs 27.50 to Rs 34, again depending on the type of bus.

Rameswaram These buses go via Tiruchirappalli and terminate at Mandapam. Fare for the 14 to 15-hour journey is Rs 47 to Rs 58.

Trivandrum Buses go via Trichy, Madurai and Nagercoil. The journey takes about 17½ hours and costs from Rs 80.

Tiruvalluvar and the Andhra Pradesh State Road Transport Corporation (APSRTC) operate numerous buses every day to Tirupathi. Some of them take circuitous routes to get there, so make sure you get an express bus. The journey takes about four hours and costs

Rs 15.50 to Rs 18. The APSRTC buses also depart from the Tiruvalluvar terminal.

While you're at the Tiruvalluvar terminal, it's worth picking up a copy of the *Bus Route Map*, which not only lists all the Tiruvalluvar services, journey times and fares – though not the schedules – but provides you with an excellent map of Tamil Nadu and Kerala.

Boat The Shipping Corporation of India operates a service to the Andaman & Nicobar islands (see that section for details) and used to operate a service to Penang in Malaysia. The Penang ship *MV Chidambaram* sank, caught fire or suffered some total catastrophe and at present a replacement is still only an indefinite possibility. Check with their agent K P V Sheikh Mohammed Rowther & Co (tel 25756-7-8), 202 (or 41) Linghi Chetty St.

When the Penang service was operating the journey took 4½ days, and although sailing to Penang might seem like a pleasant alternative to flying we seemed to get nothing but shock-horror stories about the trip:

Tourist Class 1, which is two grades below deluxe, is down among the migrant workers, most of whom sleep literally in cages, who are not toilet-trained and were prone to use the corridor outside our cabin. We had been told in advance by KPV Sheikh Mohammed Rowther that we would be sharing a four-berth cabin, the toilet would be shared with another similar cabin, and we would have only Indian food.

We thought this well worth putting up with for three days to save Rs 800 each. What they didn't tell us was that (a) the food would be disgusting, (b) we would be sharing with people who didn't know what to do with a western toilet, and (c) we would be down amongst the cages. We chickened out and changed to 1st class before the boat sailed. But we did meet some westerners who survived the trip. Their advice to anyone who absolutely can't afford to spend the extra is to bring three days' food with them and to ignore the ship's notices regarding segregation of classes ....

The food in 1st class was dreadful, and being a 1st-class passenger is no help at all in getting through immigration.

On the other hand Gavin Young's book *Slow Boats to China* has a chapter on travelling Madras-Penang-Singapore on the *Chidambaram* and he doesn't make it sound too bad.

Getting Around

Airport There are separate domestic (new) and international (old) airport terminals at Madras. A bus runs between them for Rs 2. The regular airport bus into town costs Rs 15. It stops at the major hotels and at Egmore Station and terminates at the Indian Airlines office on Marshall Rd. An auto-rickshaw will cost Rs 35 to Rs 40, a taxi Rs 70 to Rs 80.

For those on a very tight budget the cheapest way of getting from the airport at Meenambakkam to the city is to walk to Ninambakkam railway station (about 10 minutes) and take a commuter train into the city. The train passes through Egmore Station and the last stop is Beach Station, opposite the GPO. There are frequent trains from 4 am to midnight. If you're heading for the Youth Hostel, get off the train at Saidapet Station and take a bus from there to Adyar.

Bus If you're spending long in Madras and will be using city buses, then a copy of *Madras City Tourist Guide* will be useful as it contains a full list of all the city bus routes. Some of the more useful buses include:

Nos 9 & 10 – Parry's Corner to Central and Egmore Stations. Other buses which pass through Egmore include Nos 4D, 16, 17, 17D, 17E, 22, 23A, 27, 27B, 27D, 29A, 29D, 38B, 40, 43 & 71A.
Nos 11A & 18 – Parry's Corner to Mount Rd (Anna Salai). Other buses which run along the city end of Mount Rd include Nos 3A, 4G, 5A, 11D, 11E, 17A, 17C, 18, 18B, 18C, 18D, 18E, 19S, 23, 23B, 23C, 25,

25B, 27A, 27D, 36 & 36A.

No 27D – Mount Rd to Egmore Station.

Taxi Taxis take up to five people and cost Rs 3 for the first 1.6 km followed by Rs 1.70 for each subsequent km. Waiting costs Rs 2.40 per hour. Most drivers will use the meters without being reminded of their existence.

Auto & Cycle Rickshaw Auto-rickshaws cost Rs 2 for the first 1.6 km, followed by Rs 1.20 for each subsequent km. A little persuasion may be required before they use the meter. You have to be firm with the cycle-rickshaw wallahs, as they are inclined to ask for more than the agreed fare on arrival. You can hire bicycles from Broadlands or other bicycle-hire places for Rs 5 a day.

Things to Buy

Traditional crafts of the south you can look for in Madras include wooden temple carvings and the bronze cast figures of gods which are a speciality of Tanjore. Poompuhar at 818 Anna Salai is the Tamil Nadu state handicraft emporium. The Cottage Industries Emporium across from the Taj Coromandel Hotel is also good. You'll find more interesting crafts in the shops at first-class hotels including, of course, the Connemarra. For more mundane goods Spencer's on Anna Salai has a supermarket department.

Tony's Notebook

Indian Airlines

Flying Indian Airlines is a much more restful experience since they've computerised. Well, booking Indian Airlines flights is much more restful, anyway. At their Calcutta office each terminal has a floor fan standing behind it since somebody forgot to design a cooling fan into the computer terminals!

New computers or not, they can still dish up some truly terrible food though. They get it right on some of the longer flights, but on short hops 'meals' are usually sandwiches which look as dreadful as they taste. The real surprise, however, is that often they're not prepared by Indian Airlines but by the local top-notch hotel which, with commendable honesty but considerable lack of marketing sense, even add their name card to the junk they prepare. Would anybody deign to eat at the Taj Mahal Hotel in Bombay after they'd see a Taj cheese sandwich on an IA flight?

Watch Out

You've got to be on your toes in India. Officially they drive on the left but in practice it's more usually optional, so don't just look for traffic the way it *should* be coming. There will often be a bicycle, rickshaw or even truck sneaking down in the opposite direction. They'll create a third line of traffic right over on the opposite side of the road or take short cuts along the wrong lane of divided roads.

Watch out for your head too. Many Indian buildings seem to have been constructed without recourse to preliminary drawings or plans. Half-way up the flight of steps the builders have suddenly realised it's not going to get to the next level in time so a corner is hurriedly inserted. But oops, that hasn't been allowed for down below (or up above) and we now have (as Californians would say) 'radically impaired vertical clearance'. For tall and unwary westerners this means frequent cracks on the skull at turns in the stairs.

Tamil Nadu

Population: 46 million
Area: 130,069 square km
Capital: Madras
Main language: Tamil

The southern state of Tamil Nadu is the most 'Indian' part of India. The Aryans never brought their meat-eating influence to the extreme south so this is the true home of Indian vegetarianism. The early Muslim invaders and the later Moghuls made only fleeting incursions into the region, so Hindu architecture here is at its most vigorous and the Muslim architecture virtually non-existent. Even the British influence was a minor one, although Madras was their earliest real foothold on the subcontinent. There were a number of early Dravidian kingdoms in the south. The Pallavas, with their capital at Kanchipuram, were the earliest and they were superseded by the Cholas, centred at Tanjore. Further south the Pandyas ruled from Madurai while in the neighbouring region of Karnataka the Chalukyans were the main power.

Tamil Nadu is the home of Dravidian art and culture, characterised best by the amazingly ornate temples with their soaring towers known as *gopurams*. A trip through Tamil Nadu is very much a temple hop between places like Kanchipuram, Chidambaram, Tiruchirappalli, Tanjore, Madurai and Rameswaram. There are also earlier temples in Tamil Nadu, particularly the ancient shrines of Mahabalipuram. In addition, the state has an important group of wildlife reserves, some fine beaches and a number of pleasant hill stations like the well-known Ooty.

The people of Tamil Nadu, the Tamils, are familiar faces far from their home state. Many Tamils have immigrated to Singapore, Malaysia and Sri Lanka. Despite their reputation as hard workers

Tamil Nadu is an easygoing, relaxed state. Things drift by here and even Madras, India's fourth largest city, is a laid-back, unhurried and uncrowded place compared to the northern cities of Calcutta and Bombay.

For the traveller Tamil Nadu offers excellent value, particularly in accommodation. Prices are generally lower than they are further north and in addition standards are often higher. There are many modern, low-priced hotels in Tamil Nadu. Food is also good; you may get heartily sick of thalis while you're here, but they are consistently good and consistently low priced.

Architecture

The Dravidian temples of the south, found principally in Tamil Nadu, are unlike the classic temple designs found further north. The central shrine is topped by a pyramidal tower of several storeys known as the *vimana*. One or more entrance porches, the *mandapams*, lead to this shrine. Around the central shrine there is a series of courts, enclosures, even tanks. Many of the larger temples

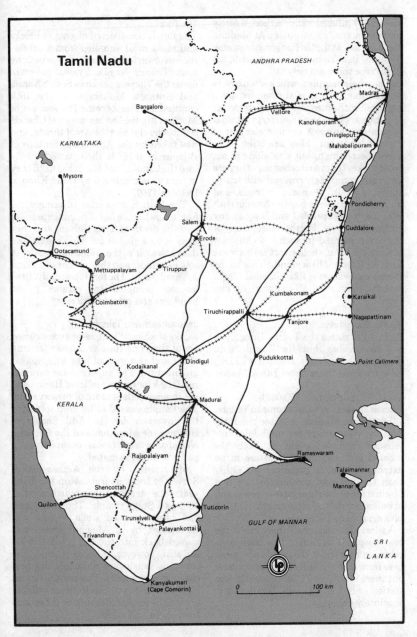

have '1000-pillared halls', although rarely are there actually 1000 pillars. At Madurai there are 997, at the Sri Ranganathaswamy Temple in Trichy there are 940, at Tiruvarur there are only 807.

The whole complex, which often covers an enormous area, is surrounded by a high wall with entrances through towering gopurams. These rectangular, pyramidal towers are the most notable element of Dravidian design. They are often 50 or more metres high, but size alone is not what makes them so interesting – they are generally completely covered with sculptures of gods, demons, mortals and animals. The towers positively teem with life; they're as crowded and busy as any Indian city street. Furthermore, many of them are painted in such a technicolor fashion that the whole effect is like some sort of Hindu Disneyland. This is no recent innovation – like classical Greek statues they were all painted at one time.

Tourist Bungalows

As in other states the Tourist Bungalows are good value, but the Tamil Nadu Tourist Development Council (TTDC) have renamed theirs *Hotel Tamil Nadus*.

VELLORE (population 150,000)

Almost the only reason to come to Vellore, 145 km from Madras, is to see the 16th-century Vijayanagar fort and Jalakanteshwara Temple inside it. Both the moated fort and the temple are in an excellent state of preservation. Other than the fort and temple, Vellore is a fascinating semi-rural bazaar town, full of bullock carts and street markets. It's a photographer's paradise.

Vellore also has, surprisingly, one of the best hospitals in India. The town feels cosmopolitan due to the people who come here from all over India for medical care, but there is no Tourist Office and the bus station only has signs in Tamil and is absolutely chaotic.

The Fort

The fort is constructed of granite blocks and has a moat supplied from a subterranean drain fed by a tank. It was built by Sinna Bommi Nayak, a vassal chieftain under the Vijayanagar kings Sada Sivaraja and Sriranga Maharaja, in the 16th century. It later became the fortress of Mortaza Ali, the brother-in-law of Chanda Sahib who claimed the Arcot throne, and was taken by the Adil Shahi Sultans of Bijapur in 1676. It then passed briefly into the hands of the Marathas until they in turn were displaced by Daud Khan of Delhi in 1760.

The British were next to occupy the fort, following the fall of Srirangapatnam and the death of Tipu Sultan, and they used it as a prison for Tipu's sons and daughters. It's the Windsor Castle of southern India and the only one of its kind in Tamil Nadu. The fort (open daily, free) is now occupied by various public buildings and private offices.

Jalakanteshwara Temple

Jalakanteshwara Temple was constructed about the same time as the fort (around 1566) and is a gem of late Vijayanagar architecture. The superb stone carvings rival the Vijayanagar relics of Hampi and are in an excellent state of preservation. The temple ceased to be used following the invasions by the Adil Shahis of Bijapur, the Marathas and the Carnatic Nawabs, when it was occupied as a garrison and desecrated.

Maintained by the Archaeological Survey of India as a museum for many years, the structure was rededicated in 1981 as a Shiva temple. The idol, which had been removed when Vellore was threatened by a Muslim army, was moved back into the fort. Non-Hindus are still, however, allowed to enter the sanctum sanctorum although the best carvings are outside. The temple has an elephant which you can often see walking around the market area, taking collections from shops and stalls.

Christian Medical College Hospital

This hospital is a surprising find in such a small town. There are over 1000 beds in the main buildings alone and patients come from as far away as Malaysia, Sri Lanka and the Middle East. It was founded by an American missionary in 1900 and has nearly 300 staff members and over 1000 students and trainees. It is supported by 74 churches and organisations worldwide. Karigiri, near Vellore, is a centre for leprosy research.

Church

The modern church is built in an old

British cemetery, where there is the tomb of a captain who died in 1799 'of excessive fatigue incurred during the glorious campaign which ended in the defeat of Tipoo Sultaun'. There is also a memorial to the victims of the little-known 'Vellore Mutiny' of 1856, the year before the great Indian Mutiny. It was instigated by the second son of Tipu Sultan, who was incarcerated in the fort at that time, and was put down by a task force sent from Arcot.

Places to Stay

Vellore's best budget hotel is the *India*

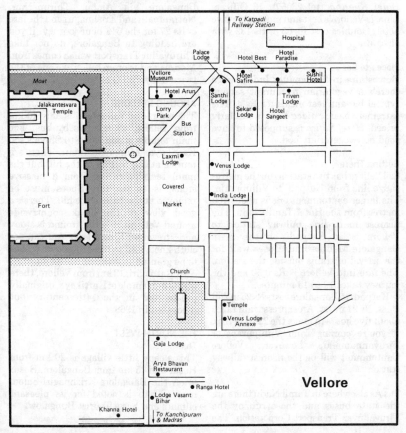

Lodge opposite the clock tower which was built for George V! Rooms with attached bathroom are Rs 15/25. The hotel is secure, the management are friendly and it's the most likely place in town to meet other westerners. Downstairs a vegetarian restaurant serves typical banana-leaf meals for Rs 4.

Gaja Lodge is a comfortable place with rooms at Rs 20/30. If you need to be close to the hospital, *Hotel Susheel* is convenient and has singles/doubles for Rs 25/40. Most of the other 'lodges' are very basic.

At the other end of the price scale the *Hotel Khanna* (tel 23060), 16 Officers Line, is Vellore's best and most expensive hotel. Doubles cost Rs 63 or Rs 132 with air-con.

Places to Eat

Downstairs in the popular *India Lodge* there's a vegetarian restaurant serving typical banana-leaf meals for Rs 4. The extremely basic *Palace Café* is similarly priced. *Hotel Safire* is supposed to have good non-vegetarian food.

Getting There

Rail Vellore has two stations on the metre-gauge line from Katpadi to Villupuram. The larger cantonment one is about 100 metres from the Hotel Tamil Nadu. The nearest main line railway station to Vellore is at Katpadi on the main Bangalore-Madras line. Buses wait for the arrival of trains outside the station. The fare into Vellore is Rs 0.50 and the journey takes 10 to 15 minutes.

Katpadi to Bangalore costs Rs 25 in 2nd class, Rs 97 in 1st. An express train takes about five hours to make the 228-km trip. If you're coming from Villupuram or Tiruvannamalai, however, Vellore Cantonment will be the nearest railway station.

Bus As elsewhere in Tamil Nadu there are the state buses and those run by the Tiruvalluvar Transport Corporation. The former are cheaper but the latter are generally faster and a good deal less degenerate.

There are a dozen buses daily to Madras via Arcot, Kanchipuram and Poonamallee. There is also a daily nonstop air-con bus but you must get a 'priority booking ticket' the day before and be at the depot half an hour early at the latest for this bus – at least in theory. The bus I was on was not only empty but stopped for a (very welcome) chai break at Kanchipuram. The buses cost Rs 10 and the journey takes about three hours.

There are a half dozen buses daily to Bangalore via Ambu, Thirupathur, Natrampalli and Krishnagiri and the fare is Rs 27 for the 5½-hour journey. If you are heading to Bangalore, do not take Thiruvallur Transport which comes from Madras and is often full. Take one of the twice-daily PATC buses.

AROUND VELLORE

The temple of Vellamalai is only 10 km from Vellore, 45 minutes by bus. The main temple is dedicated to Shiva's son Kartikaya, Murga in Tamil. There's a temple at the bottom of the hill but the main temple, carved from a massive stone, is at the top. Shoes must be removed at the base of the hill. There's a good view of the bleak countryside around Vellamalai – the ground is stony and strewn with boulders. You can see cloth knots tied to trees to ask for wishes to be granted.

At Ratnagiri, 12 km from Vellore, there is another temple of Kartikaya, originally constructed in the 14th century but renovated in 1968.

THE NORTH-WEST
Thali

This sleepy little village is 20 km from Hosur and 45 km from Bangalore. Hosur is on the Bangalore-Krishnagiri-Salem route. Thali is noted for its pleasant climate and has a Tourist Bungalow.

Hogenekkal

This beautiful and quiet waterfall is 25 km from Dharampuri and 80 km from Bangalore on the Bangalore-Salem route. Here the Cauvery River enters the plains and the river dashing against the rocks is a great sight. It's most impressive in July-August. A huge weekly fair is held in the nearby village of Pennagaram.

Places to Stay *Hotel Tamil Nadu* (tel 47) in Dharamapuri has rooms and dorm beds.

Yercaud

This quiet and low-priced hill town with its many coffee plantations is 33 uphill km from Salem. It's a good place for trekking and boating.

Places to Stay *Hotel Tamil Nadu* has rooms and dorm beds. *Hotel Shevaroy* is more expensive.

KANCHIPURAM (population 125,000)

Sometimes known as Siva Vishnu Kanchi, this is one of the seven sacred cities of India and was successively the capital of the Pallavas, Cholas and Rajas of Vijayanagar. During Pallava times it was, on occasion, briefly occupied by the Chalukyans of Badami and the Rashtrakutas when the battle fortunes of the Pallava kings hit a low spot.

Kanchipuram is one of India's most spectacular temple cities and its many gopurams can be seen from miles away. Many of the temples are the work of the later Cholas and of the Vijayanagar kings. They're spread out all across the city and you'll need at least a whole day to see them. The best way to do this is to hire a bicycle or to take on a rickshaw driver for the whole day (this should cost around Rs 15). There are no taxis or autorickshaws.

You should have plenty of small change handy when visiting the temples to mollify various demands for baksheesh by 'temple watchmen', 'shoe watchers', 'guides' and assorted priests. As it's a famous temple city, plenty of pilgrims and tourists come here and the army of hangers-on is legion. Almost to a man, the people who attach themselves to you as 'guides' are a complete waste of time and will bore you shitless. They'll hustle you round at the speed of light, fill your ears with nonsense and then demand you pay them up to Rs 10 for the unsolicited pain of their tedious company.

Kanchi is also famous for its handwoven silk fabrics. This industry has roots going back to Pallava times, when the weavers were employed to produce clothing and other fabrics for the kings.

Kailasanatha Temple

Dedicated to Shiva, this is one of the earliest temples and was built by the Pallava king, Rayasimha, in the late 7th century, though its front was added later by King Mahendra Varman III. It's the only temple at Kanchi which hasn't been cluttered with more recent additions by the Cholas and Vijayanagar kings, and so reflects the freshness and simplicity of early Dravidian architecture, of which other examples can be seen at Mahabalipuram.

A few fragments of the 8th-century murals which used to grace the alcoves are still visible and are a reminder of how magnificent the temple must have looked when it was first built. If you have any interest in archaeology, the Archaeological Survey of India has an office opposite the temple and the staff are most willing to tell you more about the history of Kanchipuram.

Vaikuntaperumal Temple

Dedicated to Vishnu, this temple was built between 674 and 800 AD by Parameshwara and Nandi Varman II, shortly after the Kailasanatha Temple. The cloisters inside the outer wall consisting of lion pillars represent the first phase in the evolution of the grand 1000-pillared halls of later temples.

Ekambareshwara Temple

Dedicated to Shiva, this is one of the largest temples in Kanchipuram and covers nine hectares. Its huge gopuram, 59 metres (192 feet) high, and massive outer stone wall were constructed by Krishna Devaraja of the Vijayanagar empire in 1509, though construction was originally started by the Pallavas and later added to by the Cholas. Inside are five separate enclosures and a 1000-pillared hall.

The name of the temple is said to be a modified form of Eka Amra Nathar – the Lord of the Mango Tree – and in one of the enclosures is a very old mango tree with four branches representing the four Vedas. The fruits of these four branches are said to have different tastes, and a plaque nearby claims that the tree is 3500 years old. Wishful thinking though this might be, it's revered as a manifestation of the god and is the only 'shrine' you'll be allowed to walk around as a non-Hindu and partake of the sacred ash (modest contributions gratefully accepted). You will not be allowed into the sanctum sanctorum as this is still a functioning Hindu temple, but you may be able to go up inside the gopuram – good views from the top. The temple elephant suffers from the worst boredom-induced eczema and running sores I've seen in India.

This is undoubtedly the worst temple for hustlers and there's also a 'camera fee' of Rs 2 which goes towards the upkeep of the temple (the income from pilgrims and tourists tops Rs 200,000 annually!). A leaflet is on sale inside the temple entitled *History of Sri Ekambaranathar Temple*. For a quick hit of esoteric nonsense and gobbledegook it's worth a rupee!

Kamakshiamman Temple

Dedicated to the goddess Parvati, this imposing temple is the site of the annual car festival which falls on the 9th lunar day in February/March. When not in use, the ornately carved wooden car is kept partially covered in corrugated iron halfway up Gandhi Rd. The temple has a golden gopuram in the centre.

A recent visitor reported that he was 'rather taken by the elephant at the temple entrance who deftly takes your offerings in his trunk, gives you a slobbery blessing with same on the head, and passes the cash to his master'.

Varadarajaperumal Temple

Like the Ekambareshwara Temple, this is another enormous monument with massive outer walls and a 1000-pillared hall. One of its most notable sculptural features is a huge chain carved out of a single piece of stone. The temple is dedicated to Vishnu and was built by the Vijayanagar kings. Entrance costs Rs 0.50 and there is a 'camera fee' of Rs 2.

Other Temples

The above are, of course, only the most famous of the Kanchipuram temples. There are many more both in the city and outside it. Walk in any direction and you will come across others. The small Kailasanatha Temple, for example, is run by the archaeology department and is very interesting. It's closed between 12.30 and 4 pm.

Places to Stay

The *Ashok Travellers' Lodge* (tel 2461), 78 Kamakshi Amman Sannathi St, is close to the railway station. This is the only middle or upper-bracket place in Kanchi; rooms (there are only three) cost Rs 75/115 plus 10% for singles/doubles. There is an attached restaurant where the food is 'healthy and copious though unexciting'. It's in a pleasant garden setting and you can book in advance through the ITDC in Madras.

Raja's Lodge, Nellukkara St, is close to the bus stand and has rooms from Rs 15 to Rs 40. The more expensive rooms have their own bathrooms. The *Palava Palace* on Gandhi Rd has doubles at Rs 20 and is very clean. Other cheap lodges include

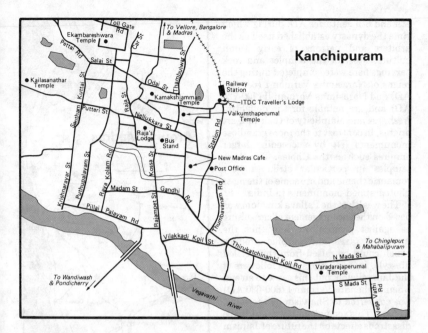

Kanchipuram

the well-kept *Sri Rama Lodge* (also on Nellukkara St), *Sri Krishna Lodge* (right opposite with rooms at Rs 17/27) and *Town Lodge*. There is also a *Municipal Rest House* (tel 2301) where rooms cost from Rs 15; advance booking is advisable.

Places to Eat
There are many small vegetarian places in the vicinity of the bus stand where you can buy a typical plate meal for around Rs 4. If you're tired of thalis there's not much else, but you could try the non-vegetarian *New Madras Café* or the *Ashok Travellers' Lodge*. On Station Rd the *Pandiyan Restaurant* serves Chinese, tandoori and other non-vegetarian food and does good breakfast toast.

Getting There
Rail Trains run from Kanchipuram to Madras, Pondicherry and Madurai. There is also a branch line to Chingleput.

Bus The timetable here, as elsewhere, is in Tamil but there is no problem finding a bus in the direction you want to go. There are frequent services to Madras, Pondicherry, Vellore, Chingleput and so on. Direct buses to Madras (2½ to three hours) cost Rs 7.50 (bus No 141), but going via Poonamallee, where you change, costs less. To Mahabalipuram, take a bus to Chingleput and then change. Vellore-Madras buses run through Kanchi; Vellore-Kanchi is about two hours for Rs 7.

MAHABALIPURAM (Mamallapuram)
Mahabalipuram was the second capital and sea port of the Pallava kings of Kanchipuram, the first Tamil dynasty of any real consequence to emerge after the fall of the Gupta empire, and is world famous for its shore temples. Though the dynasty's origins are lost in the mists of legend, it was at the height of its political power and artistic creativity between the

5th and 8th centuries AD, during which time the dynasty established itself as the arbiters and patrons of early Tamil culture. Most of the temples and rock carvings here were completed during the reigns of Narasimha Varman I (630-668 AD) and Narasimha Varman II (700-728 AD) and are notable for the delightful freshness and simplicity of their folk-art origins, in contrast to the more grandiose monuments left by succeeding larger empires such as the Cholas. The shore temples in particular strike a very romantic theme and are some of the most photographed monuments in India.

The wealth of the Pallava kingdom was based on the encouragement of agriculture as against pastoralism, and thus the increased taxes and surplus produce which could be raised from this settled lifestyle. Its early kings were followers of the Jain religion, but this came to an end when Mahendra Varman I (600-630 AD) was converted to Shaivism by the saint, Appar. This conversion was to have disastrous effects on the future of Jainism in Tamil Nadu and explains why the majority of the temples at Mahabalipuram (and Kanchipuram) are dedicated either to Shiva or Vishnu.

Today, Mahabalipuram is a small but very pleasant and easygoing village of essentially two streets at the foot of the low-lying, boulder-strewn hill where most of the temples and rock carvings are located. It's gradually becoming a travellers' haunt as people begin to rent houses and stay here for some time and restaurants are set up catering to western tastes – usually seafood. After the noise, fumes, bustle and crowding of Madras and other large cities, Mahabalipuram is like coming to another planet. It's a relaxing place with a wonderful combination of an excellent beach, cheap accommodation, good seafood *and* the fascinating remains of an ancient Indian kingdom.

The sculpture here is particularly interesting because it shows scenes of day-to-day life – women milking buffaloes,

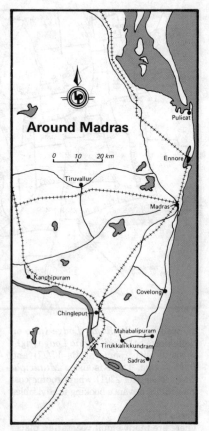

portentous city dignitaries, young girls primping and posing at street-corners or swinging their hips in artful come-ons. By contrast other carvings throughout the state represent gods and goddesses, and any images of ordinary folk are conspicuous by their absence. Stone carving is still very much a living craft in Mahabalipuram, as a visit to the School of Sculpture will show. It's diagonally opposite the bus stop and is open from 9 am to 1 pm and 2 to 6 pm, closed Tuesdays.

Information

The Tourist Office in Mahabalipuram

has a limited amount of information. It's open 10 am to 5.30 pm daily. There are good views over the whole town from the lighthouse. It's open from 2 to 4 pm and they charge a Rs 0.25 entry fee. No photography for 'security reasons'. There's a nuclear power station visible a few km south on the coast.

You can change travellers' cheques at the Indian Overseas Bank. A small library near the Tourist Office has a surprising collection of novels, history books, Hindu philosophic treatises, biographies of Gandhi and current Indian daily newspapers – excellent if you need something to read.

Mahabalipuram even has a resident guru, the Guruji Thapas Yogi, who does yoga lessons daily at his ashram on Five Rathas Rd and is only too happy to have western visitors. If you get ill try the Anna Ashram Christian Dispensary.

Arjuna's Penance

Carved in relief on the face of a huge rock is the mythical story of the River Ganges issuing from its source high up in the Himalaya. The panel depicts animals, deities and other semi-divine creatures, fables from the *Panchatantra*, and Arjuna doing a penance to obtain a boon from Lord Shiva. It's one of the freshest, most realistic and unpretentious rock carvings in India.

Krishna Mandapam

This is one of the earliest rock-cut temples with carvings of a pastoral scene depicting Lord Krishna lifting up the Govardhana mountain to protect his kinfolk from the wrath of Indra.

Mandapams

In all there are eight *mandapams* (shallow, rock-cut halls) scattered over the main hill which are of interest for their internal figure sculptures. Two of the *mandapams* have been left unfinished.

Rathas

These are the architectural prototypes of all Dravidian temples, with their imposing gopurams and *vimanas*, multi-pillared halls and sculptured walls which dominate the landscape of Tamil Nadu. The Rathas (literally temple chariots) are named after the Pandavas, the heroes of the *Mahabharata* epic, and are full-size models of different kinds of temples known to the Dravidian builders of the 7th century AD. With one exception, the Rathas depict structural types which recall the earlier architecture of the Buddhist temples and monasteries. Though they are popularly known as the 'Five Rathas', there are in fact eight of them.

Shore Temples

These beautiful and romantic temples ravaged by wind and sea represent the final phase of Pallava art and were built in the late 7th century during the reign of Rajasimha. The two spires of these temples, containing a shrine for Vishnu and one for Shiva, were modelled after the Dharmaraja Ratha but with considerable modification.

The temples are approached through paved forecourts with weathered perimeter walls supporting long lines of bulls and entrances guarded by mythical deities. Most of the detail of the carvings has disappeared over the centuries yet a remarkable amount remains, especially inside the shrines themselves.

Saluvan Kuppan

This cave temple complex is about a half hour's walk along the beach, north of the TTDC resort and beyond the fishing village. It's off the beach, behind the sand dunes. There are two cave temples, one with a tiger's head carved over it and a relief cut in the rock.

Places to Stay – bottom end

Mahabalipuram is a small village and cheap accommodation is in limited supply. Depending on the season, you may have little choice in where to stay for the first night or two. Very few of the hotel rooms face the sea so they miss out on the cooling sea breezes. As a result the top rooms in some of the smaller lodges can become stifling by evening, even with the fan on. Beware, however, of thieving monkeys taking advantage of open windows.

The TTDC *Youth Hostel & Cottages*, off the road to the Shore Temples, is very popular. The dormitories consist of two very large rooms, one for women and the other for men, and cost Rs 10 per night. Lock-up cupboards are available but you have to provide your own lock. The only trouble with the dorms is that there are no nets and at certain times of year they can be full of mosquitoes. The cottages are excellent value with doubles with bath for Rs 33 to Rs 50 or larger cottages for Rs 70. They have attached bathrooms and face the sea, so you get the benefit of sea breezes. There's a restaurant at the Youth Hostel, but there's no atmosphere, the food is expensive and the service is slow. Few people eat there.

Another very good place is the *Mamalla Bhavan* (tel 50) facing the bus stand. The rooms are cool, clean and well maintained, and you'll be made to feel very welcome by the affable (he hates being called that!) Raju, who has worked here for a number of years. It's largely a result of his influence that the hotel is so popular with travellers. Rooms with attached bath cost Rs 15/25. The whole of the ground floor is taken up by the best south Indian vegetarian restaurant in the village.

If the Mamalla Bhavan is full, the next best place is the *Mamalla Lodge*, run by the same people. Rooms cost Rs 10 to Rs 20 and have common showers and toilets. The staff are pretty lethargic, but somehow they manage to keep the place reasonably clean. There are also some doubles in the new extension with attached baths, which cost Rs 25.

There are a number of other small lodges in Mahabalipuram – all with rooms in the Rs 10 to Rs 30 bracket but prices are generally negotiable depending on demand. They include the *Merina Lodge, Pallava Lodge, Royal Lodge* and *Chitra Lodge*. At most of these places the standards are abysmal. It would be generous, but dishonest, to describe them as 'very basic'. In fact, most of them are filthy, depressing hovels with walls blathered with the dessicated spittle of what appears to be generations of slobs; the beds have the appearance of tussocks of paspalum grass and the sheets (where they exist) bear the indelible stains of numberless nuptials and execrable practices. How much does a new sheet and a can of whitewash cost you idle money-grabbers?

If you don't want to stay in a hotel at all, but prefer to rent a room in one of the houses of the local people, you'll have no difficulty finding one. You'll pay around Rs 70 a week, but don't expect electricity, fans and toilets for this. Most rooms of this type are in the Five Rathas village.

Places to Stay – top end

Scattered over several km, north of Mahabalipuram, is a string of beach resorts ranging from the very expensive to the surprisingly reasonable. They all offer fairly similar facilities – swimming pool, bar, restaurant catering to both western and Indian tastes, games, sometimes a discotheque – but vary a lot in terms of the quality and siting of the rooms. Some are obviously pitched at those whose major concern is sun-n-sand activities; others are more for the businessperson in search of a congenial place to relax or conclude a deal. Occasionally you get remarkable mixtures of people at some of the resorts. I came across a bunch of very reserved Russian functionaries on annual leave, a group of college kids from the American Midwest out for a good time, and an Indian table-tennis team!

Going north from Mahabalipuram, the first of the resorts is the *Temple Bay*

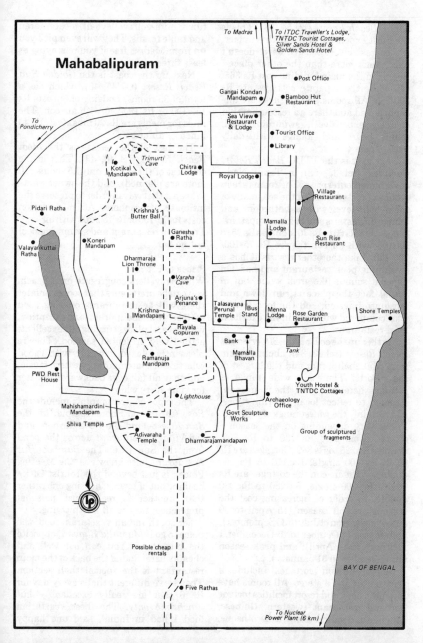

Mahabalipuram

To Madras
To ITDC Traveller's Lodge, TNTDC Tourist Cottages, Silver Sands Hotel & Golden Sands Hotel
Post Office
Gangai Kondan Mandapam
Bamboo Hut Restaurant
Sea View Restaurant & Lodge
To Pondicherry
Tourist Office
Library
Trimurti Cave
Kotikal Mandapam
Chitra Lodge
Royal Lodge
Village Restaurant
Pidari Ratha
Krishna's Butter Ball
Ganesha Ratha
Mamalla Lodge
Valayankuttai Ratha
Koneri Mandapam
Sun Rise Restaurant
Dharmaraja Lion Throne
Varaha Cave
Arjuna's Penance
Krishna Mandapam
Talasayana Perunal Temple
Bus Stand
Menna Lodge
Rose Garden Restaurant
Shore Temples
Rayala Gopuram
Ramanuja Mandpam
Bank
Mamalla Bhavan
Tank
PWD Rest House
Lighthouse
Youth Hostel & TNTDC Cottages
Archaeology Office
Mahishamardini Mandapam
Shiva Temple
Govt Sculpture Works
Adivaraha Temple
Dharmarajamandapam
Group of sculptured fragments
Possible cheap rentals
BAY OF BENGAL
Five Rathas
To Nuclear Power Plant (6 km)

Ashok Beach Resort (tel 51, 58). This is the most expensive of them all – in fact, it's excessively expensive as it doesn't offer much more than the other places. Rooms in the main building cost Rs 365/440 while the separate cottages are Rs 300/385. All rooms and cottages are air-conditioned and there's a restaurant, bar (fiercely expensive!), swimming pool, tennis court and lounge with daily newspapers.

Next to it is the TTDC *Beach Resort Complex* (tel 35, 68), a Tamil Nadu government enterprise. The rooms are in groups of cottages facing the sea, many of them split-level with a bathroom and lounge downstairs and bedroom upstairs. Singles are Rs 60 to Rs 70, doubles Rs 75 to Rs 100; with air-con they're Rs 75-100/100-150. Like the other resorts it has a swimming pool, restaurant and bar. On paper it sounds like great value, but in actual fact the place is run down and mosquito infested, and the food is very poor compared with that in the excellent local restaurants.

Further up the coast is the *Silver Sands Beach Resort* (tel 83, 84), about two km from Mahabalipuram and the largest of the resorts. There's a wide range of cottages here; many of them are constructed to reflect local building styles, and certainly the widest range of facilities. Prices vary depending on the season – single rooms cost Rs 180 to Rs 300, doubles Rs 225 to Rs 380. Cottages are Rs 80 to Rs 100 single, Rs 110 to Rs 150 double. With air-con the cottages are Rs 190 to Rs 300 single, Rs 280 to Rs 380 double. In order of increasing cost the seasons are: off season (15 April to 30 June); low season (1 July to 30 September); high season (1 October to 15 December/1 February to 14 April); and peak season (16 December to 31 January).

Deluxe air-con cottages include a refrigerator and a stereo. All rooms have mosquito nets, and resort facilities include bar and restaurant (western, Chinese, Mughlai and south Indian), a discotheque, films, mini-golf, volleyball, a catamaran and table tennis. They will even pick you up from Madras free if you're staying at least three nights.

Next up the coast is the *Golden Sun Beach Resort* (tel 45, 46), which has a total of 35 rooms. Lodging only costs Rs 150/190 or Rs 190/240 with air-con. The rates for meals are Rs 20 breakfast, Rs 40 lunch or dinner.

The last of the resorts is the *Ideal Beach Resort* (tel 40, 43). This is the smallest of them with only 15 rooms (10 more are planned), and the owner wants to keep it that way in order to preserve the intimate atmosphere. Accommodation costs Rs 75/100 or Rs 150/200 with air-con. There is a restaurant and swimming pool but no bar.

Places to Eat

When travellers congregate on a beach, you can be pretty sure that sooner or later there will be restaurants offering good seafood. Mahabalipuram is no exception, with several places turning out excellent, attractively presented seafood. They're pleasantly relaxed, generally with a good selection of contemporary western music, and they all fall over backwards to cater for your every whim.

These popular restaurants include the *Rose Garden* on Shore Temple Rd, the *Sun Rise* behind the Rose Garden, and the *Village Restaurant* across the pond from the Sun Rise. The *Bamboo Hut Restaurant*, also known as 'the Meeting Place', is just beyond the Tourist Office heading out of town. Choosing one rather than another is really just personal preference; they're all worth trying.

For south Indian vegetarian food, the place to go is *Mamalla Bhavan*, opposite the bus stand. You can eat well and cheaply here. Round the back of the main restaurant is the special thali section. They serve different thalis every day for Rs 6 that are really excellent – but *lunchtime only*. The 'best vegetarian food I had in India', said one happy traveller. When all the seafood restaurants are pulling down the shutters, and even the 'Wine Store' has closed, you'll find many travellers and local people gathering for a final nightcap just round the corner from the Mamalla Bhavan at the chai stall at the top of the road which leads down to the Shore Temples.

Getting There

Bus Bus Nos 19A, 19C and 68 go to Madras. The 2½-hour journey costs Rs 5.70 or Rs 6.70 depending on whether you go by the coast route or the Chingleput route, and there are frequent departures. Sometimes you can get a seat in a share-taxi for only a few rupees more.

Direct buses leave for Pondicherry five times daily. The 2½-hour journey costs Rs 8 to Rs 9. Get there early if you want a seat. Every one to two hours a bus departs for Chingleput; the one-hour journey costs Rs 3. This is the bus to take if you want to go to Tirukkalikundram.

It's theoretically possible to get to Pondicherry via Chingleput rather than taking the direct bus, but you should resist the temptation. The buses all arrive full from Madras and most of them don't even stop. You'll be stuck there for hours.

Getting Around

Bicycles are available for hire in the village if you want to visit Tirukkalikundram or the Crocodile Farm. There's a cycle shop about half-way between the Mamalla Lodge and the Mamalla Bhavan. They cost Rs 6 per day and there's no fuss, no deposit – just write your name and passport number in the book.

Things to Buy

Mahabalipuram has revived the ancient crafts of the Pallava stone masons and sculptors, and the town awakes every day to the sound of chisels chipping away at pieces of granite. Some excellent work is turned out. The yards have contracts to supply images of deities and restoration

pieces to many temples throughout India and Sri Lanka. Some of the smaller works are available for sale in the crafts shops which line the road from the bus stand to the Rose Garden Restaurant.

Also for sale in these shops are soapstone images of Hindu gods, woodcarvings, jewellery and bangles made from sea shells and other similar products. This is one of the best places to buy soapstone work.

OTHER PLACES AROUND MADRAS
Chingleput & Kovelong

Chingleput is on the Mahabalipuram-Madras road and has the ruins of an ancient Vijayanagar fort which had a chequered history during the British period. On the coast, Kovelong is a fishing settlement with a fine beach and the expensive *Fisherman's Cove Resort* (tel 947, 268) with rooms at Rs 325 to Rs 500 for singles, Rs 400 to Rs 500 for doubles as well as some cheaper lodges. Food at the Fisherman's Cove is very good and surprisingly reasonably priced.

Tirukkalikundram (Tirukazhukundram)

This pilgrimage centre, with its hilltop temple 14 km from Mahabalipuram, is famous as the place where two eagles come to be fed by a priest every day. Legend has it that they come from Varanasi (Benares). India, of course, is full of such legends. There are 500 very steep steps to the top of the hill, the soft drink sellers at the top do a brisk trade when it's hot! Some less-fit Indians get themselves carried up in baskets. What most guidebooks ignore about this place, however, is the amazing temple complex with its enormous gopurams at the base of the hill. It's very impressive yet seemingly little visited – you can get here from Mahabalipuram either by bus or by bicycle.

Crocodile Farm

About 15 km from Mahabalipuram on the road to Madras, this farm is engaged in breeding crocodiles to augment their population in the wildlife sanctuaries of India. There are now only several hundred of these reptiles left. Visitors are welcome and you can see all sizes from the newly-hatched to the adults. The farm is signposted so you can't miss it. Probably the best way to get there is by bicycle, although you can take any Madras bus from Mahabalipuram.

Vedanthangal

This is one of India's major bird sanctuaries, 80 km from Madras. There's a *Rest House* and an observatory tower. Immediately after the rainy season great numbers of aquatic birds flock here. Between 3 and 6 pm is the best time to see them.

Tiruvannamalai

Further south towards Pondicherry, a 66-km detour inland from Tindivanam will bring you to this temple town. There are over 100 temples here, but the Shiva-Parvati temple of Arunachaleswar is said to be the largest in India. The main gopuram is 66 metres high and has 13 storeys, and there is a 1000-pillared hall. The splendid old fortress of Gingee can be visited between here and Pondicherry.

Places to Stay You can stay at the *Park Hotel* or the *Modern Café* in Tiruvannamalai.

Gingee

About 150 km south-east of Madras, Gingee (pronounced 'shingee') is on the road to Tiruvannamalai. There is an interesting complex of forts, built mainly around 1200 AD by the Vijayanagar empire. On three separate hills, the fort is joined by three km of fortified walls. The buildings – a granary, audience hall, Shiva temple, mosque in memory of a favourite general – are fairly ordinary but the landscape is impressive. The mountains are all covered by huge boulders.

Gingee is pleasantly free of postcard sellers and the like; in fact it's deserted.

You can easily spend a whole day here exploring. There's an uneven staircase of stone slabs up Krishnagiri Hill but the route up to Rajagiri Fort is much more difficult to follow. A rickshaw from the town to the hills and back, waiting for you while you explore, will be about Rs 15.

PONDICHERRY (population 600,000)

Formerly a French colony which was settled in the early part of the 18th century, Pondicherry became part of the Indian Union in the early '50s when the French voluntarily relinquished control. Together with the other former French enclaves of Karaikal (also in Tamil Nadu), Mahe (Kerala) and Yanam (Andhra Pradesh), it now forms the Union Territory of Pondicherry.

The tourist literature will give you the impression that Pondicherry is an enduring pocket of French culture on the Indian sub-continent, but it's nothing of the sort. The only visible French influence which remains are the red *kepis* and belts worn by the local police, the huge French Consulate-General which, together with the predictable Hotel de Ville, dominates the waterfront, and a few streets around the central square which exude a Mediterranean ambience. Apart from that, Pondicherry is as Indian as anywhere else in India although it is relatively well lit, paved and laid out. It certainly doesn't compare with Goa's Portuguese or Darjeeling's English flavour. English is spoken everywhere; even the signs are in English or Tamil – not French. The name Pondicherry itself may soon be replaced by the older name, Puducherry, if a recent state government resolution is put into effect.

The main reason people visit Pondicherry is to see the Sri Aurobindo Ashram and its offshoot, Auroville, 10 km outside of town. The ashram, founded by Sri Aurobindo in 1926, is one of the most popular with westerners in India, and also one of the most affluent. Its spiritual tenets are based on a synthesis of yoga

Pondicherry

To Auroville & Madras

To Youth Hostel & Hotel L'Abri

Thiyaga Raja St
P Covil St
MA Covil St
ID Covil St
KA Covil St
Sri Aurobindo St
Supraya Chettiar St
C Covil St
AH Madam St
J Nehru St
Rangapillai St
Nidarajapayer St

North Boulevard
B Derichemont St
L Thollendal St
Dupuy St

St Louis St

French Consulate-General

Bliss Restaurant
Sri Aurobindo Ashram

To Auroville & Madras

Geekay Lodge
Amala Lodge (annex)
Market

Aristo Hotel
India Coffee House

Auroville Shop

Auroville Information Centre

Amala Lodge (main building)

Ellora Hotel

Venus Bar

Barathi St

Mahatma Gandhi Rd

International Guest House (Ashram accommodation)

GPO

François Martin St

Romain Roland Library

Compagnie St
St Martin St

Ashram Beach Office

Old Lighthouse

St Theresa St

Sinna Pappara St
Lapporth St
Monthorsier St
C Mudhaliar St

West Boulevard

Cathedral St
Canteen St
Capt Xavier St
Gingy St

Govt Square

Vict Simonel St

French Library

Tourist Office

India Coffee House

Gandhi Memorial

Foreigner's Registration Office

Air India

To Express Bus Stand, Villupuram & Cuddalore

Bus Station

Bank

Lal Bahabhur Gi

Romain Roland St
Dumas St
Goubert Ave

Botanical Gardens

Eai Amman Covil St

Labour Donnai St
Suffren St

South Boulevard

Canal

French Institute

Park Guest House (Ashram accommodation)

0 1 2km

Govt Tourist Home

Water Tower

Fiesta Restaurant

To TV Station

To New Lighthouse

Main Wharf

and modern science. After Aurobindo's death, spiritual authority passed to one of his devotees, a French woman known as 'The Mother', who herself died in 1973, aged 97. Although the ashram underwrites and promotes a lot of cultural and educational activities in Pondicherry, it's very unpopular with local people since it owns virtually everything worth owning in the union territory but refuses to allow local participation in the running of the society.

Orientation

The town is constructed on a grid plan surrounded by a more-or-less circular boulevard so it's easy to find your way around. The town is divided by a canal between an eastern and a larger western part. In colonial days it was the dividing line between the European and Indian parts of the town. The French residential area was near the present-day harbour. The main street is now known as Rue Nehru. At the southern end of the beach road (near the Park Guest House) there is a statue of Duplexis.

The Aurobindo Ashram, its offices, educational institutes and guest houses are all clustered around the streets between the waterfront and the drain to the left of the central Government Square. The French Consulate-General is also in this area. The streets in this part of town are very attractive and strongly reflect French influence.

Most of the hotels are to be found along Rangapillai St, which connects West Boulevard with the Government Tourist Home (the best of the mid-range) and the super-cheap Youth Hostel next door. These are on the southern edge of town close to the railway station. Auroville lies 10 km to the north-west of town.

There's a good deal of Indianisation of street names taking place in Pondicherry, so these may change slightly. For example, Rangapoulle has been changed to Rangapillai.

Information

The Tourist Office is on Government Square. The Ashram Beach Office and Auroville Information Office, Goubert Avenue, have information about the Sri Aurobindo Ashram and Auroville as well as maps of Pondicherry and Auroville.

The Auroville Information & Reception Centre is at Bharat Nivas in Auroville, together with their handicrafts shop. It's closed on Saturdays and Sundays. There's very little printed information about Auroville here – they mostly seem to sell books on and by Sri Aurobindo and The Mother. This is where you book accommodation in Auroville's International Guest House.

Sri Aurobindo Ashram

The main ashram building is on Rue de la Marine and is surrounded by others given over to the various educational and cultural activities of the Aurobindo Society. It's open every day and there are always people hanging about in the entrance lobby who will show you around if you're interested. The room where Aurobindo and The Mother used to meditate (Aurobindo's Samadhi) is open for viewing by appointment daily between 11.30 and 11.45 am only. Personally, I found its air of self-conscious other-worldliness somewhat contrived.

Opposite this main building is the main educational centre where you can catch a film, slide-show, play or lecture virtually every night of the week. These events are open to all and are very popular. Audiences are usually half-western and half-Indian. For most there's no entry charge but a donation is sometimes collected.

On the seafront is the Ashram Beach Office and Auroville Information Office. On sale are books on and by Sri Aurobindo and The Mother, jewellery and hand-made paper. There's also a photographic exhibition (which isn't that good) and information sheets, both on Auroville.

Auroville

The brainchild of The Mother and designed by French architect Roger Anger, Auroville was meant to be 'an experiment in international living where men and women could live in peace and progressive harmony with each other above all creeds, politics and nationalities'. It took off at a ceremony on 28 February 1968 when the president of India and representatives of 121 countries came to pour the soil of their lands into an urn to symbolise universal oneness. For a time, idealism ran high. The project attracted many foreigners, particularly from France, Germany, the UK, Holland and Mexico, and money poured in from various state governments, the central Indian government and UNESCO. Construction of living quarters, schools, an enormous meditation hall (the Matri Mandir), dams, reafforestation, orchards and other agricultural projects were begun. The amount of energy and effort which went into Auroville in those days is obvious even now, and the idealism with which the place kicked off still surfaces in conversations with Aurovillians.

Unfortunately, in 1973 The Mother, who was the undisputed spiritual and administrative head of the Sri Aurobindo Society and Auroville, died and a power struggle ensued for control of Auroville. In support of its case for control, the society quoted The Mother as having said that 'the township with all its property will belong to the Sri Aurobindo Society', but the Aurovillians countered this with another of her statements which was that 'Auroville belongs to nobody in particular, (it) belongs to humanity as a whole'.

The struggle soon developed into bitter acrimony with both sides trading accusations. On the one hand the Aurovillians accused the society of diverting and misusing funds meant for the project and of creating obstacles over the renewal of visas for the foreigners at Auroville. On the other hand, the society accused the Aurovillians of corrupting The Mother's concept by indulging in free sex and drugs. On two occasions in 1977 and 1978 the cold war erupted into violence and led to police intervention. Though the Aurovillians retained the sympathy of the Pondicherry administration, the odds were stacked against them since all funds for the project were channelled through the society. The society also had the benefit of powerful friends in the Indian Government – including three former cabinet ministers – who consistently sided with the ashram. In order to demonstrate their hold over Auroville the society began to hold up funds, which resulted in the abandonment of construction work, particularly on the Matri Mandir, and is why there are so many moss-covered, half-completed buildings.

The Aurovillians reacted to this take-over bid with admirable resourcefulness, pooling their assets to take care of the food and financial needs of the residents and setting up 'Auromitra', a friends-of-Auroville organisation to raise funds. Nevertheless, things got so serious in early 1976 that the ambassadors of France, Germany and the USA were forced to step in with offers of help from their governments to prevent the residents from starving.

Finally an Indian government committee recommended that the powers of the Aurobindo Society be transferred to a committee made up of representatives of the various interest groups including the Aurovillians, and that there should be greater local participation. Despite news (greeted with cautious optimism by the Aurovillians) in 1980 that the central government would take over the project, Auroville remains independent and the Aurobindo Ashram is not a part of Auroville at the present time.

The project has 14 settlements and about 1100 resident foreigners including children. The settlements include: *Promesse*, on the road to Madras; *Hope*, a 25-hectare farm with orchards set up as an experiment in organic farming; *Udavi*,

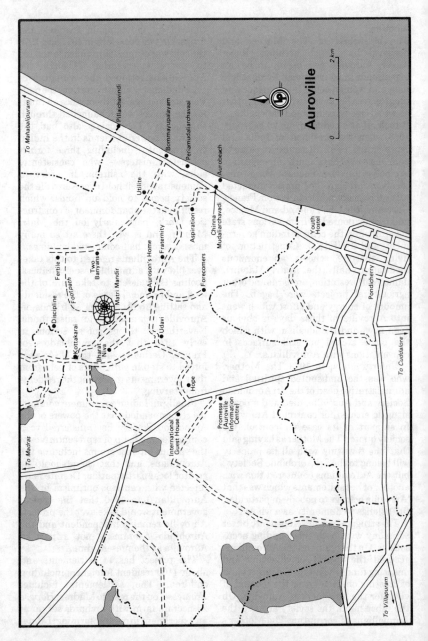

Auroville

To Mahabalipuram

Pillaichavindi

Bommayupalayam

Periamudaliarchavaai

Aurobeach

Utilite

Aspiration

Chinna
Mudaliarchavadi

Youth
Hostel

Fertile

Fraternity

Auroson's Home

Forecomers

Pondicherry

Discipline

Footpath

Two
Banyans

Matri Mandir

Udavi

Kottakarai

Bharat
Niva

To Cuddalore

Hope

To Madras

International
Guest House

Promesse
(Auroville
Information
Centre)

To Villupuram

2 km

where Aurovillians helping in the development of the nearby Tamil village of Edayanchavadi live; *Auroson's Home*, south of the Matri Mandir, which is involved with environmental research and the utilisation of natural sources of energy; *Discipline*, an agricultural project; *Fertile, Two Banyans* and *Utility*, all engaged in tree planting and agriculture; *Fraternity*, a handicrafts community which works in close operation with local Tamil villagers; and *Aspiration*, at present the largest community, which is an educational, health care and village industry project.

The huge Matri Mandir, designed to be the spiritual and physical centre of Auroville, is clearly visible from many points but its construction had to be abandoned when the Aurobindo Society cut off funds. Building will no doubt be resumed when the central government has sorted out funds for the project. Just off to one side of the Matri Mandir is a very pleasant communal kitchen and dining hall where you can get a meal for a small donation and have a chance to talk to the residents.

The best ways to enter Auroville are: From the coast road at the village of Chinna Mudaliarchavadi, head towards *Aspiration* (don't worry about missing this turning because all the local people will point it out for you); or from the main road to Madras take the first right turn past Promesse.

Aquarium

Situated in the Botanical Gardens at the junction of West Boulevard and Lal Bahadhur St, the aquarium has some rare ornamental fish.

French Institute

Located on Dumas St, the institute was established in 1955 primarily as a research centre for Indian culture. Its vegetation maps are universally acclaimed.

Tours

The Tourist Information Centre is opposite Gandhi Statue behind All India Radio. They expect to open a branch near the Bus Stand. The centre conducts sightseeing tours of Pondicherry and Auroville when there are more than 10 wanting to go. The all-day tour at 9 am takes you to such city landmarks as the museum, War Memorial, Botanical Gardens and places connected with the ashram. The tour is not very good value; in a small place like Pondicherry you can do it on your own unless your time is limited.

The ashram conducts its own tour of such ashram-run enterprises as the Handloom Centre, Ayurvedic Medicine Center and Art Gallery. They charge Rs 7 (compared with Rs 10 for the Tourist Office tour). If you are deeply interested in ashram activities it may be worthwhile; otherwise skip it.

Places to Stay

Whatever the locals may think about the Sri Aurobindo Ashram, they do have the best hotel in Pondicherry. And there are always a lot of travellers staying there (though tobacco smokers will have to severely curtail their filthy habit – there are not only people breathing here, but notices in all the public areas saying 'No Smoking'). It's the *Park Guest House* at the south end of Goubert Avenue in a superb location right next to the beach, but more than a km from the ashram. Doubles range from Rs 50 to Rs 100 and there's a restaurant.

The other hotel owned by the ashram is the *International Guest House* (tel 2200), Gingy Salai St, but it's often full due to long-term group bookings. If there is room, singles cost Rs 20, doubles Rs 30 and Rs 50 and triple rooms Rs 50. There is a 10% discount for ashram members. It is near the ashram, two blocks from the sea and a block from the main market. Rooms are spotlessly clean and have a photo of The Mother. The only thing I want to know about this place is what petulant, other-worldly wanker pinned to the noticeboard the following sign: 'Cleanliness is the first indispensible step towards the supramental manifestion. We cannot shelter hippies in our guest house'. I probably wouldn't even have noticed it had it not been done in gold-tinted paint in a virtually illegible and pretentious pseudo-artistic scrawl!

Auro Ashraya in 10 Shetty St, one block from the Canal and Nehru St, has cheaper and more basic accommodation. Single rooms cost as little as Rs 15 and there is also a Rs 4 dormitory. The manager is a good source of information on Indian holy men who have lived in Europe and America.

If the ashram guest houses are full or you want somewhere cheaper to stay, head for the *Government Tourist Home* (tel 694), Uppalam Rd, which is excellent value at Rs 20/30 and is similar to the Tourist Bungalows in other states. All rooms have attached bath; there are a few air-con rooms. It's quiet and surrounded by lawns and gardens but the standards of cleaning have fallen of late.

Seaside Guest House (tel 6494) is on the coast east of the Gandhi statue at 10 Goubert Avenue and has nice rooms facing the sea. Doubles cost Rs 50 to Rs 100. There's a wide range of places along Rangapillai St. At the top end of the market is the *Hotel Ellora* (tel 2111) near the junction with Cathedral St, which offers singles with attached bath for Rs 15 to Rs 30, doubles for Rs 50 and air-con doubles with attached bath for Rs 90. The *Hotel Seker*, 48 Rangapillai St, has rooms with attached bath for Rs 25/40. *Shanti Guest House*, in pleasant surroundings opposite the State Bank of India, has some nice rooms on the upper floor which are rented to long-term residents. Other rooms cost Rs 35 a double.

Similar in standard, but with fewer pretensions, is the *Ajantha Lodge*, 144 Rangapillai St, which is good value and secure at Rs 35 for a double. *Hotel L'Abri* (tel 5673) at Zamindar Gardens on the northern edge of town is in a modern four-storey building. Doubles are Rs 55 or Rs 90 with air-con. At *Hotel Aristo* rooms are Rs 35/40 or Rs 100/125 with air-con. *Cottage Guest House* (Gingy Salai and Rangapillai) is good value at just Rs 20/30. This new hotel is two blocks from the Ashram Dining Hall.

The cheapest place in town is the excellent *Youth Hostel* (tel 3495) out at Solaithandavankuppam in the northern suburbs, which has dormitory rooms with beds at Rs 6, lock-up cupboards, bedside tables with lamps, a restaurant and cooking facilities for those who want to put their own food together. Not only that, but it's right on the seashore, so you get the benefit of cooling sea breezes. The only problem with this place is its distance from town – and perhaps the pronunciation of the name of the suburb! – but it's easy enough to get there on a rented bicycle. A rickshaw should cost you Rs 5 each way. If you're only staying overnight, it's probably not worth the adventure. Also it's often full with Indian students staying on a permanent basis.

There are nine guest houses attached to the villages at Auroville. They cost Rs 30 to Rs 50.

Places to Eat

Hotel Aristo is probably the best restaurant in town. It has a 207-item menu with everything made to order, so expect to have to wait at least 20 minutes before your food arrives. They put a lot of effort into the preparation and presentation but unfortunately it's quite expensive. The *Shamiyana Restaurant*, just south of Government Square on Rue Victor Simonet, has excellent food and another amazingly long menu.

Chinatown Restaurant, opposite the Alliance Francaise library, seems popular but I was not impressed by the food. The *India Coffee House*, near the Gandhi statue on the beach, has good views of Pondicherry. At the *Bliss Restaurant*, along the canal and Rangapillai St, you can get straightforward thalis for Rs 7. In the first block after the canal, in a side street off Nehru Rd, *Jalram* does a Rs 9 thali. Try *Ashirvad* for good vegetarian food, or *Patisserie* next to the ashram dining hall.

Lunch, breakfast and dinner cost just Rs 8 for the day in the ashram cafeteria. Dinner consists of rice, vegetables, bread and milk but it's very basic. You buy coupons from one of the ashram-run lodges.

After Tamil Nadu's steep beer prices it's with a sense of relief that the quaffer of ale crosses the state border into either Pondicherry or Karaikal, where the cheapest brands (Burtons of Bangalore) sell for a mere Rs 7.50 per cold 750-ml bottle. Even Golden Eagle and Kingfisher are only Rs 8.25 (bottles of the latter can cost over Rs 20 in hotel bars in Tamil Nadu and Rs 13 from a 'wine store'). Pondicherry is full of bars, but many of them would be at home in a Charles Dickens novel. However, there are a few reasonable places where you won't feel an urgent need for penicillin after visiting. Try, for instance, the *Venus Bar* on Mahatma Gandhi Rd near the junction with Rangapillai St.

Getting There

Rail There is one direct train to Madras each day (the Pondicherry Express) but, since the line to Pondicherry is a branch line, all other journeys by rail involve changing at Villupuram. There are several trains to Villupuram each day from Pondicherry. If you're heading south or coming back from there, you can avoid having to back-track from Villupuram by going via Thiruppapuliyar Railway Station, a short Rs 1 bus journey from Pondi.

Bus There are two bus stations in Pondicherry: the local bus stand is at the back of the roundabout where West Boulevard Rd becomes South Boulevard Rd opposite the Botanical Gardens; the express bus stand is about half a km out on the Villupuram Rd, past the Botanical Gardens. At the local bus stand you get buses for Mahabalipuram and Vellore. It is utter chaos; there are no signs in English and no inquiry window. At the express bus stand you get buses for Trichy, Madurai, Kanchipuram, Madras and Tanjore. The Mahabalipuram bus trip is a pleasant ride along the coast.

Tiruvalluvar and a few other private carriers operate out of the express bus stand. Madras buses depart hourly and cost Rs 16. There are two a day to Trichy and Tanjore (six-hour trip). There are four Vellore buses a day. Other buses go to Coimbatore and to Kanyakumari via Madurai and Nagercoil.

Getting Around

As there is no public transport, rickshaws seem to be the only way of getting around. There seems to be an oversupply of them and the drivers will try very hard to get you aboard.

There's no chance of walking round Auroville in a day – it's too spread out. The best way to visit it is to rent a bicycle for the day through your hotel in Pondicherry – average cost is Rs 5, no deposit necessary. At present there are no good guided tours to Auroville. The Tourist Office's one-hour tour is not very good and the Auroville Information tours are not currently operating. A round trip by taxi should cost about Rs 20.

TANJORE (Thanjavur)
(population 140,000)
Tanjore was the ancient capital of the Chola kings whose origins, like those of the Pallavas, Pandyas and Cheras with whom they shared the tip of the Indian peninsula, go back to the beginning of the Christian era. Power struggles between these groups were a constant feature of their early history, with one or another gaining the ascendant from time to time. The Cholas' turn for empire building came between 850 and 1270 AD and, at

THE DEVOTIONAL BELL AT SOME TEMPLES DOES NOT FAVOR THE DIMINUTIVE DEVOTEE...

the height of their power, they controlled the greater part of the Indian peninsula south of a line drawn between Bombay and Puri, including parts of Sri Lanka and even, for a while, the Srivijaya kingdom of the Malay peninsula and Sumatra.

Probably their greatest emperors were Raja Raja (985-1014 AD), who was responsible for building the Brihadeshwara Temple (Tanjore's main attraction), and his son Rajendra I (1012-1044 AD), whose navies competed with the Arabs for control of the trade routes across the Indian Ocean and who was responsible for bringing Srivijaya under Chola control. Most of the Chola emperors were generous patrons of the arts and it was during their rule that Dravidian culture reached the pinnacle of its development. The temples, forts and palaces of Tanjore are superb examples of this cultural explosion which had its roots in the early folk-art traditions developed by the Pallavas at Kanchipuram and Mahabalipuram. The wealth which underwrote this seemingly endless construction came originally from the rich, fertile rice-growing area of the Cauvery River delta which is the rice bowl of southern India even today. It was later augmented by the profits which accrued from control of the lucrative trade between China and India, following Rajendra I's conquest of Srivijaya.

Tanjore wasn't the only place graced with Chola patronage. There are numerous others within easy reach of Tanjore, with enormous Chola temples. The main ones are at Kumbakonam (40 km), Thiruvaiyaru (13 km), Thirukandiyur (10 km) and Gangakondacholapuram (71 km). There is also the enormous temple complex – probably India's largest – at Srirangam near Tiruchirappalli in which the Cholas had a hand. It's well worth putting aside several days to see Tanjore and its surrounding temple towns.

Orientation & Information

Tanjore is dominated by the enormous

gopurams of the Brihadeshwara Temple. The temple itself, surrounded by fortified walls and a moat, is between the Grand Anicut Canal and the old town. The old town, with its winding streets and alleys and the extensive ruins of the palace of the Nayaks of Madurai, stands between the Grand Anicut Canal and the Vadavar River. It was at one time surrounded by a fortified wall and moat, though most of this has now disappeared. Between the bus stand at the edge of the old city and the railway station runs Gandhiji Rd, along which are most of the hotels, a number of restaurants, the State Arts & Crafts Emporium and the GPO. Most of the other hotels are at the back of the railway station on Trichy Rd.

The Tourist Office (tel 613001) is in front of the Hotel Tamil Nadu on Gandhiji Rd. It is open daily except Wednesdays and Fridays between 8 am and 8 pm. On Wednesdays and Fridays the hours are 8 to 11 am and 4 to 6 pm. The Hotel Tamil Nadu on Gandhiji Rd has good maps of Tamil Nadu showing all the main places of interest. If you're going to be spending any amount of time visiting the state's numerous temple cities, it's a good idea to get a copy of this Rs 3 map.

Brihadeshwara Temple & Fort

Built by Raja Raja (985-1014 AD), this is the crowning glory of Chola temple architecture. It's a superb and fascinating monument which you could spend days exploring. The dome on top of the apex of the 63-metre (206-foot) high temple, which encloses an enormous Shiva lingam (Hindus only!), is a single piece of granite weighing an estimated 81 tonnes. It was put in place by hauling it along an earthwork ramp six km long in a manner similar to the one used for the Egyptian pyramids, and has been worshipped continuously for more than 1000 years.

The gateway to the inner courtyard is guarded by one of the largest Nandis (Shiva's bull) in India, also carved out of a single piece of rock. The carved stonework of the temple, gopurams and adjoining structures is rich in detail and reflects not only Shaivite influences but Vaishnavite and Buddhist themes. Recently discovered frescoes adorn much of the walls and ceilings of the inner courtyard surround. They have been dated to Chola times and were executed with the same techniques used in European fresco work.

Inside the inner courtyard off to the left is a well-arranged Archaeological Museum, with some interesting exhibits as well as wall charts and maps detailing the history of the Chola empire. It's open daily from 9 am to 12 noon and 4 to 9 pm and they have an interesting little booklet titled *Chola Temples* for Rs 2.

The temple and fort are open every day and there is no charge for entry, but as this is still a functioning Hindu temple non-Hindus are not allowed to enter the sanctum sanctorum. This is really no great loss.

Palace, Art Gallery & Saraswati Mahal Library

This vast, labyrinthine building of huge corridors, spacious halls, observation towers and shady courtyards in the centre of the old town was built partly by the Nayaks of Madurai around 1550 and partly by the Marathas. Some sections of it are now in ruins, but a substantial amount remains intact.

In this building the Art Gallery has granite and wonderful bronze statues from the 9th to 12th centuries. The Saraswati Mahal library, established around 1700 AD, contains a collection of over 30,000 palm-leaf and paper manuscripts in Indian and European languages and a set of prints of Chinese tortures of prisoners on its walls!

The Tamil Nadu Museum contains examples of Tamil folk arts, music and other arts and undertakes research on the Tamil people.

Opening hours are 10 am to 1 pm and 2

or 3 to 5 pm. Entry to the museum is Rs 1.

Other Temples

Brihadeshwara Temple, though undoubtedly the most impressive and interesting, is only one of more than 70 temples in Tanjore! Many of these may be seen by walking around the old town.

Places to Stay

Many of the hotels are either along Gandhiji Rd between the bus and railway stations, or at the back of the railway station itself along Tiruchirappalli Rd – otherwise known as Vallam Rd. You're not going to find better value in Tanjore than the *Hotel Tamil Nadu* (tel 57 or 601) on Gandhiji Rd. Run by the State Government Tourist Corporation, it's spacious, spotless and very pleasantly decorated; the rooms have curtains, fan, desk, wardrobe, comfortable beds, blankets and their own bathroom with hot water in the mornings. The rooms surround a quiet, leafy courtyard, and the staff bend over backwards to make you feel happy and comfortable. All this for just Rs 40 to Rs 75. A few more expensive air-con rooms are also available. There is an attached restaurant and a 'permit room' with very expensive beer. The hotel is an easy 10 minutes' walk from the bus station.

Similar in standard, but more expensive, is the *Ashok Traveller's Lodge* (tel 613007), two km from the city centre. Like the Hotel Tamil Nadu, it has pleasant gardens, but singles/doubles with attached bathroom and hot water are Rs 65/100. The restaurant normally only prepares meals for groups and the food is not so good anyway.

The *Ashoka Lodge* (tel 593-4), Abraham Panjithar Rd, has rooms with common bath for Rs 15/20 or with attached bath for Rs 25/40. There are also two air-con doubles for Rs 75. This is a large and modern hotel with 76 rooms but there is no attached restaurant. *Shri Mahalakshmi Lodge* (tel 369) on South Rampart near the bus stand has spotless rooms with attached bathrooms for Rs 19/37 and a good vegetarian restaurant. On the same street the *Hotel Karthik* has doubles with air-con for Rs 50.

If you are looking for the real cheapies, try *Raja's Rest House* (tel 501), right at the back of Hotel Tamil Nadu, which has 30 singles with common bath for Rs 10 and a cottage with attached bath for Rs 20. Also at the bottom end of the market, the very basic and spartan *Rajarajan House* (it used to be Hotel Bilal) on Gandhiji Rd, and the *Ajanta Lodge* (tel 736) at 1306 South Main St, have singles from Rs 15. Tanjore has excellent *Railway Retiring Rooms* at Rs 20 per person.

Places to Eat

There are plenty of simple vegetarian restaurants around the bus stand and along the beginning of Gandhiji Rd with plate meals for Rs 4. *Padma Restaurant* serves good vegetarian meals. Another good vegetarian restaurant is the *Ananth Bhavan*, Gandhiji Rd, which has midday banana-leaf thalis with curd. In the evenings it's a good place for tiffin (no meals in the evenings).

Sri Vasavi Café at 1367 South Rampart also does excellent thalis. The *Saraswhadhi Restaurant* on Ghandiji Rd next to the bus station has good meals for just Rs 3. The *Bilal Restaurant* has non-vegetarian food and is cheap and good – excellent chicken and mutton dishes. *Sathars* opposite the hospital is also good.

The *Hotel Tamil Nadu's* restaurant has improved of late although one visitor reported that 'if this is improvement it must have been woeful before'. In general, however, in Tanjore it's thalis or nothing.

Getting There

Rail It's 8½ hours and 351 km between Tanjore and Madras (Egmore) at a fare of Rs 35 in 2nd class, Rs 138 in 1st. The 50-km trip to Trichy takes only 1½ hours at a

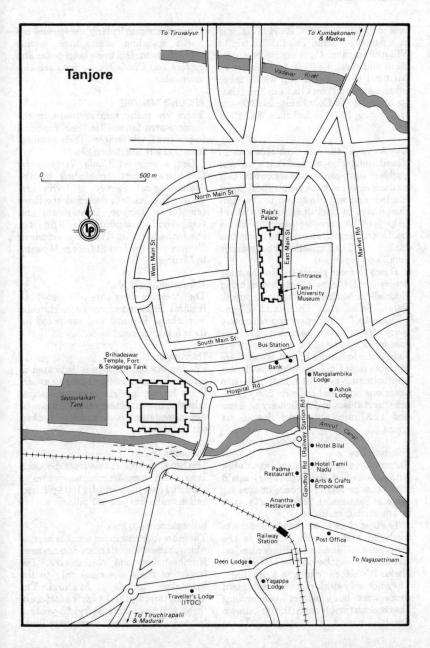

cost of Rs 5 in 2nd class, Rs 34 in 1st, less in a passenger train. The 192-km trip to Villupuram takes 4½ hours at a cost of Rs 23 in 2nd class, Rs 83 in 1st. Tanjore to Madurai is a 205-km trip which takes seven hours and costs Rs 24 in 2nd class, Rs 88 in 1st. To Coimbatore is a 300-km trip costing Rs 30 in 2nd class, Rs 120 in 1st.

Bus As usual the bus timetables are in Tamil, but (also as usual) it's no real problem since conductors shout out their destinations and most people speak some English and will direct you to the right bus. A sign in English announces 'Can I help you?' A traveller reported that a traffic policeman 'escorted us to the bus for Trichy!' The Tiruvalluvar bus stand is small and organised.

Buses to most places within the state are frequent, the main destinations being Courtallim, Madras, Madurai, Nagarcoil, Palani, Shencottah, Trichy and Vellore.

Buses to Trichy depart approximately every 10 minutes from bay 11. The journey takes one to 1½ hours and costs Rs 5. Buses to Kumbakonam, where there are more huge Chola temples, also depart approximately every 10 minutes. The trip takes one hour and costs Rs 2.75. There are direct buses to Pondicherry at 6 am and 12.30 pm; they take five to six hours.

Things to Buy

Tanjore is famous for *repoussé* (metalwork with raised relief) and copperwork inlaid with brass and silver. Bronze images are made at Samimalai, 72 km from Tanjore, by traditional craftspeople.

The best place to see the range of crafts made in and around Tanjore is the Poompuhar Handicrafts Emporium on Gandhiji Rd, just beyond the Hotel Tamil Nadu. It's closed from 1 to 3 pm daily. They not only stock repoussé and inlaid copperwork, but excellent woodcarvings like those on temple carts (the type drawn through streets at festivals). These

carvings are particularly cheap, and it's worth spending some time sorting through them. Old brass betel boxes and cutters and Chola bronze pots are also interesting.

AROUND TANJORE

There are many smaller towns in the Tanjore area famous for their huge and impressive Chola temples. Their distances from Tanjore are in brackets.

Get a copy of *Chola Temples* by C Sivaramamurti, published by the Archaeological Survey of India and costing just Rs 2. It describes the three temples in Tanjore, Dharasuram and Gangakondacholapuram. You'll find it in the Brihadeshwara Temple museum in Tanjore or in the Fort St George Museum in Madras.

Thirukandiyur (10 km)

The temples here are dedicated to Brahma Sirakandeshwara and Harsaba Vimochana Perumal and are noted for their fine sculptural work.

Thiruvaiyaru (13 km)

The famous temple here is dedicated to Shiva and known as Panchanatheshwara. Every January an eight-day music festival is held in honour of the saint, Thiagaraja. Accommodation is completely booked out at this time.

Thiruvarur

The Shiva temple at this town, between Tanjore and Nagapattinam, was gradually extended over the years. Its 1000-pillared hall actually has just 807 pillars.

Kumbakonam (40 km)

There are four enormous temples here, of which the most important are Sarangapani, Kumbeshwara and Nageshwara. The largest of these is second only to the Meenakshi Temple at Madurai. The semi-erotic sculptural work is a feature of these temples. Once every 12 years a festival is held at the Mahamaham Tank.

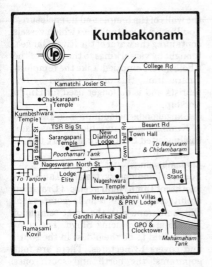

Kumbakonam

College Rd
Kamatchi Josier St
Chakkarapani Temple
Kumbeshwara Temple
TSR Big St
Besant Rd
Town Hall
Sarangapani Temple
New Diamond Lodge
To Mayuram & Chidambaram
Poothamari Tank
Nageswaran North St
Lodge Elite
Bus Stand
To Tanjore
Nageshwara Temple
New Jayalakshmi Villas & PRV Lodge
Gandhi Adikal Salai
Ramasami Kovil
GPO & Clocktower
Mahamaham Tank

Thousands of devotees flock here, as the waters of the Ganges are said to flow into the tank at that time! The next festival will take place in 1992. One traveller reported that all the temples in Kumbakonam were closed between 11.30 am and 4 pm.

Of all the temple towns around Tanjore, this is perhaps the best to visit if your time is limited. It makes an excellent base to visit the nearby and very interesting towns of Dharasuram and Gangakondacholapuram. Kumbakonam is a typical small south Indian town and very interesting to stay in.

Places to Stay & Eat The *New Diamond Lodge* at 93 Nageswaran North St is very clean with doubles with shower and toilet for Rs 25. The *P R V Lodge* and *Lodge Elite* at 106 Nageswaran North St are comparable. At the recently opened *Hotel A R R* (tel 21234) at 21 T S R Big St rooms cost from Rs 50/75.

Excellent vegetarian meals are available at the *New Jayalakshmi Vilas* and at the *P R V Lodge*. *Hotel A R R* does Indian, Chinese and western food and has a bar.

Getting There A bus from Tanjore (there are plenty of them) takes about an hour and costs Rs 4. There are few direct buses from Trichy; it may be easier to go first to Tanjore. The bus stops by the temples; they are all a couple of blocks from each other. To avoid full buses on the return, take a rickshaw to the bus stand further on. There are plenty of places to hire bicycles in Kumbakonam, including one just opposite the New Diamond Lodge.

Dharasuram
Dharasuram is a small town four km west of Kumbakonam. The Dharasuram or Airatesvara Temple is a superb example of 12th-century Chola architecture built by Raja Raja II (1146-1163). The temple is set behind the village. It is in a fine state of preservation and is fronted by columns with unique miniature sculptures. In the 14th century the row of largest statues around the temple was replaced by brick and concrete statues similar to those found at the Tanjore temple – many of these have been removed to the art gallery in the Raja's Palace in Tanjore but are scheduled to be returned to Dharasuram in the near future. The sculptures representing Shiva as Kankala-murti (the mendicant) and a number of wives of sages who stand by, dazzled by his beauty, are remarkable.

The temple is little used at present but a helpful and knowledgeable priest speaks good English. This 'wrinkled old retainer must be the only guide in India who is truly in love with his treasure', was one report. The town is also a silk-weaving centre and is easily reached from Kumbakonam by bicycle.

Gangakondacholapuram (71 km)
The gopurams of this enormous temple dominate the landscape for far around. It was built by the Chola emperor Rajendra I (1012-1044) in imitation of the style of Brihadeshwara Temple at Tanjore, built by his father, and is dedicated to Shiva. There are many beautiful sculptures on

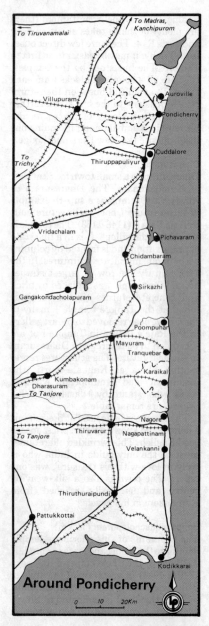

Around Pondicherry

0   10   20Km

the walls of the temple and its enclosures. You'll see a huge tank into which vessels containing the water of the River Ganges, brought by vassal kings to the court of the Cholas, were emptied. Like the temple at Dharasuram, this one is visited by few tourists and is no longer used for Hindu worship.

Gangakondacholapuram is 35 km north of Kumbakonam and, like Dharasuram, easily visited from there as a day trip.

Chidambaram

South of Pondicherry, towards Tanjore, is another of Tamil Nadu's gems of Dravidian architecture – the temple complex of Chidambaram with the great temple of Nataraja, the dancing Shiva. The complex is said to be the oldest in the south and covers 13 hectares. There are four gopurams, the north and south ones towering 49 metres high. Two of the gopurams are carved with the 108 classical postures of Nataraja, Shiva in his role as the cosmic dancer.

Other notable features of the temple include the 1000-pillared hall, the Nritta Sabha court carved out like a gigantic chariot, and the image of Nataraja himself in the central sanctum. There are other, lesser, temples in the complex including ones to Parvati, Subrahmanya and Ganesh, and a newer Vishnu temple. Chidambaram was a Chola capital from 907 to 1310 and the Nataraja temple was erected during the reign of Vira Chola Raja (927-997).

'This is', reported one visitor, 'one of the few places where you can get all the way in the temple and watch with the Hindus the fantastic fire rituals. I got there on a Saturday afternoon and from 6 to 8.30 pm had the greatest experience of my Indian trip'. The ceremony takes place every Friday and Saturday – very good days for prayer.

... the pace of the music was wild, the bells started ringing, a deafening sound filled the temple and the silver doors opened. In a quick succession priests moved their burning candelabras and other flames in front of the idols. The crowd raised their hands in prayer. Then sound came from the next sanctuary and a curtain dropped, the bells rang again and the ritual was repeated while the silver doors closed. Again and again the ritual is repeated in other sanctuaries.

Places to Stay The *Hotel Tamil Nadu* is good value at Rs 40 and there are a couple of other hotels around. At the *P V Lodge* by the temple entrance, clean singles are Rs 10 or with attached bathroom Rs 15. *Hotel Raja Raja* at 162 West Car St backs onto the temple and is very convenient for observing temple life. Clean rooms are Rs 35/50.

Places to Eat Meals at the *Hotel Tamil Nadu* are Rs 10. The *Udipi Sri Krishna Vilas* has good south Indian food.

Getting There
Buses to all the above places can be found at the bus stand in Tanjore and services are frequent.

Pichavaram
This sea resort with its backwaters and unique mangrove forest is 15 km east of Chidambaram. There is a Marine Research Institute at nearby Porto Novo, a former Portuguese and Dutch port. The TTDC has built a *Youth Hostel* with dorm facilities here.

Other Places
Nagore (45 km) is an important Muslim pilgrimage centre. Velankanni (90 km) has the famous Roman Catholic Church of Our Lady of Good Health. People of all religions flock here, many donate gold or silver models of parts of the body which have been cured! There's a major festival here on 8 September. There's a *PWD Rest House* at Ettukudi, six km away, or write to the vicar of St Mary's Church, Velankanni, about accommodation.

At the mouth of the Cauvery River, Poompuhar was a major Chola empire

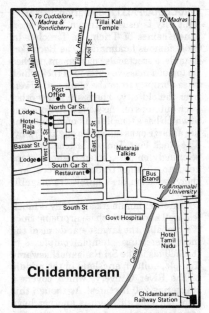

Chidambaram

seaport but only a small village stands there today. Trade was once carried on with Rome as well as other centres in the east. There's a fine beach, a good *Rest House* and some south Indian vegetarian restaurants which are very cheap.

Tranquebar
South of Poompuhar, this was a Danish trading post in the 1700s and has a church built by the Lutherans. Later it came under British rule but Danesborg Fort still looks out to sea – impressive and decaying. There are some fine old colonial houses, plus lots of children pestering you to buy Danish coins.

Karaikal
This enclave was part of Pondicherry and is full of French buildings, French gendarmes' capes and so on. There's a well-maintained old Catholic church but the population is predominantly Muslim. You can easily hire bicycles.

TIRUCHIRAPPALLI (population 340,000)
This city is usually known by its shortened names of Trichy or Tiruchy. Its most famous landmark is the Rock Fort Temple, a spectacular monument perched on top of a massive outcrop of rock which rises abruptly from the plain and towers over the old city. There are a few other such outcrops on the way to Tanjore, one of which has a temple built on it, but none are as large or as tall as the one at Trichy. The Rock Fort Temple is reached by a seemingly endless, steep flight of steps cut into a tunnel through the rock, and the views from the summit are magnificent.

The other landmark at Trichy is much less well known, which is surprising since it's probably the largest – and one of the most interesting – temple complexes in India. This is the Sri Ranganathaswamy Temple, built on an island in the middle of the River Cauvery, which covers a staggering 250 hectares! As though this were not enough there is another huge temple complex nearby – the Sri Jambukeshwara Temple. Both are visible from the summit of the Rock Fort Temple, shrouded in coconut palms, and both are worth spending a whole day exploring. Very few travellers seem to find their way to Srirangam, probably because of the fame of the other Tamil Nadu temples at Tanjore, Madurai and Rameswaram, which is a pity since the temples at Trichy are fascinating and deserve far more recognition.

Trichy itself has a long history going back to the centuries before the Christian era when it was a Chola citadel. In the first millenium AD, it changed hands many times between the Pallavas and Pandyas until taken by the Cholas in the 10th century AD. When the Chola empire finally decayed it passed into the hands of the Vijayanagar kings of Hampi, and remained with them until they were defeated by the forces of the Deccan Sultans in 1565 AD. The town and fort, as it stands today, was built by the Nayaks of Madurai, and was one of the main centres around which the wars of the Carnatic were fought in the 18th century when the British and French were struggling for supremacy in India.

Other than the monuments, the city is a pleasant place to stay with a good range of hotels and facilities. Though spread out, it has an excellent local bus system which doesn't demand the strength of an ox and the skin of an elephant to make use of.

Orientation & Information
Trichy is spread out over a considerable area and you will need transport to get from one part to another, but most of the hotels, restaurants, bus stand, railway station, Tourist Office, airline offices and GPO are within two or three minutes' walk of each other in the cantonment area. The Rock Fort Temple is several km north of this area near the banks of the River Cauvery. Further north, on an island in the Cauvery, stand the two temples at Srirangam, on opposite sides of the main road to Madras and Salem.

The Tourist Office is at the front of the Hotel Tamil Nadu within sight of the bus terminal. It's open daily except Sundays and public holidays between 10.30 am and 5.30 pm.

Rock Fort Temple
This monument tops a massive outcrop of rock, 83 metres (273 feet) high, and is reached by climbing 437 steps cut into a tunnel through the rock. It's a stiff climb but well worth it for the views from the top. Non-Hindus are not allowed into the sanctum sanctorum at the summit or into the Sri Thayumanaswamy Temple dedicated to Shiva, half-way up, so a visit here tends to be a brief affair.

Hours are daily from 6 am until 8 pm and entrance is Rs 0.10 plus an outrageous Rs 5 if you have a camera (the only photographically interesting vista is the one to the north over the temples at Srirangam). You must leave your shoes at

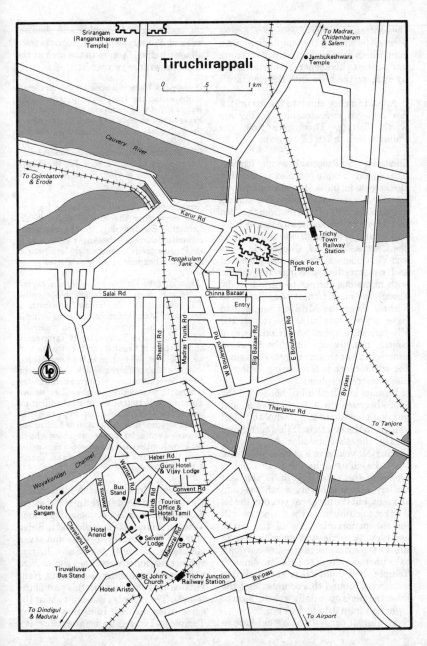

the entrance, where you can amuse yourself by offering the temple elephant a coin, which he takes in the tip of his trunk and passes to his keeper. You're rewarded by a tap on the head with the elephant's trunk.

Apart from the climb to the summit, a few rock-cut cave temples nearby are worth visiting. They date from the Pallavas (6th to 7th centuries).

Srirangam – Sri Ranganathaswamy Temple

This superb temple complex is probably the largest in India. It's surrounded by seven concentric walls and has 21 gopurams in total. The bulk of it dates from the 14th to 17th centuries and many people have had a hand in its construction, including the Cheras, Pandyas, Cholas, Hoysalas and Vijayanagars. It's very well preserved and has excellent carvings throughout with numerous shrines to various gods, though the main temple is dedicated to Vishnu. Even the Muslims are said to have prayed here after the fall of the Vijayanagar empire. Non-Hindus are, of course, not allowed into the sanctum sanctorum but this is really no loss since the whole place is fascinating. There is also a temple elephant.

Bazaars and Brahmins' houses fill the space between the outer four walls, and you don't have to take your shoes off until you get to the fourth wall (it's customary to tip the shoe minder 10 paise on leaving). If you have a camera with you, you'll be charged Rs 10 at this point. Opposite the shoe deposit is the 'Art Gallery' which is hardly worth a second thought, but it's here that you buy the Rs 2 ticket to climb up to the top of the wall for the panoramic view of the entire complex. A guide will go with you to unlock the gates and make sure you don't take photographs of the golden Vinanan Temple. You could easily spend all day wandering around this complex, but the inner temple is open daily from 6.15 am to 1 pm and from 3.15 to 8.45 pm.

An annual car festival is held here in the last week of December and the first week of January, drawing pilgrims from all over India. If you're in the area at the time, make sure you see it.

Guidebooks There is a book for sale in certain shops within the temple complex called *Sri Ranga Kshetra Mahatmyam* by R Narasimhan Praveen, which costs Rs 1.50. The intention of the author was probably to create a guidebook and collection of legends about the temple, but it's full of the most incomprehensible nonsense you're likely to come across. For this reason alone it's worth buying. Some gems from it include:

'Pavithrotsava is conducted to the Lord for nine days from the Sukla-Paksha (bright fortnight) Ekadasi day. To the negligence committed during all these days in the years in the Pujas, remedy is being sought for otherwise Aparadakshanpana is being sought for'.

'Thondar-Adi – He is called as Vipra Narayana – He was born in a sacred place called Thirumadangudi. His Janma Nakashatra is Jyeshta in Margazhi month. He was living in Srirangam and engaged himself in presenting Thiru Thuzhai or Thulasi to Sri Tanganatha and garlands of beautiful and scented flowers were daily offered by him to the Lord. He has sung the famous Thirumalai, which is especially in devotion to Lord Sri Ranganatha and no others. His another prabandha named Thiruppalli Yezhuchi is the most important part of the Thirumozhi group to wake up the Lord everyday. It is also spoken as Thirumalai Ariyar – Perumalai Ariyar – ie Those who do not know Lord Sri Ranganatha. Sri Vanamal of Lord Vishnu took the avathar of this Tondar Adi Podi Alwar'.

Srirangam – Sri Jambukeshwara Temple

On the opposite side of the main Madras-Salem road from Sri Ranganathaswamy Temple, this temple is dedicated to Shiva and has five concentric walls and seven gopurams. Its deity is a Shiva lingam submerged under water that comes from a spring in the sanctum sanctorum. Non-Hindus are not allowed in this part of the temple. The complex was built about the same time as Sri Ranganathaswamy Temple and is equally as interesting. It's open daily between 6 am and 1 pm and between 4 and 9.30 pm, and there's another Rs 10 camera fee.

Getting There Getting to any of the above monuments from the bus stand/railway station area is simplicity itself. Just take bus No 1 from either the railway station or the bus stand. The fare from the railway station to Srirangam is Rs 1. Buses are rarely full and the service runs approximately every five minutes.

St John's Church

Trichy has some interesting Raj-era monuments as well. Built in 1812, St John's Church has louvered side doors which can be opened to turn the church into an airy pavilion. It's interesting for its setting and architecture and also for the surrounding cemetery. Rouse the watchman to let you in.

Tours

The Tourist Office has a morning tour of Trichy and an afternoon tour to Tanjore.

Places to Stay – bottom end

Hotel Tamil Nadu (tel 253383) is opposite the bus stand. All rooms have attached bathrooms and cost Rs 30/40 or Rs 60/90 with air-con. There is also an eight-bed dormitory at Rs 5 per bed. It is nowhere near as palatial as the Tanjore Tourist Bungalow, but the Tourist Office is in this hotel and there is a good restaurant and bar.

Hotel Anand (tel 26545), 1 Racquet Court Lane, is probably the most attractive of the cheaper places although it's a bit grubby. Rooms cost Rs 30/50; with air-con doubles/triples are Rs 75/100. There are no air-con singles. All rooms have their own bathrooms and there is a good restaurant. The *Arun Hotel* at 24 State Bank Rd near the bus stand and the junction railway station has very clean and pleasant rooms which are excellent value at Rs 50; doubles with air-con are Rs 75. *Hotel Rajasugam*, opposite the bus

stand, is clean and has a restaurant which serves great coffee and good thalis and bread. Doubles with bath are Rs 47.

Opposite the bus stand at 13A Royal Rd, the *Guru Hotel* (tel 25298) is a pleasant place at Rs 25/40 for singles/doubles, all with attached bathrooms. It also has some deluxe doubles and a good vegetarian restaurant in the basement. Just beyond the Guru is the slightly more expensive but also pleasant *Hotel Lakshmi* (tel 25298), at 3A Alexander Rd. It also has a restaurant.

Hotel Ajanta (tel 24501), Junction Rd, is a huge place with its own vegetarian restaurant and with rooms at Rs 30/50 or at Rs 70/80 with air-con. You even get a newspaper in your room in the morning in this recommended hotel. *Vijay Lodge* (tel 24511), next to the Guru Hotel at 13B Royal Rd, is good value too and again there's a restaurant – the pleasant outdoor *Uma Shankar Hotel*.

There are a number of very cheap budget hotels along Junction Rd, which stretches from the railway station to the bus stand. Although there's not a lot to choose between them, the *Selvam Lodge* (tel 23114) has been the most popular with travellers for years. The rooms are very basic and cell-like, and sheets are not provided. Costs are Rs 15/25 for singles/doubles with common bath, or Rs 20/35 with attached bath.

If you'd prefer to stay near the Rock Fort, try the *City Lodge* (tel 23452), 69 West Boulevard Rd, which has rooms from Rs 10.

Places to Stay – top end

Sangam Hotel (tel 25202) on Collector's Office Rd is the best hotel in town, although it is not well appointed or maintained. Rooms are Rs 125/175 or Rs 145/300 with air-con. The hotel has one of the few bars in Trichy but beers are a mite expensive and the restaurant is too. Other hotels with bars are the Hotel Tamil Nadu, the Ashok Lodge and the Ashby.

The *Ashok Travellers' Lodge* (tel 23498) on Race Course Rd is somewhat inconveniently situated south of the railway station on the way to the airport. Rooms are Rs 65/120 without air-con.

Rooms at the *Hotel Aristo* (tel 26565), 2 Dindigul Rd, are Rs 50/70 or Rs 65/90 with air-con. There are also air-con cottages at Rs 140/220. It's good value and has its own restaurant. *Hotel Rajali* is a brand-new and luxurious hotel with doubles at Rs 120. It's just past the Hotel Tamil Nadu on McDonald Rd, but one visitor wrote that 'every time you ask what time it is there's a hand out for a tip and they won't give up until they get it!'

Hotel Ashby (tel 23652), 17A Junction Rd, merits description as Trichy's only faded touch of the Raj. If you like the Fairlawn in Calcutta, try this place. Rooms with attached bathroom are Rs 45/75 or Rs 75/110 with air-con. The hotel has its own restaurant and bar.

Places to Eat
There are plenty of vegetarian meals cafés around the bus stand and along Junction Rd. One of the best is at the *Guru Hotel*, and another good one is the rooftop of the *Selvam Lodge*, both mentioned above.

If you're looking for something other than a thali, then try the *Vijay Lodge* or the vegetarian *Hotel Anand* where the food is good. Almost opposite the Hotel Anand is the *Karitha*, a vegetarian restaurant that does excellent, highly elaborate thalis for Rs 7, and has an air-con room. The *Ashby* also has good thalis and drinks and excellent service.

The *Selvam Lodge* has a rooftop restaurant which is an excellent place for south Indian food in the evenings. There is also a south Indian vegetarian restaurant on the ground floor and a dimly-lit, prison-like, air-conditioned restaurant on the 1st floor.

The *Victoria Restaurant* gets mixed reactions for its non-vegetarian food. Some find the food too spicy, others like

it. It's often crowded. The restaurant in the *Hotel Ajanta* is good.

Getting There
Air Trichy has an airport and is connected every day with Madras (Rs 296) and Trivandrum (Rs 296) by Indian Airlines. Indian Airlines and Air Lanka each have two flights to Colombo every week for Rs 502. The Rameswaram ferry service to Sri Lanka is currently suspended due to disturbances in the north of Sri Lanka; the cheapest route there is to fly from either Trichy or Trivandrum.

Indian Airlines (tel 620001) are in the Railway Cooperative Mansion, Dindigul Rd. The Air Lanka office (tel 27952) is in Hotel Laxmi.

Rail Trichy is on the main Madras-Madurai rail line. Some trains run directly from Madras (337 km, five to eight hours, Rs Rs 34 in 2nd class, Rs 134 in 1st), while others go via Chidambaram and Tanjore, 64 km further. Madras-Madurai and Madras-Rameswaram trains also go through Trichy. It's about seven hours from Trichy to Rameswaram.

From Trichy it's 155 km on to Madurai, taking 2½ to four hours at a cost of Rs 19 in 2nd class, Rs 71 in 1st. There are many passenger trains as well as express services Trichy-Madurai, but during the day you cannot reserve 2nd-class seats so there's the usual battle for a space.

Bus Trichy has a state transport bus stand and a Tiruvalluvar bus stand only two minutes' walk away. As usual the state bus stand timetables are only in Tamil. Express buses are distinguished from ordinary buses by the word 'Fast' (in English) on the direction indicator at the front. Services to most places are frequent and tickets are sold by the conductor as soon as the bus arrives. Just buy your ticket and hop on.

A daily direct bus to Kodaikanal takes six hours and costs Rs 17. Trichy to Madurai takes three or four hours and costs Rs 12. The 'Fast' bus only stops twice, once at Dindigul for chai. There is a service about every half hour,

Tiruvalluvar theoretically has buses to Madras, Madurai, Nagarcoil and Villupuram hourly all day and night. There are 15 buses to Coimbatore. There are now two direct buses from Trichy to Pondicherry daily.

Getting Around

Trichy has an excellent privately run local bus service. It's comparatively easy to use and uncrowded. Take a bus No 7, 63, 63A, 122 or 128 to the airport. Allow about half an hour to get there. When travelling on local buses (at Madurai too) males seem to sit on one side, females on the other. Couples tend to stick to the male side although western couples are accepted on either!

MADURAI (population 817,000)

This bustling city of over half a million people – packed with pilgrims, beggars, businesspeople, bullock carts and legions of under-employed rickshaw wallahs – is one of southern India's oldest, and has been a centre of learning and pilgrimage for centuries. Unlike those in many big cities in south India, few people here seem to understand English. Madurai's main attraction is the famous Shree Meenakshi Temple in the heart of the old town, a riotously baroque example of Dravidian architecture with gopurams covered from top to bottom with a breathless profusion of multi-coloured images of gods, goddesses, animals and mythical figures. Nothing quite like it exists outside Disneyland! The temple seethes with activity from dawn till dusk and its many shrines attract pilgrims from all over India and tourists from all over the world. On any one day it's been estimated that there are 10,000 visitors!

Madurai's history falls into roughly four periods beginning over 2000 years ago, when it was the capital of the Pandyan kings and known to the 4th-century BC Greeks via Megasthenes, their ambassador at the court of Chandragupta Maurya. In the 10th century AD it was taken by the Chola emperors and remained theirs until the Pandyas briefly regained their independence in the 12th century, only to lose it again in the 14th to the Muslim invaders under Malik Kafur, a general in the service of the Delhi Sultanate. Malik Kafur set up his own dynasty here which ruled for a while before being overthrown by the Hindu Vijayanagar kings of Hampi. After the fall of Vijayanagar in 1565, Madurai was taken over by the Nayaks who ruled from 1559 until 1781 AD. It was during the reign of Tirumalai Nayak (1623-55) that the bulk of the Meenakshi Temple was built. Madurai became the cultural centre of the Tamil people and played an important role in the development of the Tamil language.

Madurai passed into British hands in the form of the East India Company, who took over the revenues of the area after the wars of the Carnatic in 1781. In 1840, the company razed the fort which had previously surrounded the city and filled in the moat. Four broad streets – the Veli streets – were constructed on top of this fill and define the limits of the old city to this day.

Madurai is one huge, non-stop bazaar crammed full of shops, street markets, temples, pilgrims' *choultries*, hotels, restaurants and small industries. It's one of the south's liveliest cities, yet small enough not to be overwhelming, and it's very popular with travellers. You'll love it!

Orientation

The old town of Madurai is contained within the almost square enclosure marked out by the Veli streets (South Veli St, East Veli St, etc) on the south bank of the River Vaigai. Within this area are found almost all the main points of interest, the transport services, mid-range and budget hotels, restaurants, Tourist Office and

GPO. Most of the hotels and restaurants used by travellers are west of the Meenakshi Temple between North Masi and South Masi Sts, but particularly along Town Hall Rd and West Masi St. Two of the three bus stations, the railway station and the GPO are on West Veli St, as is the Tourist Office which is close to the Hotel Tamil Nadu near the junction with South Veli St.

Outside this area, on the north bank of the River Vaigai in the cantonment area, are several larger hotels, the YWCA, the Circuit House and the Gandhi Museum. The Mariamman Teppakkulam tank and temple stand on the south bank of the Vaigai several km east of the old city.

Information
The Tourist Office, 180 West Veli St, is close to the Hotel Tamil Nadu. The staff are friendly and helpful, and maps of Madurai backed with some information about the city are available free. There are also branch offices at Madurai Junction Station and at the airport.

East of the temple there's an interesting and popular tailor's market. They make up clothes in less than 24 hours.

Shree Meenakshi Temple
The Meenakshi Temple attracts pilgrims from all over India in their thousands every day. Its enormous gopurams, profusely covered with gaily coloured statues, dominate the landscape for far around, and are visible from many of the rooftops in Madurai. It is named after the daughter of a Pandyan king who, legend has it, was born with three breasts. The king was told at the time of her birth that the extra breast would disappear when she met the man she was to marry, and this duly happened when she met Lord Shiva on Mt Kailas. Shiva told her to return to Madurai, and eight days later arrived there himself in the form of Lord Sundareshwara to marry her.

The present temple was designed in 1560 by Vishwanatha Nayak and substan-

tially built during the reign of Tirumalai Nayak (1623-55 AD), but it has a history going back 2000 years to the times when Madurai was the capital of the Pandya kings. There are four entrances to the temple, which occupies six hectares and has 12 towers ranging in height from 45 to 50 metres. The tallest of the four outer-rim nine-storey towers is the 50-metre-high southern tower. The hall of 1000 columns actually has 985.

Depending on the time of day, you can bargain for bangles, spices or saris in the bazaar between the outer and inner walls of the temple, watch pilgrims bathing in the tanks, listen to temple music in front of the Meenakshi Amman shrine (which is relayed through the whole complex on a PA system), wander through the interesting museum or climb to the top of a gopuram. It's a city within a city and many travellers spend days exploring its labyrinthine corridors and halls. Only the inner sanctum is off-limits to non-Hindus and 90% of the remaining temple can be visited.

Part of the temple complex has been converted into a museum – the Temple Art Gallery – which is worth a visit even though it's decidedly dilapidated and many labels are missing. It contains some beautiful stone and brass images, examples of ancient south Indian scripts, friezes and various attempts to explain the Hindu pantheon and the many legends associated with it, as well as one of the best exhibits on Hindu deities anywhere. Entrance to the Art Gallery costs Rs 0.50 plus (officially) Rs 5 for a camera if you intend to use it.

You can climb to the top of the south-facing gopuram between 6 am and 5.30 pm. Buy a Rs 0.50 ticket from the office on the left as you enter the temple. A guide takes you up there via the many winding, grimy and gradually narrower and narrower stairways. If you suffer from vertigo this climb is not for you, since you emerge on the very top of the gopuram where there are no restraining rails and very little else to hold onto – but the views are excellent! On the way down the guide will hassle you for a 'tip'.

On most evenings between 6 and 7.30 and 9 and 10 pm temple music is played outside the Meenakshi Amman shrine – mantras, fiddle, squeeze box, tabla and bells. There are some excellent musicians among those who play.

The temple in general is open between 5 am and 12.30 pm and again between 4 and 10 pm. Photography is allowed inside only between 12.30 and 4 pm on payment of Rs 5. You can leave your shoes at any of the four entrances, except the southern one, and they will be looked after for Rs 0.15. Many of the priests inside are very friendly and will take the trouble to show you around and explain what's happening. Licensed guides charge Rs 10 for an hour.

There's a wonderful procession around 7 pm on the first day of the Tamil month – or whenever a devotee pays Rs 1001! It consists of a caparisoned bull carrying drums, two caparisoned camels, the painted temple elephant, a wild band and an ornate shrine illuminated garishly with power from a generator in a trailer, the shrine being pulled by the devotees who gave the Rs 1001! The procession goes around the temple so you can follow it around or double back to see it again.

Tom Harriman & Jan King, USA

At 9.15 each evening there's also a closing ceremony when an image of Shiva is carried in procession to Parvati's bedroom – and taken back at about 6 am the next morning.

Tirumalai Naick Palace
About a km from the Meenakshi Temple (Rs 2 by rickshaw), this Indo-Saracenic palace was built in 1636 by the ruler of the same name. Much of it has fallen into ruin and the pleasure gardens and surrounding defensive wall have disappeared, but it was partially restored by Lord Napier, the governor of Madras, in 1866-72 and further restoration work is in progress at present. Only the entrance gate, main hall, dance hall and a small museum remain today.

The palace is open daily, 9 am to 12.30 pm and 2 to 4 or 5 pm, and entrance costs Rs 0.40. You can get there on a No 11, 11A or 17 bus from the Central Bus Stand. There's no charge for photography. There is a *son et lumière* in English at 6.45 pm daily. Tickets cost Rs 1, 2 and 3 and it's excellent entertainment telling the history of the city with sound and coloured lights on the temple carvings.

Gandhi Museum
Housed in the old palace of the Rani Mangammal, this oddly moving museum tells a few little-known facts about the Mahatma although the only real Gandhi memorabilia is the blood-stained dhoti from the assassination, behind a bulletproof screen. There's also a library and an

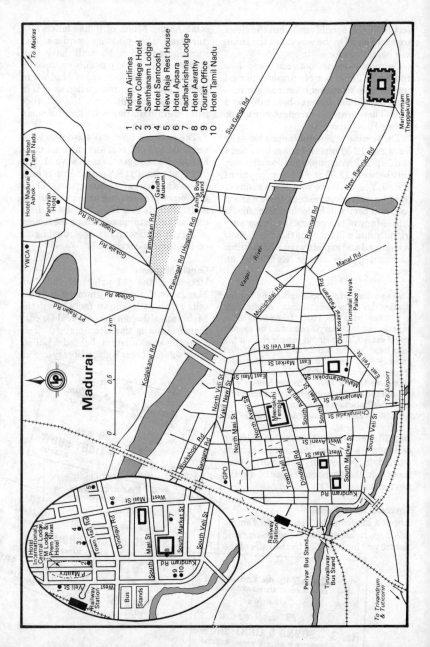

Madurai

1 Indian Airlines
2 New College Hotel
3 Santhanam Lodge
4 Hotel Santoosh
5 New Raja Rest House
6 Hotel Apsara
7 Radhakrishna Lodge
8 Hotel Aarathy
9 Tourist Office
10 Hotel Tamil Nadu

exhibition of crafts produced by village industry concerns in south India. Not to mention an 'everything you want to know about latrines' display. Part of the museum is used for lectures and seminars. It's open daily between 10 am and 1 pm, and 2 to 4 pm, except Wednesdays. Get there on a bus No 3 from the Central Bus Stand.

Mariamman Teppakkulam Tank

This tank, several km east of the old city, covers an area almost equal to that of the Meenakshi Temple and is the site of the Teppam Festival (Float Festival) in January and February. The festival attracts thousands of pilgrims from all over India – at other times of year the tank is not really worth a visit. It was built in 1646 by Tirumalai Nayak and is connected to the River Vaigai by underground channels.

Other Temples

Besides the Meenakshi Temple there are several other important temples worth visiting in Madurai, all of them built in the typical late Dravidian style. Try the two along South Masi St between Kundram Rd and West Masi St. One of them has a temple elephant, the other offers some fine music in the evening. The Femina Fabric Store at 10-12 West Chitrai St will let you view the temples from their roof.

Festivals

Madurai's principal festivals are:

Teppam (Float) Festival A very popular festival which attracts pilgrims from all over India. The images of Shree Meenakshi and Lord Sundareshwara (Shiva) are mounted on floats and taken to the Mariammam Theppakkulam Tank, where they are pulled back and forth across the water to the island temple in the tank's centre for several days before being taken back to Madurai. The festival takes place in January or early February.

Chithirai Festival Takes place in late April/early May and celebrates the marriage of Shree Meenakshi to Lord Sundareshwara.

Avanimoola Festival Takes place in late August/early September. Temple cars are drawn round the streets of Madurai.

Places to Stay – bottom end

Madurai is another town where finding a room can sometimes be difficult. In a pilgrim city the size and importance of Madurai, there are lots of cheap hotels and lodges offering basic accommodation. Many of them are just flop houses which bear the scars of previous occupants' bad habits. They're OK for a night, but not for much longer. On the other hand, there are a few – mostly along Town Hall Rd and Dindigul Rd – which are clean and very good value.

Along Town Hall Rd between West Masi St and West Veli St you can try any one of the following: The *Subham Hotel* is a good, clean, comfortable place with big bathless doubles for Rs 20. The *Ravi Lodge* and the *Hotel Santoosh* both cost Rs 30.

New College Hotel is an enormous place where you'll always be able to find a room. Singles/doubles, all with attached bath, cost Rs 25/40, and there are a few air-con rooms. The hotel has an attached vegetarian restaurant, bookshop and general store. Ask for a room on the top floor – excellent views of Meenakshi Temple. The similarly priced *Hotel KPS* at 8-9 West Masi St also has good views over the temple.

The *TM Lodge* on West Perumal Maistry St has beautifully clean rooms with attached bath for Rs 21/45. The staff are attentive and it's excellent value. Next to the Thangkam Theatre on the first road parallel to West Veli St from the station, the *KP Lodge* is clean and pleasant. Doubles with fan are Rs 20 and you can sleep on the roof.

The *New Raja Rest House*, off Dindigul Rd, is reasonably good value. It's a huge place which caters mainly for pilgrims, and the bathrooms consist of a tap, bucket and toilet. The *Rahakrishna Lodge*, Koodalalagarkoil St, used to be popular with travellers due to its rock-bottom prices. It's dingy and the hardboard-partitioned rooms aren't too clean.

Places to Stay – middle

There are three hotels at the top end of the middle range. *Hotel Prem Nivas* (tel 625 001), 102 West Perumal Maistry St, has been recommended by a lot of travellers. It's fairly new and very well maintained. All rooms have their own bath with hot and cold running water. Rooms without air-con cost Rs 37/66; with air-con they are Rs 110 a double. There are no singles. It's less than five minutes' walk from the railway station.

The new *Hotel Aarathy* (tel 31571), 9 Perumalkoil West Mada St, is similar in standard to the Prem Nivas and is just a few minutes' walk from the bus station. Rooms all have attached bathrooms with hot water and cost Rs 40/70 or Rs 80/120 with air-con. It is very popular, comfortable and has a restaurant. You even get a complimentary paper in the morning.

The last of the three, the *Hotel Tamil Nadu* (tel 31435), is on West Veli St, opposite the bus terminal. It's a State Tourist Development Corporation undertaking and good value at Rs 35/50 or Rs 70/100 with air-con. All the rooms have their own bathroom and the hotel is conveniently situated directly opposite the bus station. On the other hand, it's often full, and even if you made a booking you shouldn't rely on having a room when you arrive. Mosquitoes inhabit the rooms in large numbers, even in winter.

Places to Stay – top end

Madurai's three best hotels are clustered together well out of the centre of town across the Vaigai River, along Alagarkoil Rd. An auto-rickshaw should cost Rs 7 to Rs 9, although the price will double when they hear where you want to go! City bus

Nos 2, 16 or 20 (among others) will get you there for less than a rupee.

Hotel Madurai Ashok (tel 42531) and the *Pandyan Hotel* (tel 26671) are both on Alagarkoil Rd, four km from the centre. They're centrally air-conditioned, the rooms have all mod cons, and there are bars and restaurants offering a variety of cuisine (Indian, Chinese and western). The 43-room Ashok costs from Rs 290/375 for singles/doubles and claims to be Madurai's best hotel. The 60-room Pandyan Hotel has rooms for Rs 280/330.

Also on Alagarkoil Rd but cheaper than these is the second state-government operated *Hotel Tamil Nadu* (tel 42461). Having two different hotels with the same name is somewhat confusing. It's a slightly smaller hotel with a choice of air-con or non-air-con rooms. They all have attached bath, hot and cold running water and a telephone. Rooms are Rs 75/100 or Rs 100/150 with air-con. There is a bar and restaurant (Indian, Chinese and western cuisine) and the staff is pleasant and friendly.

Places to Eat

There are many typical south Indian vegetarian restaurants around the Meenakshi Temple and along Town Hall Rd, Dindigul Rd and West Masi St. These serve thalis for Rs 4 or Rs 5 and masala dosa and coffee for Rs 2 to Rs 3. Some of the best include the *New Arya Bhawan* and other restaurants at the junction of Dindigul Rd and West Masi St. The names may only be in Tamil.

Inexpensive vegetarian food can also be found at the *New College Hotel* – it's large and impersonal but the food is great. The *Sri Ram Mess Restaurant* has excellent all-you-can-eat vegetarian meals at lunchtime for Rs 8.

On Town Hall Rd the *Amutham Restaurant* and the very good *Taj Restaurant* are popular and crowded places with non-vegetarian dishes, unusual in very vegetarian Madurai!

Other places with non-vegetarian food include the restaurant in the *Hotel Tamil Nadu*, West Veli St, which has a variety of dishes including western breakfasts (toast and jam, omelettes, fried and scrambled eggs, etc) and very slow service. The *Indo-Ceylon Restaurant*, Town Hall Rd close to New College House, has vegetarian and non-vegetarian meals and excellent curd. *Bamboo Cove* has good Chinese food. The *Railway Station Restaurant* has good food and is conveniently located.

At the Pandyan Hotel's *Jasmine Restaurant* the food is, according to a recent visitor, 'expensive and not very good, the service is bad and there is a band which spent five minutes rehearsing before *each* number'.

Getting There

Air There is a daily flight Madras-Madurai-Cochin and return, and less frequent connections with Bangalore. Fares to Madurai are Bangalore Rs 342, Cochin Rs 263 and Madras Rs 398.

Rail It's 492 km from Madras to Madurai and the journey takes eight hours via Trichy, longer via Chidambaram and Tanjore. Fares are Rs 45 in 2nd class, Rs 181 in 1st. The new all-2nd-class Vagai Express is particularly fast and comparatively luxurious. To Rameswaram it takes six hours to cover the 164 km. Fares are Rs 20 in 2nd class, Rs 74 in 1st.

If you're heading for Kerala, the best train to take is the morning Madras-Quilon Mail, as the line crosses the Western Ghats through some spectacular mountain terrain, and there are some superb gopurams to be seen at Srivilliputur (between Sivaksi and Rajapalaryam) and Sankarankovil. This train takes eight hours and the 268-km journey costs Rs 27 in 2nd class, Rs 110 in 1st. It gets into Quilon in plenty of time for you to make it to Trivandrum or Kovalam Beach later in the afternoon.

Sleeping berths and seats can only be booked on the night trains out of Madurai. You cannot book a seat on a day train which does not start from Madurai, but it's easy to get one from the compartment attendant when a train arrives. Many of the through trains are half empty.

Bus There are three bus stands in Madurai. Two are next to each other, but the third is across the river in the suburban part of the town. Central bus stand (also called Periyar bus stand) is for local city and short-distance buses. Tiruvalluvar bus stand is for long-distance buses, such as Madras or Cape Comorin. The third is the Anna bus stand, from where buses go to Tanjore or Trichy. If your bus terminates here you will have to take bus No 3 or 3A to Central bus stand.

If you're heading for Kanyakumari, take the early-morning buses because they start from Madurai and you're more or less assured of a seat. Later buses start from other places and go via Madurai, so you can't be sure of a seat until the bus arrives. The super-deluxe buses cost Rs 40 and take six hours.

To Madras (447 km) ordinary buses cost Rs 40. The six-hour trip to Kodai (120 km) costs Rs 9.50. There are buses every two hours from 5 am to 4 pm. A direct bus to Trichy (128 km) leaves Madurai at 4 pm and takes six hours.

There are four Tiruvalluvar buses daily to Kottayam in Kerala. The pleasant, scenic trip takes about 8½ hours. The 9 am departure may stop for lunch in the new and very attractive *Hotel Ambadi* between Kumili and Thekkady. If you've got time to kill at the bus station a reader suggested that you 'go and admire the 1968 Chevrolet Impala at BISMI Auto Consultants, 112 TPK Rd, three minutes' walk from the station. It's huge – you could seat a banquet of 20 around the bonnet (hood). It's normally hired out for wedding processions'.

Getting Around

Airport The airport is six km from the city centre. A Rs 10 airport bus goes to the big hotels, the Hotel Tamil Nadu and close to the budget-hotel area.

Bus Some useful local buses include Nos 3 and 4 to the Gandhi Museum (the No 2 nearly gets there!), No 4 to Mariammam Theppakkulam Tank, No 5 to the Tiruparankundram rock-cut temple (eight km outside Madurai) and No 44 to the Alagarkoil Vaishnavite shrine (21 km from Madurai). See the note above about the three bus stations in Madurai.

RAMESWARAM (population 11,000)

Rameswaram is the Varanasi of the south and a major pilgrimage centre both for Saivaites and Vaishnavites. Ramanatha-swamy Temple is one of the most important temples in the south. This is also the port from which the ferry to Talaimannar (Sri Lanka) used to depart before it was suspended due to the turmoil in that country.

Orientation & Information

Rameswaram is an island in the Gulf of Mannar which is connected to the mainland at Mandapam by rail, although a road bridge is being constructed. It's a small town and most of the hotels and restaurants, ferry jetty, railway station and post office are clustered around the Ramanathaswamy Temple.

Accommodation is often very difficult to find, especially late in the day.

Ramanathaswamy Temple

The town's most famous monument is the Ramanathaswamy Temple, a gem of late Dravidian architecture. Its most renowned features are the magnificent corridors lined with massive sculptured pillars, which are noted for their elaborate design, style and rich carving. One of these corridors is an incredible 1220 metres (4000 feet) in length! – the longest in India.

Legend has it that Rama (of the Indian epic the *Ramayana*) sanctified this place by worshipping Lord Shiva here after the battle of Sri Lanka. Rama sent his most devout disciple, Hanuman (the monkey god), to Mt Kailas to bring a lingam but the monkey god was delayed. As Shiva had to be worshipped at a certain time, Rama's wife Sita moulded one herself which subsequently became known as the Ramanatha. On Hanuman's return, Rama was forced to console the monkey god by having the lingam which he had brought from Mt Kailas installed near the Ramanatha, and decreeing that the Hanuman lingam should have precedence over the Ramanatha.

The temple was begun in the 12th century AD and added to by various rulers over the succeeding centuries so that today its gopuram is 53.6 metres (176 feet) high. Only Hindus are allowed into the inner sanctum.

Kothandaraswamy Temple

This is another famous temple at Dhanushkodi on the extreme tip of the island. Kothandaraswamy Temple was the only structure to survive the 1964 cyclone which washed the rest of the village away. Legend has it that Vibishana, brother of Ravana, the kidnapper of Sita, surrendered to Rama at this spot. Dhanushkodi can be reached by road from Rameswaram. Buses go there every two hours, the last one back at 8 pm.

Other

Rameswaram's other attractions are its coral reefs and beaches fringed with swaying coconut palms and tamarind trees. From Gandhamathana Parvathum, a hillock to the north of Rameswaram and the highest point on the island, an excellent view over the whole island can be had. At Dhanushkodi, at the very tip of the peninsula, is a lovely bathing pool. There's nobody there except friendly fishermen.

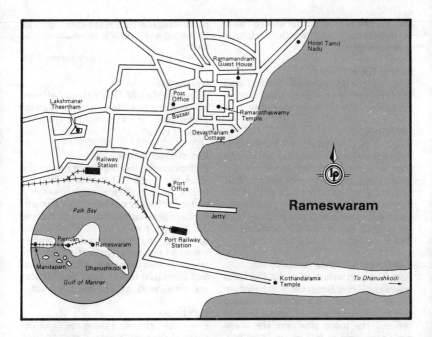

Places to Stay

Accommodation can be a real problem at Rameswaram and you should try to make advance bookings at the *Hotel Tamil Nadu* (tel 77) if you want a reasonable place to stay. If you cannot do this then you must be prepared to take whatever is available. This TTDC-operated place is without doubt the best place to stay but is almost always full. The rooms are quite luxurious at Rs 50/70 with their own bathroom and balcony overlooking the sea, and there's also a dormitory. The food, on the other hand, is ghastly and you should eat elsewhere. A rickshaw from the railway station to the hotel should cost about Rs 5.

Nadar Mahajana Sangam Lodge, New St, is about 15 minutes' walk from the railway station. Rooms with bathroom cost from Rs 20. It's clean and quiet and the next best place after the tourist bungalow. The *Alanka Tourist Home* is a new hotel near the temple entrance on the town side with doubles at Rs 30. The new *Hotel Maharaja* (tel 71) has rooms from Rs 15 to Rs 50, plus more expensive rooms with air-con. If you get a room with a balcony in this friendly and well-kept hotel you can sit for hours watching the street activity below.

At the station there are *Railway Retiring Rooms* and also dorm facilities. Other places to stay include the *Lakshmi Lodge, Meenakshi Lodge, Devasthanam Cottage, Vivekananda Illam, Rama Mandiram Guest House* and *Tirupati Devasthanam Bungalow* with prices from Rs 10 to Rs 30. If you're really stuck there is a covered roof at the *Lakshmi Lodge*, near the temple, where you can sleep for Rs 5 a night.

Places to Eat

There are a number of vegetarian restaurants serving typical south Indian thalis. They're all of similar quality; none is outstanding and worth particular recommendation.

Getting There
Some of the trains from Madras and Madurai arrive pre-dawn, ideal for the Sri Lanka ferry if it were operating.

TIRUCHENDUR
South of Rameswaram and Tuticorin is this impressive temple where you may be able to enter the inner sanctums and watch the enthusiastic proceedings. Just be careful if they offer you a gulp of the holy water. Pouring it over your hands and rubbing them together joyously is an acceptable substitute for drinking it! There is a *Hotel Tamil Nadu* here.

KANYAKUMARI (Cape Comorin)
Kanyakumari is the 'Land's End' of India where the Bay of Bengal meets the Indian Ocean, and where it's possible to enjoy the unique experience of seeing the sun set and the moon rise over the ocean simultaneously at full moon. It's also a popular pilgrimage destination for Hindus, for whom it is of great spiritual significance. It is dedicated to the goddess Kanyakumari, an incarnation of Parvati, Shiva's consort.

Other than that, Kanyakumari is highly over-rated – trinket stalls, a lousy beach and one of those places with megaphones at the end of each street which rip your ear drums apart between 4 am and 10 pm. Do Indians collectively suffer from some congenital disability which makes them incapable of perceiving the excruciating level of noise pollution in some places, or is it a perverse form of merit-garnering penance? No, you can safely give this place a miss if your time is limited. The real show is the pilgrims from all over, a good cross-section of India.

The villagers on the north of town are really friendly though – naked teenagers on miniscule bits of plywood flotsam trying to surf the placid ocean. Computer buffs might want to get a Rs 10 bamboo mat with CPM 86 written on it, in shells.

Ray Spears, USA

Information
There is a Tourist Office about half-way between the Bus Stand and the Gandhi Mandapam – but what could you possibly want to know?

Kanyakumari Temple
Picturesquely located overlooking the shore, the Kumari Ghat attracts pilgrims from all over India, who come to worship and to bathe. Legend has it that Parvati, in one of her incarnations as Devi Kanya, did penance here to secure Shiva's hand in marriage but was unsuccessful, and so vowed to remain a virgin (Kanya). The temple is open daily from 4.30 to 11.30 am and from 5.30 to 8.30 pm. Non-Hindus are not allowed into the inner sanctum.

Lighthouse
From the lighthouse there are excellent views of the countryside. It is open from 3 to 7 pm and entry costs Rs 0.25. Unfortunately, no photos can be taken.

Vivekananda Memorial
This memorial is on two rocky islands which project from the sea about 200 metres from the shoreline. The Indian philosopher Swami Vivekananda came here in 1892 and sat on the rock meditating before setting out as one of India's most important religious crusaders. The *mandapam* which stands here in his memory was built in 1970 and employs architectural styles from all over India. There's a ferry service to the island every half hour for Rs 3 per person plus an entry fee of Rs 1 to the Rock Temple. The islands are open to visitors 7 to 11 am and 2 to 5 pm.

If you're looking for a quiet beach, one of the finest in Tamil Nadu, before heading north into Kerala try the one at Kolachal about half-way between Kanyakumari and Trivandrum.

Kanyakumari

Suchindram Temple

This temple to Indra is about 10 minutes from Kanyakumari by auto-rickshaw and can be visited by non-Hindus. It's very interesting with (reported one visitor) 'marvellous carved pillars, some depicting extremely rude scenes'! If you go there immediately after the sunset-bathing ceremonies at the cape you can watch the evening sacred-flame ceremonial.

Places to Stay

Hotels can be heavily booked and as a result prices can be pushed up. At the bottom end of the market there are a bunch of cheap hotels clustered at the back of the bus stand close to Vinayakar Koil. They include the *Raja Tourist Lodge* and the *Gopi Nivas Lodge*, both offering rooms with attached bathroom from Rs 20. Close to them and of similar standard is *Sri Bhagavathi Lodge*.

Devi Cottage, opposite the Sri Bhagavathi, is cheaper and has rooms with three, four and five beds, but no singles. You need to bargain here, as they quote whatever they think you're silly enough to pay. Near the bus stand the *Township Lodge* has rooms with common bathroom for Rs 10 to Rs 20 as well as a large hall – no beds – which will fit 50 people.

Right in the centre of town, the best middle-range hotel is the *Darsana Tourist Home* with good doubles with bathroom for Rs 40. Similar in standard but not quite as good is the *Jothi Lodge*, two or three doors up from the Darsana. Again, there are no singles. The *Tri-Sea Lodge*, opposite the Darsana Tourist Home, is largely for families and groups who are going to share large rooms, and it's not at all cheap.

Also in this bracket, the *Parvathi Nivas Lodge* is very close to the expensive Hotel Sangam and has a solitary single at Rs 20; the other rooms are doubles at Rs 40. All rooms in this pleasant, older-style building have attached bath. The *Youth Hostel* has dorm beds for Rs 7.50 or doubles for Rs 25. *Vivekananda Kendra* is a km north of Kanyakumari and has singles at Rs 15 to Rs 20, a pictorial exhibition on the life of Vivekananda and lessons in yoga.

The hotels that overlook the sea to the west of the bus stand are particularly pleasant. They include *Hotel Tamil Nadu* (tel 22, 57), which offers really pleasant rooms with balcony – some of which overlook the sea – and attached bath. A double room costs Rs 50 or Rs 40 for single occupancy. There is an attached restaurant and bar but a traveller complained that 'my vegetable fried rice was rice, three peas and two slivers of carrot, honest, I counted'. Also overlooking the sea, *Kerala House* (tel 29) is a huge building but contains only eight rooms which cost Rs 50 a double, plus Rs 8 for each additional person. Again, there is an attached restaurant. *Manickum Tourist Home* is another place with balconied rooms overlooking Vivekananda rock. Doubles with bath are Rs 60 to Rs 80 depending on the floor, and the restaurant has good food.

Sankar's Guest House is one of the first hotels you will come to on your way from the railway station to the centre of town. Rooms with attached bathrooms cost from Rs 40. Finally, the new *Hotel Sangam* (tel 62) is opposite the post office, 200 metres from the bus stand on Main Rd. Air-con rooms with attached bathroom cost from Rs 75. The rooms are well fitted out and some have a verandah.

Getting There

Rail There is now a railway line direct to Kanyakumari, and trains run to Nagarcoil Junction, Trivandrum and Tirunelvelli. Trivandrum is only 87 km away and the fare is Rs 10 in 2nd class, Rs 48 in 1st on an express train.

Bus Buses go from Kanyakumari to Coimbatore (six daily, 11½ hours), Madras (four daily, 16 hours), Madurai (one daily, six hours), Pondicherry (daily, 14 hours), Rameswaram (six daily, 7½ hours) and Trivandrum (four daily, 2½ hours, Rs 9.50).

AROUND KANYAKUMARI

Padmanabhapuram

Near Nagarcoil, this was once the capital of the state of Travancore. There's an old fort and a pagoda-shaped palace with fine 17th and 18th-century murals on the topmost floor – even finer than those at Matancherry in Cochin, reported one visitor. They are 'less restored, in better condition and staggeringly beautiful'. Padmanabhapuram was once the seat of the rulers of Travancore – a princely state during the days of the Raj which included a large part of present-day Kerala and the western littoral of Tamil Nadu. The palace is close to the Kerala border, 55 km south of Trivandrum, and conveniently visited between Kanyakumari and Trivandrum. It's closed Mondays.

Courtallam

Further north, three km from Tenkasi Junction on the Madurai-Trivandrum railway route, there are seven sparkling waterfalls, among the best in India. The best time to visit is June-September; avoid Sundays.

KODAIKANAL (population 20,500)

Of the three main hill stations of the south – Ootacamund, Kodaikanal and Yercaud – Kodaikanal is undoubtedly the most beautiful and has the advantage over Ooty that the temperature – even in winter – rarely drops to the point where you need to wear heavy clothing. It's on the southern crest of the Palani Hills, about 120 km north-west of Madurai among thickly wooded slopes, waterfalls and precipitous rocky outcrops. Some of the views to the south are the most spectacular you will find anywhere in India, and are within a few minutes' walking distance of the centre of town – unlike Ooty where you have to walk several km to find them.

Kodaikanal isn't just for those who want to get away from the heat of the plains during the summer months, but for those who are looking for a relaxing place to put up their feet for a while, and do some hiking now and again. Like Ooty, Kodaikanal has its own landscaped, artificial lake with boating facilities.

Having said that, once you've rowed around the lake, admired the views and put in a few days' hiking, there isn't a great deal else to do, especially if you're travelling alone. Apart from one or two restaurants down Hospital Rd, there's really nowhere that people gather in the evenings, so it's back to your hotel and early to bed, unless you happen to be lucky enough to break into the 'expatriate' resident community here. It certainly exists but I got the distinct impression that it was composed almost entirely of affluent Sinhalese Tamils looking for a suitable school for their offspring, loud-mouthed American teenagers doing a term at the prestigious Kodai School, and snobby hipppies who'd set up house and home in the area.

Information

There is a Tourist Office next to the bus stand – or rather there's a sign for one – but it's a joke. If you want literature about Kodai, try the bookshop more or less opposite this so-called Tourist Office.

The best times to visit Kodaikanal are during the months of April to June or August to October. The main rainy season is between November and December. The temperature ranges between 11 and 20°C in summer and 8 and 17°C in winter, and the altitude is 2133 metres (7000 feet).

Things to See

Obviously the main thing to do in Kodai is walk around and enjoy the sights and views. There are numerous stone and wood cottages from the British period with rolling lawns edged with flowering shrubs and trees.

Two of the most spectacular views in India can be enjoyed from Coaker's Walk, where there's an observatory with telescope available if you feel the need, and from Pillar Rocks, the latter a seven-km hike. These places offer two of the most spectacular views in India. Bryant Park is also worth a visit, especially if you have any interest in botany. It was laid out, landscaped and stocked over many, many years by a British colonial administrator of the same name. Also worth a visit are the Flora & Fauna Museum at the Sacred Heart College and the adjoining orchid collection at nearby Shembaganur. The museum is open 10 to 11.30 am and 3.30 to 5 pm, closed Sundays. There are numerous waterfalls in the area, though you will pass the main one – Silver Cascade – on the road up to Kodai.

The lake at Kodai has been wonderfully landscaped, and rowboats are available for Rs 15 per hour plus a returnable deposit. Down by the boathouse you'll be accosted by people who want to rent you horses. They are not cheap, and you'll be quoted as much as they think you're silly enough to pay; Rs 20 per hour seems to be the prevailing rate. You can ride them accompanied or unaccompanied. The saddles aren't too hot either, especially if you're used to your own – in fact they're bloody awful.

Places to Stay – bottom end

The buses which go up to Kodaikanal follow Law's Ghat Rd all the way round past the lake, past Kodai School up to the top of the hill and down Bazaar Rd to the bus stand. If you want the Hotel Tamil Nadu/Youth Hostel, MNS Lodge or Carlton Hotel, tell the driver where you want to get off; otherwise you'll have to do a lot of unnecessary walking back from the bus stand. They're willing to stop just about anywhere.

Many of the budget hotels are to be found along Bazaar Rd downhill from the post office. Only the big hotels have fixed prices during the summer season; others charge what they think the traffic will bear. There isn't a great deal to choose from among them and they're all pretty good value for what they offer. They include the *Lodge Siraaj*, *Lodge Everest* and the slightly better *Hotel Amar* and *Hotel Guru*, all with singles/doubles for Rs 20/25.

Another popular place is *Zum Zum Lodge* at the top end of Bryant Park where Coaker's Walk starts. The rooms are spartan and somewhat primitive, but you can get doubles for Rs 15 and the price is negotiable if you are staying longer. There is a sort of common room with a log fire going in the evening that is a good place to meet other travellers. At the bottom of the hill, past the Zum Zum, the *Globe Lodge* has doubles with bath for Rs 20 to Rs 25. The lodge has great views and the rooms are OK although it's not the cleanest place around. *MNS Lodge*, below the Hotel Jaya, has doubles with common showers for Rs 40.

Near the start of Coaker's Walk, *Tai Lodge* has some rooms with good views. Doubles at Rs 25 are partitioned in such a way that there is really no privacy.

Yagappa Lodge charges Rs 50 for a double off season. *Lilly's Valley Resort* at 17/178 Sivanadi Rd is a little bit out of town but it's clean, well kept and friendly and the cottages are good value at Rs 25. Rooms are also available in private homes, usually with full board either by the day or for longer periods – you'll get a few offers while you're here.

At the *Hotel Tamil Nadu* (see top end below) there's a *Youth Hostel* with dorm beds for Rs 12; Rs 10 off season. At the end of Coaker's Walk the *Greenlands Youth Hostel* is better, costs Rs 7.50 per night and has good views and even a hot shower. The staff will serve tea or coffee almost any time of the day or night, and if it's too cold they'll make a fire. It's also got a resident cook who'll perform miracles in the kitchen for a small fee.

Places to Stay – top end

Kodaikanal's most prestigious hotel is the *Carlton Hotel* (tel 252), Boathouse Rd, which overlooks the lake and has its own restaurant and bar. Singles/doubles are Rs 220/335 plus 10%! Bundles of firewood are available at Rs 10 each but all rooms have hot water. Their Rs 55 buffet dinner is excellent. Opposite the Carlton the *New Garden Manor Hotel* has doubles at Rs 180.

Less expensive than the Carlton, but without the advantage of lake views, is the *Hotel Tamil Nadu & Youth Hostel* (tel 481), Fern Hill Rd. Like the other Hotel Tamil Nadus, this is a state government project. In the high season (April, May, June) singles/doubles cost Rs 70/110. There are also family rooms with five beds. In the low season (July to March) rooms cost Rs 40/70. The hotel has a restaurant and bar but is inconveniently located unless you have a car because it is a 15-minute walk from the bus stand, Rs 15 for a taxi.

Hotel Jaya (tel 462) is a modern hotel within a stone's throw of the bus stand and of similar standard to the Hotel Tamil Nadu. All the rooms have attached

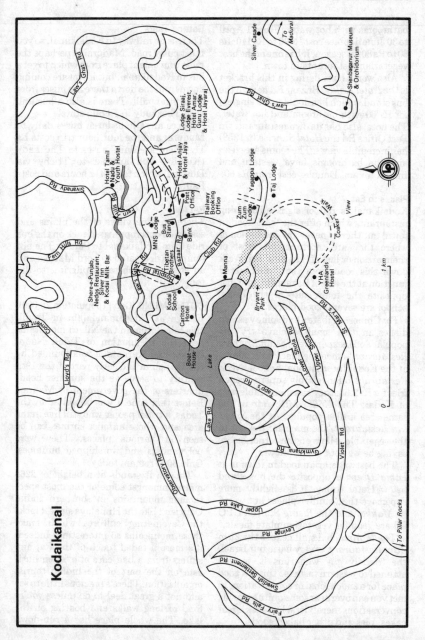

Kodaikanal

To Madurai

Silver Cascade

Shenbaganur Museum & Orchidorium

Law's Ghat Rd

Law's Ghat Rd

Hotel Tamil Nadu Youth Hostel

Sivanady Rd

Fern Hills Rd

Hills Rd

Plum

Lodge Siraaj, Lodge Everest, Hotel Amar, Guru Lodge & Hotel Jayaraj

Hotel Anjay & Hotel Jaya

Post Office

Railway Booking Office

Yagappa Lodge

Taj Lodge

Zum Zum Lodge

Coaker's Walk

View

MNS Lodge

Bus Stand

Bank

Bazaar Rd

Club Rd

Convent Rd

Shere-e-Punjab, Nedos Restaurant, Silver Inn & Kodai Milk Bar

Tibetan Brothers

Hospital

MNS Ghat Rd

Manna

YHA Greenlands Hostel

St Mary's Rd

Kodai School

Carlton Hotel

Bryant Park

Boat House

Lake

Lower Shola Rd

Upper Shola Rd

Lloyd's Rd

Lake Rd

Tapp's Rd

Gymkhana Rd

Violet Rd

Observatory Rd

Upper Lake Rd

Lower Lake Rd

Levinge Rd

Swedish Settlement Rd

Fairy Falls Rd

To Pillar Rocks

0   1 km

bathrooms with hot water. From 1 April to 30 June doubles cost Rs 90 to Rs 110; Rs 60 to Rs 80 off season. It has one of the best vegetarian restaurants in town.

Also worth considering in this bracket is the *Hotel Anjay*, Bazaar Rd next to the bus stand, which has doubles (no singles) for Rs 60 with bathroom and hot water. The hotel also has its own restaurant. On Post Office Rd the *Hotel Sunrise* (tel 358) has incredible views. The rooms are clean and the bathrooms have western and Indian toilets! Doubles cost from Rs 60.

Places to Eat

Kodaikanal is full of signs advertising restaurants which offer the 'best' food in town, but there's never any indication of where they are. Fortunately, most of them are on or just off Hospital Rd. Walk down this road from the five-cornered junction at the end of Bazaar Rd, and just opposite the main gate of the Kodai school are several good places.

For Chinese, Tibetan and some western dishes in this small enclave try the popular and inexpensive *Tibetan Brothers Restaurant*, a meeting place for students at the Kodai International School. *Nedo Restaurant* offers simply superb French fries for Rs 2.50; they're a memorable part of Kodai! The *Kodai Milk Bar* in the same area is also popular. At the *Silver Inn Restaurant* 'the manager ran out to the vegetable sellers on the corner before saying he was out of cauliflower!'

The best vegetarian food in town is at *Pakia Deepam* opposite the bus stand below Hotel Anjay. It is slightly more expensive than similar places but worth it. *Makkal* and the *Rising Star* on GPO Rd are good for vegetarian plate meals.

The *Manna* chai stall next to the *Zum Zum Restaurant* is very basic but Israel, the friendly guy who runs it, is well attuned to western tastes so this is a good place for a snack, chai or conversation. In fact you can overhear some quite amazing conversations here! Israel makes great cakes, pies and other baked goods.

Getting There

There is no railway to Kodaikanal, so you must go by road. Madurai is perhaps the most convenient place from which to get a bus to Kodaikanal, but if you are coming down from the north there are buses from Tiruchirappalli. There is also a bus link with Thekkady in Kerala state.

There are a half dozen buses daily to Madurai and the four-hour trip costs Rs 11. There are daily buses to Thekkady (Kumily) and another to Trichy via Dindigul which takes 4½ hours and costs Rs 15.

PALANI

There are fine views of the plains and scattered outcroppings of rock on the bus ride from Kodaikanal to Palani. The hill temple is dedicated to Lord Maruga and an electric winch takes pilgrims to the top.

OOTACAMUND (Ooty) (population 78,000)

Known as Udagamandalam in Tamil, this hill station in the Nilgiri mountains near the tri-junction of Tamil Nadu, Kerala and Karnataka was founded by the British in the early part of the 19th century to serve as the summer head-quarters of the government of Madras. Before that time it was inhabited by the Todas, a tribal people who still live in the area and whose animist shrines can be seen at various places. They were polygamists and worshipped buffaloes. Only 3000 remain today.

Though it stands at a height of 2268 metres amongst some of the most spec-tacular mountains in southern India, Ooty isn't like the Himalaya since it lacks the fascinating cultures which make those mountains so interesting. Indeed, it's more a faded touch of the Raj and suffers from a bad case of over-enthusi-asm on the part of the Indian tourist organisation. There's precious little to see and not a great deal to do unless you're fond of long walks and boating on the lake. The whole place has a run-down feeling about it, not unusual in India. The best part of Ootacamund is the journey there along a narrow, winding and very steep mountain road which passes through luxuriant rain forest and tea plantations.

Despite the tourist literature Ooty is very pleasant and relaxing, ideal as an escape from the heat of the lowlands. In winter and during the monsoon it can be cold and you will need warm clothing. As far as general appearances go, it's an unlikely combination of southern England and Australia with single-storey stone cottages surrounded by twee, fenced flower gardens scattered along leafy, winding lanes with tall eucalypt stands covering the otherwise barren hilltops. Since they were introduced back in the 19th century, the eucalypts have spawned a small oil-extraction industry in the area and bottles of eucalyptus oil can be bought in many shops in the town.

The other main reminders of the British period are the stone churches and the huge boys' school in its own landscaped gardens at the bottom end of the lake. There's also the terraced and very English Botanical Gardens in which Government House stands on the lower slopes of Doddabetta (2623 metres), the highest peak in Tamil Nadu. From the top of Doddabetta you can see Coonoor, Wellington, Coimbatore, Mettupalayam and even to Mysore on a clear day.

Ootacamund, although it quickly became the principal hill station in southern India during the Raj, was not the first in this area. As early as 1819 the British had begun to build houses at nearby Kotagiri. This much smaller town still survives as a minor hill station and has a climate mid-way between that of Ooty and Coonoor.

....the Ooty Club must have the best preserved artefacts of the British colonial past in all of India. The men's bar, billiards room, rummy room and library still gleam in all their finery. Hunting boards, trophies, portraits of Winston and Queen Vic decorate the walls, photographs of the hunt and the hunt masters from 1870 to 1929 adorn the dining room with its polished tables and signing-out book, still in use. It's now a living museum patronised by the Indian upper class – permission to view it can be obtained from the manager who will have someone show you round. One of the bar rooms is 'Colonel Jaco's Room' – in gold lettering over the door. Inside, an enormous portrait of the man himself presides over the plush armchairs and dark wood tables – his riding stick ensconced in a glass case below the portrait.

Orientation

Ooty is spread out over a large area amongst rolling hills and valleys and connected by a complicated system of narrow, winding lanes and flights of steps through the main area of town containing the railway station, bus stand, bazaar, Tourist Office, restaurants and GPO. Most of the hotels are between the eastern end of the lake and the so-called Charing Cross (the junction of Coonoor, Kelso and Commercial Rds).

Ooty can be divided into two areas. The bus stand and railway stations are near the artificial lake and there are a number of hotels in the area. About two km from the bus stand, the Charing Cross area is near the Botanical Gardens, Hotel Tamil Nadu and Tourist Office. The budget hotels and cafés are scattered around in the bazaar which stretches between Hospital and Commercial Rds with a few others in the streets below Commercial Rd, east of the racecourse. Other hotels are strung out along High Level and Avalanche Rds.

Information

The Tourist Office on Commercial Rd is opposite the Nahar Tourist Home. The only literature available here is a leaflet with a map of Ooty and details of the current hotel prices. The office is staffed by three idle layabouts, who know nothing more than the leaflet they hand you. This must be one of the worst tourist offices in south India.

Higginbotham's, just across the road

from Chellaram's Department Store in the Charing Cross area, is an excellent bookshop. If you intend to visit Mudumalai it's wise to book accommodation in advance if you want to be sure of a bed for the night. This can be booked at the office of the District Forest Officer on Coonoor Rd.

Things to See & Do

Ooty is a place for outdoor activities. Any number of long walks can be made and some superb views over Ooty and the Nilgiris can be found – just head out in any direction you like. If you'd prefer to go on horseback, horses can be rented next to the boathouse on the north side of the lake for about Rs 10 to Rs 15 per hour depending on the season. They can be delivered to your hotel for no extra charge. You can take them off on your own or hire one of the owners as a guide.

Rowboats and motor boats can be hired for use on the lake. Costs depend on the boat and the season, but rowboats are Rs 4 to Rs 15 per hour, motor boats rather more expensive. The off season is July-August and November-February; high season is March-June and September-October. The noticeboard which used to stand at the lake included this gem of Indian-English: 'Rowers are available for rowing capacity including rower's rowing cooly charges extra'. Work that one out! If you want to go out on the lake do it soon; water hyacinth has already claimed half of it and will soon take over completely.

In the town itself the bazaar is worth a visit and you may come across some interesting crafts produced by the hill tribes in the area. See Chellaram's Department Store for literally dozens of reminders of British occupancy. Other oddities around Ooty include the police's 'Single Digit Finger Print Section' and the 'Co-operative Society of Ooty – Potato Chip Division'.

Tours

Kings Travel (tel 3137), Nahar Tourist Home, Commercial Rd, offer two tours. The first covers Doddabetta Peak, Kotagiri, Kodanad View Point, Coonoor, Dolphin's Nose, Lamb's Rock and Sims Park. The other tour goes to Doddabetta Peak, the Botanical Gardens and Ooty Lake in the morning, then to the Mudumalai Wildlife Sanctuary in the afternoon.

The tours take all day and cost about Rs 75. Charges include a vegetarian lunch, snacks, entrance fees, a guide and a group photograph (!). If you're hoping to see very much of Mudumalai, forget the second tour as you spend precisely 2¼ hours there.

Places to Stay

Rock-bottom places vary widely in quality and prices can increase dramatically in the high season. Do some shopping around; prices don't necessarily equate with quality – many of them are very dingy, some revoltingly filthy. On the other hand, the mid-range and top-end places may offer considerable reductions in the off season.

Places to Stay – bottom end

Charing Cross Area The best value in the Charing Cross area is the *Co-operative Guest House* which has doubles for Rs 25 but is likely to be full most of the time. At the *Hotel Tamil Nadu* (see top end below) a *Youth Hostel* charges Rs 5 per bed off season and Rs 7.50 high season.

Bus Stand Area *Hotel Dasaprakash* (tel 2434-5), on the hill south of the bus station, was once a grand building but has now gone to seed. Mouldy old moth-eaten photographs of the Maharaja of Mysore being shown around in better days attempt to recapture that old grandeur, but it's no longer in that bracket. If you want to stay close to the bus stand this is perhaps the best place for the price. Rooms start at Rs 35/60 and go on up to Rs

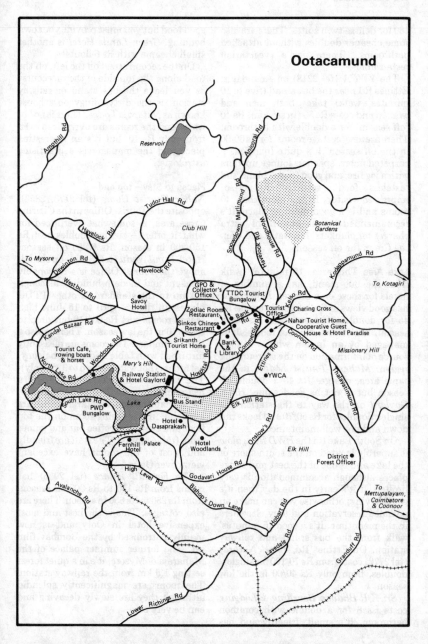

Ootacamund

160 for deluxe twin suites. There are also some cheaper doubles without attached bathrooms. There is a vegetarian restaurant.

The *YWCA* (tel 2218) on Anandagiri Ettines Rd near the bus stand (five to 10 minutes' walk) takes both men and women and costs Rs 80 (in season), Rs 40 (off season) for a double with bathroom. There are also 'cottage rooms' for Rs 50/60 in the off season. It's quite luxurious – carpeted floors, spacious lounge upstairs with a log fire, and good food – 'bland and tasteless food', reported a not-so-impressed visitor. It has more than 40 rooms and is a good meeting place. It's recommended – but beware of extra charges for blankets, hot water and even the fire in the off season!

Lake Area This area, 15 minutes' walk from the bus stand, has a number of hotels for those on a budget. *Reflections* has good views of the lake and charges Rs 45 for doubles off season and Rs 90 in season, but it has only six rooms. It is managed by an Indian who is a good source of information on the surrounding region. *Mahesh Tourist Lodge*, in the same area, charges Rs 40 a double off season but is not as good value. *Hotel Gaylord* on the way to the station has singles/doubles for Rs 50/70 and looks run down and not well maintained.

On South Lake Rd the *PWD Bungalow* is superbly located on the south shore of the lake and is one of the best mid-range places although accommodation is very limited. If it's early in the day then it's worth trying; otherwise you can make an advance reservation and stay elsewhere in the meantime. It's a good 15 minutes' walk from the bus stand and railway station. On Ettines Rd, *Hotel Nataraj* (tel 2772) costs from Rs 70/100 for singles/doubles, from only Rs 40/60 in the low season.

Sri K R Bhavan Boarding & Lodging costs Rs 8 for a double with common bathroom. It's small, friendly and has good food but you must provide your own bedding. *Green Lands Hotel* is another small cheapie with Rs 6 doubles.

On the second street on the left, off the road along the top side of the racecourse as you leave the bus stand or railway station, is the dirty, dingy doss house known as *Nataraja Lodge*. There is no hot water and the rooms are overpriced even from only Rs 10, but it's an interesting place and the manager is a practising astrologist.

Places to Stay – top end
Nahar Tourist Home (tel 2173, 2853), opposite the Tourist Office in the Charing Cross area, is somewhat overpriced for what it offers – singles/doubles cost Rs 150/200 in season, Rs 60/80 off season. *Hotel Tamil Nadu* (tel 2543-4) on the hill above the Tourist Office is a reasonably pleasant and modern building although not up to the standard of other TTDC places. In the 15 April to 15 June high season rooms cost Rs 60/110 but drop to Rs 40/70 in the low season. There is also a Rs 12 dormitory. The rooms are pleasantly furnished with table and chair, balcony, bathroom (hot water from 6 to 9 am only). The radio doesn't work though, and a heater in the room will cost an extra Rs 15. Vegetarian and non-vegetarian meals are available in the dining room on the top floor and there is a coffee bar and games room (table tennis). The staff are friendly and most of the rooms have excellent views over Ooty.

The *Fernhill Palace* (tel 2055) has rooms from Rs 150 to Rs 300 off season, from Rs 250 to Rs 650 in season. There are also cottages. This is the best and most expensive hotel in Ooty and is now mainly patronised by the Bombay film set. The former summer palace of the Maharaja of Mysore, it's in a quiet forest setting 1.5 km from the railway station. The rooms are magnificently splendid although they are slowly decaying and can be very cold.

The Fernhill Palace is decorated with hunt photographs (of the hunt assembled on the lawn outside). The ballroom, now the restaurant, is a huge grand affair, bordered by a balcony on which the old snooker table sits, balls cracked with age, and hung with decidedly moth-eaten velvet drapes. The bookcase is not to be missed, housing gems such as *Juvenile Crime in Southern India* by J W Combes in 1890, condoning flogging as the best form of punishment and comparing the physical features of young criminals with apes. Others of interest are *Polo in India* from 1907, *Lord Curzon in India 1898-1905* and so on. You can have coffee here for Rs 6, served in solid silver by uniformed waiters.

In the same area as the Fernhill Palace, but much smaller and less impressive, is *Hotel Palace* (tel 2866), which belonged to the former Nizam of Hyderabad. Double rooms cost Rs 250, less off season. The adjacent building known as 'The Cedars' was the Nizam's former harem!

The new *Hotel Lake View* at the southwest corner of the lake is good value with doubles for Rs 210 in season, Rs 135 out of season. *Hotel Savoy* (tel 2572, 2463) costs Rs 215/310 in season and Rs 175/260 off season. The cheaper *Hotel Brindavan* (tel 2061-2-3) on Woodcock Rd costs from Rs 60/120 in the high season.

Places to Eat

Many hotels have their own restaurants, open to non-residents. In the Charing Cross area, *Tandoor* has good non-vegetarian dishes and a doorman who salutes you as you pass by. In the same area, *Blue Hill* is also popular and less expensive. The restaurant in the *Nahar Tourist Home* has good thalis. Try their Rs 12 Madras thali. *Hotel Paradise* in Commercial Rd near the Tourist Office has north Indian food at reasonable prices.

There is a good Chinese restaurant called *Shinkowi* near the Collectorate. In the bus stand area, the restaurant in *Hotel Dasaprakash* has excellent thalis for Rs 13. The *Tudor Cheese Company* has superb cheddar cheese. The *Railway Station Restaurant* also does quite good food.

Getting There

Rail Ooty has its own miniature railway connecting it with the lowlands. The trains, with their quaint yellow and blue carriages, are not quite as small as the Darjeeling toy train, but they're not as big as those on the main lines. The unique feature of this line is the toothed central rail which the locomotives lock onto on the steeper slopes.

Wellington, just above Coonoor, is a good place to watch the train climb one side of the valley, cross it by bridge and then double back to climb the opposite side. Like the journey up to Darjeeling by train, this is an excellent way of getting to Ooty and affords some spectacular views of the precipitous eastern slopes of the rainforest-covered Nilgiris. Views are best from the right on the way up, from the left on the way down.

The miniature railway starts at Mettupalayam, north of Coimbatore, and goes via Coonoor to Ooty. The departures and arrivals at Mettupalayam connect with the Nilgiri Express, which runs between Mettupalayam and Madras. If you're heading for Ooty, the Nilgiri Express departs Madras at 9 pm and arrives at Mettupalayam at 7.10 am. The miniature trains depart Mettupalayam for Ooty at 7.35 am and arrives in Ooty at 12 noon. There's a 2.55 pm departure from Ooty to connect with the Nilgiri Express when it leaves Mettupalayam at 7.10 pm. The 46-km journey takes about 4½ hours up to Ooty, about 3½ hours going down. There are also trains between Ooty and Coonoor.

Bus There are local buses hourly for the 1¼-hour, Rs 3 trip to Kotagiri. There are a dozen buses daily to Coonoor and the one-hour trip costs Rs 1.75. Four buses daily go to Dandabitta.

The trip to Bangalore by long-distance bus takes nine hours and costs Rs 24. The trip to Calicut is very fine – 'our favourite journey in the whole of southern India (sit on the left side)', wrote a traveller. Buses also depart regularly to Gudalur, Gundulpet and Hassan.

The 5½-hour trip to Mysore costs Rs 18. This is the bus to take if you're heading for the Mudumalai Wildlife Sanctuary under your own steam. Get off at Theppukady, where the reception centre is. The journey this far from Ooty takes about 2½ hours and costs Rs 10.

Getting Around

If you take an auto-rickshaw from the bus stand to Charing Cross, the 'fixed rate' is Rs 5, while taxis charge Rs 10, which is high for this distance. They seem used to overcharging vacationing Indians. There is a bus service between the bus stand and Charing Cross, although the locals seem reluctant to tell you about it. The bus is marked 'Talkonda' and charges only Rs 0.50. From Charing Cross the local buses start near the Co-operative Bank.

AROUND OOTY

Kotagiri is a much smaller and quieter hill station about 28 km from Ooty. From here you can visit Catherine Falls (eight km), Elk Falls (eight km) and Kodanad View Point (16 km), where there there is a fine panoramic view over the eastern slope of the Nilgiris and the plains.

Places to Stay

There are a few basic lodges in Kotagiri, such as the *Hotel Ram Vihar* where rooms cost from Rs 25. In Coonoor the *Hampton Manor Hotel* (tel 244, 961-4) has rooms from Rs 100 to Rs 250. Or there's the *Ritz Hotel* (tel 6242) on Orange Grove Rd with rooms at Rs 75/150. In Mettupalayam there's a very pleasant two-bed *Retiring Room* spanning the width of the platform so you can hear the steam engines on one side and the Nilgiri Express on the other in the evening.

COIMBATORE (population 380,000)

Coimbatore is a large and busy city at the foot of the Nilgiri mountains, full of 'shirting & suiting' shops. Its only interest for travellers is as a way station to Ootacamund and the other Nilgiri hill stations.

Orientation

The bus and railway stations are a considerable distance from each other and both are well outside the city centre. You'll need an auto-rickshaw to get from one to the other. A number of mid-range and budget hotels are clustered around the bus station – adequate for a night's stay.

Places to Stay

Hotel Sree Shakti (tel 34225, 34229), 11/148 Sastri Rd, is a large, modern hotel opposite the bus station. Rooms cost from Rs 35 and are pleasantly decorated, reasonably clean and have fan and attached bathrooms. The staff are very friendly and room service is available.

The *Zakin Hotel*, Sastri Rd, is a few doors up from the Shakti and also opposite the bus station. Rooms cost from Rs 20, more with attached bathroom, and it's of similar quality to the Shakti. Round the corner from the Sree Shakti and the Zakin, *Hotel Samnathdram* has rooms for Rs 40. *Hotel Anand Vihar* at 6 State Bank Rd opposite the railway junction is spotlessly clean, cheap and very pleasant. *Hotel Alankar* (tel 26293) at 10 Sivaswamy Rd has rooms with attached bathroom at Rs 45/80, with air-con at Rs 90/150.

Hotel Tamil Nadu on Dr Nanjappa Rd, across from the bus station, has rooms from Rs 75 or from Rs 100 with air-con. It has a restaurant and bar. *Hotel Anand Vihar* (tel 22580) is at 6 State Bank Rd opposite the Railway Junction and has singles at Rs 18 or with bath from Rs 20 to Rs 35, doubles with bath Rs 30 to Rs 50. The *Railway Retiring Rooms* at the station are dirty and noisy.

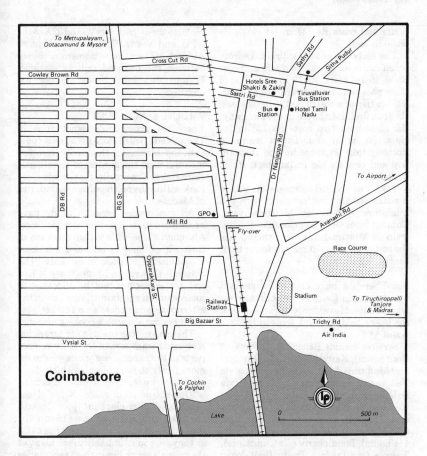

Coimbatore

Places to Eat

The *Zakin Hotel* has an attached restaurant on the ground floor which serves non-vegetarian food. There are a number of other vegetarian and non-vegetarian restaurants where you can get a good meal opposite the bus station along Sastri Rd. There's a cheap place in the bus station itself. By the railway junction the *Sunrise Biriyani Hotel* does good non-vegetarian food if you can ignore the kitchen smoke which somehow finds its way down from the floor above and gets sucked in the windows.

Getting There

Air There are flights between Coimbatore and Bangalore (Rs 236), Bombay (Rs 819) and Madras (Rs 468).

Rail Coimbatore is a major rail junction and there are services to most major centres. The direct Karnataka Kerala Express operates twice a week from New Delhi and makes the 2627-km trip in 38 hours at a cost of Rs 522 in 1st class, Rs 133 in 2nd. There are numerous daily trains between Madras (Central) and Coimbatore. The 494-km trip takes seven to nine hours and costs Rs 143 in 1st class, Rs 36.50 in 2nd.

The daily trains to Madurai take from seven hours for the 229-km trip and cost Rs 75 in 1st class, Rs 19 in 2nd. One of them goes on to Rameswaram, a 14-hour, 393 km trip at a cost of Rs 120 in 1st class, Rs 31 in 2nd. Bangalore is 424 km away; the eight-hour trip costs Rs 128 in 1st class, Rs 33 in 2nd. Direct trains to Bombay take 33 hours for the 1635-km trip and cost Rs 358 in 1st class, Rs 92 in 2nd.

Take the Nilgiri Express if you're heading for Ooty; it connects with the miniature railway at Mettupalayam. Coming from Ooty you can take the toy train to Mettupalayam and then a bus the rest of the way – it may be faster than continuing by train.

Bus There's a huge and well-organised bus station in Coimbatore, but as elsewhere timetables are only in Tamil except for buses to Ooty and some interstate buses.

Services include Bangalore, Guruvayur (four hours), Kanyakumari (via Dindigul and Madurai), Madras (some services via Vellore and Kanchipuram), Madurai (via Palani, Dinigul and Kodai Rd), Mysore (6½ hours), Naggapattinam (via Trichy and Tanjore), Nagarcoil (via Dindigul and Madurai), Palghat (several hourly, 1¼ hours), Pondicherry (via Cuddalore), Tanjore (via Trichy), Trichy (half dozen buses daily, 5½ hours) and Trichur (3¼ hours).

There are 20 to 30 buses daily to Ooty and the three-hour Rs 10 journey is one of the most spectacular bus trips in southern India. Don't expect to get on the first bus which arrives, because even in the off season there will be a long queue. You generally can expect to get on the second or third bus to arrive after you join the queue.

Getting Around
Useful buses around Coimbatore include No 20 to the airport, Nos 25 and 32A to the GPO, and Nos 1A, 7, 65 and 75 to Indian Airlines. There are numerous buses between the bus and railway stations. Coimbatore's local buses are not too crowded.

WILDLIFE SANCTUARIES
There are six wildlife sanctuaries in Tamil Nadu, three close to the east coast and the others in the richly forested mountains on the borders of Kerala and Karnataka. The smallest is Guindy Deer Park within the metropolitan boundaries of Madras.

All sanctuaries except Guindy have accommodation and transport facilities. Although it's possible to turn up at any of them without making prior arrangements, it's advisable to book in advance. The reason is that rooms in sanctuary lodges and rest houses cannot be allocated to unannounced guests until very late in the afternoon, when there's no further possibility of anyone with a booking arriving.

There's also the question of arranging motorised transport to the more remote parts of the sanctuaries where you're far more likely to see animals, which don't often venture too close to areas of human settlement or main roads. Some of the sanctuaries offer elephant rides through the forest and, although these needn't be booked in advance and are great fun as far as they go, you're unlikely to see many of the animals which live in these sanctuaries from the back of an elephant.

At present, most of the sanctuaries are geared to groups who arrive with their own transport and who have pre-booked at least a few days ahead. If you're alone and haven't booked, you could find that a lot of your time is taken up waiting for arrival of a group to which you can attach yourself. Without transport, too, your choice of accommodation is limited unless you can get a lift. It's time the Indian tourist organisation gave some thought to catering for visitors without their own transport and who can't,

Wildlife Sanctuaries

ANDHRA PRADESH
Madras
Guindy Sanctuary
KARNATAKA
Vedanthangal Sanctuary
Pondicherry
Mudumalai Sanctuary
Ootacamund
Anamalai Sanctuary
Tiruchirappalli
Tanjore
Point Calimere Sanctuary
KERALA
Madurai
Mundanthurai Sanctuary
Tirunelveli

at night, if you're lucky, tiger. The Reception Centre has a board on which they record which animals were sighted and where. There's also a visitors' book which makes interesting reading, especially the accounts of those who (perhaps foolishly) have gone out walking at night and met tigers!

The main service area in this sanctuary is the village of Theppukadu on the main road between Ootacamund and Mysore, where the Wildlife Sanctuary Reception Centre, Sylvan Lodge, chai shops and elephant camp are. Any of the buses which run between Ooty and Mysore will take you there; from Ooty it's a 2½-hour journey. It's advisable to book accommodation and transport in the sanctuary in advance, either with the Forest Officer in Ooty on Coonoor Rd or at a Tamil Nadu Tourist Office. There are entry fees for visitors, vehicles and cameras. Jeeps and minibuses can be hired in the park, and elephant rides are available. The elephants go crashing through the bush over a four to five km circuit and are great fun, but you'll be lucky to see anything other than spotted deer, warthogs, buffaloes and monkeys.

The best time to visit the sanctuary is between February and May, though you can visit at any time of the year except possibly in the dry season when it may be closed. Heavy rain is common in October and November.

because of the way they travel, make bookings weeks in advance. Nevertheless, visiting at least one of the sanctuaries can still be a very rewarding experience.

Mudumalai Wildlife Sanctuary

In the luxuriantly forested foothills of the Nilgiris, Mudumalai is part of a much larger sanctuary which includes those of Bandipur and Wynad in neighbouring Karnataka and Kerala. The main attractions here are the herds of spotted deer, gaur (Indian bison) and elephant; tiger; panther; wild pig; sloth; and the otters and crocodiles which live in the River Moyar. It's possible to see all of these if you have made arrangements with the forest department for a vehicle to take you to the more remote parts of the sanctuary.

Even around Theppukadu, where the Reception Centre is located, you will see spotted deer, elephant and wild pig, and

Places to Stay If you're relying on public transport, you'll have to stay either at Theppukadu or at Abhayaranyam, which are both on the bus route. In any event, you first have to call the Reception Centre to find out whether you have a booking.

The *Abhayaranyam Rest House* has rooms from Rs 25 and there's a dormitory at the Range Office a short way from the Rest House. Catering facilities are available.

At Theppukadu Village the *Sylvan Lodge* has rooms from Rs 40 and a dormitory. Good meals are available

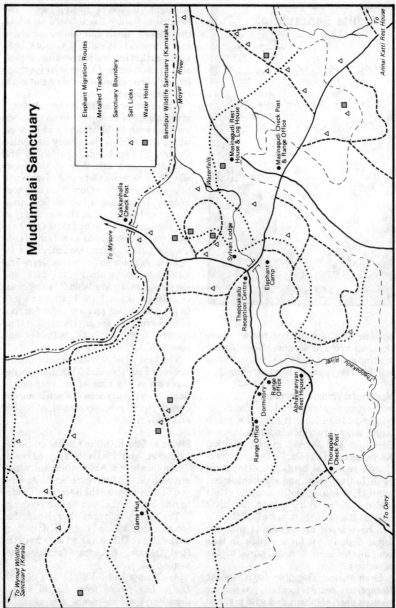

Mudumalai Sanctuary

Legend:
- ······· Elephant Migration Routes
- ━ ━ ━ Metalled Tracks
- ── Sanctuary Boundary
- △ Salt Licks
- ▢ Water Holes

To Annai Katti Rest House

Moyar River

Bandipur Wildlife Sanctuary (Karnataka)

Masinagudi Rest House & Log House

Masinagudi Check Post & Range Office

Waterfalls

Kakkanhalla Check Post

To Mysore

Sylvan Lodge

Elephant Camp

Theppakadu Reception Centre

Theppakadu River

Range Office

Dormitory

Abhayaranyan Rest House

Thorappalli Check Post

To Ooty

Game Hut

To Wynad Wildlife Sanctuary (Kerala)

whether you are staying there or not.

The *Reception Centre* has a dormitory with eight beds (four per room) and an attached toilet and shower but no catering facilities. If you're staying here you can eat at the chai shops in the village or at the Sylvan Lodge. Baggage can be left safely at the Reception Centre whether you have a booking or not, if you're planning on staying for the night.

There's a dorm at Kargundi, three km south of Theppukadu. Dinner and breakfast are available but you still must get permission from Theppukadu to stay there. There's a watchtower half a km from Kargundi on the river and two others about seven km into the park.

At Masinagudi Village the *Masinagudi Rest House* has rooms from Rs 15 and catering facilities are available. *Bamboo Banks Farm* (tel 22) is more expensive from Rs 75 including breakfast. *Mountania Rest House* (tel 37) has cottages from Rs 150, all with attached bathrooms. They also have a log cabin with dormitory facilities. Meals are available, the food is excellent, and there's a bar. Bookings can be made in advance at Safari Travels (tel 3141) opposite Union Church, Ooty.

Getting There The Ooty-Mysore and Ooty-Hassan buses both stop at Theppukadu if there's anyone getting off or if they have spare seats. If not, they tend to drive straight through. If you're leaving the sanctuary, you have to make a determined effort to flag the bus down. On the other hand, it's relatively easy to have a word with people who arrive in their own transport and get yourself a lift back to Ooty or Mysore, or even to Masinagudi if you don't want to stay at Theppukadu for the night. Ooty-Gundalpet buses also pass the sanctuary and are more easily flagged down.

You can visit the sanctuary on tours from Ooty. A writer reported seeing two herds of elephants, Indian bison, deer and peacocks from his perch on the roof of the tour minibus.

Vedanthangal Water Birds Sanctuary

This is one of the most spectacular breeding grounds in India. Water fowl gather here for about six months of the year from October/November to March, depending on the monsoons, and their numbers peak in December and January. At the height of the breeding season it's possible to see up to 30,000 birds at one time. The best times to visit are early morning and late afternoon.

The main types of birds which come here to breed and nest include cormorants, egrets, herons, storks, ibises, spoonbills, grebes and pelicans. Many other species of migratory birds also visit the sanctuary.

The best way to get there is via bus from Madras to Chingleput, but you will have to hire transport to take you to the *Forest Rest House*; it's the only place to stay, with rooms from Rs 25.

Calimere Wildlife Sanctuary

On the east coast just south of the Pondicherry territory of Karaikal in Tanjore district, Point Calimere is noted for its congregation of black buck, spotted deer, wild pig and vast flocks of migratory water fowl, especially flamingoes. Every year in winter the tidal mud flats and marshes are covered with masses of birds – teals, shovellers, curlews, gulls, terns, plovers, sandpipers, shanks and herons. It's possible to see up to 30,000 flamingoes at one time. In the spring a different set of birds – koels, mynas and barbets – are drawn here by the profusion of wild berries.

The best time to visit is between November and January. From April to June there is very little activity. The main rainy season is from October to December. You can get to Point Calimere either by rail on the Mayavaram-Thiruthuraipoondi section or by regular bus from either Tanjore or Mayavaram. A *Forest Rest House* has rooms from Rs 10 but facilities are very basic and no meals are available.

Mundanthurai Tiger Sanctuary

Mundanthurai is in the mountains near the border with Kerala. The nearest railway station is at Amabasamudram and there are regular buses from there to the sanctuary. As the name implies, this is principally a tiger sanctuary and the best time to visit is between January and September, though you can visit at any time of year. The main rainy season is between October and December. Since you're most likely to see tigers in the very early morning or late evening, you should stay here for the night. The Forest Department will arrange to take you around the sanctuary.

Accommodation is in a *Forest Rest House* which has rooms from Rs 20 plus a small charge for electricity.

Anamalai Wildlife Sanctuary

This is the third of the wildlife sanctuaries in the mountains along the Tamil Nadu-Kerala border. Anamalai is south of Coimbatore and can be reached either by regular bus from Coimbatore or by rail to Pollachi and then by bus to the sanctuary. The Reception Centre is at Parambikulam Dam. The major attractions at Anamalai are elephant, gaur, tiger, panther, spotted deer, wild boar, bear, porcupine and civet cat. The Nilgiri tahr, commonly known as ibex, can also be seen here. Transport through the sanctuary can be arranged by the Forest Department.

Accommodation is available at three places: the *Forest Rest House* at Topslip with six rooms; *Varagaliar Rest House* deep inside the forest with basic accommodation (but you must take your own provisions as there are no catering facilities); *Mount Stuart Rest House* with two rooms and meals available. The sanctuary can be visited at any time of the year, but the best times are very early morning or late evening.

Guindy Deer Park

See the Madras section.

Tony's Notebook

Tamil Ingenuity

The Tamils have a reputation as an ingenious lot and they seem to have been the first with another feat of mechanical ingenuity – the moped rickshaw. Some of Madras' cycle-rickshaws have a small moped engine tacked on the back, behind the axle. The rider pedals it into action and it putt-putts off at a dignified speed but still faster than your average man-powered machine. Presumably it helps on hills too.

Life is Cheap Department

In early '86 a train ran into a crowd of spectators standing on the railway lines to watch a fireworks display at Tellicherry in the south of India. At least 27 people were killed and the engine driver, after stopping briefly, wisely 'proceeded on the journey'. Later Southern Railways announced that it was 'not a train accident . . . . (but) an unfortunate case of running over and killing trespassers'.

Andaman & Nicobar

Population: 188,000
Area: 8293 square km
Capital: Port Blair
Main languages: various tribal

In the middle of the Bay of Bengal, half-way between India and Burma, lies this string of over 300 richly forested tropical islands which reach almost to the tip of Sumatra. Ethnically they are not a part of India, and until fairly recently were peopled by several distinct tribes having different physiognomies and speaking different languages.

The tribes fall into three main groups. The Onges, concentrated mainly on Little Andaman, are a small, dark-complexioned tribe of hunters and gatherers, who wear no clothes other than tassled genital decorations and are fond of colourful make-up. The Nicobaris, whose home is on Car Nicobar, are a fair-complexioned people who have begun to adapt to contemporary Indian society. They live mainly on fish, coconuts and pigs and are organised into villages controlled by a village headman. The last group, the Shompens, are found on Great Nicobar. So far they have resisted integration into Indian society and tend to shy away from areas occupied by Indian immigrants from the mainland, preferring to lead their lives according to their own traditions.

The Indian government is fond of eulogising its efforts to bring civilisation to these islands but, reading between the lines, it's obvious it regards these indigenous tribes as stone-age people and its attitude towards them is condescending. In an effort to develop the islands economically, the Indian government has completely disregarded the needs and land rights of the tribes and has encouraged massive immigration from the mainland – mainly of Tamils who were expelled

from Sri Lanka – which has pushed the population from 50,000 to 150,000 in just 15 years. The original islanders' culture is being swamped. If you want to see it before it's gone, you need a special permit for the islands and there are numerous restrictions as to which parts you can visit on arrival.

The Andaman & Nicobar islands were annexed by the Marathas from the mainland of India in the late 17th century. In the early 18th century they were the base of the Maratha admiral, Kanhoji Angre, whose navy harassed and frequently captured British, Dutch and Portuguese merchant vessels. Angre even managed to capture the yacht of the British governor of Bombay in 1713, and released it only after a ransom of powder and shot was delivered. Though attacked by the British, and later by a combined British-Portuguese naval task force, Angre remained undefeated right up to his death in 1729.

The islands were finally annexed by the British in the 19th century and used as a penal colony for Indian freedom fighters. The notorious 'cellular jail', one of the

779

'tourist attractions' of Port Blair where many of the inmates were executed either judicially or clandestinely, was begun in the last decade of the 19th century and finished in 1908. During WW II the islands were occupied for a time by the Japanese, but they were not welcomed as liberators and the local tribes took up guerrilla activities against them. When independence came to India the islands were incorporated into the Indian Union.

At present a big effort is being made to develop the islands, and vast tracts of forest have been cut down. There has been some replanting with 'economic' timber like teak, but much of it has been turned over to rubber plantations.

Climate

There is little seasonal variation. Continuous sea breezes keep temperatures within the range of 23 to 31°C and humidity around 80% all year. The southwest monsoons come to the islands between mid-May and October and the north-east monsoons between November and January. The best times to visit are mid-November and mid-May.

Permits

Foreigners need a permit to visit the Andaman & Nicobar islands, but this can now be obtained on arrival at Port Blair whether you go by ship or air. The only trouble is that the government has introduced this new ruling but not bothered to tell the shipping lines or most other people who could usefully know!

The permit, which is normally valid for 15 days, only allows foreign visitors to visit the North, Middle and South Andamans. Certain other islands can be visited with an additional permit obtainable in Port Blair, but foreign visitors are not allowed to visit the Nicobar and other southern islands at all. The permit can usually be extended for a further 15-day period.

Alternatively you can apply in India or from overseas (allow at least six weeks) to the Deputy Secretary, Government of India, Ministry of Home Affairs, North Block, New Delhi, India, or to your nearest Indian embassy or consulate.

In Madras you can obtain a permit in three days from the Chief Immigration Officer, 9 Village Rd, just off Nungambakkan Rd, before the junction with Sterling Rd (bus route No 10).

Information

The Government of India Tourist Office is at Middle Point. There is also the state government Directorate of Information, Publicity & Tourism (tel 2596) at Port Blair.

Foreign-exchange facilities are available at banks in Port Blair. There is a hospital. Four days a week are dry days, but until recently the Andaman & Nicobar islands used to have total prohibition.

Things to See

There is not a great deal of sightseeing on these islands – their attraction is the beaches and reefs, or as a place to relax or to visit the various tribes. Places of interest include the Anthropological Museum, Marine Museum, Cellular Jail (once used to imprison opponents of British rule), Mini Zoo and Herbarium.

Corbyn's Cove is the nearest beach to Port Blair, 10 km from the town or four km beyond the airport. Chiriya Tapu is the southernmost point of the South Andamans and has beaches noted for their butterflies. From here you can visit Cinque Island, although a further permit is required. Wandoor Beach is on the west coast and from here boats can be hired to Grub, Redskin, Jolly Buoy and Snob islands. A permit is required to visit these islands, and except for Jolly Buoy you must travel in an organised group. Ross Island is not open to foreigners.

Tours are organised from the Tourist Information Centre in Haddo, and three days a week there is a two-hour afternoon harbour cruise on the *MV Dweep Verharnee* for Rs 20 (children Rs 10).

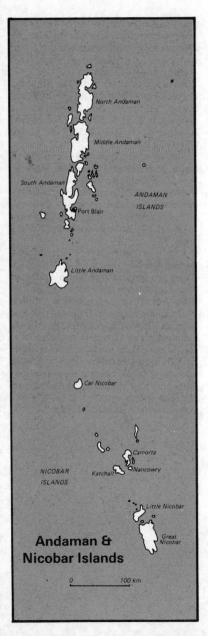

North Andaman

Middle Andaman

South Andaman

ANDAMAN
ISLANDS

Port Blair

Little Andaman

Car Nicobar

Camorta

NICOBAR   Nancowry
ISLANDS   Katchall

Little Nicobar

**Andaman &
Nicobar Islands**

Great
Nicobar

0   100 km

Places to Stay & Eat
South Andaman At Corbyn's Cove the *Andaman Beach Resort* (tel 2599, 2781) has rooms at Rs 200/240 or with meals at Rs 280/400. This attempt to run an Andaman 'beach resort' has been less than wildly successful! The *Welcomgroup Bay Island* (tel 2881-91) at Marine Hill, Port Blair has rooms at Rs 225/325 or rooms with air-con for an additional Rs 50.

There are three places all booked through the Deputy Director of Tourism (tel 2596) in Port Blair. The *Nicobarese Cottages* are Rs 130 for a cottage, Rs 160 with air-con. The *Megapode Nest* (tel 2207) costs Rs 40 per person, Rs 55 with air-con and is good value *if* you can get in. There is also the *Tourist Home*, which costs Rs 10 per person.

Four other places can be booked through the Executive Engineer of Port Blair North Division. *Guest House No 1* and *No 2* cost Rs 10 per bed. The *Municipal Guest House* at Dilanipur costs Rs 10 per room. The *Municipal Guest House* at Manuar Park costs Rs 7 per room plus Rs 3.50 per bed.

Port Blair has a *Youth Hostel* with dorm beds at Rs 8 or rooms at Rs 20. In addition, there are *Forest Rest Houses* at Rs 5 per person at Chiriya Tapu and Wandoor Beach.

The Andamans don't seem totally ready for mass travel yet:

We were dropped at the very basic *Tourist Cottage* in Aberdeen Bazaar. Three Swiss girls with us managed to get a small room for Rs 50 with shower and toilet, while Gerd and I were assigned to an incomplete dormitory. Only two walls were properly built, with piles of timber and wood shavings all over the floor and three solid wooden beds – no mattresses, sheets or pillows provided. We were eaten alive by mosquitoes which proliferate in numerous sewers and open drains in the area and which were swarming in through large gaps in the unfinished walls. For this we were charged a pricey Rs 10 each. There was nowhere to sit and no food available.   *Robin Chakrabarti, UK*

There's also very little food available outside of the expensive resorts – there are virtually no restaurants and the shops have little other than bread and eggs.

Middle & North Andaman On Middle Andaman there are *Rest Houses* at Betapur, Kandamtala and Rangat. North Andaman has *Rest Houses* at Aerial Bay, Diglipur, Kandamtala, Mayabunder, Parangara and Tugapur. These Rest Houses are comfortable and inexpensive.

Getting There

Air Indian Airlines have three-times-weekly flights between Port Blair and Madras (Rs 1180) or Calcutta (Rs 1167). The flights take two hours.

Boat The ships *MV Andamans, TSS Nancowry, MV Harshavardhana* and *MV Akbar* operate to Port Blair from Calcutta, Madras and Vizag. The *MV Harshavardhana* is the fastest and most modern of the ships. The crossing takes two to three days but schedules are irregular. Fares are Rs 69 bunk class, Rs 100 air-con bunk, Rs 355, 389, 500 or 558 for the various cabins from class C to A or air-con.

Food is additional; it's cheaper in bunk class (Indian food only) than in cabin class (Indian or western), where a four-day crossing will cost about Rs 150. For that you get tea and two biscuits at 6 am, a big western-style breakfast at 9 am, an enormous non-vegetarian lunch at 1 pm, tea again at 4 pm and and equally large evening meal at 7 pm.

In Calcutta check with the Shipping Corporation of India (tel 239456), Shipping House, 13 Strand Rd. In Madras the agents are K P V Sheikh Mohammed Rowther & Co (tel 510346), 41 Linghi Chetty St.

Slow Boats to China by Gavin Powell has a description of travelling Madras-Port Blair-Calcutta with a short stay in the Andamans. Recent visitors report it's an interesting and enjoyable crossing, although solo women travellers may have to avoid the attention of some of the crew.

Getting Around

There is a ferry around South Andaman Island three times daily from the Fisheries Jetty, Port Blair, which calls at Bamboo Flat, Haddo Harbour, Dandus Point and Junglee Ghat. Check with the Marine Department or Oceanic Company, M G Rd, Middle Point for local boat charters to Jolly Buoy, Redskin, Grub or Cinque islands. Ferries operate between Port Blair and other islands in the Andaman & Nicobar group but foreigners are not permitted to visit most of them.

Glossary

Indian English is full of interesting little everyday expressions. Where in New York you might get robbed by a mugger, in India it will be a *dacoit* who relieves you of your goods. Politicians may employ strong-arm heavies known in India as *goondas*. There is a plethora of Indian terms for strikes, lock-outs and sit-ins – Indians can have *hartals, bhands* and *gheraos* for example. And then there are all those Indian servants – children get looked after by *ayahs*, your house (and your *godown* if you have one) is guarded by a *chowkidah* (but they're reputed to be a lazy bunch much given to lying around on *charpois*), and when the toilet needs cleaning there is no way your *bearer* is going to do it, that requires calling in a *sweeper*.

Then there are all the religious terms, the numerous Hindu gods, their attendants, consorts, vehicles and symbols. The multiplicity of religions in India also provides a whole series of terms for temples, shrines, tombs or memorials. It's surprising how many Indian terms have crept into everyday English usage. We can sit out on a *verandah*, wear *pyjamas* or *sandals* and *dungarees* (which may well be *khaki*), *shampoo* our hair, visit the *jungle*, worry about protecting our *loot* – they're all Indian words.

The glossary that follows is just a sample of words you may come across during your Indian wanderings. See Food and Religion for lots more.

Acha – OK.
Acharya – revered teacher, originally a spiritual guide or preceptor.
Anikut – weir or dam.
Anna – one sixteenth of a rupee, now extinct but still used in marketplace conversation, ie eight annas are 50 paise, four annas are 25 paise.
Arrack – spirit drink made from coconut sap or rice wine.

Ashram – spiritual college cum retreat.
Astrology – far more than just a newspaper space filler; marriages are not arranged, flights not taken, elections not called without checking the astrological charts.
Avalokitesvara – one of the Buddha's most important disciples.
Ayah – children's nurse or nanny.
Ayurvedic – Indian natural and herbal medicine.

Baba – religious master but also used in a more everyday manner.
Babu – lower-level clerical worker.
Bagh – garden.
Bahadur – brave or chivalrous, honorific title.
Baksheesh – tip, bribe or donation to a beggar.
Bandar – port or harbour.
Bandh – general strike.
Banian – T-shirt or under-vest.
Baniya – money-lender.
Banyan – Indian fig tree.
Baoli – well, particularly a step well with landings and galleries.
Basti – Jain temple.
Bazaar – market area. A market town is called a bazaar.
Bearer – rather like a butler.
Beedis (bidis) – small, hand-rolled cigarettes – really just a rolled-up tobacco leaf.
Begum – Muslim woman of high rank.
Betel – nut of the betel tree, chewed as a mild intoxicant.
Bhagvadgita – Krishna's lessons to Arjuna, part of the *Mahabharata*.
Bhang – dried leaves and flowering shoots of the marihuana plant.
Bhang-lassi – a blend of lassi with bhang, a drink with a kick.
Bhisti (bheesti) – water carrier.
Black money – undeclared, untaxed money. There's lots of it in India.
Bodhisattva – near Buddha, follower of Buddha.
Bo-tree – *ficus religiosa*, the tree under which the Buddha attained enlightenment.
Brahmin – highest Indian caste.
Bund – embankment or dyke.
Burka – one-piece garment which totally covers Muslim women.

Bustee – slum areas of Calcutta.

Cantonment – administrative and military area of a British Raj-era town.
Caste – one's station in life.
Chaitya – Buddhist temple.
Chakra – focus of one's spiritual power, disc-like weapon of Vishnu.
Chalo, chalo, chalo – 'let's go, let's go, let's go' – what you yell as the bus leaves.
Chance List – the wait list on Indian Airline flights.
Chang – Tibetan rice beer.
Chaoultries – dharamsalas in the south.
Chappals – sandals.
Chappati – unleavened Indian bread.
Charas – resinous exudate of the marihuana plant, hashish.
Charpoi – Indian rope bed.
Chat – general term for small snacks, papris, etc.
Chhatri – tomb or mausoleum.
Chauri – fly whisk.
Chela – pupil or follower, as George Harrison was to Ravi Shankar.
Chillum – pipe part of a hookah, commonly used to describe the small pipes for smoking ganja.
Chorten – Tibetan word for stupa.
Chowk – courtyard or marketplace.
Chowkidah – nightwatchman, often a cook as well.
Cong (I) – Congress Party (India) or Congress Party (Indira) depending on how cynical you are.
Country Liquor – locally produced liquor.
CPI – Communist Party of India.
CPI (M) – the Communist Party of India (Marxist). It's the bigger, more powerful party and is currently in power in West Bengal (Calcutta).
Crore – 10 million.
Curd – yoghurt.
Cutcherry – office or building for public business.

Dacoit – robber, particularly armed robber.
Dacoity – to suffer at the hands of a dacoit.
Dargah – shrine or place of burial of a Muslim saint.
Darshan – offering or audience with someone, usually a guru.
Darwaza – gateway or door.
Dhaba – hole-in-the-wall restaurant or snack bar.

Dhal – lentil soup, what most of India lives on.
Dharamsala – religious guest house.
Dharma – Buddhist teachings.
Dhobi – clothes washerman.
Dhopalta – scarf worn by Punjabi women.
Dhoti – like a longhi, but the cloth is then pulled up between the legs.
Digambara – 'sky-clad' Jain sect who extend their disdain for worldly goods to include not wearing clothes.
Diwan – principal officer in a princely state, royal court or council.
Diwan-i-Am – Hall of Public Audience.
Diwan-i-Khas – Hall of Private Audience.
Dooli – covered litter or stretcher. You may still see elderly tourists being carried around some sights in a dooli.
Dowry – it's illegal but no arranged marriage (and most marriages are arranged) can be made without it.
Dravidian – ornate southern Indian architectural style, also southern Indian race.
Durbar – royal court, also used to describe a government.
Durga – same as Kali, terrible manifestation of Parvati.
Dwarpal – door-keeper, sculpture beside the doorways to Hindu or Buddhist shrines.

Election symbols – identifying symbols for the various political parties, since so many voters are illiterate.
Emergency – the period during which Indira Gandhi suspended many rights and many observers assumed she was intent on establishing a dictatorship.
Eve-teasing – the Indian equivalent of Italian bottom pinching.
Export gurus – gurus whose following is principally from the west.

Fakir – accurately a Muslim who has taken a vow of poverty, but also applied to Hindu ascetics such as sadhus.
Fenni – spirit drink made from cashews, found in Goa.
Firman – a royal order or grant.
Freaks – young westerners wandering India. The '60s live!

Gaddi – throne of a Hindu prince.
Ganesh – god of learning, elephant-headed son of Shiva and Parvati, probably the most popular god in the whole Hindu pantheon.

Ganga – Ganges River.
Ganja – dried flowering tips of marihuana plant.
Garuda – man-bird vehicle of Vishnu.
Ghari – horse carriage.
Ghat – steps or landing on a river, place where corpses are cremated.
Ghazal – Urdu songs, sad love themes.
Ghee – all-purpose cooking oil, clarified butter.
Gherao – lock in, where the workers lock the management in!
Godmen – commercial-minded gurus, see export gurus.
Godown – warehouse.
Gompa – Tibetan-Buddhist monastery.
Gonds – aboriginal Indian race, now mainly found in the jungles in central India.
Goondas – ruffians or toughs. Political parties often have gangs of goondas.
Gopis – cowherd girls. Krishna was very fond of them.
Gopuram – soaring pyramidal gateway tower of a Dravidian temple.
Gurdwara – Sikh temple.
Guru – teacher or holy man.

Haji – a Muslim who has made the pilgrimage (haj) to Mecca.
Hanuman – monkey god.
Harijan – literally 'Children of God', but actually it still means the lowest caste, the untouchables.
Hartal – strike.
Haveli – traditional mansions with interior courtyards, particularly in Rajasthan and Gujarat.
Hookah – water pipe for smoking tobacco.
Howdah – framework for carrying people on an elephant's back.
Hypothecated – Indian equivalent of leased or mortgaged. You often see small signs on taxis or auto-rickshaws stating that the vehicle is 'hypothecated' to some bank or other.

Idgah – open enclosure to the west of a town where prayers are offered during the Muslim festival of Id.
Imam – Muslim leader.
Imambara – tomb of a Shi'ite Muslim holy man.
IMFL – Indian Made Foreign Liquor – beer or spirits produced in India.
Indra – king of the Vedic gods.

Jaggery – hard, brown sugar-like sweetener made from kitul palm sap.
Janata – people, thus the Janata Party is the People's Party.
Jatakas – tales from the Buddha's various lives.
Jauhar – ritual mass suicide by immolation, traditionally performed by Rajput women at times of military defeat to avoid being dishonoured by their captors.
Ji – honorific title that can be added to the end of almost anything – thus Babaji, Gandhiji.
Juggernauts – huge, extravagantly decorated temple 'cars' dragged through the streets during Hindu festivals.
Jumkahs – ear-rings.
Jyotorlinga – 12 holy Shiva shrines in India are known as the 12 Jyotorlingas.

Kachahri – see Cutchery.
Kadi – homespun cloth. Mahatma Gandhi spent much energy in encouraging people to spin their own Kadi cloth rather than buy imported English material.
Kali – Parvati's terrible side.
Karmachario – university term.
Kartikiya – god of war, Shiva's son.
Kata – Tibetan prayer shawl, traditionally given to a lama when one is brought into his presence.
Khalistan – independent Punjab campaigned for by Sikh extremists.
Khan – Muslim honorific title.
Kibla – niche in the wall to which Muslims look when praying in order to face Mecca.
Kothi – residence, house or mansion.
Kotwali – police station.
Krishna – Vishnu's eighth incarnation, often coloured blue.
Kundalini – coiled serpent, the manifestation of Kali, the place at the base of your spine where your shakti resides.

Lakh – 100,000.
Lama – Tibetan-Buddhist priest or holy man.
Lassi – very refreshing yoghurt and iced-water drink.
Lathi – baton, what Indian police hit you with if you get in the way of a lathi charge.
Laxmi (or Lakshmi) – Vishnu's consort, goddess of wealth, very popular in Bombay.
Lingam – phallic symbol, symbol of Shiva.
Lok – people.
Lok Dal – political party, one of the components of the Janata party.

Lok Sabha – lower house in the Indian parliament, comparable to the House of Representatives or House of Commons.

Longhi – loin cloth wrapped around the thighs.

Mahabharata – Vedic epics, one of the two major Hindu epics.

Mahal – house or palace, queen.

Maharaja – Raja, Hindu king or prince.

Mahatma – literally 'great soul'.

Mahayana – large-vehicle Buddhism.

Mahout – elephant rider/master.

Maidan – open place or square.

Mali – gardener.

Mandala – Tibetan geometrical and astrological representation of the world.

Mandir – temple.

Mandapam – pillared pavilion in front of a temple.

Mani stone – stone carved with the Tibetan-Buddhist chant 'Om mani padme hum' or 'Hail to the jewel in the lotus'.

Mantra – prayer formula or chant.

Mara – Buddhist god of death, has three eyes and holds the wheel of life.

Maratha (Mahratta) – war-like central Indian race who often controlled much of India and gave the Moghuls a lot of trouble.

Masjid – mosque. Jami Masjid is the Friday Mosque or main mosque.

Maund – now largely superseded unit of weight.

Math – monastery.

Mela – a fair.

Memsahib – European married lady, from 'madam-sahib', still more widely used than you'd think.

Mendi – ornate patterns painted on women's hands and feet for important festivals, particularly in Rajasthan. Beauty parlours and bazaar stalls will do it for you, about Rs 30 for the feet and both sides of the hands!

Mihrab – see Kibla.

Moghul – golden period of Indian history from the emperor Babur to Aurangzeb, the last powerful Moghul ruler.

Monsoon – rainy period from around June to October, when it rains virtually every day.

Moorcha – mob march or protest march.

Mughal – same as Moghul.

Muezzin – one who calls Muslims to prayer from the minaret.

Mullah – Muslim priest.

Munshi – writer, secretary or language teacher.

Naga – snake or a person from Nagaland.

Nandi – bull, vehicle of Shiva and usually found at Shiva temples.

Narayan – an incarnation of Vishnu.

Narsimha (Narsingh) – man-lion incarnation of Vishnu.

Nautch Girls – dancing girls, a nautch is a dance.

Nawab – nobleman or governor.

Naxalites – ultra-leftist political movement, started in northern part of West Bengal where it appeared as a rebellion against landlords by peasants. Characterised by extreme violence, it originated in the village of Naxal and is now fairly subdued in West Bengal, but still exists in Uttar Pradesh.

Nilakantha – form of Shiva with blue throat from swallowing poison that would have destroyed the world.

Nirvana – the ultimate aim of Buddhist existence, a state where one leaves the cycle of existence and does not have to suffer further rebirths.

Nizam – hereditary title of the rulers of Hyderabad.

Nullah – ditch or small stream.

Padyatra – 'foot journey' made by politicians to raise support at the village level.

Pagoda – Buddhist religious monument composed of a solid hemisphere containing relics of the Buddha – also known as a dagoba, stupa or chedi.

Palanquin – box-like enclosure carried on poles on four men's shoulders; the occupant sits inside on a seat.

Pali – the original language in which the Buddhist scriptures were recorded. Scholars still look to the original Pali texts for the true interpretations.

Pan – betel nut plus the chewing additives.

Pandit – teacher or wise man. The word is often used in Kashmir where there are many of these. Sometimes used deprecatingly to mean a bookworm.

Peepul – fig tree, especially a Bo tree.

Peon – lowest grade clerical worker.

Pice – a quarter of an anna.

Pinjrapol – animal hospital maintained by Jains.

Pooja – offering or prayers.

Pranayama – study of breath control.

Prasad – food offering, something you can eat.

Pukkah – proper, very much a Raj-era term.

Punkah – cloth fan, swung by pulling a cord.
Puranas – the ancient Hindu scriptures.
Purdah – isolation in which Muslim women are kept.

Raga – somewhat equivalent to a piece, division or movement of western music.
Railhead – station or town at the end of a railway line, termination point.
Raj – rule or sovereignty, but specifically applied to the period of British rule in India.
Raja – king.
Rajput – Hindu warrior caste, royal rulers of Rajasthan.
Ramayana – the story of Rama and Sita and their conflict with Rawana, one of the longest lasting of Indian legends and retold in various forms throughout almost all South-East Asia.
Rani – wife of a princely ruler or a ruler in her own right.
Rasta Roko – road block for protest purposes.
Rath – temple chariot or car used in religious festivals.
Raths – rock-cut Dravidian temples at Mahabalipuram.
Rickshaw – two-wheeled vehicle in which one or two passengers are pulled. Only in Calcutta and one or two hill stations do the old man-powered rickshaws still exist. In towns they are now generally bicycle-rickshaws.
Rishis – great sages of old, nowadays applied to any distinguished poet, philosopher or spiritual personality.
Road – railway town which serves as a communication point to a larger town off the line, ie Mt Abu and Abu Road.

Sadhu – wandering holy man, generally Saivaites, mostly laymen who have given everything up to seek religious salvation. They will usually be addressed as 'swamiji' or 'babaji.
Sahib – 'lord', title applied to any gentlemen and most Europeans.
Saivaite – (or Shaivaite) follower of Lord Shiva.
Salwar – blouse worn by Punjabi women.
Samadhi – an ecstatic state, sometimes defined as 'ecstasy, trance, communion with God' or 'ecstatic state of mystic consciousness'. Another definition is the place where a holy man was cremated, usually venerated as a shrine.
Sati – 'honourable woman', what a woman becomes if she throws herself on her husband's funeral pyre. Although banned a century or so ago, occasionally satis are still performed.
Satsang – discourse by a swami.
Satyagraha – non-violent protest involving a fast, popularised by Gandhi. From Sanskrit, literally 'insistence on truth'.
Sepoy – private in the infantry.
Serai – place for accommodation of travellers, specifically a caravanserai where camel caravans once stopped.
Shakti – spiritual energy, life force or strength.
Shikar – hunting expedition, now virtually extinct.
Shikara – gondola-like boat used on Dal Lake in Kashmir.
Shirting – material shirts are made out of.
Sikhara – Hindu temple spire or temple.
Sirdar – leader or commander.
Sitar – Indian stringed instrument, very difficult to tune – which did not prevent it from becoming a '60s craze.
Sof – aniseed seeds, comes with the bill after a meal and you chew a pinch of it as a digestive.
Sonam – karma built up in successive reincarnations.
Sufi – ascetic Muslim mystic.
Suiting – material suits are made out of.
Swami – title given to initiated monks, means 'lord of the self'.
Sweeper – lowest caste servant, who performs the most menial of tasks.
Syce – groom.

Tabla – small drums, almost like bongo drums.
Tamil – people of south-east India.
Tank – artificial water-storage lake.
Tanka – rectangular Tibetan painting on cloth.
Tantric Buddhism – Tibetan Buddhism with strong sexual and occult overtones.
Tatty – woven grass screen which is wetted and hung outside windows in the hot season to provide a remarkably effective system of air-cooling.
Tempo – noisy three-wheeler public transport vehicle.
Thali – traditional south Indian 'all-you-can-eat' vegetarian meal, very widespread and an excellent, tasty meal – the name derives from the 'thali' plate the food is served on.
Theravada – small-vehicle Buddhism.

Thirthayatara – sort of pilgrimage.

Thug – follower of thuggee, religious-inspired ritual murderers in the last century.

Tiffin – snack, particularly around lunchtime.

Tirthankars – the 24 great Jain teachers.

Toddy – mildly alcoholic drink, tapped from the palm tree.

Tonga – two-wheeled horse or pony carriage.

Tope – grove of trees, usually mangoes.

Topi – sun hat, much used by the British in the Raj era.

Torana – architrave over temple entrance.

Trimurti – three-faced Shiva image.

Tripitaka – the classical Theravada Buddhist scriptures, which are divided into three categories, hence its name the 'three baskets'. The Mahayanists have other scriptures in addition.

Untouchable – lowest caste for whom the most menial tasks are reserved. The name derives from the belief that higher castes risk defilement if they touch one.

Upanishads – ancient Vedic scripts, the last part of the Vedas.

Vanaspati – cooking oil, edible oils.

Varuna – supreme Vedic god.

Vedas – ancient spiritual texts, the orthodox Hindu scriptures.

Vihar – monastery.

Vimana – principle part of a Hindu temple.

Wallah – person. Can be added onto almost anything – thus dhobi-wallah (clothes washer), taxi-wallah (taxi driver).

Wazir – prime minister.

Yagna – religious self-mortification, such as a snake-yagna where you sit in a cage full of snakes trying to get yourself in the Guinness Book of Records. Being interred alive is another popular yagna feat.

Yoni – vagina, female fertility symbol.

Zamindar – landowner.

Zenana – area of a high-class Muslim household where the women are secluded.

Index

Abbreviations

Map references are in **bold** type

THANKS

Writers (apologies if we've mis-spelt your names) to whom thanks must go include:

Karl Abbott (USA); J L Abraham (Aus); M Addis; Jagdish Agarwal (I); Dr A K Aggarwal (UK); Adi Ahamoni (Isr); Gary Ahearn (Aus); Bill Aitken; Nick & Claudia Alexander; Penny Allen; R Allot (UK); Margaret Allsebrook (USA); David Alowinckle (USA); Yuval Amir (I); Chuck & Karen Amital (USA); Frank Amnon Menachem (Isr); Iver Houmark Anderson (Dk); Felise Ansell; Irene Asao-Wells (USA); June Atkinson (UK); Deena Atlas (USA); Alan Avchalom (Isr); Charles Bado (Aus); Colin Bailey (NZ); Frank Bailey (NZ); Andrew Baily; Nigel Baker; Ruth & Joel Baks (Isr); Professor & Miss J G Ball (UK); Greg Banks (USA); Evelyne Barbet (F); Michael Barkai (Isr); G Bartholomew (UK); Bonnie Baskin (USA); Peter Bauer (A); Bhikku Josh Beattie (UK); A Bell (UK); Carl Bengstrom-Nielsen (Dk); Steve Bennett (UK); Alison Bentley (Aus); Catherine Bernaud (F); N Beschorner (UK); J H Beveridge (USA); Jagmohan Bhatia (Aus); Elsie Bishoff (It); Grant Blackwell (UK); Windy Blake (Aus); Anders Blomquist (Sw); Deb Bloom; Steve Bonley (USA); Trevor Boone (UK); Robert Booth (UK); Annie Borden (UK); Tom Borden; Magnus Bowles (UK); Jenepher Bramble; Claudine Breton; Denise Brosman (Aus); Joan Brown (Aus); Leo Buccelato; Joss Buchanan (UK); John Bucklow (UK); Rick Bugges (USA); Paul Buhagiar (UK); Tony Bullock (USA); John Bungey (UK); Sue Bush (UK); Asim Butt (UK); Jane & Ashley Butterfield (UK); Roy Butterfield (UK); Janet Camac (Aus); Sylvia Caras (USA); Annie Caswell (C); Anthony Cauchi (I); Diego Ceradis (F); Robin Chakrabarti (UK); Nick J Chamchuk (C); Chan Wai Kay (HK); L Charlesworth; Calum Chase (UAE); Anil Chawla (I); Deborah Chinn (UK); Charlie Chiyako; Dan, Charlotta & Victoria Chorian (I); Chris Robert J Christopher (C); Mickie Chronister (USA); Ms J Clarence (Aus); Tim Clark; Benjamin Clifford (USA); H Cobbett (UK); Diana M Cohen (N); Andum Collins (I); Gabriele & Brett Collins (USA); J Connellan (Aus); Dave Cooke (UK); Debbie Cordingley (HK); David Corley; Joe Corrigan (UK); Tim Court (UK); Sarah Courtenay (UK); Paul Covill (UK); Dan Cox (C); Helen Craig (Aus); Maggie Cray (UK); Mark Crean (UK); Sara Crisp (USA); Martin Crone (Nl); Catherine Cross (Aus); Jeanne Culf (Aus); Peter Culross (Aus); Michael Cunningham (UK); Steve Currie (Aus); Nicholas Curtis (UK); Gerard Custer (USA); Michael Dalby (USA); David & Srada (UK); David & Sue Mark C Davidar; Neil Davies (UK); Ged Davies (USA); Richard Davies-Sherwood (US); Peter Davis (Aus); Paul Davis (USA); Dr Penny Dawson; Guy de Beaujeu (UK); Jola de Horst; Jan Martin de Jager (Nl); José de Waard (Nl); Hans de Wit (Nl); Desh Deepak (I); Neel Prabha Deepak (I); Steve Deiné (USA); Steve Derne (USA); Paula Deutsch (USA); Aires Dias; Kenneth Dick (I); Rowena Dique (I); Bruce Dodson (USA); Sue Dossa (UK); Nigel Dudley (UK); Maxine Dunkelman (USA); Leoni Dunning; R Dyke (C); Roger Edmonds (UK); Dr N C Edul (I); Robert Egg (D); Anne-Marie Ehrnhoffer; Mark Eilen (UK); Jim Ellison (USA); Ruth Ennals (UK); Kathleen Erwin (USA); Howard Esler (Aus); J A Evers (Aus); Rosalind Eyben (I); Julian Eyears (UK); Margarete Falbe (D); Jenny Farrer; David Feith (Aus); Andy Fenton (UK); Irene Finne (Sw); R J Fisher (Aus); Leslie & Andrew Fisher (UK); Andy Fisk (UK); Peter & Gill Flegg (UK); Samuel Fleischaetoer (USA); Ron Fontana (USA); Al & Joan Forster; Veronica Forwood; Hugh Fox (UK); Loren Franklin; Dirk & Nel Frans; Per Frederiksen (Dk); Gerhard Friesenecker (A); Anne Froger (Aus); Aileen Furphy (Ir); Akyazili Fuson (B); Alan Gardner (UK); Roger Gariun-Michaud (Aus); George & Mabel Garside (NZ); Niranjan Gaur (I); Marc Gautering (B); D A Gaw (UK); Susan Gellner (UK); Thomas George (UK); Bruno Ghise (B); Glyn & Elizabeth Gibson (UK); G S Gimson (UK); Pia Giossi (CH); Paul & Maree Girdler (Aus); Kay & Geoffrey Gladstone (Aus); Pia Glossi (CH); Pat & Ray Glover (UK); Barry Goddard (UK); Tim Gokey (UK); Terry Goldberg (Aus); Ron Goldstein (USA); Dave Goldstraw (Aus); Karen Gooch (UK); John Good (UK); Anne Goodwin (UK); Mark Goodwin (USA); Peter Gordon (NZ); Rudolf Gossenreiter (A); Andrew Grace (UK); Patricia Gracey (UK); Sibylle Gradnitzer (D); Christopher Gray (UK); David Gray (UK); Kenny Gray (UK); Alice & Dave Green (Cy); Dane Green (UK); Jim Greenblatt (USA); Russel Greene (UK); C A Gregory (Aus); Kate Morgudge Greswold (UK); Grovers; Marc Grutering (B); N Gustafsson (Aus); J Haigh (Can); Sara Hall (UK); Nerida & Robert Hall; David Halperin (USA); Lisa Haney (USA);

Bjarne Stig Hansen (Dk); Christian Sylvest Hansen (Dk); C J Harding (UK); June Harnest (USA); Suzanne Harris (Aus); Tracy Harris (UK); Mark & Katrina Harris; R Hartley (UK); Peter Hatswell (Aus); Howard Deng Hausen (USA); M B Hausler (USA); Sparkle Hayter (C); Julian & Lyndie Heather; Beryl Heitzman (UK); Eva Helgstrand (Sw); Chris Hellier; R & K Helm (USA); Herbert Henke (Aus); Peter Hill (UK); Michelle Hills (B); David Hipgrave (Aus); Dorothy Hirschland (USA); Andrea Hobi (CH); Monica Hocking (Aus); Jane Hockley (UK); J C Hodder (USA); Miriam Hoffman (USA); Christopher Hogan (Aus); Josh & Claracy Holehouse (USA); Sally Holt (UK); Steve Hopkins; Patrick Hosking (UK); Felicity Hourist (UK); T Howard (UK); Heidi Howell (USA); D Hows (UK); John Hudson (UK); Mike Hudson (UK); William B Hughson (USA); Erik Huizer (Nl); Cornille Hulse (UK); Peter Hunt; Johnny Hylthoff (Dk); Paul Ishikama (USA); Santosh Iyer (I); Mick Jackson (UK); Faith James (UK); Derek Jeffrey (UK); Michael Jennings (US); Paul-Erik Jensen (Dk); Randall Clay Jeter-Ganesh; Robyn Johnson (Aus); David Johnston (Ir); Mark Johnston (USA); Peter Jones (Aus); Adrian Jones (UK); T L Jones (UK); Babli Jose (I); P J Joske (Aus); Emma Joynson (D); Mark Kalish (USA); W Kasper (Aus); Brian Kearns (UK); Lois Keogh (Aus); Simon Kettley (UK); Andrew Killick (UK); Edward Kim (USA); T Kimball (Aus); C J Kimberley (USA); Don Kinsella (USA); Donna Kirkland (USA); S Kitson (I); Hans Klomp (NN); Roger Knipp (USA); Wolfgang Koeth (D); Audrey Koh (USA); Stephanie Koutsapis (USA); Sue Krusher (Aus); S Kumar; Umesh Kumar; Michael Kutter (Dk); Julie Kynoch (Aus); Sophia Lambert (UK); Eric Langhammer (UK); Torben B Larsen (Dk); Annette Larson (Dk); Robin & Peter Lather (Aus); J J Latimer (Aus); Jeanne Le Roux (F); Steve Leathers (USA); Sarah Lee (UK); Henk & Rini Leenen (Nl); Mark Lennon (USA); Margaret Lesjak (Aus); Michael Levin (UK); Nicola Levitt (UK); Liz Lewis (Aus); Susanne Liden (Aus); John Limemeier; Vivienne Linder (NZ); Amanda Lindley (UK); Chris Link (D); John Linnemeier; Lauren Linowitz (USA); Marie Lippens (B); Greg Lipton (USA); Alison & Andrew Livatad; A Lodge (UK); Julian Longley (UK); Lia Strange Lorrenzes (Dk); Max Loveridge (Aus); Dr Newton Luiz (I); Finn Lundorf (Dk); Sandy MacDonald (C); Betty Macintosh (Aus); James Macintosh (Can); Denys Maggie (B); David W Mahoney (HK); Paul Maine (UK); A Maley (Aus); Julie Mantello (Aus); Andrew Markham (UK); Sabrina Marks; Geoffrey J Martyn (USA); Annie & Gerry Marucci; Christ Matthews (Aus); Elizabeth Maudslay (UK); Mark & Carl Maxey (USA); Debbie Mayling (UK); Mikkel McAlinder; Bruce McCluitic (USA); Ros McConaghy (Aus); Mike McDermott (Aus); Robert McDougall (Aus); Amanda McIntosh (Aus); Helen McLean (UK); Sian McLean; J McNally (Aus); Fiona McRae (UK); I L Meers (UK); Eloise Meneses; Helen Menezer (UK); Bill Menzies (NZ); Stephen Merrett (Aus); P Merriam (UK); Chrissy Merton (UK); Michael (USA); Michelle Fransesca Mills (UK); Ian J Mills; Ray Milner (UK); Kenny Mitchell (UK); Lino Monteiro (I); Moses Moon (USA); Catherine Mooney; Tim Moore (USA); Christine Moore; Shirley Morris (Aus); Rosenzverg Moshe (Isr); Barbara Moss (Aus); Danny Moss; W E Muir (C); Constance S Mukhererjee (USA); Berthy Muller (CH); I Mullick; Nicola & George Munro (UK); Bruce Munro (USA); William Munsey; Fraser Murdoch (UK); Patrick Murphy (UK); Simon Murray (Aus); Simon Murray (UK); Jon Murray; Wayne Myers (USA); Paul Mynott (UK); Felicity Neilson (F); S Ness (Aus); Mark Newell; Bob & Florence Newnham (Aus); Nick the Aussie; Anders Nielsen (Dk); Eva Nielsen (Dk); Sally Noble (UK); Edith Nolot (F); Niels Norlinger (Dk); Joe S Nyor (UK); T O'Gorman (C); Maeve & Matthew O'Meara (Aus); Peter O'Roushe; David Oakley; Pascal & Sabera Oberson (CH); James Obome; Marianne Olesen (Dk); Jan Orleañski (P); Benthe Oseth; Giampero Pani; Alison Parfitt (UK); Margie Parith (Can); Jenny Parker; Karen Partridge (Aus); Wilma Pastro (Aus); Robin & Peter Payne (Aus); Robert Peel (UK); Dan Peha (USA); Peter Penders (Nl); Sunny & Doug Pendleton-Mavor (USA); Adam Penenberg (USA); Ralph Penglis (Aus); Kevin Perret (UK); Benjamin Pessok (UK); Al & Charlotte Peters (USA); Jill Phillips (Aus); John & Tomris Phillips (Aus); Martin Phillips (UK); Michael Phillips; Dave & Maggie Pidwell; Bruce Pink; Kate Pitman (UK); M V Pitt; Herman Planter (USA); Robert Plumb (UK); Jan Pope (USA); William Pope (USA); Diane Porter (Ir); Om Prakash (I); Jenny Pratt (Aus); Isabella Pratt; Tim Prentico (UK); Stephanie Price (Aus); Amy Prince (USA); R C Putnam (UK); Stephen Quinn (UK); Neil

Quinton (D); Nancy Randall (USA); Adam Randolph (USA); Bo Rasmussen (Dk); Aurora Rausa (USA); R C Rawlings; Steven Rawlins (UK); V Krishna Reddy (I); Tommy & Peter Reeves (UK); Linda Reinke (C); Byron Render; Kay Renius (USA); Zara Reynell (Aus); Sarah Reynolds (UK); Tim Rhodes (Aus); J Richen (PNG); Dr C M Ridley (UK); Johanna Rieqelhofer (A); Chris Riley; Andrew Robb (UK); Max Robenstone (Aus); James Roberts (UK); A Robertson (Aus); Anthony Robins (NZ); Jean Robinson (UK); Matthew Robson (UK); Prof Robert Rodger (Aus & C); Bob Rodgers (HK); Marlene Roeder (USA); Neil Rokison (UK); Leigh Rollara (Aus); M Romberg (UK); Lisa Roscoe; Mr & Mrs Rose (Aus); B Rose (UK); Peter J Rosenlrantz (Dk); Michael Ross (Aus); Sarah Roth (USA); Peter Rowlands (UK); R H Rudkin (Aus); Darren Russell (Aus); Geoff Russell (Aus); Julie Russell (UK); Peter Russenberger; D'Arcy Ryan (Aus); J Ryan (C); Margaret Saunders (UK); Rian & Aleks Scheffer (Nl); Halvard Scheutz (Sw); Anyu Schiffrin (USA); Denni Schnapp (Dk); Bernard Schneider (F); Jan R Schroder (D); Robert Sebes (Aus); P N Sehroeter (Aus); Robert Seljak (Can); Mark Seltzer (C); Toms Sendey; Brenda Senger (C); Daphna & Ilan Shacham (Isr); Lochan Vishal Sharma (I); Chris Shaw (Can); Sarah & Julia Shaw; Gary Siegel (USA); Lincoln Siliakus (Aus); J Christopher Sill (USA); Matthew J Simmonds; Dr S C Singal (I); Balwant Singh (S); Auyan Sinha (I); D Skeggs (C); Suscen Slowinslev (USA); Teresa Smallbone; Fred & Sheila Smart (Aus); Clive Smith (Aus); Lyn Smith (Aus); Danny Smith; Anette Sode (Dk); Anita Soley (UK); Rob Someone (UK); Ray Spears (USA); Jennifer Spiller (UK); V Spooner (PNG); Peter Steffensen-Solvejg (Dk); Marcel Steggerda (Nl); Meg Stenger (USA); E G Stern; Anne Stevens (USA); Evan Stewart (Can); Sally Stibbard (UK); Monika Stocker (CH); Adam Stone (UK); Greg Stonehouse (Aus); Denise Storey; Glyn Strange (NZ); Franz Stransky (D); Tracey Strath (Aus); Sita Stuhlmiller (USA); Paul Suhler (USA); E E Sumesh (I); Mark Svensson (UK); Kees Swart (Nl); Mark Swimelar (USA); Martha Takaro (USA); Richard Tanner (F); Bruce Taylor (Aus); John Taylor (UK); Keith Taylor (UK); Tony Tedesco (USA); Fayna Teeters (USA); Sven Terno (D); Nina Ternov (D); Bhikkhu Thitinyana (SL); Vicki Thompson (Aus); Susan & Glen Thrasher (NZ); Brian Threlkeld (USA); Cherie Thurston (NZ); Leann Tilley (Aus); Tineke; Grant Tokely (Aus); Ted Town (Can); Clive & Linda Towsey (Aus); Pranav Tripathi (I); Fiona Tronnson (UK); Robert Trudel (C); A J Truelove (Aus); John Truran (Aus); Colin H Turner (UK); Hashim Tyabji; Howard Ubalier (HK); Dr Jamie Uhrig; Peter Ujlaki; Jack Urner; Get van de Haterd (Aus); van Keuk (Nl) Chiel van Soelen (Nl); Jos van Sonderen (Nl); S Venkateswaran (I); Steven Verplanken (B); Ludovica Villa (It); Ilka Viyse (Aus); Wim Voerman; Bettina Vogel (D); Dietrich von Blanckenburg (D); Edith Vossebrecker; Frieda Wachsmann (Aus); Tim Waggett; Paul Wagner (Aus); Thomas B Wahl (D); Eric Wakin (USA); Tim Walker (CH); Chris Walker (UK); Robyne & Nick Walker-Jonson; Hugh Waller (UK); S D Walter (C); Susan Wanning (USA); Sarah Waterhouse (UK); Jonathon Weiland (USA); William Weir (USA); Peter Wells (UK); Derek & Jennifer Werner (USA); Andes Westlund (N); Dieter Wettig; Gerard Whelan; Jane White (UK); Simon J Wickenden (Aus); Manfred Wiesinger (A); Phil Wigglesworth (UK); Helen Wilder; Tony Wilford (UK); Joseph Wilken (Nl); Evan Williams (Aus); K A Williams; Neil Williamson (UK); Buzz Willits (USA); J & K Wilson (G); K K Wilson (UK); Joan Wilson; Gillian Witchard (Aus); Hutty Woah Manau; Susan Woldenburg (USA); Tahanga alias Boxholder alias Wombat (Aus); Jack Wood (USA); Michael Woodhouse; Mary Woodward (Aus); Gary Worthington (USA); Sam Wright; Anne Wurr (USA); Peter D Young (UK); Coralie Younger (Aus); R A Zambardino (UK); Bhakti Ziek (USA); Marek Zyromzki (P)

A – Austria; Aus – Australia, B – Belgium, C – Can, CH – Switzerland, Cy – Cyprus, D – West Germany, Dk – Denmark, F – France, G – Greece, HK – Hong Kong, I – India, Ir – Ireland; Isr – Israel, It – Italy, N – Norway, Nl – Netherlands, NZ – New Zealand, P – Poland, PNG – Papua New Guinea, S – Singapore, SL – Sri Lanka, Sw – Sweden, UAE – United Arab Emirates; UK – UK, USA – USA

Lonely Planet Newsletter

We collect an enormous amount of information here at Lonely Planet. Apart from our research there's a steady stream of letters from people out on the road. To make the most of all this info we produce a quarterly Newsletter (approx Feb, May, Aug, and Nov).

The Newsletter is packed with down-to-earth information from the pens of hundreds of travellers who write from first-hand experience. Whether you want the latest facts, travel stories, or simply to reminisce, the Newsletter will keep you in touch with what is going on.

Where else could you find out:
- about boat trips on the Yalu River?
- where to stay if you want to live in a typical Thai village?
- how long it takes to get a Nepalese trekking permit?
- that Israeli youth hostel stamps will get you deported from Syria?

One year's subscription is \$10.00 (that's US\$ in the USA or A\$ in Australia), payable by cheque, money order, Amex, Visa, Bankcard or MasterCard.

Order Form

Please send me four issues of the Lonely Planet Newsletter. (Subscription starts with next issue. 1987 price – subject to change.)

Name and address (print) ....

....

....

Tick one

☐ Cheque enclosed (payable to Lonely Planet Publications)
☐ Money Order enclosed (payable to Lonely Planet Publications)
Charge my ☐ Amex, ☐ Visa, ☐ Bankcard, ☐ MasterCard for the amount of \$............

Card No ....   Expiry Date ....

Cardholder's Name (print) ....

Signature ....   Date ....

Return this form to:
Lonely Planet Publications   *or*   Lonely Planet Publications
PO Box 2001A   PO Box 88
Berkeley   South Yarra
CA 94702   Victoria 3141
USA   Australia

Guides to the Indian sub-continent

Kashmir, Ladakh & Zanskar – a travel survival kit
This book contains detailed information on three contrasting Himalayan regions in the Indian state of Jammu and Kashmir – the narrow valley of Zanskar, reclusive Ladakh, and the beautiful Vale of Kashmir.

Trekking in the Indian Himalaya
The Indian Himalaya offers some of the world's most exciting treks. This book has advice on planning and equipping a trek, plus detailed route descriptions.

Kathmandu & the Kingdom of Nepal – a travel survival kit
Few travellers can resist the lure of magical Kathmandu and its surrounding mountains. This guidebook takes you round the temples, to the foothills of the Himalaya, and to the Terai.

Trekking in the Nepal Himalaya
Complete trekking information for Nepal, including day-by-day route descriptions and detailed maps – this book has a wealth of advice for both independent and group trekkers.

Pakistan – a travel survival kit
Pakistan has been called 'the unknown land of the Indus' and many people don't realise the great variety of experiences it offers – from bustling Karachi, to ancient cities and tranquil mountain valleys.

Bangladesh – a travel survival kit
The adventurous traveller in Bangladesh can explore tropical forests and beaches, superb hill country, and ancient Buddhist ruins. This guide covers all these alternatives – and many more.

Sri Lanka – a travel survival kit
This guide takes a complete look at the island Marco Polo described as 'the finest in the world'. In one handy package you'll find ancient cities, superb countryside, and beautiful beaches.

Language survival kits

Nepal phrasebook
Nepali is spoken in parts of India, Sikkim and Bhutan as well as Nepal. This phrasebook, which includes a special trekking chapter, will be especially useful for people who travel off the beaten track.

Sri Lanka phrasebook
This phrasebook covers Sinhala, the official national language of Sri Lanka. It's an ancient language with a complicated script but its pronunciation is not difficult.

Tibet phrasebook
Few Tibetans speak English, so it is important to be able to communicate in Tibetan. This language is also spoken in other parts of China, Nepal, Sikkim and Ladakh. Tibetan script is included to enable you to 'point and show'.

China phrasebook
China's official language, Mandarin (*Putonghua*) is covered in this phrasebook. It includes both conventional *pinyin* spellings and Chinese characters for all phrases.

Thailand phrasebook
This phrasebook uses easy-to-follow pronunciation symbols but also includes Thai script. This allows you to 'point and show' when the complexities of a tonal language defeat you!

Indonesia phrasebook
A little Indonesian is easy to learn, and it's almost identical to Malay so this book is doubly useful. The rewards for learning some *Bahasa* are far greater than the effort involved!

Papua New Guinea phrasebook
Pidgin is PNG's lingua franca, also spoken with minor variations in the Solomon Islands and Vanuatu. Pidgin will be especially useful in the countryside and on the islands.

Forthcoming
Hindi/Urdu phrasebook
Burma phrasebook
Philippine phrasebook
Swahili phrasebook

Temperature

To convert °C to °F multipy by 1.8 and add 32

To convert °F to °C subtract 32 and multipy by 5/9

Length, Distance & Area

	multipy by
inches to centimetres	2.54
centimetres to inches	0.39
feet to metres	0.30
metres to feet	3.28
yards to metres	0.91
metres to yards	1.09
miles to kilometres	1.61
kilometres to miles	0.62
acres to hectares	0.40
hectares to acres	2.47

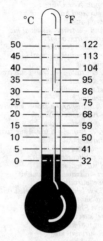

Weight

	multipy by
ounces to grams	28.35
grams to ounces	0.035
pounds to kilograms	0.45
kilograms to pounds	2.21
British tons to kilograms	1016
US tons to kilograms	907

A British ton is 2240 lbs, a US ton is 2000 lbs

Volume

	multipy by
imperial gallons to litres	4.55
litres to imperial gallons	0.22
US gallons to litres	3.79
litres to US gallons	0.26

5 imperial gallons equals 6 US gallons
a litre is slightly more than a US quart, slightly less
than a British one

Lonely Planet travel guides

Africa on a Shoestring
Alaska – a travel survival kit
Australia – a travel survival kit
Bali & Lombok – a travel survival kit
Bangladesh – a travel survival kit
Burma – a travel survival kit
Bushwalking in Papua New Guinea
Canada – a travel survival kit
China – a travel survival kit
Chile & Easter Island – a travel survival kit
East Africa – a travel survival kit
Ecuador & the Galapagos Islands
Egypt & the Sudan – a travel survival kit
Fiji – a travel survival kit
Hong Kong, Macau & Canton – a travel survival kit
India – a travel survival kit
Indonesia – a travel survival kit
Japan – a travel survival kit
Kashmir, Ladakh & Zanskar – a travel survival kit
Kathmandu & the Kingdom of Nepal
Korea & Taiwan – a travel survival kit
Malaysia, Singapore & Brunei – a travel survival kit
Mexico – a travel survival kit
New Zealand – a travel survival kit
North-East Asia on a Shoestring
Pakistan – a travel survival kit kit
Papua New Guinea – a travel survival kit
Philippines – a travel survival kit
Raratonga & the Cook Islands – a travel survival kit
South America on a Shoestring
South-East Asia on a Shoestring
Sri Lanka – a travel survival kit
Tahiti – a travel survival kit
Thailand – a travel survival kit
Tibet – a travel survival kit
Tramping in New Zealand
Travel with Children
Travellers Tales
Trekking in the Indian Himalaya
Trekking in the Nepal Himalaya
Turkey – a travel survival kit
West Asia on a Shoestring

Lonely Planet phrasebooks

Indonesia Phrasebook
China Phrasebook
Nepal Phrasebook
Papua New Guinea Phrasebook
Sri Lanka Phrasebook
Thailand Phrasebook
Tibet Phrasebook

Lonely Planet Distribution

Lonely Planet travel guides are available round the world. If you can't find them, ask your bookshop to order them from one of the distributors listed below. For countries not listed, or if you would like a free copy of our latest booklist write to Lonely Planet in Australia.

Australia
Lonely Planet Publications, PO Box 88, South Yarra, Victoria 3141.
Canada
Raincoast Books, 112 East 3rd Avenue, Vancouver, British Columbia V5T 1C8.
Denmark, Finland & Norway
Scanvik Books aps, Store Kongensgade 59 A, DK-1264 Copenhagen K.
Hong Kong
The Book Society, GPO Box 7804.
India & Nepal
UBS Distributors, 5 Ansari Rd, New Delhi - 110002.
Israel
Geographical Tours Ltd, 8 Tverya St, Tel Aviv 63144.
Japan
Intercontinental Marketing Corp, IPO Box 5056, Tokyo 100-31.
Netherlands
Nilsson & Lamm bv, Postbus 195, Pampuslaan 212, 1380 AD Weesp.
New Zealand
Roulston Greene Publishing Associates Ltd, Private Bag, Takapuna, Auckland 9.
Papua New Guinea see Australia.
Singapore & Malaysia
MPH Distributors, 601 Sims Drive #03-21, Singapore 1438.
Spain
Altair, Balmes 69, 08007 Barcelona.
Sweden
Esselte Kartcentrum AB, Vasagatan 16, S-111 20 Stockholm.
Thailand
Chalermnit, 108 Sukhumvit 53, Bangkok, 10110.
UK
Roger Lascelles, 47 York Rd, Brentford, Middlesex, TW8 OQP.
USA
Lonely Planet Publications, PO Box 2001A, Berkeley, CA 94702.
West Germany
Buchvertrieb Gerda Schettler, Postfach 64, D3415 Hattorf a H.